(ex•pl|)

1. Investigating in a systematic way: exami   ning
into or ranging over for the purpose of disco

(ex·plor·ing)

SERIES

(ex•ploring)

1. Investigating in a systematic way: examining. 2. Searching
into or ranging over for the purpose of discovery.

Microsoft® Office 2010
Volume 1

Robert T. Grauer

Mary Anne Poatsy | Keith Mulbery |

Michelle Hulett | Cynthia Krebs | Keith Mast

Prentice Hall
Upper Saddle River   London   Singapore
Toronto   Tokyo   Sydney   Hong Kong   Mexico City

Library of Congress Cataloging-in-Publication Data
Microsoft Office 2010 / Robert T. Grauer . . . [et al.].
    v. cm. — (Exploring Microsoft Office 2010 series)
  Includes index.
  ISBN-13: 978-0-13-612232-6
  ISBN-10: 0-13-612232-9
  1. Microsoft Office.   2. Business—Computer programs.   I. Grauer, Robert T., 1945-
  HF5548.4.M525M52498 2011
  005.5—dc22

                                                    2010013087

Editor in Chief: Michael Payne
Acquisitions Editor: Samantha McAfee
Product Development Manager: Eileen Bien Calabro
Editorial Project Manager: Meghan Bisi
Development Editors: Laura Town and Jennifer Campbell
Editorial Assistant: Erin Clark
AVP/Director of Product Development: Lisa Strite
Editor-Digital Learning & Assessment: Paul Gentile
Product Development Manager-Media: Cathi Profitko
Editorial Media Project Manager: Alana Coles
Production Media Project Manager: John Cassar
Director of Marketing: Kate Valentine
Marketing Manager: Tori Olson Alves

Marketing Coordinator: Susan Osterlitz
Marketing Assistant: Darshika Vyas
Senior Managing Editor: Cynthia Zonneveld
Associate Managing Editor: Camille Trentacoste
Production Project Manager: Ruth Ferrera-Kargov
Manager of Rights & Permissions: Hessa Albader
Senior Operations Specialist: Diane Peirano
Senior Art Director: Jonathan Boylan
Cover Design: Jonathan Boylan
Cover Illustration/Photo: Courtesy of Shutterstock® Images
Composition: PreMediaGlobal
Full-Service Project Management: PreMediaGlobal
Typeface: 10.5/12.5 Minion

Photos in the PowerPoint chapters are reprinted courtesy of: Andy Sorensen Photography, Ryan Phillips at Xeric Landscape and Design, Jo Porter Photography, David and Ali Valeti, Brad and Jenalee Behle, Katherine Hulse Photography, Shanna Michelle Photography, Alan Jensen Photography, and Jaron and Jennifer Krebs.

YouTube screenshot on page 945 is reprinted by permission of Common Craft, LLC.

Images reprinted by permission of Shutterstock.com appear in the text on pages 771, 816, 826, 831, and 834.

Screenshot on page 532 is reprinted with permission of Columbia Sportswear Company.

Selected content in the PowerPoint chapters is used with permission from: Cameron Martin, Ph.D., Utah Valley University; Quinn Foote, Dustin Miller, and Tyler Fox, Utah Valley University DGM Students; Bryan Stinson, Survival Solutions; and Jan Bentley, Kathleen Richards, and Diane Hartman, Utah Valley University.

Microsoft® and Windows® are registered trademarks of the Microsoft Corporation in the U.S.A. and other countries. Screen shots and icons reprinted with permission from the Microsoft Corporation. This book is not sponsored or endorsed by or affiliated with the Microsoft Corporation.

Pearson Prentice Hall™ is a trademark of Pearson Education, Inc.
Pearson® is a registered trademark of Pearson plc
Prentice Hall® is a registered trademark of Pearson Education, Inc.

Pearson Education Ltd., London
Pearson Education Singapore, Pte. Ltd.
Pearson Education, Canada, Ltd.
Pearson Education–Japan
Pearson Education Australia PTY, Limited

Pearson Education North Asia Ltd., Hong Kong
Pearson Educación de Mexico, S.A. de C.V.
Pearson Education Malaysia, Pte. Ltd.
Pearson Education, Upper Saddle River, New Jersey

Many of the designations by manufacturers and seller to distinguish their products are claimed as trademarks. Where those designations appear in this book, and the publisher was aware of a trademark claim, the designations have been printed in initial caps or all caps.

10 9 8 7 6 5 4 3 2

Prentice Hall
is an imprint of

www.pearsonhighered.com

ISBN-13: 978-0-13-612232-6
ISBN-10: 0-13-612232-9

DEDICATIONS

For my husband Ted, who unselfishly continues to take on more
than his fair share to support me throughout this process; and for
my children, Laura, Carolyn, and Teddy, whose encouragement and
love have been inspiring.

Mary Anne Poatsy

I dedicate this book in loving memory to Grandma Ida Lu Etta (Billie) Hort,
who was a positive role model for me through her patience, caring personality,
and perseverance through challenging situations. I treasure her support and
encouragement throughout my personal and professional endeavors,
including years of textbook writing.

Keith Mulbery

I would like to dedicate this book to my wonderful husband John
and my sweet baby girl Dakota. They have shown an amazing amount
of patience and support as I put in hours and hours of work on this project.
And to my amazing friends, family, and students who offer encouragement
and motivate me to be the best I can be. God bless you all.

Michelle Hulett

To my precious children—your strength, and the love and support
you share with one another amazes me. Your love sustains me. To my family
(those who have been, those who are now, and those who will be)—we are one,
and our love endures forever.

Cynthia Krebs

I would like to dedicate this book to my parents, John and Millie,
who have given me all the love and support that a son could ever ask for.

Keith Mast

I wholeheartedly dedicate this book to my father in recognition
of his support, guidance, and encouragement. His steady influence
and unwavering confidence continue to be an inspiration in my life.
He is truly my hero.

Lynn Hogan

ABOUT THE AUTHORS

Mary Anne Poatsy, Series Editor

Mary Anne is a senior faculty member at Montgomery County Community College, teaching various computer application and concepts courses in face-to-face and online environments. She holds a B.A. in psychology and education from Mount Holyoke College and an M.B.A. in finance from Northwestern University's Kellogg Graduate School of Management.

Mary Anne has more than 12 years of educational experience. She is currently adjunct faculty at Gwynedd-Mercy College and Montgomery County Community College. She has also taught at Bucks County Community College and Muhlenberg College, as well as conducted professional training. Before teaching, she was vice president at Shearson Lehman in the Municipal Bond Investment Banking Department.

Dr. Keith Mulbery, Consulting Series Editor and Excel Author

Dr. Keith Mulbery is the Department Chair and an Associate Professor in the Information Systems and Technology Department at Utah Valley University (UVU), where he teaches computer applications, C# programming, systems analysis and design, and MIS classes. Keith also served as Interim Associate Dean, School of Computing, in the College of Technology and Computing at UVU.

Keith received the Utah Valley State College Board of Trustees Award of Excellence in 2001, School of Technology and Computing Scholar Award in 2007, and School of Technology and Computing Teaching Award in 2008. He has authored more than 15 textbooks, served as Series Editor for the Exploring Office 2007 series, and served as developmental editor on two textbooks.

Keith received his B.S. and M.Ed. in Business Education from Southwestern Oklahoma State University and earned his Ph.D. in Education with an emphasis in Business Information Systems at Utah State University. His dissertation topic was computer-assisted instruction using Prentice Hall's Train and Assess IT program to supplement traditional instruction in basic computer proficiency courses.

Michelle Hulett, Word Author

Michelle Hulett received a B.S. degree in CIS from the University of Arkansas and an M.B.A. from Missouri State University. She has worked for various organizations as a programmer, network administrator, computer literacy coordinator, and educator. She currently serves as a Senior Instructor in the CIS department and Director of International Business Programs at Missouri State University.

When not teaching or writing, she enjoys flower gardening, traveling (Alaska and Hawaii are favorites), hiking, canoeing, and camping with her husband John, dog Dakota, and any friends or neighborhood kids who tag along.

Cynthia Krebs, PowerPoint Author

Cynthia Krebs is the Director of Business and Marketing Education and a professor in the Digital Media Department at Utah Valley University (UVU). In 2008, she received the UVU College of Technology and Computing Scholar Award. She has also received the School of Business Faculty Excellence Award twice during her tenure at UVU. Cynthia teaches the Methods of Teaching Digital Media class to future teachers, as well as classes in basic computer proficiency, business presentations, business graphics, and introduction to digital media.

Cynthia is active in Utah Business and Computer Education Association, Western Business Education Association, the National Business Education Association, and the Utah Association of Career and Technical Educators. In 2009/2010, she served on the Executive Board of UACTE, as President of UBCEA, and as Computer Workshop Chair for WBEA. She was awarded the WBEA Outstanding Educator at the University Level in 2009. Cynthia has written multiple texts on Microsoft Office software, consulted with government and business, and has presented extensively at the local, regional, and national levels to professional and business organizations.

Cynthia lives by a peaceful creek in Springville, Utah. When she isn't teaching or writing, she enjoys spending time with her children, spoiling Ava and Bode, traveling with friends, and reading.

Keith Mast, Access Author

Keith A. Mast develops a wide range of Access applications that solve challenging business problems and improve efficiency. His solutions help businesses and organizations in manufacturing, pharmaceutical, financial services, and agriculture, among other industries. Clients include Visible Filing Concepts, Inc.; Moyer's Chicks, Inc.; Marcho Farms, Inc.; TCM America, Inc.; LANsultants, Inc.; Spector, Roseman, Kodroff, & Willis, PC; Heinz, Inc.; DuPont; and Sony Entertainment.

He is an adjunct faculty member at Montgomery County Community College, Blue Bell, Pennsylvania, continuing his long-standing love of teaching and exemplified by his prior experience as a high school teacher, business school instructor, and Access seminar leader.

Keith promotes the ethical standards of the consulting profession both in how Mast Consulting, LLC deals with its clients and as an active volunteer leader of the Independent Computer Consultants Association of the Delaware Valley.

Keith resides in Norristown, PA, a suburb of Philadelphia. In his free time, he enjoys biking, running, kayaking, ballroom dancing, and being in nature.

For more information, visit him on Facebook, LinkedIn, or at www.keithmast.com.

Dr. Lynn Hogan, Office Fundamentals and File Management and Windows 7 Author

Lynn Hogan has taught in the Computer Information Systems area at Calhoun Community College for 29 years. She is the author of *Practical Computing* and has contributed chapters for several computer applications textbooks. Primarily teaching in the areas of computer literacy and computer applications, she was named Calhoun's outstanding instructor in 2006. She received an M.B.A. from the University of North Alabama and a Ph.D. from the University of Alabama. Lynn resides in Alabama with her husband and two daughters.

Dr. Robert T. Grauer, Creator of the Exploring Series

Bob Grauer is an Associate Professor in the Department of Computer Information Systems at the University of Miami, where he is a multiple winner of the Outstanding Teaching Award in the School of Business, most recently in 2009. He has written numerous COBOL texts and is the vision behind the Exploring Office series, with more than three million books in print. His work has been translated into three foreign languages and is used in all aspects of higher education at both national and international levels. Bob Grauer has consulted for several major corporations including IBM and American Express. He received his Ph.D. in operations research in 1972 from the Polytechnic Institute of Brooklyn.

BRIEF CONTENTS

WINDOWS 7

| CHAPTER ONE | Getting Started with Windows 7 | 1 |

OFFICE FUNDAMENTALS AND FILE MANAGEMENT

| CHAPTER ONE | Office Fundamentals and File Management | 51 |

WORD

CHAPTER ONE	Introduction to Word	117
CHAPTER TWO	Document Presentation	163
CHAPTER THREE	Collaboration and Research	217
CHAPTER FOUR	Document Productivity	261

EXCEL

CHAPTER ONE	Introduction to Excel	311
CHAPTER TWO	Formulas and Functions	373
CHAPTER THREE	Charts	421
CHAPTER FOUR	Datasets and Tables	473

ACCESS

CHAPTER ONE	Introduction to Access	531
CHAPTER TWO	Relational Databases and Queries	579
CHAPTER THREE	Customize, Analyze, and Summarize Query Data	649
CHAPTER FOUR	Creating and Using Professional Forms and Reports	693

POWERPOINT

CHAPTER ONE	Introduction to PowerPoint	759
CHAPTER TWO	Presentation Development	809
CHAPTER THREE	Presentation Design	851
CHAPTER FOUR	PowerPoint Rich Media Tools	919

GLOSSARY 981

INDEX 992

CONTENTS

WINDOWS 7

CHAPTER ONE ➤ Getting Started with Windows 7   1

CASE STUDY: CEDAR COVE ELEMENTARY SCHOOL	1	Performing a Search	34
OBJECTIVES	1	Getting Help	37
WINDOWS 7 FUNDAMENTALS	2	HANDS-ON EXERCISE 3:	
Understanding the Desktop	2	Windows Search and Help	40
Managing Windows	12		
HANDS-ON EXERCISE 1:		CHAPTER OBJECTIVES REVIEW	43
Windows 7 Fundamentals	16	KEY TERMS	43
WINDOWS PROGRAMS AND SECURITY FEATURES	23	MULTIPLE CHOICE	44
Identifying Windows Accessories	23	PRACTICE EXERCISES	45
Working with Security Settings and Software	26	MID-LEVEL EXERCISES	48
HANDS-ON EXERCISE 2:		CAPSTONE EXERCISE	49
Windows Programs and Security Features	31	BEYOND THE CLASSROOM	50
WINDOWS SEARCH AND HELP	34		

OFFICE FUNDAMENTALS AND FILE MANAGEMENT

CHAPTER ONE ➤ Office Fundamentals and File Management   51

CASE STUDY: RAILS AND TRAILS	51	Using the Clipboard Group Tasks	87
OBJECTIVES	51	Using the Editing Group Tasks	90
FILES AND FOLDERS	52	HANDS-ON EXERCISE 4:	
Using Windows Explorer	52	Home Tab Tasks	92
Working with Folders and Files	56	INSERT TAB TASKS	97
Selecting, Copying, and Moving Multiple		Inserting Objects	97
Files and Folders	58	REVIEW TAB TASKS	99
HANDS-ON EXERCISE 1:		Reviewing a File	99
Files and Folders	60	PAGE LAYOUT TAB TASKS	101
MICROSOFT OFFICE SOFTWARE	64	Changing Page Settings	102
Identifying Common Interface Components	64	HANDS-ON EXERCISE 5:	
Getting Office Help	69	Tasks on the Insert Tab, Page Layout Tab,	
HANDS-ON EXERCISE 2:		and Review Tab	104
Microsoft Office Software	71		
BACKSTAGE VIEW TASKS	76	CHAPTER OBJECTIVES REVIEW	108
Opening a File	76	KEY TERMS	109
Printing a File	79	MULTIPLE CHOICE	110
Closing a File and Application	80	PRACTICE EXERCISES	111
HANDS-ON EXERCISE 3:		MID-LEVEL EXERCISES	114
Backstage View Tasks	81	CAPSTONE EXERCISE	115
HOME TAB TASKS	84	BEYOND THE CLASSROOM	116
Selecting and Editing Text	84		

CHAPTER ONE ➤ Introduction to Word 117

CASE STUDY: FIRST RIVER OUTFITTER 117
OBJECTIVES 117
INTRODUCTION TO WORD PROCESSING 118
Understanding How Word Processors Work 119
Customizing Word 124
HANDS-ON EXERCISE 1:
Introduction to Word Processing 126
DOCUMENT ORGANIZATION 131
Using Features That Improve Readability 131
Checking Spelling and Grammar 135
Displaying a Document in Different Views 136
HANDS-ON EXERCISE 2:
Document Organization 139
FINALIZE A DOCUMENT 144
Preparing a Document for Distribution 144
Modifying Document Properties 149

HANDS-ON EXERCISE 3:
Finalize a Document 151

CHAPTER OBJECTIVES REVIEW 155
KEY TERMS 155
MULTIPLE CHOICE 156
PRACTICE EXERCISES 157
MID-LEVEL EXERCISES 160
CAPSTONE EXERCISE 161
BEYOND THE CLASSROOM 162

CHAPTER TWO ➤ Document Presentation 163

CASE STUDY: SIMSERV-PITKA ENTERPRISES 163
OBJECTIVES 163
TEXT FORMATTING FEATURES 164
Applying Font Attributes Through the Font Dialog Box 164
Controlling Word Wrap 168
HANDS-ON EXERCISE 1:
Text Formatting Features 169
PARAGRAPH FORMATTING FEATURES 172
Setting Off Paragraphs with Tabs, Borders, Lists, and Columns 172
Applying Paragraph Formats 178
HANDS-ON EXERCISE 2:
Paragraph Formatting Features 182
STYLES 187
Understanding Styles 187
Creating and Modifying Styles 187

HANDS-ON EXERCISE 3:
Styles 192
GRAPHICAL OBJECTS 197
Formatting a Graphical Object 197
Inserting Symbols into a Document 201
HANDS-ON EXERCISE 4:
Graphical Objects 202

CHAPTER OBJECTIVES REVIEW 206
KEY TERMS 207
MULTIPLE CHOICE 208
PRACTICE EXERCISES 209
MID-LEVEL EXERCISES 213
CAPSTONE EXERCISE 215
BEYOND THE CLASSROOM 216

CHAPTER THREE ➤ Collaboration and Research 217

CASE STUDY: MARKETING PLAN FOR TAKE NOTE PAPERIE 217
OBJECTIVES 217
DOCUMENT REVISIONS 218
Inserting Comments in a Document 218
Tracking Changes in a Document 221
HANDS-ON EXERCISE 1:
Document Revisions 224
RESEARCH PAPER BASICS 229
Acknowledging a Source 229
Creating and Modifying Footnotes and Endnotes 232
HANDS-ON EXERCISE 2:
Research Paper Basics 234
RESEARCH PAPER ENHANCEMENTS 237
Inserting a Table of Contents and Index 237
Adding Other Reference Tables 241
Creating Cross-References 243

HANDS-ON EXERCISE 3:
Research Paper Enhancements 245

CHAPTER OBJECTIVES REVIEW 252
KEY TERMS 252
MULTIPLE CHOICE 253
PRACTICE EXERCISES 254
MID-LEVEL EXERCISES 257
CAPSTONE EXERCISE 259
BEYOND THE CLASSROOM 260

CHAPTER FOUR > Document Productivity

CASE STUDY: COMMUNITY DISASTER RELIEF CENTER	261
OBJECTIVES	261
TABLES	262
Inserting a Table	262
Formatting a Table	264
HANDS-ON EXERCISE 1:	
Tables	267
ADVANCED TABLE FEATURES	273
Sorting and Applying Formulas to Table Data	273
Converting Text to a Table	275
HANDS-ON EXERCISE 2:	
Advanced Table Features	276
MAIL MERGE	281
Selecting a Main Document	282
Selecting or Creating Recipients	283

Inserting Merge Fields	287
Merging a Main Document and a Data Source	288
HANDS-ON EXERCISE 3:	
Mail Merge	291
CHAPTER OBJECTIVES REVIEW	299
KEY TERMS	299
MULTIPLE CHOICE	300
PRACTICE EXERCISES	301
MID-LEVEL EXERCISES	305
CAPSTONE EXERCISE	308
BEYOND THE CLASSROOM	310

MICROSOFT OFFICE EXCEL 2010

CHAPTER ONE > Introduction to Excel

CASE STUDY: OK OFFICE SYSTEMS	311
OBJECTIVES	311
INTRODUCTION TO SPREADSHEETS	312
Planning for Effective Workbook and Worksheet Design	312
Exploring the Excel Window	313
Entering and Editing Cell Data	316
HANDS-ON EXERCISE 1:	
Introduction to Spreadsheets	318
MATHEMATICS AND FORMULAS	321
Using Symbols and the Order of Precedence	321
Using Auto Fill	323
Displaying Cell Formulas	324
HANDS-ON EXERCISE 2:	
Mathematics and Formulas	325
WORKBOOK AND WORKSHEET MANAGEMENT	330
Managing Worksheets	330
Managing Columns and Rows	333
Selecting, Moving, Copying, and Pasting	337
HANDS-ON EXERCISE 3:	
Workbook and Worksheet Management	341

FORMATTING	346
Applying Alignment and Font Options	346
Applying Number Formats	348
HANDS-ON EXERCISE 4:	
Formatting	350
PAGE SETUP AND PRINTING	354
Selecting Page Setup Options	354
Printing a Worksheet	357
HANDS-ON EXERCISE 5:	
Page Setup and Printing	358
CHAPTER OBJECTIVES REVIEW	362
KEY TERMS	362
MULTIPLE CHOICE	363
PRACTICE EXERCISES	364
MID-LEVEL EXERCISES	369
CAPSTONE EXERCISE	371
BEYOND THE CLASSROOM	372

CHAPTER TWO > Formulas and Functions

CASE STUDY: DENVER MORTGAGE COMPANY	373
OBJECTIVES	373
FORMULA BASICS	374
Using Semi-Selection to Create a Formula	374
Using Relative, Absolute, and Mixed Cell References in Formulas	374
Avoiding Circular References	376
HANDS-ON EXERCISE 1:	
Formula Basics	377
FUNCTION BASICS	382
Inserting a Function	382
Totaling Values with the SUM Function	384

Inserting Basic Statistical Functions	385
Using Date Functions	387
HANDS-ON EXERCISE 2:	
Function Basics	389
LOGICAL, LOOKUP, AND FINANCIAL FUNCTIONS	394
Determining Results with the IF Function	394
Using Lookup Functions	396
Calculating Payments with the PMT Function	398
HANDS-ON EXERCISE 3:	
Logical, Lookup, and Financial Functions	399

RANGE NAMES 403
Creating and Maintaining Range Names 403
Using Range Names in Formulas 405
HANDS-ON EXERCISE 4:
Range Names 406

CHAPTER OBJECTIVES REVIEW 409

KEY TERMS 409
MULTIPLE CHOICE 410
PRACTICE EXERCISES 411
MID-LEVEL EXERCISES 416
CAPSTONE EXERCISE 419
BEYOND THE CLASSROOM 420

CHAPTER THREE ➤ Charts 421

CASE STUDY: HORT UNIVERSITY MAJORS 421
OBJECTIVES 421
CHART BASICS 422
Deciding Which Chart Type to Create 422
Creating a Chart 432
HANDS-ON EXERCISE 1:
Chart Basics 436
CHART DESIGN 441
Changing the Chart Type 441
Changing the Data Source and Structure 442
Applying a Chart Layout and a Chart Style 442
Moving a Chart 443
Printing Charts 444
Inserting and Customizing a Sparkline 444
HANDS-ON EXERCISE 2:
Chart Design 446

CHART LAYOUT 451
Selecting and Formatting Chart Elements 451
Customizing Chart Labels 453
Formatting the Axes and Gridlines 455
Adding a Trendline 456
HANDS-ON EXERCISE 3:
Chart Layout 457

CHAPTER OBJECTIVES REVIEW 462
KEY TERMS 463
MULTIPLE CHOICE 464
PRACTICE EXERCISES 465
MID-LEVEL EXERCISES 469
CAPSTONE EXERCISE 471
BEYOND THE CLASSROOM 472

CHAPTER FOUR ➤ Datasets and Tables 473

CASE STUDY: THE SPA EXPERTS 473
OBJECTIVES 473
LARGE DATASETS 474
Freezing Rows and Columns 475
Printing Large Datasets 476
HANDS-ON EXERCISE 1:
Large Datasets 479
EXCEL TABLES 484
Understanding Table Design 484
Creating a Table 485
Applying a Table Style 487
HANDS-ON EXERCISE 2:
Excel Tables 489
TABLE MANIPULATION AND AGGREGATION 493
Sorting Data 493
Filtering Data 495
Using Structured References and a Total Row 498

HANDS-ON EXERCISE 3:
Table Manipulation and Aggregation 501
CONDITIONAL FORMATTING 509
Applying Conditional Formatting 509
Creating a New Rule 512
Sorting and Filtering Using Conditional Formatting 514
HANDS-ON EXERCISE 3:
Conditional Formatting 515

CHAPTER OBJECTIVES REVIEW 519
KEY TERMS 519
MULTIPLE CHOICE 520
PRACTICE EXERCISES 521
MID-LEVEL EXERCISES 525
CAPSTONE EXERCISE 528
BEYOND THE CLASSROOM 530

CHAPTER ONE > Introduction to Access   531

CASE STUDY: MANAGING A BUSINESS IN THE GLOBAL
   ECONOMY   531
OBJECTIVES   531
DATABASES ARE EVERYWHERE!   532
   Navigating Among the Objects in an Access Database   533
   Understanding the Difference Between Working in
   Storage and Memory   540
   Practicing Good Database File Management   541
   Backing Up, Compacting, and Repairing Access Files   541
HANDS-ON EXERCISE 1:
   Databases Are Everywhere!   543
FILTERS, SORTS, AND ACCESS VERSUS EXCEL   549
   Creating Filters   549
   Sorting Table Data on One or More Fields   552
   Knowing When to Use Access or Excel to Manage Data   553

HANDS-ON EXERCISE 2:
   Filters, Sorts, and Access Versus Excel   555
RELATIONAL DATABASE   560
   Using the Relationships Windows   560
   Understanding Relational Power   561
HANDS-ON EXERCISE 3:
   Relational Database   563

CHAPTER OBJECTIVES REVIEW   568
KEY TERMS   569
MULTIPLE CHOICE   570
PRACTICE EXERCISES   571
MID-LEVEL EXERCISES   575
CAPSTONE EXERCISE   577
BEYOND THE CLASSROOM   578

CHAPTER TWO > Relational Databases and Queries   579

CASE STUDY: BANK AUDITOR UNCOVERS MIDHANDLED
   FUNDS   579
OBJECTIVES   579
TABLE DESIGN, PROPERTIES, VIEWS, AND WIZARDS   580
   Designing Data   580
   Creating Tables   584
HANDS-ON EXERCISE 1:
   Table Design, Properties, Views, and Wizards   590
MULTIPLE TABLE DATABASES   596
   Understanding Table Relationships   596
   Sharing Data with Excel   598
   Establishing Table Relationships   602
HANDS-ON EXERCISE 2:
   Multiple Table Databases   605
SINGLE-TABLE QUERIES   613
   Creating a Single-Table Query   613
   Specifying Criteria for Different Data Types   616

   Copying and Running a Query   619
   Using the Query Wizard   619
HANDS-ON EXERCISE 3:
   Single-Table Queries   622
MULTI-TABLE QUERIES   625
   Creating a Multi-Table Query   625
   Modifying a Multi-Table Query   626
HANDS-ON EXERCISE 3:
   Multi-Table Queries   630

CHAPTER OBJECTIVES REVIEW   634
KEY TERMS   635
MULTIPLE CHOICE   636
PRACTICE EXERCISES   637
MID-LEVEL EXERCISES   642
CAPSTONE EXERCISE   645
BEYOND THE CLASSROOM   647

CHAPTER THREE > Customize, Analyze, and Summarize Query Data   649

CASE STUDY: HOUSING SLUMP MEANS OPPORTUNITY
   FOR COLLEGE STUDENTS   649
OBJECTIVES   649
CALCULATIONS, EXPRESSIONS, AND FUNCTIONS   650
   Understanding the Order of Operations   650
   Creating a Calculated Field in a Query   651
HANDS-ON EXERCISE 1:
   Calculations, Expressions, and Functions   654
EXPRESSION BUILDER, FUNCTIONS, AND
   DATE ARITHMETIC   660
   Creating Expressions with the Expression Builder   660
   Using Built-In Functions in Access   662
   Performing Date Arithmetic   665
HANDS-ON EXERCISE 2:
   Expression Builder, Functions, and Date Arithmetic   667

AGGREGATE FUNCTIONS   675
   Adding Aggregate Functions to Datasheets and Queries   675
HANDS-ON EXERCISE 3:
   Aggregate Functions   679

CHAPTER OBJECTIVES REVIEW   683
KEY TERMS   683
MULTIPLE CHOICE   684
PRACTICE EXERCISES   685
MID-LEVEL EXERCISES   688
CAPSTONE EXERCISE   690
BEYOND THE CLASSROOM   692

CHAPTER FOUR > Creating and Using Professional Forms and Reports 693

CASE STUDY: COFFEE SHOP STARTS NEW BUSINESS 693
OBJECTIVES 693
FORM BASICS 694
Creating Forms Using the Form Tools 694
Modifying a Form 699
Sorting Records in a Form 700
HANDS-ON EXERCISE 1:
Form Basics 702
FORM SECTIONS, VIEWS, AND CONTROLS 709
Identifying Form Sections 709
Revising Forms Using Form Views 710
Identifying Control Types in Forms 712
HANDS-ON EXERCISE 2:
Form Sections, Views, and Controls 715
REPORT BASICS 721
Creating Reports Using Report Tools 721
Modifying a Report 728
Sorting Records in a Report 730

HANDS-ON EXERCISE 3:
Report Basics 731
REPORT SECTIONS, VIEWS, AND CONTROLS 737
Identifying Report Sections 737
Revising Reports Using Report Views 741
Identifying Control Types in Reports 742
HANDS-ON EXERCISE 3:
Report Sections, Views, and Controls 743

CHAPTER OBJECTIVES REVIEW 748
KEY TERMS 749
MULTIPLE CHOICE 750
PRACTICE EXERCISES 751
MID-LEVEL EXERCISES 754
CAPSTONE EXERCISE 757
BEYOND THE CLASSROOM 758

MICROSOFT OFFICE POWERPOINT 2010

CHAPTER ONE > Introduction to PowerPoint 759

CASE STUDY: BE A TRAINER 759
OBJECTIVES 759
INTRODUCTION TO POWERPOINT 760
Using PowerPoint Views 761
Saving as a Slide Show 765
HANDS-ON EXERCISE 1:
Introduction to PowerPoint 766
PRESENTATION CREATION 769
Planning a Presentation 769
Assessing Presentation Content 772
Using Slide Layouts 772
Applying Themes 773
Reviewing the Presentation 774
HANDS-ON EXERCISE 2:
Presentation Creation 775
PRESENTATION DEVELOPMENT 780
Inserting Media Objects 780
Adding a Table 781

Using Animations and Transitions 781
Inserting a Header or Footer 784
HANDS-ON EXERCISE 3:
Presentation Development 786
NAVIGATION AND PRINTING 791
Running and Navigating a Slide Slow 791
Printing in PowerPoint 793
HANDS-ON EXERCISE 4:
Navigation and Printing 796

CHAPTER OBJECTIVES REVIEW 798
KEY TERMS 798
MULTIPLE CHOICE 799
PRACTICE EXERCISES 800
MID-LEVEL EXERCISES 804
CAPSTONE EXERCISE 806
BEYOND THE CLASSROOM 808

CHAPTER TWO > Presentation Development 809

CASE STUDY: THE WELLNESS EDUCATION CENTER 809
OBJECTIVES 809
TEMPLATES 810
Creating a Presentation Using a Template 810
Modifying a Template 812
HANDS-ON EXERCISE 1:
Templates 813
OUTLINES 817
Creating a Presentation in Outline View 817
Modifying an Outline Structure 818
Printing an Outline 819

HANDS-ON EXERCISE 2:
Outlines 821
DATA IMPORTS 825
Importing an Outline 825
Adding Existing Content to a Presentation 825
HANDS-ON EXERCISE 3:
Data Imports 827
DESIGN 830
Using Sections 830
Examining Slide Show Design Principles 831
Modifying a Theme 833

HANDS-ON EXERCISE 4:
Design   835

CHAPTER OBJECTIVES REVIEW   838
KEY TERMS   838
MULTIPLE CHOICE   839

PRACTICE EXERCISES   840
MID-LEVEL EXERCISES   844
CAPSTONE EXERCISE   849
BEYOND THE CLASSROOM   850

CHAPTER THREE ➤ Presentation Design   851

CASE STUDY: ILLUSTRATIONS AND INFOGRAPHICS
MINI-CAMP   851
OBJECTIVES   851
SHAPES   852
Creating Shapes   852
Applying Quick Styles and Customizing Shapes   857
HANDS-ON EXERCISE 1:
Shapes   865
SMARTART AND WORDART   873
Creating SmartArt   873
Modifying SmartArt   877
Creating WordArt   881
Modifying WordArt   881
HANDS-ON EXERCISE 2:
SmartArt and WordArt   883

OBJECT MANIPULATION   887
Modifying Objects   887
Arranging Objects   892
HANDS-ON EXERCISE 3:
Object Manipulation   897

CHAPTER OBJECTIVES REVIEW   903
KEY TERMS   903
MULTIPLE CHOICE   904
PRACTICE EXERCISES   905
MID-LEVEL EXERCISES   909
CAPSTONE EXERCISE   913
BEYOND THE CLASSROOM   916

CHAPTER FOUR ➤ PowerPoint Rich Media Tools   919

CASE STUDY: WEDDING ALBUMS   919
OBJECTIVES   919
PICTURES   920
Inserting a Picture   920
Transforming a Picture   922
Using the Internet as a Resource   933
HANDS-ON EXERCISE 1:
Pictures   936
VIDEO   943
Adding Video   943
Using Video Tools   946
HANDS-ON EXERCISE 2:
Video   950
AUDIO   953
Adding Audio   953
Changing Audio Settings   955

HANDS-ON EXERCISE 3:
Audio   957
PHOTO ALBUMS   961
Creating a Photo Album   961
Setting Photo Album Options   962
HANDS-ON EXERCISE 3:
Photo Albums   963

CHAPTER OBJECTIVES REVIEW   967
KEY TERMS   967
MULTIPLE CHOICE   968
PRACTICE EXERCISES   969
MID-LEVEL EXERCISES   973
CAPSTONE EXERCISE   976
BEYOND THE CLASSROOM   980

GLOSSARY 981

INDEX 992

ACKNOWLEDGMENTS

The Exploring team would like to acknowledge and thank all the reviewers who helped us prepare for the Exploring Office 2010 revision by providing us with their invaluable comments, suggestions, and constructive criticism:

Allen Alexander
Delaware Technical & Community College

Andrea Marchese
Maritime College, State University of New York

Andrew Blitz
Broward College, Edison State College

Angela Clark
University of South Alabama

Astrid Todd
Guilford Technical Community College

Audrey Gillant
Maritime College, State University of New York

Barbara Stover
Marion Technical College

Barbara Tollinger
Sinclair Community College

Ben Brahim Taha
Auburn University

Beverly Amer
Northern Arizona University

Beverly Fite
Amarillo College

Bonnie Homan
San Francisco State University

Brad West
Sinclair Community College

Brian Powell
West Virginia University

Carol Buser
Owens Community College

Carol Roberts
University of Maine

Cathy Poyner
Truman State University

Charles Hodgson
Delgado Community College

Cheryl Hinds
Norfolk State University

Cindy Herbert
Metropolitan Community College–Longview

Dana Hooper
University of Alabama

Dana Johnson
North Dakota State University

Daniela Marghitu
Auburn University

David Noel
University of Central Oklahoma

David Pulis
Maritime College, State University of New York

David Thornton
Jacksonville State University

Dawn Medlin
Appalachian State University

Debby Keen
University of Kentucky

Debra Chapman
University of South Alabama

Derrick Huang
Florida Atlantic University

Diana Baran
Henry Ford Community College

Diane Cassidy
The University of North Carolina at Charlotte

Diane Smith
Henry Ford Community College

Don Danner
San Francisco State University

Don Hoggan
Solano College

Elaine Crable
Xavier University

Erhan Uskup
Houston Community College–Northwest

Erika Nadas
Wilbur Wright College

Floyd Winters
Manatee Community College

Frank Lucente
Westmoreland County Community College

G. Jan Wilms
Union University

Gail Cope
Sinclair Community College

Gary DeLorenzo
California University of Pennsylvania

Gary Garrison
Belmont University

Gerald Braun
Xavier University

Gladys Swindler
Fort Hays State University

Heith Hennel
Valencia Community College

Irene Joos
La Roche College

Iwona Rusin
Baker College; Davenport University

J. Roberto Guzman
San Diego Mesa College

Jan Wilms
Union University

Janet Bringhurst
Utah State University

Jim Chaffee
The University of Iowa Tippie College of Business

Joanne Lazirko
University of Wisconsin–Milwaukee

Jodi Milliner
Kansas State University

John Hollenbeck
Blue Ridge Community College

John Seydel
Arkansas State University

Judith A. Scheeren
Westmoreland County Community College

Judith Brown
The University of Memphis

Karen Priestly
Northern Virginia Community College

Karen Ravan
Spartanburg Community College

Kathleen Brenan
Ashland University

Ken Busbee
Houston Community College

Kent Foster
Winthrop University

Kevin Anderson
Solano Community College

Kim Wright
The University of Alabama

Kristen Hockman
University of Missouri–Columbia

Kristi Smith
Allegany College of Maryland

Laura McManamon
University of Dayton

Leanne Chun
Leeward Community College

Lee McClain
Western Washington University

Linda D. Collins
Mesa Community College

Linda Johnsonius
Murray State University

Linda Lau
Longwood University

Linda Theus
Jackson State Community College

Lisa Miller
University of Central Oklahoma

Lister Horn
Pensacola Junior College

Lixin Tao
Pace University

Loraine Miller
Cayuga Community College

Lori Kielty
Central Florida Community College

Lorna Wells
Salt Lake Community College

Lucy Parakhovnik (Parker)
California State University, Northridge

Marcia Welch
Highline Community College

Margaret McManus
Northwest Florida State College

Margaret Warrick
Allan Hancock College

Marilyn Hibbert
Salt Lake Community College

Mark Choman
Luzerne County Community College

Mary Duncan
University of Missouri – St. Louis

Melissa Nemeth
Indiana University Purdue University
Indianapolis

Melody Alexander
Ball State University

Michael Douglas
University of Arkansas at Little Rock

Michael Dunklebarger
Alamance Community College

Michael G. Skaff
College of the Sequoias

Michele Budnovitch
Pennsylvania College of Technology

Mike Jochen
East Stroudsburg University

Mike Scroggins
Missouri State University

Nanette Lareau
University of Arkansas Community College–
Morrilton

Pam Uhlenkamp
Iowa Central Community College

Patrick Smith
Marshall Community and Technical College

Paula Ruby
Arkansas State University

Peggy Burrus
Red Rocks Community College

Peter Ross
SUNY Albany

Philip H Nielson
Salt Lake Community College

Ralph Hooper
University of Alabama

Ranette Halverson
Midwestern State University

Richard Cacace
Pensacola Junior College

Robert Dušek
Northern Virginia Community College

Robert Sindt
Johnson County Community College

Rocky Belcher
Sinclair Community College

Roger Pick
University of Missouri at Kansas City

Ronnie Creel
Troy University

Rosalie Westerberg
Clover Park Technical College

Ruth Neal
Navarro College

Sandra Thomas
Troy University

Sophie Lee
California State University, Long Beach

Steven Schwarz
Raritan Valley Community College

Sue McCrory
Missouri State University

Susan Fuschetto
Cerritos College

Susan Medlin
UNC Charlotte

Suzan Spitzberg
Oakton Community College

Sven Aelterman
Troy University

Terri Holly
Indian River State College

Thomas Rienzo
Western Michigan University

Tina Johnson
Midwestern State University

Tommy Lu
Delaware Technical and Community College

Troy S. Cash
NorthWest Arkansas Community College

Vicki Robertson
Southwest Tennessee Community College

Weifeng Chen
California University of Pennsylvania

Wes Anthony
Houston Community College

William Ayen
University of Colorado at Colorado Springs

Wilma Andrews
Virginia Commonwealth University

Yvonne Galusha
University of Iowa

We'd also like to acknowledge the reviewers of previous editions of Exploring:

Aaron Schorr
Fashion Institute of Technology

Alan Moltz
Naugatuck Valley Technical Community College

Alicia Stonesifer
La Salle University

Allen Alexander
Delaware Tech & Community College

Alok Charturvedi
Purdue University

Amy Williams
Abraham Baldwin Agriculture College

Andrea Compton
St. Charles Community College

Annette Duvall
Central New Mexico Community College

Annie Brown
Hawaii Community College

Antonio Vargas
El Paso Community College

Barbara Cierny
Harper College

Barbara Hearn
Community College of Philadelphia

Barbara Meguro
University of Hawaii at Hilo

Barbara Sherman
Buffalo State College

Barbara Stover
Marion Technical College

Bette Pitts
South Plains College

Beverly Fite
Amarillo College

Bill Daley
University of Oregon

Bill Morse
DeVry Institute of Technology

Bill Wagner
Villanova

Bob McCloud
Sacred Heart University

Bonnie Homan
San Francisco State University

Brandi N. Guidry
University of Louisiana at Lafayette

Brian Powell
West Virginia University–Morgantown Campus

Carl Farrell
Hawaii Pacific University

Carl M. Briggs
Indiana University School of Business

Carl Penzuil
Ithaca College

Carlotta Eaton
Radford University

Carole Bagley
University of St. Thomas

Carolyn DiLeo
Westchester Community College

Cassie Georgetti
Florida Technical College

Catherine Hain
Central New Mexico Community College

Charles Edwards
University of Texas of the Permian Basin

Cheryl Slavik
Computer Learning Services

Christine L. Moore
College of Charleston

Cody Copeland
Johnson County Community College

Connie Wells
Georgia State University

Dana Johnson
North Dakota State University

Dan Combellick
Scottsdale Community College

Daniela Marghitu
Auburn University

David B. Meinert
Southwest Missouri State University

David Barnes
Penn State Altoona

David Childress
Ashland Community College

David Douglas
University of Arkansas

David Langley
University of Oregon

David Law
Alfred State College

David Rinehard
Lansing Community College

David Weiner
University of San Francisco

Delores Pusins
Hillsborough Community College

Dennis Chalupa
Houston Baptist

Diane Stark
Phoenix College

Dianna Patterson
Texarkana College

Dianne Ross
University of Louisiana at Lafayette

Don Belle
Central Piedmont Community College

Douglas Cross
Clackamas Community College

Dr. Behrooz Saghafi
Chicago State University

Dr. Gladys Swindler
Fort Hays State University

Dr. Joe Teng
Barry University

Dr. Karen Nantz
Eastern Illinois University

Duane D. Lintner
Amarillo College

Elizabeth Edmiston
North Carolina Central University

Erhan Uskup
Houston Community College

Ernie Ivey
Polk Community College

Fred Hills
McClellan Community College

Freda Leonard
Delgado Community College

Gale E. Rand
College Misericordia

Gary R. Armstrong
Shippensburg University of Pennsylvania

Glenna Vanderhoof
Missouri State

Gregg Asher
Minnesota State University, Mankato

Hank Imus
San Diego Mesa College

Heidi Gentry-Kolen
Northwest Florida State College

Helen Stoloff
Hudson Valley Community College

Herach Safarian
College of the Canyons

Hong K. Sung
University of Central Oklahoma

Hyekyung Clark
Central New Mexico Community College

J Patrick Fenton
West Valley College

Jack Zeller
Kirkwood Community College

James Franck
College of St. Scholastica

James Gips
Boston College

Jana Carver
Amarillo College

Jane Cheng
Bloomfield College

Jane King
Everett Community College

Janis Cox
Tri-County Technical College

Janos T. Fustos
Metropolitan State College of Denver

Jean Kotsiovos
Kaplan University

Jeffrey A Hassett
University of Utah

Jennifer Pickle
Amarillo College

Jerry Chin
Southwest Missouri State University

Jerry Kolata
New England Institute of Technology

Jesse Day
South Plains College

Jill Chapnick
Florida International University

Jim Pepe
Bentley College

Jim Pruitt
Central Washington University

John Arehart
Longwood University

John Lee Reardon
University of Hawaii, Manoa

John Lesson
University of Central Florida

John Shepherd
Duquesne University

Joshua Mindel
San Francisco State University

Judith M. Fitspatrick
Gulf Coast Community College

Judith Rice
Santa Fe Community College

Judy Brown
The University of Memphis

Judy Dolan
Palomar College

Karen Tracey
Central Connecticut State University

Karen Wisniewski
County College of Morris

Karl Smart
Central Michigan University

Kathleen Brenan
Ashland University

Kathryn L. Hatch
University of Arizona

Kevin Pauli
University of Nebraska

Kim Montney
Kellogg Community College

Kimberly Chambers
Scottsdale Community College

Krista Lawrence
Delgado Community College

Krista Terry
Radford University

Lancie Anthony Affonso
College of Charleston

Larry S. Corman
Fort Lewis College

Laura McManamon
University of Dayton

Laura Reid
University of Western Ontario

Linda Johnsonius
Murray State University

Lisa Prince
Missouri State University

Lori Kelley
Madison Area Technical College

Lucy Parker
California State University, Northridge

Lynda Henrie
LDS Business College

Lynn Band
Middlesex Community College

Lynn Bowen
Valdosta Technical College

Malia Young
Utah State University

Margaret Thomas
Ohio University

Margie Martyn
Baldwin Wallace

Marguerite Nedreberg
Youngstown State University

Marianne Trudgeon
Fanshawe College

Marilyn Hibbert
Salt Lake Community College

Marilyn Salas
Scottsdale Community College

Marjean Lake
LDS Business College

Mark Olaveson
Brigham Young University

Martin Crossland
Southwest Missouri State University

Mary McKenry Percival
University of Miami

Meg McManus
Northwest Florida State College

Michael Hassett
Fort Hayes State University

Michael Stewardson
San Jacinto College–North

Midge Gerber
Southwestern Oklahoma State University

Mike Hearn
Community College of Philadelphia

Mike Kelly
Community College of Rhode Island

Mike Thomas
Indiana University School of Business

Mimi Duncan
University of Missouri–St. Louis

Minnie Proctor
Indian River Community College

Nancy Sardone
Seton Hall University

Pam Chapman
Waubonsee Community College

Patricia Joseph
Slippery Rock University

Patrick Hogan
Cape Fear Community College

Paul E. Daurelle
Western Piedmont Community
College

Paula F. Bell
Lock Haven University of Pennsylvania

Paulette Comet
Community College of Baltimore County,
Catonsville

Pratap Kotala
North Dakota State University

Ranette Halverson
Midwestern State University

Raymond Frost
Central Connecticut State University

Richard Albright
Goldey-Beacom College

Richard Blamer
John Carroll University

Richard Herschel
St. Joseph's University

Richard Hewer
Ferris State University

Robert Gordon
Hofstra University

Robert Marmelstein
East Stroudsburg University

Robert Spear
Prince George's Community College

Robert Stumbur
Northern Alberta Institute of Technology

Roberta I. Hollen
University of Central Oklahoma

Roland Moreira
South Plains College

Ron Murch
University of Calgary

Rory J. de Simone
University of Florida

Rose M. Laird
Northern Virginia Community College

Ruth Neal
Navarro College

Sally Visci
Lorain County Community College

Sandra M. Brown
Finger Lakes Community College

Sharon Mulroney
Mount Royal College

Shawna DePlonty
Sault College of Applied Arts and Technology

Stephen E. Lunce
Midwestern State University

Steve Schwarz
Raritan Valley Community College

Steven Choy
University of Calgary

Stuart P. Brian
Holy Family College

Susan Byrne
St. Clair College

Susan Fry
Boise State University

Suzan Spitzberg
Oakton Community College

Suzanne Tomlinson
Iowa State University

Thomas Setaro
Brookdale Community College

Todd McLeod
Fresno City College

Vernon Griffin
Austin Community College

Vickie Pickett
Midland College

Vipul Gupta
St. Joseph's University

Vivek Shah
Texas State University–San Marcos

Wei-Lun Chuang
Utah State University

William Dorin
Indiana University Northwest

Additionally, we'd like to thank our Instructor Resource authors:

Anci Shah
Houston Community College

Ann Rovetto
Horry-Georgetown Technical College

Arlene Eliason
Minnesota School of Business

Barbara Stover
Marion Technical College

Carol Roberts
University of Maine

David Csuha
Passaic County Community College

James Powers
University of Southern Indiana

Jayne Lowery
Jackson State Community College

Julie Boyles
Portland Community College

Kyle Stark
Macomb Community College

Linda Lau
Longwood University

Lisa Prince
Missouri State University

Lynn Bowen
Valdosta Technical College

Lynn Hogan
Calhoun Community College

Mary Lutz
Southwestern Illinois College

Meg McManus
Northwest Florida State College

Sally Baker
DeVry University

Sharon Behrens
Mid-State Technical College

Stephanie Jones
Texas Tech University

Steve Rubin
California State University, Monterey Bay

Suzan Spitzberg
Oakton Community College

Tom McKenzie
James Madison University

Finally, we'd like to extend our thanks to the Exploring 2010 technical editors:

Chad Kirsch	Janice Snyder	Lori Damanti
Cheryl Slavik	Joyce Nielsen	Sandra Swinney
Elizabeth Lockley	Julie Boyles	Sean Portnoy
Janet Pickard	Lisa Bucki	

PREFACE

The Exploring Series and You

Exploring is Pearson's Office Application series which requires students like you to think "beyond the point and click." With Office 2010, Exploring has embraced today's student learning styles to support extended learning beyond the classroom.

The goal of Exploring is, as it has always been, to go further than teaching just the steps to accomplish a task—the series provides the theoretical foundation for you to understand when and why to apply a skill. As a result, you achieve a deeper understanding of each application and can apply this critical thinking beyond Office and the classroom.

You are plugged in constantly, and Exploring has evolved to meet you half-way to work within your changing learning styles. Pearson has paid attention to the habits of students today, how you get information, how you are motivated to do well in class, and what your future goals look like. We asked you and your peers for acceptance of new tools we designed to address these points, and you responded with a resounding "YES!"

Here Is What We Learned About You

You go to college now with a different set of skills than students did five years ago. The new edition of Exploring moves you beyond the basics of the software at a faster pace, without sacrificing coverage of the fundamental skills that you need to know. This ensures that you will be engaged from page 1 to the end of the book.

You and your peers have diverse learning styles. With this in mind, we broadened our definition of "student resources" to include Compass, an online skill database; movable Visual Reference cards; relevant Set-Up Videos filmed in a familiar, commercial style; and the most powerful online homework and assessment tool around, my**it**lab. Exploring will be accessible to all students, regardless of learning style.

You read, prepare, and study differently than students used to. You use textbooks like a tool—you want to easily identify what you need to know and learn it efficiently. We have added key features that make the content accessible to you and make the text easy to use.

You are goal-oriented. You want a good grade and you want to be successful in your future career. With this in mind, we used motivating case studies and Set-Up Videos to aid in the learning now and to show the relevance of the skills to your future careers.

Moving Beyond the Point and Click and Extending Your Learning Beyond the Classroom

All of these additions will keep you more engaged, helping you to achieve a higher level of understanding and to complete this course and go on to be successful in your career. In addition to the vision and experience of the series creator, Robert T. Grauer, we have assembled a tremendously talented team of Office Applications authors who have devoted themselves to teaching you the ins and outs of Microsoft Word, Excel, Access, and PowerPoint. Led in this edition by series editor Mary Anne Poatsy, the whole team is equally dedicated to the Exploring mission of **moving you beyond the point and click, and extending your learning beyond the classroom**.

Key Features of Exploring Office 2010

- **White Pages/Yellow Pages** clearly distinguish the theory (white pages) from the skills covered in the Hands-On Exercises (yellow pages) so students always know what they are supposed to be doing.

- **Objective Mapping** enables students to skip the skills and concepts they know and quickly find those they do not know by scanning the chapter opener pages for the page numbers of the material they need.

- **Pull Quotes** entice students into the theory by highlighting the most interesting points.

- **Case Study** presents a scenario for the chapter, creating a story that ties the Hands-On Exercises together.

- **FYI Icon** indicates that an exercise step includes a skill that is common to more than one application. Students who require more information on that skill may utilize the Office Fundamentals and File Management chapter, the Visual Reference Cards, or Compass for assistance.

- **Set-Up Video** introduces the chapter's Case Study to generate student interest and attention and shows the relevance of the skills to students' future work.

- **Key Terms** are defined in the margins to ensure student comprehension.

- **End-of-Chapter Exercises** offer instructors several options for assessment. Each chapter has approximately 12–15 exercises ranging from multiple choice questions to open-ended projects.

CREATIVE CASE   DISCOVER

- **Enhanced Mid-Level Exercises** include a **Creative Case**, which allows students some flexibility and creativity, not being bound by a definitive solution, as well as **Discover Steps**, which encourage students to use Help or to problem-solve to accomplish a task.

Instructor Resources

The Instructor's Resource Center, available at www.pearsonhighered.com includes the following:
- **Annotated Solution Files with Scorecards** assist with grading the Hands-On Exercises and end-of-chapter exercises.

- **Data and Solution Files**

- **Capstone Production Tests** allow instructors to assess all skills covered in a chapter with a single project.

- **Rubrics** for Mid-Level Creative Cases and Beyond the Classroom Cases in Microsoft® Word format enable instructors to customize the assignments for their classes.

- **PowerPoint® Presentations** with notes for each chapter are included for out-of-class study or review.

- **Audio PowerPoint Presentations** provide an alternate version of the PowerPoint presentations in which all the lecture notes have been prerecorded.

- **Lesson Plans** provide a detailed blueprint to achieve chapter learning objectives and outcomes.

- **Objectives List** maps chapter objectives to Hands-On Exercises and end-of-chapter exercises.

- **Multiple Choice Answer Key**

- **Complete Test Bank**, also available in TestGen format.

- **Set-Up Video Exercises** provide companion exercises for the Set-Up Video for each chapter.

- **Syllabus templates** for 8-week, 12-week, and 16-week courses.

- **Grader projects** provide live-in-the-application assessment for each chapter's Capstone Exercise and additional capstone exercises.

- **Instructor Reference Cards**, available electronically and as printed cards, for each chapter, include:
  - **Concept Summary** outlines the KEY objectives to cover in class with tips on where students get stuck as well as how to get them unstuck.
  - **Scripted Lecture** provides instructors with a lecture outline that mirrors the Hands-On Exercises.

Online Course Cartridges

Flexible, robust, and customizable content is available for all major online course platforms that include everything instructors need in one place. Please contact your Sales Representative for information on accessing course cartridges for WebCT, Blackboard, or CourseCompass.

Student Resources

Student Data CD

- Student Data Files

- Set-Up Videos introduce the chapter's Case Study to generate student interest and attention and show the relevance of the skills to students' future work.

- Compass access for PC and mobile phone

Visual Reference Cards

A two-sided reference card for each application provides students with a visual summary of information and tips specific to each application that provide answers to the most common student questions. The cards can be easily attached to and detached from the book's spiral binding to be used as a bookmark, and all cards are clearly color-coded by application.

Compass

Compass is a searchable database of Microsoft Office 2010 skills that is available for use online on a computer or on your mobile phone. Using a keyword look-up system on your computer, the database provides multimedia instructions via videos and at-a-glance frames to remind students how to perform a skill. For students on the go, you can use your mobile phone to search and access a brief description of a skill and the click-stream instructions for how to perform the skill. This is a resource for the tech savvy student, who wants help and answers right away. Students get access to Compass through my**it**lab and/or the Student CD.

Prentice Hall's Companion Web Site

www.pearsonhighered.com/exploring offers expanded IT resources and downloadable supplements. Students can find the following self-study tools for each chapter:

- Online Study Guide

- Chapter Objectives

- Glossary

- Chapter Objectives Review

- Web Resources

- Student Data Files

myitlab my**it**lab for Office 2010 is a solution designed by professors for professors that allows easy delivery of Office courses with defensible assessment and outcomes-based training. The new *Exploring Office 2010* system will seamlessly integrate online assessment, training, and projects with my**it**lab for Microsoft Office 2010!

myitlab for Office 2010 Features. . .

- **Assessment and training built to match** *Exploring Office 2010* instructional content so that my**it**lab works with *Exploring* to move students beyond the point and click.

- **Both project-based and skill-based assessment and training** allow instructors to test and train students on complete exercises or individual Office application skills.

- **Full course management functionality** includes all instructor and student resources, a complete Gradebook, and the ability to run a variety of reports including detailed student clickstream data.

- **The most open, realistic, high-fidelity simulation** of Office 2010 so students feel like they are learning Office, not just a simulation.

- **Grader, a live-in-the-application project-grading tool**, enables instructors to assign projects taken from the end-of-chapter material and additional projects included in the instructor resources. These are graded automatically, with detailed feedback provided to both instructors and students.

WINDOWS 7

1 GETTING STARTED WITH WINDOWS 7

An Introduction to the Operating System

Watch the
**Set-up
Video**
for this
Case Study!

CASE STUDY | Cedar Cove Elementary School

A good friend recently graduated with a degree in Elementary Education and is excited to begin her first job as a fifth-grade teacher at Cedar Cove Elementary School. The school has a computer lab for all students as well as a computer system in each classroom. The computers were acquired through a state technology grant so they are new models running Windows 7. Your friend's lesson plans must include a unit on operating system basics and an introduction to application software. Because you have a degree in Computer Information Systems, she has called on you for assistance with the lesson plans. She also hopes you will occasionally visit her classroom to help present the material.

The elementary school is located in a low-income area of the city, so you cannot assume that all students have been exposed to computers at home, especially to those configured with Windows 7. Your material will need to include very basic instruction in Windows 7, along with a general overview of application software. You will probably focus on application software that is included with Windows 7, including WordPad, Paint, and Calculator. Your friend's lesson plans must be completed right away, so you are on a short timeline but are excited about helping students learn!

OBJECTIVES AFTER YOU READ THIS CHAPTER, YOU WILL BE ABLE TO:

1. Understand the desktop *p.2*
2. Manage windows *p.12*
3. Identify Windows accessories *p.23*
4. Work with security settings and software *p.26*
5. Perform a search *p.34*
6. Get help *p.37*

Windows 7 Fundamentals

Computer activities that you enjoy might include e-mail, games, social networking, and digital photo management. If you have a computer at work, you probably use such software as spreadsheet, database, word processing, and other job-specific applications. Those applications are necessary for your enjoyment or career, but they would not be possible without an *operating system*. The operating system is software that directs such computer activities as checking all components, managing system resources, and communicating with application software.

> Windows 7 is a Microsoft operating system produced in 2009 and available on most new microcomputer systems.

Windows 7 is a Microsoft operating system produced in 2009 and available on most new microcomputer systems. Because you are likely to encounter Windows 7 on computers at school, work, and home, it is well worth your time to explore it and learn to appreciate its computer management and security features. In this section, you will explore the desktop and its components, including the Start menu and taskbar. You will also learn to customize the desktop with a background and color scheme of your choice.

An **operating system** is software that directs computer activities such as recognizing keyboard input, sending output to a display, and keeping track of files and folders.

Understanding the Desktop

The **desktop** is the screen that displays when you turn on a computer. It contains icons and a taskbar.

A **window** is an onscreen rectangular area representing a program or system resource, or data.

The *desktop* is the display that you see after you turn on a computer and respond to any username and password prompts. The Windows 7 desktop includes components that enable you to access system resources, work with software, and manage files and folders. It is called a *desktop* because it serves the purpose of a desk, on which you can manage tasks and complete paperwork. Just as you can work with multiple projects on a desk, you can work with several software applications, each occupying a *window*, or area of space, on the desktop.

Identify Desktop Components

An **icon** is a small picture on the desktop representing a program, file, folder, or other item.

One of the first things that you will notice about the desktop is the presence of a few small pictures, each with a description underneath. Those pictures, or *icons*, represent programs, files, folders, or other items related to your computer. The desktop that you see on your home computer might differ from the one that you use at school or work because each computer has a unique configuration of installed programs and files. Invariably, most desktops contain one or more icons such as the one shown in Figure 1.1. You can easily add and remove icons so

FIGURE 1.1 Desktop ➤

that the desktop includes only those items that are important to you or that you access often. You can even include desktop folders in which you can organize files and programs.

As you work with a computer, you will find that you access some programs, or software, more often than others. Instead of searching for the program on a program list, you will find it convenient to add a program icon to the desktop. The icon is not actually the program, but a link to the program, called a ***shortcut***. Such shortcut icons are identified by a small arrow in the bottom-left corner of the icon. Figure 1.2 shows a shortcut icon. A computer provides a large amount of storage space, some of which you might use to house files, such as documents, worksheets, and digital photos related to particular projects or work-related activities. Because the desktop is so convenient to access, you could create a folder, identified by a folder icon, on the desktop to organize such files. See the folder icon in Figure 1.2. If you save files to the desktop, you should organize them in desktop folders. That way, the desktop will not become too cluttered and you can easily find related files later. Keep in mind that just as you strive to keep a desk relatively clear, you will also want to maintain order on the Windows desktop.

A **shortcut** is a pointer, or link, to a program or computer resource.

Folder icon

Shortcut icon

FIGURE 1.2 Icons ➤

You can easily add icons to the desktop, but the way in which you add an icon depends on the icon's purpose.

- **To add a program shortcut to the desktop**, you must first locate the program. Most often, you can simply click the Start button (located in the bottom-left corner of the desktop). Point to All Programs. Navigate the menu to display the program, but do not open it. Instead, right-click and drag the program name to the desktop. Release the mouse button. Click Create shortcuts here.
- **To add a folder to the desktop**, right-click an empty area of the desktop. Point to New and click Folder. Type a folder name and press Enter.

You can also delete and rename icons, as described below.

- **To delete an icon**, right-click the icon and click Delete. Respond affirmatively if asked whether to place the icon in the Recycle Bin. Remember that deleting a program shortcut icon does not remove, or uninstall, the program itself. You simply remove the desktop pointer (shortcut) to the program.
- **To rename an icon**, right-click the icon and click Rename. Type the new name and press Enter.

A **gadget** is a desktop item that represents such items as games or puzzles, or constantly changing data, such as a clock or a calendar. Gadgets can be selected or downloaded and opened on the desktop.

Another item that can be placed on the desktop is a desktop *gadget*. A gadget represents data that is constantly changing, or an item such as a game or puzzle. Although some gadgets are available when you install Windows 7, you can add additional gadgets from the Microsoft Windows Web site. To view the gadgets that are available within Windows, right-click an empty area of the desktop and click Gadgets. The gallery shown in Figure 1.3 displays. Double-click a gadget to place it on the desktop. Click Get more gadgets online to download others. To remove a gadget from the desktop, right-click the gadget and click Close gadget.

Gadget

Click here to get gadgets online

FIGURE 1.3 Gadgets Gallery ➤

By default, gadgets are grouped together on the right side of the desktop. By changing a few settings, you can resize gadgets, cause them to always appear on top of any open windows, adjust the opacity level, and move them. All of these options are available when you right-click a gadget on the desktop.

Explore the Taskbar

You can have several projects, papers, and other items on a desk. In fact, you can have so many things on a desk that it becomes difficult to sort through them all. Similarly, you can have several windows, or applications, open on a computer desktop at one time. Unlike a desk, however, the Windows

The Windows desktop provides a tool for keeping track of open computer projects—the taskbar.

The **taskbar** is the horizontal bar at the bottom of the desktop that enables you to move among open windows and provides access to system resources.

The **Start button**, located on the left side of the taskbar, is the place to begin when you want to open programs, get help, adjust computer settings, access system resources, or even shut down a computer.

The **Notification area**, on the right side of the taskbar, displays icons for background programs and system resources. It also provides status information in pop-up windows.

desktop provides a tool for keeping track of open computer projects—the ***taskbar***. The taskbar is a long horizontal bar located at the bottom of the desktop. The taskbar is the location of the ***Start button***, toolbars, open window buttons, and the ***Notification area***.

When you open a program or work with a file, the item will display in a window on the desktop. It is not unusual to have several windows open at one time. When that happens, the windows sometimes overlap, making it difficult to see what is underneath or to remember what you have open. The taskbar simplifies the task of keeping track of the desktop. Every open window has a corresponding icon on the taskbar. Icons often represent programs, such as Excel and Word. To move from one window to another, simply click the taskbar icon representing the window. It works much like shifting paper on a desk but is easier. Figure 1.4 shows two windows open on the desktop, with corresponding taskbar program icons. Although several windows can be open at one time, only one is active (in front of other windows).

Program icons

FIGURE 1.4 Program Icons on the Taskbar ➤

Aero Peek provides a preview of an open window without requiring you to click away from the window that you are currently working on. Place the mouse pointer over any icon that represents an open window to view its contents.

Windows 7 taskbar icons are large and unlabeled, unlike icons found in earlier Windows versions. The size and simplicity gives a clean uncluttered feel to the taskbar. Even if you have multiple files open for one icon, such as when you have several word processing documents open, you will see only one program icon. If several programs are open, you will see a taskbar icon for each open window. To get a sneak preview of any open window, even if it is obscured by another, place the mouse pointer over the program's icon on the taskbar. The resulting preview is called ***Aero Peek***. Place the mouse pointer over the thumbnail (previewed window), without clicking, to temporarily view the window in full size. When you move the mouse pointer away, the active window reappears. If you click the thumbnail (window preview) you will switch to the previewed window. See Figure 1.5 for an example of Aero Peek.

Aero Peek preview

FIGURE 1.5 Aero Peek ➤

The **Start menu** is a list of programs, folders, and utilities that displays when you click the Start button.

When you click the Start button, you will see the ***Start menu***, as shown in Figure 1.6. As its name implies, the Start menu is the place to begin when you want to open programs, get help, adjust computer settings, access system resources, or even shut down your computer. The Start menu is comprised of three areas. The *left pane* displays a short list of commonly accessed programs on your computer. When you point to All Programs, you will see a more complete list of programs. The *right pane* provides access to system folders, such as Documents, Pictures, and Music. It also enables you to adjust system settings, log off a user account, shut down the computer, and get help. The Search box, located at the bottom of the left side of the Start menu (see Figure 1.6), is where you can type keywords of an item you are looking for, such as a file or folder. You will explore the topic of searching later in this chapter.

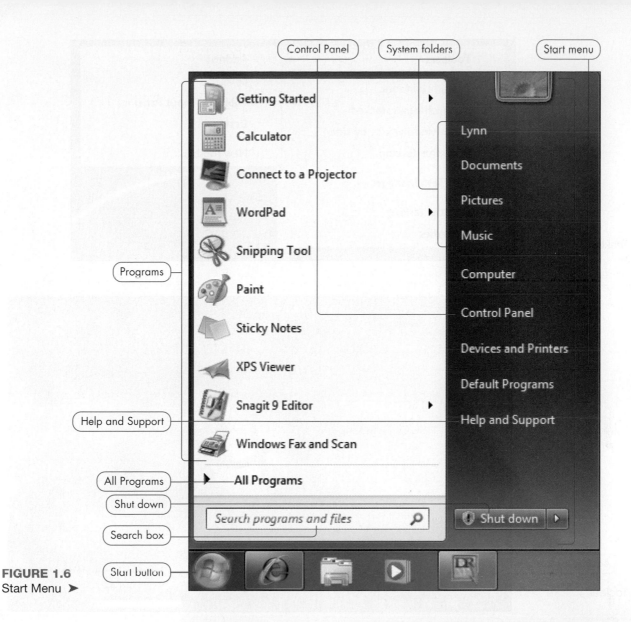

Control Panel   System folders   Start menu

Getting Started ▶

Calculator

Connect to a Projector

WordPad ▶

Snipping Tool

Programs

Paint

Sticky Notes

XPS Viewer

Snagit 9 Editor ▶

Help and Support

Windows Fax and Scan

All Programs   ▶ All Programs

Shut down

Search box   Search programs and files 🔍

Lynn

Documents

Pictures

Music

Computer

Control Panel

Devices and Printers

Default Programs

Help and Support

⏻ Shut down ▶

FIGURE 1.6
Start Menu ➤

Start button

TIP Hide the Taskbar

Although it is very helpful, the taskbar can occupy space on your work area that you need. To temporarily hide the taskbar, right-click an empty area of the taskbar. Click Properties. In the Taskbar appearance area of the Taskbar and Start Menu Properties window, click to select Auto-hide the taskbar, and then click OK. The taskbar immediately disappears. When you move the mouse pointer to the previous location of the taskbar, it will appear, but only until you move the mouse pointer away. To return the taskbar to view, reverse the process described above, clicking to deselect Auto-hide the taskbar.

A **toolbar** is an area of items that you can select, usually displayed on the taskbar or within an application.

The taskbar is a convenient place to display *toolbars*, which provide shortcuts to Web resources and enable you to quickly move to a specified address. Specifically the Links and Address toolbars are handy additions to the taskbar but are not automatically displayed. To see a list of available toolbars, right-click an empty part of the taskbar and point to Toolbars. See Figure 1.7 for an example of a toolbar list. Click any item in the list to add or remove it. If you see a checkmark beside a toolbar, the toolbar is already open on the taskbar. Figure 1.8 shows a taskbar that includes an Address toolbar.

FIGURE 1.7 Taskbar Toolbars List ➤

Address toolbar

FIGURE 1.8 Toolbar Example ➤

When you **pin** an item, it becomes a permanent part of the taskbar, accessible with a single click.

A **Jump List** is a list of actions or resources associated with an open window button or pinned item on the taskbar.

You can place, or ***pin***, icons of frequently used programs on the taskbar for quick access later. When you pin a program, the program icon becomes a permanent part of the taskbar, as shown in Figure 1.9. You can then open the program by single-clicking its icon. If the program that you want to pin is not already open, click Start, browse to the program name, right-click the name, and click Pin to Taskbar. If the program that you want to pin is already open, right-click the program icon on the taskbar to open its ***Jump List*** (see Figure 1.9). Click Pin this program to taskbar. A Jump List is a list of shortcuts to pinned items, most often simply the program name, an option to pin or unpin an item, and a close option.

Jump List

Tasks

🎵 Go to iTunes Store

🎵 Search iTunes Store

🎵 iTunes

📌 Pin this program to taskbar

❌ Close window

Currently open programs

Pinned programs

FIGURE 1.9 Pinned Programs ➤

TIP Pin Items to the Start Menu

Just as you can pin programs to the taskbar, you can pin items to the Start menu. When you pin a program to the Start menu, it becomes a permanent selection on the left side of the Start menu. A pinned program always shows on the Start menu so that you can find the program easily and open it with a single click. To pin a program, locate its name on the Start menu, right-click it, and click Pin to Start Menu. You can pin a program from the Start menu to both the Start menu and the taskbar, but you cannot pin a program from the taskbar to the Start menu.

A major purpose of the Notification area is providing important status information that appears in a pop-up window when you click the Action Center icon.

You will find the Notification area (see Figure 1.10) on the right side of the taskbar. It displays icons for programs running in the background, such as a virus scanner, and provides access to such system activities as managing wireless networks and adjusting volume. A major purpose of the Notification area is to provide important status information that appears in a pop-up window when you click the Action Center icon. Status information could include the detection of new devices, the availability of software updates, or

🚩 2 important messages

Find an antivirus program online (Important)

Windows will install updates as scheduled (Important)

Open Action Center

Pop-up window

Notification area

Action Center icon

1:35 PM
10/18/2009

FIGURE 1.10 Notification Area ➤

The **Action Center** monitors maintenance and security settings, providing alerts when necessary.

recommended maintenance and security tasks. An example of a pop-up notification is given in Figure 1.10. If the notification is of a recommended update or maintenance task, you can click the message to perform the recommended task. If you see an *Action Center* icon associated with the notification, click it to open the Action Center for additional details. You will find more information about the Action Center later in this chapter.

Customize the Desktop

Each time you turn on your computer, you see the desktop. For a little variety you can customize the desktop with a different background or color theme. You can even include a slide show of favorite photos to display when your computer is idle. Customizing the desktop can be fun and creative. Windows 7 provides a wide selection of background and color choices.

To change the desktop background, add moving images, or change the color theme, right-click an empty area of the desktop and click Personalize. Make a selection from those shown in Figure 1.11. If you choose to change the background, click Desktop Background (see Figure 1.11). Then select or confirm the picture location (see Figure 1.12). You can choose from built-in categories such as Windows Desktop Backgrounds, or you can browse for a folder containing your personal pictures. If you select Windows Desktop Backgrounds, you can select from several categories (nature, architecture, etc.). Click Window Color (see Figure 1.11) to change the color of window borders, the Start menu, and the taskbar. You can also select a *screen saver* (see Figure 1.11). A screen saver is a moving series of pictures or images that appears when your computer has been idle for a specified period of time. You might use a screen saver for privacy, so that when you are away from your desk, the display is obscured by the moving images. Figure 1.13 shows the Screen Saver Settings dialog box from which you can select a screen saver and adjust settings. Settings include how long the computer must be idle before a screen saver is displayed, as well as the option to require a log on before the screen saver disappears. Click Save Changes (see Figure 1.12) after making any of the above selections or Cancel to ignore changes. Close any open windows.

A **screen saver** is a series of moving images that appears on the desktop when a computer has been idle for a specified period of time.

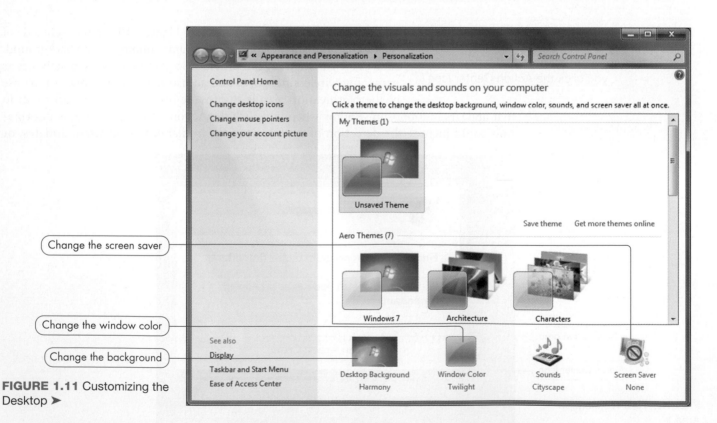

Change the screen saver

Change the window color

Change the background

FIGURE 1.11 Customizing the Desktop ➤

Select a picture location

Browse for your own pictures

FIGURE 1.12 Selecting a Picture Location ➤

Select a screen saver

Adjust the wait time

Require logon to remove screen saver from view

FIGURE 1.13 Screen Saver Settings ➤

Managing Windows

When you open a program, file, or folder, it opens in a window. You can have many windows open at the same time. If that is the case, the windows will begin to overlap and obscure each other. Although Windows 7 can work with multiple open windows within its multitasking environment, you might find it difficult to manage the windows and projects effectively. Using the taskbar, you can move among open windows with ease, but you will also need to know how to move, resize, and close windows. Windows 7 makes it easy to automatically arrange windows, even snapping them quickly to the desktop borders.

> Using the taskbar, you can move among open windows with ease, but you will also need to know how to move, resize, and close windows.

Identify Window Components

All windows share common elements including a title bar and control buttons. Although each window's contents vary, those common elements make it easy for you to manage windows appropriately so that you make the best use of your time and computer resources.

> The **title bar** is the long bar at the top of each open window, containing the file or folder name and the program name.

The *title bar* is the long bar at the top of each window, as shown in Figure 1.14. The title bar always displays the name of the file and the program (or the name of the folder if you are viewing folder contents). Control buttons are found on the right side of the title bar. Those control buttons enable you to minimize, maximize (or restore down), and close any open window.

FIGURE 1.14 Windows Components ➤

When you minimize a window, you hide it from view but do not close it. That means that the window becomes a taskbar icon that you can click to return the window to its original size. See the Minimize button in Figure 1.14.

The middle control button shares two functions depending on the current size of the window. One is to maximize a window and one is to restore down to a smaller size. If a window is less than full size, click the middle button to maximize the window so that it occupies the entire desktop. The Maximize button looks like a small box. The Restore Down button appears as two overlapped boxes. The middle button in Figure 1.14 is the Maximize button. You can also maximize or restore down a window by double-clicking the title bar of the open window.

> ### TIP Maximize a Window and Expand a Window Vertically
>
> You can quickly maximize a window by dragging the title bar to the top of the desktop. The window immediately becomes full sized. To expand a window vertically without changing the window's width, drag a top or bottom border to the corresponding top or bottom edge of the desktop. When you place the mouse pointer on a border of a window, the pointer assumes the shape of a double-headed arrow. Only then should you drag the window to the top or bottom edge of the desktop. Release the mouse button to expand the window vertically.

The button on the far right side of the title bar is used to close a window. It is always displayed as an X. When you close a window, you remove the file or program from memory. If you have not saved a file that you are closing, Windows 7 will prompt you to save it before closing.

Work with Windows

It is sometimes necessary to move or resize a window. If multiple windows are open, you will need to know how to switch between windows and how to rearrange them. Windows 7 provides easy ways to select among windows, including the Aero Flip 3D experience.

If a window is obscuring something that you need to see, you can move or resize the window to reveal what is behind. You can only move or resize a window that is not maximized. To move a window, drag the title bar. To resize a window, place the mouse pointer on a border of the window. The pointer will become a double-headed arrow. Drag to make the window larger or smaller. If the pointer is on a corner of the window, forming a diagonal double-headed arrow, you can resize two adjacent sides of the window at once by dragging.

You can also use the keyboard to switch to another window. To cycle through all open windows, stopping at any one, hold down Alt on the keyboard and repeatedly press Tab. Release Alt when you see the window that you want to display. *Aero Flip 3D* arranges all open windows in a three-dimensional stack that you can quickly flip through. Figure 1.15 shows a sample Aero Flip 3D stack. Hold down the Windows logo key and press Tab to cycle through open windows. Release the Windows logo key to stop on any window. You can also click any window in the stack to display it.

Given what you know about resizing and moving windows, you can rearrange windows to suit your purposes. You can minimize or close those that are not necessary, returning to them later. Even so, you might prefer to let Windows 7 arrange your windows automatically. Windows 7 can arrange windows in a cascading fashion, vertically stacked, or side by side. If multiple windows are open on the desktop, right-click an empty part of the taskbar. Click Cascade windows, Show windows stacked, or Show windows side by side.

If a window is obscuring something that you need to see, you can move or resize the window to reveal what is behind.

Aero Flip 3D is a feature that shows windows in a rotating 3D stack so that you can select a window.

FIGURE 1.15 Aero Flip 3D Stack ➤

Snap arranges windows automatically along the left and right sides of the desktop.

Snap is a Windows 7 feature that will automatically place a window on the side of the desktop, resulting in a well-ordered arrangement of windows. Simply drag the title bar of a window to the left or right side of the desktop until an outline of the window appears. Release the mouse button. Do the same with another window.

Earlier in this section, you learned that Aero Peek is a Windows 7 feature that enables you to preview open windows, switching to them if you like. Another function of Aero Peek is to provide a quick way to show the desktop without actually removing or minimizing windows. Simply point to the Show desktop button, shown in Figure 1.16. A quick way to show the desktop without actually removing or minimizing windows is to point to the Show desktop button, shown in Figure 1.16. If you simply want to see the desktop temporarily, do not click the Show desktop button—just point to it; the desktop displays. When you move away from the button, windows reappear as they were previously. If you do want to minimize all open windows, click the Show desktop button. Click the button again to return the windows to view (or click the corresponding icons on the taskbar).

A **dialog box** is a special window that opens when you are accomplishing a specific task and when your confirmation or interaction is required.

The preceding discussion of windows focused on those windows that represent programs, files, or folders. Those could be considered standard windows. A *dialog box* is a special window that displays when an operation requires confirmation or additional information. Figure 1.17

Show desktop button

FIGURE 1.16 Showing the Desktop ➤

shows a typical dialog box. By responding to areas of the dialog box, you can indicate how you want an operation to occur and how the program should behave. In effect, a dialog box asks for interaction with you before completing a procedure. You cannot minimize or maximize a dialog box, but you can move it. You can close it or make selections, get help by clicking the ? button (if present), and click OK (or Cancel if you want to ignore any selections you might have made). Print dialog box selections are shown in Figure 1.17 and summarized below.

- *Option buttons* indicate mutually exclusive choices, one of which *must* be chosen, such as the page range. In this example, you can print all pages, the selection (if it is available), the current page, or a specific set of pages (such as pages 1–4), but you must choose *one and only one* option. When you select an option, any previously selected option is deselected.
- A *text box*, such as the one shown beside the *Pages* option in Figure 1.17, enables you to enter specific information. In this case, you could type 1–5 in the text box if you wanted only the first five pages to print.
- A *spin arrow* is a common component of a dialog box, providing a quick method of increasing or decreasing a setting. For example, clicking the spin arrow (or spinner) beside *Number of copies* enables you to increase or decrease the number of copies of the document to print.
- *Check boxes* are used instead of option buttons if the choices are not mutually exclusive. You can select or clear options by clicking the appropriate check box, which toggles the operation on and off. In Figure 1.17, you can select either or both options of printing to a file or using manual duplex. Unlike an option button, check boxes enable you to make several selections at the same time.
- A *list box* displays some or all of the available choices, any of which can be selected by clicking the list item. For example, you can choose from several print options, including printing all pages, or only odd or even pages.
- All dialog boxes also contain one or more *command buttons* that provide options to either accept or cancel your selections. OK, for example, initiates the printing process shown in Figure 1.17. Cancel does just the opposite and ignores (cancels) any changes made to the settings, closing the dialog box.

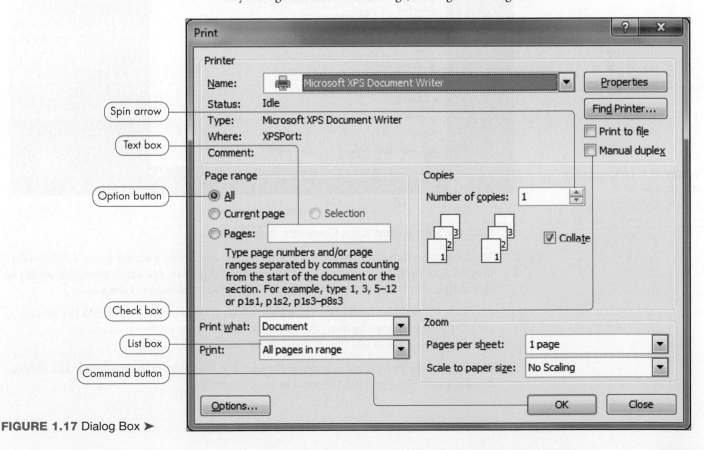

FIGURE 1.17 Dialog Box ➤

1 Windows 7 Fundamentals

Tomorrow, you will meet with the Cedar Cove class to present an introduction to Windows 7. Only one computer is present in the classroom, and it is connected to a projector. You plan to demonstrate a few basics of working with the operating system including managing windows, adding gadgets, and working with the taskbar and Start menu. Above all, you want to keep it simple so that you encourage class enthusiasm. You have prepared a script that you plan to follow and you will practice it in the steps that follow.

Skills covered: Open, Resize, Move, and Close a Window • Manage Multiple Windows, Arrange Windows Automatically, Arrange Windows Using *Snap* • Add and Remove Gadgets, Add Shortcuts to the Desktop, Identify Icons • Explore the Start Menu, Pin Items to the Start Menu, Customize the Taskbar, Pin Items to the Taskbar • Change the Desktop Background and Screen Saver

---

STEP 1 ▶ **OPEN, RESIZE, MOVE, AND CLOSE A WINDOW**

Before the students can work with software, they must learn to work with windows. Specifically, they must understand that software and other system settings will display in a window and they must become comfortable opening, closing, resizing, and moving windows. You will stress the importance of the desktop as the location of all windows. Refer to Figure 1.18 as you complete Step 1.

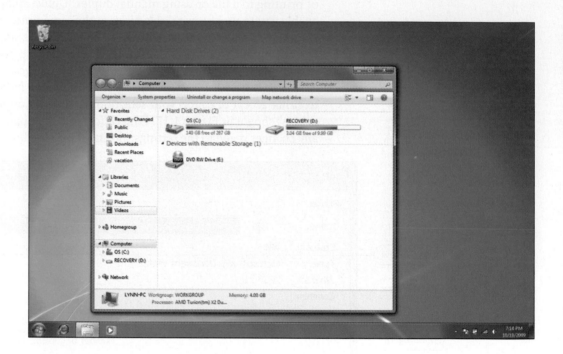

FIGURE 1.18 Computer Window ▶

a. Click the **Start button**. Click **Computer** in the right pane.

   You have opened the Computer window, giving a summary of your computer's disk configuration. The window contents are not important at this time; you are interested in it only as an example of a window that you can use to demonstrate Windows basics.

b. Compare the window to that shown in Figure 1.18. If the window already fills the desktop, click the **Restore Down button** (the middle button) to restore the window to a smaller size. If it is less than full size, leave it as is.

c. Place the mouse pointer on a corner of the window. The pointer should appear as a double-headed arrow. Drag to make the window slightly smaller.

    d. Place the mouse pointer on the title bar of the window. Drag to move it to another location on the desktop.

    e. Place the mouse pointer on the top border of the window. Drag to make the window slightly larger.

    f. Click the **Close button** (shown as an X) in the top-right corner of the window to close it.

MANAGE MULTIPLE WINDOWS, ARRANGE WINDOWS AUTOMATICALLY, ARRANGE WINDOWS USING *SNAP*

Because there will be occasions when several windows are open simultaneously, students must learn to arrange them. You will show them various ways that Windows 7 can help arrange open windows. Refer to Figure 1.19 as you complete Step 2.

FIGURE 1.19 Working with Two Windows ➤

    a. Click the **Start button**. Click **Documents** in the right pane. Click the **Start button**. Click **Pictures** in the right pane.

> **TROUBLESHOOTING:** If the two windows open so that one is directly on top of the other, obscuring the lower window, drag the title bar of the topmost window to move the window so that you can see both.

You have opened two windows—Pictures and Documents. You are going to show students various ways to arrange the open windows. The two open windows are most likely overlapped, but if yours are not, that's OK. Just make sure both windows are open.

    b. Right-click an empty part of the taskbar. Click **Show windows stacked**. Compare your desktop with Figure 1.19.

The contents of the windows will vary, but the arrangement should be similar.

> **TROUBLESHOOTING:** If your desktop displays more than two stacked windows, you have more than two windows open. You should make sure that only the Pictures and Documents windows are open. Close any others by right-clicking the corresponding taskbar icon and clicking Close window.

c. Right-click an empty part of the taskbar. Click **Show windows side by side**.

The two windows should line up vertically.

d. Click the **Close button** in both windows to close them.

e. Click the **Start button**. Click **Computer**. Click the **Start button**. Click **Control Panel**.

> **TROUBLESHOOTING:** If either window opens at full size (maximized), click the Restore Down button (middle button) at the top-right side of the title bar to make the window smaller.

You have opened two windows—Computer and Control Panel. You will use the Windows Snap feature to position each window on a side of the desktop.

f. Drag the title bar of one of the windows to one side of the desktop. Keep dragging the window, even beyond the desktop edge, until a window outline appears. Release the mouse button. Do the same for the other window, snapping it to the opposite side of the desktop.

Both windows should be evenly spaced, each occupying half of the desktop.

g. Close both windows. (Click the **Close button** in the top-right corner of each.)

STEP 3 **ADD AND REMOVE GADGETS, ADD SHORTCUTS TO THE DESKTOP, IDENTIFY ICONS**

Not only do you want students to understand the basics of managing windows, but you know that they will also enjoy customizing the desktop. They need to know how to identify icons. They will also benefit from creating program shortcuts and adding gadgets for constantly changing items like the weather or a clock. Refer to Figure 1.20 as you complete Step 3.

FIGURE 1.20 Taskbar and Start Menu Properties ➤

a. Note any icons on the desktop that have an arrow in the bottom-left corner. They represent programs or system resources. Double-click an icon to open the item window. Close the window by clicking the **Close button** in the top-right corner.

b. Right-click an empty area of the taskbar. Click **Properties**. Click the **Auto-hide the taskbar check box** (unless a checkmark already appears), as shown in Figure 1.20. Click **OK**.

The taskbar will only show if you place the mouse pointer near where it should show. When you move the mouse pointer away, the taskbar disappears. You will explain to students that they can use the Taskbar and Start Menu Properties dialog box to customize the appearance and behavior of the taskbar.

c. Move the mouse pointer to the location of the taskbar. Right-click an empty area of the taskbar. Click **Properties**. Click to deselect the **Auto-hide the taskbar check box**. Click **OK**.

d. Click the **Start button**. Point to **All Programs**. Click **Accessories**. Right-click and drag Paint to the desktop. Release the mouse button. Click **Create shortcuts here**.

> **TROUBLESHOOTING:** To create a shortcut on the desktop, you must be able to see the desktop. Therefore, all windows should be closed before you drag the program from the Start menu. Also, be sure to use the right mouse button to drag, not the left.

You have placed a program shortcut on the desktop so that you can easily find it later. The arrow in the lower-left corner of the Paint icon indicates that it is a shortcut.

e. Right-click the **Paint shortcut icon** on the desktop. Click **Delete**. Click **Yes** to confirm the deletion.

Because you want to leave the classroom's computer just as you found it, you will delete the Paint shortcut from the desktop.

f. Right-click an empty area of the desktop. Click **Gadgets**. Double-click **Clock**. The Clock gadget appears on the right side of the desktop. Double-click **Weather** to add a Weather gadget.

> **TROUBLESHOOTING:** You must be connected to the Internet for the Weather gadget to display. If you are not connected, you will see a note to that effect where the gadget would have been placed.

g. Right-click the **Clock gadget**, and then click **Close gadget**. Do the same for the Weather gadget.

Because you want to leave the classroom's computer as you found it, you will close the Clock and Weather gadgets.

h. Click the **Close button** to close the Gadgets window.

STEP 4 **EXPLORE THE START MENU, PIN ITEMS TO THE START MENU, CUSTOMIZE THE TASKBAR, PIN ITEMS TO THE TASKBAR**

Upon completing the fifth grade, the students with whom you are working will advance to middle school. There, they will be expected to be comfortable with Windows 7. You will be with them for only a couple of class sessions, so you want to use your time to make sure they are introduced to the Start menu, understand the purpose of icons, and are confident with customizing the taskbar. With just a little practice, they will be well-prepared for middle school computer work. Refer to Figure 1.21 as you complete Step 4.

FIGURE 1.21 Pin a Program to Start Menu ➤

a. Click the **Start button**. Note the programs that display on the left side of the menu. Take a look at the right side of the menu. Click **Pictures**. Close the window that represents the Pictures folder.

You will explain to students that the left side of the Start menu contains commonly accessed programs or those that have been pinned to the Start menu. The right side includes system folders, such as Pictures, Documents, and Music; the Control Panel; and Help and Support. The Search box, located at the bottom-left side of the Start menu, enables searches based on keywords.

b. Click the **Start button**. Point to **All Programs**. Click **Accessories**. Scroll, if necessary, to show Paint. Right-click **Paint**. Click **Pin to Start Menu**, as shown in Figure 1.21. Click outside the Start menu to remove it from view.

The example you will give students is that in some classes they will have a recurring need to open the Paint program. You want them to practice pinning the program to the Start menu.

c. Click the **Start button**. Check to make sure Paint appears on the left side of the menu. Click **Paint** to open it. Click the **Close button** to close the program.

> **TROUBLESHOOTING:** If you have recently opened Paint files, you might find it necessary to click Paint twice to open the program.

d. Click the **Start button**. Note that because Paint is a pinned program, it appears above the line on the left side of the Start menu. Right-click **Paint**. Click **Unpin from Start Menu**. Click outside the Start menu to remove it from view.

Because you want to leave the classroom's computer as you found it, you will unpin the Paint program from the Start menu.

e. Click the **Start button**. Point to **All Programs**. Click **Accessories**. Point to **WordPad** and right click. Click **Pin to Taskbar**. Click outside the Start menu to remove the menu from view.

Students will need to know that if they open a program often, it is easy to pin it to the taskbar for quick access. That way, they won't have to find it on the Start menu or double-click an icon on the desktop. Instead, they can single-click the icon on the taskbar.

f. Click the **WordPad icon** on the taskbar. If you are not sure which icon is WordPad, place the mouse pointer over any icon and see the program name. Then locate WordPad. After WordPad opens, close it. Right-click the **WordPad icon** on the taskbar, and then click **Unpin this program from taskbar**.

After demonstrating the use of a pinned icon (by opening the associated program), you remove the pinned icon from the taskbar.

STEP 5 | **CHANGE THE DESKTOP BACKGROUND AND SCREEN SAVER**

To end the class session on a creative note, you want the students to have fun changing the desktop background and experimenting with screen savers. Refer to Figures 1.22 and 1.23 as you complete Step 5.

> **TROUBLESHOOTING:** If you are working in a campus lab, you might not be able to change the desktop background or screen saver. In that case, you cannot complete this step of the Hands-On Exercise.

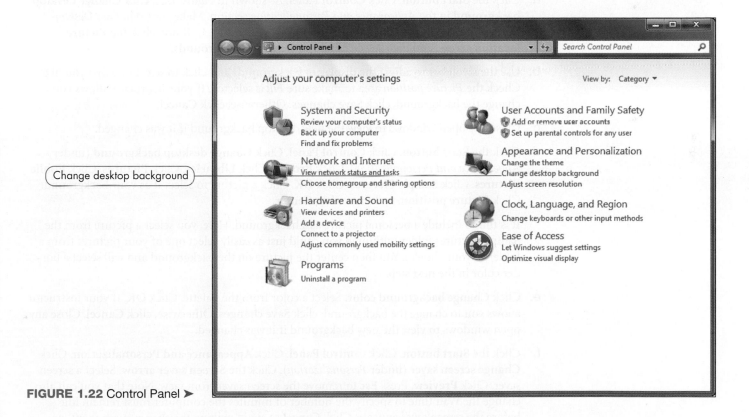

FIGURE 1.22 Control Panel ➤

Select Picture location

Scroll bar

Select Picture position

FIGURE 1.23 Selecting a background ➤

a. Click the **Start button**. Click **Control Panel**. As shown in Figure 1.22, click **Change desktop background** in the *Appearance and Personalization* section. Make sure *Windows Desktop Backgrounds* appears in the Picture location (see Figure 1.23). If not, click the **Picture location arrow**, and then select **Windows Desktop Backgrounds**.

b. Use the scroll bar to adjust the display of backgrounds and click to select one that you like. Check the *Picture position* area to make sure *Fill* is selected. If your instructor allows you to change the background, click **Save changes**. Otherwise, click **Cancel**.

c. Close any open windows to view the new desktop background if it was changed.

d. Click the **Start button**. Click **Control Panel**. Click **Change desktop background** (under *Appearance and Personalization*). Click **Browse**. Click **Libraries**. Click **Pictures**. Click **Public Pictures**. Click **Sample Pictures**. Click **OK**. Click a picture to select it as your background. Click **Picture position**, and then select **Center**.

It is fun to include a personal picture as a background. Here, you select a picture from the Sample Pictures folder (although you could just as easily select one of your pictures from a folder of your choice). You then center the picture on the background and will select a border color in the next step.

e. Click **Change background color**. Select a color from the palette. Click **OK**. If your instructor allows you to change the background, click **Save changes**. Otherwise, click **Cancel**. Close any open windows to view the new background if it was changed.

f. Click the **Start button**. Click **Control Panel**. Click **Appearance and Personalization**. Click **Change screen saver** (under *Personalization*). Click the **Screen saver arrow**. Select a screen saver. Click **Preview**. Press **Esc** to remove the screen saver from view. Note that you can also change the Wait time to specify the number of minutes the computer must remain idle before the screen saver appears. Click **Cancel** to avoid making the change permanent, or click **OK** if you are allowed to change the screen saver. Close any open windows.

Unless you saved the screen saver change and unless you wait the required wait time for the screen saver to appear, you will see no changes.

Windows Programs and Security Features

Windows 7 is a full-featured operating system, including built-in programs for such tasks as word processing, creating graphics, and system security. With only a little effort, you can learn to use those programs. Regardless of how many programs you install on your computer system, you can take comfort in knowing that you will always have access to software supporting basic tasks and that your computer is protected against spyware and hacking. In this section, you will learn to work with Windows 7 accessory and security programs.

> You can take comfort in knowing that you will always have access to software supporting basic tasks and that your computer is protected against spyware and hacking.

Identifying Windows Accessories

You use a computer for many purposes, but a primary reason to enjoy a computer is to run programs. A program is software that accomplishes a specific task. You use a word processing program to prepare documents, an e-mail program to compose and send e-mail, and a database program to maintain records. You can customize a computer by installing programs of your choice. Windows 7 provides a few programs for basic tasks, as well. Those programs include WordPad, Notepad, Paint, Snipping Tool, and Calculator.

Use Notepad and WordPad

Notepad is a text editing program built in to Windows 7.

WordPad is a basic word processing program built in to Windows 7.

Notepad and *WordPad* are programs that enable you to create and print documents. Notepad is a basic text editing program used primarily to edit text files, files that are identified with a .txt extension. Programmers sometimes use Notepad to prepare basic program statements. Notepad is not at all concerned with style and does not include the features of typical word processing software such as document formatting and character design.

WordPad, on the other hand, is a basic word processing program, and includes the capability of formatting text and inserting graphics. Not as full-featured as Microsoft Word, WordPad is still a handy alternative when you do not have access to Word or when you want to quickly create a simple document. WordPad saves documents in a Microsoft Word format, so you can open WordPad files in Word.

Figure 1.24 shows both WordPad and Notepad windows. Note the bare-bones appearance of Notepad when compared with WordPad. Access either program by clicking the Start button. Point to All Programs. Click Accessories. Make a program selection.

Notepad

WordPad

FIGURE 1.24 WordPad and Notepad ➤

Use Paint

Paint is a Windows 7 program that enables you to create drawings and to open digital pictures. You will recall that you opened Paint in Hands-On Exercise 1. Figure 1.25 shows the Paint interface. Note the Ribbon at the top of the Paint window that includes such items as the Pencil tool, Brushes, Colors, and Shapes. Open Paint by clicking the Start button, All Programs, Accessories, and Paint. The palette in the center of the Paint window acts as an easel on which you can draw.

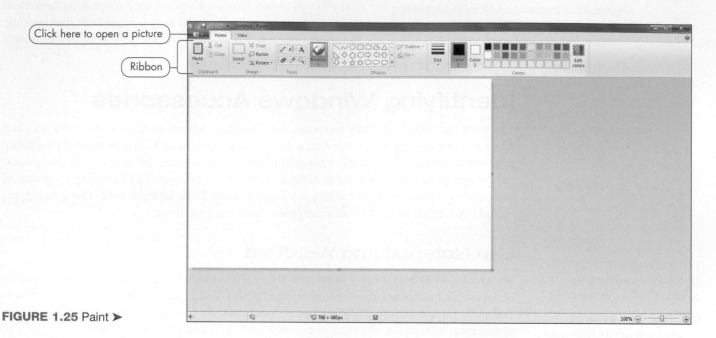

Click here to open a picture

Ribbon

FIGURE 1.25 Paint ➤

When you open Paint, you can create and save a colorful drawing, including text, shapes, and background color. You can also open a digital photo and add comments, shapes, or drawings. If you want to work with an existing picture, open the photo by clicking the button in the top-left corner of the Paint window (see Figure 1.25). Click Open, browse to the location of the picture, and double-click the picture. Then use Paint tools to add to the picture, saving it when done.

Use the Calculator

Just as you might use a handheld calculator, you can take advantage of the Windows 7 *Calculator* accessory. From simple addition, subtraction, multiplication, and division to advanced scientific, programming, and statistical functions, Calculator is a very handy tool to be aware of. Open Calculator by clicking the Start button, All Programs, Accessories, and Calculator. Figure 1.26 shows all four Calculator versions. Change from one version to another by clicking View and making a selection.

When using Calculator, you can either type numeric entries and operators (+, −, *, and /) or you can click corresponding keys on the calculator. You can also use the numeric keypad, usually found to the right of the keyboard on a desktop computer. Laptops do not typically have a numeric keypad but often include a function key that you can press to use alternate keys as a numeric keypad.

Scientific view

Standard view

Statistics view

Programmer view

FIGURE 1.26 Calculator
Views ➤

Use the Snipping Tool

The **Snipping Tool** is a Windows
7 accessory that enables you to
capture and save a screen display.

A **snip** is a screen display that
you have captured with the
Snipping Tool.

The *Snipping Tool* is a Windows 7 accessory program that enables you to capture, or *snip*, a
screen display so that you can save, annotate, or share it. On occasion, you might need to
capture an image of the screen for use in a report or to document an error for later troubleshooting. Using the Snipping Tool (see Figure 1.27), you can capture screen elements in a
rectangular, free-form, window, or full-screen fashion. Then you can draw on or annotate
the screen captures, save them, or send them to others.

FIGURE 1.27 Snipping Tool ➤

Open the Snipping Tool by clicking the Start button, All Programs, Accessories, and
Snipping Tool. Click the New arrow and select a snip type (rectangular, free-form, etc.). If
you select a window snip type, you will click the window to capture. If you select rectangular
or free-form, you must drag to identify the area to capture. Of course, it is not necessary to
specify an area when you select full-screen capture.

After you capture a snip, it is displayed in the mark-up window, where you can write or draw on it. The screen capture is also copied to the Clipboard, which is a temporary holding area in your computer's memory. You can then paste the screen capture in a word processing document when the document is displayed by clicking Paste on the word processor's toolbar. The Clipboard is temporary storage only. Because the Clipboard's contents are lost when your computer is powered down, you should immediately paste a copied screen image if it is your intention to include the screen capture in a document or other application. Otherwise, you can save a screen capture by clicking Save Snip and indicating a location and file name for the snip.

Working with Security Settings and Software

So that you can enjoy your computer for a long time, you will want to protect it from security threats such as viruses, spyware, and hacking. Windows 7 monitors your security status,

> Windows 7 monitors your security status, providing recommendations for security settings and software updates as needed.

providing recommendations for security settings and software updates as needed. Although Windows 7 provides a firewall and antispyware software, you should make sure your computer is also protected against viruses. Such protection requires that you install antivirus software that is not included with Windows 7. Although you are not protected against viruses automatically,

Windows Defender is a program that identifies and removes spyware.

Spyware is software that gathers information through a user's Internet connection, usually for advertising purposes. Spyware is most often installed without a user's permission.

A **firewall** is software or hardware that protects a computer or network from unauthorized access.

Windows 7 does have security features. *Windows Defender* is antispyware software included with Windows 7. It identifies and removes *spyware*, which is software that is usually downloaded without your awareness, collecting personal information from your computer. Windows 7 also includes a *firewall* to protect against unauthorized access (hacking).

Understand the Action Center

Windows 7 monitors your system for various maintenance and security settings, recommending action through the Action Center when necessary. Open the Action Center by clicking the Start button, Control Panel, System and Security, and then Action Center. In

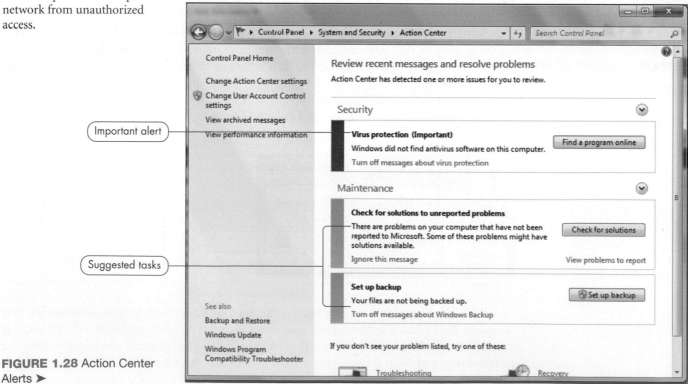

FIGURE 1.28 Action Center Alerts ➤

Figure 1.28, the Action Center gives several messages in order of severity. Red flags are for potentially serious or important alerts that should be addressed soon. Yellow items are suggested tasks, usually maintenance such as backing up files. For a quick summary of Action Center items, you can click the Action Center icon in the Notification area. Click a link on the summary list to explore a recommended action. When the status of a monitored item changes, perhaps when antivirus software becomes out of date, Action Center will display a message in a balloon (pop-up) on the Notification area (see Figure 1.29).

Recommended actions

Action Center icon

FIGURE 1.29 Notification Area Alert ➤

Use Windows Defender

You probably enjoy accessing Web sites and downloading programs. Although such activity is a great way to have fun, it carries a serious risk—downloading spyware along with the program. Actually, spyware can be installed on your computer whenever you connect to the Internet, regardless of whether you download anything. Spyware is usually installed without your knowledge. It can do anything from keeping track of Web sites you visit (for marketing purposes) to changing browser settings to recording keystrokes. Obviously, spyware is unwelcome and a potential security risk.

Windows Defender is antispyware software that is included with Windows 7. Windows Defender can be set to run in real time, which means that it is always on guard against spyware, alerting you when spyware attempts to install itself or change your computer settings. You can also schedule routine scans so that Windows Defender checks your system for malicious software. Open Windows Defender by clicking the Start button, typing Windows Defender in the Search box, and pressing Enter (or clicking the corresponding link in the Results list). Figure 1.30 shows the Windows Defender program window.

Customize User Account Control

User Account Control (UAC) is a Windows feature that asks for your permission before enabling a program to make a change to your system settings. Although such information is sometimes helpful, you might prefer to be notified only when substantial changes are attempted; that way, you are not interrupted quite as often. Windows Vista, the previous version of Windows, was noted for what some users considered excessive UAC prompts.

If you have only one user account on your computer, it is an administrator-level account. Most likely, you are the administrator, which means that only you can respond to UAC messages. Other user accounts are considered standard accounts, with varying levels of permissions that you can choose to grant.

User Account Control (UAC) is a Windows feature that asks for your permission before enabling any changes to your computer settings.

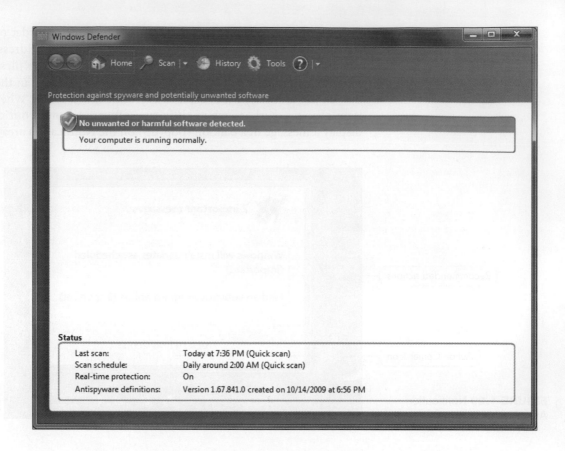

FIGURE 1.30 Windows
Defender ➤

You might want to be informed of any changes that occur, even those that you initiate, that change your Windows settings. Or perhaps you prefer to know of only those changes attempted by programs. In either case, you can modify the level of UAC through the Action Center. Click the Start button, Control Panel, System and Security, and then Action Center. Click Change User Account Control settings. Adjust the bar in the dialog box shown in Figure 1.31.

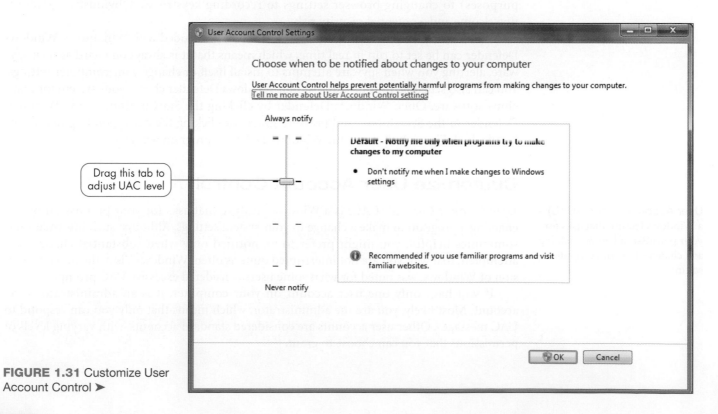

FIGURE 1.31 Customize User
Account Control ➤

CHAPTER 1 • Getting Started with Windows 7

Access Windows Update

As you are probably well aware, there is no perfect product. Windows 7 is no exception. Even long after the operating system is produced, Microsoft will undoubtedly identify ways to enhance its security or fix problems that occur. You do not need to download or purchase an updated operating system each time changes are necessary; instead, you can simply make sure that your computer is set to automatically download any updates (fixes). Such modifications to the operating system are called *Windows Updates*.

Microsoft strongly recommends that you configure your computer to automatically download and install any updates. That way, you do not have to remember to check for updates or manually download them. To schedule automatic updates, click the Start button, All Programs, and then Windows Update. Click Change settings. As shown in Figure 1.32, you can click to select the level of updates. You can have Windows both download and install updates automatically (strongly recommended), only download but let you install them, or never check for updates (certainly not recommended!). You can also schedule a time for updates to occur.

A **Windows Update** is an addition to the operating system that prevents or corrects problems, including security concerns.

Select the level of update

FIGURE 1.32 Windows Update ➤

Even between scheduled downloads, you can have your computer check for updates. Click the Start button, All Programs, Windows Update, and then Check for updates. If you want to check for updates for other Microsoft products, such as Microsoft Office, open Windows Update, and click Change settings. Select Give me updates for Microsoft products and check for new optional Microsoft software when I update Windows.

Use Windows Firewall

When you work with the Internet, the possibility that a self-replicating virus or another user could disable your computer or view its contents always exists. To keep that from occurring, it is imperative that you use firewall software. Windows 7 includes firewall software that is active when the operating system is installed. It remains on guard whenever your computer is on, protecting against both unauthorized incoming traffic and outgoing. That means that other people, computers, or programs are not allowed to communicate with your computer unless you give permission. Also, programs on your system are not allowed to communicate online unless you approve them.

Periodically, you might want to check to make sure your firewall has not been turned off accidentally. Click the Start button, Control Panel, System and Security, and then Check firewall status (under Windows Firewall). From the dialog box (see Figure 1.33), you can turn the firewall on or off. You can also adjust other firewall settings.

FIGURE 1.33 Windows Firewall ➤

Click here to turn the firewall on or off

TIP Set Up Parental Controls

If children in your household have user accounts on your computer, you can set up parental controls to limit the hours they can use the computer, the types of games they can play, and the programs they can run. User accounts that you limit must be standard accounts. You cannot apply parental controls to a guest account, which is an account type reserved for people who use your computer on a temporary basis. If you plan to use parental controls, it is a good idea to turn off the guest account (open the Control Panel, click Add or remove user accounts, click Guest, click Turn off the guest account). Open the Control Panel to create user accounts and assign standard privileges. To assign parental controls, open the Control Panel and click Set up parental controls for any user (under User Accounts and Family Safety). After selecting the user account to limit, apply any parental controls.

2 Windows Programs and Security Features

Windows is a gateway to using application software. You know that the fifth-grade students are most interested in the "fun" things that can be done with software. You want to excite them about having fun with a computer but you also want them to understand that along with the fun comes some concern about security and privacy. In this section of your demonstration, you will encourage them to explore software and to understand how Windows can help address security concerns.

Skills covered: Create a WordPad Document, Use Calculator • Use the Action Center to Check Security and Privacy Settings • Use the Snipping Tool

STEP 1 ▶ CREATE A WORDPAD DOCUMENT, USE CALCULATOR

Because all computers are configured with different software, your demonstration to the class will focus on only those programs (software) that are built in to Windows (those that students are most likely to find on any computer). Specifically, you will use WordPad and Calculator for your brief discussion. Refer to Figure 1.34 as you complete Step 1.

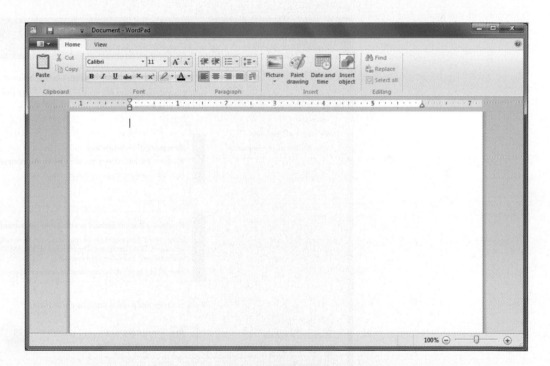

FIGURE 1.34 WordPad ➤

a. Click the **Start button**. Point to **All Programs**. Click **Accessories**. Click **WordPad**. The WordPad window opens, as shown in Figure 1.34.

   WordPad is a word processing program that is installed along with Windows 7 (and earlier Windows versions).

b. Be sure the insertion point is located in the WordPad window. Type your first and last names. Press **Enter**. Type your street address. Press **Enter**. Type your city, state, and zip.

> **TROUBLESHOOTING:** Before typing your name, you should see a blinking black bar (insertion point) in the white WordPad document area. If you do not, click in the document area to position the insertion point.

c. Close the WordPad document. Click **Don't Save** when prompted to save your changes.

Having demonstrated the use of a word processor, you will close the document without saving it.

d. Click the **Start button**. Point to **All Programs**. Click **Accessories**. Click **Calculator**. Click **View**. If you do not see a bullet beside *Standard*, click **Standard**. If you do see a bullet beside *Standard*, press **Esc** (on the keyboard).

e. Click the corresponding keys on the calculator to complete the following formula: **87+98+100/3**. Click the = sign when you have typed the formula.

You use the calculator to show how a student might determine his average, assuming he has taken three exams (weighted equally) with scores of 87, 98, and 100. The result should be 95.

f. Close the Calculator.

<hr>

STEP 2 ▶ USE THE ACTION CENTER TO CHECK SECURITY AND PRIVACY SETTINGS

The Action Center will occasionally display messages regarding security and privacy settings. You want the Cedar Cove students to be aware of how important those messages are, so you will show them how to use the Action Center. Refer to Figure 1.35 as you complete Step 2.

> **TROUBLESHOOTING:** If you are working in a campus lab, you might not have access to the Action Center or Windows Update. In that case, you should proceed to Step 3 of this Hands-On Exercise.

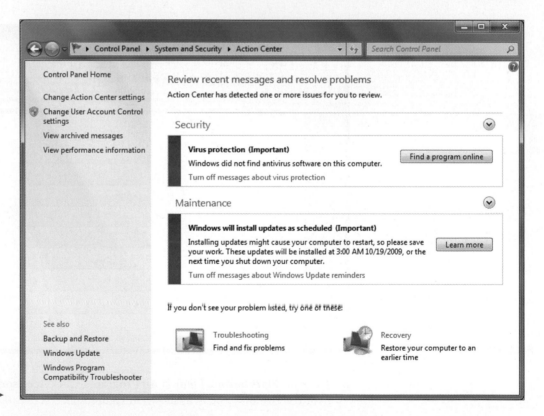

FIGURE 1.35 Action Center ➤

a. Click the **Start button**. Click **Control Panel**. Click **System and Security**. Click **Action Center**.

Although any alerts displayed on your computer may vary from those shown in Figure 1.35, the general appearance should be similar.

b. Click **Change Action Center settings**. Take a look at the items monitored by the Action Center. Note that you can select or deselect any of them. Click **Cancel**. Close the Action Center.

c. Click the **Start button**. Point to **All Programs**. Scroll through the list of programs if necessary and click **Windows Update**. Click **Change settings**. Is your system scheduled for a routine check for or installation of updates? Click **Back** (arrow pointing left at the top-left corner of the window).

d. Click **View update history**. You should see a summary of recent updates and their level of importance. Click **OK**. Close any open windows.

USE THE SNIPPING TOOL

As students progress and are required to use a computer in many facets of their education, they might find occasion to include screen captures in reports or presentations. Windows 7 includes a Snipping Tool that enables you to select any part of the screen and save it as a picture file. You plan to present the Snipping Tool to the Cedar Cove class. Refer to Figures 1.36 and 1.37 as you complete Step 3.

FIGURE 1.36 Snipping Tool ➤

FIGURE 1.37 Saving a Snip ➤

a. Click the **Start button**. Click **Computer**. If the Computer window opens in full size (maximized), click the **Restore Down button** to reduce the window size.

Assume that as part of a report, students are to insert a picture of the Computer window. After opening the Computer window, you will illustrate the use of the Snipping Tool to capture the screen in a picture file.

b. Click the **Start button**. Point to **All Programs**. Click **Accessories**. Click **Snipping Tool**. The Snipping Tool displays as shown in Figure 1.36. Click the **New arrow**. Click **Window Snip**. Click in the Computer window to select it.

You have selected a window as a screen capture.

c. Click the **Save Snip icon** in the Snipping Tool window (see Figure 1.37). Scroll up in the left pane of the Save As dialog box, if necessary, and then click **Favorites**. Click **Desktop** (in the left pane, not the right). Click in the **File name box** (where you most likely see the word *Capture*). Drag to select the word *Capture* (if it is not already selected). Type **Computer window** (to change the file name). Click **Save**.

You have saved the picture of the Computer window to the desktop.

d. Close any open windows. You should see the *Computer window* file on the desktop. Double-click to open it. Close the file.

e. Right-click **Computer window** on the desktop. Click **Delete**. Confirm the deletion.

You will remove the file from the desktop.

Windows Search and Help

No matter how well prepared you are or how much you know about your computer, you will occasionally have questions about a process or tool. And no matter how careful you are to save files in locations that will be easily located later, you will sometimes lose track of a file or folder. In those cases, Windows 7 can help! You can take advantage of an extensive Help and Support library to get some questions answered and you can search for items, using anything that you know—part of the file name, the file type, or even a bit of the contents. In this section, you will learn to search for items such as files, folders, and programs. You will also explore the Help and Support feature.

> You can take advantage of an extensive Help and Support library to get some questions answered and you can search for items, using anything that you know.

Performing a Search

If you know anything about an item you are looking for, you are likely to find it if it is on your computer. Windows 7 provides several ways to search. You can use the Search box found on the Start menu or you can use the Search box located at the top-right corner of some open windows. You can customize a search to look at specific folders, libraries, or storage media, and you can narrow the search by filters (file type, date modified, etc.). After conducting a search, you can save it so that you can access it later without recreating search criteria.

Conduct a Search

> A **tag** is a custom file property that you create to further identify a file. A tag could be a rating that you apply to a file. You can set tags and view file properties in the details pane of a window.

You will find a Search box on the Start menu and at the top-right corner of most open windows (see Figure 1.38). You will probably find the Search box on the Start menu the most convenient place to begin a search. You can find files, folders, programs, and e-mail messages saved on your computer by entering one or more keywords in the Search box. As you type, items that match your search will appear in the list above the Search box. Click any item to be directed to that location or file. The search will occur based on text in the file, text in the file name, *tags*, and other *file properties*.

> You can find files, folders, programs, and e-mail messages saved on your computer by entering one or more keywords in the Search box.

If you are certain a program is installed on your computer, but you cannot find the program on the Start menu or elsewhere, or perhaps you just don't know where to find the program, you can type some or all of the program name in the Search box on the Start menu. Immediately, you will see any matching program names in the list above. Simply click the name in the list to open the program.

> A **file property** is an identifier of a file, such as author or date created. You can find file properties in the details pane of a window.

Search box in a window

Search box on the Start menu

FIGURE 1.38 Search Box on the Start Menu and in a Window ➤

When you perform a search, Windows 7 searches quickly through indexed locations. All folders in Libraries are automatically included in an index. If you search in locations that are not indexed, the search can be much slower than it would be otherwise. To get a list of indexed locations and to add additional folders or disk drives to the index, click the Start button and type Indexing Options in the Search box. Click Indexing Options from the list that displays above. If you want to add locations, click Modify.

Suppose you cannot find a document that you feel sure you saved in the Documents folder. Open the Documents folder (click the Start button and click Documents). Click in the Search box at the top-right corner of the Documents window. Type any identifier (part or all of the file name, some file contents, or a file tag or property). As you type, any matching file in the Documents folder is displayed.

When you conduct a search through a window (not the Start menu), only the contents of the current folder are searched. You can expand the search to include other folders or libraries and other storage media. You can also narrow the search to seek only specific file types or for properties specific to the folder. For example, if you are searching for music in the Music folder, you might want to narrow the search to a particular artist.

Expand or Narrow a Search

To expand the search, begin typing a search term in the Search box of a window and then scroll to the bottom of the list of search results. Point to a selection in the Search again in area (see Figure 1.39) and select another area to search. Selecting Computer searches the entire computer system, even those areas that are not indexed, as well as Libraries (including Documents, Music, Pictures, and Videos). Use Custom to search a specific location, or Internet to search online.

To narrow a search, click in the Search box of a window and click the appropriate search filter below the search area. Depending on the folder or file type you are searching for, specific filters will vary. Figure 1.40 shows a search of the Pictures folder for any files containing

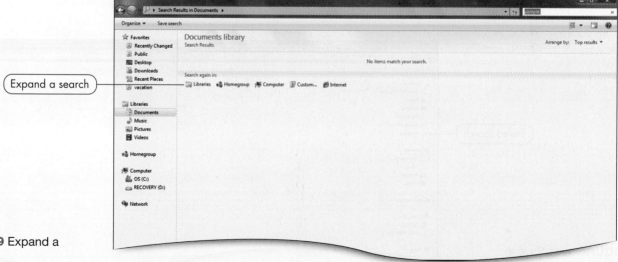

FIGURE 1.39 Expand a Search ➤

the word *Vacation.* The search will be narrowed by selecting the Date Taken filter. Simply click an option to filter by and indicate the criteria. The way you enter criteria depends on the filter selected. For example, you might simply click to select an artist in the Music folder, whereas you could indicate a range of dates to narrow a search of Pictures.

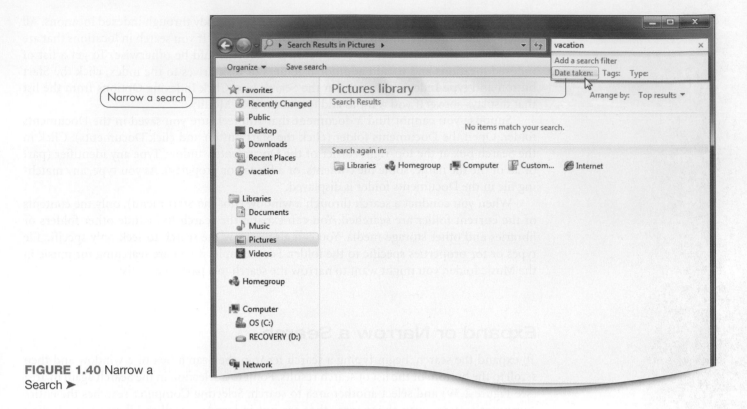

FIGURE 1.40 Narrow a Search ➤

Save a Search

If you know that you will conduct the same search often, you might find it helpful to save the search so that you do not have to continually enter the same search criteria. Perform the search once. On the toolbar, click Save search. Type a name for the search and click Save. The next time you want to conduct the search, open the Computer window. The saved search name is displayed in the Favorites section, as shown in Figure 1.41. Simply click the link to get new results.

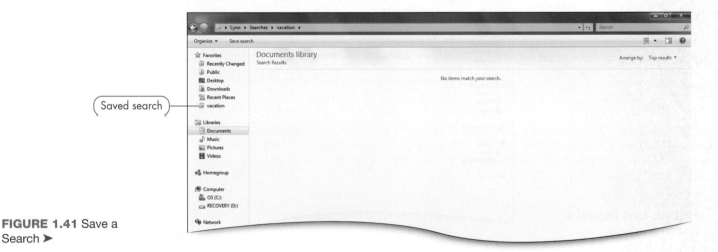

FIGURE 1.41 Save a Search ➤

Getting Help

Help and Support is available from the Start menu, providing assistance with specific questions or providing broad discussions of Windows features.

Help on almost any Windows topic is only a click away using **Help and Support.** As you find that you need assistance on a topic or procedure, click the Start button and click Help and Support. You can then browse the help library by topic or search the library by typing keywords. Use the Remote Assistance feature (accessible after you click More support options in the lower-left corner of the Windows Help and Support window) if you want to ask someone to help with a computer problem from a distance. You can even take advantage of Microsoft's extensive online help. Help is also available within a dialog box and within a software application. Obviously, help can be found wherever you need it!

> Help on almost any Windows topic is only a click away using Help and Support.

Search and Browse Help

Most often, you know exactly what you need assistance with. In that case, click in the Search box of Help and Support (see Figure 1.42), and type your topic. For example, if you are seeking information on resizing desktop icons, type *resize desktop icons*. Press Enter. A list of results displays, arranged in order of usefulness. Click any topic to view more detail. You can print results by clicking Print.

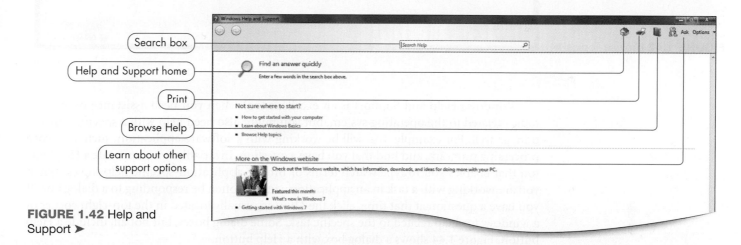

FIGURE 1.42 Help and Support ➤

Help topics are also available when you browse help by clicking Browse Help (see Figure 1.42). By browsing the subsequent list of topics, you can learn a lot about Windows. You might browse Help and Support when you have no particular need for topic-specific assistance or when your question is very general. Figure 1.43 summarizes topics that you can select from when you browse Help.

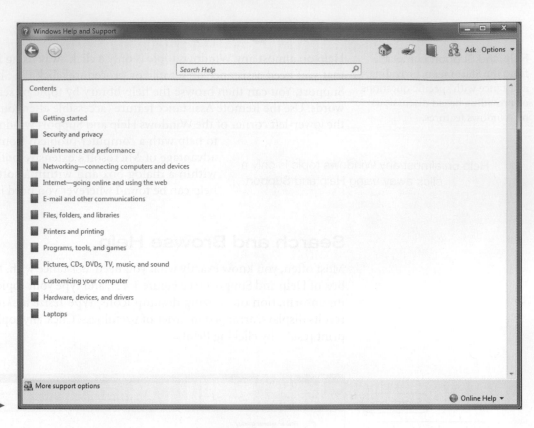

FIGURE 1.43 Browse Topics ➤

Windows Help and Support is an excellent tool when you need assistance on general topics related to the operating system, but you might also need help with a specific application, as well. For example, you will be working with a software application, such as a word processing program, and find that you have a question. Invariably, you can locate a Help button that enables you to type search terms or browse application-specific help topics. When you are working with a task in an application, you will often be responding to a dialog box. If you have a question at that time, click the ? button, usually located in the top-right corner of a window, for help related to the specific task. Some dialog boxes, but not all, include a Help button. Figure 1.44 shows a dialog box with a Help button.

Help button

FIGURE 1.44 Dialog Box Help ➤

Get Remote Assistance

Undoubtedly, you will have trouble with your computer at some time and need some assistance. You might consider getting someone to help you by letting them connect to your computer remotely to determine the problem. Of course, you will only want to ask someone that you trust because that person will temporarily have access to your files.

Remote Assistance is available through Windows 7 Help and Support. Click the Start button, and then Help and Support. Click More support options, in the lower-left corner of the Windows Help and Support window. Click Windows Remote Assistance. Click an option to either invite someone you trust to help you or to help someone who has invited you. If the person who is helping you is also using Windows 7, you can use a method called Easy Connect. The first time you use Easy Connect to request assistance, you will receive a password that you then give to the person offering assistance. Using that password, the helper can remotely connect to your computer and exchange information. Thereafter, a password is not necessary—you simply click the contact information for the helper to initiate a session. If the person providing assistance is using another Windows operating system, you can use an invitation file, which is a file that you create that is sent (usually by e-mail) to the person offering assistance. The invitation file includes a password that is used to connect the two computers.

Get Online Help

So that you are sure to get the latest help, you will probably want to include online Help files in your searches for assistance. To make sure that is happening, open Help and Support, click Options, and then click Settings. Click to select Improve my search results by using online Help (recommended). Click OK. Of course, you must be connected to the Internet before accessing online Help.

HANDS-ON EXERCISES

3 Windows Search and Help

As you close your presentation to the Cedar Cove class, you want the students to be confident in their ability but well aware that help is available. You plan to demonstrate several ways they can get assistance. You also want them to know how to conduct searches for files and folders. Although they might not give it much thought, you know that there will be many times when they will forget where they saved a very important file. Therefore, it is imperative that you include the topic of searching in your presentation.

Skills covered: Explore Windows Help, Search Using Keywords • Use the Search Box to Conduct a Search, Expand a Search • Get Help in an Application, Get Help in a Dialog Box.

STEP 1 ▶ EXPLORE WINDOWS HELP, SEARCH USING KEYWORDS

As students in your class progress to middle and high school, they may have opportunities to use laptops for class work. They also are likely to find themselves in locations where they can connect to the Internet wirelessly. Using that example, you will help the class understand how to use Windows Help and Support to learn how to find and safely connect to an available wireless network. Refer to Figure 1.45 as you complete Step 1.

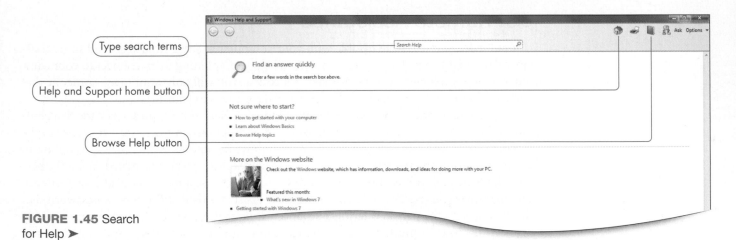

FIGURE 1.45 Search for Help ➤

a. Click the **Start button**. Click **Help and Support** in the right pane. Maximize the Windows Help and Support window.

> **TROUBLESHOOTING:** Your computer should be connected to the Internet before completing this exercise. That way, you can include online help resources.

b. Click the **Browse Help button**. Click **Networking—connecting computers and devices**. Click **Connecting to a network**. Click **View and connect to available wireless networks**. Read through the topic. Pay close attention to any warning about safely connecting to a wireless network.

You will show students how to use Help and Support browsing to locate help on a topic—in this case, connecting to a wireless network..

c. Click the **Help and Support home button**. Click in the **Search Help box**, and then type **Connect to a wireless network**. Press **Enter**. Click **View and connect to available wireless networks**.

Note that you arrived at the same topic as in the previous step, but took a different route. Close the Windows Help and Support window.

d. Use any method of getting Help and Support to answer the question "How can I make sure a wireless connection is secure?" What did you find?

STEP 2 ▶ USE THE SEARCH BOX TO CONDUCT A SEARCH, EXPAND A SEARCH

You want to show students how to search for files, but you are not familiar enough with the classroom computer to know what files to search for. You know, however, that Windows-based computers will include some picture files so you feel certain you can use the example of searching for files with a .jpg (picture) type. You will also illustrate expanding and narrowing a search. Refer to Figure 1.46 as you complete Step 2.

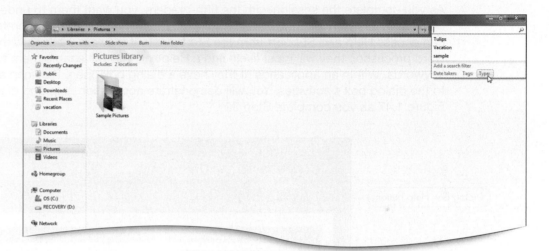

FIGURE 1.46 Narrow a Search ➤

a. Click the **Start button**. Click **Pictures**. Maximize the window. Click in the **Search Pictures box**, and then type **Tulips**. Double-click the *Tulips* file to open it. Close any open windows.

> **TROUBLESHOOTING:** If you do not find a Tulips file, place the student file CD in the CD drive. Wait a few seconds and close any dialog box that opens. In the Search again area, click Custom. Click the Computer arrow. Click the CD drive containing your student CD. Click OK. Navigate to the student data file for this chapter and double-click Tulips.

You search for a file by name—Tulips. Because one of the desktop backgrounds provided by Windows 7 is a file named Tulips, you should be able to find it on the classroom computer in the Pictures folder.

b. Click the **Start button**. Click **Pictures**. Maximize the window, if necessary. Click in the **Search Pictures box**. Look beneath the *Search* box to find the *Add a search filter* area. Click **Type**, as shown in Figure 1.46. Click **.jpg**. All files of that type should display to the left. Double-click any file to open it. Close the picture.

You want to find a few picture files that are saved in the Pictures folder. Because you know that many picture files are of the .jpg file type, you can limit the search to that file type.

c. Click **Documents** in the left pane. Click in the **Search Documents box**, and then type **Sample**. Regardless of whether any results are found, expand the search to include Libraries. Click **Libraries** in the *Search again in* area. Double-click the **Sample Music folder** to view the folder contents. Close all open windows.

d. Click the **Start button**. Click in the **Search box** on the Start menu, and then type **Getting Started**. If more than one Getting Started link appears, place the mouse pointer over each link. Click the one with a ScreenTip that reads *Learn about Windows features and start* *using them*. Click **Go online to learn more**. You will be directed to a Microsoft Web page that provides information on Windows 7. Take a look, click any links that look interesting, and then close any open windows.

> **TROUBLESHOOTING:** After clicking Go online to learn more, you will view a Web page only if your computer is currently connected to the Internet.

Windows 7 provides a Getting Started tip box, but since you are not sure where that information resides, you will use the Search box on the Start menu to find it.

STEP 3 **GET HELP IN AN APPLICATION, GET HELP IN A DIALOG BOX**

As you complete the session with the fifth-graders, you want them to understand that they will never be without assistance. If they need help with general computer and operating system questions, they can access Help and Support from the Start menu. If they are working with an application, such as a word processor, they will most likely find a Help link that will enable them to search for help related to keywords. Within an application, if they have a dialog box open, they can sometimes get help related to the dialog box's activities. You will demonstrate application help and dialog box help. Refer to Figure 1.47 as you complete Step 3.

FIGURE 1.47 Dialog Box Help ➤

a. Click the **Start button**. Click in the **Search box** on the Start menu. Type **Windows Defender**. Click the **Windows Defender link** that appears in the results list.

b. Click the question mark (**?**) shown in Figure 1.47 on the right side of the Windows Defender toolbar. Maximize the Windows Help and Support window. Click **Scan for spyware and other potentially unwanted software**. Read about how to conduct a Windows Defender scan. Close all open windows.

c. Click the **Start button**. Click **Control Panel**. Click **Appearance and Personalization**. Click **Change the theme** in the *Personalization* section. Click the **?** in the top-right corner of the dialog box to open dialog box Help. Read about themes. Close any open windows.

CHAPTER OBJECTIVES REVIEW

After reading this chapter, you have accomplished the following objectives:

1. **Understand the desktop.** The desktop is the display that appears when you turn on a computer. It contains icons (small pictures) that represent programs, files, folders, and system resources. The taskbar is the horizontal bar along the bottom of the desktop. It includes a Start button, pinned icons, icons of open windows, and the Notification area. You can customize the desktop to include a background and a screen saver.

2. **Manage windows.** Programs, folders, and other computer projects open in individual windows on the desktop, much like papers on a desk. You can manage windows by moving, resizing, stacking, or snapping them into position so that multiple windows are easier to work with and identify.

3. **Identify Windows accessories.** Windows 7 provides several accessory programs, including a word processor (WordPad), text editor (Notepad), calculator (Calculator), and screen capture tool (Snipping Tool). You will find accessory programs when you click the Start button, All Programs, and Accessories.

4. **Work with security settings and software.** Windows 7 takes computer security seriously, providing monitoring and software that helps keep your computer safe from spyware and hackers. Windows Defender, an antispyware program, is included with Windows and works to identify and remove instances of spyware. Spyware is unsolicited and unwelcome software that is often installed on your computer without your knowledge or permission. It can then track your Internet travel and modify your computer settings. The Action Center monitors the status of your security and maintenance settings,

alerting you when maintenance tasks (such as backing up your system) are overlooked or when your security is at risk (when antivirus software is out of date, for example). A Windows firewall protects against unauthorized access to your computer from outside entities and prohibits Internet travel by programs from your computer without your permission.

5. **Perform a search.** As you work with a computer, it is inevitable that you will forget where you saved a file or that you misplace a file or folder. Windows 7 provides ample support for finding such items, providing a Search box on the Start menu and in every open window. As you type search keywords in either of those areas, Windows immediately begins a search, showing results. From an open window, you can begin a search and then narrow it by file type or other criteria unique to the searched folder. You might, for example, narrow a search by Date Taken if you are searching in the Pictures folder. You can also expand a search to include more search areas than the current folder.

6. **Get Help.** You can learn a lot about Windows by accessing the Help and Support features available with Windows 7. Get help when you click the Start button and Help and Support. If you are looking for specific answers, you can type search keyword(s) in the Search box and then click any resulting links. If your question is more general, you can browse Help by clicking the Browse Help button, and then working through various links, learning as you go. Help is also available within an application by clicking a Help button and phrasing a search. If you are working with a dialog box, you can click a ? button for specific assistance with the task at hand.

KEY TERMS

Action Center *p.10*
Aero Flip 3D *p.13*
Aero Peek *p.5*
Calculator *p.24*
Desktop *p.2*
Dialog box *p.14*
File property *p.34*
Firewall *p.26*
Gadget *p.4*
Help and Support *p.37*
Icon *p.2*
Jump List *p.8*

Notepad *p.23*
Notification area *p.5*
Operating system *p.2*
Paint *p.24*
Pin *p.8*
Screen saver *p.10*
Shortcut *p.3*
Snap *p.14*
Snip *p.25*
Snipping Tool *p.25*
Spyware *p.26*
Start button *p.5*

Start menu *p.6*
Tag *p.34*
Taskbar *p.5*
Title bar *p.12*
Toolbar *p.7*
User Account Control (UAC) *p.27*
Window *p.2*
Windows Defender *p.26*
Windows Update *p.29*
WordPad *p.23*

MULTIPLE CHOICE

1. The Windows 7 feature that alerts you to any maintenance or security concerns is the:
   (a) Action Center.
   (b) Security Center.
   (c) Windows Defender.
   (d) Control Pane.

2. Snapping windows means that you:
   (a) Minimize all open windows simultaneously so that the desktop displays.
   (b) Auto arrange all open windows so that they are of uniform size.
   (c) Manually reposition all open windows so that you can see the content of each.
   (d) Move any open windows to an opposing side of the desktop until they snap into place.

3. Which of the following accessory programs is primarily a text editor?
   (a) Notepad
   (b) Snipping Tool
   (c) Journal
   (d) Calculator

4. A calendar, which is an example of a constantly changing desktop item, is a(n):
   (a) Icon.
   (b) Thumbnail.
   (c) Gadget.
   (d) Action.

5. Open windows are displayed as icons, or buttons, on the:
   (a) Desktop
   (b) Taskbar.
   (c) Notification area.
   (d) Start menu.

6. A shortcut icon on the desktop is identified by:
   (a) An arrow at the lower-left corner of the icon.
   (b) The word *shortcut* included as part of the icon name.
   (c) A checkmark at the lower-left corner of the icon.
   (d) Its placement on the right side of the desktop.

7. Help and Support is available from which of the following?
   (a) Start menu
   (b) Desktop icon
   (c) Notification area
   (d) Taskbar

8. Which of the following is NOT a method of switching between open windows?
   (a) Alt+Tab
   (b) Shift+Tab
   (c) Click an open window icon on the taskbar.
   (d) Windows logo+Tab

9. When you maximize a window, you:
   (a) Fill the screen with the window.
   (b) Prioritize the window so that it is always placed on top of all other open windows.
   (c) Expand the window's height but leave its width unchanged.
   (d) Expand the window's width but leave its height unchanged.

10. When you enter search keywords in the Search box of a folder window (such as the Documents window):
    (a) The search is not limited to the selected folder.
    (b) The search cannot be further narrowed.
    (c) The search is automatically expanded to include every folder on the hard drive.
    (d) The search is limited to the selected folder, but can be expanded if you like.

1 Senior Academy

As a requirement for completing graduate school, you must submit a thesis, which is a detailed research report. Your degree is in Education with a minor in Information Technology. Your thesis will center on generational learning styles, comparing the way students learn across the generations. Although you have not yet conducted your research, you suspect that students aged 55 and older have a very different way of learning than do younger students. You expect the use of technology in learning to be much more intimidating to older students who have not been exposed to such learning at a high level. As a researcher, however, you know that such suppositions must be supported or proven incorrect by research. As part of your thesis preparation, you are surveying a group of senior adults and a group of college students who are less than 25 years old. The local senior center will distribute your survey to seniors who are currently enrolled in a non-credit computer literacy course sponsored by the senior center. The same survey will be given to students enrolled in a computer literacy college course. The survey covers Windows 7 basics and includes the following steps. You should go over the steps before finalizing the survey instrument. This project follows the same set of skills as used in Hands-On Exercises 1, 2, and 3 in the chapter. Refer to Figure 1.48 as you complete this exercise.

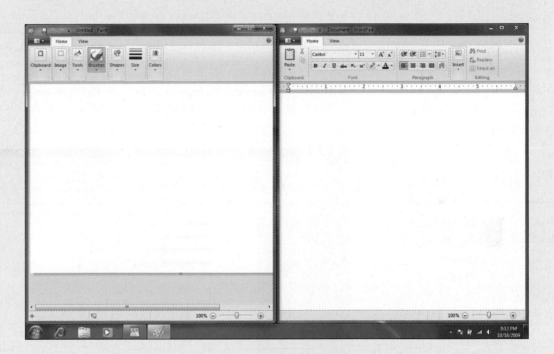

FIGURE 1.48 Paint and WordPad windows ➤

a. Click the **Start button**. Click **Control Panel**. Click **Change desktop background**. Make sure Picture location shows Windows Desktop Backgrounds. Scroll through the picture choices and select one. Click **Save Changes** if you are allowed to make a change to the desktop, or **Cancel** if you are not. Close all open windows.

b. Click the **Start button**. Point to **All Programs**. Click **Accessories**. Right-click **WordPad**, and then click **Pin to Taskbar**. Click outside the Start menu to remove it from view.

c. Click the **Start button**. Point to **All Programs**. Click **Accessories**. Right-click **Paint**. Click **Pin to Start Menu**. Click outside the Start menu to remove it from view.

d. Click the **Start button**. Point to **All Programs**. Click **Accessories**. Right-click and drag **Notepad** to the desktop. Release the mouse button. Click **Create shortcuts here**.

e. Click the **WordPad icon** on the taskbar. With WordPad still open, click the **Start button**. Click **Paint**. If you have recently opened Paint files, you may have to click Paint twice to open it.

f. Right-click an empty area of the taskbar. Click **Show windows side by side**. Compare your screen to Figure 1.48.

g. Click the **Close button** at the top-right corner of the Paint window to close the program.

h. Click the **Maximize button** (middle control button) on the right side of the WordPad window to maximize the window.

i. Click the **Start button**. Click **Help and Support**. Click **Browse Help**. Click **Security and privacy**. Scroll down the list if necessary and click **Helping to protect your computer from viruses**. Click **How can I tell if my computer has a virus?**. Identify some symptoms of a virus.

j. Right-click an empty area of the taskbar. Click **Show windows stacked**. Click in the WordPad window and in your own words, list at least three virus symptoms.

k. Click the **Start button**. Point to **All Programs**. Click **Accessories**. Click **Snipping Tool**. Click the **New arrow**. Click **Full-screen Snip**. Click **Save Snip**. Scroll down the left side of the **Save As dialog box**, and then click to select the disk drive where you will save your student files. Click in the **File name box**, and then type **win01p1survey_LastnameFirstname**. Click **Save**.

l. Close all open windows without saving.

m. Right-click the **WordPad icon** on the taskbar. Click **Unpin this program from taskbar**. Click the **Start button**. Right-click **Paint**. Click **Unpin from Start Menu**. Click outside the Start menu to remove it from view.

n. Right-click the **Notepad icon** on the desktop. Click **Delete**. Confirm the deletion.

2 Silent Auction

As part of your responsibility as vice president of the National Youth Assembly of College Athletes, you are soliciting donated items for a silent auction at the national conference. You accept items and tag them with an estimated value and a beginning bid requirement. You will use a computer to keep a record of the donor, value, and minimum bid requirement. Because you will not always be in the office when an item is donated, you will configure the desktop and taskbar of the computer to simplify the job of data entry for anyone who happens to be at the desk. This project follows the same set of skills as used in Hands-On Exercises 1, 2, and 3 in the chapter. Refer to Figure 1.49 as you complete this exercise.

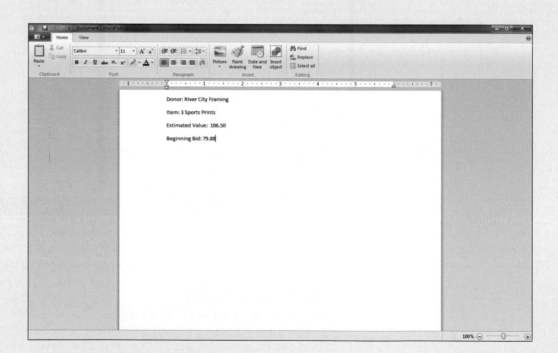

FIGURE 1.49 Silent Auction Items ➤

a. Click the **Start button**. Point to **All Programs**. Click **Accessories**. Right-click and drag **WordPad** to the desktop. Click **Create shortcuts here**.

b. Right-click an empty area of the taskbar. Click **Properties**. Click the **Auto-hide the taskbar check box** (if no check mark appears). Click **OK**.

c. Double-click the **WordPad icon** on the desktop. WordPad will open.
- Click the **Maximize button**. If no insertion point (blinking bar) appears in the upper-left corner of the white space, click to position it there.
- Type **Donor: River City Framing**. Press **Enter**.
- Type **Item: 3 Sports Prints**. Press **Enter**.
- Type **Estimated Value:**. Press **Spacebar**.

d. Click the **Start button**. Point to **All Programs**. Click **Accessories**. Click **Calculator**.

The estimated value of each print is $35.50, but the frames will be sold as a unit. Therefore, you need to determine the total value ($35.50 multiplied by 3). Because you are in the middle of typing a WordPad document, you do not want to close it. Instead, you will open the Calculator program and compute the value.

e. Use the mouse to click **35.50*3** and click =. The total value should show on the calculator. Minimize the Calculator.

f. Type the total in the WordPad document. Press **Enter**. Type **Beginning Bid:**. Press the spacebar.

g. Click the **Calculator icon** on the taskbar. The amount from step (e) should still be displayed on the Calculator. Click the **multiplication key** (*) and **.75**. Click =. Jot down the value shown on the Calculator and close the Calculator.

The beginning bid will be 75% of the estimated value. So the calculation should be Estimated Value multiplied by .75.

h. Click after the word *Bid:* in the WordPad window, if necessary. Type the value that you recorded in step (g), rounded up to the nearest hundredth. Press **Enter**. Compare your screen to Figure 1.49.

i. Click the **Start button**. Click **Help and Support**. Maximize the Windows Help and Support window. Click in the **Search box**, and then type **WordPad**. Press **Enter**. Click **Using WordPad**. Click **Create, open, and save documents** on the right side. If necessary, click **Create, open, and save documents** to expand the detail. Look at the displayed table to determine how to save a document. Close Windows Help and Support.

j. Click **WordPad** (just to the left of the Home tab) as you were directed in the Help and Support tip.
- Click **Save**.
- Scroll down the left side of the dialog box to Computer and click the disk drive where you save your student files. Proceed through any folder structure, as directed by your instructor.
- Click in the **File name box**, and then type **win01p2auction_LastnameFirstname**. You might first need to remove the current file name before typing the new one.
- Click **Save**.
- Close WordPad.

k. Right-click the taskbar. Click **Properties**. Click **Auto-hide the taskbar**. Click **OK**.

l. Right-click the **WordPad icon** on the desktop. Click **Delete**. Confirm the deletion.

1 Junk Business

You and a college friend have signed on as a franchise for JUNKit, a company that purchases unwanted items and disposes of or recycles them. A recent pickup included a desktop computer that appeared to be reusable. Because you had a few spare parts and some hardware expertise, you rebuilt the computer and installed Windows 7. Now you will check the system to verify that it is workable and configured correctly.

a. Open WordPad and type as directed when you complete the following items.

b. Open the Action Center. Are there any alerts? Make note of them and close the Action Center. In the WordPad document, type **Step b:** and then list any alerts or indicate that there are none. Press **Enter**.

c. Open Windows Defender and check to see when the last scan occurred. Click the WordPad icon on the taskbar, click in the document on the line following your response for Step b, type **Step c:** and then record when the last scan occurred. Press **Enter**. Right-click the **Windows Defender** icon on the taskbar, and then click **Close window**.

d. Check the firewall status. Is the firewall on? Close the System and Security window. If necessary, click in the WordPad document on the line following your response for Step c. Type **Step d:** and then record whether the firewall is on or off. (Note that the firewall may not be on for the lab computer because the campus lab is likely to be behind another campus-wide firewall. Your computer at home is more likely to have the firewall turned on.) Press **Enter**.

e. Check Windows Update. When did the last update occur? Click the **WordPad icon** on the taskbar. If necessary, click in the WordPad document on the line following your response for Step d. Type **Step e:** and then record the date of the last update. Press **Enter**. Right-click the **Windows Update icon** on the taskbar, and then click **Close window**.

f. Check for available desktop backgrounds. Identify one that you plan to use, but click **Cancel** without selecting it. Close any open windows other than WordPad. If necessary, click in the WordPad document on the line following your response for Step e. Type **Step f:** and then list the name of the background that you would have selected in the WordPad document. Press **Enter**.

g. Open Help and Support. Find information on the Aero desktop. Specifically, identify a definition of the Aero desktop and requirements for its use (computer specifications and Windows 7 versions that support Aero). Going a little further, find out what Aero Shake is and how it could be beneficial in managing a desktop. Click the **WordPad icon** on the taskbar, type **Step g:** and then summarize your findings in the WordPad document. Press **Enter**.

h. Click the **Restore Down button** to reduce the size of the WordPad window. Snap the Windows Help and Support window to one side of the desktop and the WordPad document to the other.

i. Close the Windows Help and Support window. Save the WordPad document by clicking **Save** (second from left on the topmost row of the WordPad window). Scroll down in the left pane of the dialog box and click **Computer**. Double-click the disk drive where you save your student files (as directed by your instructor). Click in the **File name box**, and then type **win01m1junk_LastnameFirstname**. Click **Save**. Close WordPad.

2 Technical Writing

You are employed as a software specialist with Wang Design, a firm that provides commercial and residential landscape design and greenscape services. The landscape designers use a wide array of software that assists with producing detailed plans and lawn layouts. The firm has just purchased several new computers, configured with Windows 7. Because the operating system is new to all employees, you have been assigned the task of producing a small easy-to-follow manual summarizing basic Windows 7 tasks. Use WordPad or Microsoft Word to produce a report, no more than 10 pages, based on the following topic outline. Where appropriate, use the Snipping Tool to include screen captures that illustrate a topic or process. Use this chapter and Windows Help and Support to find information for your report. Save your report as **win01m2writing_LastnameFirstname**.

1. Desktop Components
2. Customizing the Desktop
3. Windows Accessories
4. Windows Search

CAPSTONE EXERCISE

You are enrolled in a Directed Studies class as one of the final courses required for your degree. The class is projects-based, which means that the instructor assigns open-ended cases for students to manage and report on. You will prepare teaching materials for a Windows 7 community education class. The class is a new effort for the college, and given early enrollment figures, it appears that most students are over the age of 45 with very little computer background. Most students indicate that they have recently purchased a computer with Windows 7 and want to learn to work with the operating system at a minimal level. The class is short, only a couple of Saturday mornings, and it is fast approaching. In this exercise, you will prepare and test class material introducing students to the desktop, managing windows, working with accessory programs and security settings, getting help, and finding files. Your instructor wants screen shots of your progress, so you will use the Snipping Tool to prepare those.

Explore the Desktop and Manage Windows

The instructor will spend the first hour of class introducing students to the Windows 7 desktop and to the concept of windows. He will assume that students are complete novices, so he wants an outline that begins with the basics. You have prepared the series of steps given below. You will go through those steps, preparing a screen shot to accompany your submission.

a. Auto arrange icons on the desktop (if they are not already set to auto arrange).

b. Create a desktop shortcut for the Notepad program.

c. Pin the WordPad program to the taskbar.

d. Open the Notepad shortcut. If necessary, restore down the window so that it is not maximized.

e. Open WordPad from the taskbar. If necessary, restore down the window so that it is not maximized.

f. Snap each window to opposing sides of the desktop.

g. Show the windows stacked.

h. Use the Snipping Tool to capture a copy of the screen. Save it as **win01c1desktop_LastnameFirstname**.

i. Close all open windows.

Work with Accessory Programs and Security Settings

The instructor wants to make sure students understand that some software is included with a Windows 7 installation. Because using any type of software most often involves Internet access, you know that the class must include instruction on security risks and solutions. You have prepared some notes and will test them in the steps that follow.

a. Open WordPad. Maximize the window, if necessary. Students in class will be instructed to type a paragraph on Windows 7 security features. Use Windows 7 Help and Support if necessary to identify Windows 7 security features, and then compose a paragraph in the WordPad document. Minimize WordPad but do not close it.

b. Open Paint. Maximize the window, if necessary. Click the top half of **Brushes**. Click and drag to write your name in the *Paint* area. Click the top half of **Select**. Click and drag in a rectangle around your name. Click **Copy**. Close Paint without saving.

c. Click the **WordPad icon** on the taskbar. Click the top half of **Paste** to add your "signature" to the paragraph.

d. Save the WordPad document as **win01c1paragraph_LastnameFirstname**.

e. Close WordPad.

Get Help and Find Files

You know from personal experience that things usually work well when an instructor is available to help. You also know that as students leave the Windows 7 class, they will have questions and must know how to find help themselves. They will also undoubtedly misplace files. The steps that follow should help them understand how to get help and how to find files, programs, and folders.

a. Browse Help and Support to find information on the Start menu.

b. Search Help and Support to find a description of remote assistance.

c. Minimize the Windows Help and Support window.

d. Click the **Start button**, click in the **Start menu Search box**, and then type **Word**. You will search for any program with the word *word* in the program name. At the very least, you should see *WordPad* in the results list. Click the program name to open it. If WordPad is maximized, restore it down to less than full size.

e. Click the **Help and Support icon** on the taskbar to open the window.

f. Show the windows stacked.

g. Use the Snipping Tool to capture the screen, saving it as **win01c1help_LastnameFirstname**. Close all open windows.

h. Unpin the **WordPad icon** from the taskbar.

i. Delete the **NotePad icon** from the desktop.

Speech Class

GENERAL CASE

You are taking a Speech class and must develop a demonstration speech, complete with a sheet of notes. A demonstration speech is one in which you teach or direct the class on how to do something. Because Windows 7 is a relatively new operating system, you decide to demonstrate some of its features. You will use WordPad to record a few notes that will help you make your presentation. After completing your notes, save the document as **win01b1speech_LastnameFirstname** in a location as directed by your instructor. In a 1, 2, 3 fashion (listing your points in numerical order), provide directions to the class on how to:

- Customize the desktop with a background and screen saver.
- Pin programs to the taskbar and the Start menu.
- Use the Start menu Search box to find and open a program that you think is installed on your computer system.
- Get Help on an item related to Windows 7.
- Make sure your computer is protected against spyware and hacking.

Campus Chatter

RESEARCH CASE

As a reporter for the college newspaper *Campus Chatter,* you are responsible for the education section. Each month, you contribute a short article on an educational topic. This month, you will summarize a feature of Windows 7. You are having writer's block, however, and need a nudge, so you will use the Internet for an idea. Click Start, All Programs, Accessories, Getting Started. Click Go online to learn more. You will be directed to the Windows 7 Web site. Peruse some links, locate a topic of interest, and use WordPad to write a minimum one-page typed report on a topic related to Windows 7. Save the report as **win01b2chatter_ LastnameFirstname** in a location as directed by your instructor.

Laptop Logic

DISASTER RECOVERY

Your job in sales with an educational software company requires a great deal of travel. You depend on a laptop computer for most of what you do, from keeping sales records to connecting with an overhead projector when you make presentations to groups. In short, you would be lost without your computer. A recent scare, when you temporarily misplaced the laptop, has led you to consider precautions you can take to make sure your computer and its data are protected. Since you have a little free time before leaving for your next trip, you will use Windows 7 Help and Support to explore some suggestions on protecting your laptop. Open Help and Support and search for information on *protecting a laptop*. Create a one- to two-page typed report covering two topics. First, describe how you would protect data (including passwords and financial information) on your laptop. Second, provide some suggestions on steps you can take to make sure you do not lose your laptop or have it stolen. Use WordPad to record the report, saving the report as **win01b3laptop_LastnameFirstname** in a location as directed by your instructor.

1 OFFICE FUNDAMENTALS AND FILE MANAGEMENT

Taking the First Step

CASE STUDY | Rails and Trails

Watch the **Set-up Video** for this Case Study!

You are an administrative assistant for a local historical preservation project. The project involves creating a series of trails designed for hikers, bikers, and horseback riders. The trails generally follow the route of a historic railroad line that traversed the northwestern corner of Kentucky from the early 1900s until it was discontinued in 1991. The 78 miles of trails follow the original rail route, which passed through natural hardwood forests and open meadows. Considered a major impetus of the Kentucky Historical Preservation Society, the project has received both public and private funding through legislative appropriations and private and federal grants.

As the administrative assistant, you are responsible for overseeing the production of documents, spreadsheets, newspaper articles, and presentations that will be used to increase public awareness of the Rails and Trails project. Other clerical assistants who are familiar with Microsoft Office will prepare the promotional materials, and you will proofread, make necessary corrections, adjust page layouts, save and print documents, and identify appropriate templates to simplify tasks. Your experience with Microsoft Office 2010 is limited, but you know that certain fundamental tasks that are common to Word, Excel, and PowerPoint will help you accomplish your oversight task. You are excited to get started on the project!

OBJECTIVES   AFTER YOU READ THIS CHAPTER, YOU WILL BE ABLE TO:

1. Use Windows Explorer *p.52*
2. Work with folders and files *p.56*
3. Select, copy, and move multiple files and folders *p.58*
4. Identify common interface components *p.64*
5. Get Office Help *p.69*
6. Open a file *p.76*
7. Print a file *p.79*
8. Close a file and application *p.80*
9. Select and edit text *p.84*
10. Use the Clipboard group tasks *p.87*
11. Use the Editing group tasks *p.90*
12. Insert objects *p.97*
13. Review a file *p.99*
14. Change page settings *p.102*

Files and Folders

If you stop to consider why you use a computer, you will most likely conclude that you want to produce some type of output. That output could be games, music, or the display of digital photographs. Perhaps you use a computer at work to produce reports, financial worksheets, or schedules. All of those items are considered computer *files*. Files include electronic data such as documents, databases, slide shows, and worksheets. Even digital photographs, music, videos, and Web pages are saved as files.

> Windows 7 provides tools that enable you to create folders and to save files in ways that make locating them simple.

You use software to create and save files. For example, when you type a document on a computer, you first open a word processor such as Microsoft Word. Similarly, you could use a type of Web-authoring software to create a Web page. In order to access files later, you must save them to a computer storage medium such as a hard drive or flash drive. And just as you would probably organize a filing cabinet into a system of folders, you can organize storage media by *folders* that you name and into which you place data files. That way, you can easily retrieve the files later. Windows 7 provides tools that enable you to create folders and to save files in ways that make locating them simple. In this section, you will learn to use Windows Explorer to manage folders and files.

A **file** is a document or item of information that you create with software and to which you give a name.

A **folder** is a named storage location where you can save files.

Using Windows Explorer

Windows Explorer is a Windows component that can be used to create and manage folders.

A **subfolder** is a folder that is housed within another folder.

Windows Explorer is a component that can be used to create and manage folders. The sole purpose of a computer folder is to provide a labeled storage location for related files so that you can easily organize and retrieve items. A folder structure can occur across several levels, so you can create folders within other folders (called *subfolders*), arranged according to purpose. Windows 7 introduces the concept of libraries, which are folders that gather files from different locations and display the files as if they were all saved in a single folder, regardless of where they are physically stored. Using Windows Explorer, you can manage folders, work with libraries, and view favorites (areas or folders that are frequently accessed).

Understand and Customize the Interface

To open Windows Explorer, click Windows Explorer on the taskbar as shown in Figure 1.1. You can also right-click the Start button and click Open Windows Explorer. Figure 1.2 shows the Windows Explorer interface containing several areas. Some of those areas are described in Table 1.1.

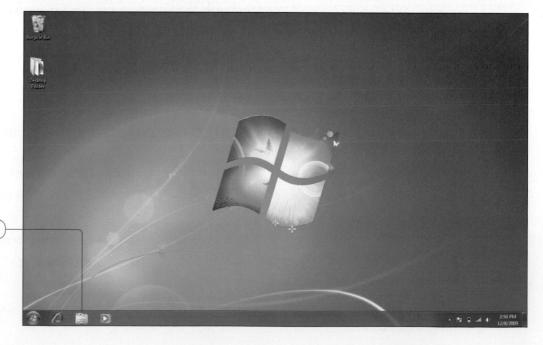

FIGURE 1.1 Windows Explorer ➤

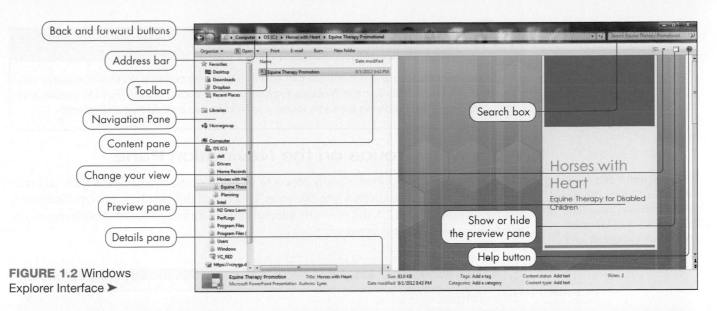

Back and forward buttons

Address bar

Toolbar

Navigation Pane

Content pane

Change your view

Preview pane

Details pane

Search box

Horses with Heart

Equine Therapy for Disabled Children

Show or hide the preview pane

Help button

FIGURE 1.2 Windows Explorer Interface ➤

TABLE 1.1	Windows Explorer Interface
Navigation Pane	The Navigation Pane contains five areas: Favorites, Libraries, Homegroup, Computer, and Network. Click an item in the Navigation Pane to display contents and to manage files that are housed within a selected folder.
Back and Forward Buttons	Use these buttons to visit previously opened folders or libraries.
Toolbar	The Toolbar includes buttons that are relevant to the currently selected item. If you are working with a music file, the toolbar buttons might include one for burning to a CD, whereas if you have selected a document, the toolbar would enable you to open or share the file.
Address Bar	The Address bar enables you to navigate to other folders or libraries.
Content Pane	The Content pane shows the contents of the currently selected folder or library.
Search Box	Find files and folders by typing descriptive text in the Search box. Windows immediately begins a search after you type the first character, further narrowing results as you type.
Details Pane	The Details pane shows properties that are associated with a selected file. Common properties include information such as the author name and the date the file was last modified.
Preview Pane	The Preview pane provides a snapshot of a selected file's contents. You can see file contents before actually opening the file. The Preview pane does not show the contents of a selected folder.

As you work with Windows Explorer, you might find that the view is not how you would like it. The file and folder icons might be too small for ease of identification, or you might want additional details about displayed files and folders. Modifying the view is easy. To make icons larger or to provide additional detail, click the Change your view arrow (see Figure 1.2), and select from the views provided. If you want additional detail, such as file type and size, click Details. You can also change the size of icons by selecting Small, Medium, Large, or Extra Large icons. The List view shows the file names without added detail, whereas Tiles and Content views are useful to show file thumbnails (small pictures describing file contents) and varying levels of detail regarding file locations. To show or hide Windows Explorer panes, click Organize (on the Toolbar), point to Layout, and then select the pane to hide or show. You can widen or narrow panes by dragging a border when the mouse changes to a double-headed arrow. When you click Show or hide the Preview pane, you toggle—or change between— views. If the Preview pane is not shown, clicking the button shows the pane. Conversely, if the pane is already open, clicking the button will hide it.

Work with Groups on the Navigation Pane

The **Navigation Pane** is located on the left side of the Windows Explorer window, providing access to Favorites, Libraries, Homegroup, Computer, and Network areas.

The *Navigation Pane* provides ready access to computer resources, folders, files, and networked peripherals. It is divided into five areas: Favorites, Libraries, Homegroup, Computer, and Network. In Figure 1.3, the currently selected area is Libraries. Each of those components provides a unique way to organize contents.

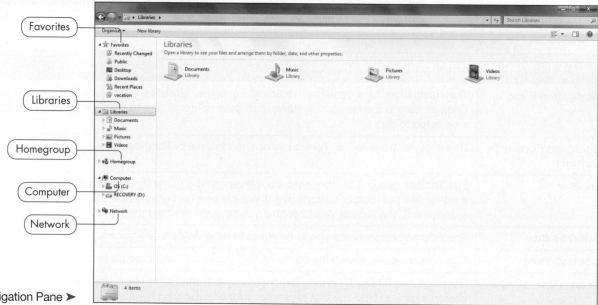

FIGURE 1.3 Navigation Pane ➤

A **library** is an organization method that collects files from different locations and displays them as one unit.

Earlier, we used the analogy of computer folders to folders in a filing cabinet. Just as you would title folders in a filing cabinet according to their contents, computer folders are also titled according to content. Folders are physically located on storage media such as a hard drive or flash drive. You can also organize folders into *libraries*, which are collections of files from different locations that are displayed as single units. For example, the Pictures library includes files from the Pictures folder and from the Public Pictures folder, both of which are physically housed on the hard drive. Although the library content comes from two separate folders, contents are displayed as a unit.

Windows 7 includes several libraries that include default folders or devices. For example, the Documents library includes the My Documents and Public Documents folders, but you can add other folders if you wish so that they are also housed within the Documents library. To add a folder to a library, right-click the folder, and then point to Include in library. Then select a library, or select Create new library and create a new one. To remove a folder from a library, open Windows Explorer, and then click the library from which you want to remove the folder. In the Library pane shown at the right side of the Windows Explorer window, click the locations link (next to the word *Includes*). The link will indicate the number of physical locations in which the folders are housed. For example, if folders in the Pictures library are drawn from two locations, the link will read *2 locations*. Click the folder that you want to remove, click Remove, and then click OK.

The Computer area provides access to specific storage locations, such as a hard drive, CD/DVD, and removable media (including a flash drive). Files and folders housed on those storage media are accessible when you click Computer. For example, click drive C, shown under Computer in the Navigation Pane, to view its contents in the Content pane on the right. If you simply want to see the subfolders of the hard drive, click the arrow to the left of drive C to expand the view, showing all subfolders. Click the arrow again to collapse the view, removing subfolder detail. It is important to understand that clicking the arrow (as opposed to clicking the folder or area name) does not actually select an area or folder. It merely displays additional levels contained within the area. Clicking the folder or area, however, does select the item. Figure 1.4 illustrates the difference between clicking the area in the Navigation Pane and clicking the arrow to the left.

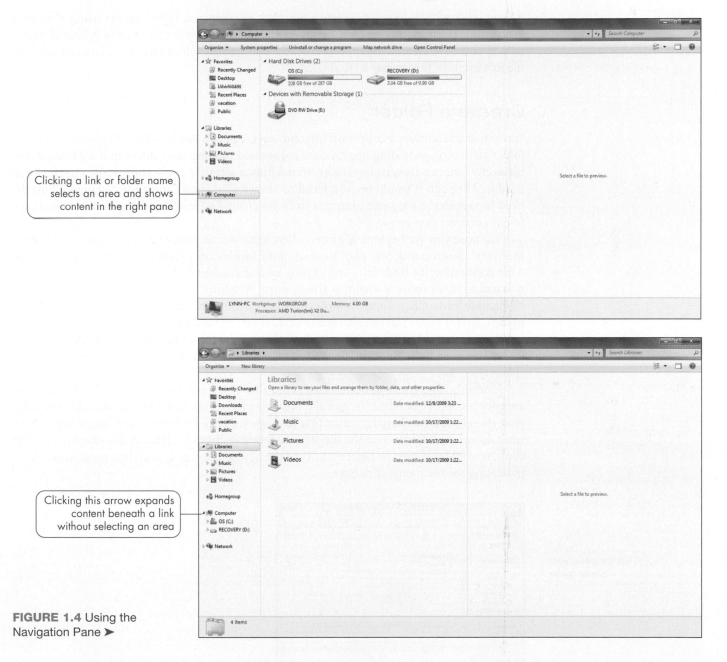

Clicking a link or folder name selects an area and shows content in the right pane

Clicking this arrow expands content beneath a link without selecting an area

FIGURE 1.4 Using the Navigation Pane ➤

Click the drive in the Navigation Pane (or double-click the drive in the Content pane). Continue navigating through the folder structure until you find the folder that you seek. Double-click the folder (in the Content pane) or single-click the folder (in the Navigation Pane) to view its contents.

The Favorites area contains frequently accessed folders and recent searches. You can drag a folder, a saved search, a library, or a disk drive to the Favorites area. To remove a favorite, simply right-click the favorite, and then click Remove. You cannot add files or Web sites as favorites.

Homegroup is a Windows 7 feature that enables you to share resources on a home network. You can easily share music, pictures, videos, and libraries with other people in your home through a homegroup. It is password protected, so you do not have to worry about privacy.

Windows 7 makes creating a home network easy, sharing access to the Internet and peripheral devices such as printers and scanners. The Network area provides quick access to those devices, enabling you to see the contents of network computers.

Working with Folders and Files

As you work with software to create a file, such as when you type a report using Microsoft Word, your primary concern will be saving the file so that you can retrieve it later if necessary. If you have created an appropriate and well-named folder structure, you can save the file in a location that is easy to find later.

Create a Folder

You can create a folder a couple of different ways. You can use Windows Explorer to create a folder structure, providing appropriate names and placing the folders in a well-organized hierarchy. You can also create a folder from within a software application at the time that you need it. Although it would be wonderful to always plan ahead, most often you will find the need for a folder at the same time that you have created a file. The two methods of creating a folder are described below.

Suppose you are beginning a new college semester and are taking four classes. To organize your assignments, you plan to create four folders on a flash drive, one for each class. After connecting the flash drive and closing any subsequent dialog box (unless the dialog box is warning of a problem with the drive), open Windows Explorer. Click Computer in the Navigation Pane. Click the removable (flash) drive in the Navigation Pane, or double-click it in the Content pane. You can also create a folder on the hard drive in the same manner, clicking drive C instead of the removable drive. Click New folder on the Toolbar. Type the new folder name, such as English 101, and press Enter. Repeat the process for the other three classes.

Undoubtedly, you will occasionally find that you have just created a file but have no appropriate folder in which to save the file. You might have just finished the slide show for your speech class but have forgotten first to create a speech folder for your assignments. Now what do you do? As you save the file, a process that is discussed later in this chapter, you can click New folder shown in Figure 1.5. Type the new folder name, and then press Enter. After indicating the file name, click Save.

Click here to create a new folder

FIGURE 1.5 Create a New Folder ➤

Open, Rename, and Delete Folders and Files

You have learned that folders can be created in Windows Explorer but that files must be created in other ways, such as within a software package. Although Windows Explorer cannot create files, you can use it to open, rename, and delete files just as you use it for folders.

Using the Navigation Pane, you can locate and select a folder containing a file that you want to open. For example, you will want to open the speech slide show so that you can practice before giving the presentation to the class. Open Windows Explorer, and navigate to the speech folder on your removable drive (flash drive). The file will display in the right pane. Double-click the file. The program that is associated with the file will open the file. For example, if you used PowerPoint to create the slide show, then PowerPoint will open the file. To open a folder and display the contents, just single-click the folder in the Navigation Pane or double-click it in the Content pane.

At times, you may find a more suitable name for a file or folder than the one that you originally gave it. Or perhaps you made a typographical mistake when you entered the name. In these situations, you should rename the file or folder. In Windows Explorer, move through the folder structure to find the folder or file. Right-click the name, and then click Rename. Type the new name, and then press Enter. You can also rename an item when you click the name twice, but much more slowly than a double-click. Type the new name, and then press Enter. Finally, you can click a file or folder once to select it, click Organize, click Rename, type the new name, and then press Enter.

It is much easier to delete a folder or file than it is to recover it if you remove it by mistake. Therefore, be very careful when deleting items so that you are sure of your intentions before proceeding. When you delete a folder, all subfolders and all files within the folder are also removed. If you are certain you want to remove a folder or file, the process is simple. Right-click the item, click Delete, and then click Yes if asked to confirm removal to the Recycle Bin. Items are only placed in the Recycle Bin if you are deleting them from a hard drive. Files and folders deleted from a removable storage medium, such as a flash drive, are permanently deleted, with no easy method of retrieval. You can also delete an item (file or folder) when you click to select the item, click Organize, and then click Delete.

Save a File

As you create or modify a project such as a document, presentation, or worksheet, your work is placed in RAM, which is the computer's temporary memory. When you shut down the computer or inadvertently lose electrical power, the contents of RAM are erased. Even with a loss of electrical power, however, RAM on a laptop will not be erased until the battery runs down. Because you will most likely want to continue the project at another time or keep it for later reference, you need to save it to a storage medium such as a hard drive, CD, or flash drive. When you save a file, you will be working within a software package. Therefore, you must follow the procedure dictated by that software to save the file. Thankfully, most software requires that you save files in a similar fashion, so you can usually find your way through the process fairly quickly.

The first time that you save a file, you must indicate where the file should be saved, and you must assign a file name. Of course, you will want to save the file in an appropriately named folder so that you can find it easily later. Thereafter, you can quickly save the file with the same settings, or you can change one or more of those settings, perhaps saving the file to a different storage device as a backup copy. Figure 1.6 shows a typical Save As dialog box that enables you to confirm or change settings before finally saving the file.

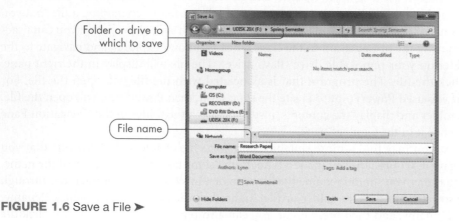

FIGURE 1.6 Save a File ➤

Selecting, Copying, and Moving Multiple Files and Folders

On occasion, you will want to select folders and files, such as when you need to rename, delete, copy, or paste them. You might want to open files and folders so that you can view the contents. Single-click a file or folder to *select* it; double-click a file or folder (in the Content pane) to *open* it. When you want to apply an operation to several files at once, such as deleting or moving them, you will want to select all of them. Knowing how to select several files and folders at one time makes the process of copying, or moving, items quick and simple.

Select Multiple Files and Folders

You can select several files and folders, regardless of whether they are adjacent to each other in the file list. Suppose that your digital pictures are contained in the Pictures folder. You might want to delete some of the pictures because you have already copied them to a CD and you want to clear up some hard drive space. To select certain pictures in the Pictures folder, open Windows Explorer, and then click the Pictures library. You will recall that the Pictures library groups and displays pictures from multiple folders. Navigate through any folder structure to locate the desired pictures in the Content pane. Assume that you want to select the first four pictures displayed. Because they are adjacent, you can select the first picture, hold down Shift, and click the fourth picture. All four pictures will be highlighted, indicating that they are selected. At that point, you can delete, copy, move, or rename the selected pictures. The next section of this chapter explains how to copy and move selections.

If the files or folders to be selected are not adjacent, simply click the first item. Hold down Ctrl while you click all other files or folders, one at a time, releasing Ctrl only when you have finished selecting all files or folders. All files or folders will be selected.

To select all items in a folder or disk, use Windows Explorer to navigate to the desired folder. Open the folder, then hold down Ctrl, and press A on the keyboard. You can also click Organize, and then Select All to select all items.

> **TIP** Using a Check Box to Select Items
>
> Windows 7 includes a file selection technique that makes it easy to make multiple selections, regardless of whether the items are adjacent. To activate the option, open Windows Explorer, and then change the view to Details. Click Organize, and then select Folder and search options. The Folder Options dialog box opens. Click the View tab, scroll down in the Advanced settings box, click Use check boxes to select items (see Figure 1.7), and then click OK. As you move the mouse pointer along the left side of files and folders, a check box appears. Click in the check box to select the file. In this manner, you can select multiple files and folders. If you want to quickly select all items in the folder, click the check box that appears in the Name column.

Click here to select items with check boxes

FIGURE 1.7 Use Check Boxes to Select Items ➤

Copy and Move Files and Folders

When you copy or move a folder, both the folder and any files that it contains are affected. You can move or copy a folder or file to another location on the same drive or to another drive. If your purpose is to make a *backup* copy of an important file or folder, you will probably want to copy it to another drive.

A **backup** is a copy of a file, usually on another storage medium.

Using a shortcut menu is one of the most foolproof ways to move or copy an item. In Windows Explorer, select the file or folder that you want to move or copy. If you want to copy or move multiple items, follow the directions in the previous section to select them all at once. Right-click the item, and select either Cut or Copy. Scroll through the Navigation Pane to locate the drive or folder to which you want to move or copy the selected item. Right-click the destination drive or folder, and then click Paste. If the moved or copied item is a folder, it should appear as a subfolder of the selected folder. If the moved or copied item is a file, it will be placed within the selected folder.

1 Files and Folders

You will soon begin to collect files from volunteers who are preparing promotional and record-keeping material for the Rails and Trails project. It is important that you save the files in appropriately named folders so that you can easily access them later. Therefore, you plan to create folders. You can create folders on a flash drive or a hard drive. You will select the drive on which you plan to save your student files. As you create a short document, you will save it in one of the folders. You will then make a backup copy of the folder structure, including all files, so that you do not run the risk of losing the material if the drive is damaged or misplaced.

Skills covered: Create Folders and Subfolders • Create and Save a File • Rename and Delete a Folder • Open and Copy a File

STEP 1 ▶ CREATE FOLDERS AND SUBFOLDERS

You decide to create a folder titled *Rails and Trails Project*, and then subdivide it into subfolders that will help categorize the project files. Refer to Figure 1.8 as you complete Step 1.

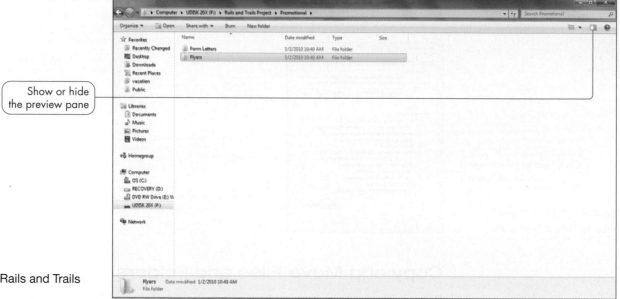

FIGURE 1.8 Rails and Trails Folders ➤

a. Insert your flash drive (if you are using a flash drive for your student files), and close any dialog box that opens (unless it is informing you of a problem with the drive). Click **Windows Explorer** on the taskbar. Click **Show the preview pane** unless the Preview pane is already displayed.

The removable drive shown in Figure 1.8 is titled UDISK 20X (F:), describing the drive manufacturer and the drive letter. Your removable drive will be designated in a different manner, perhaps also identified by manufacturer. The drive letter identifying your flash drive is likely to be different because the configuration of disk drives on your computer is unique.

> **TROUBLESHOOTING:** If you do not have a flash drive, you can use the hard drive. In the next step, simply click drive C in the Navigation Pane instead of the removable drive.

b. Click the removable drive in the Navigation Pane (or click **drive C** if you are using the hard drive). Click **New folder** on the Toolbar, type **Rails and Trails Project**, and then press **Enter**.

You create a folder where you can organize subfolders and files for the Rails and Trails project.

c. Double-click **Rails and Trails Project** in the Content pane (middle pane). The Address bar should show that it is the currently selected folder. Click **New folder**, type **Promotional**, and then press **Enter**.

You decide to create subfolders of the Rails and Trails Project folder to contain promotional material, presentations, and office records. You create three subfolders, appropriately named.

d. Check the Address bar to make sure *Rails and Trails Project* is still the current folder. Click **New folder**, type **Presentations**, and then press **Enter**.

e. Click **New folder**, type **Office Records**, and then press **Enter**.

f. Double-click **Promotional** in the middle pane. Click **New folder**, type **Form Letters**, and then press **Enter**. Click **New folder**, type **Flyers**, and then press **Enter**.

To subdivide the promotional material further, you create two subfolders, one to hold form letters and one to contain flyers. Your screen should appear as in Figure 1.8.

g. Close Windows Explorer.

STEP 2 ► **CREATE AND SAVE A FILE**

As the project gears up, you assign volunteers to take care of certain tasks. After creating an Excel worksheet listing those responsibilities, you will save it in the Office Records folder. Refer to Figure 1.9 as you complete Step 2.

FIGURE 1.9 Volunteers Worksheet ➤

a. Click the **Start button**, and then point to **All Programs**. Scroll down the program list, if necessary, and then click **Microsoft Office**. Click **Microsoft Excel 2010**.

You use Microsoft Excel to create the volunteers worksheet.

b. Type **Rails and Trails Assignments** in **cell A1**. Press **Enter** twice.

Your cursor will be in cell A3.

c. Type **Category**. Press **Tab** to move the cursor one cell to the right, and then type **Volunteer**. Press **Enter**. Complete the remaining cells of the worksheet as shown in Figure 1.9.

d. Click the **File tab** (in the top-left corner of the Excel window). Click **Save**.

The Save As dialog box displays. The Save As dialog box is where you determine the location, file name, and file type of any document. You can also create a new folder in the Save As dialog box.

e. Scroll down if necessary, and then click **Computer** in the left pane. In the Content pane, double-click the drive where you will save the file. Double-click **Rails and Trails Project** in the Content pane. Double-click **Office Records**. Click in the **File name box**. Type **f01h1volunteers_LastnameFirstname** in the **file name box**, replacing *LastnameFirstname* with your own last name and first name. Click **Save**.

The file is now saved as *f01h1volunteers_LastnameFirstname*. You can check the title bar of the workbook to confirm the file has been saved with the correct name.

f. Click the **Close button** in the top-right corner of the Excel window to close Excel.

> **TROUBLESHOOTING:** If you click the lower X instead of the one in the top-right corner, the current Excel worksheet will close, but Excel will remain open. In that case, click the remaining X to close Excel.

The Volunteers workbook is saved in the Office Records subfolder of the Rails and Trails Project folder.

STEP 3 ▶ RENAME AND DELETE A FOLDER

As often happens, you find that the folder structure is not exactly what you need. You will remove the Flyers folder and the Form Letters folder and will rename the Promotional folder to better describe the contents. Refer to Figure 1.10 as you complete Step 3.

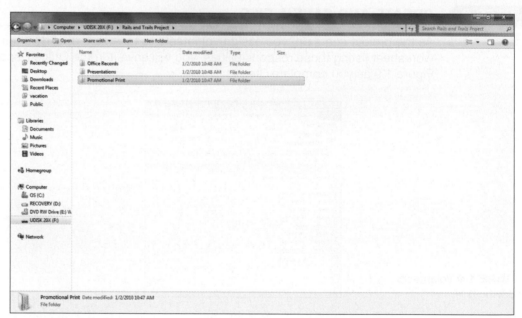

FIGURE 1.10 Rails and Trails Project Folder Structure ➤

a. Right-click the **Start button**. Click **Open Windows Explorer**. Click the disk drive where you save your files (under Computer in the Navigation Pane). Double-click **Rails and Trails Project** in the Content pane.

b. Click the **Promotional folder** to select it.

> **TROUBLESHOOTING:** If you double-click the folder instead of using a single-click, the folder will open and you will see its title in the Address bar. To return to the correct view, click Rails and Trails Project in the Address bar.

c. Click **Organize**, click **Rename**, type **Promotional Print**, and then press **Enter**.

Since the folder will be used to organize all of the printed promotional material, you decide to rename the folder to better reflect the contents.

d. Double-click **Promotional Print**. Click **Flyers**. Hold down **Shift**, and then click **Form Letters**. Both folders should be selected (highlighted). Right-click either folder, and then click **Delete**. If asked to confirm the deletion, click **Yes**. Click **Rails and Trails Project** in the **Address bar**. Your screen should appear as shown in Figure 1.10. Leave Windows Explorer open for the next step.

You decide that dividing the promotional material into flyers and form letters is not necessary, so you delete both folders.

STEP 4 **OPEN AND COPY A FILE**

You hope to recruit more volunteers to work with the Rails and Trails project. The Volunteers worksheet will be a handy way to keep up with people and assignments, and as the list grows, knowing exactly where the file is saved will be important for easy access. You will modify the Volunteers worksheet and then make a backup copy of the folder hierarchy. Refer to Figure 1.11 as you complete Step 4.

FIGURE 1.11 Rails and Trails Folder Structure ➤

a. Double-click the **Office Records folder**. Double-click *f01h1volunteers_LastnameFirstname*.

Because the file was created with Excel, that program opens, and the volunteers worksheet is displayed.

b. Click **cell A11**, and then type **Office**. Press **Tab**, type **Adams**, and then press **Enter**. Click the **File tab** in the top-left corner of the Excel window, and then click **Save**. The file is automatically saved in the same location with the same file name as before. Close Excel.

A neighbor, Samantha Adams, has volunteered to help in the office. You record that information on the worksheet and save the updated file in the Office Records folder.

c. Click the location where you save files in the Navigation Pane in Windows Explorer. Right-click **Rails and Trails Project** in the right pane. Click **Copy**.

d. Right-click **Desktop** in the Favorites group on the Navigation Pane, and then click **Paste**. Close Windows Explorer. If any other windows are open, close them also.

You make a copy of the Rails and Trails Project folder on the desktop.

e. Double-click **Rails and Trails Project** on the desktop. Double-click **Office Records**. Is the volunteers worksheet in the folder? Your screen should appear as shown in Figure 1.11. Close Windows Explorer.

f. Right-click the **Rails and Trails Project folder** on the desktop, click **Delete**, and then click **Yes** when asked to confirm the deletion.

You delete the Rails and Trails Project folder from the desktop of the computer because you may be working in a computer lab and want to leave the computer as you found it.

Microsoft Office Software

Organizations around the world rely heavily on *Microsoft Office* software to produce documents, spreadsheets, presentations, and databases. Microsoft Office is a productivity software suite including four primary software components, each one specializing in a particular type of output. You can use *Word* to produce all sorts of documents, including memos, newsletters, forms, tables, and brochures. *Excel* makes it easy to organize records, financial transactions, and business information in the form of worksheets. With *PowerPoint*, you can create dynamic presentations to inform groups and persuade audiences. *Access* is relational database software that enables you to record and link data, query databases, and create forms and reports. You will sometimes find that you need to use two or more Office applications to produce your intended output. You might, for example, find that a Word document you are preparing for your investment club should also include a summary of stock performance. You can use Excel to prepare the summary and then incorporate the worksheet in the Word document. Similarly, you can integrate Word tables and Excel charts in a PowerPoint presentation. The choice of which software component to use really depends on what type of output you are producing. Table 1.2 describes the major tasks of the four primary programs in Microsoft Office.

> Microsoft Office is a productivity software suite including four primary software components, each one specializing in a particular type of output.

Microsoft Office is a productivity software suite that includes word processing, spreadsheet, presentation, and database software components.

Word is a word processing program included in Microsoft Office.

Excel is software that specializes in organizing data in worksheet form. It is included in Microsoft Office.

PowerPoint is a Microsoft Office software component that enables you to prepare slideshow presentations for audiences.

Access is a database program included in Microsoft Office.

TABLE 1.2 Microsoft Office Software	
Office 2010 Product	**Application Characteristics**
Word 2010	Word processing software is used with text to create, edit, and format documents such as letters, memos, reports, brochures, resumes, and flyers.
Excel 2010	Spreadsheet software is used to store quantitative data and to perform accurate and rapid calculations with results ranging from simple budgets to financial analyses and statistical analyses.
PowerPoint 2010	Presentation graphics software is used to create slide shows for presentation by a speaker, to be published as part of a Web site, or to run as a stand-alone application on a computer kiosk.
Access 2010	Relational database software is used to store data and convert it into information. Database software is used primarily for decision-making by businesses that compile data from multiple records stored in tables to produce informative reports.

As you become familiar with Microsoft Office, you will find that although each software component produces a specific type of output, all components share common features. Such commonality gives a similar feel to each software application so that learning and working with primary Microsoft Office software products is easy. In this section, you will identify features common to Microsoft Office software, including such interface components as the Ribbon, the Backstage view, and the Quick Access Toolbar. You will also learn how to get help with an application.

Identifying Common Interface Components

A **user interface** is a collection of onscreen components that facilitates communication between the software and the user.

As you work with Microsoft Office, you will find that each application shares a similar *user interface*. The user interface is the screen display through which you communicate with the software. Word, Excel, PowerPoint, and Access share common interface elements, as shown in Figure 1.12. As you can imagine, becoming familiar with one application's interface makes it that much easier to work with other Office software.

FIGURE 1.12 Microsoft Office Interface ➤

Use the Backstage View and the Quick Access Toolbar

The **Backstage view** is a new component of Office 2010 that provides a concise collection of commands related to an open file. Using the Backstage view, you can print, save, open, close, and share a file. In addition, you can view properties and other information related to the file. A file's properties include the author, file size, permissions, and date modified. You can access the Backstage view by clicking the File tab. The **Quick Access Toolbar**, located at the top-left corner of the Office window, provides handy access to commonly executed tasks such as saving a file and undoing recent actions. The **title bar** identifies the current file name and the application in which you are working. It also includes control buttons that enable you to minimize, maximize, restore down, or close the application window. Refer to Figure 1.12 for the location of those items on the title bar.

> Using the Backstage view, you can print, save, open, close, and share a file.

The **Backstage view** displays when you click the File tab. It includes commands related to common file activities and provides information on an open file.

The **Quick Access Toolbar** provides one-click access to commonly used commands.

The **title bar** contains the current file name, Office application, and control buttons.

When you click the File tab, you will see the Backstage view, as shown in Figure 1.13. Primarily focusing on file activities such as opening, closing, saving, printing, and beginning new files, the Backstage view also includes options for customizing program settings, getting help, and exiting the program. It displays a file's properties, providing important information on file permission and sharing options. When you click the File tab, the Backstage view will occupy the entire application window, hiding the file with which you might be working. For example, suppose that as you are typing a report you need to check the document's properties. Click the File tab to display a Backstage view similar to that shown in Figure 1.13. You can return to the application—in this case, Word—in a couple of ways. Simply click the File tab again (or any other tab on the Ribbon). Alternatively, you can press Esc on the keyboard. The Ribbon is described in the next section.

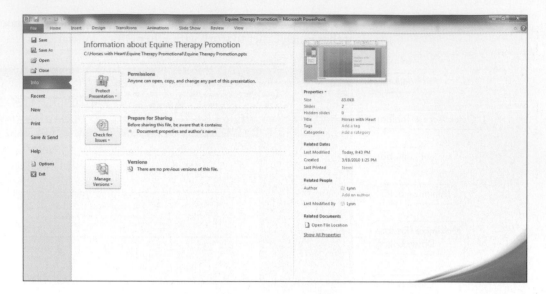

FIGURE 1.13 Backstage View ➤

The Quick Access Toolbar provides one-click access to common activities. Figure 1.14 describes the Quick Access Toolbar. By default, the Quick Access Toolbar includes buttons for saving a file and for undoing or redoing recent actions. You will probably perform an action countless times in an Office application and then realize that you made a mistake. You can recover from the mistake by clicking Undo on the Quick Access Toolbar. If you click the arrow beside Undo, you can select from a list of previous actions in order of occurrence. The Undo list is not maintained when you close a file or exit the application, so you can only erase an action that took place during the current Office session. Similar to Undo, you can also Redo (or Replace) an action that you have just undone. You can customize the Quick Access Toolbar to include buttons for frequently used commands such as printing or opening files. Because the Quick Access Toolbar is onscreen at all times, the most commonly accessed tasks are just a click away.

FIGURE 1.14 Quick Access Toolbar ➤

> **TIP** Customizing the Quick Access Toolbar
>
> To customize the Quick Access Toolbar, click Customize Quick Access Toolbar, as shown in Figure 1.14, and select from a list of commands. If a command that you want to include on the toolbar is not on the list, you can simply right-click the command on the Ribbon, and then click Add to Quick Access Toolbar. Similarly, remove a command from the Quick Access Toolbar by right-clicking the icon on the Quick Access Toolbar, and then clicking Remove from Quick Access Toolbar. If you want to display the Quick Access Toolbar beneath the Ribbon, click Customize Quick Access Toolbar (Figure 1.14), and then click Show Below the Ribbon.

Familiarize Yourself with the Ribbon

The **Ribbon** is the long bar of tabs, groups, and commands located just beneath the Title bar.

Each **tab** on the Ribbon contains groups of related tasks.

A **group** is a subset of a tab that organizes similar tasks together.

A **command** is a button or area within a group that you click to perform tasks.

The ***Ribbon*** is the command center of Office applications. It is the long bar located just beneath the Title bar, containing tabs, groups, and commands. Each ***tab*** is designed to appear much like a tab on a file folder, with the active tab highlighted. The File tab is always a darker shade than the other tabs, and a different color depending on the application. Remember that clicking the File tab opens the Backstage view. Other tabs on the Ribbon enable you to create and modify a file. The active tab in Figure 1.15 is the Home tab.

When you click a tab, the Ribbon displays several task-oriented ***groups***, with each group containing related ***commands***. Microsoft Office is designed to provide the most functionality possible with the fewest clicks. For that reason, the Home tab, displayed when you first open an Office software application, contains groups and commands that are commonly used. For example, because you will often want to change the way text is displayed, the Home tab in each Office application includes a Font group with activities related to modifying text. Similarly, other tabs contain groups of related actions, or commands, many of which are unique to the particular Office application.

FIGURE 1.15 Ribbon ➤

Because Word, PowerPoint, Excel, and Access all share a similar Ribbon structure, you will be able to move at ease among those applications. Although the specific tabs, groups,

> Because Word, PowerPoint, Excel, and Access all share a similar Ribbon structure, you will be able to move at ease among those applications.

and commands vary among the Office programs, the way in which you use the Ribbon and the descriptive nature of tab titles is the same regardless of which program you are working with. For example, if you want to insert a chart in Excel, a header in Word, or a shape in PowerPoint, you will click the Insert tab in any of those programs. The first thing that you should do as you begin to work with an Office application is to study the Ribbon. Take a look at all tabs and their contents. That way, you will have a good idea of where to find specific commands and how the Ribbon with which you are currently working differs from one that you might have used previously in another application.

> ### TIP Hiding the Ribbon
>
> The Ribbon occupies a good bit of space at the top of the Office interface. If you are working with a large project, you might want to maximize your workspace by temporarily hiding the Ribbon. You can hide the Ribbon in several ways. Double-click the active tab to hide the Ribbon, and then double-click any tab to redisplay it. Alternatively, you can press Ctrl+F1 to hide the Ribbon, with the same shortcut key combination redisplaying it. Finally, you can click Minimize the Ribbon (see Figure 1.15), located at the right side of the Ribbon, clicking it a second time to redisplay the Ribbon.

A **dialog box** is a window that enables you to make selections or indicate settings beyond those provided on the Ribbon.

A **Dialog Box Launcher** is an icon in Ribbon groups that you can click to open a related dialog box. It is not found in all groups.

The Ribbon provides quick access to common activities such as changing number or text formats or aligning data or text. Some actions, however, are not so common but are related to commands displayed on the Ribbon. For example, you might want to change the background of a PowerPoint slide to include a picture. In that case, you will need to work with a ***dialog box*** that provides access to more precise, but less frequently used, commands. Figure 1.16 shows a dialog box. Some commands display a dialog box when they are clicked. Other Ribbon groups include a ***Dialog Box Launcher*** that, when clicked, opens a corresponding dialog box. Figure 1.15 shows a Dialog Box Launcher.

Dialog box Help button

FIGURE 1.16 Dialog Box ➤

A **gallery** is a set of selections that appears when you click a More button, or in some cases when you click a command, in a Ribbon group.

The Ribbon contains many selections and commands, but some selections are too numerous to include in the Ribbon's limited space. For example, Word provides far more text styles than it can easily display at once, so additional styles are available in a *gallery*. A gallery also provides a choice of Excel chart styles and PowerPoint transitions. Figure 1.17 gives an example of a PowerPoint Themes gallery. Most often, you can display a gallery of additional choices by clicking the More button that is found in some Ribbon selections. Figure 1.15 shows a More button.

Themes gallery

FIGURE 1.17 PowerPoint Themes Gallery ➤

Live Preview is an Office feature that provides a preview of the results of a selection when you point to an option in a list. Using Live Preview, you can experiment with settings before making a final choice.

A **contextual tab** is a Ribbon tab that displays when an object, such as a picture or clip art, is selected. A contextual tab contains groups and commands specific to the selected object.

When editing a document, worksheet, or presentation, it is helpful to see the results of formatting changes before you make final selections. You might be considering changing the font color of a selection in a document or worksheet. As you place the mouse pointer over a color selection in a Ribbon gallery or group, the selected text will temporarily display the color to which you are pointing. Similarly, you can get a preview of how color designs would appear on PowerPoint slides by pointing to specific themes in the PowerPoint Themes group and noting the effect on a displayed slide. When you click the item, such as the font color, the selection is applied. The feature enabling a preview of the results of a selection is called *Live Preview*. It is available in various Ribbon selections among the Office applications.

Office applications make it easy for you to work with objects such as pictures, clip art, shapes, charts, and tables. When you include such objects in a project, they are considered separate components that you can manage independently. To work with an object, you must click to select it. When you select an object, the Ribbon is modified to include one or more *contextual tabs* containing groups of commands related to the selected object. Figure 1.18 shows a contextual tab related to a selected object in a Word document. When you click outside the selected object, the contextual tab disappears.

Contextual tab

FIGURE 1.18 Contextual Tab ➤

A **Key Tip** is the letter or number that displays over features on the Ribbon and Quick Access Toolbar. Typing the letter or number is the equivalent of clicking the corresponding item.

Use the Status Bar

The *status bar* is found at the bottom of the program window and contains information relative to the open file. It also includes tools for changing the view of the file and for changing the size of onscreen file contents. Contents of the status bar are unique to each specific application. When you work with Word, the status bar informs you of the number of pages and words in an open document. Excel's status bar displays summary information, such as average and sum, of selected cells. The PowerPoint status bar shows the slide number, total slides in the presentation, and the applied theme.

The **status bar** is the horizontal bar located at the bottom of an Office application containing information relative to the open file.

Regardless of the application in which you are working, the status bar includes view buttons and a Zoom slider. You can also use the View tab on the Ribbon to change the current view or zoom level of an open file. The status bar's view buttons, shown in Figure 1.19, enable you to change the *view* of the open file. You might, for example, view a PowerPoint slide presentation with multiple slides displayed (Slide Sorter view) or with only one slide in large size (Normal view). In Word, you could view a document in Print Layout view (showing margins, headers, and footers), Full Screen Reading view, Web Layout view, or Draft view (with the greatest amount of typing space possible). As you learn more about Office applications in the following chapters, you will become aware of the views that are specific to each application.

Changing the **view** of a file changes the way it appears onscreen.

FIGURE 1.19 Word Status Bar ➤

The **Zoom slider** enables you to increase or decrease the size of file contents onscreen.

The *Zoom slider* always displays at the far right side of the status bar. You can drag the tab along the slider in either direction to increase or decrease the magnification of the file. Be aware, however, that changing the size of text onscreen does not increase the font size when the file is printed or saved.

Getting Office Help

One of the most frustrating things about learning new software is determining how to complete a task. Thankfully, Microsoft includes comprehensive help in Office so that you are less likely to feel such frustration. As you work with any Office application, you can access help online as well as within the current software installation. Help is also available through a short description that displays when you rest the mouse pointer on a command. Additionally, you can get help related to a currently open dialog box by clicking a question mark in the top-right corner of the dialog box or when you click the Help button in the Backstage view.

Use Office Help

To access the comprehensive library of Office Help, click the Help button, displayed as a question mark, on the far right side of the Ribbon (see Figure 1.15). You can get the same help by pressing F1 on the keyboard. The Backstage view also includes a Help feature, providing assistance with the current application as well as a direct link to online resources and technical support. Figure 1.20 shows the Help window that will display when you press F1, when you click the Help button, or when you click File, Help, Microsoft Office Help. For general information on broad topics, click a link in the window. However, if you are having difficulty with a specific task, it might be easier to simply type the request in the Search box. Suppose you are seeking help with using the Goal Seek feature in Excel. Simply type *Goal Seek* or a phrase such as *find specific result by changing variables* in the Search box, and press Enter (or click the magnifying glass on the right). Then select from displayed results for more information on the topic.

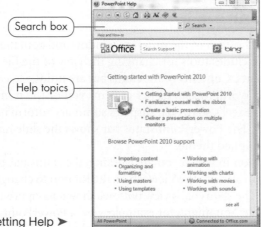

FIGURE 1.20 Getting Help ➤

Use Enhanced ScreenTips

An **Enhanced ScreenTip** provides a brief summary of a command when you place the mouse pointer over the command button.

For quick summary information on the purpose of a command button, place the mouse pointer over the button. An ***Enhanced ScreenTip*** displays, giving the purpose of the command, short descriptive text, and a keyboard shortcut if applicable. Some ScreenTips include a suggestion for pressing F1 for additional help. The Enhanced ScreenTip in Figure 1.21 provides context-sensitive assistance.

FIGURE 1.21 Enhanced ScreenTip ➤

Get Help with Dialog Boxes

Getting help while you are working with a dialog box is easy. Simply click the Help button that appears as a question mark in the top-right corner of the dialog box (see Figure 1.16). The subsequent Help window will offer suggestions relevant to your task.

HANDS-ON EXERCISES

myitlab
HOE2 Training

2 Microsoft Office Software

As the administrative assistant for the Rails and Trails project, you need to get the staff started on a proposed fund-management worksheet. Although you do not have access to information on current donations, you want to provide a suggested format for a worksheet to keep up with donations as they come in. You will use Excel to begin design of the worksheet.

Skills covered: Open an Office Application, Get Enhanced ScreenTip Help, and Use the Zoom Slider • Get Help, Use the Backstage View • Change the View and Use Live Preview • Use the Quick Access Toolbar and Explore PowerPoint Views

---

STEP 1 ▶ **OPEN AN OFFICE APPLICATION, GET ENHANCED SCREENTIP HELP, AND USE THE ZOOM SLIDER**

Because you will use Excel to create the fund-raising worksheet, you will open the application. You will familiarize yourself with items on the Ribbon by getting Enhanced ScreenTip Help. For a better view of worksheet data, you will use the Zoom slider to magnify cell contents. Refer to Figure 1.22 as you complete Step 1.

FIGURE 1.22 Fund-Raising Worksheet ▶

a. Click the **Start button** to display the Start Menu. Point to **All Programs**. Scroll down the list, if necessary, and click **Microsoft Office**. Click **Microsoft Excel 2010**.

You have opened Microsoft Excel because it is the program in which the fund-raising worksheet will be created.

b. Type **Date**. As you type, the text appears in the current worksheet cell, **cell A1**. Press **Tab**, and then type **Contact**. Press **Tab**, and then type **Amount**. Press **Enter**. Your worksheet should look like the one in Figure 1.22.

The worksheet that you create is only a beginning. Your staff will later suggest additional columns of data that can better summarize the hoped-for donations.

c. Hover the mouse pointer over any command on the Ribbon and note the Enhanced ScreenTip that displays, informing you of the purpose of the command. Explore other commands and identify their purpose.

d. Click the **Page Layout tab**, click **Orientation** in the Page Setup group, and then click **Landscape**.

The Page Layout tab is also found in Word, enabling you to change margins, orientation, and other page settings. Although you will not see much difference in the Excel screen display after you change the orientation to landscape, the worksheet will be oriented so that it is wider than it is tall when printed.

e. Drag the tab on the **Zoom slider**, located at the far right side of the status bar, to the right to temporarily magnify the text. Click the **View tab**, and then click **100%** in the Zoom group to return the text to its original size. Keep the workbook open for the next step in this exercise.

When you change the zoom, you do not change the text size that will be printed or saved. The change merely magnifies or decreases the view while you work with the file.

STEP 2 GET HELP, USE THE BACKSTAGE VIEW

Because you are not an Excel expert, you occasionally rely on the Help feature to provide information on tasks. You need assistance with saving a worksheet, previewing it before printing, and printing the worksheet. From what you learn, you will find that the Backstage view enables you to accomplish all of those tasks. Refer to Figure 1.23 as you complete Step 2.

Search box

FIGURE 1.23 Getting Help ➤

a. Click the **Help button**, which is the question mark in the top-right corner of the Ribbon.

The Help dialog box displays.

b. Click in the white text box to the left of the word *Search* in the Help dialog box, as shown in Figure 1.23. Type **preview before printing** and click **Search**. In the Help window, click **Preview worksheet pages before printing**. Read about how to preview a worksheet before printing. From what you read, can you identify a keyboard shortcut for previewing worksheets? Click the **Close button**.

Before you print the worksheet, you would like to see how it will look when printed. You can use Help to find information on previewing before printing.

> **TROUBLESHOOTING:** You must be connected to the Internet to get context-sensitive help.

c. Click the **File tab**, and then click **Print**.

Having used Office Help to learn how to preview before printing, you follow the directions to view the document as it will look when printed. The preview of the worksheet displays on the right. To print the worksheet, you would click Print. However, you can first select any print options, such as the number of copies, from the Backstage view.

d. Click the **Help button**. Excel Help presents several links related to the worksheet. Explore any that look interesting. Return to previous Help windows by clicking **Back** at the top-left side of the Help window. Close the Help dialog box.

e. Click the **Home tab**. Point to **Bold** in the Font group.

You will find that, along with Excel, Word and PowerPoint also include formatting features in the Font group, such as Bold and Italic. When the Enhanced ScreenTip appears, identify the shortcut key combination that could be used to bold a selected text item. It is indicated as Ctrl plus a letter. What is the shortcut?

f. Click the **Close button** in the red box in the top-right corner of the Excel window to close both the workbook and the Excel program. When asked whether you want to save changes, click **Don't Save**.

You decide not to print or save the worksheet right now. Instead, you will get assistance with its design and try it again later.

> **TROUBLESHOOTING:** If you clicked the Close button on the second row from the top, you closed the workbook but not Excel. Click the remaining Close button to close the program.

STEP 3 ▶ CHANGE THE VIEW AND USE LIVE PREVIEW

It is important that the documents you prepare or approve are error-free and as attractive as possible. Before printing, you will change the view to get a better idea of how the document will look when printed. In addition, you will use Live Preview to experiment with font settings before actually applying them. Refer to Figure 1.24 as you complete Step 3.

FIGURE 1.24 Word Views ➤

a. Click the **Start button**, and then point to **All Programs**. Scroll down, if necessary, and click **Microsoft Office**. Click **Microsoft Word 2010**.

You have opened a blank Word document. You plan to familiarize yourself with the program for later reference.

b. Type your full name, and then press **Enter**. Drag to select your name (or position the mouse pointer immediately to the left of your name so that the pointer looks like a white arrow, and then click). Your name should be shaded, indicating that it is selected.

You have selected your name because you want to experiment with using Word to change the way text looks.

c. Click the **Font Size arrow** in the Font group on the Home tab. If you need help locating Font Size, check for an Enhanced ScreenTip. Place the mouse pointer over any number in the subsequent list, but do not click. As you move to another number, notice the size of your name change. The feature you are using is called Live Preview. Click any number in the list to change the text size of your name.

d. Click **Draft** in the View Shortcuts group on the status bar to change the view (see Figure 1.24).

When creating a document, you might find it helpful to change the view. Word's Print Layout view is useful when you want to see both the document text and such features as margins and page breaks. Draft view provides a full screen of typing space without displaying margins or other print features, such as headers or footers. PowerPoint, Excel, and Access also provide view options, although they are unique to the application. The most common view options are accessible from View Shortcuts on the status bar of each application.

e. Click the **Close button** in the top-right corner of the Word window to close both the current document and the Word program. When asked whether you want to save the file, click **Don't Save**.

During the course of the Rails and Trails project, you will be asked to review documents, presentations, and worksheets. It is important that you explore each application to familiarize yourself with operations and commonalities. Specifically, you know that the Quick Access Toolbar is common to all applications and that you can place commonly used commands there to streamline processes. Also, learning to change views will enable you to see the project in different ways for various purposes. Refer to Figure 1.25 as you complete Step 4.

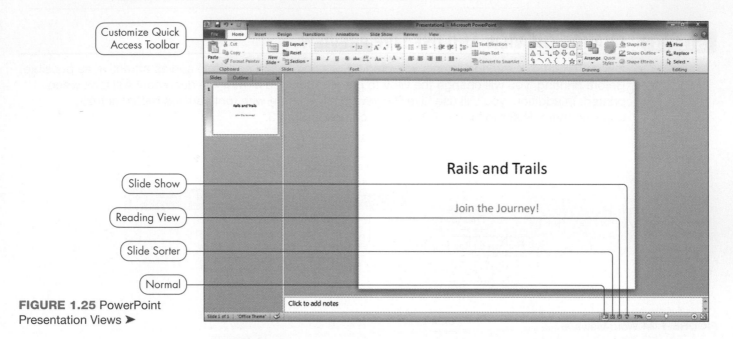

FIGURE 1.25 PowerPoint Presentation Views ➤

a. Click the **Start button**, and then point to **All Programs**. Scroll down, if necessary, and click **Microsoft Office**. Click **Microsoft PowerPoint 2010**.

You have opened PowerPoint. You see a blank presentation.

b. Click **Click to add title**, and then type **Rails and Trails**. Click in the bottom, subtitle box, and then type **Join the Journey!** Click the bottom-right corner of the slide to deselect the subtitle. Your PowerPoint presentation should look like that shown in Figure 1.25.

c. Click **Undo** on the Quick Access Toolbar.

The subtitle on the current slide is removed because it is the most recent action.

d. Click **Slide Sorter** in the View Shortcuts group on the status bar.

The Slide Sorter view shows thumbnails of all slides in a presentation. Because this presentation has only one slide, you see a small version of one slide.

e. Move the mouse pointer to any button on the Quick Access Toolbar and hold it steady. See the tip giving the button name and the shortcut key combination, if any. Move to another button and see the description.

The Quick Access Toolbar has at least three buttons, Save, Undo, and Redo (or Repeat). In addition, a small arrow is included at the far-right side. If you hold the mouse pointer steady on the arrow, you will see the ScreenTip Customize Quick Access Toolbar.

f. Click **Customize Quick Access Toolbar**. From the menu, click **New**. The New button enables you to quickly create a new presentation (also called a document).

g. Click **Customize Quick Access Toolbar**, and then click **New**. The button is removed from the Quick Access Toolbar.

You can customize the Quick Access Toolbar by adding and removing items.

h. Click **Normal** in the View Shortcuts group on the status bar.

The presentation returns to the original view in which the slide displays in full size.

i. Click **Slide Show** in the View Shortcuts group on the status bar.

The presentation is shown in Slide Show view, which is the way it will be presented to audiences.

j. Press **Esc** to end the presentation.

k. Close the presentation without saving it. Exit PowerPoint.

Backstage View Tasks

When you work with Microsoft Office files, you will often want to open previously saved files, create new ones, print items, and save and close files. You will also find it necessary to indicate options, or preferences, of settings. For example, you might want a spelling check to occur automatically, or you might prefer to initiate a spelling check only occasionally. Getting Help is also a common selection that you want to find easily. Because those tasks are applicable to each software application within the Office 2010 suite, they are accomplished through a common area in the Office interface—the Backstage view. Open the Backstage view by clicking the File tab. Figure 1.26 shows the area that displays when you click the File tab. The Backstage view also enables you to exit the application and to identify file information, such as the author or date created. In this section, you will explore the Backstage view, learning to create, open, close, and print files.

FIGURE 1.26 Backstage View ➤

Opening a File

When working with an Office application, you can begin by opening an existing file that has already been saved to a storage medium, or you can begin work on a new file. Both actions are available when you click the File tab. When you first open Word, Excel, or PowerPoint, you will be presented with a new blank work area that you can begin using immediately. When you first open Access, you will need to save the file before you can begin working with it. You can also open a project that you previously saved to a disk.

Create a New File

After opening an Office application, such as Word, Excel, or PowerPoint, you will be presented with a blank document area. The word *document* is sometimes used generically to refer to any Office file, including a Word document, an Excel worksheet, or a PowerPoint presentation. Perhaps you are already working with a document in an Office application but want to create a new file. Simply click the File tab, and then click New. Double-click Blank document (or Blank presentation or Blank workbook, depending on the specific application). You can also single-click Blank document, and then click Create.

Open a File Using the Open Dialog Box

If you choose to open a previously saved file, as you will need to do when you work with the data files for this book, you will work with the Open dialog box as shown in Figure 1.27. That dialog box appears after you select Open from the File tab. Using the Navigation Pane, you will make your way to the file to be opened. Double-click the file or click the file name once, and then click Open. Most likely, the file will be located within a folder that is appropriately named to make it easy to find related files. Obviously, if you are not well aware of the file's location and file name, the process of opening a file could become quite cumbersome. However, if you have created a well-designed system of folders, as you learned to do in the *Files and Folders* section of this chapter, you will know exactly where to find the file.

FIGURE 1.27 Open Dialog Box ➤

Open a File Using the Recent Documents List

You will often work with a file, save it, and then continue the project at a later time. Office simplifies the task of reopening the file by providing a Recent Documents list with links to your most recently opened files. See Figure 1.28 for an example of a Recent Documents list. To access the list, click the File tab, and then click Recent. Select from any files listed in the right pane. The list constantly changes to reflect only the most recently opened files, so if it has been quite some time since you worked with a particular file, you might have to work with the Open dialog box instead of the Recent Documents list.

Pushpin icon

FIGURE 1.28 Recent Documents List ➤

TIP Keeping Files on the Recent Documents List

The Recent Documents list displays a limited list of only the most recently opened files. You might, however, want to keep a particular file in the list regardless of how recently it was opened. In Figure 1.28, note the pushpin icon that appears to the right of each file. Click the icon to cause the file to remain in the list. At that point, you will always have access to the file by clicking the File tab and selecting the file from the Recent Documents list. The pushpin of the "permanent" file will change direction so that it appears to be inserted, indicating that it is a pinned item. If later you want to remove the file from the list, simply click the inserted push-pin, changing its direction and allowing the file to be bumped off the list when other, more recently opened, files take its place.

Open a File from the Templates List

A **template** is a predesigned file that you can modify to suit your needs.

You do not need to create a new file if you can access a predesigned file that meets your needs or one that you can modify fairly quickly to complete your project. Office provides such files, called *templates*, making them available when you click the File tab and then New. Refer to Figure 1.29 for an example of a Templates list. The top area is comprised of template groups

> You do not need to create a new file if you can access a predesigned file that meets your needs or one that you can modify fairly quickly to complete your project. Office provides such files, called templates.

available within the current Office installation on your computer. The lower category includes template groups that are available from Office.com. When you click to select a group, you are sometimes presented with additional choices to narrow your selection to a particular file. For example, you might want to prepare a home budget. After opening Excel, click the File tab, and then click New. From the template categories, you could click Budgets from the Office.com Templates area, click Monthly Family

Budget, and then click Download to display the associated worksheet (or simply double-click Monthly Family Budget). If a Help window displays along with the worksheet template, click to close it, or explore Help to learn more about the template. If you know only a little bit about Excel, you could then make a few changes so that the worksheet would accurately represent your family's financial situation. The budget would be prepared much more quickly than if you began the project with a blank workbook, designing it yourself.

Templates available in a typical Office installation

Templates available from Office.com

FIGURE 1.29 Working with Templates ➤

Printing a File

There will be occasions when you will want to print an Office project. Before printing, you should preview the file to get an idea of how it will look when printed. That way, if there are obvious problems with the page setup, you can correct them before wasting paper on something that is not correct. When you are ready to print, you can select from various print options, including the number of copies and the specific pages to print. If you know that the page setup is correct and that there are no unique print settings to select, you can simply print the project without adjusting any print settings.

It is a good idea to take a look at how your document will appear before you print it. The Print Preview feature of Office enables you to do just that.

It is a good idea to take a look at how your document will appear before you print it. The Print Preview feature of Office enables you to do just that. In Print Preview, you will see all items, including any headers, footers, graphics, and special formatting. To view a project before printing, click the File tab, and then click Print. The subsequent Backstage view shows the file preview on the right, with print settings located in the center of the Backstage screen. Figure 1.30 shows a typical Backstage print view.

Print Preview

Print

Print Settings

Zoom to Page

Zoom slider

FIGURE 1.30 Backstage Print View ➤

To increase the size of the file preview, drag the Zoom slider to the right. The Zoom slider is found on the right side of the status bar, beneath the preview. Remember that increasing the font size by adjusting the zoom only applies to the current display. It does not actually increase the font size when the document is printed or saved. To return the preview to its original size, click Zoom to Page found at the right of the Zoom slider. See Figure 1.30 for the location of the Zoom slider and Zoom to Page.

Other options on the Backstage Print view vary, depending on the application in which you are working. Regardless of the Office application, you will be able to access Print Setup options from the Backstage view, including page orientation (landscape or portrait), margins, and page size. You will find a more detailed explanation of those settings in the *Page Layout Tab Tasks* section later in this chapter. To print a file, click Print (shown in Figure 1.30).

The Backstage Print view shown in Figure 1.30 is very similar across all Office applications. However, you will find slight variations specific to each application. For example, PowerPoint's Backstage Print view includes options for printing slides and handouts in various configurations and colors, whereas Excel's focuses on worksheet selections and Word's includes document options. Regardless of software, the manner of working with Backstage's print options remains consistent.

Closing a File and Application

Although you can have several documents open at one time, limiting the number of open files is a good idea. Office applications have no problem keeping up with multiple open files, but you can easily become overwhelmed with them. When you are done with an open project, you will need to close it along with the application itself.

You can easily close any files that you no longer need. With the desired file on the screen, click the File tab, and then click the Close button. Respond to any prompt that might appear suggesting that you save the file. The application remains open, but the selected file is closed. To close the application, click the File tab, and then click Exit.

> **TIP** Closing a File and an Application
>
> When you close an application, all open files within the application are also closed. You will be prompted to save any files before they are closed. A quick way to close an application is to click the X in the top-right corner of the application window.

3 Backstage View Tasks

Projects related to the Rails and Trails project have begun to come in for your review and approval. You have received an informational flyer to be distributed to civic and professional groups around the city. It contains a new logo along with descriptive text. Another task on your agenda is to keep the project moving according to schedule. You will identify a calendar template to print and distribute. You will explore printing options, and you will save the flyer and the calendar to a disk as directed by your instructor.

Skills covered: Open and Save a File • Preview and Print a File • Open a File from the Recent Documents List and Open a Template

STEP 1 ▶ OPEN AND SAVE A FILE

You have asked your staff to develop a logo that can be used to promote the Rails and Trails project. You will open a Word document that includes a proposed logo and you will save the document to a disk drive. Refer to Figure 1.31 as you complete Step 1.

FIGURE 1.31 Promotional Flyer (Word Document) ▶

a. Click the **Start button** to display the Start Menu, and then click **All Programs**. Scroll down the list, if necessary, and then click **Microsoft Office**. Click **Microsoft Word 2010**.

You have opened Microsoft Word because it is the program in which the promotional flyer is saved.

b. Click the **File tab**, and then click **Open**. Navigate to the location of your student files. Because you are working with Microsoft Word, the only files listed are those that were created with Microsoft Word. Double-click *f01h3flyer* to open the file shown in Figure 1.31. Familiarize yourself with the document.

The logo and the flyer are submitted for your approval. A paragraph underneath the logo will serve as the launching point for an information blitz and the beginning of the fund-raising drive.

c. Click the **File tab**, and then click **Save As**.

You choose the Save As command because you know that it enables you to indicate the location to which the file should be saved, as well as the file name.

d. Click the drive where you save your files, and then double-click **Rails and Trails Project**. Double-click **Office Records**, click in the **File name box**, type **f01h3flyer_ LastnameFirstname**, and then click **Save**. Keep the file open for the next step in this exercise.

PREVIEW AND PRINT A FILE

You approve of the logo, so you will print the document for future reference. You will first preview the document as it will appear when printed. Then you will print the document. Refer to Figure 1.32 as you complete Step 2.

FIGURE 1.32 Backstage Print ➤

a. Click the **File tab**, and then click **Print**.

Figure 1.32 shows the flyer preview. It is always a good idea to check the way a file will look when printed before actually printing it.

b. Drag the **Zoom slider** to increase the document view. Click **Zoom to Page** to return to the original size.

c. Click **Portrait Orientation** in the Print settings area in the center of the screen. Click **Landscape Orientation** to show the flyer in a wider and shorter view.

d. Click **Landscape Orientation**, and click **Portrait Orientation** to return to the original view.

You decide that the flyer is more attractive in portrait orientation, so you return to that setting.

e. Click the **Copies arrow** repeatedly to increase the copies to **5**.

You will need to print five copies of the flyer to distribute to the office assistants for their review.

f. Press **Esc** to leave the Backstage view.

You choose not to print the flyer at this time.

g. Click the **File tab**, and then click the **Close button**. When asked, click **Don't Save** so that changes to the file are not saved. Leave Word open for the next step in this exercise.

OPEN A FILE FROM THE RECENT DOCUMENTS LIST AND OPEN A TEMPLATE

A large part of your responsibility is proofreading Rails and Trails material. You will correct a typo in a phone number in the promotional flyer. You must also keep the staff on task, so you will identify a calendar template on which to list tasks and deadlines. Refer to Figure 1.33 as you complete Step 3.

Recently opened flyer

FIGURE 1.33 Recent Documents List ➤

a. Click the **File tab**, click **Recent** if necessary, and then click *f01h3flyer_LastnameFirstname* in the **Recent Documents list**.

Figure 1.33 shows the Recent Documents list. After clicking the document, the promotional flyer opens.

b. Scroll down, and then click after the number 1 in the telephone number in the contact information. Press **Backspace** on the keyboard, and then type **2**.

You find that the phone number is incorrect, so you make a correction.

c. Click **Save** on the Quick Access Toolbar, click the **File tab**, and then click the **Close button**.

When you click Save on the Quick Access Toolbar, the document is saved in the same location with the same file name as was indicated in the previous save.

d. Click the **File tab**, and then click **New**. From the list of template categories available from Office.com, click **Calendars**, and then click the current year's calendar link.

Office.com provides a wide range of calendar choices. You will select one that is appealing and that will help you keep projects on track.

e. Click a calendar of your choice from the gallery, and then click **Download**. Close any Help window that may open.

The calendar that you selected opens in Word.

> **TROUBLESHOOTING:** It is possible to select a template that is not certified by Microsoft. In that case, you might have to confirm your acceptance of settings before you click Download.

f. Click **Save** on the Quick Access Toolbar. If necessary, navigate to **Office Records** (a subfolder of Rails and Trails Project) on the drive where you save your student files. Save the document as **f01h3calendar_LastnameFirstname**. Click **OK**, if necessary. Close the document, and then exit Word.

Because this is the first time to save the calendar file, the Save button on the Quick Access Toolbar opens a dialog box in which you must indicate the location of the file and the file name.

Home Tab Tasks

You will find that you will repeat some tasks often, whether in Word, Excel, or PowerPoint. You will frequently want to change the format of numbers or words, selecting a different font or changing font size or color. You might also need to change the alignment of text or worksheet cells. Undoubtedly, you will find a reason to copy or cut items and paste them elsewhere in the document, presentation, or worksheet. And you might want to modify file contents by finding and replacing text. All of those tasks, and more, are found on the Home tab of the Ribbon in Word, Excel, and PowerPoint. The Access interface is unique, sharing little with other Office applications, so this section will not address Access. In this section, you will explore the Home tab, learning to format text, copy and paste items, and find and replace words or phrases. Figure 1.34 shows Home tab groups and tasks in the various applications. Note the differences and similarities between the groups.

FIGURE 1.34 Home Tab in Word, Excel, and PowerPoint ➤

Selecting and Editing Text

After creating a document, worksheet, or presentation, you will probably want to make some changes. You might prefer to center a title, or maybe you think that certain worksheet totals should be formatted as currency. You can change the font so that typed characters are larger or in a different style. You might even want to underline text to add emphasis. In all Office applications, the Home tab provides tools for selecting and editing text. You can also use the Mini toolbar for quick changes to selected text.

Select Text to Edit

Before making any changes to existing text or numbers, you must first select the characters. A general rule that you should commit to memory is "Select, then do." A foolproof way to select text or numbers is to place the mouse pointer before the first character of the text you want to select, and then drag to highlight the intended selection. Before you drag, be sure that the mouse pointer takes on the shape of the letter *I*, called the I-bar. Although other methods for selecting exist, if you remember only one way, it should be the click-and-drag method. If your attempted selection falls short of highlighting the intended area, or perhaps highlights too much, simply click outside the selection and try again.

> Before making any changes to existing text or numbers, you must first select the characters. A general rule that you should commit to memory is "Select, then do."

Sometimes it can be difficult to precisely select a small amount of text, such as a single character or a single word. Other times, the task can be overwhelming, such as when selecting an entire 550-page document. Shortcut methods for making selections in Word and PowerPoint are shown in Table 1.3. When working with Excel, you will more often need to select multiple cells. Simply drag the intended selection, usually when the mouse pointer appears as a large white plus sign. The shortcuts shown in Table 1.3 are primarily applicable to Word and PowerPoint.

TABLE 1.3 Shortcut Selection in Word and PowerPoint

Item Selected	Action
One Word	Double-click the word.
One Line of Text	Place the mouse pointer at the left of the line, in the margin area. When the mouse changes to a right-pointing arrow, click to select the line.
One Sentence	Press and hold Ctrl while you click in the sentence to select.
One Paragraph	Triple-click in the paragraph.
One Character to the Left of the Insertion Point	Press and hold Shift while you press ←.
One Character to the Right of the Insertion Point	Press and hold Shift while you press →.
Entire Document	Press and hold Ctrl while you press the letter A on the keyboard.

After having selected a string of characters, such as a number, word, sentence, or document, you can do more than simply format the selection. Suppose you have selected a word. If you begin to type another word, the newly typed word will immediately replace the selected word. With an item selected, you can press Delete to remove the selection. You will learn later in this chapter that you can also find, replace, copy, move, and paste selected text.

Use the Mini Toolbar

The **Mini toolbar** is an Office feature that provides access to common formatting commands. It is displayed when text is selected.

You have learned that you can always use commands on the Ribbon to change selected text within a document, cell, or presentation. All it takes is locating the desired command on the Home tab and clicking to select it. Although using Home tab commands is simple enough, an item called the ***Mini toolbar*** provides an even shorter way to accomplish some of the same formatting changes. When you select any amount of text within a worksheet, document, or presentation, you can move the mouse pointer only slightly within the selection to display the Mini toolbar, as shown in Figure 1.35. The Mini toolbar provides access to the most common formatting selections, such as boldfacing, italicizing, or changing font type or color. Unlike the Quick Access Toolbar, the Mini toolbar is not customizable, which means that you cannot add or remove options from the toolbar. The Mini toolbar will only appear when text is selected. The closer the mouse pointer is to the Mini toolbar, the darker the toolbar. As you move the mouse pointer away from the Mini toolbar, it becomes almost transparent. Make any selections from the Mini toolbar by clicking the corresponding button.

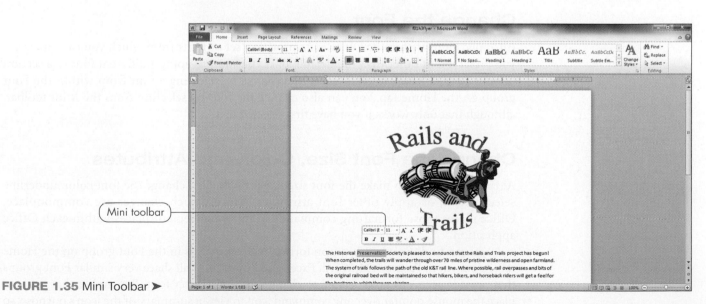

Mini toolbar

FIGURE 1.35 Mini Toolbar ➤

To temporarily remove the Mini toolbar from view, press Esc. If you want to permanently disable the Mini toolbar so that it does not appear in any open file when text is selected, click the File tab and click Options. As shown in Figure 1.36, click General, if necessary. Deselect the Show Mini Toolbar on selection setting by clicking the check box to the left of the setting and clicking OK.

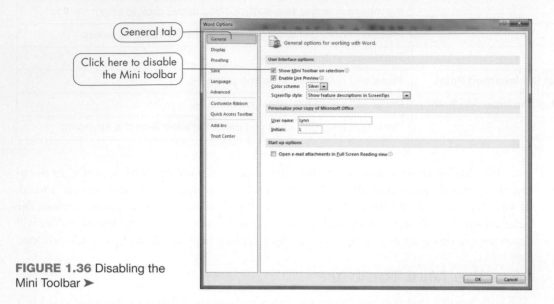

FIGURE 1.36 Disabling the Mini Toolbar ➤

Apply Font Attributes

A **font** is a character design that includes size, spacing, and shape.

A *font* is a character design. More simply stated, it is the way characters appear onscreen, including qualities such as size, spacing, and shape. Each Office application has a default font, which is the font that will be in effect unless you change it. Other font attributes include boldfacing, italicizing, and font color, all of which can be applied to selected text. Some formatting changes, such as Bold and Italic, are called *toggle* commands. They act somewhat like light switches that you can turn on and off. For example, after having selected a word that you want to boldface, click Bold in the Font group of the Home tab to turn the setting "on." If at a later time you want to remove boldface from the word, select it again, and then click Bold. This time, the button turns "off" the bold formatting.

To **toggle** is to switch from one setting to another. Several Home tab tasks, such as Bold and Italic, are actually toggle commands.

Change the Font

All applications within the Office suite provide a set of fonts from which you can choose. If you prefer a font other than the default, or if you want to apply a different font to a section of your project, you can easily make the change by selecting a font from within the Font group on the Home tab. You can also change the font by selecting from the Mini toolbar, although that only works if you have first selected text.

Change the Font Size, Color, and Attributes

At times, you want to make the font size larger or smaller, change the font color, underline selected text, or apply other font attributes. Because such changes are commonplace, Office places those formatting commands in many convenient places within each Office application.

You can find the most common formatting commands in the Font group on the Home tab. As shown in Figure 1.34, Word, Excel, and PowerPoint all share very similar Font groups that provide access to tasks related to changing the character font. Remember that you can place the mouse pointer over any command icon to view a summary of the icon's purpose, so although the icons might at first appear cryptic, you can use the mouse pointer to quickly determine the purpose and applicability to your desired text change. You can also find a subset of those commands plus a few additional choices on the Mini toolbar, which becomes available when you make a text selection.

If the font change that you plan to make is not included as a choice on either the Home tab or the Mini toolbar, you can probably find what you are looking for in the Font dialog box. Click the Dialog Box Launcher in the bottom-right corner of the Font group. Figure 1.37 shows a sample Font dialog box. Since the Font dialog box provides many formatting choices in one window, you can make several changes at once. Depending on the application, the contents of the Font dialog box vary slightly, but the purpose is consistent—providing access to choices related to modifying characters.

FIGURE 1.37 Font Dialog Box ➤

Using the Clipboard Group Tasks

The **Clipboard** is an Office feature that temporarily holds selections that have been cut or copied. It also enables you to paste those selections in other locations within the current or another Office application.

When you **cut** a selection, you remove it from the original location and place it in the Office Clipboard.

When you **copy** a selection, you duplicate it from the original location and place the copy in the Office Clipboard.

> The Clipboard group enables you not only to copy and cut text, but also to copy formatting.

When you **paste** a selection, you place a cut or copied item in another location.

The **Format Painter** is a Clipboard group command that copies the formatting of text from one location to another.

A **shortcut menu** provides choices related to the selection or area at which you right-click.

On occasion, you will want to move or copy a selection from one area to another. Suppose that you have included text on a PowerPoint slide that you believe would be more appropriate on a previous slide. Or perhaps an Excel formula should be copied from one cell to another because both cells should be totaled in the same manner. You can easily move the slide text and copy the Excel formula by using options found in the Clipboard group on the Home tab. The *Clipboard* is an area of memory reserved to temporarily hold selections that have been *cut* or *copied*. Although the Clipboard can hold up to 24 items at one time, the usual procedure is to *paste* the cut or copied selection to its final destination fairly quickly. When the computer is shut down or loses power, the contents of the Clipboard are erased, so it is important to finalize the paste procedure during the current session.

The Clipboard group enables you not only to copy and cut items, but also to copy formatting. Perhaps you have applied a font style to a major heading of a report and you realize that the same formatting should be applied to other headings. Especially if the heading includes multiple formatting features, you will save a great deal of time by copying the entire package of formatting to the other headings. In so doing, you will ensure the consistency of formatting for all headings because they will appear exactly alike. Using the Clipboard group's *Format Painter*, you can quickly and easily copy all formatting from one area to another in Word, PowerPoint, and Excel.

TIP Using a Shortcut Menu

In Office, you can usually accomplish the same task in several ways. Although the Ribbon provides ample access to formatting and Clipboard commands (such as Format Painter, cut, copy, and paste), you might find it convenient to access the same commands on a *shortcut menu*. Right-click a selected item or text to open a shortcut menu such as the one shown in Figure 1.38. A shortcut menu is also sometimes called a *context menu* because the contents of the menu vary depending on the location at which you right-clicked.

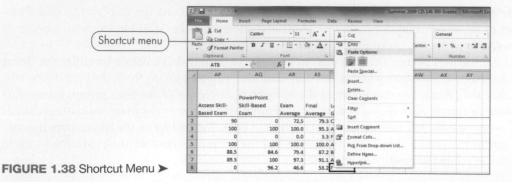

FIGURE 1.38 Shortcut Menu ➤

Copy Formats with the Format Painter

As described earlier, the Format Painter makes it easy to copy formatting features from one selection to another. You will find the Format Painter command conveniently located in the Clipboard group of the Home tab. Figure 1.39 shows Clipboard group tasks. To copy a format, you must first select the text containing the desired format. If you want to copy the format to only one other selection, *single-click* Format Painter. If, however, you plan to copy the same format to multiple areas, *double-click* Format Painter. As you move the mouse pointer, you will find that it has the appearance of a paintbrush with an attached I-bar. Select the area to which the copied format should be applied. If you single-clicked Format Painter to copy the format to one other selection, Format Painter turns off once the formatting has been applied. If you double-clicked Format Painter to copy the format to multiple locations, continue selecting text in various locations to apply the format. Then, to turn off Format Painter, click Format Painter again, or press Esc.

FIGURE 1.39 Clipboard
Group Tasks ➤

Move and Copy Text

Undoubtedly, there will be times when you want to revise a project by moving or copying items such as Word text, PowerPoint slides, or Excel cell contents, either within the current application or among others. For example, a section of a Word document might be appropriate as PowerPoint slide content. To keep from retyping the Word text in the PowerPoint slide, you can copy the text and paste it in a blank PowerPoint slide. At other times, it might be necessary to move a paragraph within a Word document or to copy selected cells from one Excel worksheet to another. The Clipboard group contains a Cut command with which you can select text to move. You can also use the Copy command to duplicate items and the Paste command to place moved or copied items in a final location. See those command icons in Figure 1.39.

> **TIP** Using Ribbon Commands with Arrows
>
> Some commands, such as Paste in the Clipboard group, contain two parts: the main command and an arrow. The arrow may be below or to the right of the command, depending on the command, window size, or screen resolution. Instructions in the Exploring series use the command name to instruct you to click the main command to perform the default action (e.g., Click Paste). Instructions include the word *arrow* when you need to select an additional option (e.g., Click the Paste arrow).

The first step in moving or copying text is to select the text. After that, click the appropriate icon in the Clipboard group either to cut or copy the selection. Remember that cut or copied text is actually placed in the Clipboard, remaining there even after you paste it to another location. It is important to note that you can paste the same item multiple times because it will remain in the Clipboard until you power down your computer or until the Clipboard exceeds 24 items. To paste the selection, click the location where you want the text to be placed. The location can be in the current file or in another open file within any Office application. Then click Paste in the Clipboard group. In addition to using the Clipboard group icons, you can also cut, copy, and paste in any of the ways listed in Table 1.4.

TABLE 1.4	Cut, Copy, and Paste Options
Result	**Actions**
Cut	• Click Cut in Clipboard group. • Right-click selection, and then click Cut. • Press Ctrl+X
Copy	• Click Copy in Clipboard group. • Right-click selection, and then click Copy. • Press Ctrl+C.
Paste	• Click in destination location, and then click Paste in Clipboard group. • Right-click in destination location, and then click Paste. • Click in destination location, and then press Ctrl+V. • Click the Clipboard Dialog Box Launcher to open the Clipboard task pane. Click in destination location. With the Clipboard task pane open, click the arrow beside the intended selection, and then click Paste.

Use the Office Clipboard

When you cut or copy selections, they are placed in the Office Clipboard. Especially if you cut or copy multiple items, you might need to view the contents of the Clipboard so that you can select the correct item to paste. Regardless of which Office application you are using, you can view the Clipboard by clicking the Clipboard Dialog Box Launcher as shown in Figure 1.40.

Clipboard Dialog Box Launcher

Clipboard task pane

FIGURE 1.40 Clipboard Task Pane ➤

Unless you specify otherwise when beginning a paste operation, the most recently added Clipboard item is pasted. You can, however, select an item from the Clipboard task pane to paste. Similarly, you can delete items from the Clipboard by making a selection in the Clipboard task pane. You can remove all items from the Clipboard by clicking Clear All. The Options button in the Clipboard task pane enables you to control when and where the Clipboard is displayed. Close the Clipboard task pane by clicking the Close button in the top-right corner of the task pane or by clicking the arrow in the title bar of the Clipboard task pane and selecting Close.

Using the Editing Group Tasks

The process of finding and replacing text is easily accomplished through options in the Editing group of the Home tab. You will at times find it necessary to locate each occurrence of a text item so that you can replace it with another or so that you can delete, move, or copy it. If you have consistently misspelled a person's name throughout a document, you can find the misspelling and replace it with the correct spelling in a matter of a few seconds, no matter how many times the misspelling occurs in the document. The Editing group also enables you to select all contents of a project document, all text with similar formatting, or specific objects, such as pictures, clip art, or charts. The Editing group is found at the far-right side of the Home tab in all Office applications except Access.

The Excel Editing group is unique in that it also includes provisions for sorting, filtering, and clearing cell contents; filling cells; and summarizing numeric data. Because those commands are relevant only to Excel, this chapter will not address them specifically. Figure 1.41 shows the Editing group of Excel, Word, and PowerPoint. Note the differences.

FIGURE 1.41 Editing Group ➤

Find and Replace Text

Find locates a word or phrase that you indicate in a document.

Replace finds text and replaces it with a word or phrase that you indicate.

Especially if you are working with a lengthy project, manually seeking a specific word or phrase can be time-consuming. Office enables you not only to *find* each occurrence of a series of characters, but also to *replace* what it finds with another series.

To begin the process of finding a specific item, click Replace in the Editing group on the Home tab of Word or PowerPoint. To begin a find and replace procedure in Excel, you must click Find & Select, and then click Replace. The subsequent dialog box enables you to indicate a word or phrase to find and replace. See Figure 1.42 for the Find and Replace dialog box in each Office application.

FIGURE 1.42 Find and Replace Dialog Box ➤

Ctrl+F is a shortcut to finding items in a Word, Excel, or PowerPoint file. When you press Ctrl+F, the Find and Replace dialog box shown in Figure 1.42 displays in Excel and PowerPoint. Pressing Ctrl+F in Word displays a feature—the Navigation task pane—at the left side of a Word document. When you type a search term in the Search Document area, Word finds and highlights all occurrences of the search term. The Navigation task pane also makes it easy to move to sections of a document based on levels of headings. The Navigation task pane is only found in Word 2010.

To find and replace selected text, type the text to locate in the *Find what* box and the replacement text in the *Replace with* box. You can narrow the search to require matching case or find whole words only. If you want to replace all occurrences of the text, click Replace All. If you want to replace only some occurrences, click Find Next repeatedly until you reach the occurrence that you want to replace. At that point, click Replace. Click the Close button (or Cancel).

An Excel worksheet can include more than 1,000,000 rows of data. A Word document's length is unlimited. Moving to a specific point in large files created in either of those applications can be a challenge. That task is simplified by the Go To option, found in the Editing group as an option of the Find command (or under Find & Select in Excel). Click Go To and enter the page number (or other item, such as section, comment, bookmark, or footnote) or the specific Excel cell. Click Go To (in Word) or OK in Excel.

HANDS-ON EXERCISES

4 Home Tab Tasks

You have created a list of potential contributors to the Rails and Trails project. You have used Excel to record that list in worksheet format. Now you will review the worksheet and format its appearance to make it more attractive. You will also modify the promotional flyer that you reviewed in the last Hands-On Exercise. In working with those projects, you will put into practice the formatting, copying, moving, and editing information from the preceding section.

Skills covered: Move, Copy, and Paste Text • Select Text, Apply Font Attributes, and Use the Mini Toolbar • Use Format Painter and Work with a Shortcut Menu • Use the Font Dialog Box and Find and Replace Text

STEP 1 ▶ MOVE, COPY, AND PASTE TEXT

Each contributor to the Rails and Trails project is assigned a contact person from the project. You manage the worksheet that keeps track of those assignments, but the assignments sometimes change. You will copy and paste some worksheet selections to keep from having to retype data. You will also reposition a clip art image to improve the worksheet's appearance. Refer to Figure 1.43 as you complete Step 1.

FIGURE 1.43 Contributor List (Excel) ➤

a. Click the **Start button** to display the Start menu, point to **All Programs**, scroll down the list if necessary, and then click **Microsoft Office**. Click **Microsoft Excel 2010**.

The potential contributors list is saved as an Excel worksheet. You will first open Excel.

b. Open the student data file *f01h4contacts*. Save the file as **f01h4contacts_LastnameFirstname** in the Office Records folder on the drive where you save your files.

The potential contributors list shown in Figure 1.43 is displayed.

c. Click **cell C7** to select the cell that contains *Alli Nester*, and then click **Copy** in the Clipboard group on the Home tab. Click **cell C15** to select the cell that contains *Roger Sammons*, click **Paste** in the Clipboard group, and then press **Esc** to remove the selection from *Alli Nester*.

Alli Nester has been assigned as the Rails and Trails contact for Harris Foster, replacing Roger Sammons. You make that replacement on the worksheet by copying and pasting Alli Nester's name in the appropriate worksheet cell.

d. Click the picture of the train. A box displays around the image, indicating that it is selected. Click **Cut** in the Clipboard group, click **cell A2**, click **Paste**, and then click anywhere outside the train picture to deselect it.

> **TROUBLESHOOTING:** A Paste Options icon might appear in the worksheet after you have moved the train picture. It offers additional options related to the paste procedure. You do not need to change any options, so ignore the button.

You decide that the picture of the train will look better if it is placed on the left side of the worksheet instead of the right. You move the picture by cutting and pasting the object.

e. Click **Save** on the Quick Access Toolbar. Click the **Minimize button** to minimize the worksheet without closing it.

STEP 2 ▶ SELECT TEXT, APPLY FONT ATTRIBUTES, AND USE THE MINI TOOLBAR

As the opening of Rails and Trails draws near, you are active in preparing promotional materials. You are currently working on an informational flyer that is almost set to go. You will make a few improvements before approving the flyer for release. Refer to Figure 1.44 as you complete Step 2.

FIGURE 1.44 Promotional Flyer (Word) ➤

a. Click the **Start button** to display the Start menu. Click **All Programs**, scroll down if necessary, and then click **Microsoft Office**. Click **Microsoft Word 2010**. Open *f01h4flyer* and save the document as **f01h4flyer_LastnameFirstname** in the Promotional Print folder (a subfolder of Rails and Trails project) on the drive where you save your files.

You plan to modify the promotional flyer slightly to include additional information about the Rails and Trails project.

> **TROUBLESHOOTING:** If you make any major mistakes in this exercise, you can close the file without saving it, open *f01h4flyer* again, and start this exercise over.

b. Click after the period after the word *sharing* at the end of the first paragraph. Press **Enter**, and then type the text below. As you type, do not press Enter at the end of each line. Word will automatically wrap the lines of text.

Construction of the trail will be funded in several ways. Thanks to the persistent efforts of local interest groups and individuals, we have secured $13.5 million through local, state, and federal departments and grants. The journey has only begun, however. At its completion, the

trail is estimated to cost $15 million. In an effort to fully fund the project, we need private contributions. Will you help us create an everlasting tribute to our community's history? Please consider donating any amount that is within your means, as every donation counts. For further information, please contact Rhea Mancuso at (335)555-9813.

> **TROUBLESHOOTING:** If you make any mistakes while typing, press Backspace and correct them.

c. Scroll down and select all of the text at the end of the document, beginning with **For more information, contact:**. Press **Delete**.

   When you press Delete, selected text (or characters to the right of the cursor) are removed. Deleted text is not placed in the Clipboard.

d. Select the words *Join us on the journey!* Click **Italic** in the Font group, and then click anywhere outside the selection to see the result.

e. Select both paragraphs but not the final italicized line. While still within the selection, move the mouse pointer slightly to display the Mini toolbar, click the **font arrow** on the Mini toolbar, and then select **Arial**.

> **TROUBLESHOOTING:** If you do not see the Mini toolbar, you might have moved too far away from the selection. In that case, click outside the selection, and then drag to select it once more. Without leaving the selection, move the mouse pointer slightly to display the Mini toolbar.

   You have changed the font of the two paragraphs.

f. Click after the period following the word *counts* before the last sentence in the second paragraph. Press **Enter**, and then press **Delete** to remove the extra space before the first letter, if necessary. Move the mouse pointer to the margin area at the immediate left of the new line. The mouse pointer should appear as a white arrow. Click once to select the line, click **Underline** in the Font group, and then click anywhere outside the selected area. Your document should appear as shown in Figure 1.44.

   You have underlined the contact information to draw attention to the text.

g. Save the document and keep it open for the next step in this exercise.

STEP 3 ▶ USE FORMAT PAINTER AND WORK WITH A SHORTCUT MENU

You are on a short timeline for finalizing the promotional flyer, so you will use a few shortcuts to avoid retyping and reformatting more than is necessary. You know that you can easily copy formatting from one area to another using Format Painter. Shortcut menus can also help make changes quickly. Refer to Figure 1.45 as you complete Step 3.

FIGURE 1.45 Promotional Flyer (Word) ▶

a. Select the words **Rails and Trails** in the first paragraph, and then click **Bold** in the Font group.

b. Click **Format Painter** in the Clipboard group, and then select the second to last line of the document, containing the contact information. Click anywhere outside the selection to deselect the line.

The format of the area that you first selected (Rails and Trails) is applied to the line containing the contact information.

c. Select the text *Join us on the journey!* Right-click in the selected area, click **Font** on the shortcut menu, click **22** in the **Size box** to reduce the font size slightly, and then click **OK**. Click outside the selected area.

Figure 1.45 shows the final document as it should now appear.

d. Save the document and close Word.

The flyer will be saved with the same file name and in the same location as it was when you last saved the document in Step 2. As you close Word, the open document will also be closed.

STEP 4 ▶ USE THE FONT DIALOG BOX AND FIND AND REPLACE TEXT

The contributors worksheet is almost complete. However, you first want to make a few more formatting changes to improve the worksheet's appearance. You will also quickly change an incorrect area code by using Excel's Find and Replace feature. Refer to Figures 1.46 and 1.47 as you complete Step 4.

FIGURE 1.46 Excel Dialog Box Launcher ➤

FIGURE 1.47 Excel Format Cells Dialog Box ➤

a. Click the **Excel icon** on the taskbar to redisplay the contributors worksheet that you minimized in Step 1.

The Excel potential contributors list displays.

b. Drag to select **cells A6 through C6**.

> **TROUBLESHOOTING:** Make sure the mouse pointer looks like a large white plus sign before dragging. It is normal for the first cell in the selected area to be a different shade. If you click and drag when the mouse pointer does not resemble a white plus sign, text may have been moved or duplicated. In that case, click Undo on the Quick Access Toolbar.

c. Click the **Dialog Box Launcher** in the Font group as shown in Figure 1.46. Click the **Fill tab**, and then click **Fill Effects** as shown in Figure 1.47. Click any style in the Variants group, click **OK**, and then click **OK** once more to close the Format Cells dialog box. Click outside the selected area to see the final result.

The headings of the worksheet are shaded more attractively.

d. Click **Find & Select** in the Editing group, click **Replace**, and then type **410** in the **Find what box**. Type **411** in the **Replace with box**, click **Replace All**, and then click **OK** when notified that Excel has made 10 replacements. Click **Close**.

You discover that you consistently typed an incorrect area code. You use Find and Replace to make a correction quickly.

e. Save the *f01h4contacts_LastnameFirstname* workbook. Close the workbook and exit Excel.

The workbook will be saved with the same file name and in the same location as it was when you last saved the document in Step 1. As you exit Excel, the open workbook will also be closed.

Insert Tab Tasks

As its title implies, the Insert tab enables you to insert, or add, items into a file. Much of the Insert tab is specific to the particular application, with little commonality to other Office applications. Word's Insert tab includes text-related commands, whereas Excel's is more focused on inserting such items as charts and tables. PowerPoint's Insert tab includes multimedia items and links. Despite their obvious differences in focus, all Office applications share a common group on the Insert tab—the Illustrations group. In addition, all Office applications enable you to insert headers, footers, text boxes, and symbols. Those options are also found on the Insert tab in various groups, depending on the particular application. In this section, you will work with common activities on the Insert tab, including inserting pictures and clip art.

> Despite their obvious differences in focus, all Office applications share a common group on the Insert tab—the Illustrations group.

Inserting Objects

With few exceptions, all Office applications share common options in the Illustrations group of the Insert tab. PowerPoint places some of those common features in the Images group. You can insert pictures, clip art, shapes, screenshots, and SmartArt. Those items are considered objects, retaining their separate nature when they are inserted in files. That means that you can select them and manage them independently of the underlying document, worksheet, or presentation.

After an object has been inserted, you can click the object to select it or click anywhere outside the object to deselect it. When an object is selected, a border of small dots, or "handles," surrounds it, appearing at each corner and in the middle of each side. Figure 1.48 shows a selected object, surrounded by handles. Unless an object is selected, you cannot change or modify it. When an object is selected, the Ribbon expands to include one or more contextual tabs. Items on the contextual tabs relate to the selected object, enabling you to modify and manage it.

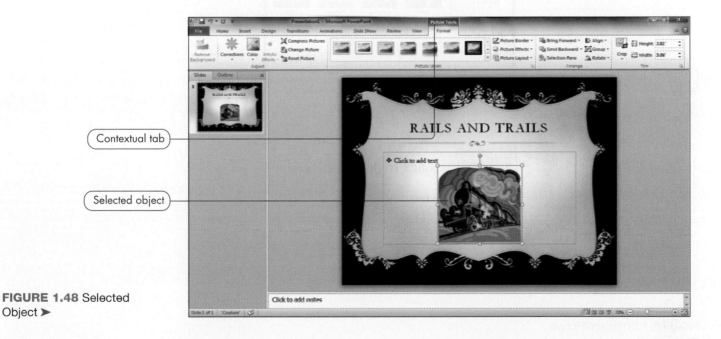

FIGURE 1.48 Selected Object ➤

TIP Resizing and Moving a Selected Object

You can resize and move a selected object. Place the mouse pointer on any handle, and then drag (when the mouse pointer looks like a two-headed arrow) to resize the object. Be careful! If you drag a side handle, the object is likely to be skewed, possibly resulting in a poor image. Instead, drag a corner handle to proportionally resize the image. To move an object, drag the object when the mouse pointer looks like a four-headed arrow.

Insert Pictures

Documents, worksheets, and presentations can include much more than just words and numbers. You can easily add energy and description to the project by including pictures and other graphic elements. Although a *picture* is usually just that—a digital photo—it is actually defined as a graphic element retrieved from storage media such as a hard drive or a CD. A picture could actually be a clip art item that you saved from the Internet onto your hard drive.

A **picture** is a graphic file that is retrieved from storage media and placed in an Office project.

The process of inserting a picture is simple. First, click in the project where you want the picture to be placed. Make sure you know where the picture that you plan to use is stored. Click the Insert tab. Then, in the Illustrations group (or Images group in PowerPoint), click Picture. The Insert Picture dialog box shown in Figure 1.49 displays. Select a picture and click Insert (or simply double-click the picture). In addition, on some slide layouts, PowerPoint displays an Insert Picture from File button (Figure 1.50) that you can click to select and position a picture on the slide.

FIGURE 1.49 Insert Picture Dialog Box ➤

FIGURE 1.50 Insert Picture from File ➤

Insert Clip Art

Clip art is an electronic illustration that can be inserted into an Office project.

A large library of *clip art* is included with each Office installation. Office.com, an online resource providing additional clip art and Office support, is also available from within each Office application. To explore available clip art, click the Insert tab within an Office program, and then click Clip Art in the Illustrations group (or the Images group in PowerPoint). Figure 1.51 shows the Clip Art task pane that displays. Suppose that you are looking for some clip art to support a fund-raising project. Having opened the Clip Art task pane, you could click in the *Search for* box and type a search term, such as *money*. To limit the results to a particular media type, click the arrow beside the *Results should be* box, and make a selection. Click Go to initiate the search.

FIGURE 1.51 Clip Art Task Pane ➤

You can resize and move clip art just as you have learned to similarly manage pictures. All Office applications enable you to insert clip art from the Illustrations group. However, PowerPoint uses a unique approach to working with graphics, including the ability to insert clip art by selecting from a special-purpose area on a slide.

Review Tab Tasks

As a final touch, you should always check a project for spelling, grammatical, and word-usage errors. If the project is a collaborative effort, you and your colleagues might add comments and suggest changes. You can even use a thesaurus to find synonyms for words that are not quite right for your purpose. The Review tab in each Office application provides all these options and more. In this section, you will learn to review a file, checking for spelling and grammatical errors. You will also learn to use a thesaurus to identify synonyms.

Reviewing a File

As you create or edit a file, you will want to make sure no spelling or grammatical errors exist. You will also be concerned with wording, being sure to select words and phrases that best represent the purpose of the document, worksheet, or presentation. On occasion, you might even find yourself at a loss for an appropriate word. Not to worry. Word, Excel, and PowerPoint all provide standard tools for proofreading, including a spelling and grammar checker and a thesaurus.

Check Spelling and Grammar

In general, all Office applications check your spelling and grammar as you type. If a word is unrecognized, it is flagged as misspelled or grammatically incorrect. Misspellings are identified with a red wavy underline, grammatical problems are underlined in green, and word usage errors (such as using *bear* instead of *bare*) have a blue underline. If the word or phrase is truly in error—that is, it is not a person's name or an unusual term that is not in the application's dictionary—you can correct it manually or you can let the software correct it for you. If you right-click a word or phrase that is identified as a mistake, you will see a shortcut menu similar to that shown in Figure 1.52. If the application's dictionary can make a suggestion as to the correct spelling, you can click to accept the suggestion and make the change. If a grammatical rule is violated, you will have an opportunity to select a correction. However, if the text is actually correct, you can click Ignore (to bypass that single occurrence) or Ignore All (to bypass all occurrences of the flagged error in the current document). Click Add to Dictionary if you want the word to be considered correct whenever it appears in all documents. Similar selections on a shortcut menu enable you to ignore grammatical mistakes if they are not errors.

> In general, all Office applications check your spelling and grammar as you type.

FIGURE 1.52 Correcting Misspelling ➤

You might prefer the convenicnce of addressing possible misspellings and grammatical errors without having to examine each underlined word or phrase. To do so, click Spelling & Grammar in the Proofing group of the Review tab. Beginning at the top of the document, each identified error is highlighted in a dialog box similar to Figure 1.53. You can then choose how to address the problem by making a selection in the dialog box.

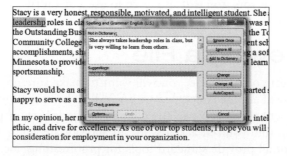

FIGURE 1.53 Checking for Spelling and Grammatical Errors ➤

Many Office settings are considered *default* options. Thus, unless you specify otherwise, the default options are in effect. One such default option is the automatic spelling and grammar checker. If you prefer to enable and disable certain options or change default settings in an Office application, you can click the File tab and click Options. From that point, you can work through a series of categories, selecting or deselecting options at will. For example, if you want to change how the application corrects and formats text, you can select or deselect settings in the Proofing group.

A **default** setting is one that is in place unless you specify otherwise.

Use the Thesaurus

As you write, there will be times when you are at a loss for an appropriate word. Perhaps you feel that you are overusing a word and want to find a suitable substitute. The Thesaurus is the Office tool to use in such a situation. Located in the Proofing group of the Review tab, Thesaurus enables you to search for synonyms, or words with similar meanings. Select a word, then click Thesaurus, in the Proofing group on the Review tab. A task pane displays on the right side of the screen, and synonyms are listed similar to those shown in Figure 1.54. You can also use the Thesaurus before typing a word to find substitutes. Simply click Thesaurus and type the word for which you are seeking a synonym in the Search for box. Press Enter or click the green arrow to the right of the Search box for some suggestions. Finally, you can also identify synonyms when you right-click a word and point to Synonyms (if any are available). Click any word to place it in the document.

Thesaurus task pane

FIGURE 1.54 Thesaurus Task Pane ➤

Page Layout Tab Tasks

When you prepare a document or worksheet, you are concerned with the way the project appears onscreen and possibly in print. Unlike Word and Excel, a PowerPoint presentation is usually designed as a slide show, so it is not nearly as critical to concern yourself with page layout settings. The Page Layout tab in Word and Excel provides access to a full range of options such as margin settings and page orientation. In this section, you will identify page layout settings that are common to Office applications. These settings include margins and page orientation.

The Page Layout tab in Word and Excel provides access to a full range of options such as margin settings and page orientation.

Changing Page Settings

Because a document is most often designed to be printed, you will want to make sure it looks its best in printed form. That means that you will need to know how to adjust margins and how to change the page orientation. Perhaps the document or spreadsheet should be centered on the page vertically or the text should be aligned in columns. By adjusting page settings, you can do all these things and more. You will find the most common page settings, such as margins and page orientation, in the Page Setup group of the Page Layout tab. For less common settings, such as determining whether headers should print on odd or even pages, you can use the Page Setup dialog box.

Change Margins

A **margin** is the blank space around the sides, top, and bottom of a document or worksheet.

A *margin* is the area of blank space that appears to the left, right, top, and bottom of a document or worksheet. Margins are only evident if you are in Print Layout or Page Layout view or if you are in the Backstage view, previewing a document to print. To change or set margins, click the Page Layout tab. As shown in Figure 1.55, the Page Setup group enables you to change such items as margins and orientation. To change margins, click Margins. If the margins that you intend to use are included in any of the preset margin options, click a selection. Otherwise, click Custom Margins to display the Page Setup dialog box in which you can create custom margin settings. Click OK to accept the settings, and close the dialog box. You can also change margins when you click Print on the File tab.

FIGURE 1.55 Page Setup Group ➤

Change Page Orientation

A page or worksheet displayed in **portrait** orientation is taller than it is wide.

A page or worksheet displayed in **landscape** orientation is wider than it is tall.

Documents and worksheets can be displayed in *portrait* orientation or in *landscape*. A page displayed or printed in portrait orientation is taller than it is wide. A page in landscape orientation is wider than it is tall. Word documents are usually more attractive displayed in portrait orientation, whereas Excel worksheets are often more suitable in landscape. To select page orientation, click Orientation in the Page Setup group on the Page Layout tab. See Figure 1.55 for the location of the Orientation command. Orientation is also an option in the Print area of the Backstage view.

Use the Page Setup Dialog Box

The Page Setup group contains the most commonly used page options in the particular Office application. Some are unique to Excel, and others are more applicable to Word. Other less common settings are only available in the Page Setup dialog box, displayed when you click the Page Setup Dialog Box Launcher. The subsequent dialog box includes options for customizing margins, selecting page orientation, centering vertically, printing gridlines, and creating headers and footers, although some of those options are only available when working with Word, and others are unique to Excel. Figure 1.56 gives a glimpse of both the Excel and Word Page Setup dialog boxes.

Word

Excel

FIGURE 1.56 Page Setup
Dialog Boxes ➤

5 Tasks on the Insert Tab, Page Layout Tab, and Review Tab

The Rails and Trails project is nearing kickoff. You are helping plan a ceremony to commemorate the occasion. To encourage interest and participation, you will edit a PowerPoint presentation that is to be shown to civic groups, the local retiree association, and to city and county leaders. You know that pictures and clip art add energy to a presentation when used appropriately, so you will check for those elements, adding whatever is necessary. A major concern is making sure the presentation is error free and that it is available in print so that meeting participants can review it later. As a reminder, you also plan to have available a handout giving the time and date of the dedication ceremony. You will use the Insert tab to work with illustrations and the Review tab to check for errors, and you will use Word to generate an attractive handout as a reminder of the date.

Skills covered: Check Spelling and Use the Thesaurus • Insert Clip Art and Pictures • Select Margins and Page Orientation

---

STEP 1 ▶ CHECK SPELLING AND USE THE THESAURUS

As you check the PowerPoint presentation that will be shown to local groups, you make sure no misspellings or grammatical mistakes exist. You also use the Thesaurus to find a suitable substitution for a word you feel should be replaced. Refer to Figure 1.57 as you complete Step 1.

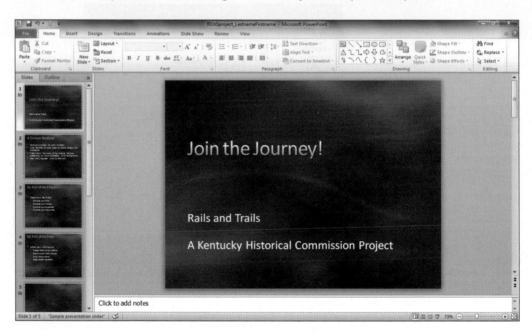

FIGURE 1.57 Project Presentation ▶

a. Click the **Start button** to display the Start menu, and then point to **All Programs**. Click **Microsoft Office**, and then click **Microsoft PowerPoint 2010**. Open *f01h5project* and save it as **f01h5project_LastnameFirstname** in the Presentations folder (a subfolder of Rails and Trails Projects) on the drive where you save your files. The presentation displays as shown in Figure 1.57.

The PowerPoint presentation opens, with Slide 1 shown in Normal view.

b. Click **Slide Show** and the **Slide Show tab**, and then click **From Beginning** in the Start Slide Show group to view the presentation. Click to advance from one slide to another. After the last slide, click to return to Normal view.

c. Click the **Review tab**, and then click **Spelling** in the Proofing group. The first misspelling is not actually misspelled. It is the name of a city. Click **Ignore** to leave it as is. The next flagged misspelling is truly misspelled. With the correct spelling selected, click **Change** to correct the mistake. Correct any other words that are misspelled. Click **OK** when the spell check is complete.

d. Click **Slide 2** in the Slides pane on the left. Double-click the word *route*, click **Thesaurus** in the Proofing group, point to **path** in the Research pane, click the arrow to the right of the word path, and then click **Insert**. Press the **Spacebar**.

The word *route* is replaced with the word *path*.

e. Click the **Close button** in the top-right corner of the Research pane.

f. Save the presentation and keep it open for the next step.

STEP 2 **INSERT CLIP ART AND PICTURES**

Although the presentation provides the necessary information and encourages viewers to become active participants in the project, you believe that pictures and clip art might make it a little more exciting. Where appropriate, you will include clip art and a picture. Refer to Figures 1.58 and 1.59 as you complete Step 2.

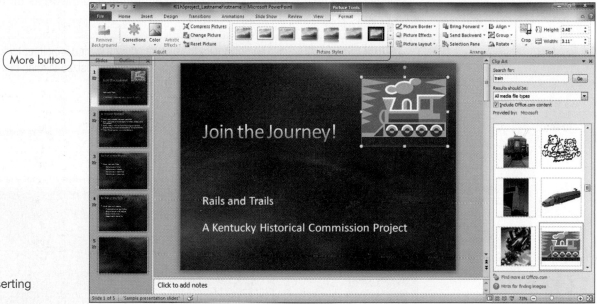

FIGURE 1.58 Inserting Clip Art ➤

a. Display Slide 1, click the **Insert tab**, and then click **Clip Art**.

The Clip Art task pane opens on the right side of the screen.

b. Type **train** in the **Search for box** in the Clip Art task pane. Click the check box beside *Include Office.com content* (unless it is already checked), click the arrow beside *Results should be*, and then click the check box beside *All media types* (unless it is already checked). Narrow results to illustrations by clicking the check box beside *Illustrations*, and then click **Go**.

You will identify clip art to be displayed on Slide 1.

c. Click to select any clip art image of a train.

> **TROUBLESHOOTING:** Be sure to click the clip art image, not the arrow to the right. If you click the arrow, you will then need to click Insert to place the clip art image on the slide.

> **TROUBLESHOOTING:** It is very easy to make the mistake of inserting duplicate clip art images on a slide, perhaps because you clicked the image more than once in the Clip Art task pane. If that should happen, you can remove any unwanted clip art by clicking to select it on the slide and pressing Delete.

The clip art image probably will not be placed as you would like, but you will move and resize it in the next substep. Also, the clip art is selected, as indicated by the box and handles surrounding it.

d. Click a corner handle (small circle) on the border of the clip art. Make sure the mouse pointer appears as a double-headed arrow. Drag to resize the image so that it appears similar to that shown in Figure 1.58. Click in the center of the clip art. The mouse pointer should appear as a four-headed arrow. Drag the clip art to the top-right corner of the slide. Make sure the clip art is still selected (it should be surrounded by a box and handles). If it is not selected, click to select it.

e. Click the **More button** of the Picture Styles group (see Figure 1.58) to reveal a gallery of styles. Position the mouse pointer over any style to see a preview of the style applied to the clip art. Click to apply a style of your choice. Close the Clip Art task pane.

f. On Slide 5, type **The Journey Begins** in the **Title box**. Click **Insert Picture from File** in the Content Placeholder (see Figure 1.50), navigate to the student data files, and then double-click *f01h5rails*.

A picture is placed on the final slide.

g. Click to select the picture, if necessary. Drag a corner handle to resize the picture. Click the center of the picture and drag the picture to reposition it in the center of the slide as shown in Figure 1.59.

> **TROUBLESHOOTING:** You can only move the picture when the mouse pointer looks like a four-headed arrow. If instead, you drag a handle, the picture will be resized instead of moved. Click Undo on the Quick Access Toolbar and try it again.

FIGURE 1.59 Inserting a Picture ➤

h. Click **Picture Effects** in the Picture Styles group on the Format tab, point to **Soft Edges**, and then click **5 Point**.

i. Click the **Slide Show tab**, and then click **From Beginning** in the Start Slide Show group. Click to advance from one slide to another. After the last slide, click to return to Normal view.

j. Save the presentation and exit PowerPoint.

You are ready to finalize the flyer, but before printing it you want to see how it will look. You wonder if it would be better in landscape or portrait orientation, so you will try both. After adjusting the margins, you are ready to save the flyer for later printing and distribution. Refer to Figure 1.60 as you complete Step 3.

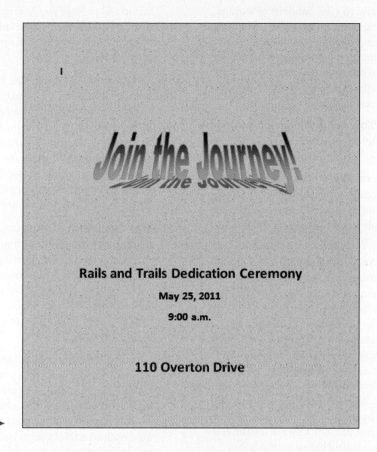

FIGURE 1.60 Word Handout ➤

a. Click the **Start button** to display the Start menu, and then point to **All Programs**. Click **Microsoft Office**, and then click **Microsoft Word 2010**. Open *f01h5handout* and save it as **f01h5handout_LastnameFirstname** in the Promotional Print folder on the drive where you save your files. The handout that you developed to help publicize the dedication ceremony displays as shown in Figure 1.60.

b. Click the **Page Layout tab**, click **Orientation** in the Page Setup group, and then click **Landscape** to view the flyer in landscape orientation.

   You want to see how the handout will look in landscape orientation.

c. Click the **File tab**, click **Print**, and then click **Next Page** (right-directed arrow at the bottom center of the preview page).

   The second page of the handout shows only the address. You can see that the two-page layout is not an attractive option.

d. Click the **Home tab**. Click **Undo** on the Quick Access Toolbar. Click the **File tab**, and then click **Print**.

   The document fits on one page. Portrait orientation is a much better choice for the handout.

e. Click the **Page Layout tab**, click **Margins**, and then select **Custom Margins**. Click the **spin arrow** beside the Left margin box to increase the margin to **1.5**. Similarly, change the right margin to **1.5**. Click **OK**.

f. Save the document and exit Word.

After reading this chapter, you have accomplished the following objectives:

1. **Use Windows Explorer.** You can use Windows Explorer to manage files and folders and to view contents of storage media. In addition to viewing the contents of physical folders, you can also manage libraries, which are collections of related data from various physical locations. Windows Explorer provides information on networked resources and shared disk drives, as well. Using the Favorites area of Windows Explorer, you can locate areas of frequent access.

2. **Work with folders and files.** Using Windows Explorer, you can create folders and rename, delete, move, and copy files and folders. You can also open files through Windows Explorer.

3. **Select, copy, and move multiple files and folders.** Backing up, or copying, files and folders is necessary to ensure that you do not lose important data and documents. You can quickly move or copy multiple items by selecting them all at one time.

4. **Identify common interface components.** You can communicate with Office software through the Microsoft Office user interface. Common interface components, found in all Microsoft Office applications, include the Ribbon, Quick Access Toolbar, title bar, status bar, and the Backstage view. The Ribbon is organized by commands within groups within tabs on the Ribbon. The Quick Access Toolbar provides one-click access to such activities as Save, Undo, and Repeat (Redo). The Backstage view is an Office feature that enables such common activities as opening, closing, saving, and printing files. It also provides information on an open file. The status bar contains information relative to the open file. The title bar identifies the open file's name and contains control buttons (minimize, maximize/restore down, and close).

5. **Get Office Help.** You can get help while you are using Microsoft Office by clicking the Help button, which appears as a question mark in the top-right corner of the Ribbon. You can also click the File tab to open the Backstage view, and then click the Help button. Assistance is available from within a dialog box by clicking the Help button in the top-right corner of the dialog box. When you rest the mouse pointer over any command on the Ribbon, you will see an Enhanced ScreenTip that provides a brief summary of the command.

6. **Open a file.** After a file has been saved, you can open it by clicking the File tab and selecting Open. If you recently worked with a file, you can reopen it from the Recent Documents list, which is displayed when you click Recent on the Backstage view. Finally, you can open a file from a template. Templates are predesigned files supplied by Microsoft from within the current Office installation or from Office.com.

7. **Print a file.** Often, you will want to print a file (a document, worksheet, or presentation). The Backstage view makes it easy to preview the file, change print settings, and print the file.

8. **Close a file and application.** When you close a file, it is removed from memory. If you plan to work with the file later,

you will need to save the file before closing it. The Office application will prompt you to save the file before closing if you have made any changes since the last time the file was saved. When you close an application, all open files within the application are also closed.

9. **Select and edit text.** The Home tab includes options to change the appearance of text. You can change the size, color, and type of font, as well as other font attributes. The font is the typeface, or the way characters appear and are sized. Before changing existing text, you must select what you want to change. Although shortcuts to text selection exist, you can always select text by dragging to highlight it. Any formatting changes that you identify apply only to selected text or to text typed after the changes are invoked.

10. **Use the Clipboard group tasks.** The Clipboard is a holding area for selections that you have cut or copied. Although you can view the Clipboard by clicking the Dialog Box Launcher in the Clipboard group, doing so is not necessary before pasting a cut or copied item to a receiving location. Another option in the Clipboard group is Format Painter, which enables you to copy formatting from one area to another within a file.

11. **Use the Editing group tasks.** You can easily find selected words or phrases and replace them, if necessary, with substitutions. There may be occasions when you simply want to find an occurrence of selected text without replacing it, whereas at other times you want to make replacements immediately. The Find option enables you to locate text, whereas Replace enables you to find all occurrences of an item quickly and replace it with another.

12. **Insert objects.** Pictures, clip art, shapes, screenshots, headers and footers, and text boxes are objects that you can insert in Office projects. After you have inserted an object, you can click to select it and manage it independently of the underlying worksheet, document, or presentation. When you select an object, a contextual tab appears on the Ribbon to provide formatting options specific to the selected object.

13. **Review a file.** You can check spelling, grammar, and word usage using any Office application. In fact, applications are usually set to check for such errors as you type, underlining possible misspellings in red, grammatical mistakes in green, and incorrect word usage in blue. Errors are not always correctly identified, as the Office application might indicate a misspelling when it is simply a word that is not in its dictionary. You can also check spelling and grammar by selecting Spelling & Grammar in the Proofing group on the Review tab.

14. **Change page settings.** You can change margins and page orientation through commands in the Page Setup group of the Page Layout tab. The Page Setup dialog box, accessible when you click the Dialog Box Launcher in the Page Setup group, provides even more choices of page settings.

KEY TERMS

Access *p.64*
Backstage view *p.65*
Backup *p.59*
Clip art *p.99*
Clipboard *p.87*
Command *p.67*
Contextual tab *p.68*
Copy *p.87*
Cut *p.87*
Default *p.101*
Dialog box *p.67*
Dialog Box Launcher *p.67*
Enhanced ScreenTip *p.70*
Excel *p.64*
File *p.52*
Find *p.90*

Folder *p.52*
Font *p.86*
Format Painter *p.87*
Gallery *p.68*
Group *p.67*
Key Tip *p.69*
Landscape *p.102*
Library *p.54*
Live Preview *p.68*
Margin *p.102*
Microsoft Office *p.64*
Mini toolbar *p.85*
Navigation Pane *p.54*
Paste *p.87*
Picture *p.98*
Portrait *p.102*

PowerPoint *p.64*
Quick Access Toolbar *p.65*
Replace *p.90*
Ribbon *p.67*
Shortcut menu *p.87*
Status bar *p.69*
Subfolder *p.52*
Tab *p.67*
Template *p.78*
Title bar *p.65*
Toggle *p.86*
User interface *p.64*
View *p.69*
Windows Explorer *p.52*
Word *p.64*
Zoom slider *p.70*

1. The Recent Documents list:
   (a) Shows documents that have been previously printed.
   (b) Shows documents that have been previously opened.
   (c) Shows documents that have been previously saved in an earlier software version.
   (d) Shows documents that have been previously deleted.

2. Which of the following Windows Explorer features collects related data from folders and gives them a single name?
   (a) Network
   (b) Favorites
   (c) Libraries
   (d) Computer

3. When you want to copy the format of a selection, but not the content:
   (a) Double-click Copy in the Clipboard group.
   (b) Right-click the selection, and then click Copy.
   (c) Click Copy Format in the Clipboard group.
   (d) Click Format Painter in the Clipboard group.

4. Which of the following is not an object that can be inserted in an Office document?
   (a) Picture
   (b) Clip art
   (c) Paragraph box
   (d) Text box

5. What does a red wavy underline in a document, spreadsheet, or presentation mean?
   (a) A word is misspelled or not recognized by the Office dictionary.
   (b) A grammatical mistake exists.
   (c) An apparent word-usage mistake exists.
   (d) A word has been replaced with a synonym.

6. When you close a file:
   (a) You are prompted to save the file (unless you have made no changes since last saving it).
   (b) The application (Word, Excel, or PowerPoint) is also closed.
   (c) You must first save the file.
   (d) You must change the file name.

7. Live Preview:
   (a) Opens a predesigned document or spreadsheet that is relevant to your task.
   (b) Provides a preview of the results of a choice you are considering before you make a final selection.
   (c) Provides a preview of an upcoming Office version.
   (d) Enlarges the font onscreen.

8. You can get help when working with an Office application in which one of the following areas?
   (a) Help tab
   (b) Status bar
   (c) The Backstage view
   (d) Quick Access Toolbar

9. The Find and Replace feature enables you to do which of the following?
   (a) Find all instances of misspelling and automatically correct (or replace) them.
   (b) Find any grammatical errors and automatically correct (or replace) them.
   (c) Find any specified font settings and replace them with another selection.
   (d) Find any character string and replace it with another.

10. A document or worksheet printed in portrait orientation is:
    (a) Taller than it is wide.
    (b) Wider than it is tall.
    (c) A document with 2″ left and right margins.
    (d) A document with 2″ top and bottom margins.

1 Editing a Menu

You have gone into partnership with a friend to open a health food restaurant in a golf and tennis community. With the renewed emphasis on healthy living and the large number of high-income renters and condominium owners in the community, the specialty restaurant should do well. In preparation for the opening, your partner has begun a menu that you will review and edit. This exercise follows the same set of skills as used in Hands-On Exercises 1, 2, 3, 4, and 5 in the chapter. Refer to Figure 1.61 as you complete this exercise.

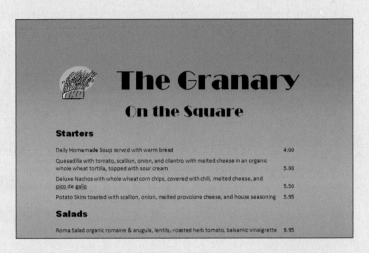

FIGURE 1.61 Restaurant Menu ➤

a. Click **Windows Explorer** on the taskbar, and then select the location where you save your files. Click **New folder**, type **The Granary**, and then press **Enter**. Close Windows Explorer.

b. Start Word. Open *f01p1menu* and save it as **f01p1menu_LastnameFirstname** in the The Granary folder.

c. Click the **Review tab**, and then click **Spelling & Grammar** in the Proofing group. The words *pico*, *gallo*, and *mesclun* are not misspelled, so you should ignore them when they are flagged. Other identified misspellings should be changed.

d. Click after the word *bread* in the first item under *Starters*. Press the **Spacebar**, and then type **or cornbread**.

e. Double-click **Desserts** on page 2 to select the word, and then type **Sweets**.

f. Drag to select the **Sandwiches section**, beginning with the word *Sandwiches* and ending after *8.75*. Click the **Home tab**, click **Cut** in the Clipboard group, click to place the insertion point before the word *Salads*, and then click **Paste** in the Clipboard group. The *Sandwiches* section should be placed before the *Salads* section.

g. Click **Undo** twice on the Quick Access Toolbar to return the *Sandwiches* section to its original location.

h. Change the price of Daily Homemade Soup to **4.95**.

i. Press **Ctrl+End** to place the insertion point at the end of the document, and then type your name.

j. Click the **Page Layout tab**, click **Orientation**, and then click **Landscape**. Click the **File tab**, and then click **Print** to see a preview of the document. Click the **Home tab**. Because the new look does not improve the menu's appearance, click **Undo** to return to the original orientation.

k. Press **Ctrl+Home** to move to the top of the document. Compare your results to Figure 1.61.

l. Drag the **Zoom slider** on the status bar slightly to the right to magnify text. Click the **View tab**, and then click **100%** in the Zoom group to return to the original size.

m. Save and close the file, and submit based on your instructor's directions.

You have always been interested in Web design and have worked in the field for several years. You now have an opportunity to devote yourself full-time to your career as the CEO of a company dedicated to designing and supporting Web sites. One of the first steps in getting the business off the ground is developing a business plan so that you can request financial support. You will use PowerPoint to present your business plan. This exercise follows the same set of skills as used in Hands-On Exercises 2, 3, and 4 in the chapter. Refer to Figure 1.62 as you complete this exercise.

FIGURE 1.62 Business Plan Presentation ➤

a. Start PowerPoint. Open *f01p2business* and save it as **f01p2business_ LastnameFirstname**.

b. Click the **Slides tab** in the Slides pane (on the left), if necessary. Slide 1 should be displayed. If not, click the first slide in the left pane.

c. Position the mouse pointer to the immediate left of the word *Company*. Drag to select the words *Company Name*, and then type **Inspire Web Design**.

d. Click the **Insert tab**, and then click **Clip Art** in the Images group.
   • Click in the **Search for box** in the Clip Art task pane, remove any text that might be in the box, and then type **World Wide Web**. Make sure *Include Office.com content* is checked, and then click **Go**.
   • Select any image (or the one shown in Figure 1.62). Resize and position the clip art as shown. *Hint: To reposition clip art, drag when the mouse pointer is a four-headed arrow.*
   • Click the **Format tab**, click the **More button** in the Picture Styles group, and then click the **Reflected Rounded Rectangle picture style** (fifth from the left on the top row).
   • Click outside the clip art and compare your slide to Figure 1.62. Close the Clip Art task pane.

e. On Slide 2, click after the period on the bulleted point ending with *them*, and then press **Enter**. Type **Support services will include continued oversight, modification, and redesign of client Web sites.**

f. Press **Enter**, and then type **Web hosting services will ensure uninterrupted 24/7 Web presence for clients.**

g. On Slide 3, complete the following steps:
   • Position the mouse pointer over the first bullet so that the pointer appears as a four-headed arrow, and then click the bullet. All of the text in the bullet item is selected. As you type text, it will replace the selected text.
   • Type *your name* **(CEO)** [replacing *your name* with your first and last names]**, Margaret Atkins (Financial Manager), Daniel Finch (Web Design), Susan Cummings (Web Support and Web Hosting).**

h. Click the second bullet, and then type **Team members collectively possess over 28 years' experience in Web design and business management. All have achieved success in business careers and are redirecting their efforts to support Inspire Web Design as full-time employees.**

i. Click to select the third bullet, and then press **Delete**, removing the bullet and text.

j. On Slide 1, click **Slide Show** on the status bar. After viewing a slide, click the mouse button to proceed to the next slide. Continue to click until the slide show ends.

k. Click **Slide Sorter** on the status bar. You and your partners have decided to rename the company. The new name is **Inspired Web Design**.
   - Click the **Home tab**, and then click **Replace** in the Editing group. Be careful to click the button, not the arrow to the right.
   - Type **Inspire** in the **Find what box**. Type **Inspired** in the **Replace with box**.
   - Click **Replace All**. Three replacements should be made. Click **OK**, and then click **Close** in the Replace dialog box.

l. Save and close the file, and submit based on your instructor's directions.

3 Planning Ahead

You and a friend are starting a lawn care service and have a few clients already. Billing will be a large part of your record keeping, so you are planning ahead by developing a series of folders to maintain those records. This exercise follows the same set of skills as used in Hands-On Exercises 1 and 4 in the chapter. Refer to Figure 1.63 as you complete this exercise.

FIGURE 1.63 N2 Grass Folder Structure ➤

a. Click **Windows Explorer** on the taskbar, and then select the location where you save your files. Click **New folder**, type **N2 Grass Lawn Care**, and then press **Enter**.

b. Double-click **N2 Grass Lawn Care** in the Content pane.
   - Click **New folder**, type **Business Letters**, and then press **Enter**.
   - Click **New folder**, type **Billing Records**, and then press **Enter**. Compare your results to Figure 1.63. Close Windows Explorer.

c. Start Word. Open *f01p3lawn*. Use Find and Replace to replace the text *Your Name* with your name.

d. Click the **File tab**, and then click **Save As**.
   - Click **Computer** in the left pane.
   - Click the drive (in the Navigation Pane) where you save your student files. Double-click **N2 Grass Lawn Care**, and then double-click **Business Letters**.
   - Save the file as **f01p3lawn_LastnameFirstname**. Click **OK**, if necessary. Close the document and exit Word.

e. Open Windows Explorer.
   - Click **Computer** in the Navigation Pane.
   - In the Content pane, double-click the drive where you earlier placed the N2 Grass Lawn Care folder. Double-click **N2 Grass Lawn Care**.
   - Right-click **Billing Records**, click **Rename**, type **Accounting Records,** and then press **Enter**.

f. Click the **Start button**, click **All Programs**, click **Accessories**, and then click **Snipping Tool**. You will use the Snipping Tool to capture the screen display for submission to your instructor.
   - Click the **New arrow**, and then click **Full-screen Snip**.
   - Click **File**, and then click **Save As**.

g. Save the file as **f01p3snip_LastnameFirstname**. Close the file and submit based on your instructor's directions.

MID-LEVEL EXERCISES

1 Reference Letter

You are an instructor at a local community college. A student has asked you to provide her with a letter of reference for a job application. You have used Word to prepare the letter, but now you need to make a few changes before it is finalized.

a. Open Windows Explorer. Create a new folder on the drive where you save your student files, naming it **Letters of Reference**. Close Windows Explorer.

b. Start Word. Open *f01m1letter* and save it in the Letters of Reference folder as **f01m1letter_LastnameFirstname**.

c. Type your name, address, and the current date in the address area, replacing the generic text. The letter is to go to **Ms. Samantha Blake, CEO, Ridgeline Industries, 410 Wellington Parkway, Huntsville AL 35611**. The salutation should read **Dear Ms. Blake:**.

d. Bold the student's first and last names in the first sentence.

e. Find each occurrence of the word *Stacy* and replace it with **Stacey**.

f. Find and insert a synonym for the word *intelligent* in the second paragraph.

g. Move the last paragraph (beginning with *In my opinion*) to position it before the third paragraph (beginning with *Stacey*).

h. Press **Ctrl+Home** to move the insertion point to the beginning of the document. Check spelling, selecting a correction for each misspelled word and ignoring spelling or grammatical mistakes that are not actually incorrect.

i. Type your name and title in the area beneath the word *Sincerely*.

j. Preview the document as it will appear when printed.

k. Save and close the file, and submit based on your instructor's directions.

2 Medical Monitoring

You are enrolled in a Health Informatics program of study in which you learn to manage databases related to health fields. For a class project, your instructor requires that you monitor your blood pressure, recording your findings in an Excel worksheet. You have recorded the week's data and will now make a few changes before printing the worksheet for submission.

a. Start Excel. Open *f01m2tracker* and save it as **f01m2tracker_LastnameFirstname**.

b. Preview the worksheet as it will appear when printed.

c. Change the orientation of the worksheet to **Landscape**. Preview the worksheet again. Click the **Home tab**.

d. Click in the cell beside *Name*, and then type your first and last names. Press **Enter**.

e. Change the font of the text in **cell C1** to **Verdana** and the font size to **20**.

f. Copy the function in **cell E22** to **cells F22 and G22**. *Hint: After selecting cell E22 and clicking Copy, drag cells F22 and G22. Before you drag, be sure the mouse pointer has the appearance of a large white plus sign. Then click Paste to copy the formula to those two cells. Press* **Esc** *to remove the selection from around* **cell E22**.

g. Get Help on showing decimal places. You want to increase the decimal places for the values in **cells E22, F22, and G22**, so that each value shows two places to the right of the decimal. Use Excel Help to learn how to do that. You might use *Increase Decimals* as a Search term. When you find the answer, select the three cells and increase the decimal places to **2**.

h. Click **cell A1**, and insert a clip art image of your choice related to blood pressure. Be sure the images include content from Office.com. If necessary, resize and position the clip art attractively. *Hint: To resize clip art, drag a corner handle (small circle). To reposition, drag the clip art when the mouse pointer is a four-headed arrow.*

i. Open the Backstage view, and adjust print settings to print two copies. You will not actually print two copies unless directed by your instructor.

j. Save and close the file, and submit based on your instructor's directions.

You are a member of the Student Government Association (SGA) at your college. As a community project, the SGA is sponsoring a "Stop Smoking" drive designed to provide information on the health risks posed by smoking cigarettes and to offer solutions to those who want to quit. The SGA has partnered with the local branch of the American Cancer Society as well as the outreach program of the local hospital to sponsor free educational awareness seminars. As the SGA Secretary, you will help prepare a PowerPoint presentation that will be displayed on plasma screens around campus and used in student seminars. You will use Microsoft Office to help with those tasks.

Manage Files and Folders

You will open, review, and save an Excel worksheet providing data on the personal monetary cost of smoking cigarettes over a period of years.

a. Create a folder called **SGA Drive** on the drive where you save your files.

b. Start Excel. Open *f01ccost* from the student data files and save it in the SGA Drive folder as **f01ccost_LastnameFirstname**.

c. Click **cell A10**, and then type your first and last names. Press **Enter**.

Modify Font

To highlight some key figures on the worksheet, you will format those cells with additional font attributes.

a. Draw attention to the high cost of smoking for 10, 20, and 30 years by changing the font color in **cells G3 through I4** to **Red**.

b. Italicize the Annual Cost cells (**F3 and F4**).

c. Click **Undo** on the Quick Access Toolbar to remove the italics. Click **Redo** to return the text to italics.

Insert Clip Art

You will add a clip art image to the worksheet and then resize it and position it.

a. Click **cell G7**, and then insert clip art appropriate for the topic of smoking.

b. Resize the clip art and reposition it near cell B7, if necessary.

c. Click outside the clipart to deselect it. Close the Clip Art task pane.

Preview Print, Change Page Layout, and Print

To get an idea of how the worksheet will look when printed, you will preview the worksheet. Then you will change the orientation and margins before printing it.

a. Preview the document as it will appear when printed.

b. Change the page orientation to **Landscape**. Click the **Page Layout tab**, and then change the margins to **Narrow**.

c. Preview the document as it will appear when printed.

d. Adjust the print settings to print two copies. You will not actually print two copies unless directed by your instructor.

e. Save the workbook and exit Excel.

Find and Replace

You have developed a PowerPoint presentation that you will use to present to student groups and for display on plasma screens across campus. The presentation is designed to increase awareness of the health problems associated with smoking. The PowerPoint presentation has come back from the reviewers with only one comment: A reviewer suggested that you spell out Centers for Disease Control and Prevention, instead of abbreviating it. You do not remember exactly which slide or slides the abbreviation might have been on, so you use Find and Replace to make the change quickly.

a. Start PowerPoint. Open *f01c1quit* and save it in the SGA Drive folder as **f01c1quit_LastnameFirstname**.

b. Replace all occurrences of *CDC* with **Centers for Disease Control and Prevention**.

Cut and Paste and Insert a Text Box

The Mark Twain quote on Slide 1 might be more effective on the last slide in the presentation, so you will cut and paste it there in a text box.

a. On Slide 1, select the entire Mark Twain quote, including the author name, and then cut it.

b. On Slide 22, paste the quote, reposition it more attractively, and then format it in a larger font size.

Check Spelling and Change View

Before you call the presentation complete, you will spell check it and view it as a slide show.

a. Check spelling. The word *hairlike* is not misspelled, so it should not be corrected.

b. View the slide show, and then take the smoking quiz. Click after the last slide to return to the presentation.

c. Save and close the presentation. Exit PowerPoint. Submit both files included in this project as directed by your instructor.

Employment Résumé

GENERAL CASE

You have recently graduated from a university and are actively seeking employment. You know how important it is to have a comprehensive résumé to include with job applications, so you will use Word to prepare one. Instead of beginning a new document, you will modify a résumé template that is installed with Word. You can locate an appropriate résumé template by clicking the File tab and then clicking New. Select a résumé template from the Office.com area. Save the résumé as **f01b1resume_LastnameFirstname** in an appropriately named folder where you save your student files. Modify the résumé in any way you like, but make sure to complete the following activities:

- Include your name on the résumé. All other information, including address, education, employment history, and job objective, can be fictional.
- Format some text differently. The choice of text is up to you, but you should change font size and type and apply appropriate character attributes to improve the document's appearance.
- Find and replace all occurrences of the word *education* with **academic preparation**.
- Check the document for spelling errors, correcting or ignoring any that you find.
- Change the margins to **1.5"** right and left. Preview the document as it will appear when printed. Save and close the document. Keep Word open.
- Open a new blank document. Create a cover letter that will accompany the résumé. You can use a template for the cover letter if you find an appropriate one. The letter should serve as your introduction, highlighting anything that you think makes you an ideal employee.
- Save the cover letter as **f01b1cover_LastnameFirstname** and exit Word. Submit the file as directed by your instructor.

Fitness Planner

RESEARCH CASE

Microsoft Excel is an excellent organizational tool. You will use it to maintain a fitness planner. Start Excel. Open *f01b2exercise*, and then save it as **f01b2exercise_LastnameFirstname**. The fitness planner is basically a template, which means that all exercise categories are listed, but without actual data. To personalize the planner to improve its appearance, complete the following activities:

- Change the orientation to **Landscape**. Preview the worksheet as it will appear when printed.
- Move the contents of **cell A2** (*Exercise Planner*) to **cell A1**.
- Click **cell A8**, and then use **Format Painter** to copy the format of that selection to **cells A5 and A6**. Increase the font size of **cell A1** to **26**.
- Use Excel Help to learn how to insert a header. Then insert a header on the worksheet with your first and last names.
- Insert a fitness-related clip art item in **cell A21**, positioning and sizing it so that it is attractive. Click outside the clip art to deselect it.
- Begin the fitness planner, entering at least one activity in each category (warm-up, aerobics, strength, and cool-down). Use **Find and Select** to replace all occurrences of *Exercises* with **Activities**. Save and close the file, and submit as directed by your instructor.

Household Records

DISASTER RECOVERY

You recently received a newsletter from the insurance company with which you have homeowners insurance. An article in the newsletter suggested that you maintain detailed records of your household appliances and other items of value that are in your home. In case of burglary or disaster, an insurance claim is expedited if you are able to itemize what was lost along with identifying information such as serial numbers. You will use Excel to prepare such a list. You will then make a copy of the record on another storage device for safekeeping outside your home (in case your home is destroyed by a fire or weather-related catastrophe).

- Connect a flash drive to your computer, and then close any dialog box that may appear (unless it is informing you of a problem with the drive). Use Windows Explorer to create a folder on the hard drive titled **Home Records**.
- Start Excel. Design a worksheet listing at least five fictional appliances and electronic equipment along with the serial number of each. Design the worksheet in any way you like. Save the workbook as **f01b3household_LastnameFirstname** in the Home Records folder of the hard drive. Close the workbook and exit Excel.
- Use Windows Explorer to copy the Home Records folder from the hard drive to your flash drive. Click the **flash drive** in the Navigation Pane of Windows Explorer. Double-click the **Home Records folder** in the Content pane.
- Click the **Start button**, click **All Programs**, click **Accessories**, and then click **Snipping Tool**. Click the **New arrow**, and then click **Full-screen Snip**. Click **File**, and then click **Save As**. Save the screen display as **f01b3disaster_LastnameFirstname**.
- Close all open windows and submit the files as directed by your instructor.

1 INTRODUCTION TO WORD

Organizing a Document

Watch the **Set-up Video** for this Case Study!

CASE STUDY | First River Outfitter

Maneuvering a canoe through a series of rolling rapids on a fast-flowing river is an exhilarating experience. Lawson Templeton, your best friend and canoeing partner, is opening a business called First River Outfitter that provides canoe and kayak rentals, guided float trips, and shuttle services to floaters and tourists who visit the Buffalo National River near Ponca, Arkansas. Lawson wants you to work part-time as an office manager generating documents for marketing, reporting, and contracts because of your experience with Microsoft Office applications.

Preparation for the new business includes acquiring real estate and equipment, but it also demands the development of marketing materials that generate new business. Your first project is to transform the rough draft of a document about river distances, safety precautions, and rental fees into a professional-looking article. This article will not only be posted on the First River Outfitter's Web site, but also printed and mailed to customers after they book a trip or reserve a rental. Your training in Microsoft Office Word 2010 enables you to modify the document easily and efficiently. After you complete the modifications, you both can go float the river!

OBJECTIVES AFTER YOU READ THIS CHAPTER, YOU WILL BE ABLE TO:

1. Understand how word processors work *p.119*

2. Customize Word *p.124*

3. Use features that improve readability *p.131*

4. Check spelling and grammar *p.135*

5. Display a document in different views *p.136*

6. Prepare a document for distribution *p.144*

7. Modify document properties *p.149*

Introduction to Word Processing

Word processing software is the most commonly used type of software. You can create letters, reports, research papers, newsletters, brochures, and other documents with Word. You can even create and send e-mail, produce Web pages, and update blogs with Word.

Word processing software, often called a word processor, is the most commonly used type of software. People around the world—students, office assistants, managers, and professionals in all areas—use word processing programs such as Word for a variety of tasks. You can create letters, reports, research papers, newsletters, brochures, and other documents with Word. You can even create and send e-mail, produce Web pages, and update blogs with Word. Figure 1.1 shows examples of documents created in Word.

Word processing software enables you to produce documents such as letters, reports, and research papers.

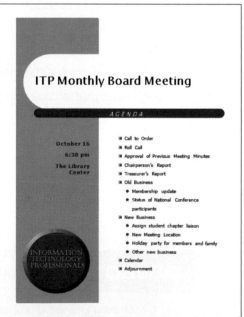

FIGURE 1.1 Versatility of Microsoft Office Word 2010 ➤

Word provides several features that enable you to enhance documents with only a few clicks of the mouse. You can change colors, add interesting styles of text, insert graphics, use a table to present data, track changes made to a document, view comments made about document content, combine several documents into one, and quickly create reference pages such as a table of contents, an index, or a bibliography.

This chapter provides a broad-based introduction to word processing and Word in general. All word processors adhere to certain basic concepts that must be understood to use the program effectively.

In this section, you will learn about the Word interface and word wrap. You will also learn how to move around quickly in a document and how to turn features on and off quickly by toggling. Finally, you will learn about breaks in a document, how to add page numbers, how to insert cover pages quickly, and how to customize Word.

Understanding How Word Processors Work

The Exploring series authors used Word to write this book. You will use Word to complete the exercises in this chapter. When you start Word, your screen might look different than the screen shown in Figure 1.2. This is because the commands are customizable, and elements that display will be affected. However, you should recognize the basic elements emphasized in Figure 1.2.

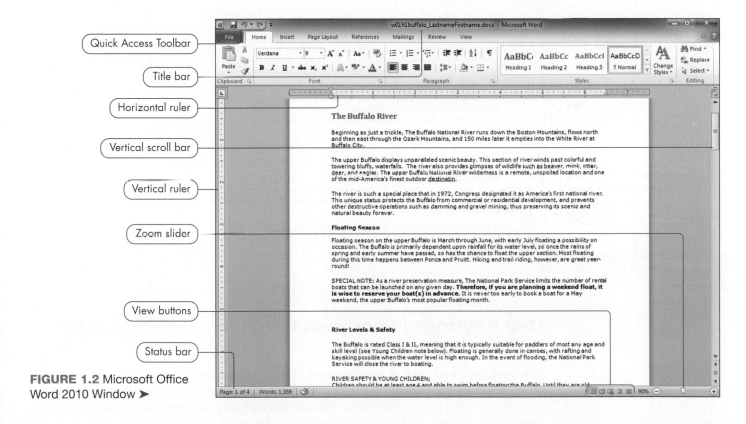

Quick Access Toolbar
Title bar
Horizontal ruler
Vertical scroll bar
Vertical ruler
Zoom slider
View buttons
Status bar

FIGURE 1.2 Microsoft Office Word 2010 Window ➤

When Word opens, several basic features are available. These features include the Ribbon, the Quick Access Toolbar, vertical and horizontal scroll bars, and the status bar, which you learned about in the Office Fundamentals chapter. The status bar at the bottom of the window displays information about the open Word document such as the page number where the insertion point is currently positioned, the total number of pages in the document, and the total number of words in the document.

Learn About Word Wrap

Whether you are new to using a word processor or have been using one for a period of time, you will notice that certain functions seem to happen automatically. As you type, you probably do not think about how much text can fit on one line or where the sentences roll from

Word wrap moves words to the next line if they do not fit on the current line.

A **hard return** is created when you press Enter to move the insertion point to a new line.

A **soft return** is created by the word processor as it wraps text to a new line.

one line to the other. Fortunately, Word takes care of that for you. This feature is called *word wrap* and enables you to type continuously without pressing Enter at the end of a line within a paragraph. The only time you press Enter is when you want the insertion point to move to the next line.

Word wrap is closely associated with another concept: the hard and soft return. A *hard return* is created when you press Enter at the end of a line or paragraph. A *soft return* is created by the word processor as it wraps text from one line to the next. The locations of the soft returns change automatically as text is inserted or deleted. Only the user, who must intentionally insert or delete each hard return, can change the location of such returns.

The paragraphs at the top of Figure 1.3 show two hard returns, one at the end of each paragraph. Figure 1.3 also includes four soft returns in the first paragraph (one at the end of every line except the last) and three soft returns in the second paragraph. Now, assume the margins in the document are made smaller (that is, the line is made longer), as shown in the bottom paragraphs of Figure 1.3. The number of soft returns decreases as more text fits on a line and fewer lines are needed. The revised document still contains the two original hard returns—one at the end of each paragraph.

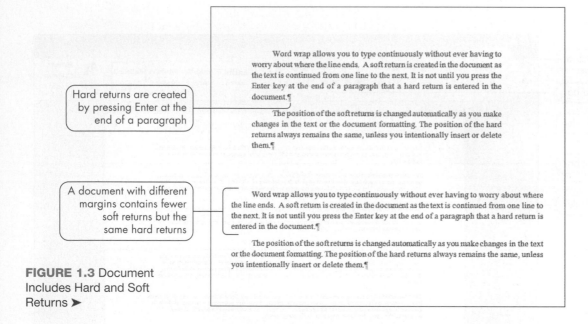

FIGURE 1.3 Document Includes Hard and Soft Returns ➤

Use Keyboard Shortcuts to Move Around a Document

The horizontal and vertical scrollbars and the scroll arrows are frequently used to view different pages in a document. However, clicking the scrollbars or arrows does not move the insertion point; it merely lets you see different parts of the document and leaves the insertion point where it was last positioned. To move the insertion point in a document you use the mouse or the keyboard. Table 1.1 shows useful keyboard shortcuts for navigating a document and relocating the insertion point.

TABLE 1.1 Keyboard Navigation Controls

Keys	Moves the Insertion Point	Keys	Moves the Insertion Point
←	One character to the left	Ctrl+Home	To the beginning of the document
→	One character to the right	Ctrl+End	To the end of the document
↑	Up one line	Ctrl+←	One word to the left
↓	Down one line	Ctrl+→	One word to the right
Home	To the beginning of the line	Ctrl+↑	Up one paragraph
End	To the end of the line	Ctrl+↓	Down one paragraph
Page Up	Up to the previous page	Ctrl+Page Up	To the top of the previous page
Page Down	Down to the next page	Ctrl+Page Down	To the top of the next page

Discover Toggle Switches

To **toggle** is to switch from one setting to another.

A *toggle*, when pressed or clicked, causes the computer to switch from one setting to another. Caps Lock is an example of a toggle button. Each time you press it, newly typed text will change from uppercase to lowercase, or vice versa. In the Office Fundamentals chapter you read about other toggle buttons. Sometimes you can invoke a toggle by pressing keys on the keyboard, such as Caps Lock. You invoke many toggle features, such as the Bold, Italic, and Underline commands, by clicking a combination of keys or a ribbon command to turn the feature on and off.

The **Show/Hide feature** reveals where formatting marks, such as spaces, tabs, and returns, are used in the document.

A toggle that enables you to reveal formatting applied to a document is the *Show/Hide feature*. Click Show/Hide (¶) in the Paragraph group on the Home tab to reveal where formatting marks, such as spaces, tabs, and hard returns, are in the document. Figure 1.4 displays formatting marks when the Show/Hide (¶) feature is on.

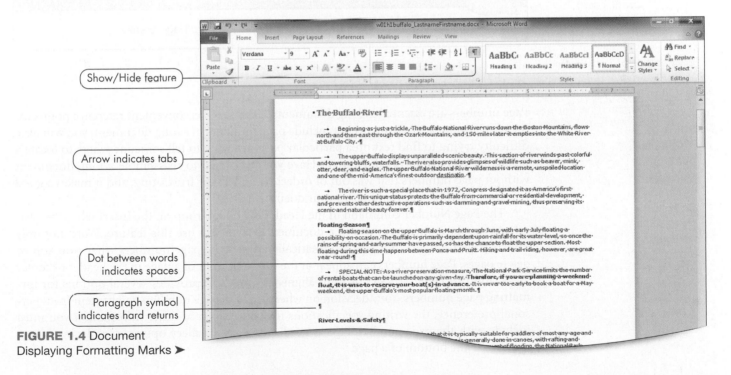

FIGURE 1.4 Document Displaying Formatting Marks ➤

Insert Page Breaks

A **soft page break** is inserted when text fills an entire page, then continues onto the next page.

When you type more text than can fit on a page, Word continues the text on another page using soft and hard page breaks. The *soft page break* is a hidden marker that automatically continues text on the top of a new page when text no longer fits on the current page. These breaks adjust automatically when you add and delete text. For the most part, you rely on soft page breaks to prepare multiple-page documents. However, at times you need to start a new page before Word inserts a soft page break.

When this occurs, you can insert a ***hard page break***, a hidden marker, to force text to begin on a new page. You can insert a hard page break into a document using the Breaks command in the Page Setup group on the Page Layout tab or using Page Break in the Pages group on the Insert tab. To view the page break markers in Print Layout view you must click Show/Hide (¶) on the Home tab to toggle on the formatting marks, as shown in Figure 1.5. You can view the page break markers without Show/Hide toggled on when you switch to Draft view.

A **hard page break** forces the next part of a document to begin on a new page.

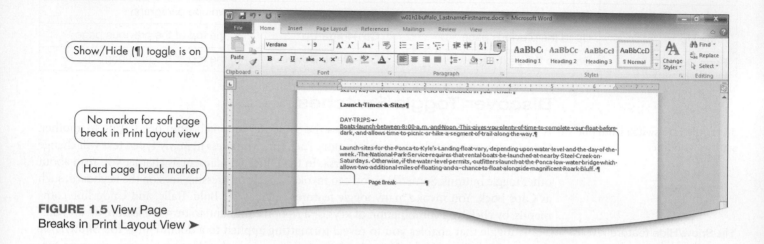

Show/Hide (¶) toggle is on

No marker for soft page break in Print Layout view

Hard page break marker

FIGURE 1.5 View Page Breaks in Print Layout View ➤

> **TIP** Hard Page Break Shortcut
>
> You can use the keyboard shortcut Ctrl+Enter to insert a hard page break.

Add Page Numbers

Page numbers are essential in long documents. They serve as convenient reference points for the writer and reader. If you do not include page numbers in a long document, you will have difficulty trying to find text on a particular page or trying to tell someone where to locate a particular passage in the document. Have you ever tried to reassemble a long document without page numbers that was out of order? It can be very frustrating, and it makes a good case for inserting page numbers in your documents.

The Page Number command in the Header & Footer group on the Insert tab is the easiest way to place page numbers in a document. When you use this feature, Word not only inserts page numbers, but also automatically adjusts the page numbers when you add or delete pages. Page numbers can appear at the top or bottom of a page in the header or footer areas, and can be left, center, or right aligned. Word 2010 provides several options for formatting page numbers. Your decision on where to place page numbers might stem from personal preference, the writing specifications for your paper, or other information you must include with the page number. Figure 1.6 displays a few gallery options for placing a page number at the bottom of a page.

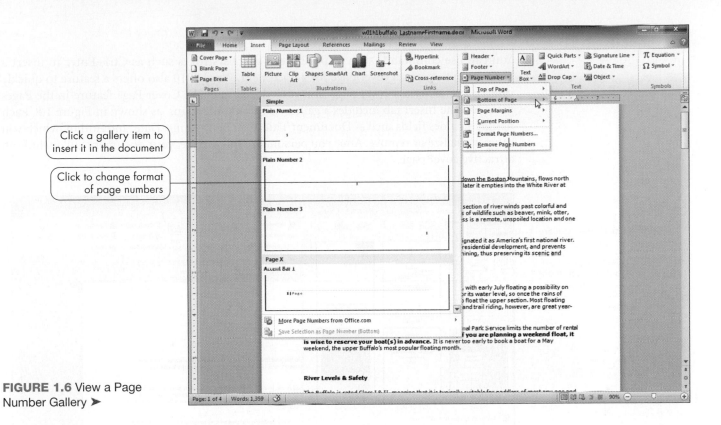

Click a gallery item to insert it in the document

Click to change format of page numbers

FIGURE 1.6 View a Page Number Gallery ➤

Word enables you to customize the format of page numbers. For example, at the beginning of a document you can use Roman numerals instead of Arabic numerals for preface pages. You also can adjust the page numbering so that it starts numbering on a page other than the first. This is useful when you have a report with a cover page; you typically do not consider the cover as page one and therefore begin numbering the page that follows it. You use the Format Page Number feature to display the Page Number Format dialog box (see Figure 1.7). If you are not satisfied with the page numbering in a document, use the Remove Page Numbers command to remove them.

Click to change page number options

Click to display page number in Roman numerals

Specify number if not 1

FIGURE 1.7 Page Number Format Dialog Box ➤

Insert a Cover Page

You can use commands such as page break and keystrokes such as Ctrl+Enter to insert a blank page to use as a cover page for a document. Word 2010 also offers a feature to quickly insert a preformatted cover page into your document. The Cover Page feature in the Pages group on the Insert tab includes a gallery with several designs, as shown in Figure 1.8. Each design includes fields such as Document Title, Company Name, Date, and Author, which you can personalize or remove. After you personalize this feature, your document will include an attractive cover page.

FIGURE 1.8 Insert a Cover Page ➤

Customizing Word

As installed, Word is immediately useful. However, you might find options that you would prefer to customize, add, or remove from the document window. For example, you can add commands to the Quick Access Toolbar (QAT) that do not currently display on any tab. You can also add frequently used commands to the QAT.

You can customize Word in many different ways. To begin the process, click the File tab, and then click Options. From there, you can view the options that are customizable. Table 1.2 describes the main categories that you can customize and some of the features in each category. You should take time to glance through each category as you continue to read this chapter. Keep in mind that if you are working in a school lab, you might not have permission to change options permanently.

TABLE 1.2 Word Options

Menu Category	Description	Sample of Options to Change
General	Change options that customize the window area and identify the user.	Show Mini toolbar; show Enhanced ScreenTips; change color scheme; change user name and initials.
Display	Change how documents are displayed on the screen and in print.	Show white space between pages in Print Layout view; always show formatting marks such as spaces on the screen; print document properties.
Proofing	Modify how Word corrects and formats your text.	Ignore words in uppercase (don't flag as incorrect in your text); use spelling checker; use contextual spelling and mark grammatical errors.
Save	Customize how documents are saved.	Default locations and format to save files; AutoRecover file location; Web server location.
Language	Set preference for one or more languages to use, which also invokes supporting resources such as dictionaries and grammar checking.	Editing language, language priority order.
Advanced	Specify editing options; cut, copy, and paste options; show document content options; display options; print options; and save options.	Enable text to be dragged and dropped; enable click and type; default paragraph style; show paste option buttons; show smart tags; number of recent documents to show in file menu; print pages in reverse order; always create backup copy; embed smart tags; update automatic links at open; compatibility options.
Customize Ribbon	Customize the existing Ribbon or create a new tab.	Add or remove tasks from the default tabs; create a new tab; reset all tabs to default tasks.
Quick Access Toolbar	Customize the Quick Access Toolbar and other keyboard shortcuts.	Add or remove buttons from the QAT; determine location of QAT; customize keyboard shortcuts.
Add-Ins	View the add-ins previously installed, customize settings for add-ins, and install more add-ins.	View settings for active and inactive application add-ins; manage smart tags, templates, and disabled items.
Trust Center	View online documentation about security and privacy and change settings to protect documents from possible infections.	Enable and disable macros; change ActiveX settings; set privacy options; select trusted publishers and locations.

As you can see, you are able to customize dozens of settings in Word. Table 1.2 offers only a small sample of what can be customized. You may not need to make any changes at all! But as you become more familiar with features in Word, you may want to use options to customize the application to fit your specific needs.

HANDS-ON EXERCISES

1 Introduction to Word Processing

As the new office manager for First River Outfitter, you must preview the document Lawson drafted for use as a marketing brochure. You will proofread the current document and make modifications to improve readability and the way the document looks in print.

Skills covered: Use Keyboard Shortcuts to Navigate a Document and Insert a Page Break • Insert a Page Number • Add a Cover Page and Revise Page Numbers • Change Word Options

---

STEP 1 ▷ USE KEYBOARD SHORTCUTS TO NAVIGATE A DOCUMENT AND INSERT A PAGE BREAK

When you open the file that contains information about the Buffalo River, you look to see if paragraph breaks are in odd places, making the content difficult to read. When you find them, you insert page breaks to improve readability. Refer to Figure 1.9 as you complete Step 1.

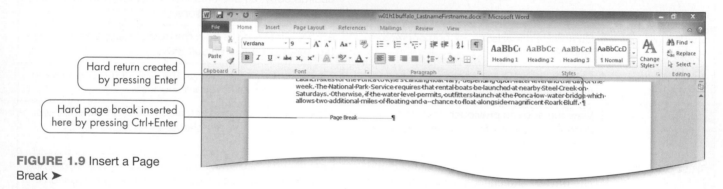

Hard return created by pressing Enter

Hard page break inserted here by pressing Ctrl+Enter

FIGURE 1.9 Insert a Page Break ➤

 FYI

a. Start Word. Open *w01h1buffalo* and save it as **w01h1buffalo_LastnameFirstname**.

> **TROUBLESHOOTING:** If you make any major mistakes in this exercise, you can close the file, open *w01h1buffalo* again, and then start this exercise over.

When you save files, use your last and first names. For example, as the Word author, I would name my document w01h1buffalo_HulettMichelle.

> **TIP** Save and Save Again
>
> You should practice saving your files often. If you open a document and you do not want to change its name or where it is stored, the easiest way to save it is to click Save on the Quick Access Toolbar. You can also click the File tab and then click Save, or you can press the keyboard command Ctrl+S to save quickly and often.

b. Press **Page Down** five times, stopping on each page to view the document contents. Press **Ctrl+Home** to return to the top of the document.

c. Scroll down until you can view the last line of the second page.

d. Click **Show/Hide** (¶) in the Paragraph group on the Home tab.

This toggle enables you to see exactly where the paragraphs and other text break on each line and across pages.

e. Click to the left of the *Glass, Trash, & Other Regulations* paragraph title.

This paragraph begins at the bottom of page 2 and continues to the top of page 3. It would be best if the heading and each paragraph below the heading displays together on one page, so inserting a hard return will move them all together.

f. Press **Ctrl+Enter** to insert a hard page break.

The hard page break is marked as a Page Break. Now the paragraph heading displays on the same page as the paragraph, as shown in Figure 1.9.

g. Click **Save** in the Quick Access Toolbar.

STEP 2 ▶ INSERT A PAGE NUMBER

The next step you take to improve readability of this document is the addition of page numbers. If someone prints the document and the pages become scattered, he or she should be able to use page numbers to reassemble it in the proper order. Refer to Figure 1.10 as you complete Step 2.

FIGURE 1.10 Add a Page Number ▶

a. Click the **Insert tab**. Click **Page Number** in the Header & Footer group, and then point to **Bottom of Page**. Scroll down the gallery, and then click **Thick Line**, as shown in Figure 1.10.

A dark line and the page number display on the bottom of each page. The Header & Footer Tools tab displays in the Ribbon area.

b. Click the **Footer from Bottom arrow** in the Position group until **0.3** displays.

You make this modification to enable the footer to rest closer to the bottom of the page and reduce the white space that displays. Reducing this number is one way to utilize the paper more efficiently and display more text on a page. In the case of very long documents, this can reduce the number of sheets of paper used for printing.

c. Click **Close Header and Footer**. Click the **Home tab**, and then click **Show/Hide** (¶) in the paragraph group to turn off formatting marks.

d. Press **Ctrl+S** to save the document.

ADD A COVER PAGE AND REVISE PAGE NUMBERS

Because you are working with a document that will be used for advertising purposes, you want to add an attractive cover page. You will use a Word feature to insert a cover page very quickly and easily. You will then make adjustments to the page numbering to reflect the addition of the cover page. Refer to Figure 1.11 as you complete Step 3.

Document title field

Subtitle field

Author field

FIGURE 1.11 New Cover Page ➤

a. Click the **Insert tab**, click **Cover Page** in the Pages group, and then click **Mod** from the gallery.

Now that the cover page displays, the rest of the document begins at the top of page 2. The insertion point does not have to be at the beginning of a document to insert a cover page; it inserts automatically as the first page.

b. Type **Floating the Buffalo National River** to replace the text *Type the document title*.

> **TROUBLESHOOTING:** If you begin to type and the existing text remains, just click inside the title area to position your cursor there, and then begin to type. You can also scroll to select the existing text, and then replace it when you type.

c. Press **Tab** to select the **Subtitle field**, and then replace the text *Type the document subtitle* with **with First River Outfitter**. Replace the capital *W* with a lower case *w* on the word *with*, if necessary.

When you fill in the document subtitle, Word automatically capitalizes the first letter of the first word. In this case, it is inappropriate to capitalize the word *with*, so you must revise the subtitle to remove the capitalization.

d. Right-click the **Abstract field** below the subtitle, and then select **Cut**. Press **Tab** two times to select the **Author field**, and then type your name. Right-click the **Date field**, and then select **Cut**. Compare your cover page to Figure 1.11.

e. Look at the status bar at the bottom of the page to determine the page where the insertion point is located. If necessary, scroll to page 2, and then double-click the white space at the top of the second page to place your insertion point in the header.

Notice that the Different First Page option is selected in the Options group on the Header & Footer Tools Design tab. The cover page you created does not require a header or footer, and this setting prevents them from displaying on the first page. This setting is checked automatically when you insert a cover page.

f. Click **Close Header and Footer**.

When you scroll to view the bottom of the second page, the number 1 displays.

g. Save the document.

STEP 4 CHANGE WORD OPTIONS

You remember that the Word Options dialog box has a few settings that you want to change or confirm. First, you want to make sure your name is applied to this installation of Word. Your next concern is that backups occur in a timely manner so that you will lose minimal information in the event of a system crash; therefore, you decide to reduce the time between backups. You often preview your document to see how it looks for printing, so you add the Print Preview command to the Quick Access Toolbar. Refer to Figure 1.12 as you complete Step 4.

FIGURE 1.12 Add Print Preview to the Quick Access Toolbar ➤

a. Click the **File tab**, and then click **Options** near the bottom of the menu.

b. Type your name in the **User name box** that displays in the General category of options.

When you change this setting, your name is attached to a file as the author of that document. Other features presented later also use this setting.

c. Click **Save** on the left side of the Word Options dialog box. Reduce the time that currently displays next to *Save AutoRecover information every 10 minutes* to **3**.

You do a lot of work within the time span of a few minutes, so you may prefer to have the backups happen every three minutes instead of every ten minutes.

d. Click **Quick Access Toolbar** on the left side of the Word Options dialog box.

e. Scroll down the list of commands on the left side until *Print Preview and Print* displays. Click **Print Preview and Print**, and then click **Add** to copy the Print Preview and Print command, as shown in Figure 1.12.

f. Click **OK** to close the Word Options dialog box.

The Print Preview and Print command now displays on the Quick Access Toolbar at the top of the page on the title bar.

> **TROUBLESHOOTING:** If you work in a lab environment, you might not have permission to modify the Word settings. Accept any error messages you might see when saving the Word options, and then proceed to the next step.

g. Save the document and keep it onscreen if you plan to continue with the next Hands-On Exercise. If not, close the document, and then exit Word.

Document Organization

Throughout your college and professional career, you will create a variety of documents. As you compose and edit you want to set the documents up so that some parts display differently than others when you view or print them. Word has settings that enable you to segment a document just for this purpose.

In this section, you will learn how to make changes to a Word document, such as inserting section breaks, adding headers and footers, and displaying watermarks. You will also learn about features that help you monitor spelling and grammar, and you will learn about different view modes.

Using Features That Improve Readability

When you create a document you consider the content you will insert, but you also should consider how you want the document to look when you print or display it. Many of the settings you use for this purpose are on the Page Layout tab. For example, when you create a short business letter, you want to increase the margins to a width such as 1.5" on all sides, so the letter contents are balanced on the printed page. If you print a formal or research paper, you want to use a 1.5" left margin and a 1" right margin to provide extra room on the left for binding.

> When you create a document, you consider the content you will insert, but you also should consider how you want the document to look when you print or display it.

Another setting to consider for a document is orientation. Most documents, such as letters and research papers, use portrait orientation. However, a brochure, large graphic, chart, or table might display better on a page with landscape orientation.

If you need to print a document on special paper, such as legal size (8½" x 14") paper or an envelope, you should select the paper size before you create the document text. The Size command in the Page Setup group on the Page Layout tab contains several different document sizes that you can use. If you have special paper requirements, you can select More Paper Sizes to enter your own custom size. If you do not select the special size before you print, you will waste paper and find yourself with a very strange-looking printout.

Insert Headers and Footers

A **header** is information that displays at the top of each document page.

A **footer** is information that displays at the bottom of each document page.

Headers and footers give a professional appearance to a document. A *header* consists of one or more lines at the top of each page. A *footer* displays at the bottom of each page. The advantage of using a header or footer is to specify the content only once, after which it appears automatically on all pages. Although you can type the text yourself at the top or bottom of every page, it is time-consuming, and the possibility of making a mistake is great. You also can insert a field, such as a page number or file name, and Word will automatically insert the correct information. A document may display headers but not footers, footers but not headers, both headers and footers, or neither. A page number is a simple header or footer and can be created by clicking Page Number, selecting the location where it will display, and selecting the style you prefer. Footers might also contain the date the document was created or the file name. Headers might contain the name of an organization, the author, or the title of the document. Take a moment to notice the type of information you see in the headers and footers of the books or magazines you are reading.

Headers and footers are added from the Insert tab and are formatted like any other paragraph. They can be center, left, or right aligned. You can format headers and footers in any typeface or point size and can include special fields to insert automatically information such as author, date, or time a document is saved. The content of the headers and footers is adjusted for changes in page breaks caused by modifications to the body of the document. This happens most often for page numbers because the addition or deletion of information in a document can alter the page numbering.

Word 2010 offers many built-in formatting options that enable you to add a professional look quickly. It also enables you to control how headers and footers display throughout a document. These options display on the Header & Footer Tools Design tab (see Figure 1.13). For instance, you can specify a different header or footer for the first page; this is advisable when you have a cover page and do not want the header (or footer) to display on that page. You can also have different headers and footers for odd and even pages. This feature is useful when you plan to print a document that will be bound as a book. Notice the different information this book prints on the footer of odd versus even pages and how the page numbers display in the corners of each page. If you want to change the header (or footer) midway through a document, you need to insert a section break at the point where the new header (or footer) is to begin. These breaks are discussed in the next section.

FIGURE 1.13 Header and Footer Tools Commands ➤

Create Sections

Formatting in Word occurs on three levels: character, paragraph, and section. Formatting at the section level controls headers and footers, page numbering, page size and orientation, margins, and columns. Most documents you work with, unless intentionally changed, probably consist of a single section, and thus any formatting is applied to the entire document. You can, however, divide a document into sections and format each section independently.

A **section break** is a marker that divides a document into sections, thereby enabling different formatting in each section.

You determine where one section ends and another begins by clicking Breaks in the Page Setup group on the Page Layout tab. A *section break* is a marker that divides a document into sections. It enables you to control where text is placed and how it will be formatted on the printed page; that is, you can specify that text in the new section displays on the same page or on a new page. Formatting at the section level gives you the ability to create more sophisticated documents. Word stores the formatting characteristics of each section within the section break at the end of a section. Thus, deleting a section break also deletes the section formatting, causing the text above the break to assume the formatting characteristics of the next section.

Word has four types of section breaks, as shown in Table 1.3.

TABLE 1.3 Section Breaks

Type	Description	Example
Next Page	When inserted, text that follows must begin at the top of the next page.	Use to force a chapter to start at the top of a page.
Continuous	When inserted, text that follows can continue on the same page.	Use to format text in the middle of the page into columns.
Even Page	When inserted, text that follows must begin at the top of the next even-numbered page.	Use to force a chapter to begin at the top of an even-numbered page.
Odd Page	When inserted, text that follows must begin at the top of the next odd-numbered page.	Use to force a chapter to begin at the top of an odd-numbered page.

When you use section breaks, you can do the following:

- Change the margins within a multipage letter, where the section containing only the first page (the letterhead) requires a larger top margin than the other pages in the letter.
- Change the orientation in one section from portrait to landscape to accommodate a wide table or graphic in the middle or end of the document.
- Change the page numbering in one section to use Roman numerals for a table of contents and Arabic numerals thereafter on pages in remaining sections.
- Change the number of columns in a newsletter, which may contain a section with a single column at the top of a page for the masthead and another section with two or three columns in the body of the newsletter.

Figure 1.14 displays the last page of the Buffalo River document. The document has been divided into two sections, and the insertion point is currently on the last page of the document, which is also the first page of the second section. Note the difference in page number on the footer and in the status bar.

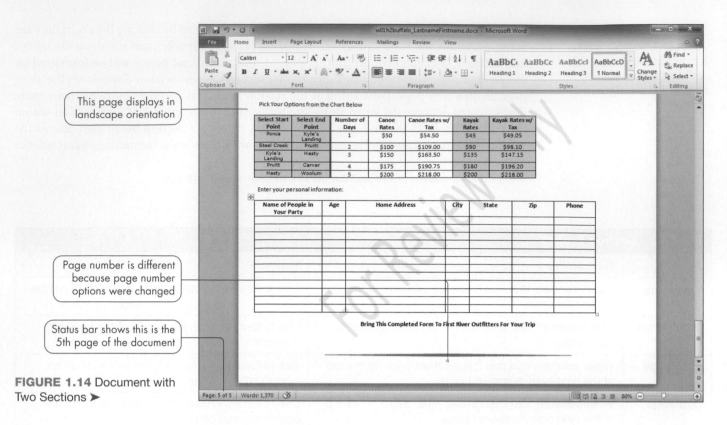

This page displays in landscape orientation

Page number is different because page number options were changed

Status bar shows this is the 5th page of the document

FIGURE 1.14 Document with Two Sections ➤

When a document has multiple sections, the Link to Previous feature in the Header & Footer Tools tab is important to consider. If you want page numbering to continue sequentially so the numbering is not interrupted from section to section, activate the Link to Previous toggle. It displays with an orange color when active. If you want to restart page numbering when a section changes, turn off the Link to Previous toggle. Additionally, you can move from the header or footer of one section to another section by clicking Next or Previous in the Navigation group on the Design tab, as shown in Figure 1.15.

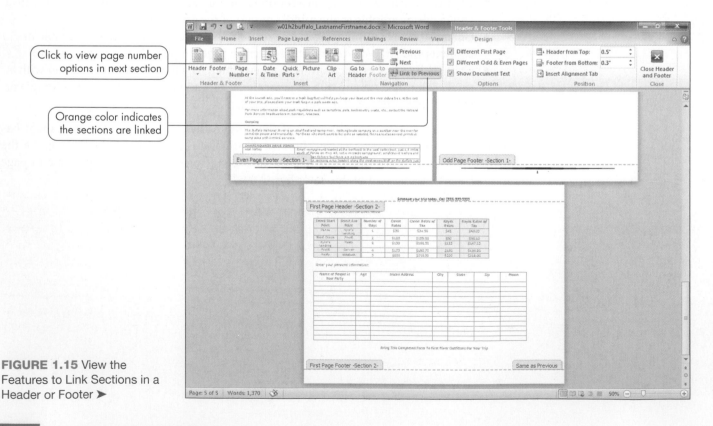

Click to view page number options in next section

Orange color indicates the sections are linked

FIGURE 1.15 View the Features to Link Sections in a Header or Footer ➤

Insert a Watermark

A **watermark** is text or a graphic that displays behind text.

A *watermark* is text or a graphic that displays behind text. Watermarks are often used to display a very light, washed-out logo for a company. They are also frequently used to indicate the status of a document, such as *FOR REVIEW ONLY*, as shown in Figure 1.16. Watermarks do not display on a document that is saved as a Web page, nor will they display in Web Layout view.

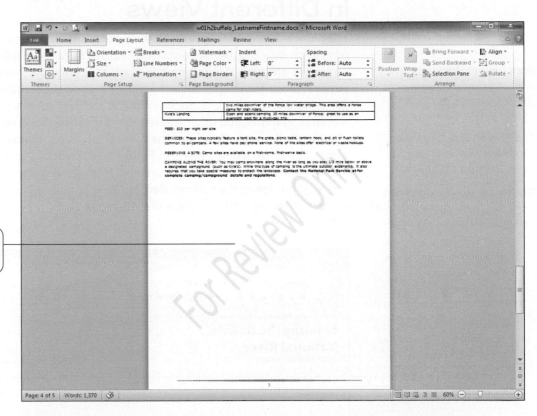

For Review Only displays as a watermark behind text on the page

FIGURE 1.16 Document That Includes a Watermark ➤

Checking Spelling and Grammar

It is important to create a document that is free of typographical and grammatical errors. With the automated spelling and grammar checker tools in Word, it is relatively easy to do so. However, you should always proofread a document because the spelling and grammar checker will not always find every possible error.

In addition to spelling and grammar checking, Word provides many features that correct a variety of grammatical mistakes. Word has a contextual spelling feature that attempts to locate a word that is spelled correctly but used incorrectly. For example, many people confuse the usage of words such as *their* and *there*, *two* and *too*, and *which* and *witch*. The visual indication that a contextual spelling error exists is a blue wavy line under the word, as shown in Figure 1.17.

When you invoke the spelling and grammar checking feature, contextual spelling mistakes will also display, and you can change them during this process.

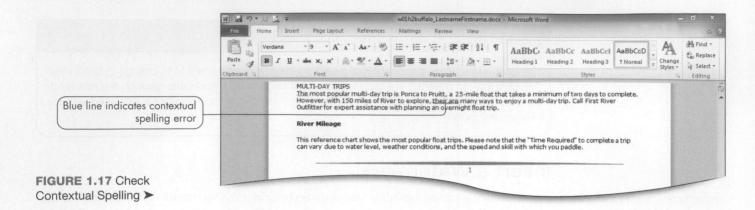

Blue line indicates contextual spelling error

FIGURE 1.17 Check Contextual Spelling ➤

Displaying a Document in Different Views

Print Layout view is the default view and closely resembles the printed document.

Full Screen Reading view eliminates tabs and makes it easier to read a document.

Draft view shows a simplified work area, removing white space and other elements from view.

The View tab provides options that enable you to display a document in many different ways. Each view can display your document at a different magnification, which in turn determines the amount of scrolling necessary to see remote parts of a document. The *Print Layout view* is the default view and is the view you use most frequently. It closely resembles the printed document and displays the top and bottom margins, headers and footers, page numbers, graphics, and other features that do not appear in other views.

The *Full Screen Reading view* hides the Ribbon, making it easier to read your document. The *Draft view*, shown in Figure 1.18, creates a simple area in which to work; it removes white space and certain elements from the document, such as headers, footers, and graphics, but leaves the Ribbon. Because view options are used frequently, buttons for each are located on the status bar, as shown in Figure 1.18.

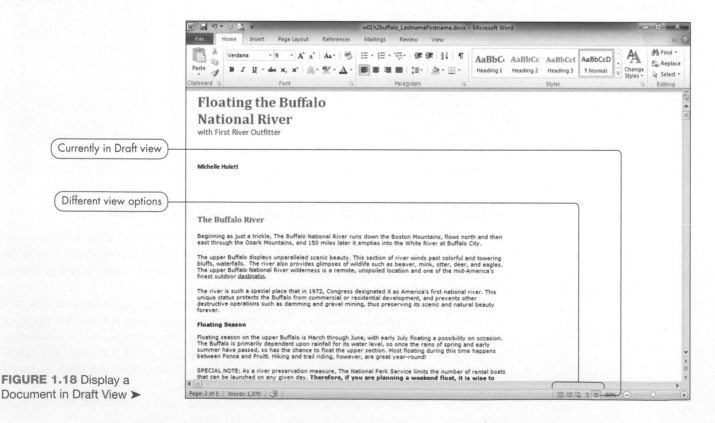

Currently in Draft view

Different view options

FIGURE 1.18 Display a Document in Draft View ➤

When you click Zoom in the Zoom group on the View tab, the Zoom dialog box displays with several options (see Figure 1.19). You can use the Zoom controls to display the document onscreen at different magnifications—for example, 75%, 100%, or 200%. This command does not affect the size of the text on the printed page. It is helpful to be able to zoom in to view details or to zoom out and see the effects of your work on a full page.

View three pages at once

Preview current Zoom option

FIGURE 1.19 Zoom Dialog Box ➤

Word will automatically determine the magnification if you select one of the Zoom options—Page width, Text width, Whole page, or Many pages (Whole page and Many pages are available only in the Print Layout view). Figure 1.20, for example, displays the Buffalo River document in Print Layout view. The 27% magnification is determined automatically after you specify the number of pages, in this case 2 × 2. If you use a wide screen, the magnification size might differ slightly.

Click and drag Zoom slider to decrease or increase the zoom

Magnification is determined after selecting 2x2 page view in the Zoom dialog box

Orange shading indicates Print Layout view is selected

FIGURE 1.20 View Four Pages of a Document ➤

TIP Use the Status Bar to Change View Options

The status bar repeats commands from the View tab in a handy location for quick access. You can switch to Print Layout, Full Screen Reading, Web Layout, Outline, or Draft view from the buttons on the status bar. You also can use the Zoom slider to change the zoom of the current document or click the Zoom command to display the Zoom dialog box, which contains more viewing options.

The **Outline view** displays a structural view of the document that can be collapsed or expanded.

The **Web Layout view** is used when creating a Web page.

The View tab also provides access to two additional views—the Outline view and the Web Layout view. The *Outline view* does not display a conventional outline, but rather a structural view of a document that can be collapsed or expanded as necessary. The *Web Layout view* is used when you are creating a Web page.

<head>
</head>

HANDS-ON EXERCISES

2 Document Organization

You have made some introductory edits to the document that will be used in marketing the First River Outfitter, but you plan to make more changes that will improve organization and readability. These improvements require a section break at the end that will enable you to format the last page differently from the others. You also remember to check spelling and grammar.

Skills covered: Change Page Margins and Insert a Page Break • Insert Headers in Sections • Add a Watermark • Check Spelling and Grammar

---

STEP 1 ▶ CHANGE PAGE MARGINS AND INSERT A PAGE BREAK

One step in conserving the amount of paper used in marketing materials is to reduce the margins on the pages that will print. In this step you change margins and insert a page break to create a new section at the end of the document. Then you change orientation on the last page to make it easier to view a lengthy table. Refer to Figure 1.21 as you complete Step 1.

Click to insert a section break that starts on the next page

FIGURE 1.21 Insert a Section Break ➤

a. Open *w01h1buffalo_LastnameFirstname* if you closed it at the end of Hands-On Exercise 1. Save the document with the new name **w01h2buffalo_LastnameFirstname**, changing *h1* to *h2*.

b. Click the **Page Layout tab**, and then click **Margins** in the Page Setup group. Click **Custom Margins**.

The Page Setup dialog box displays.

c. Click the **Margins tab**, if necessary. Type **.5** in the **Top margin box**. Press **Tab** to move the insertion point to the Bottom margin box. Type **.5** and press **Tab** to move to the Left margin box.

0.5″ is the equivalent of 1/2 of one inch.

d. Click the **Left margin arrow** to set the left margin at **0.6**, and then repeat the procedure to set the right margin to **0.6**.

The top and bottom margins are now set at 0.5″, and the left and right margins are set at 0.6″.

e. Check that these settings apply to the **Whole document**, located in the lower portion of the dialog box. Click **OK** to close the dialog box.

You can see the change in layout as a result of changing the margins. The content now displays with less white space around the text. And the page break at the beginning of the *Glass, Trash, & Other Regulations* section that you inserted earlier is no longer needed.

f. Scroll down and position the insertion point on the left side of the *Glass, Trash, & Other Regulations* title. Press **Backspace**.

> **TROUBLESHOOTING:** If the page break does not disappear immediately, you might have to press Backspace a second time.

g. Scroll down and place the insertion point on the left side of the heading *Plan Your Trip Now!* Click **Breaks** in the Page Setup group, and then click **Next Page** under *Section Breaks*, as shown in Figure 1.21.

The table for personal information that displays on the last page is very wide and does not show the entire table in the portrait orientation. By inserting this section break you can now make modifications, such as turning this page to landscape orientation, without changing the previous pages. Those changes will occur in the next steps.

h. Click **Orientation**, and then select **Landscape**.

The table of personal information now displays completely.

i. Press **Ctrl+S** to save the document.

STEP 2 ▶ **INSERT HEADERS IN SECTIONS**

The document you are preparing will be read by potential customers. To make sure you maximize all areas of the document to market the company, you decide to use the area at the top of a page to add a small amount of information, such as phone numbers for the business. Refer to Figure 1.22 as you complete Step 2.

Different First Page setting in use for this section also

Indicates you created a new section

FIGURE 1.22 Document Header ➤

a. Click the **Insert tab**, click **Header** in the Header & Footer group, and then click **Edit Header**.

The Insertion point displays in the header of the last page, and the Header & Footer Tools Design tab displays in the Ribbon. Notice also that the Header tab for this page indicates this is Section 2, as seen in Figure 1.22.

b. Scroll up and click in a header or footer in Section 1. Click **Different Odd & Even Pages** in the Options group to turn on this feature.

c. Scroll and click to position the insertion point in a header identified as *Even Page Header -Section 1-*, if necessary.

Any information you insert in this header will only show up on even-numbered pages. It looks more professional to omit headers from the first page of text and add them on following pages. This enables you to place information on only even-numbered pages throughout the document. The setting can be used in addition to the Different First Page feature, which is already being used to prevent any header or footer from displaying on the cover page.

d. Press **Tab** two times to move the insertion point to the right side of the header. Type **Schedule your trip today. Call (555) 555-5555.**

The text and phone number display in the header. Scroll down and notice the header displays on this page only.

e. Scroll down and position the insertion point in the header for Section 2. Click **Link to Previous** in the Navigation group to turn that setting off.

The creation of the new section automatically invokes the Link to Previous command. When turned on, it enables the same header or footer to display on the first page in each section. To prevent this contact information from displaying on the cover page you disable that setting in Section 2.

f. Press **Tab** two times, and then type **Schedule your trip today. Call (555) 555-5555.**

Because you insert a separate section for the last page, the headers and footers in the previous section do not automatically display there. To continue the trend of placing the contact information at the top of every even-numbered page, you must insert it again in the new section.

g. Scroll up to the previous page, select the entire odd page footer from Section 1, and then click **Ctrl+C**.

Another consequence of invoking the Different Odd & Even Pages setting is that the footers for the even pages in Section 1 were removed. The next steps copy the footer from the odd pages and insert it into the even pages.

h. Scroll up to the *Even Page Footer -Section 1-*, and then place the insertion point in the footer. Press **Ctrl+V** to insert the page number and heavy line.

> **TROUBLESHOOTING:** If you insert an extra line return and the cursor displays on the line below the page number at the end of the paste operation, press Backspace to remove the extra line return so it does not needlessly extend the space for the footer.

i. Scroll through the document and notice the sequential page numbering only on the middle pages, not the cover sheet or last page. Click **Close Header and Footer**.

j. Save the document.

You plan to send a copy of your current work to Lawson for review. You want to make sure this document is marked so anyone who views it will know it is not complete or ready to distribute to customers. You insert a watermark that will display faintly on each page. Later, when the document is complete, you will remove the watermark. Refer to Figure 1.23 as you complete Step 3.

Click to view Watermark gallery

Click Text watermark to customize

Type the text you want to display on the page

Customize your watermark with these settings

FIGURE 1.23 Type Text to Display as a Watermark ➤

a. Click the **Page Layout tab**. Click **Watermark** in the Page Background group, and then click **Custom Watermark**.

The Watermark dialog box displays with several options available. You decide to enter your own words to communicate the message that displays as a watermark on this page.

b. Click **Text watermark**.

c. Select the text *ASAP* that displays beside *Text*, and then type **For Review Only** to replace *ASAP*, as shown in Figure 1.23. Click **OK**. Scroll to page 4, which displays 3 as the page number in the footer, to get a better view of the watermark.

The watermark is in place and displays on each page in each section. It is easier to see it on page 4 because this page has less text.

> **TIP** Frequently Used Watermarks
>
> When you click Watermark in the Page Background group, several of the most commonly used watermark statements display, such as *DRAFT* or *CONFIDENTIAL*. You can also select the option to view more Watermarks from Office.com.

d. Click **Print Preview** in the Quick Access Toolbar, and notice the watermark in the preview of the document.

e. Click the **File tab** to close Print Preview. Press **Ctrl+S** to save the document.

STEP 4 ▶ CHECK SPELLING AND GRAMMAR

You are always careful to check spelling and grammar before distributing a document for others to read. After several edits, you decide it is time to run the spelling and grammar check feature in Word and make changes to remove any mistakes. Refer to Figure 1.24 as you complete Step 4.

Click to retain the word in current form

Possible incorrect usage of word

Select from suggestions in this box

Click to replace word with highlighted suggestion

Also checks grammar when selected

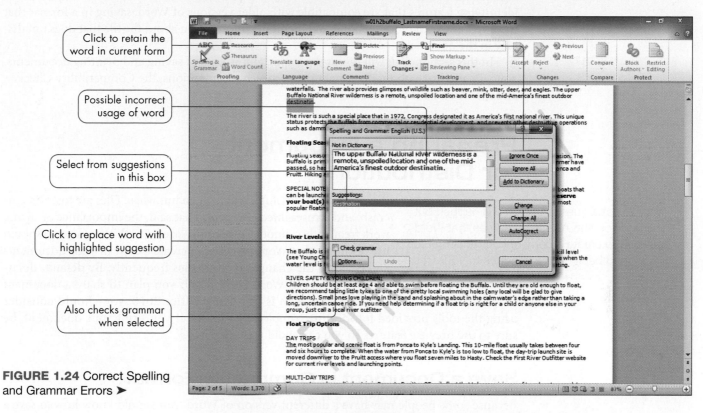

FIGURE 1.24 Correct Spelling and Grammar Errors ➤

 FYI

a. Place the cursor at the top of page 2, on the left side of the text *The Buffalo River*. Click the **Review tab**, and then click **Spelling & Grammar** in the Proofing group.

The Spelling and Grammar dialog box displays with the first error indicated in red text, as shown in Figure 1.24.

b. Remove the check from the *Check grammar* option. If necessary, click **Yes** in the dialog box that asks if you want to continue checking the document.

Many of the headings in the document will be flagged for incorrect grammar, so this will let you bypass all of them and check the spelling only.

> **TROUBLESHOOTING:** If additional text is flagged, such as *you've*, click Ignore All. This indicates that Word is checking grammar and style. To do a simple spelling and grammar check, click the File tab, click Options, click Proofing, click the Writing Style arrow, choose Grammar Only, and then click OK.

c. Click **Change All** to replace all misspellings of the word *destinatin* with the correct *destination*, and then view the next error.

d. Click **Change** to replace the contextual spelling error *their are* with *there are* near the bottom of the first page.

e. Click **Ignore once** to the remaining spelling errors in the document. These words are spelled correctly, but are not included in the spelling checker dictionary, and therefore, are flagged as spelling errors. Click **OK** in the box that informs you the spelling and grammar check is complete.

f. Save the document and keep it onscreen if you plan to continue with the next Hands-On Exercise. If not, close the document and exit Word.

Finalize a Document

After you organize your document and make all the formatting changes you desire, you need to save the document in its final form and prepare it for use by others. You can take advantage of features in Word that enable you to manipulate the file in a variety of ways, such as identifying features that are compatible with older versions of Word, saving in a format that is compatible with older versions, and including information about the file that does not display in the document.

In this section, you will revisit the important process of saving and printing documents. You will also learn about document properties, backup options, the Compatibility Checker, and the Document Inspector.

Preparing a Document for Distribution

> It is not a question of *if* it will happen but *when*. You should use resources that Word provides to create a copy of your documents and back up the changes to your files at every opportunity.

It is not a question of *if* it will happen but *when*. Files are lost, systems crash, and viruses infect a system. That said, the importance of saving work frequently cannot be overemphasized. For this reason, you should use resources that Word provides to create a copy of your documents and back up the changes to your files frequently. By default, documents will save as Word 2010 files. If you plan to share a document with someone who is not using Office 2010, you should consider using the tools provided for locating compatibility issues. If you print your document, be sure to use preview features so you can avoid wasting paper.

Save a Document in Compatible Format

Because some people may have a different version of Word, you should know how to save a document in a format that they can use. People cannot open a Word 2010 document in the 97-2003 versions of Word unless they install the Compatibility Pack that contains a converter. If you are sure they have not installed the Compatibility Pack, you should save the document in Word 97-2003 format.

After reading the Office Fundamentals chapter, you know the Save and Save As commands are used to copy your documents to disk and should be used frequently to avoid loss of work and data. To save a document so that someone with a 97-2003 version of Office can open it, do the following:

1. Click the File tab.
2. Click Save As.
3. Select the Save as type arrow, and then select Word 97-2003 (see Figure 1.25).
4. Enter a name for your file in the Save As dialog box. The saved file will have the .doc extension instead of the Word 2010 extension, .docx.

FIGURE 1.25 Save a Document in Compatible Format ➤

If you open a Word document created in an earlier version, such as Word 2003, the title bar will include *(Compatibility Mode)* at the top. You can still work with the document and even save it back in the same format for Word 97-2003 users. However, some features introduced in Word 2007 and used in Word 2010, such as SmartArt and graphic enhancement options used in the cover page, are not viewable or available for use in compatibility mode.

To remove the file from compatibility mode, click the File tab, and then click Convert. It will convert the file and remove the *(Compatibility Mode)* designator, but the .doc extension will still display. The next time you click Save, the extension will change to .docx, indicating that the file is converted into a Word 2010 file; you will then be able to use all of the Word 2010 features.

Understand Backup Options

AutoRecover enables Word to recover a previous version of a document.

Word enables you to back up files in different ways. One option is to use a feature called **AutoRecover**. If Word crashes when AutoRecover is enabled, the program will be able to recover a previous version of your document when you restart the program. The only work you will lose is anything you did between the time of the last AutoRecover operation and the time of the crash, unless you happen to save the document in the meantime. The default *Save AutoRecover information every 10 minutes* ensures that you will never lose more than 10 minutes of work. AutoRecover is enabled from the Save category in the Word Options menu.

You can also set Word to create a backup copy with every save. Assume that you have created the simple document with the phrase *The fox jumped over the fence*, and have saved it under the name *Fox*. Assume further that you edit the document to read *The quick brown fox jumped over the fence*, and that you save it a second time. The second Save command changes the name of the original document from *Fox* to *Backup of Fox*, then saves the current contents of memory as *Fox*. In other words, the disk now contains two versions of the document: the current version *Fox* and the most recent previous version *Backup of Fox*.

The cycle goes on indefinitely, with *Fox* always containing the current version and *Backup of Fox* the most recent previous version. So, if you revise and save the document a third time, the original (first) version of the document disappears entirely because only two versions are kept. The contents of *Fox* and *Backup of Fox* are different, but the existence of the latter enables you to retrieve the previous version if you inadvertently edit beyond repair or accidentally erase the current *Fox* version. You set this valuable backup option from the Advanced category in the Word Options menu; it is not automatically enabled.

Run the Compatibility Checker

The **Compatibility Checker** looks for features that are not supported by previous versions of Word.

The *Compatibility Checker* is a feature in Word 2010 that enables you to determine if your document includes features that are not supported by Word 97-2003 versions. After you complete your document, do the following:

1. Click the File tab.
2. Click Check for Issues.
3. Click Check Compatibility.

If the document contains anything that could not be opened in a different version of Word, the Microsoft Word Compatibility Checker dialog box lists it. From this dialog box you also can indicate that you want to always check compatibility when saving this file (see Figure 1.26). If you are saving the document in a format to be used by someone with an earlier version, you will want to make corrections to the items listed in the dialog box before saving again and sending the file.

List of incompatible items in the document

Always check compatibility of this file

FIGURE 1.26 Compatibility Checker ➤

Run the Document Inspector

The **Document Inspector** checks for and removes different kinds of hidden and personal information from a document.

Before you send or give a document to another person, you should run the *Document Inspector* to reveal any hidden or personal data in the file. For privacy or security reasons, you might want to remove certain items contained in the document such as author name, comments made by one or more persons who have access to the document, or document server locations. Some inspectors are specific to individual Office applications, such as Excel and PowerPoint. Word provides inspectors that you can invoke to reveal different types of information, including the following:

- Comments, Revisions, Versions, and Annotations
- Document Properties and Personal Information
- Custom XML Data
- Headers, Footers, and Watermarks
- Invisible Content
- Hidden Text

The inspectors can also locate information in documents created in older versions of Word. Because some information that the Document Inspector might remove cannot be recovered with the Undo command, you should save a copy of your original document, using a different name, just before you run any of the inspectors. After you save the copy, do the following:

1. Click the File tab.
2. Click Check for Issues.
3. Click Inspect Document.

The Document Inspector dialog box displays first, enabling you to select the types of content you want it to check (see Figure 1.27). When the check is complete, Word lists the results and enables you to choose whether to remove the content from the document. If you forget to save a backup copy of the document, you can use the Save As command to save a copy of the document with a new name after you run the inspector.

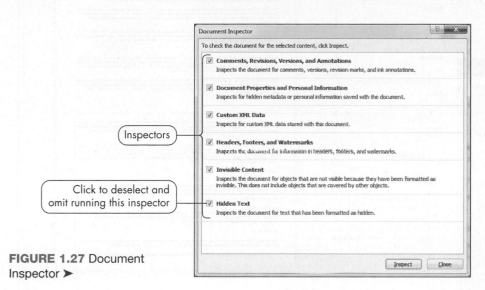

FIGURE 1.27 Document Inspector ➤

Select Printing Options

People often print an entire document when they want to view only a few pages. All computer users should be mindful of the environment, and limiting printer use is a perfect place to start. Millions of sheets of paper have been wasted because someone did not take a moment to preview his or her work and then had to reprint due to a minor error that is easily noticed in a preview window.

Click the File tab, and click Print to view the Backstage view settings and options for printing. Fortunately, the print preview displays automatically, so you know how your document will print in its current form. You see one page at a time, but you can use the Previous Page and Next Page arrows to navigate to other pages. You can also use the zoom slider or Zoom to Page setting at the bottom of the Preview pane to magnify the page or preview several pages at once.

After evaluating the preview carefully, you can select from many print options in the Backstage view, as shown in Figure 1.28. At the top of the screen you can scroll to select the number of copies. To select a different printer, if you have access to more than one, click the Printer arrow. Word has other print settings; Table 1.4 lists a sampling of options available for each setting. Settings might vary from one computer to another because of the difference in printers.

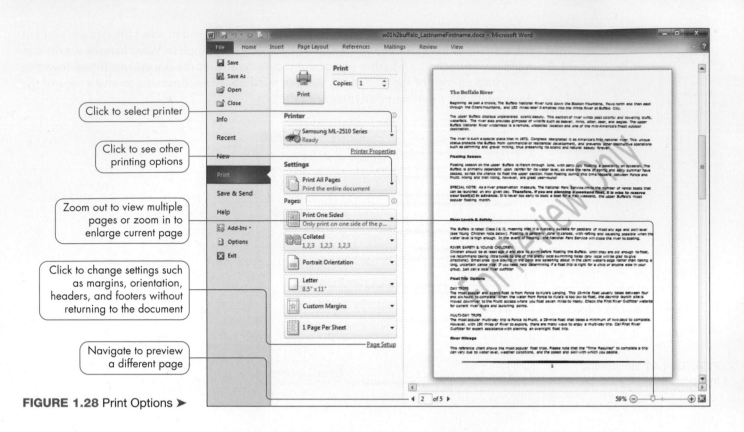

Click to select printer

Click to see other printing options

Zoom out to view multiple pages or zoom in to enlarge current page

Click to change settings such as margins, orientation, headers, and footers without returning to the document

Navigate to preview a different page

FIGURE 1.28 Print Options ➤

TABLE 1.4	Print Settings
Setting	**Options**
Print All Pages	Print Selection Print Current Page Print Custom Range Document Properties Only Print Odd Pages Only Print Even Pages
Print One Sided	Print Both Sides (only listed if your printer is capable of duplex printing) Manually Print on Both Sides
Collated	Collated (1,2,3; 1,2,3; 1,2,3) Uncollated (1,1,1; 2,2,2; 3,3,3)
Portrait Orientation	Portrait Orientation Landscape Orientation
Letter	Legal (8.5″ × 14″) A4 (8.27″ × 11.69″) More Paper Sizes
Normal Margins	Normal Narrow Custom Margins
1 Page Per Sheet	2 Pages Per Sheet 4 Pages Per Sheet 16 Pages Per Sheet Scale to Paper Size

Modifying Document Properties

Sometimes, you want to record detailed information about a document but do not want to display the information directly in the document window. You use the Document Panel to store descriptive information such as a title, subject, author, keywords, and summary.

Sometimes, you want to record detailed information about a document but do not want to display the information directly in the document window. For example, you might want to record some notes to yourself about a document, such as the document's author, purpose, or intended audience. You use the *Document Panel* to store descriptive information such as a title, subject, author, keywords, and summary.

The **Document Panel** enables you to enter descriptive information about a document.

When you click the File tab and display the Backstage view, you see a thumbnail version of the current page. Below that thumbnail you see information about the document such as the size, number of pages, word count, title, date modified, and author. You can modify some document information in this view, but you can also display the full Document Panel to view and edit other properties. To display the Document Panel, as shown in Figure 1.29, do the following:

1. Click the File tab.
2. Click the Properties arrow.
3. Click Show Document Panel.

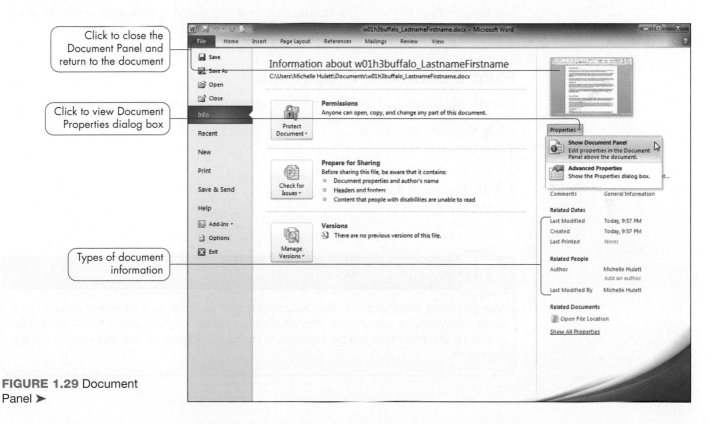

Click to close the Document Panel and return to the document

Click to view Document Properties dialog box

Types of document information

FIGURE 1.29 Document Panel ➤

When you save the document, Word saves this information with the document. You can update the descriptive information at any time by opening the Document Panel for the respective document.

Customize Document Properties

In addition to creating, modifying, and viewing a document summary, you may want to customize the document properties in the Document Panel. For example, you might want to add a *Date completed* property and specify an exact date for reference. This date would reflect the completion date, not the date the file was last saved—in case someone opens a file and saves it without making changes. You also might create a field to track company information such as warehouse location or product numbers.

When you click Document Properties and then click Advanced Properties, the Properties dialog box displays. Most commonly used properties display in the General tab. The Custom tab of the Properties dialog box enables you to add custom property categories and assign values to them. The Statistics tab provides useful information about the document, such as the creation date, the total editing time, and the word count.

Print Document Properties

You can print document properties to store hard copies for easy reference. To do this,

1. Click the File tab.
2. Click Print.
3. Click Print All Pages.
4. Click Document Properties.
5. Click Print.

3 Finalize a Document

As office manager for First River Outfitter, you are responsible for the security, management, and backup of all documents the business uses. Your formatting changes to the marketing document make it look more professional; now you must perform last-minute checks before sending it to Lawson for a final check. You also change document properties so it will be easy to locate and identify from your system storage device.

Skills covered: Modify Document Properties • Run the Document Inspector and a Compatibility Check • Save in a Compatible Format • Use Print Preview Features

STEP 1 MODIFY DOCUMENT PROPERTIES

You want to add data to your document so you can identify information such as the author, title, purpose, and date that it was completed—not just the last revision date, which is assigned by the computer. Since you don't want this information to show up in your document, you include it in the Document Properties. Refer to Figure 1.30 as you complete Step 1.

Click Custom tab to create special document properties

Click Summary tab to insert general document information

List of custom fields added to document

Click to attach Project field to document properties

Custom setting is not applied until added

FIGURE 1.30 Create Custom Document Properties ➤

a. Open *w01h2buffalo_LastnameFirstname* if you closed it at the end of Hands-On Exercise 2. Save the document with the new name **w01h3buffalo_LastnameFirstname**, changing *h2* to *h3*.

b. Click the **File tab**, click **Properties**, and then click **Show Document Panel**.

The Document Panel displays above your document. The document title and author name you entered on the cover page display in their respective boxes here. The subtitle you entered on the cover page displays in the Subject box.

> **TROUBLESHOOTING:** If the Document Panel disappears, repeat step b above to display it again.

c. Click one time in the **Comments box**, and then type **General Information**.

d. Click the **Document Properties arrow** in the top-left of the Document Properties panel, and then select **Advanced Properties** to display the w01h3buffalo_LastnameFirstname.docx Properties dialog box.

e. Create a custom property by completing the following steps:
- Click the **Custom tab**, and then select **Project** in the **Name list**.
- Type **Marketing Information** in the **Value box**, as shown in Figure 1.30, and then click **Add**.
- Click **OK** to close the dialog box.

You want to catalog the documents you create for First River Outfitter, and one way to do that is to assign a project scope using the custom properties that are stored with each document. Because you set up a custom field in the Document Properties, you can later perform searches and find all documents in that Project category.

f. Click **Close the Document Information Panel** in the top-right corner of Document Properties. Save the document.

> **TIP** Document Properties and Windows Explorer
>
> When you hover your mouse over a document in Windows Explorer, information stored as Document Properties will display.

STEP 2 ▶ RUN THE DOCUMENT INSPECTOR AND A COMPATIBILITY CHECK

You cannot remember if Lawson is using Office 2010 or an earlier version of Word. You decide to take precautions and run the Document Inspector and Compatibility check prior to saving the file in a compatible version. Refer to Figure 1.31 as you complete Step 2.

FIGURE 1.31 Document Inspector Results ➤

a. Click the **File tab**, click **Check for Issues** in the center part of the window, and then select **Check Compatibility**.

Any noncompatible items in the document will display in the Microsoft Office Word Compatibility Checker dialog box. For this document, 17 occurrences of a feature are not compatible with earlier versions of Word.

b. Click **OK** after you view the incompatible listings.

c. Click the **File tab**, and then click **Save As**. Save the document as **w01h3buffalo2_LastnameFirstname**, adding the number *2* at the end of *buffalo*.

Before you run the Document Inspector, you save the document with a different name in order to have a backup. You should always create a backup of the document because the Document Inspector might make changes that you cannot undo.

d. Click the **File tab**, click **Check for Issues**, and then select **Inspect Document**.

> **TROUBLESHOOTING:** An informational window might display with instructions to save the document before you run the Document Inspector. You should always create a backup of the document because the Document Inspector might make changes that you cannot undo.

e. Click to select any inspector check box that is not already checked. Click **Inspect**.

The Document Inspector results display and enable you to use Remove All buttons to eliminate the items found in each category.

f. Click the **Close button**; do not remove any items at this time.

g. Save the document as **w01h3buffalo_LastnameFirstname**, deleting the *2* at the end of *buffalo* and reverting back to the previous name. Click **OK** to replace the existing file with the same name.

STEP 3 ▶ SAVE IN A COMPATIBLE FORMAT

You know Lawson is anxious to review a copy of this document. You have learned that Lawson is running Word 2000 in his office, so you decide to convert the file so he will be able to open and view it easily. After you save it in compatible mode, you convert it again so Lawson can view your work using the current version. Refer to Figure 1.32 as you complete Step 3.

Extension .doc indicates file is saved as a Word 97-2003 document

Compatibility Mode displays in title bar

FIGURE 1.32 File Saved in Word 97-2003 Format ➤

a. Click the **File tab**, click **Save As**, click the **Save as type arrow**, and then select **Word 97-2003 Document**.

b. Confirm the Save as type box displays *Word 97-2003 Document (*.doc)*, and then click **Save**.

The Microsoft Word Compatibility Checker dialog box displays to confirm the compatibility issues you have already seen.

c. Click **Continue** to accept the alteration.

The title bar displays *(Compatibility Mode)* following the file name *w01h3buffalo_LastnameFirstname.doc*. If you set the option to display file extensions on your computer, the document extension .doc displays in the title bar, as shown in Figure 1.32.

d. Click the **File tab**, and then click **Convert**.

The Compatibility Mode designation is removed from the title bar. If a dialog box displays stating the document will be converted to the newest file format, click OK. You can check the option that prevents the dialog box from displaying each time this situation occurs.

e. Click **Save** on the Quick Access Toolbar. Click **Save** in the Save As dialog box, and then click **OK** if the authorization to replace the current file displays.

The document extension has been restored to .docx.

Since you believe you have made the final changes to the document for now, you preview it onscreen. When you preview it this way, you are not wasting paper on unnecessary printouts. Refer to Figure 1.33 as you complete Step 4.

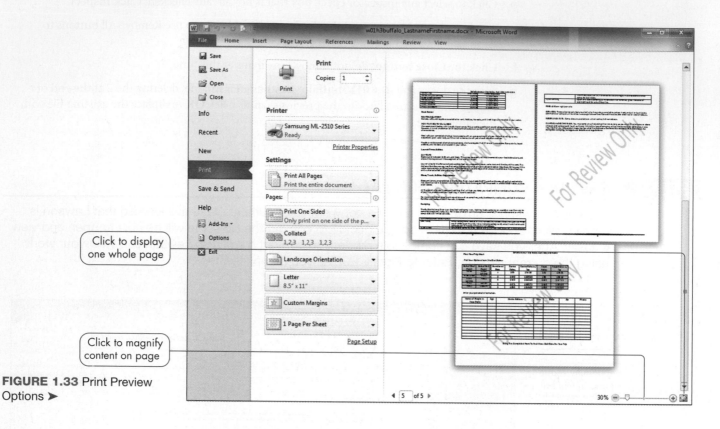

Click to display one whole page

Click to magnify content on page

FIGURE 1.33 Print Preview Options ➤

a. Click **Ctrl+Home**, if necessary, to move to the beginning of the document. Click the **File tab**, and then click **Print**.

The Print Preview window displays the first page.

b. Click **Zoom out** on the Zoom slider until the first four pages display.

The display can vary depending on your settings, but you should see four pages of the document.

c. Click the **Next Page** navigation arrow four times until the last page of the document displays.

You can see how the last page is formatted differently due to the section break inserted previously.

d. Click the **File tab** again to return to the application.

e. Close *w01h3buffalo_LastnameFirstname* and submit based on your instructor's directions.

CHAPTER OBJECTIVES REVIEW

After reading this chapter, you have accomplished the following objectives:

1. **Understand how word processors work.** Word provides a multitude of features that enable you to enhance documents easily while typing or with only a few clicks of the mouse. As you type, the word wrap feature automatically positions text for you using soft returns; however, you can insert a hard return to force text to the next page or to increase spacing between paragraphs. Keyboard shortcuts are useful for navigating a document, and toggle switches are often used to alternate between two states while you work. Page numbers are easy to add, and they serve as a convenient reference point to assist in reading through a document. Word also offers a feature to quickly insert a preformatted cover page in your document. The Cover Page feature includes a gallery with several designs.

2. **Customize Word.** Word is useful immediately. However, many options can be customized. The Word Options dialog box contains ten categories of options that you can change, including General, Proofing, and Add-Ins.

3. **Use features that improve readability.** When you create a document, you should consider how it will look when you print or display it. Margins determine the amount of white space from the text to the edge of the page, and you can set pages to display in portrait or landscape orientation. Headers and footers give a professional appearance to a document and are the best location to store page numbers. A section break is a marker that divides a document into sections, thereby enabling different formatting in each section. By using section breaks, you can change the margins within a multipage letter, where the first page (the letterhead) requires a larger top margin than the other pages in the letter. You can also change the page numbering within a document.

4. **Check spelling and grammar.** In conjunction with the spelling and grammar check feature, the contextual spelling feature attempts to locate a word that is spelled correctly but used incorrectly. For example, it looks for the correct usage of the words *there* and *their*. A contextual spelling error is underlined with a blue wavy line.

5. **Display a document in different views.** The View tab provides options that enable you to display a document in many different ways. Views include Print Layout, Full Screen Reading, Web Layout, Outline, and Draft. To change the view quickly, click a button on the status bar in the lower-right corner of the window. The Zoom dialog box includes options to change to whole page or multipage view.

6. **Prepare a document for distribution.** To prevent loss of data you should save and back up your work frequently. You should also be familiar with commands that enable you to save your documents in a format compatible with older versions of Word. Several backup options can be set, including an AutoRecover setting you can customize. You can also require Word to create a backup copy in conjunction with every save operation. Word 2010 includes a compatibility checker to look for features that are not supported by previous versions of Word, and it also offers a Document Inspector that checks for and removes different kinds of hidden or personal information from a document. The Backstage view print area contains many useful options including options to print only the current page, a specific range of pages, or a specific number of copies.

7. **Modify document properties.** You can create a document summary that provides descriptive information about a document, such as a title, subject, author, keywords, and comments. When you create a document summary, Word saves the document summary with the saved document. You also can print document properties.

KEY TERMS

AutoRecover *p.145*
Compatibility Checker *p.146*
Document Inspector *p.146*
Document Panel *p.149*
Draft view *p.136*
Footer *p.131*
Full Screen Reading view *p.136*

Hard page break *p.122*
Hard return *p.120*
Header *p.131*
Outline view *p.138*
Print Layout view *p.136*
Section break *p.133*
Show/Hide feature *p.121*

Soft page break *p.121*
Soft return *p.120*
Toggle *p.121*
Watermark *p.135*
Web Layout view *p.138*
Word processing software *p.118*
Word wrap *p.120*

1. How do you display the Backstage view Print options?

   (a) Click Print on the Quick Access Toolbar.
   (b) Click the File tab, and then click Print.
   (c) Click the Print Preview command.
   (d) Click the Home tab.

2. Which view removes white space, headers, and footers from the screen?

   (a) Full Screen Reading
   (b) Print Layout
   (c) Draft
   (d) Print Preview

3. You are the only person in your office to upgrade to Word 2010. Before you share documents with coworkers you should do which of the following?

   (a) Print out a backup copy.
   (b) Run the Compatibility Checker.
   (c) Burn all documents to CD.
   (d) Have no concerns that coworkers can open your documents.

4. A document has been entered into Word using the default margins. What can you say about the number of hard and soft returns if the margins are increased by 0.5″ on each side?

   (a) The number of hard returns is the same, but the number and/or position of the soft returns increases.
   (b) The number of hard returns is the same, but the number and/or position of the soft returns decreases.
   (c) The number and position of both hard and soft returns is unchanged.
   (d) The number and position of both hard and soft returns decreases.

5. Which of the following is detected by the contextual spelling checker?

   (a) Duplicate words
   (b) Use of the word *their* when you should use *there*
   (c) Irregular capitalization
   (d) Improper use of commas

6. If your cursor is near the bottom of a page and you want to display the next paragraph you type at the top of a new page, you should use which of the following?

   (a) Enter
   (b) Ctrl+Page Down
   (c) Ctrl+Enter
   (d) Page Layout, Breaks, Line Numbers

7. You need to insert a large table in the middle of a report that contains page numbers in the footer. The table is too wide to fit on a standard page. Which of the following is the best option to use in this case?

   (a) Put the table in a separate document, and do not worry about page numbering.
   (b) Insert a section break, and change the format of the page containing the table to landscape orientation.
   (c) Change the whole document to use landscape orientation.
   (d) Change margins to 0″ on the right and left.

8. What feature adds organization to your documents?

   (a) Print Preview
   (b) Orientation
   (c) Page Numbers
   (d) Find and Replace

9. If you cannot determine why a block of text starts at the top of the next page, which toggle switch should you invoke to view the formatting marks in use?

   (a) Word wrap
   (b) Show/Hide
   (c) Bold font
   (d) Caps Lock

10. What visual clue tells you that a document is not in Word 2010 format?

    (a) The status bar includes the text *(Compatibility Mode)*.
    (b) The file extension is .docx.
    (c) The title bar is a different color.
    (d) The title bar includes *(Compatibility Mode)* after the file name.

PRACTICE EXERCISES

1 Executive Assistant Training Tools

To prepare for a position as an executive assistant, you decide to learn more about the keyboard shortcuts that are available in Word. Keyboard shortcuts are especially useful if you are a good typist because your hands can remain on the keyboard, as opposed to continually moving to and from the mouse. Although people usually learn the shortcuts as they work in Word, it is helpful to view a list to determine which shortcuts you might be inclined to use on a more regular basis. It is nice to know the same shortcuts apply to multiple applications, such as Microsoft Office Excel, PowerPoint, and Access. This exercise follows the same set of skills as used in Hands-On Exercises 1, 2, and 3 in the chapter. Refer to Figure 1.34 as you complete this exercise.

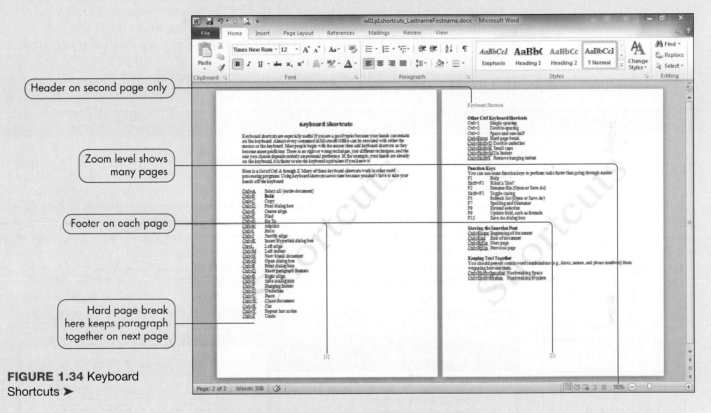

Header on second page only

Zoom level shows many pages

Footer on each page

Hard page break here keeps paragraph together on next page

FIGURE 1.34 Keyboard Shortcuts ➤

a. Open the *w01p1shortcuts* document. Click the **File tab**, click **Convert**, and then click **OK** in the dialog box that might display. Save the document as **w01p1shortcuts_LastnameFirstname**, paying special attention that it is saved in Word format (*.docx).

b. Place your cursor at the end of the first paragraph. Press **Enter** two times, and then type **Here is a list of Ctrl A through Z. Many of these keyboard shortcuts work in other word processing programs. Using keyboard shortcuts saves time because you don't have to take your hands off the keyboard.**

c. Click the **Page Layout tab**, click **Margins** in the Page Setup group, and then select **Normal**. Click **Orientation**, and then select **Portrait**.

d. Click the **Home tab**, and then click **Show/Hide** (¶) in the Paragraph group, if necessary, to display formatting marks.

e. Move the insertion point to the left side of the hard return mark at the end of the line containing *Ctrl+B*. Press **Ctrl+B**, and then type the word **Bold**. Using keyboard shortcuts prior to typing applies the format to all typed text that follows. Alternately, you can type and then select the text prior to applying the format. The format used on text is stored in the hard return mark that follows the text.

f. Move the insertion point to the left side of the hard return mark at the end of the line containing *Ctrl+I*. Press **Ctrl+I**, and then type the word **Italic**.

g. Scroll to the bottom of the first page, and then place the insertion point on the left side of the title *Other Ctrl Keyboard Shortcuts*. Press **Ctrl+Enter** to insert a hard page break and keep the group together on one page.

h. Click the **Insert tab**, click **Page Number** in the Header & Footer group, point to **Bottom of Page**, and then click **Brackets 1** from the gallery.

i. Click **Header** in the Header & Footer group, and then select **Edit Header**. Click **Different First Page** in the Options group to insert a check mark. Place the insertion point in the header area of the second page, if necessary, and then type **Keyboard Shortcuts**.

j. Move the insertion point to the first page footer. Click **Page Number** in the Header & Footer group, point to **Bottom of Page**, and then click **Brackets 1** from the gallery. Click **Close Header and Footer**. After selecting the option for Different First Page in the previous step, the headers and footers on the first page were removed. This enables you to insert information on the first page, which won't display in the header or footer of the remaining pages.

k. Click the **Page Layout tab**, click **Watermark**, and then click **Custom Watermark**. Click **Text watermark**, select the text *ASAP*, and then type **Shortcuts**. Click **OK**.

l. Click **Zoom level** in the status bar, click the **Many pages icon**, and then drag to select **1 × 2 Pages**. Click **OK** to close the Zoom dialog box. Click **Show/Hide** (¶) in the Paragraph group on the Home tab to toggle off the formatting marks. Compare your document to Figure 1.34.

m. Click the **File tab**, click **Print**, click the **1 Page per sheet arrow**, and then click **2 Pages Per Sheet**. If instructed, click **Print** to print the document.

n. Save and close the file, and submit based on your instructor's directions.

2 Aztec Computers

As the owner of Aztec Computers, you are frequently asked to provide information about computer viruses and backup procedures. You are quick to tell anyone who asks about data loss that it is not a question of if it will happen, but when—hard drives die, removable disks are lost, and viruses may infect systems. You advise customers and friends alike that they can prepare for the inevitable by creating an adequate backup before the problem occurs. Because people appreciate a document to refer to about this information, you have started one that contains information that should be taken seriously. After a few finishing touches, you will feel comfortable about passing it out to people who have questions about this topic. This exercise follows the same set of skills as used in Hands-On Exercises 1, 2, and 3 in the chapter. Refer to Figure 1.35 as you complete this exercise.

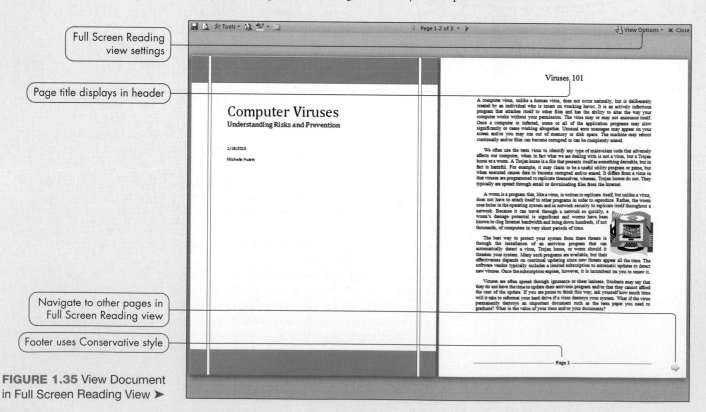

Full Screen Reading view settings

Page title displays in header

Navigate to other pages in Full Screen Reading view

Footer uses Conservative style

FIGURE 1.35 View Document in Full Screen Reading View ➤

a. Open the *w01p2virus document* and save it as **w01p2virus_LastnameFirstname**.

b. Create a cover page by completing the following steps:
   - Click the **Insert tab**, click **Cover Page** in the Pages group, and then click **Pinstripes**.
   - Click **Type the document subtitle**, and then type the text **Understanding Risks and Prevention**.
   - Click **Pick the Date**, click the arrow, and then select **Today**.
   - Right-click **Type the company name**, and then select **Cut**.
   - Click **Type the author name**, and then type your name.

c. Scroll to the bottom of the first page of the report, and then place the insertion point on the left side of the title *The Essence of Backup*. Click the **Page Layout tab**, click **Breaks**, and then click **Next Page**.

d. Set up headers and footers by completing the following steps:
   - Click the **Insert tab**, click **Footer**, and then click **Conservative**. A page number footer is added to *First Page Footer -Section 2-*.
   - Select the page number footer in *First Page Footer -Section 2-*, and then press **Ctrl+C** to copy the page number footer to the clipboard.
   - Click **Previous** in the Navigation group to place the insertion point in the Section 1 footer, and then press **Ctrl+V** to paste the page number and graphic into this footer. Since this document has two sections, you must duplicate the steps when you want to display the same footer (or header) in both.
   - Place the insertion point in *First Page Header -Section 2-*. Click **Page Number** in the Header & Footer group, click **Format Page Numbers**, and then click **Continue from Previous Section**. Click **OK**.
   - Click **Previous** in the Navigation group to place the insertion point in *Header -Section 1-*. Type **Viruses 101** and press **Ctrl+E** to center it. Use the Mini toolbar to increase the font to **20 pt**.
   - Place the insertion point in *First Page Header -Section 2-*. Click **Link to Previous** in the Navigation group to turn the setting off and enable you to create a unique header for this section instead of displaying the header from the previous section.
   - Type **The Essence of Backup**, press **Ctrl+E** to center it, and then use the Mini toolbar to increase the font to **20 pt**.
   - Click **Close Header and Footer**.

e. Delete the lines that contain the text *Viruses 101* and *The Essence of Backup* from the two pages of the report because these titles now display in the header.

f. Click the **Review tab**, and click **Spelling & Grammar**. Click **Change** to correct the contextual spelling error reported on backup, and then click **OK** when complete.

g. Complete the following steps to display the document in different views:
   - Click **Draft** in the status bar, and then scroll to view the location of the section break.
   - Click **Full Screen Reading** on the status bar.
   - Click **View Options** in the top-right corner, and then click **Show Two Pages**, if necessary.
   - Click **View Options** again, and then click **Show Printed Page**.
   - Click the arrows in the bottom corners to view each page, and then return to the first page. Compare your document to Figure 1.35.
   - Click the **Close button** to return to Print Layout view.

h. Click the **File tab**, click **Properties**, and then select **Show Document Panel**. Click in the **Comments box**, and then type **General information for understanding computer viruses**. Click **Close the Document Information Panel**.

i. Save the document. Click the **File tab**, click **Check for Issues**, and then click **Check Compatibility**. Click **OK** to close the Microsoft Word Compatibility Checker dialog box after you review the results.

j. Click the **File tab**, click **Check for Issues**, select **Inspect Document**, and then click **Inspect**. Click **Close** after you review the results.

k. Save and close the file, and submit based on your instructor's directions.

1 Heart Disease Prevention

Millions of people suffer from heart disease and other cardiac-related illnesses. Of those people, several million will suffer a heart attack this year. Your mother volunteers for the American Heart Association and has brought you a document that explains what causes a heart attack, the signs of an attack, and what you can do to reduce your risk of having one. The information in the document is very valuable, but she needs you to put the finishing touches on this document before she circulates it in the community.

a. Open the *w01m1heart document* and save it as **w01m1heart_LastnameFirstname**.

b. Convert *w01m1heart_LastnameFirstname* so it does not save in Compatibility Mode.

c. Create a cover page for the report. Use Stacks in the cover page gallery. Add text where necessary to display the report title **Heart Attacks:** and the subtitle **What You Should Know**. Insert your name as author, replacing *Exploring Series*.

d. Change the document margins to **0.75″** on all sides.

e. Create a section break between the cover page and the first page of the report.

DISCOVER f. Create a footer in Section 2 by typing the text **Page**, leave a space, and then insert a page number field. The page number should only display at the bottom of the pages in Section 2. The first page of Section 2, not the cover page, should display page number 1.

g. Create a header that displays the report title and subtitle. It should not display on the cover or first page of the report. Confirm that the headers and footers in the second section are not linked to the first section.

h. Insert hard page breaks where necessary to prevent a paragraph or list from breaking across pages. View the document in Full Screen Reading view to confirm it is formatted as instructed and ready for printing.

i. Check spelling in the document. Change the document properties to include a custom field for Date completed.

j. Check Word Options and verify that AutoRecover backups occur every five minutes or less.

k. Print the document properties if approved by your instructor.

l. Save and close the file, and submit based on your instructor's directions.

2 Career Considerations

Your Introduction to College Life teacher has requested you consider the career path you might like to follow and write a paper about it. In this paper, you decide to discuss the field of Optometry, and you even describe your experience shadowing a doctor of Optometry one day last summer. The first draft is written, but you make a few more revisions before submitting the paper to your instructor for a preliminary check on your progress.

a. Open *w01m2career* and save it as **w01m2career_LastnameFirstname**.

b. Set margins to **1″** on the top, bottom, left, and right.

c. Turn on **Show/Hide** (¶), if necessary, to view formatting marks in the document. Correct the absence of a tab that is needed to indent the first paragraph.

d. Display the document in Draft view. Use keyboard shortcuts to move to the end of the document, and then remove unnecessary page returns and breaks below the last paragraph. Return to Print Layout view when complete.

e. Insert page numbers, at the bottom of the pages, using the **Bold Numbers 3 style**. Create a header that starts on page 2 and displays the title of the paper on the left and your name on the right.

f. Insert a watermark that displays **Draft** when you print the document.

g. Use the Spelling & Grammar tool to check the document.

h. Insert Page Breaks where necessary to display the document in a manner that prevents paragraphs from breaking across a page.

i. Run the Compatibility Checker and Document Inspector, and then save the document in Word 97-2003 format.

j. Save and close the file, and submit based on your instructor's directions.

Ethical conflicts occur all the time and result when one person or group benefits at the expense of another. Your Philosophy 101 instructor assigned a class project whereby students must consider the question of ethics and society. The result of your research includes a collection of questions every person should ask him- or herself. Your paper is nearly complete but needs a few modifications before you submit it.

Spelling, Margins, and Watermarks

You notice Word displays spelling and grammar errors with the colored lines, so you must correct those as soon as possible. Additionally, you want to adjust the margins and then insert a watermark that displays when you print so that you will remember that this is not the final version.

a. Open the file *w01c1ethics* and save it as **w01c1ethics_LastnameFirstname**.

b. Display the Word Options dialog box, and then engage the Contextual Spelling feature if it is not already in use.

c. Run the Spelling & Grammar tool to correct all misspelled words and contextual errors.

d. Change the margins to use a setting of **0.75"** on all sides.

e. Insert a watermark that displays **Version 1** when printed.

Cover Page, Headers, and Footers

You want to add a cover page that will attractively introduce your paper. Then you will set up page numbering, but it must not display on the cover page. Because you are going to customize headers and footers very precisely, you must use several of the custom settings available for Headers and Footers.

a. Insert a Cover Page that uses the Puzzle style. Select **Today** in the two Date fields. Type the title of the paper in the appropriate field, and then add your name as author, but remove all other fields from the cover page.

b. Insert a page number at the bottom of the first page of the report (the page that follows the cover page) using **Accent Bar 2 style**. There should be no header on this page.

c. Display the page number in the header of the remaining page of the report using the **Accent Bar 2 style**. (Hint: Use the Different Odd & Even Pages Header & Footer option.) In the footer of this page, display the report title on the left and your name on the right.

Set Properties and Finalize Document

After improving the readability of the document, you remember that you have not yet saved it. Your professor still uses an older version of Word, so you save the document in a compatible format that will display easily. You also remove the watermark just before saving the final copy.

a. Save the document.

b. Run the Compatibility Checker and Document Inspector, but do not take any suggested actions at this time.

c. Add **Ethics**, **Responsibility**, and **Morals** to the Keywords: field in the document properties.

d. Remove the watermark.

e. Save the document again, in Word 97-2003 format, as **w01c1ethics_LastnameFirstname**.

f. Use the Print Preview and Print feature to view the document before printing. If allowed by your instructor, print one copy of the document using the 2 Pages per sheet setting.

BEYOND THE CLASSROOM

More Career Choices GENERAL CASE	Have you taken time to think about the career you wish to pursue when you complete your education? In Mid-Level Exercise 2, you modified a documentary written by a student with interest in optometry. Now it is your turn to develop a similar paper about a different career field. After you write your own documentary using Word, use the skills from this chapter to format it with a professional look, and then name the document **w01b1job_LastnameFirstname**. Save and close the file, and submit based on your instructor's directions.

Animal Concerns RESEARCH CASE	As the population of family pets continues to grow, it is imperative that we learn how to be responsible pet owners. Very few people take the time to perform thorough research on the fundamental care of and responsibility for animal populations. Open the *w01b2animal* document, and then save it as **w01b2animal_LastnameFirstname**. Search the Internet for information that will contribute to this report on animal care and concerns. Compare information from at least three sources. Give consideration to information that is copyrighted; any information you quote should be cited in the document. As you enter the information and sources into the document, you will be reminded of concepts learned in this chapter, such as word wrap and soft returns. Use your knowledge of other formatting techniques, such as hard returns, page numbers, and margin settings, to create an attractive document. Create a cover page for the document, perform a spelling check, and then view the print preview before submitting this assignment to your instructor. Create headers and/or footers to improve readability. Save and close the file, and submit based on your instructor's directions.

TMG Newsletter DISASTER RECOVERY	Open *w01b3tmgnews*, and then save it as **w01b3tmgnews_LastnameFirstname**. The document was started by an office assistant, but he quickly gave up on it after he moved paragraphs around until it became unreadable. The document contains significant errors, which cause the newsletter to display in a very disjointed way. Use your knowledge of Page Layout options and other Word features to revise this newsletter in time for the monthly mailing. Save and close the file, and submit based on your instructor's directions.

2 DOCUMENT PRESENTATION

Editing and Formatting

CASE STUDY | Simserv-Pitka Enterprises

Watch the **Set-up Video** for this Case Study!

Simserv Enterprises, a consumer products manufacturing company, has recently acquired a competitor in an effort to become a stronger company poised to meet the demands of the market. Each year, Simserv generates a corporate annual summary and distributes it to all employees and stockholders. You are the executive assistant to the president of Simserv, and your responsibilities include preparing and distributing the corporate annual summary. This year, the report emphasizes the importance of acquiring Pitka Industries to form Simserv-Pitka Enterprises.

The annual report always provides a synopsis of recent changes to upper management, and this year, it will introduce a new Chairman of the Board and Chief Executive Officer, as well as a new Chief Financial Officer. Information about these newly appointed executives and other financial data has been gathered, but the report needs to be formatted to display the information clearly and professionally before it can be distributed to employees and stockholders.

OBJECTIVES AFTER READING THIS CHAPTER, YOU WILL BE ABLE TO:

1. Apply font attributes through the Font dialog box *p.164*

2. Control word wrap *p.168*

3. Set off paragraphs with tabs, borders, lists, and columns *p.172*

4. Apply paragraph formats *p.178*

5. Understand styles *p.187*

6. Create and modify styles *p.187*

7. Format a graphical object *p.197*

8. Insert symbols into a document *p.201*

Text Formatting Features

Typography is the appearance of printed matter.

The arrangement and appearance of printed matter is called *typography*. You may also define it as the process of selecting typefaces, type styles, and type sizes. The importance of these decisions is obvious, for the ultimate success of any document depends greatly on its appearance. Typeface should reinforce the message without calling attention to itself and should be consistent with the information you want to convey. For example, a paper prepared for a professional purpose, such as a résumé, should have a standard typeface instead of one that looks funny or cute. Additionally, you want to minimize the variety of typefaces in a document to maintain a professional look.

> The ultimate success of any document depends greatly on its appearance. Typeface should reinforce the message without calling attention to itself and should be consistent with the information you want to convey.

A **typeface** or **font** is a complete set of characters.

A **serif typeface** contains a thin line at the top and bottom of characters.

A **sans serif typeface** does not contain thin lines on characters.

A *typeface* or *font* is a complete set of characters—upper- and lowercase letters, numbers, punctuation marks, and special symbols. A definitive characteristic of any typeface is the presence or absence of thin lines that end the main strokes of each letter. A *serif typeface* contains a thin line or extension at the top and bottom of the primary strokes on characters. A *sans serif typeface* (*sans* from the French meaning *without*) does not contain the thin lines on characters. Times New Roman is an example of a serif typeface. Arial is a sans serif typeface.

Serifs help the eye to connect one letter with the next and generally are used with large amounts of text. The paragraphs in this book, for example, are set in a serif typeface. A sans serif typeface is more effective with smaller amounts of text such as titles, headlines, corporate logos, and Web pages. For example, the blue heading Text Formatting Features and the quote by the first paragraph on this page are set in a sans serif font.

A **monospaced typeface** uses the same amount of horizontal space for every character.

A **proportional typeface** allocates horizontal space to each character.

Type style is the characteristic applied to a font, such as bold.

A second characteristic of a typeface is whether it is monospaced or proportional. A *monospaced typeface* (such as `Courier New`) uses the same amount of horizontal space for every character regardless of its width. A *proportional typeface* (such as Times New Roman or Arial) allocates space according to the width of the character. For example, the lowercase *m* is wider than the lowercase *i*. Monospaced fonts are used in tables and financial projections where text must be precisely lined up, one character underneath the other. Proportional typefaces create a more professional appearance and are appropriate for most documents, such as research papers, status reports, and letters. You can set any typeface in different *type styles* such as regular, **bold**, *italic*, or ***bold italic***.

In this section, you will apply font attributes through the Font dialog box, change case, and highlight text so that it stands out. You will also control word wrap by inserting nonbreaking hyphens and nonbreaking spaces between words.

Applying Font Attributes Through the Font Dialog Box

In the Office Fundamentals chapter, you learn how to use the Font group on the Home tab to apply font attributes. In addition to applying commands from the Font group, you can display the Font dialog box when you click the Font Dialog Box Launcher. Making selections in the Font dialog box before entering text sets the format of the text as you type (see Figure 2.1).

Selected font size

Selected font

Selected font style

Click arrow to select font color

Additional special effects

Preview box

FIGURE 2.1 Font Dialog Box ➤

Select Font Options

In addition to changing the font, font style, and size, you can apply other font attributes to text. Although the Font group on the Home tab contains special effects commands such as strikethrough, subscript, and superscript, the Effects section in the Font tab in the Font dialog box contains other options for applying color and effects, such as small caps and double strikethrough. From this dialog box you can change the underline options and indicate if spaces are to be underlined or just words. You can even change the color of the text and the color of the underline.

New to Office 2010 is the Text Effects feature in the Font group. When you click Text Effects you can choose from a variety of colors and styles to immediately apply to text. The feature enables you to customize the effects by selecting colors, line widths, and amount of transparency. In addition to the Home tab, you can access Text Effects from the Font dialog box. When you use that path, another dialog box opens, showing custom options for each effect. Table 2.1 gives a general description of these special effects.

TABLE 2.1	Font Effects		
Effect	**Description and Options**	**Sample of Options to Change**	**Sample of Effect**
Text Fill	Select a color to apply to the font.	No fill Solid fill Gradient fill	Sample
Text Outline	Select a color and line type to outline the font.	No line Solid line Gradient line	Sample
Outline Style	Select line width, type (solid, dashed), and cap on the font.	Width Dash type Arrow settings	Sample
Shadow	Select amount of shadow to apply to the font.	Color Transparency Angle	Sample
Reflection	Select a reflection style to apply to the font.	Presets Size Blur	Sample
Glow and Soft Edges	Select a glow or soft edge that displays around the font.	Color Size Presets	Sample
3-D Format	Select features that present the font in 3-D form.	Bevel Depth Surface	Sample

Hidden text is document text that does not appear onscreen, unless you click Show/Hide (¶) in the Paragraph group on the Home tab. You can use this special effect format to hide confidential information before printing documents for other people. For example, an employer can hide employees' Social Security numbers before printing a company roster. Note, however, that if you e-mail a document that contains hidden text, the recipient will be able to view it.

Hidden text does not appear onscreen.

Set Character Spacing

Character spacing refers to the amount of horizontal space between characters. Although most character spacing is acceptable, some character combinations appear too far apart or too close together in large-sized text when printed. If so, you might want to adjust for this spacing discrepancy. The Advanced tab in the Font dialog box contains options in which you manually control the spacing between characters. The Advanced tab shown in Figure 2.2 displays four options for adjusting character spacing: Scale, Spacing, Position, and Kerning.

Character spacing is the horizontal space between characters.

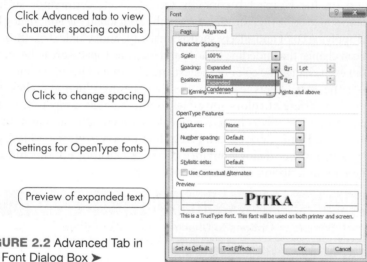

Click Advanced tab to view character spacing controls

Click to change spacing

Settings for OpenType fonts

Preview of expanded text

FIGURE 2.2 Advanced Tab in the Font Dialog Box ➤

Scale or **scaling** adjusts height and width by a percentage of the original size. For text, adjustments to scale will increase or decrease the text horizontally as a percentage of its size; it does not change the vertical height of text. You may use the scale feature on justified text, which does not produce the best-looking results—adjust the scale by a low percentage (90%–95%) to improve text flow without a noticeable difference to the reader. You may select the Expanded option to stretch a word or sentence so it fills more space; for example, use it on a title you want to span across the top of a page. The Condensed option is useful to squeeze text closer together, such as when you want to prevent one word from wrapping to another line.

Scale or **scaling** is the adjustment of height or width by a percentage of the image's original size.

Position raises or lowers text from the baseline without creating superscript or subscript size. Use this feature when you want text to stand out from other text on the same line, or use it to create a fun title by raising and/or lowering every few letters. **Kerning** automatically adjusts spacing between characters to achieve a more evenly spaced appearance. Kerning primarily enables letters to fit closer together, especially when a capital letter can use space unoccupied by a lowercase letter beside it. For example, you can kern the letters *Va* so the top of the *V* extends into the empty space above the *a* instead of leaving an awkward gap between them.

Position raises or lowers text from the baseline.

Kerning enables more even spacing between characters.

Word 2010 introduces support for OpenType fonts. **OpenType** is an advanced form of font that is designed for all platforms, including Windows and Macintosh. OpenType font technology has advantages over the commonly used TrueType Font because it can hold more

OpenType is a form of font designed for use on all platforms.

characters in a set and is more compact, enabling smaller file sizes. If you install OpenType fonts on your PC, you can use the OpenType font settings in the Advanced tab of the Font dialog box.

Change Text Case (Capitalization)

Use **Change Case** to change capitalization of text.

To change the capitalization of text in a document quickly, use *Change Case* in the Font group on the Home tab. When you click Change Case, the following list of options display:

- **Sentence case** (capitalizes only the first word of the sentence or phrase).
- **lowercase** (changes the text to all lowercase).
- **UPPERCASE** (changes the text to all capital letters).
- **Capitalize Each Word** (capitalizes the first letter of each word; effective for formatting titles, but remember to lowercase first letters of short prepositions, such as *of*).
- **tOGGLE cASE** (changes lowercase to uppercase and uppercase to lowercase).

This feature is useful when generating a list and you want to use the same case formatting for each item. If you do not select text first, the casing format will take effect on the text where the insertion point is located. You can toggle among uppercase, lowercase, and sentence case formats by pressing Shift+F3.

Apply Text Highlighting

Use the **Highlighter** to mark text that you want to locate easily.

People often use a highlighting marker to highlight important parts of textbooks, magazine articles, and other documents. In Word, you use the *Highlighter* to mark text that you want to stand out or locate easily. Highlighted text draws the reader's attention to important information within the documents you create, as illustrated in Figure 2.3. The Text Highlight Color command is located in the Font group on the Home tab and on the Mini toolbar. You can click Text Highlight Color before or after selecting text. When you click Text Highlight Color before selecting text, the mouse pointer resembles a pen that you can click and drag across text to highlight it. The feature stays on so you can highlight additional text. When you finish highlighting text, click Text Highlight Color again, or press Esc to turn it off. If you select text first, click Text Highlight Color to apply the color. To remove highlights, select the highlighted text, click the Text Highlight Color arrow, and choose No Color.

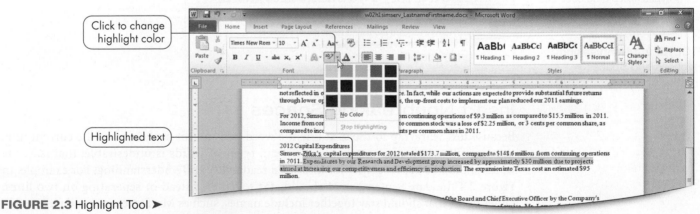

FIGURE 2.3 Highlight Tool ➤

If you use a color printer, you see the highlight colors on your printout. If you use a monochrome printer, the highlight appears in shades of gray. Use Print Preview prior to printing to be sure that you can easily read the text with the gray highlight. If not, select a lighter highlight color, and preview your document again. You can create a unique highlighting effect by choosing a dark highlight color, such as Dark Blue, and applying a light font color, such as White.

Controlling Word Wrap

In Word, text wraps to the next line when the current line of text is full. Most of the time, the way words wrap is acceptable. Occasionally, however, text may wrap in an undesirable location. To improve the readability of text, you need to proofread word-wrapping locations and insert special characters. Two general areas of concern are hyphenated words and spacing within proper nouns.

Insert Nonbreaking Hyphens

A **nonbreaking hyphen** prevents a word from becoming separated at the hyphen.

If a hyphenated word falls at the end of a line, the first word and the hyphen may appear on the first line, and the second word may wrap to the next line. However, certain hyphenated text, such as phone numbers, should stay together to improve the readability of the text. To keep hyphenated words together, replace the regular hyphen with a nonbreaking hyphen. A **nonbreaking hyphen** keeps text on both sides of the hyphen together, thus preventing the hyphenated word from becoming separated at the hyphen, as shown in Figure 2.4. To insert a nonbreaking hyphen, press Ctrl+Shift+Hyphen. When you click Show/Hide in the Paragraph group on the Home tab to display formatting symbols, a regular hyphen looks like a hyphen, and a nonbreaking hyphen appears as a wider hyphen. However, the nonbreaking hyphen looks like a regular hyphen when printed.

FIGURE 2.4 Nonbreaking Hyphens and Spaces ➤

Insert Nonbreaking Spaces

A **nonbreaking space** keeps two or more words together on a line.

Because text will wrap to the next line if a word does not fit at the end of the current line, occasionally word wrapping between certain types of words is undesirable; that is, some words should be kept together for improved readability and understanding. For example, in Figure 2.4 the date September 21 should stay together instead of separating on two lines. Other items that should stay together include names, such as Ms. Stevenson, and page references, such as page 15. To prevent words from separating due to the word wrap feature, you can insert a **nonbreaking space**—a special character that keeps two or more words together. To insert a nonbreaking space, press Ctrl+Shift+Spacebar between the two words that you want to keep together. If a space already exists, the result of pressing the Spacebar, you should delete it before you insert the nonbreaking space.

HANDS-ON EXERCISES

1 Text Formatting Features

As the executive assistant to the president at Simserv-Pitka Enterprises, you are responsible for preparing and distributing the Annual Summary. A report of this importance should be easy to read, attractive, and professional. You have the basic information to include in the report, and your first step is to change the formatting of some text so that it displays nicely in print, to include highlighting where appropriate, and to look for places where you might need to insert nonbreaking hyphens or spaces.

Skills covered: Change Text Appearance • Insert Nonbreaking Spaces and Nonbreaking Hyphens • Highlight Text

---

STEP 1 CHANGE TEXT APPEARANCE

As you begin to prepare the report for the Board and stockholders, you know the first thing that requires your attention is changing the font of the whole document so that it is easier to read. Additionally, you will change the font properties of the heading and subheading so they stand out from the rest of the text. Refer to Figure 2.5 as you complete Step 1.

Font changed to Times New Roman

Font Dialog Box Launcher

Heading using bold, small caps, shadow, and expanded font properties

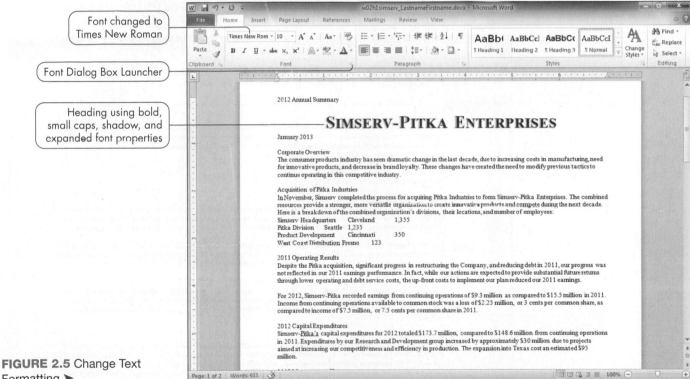

FIGURE 2.5 Change Text Formatting ➤

a. Open *w02h1simserv* and save it as **w02h1simserv_LastnameFirstname**.

> **TROUBLESHOOTING:** If you make any major mistakes in this exercise, you can close the file, open *w02h1simserv* again, and then start this exercise over.

b. Click **Ctrl+A** to select all of the text in the document. Click the **Font arrow** in the Font group on the Home tab, and then select **Times New Roman**.

You use a serif font on the whole document because it is easier to read in print.

 FYI

c. Select the second line of the document, *Simserv-Pitka Enterprises*. Click **Center** on the Mini toolbar.

d. Click the **Font Dialog Box Launcher** in the Font group.

The Font dialog box displays with the Font tab options.

e. Click the **Font tab**, if necessary, and then click **Bold** in the Font style box. Select **26** in the Size box. Click to select the **Small caps Effect**.

f. Click **Text Effects**. Click **Shadow**, click **Presets**, and then click **Offset Left** (third row, third column). Click the **Close button** to return to the Font dialog box.

g. Click the **Advanced tab**, and then click the **Spacing arrow**. Select **Expanded**, and then notice how the text changes in the preview box. Click **OK**.

Word expands the spacing between letters in the subtitle as shown in Figure 2.5. You will apply this formatting to the third line in a later exercise.

h. Save the document.

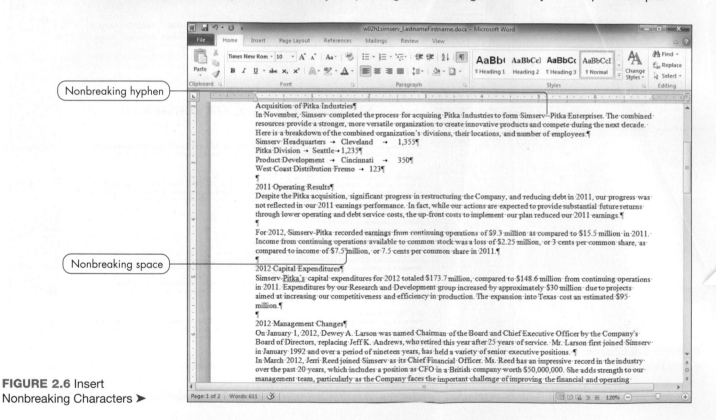

FIGURE 2.6 Insert Nonbreaking Characters ➤

STEP 2 ▶ INSERT NONBREAKING SPACES AND NONBREAKING HYPHENS

Since the company's new name, Simserv-Pitka, is hyphenated, you want to keep the name together and not split it if it appears at the end of a text line. Therefore, you will replace existing hyphens in Simserv-Pitka, as well as in other areas of the document, with nonbreaking hyphens. You will also replace existing spaces with nonbreaking spaces to make sure the information displays properly when the report is completed and ready for printing. Refer to Figure 2.6 as you complete Step 2.

a. Select the hyphen between the text *Simserv-Pitka* in the first sentence of the *Acquisition of Pitka Industries* paragraph. Press **Delete**, and then press **Ctrl+Shift+Hyphen** to insert a nonbreaking hyphen.

TROUBLESHOOTING: If text continues word wrapping between two words after you insert a nonbreaking space or nonbreaking hyphen, click Show/Hide (¶) in the Paragraph group on the Home tab to display symbols, and then identify and delete regular spaces or hyphens that still exist between words.

b. Place the insertion point between *$7.5* and *million* in the last sentence of the second paragraph under the *2011 Operating Results* heading.

Before inserting a nonbreaking space, you must position the insertion point between the two words you want to keep together.

c. Delete the existing space, and then press **Ctrl+Shift+Spacebar** to insert a nonbreaking space.

d. Click **Show/Hide** (¶) in the Paragraph group, and then notice the different format for the nonbreaking hyphen and space, as seen in Figure 2.6.

If text is enlarged, the nonbreaking space keeps *$7.5 million* together, preventing word wrapping between the two words.

e. Click **Show/Hide** (¶) again to remove the formatting marks. Save the document.

TIP Another Way to Insert Nonbreaking Spaces and Hyphens

An alternative to using keyboard shortcuts to insert nonbreaking spaces and hyphens is to use the Symbols gallery on the Insert tab. From the Insert tab, click the Symbol arrow and click More Symbols to display the Symbol dialog box. Click the Special Characters tab, select the Nonbreaking Hyphen or the Nonbreaking Space character option, and click Insert to insert a nonbreaking hyphen or a nonbreaking space, respectively. Close the Symbol dialog box after inserting the nonbreaking hyphen or nonbreaking space.

STEP 3 **HIGHLIGHT TEXT**

Some information in a document is so important that you want to be sure to draw attention to it. The Highlighting tool is useful for this purpose and you use it in the next step to make sure the reader knows about the great investment in Research and Development at Simserv-Pitka Enterprises. Refer to Figure 2.7 as you complete Step 3.

FIGURE 2.7 Highlight Important Information ➤

a. Select the second sentence in the *2012 Capital Expenditures* paragraph that starts with *Expenditures by our Research and Development group.*

b. Click **Text Highlight Color** in the Font group.

Word highlighted the selected sentence in the default highlight color, yellow, as seen in Figure 2.7.

TROUBLESHOOTING: If Word applies a color other than yellow to the selected text, that means another highlight color was selected after starting Word. If this happens, select the text again, click the Text Highlight Color arrow, and select Yellow.

c. Save the document and keep it onscreen if you plan to continue with the next Hands-On Exercise. If not, close the document and exit Word.

Paragraph Formatting Features

A change in typography is only one way to alter the appearance of a document. You also can change the alignment, indentation, tab stops, or line spacing for any paragraph(s) within the document. You can control the pagination and prevent the occurrence of awkward page breaks by specifying that an entire paragraph must appear on the same page, or that a heading should appear on the same page as the next paragraph. You can include borders or shading for added emphasis around selected paragraphs.

> A change in typography is only one way to alter the appearance of a document. You also can change the alignment, indentation, tab stops, or line spacing for any paragraph(s) within the document.

Word implements all of these paragraph formats for all selected paragraphs. If no paragraphs are selected, Word applies the formats to the current paragraph (the paragraph containing the insertion point), regardless of the position of the insertion point within the paragraph when you apply the paragraph formats.

In this section, you will set tabs, apply borders, create lists, and format text into columns to help offset text for better readability. You will also change text alignment, indent paragraphs, set line and paragraph spacing, and control pagination breaks.

Setting Off Paragraphs with Tabs, Borders, Lists, and Columns

Many people agree that their eyes tire and minds wander when they read page after page of plain black text on white paper. To break up long blocks of text or draw attention to an area of a page, you can format text with tabs, borders, lists, or columns. These formatting features enable you to modify positioning, frame a section, itemize for easy reading, order steps in a sequence, or create pillars of text for visual appeal and easy reading. For example, look through the pages of this book and notice the use of bulleted lists, tables for reference points, and borders around TIP boxes to draw your attention and enhance the pages.

Set Tabs

> A **tab** is a marker for aligning text in a document.

One way to enhance the presentation of text on a page visually is to use tabs. *Tabs* are markers that specify the position for aligning text and add organization to a document. They often are used to create columns of text within a document. When you start a new document, the default tab stops are set every one-half inch across the page and are left aligned. Every time you press Tab, the insertion point moves over .5″. You typically press Tab to indent the first line of paragraphs in double-spaced reports or the first line of paragraphs in a modified block style letter.

You can access many Tab settings from the Tabs dialog box. To view the Tabs dialog box, click the Paragraph Dialog Box Launcher in the Paragraph group on the Home tab, then click Tabs from the Indents and Spacing tab. You can also display the Tabs dialog box by double-clicking a tab setting on the ruler. Table 2.2 describes the different types of tabs.

TABLE 2.2   Tab Markers

Tab Icon on Ruler	Type of Tab	Function
⌊	*left tab*	Sets the start position on the left so as you type, text moves to the right of the tab setting.
⌄	*center tab*	Sets the middle point of the text you type; whatever you type will be centered on that tab setting.
⌋	*right tab*	Sets the start position on the right so as you type, text moves to the left of that tab setting and aligns on the right.
⌊.	*decimal tab*	Aligns numbers on a decimal point. Regardless of how long the number, each number lines up with the decimal in the same position.
⏐	*bar tab*	This tab does not position text or decimals, but inserts a vertical bar at the tab setting. This bar is useful as a separator for text printed on the same line.

A **left tab** marks the position to align text on the left.

A **center tab** marks where text centers as you type.

A **right tab** marks the position to align text on the right.

A **decimal tab** marks where numbers align on a decimal point as you type.

A **bar tab** marks the location of a vertical line between columns.

An alternative to using the Tabs dialog box is to set tabs directly on the ruler. Click the Tabs selector on the left side of the ruler (refer to Figure 2.8) until it displays the tab alignment you want. Then click the ruler in the location where you want to set the type of tab you selected. To delete a tab, click the tab marker on the ruler, and then drag it down and off the ruler.

Click to show or hide Ruler

Tab selector

Tab position on ruler

FIGURE 2.8 Tab Selector and Ruler ➤

> **TIP** Deleting Tabs
>
> When you set a new tab by clicking on the ruler, Word deletes all tab settings to the left of the tab you set. If you need to delete a single tab setting, for example the tab at 1.5″, click the 1.5″ tab marker on the ruler and drag it off of the ruler. When you release the mouse, you delete only that tab setting. If a marker does not display on the ruler for a tab, use the Tabs dialog box to adjust tab settings.

A **leader character** is dots or hyphens that connect two items of information.

In the Tabs dialog box, you also can specify a ***leader character***, typically dots or hyphens, which display on the left side of the tab and serve to draw or lead the reader's eye across the page to connect two items of information. For example, in Figure 2.9, it is easier to read the location and number of employees for each division because tab leader characters connect each piece of information. When dot characters connect items, they are often called *dot leaders* or just *leaders*. Notice also in the Tab dialog box in Figure 2.9, the default tab settings have been cleared and new tab settings are in place at .5″ and 2.5″; additionally, a right tab is set at 4″.

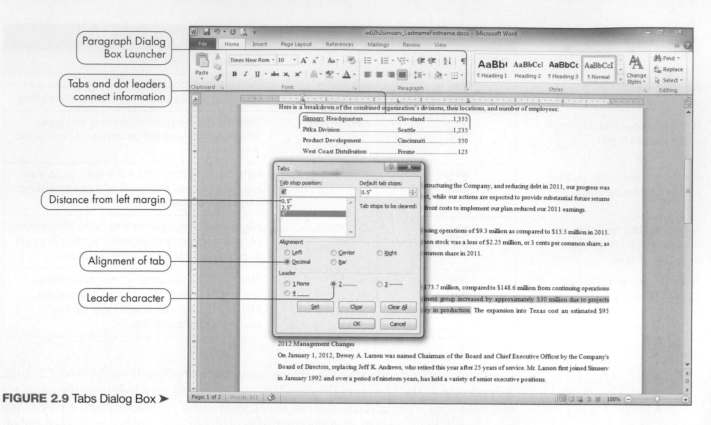

Paragraph Dialog Box Launcher

Tabs and dot leaders connect information

Distance from left margin

Alignment of tab

Leader character

FIGURE 2.9 Tabs Dialog Box ➤

Apply Borders and Shading

A **border** is a line that surrounds a paragraph, a page, a table, or an image.

Shading is background color that appears behind text.

You can draw attention to a document or an area of a document by using the Borders and Shading command. A **border** is a line that surrounds a paragraph, a page, a table, or an image, similar to how a picture frame surrounds a photograph or piece of art. **Shading** is a background color that appears behind text in a paragraph, a page, or a table. You can apply specific borders, such as top, bottom, or outside, from the Border command in the Paragraph group on the Home tab. For customized borders, click the Borders arrow in the Paragraph group on the Home tab to open the Borders and Shading dialog box (see Figure 2.10). Borders or shading is applied to selected text within a paragraph, to the entire paragraph if no text is selected, or to the entire page if the Page Border tab is selected. Even though other features can highlight text with color, you can use the Borders and Shading commands to add boxes and/or shading around text, as well as place horizontal or vertical lines around different quantities of text. A good example of this practice is used in the Exploring series: The TIP boxes are surrounded by a border with dark shading and use a white font color for the headings to attract your attention.

Borders tab

Line style

Preview box

Line color

Line width

Click to insert one horizontal line across the page

FIGURE 2.10 Apply a Border Around Text, Paragraphs, or Pages ➤

You can choose from several different line styles in any color, but remember you must use a color printer to display the line colors on the printed page. Colored lines appear in gray on a monochrome printer. Using the Box setting, you can place a uniform border around a paragraph, or you can choose a shadow effect with thicker lines at the right and bottom. You also can apply lines to selected sides of a paragraph by selecting a line style, and then clicking the desired sides as appropriate.

The horizontal line button at the bottom of the Borders and Shading dialog box provides access to a variety of attractive horizontal line designs. This is useful for displaying a horizontal line across a page to separate two elements. It also makes a nice border in a header or footer.

The Page Border tab enables you to place a decorative border around one or more selected pages. As with a paragraph border, you can place the border around the entire page, or you can select one or more sides. The page border also provides an additional option to use preselected clip art as a border instead of ordinary lines. Note that it is appropriate to use page borders on documents such as fliers, newsletters, and invitations, but not on formal documents such as research papers and professional reports.

> Use page borders on ... fliers, newsletters, and invitations, but not on formal documents such as research papers and professional reports.

Shading is applied independently of the border and is accessed from the Borders and Shading dialog box or from Shading in the Paragraph group on the Home tab. Clear (no shading) is the default. Solid (100%) shading fills in a box around the text, and in some instances, the text is turned white so you can read it. Shading of 10% or 20% generally is most effective to add emphasis to the selected paragraph (see Figure 2.11). The Borders and Shading command is implemented on the paragraph level and affects the entire paragraph unless text has been selected within the paragraph.

FIGURE 2.11 Apply Shading to Text or a Paragraph ➤

Create Bulleted and Numbered Lists

A **bulleted list** itemizes and separates paragraph text to increase readability.

A **numbered list** sequences and prioritizes items.

A **multilevel list** extends a numbered list to several levels.

A list helps you organize information by highlighting important topics. A **bulleted list** itemizes and separates paragraphs to increase readability. A **numbered list** sequences and prioritizes the items and is automatically updated to accommodate additions or deletions. A **multilevel list** extends a numbered list to several levels, and it too is updated automatically when topics are added or deleted. You create each of these lists from the Paragraph group on the Home tab.

To apply bullet formatting to a list, click the Bullets arrow and choose one of several predefined symbols in the Bullet library (see Figure 2.12). Position your mouse over one of the bullet styles in the Bullet Library and a preview of that bullet style will display in your document. To use that style, simply click the bullet. If you want to use a different bullet symbol, click the Define New Bullet option below the Bullet Library to choose a different symbol or picture for the bullet.

Click to view Bullet Library

Click to choose a different bullet symbol or to change bullet formatting

Preview of bullet as mouse hovers over the style

FIGURE 2.12 Bulleted List Options ➤

After you select text, you can click the Numbering arrow in the Paragraph group to apply Arabic or Roman numerals, or upper- or lowercase letters, for a numbered list. When you position the mouse pointer over a style in the Numbering Library, you see a preview of that numbering style in your document. As with a bulleted list, you can define a new style by selecting the Define New Number Format option below the Numbering Library. Note, too, the options to restart or continue numbering found by selecting the Set Numbering Value option. These become important if a list appears in multiple places within a document. In other words, each occurrence of a list can start numbering anew, or it can continue from where the previous list left off.

The Multilevel List command enables you to create an outline to organize your thoughts in a hierarchical structure. As with the other types of lists, you can choose one of several default styles and/or modify a style through the Define New Multilevel List option below the List Library. You also can specify whether each outline within a document is to restart its numbering, or whether it is to continue numbering from the previous outline.

Format Text into Columns

A **column** formats a section of a document into side-by-side vertical blocks.

Columns format a section of a document into side-by-side vertical blocks in which the text flows down the first column and then continues at the top of the next column. The length of a line of columnar text is shorter, enabling people to read through each document faster. To format text into columns, click the Page Layout tab and click Columns in the Page Setup group. From the Columns gallery, you can specify the number of columns or select More Columns to display the Columns dialog box. The Columns dialog box provides options for setting the number of columns and spacing between columns. Microsoft Word calculates the width of each column according to the left and right document margins on the page and the specified (default) space between columns.

The dialog box in Figure 2.13 implements a design of two equal columns. The width of each column is computed based on current left and right document margins and the spacing between columns. The width of each column is determined by subtracting the sum of the margins and the space between the columns from the page width of 8.5″. The result of the subtraction results in column widths of 3.25″.

Preset column specifications

Number of columns

Column width

Spacing between columns

Preview box

FIGURE 2.13 Columns Dialog Box ➤

One subtlety associated with column formatting is the use of sections, which control elements such as the orientation of a page (landscape or portrait), margins, page numbers, and the number of columns. Most of the documents you work with consist of a single section, so section formatting is not an issue. It becomes important only when you want to vary formatting in different parts, or sections, of the document. For example, you could use section formatting to create a document that has one column on its title page and two columns on the remaining pages. Creating this type of formatting requires you to divide the document into two sections by inserting a section break. You then format each section independently and specify the number of columns in each section.

Display Nonprinting Formatting Marks

As you type text, Word inserts nonprinting marks or symbols. While these symbols do not display on printouts, they do affect the appearance. For example, Word inserts a code every time you press Spacebar, Tab, and Enter. When you press Enter, it leaves a paragraph mark, no matter whether it is at the end of a single word, a single line, or a complete group of sentences. Word interprets the Paragraph mark as the completion of a paragraph, and so the paragraph mark (¶) at the end of a paragraph does more than just indicate the presence of a hard return. It also stores all of the formatting in effect for the paragraph. To preserve the formatting when you move or copy a paragraph, you must include the paragraph mark in the selected text. Click Show/Hide (¶) in the Paragraph group on the Home tab to display the paragraph mark and make sure it has been selected. Table 2.3 lists several common formatting marks. Both the hyphen and nonbreaking hyphen look like a regular hyphen when printed.

> Word interprets the Paragraph mark as the completion of a paragraph…. It also stores all of the formatting in effect for the paragraph.

TABLE 2.3 Nonprinting Symbols

Symbol	Description	Create by
•	Regular space	Pressing Spacebar
°	Nonbreaking space	Pressing Ctrl+Shift+Spacebar
-	Regular hyphen	Pressing Hyphen
—	Nonbreaking hyphen	Pressing Ctrl+Shift+Hyphen
→	Tab	Pressing Tab
¶	End of paragraph	Pressing Enter
... (shows under text)	Hidden text	Selecting Hidden check box in Font dialog box
↵	Line break	Pressing Shift+Enter

Applying Paragraph Formats

The Paragraph group on the Home tab contains commands to set and control several format options for a paragraph. The options include alignment, indentation, line spacing, and pagination. These features also are found in the Paragraph dialog box. All of these formatting features are implemented at the paragraph level and affect all selected paragraphs. If no paragraphs are selected, Word applies the formatting to the current paragraph—the paragraph containing the insertion point.

Change Text Alignment

Horizontal alignment refers to the placement of text between the left and right margins.

Horizontal alignment refers to the placement of text between the left and right margins. Text is aligned in four different ways, as shown in Figure 2.14. Alignment options are justified (flush left/flush right), left aligned (flush left with a ragged right margin), right aligned (flush right with a ragged left margin), or centered within the margins (ragged left and right). The default alignment is left aligned.

> We, the people of the United States, in order to form a more perfect Union, establish justice, insure domestic tranquility, provide for the common defense, promote the general welfare, and secure the blessings of liberty to ourselves and our posterity, do ordain and establish this Constitution for the United States of America.
> **Justified (flush left/flush right)**
>
> We, the people of the United States, in order to form a more perfect Union, establish justice, insure domestic tranquility, provide for the common defense, promote the general welfare, and secure the blessings of liberty to ourselves and our posterity, do ordain and establish this Constitution for the United States of America.
> **Left Aligned (flush left/ragged right)**
>
> We, the people of the United States, in order to form a more perfect Union, establish justice, insure domestic tranquility, provide for the common defense, promote the general welfare, and secure the blessings of liberty to ourselves and our posterity, do ordain and establish this Constitution for the United States of America.
> **Right Aligned (ragged left/flush right)**
>
> We, the people of the United States, in order to form a more perfect Union, establish justice, insure domestic tranquility, provide for the common defense, promote the general welfare, and secure the blessings of liberty to ourselves and our posterity, do ordain and establish this Constitution for the United States of America.
> **Centered (ragged left/ragged right)**

FIGURE 2.14 Horizontal Alignment ➤

Left-aligned text is perhaps the easiest to read. The first letters of each line align with each other, helping the eye to find the beginning of each line. The lines themselves are of irregular length. Uniform spacing exists between words, and the ragged margin on the right adds white space to the text, giving it a lighter and more informal look.

Justified text, sometimes called fully justified, produces lines of equal length, with the spacing between words adjusted to align at the margins. Look closely and you will see many books, magazines, and newspapers fully justify text to add formality and "neatness" to the text. Some find this style more difficult to read because of the uneven (sometimes excessive) word spacing and/or the greater number of hyphenated words needed to justify the lines. However, it also can enable you to pack more information onto a page when space is constrained.

Text that is centered or right aligned is usually restricted to limited amounts of text where the effect is more important than the ease of reading. Centered text, for example, appears frequently on wedding invitations, poems, or formal announcements. In research papers, first-level titles often are centered as well. Right-aligned text is used with figure captions, in short headlines, and in document headers and footers.

The Paragraph group on the Home tab contains the four alignment options: Align Text Left, Center, Align Text Right, and Justify. To apply the alignment, select text, then click the alignment option on the Home tab. You can also set alignment from the Paragraph dialog box; the Indents and Spacing tab contains an Alignment arrow in the General section from which you can choose one of the four options.

Indent Paragraphs

You can indent individual paragraphs so they appear to have different margins from the rest of a document. Indentation is established at the paragraph level; thus, it is possible to apply different indentation properties to different paragraphs. You can indent one paragraph from the left margin only, another from the right margin only, and a third from both the left and right margins. For example, the sixth edition of the *Publication Manual of the American Psychological Association,* which establishes the APA editorial style of writing, specifies that quotations consisting of 40 or more words should be contained in a separate paragraph that is indented .5″ from the left margin. Additionally, you can indent the first line of any paragraph differently from the rest of the paragraph. Finally, a paragraph may have no indentation at all, so that it aligns on the left and right margins.

Three settings determine the indentation of a paragraph: the left indent, the right indent, and a special indent (see Figure 2.15). The left and right indents are set to 0 by default, as is the special indent, and produce a paragraph with no indentation at all. Positive values for the left and right indents offset the paragraph from both margins.

A **first line indent** marks the location to indent only the first line in a paragraph.

A **hanging indent** marks how far to indent each line of a paragraph except the first.

The two types of special indentation are first line and hanging. The ***first line indent*** affects only the first line in the paragraph, and you apply it by pressing the Tab key at the beginning of the paragraph or by setting a specific measurement in the Paragraph dialog box. Remaining lines in the paragraph align at the left margin. A ***hanging indent*** aligns the first line of a paragraph at the left margin and indents the remaining lines. Hanging indents are often used with bulleted or numbered lists and to format citations on a bibliography page.

When you view the ruler, characters display to identify any special indents that are in use. A grey triangle pointing down identifies the indention for a First Line Indent, a grey arrow pointing up identifies the indention for a Hanging Indent, and a grey square identifies the Left Indent. You can slide the characters along the ruler to modify the location of the indents.

Set Line and Paragraph Spacing

Line spacing is the space between the lines in a paragraph.

Line spacing determines the space between the lines in a paragraph and between paragraphs. Word provides complete flexibility and enables you to select any multiple of line spacing (single, double, line and a half, and so on). You also can specify line spacing in terms of points (1″ vertical contains 72 pt). Click Line and Paragraph Spacing in the Paragraph group on the Home tab to establish line spacing for the current paragraph. You can also set line spacing in the *Spacing* section on the Indents and Spacing tab in the Paragraph dialog box.

Paragraph spacing is the amount of space before or after a paragraph.

Paragraph spacing is the amount of space before or after a paragraph, as indicated by the paragraph mark when you press Enter between paragraphs. Unlike line spacing that controls *all* spacing within and between paragraphs, paragraph spacing controls only the spacing between paragraphs.

Sometimes you need to single-space text within a paragraph but want to have a blank line between paragraphs. Instead of pressing Enter twice between paragraphs, you can set the paragraph spacing to control the amount of space before or after the paragraph. You can set paragraph spacing in the *Spacing* section on the Indents and Spacing tab in the Paragraph dialog box. Setting a 12-pt After spacing creates the appearance of a double-space after the paragraph even though the user presses Enter only once between paragraphs.

The Paragraph dialog box is illustrated in Figure 2.15. The Indents and Spacing tab specifies a hanging indent, 1.5 line spacing, and justified alignment. The Preview area within the Paragraph dialog box enables you to see how the paragraph will appear within the document.

FIGURE 2.15 Indents and Spacing ➤

> **TIP** Indents and Paragraph Spacing
>
> To avoid opening the Paragraph dialog box, you can quickly change Indent or Paragraph Spacing from the Paragraph group on the Page Layout tab.

Control Widows and Orphans

A **widow** is the last line of a paragraph appearing by itself at the top of a page.

An **orphan** is the first line of a paragraph appearing by itself at the bottom of a page.

Some lines become isolated from the remainder of a paragraph and seem out of place at the beginning or end of a multipage document. A **widow** refers to the last line of a paragraph appearing by itself at the top of a page. An **orphan** is the first line of a paragraph appearing by itself at the bottom of a page. You can prevent these from occurring by checking the Widow/Orphan control in the *Pagination* section of the Line and Page Breaks tab of the Paragraph dialog box.

To prevent a page break from occurring within a paragraph and ensure that the entire paragraph appears on the same page use the *Keep lines together* option in the *Pagination* section of the Line and Page Breaks tab of the Paragraph dialog box. The paragraph is moved to the top of the next page if it does not fit on the bottom of the current page. Use the *Keep with next* option in the *Pagination* section to prevent a soft page break between the two paragraphs. This option is typically used to keep a heading (a one-line paragraph) with its associated text in the next paragraph. Figure 2.16 displays the Paragraph dialog box settings to control soft page breaks that detract from the appearance of a document.

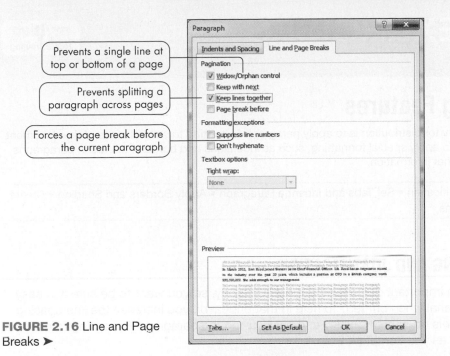

Prevents a single line at top or bottom of a page

Prevents splitting a paragraph across pages

Forces a page break before the current paragraph

FIGURE 2.16 Line and Page Breaks ➤

TIP The Section Versus the Paragraph

Line spacing, alignment, tabs, and indents are implemented at the paragraph level. Change any of these parameters anywhere within the current (or selected) paragraph(s) and you change *only* those paragraph(s). Margins, page numbering, orientation, and columns are implemented at the section level. Change these parameters anywhere within a section and you change the characteristics of every page within that section.

HANDS-ON EXERCISES

2 Paragraph Formatting Features

The next step in preparing the Annual Summary for distribution is to apply paragraph formatting to several areas of the document that will make it easier to read. You also want to apply special formatting, such as indentions and borders, to certain paragraphs for emphasis and to draw the readers' eye to that information.

Skills covered: Specify Line Spacing and Justification • Set Tabs and Indent a Paragraph • Apply Borders and Shading • Create a Bulleted and Numbered List • Create Columns

---

STEP 1 ▶ SPECIFY LINE SPACING AND JUSTIFICATION

The Annual Summary is an important document for your company, so you want to be sure it is easy to read and looks professional when printed. To help in that endeavor, you increase the line spacing and adjust justification of this document quickly and easily using the paragraph formatting features in Word. Refer to Figure 2.17 as you complete Step 1.

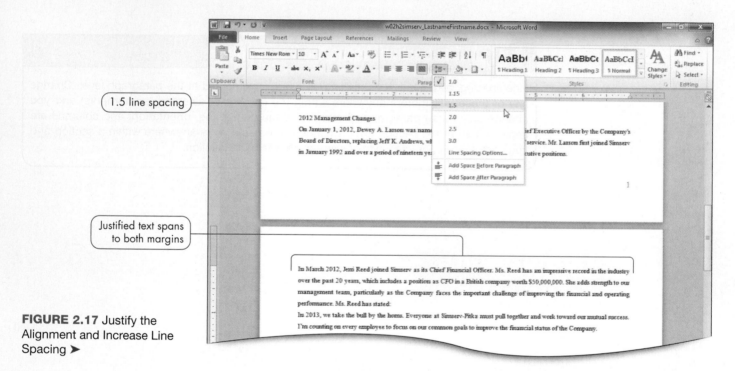

FIGURE 2.17 Justify the Alignment and Increase Line Spacing ➤

a. Open the *w02h1simserv_LastnameFirstname* document if you closed it at the end of Hands-On Exercise 1, and save it as **w02h2simserv_LastnameFirstname**, changing *h1* to *h2*.

b. Drag to select all of the text in the document, starting with the first sentence, *The consumer products industry has seen dramatic change ...*, and then click **Justify** in the Paragraph group.

c. Click **Line and Paragraph Spacing** in the Paragraph group, and then select **1.5**, as seen in Figure 2.17.

These settings align the text on the right and left margins and add spacing before and after lines of text, making it easier to read.

d. Save the document.

SET TABS AND INDENT A PARAGRAPH

You want to display the information about divisions that were acquired so that it is easy to read across the page and not jumbled together as you see it now. You decide to insert two tabs to line up the division and cities. A third tab is needed for the number of employees, and since you are aligning a number, you wisely insert a decimal tab. You also decide to indent a quotation by the new CFO so it does not blend in with the rest of the paragraph. Refer to Figure 2.18 as you complete Step 2.

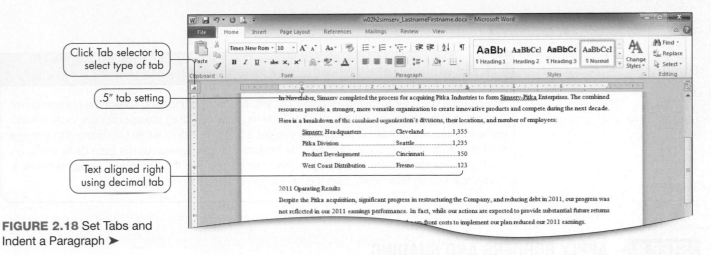

Click Tab selector to select type of tab

.5" tab setting

Text aligned right using decimal tab

FIGURE 2.18 Set Tabs and Indent a Paragraph ➤

a. Select the last four lines of the *Acquisition of Pitka Industries* paragraph.

   These lines describe facility locations and number of employees at each.

b. Click the **Paragraph Dialog Box Launcher** in the Paragraph group. Click **Tabs** in the bottom left to display the Tabs dialog box.

c. Type **.5** in the **Tab stop position box**, confirm *Left* is selected in the Alignment area, and then click **Set**.

d. Type **2.5** in the **Tab stop position box**, confirm it is a Left-aligned tab, click **2...** in the Leader area, and then click **Set** again. Click **OK** to close the Tabs dialog box.

   You set two tab stops for the Division and locations.

e. Click the **View tab**, and then click **Ruler**, if necessary, to view the Ruler at the top of the window. Select the last four lines again, if necessary, and then click the **Tab selector** at the left end of the ruler until the Decimal tab displays.

> **TROUBLESHOOTING:** If you miss the Decimal tab selector, keep clicking. All tab selections will cycle through the selector area and then repeat as you click.

f. Click the **4"** mark on the ruler to apply the Decimal tab.

   When you set the decimal tab, the numbers line up along the right edge. It is always best to display numbers aligning on the right.

g. Right-click the selected text, click **Paragraph**, and then click **Tabs**. Click the **4" tab**, click **2...** in the Leader area, and then click **OK**.

   When you add the dot leaders, it is easier to follow the information across the page for each location.

h. Click the **Home tab**, and then click **Increase Indent** in the Paragraph group to indent the list to the first tab stop.

i. Place your cursor on the left side of *Fresno* on the last line, and press **Tab** to align the data at the new tab stops, as shown in Figure 2.18.

j.   Select the quote by Jerri Reed at the end of the second paragraph following the *2012 Management Changes* heading. The quote starts *In 2013, we take the bull by the horns.*

k.   Click the **Page Layout tab**. Click the **Indent Left arrow** until *0.5"* displays.

l.   Click the **Indent Right arrow** until *0.5"* displays.

The paragraph is equally indented from the right and left margins and now displays with additional white space on the right and left sides.

m.   Save the document.

TIP   Indents and the Ruler

You can use the ruler to change the special, left, and/or right indents. Select the paragraph (or paragraphs) in which you want to change indents, and then drag the appropriate indent markers to the new location(s) on the ruler. If you get a hanging indent when you wanted to change the left indent, it means you dragged the bottom triangle instead of the box. Click Undo on the Quick Access Toolbar and try again. You can always use the Paragraph group settings or Paragraph Dialog Box rather than the ruler if you continue to have difficulty.

STEP 3   APPLY BORDERS AND SHADING

To make sure your company's financial position is recognized, you decide to place a border around that paragraph and shade it with color to make it really stand out. You know that this is another way to draw the reader's attention to important data—by highlighting with color and borders. Refer to Figure 2.19 as you complete Step 3.

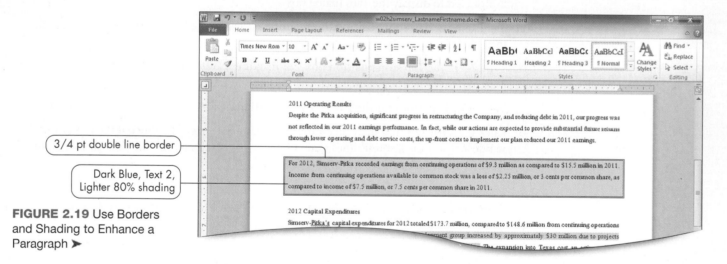

3/4 pt double line border

Dark Blue, Text 2, Lighter 80% shading

FIGURE 2.19 Use Borders and Shading to Enhance a Paragraph ➤

a.   Select the second paragraph following the *2011 Operating Results* heading, which starts *For 2012, Simserv-Pitka recorded earnings.*

b.   Click the **Home tab**, click the **Borders arrow**, and then click **Borders and Shading** to display the Borders and Shading dialog box.

c.   Click the **Borders tab**, if necessary, and then select the **double line style** in the **Style list**. Click the **Width arrow**, select **3/4 pt**, and then click **Box** in the *Setting* section.

A preview of these settings will display on the right side of the window in the Preview area.

d.   Click the **Shading tab**, click the **Fill arrow**, and then select **Dark Blue, Text 2, Lighter 80%** from the palette (second row, fourth column). Click **OK** to accept the settings for both Borders and Shading.

The paragraph is surrounded by a 3/4-pt double-line border, and light blue shading appears behind the text.

e. Click outside the paragraph to deselect it, and then compare your work to Figure 2.19.

f. Save the document.

CREATE A BULLETED AND NUMBERED LIST

The Annual Summary includes paragraphs that describe the goals for 2012. To display the key goals so each one is easily distinguishable, you decide to format them into a bulleted list. The goals described in the final paragraph should be formatted similarly, but since they are described as steps, which assume an order, you format them using a numbered list instead of simple bullets. Refer to Figure 2.20 as you complete Step 4.

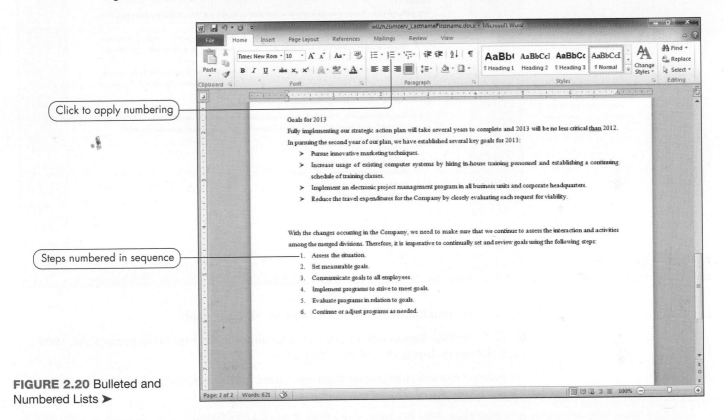

FIGURE 2.20 Bulleted and Numbered Lists ➤

a. Select the five lines of text in the first paragraph that follows the *Goals for 2013* heading, starting with *Pursue innovative marketing techniques.*

b. Click the **Home tab**, if necessary, and then click the **Bullets arrow** to display the Bullet Library.

Here you select from a variety of bullet styles. The most recently used bullets display at the top.

c. Click a bullet that is in the shape of an arrow or arrowhead. If that style does not display, click the bullet of your choice.

d. Select the last six lines of text in the last paragraph that follows the *Goals for 2013* heading.

e. Click **Numbering** in the paragraph group.

The steps are numbered in sequence from 1 to 6 as shown in Figure 2.20. Because it is important to perform these steps in this order, you use a numbered list instead of bullets.

f. Save the document.

The goals you formatted with bullets in the last step look fine, but you realize the bullets are somewhat short and would look good if displayed in columns on the page. Columns would also add an element of variety to the way the information displays on the page. Refer to Figure 2.21 as you complete Step 5.

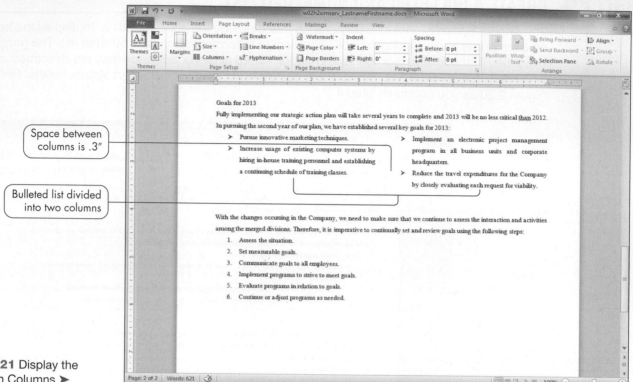

FIGURE 2.21 Display the Bullet List in Columns ▶

a. Select the four bulleted items in the *Goals for 2013* paragraph.

b. Click the **Page Layout tab**, and then click **Columns** in the Page Setup group. Click **More Columns** to display the Columns dialog box.

Because you will change several settings related to columns, you clicked the More Columns option instead of clicking the gallery option to create columns.

c. Click **Two** in the *Presets* section of the dialog box. The default spacing between columns is 0.5″, which leads to a column width of 3.25″. Change the Spacing to **.3″**, which automatically changes the column Width to *3.35″*.

d. Click **OK** to close the Columns dialog box, and compare your document to Figure 2.21.

The bulleted list is now formatted in two columns and makes efficient use of space on the page.

e. Click the **View tab**, and then click **Ruler** to turn off the ruler.

f. Save the document and keep it onscreen if you plan to continue with the next Hands-On Exercise. If not, close the document and exit Word.

Styles

As you complete reports, assignments, and projects for other classes or in your job, you probably apply the same text, paragraph, table, and list formatting for similar documents. Instead of formatting each document individually, you can create your own custom style to save time in setting particular formats for titles, headings, and paragraphs. Styles and other features in Word then can be used to automatically generate reference pages such as a table of contents and indexes. In this section, you will create and modify styles.

Understanding Styles

> Styles automate the formatting process and provide a consistent appearance to a document... Change the style and you automatically change all text defined by that style.

A **style** is a set of formatting options you apply to characters or paragraphs.

One characteristic of a professional document is the uniform formatting that is applied to similar elements throughout the document. Different elements have different formatting. For headings you can use one font, color, style, and size, and then use a completely different format design on text below those headings. The headings may be left aligned, whereas the text is fully justified. You can format lists and footnotes in entirely different styles.

One way to achieve uniformity throughout the document is to use the Format Painter to copy the formatting from one occurrence of each element to the next. If you change your mind after copying the formatting throughout a document, you have to repeat the entire process all over again. A much easier way to achieve uniformity is to store all the formatting information together, which is what we refer to as a *style*. Styles automate the formatting process and provide a consistent appearance to a document. It is possible to store any type of character or paragraph formatting within a style, and once a style is defined, you can apply it to any element within a document to produce identical formatting. Change the style and you automatically change all text defined by that style.

Creating and Modifying Styles

A **character style** stores character formatting and affects only selected text.

A **paragraph style** stores formats used on text in an entire paragraph.

Styles are created on the character or paragraph level. A *character style* stores character formatting (font, size, and style) and affects only the selected text. A *paragraph style* stores paragraph formatting such as alignment, line spacing, indents, tabs, text flow, and borders and shading, as well as the font, size, and style of the text in the paragraph. A paragraph style affects the current paragraph or, if selected, multiple paragraphs. You cannot apply a paragraph style to only part of a paragraph. You create and apply styles from the Styles group on the Home tab, as shown in Figure 2.22.

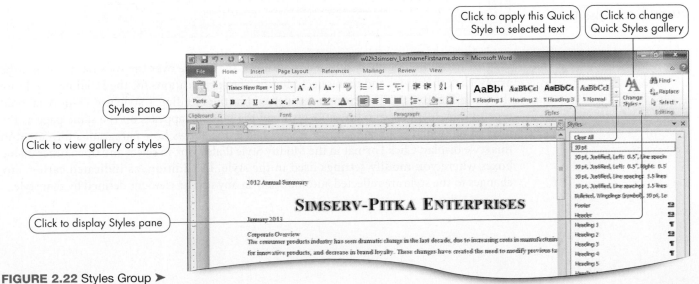

FIGURE 2.22 Styles Group ➤

The Normal template contains more than 100 styles. Unless you specify a style, Word uses the Normal style. The Normal style contains these settings: 11-pt Calibri, 1.15 line spacing, 10-pt spacing after, left horizontal alignment, and Widow/Orphan control. To apply a different style to an existing paragraph, place the insertion point anywhere within the paragraph, click the Styles Dialog Box Launcher on the Home tab to display the Styles pane, and then click the name of the style you want to use. You can create your own styles to use in a document, modify or delete an existing style, and even add your new style to the Normal template for use in other documents. The Clear All style removes all formatting from selected text.

In Figure 2.23, the task pane displays all of the styles available for use in the Simserv-Pitka Enterprises Annual Summary. The Normal style contains the default paragraph settings (left aligned, 1.15 line spacing, 10-pt spacing after, and 11-pt Calibri font) and is assigned automatically to every paragraph unless a different style is specified. It is the Heading 1 and Heading 3 styles, however, that are of interest to us, as these styles have been applied throughout the document to titles and paragraph headings. To view the style names with their styles applied, click the Show Preview check box near the bottom of the Styles pane.

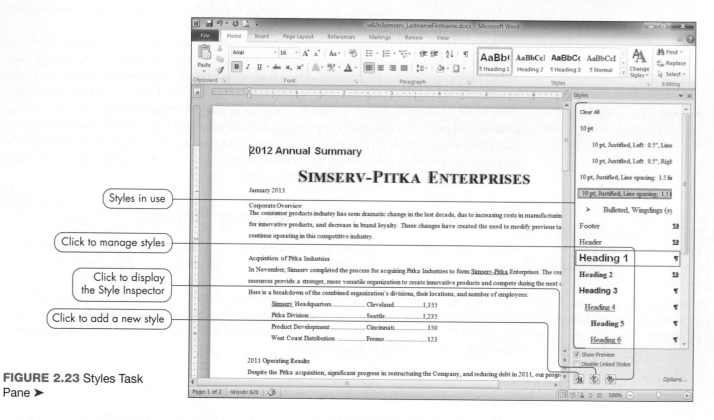

FIGURE 2.23 Styles Task Pane ➤

To change the specifications of a style, hover the mouse over the style name to view the arrow, click the arrow, and then select Modify. The specifications for the Heading 1 style are shown in Figure 2.24. The current settings within the Heading 1 style use 18-pt Arial bold type font. A 14-pt space is after the text, and the heading appears on the same page as the next paragraph. The preview frame in the dialog box shows how paragraphs formatted in this style display. Click Format in the Modify Style dialog box to select and open other dialog boxes where you modify settings used in the style. In addition, as indicated earlier, any changes to the style are reflected automatically in any text or element defined by that style.

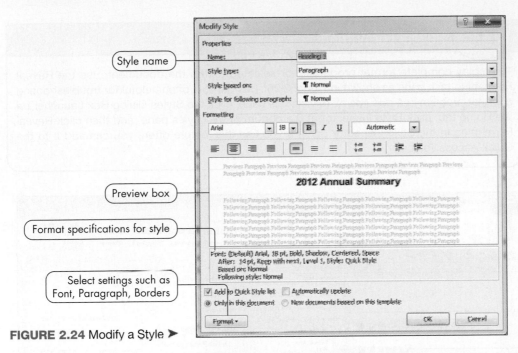

Style name
Preview box
Format specifications for style
Select settings such as Font, Paragraph, Borders

FIGURE 2.24 Modify a Style ➤

Use the Styles Pane Options

The Styles pane can display in several locations. Initially it might display as a floating window, but you can drag the title bar to move it. Drag to the far left or right side, and it will dock on that side of the window. When you display the Styles pane in your document, it might contain only the styles used in the document, as in Figure 2.23, or it might list every style in the Word document template. If the Styles pane only displays styles used in the document, you are unable to view or apply other styles.

You can change the styles that display in the Styles pane by using the Styles Pane Options dialog box, which displays when you click Options in the bottom-right corner of the Styles pane. In the *Select styles to show* box, you select from several options including Recommended, In use, In current document, and All styles, as shown in Figure 2.25. Select *In use* to view only styles used in this document; select *All styles* to view all styles created for the document template as well as any custom styles you create. Other options are available in this dialog box, including how to sort the styles when displayed, and whether to show Paragraph or Font or both types of styles.

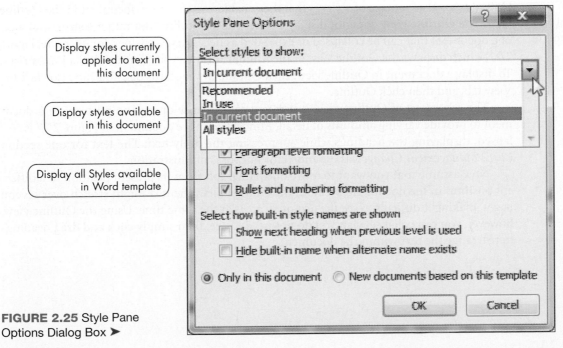

Display styles currently applied to text in this document
Display styles available in this document
Display all Styles available in Word template

FIGURE 2.25 Style Pane Options Dialog Box ➤

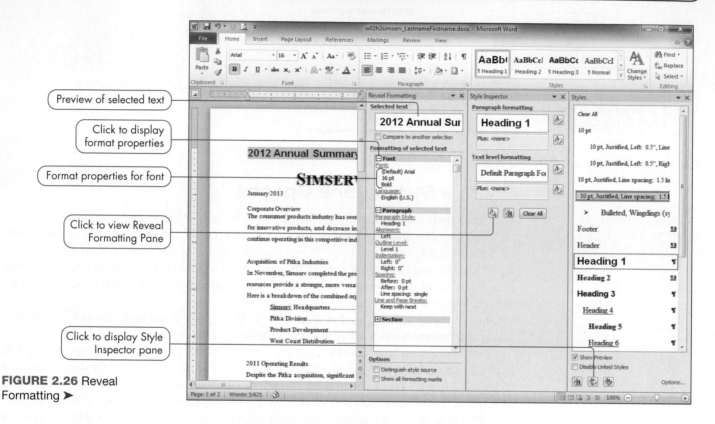

Preview of selected text

Click to display format properties

Format properties for font

Click to view Reveal Formatting Pane

Click to display Style Inspector pane

FIGURE 2.26 Reveal Formatting ➤

Use the Outline View

Outline view is a structural view that displays varying amounts of detail.

One additional advantage of styles is that they enable you to view a document in the Outline view. The *Outline view* does not display a conventional outline, but rather a structural view of a document that can be collapsed or expanded as necessary. Consider, for example, Figure 2.27, which displays the Outline view of the Annual Summary for Simserv-Pitka Enterprises. To display a document in Outline view, click Outline in the status bar. You can also click the View tab, and then click Outline.

The advantage of Outline view is that you can collapse or expand portions of a document to provide varying amounts of detail. Almost the entire document in Figure 2.27 is collapsed, displaying the headings while suppressing the body text. The text for one section (*2012 Management Changes*) is expanded for purposes of illustration.

Now assume that you want to move one paragraph from its present position to a different position in the document. Without the Outline view, the text might stretch over several pages, making it difficult to see the text of all areas at the same time. Using the Outline view, however, you can collapse what you do not need to see, then simply click and drag headings to rearrange the text within the document.

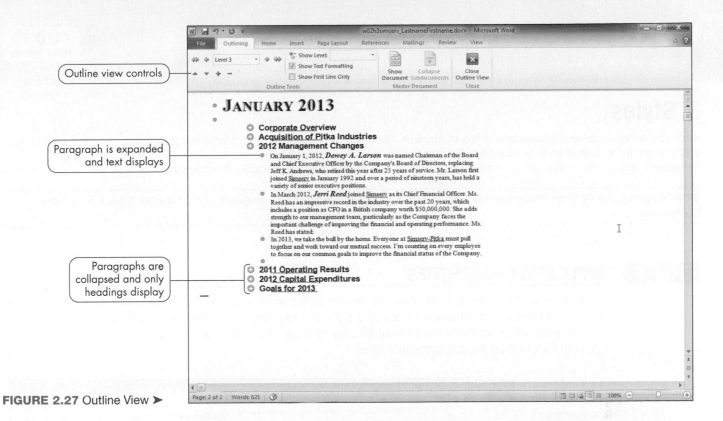

Outline view controls

Paragraph is expanded and text displays

Paragraphs are collapsed and only headings display

FIGURE 2.27 Outline View ➤

TIP The Outline Versus the Outline View

A conventional outline is created as a multilevel list using the Multilevel List command in the Paragraph group on the Home tab. Text for the outline is entered in the Print Layout view, *not* the Outline view. The latter provides a condensed view of a document that is used in conjunction with styles.

3 Styles

After you enhance several paragraphs of the document with formatting, you decide to format the paragraph headings with styles, and you create a custom style of your own. By using styles on the paragraph headings, you are certain that formatting is consistent and you have the option of making a change to all the headings in one step, if necessary.

Skills covered: Apply Style Properties • Modify the Heading 1 Style • Create a Paragraph and Character Style • Select the Outline View

---

STEP 1 ▶ APPLY STYLE PROPERTIES

For convenience, and because they are designed in a style you like, you decide to use the Heading 1 style on the document title and Heading 3 style on the paragraph headings. Fortunately, your work goes quickly when you use the Format Painter to copy the style from one heading to all the rest. Refer to Figure 2.28 as you complete Step 1.

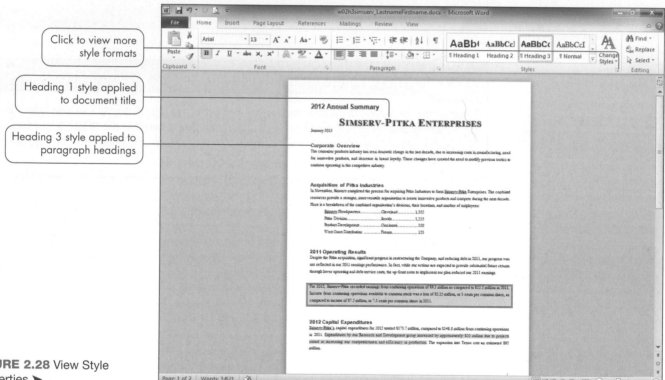

Click to view more style formats

Heading 1 style applied to document title

Heading 3 style applied to paragraph headings

FIGURE 2.28 View Style Properties ➤

a. Open *w02h2simserv_LastnameFirstname* if you closed it at the end of Hands-On Exercise 2, and save it as **w02h3simserv_LastnameFirstname**, changing *h2* to *h3*.

b. Press **Ctrl+Home** to move to the beginning of the document.

c. Select the first line of the document, *2012 Annual Summary*, click the **Home tab**, if necessary, and then click **Heading 1** from the Quick Style gallery in the Styles group.

When you hover your mouse over the different styles in the gallery, the Live Preview feature displays the style on your selected text but will not apply it until you click the style.

d. Select the paragraph heading *Corporate Overview*. Click the **More buttom** on the right side of the Quick Style gallery to display more styles, and then click the **Heading 3 style**.

e. Double-click the **Format Painter** in the Clipboard group, and then select the five remaining paragraph headings in the document to apply the **Heading 3 style**. Press **Esc** to turn off the Format Painter.

All paragraph headings in this document are formatted as shown in Figure 2.28.

f. Save the document.

STEP 2 ▸ MODIFY THE HEADING 1 STYLE

After you look at the document title, you decide it should be centered on the page and formatted to match the subtitle. Because you anticipate using that style frequently, you decide to modify the style to add center alignment and to include the font attributes used on the subtitle. Refer to Figure 2.29 as you complete Step 2.

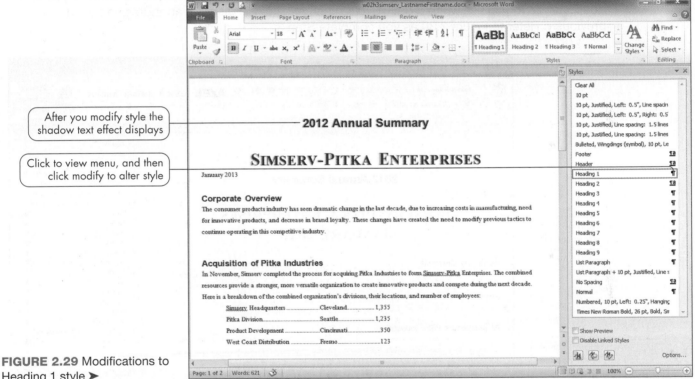

FIGURE 2.29 Modifications to Heading 1 style ➤

a. Click the **Styles Dialog Box Launcher** in the Styles group. Double-click the title bar of the Styles pane to dock it, if necessary, so it does not float on the screen.

b. Click **Ctrl+Home** to move to the beginning of the document. Notice the Heading 1 style is selected in the Styles pane. Hover your mouse over the style description in the Styles pane to display the arrow, click the arrow, and then select **Modify** to display the Modify Style dialog box.

> **TROUBLESHOOTING:** If you click the style name instead of the arrow, you will apply the style to the selected text instead of modifying it. Click Undo on the Quick Access Toolbar to cancel the command. Click the arrow next to the style name to display the associated menu, and select the Modify command to display the Modify Style dialog box.

c. Click **Center** in the *Formatting* section to change the alignment of this title. Click **Format** in the bottom-left corner of the window, and then click **Font** to display the Font dialog box. If necessary, click the **Font tab**. Change Font size to **18**, and then click **OK** to close the Font dialog box and return to the Modify Style dialog box.

d. Click **Format**, and then select **Text Effects**. Click **Shadow**, click **Presets,** and then click **Offset Left** (second row, third column). Click the **Close button**.

e. Click **Format**, and then select **Paragraph**. If necessary, click the **Indents and Spacing tab**. In the *Spacing* section, type **14** in the **After box**.

   Since 14 is not one of the predefined options you see when scrolling in the Spacing After box, you must type it in.

f. Click **OK** to close the Paragraph dialog box, and then click **OK** to close the Modify Style dialog box. Compare your results to Figure 2.29.

g. Save the document.

STEP 3 ▶ CREATE A PARAGRAPH AND CHARACTER STYLE

You decide the format used on the subtitle should also be saved as a style so you can apply it to other text. You also decide to create a character style that you use on specific text to make it stand out from other text in the paragraph. Creating the paragraph and character styles enables you to duplicate the formatting without having to remember all of the different attributes you used previously. Refer to Figure 2.30 as you complete Step 3.

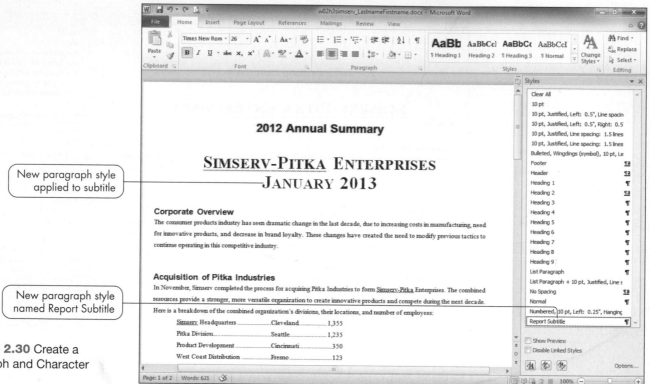

New paragraph style applied to subtitle

New paragraph style named Report Subtitle

FIGURE 2.30 Create a Paragraph and Character Style ➤

a. Move the insertion point to the left side of the subtitle *Simserv-Pitka Enterprises* that displays just below the main title. Point to the description for this subtitle on the Styles Pane (you may only be able to see the first or last few format effects listed), hover your mouse over the description to display the arrow, click the arrow, and then select **Modify Style** to display the Modify Style dialog box.

   The Styles task pane displays the specifications for this style. You have created a new style by changing the font options earlier, but the style is not yet named.

b. Click in the **Name box** in the Properties area, and then type **Report Subtitle** as the name of the new style. Click **OK**.

c. Select the third line of the document, *January 2013*, and then click **Report Subtitle** in the Styles pane to apply the new style to this line of text.

The two lines of text that make up the subtitle of the document share the same formatting, as shown in Figure 2.30. However, the shadow special effect does not save. You will modify the style to add it back and it will then display on all text that uses the Report Subtitle style.

d. Hover your mouse over the *Report Subtitle* style until the arrow displays, and then click **Modify**. Click **Format**, and then click **Text Effects**. Click **Shadow**, click **Presets**, and then click **Offset Left** (third row, third column). Click the **Close button**. Click **OK** to close the dialog box.

   Notice the shadow effect displays on both lines of text that use the Report Subtitle style. Once you apply a style, any modifications to that style will automatically show on all text that uses the style; you do not have to change text individually.

e. Select the name *Dewey A. Larson* that appears within the *2012 Management Changes* paragraph. Click **Bold** and **Italic** in the Font group. Click **Grow Font** in the Font group two times to increase the size to **12**.

f. Click **New Style** on the bottom of the Styles pane, and then type **Emphasize** as the name of the style.

g. Click the **Style type arrow**, and then select **Character**. Click **OK** to close the dialog box.

   The style named *Emphasize* is listed in the Style pane and can be used throughout your document. You create and use this character style because you only want to use it on certain words, not entire paragraphs.

h. Select the name *Jerri Reed*, also in the *2012 Management Changes* paragraph. Click **Emphasize** in the Quick Style gallery to apply the newly created Emphasize character style to the selected text.

   You can also select this character style from the Styles pane.

i. Close the Styles task pane and save the document.

STEP 4 > **SELECT THE OUTLINE VIEW**

You want to view the structure of the document quickly by looking only at titles and paragraph headings, so you invoke the Outline view in Word. By viewing the outline, you determine you should move one paragraph up, and you quickly make it so by using the Outline tools on the ribbon. Refer to Figure 2.31 as you complete Step 4.

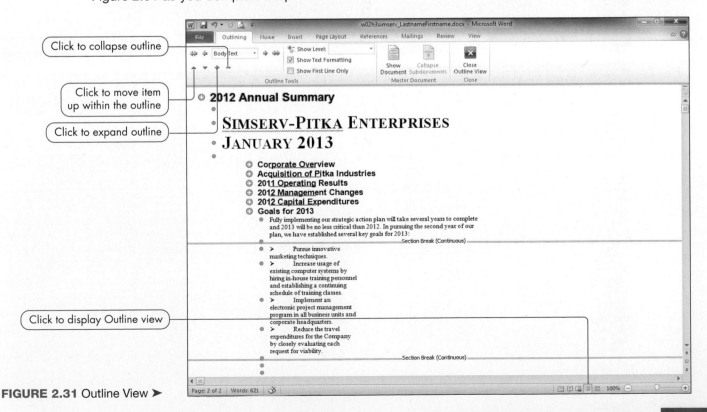

FIGURE 2.31 Outline View ➤

a. Click the **View tab**, then click **Outline** to display the document in Outline view.

b. Place the insertion point to the left of the first paragraph heading, *Corporate Overview*, and then select the rest of the document. Click the **Outlining tab**, if necessary, and then click **Collapse** in the Outline Tools group.

The entire document collapses so that only the headings display.

c. Click in the heading titled *Goals for 2013*, and then click **Expand** in the Outline Tools group to expand the subordinate paragraphs under this heading.

d. Select the paragraph heading *2012 Management Changes*, and then click **Move Up** in the Outline Tools group one time.

You moved the paragraph above the paragraph that precedes it in the outline. It now displays just below the *2011 Operating Results* paragraph, as shown in Figure 2.31. Note that you also can drag and drop a selected paragraph.

e. Click **Print Layout** in the status bar so you can view the entire document.

f. Save the document and keep it onscreen if you plan to continue with the next Hands-On Exercise. If not, close the document and exit Word.

Graphical Objects

One of the most exciting features of Word is its graphic capabilities. You can use clip art, images, drawings, scanned photographs, and symbols to visually enhance brochures, newsletters, announcements, and reports. After inserting a graphical object, you can adjust size, choose placement, and perform other formatting options.

In this section, you will format the image by changing the height and width, applying a text-wrapping style, applying a quick style, and adjusting graphic properties. Finally, you will insert symbols in a document.

> One of the most exciting features of Word is its graphic capabilities. You can use clip art, images, drawings, and scanned photographs to visually enhance brochures, newsletters, announcements, and reports.

Formatting a Graphical Object

In addition to the collection of clip art and pictures that you can access from Word, you also can insert your own pictures into a document. If you have a scanner or digital camera attached to your computer, you can scan or download a picture for use in Word. After you insert the picture, many commands are available that you can use to format the picture or any other graphical element you use in the document. Remember that graphical elements should enhance a document, not overpower it.

Adjust the Height and Width of an Image

When you insert an image in a document, it comes in a predefined size. For example, the graphic image in Figure 2.32 was very large and took up much space on the page before it was resized. Most times, you need to adjust an image's size so it fits within the document and does not greatly increase the document file size.

Word provides different tools you can use to adjust the height or width of an image, depending on how exact you want the measurements. The Picture Tools Format tab contains Height and Width commands that enable you to specify exact measurements. You can use *sizing handles*, the small circles and squares that appear around a selected object, to size an object by clicking and dragging any one of the handles. When you use the circular sizing handles in the corner of a graphic to adjust the height (or width), Word also adjusts the width (or height) simultaneously. If needed, hold down Shift while dragging the corner-sizing handle to maintain the correct proportion of the image. If you use square sizing handles on the right, left, top, or bottom, you adjust that measurement without regard to any other sides.

For more precise measurements use the scale or scaling feature. Similar to the effects on text mentioned earlier in the chapter, you can adjust the height or width of an image by a percentage of its original size. The scale adjustment is located in the Size dialog box, which you display by clicking the Size Dialog Box Launcher on the Format tab.

Sizing handles are the small circles and squares that appear around a selected object and enable you to adjust the height and width of an object.

Make manual size adjustments here

Click to display
Layout dialog box

Original size

Select to maintain height and
width proportion when
making adjustments

Size after scaling to 50%
of height and width

FIGURE 2.32 Adjusting the
Size of a Graphic Object ➤

Adjust Text Wrapping

When you first insert an image, Word treats it as a character in the line of text, which leaves a lot of empty space on the left or right side of the image. You may want it to align differently, perhaps enabling text to display very tightly around the object or even placing it behind the text. *Text wrapping style* refers to the way text wraps around an image. Table 2.4 describes the different options, which may also display as Wrap Text options.

Text wrapping style refers to the way text wraps around an image.

TABLE 2.4	Text Wrapping Styles
Wrap Text Style	**Description**
In Line with Text	Graphic displays on the line where inserted so that as you add or delete text, causing the line of text to move, the image moves with it.
Square	Enables text to wrap around the graphic frame that surrounds the image.
Tight	Enables text to wrap tightly around the outer edges of the image itself instead of the frame.
Through	Select this option to wrap text around the perimeter and inside any open portions of the object.
Top and Bottom	Text wraps to the top and bottom of the image frame, but no text appears on the sides.
Behind Text	Enables the image to display behind the text in such a way that the image appears to float directly behind the text and does not move if text is inserted or deleted.
In Front of Text	Enables the image to display on top of the text in such a way that the image appears to float directly on top of the text and does not move if text is inserted or deleted.

Apply Picture Quick Styles

The **Picture Styles** gallery contains preformatted options that can be applied to a graphical object.

Word includes a *Picture Styles* gallery that contains many preformatted picture formats. The gallery of styles you can apply to a picture or clip art is extensive, and you can modify the style after you apply it. The quick styles provide a valuable resource if you want to improve the appearance of a graphic but are not familiar with graphic design and format tools. For example, after you insert a graphic, with one click you can choose a style from the Quick Styles gallery that adds a border and displays a reflection of the picture. You might want to select a style that changes the shape of your graphic to an octagon, or select a style that applies a 3-D effect to the image. To apply a quick style, select the graphical object, then choose a quick style from the Picture Styles group on the Picture Tools Format tab. Other style formatting options, such as Soft Edges or 3-D Rotation, are listed in Picture Effects on the Picture Styles group as shown in Figure 2.33.

FIGURE 2.33 Quick Changes Using the Picture Styles Gallery ➤

Adjust Graphic Properties

Cropping (or to **crop**) is the process of trimming the edges of an image or other graphical object.

After you insert a graphic or an image, you might find that you need to edit it before using a picture style. One of the most common changes is to *crop* (also called *cropping*), which is the process of trimming edges or other portions of an image or other graphical object that you do not wish to display. Cropping enables you to call attention to a specific area of a graphical element while omitting any unnecessary detail, as shown in Figure 2.34. When you add images to enhance a document, you may find clip art that has more objects than you desire, or you may find an image that has damaged edges that you do not wish to appear in your document. You can solve the problems with these graphics by cropping. The cropping tool is located in the Size group on the Format tab.

FIGURE 2.34 Cropping a graphic ➤

Even though cropping enables you to adjust the amount of a picture that displays, it does not actually delete the portions that are cropped out. Nor does cropping reduce the size of the graphic and the Word document in which it displays. Therefore, if you want to reduce the size of an image so it does not greatly increase the size of the file, you should not use only the crop tool.

Other common adjustments to a graphical object include contrast and/or brightness. Adjusting the *contrast* increases or decreases the difference in dark and light areas of the image. Adjusting the *brightness* lightens or darkens the overall image. These adjustments often are made on a picture taken with a digital camera in poor lighting or if a clip art image is too bright or dull to match other objects in your document. Adjusting contrast or brightness can improve the visibility of subjects in a picture. You may want to increase contrast for a dramatic effect or lower contrast to soften an image. The Brightness and Contrast adjustment is combined in the Adjust group on the Format tab, as shown in Figure 2.35.

Contrast is the difference between light and dark areas of an image.

Brightness is the ratio between lightness and darkness of an image.

FIGURE 2.35 Adjust Contrast and Brightness from Dialog Box ➤

Even though graphical objects add a great deal of visual enhancement to a document, they also can increase the file size of the document. If you add several graphics to a document, you should view the file size before you copy or save it to a portable storage device, and then confirm the device has enough empty space to hold the large file. Additional consideration should be given to files you send as e-mail attachments. Many people have space limitations in their mailboxes, and a document that contains several graphics can fill their space or take a long time to download. To decrease the size of a graphic, you can use the *Compress* feature, which reduces the size of an object. After you select a graphical object, click the Compress Pictures command in the Adjust group on the Picture Tools Format tab to display the Compress Pictures dialog box. Here, you can select from options that enable you to reduce the size of the graphical elements, thus reducing the size of the file when you save. You can also select the option to compress all pictures in the document.

Compress reduces the file size of an object.

New to Office 2010 is the ability to remove the background or other portions of a picture you do not want to keep. When you select a picture and click the Remove Background tool in the Adjust group on the Format tab, Word creates automatic marquee selection area in the picture that determines the *background*, or area to be removed, and the *foreground*, or area to be kept. Word identifies the background selection with magenta coloring. You can then adjust Word's automatic selection by marking areas you want to keep, marking areas you want to remove, and deleting any markings you do not want. You can discard any changes you have made or keep your changes.

The **background** of a picture is the portion of a picture to be removed.

The **foreground** of a picture is the portion of the picture to be kept.

The Picture Tools Format tab offers many graphic editing features, some of which are described in Table 2.5.

TABLE 2.5 Graphic Editing Features

Feature	Button	Description
Height	1.5"	Height of an object in inches.
Width	1.37"	Width of an object in inches.
Crop		Remove unwanted portions of the object from top, bottom, left, or right to adjust size.
Align		Adjust edges of object to line up on right or left margin or center between margins.
Group		Process of selecting multiple objects so you can move and format them together.
Rotate		Ability to change the position of an object by rotating it around its own center.
Wrap Text		Refers to the way text wraps around an object.
Position		Specify location on page where object will reside.
Picture Border		The outline surrounding an object; it can be formatted using color, shapes, or width, or can be set as invisible.
Picture Effects		Enhance an object by adding effects such as shadow, bevel, or reflection.
Compress Pictures		Reduce the file size of an object.
Corrections		Increase or decrease brightness of an object. Increase or decrease difference between black and white colors of an object (contrast).
Color		Apply color alterations for effect, such as grayscale, sepia, or match document content colors.
Artistic Effects		Apply effects that make a picture appear as a painting or sketch.
Remove Background		Remove unwanted background in a picture. Enables customization to define unwanted areas.

Inserting Symbols into a Document

The Symbol command enables you to enter typographic symbols and/or foreign language characters into a document in place of ordinary typing—for example, ® rather than (R), © rather than (c), and ½ and ¼, rather than 1/2 and 1/4. These special characters give a document a very professional look.

You may have already discovered that some of this formatting can be done automatically through the AutoCorrect feature that is built into Word. If, for example, you type (c) it will automatically convert to the copyright symbol. You can use the Symbol command to insert other symbols, such as accented letters like the é in résumé or those in a foreign language such as ¿Cómo está usted?

The installation of Microsoft Office adds a variety of fonts onto your computer, each of which contains various symbols that can be inserted into a document. Selecting "normal text," however, as was done in Figure 2.36, provides access to the accented characters as well as other common symbols. Other fonts—especially the Wingdings, Webdings, and Symbol fonts—contain special symbols, including the Windows logo. The Wingdings, Webdings, and Symbol fonts are among the best-kept secrets in Microsoft Office. Each font contains a variety of symbols that are actually pictures. You can insert any of these symbols into a document as text, or custom bullets, or you can even select the character and enlarge the point size, change the color, then copy the modified character to create a truly original document.

Click to display Symbol gallery

Click to view Symbol dialog box

FIGURE 2.36 Insert Symbol Command ➤

HANDS-ON EXERCISES

4 Graphical Objects

To finalize the Annual Summary for Simserv-Pitka Industries, you decide to include pictures of the two new executives. As is the case with most pictures inserted into a document, they need to be resized and formatted so they will display next to the paragraphs where you insert them. You also insert a euro symbol into the document, and finish by inserting a page number in the footer.

Skills covered: Insert Picture Objects • Change Picture Formatting • Insert a Symbol

---

STEP 1 ▶ INSERT PICTURE OBJECTS

The new executives hired to lead Simserv-Pitka are important assets to the company, so you want to honor them by placing their pictures in the Annual Summary. You display the picture of each person beside the paragraph that describes his or her position and credentials. Refer to Figure 2.37 as you complete Step 1.

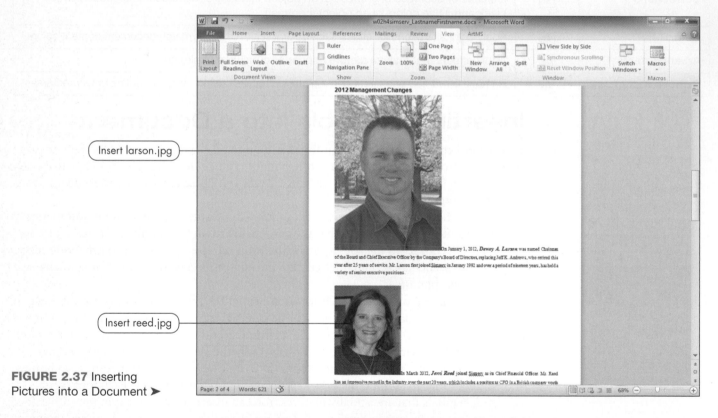

FIGURE 2.37 Inserting Pictures into a Document ➤

a. Open *w02h3simserv_LastnameFirstname* if you closed it at the end of Hands-On Exercise 3, and save it as **w02h4simserv_LastnameFirstname**, changing *h3* to *h4*.

b. Click to the left of the *2012 Management Changes* paragraph heading. Press **Ctrl+Enter** to insert a page break. Click the **Insert tab**, and then click **Picture** in the Illustrations group. Navigate to the location where files for this book are stored, and then double-click **larson.jpg** to insert the picture of Dewey A. Larson into your document.

> **TROUBLESHOOTING:** If the graphic files for these photos do not display, click the File type arrow, and then select All Files (*.*) so all file types display rather than just Word documents. Also, be certain you are clicking Insert Picture, not File, Open, to insert the graphic files.

c. Click to the left of the text *In March 2012* in the *2012 Management Changes* section. Press **Enter** to insert a blank line. Click the **Insert tab**, if necessary, and then click **Picture**. This time, double-click **reed.jpg** to insert the picture of Jerri Reed into your document. Compare your results to Figure 2.37.

d. Save the document.

CHANGE PICTURE FORMATTING

After you insert the pictures, you must adjust them, by changing size or cropping, so they are not disproportionate in size to the rest of the text in the document. You also want to adjust the wrapping style of each picture so you have the control you need to position them with the paragraphs they support. You correct colors as needed, and finally, for effect, you decide to add a border around the pictures. Refer to Figure 2.38 as you complete Step 2.

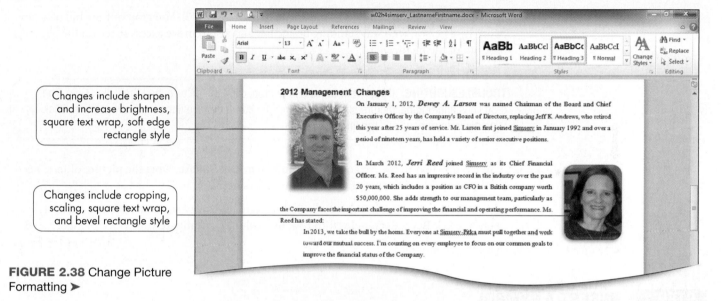

Changes include sharpen and increase brightness, square text wrap, soft edge rectangle style

Changes include cropping, scaling, square text wrap, and bevel rectangle style

FIGURE 2.38 Change Picture Formatting ➤

a. Select the picture of Dewey A. Larson. Click the **Height arrow** in the Size group on the Picture Tools Format tab until the height is reduced to *2.0"*.

The width will change in proportion to the height, which should display approximately 1.38".

b. Click **Corrections** in the Adjust group, and then click **Picture Corrections Options**. In the *Brightness and Contrast* section, decrease **Brightness** to –5%, and increase **Contrast** to 5%. Click the **Close button**.

c. Click **WrapText** in the Arrange group, and then select **Square**.

The paragraph text displays around the right side of the picture.

d. Click the **More button** in the Picture Styles group to display the entire Picture quick style gallery. Click **Soft Edge Rectangle** (second row, first column).

e. Use your mouse to drag the picture down slightly so the paragraph heading displays on the left margin and the picture displays on the left of the paragraph text only.

TIP Nudging a Picture

You can use the arrow keys on your keyboard to move a graphical image around a document in very small increments.

f. Click **Compress Pictures** in the Adjust group. Click **Apply only to this picture** to deselect the option, and then click **OK**.

Most digital picture files are quite large and can increase the size of the document substantially when you insert them. The Compression feature is vital to use in that situation. This picture of Dewey A. Larson is not extremely large, but you decide to compress the picture and make sure the size of the document stays small. By deselecting the option in this step, all graphics in the document will compress as well.

g. Select the picture of Jerri Reed. Click the **Size Dialog Box Launcher**. In the *Scale* section, click **Lock aspect ratio**, if necessary. Click the **height arrow** until *70%* displays. Click **OK**.

Because you locked the aspect ratio, which preserves proportions as the picture is resized, the Width percentage changed automatically when you reduced the height.

h. Click **Crop**, and then drag the crop lines inward from right, left, and bottom until she displays from the shoulders up. When complete, press **Crop** again to remove the crop lines.

The size of the picture should be approximately 1.6″ by 1.25″. You crop out the bill of a cap worn by a person who was standing beside her and also remove excess space on the left and bottom of the picture.

> **TROUBLESHOOTING:** If you want to revise the crop, click the picture, and then click Crop. The crop lines and original picture size display, and you can move the lines to a new position. Click Crop again to remove all crop lines.

i. Click **Wrap Text** in the Arrange group, and then click **Square**. Drag the picture of Jerri Reed to the right side of the paragraph that introduces her.

j. Click the **More button** in the Picture Styles group to display the entire Picture quick style gallery. Click **Bevel Rectangle** (fifth row, first column). Compare your work to Figure 2.38.

k. Save the document.

STEP 3 ▶ INSERT A SYMBOL

The financial manager at Simserv-Pitka reminds you that it is appropriate to use the correct currency symbols when referring to monetary assets in a document such as this, especially when the currency is not U.S. dollars. To conform to that rule, you change the symbol used to reference the value of a European company to the euro instead of using the dollar symbol. To complete the document, you insert a page number in the footer of the document. Even though it is short, page numbering helps the reader follow the order of the document. Refer to Figure 2.39 as you complete Step 3.

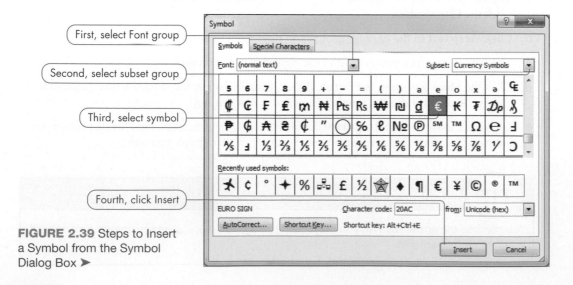

FIGURE 2.39 Steps to Insert a Symbol from the Symbol Dialog Box ➤

a. Select **$** in the second sentence in the paragraph that describes the new CFO, Jerri Reed. Press **Delete** to remove the dollar sign.

b. Click the **Insert tab**, and then click **Symbol** in the Symbols group. Click **More Symbols** to view the Symbol dialog box, as seen in Figure 2.39.

c. Change the Font group to (**normal text**), if necessary, and then change the Subset to **Currency Symbols**. Click the **Euro sign (€)**, click **Insert**, and then click the **Close button**.

When you click Insert, the symbol appears in your document at the location of your cursor. While the Symbol dialog box is open, you can return to your document, move your cursor, then return to the symbol dialog box and insert other symbols before you close.

d. Click **Page Number** in the Header and Footer group, hover the mouse over *Bottom of Page*, and then scroll down and select **Accent Bar 4**. Click **Close Header and Footer**.

e. Save and close *w02h4simserve_LastnameFirstname*, and submit based on your instructor's directions.

After reading this chapter, you have accomplished the following objectives:

1. **Apply font attributes through the Font dialog box.** Formatting occurs at the character, paragraph, or section level. The Font dialog box enables you to change the spacing of the characters and you can change attributes including font size, font color, underline color, and effects. Use the character spacing options to control horizontal spacing between letters and also adjust the scale, position, and kerning of characters. You can quickly modify the capitalization and text highlight color from the Home tab.

2. **Control word wrap.** Occasionally, text wraps in an undesirable location in your document, or you just want to keep words together for better readability. To keep hyphenated words together on one line, use a nonbreaking hyphen to replace the regular hyphen. You also can keep words together on one line by inserting a nonbreaking space instead of using the spacebar.

3. **Set off paragraphs with tabs, borders, lists, and columns.** You can change appearance and add interest to documents by using paragraph formatting options. Tabs enable you to set markers in the document to use for aligning text. Borders and shading enable you to use boxes and/or shading to highlight an area of your document. A bulleted or numbered list helps to organize information by emphasizing or ordering important topics. Columns add interest by formatting text into side-by-side vertical blocks of text.

4. **Apply paragraph formats.** The Paragraph dialog box contains many formatting options, such as alignment. Another option to adjust the distance from margins is indention. Line spacing determines the space between lines in a document, such as single or double, and can be customized. You also can specify an amount of space to insert before or after a paragraph, which is more efficient than pressing Enter. Widow/Orphan control prevents a single line from displaying at the top or bottom of a page, separate from the rest of a paragraph.

5. **Understand styles.** A style is a set of formatting instructions that has been saved under a distinct name. Styles are created at the character or paragraph level and provide a consistent appearance to similar elements throughout a document. Styles provide the foundation to use other tools such as outlines and the table of contents.

6. **Create and modify styles.** You can modify any existing style to change the formatting of all text defined by that style. You can even create a new style for use in the current or any other document.

7. **Format a graphical object.** Graphics are often added to enhance a document. After you insert one, a variety of tools can make it fit and display where you want—such as changing height and width, scaling, or cropping unwanted portions. You can position the graphic more exactly by wrapping text, and you can use the Picture Styles gallery to add borders or reflections. You can refine imperfections or add creative touches to pictures using features to sharpen, change brightness, and adjust contrast. You can compress a graphic to reduce its size as well as the size of the document.

8. **Insert symbols into a document.** Insert Symbol makes it easy to place typographic characters in a document. The symbols can be taken from any font and can be displayed in any point size.

KEY TERMS

Background *p. 200*
Bar tab *p. 173*
Border *p. 174*
Brightness *p. 200*
Bulleted list *p. 175*
Center tab *p. 173*
Change Case *p. 167*
Character spacing *p. 166*
Character style *p. 187*
Column *p. 176*
Compress *p. 200*
Contrast *p. 200*
Cropping or crop *p. 199*
Decimal tab *p. 173*
First line indent *p. 179*
Font *p. 164*
Foreground *p. 200*

Hanging indent *p. 179*
Hidden text *p. 166*
Highlighter *p. 167*
Horizontal alignment *p. 178*
Kerning *p. 166*
Leader character *p. 173*
Left tab *p. 173*
Line spacing *p. 179*
Monospaced typeface *p. 164*
Multilevel list *p. 175*
Nonbreaking hyphen *p. 168*
Nonbreaking space *p. 168*
Numbered list *p. 175*
OpenType *p. 166*
Orphan *p. 180*
Outline view *p. 190*
Paragraph spacing *p. 179*

Paragraph style *p. 187*
Picture Styles *p. 199*
Position *p. 166*
Proportional typeface *p. 164*
Right tab *p. 173*
Sans serif typeface *p. 164*
Scale or scaling *p. 166*
Serif typeface *p. 164*
Shading *p. 174*
Sizing handles *p. 197*
Style *p. 187*
Tab *p. 172*
Text wrapping style *p. 198*
Type style *p. 164*
Typeface *p. 164*
Typography *p. 164*
Widow *p. 180*

1. Which of the following is not true about typeface?

   (a) A serif typeface helps the eye connect one letter with the next.

   (b) A monospaced typeface allocates space according to the width of the character.

   (c) A san serif typeface is more effective with titles and headlines.

   (d) A typeface is a complete set of characters.

2. What is the easiest way to change the alignment of five paragraphs scattered throughout a document, each of which is formatted with the same style?

   (a) Select the paragraphs individually, then click the appropriate alignment button.

   (b) Use CTRL to select all of the paragraphs, then click the appropriate alignment button on the Home tab.

   (c) Change the format of the existing style, which changes the paragraphs.

   (d) Retype the paragraphs according to the new specifications.

3. If you want to be sure the date June 21, 2012, does not word wrap what should you do?

   (a) Use a nonbreaking hyphen in place of the comma.

   (b) Use expanded spacing on the whole number.

   (c) Use nonbreaking spaces between the month, date, and year.

   (d) Press Ctrl+Enter before you type the date.

4. Which wrap style enables text to wrap around the graphic frame that surrounds the image?

   (a) Square

   (b) Tight

   (c) Behind Text

   (d) Right and Left

5. A(n) _____ occurs when the first line of a paragraph is isolated at the bottom of a page and the rest of the paragraph continues on the next page.

   (a) widow

   (b) section break

   (c) footer

   (d) orphan

6. Which of the following is a false statement about the Outline view?

   (a) It can be collapsed to display only headings.

   (b) It can be expanded to show the entire document.

   (c) It requires the application of styles.

   (d) It is used to create a multilevel list.

7. What happens if you modify the Body Text style in a Word document?

   (a) Only the paragraph where the insertion point is located is changed.

   (b) All paragraphs in the document will be changed.

   (c) Only those paragraphs formatted with the Body Text style will be changed.

   (d) It is not possible to change a Word default style such as Body Text.

8. If you want to display text in side-by-side sections, what feature should you use to format the text?

   (a) Styles

   (b) Borders

   (c) Multilevel lists

   (d) Columns

9. Which of the following is a true statement regarding indents?

   (a) Indents are measured from the edge of the page.

   (b) The left, right, and first line indents must be set to the same value.

   (c) The insertion point can be anywhere in the paragraph when indents are set.

   (d) Indents must be set within the Paragraph dialog box.

10. The spacing in an existing multipage document is changed from single spacing to double spacing throughout the document. What can you say about the number of hard and soft page breaks before and after the formatting change?

    (a) The number of soft page breaks is the same, but the number and/or position of the hard page breaks are different.

    (b) The number of hard page breaks is the same, but the number and/or position of the soft page breaks are different.

    (c) The number and position of both hard and soft page breaks are the same.

    (d) The number and position of both hard and soft page breaks are different.

1 Engler, Guccione, & Partners

You are the Marketing Director for the Architect firm Engler, Guccione, & Partners. Lately, the firm has less work due to a reduction in construction spending. In order to bring in new business, you design a marketing plan to pursue new customers by advertising your ability to consult in legal cases. The plan is typed and in a raw form, so you use formatting features to enhance the document and impress the partners with your own skills. This exercise follows the same set of skills as used in Hands-On Exercises 1, 2, 3, and 4 in the chapter. Refer to Figure 2.40 as you complete this exercise.

FIGURE 2.40 Format a Marketing Plan ➤

a. Open *w02p1engler* and save the document as **w02p1engler_LastnameFirstname**.

b. Add a page border around the text by completing the following steps:
   - Click the **Home tab**, and then click the **Borders arrow** in the Paragraph group.
   - Select **Borders and Shading** to open the dialog box.
   - Click the **Page Border tab**, and then click **Box** in the *Setting* section.
   - Scroll down and select the **ninth** style—a double line border with a thick line outside and a thin line inside.
   - Click **OK** to close the Borders and Shading dialog box.

c. Click **Ctrl+A** to select the whole document. Click the **Font arrow** in the Font group on the Home tab, and then select **Arial**.

d. Select the first three lines, which make up the document title, and complete the following steps:
   - Click **Heading 1** in the Quick Styles gallery.
   - Right-click the **Heading 1 entry** in the Quick styles pane, and then select **Modify**.
   - Change the alignment to **Center**.
   - Change the font to **Arial**.
   - Click **Format, Font**, and then click **Small caps**. Click **OK** to close the Font dialog box.
   - Click **Format, Paragraph**, and then click the **Indents and Spacing tab**, if necessary.
   - Reduce the **Spacing Before** to **0 pt**.
   - Increase **Spacing After** to **6 pt**.

- Click **OK** to close the Paragraph dialog box.
- Click **OK** to close the Modify Style dialog box.

e. Place the insertion point on the blank line that follows the third line of the title. Click the **Borders and Shading arrow**, and then click **Horizontal Line**.

f. Select the three lines under the *Primary Tasks:* paragraph heading, and then click the **Bullets arrow** in the Paragraph group. Click **Define New Bullet**, click **Symbol** to open the Symbol dialog box, and then select **Webdings** from the **Font list**. Select the symbol that resembles a computer network (character code 194) located in the third row, third column, and then click **OK**. Click **OK** to create the bullet list, and then close the Define New Bullet dialog box.

g. Create a numbered list for the General Tasks by completing the following steps:
- Right-click the italicized word *Resumes* directly under *General Tasks*, point to *Styles* in the menu, and then click **Select Text with Similar Formatting** to select all italicized headings.
- Click the **Numbering arrow**, and then select the format that displays lowercase alphabet numbering (*a.*, *b.*, *c.*).
- Select the four sub-points for *Resumes*, and then click **Numbering** in the paragraph group. Click **Increase Indent** to display them as a multilevel list item.
- Double-click the **Format Painter** in the Clipboard group. Select each set of sub-points in the remainder of the numbered list. Press **Esc** to turn off the format painter.

h. Make the bullet lists easier to read by completing the following steps:
- Right-click the first General Task, *Resumes*. Point to *Styles* in the menu, and then click **Select Text with Similar Formatting** to select all italicized headings.
- Click the **Paragraph Dialog Box Launcher**, and then click the **Spacing Before arrow** until *12 pt* displays.
- Click **Don't add space between paragraphs of the same style** to remove the check mark from the check box. Click **OK**.
- Select item number five, *Email campaigns*. Click the **Paragraph Dialog Box Launcher**, and then click the **Line and Page Breaks tab**. Click **Keep with next**, and then click **OK**.
- Select the six sub-points for item five. Click the **Paragraph Dialog Box Launcher**, click **Keep with next**, click **Keep lines together**, and then click **OK**. This prevents the break, which enables one paragraph to split between two pages.

i. Press **Ctrl+End** to move the cursor to the end of the document. To insert a graphical image complete the following steps:
- Click the **Insert tab**, click **Picture**, browse to the data files, and then double-click **englerlogo**.
- Click the **Size Dialog Box Launcher**, and then reduce the Scale Height to **25%**. Click **OK**.
- Click **Position**, and then click **Position in Bottom Center with Square Text Wrapping**.
- Click the **More button** in the Picture Quick Styles group to display the entire Picture Styles gallery.
- Click **Reflected Perspective Right** (fifth row, third column) to apply a border and reflective effects around the graphic.
- Click **Compress Pictures** in the Adjust group, and then click **OK**.

j. Click the **Insert tab**, click **Page Number**, point to *Bottom of Page*, and select **Bold Numbers 1**. Click **Close Header and Footer**.

k. Press **Ctrl+Home**. Click the **Styles Dialog Box Launcher**. Click **Options**, and then click the **Select styles to show arrow**. Click **All styles**, and then click **OK**. Right-click the **Emphasis style** in the Styles gallery, and then select **Select All 3 Instance(s)**. Scroll down the Styles pane, and then select **Heading 2** to change all headings to a new style. Close the Style pane.

l. Place the insertion point on the left side of the paragraph under the *Goal:* heading. Press **Tab**. Press **Ctrl+T** to indent the whole paragraph the same distance as the tab setting.

m. Compare your work to Figure 2.40. Save and close the file, and submit based on your instructor's directions.

2 Queen City Medical Equipment

You are the training coordinator for Queen City Medical Equipment, and your responsibilities include tracking all employees' continuing education efforts. The company urges employees to pursue educational opportunities that add experience and knowledge to their positions, including taking any certification exams that enhance their credentials. The human resources director wants you to provide him with a list of employees who have met minimum qualifications to take an upcoming certification exam. In its present state the memo prints on two pages; you will format the memo using columns in order to save paper and display the entire list on one page. This exercise follows the same set of skills as used in Hands-On Exercises 1 and 2 in the chapter. Refer to Figure 2.41 as you complete this exercise.

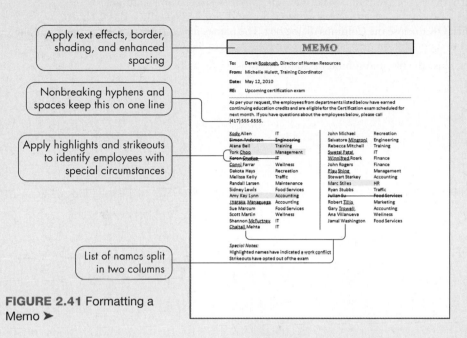

Apply text effects, border, shading, and enhanced spacing

Nonbreaking hyphens and spaces keep this on one line

Apply highlights and strikeouts to identify employees with special circumstances

List of names split in two columns

FIGURE 2.41 Formatting a Memo ➤

a. Open *w02p2memo* and save it as **w02p2memo_LastnameFirstname.**

b. Select the word *Memo,* and then complete the following steps:
   - Click **Center** in the Paragraph group, click **Change Case** in the Font group, and then select **UPPERCASE**. Click the **Font arrow**, and then select **Times New Roman**.
   - Click the **Font Size arrow**, and then select **24**. Click **Text Effects**, and then click **Gradient Fill - Gray, Outline - Gray** (third row, third column). Click the **Font Dialog Box Launcher**, click the **Advanced tab**, click the **Spacing arrow**, select **Expanded**, click **By**, and then type the number **2**. Click **OK** to close the Font dialog box.
   - Click the **Borders arrow** in the Paragraph group, and then click **Borders and Shading**. Click the **Box setting**, click the **Width arrow**, and then click **2 1/4.**
   - Click the **Shading tab**, click the **Fill arrow**, and then select **White, Background 1, Darker 5%** (second row, first column). Click **OK** to close the dialog box.

c. Select the highlighted text **Your Name Here*,* and then replace it with your name. Select the highlighted text **Insert current date*,* and then type today's date. Select the job title *director,* which follows Derek Rosbrugh's name, hold down **Ctrl**, select **human resources**, click **Change Case** in the Font group, and then select **Capitalize Each Word**.

d. Select the space between the area code *(417)* and phone number *(555),* and then press **Shift+Ctrl+Spacebar** to insert a nonbreaking space. Select the hyphen in the middle of the phone number, between *555* and *5555,* and then press **Shift+Ctrl+Hyphen** to insert a nonbreaking hyphen. Now the entire phone number should display together on one line.

e. Select the line that contains *Alana Bell* to select her name and department. On the Mini toolbar, click the **Text Highlight Color arrow**, and then click the **Yellow square**. You do this to show which employees have a work conflict and will be unable to sit for the upcoming certification exam. To identify other people who fall into that category, double-click the **Format Painter**, and then click the names *York Choo, Amy Kay Lynn,* and *Marc Stiles.* Each name is now highlighted in yellow. Press **Esc** to turn off the format painter.

f. Select *Simon Anderson*, hold down **Ctrl**, and then select *Karen Crudup* and *Julian Su.* Release Ctrl, and then click **Strikethrough** in the Font group. These employees are opting out of the exam for personal reasons, and we need to identify them as well.

g. Insert tabs to separate the names and departments by completing the following steps:
   - Click **Show/Hide (¶)** in the Paragraph group to display the tab characters.
   - Select the list of people, click the **Paragraph Dialog Box launcher**, and then click **Tabs**.
   - Type **1.5** in the **Tab stop position**, and then click **Set**.
   - Click **OK** to close the dialog box. The departments now align in a column on the right side of the employee names. Click **Show/Hide (¶)** again to turn off the formatting marks.

h. Display the list of employees in two columns, so you can print the memo on one sheet of paper instead of two, by completing these steps:
- Select all the names.
- Click the **Page Layout tab**, click **Columns**, and then select **More Columns**.
- Click **Two** in the *Presets* section in the Columns dialog box, and then check **Line between**.
- Click **OK** to close the Columns dialog box. The names now display in two columns, and the entire memo fits on one page. Compare your work to Figure 2.41.

i. Save and close the file, and submit based on your instructor's directions.

MID-LEVEL EXERCISES

1 Technology Training Conference

You created a status report to inform committee members about an upcoming conference of which you are in charge. You want the report to look attractive and professional, so you decide to create and apply your own styles rather than use those already available in Word. You create a paragraph style named Side Heading to format the headings, and then you create a character style named Session to format the names of the conference sessions and apply these formats to document text. You then copy these two styles to the Normal template.

a. Open *w02m1conference* and save it as **w02m1conference_LastnameFirstname**.

b. Create a new paragraph style named **Side Heading** using the following properties: Style based on is **Normal**, style for following paragraph is **Normal**. Font properties are **Arial, 14 pt, Bold**; and font color is **Red, Accent 2, Darker 50%.**

c. Set the following paragraph formats for this style: **12 pt Before** paragraph spacing, **6 pt After** paragraph spacing.

d. Apply the **Side Heading style** to the two-line report title, and then **Center** both lines. Apply the **Side Heading style** to the three headings *The Committee*, *Training Sessions*, and *Training Goal*.

e. Create a new character style named **Session** using the following specifications: **Bold** and **Red, Accent 2, Darker 50%** font color. Apply the **Session style** to the following words in the highlighted area: *Word*, *Web Page Development*, *Multimedia*, and *Presentation Graphics*.

f. Use the highlighted text to create a bulleted list. Remove the highlighting, and then indent the bullet list **.8"** from the right side.

g. Modify the Side Heading style to use the **Small caps font effect** and expand spacing by **1.5 pt**.

h. Save *w02m1conference_LastnameFirstname*.

i. Open the Manage Styles dialog box, and then export the **Side Heading** and **Session styles** from *w02m1conference_ LastnameFirstname.docx* to *Normal.dotm*.

j. Open a new document. Display the Styles pane, if necessary, and then verify that the Session and Side Heading styles display. After confirming they are imported, delete the two styles from the *Normal.dotm* list. If working in a computer lab, this resets the Normal template for the next user. Close the blank document without saving it.

k. Insert a nonbreaking hyphen and a nonbreaking space in the phone number that displays at the end of the report.

l. Save and close *w02m1conference_LastnameFirstname*, and submit based on your instructor's directions.

2 Association for Administrative Professionals

You are president of the Association for Administrative Professionals and you recently composed a letter to welcome new members. Now, you want to make the letter look more professional by applying paragraph formatting, such as alignment, paragraph spacing, and a paragraph border and shading. In addition, you want to create a customized bulleted list that describes plans for the organization and insert the organization's logo.

a. Open the document *w02m2welcome* and save it as **w02m2welcome_LastnameFirstname**.

b. Change the capitalization of the recipient Emily Gibson and her address so that each word is capitalized and the state abbreviation displays in uppercase. Change Ken's name to your name in the signature block.

c. Apply **Justified alignment** to each paragraph in the document. Delete the asterisk (*), and then create a customized bulleted list, selecting a picture bullet of your choice. Type the following items in the bulleted list:

Asking administrative professionals to be guest speakers at meetings.
Participating in the regional and national conferences.
Shadowing an administrative professional for a day.
Finding internships for members of the organization.

d. Select text from the salutation *Dear Emily:* through the last paragraph that ends with *next meeting.* Set **12 pt spacing After paragraph**.

e. Use the **Small Cap font effect** on *Association for Administrative Professionals* in the first paragraph.

f. Replace the word *cent* in the title of the presentation with the cent symbol found in the (normal text) Latin-1 Supplement subset.

g. Select the italicized lines of text that give date, time, and location of the meeting. Remove the italics, and then complete the following:
   - Increase left and right indents to **1.5″**, and set **0 pt spacing After paragraph**.
   - Apply a double-line border using the color **Red, Accent 2, Darker 50%**, **3/4 pt border width**, and **Red, Accent 2, Lighter 40% shading** color.

h. Click the line containing the text *Room 255*, and set **12 pt spacing After** paragraph.

i. Select the entire document, and then change the font to **12-pt Bookman Old Style**. If necessary, delete the extra tab formatting mark to the left of *Community College* to prevent it from word wrapping.

j. Use nonbreaking hyphens and nonbreaking spaces to display the telephone number on one line.

CREATIVE CASE

k. Insert the graphic **logo.jpg** and display it in the top-right corner of the document. Resize the graphic so it does not display larger than 1.6″ x 2.0″. Apply the **Reflected Round Rectangle style** to the logo. Increase the brightness settings by **15%**. Apply **Color settings** or **Artistic Effects** to your preference.

l. Save and close the file, and submit based on your instructor's directions.

In this project, you work with a document prepared for managers involved in the hiring process. This report analyzes the validity of the interview process and suggests that selection does not depend only on quality information, but on the quality of the interpretation of information. The document requires formatting to enhance readability and important information; you will use skills from this chapter to format multiple levels of headings and figures. To make it easy for readers to locate topics in your document, create and use various supplemental document components such as a table of contents and index.

Applying Styles

This document is ready for enhancements, and the styles feature is a good tool that enables you to add them quickly and easily.

a. Open *w02c1interview* and save it as **w02c1interview_LastnameFirstname**.

b. Create a paragraph style named **Title_Page_1** with these formats: **22-pt font size**, **Shadow font effect Offset Diagonal Top Right**, **character spacing expanded by 2 pt**, **horizontally centered**, using Font color **Dark Blue, Text 2, Darker 50%**. Apply this style to the first line of the document, *Understanding the Personal Interview*.

c. Create a paragraph style named **Title_Page_2** based on the first style you created, with these additional formats: **20-pt font size**, **custom color 66, 4, 66**. Apply this style to the subtitle, *A Study for Managers Involved in the Hiring Process*.

d. Replace the * in the middle of the first page with your name. Change the capitalization for your name to uppercase.

e. Select the remainder of the text in the document that follows your name, starting with *Understanding the Personal Interview*. **Justify** the alignment of all paragraphs and change line spacing to **1.15**. Place your cursor on the left side of the title *Understanding the Personal Interview*, and then insert a page break so the document starts at the top of the page.

f. Apply the **Heading 1 style** to the main headings throughout the document and the **Heading 2 style** to the paragraph headings, such as *Introduction* and *Pre-interview Impressions*.

g. Modify the Heading 2 style to use **Dark Red font color**.

Formatting the Paragraphs

Next, you will apply paragraph formatting to the document. These format options will further increase the readability and attractiveness of your document.

a. Apply a bulleted list format for the five-item list in the *Introduction*. Use the symbol of a four-sided star from the Wingdings group (symbol 170) for the bullet.

b. Select the second paragraph in the *Introduction* section that begins with *Personal interviewing continues*, and then apply these formats: **0.6″ left and right indent, 6 pt spacing after the paragraph**, **boxed 1½ pt border using the color Blue, Accent 1, Darker 25%**, and the shading color **Blue, Accent 1, Lighter 80%**.

c. Apply the first numbered-list format (1., 2., 3.) for the three phases in the *Pre-Interview Impressions* section.

d. Select the second and third paragraphs in *The Unfavorable Information Effect* section, and then display them in two columns with a line between the columns.

Inserting Graphics and Page Numbers

To put the finishing touches on your document, you will add graphics that enhance the explanations given in some paragraphs. Captions are already in place for the graphics, but final formatting must occur to display them properly. Additionally, you will create a footer to display page numbers in this long document.

a. Insert the picture file **perceptions.jpg** at the beginning of the line that contains the caption *Figure 1: Perception in the Interview* and that displays at the bottom of page 2. Center the graphic horizontally, change text wrapping, and then insert any line breaks necessary so the graphic displays on a line by itself just above the caption. Use scaling to reduce the size to 75% of the original size. Apply the **Rounded Diagonal Corner**, **White picture style**.

b. Insert the picture file **phases.jpg** at the beginning of the line that contains the caption *Figure 2: Diboye's Interview phases*. Change text wrapping, and then insert any line breaks necessary so the graphic displays on a line by itself just above the caption. Apply **Offset Center shadow effect** to the graphic.

c. Display a page number in the footer of each page using the **Accent Bar 4 format**. Prevent the footer from displaying on the title page, and then start numbering on the page that follows the title page.

d. Review the entire document, and if necessary, use **Keep Lines Together controls** to prevent headings and paragraphs from being separated across pages. Invoke the **Widow/Orphan control** also.

e. Insert nonbreaking spaces and nonbreaking hyphens where appropriate.

f. Display the document in Outline view. Collapse all paragraphs so only the headings display.

g. Save and close the file, and submit based on your instructor's directions.

Review the Skills

GENERAL CASE

You learned many skills and features of Word 2010 in this chapter. Take a few minutes to refresh yourself on these and other features by creating an outline of this chapter. Use the Multilevel list feature to type out each heading and subheading, and write a short paragraph to summarize the skills. Adjust tabs as necessary so the second and third level headings are indented at least .5″ beyond the first. Use styles for each type of heading so they appear different (as they do in the chapter). Save your work as **w02b1outline_LastnameFirstname** and submit based on your instructor's directions.

The Invitation

RESEARCH CASE

Search the Internet for an upcoming local event at your school or in your community and produce the perfect invitation. You can invite people to a charity ball, a fun run, or to a fraternity party. Your color printer and abundance of fancy fonts, as well as your ability to insert page borders, enable you to do anything a professional printer can do. Save your work as **w02b2invitation_LastnameFirstname** and submit based on your instructor's directions.

A Fundraising Letter

DISASTER RECOVERY

Each year, you update a letter to several community partners soliciting support for an auction. The auction raises funds for your organization, and your letter should impress your supporters. Open *w02b3auction* and notice how unprofessional and unorganized the document looks so far. You must make changes immediately to improve the appearance. Consider replacing much of the formatting that is in place now and instead using columns for auction items, bullets to draw attention to the list of forms, page borders, and pictures or Clip Art—and that is just for starters! Save your work as **w02b3auction_LastnameFirstname** and submit based on your instructor's directions.

3 COLLABORATION AND RESEARCH

Communicating Easily and Producing Professional Papers

CASE STUDY | Marketing Plan for Take Note Paperie

Watch the **Set-up Video** for this Case Study!

Your marketing professor assigned you to work with Rachel Starkey and your team project is to create a marketing plan for a new small business. You and Rachel have chosen a custom printing service named Take Note Paperie as the company for which you will develop a plan.

The research is complete, and the document is typed. Rachel last updated the document and has sent it to you to view and modify as you see fit. You check the comments Rachel made and perform modifications based on her notes. You also notice it is lacking vital features of a research paper that all professors require, such as the table of contents, bibliography, and table of figures, so you plan to add those. However, you also want to provide Rachel the opportunity to view your changes to the document and to provide feedback before you submit it for grading, so you leave a note for her as well. You hope this is the last round of changes before you turn it in and earn an A!

OBJECTIVES AFTER YOU READ THIS CHAPTER, YOU WILL BE ABLE TO:

1. Insert comments in a document *p.218*

2. Track changes in a document *p.221*

3. Acknowledge a source *p.229*

4. Create and modify footnotes and endnotes *p.232*

5. Insert a table of contents and index *p.237*

6. Add other reference tables *p.241*

7. Create cross-references *p.243*

Document Revisions

This chapter introduces several Word features that you can use for research papers while in school. These same skills will also be useful as you work with others on collaborative projects. One of the first things you need to do when working on a collaborative project is workgroup editing, where suggested revisions from one or more individuals can be stored electronically within a document. This feature enables the original author to review each suggestion individually before it is incorporated into the final version of the document, and further, enables multiple people to work on the same document in collaboration with one another. Another feature that is useful in workgroup settings enables you to insert comments in a document for other editors to view and respond to.

In this section, you will insert comments to provide feedback or to pose questions to the document author. Then you will track editing changes you make so that others can see your suggested edits.

Inserting Comments in a Document

> In today's organizational environment, teams of people with diverse backgrounds, skills, and knowledge prepare documentation.... When you work with a team, you can use collaboration tools in Word such as the Comments feature.

In today's organizational environment, teams of people with diverse backgrounds, skills, and knowledge prepare documentation. Team members work together while planning, developing, writing, and editing important documents. If you have not participated in a team project yet, most likely you will. When you work with a team, you can use collaboration tools in Word such as the Comments feature. A *comment* is a note or annotation that appears in the document to ask a question or provide a suggestion about the content of a document. Frequently, the comment appears in a balloon on the side of the document.

A comment is a note or annotation about the content of a document.

Before you use the comments and other collaboration features, you should click File, click Options, and then view the General section of the Word Options dialog box to confirm that your name and initials display as the user. Word uses this information to identify the person who uses collaboration tools, such as Comments. If you are in a lab environment, you might not have permission to modify settings or change the User name; however, you should be able to change these settings on a home computer.

Add a Comment

You add comments to a document to remind a reviewer, or yourself, of action that needs to be taken. To insert a comment, select a word or phrase where you want it to appear, display the Review tab, click New Comment in the Comments group to open the markup balloon (see Figure 3.1), and then type the text of the comment. If you do not select anything prior to clicking New Comment, Word assigns the comment to the word or object closest to the insertion point. When you click outside the comment area, the comment is recorded in the document. Most comments display in *markup balloons*, which are colored circles in the margin with a line drawn to the object of the comment. After you complete the comment, the text and markup balloon are highlighted in the color assigned to the reviewer.

A markup balloon is a colored circle that contains comments and displays in the margin.

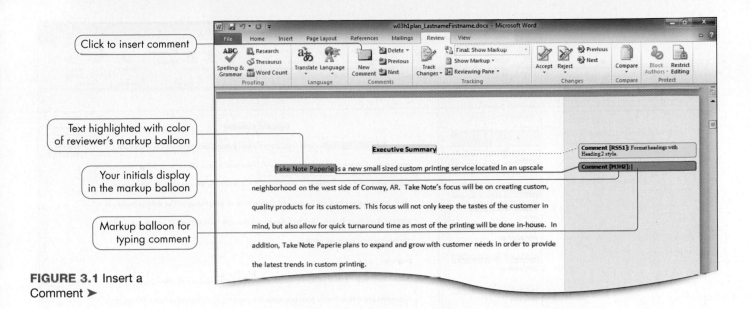

Click to insert comment

Text highlighted with color of reviewer's markup balloon

Your initials display in the markup balloon

Markup balloon for typing comment

FIGURE 3.1 Insert a Comment ➤

TIP Response Comments

You can build a dialog through comments. If you select or put the insertion point in a comment markup balloon, and then click New Comment, a new markup balloon displays adjoining the first balloon, and *R1* will follow the reviewer's initials that display inside. The *R* stands for response, so the reader knows it is a response to the original comment.

View, Modify, and Delete Comments

The **Reviewing Pane** displays comments and changes made to a document.

Comments appear in markup balloons in Print Layout, Full Screen Reading, and Web Layout views. In Draft view, comments appear as tags embedded in the document; when you hover the cursor over the tag, it displays the comment. In any view, you can display the *Reviewing Pane*, which displays all comments and editorial changes made to the main document. To display the Reviewing Pane vertically on the left side of the document, as shown in Figure 3.2, click Reviewing Pane on the Review tab. To hide the Reviewing Pane click Reviewing Pane again—it is a toggle. You can display the Reviewing Pane horizontally at the bottom when you click the Reviewing Pane arrow. The Reviewing Pane is useful when the comments are too long to display completely in a markup balloon.

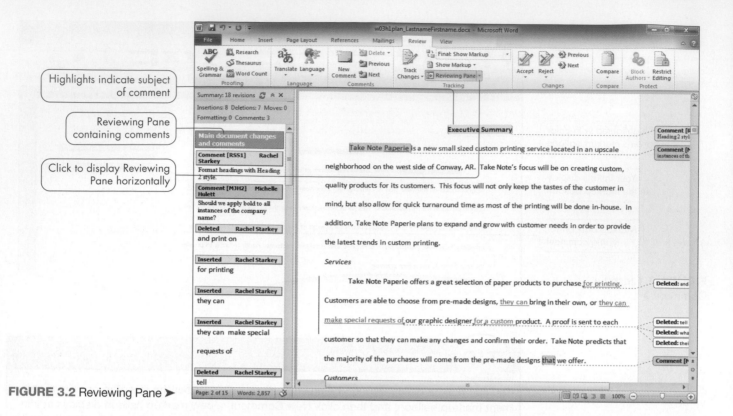

Highlights indicate subject of comment

Reviewing Pane containing comments

Click to display Reviewing Pane horizontally

FIGURE 3.2 Reviewing Pane ➤

Show Markup enables you to view document revisions by reviewers.

If you do not see comments initially, click Show Markup on the Review tab and confirm that Comments is toggled on. The *Show Markup* feature enables you to view document revisions by reviewers. It also enables you to choose which type of revisions you want to view such as Comments, Ink annotations (made on a tablet PC), insertions and deletions, or formatting changes. Each can be toggled on or off, and you can view several at the same time, as shown in Figure 3.3. Show Markup also color-codes each revision or comment by using a different color for each reviewer. If you want to view only changes by a particular reviewer, click Show Markup, click Reviewers, and deselect all reviewers except the one you prefer.

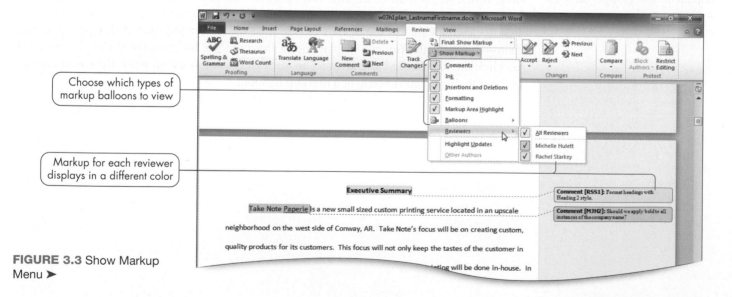

Choose which types of markup balloons to view

Markup for each reviewer displays in a different color

FIGURE 3.3 Show Markup Menu ➤

You can modify comments easily. When you click inside a markup balloon, the insertion point will relocate in the balloon, and you can use word processing formatting features, such as bold, italic, underline, and color, in the comment. If a document contains many comments, or the document is lengthy, you can click Previous and Next in the Comments group on the Review tab to navigate from comment to comment. This is a quick way to move between comments without scrolling through the entire document, and it places the insertion point in the comment automatically. You can edit comments when viewing them in the Reviewing Pane also.

After reading or acting on comments, you can delete them from the document or the Reviewing Pane by clicking Delete in the Comments group on the Review tab. When you click the Delete arrow, your options include deleting the current comment, all comments shown, or deleting all comments in the document at one time. You also can right-click a comment markup balloon and select Delete Comment from the shortcut menu. If you print a document that has comments, the comments also print. To omit the comments from the printout, click File, click Print, click the first Settings arrow (which shows Print All Pages by default), and then click Show Markup to remove the checkmark.

Tracking Changes in a Document

Whether you work individually or with a group, you can monitor any revisions you make to a document. The *Track Changes* feature monitors all additions, deletions, and formatting changes you make. It is useful in situations where a document must be reviewed by several people—each of whom can offer suggestions or changes—and then returned to one person who will finalize the document.

Use **Track Changes** to insert revision marks and markup balloons for additions, deletions, and formatting changes.

When Track Changes is not active, any change you make to a document is untraceable and no one will know what you change unless he or she compares your revised document with the previous version. When Track Changes is active, it applies *revision marks*, which indicate where a person added, deleted, or formatted text. Like Comments, the revision marks will be colored differently for each reviewer. Revision marks can vary depending on your preference in viewing them, but include strikeout lines for deleted text, underlines for inserted text, markup balloons, and changed lines. *Changed lines* are vertical bars that display in the right or left margins to specify the line that contains revision marks. You can position the mouse pointer over revision marks or markup balloons to see who made the change and on what date and time, as shown in Figure 3.4.

A **revision mark** indicates where text is added, deleted, or formatted while the Track Changes feature is active.

A **changed line** is a vertical bar in the margin to pinpoint the area where changes are made.

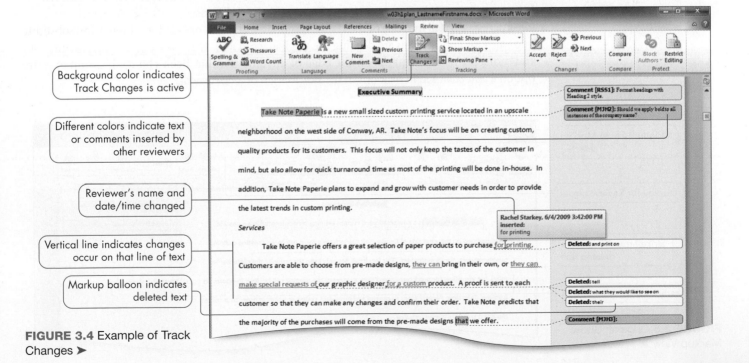

FIGURE 3.4 Example of Track Changes ➤

Word also includes markup tools, which enable you to accept or reject changes indicated by revision marks. The Changes group on the Review tab includes Accept, to accept a suggested change, and Reject, to remove a suggested change. When you accept or reject a change, the revision marks, markup balloon, and changed lines disappear. The Changes group also includes Previous and Next. When you click Previous, the insertion point moves to the beginning of any comment or change that occurs just prior to the current position. Similarly, clicking Next will move the insertion point to the beginning of the next comment or change.

If the review process takes place using paper copies of a document, it is difficult to visualize all the suggested changes at one time, and then the last person must manually change the original document. While writing the Exploring series, the authors, editors, and reviewers each inserted comments and tracked changes to the manuscript for each chapter using Word. Each person's comments or changes displayed in different colored balloons, and because all edits were performed in the same document, the Series Editor could accept and reject changes before sending the manuscript to the production department.

> **TIP** Accepting or Rejecting All Changes
>
> To accept all changes in a document at once, click the Accept arrow on the Review tab and select Accept All Changes in Document. To delete all changes in a document at once, click the Reject arrow on the Review tab and select Reject All Changes in Document.

Select Markup Views

Original: Show Markup view shows a line through deleted text and puts inserted text in a markup balloon.

Final: Show Markup view shows inserted text in the body and puts deleted text in a markup balloon.

The suggested revisions from the various reviewers display in one of two ways, as the Original Showing Markup or as the Final Showing Markup. The **Original: Show Markup** view shows the deleted text within the body of the document (with a line through the deleted text) and displays the inserted text in a balloon to the right of the actual document, as shown in Figure 3.5. The **Final: Show Markup** view is the opposite; that is, it displays the inserted text in the body of the document and shows the deleted text in a balloon. The difference is subtle and depends on personal preference with respect to displaying the insertions and deletions in a document. You can change the way markups display by clicking Show Markup, Balloons, and selecting from three choices: Show Revisions in Balloons, Show All Revisions Inline, or Show Only Comments and Formatting in Balloons.

All revisions fall into one of these two categories: insertions or deletions. Even if you substitute one word for another, you are deleting the original word and then inserting its replacement. Both views display revision marks on the edge of any line that has been changed. Comments are optional and enclosed in balloons in the side margin of a document.

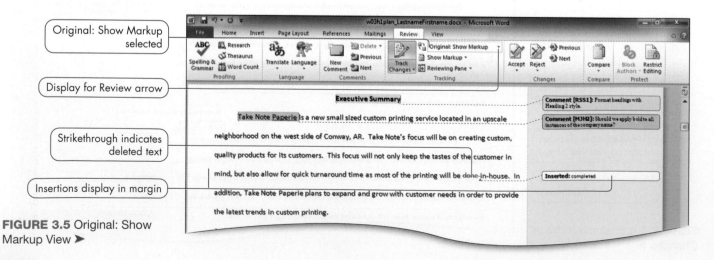

FIGURE 3.5 Original: Show Markup View ➤

To select one of the markup views you click the Display for Review arrow in the Tracking group on the Review tab (see Figure 3.5). When you click the Display for Review arrow, two additional view options are listed—Final and Original. Final shows how the document looks if you accept and incorporate all tracked changes. Original shows the document prior to using the Track Changes feature.

Customize Track Changes Options

The Track Changes feature has many options for viewing and displaying changes, which you can customize. When you click Change Tracking Options from the Track Changes arrow, the Track Changes Options dialog box displays with many features you can change. For example, you can choose the type of underline to display under inserted text (single line or double line). You can choose the type of strikethrough line to display on deleted text (strikethrough or double strikethrough). You can choose the location where the balloons display (right or left margins), and you can even choose the size of the balloons.

The beginning of this chapter mentioned that you should check the Word Options, making changes if necessary, so your name and initials are associated with any tracked changes you make in the document. You also can access those settings from the Review tab when you click the Track Changes arrow and select Change User Name, as shown in Figure 3.6. This step takes you to the General category of the Word Options dialog box, where you have the opportunity to enter your name and initials in the *Personalize your copy of Microsoft Office* section.

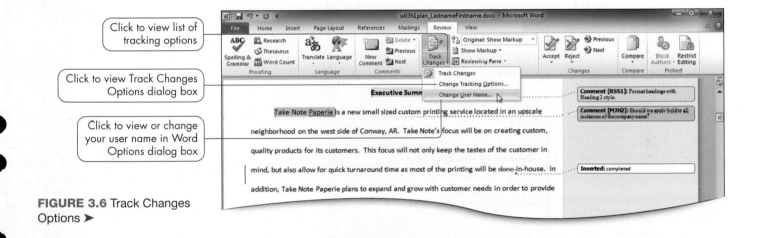

FIGURE 3.6 Track Changes Options ➤

1 Document Revisions

You open the document that Rachel Starkey prepared and find the comments she left for you. You also see her recent edits because she tracked her changes. Your task is to address any questions or requests in the comment balloons and also accept or reject the changes she made when revising the document.

Skills covered: Set User Name and Customize the Track Changes Options • Track Document Changes • View, Add, and Delete Comments • Accept and Reject Changes

---

STEP 1 ▶ SET USER NAME AND CUSTOMIZE THE TRACK CHANGES OPTIONS

You want to make sure the Word Options are customized so your name displays when comments are added or changes are tracked in a document. Then you decide to modify some of the track changes options to use settings that are distinguishable from those other editors might use. Refer to Figure 3.7 as you complete Step 1.

FIGURE 3.7 Track Changes Options Dialog Box ➤

a. Open *w03h1plan* and save it as **w03h1plan_LastnameFirstname**.

> **TROUBLESHOOTING:** If you make any major mistakes in this exercise, you can close the file, open *w03h1plan* again, and then start this exercise over.

b. Delete the text *YourName* in the subtitle and insert your first and last names. Click the **Review tab**, and then click **Track Changes** in the Tracking group.

> **TROUBLESHOOTING:** Track Changes in the Tracking group, like some other commands in Word, contain two parts: the main command icon and an arrow. Click the main command icon when instructed to click Track Changes and turn on the feature. Click the arrow when instructed to click the Track Changes arrow for additional command options.

The command displays with an orange background color, indicating the feature is turned on. When you click Track Changes, you toggle the feature on or off.

c. Click the **Track Changes arrow**, and then click **Change User Name**. In the *Personalize your copy of Microsoft Office* section, type your name in the **User name box**, and then type your initials in the **Initials box**, if necessary. Click **OK** to close the Word Options dialog box.

You want to be sure your name and initials are correct before you add any comments or initiate any changes in the document. After you update the user information, your initials display with all comments or changes you make.

> **TROUBLESHOOTING:** Personalizing your copy of Microsoft Office might not be possible in a lab environment. If you cannot make the change, just continue with the exercise.

d. Click the **Track Changes arrow**, and then click **Change Tracking Options** to open the dialog box. In the *Markup* section, click the **Insertions arrow**, and then click **Double underline**. In the *Formatting* section, click the **Track formatting check box**, if necessary, to turn on this feature.

Your revisions to the Track Changes options enable you to view any additions to the document quickly because they will be identified in balloons and your insertions will display with a double underline. Markups on formatting may not display automatically, but you confirm that option is on so you will see marks next to formatting changes that you make.

e. Click the **Use Balloons (Print and Web Layout) arrow** in the *Balloons* section, and then click **Always**, if necessary. Click the **Preferred width arrow** until **1.8"** displays. Click the **Margin arrow**, and then select **Left**, as shown in Figure 3.7. Click **OK** to close the Track Changes Options dialog box.

You altered the location of all comment and editing balloons to display on the left side of your document instead of on the right, which is the default. You also decreased the width of the markup balloons so they will take up less space in the margins.

f. Save the document.

STEP 2 ▶ TRACK DOCUMENT CHANGES

Now that the settings are set to your preference, you make a few changes so you can see how your editing is tracked separately from Rachel's. You first change the views so you can see the tracked changes made by both of you while you work, and then you later change the view so you see how the document looks as a final version. Refer to Figure 3.8 as you complete Step 2.

FIGURE 3.8 View Changes in a Document ➤

a. Click the **Display for Review arrow** in the Tracking group on the Review tab, and then select **Final: Show Markup**, if necessary. Scroll down the document until you see the heading *Executive Summary* on the second page of the document.

One comment displays in a balloon and several changes are marked in color. Because of the changes you made in Step 1, any future changes you make in the document also display in balloons in the margin of the document.

b. Replace the word *done* with **completed** in the third sentence of the first paragraph that follows the *Executive Summary* heading.

The text you inserted is colored and has a double underline beneath it.

> **TROUBLESHOOTING:** If a balloon does not display, indicating the word replacement, make sure Track Changes is on. When on, Track Changes is highlighted in an orange color on the Review tab. If necessary, click Undo, click Track Changes again to turn it on, and then repeat Step 2b.

c. Select the **Executive Summary heading**, click the **Home tab**, and then apply the **Heading 1 style** from the Styles gallery.

The heading is now left justified, and a changed line appears on the left side. A markup balloon describes the formatting change, as seen in Figure 3.8.

d. Click the **Review tab**, click the **Display for Review arrow** in the Tracking group, and then select **Final**.

The formatting change indicators do not display, and the *Executive Summary* heading displays in the new style.

e. Save the document.

STEP 3 ▶ VIEW, ADD, AND DELETE COMMENTS

As you work through the document, you think of a question you would like to ask Rachel before the plan is finalized, so you insert a comment of your own. You also remove one of her comments about an issue that is resolved. Refer to Figure 3.9 as you complete Step 3.

FIGURE 3.9 Deleting Comments ➤

a. Click the **Display for Review arrow** in the Tracking group, and then select **Final: Show Markup**.

b. Select **Take Note Paperie** at the beginning of the first sentence under the *Executive Summary* heading. Click **New Comment** in the Comments group, and then type **Should we apply bold to all instances of the company name?** in the markup balloon.

If you do not select anything prior to clicking New Comment, Word selects the word or object nearest the insertion point for the comment reference.

c. Click inside the markup balloon you created. Place your cursor to the left of the word *to*, edit the comment by typing **and italic**, and then press **Spacebar**. Click outside of the balloon to deselect it.

Your comment now displays *Should we apply bold and italic to all instances of the company name?*

d. Position the mouse pointer over the comment balloon attached to the *Executive Summary* heading.

When you position the mouse pointer over a markup balloon, Word displays a ScreenTip that tells you who created the comment and when.

e. Click Rachel Starkey's comment one time to select it, and then click **Delete** in the Comments group.

You removed the selected comment and the markup balloon. If you click the arrow on the right side of Delete in the Comments group, you can select from several options, including Delete all Comments in Document (see Figure 3.9). You can also right-click a comment and select Delete Comment.

f. Save the document.

STEP 4 ACCEPT AND REJECT CHANGES

Now you are ready to consider the changes that Rachel made and tracked. Some are good and will improve the readability of the paper; some will not. You remember how quick and easy it is to accept and reject changes by using features on the Review tab and that makes you smile. Refer to Figure 3.10 as you complete Step 4.

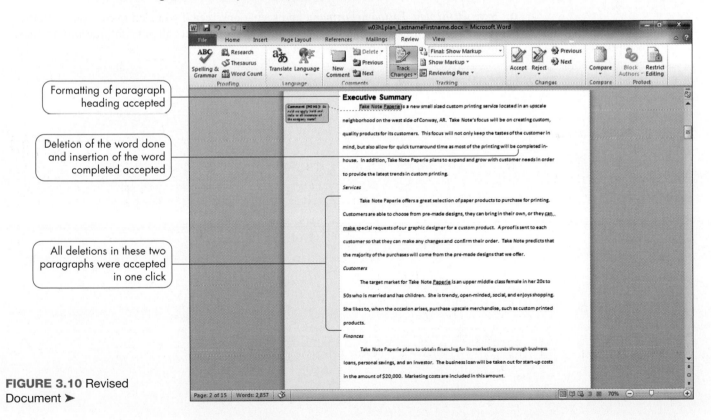

Formatting of paragraph heading accepted

Deletion of the word done and insertion of the word completed accepted

All deletions in these two paragraphs were accepted in one click

FIGURE 3.10 Revised Document ➤

a. Press **Ctrl+Home** to place the insertion point at the beginning of the document.

b. Click **Next** in the Changes group to highlight the first change, and then position the mouse pointer over the tracked change.

The formatting change to the *Executive Summary* heading is highlighted. When you position the mouse pointer on the revision, a ScreenTip appears that tells you who made the change and the date and time the change was made.

> **TROUBLESHOOTING:** If you click Next in the Comments group instead of Next in the Changes group, click Previous in the Comments group to return the cursor to the beginning of the document, and then click Next in the Changes group.

c. Click **Accept** in the Changes group.

   The formatting change is accepted. When the suggested change is accepted, the markup balloons and other Track Changes markups disappear. Additionally, the markup balloon for the next change or comment is highlighted. As with other commands, you can click Accept to accept this change only, or you can click the Accept arrow to view options for accepting changes.

d. Click **Next** in the Changes group to pass the comment and view the next markup balloon. Click **Accept** two times to accept the replacement of *done* to *completed*.

   The first time you accept the change it applies to the deletion of the word *done*. The second time you accept the change it applies to the insertion of *completed*.

e. Select the entire second and third paragraphs in the *Executive Summary* section. Click **Accept** to retain all revisions in the paragraphs. Click **Reject** to remove the empty comment that displays in this paragraph.

   All the changes in those paragraphs are accepted, the blank comment is removed, and the next change, a deletion of a complete section of the report, is highlighted. Figure 3.10 shows the first page after accepting changes.

f. Click **Reject** in the Changes group to retain the *Goals* heading and following paragraphs.

g. Save *w03h1plan_LastnameFirstname* and keep it onscreen if you plan to continue with the next Hands-On Exercise. Close the file and exit Word if you will not continue with the next exercise at this time.

Research Paper Basics

Well-prepared documents often include notes that provide supplemental information or citations for sources quoted in the document. Some documents also contain other valuable supplemental components, such as a list of figures or legal references. Word includes many features that can help you create these supplemental references, as well as many others described in the following paragraphs.

In this section, you will use Word to create citations used for reference pages, create a bibliography page that displays works cited in the document, and select from a list of writing styles that are commonly used to dictate the format of reference pages. You will also create and modify footnote and endnote citations, which display at the bottom of a page or the end of the document.

Acknowledging a Source

Plagiarism is the act of using and documenting the works of another as one's own.

It is common practice to use a variety of sources to supplement your own thoughts when writing a paper, report, legal brief, or many other types of document. Failure to acknowledge the source of information you use in a document is a form of plagiarism. *Webster's New Collegiate Dictionary* defines **plagiarism** as the act of using and documenting the ideas or writings of another as one's own. It may also apply to spoken words, multimedia works, or graphics. Plagiarism has serious moral and ethical implications and is taken seriously in the academic community; it is often classified as academic dishonesty.

> Failure to acknowledge the source of information you use in a document is a form of plagiarism.... Word includes a robust feature for tracking sources and producing the supplemental resources to display them.

To assist in your efforts to avoid plagiarism, which is frequently a thoughtless oversight rather than a malicious act, Word includes a robust feature for tracking sources and producing the supplemental resources to display them.

Create a Source

A **citation** is a note recognizing a source of information or a quoted passage.

Word provides the citation feature to track, compile, and display your research sources for inclusion in several types of supplemental references. To use this feature you use the Insert Citation command in the Citations & Bibliography group on the References tab to add data about each source, as shown in Figure 3.11. A **citation** is a note recognizing the source of information or a quoted passage. The Create Source dialog box includes fields to catalog information, such as author, date, publication name, page number, or Web site address, from the following types of sources:

- Book
- Book Section
- Journal Article
- Article in a Periodical
- Conference Proceedings
- Report
- Web site
- Document from Web site
- Electronic Source
- Art
- Sound Recording
- Performance
- Film
- Interview
- Patent
- Case
- Miscellaneous

After you create the citation sources, you can insert them into a document using the Insert Citation command. When you click the command, a list of your sources displays; click a source from the list, and the proper citation format is inserted in your document.

Click to display Source Manager dialog box

Click to change type of source

Example of entry for Web page

Click to display Create Source dialog box

FIGURE 3.11 Add a Source Citation ➤

Share and Search for a Source

The **Master List** is a database of all citation sources created in Word.

The **Current List** includes all citation sources you use in the current document.

After you add sources, they are saved in a Master List. The *Master List* is a database of all citation sources created in Word on a particular computer. The source also is stored in the *Current List*, which contains all sources you use in the current document. Sources saved in the Master List can be used in any Word document. This feature is helpful to those who use the same sources on multiple occasions. Master Lists are stored in XML format, so you can share the Master List file with coworkers or other authors, eliminating the need to retype the information and ensuring accuracy. The Master List file is stored in \AppData\Roaming\Microsoft\Bibliography, which is a subfolder of the user account folder stored under C:\Users. For example, a path to the Master File might be C:\Users\MichelleHulett\AppData\Roaming\Microsoft\Bibliography\Sources.xml.

The Source Manager dialog box (see Figure 3.12) displays the Master List you created, and you also can browse to find other XML files that contain source information. After you open a Master List, you can copy sources to your Current List. You can also copy, delete, or edit sources in either the Master or Current List from the Source Manager.

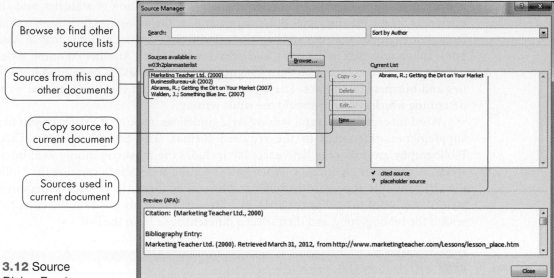

Browse to find other source lists

Sources from this and other documents

Copy source to current document

Sources used in current document

FIGURE 3.12 Source Manager Dialog Box ➤

A **bibliography** is a list of works cited or consulted by an author in a document.

Creating a Bibliography

A *bibliography* is a list of works cited or consulted by an author and should be included with the document when published. Some reference manuals use the terms Works Cited or References instead of Bibliography. A bibliography is just one form of reference that gives credit to the sources you consulted or quoted in the preparation of your paper. The addition of a bibliography to your completed work demonstrates respect for the material consulted. In addition to the bibliography, you should cite your source within a document, near any quotations or excerpts, to avoid plagiarizing. It also gives the reader an opportunity to validate your references for accuracy.

Word includes a bibliography feature that makes the addition of this reference page very easy. After you add the sources using the Insert Citation feature, you click Bibliography in the Citations & Bibliography group on the References tab, and then click Insert Bibliography. Any sources used in the current document will display in the appropriate format as a bibliography, as shown in Figure 3.13.

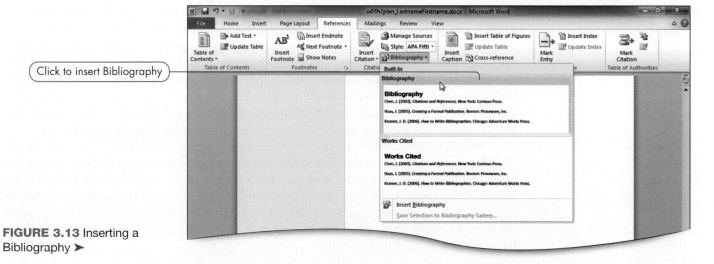

Click to insert Bibliography

FIGURE 3.13 Inserting a Bibliography ➤

Selecting the Writing Style

When research papers are prepared the author often must conform to a particular writing style. The writing style, also called an editorial style, consists of rules and guidelines set forth by a publisher of a research journal to ensure consistency in presentation of research documents. Some of the presentation consistencies that a style enforces are use of punctuation and abbreviations, format of headings and tables, presentation of statistics, and citation of references. The style guidelines differ depending on the discipline the research topic comes from. For example, the APA style originates with the American Psychological Association, but is frequently used in the social and behavioral sciences. Another common style is MLA, which is sanctioned by the Modern Language Association and is often used in the humanities and business disciplines. The topic of your paper and the audience you write to will determine which style you should use while writing.

Word incorporates several writing style guidelines, making it easier for you to generate supplemental references in the required format. The Style list in the Citations & Bibliography group on the References tab includes the most commonly used international styles, as shown in Figure 3.14. When you select the style before creating the bibliography, the citations that appear in the bibliography will be formatted exactly as required by that style. If you want to change the style after creating it, simply position the cursor anywhere within the bibliography, and then select a different style from the list.

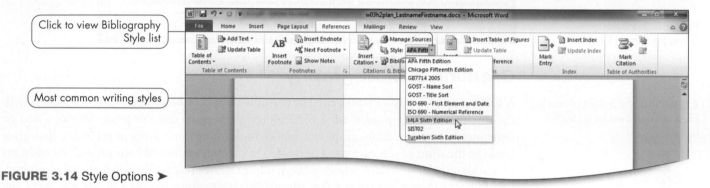

FIGURE 3.14 Style Options ➤

Creating and Modifying Footnotes and Endnotes

A **footnote** is a citation that appears at the bottom of a page.

An **endnote** is a citation that appears at the end of a document.

A **footnote** is a citation that appears at the bottom of a page, and an **endnote** is a citation that appears at the end of a document. You use footnotes or endnotes to credit the sources you quote or cite in your document. You also can use footnotes or endnotes to provide supplemental information about a topic that is too distracting to include in the body of the document. Footnotes, endnotes, and bibliographies often contain the same information. Your use of these citation options is determined by the style of paper (MLA, for example) or by the person who oversees your research. When you use a bibliography, the information about a source is displayed only one time at the end of the paper, and the exact location in the document that uses information from the source may not be obvious. When you use a footnote, the information about a source displays on the specific page where a quote or information appears. When you use endnotes, the information about a source displays only at the end of the document; however, the number that identifies the endnote displays on each page.

The References tab includes the Insert Footnote and Insert Endnote commands. If you click the Footnote and Endnote Dialog Box Launcher, the Footnote and Endnote dialog box opens, and you can modify the location of the notes and the format of the numbers. By default, Word sequentially numbers footnotes with Arabic numerals (1, 2, and 3) as shown in Figure 3.15. Endnotes are numbered with lowercase Roman numerals (i, ii, and iii) based on the location of the note within the document. If you add or delete notes, Word renumbers the remaining notes automatically.

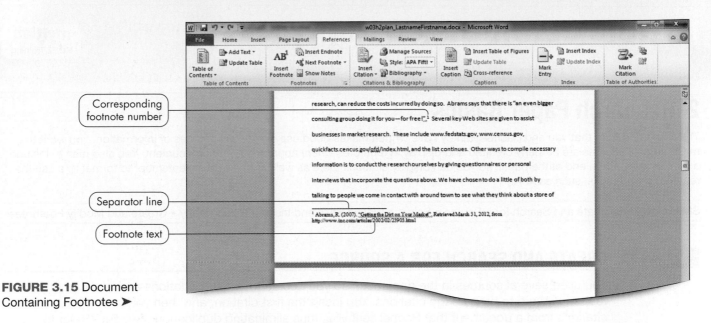

Corresponding footnote number

Separator line

Footnote text

FIGURE 3.15 Document Containing Footnotes ➤

You can easily make modifications to footnotes and endnotes. In Print Layout view, scroll to the bottom of the page (or for endnotes, to the end of the document or section), click inside the note, and then edit it. In Draft view, double-click the footnote or endnote reference mark to display the Footnotes or Endnotes pane, and then you can edit the note.

TIP Relocating a Footnote or Endnote

If you created a note in the wrong location, select the note reference mark within the text, cut it from its current location, and then paste it in the correct location within the document text. You also can use the drag-and-drop method to move a selected note reference mark to a different location.

HANDS-ON EXERCISES

2 Research Paper Basics

The Marketing Plan that you and Rachel Starkey have written makes good use of external sources of information. You want to make sure all sources are properly credited and display in footnotes where appropriate in the document. You also plan to include a bibliography at the end of the paper, so you can display citations there as well, and you must remember to format it to use the required writing style, such as APA.

Skills covered: Create and Search for a Source • Select a Writing Style and Insert a Bibliography • Create and Modify Footnotes

---

STEP 1 ▶ **CREATE AND SEARCH FOR A SOURCE**

You used several sources in the document, so you decide to use the Citations and Bibliography feature in Word to prepare the citations. You insert the first citation, and then you import the other citations from a document that Rachel sent you, thus eliminating duplication of efforts. Refer to Figure 3.16 as you complete Step 1.

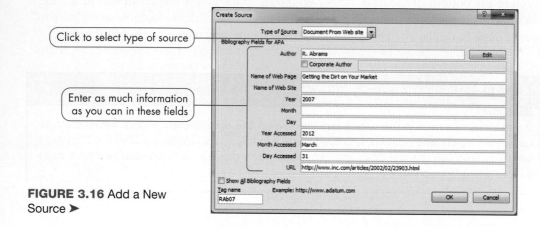

FIGURE 3.16 Add a New Source ▶

a. Open the *w03h1plan_LastnameFirstname* document if you closed it after the last Hands-On Exercise, and save it as **w03h2plan_LastnameFirstname**, changing *h1* to *h2*.

b. Click the **Display for Review arrow** in the Tracking group on the Review tab, and then select **Final**.

   You are still tracking changes in the document, but the information that displays can distract your attention, so you change the view to display it as if all your changes are accepted.

c. Click the **References tab**, click **Manage Sources** in the Citations & Bibliography group, and then click **New** in the middle of the dialog box.

   The Source Manager dialog box displays, as shown in Figure 3.16. Because you want to create a citation source without inserting the citation directly into the document, you use the Source Manager instead of clicking Insert Citation, Add New Source. After you click New in the Source Manager, the Create Source dialog box displays.

d. Click the **Type of Source arrow**, and then select **Document From Web site**. Type the source information as noted in the following table and as seen in Figure 3.16. After you enter each entry, click **OK** to add the source to your document and return to the Source Manager dialog box.

Author	R. Abrams
Name of Web Page	Getting the Dirt on Your Market
Year	2007
Year Accessed	2012
Month Accessed	March
Day Accessed	31
URL	http://www.inc.com/articles/2002/02/23903.html

To cite a source properly, you need as much information as you can provide, but you do not have to fill out all of the boxes in the Create Source dialog box. In some sources, such as the one above, the URL is more descriptive than the Web site name, and therefore more informative to anyone who wants to check your source.

e. Click **Browse** in the Source Manager dialog box to display the Open Source List dialog box. Click the drive and folder in the Folders list on the left side of the Open Source List dialog box where the student data files that accompany this book are located. Select *w03ho2planmasterlist*, and then click **OK**.

You return to the Source Manager dialog box, and three sources that Rachel Starkey had created in a separate document display in the *Sources available in* box along with the source you just created.

f. Click the first source entry, if necessary, to select it. Then press and hold **Ctrl** and select the other two new entries. Click **Copy** to insert the sources into the current document.

The three sources you copied and the one source you created display in the Current List box as well as in the Master List.

g. Click **Close** to return to the document. Save the document.

STEP 2 ▶ SELECT A WRITING STYLE AND INSERT A BIBLIOGRAPHY

Now that sources are cited and stored in the document, you can quickly insert the bibliography at the end. You also select the writing style, which affects the way each source displays in the bibliography listing. Luckily, you can select the style before or after inserting the bibliography and Word changes it accordingly. Refer to Figure 3.17 as you complete Step 2.

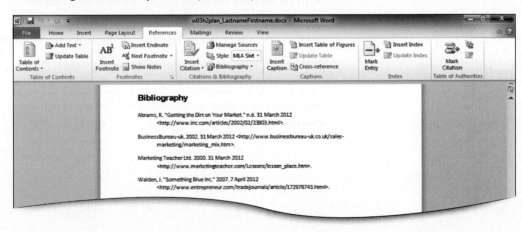

FIGURE 3.17 Bibliography in MLA Style ▶

a. Click the **Style arrow** in the Citations and Bibliography group, and then select **MLA Sixth Edition**.

b. Press **Ctrl+End** to position the insertion point at the end of the document, press **Ctrl+Enter** to add a blank page, and then type **Bibliography** at the top of the new page. Click the **Home tab**, and then apply the **Heading 1 style** from the Styles gallery. Press **End**, and then press **Enter** two times.

c. Click the **References tab**, click **Bibliography** in Citations & Bibliography, and then click **Insert Bibliography**.

The sources cited in the document display in the MLA format for bibliographies, as shown in Figure 3.17.

d. Click the **Style arrow** again, and then select **APA Fifth Edition**.

The format of the bibliography changes to reflect the standards of the APA style.

e. Save the document.

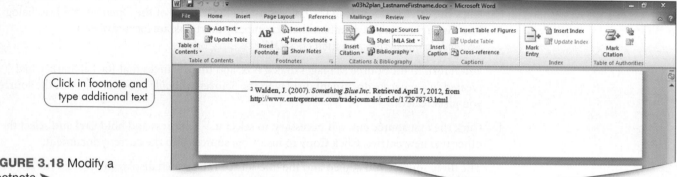

STEP 3 · CREATE AND MODIFY FOOTNOTES

Rachel inserted some footnotes, but you realize she forgot one, so you add it. You also notice one footnote needs revising so that it accurately reflects the source information. Refer to Figure 3.18 as you complete Step 3.

FIGURE 3.18 Modify a Footnote ➤

a. Scroll to the middle of page 4. Click one time at the end of the sentence that ends with *doing it for you—for free!* to relocate the insertion point. Click **Insert Footnote** in the Footnotes group.

The insertion point displays at the bottom of the page, below a horizontal line. This is where your footnote displays in the document.

b. Type **Abrams, R. (2007). "Getting the Dirt on Your Market". Retrieved March 31, 2012, from http://www.inc.com/articles/2002/02/23903.html**. Format the footnote as displayed with periods and commas, but do not bold the citation.

c. Scroll to the bottom of page 6. Click one time at the end of the footnote, a reference to an article written by J. Walden in 2007. Replace the date of retrieval with the date **April 7, 2012**.

You edited the footnote as shown in Figure 3.18.

d. Save *w03h2plan_LastnameFirstname* and keep it onscreen if you plan to continue with the next Hands-On Exercise. Close the file and exit Word if you will not continue with the next exercise at this time.

Research Paper Enhancements

The previous section mentioned several types of reference features that should be used when a document refers to outside information or sources. Some reference features are used less frequently, yet are valuable for creating professional quality documents. These supplements include a list of captions used on figures, a list of figures presented in a document, references to other locations in a document, and a list of legal sources referenced. You also can attach information that refers to the contents and origin of a document.

In this section, you will generate a table of contents at the beginning of a document. You will then learn how to designate text to include in an index and then generate the index at the end of a document. You will add captions to visual elements and create a list of the visuals used in a document, and you will create a list of references from a legal document. Finally, you will create a cross-reference, or note that refers the reader to another location in the document.

Inserting a Table of Contents and Index

Well-prepared long documents include special features to help readers locate information easily. For example, people often refer to the table of contents or the index in a long document—such as a book, reference manual, or company policy—to locate particular topics within that document. You can use Word to help you create these supplemental document components with minimal effort.

> Well-prepared long documents include special features to help readers locate information easily.... You can use Word to help you create these supplemental document components with minimal effort.

Create a Table of Contents

A *table of contents* lists headings in the order they appear in a document and the page numbers where the entries begin. Word can create the table of contents automatically, if you apply a style to each heading in the document. You can use built-in styles, Heading 1 through Heading 9, or identify your own custom styles to use when generating the table of contents. Word also will update the table to accommodate the addition or deletion of headings or changes in page numbers brought about through changes in the document.

The table of contents feature is located on the References tab. After you apply a heading style to selected text in the document, you click the References tab and click Table of Contents to insert a predefined table of the styled text and page numbers. If you want more control over the way the table of contents displays in your document, you can click the Insert Table of Contents command to select from other styles such as Classic and Formal, as well as determine how many levels to display in the table; the latter correspond to the heading styles used within the document using the custom feature. You can determine whether to right-align the page numbers, and you also can choose to include a leader character to draw the reader's eyes across the page from a heading to a page number. Table 3.1 shows the variety of styles you can choose for your table of contents.

A **table of contents** lists headings and the page numbers where they appear in a document.

TABLE 3.1 Table of Contents Styles

Fancy Format

Table of Contents

EXECUTIVE SUMMARY 3

ORGANIZATIONAL OVERVIEW 4

MISSION STATEMENT 4

GOALS 4

IMPLEMENTATION 5

EVALUATION 5

APPENDIX A. DETAILED TABLES AND CHARTS 7

BIBLIOGRAPHY 10

Formal Format

Table of Contents

EXECUTIVE SUMMARY 3
ORGANIZATIONAL OVERVIEW 4
MISSION STATEMENT 4
GOALS 4
IMPLEMENTATION 5
EVALUATION 5
APPENDIX A. DETAILED TABLES AND CHARTS..7
BIBLIOGRAPHY..10

Modern Format

Table of Contents

Executive Summary 3

ORGANIZATIONAL OVERVIEW 4

MISSION STATEMENT 4

GOALS 4

IMPLEMENTATION 5

EVALUATION 5

Appendix A. Detailed Tables and Charts 7

Bibliography 10

Simple Format

Table of Contents

Executive Summary 3

ORGANIZATIONAL OVERVIEW 4

MISSION STATEMENT 4

GOALS 4

IMPLEMENTATION 5

EVALUATION 5

Appendix A. Detailed Tables and Charts 7

Bibliography 10

Create an Index

An **index** is a listing of topics and the page numbers where the topics are discussed.

An index puts the finishing touch on a long document. The *index* provides an alphabetical listing of topics covered in a document, along with the page numbers where the topic is discussed. Typically, the index appears at the end of a book or document. Word will create an index automatically, provided that the entries for the index have been previously marked. This requires you to go through a document, select the terms to be included in the index, and mark them accordingly. You can select a single occurrence of an entry and select an option to mark all occurrences of that entry for the index. You also can refer the reader to a different location in the document when you create an index entry, such as "see also Internet."

To mark an Index entry you follow these steps:

1. Select the word or phrase in your document that you want to display in the Index.
2. Click the References tab, and then click Mark Entry in the Index group. You can also use the shortcut Alt+Shift+X.
3. If necessary, revise the Main Entry text that displays in the Mark Index Entry dialog box. For example, if you mark a word that is not capitalized in the document, you want to revise the Main Entry so it is capitalized in the Index. The text that displays in the Main Entry box will display in the Index.
4. Click Mark for this selected word or phrase or click Mark All to include all occurrences of this word or phrase in the Index.
5. In a long document, it is helpful to use the Find feature to locate the next word or phrase to mark.
6. When all words or phrases are marked, close the Mark Entry dialog box.

After you specify the entries, create the index by choosing Insert Index in the Index group on the References tab. You can choose a variety of styles for the index, just as you can for the table of contents, as shown in Table 3.2. Word arranges the index entries in alphabetical order and enters the appropriate page references. You also can create additional index entries or move text within a document, then update the index with the click of a mouse.

TABLE 3.2   Index Styles

Fancy Format

Index		
C		**P**
Custom printing, 3, 4		Product, 3
M		**Q**
Marketing plan, 5		Quality, 3

Formal Format

Index

C		P	
Custom printing 3, 4		Product 3	
M		Q	
Marketing plan 5		Quality 3	

Modern Format

Index

C		P	
Custom printing · 3, 4		Product · 3	
M		Q	
Marketing plan · 5		Quality · 3	

Simple Format

Index

Custom printing, 3, 4	Product, 3
Marketing plan, 5	Quality, 3

To modify an Index entry, you must display the index fields by clicking Show/Hide (¶) in the Paragraph group on the Home tab. Locate the entry that you wish to modify and edit the text inside the quotation marks. Do not change the entry in the finished Index, or the next time you update the index, your changes will be lost. To delete an entry, select the entire entry field, including the braces {}, and then press Delete. After you modify or delete a marked entry, click Update Index in the Index group on the References tab to display the changes in the table.

TIP AutoMark Index Entries

When you have a lengthy list of words to mark for index entries, you can use a separate Word document as a source to help you automatically mark all occurrences of each word. When you select the AutoMark command from the Index dialog box it prompts you to open the Word document that contains a list of terms you want to mark for an index. It then marks the entries automatically. The advantage is that it is fast. The disadvantage is that every occurrence of an entry is marked and displays in the index so that a commonly used term may have too many page references. You can, however, delete superfluous entries by manually deleting the field codes. Click Show/Hide (¶) in the Paragraph group of the Home tab if you do not see the entries in the document.

Adding Other Reference Tables

You will likely use the Table of Contents and Index features most often in your research and other long documents. However, you can include additional reference tables to highlight other important information in your document. Some documents might contain so many tables or pictures that listing each one in a format similar to a table of contents can be helpful. Legal documents also often include a listing of the documents they use as a reference. Word includes features to enable you to include reference tables correctly for these situations.

Assign Figure Captions

A **caption** is a descriptive title for an equation, a figure, or a table.

Documents and books often contain several images, charts, or tables. For example, this text-book contains several screenshots in each chapter. To help readers refer to the correct image or table, you can add a caption. A *caption* is a descriptive title for an image, a figure, or a table. To add a caption click Insert Caption in the Captions group on the References tab. By default, Word assigns a number to the equation, figure, or table at the beginning of the caption. When you click Insert Caption, the Caption dialog box appears, as shown in Figure 3.19, and you can edit the default caption by adding descriptive text.

Click to display Caption dialog box

Caption will be applied to selected object

Figure or table number displays automatically and keeps track of the number of figures

Select type of object

Click to change numbering format

Click to generate captions automatically

FIGURE 3.19 Caption Dialog Box ➤

To automatically generate captions, click AutoCaption in the Caption dialog box. In the *Add caption when inserting* list, in the AutoCaption dialog box, click the check box next to the element type for which you want to create AutoCaptions. Specify the default caption text in the *Use label* box, and specify the location of the caption by clicking the Position arrow. If your document will contain several captions, this feature helps to ensure each caption is named and numbered sequentially.

Insert a Table of Figures

A **table of figures** is a list of the captions in a document.

If your document includes pictures, charts and graphs, slides, or other illustrations along with a caption, you can include a *table of figures*, or list of the captions, as a reference. To build a table of figures, Word searches a document for captions, sorts the captions by number, and displays the table of figures in the document. A table of figures is placed after the table of contents for a document. The Insert Table of Figures command is in the Captions group on the References tab. The Table of Figures dialog box, shown in Figure 3.20, enables you to select page number, format, and caption label options.

Click to display Table of Figures dialog box

Click to select tab leader style

Click to select format

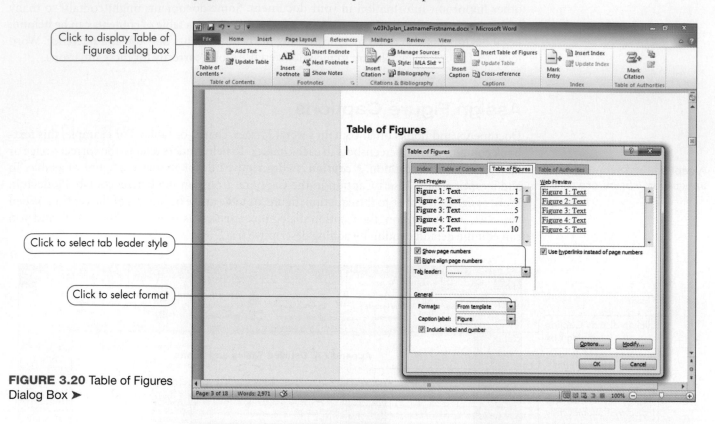

FIGURE 3.20 Table of Figures Dialog Box ➤

> **TIP** Update a Table of Figures
>
> If the figures or figure captions in a document change or are removed, you should update the table of figures. To update the table, right-click any table entry to select the entire table and display a menu. Click Update Field, and then choose between the options Update Page Numbers only or Update entire table. If significant changes have been made, you should update the entire table.

Insert a Table of Authorities

A **table of authorities** is used in legal documents to reference cases and other documents referred to in a legal brief.

A *table of authorities* is used in legal documents to reference cases, rules, treaties, and other documents referred to in a legal brief. You typically compile the table of authorities on a separate page at the beginning of a legal document. Word's Table of Authorities feature enables you to track, compile, and display citations, or references to specific legal cases and other legal documents, to be included in the table of authorities. Before you generate the table of authorities, you must indicate which citations you want to include using the Mark Citation command in the Table of Authorities group on the References tab. To mark citations, select text, and then click Mark Citation. The Mark Citation dialog box displays, as shown in Figure 3.21, and you can choose to mark this one case or mark all references to this case in the document. After you mark the citations in your document, click Insert Table of Authorities in the Table of Authorities group to generate the table at the location of your insertion point.

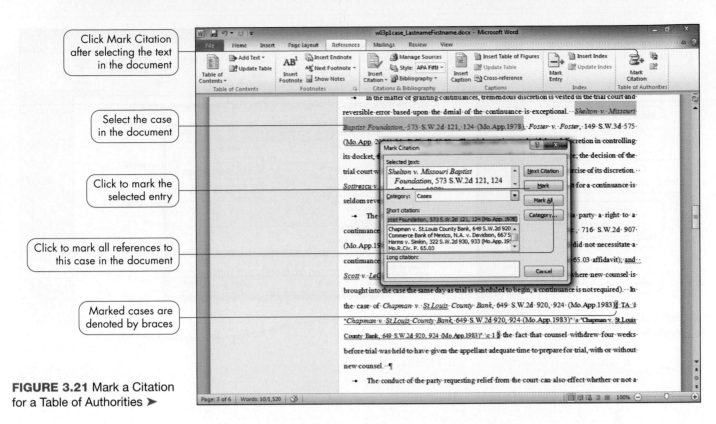

Click Mark Citation after selecting the text in the document

Select the case in the document

Click to mark the selected entry

Click to mark all references to this case in the document

Marked cases are denoted by braces

FIGURE 3.21 Mark a Citation for a Table of Authorities ➤

To modify an entry in the table of authorities, you must display the table of authorities fields by clicking Show/Hide (¶) in the Paragraph group on the Home tab. Locate the entry that you wish to modify and edit the text inside the quotation marks. Do not change the entry in the finished table of authorities, or the next time you update the table of authorities, your changes will be lost.

To delete a table of authorities entry, select the entire entry field, including the braces {}, and press Delete. After you modify or delete a marked entry, click Update Table in the Table of Authorities group on the References tab to display the changes in the table.

Creating Cross-References

A **cross-reference** is a note that refers the reader to another location for more information about a topic.

A *cross-reference* is a note that refers the reader to another location for more information about a topic. You can create automated cross-references to headings, bookmarks, footnotes, endnotes, captions, and tables. A typical cross-reference looks like this: *See page 4 for more information about local recreation facilities.* When using the automated cross-reference feature, Word tracks the location of the reference and inserts the correct page number in the place you designate in the document. For files you make available via e-mail or on an intranet, this creates an electronic cross-reference that enables the reader to hyperlink to that location.

To create a cross-reference, position the insertion point in the location where the reference occurs. On the References tab click Cross-reference in the Captions group. When the Cross-reference dialog box displays, as shown in Figure 3.22, you choose the type of reference (such as Heading, Bookmark, Figure, or Footnote) and then the reference element to display (such as page number or paragraph text). You can specify whether it displays as a hyperlink in the document, causing a ScreenTip to appear when the mouse pointer is over the cross-reference and moving you to that location when clicked, or as a static entry that simply displays a page number.

Cross-reference page number displays at insertion point

Click to insert cross-reference

Reference type (such as Heading, Bookmark, or Figure)

Create a hyperlink to the cross-referenced element

Click to choose the reference element (such as Page Number)

List changes based on selected reference type

FIGURE 3.22 Insert a Cross-Reference ➤

HANDS-ON EXERCISES

3 Research Paper Enhancements

This version of the marketing plan is nearly done. Only a few more enhancements will make it complete, so you decide to add a table of contents to the beginning of the document. Because of the number of graphic elements, you also decide to include a table of figures. An index will help the reader find information in this lengthy document, and you insert a cross-reference as well.

Skills covered: Apply Styles and Insert a Table of Contents • Define an Index Entry • Create the Index and Add Page Numbers • Add Captions and Create a Table of Figures • Create a Cross-Reference • Update the Table of Contents and View the Completed Document

---

STEP 1 APPLY STYLES AND INSERT A TABLE OF CONTENTS

Adding a table of contents (ToC) will enhance the professionalism of the marketing plan you and Rachel have developed for your class. You know that a table of contents is easy to insert if you apply styles to text first, so you take care of that and then insert the ToC. Refer to Figure 3.23 as you complete Step 1.

FIGURE 3.23 Create a Table of Contents ➤

a. Open the *w03h2plan_LastnameFirstname* document if you closed it after the last Hands-On Exercise. Save the document as **w03h3plan_LastnameFirstname**, changing *h2* to *h3*.

b. Click to the left of the *Executive Summary* title on the second page. Type **Table of Contents** and press **Enter** two times. Press **Ctrl+Enter** to insert a page break.

The ToC displays on a page between the title page and the body of the document using the Heading 1 style you applied in the previous exercise.

> **TROUBLESHOOTING:** If the Heading 1 style does not display, apply Heading 1 from the Quick Style gallery on the Home Tab to the *Table of Contents* heading.

c. Select the entire **Table of Contents heading**. Click the **Home tab**, and then apply the **Strong style**. **Center** the heading.

If you continue to use the Heading 1 style, the *Table of Contents* heading will display in the ToC itself.

d. Apply the **Heading 1 style** to the paragraph heading *Organizational Overview* on the fourth page. Continue to apply the **Heading 1 style** to the paragraph headings on the next three pages using the Format Painter.

e. Scroll up and place the insertion point on the line following the *Table of Contents* title.

f. Click the **References tab**, and then click **Table of Contents** in the Table of Contents group. Select **Insert Table of Contents.**

The Table of Contents dialog box displays (see Figure 3.23). You will see several preformatted styles provided when you click Table of Contents, but you are not using them because you want to customize the table. To customize you will select features in the Table of Contents dialog box, which you do in the next steps.

g. Click the **Show page numbers check box** and the **Right align page numbers check box**, if necessary.

h. Click the **Formats arrow** in the *General* section, and then select **Distinctive**. Click the **Tab leader arrow** in the *Print Preview* section, and then choose a dot leader. Click **OK.**

Word takes a moment to create the table of contents and then displays all paragraph headings and their associated page numbers in the location of your insertion point.

> **TROUBLESHOOTING:** If your Table of Contents includes text from the paragraphs instead of just paragraph headings, check the style applied to the text. Remove the Heading 1 or 2 styles, if they are in use, and apply a different one to avoid inclusion in the ToC. Press F9 to update your table to reflect the change.

i. Save the document.

STEP 2 ▶ DEFINE AN INDEX ENTRY

Rachel has marked several words already that will display in the index of your marketing plan. You decide to add the word *customer*, so you take steps to mark all occurrences of it; you use the Find feature to speed up the process of locating it in the document. Refer to Figure 3.24 as you complete Step 2.

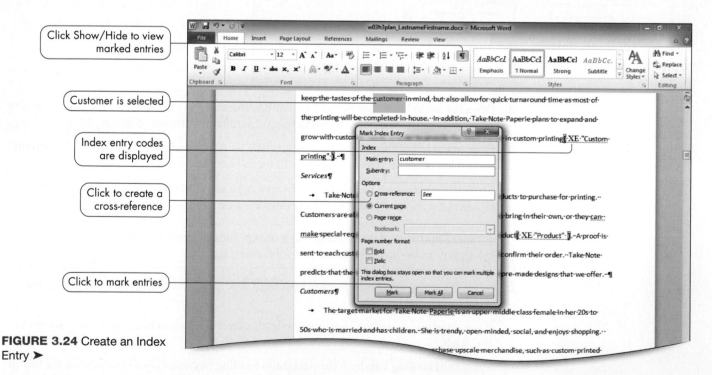

FIGURE 3.24 Create an Index Entry ➤

a. Press **Ctrl+Home** to move to the beginning of the document. Click **Ctrl+F** to display the Navigation Pane, and type **Customer** in the **text box**. Click the second entry in the results list.

You click the second occurrence because it is in singular form. The first occurrence is in plural form, but that is not what you want to mark for the index.

b. Click the **Home tab**, if necessary, and then click **Show/Hide** (¶) in the Paragraph group so you can see the nonprinting characters in the document.

The index entries already created by Rachel appear in curly brackets and begin with the letters *XE*.

c. Confirm that the entry for *customer* you just found is selected within the document. Click the **References tab**, and then click **Mark Entry** to display the Mark Index Entry dialog box, as shown in Figure 3.24.

d. Replace the lowercase *c* in the **Main Entry box** with a capital **C** so the word *Customer* displays capitalized.

The word that displays in the dialog box, and later as a hidden mark in the document text, will display in the index, so you want it to be capitalized. Capitalizing it in the index entry does not affect the way it displays in the document.

e. Click **Mark** to create the index entry.

After you create the index entry, you see the field code *{XE "Customer"}* to indicate that the index entry is created. The Mark Index Entry dialog box stays open so that you can create additional entries by selecting additional text.

f. Type **customer** in the **text box** in the Navigation Pane, if necessary, and then click the fourth entry, which is the next occurrence of the word *customer* in the document. Close the Navigation Pane.

g. Click anywhere on the Mark Index Entry dialog box, change capitalization to display *Customer* in the **Main Entry box**, and then click **Mark All** to create the index entry on all instances of the word in the remainder of the document.

You know this word occurs many times in the document and each should be referenced in the Index; this is the most efficient way to mark all occurrences simultaneously.

h. Click **Close** to close the Mark Index Entry dialog box. Click the **Home tab**, and then click **Show/Hide** (¶) to hide the formatting marks.

i. Save the document.

STEP 3 **CREATE THE INDEX AND ADD PAGE NUMBERS**

You have just marked all the words you want to include in the Index, so it is time to add it. You remember to insert the index on a blank page at the end of the document, after the bibliography, You also decide it is time to add page numbers, which are appropriate to display in a multi-page document. Refer to Figure 3.25 as you complete Step 3.

Click to view Index dialog box

Specify number of columns

Preview what the index will look like

Click arrow to select index format

FIGURE 3.25 Create the Index ➤

a. Press **Ctrl+End** to move to the end of the document, and then press **Ctrl+Enter** to add a new blank page.

   This is where you will insert the index.

b. Type **Index** and press **Enter** one time. Select **Index**, and then click **Heading 1** in the Styles gallery. Position your cursor on the line that follows the *Index* heading.

c. Click the **References tab**, and then click **Insert Index** in the Index group.

   The Index dialog box displays as shown in Figure 3.25.

d. Click the **Formats arrow**, and then select **Classic**. If necessary, click the **Columns arrow** until 2 displays. Click **OK** to create the index.

> **TROUBLESHOOTING:** Click Undo on the Quick Access Toolbar if the index does not display at the end of the document, reposition the cursor, and then repeat Steps 3c and 3d.

TIP Check the Index Entries

Every entry in the index should begin with an uppercase letter. If this is not the case, it is because the original entry within the body of the document was marked improperly. Click Show/Hide (¶) in the Paragraph group on the Home tab to display the indexed entries within the document, which appear within brackets, e.g., {XE "Customer"}. Change each entry to begin with an uppercase letter as needed.

---

e. Click the **Insert tab**, click **Page Number** in the Header & Footer group, point to **Bottom of Page**, and then click **Plain Number 3**. Click **Close Header and Footer**.

f. Save the document.

Because the marketing plan contains multiple tables and a graphic, you take steps to insert a table of figures. Similar to other reference items you insert, before you create this table you must do some preliminary work by adding captions to the tables and graphic first, which are then used in the table. Refer to Figure 3.26 as you complete Step 4.

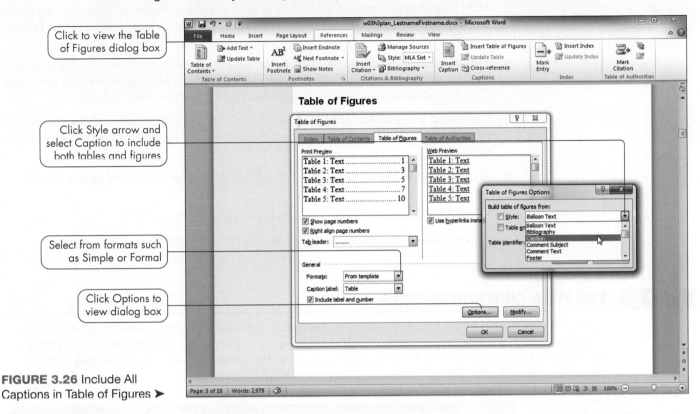

Click to view the Table of Figures dialog box

Click Style arrow and select Caption to include both tables and figures

Select from formats such as Simple or Formal

Click Options to view dialog box

FIGURE 3.26 Include All Captions in Table of Figures ➤

a. Go to page 14 where Appendix A begins. Hold your mouse over the top-left corner of the table until the cursor turns into a crosshair with arrows on each end. Click once to select the entire table. Click the **References tab**, and then click **Insert Caption** in the Captions group.

> **TROUBLESHOOTING:** Your page numbers may vary slightly. If so, find the page where *Appendix A* displays.

The Caption dialog box displays, and the insertion point is positioned at the end of the caption text that displays automatically.

b. Press the **Colon key (:)**, and then press **Spacebar** two times. Type **Initial Advertising Plan Budget** in the **Caption box**. Click the **Position arrow**, and then select **Above selected item**, if necessary. Click **OK**.

The caption *Table 1: Initial Advertising Plan Budget* displays above the chart. By default, captions for tables are placed above the table, and captions for images are placed below the image. However, you can relocate them by making a change in the Caption dialog box.

c. Scroll to the top of the next page, and then select the organization chart. Click **Insert Caption** in the Captions group to open the Caption dialog box.

d. Click the **Label arrow**, and then select **Figure**. Click to place the cursor after *Figure 1* in the **Caption box**, press the **Colon key (:)**, press **Spacebar** two times, and then type **Marketing Organization**. Click the **Position arrow**, and then click **Above selected item**. Click **OK** to close the dialog box.

The caption for this figure now displays *Figure 1: Marketing Organization*.

e. Scroll to the top of the next page, and then select the chart. Click **Insert Caption**, press the **Colon key (:)**, press **Spacebar** one time, and then type **Take Note Paperie—Price List** in the **Caption box**. Click the **Label arrow**, and then select **Table**. Click the **Position arrow**, and then select **Above selected item**, if necessary. Click **OK** to close the dialog box.

You have now created three captions in this paper—two for tables and one for a figure.

f. Move your insertion point to the bottom of page 2, which contains the ToC. Click the **Home tab**, and then click **Show/Hide (¶)**. Press **Ctrl+Enter** to insert a page, and then type **Table of Figures**. Press **Enter** two times.

g. Click the **References tab**, and then click **Insert Table of Figures** in the Captions group to display the Table of Figures dialog box. Click **Options** to display the Table of Figures Options dialog box. Click the **Style arrow**, and then select **Caption**, as shown in Figure 3.26. Click **OK**.

This option forces the table of figures to include all elements that have a caption. In our case, we apply captions to both tables and figures, so we want to be sure both types display in the table.

h. Click **OK** to close the Table of Figures dialog box and display the table of figures in your document.

The table shows two entries for tables and one entry for a figure.

i. Click the **Home tab**, and then click **Show/Hide (¶)** to remove the formatting marks.

j. Save the document.

STEP 5 ▶ CREATE A CROSS-REFERENCE

Rachel suggests you add a cross-reference in the document where the first reference to Appendix A occurs, which will enable your instructor to jump quickly to the page where the appendix starts. By using the cross-reference tool, the page number can be updated if you make changes in the document that affect it. Refer to Figure 3.27 as you complete Step 5.

When you hover over the cross-reference a ScreenTip displays

Cross-reference displays in a grey box when you click the page number

FIGURE 3.27 Insert Cross-Reference ▶

a. Scroll to page 11, and then place the insertion point on the right side of the text *Appendix A* in the last sentence of the *Price* section.

b. Press **Spacebar**, and then type (**See page** . Click the **References tab**, if necessary, and then click **Cross-reference** in the Captions group. Click the **Reference type arrow**, and then select **Heading**. Click **Appendix A. Detailed Tables and Charts** in the **For which heading list**. Click the **Insert reference to arrow**, select **Page number**, and then click **Insert**. Click **Close** to close the Cross-reference dialog box.

The cross-reference displays the number *15*, which is the page where the chart displays.

c. Type) to close the parenthesis around the cross-reference. Click one time on the number *15* in the cross-reference, and then notice it is shaded with a dark grey box. Hold your mouse over the cross-reference page number, and then view the ScreenTip, as shown in Figure 3.27.

The ScreenTip instructs you to press *Ctrl+Click to follow link* while you click the number *15*; if you do, Word will move the insertion point to the location of the chart on page 15.

d. Save the document.

STEP 6 ▸ UPDATE THE TABLE OF CONTENTS AND VIEW THE COMPLETED DOCUMENT

Before you finish you want to make sure the additions of the table of figures, bibliography, and index display in your table of contents, so you take steps to update it and all page numbers. Then you view the marketing plan as a final copy without markup. Then you save it so Rachel can look at it before you submit it to your professor. Refer to Figure 3.28 as you complete Step 6.

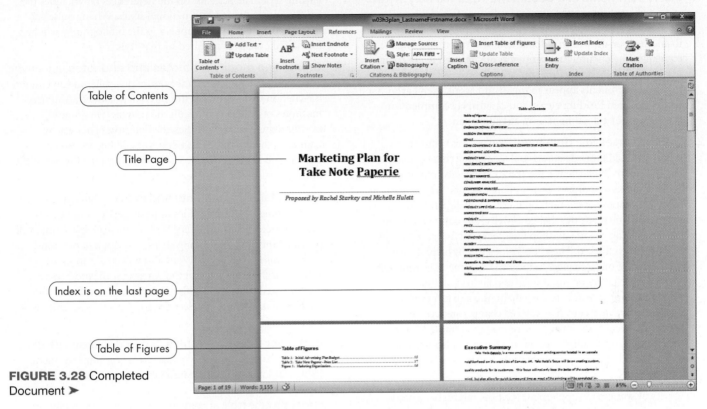

FIGURE 3.28 Completed Document ➤

a. Scroll to view the page that contains the *Table of Contents*. Right-click anywhere in the ToC, click **Update Field**, click **Update Entire Table**, and then click **OK**.

The entries for *Table of Figures*, *Bibliography*, and *Index* display, and page numbers adjust throughout the ToC to reflect these additions.

> **TROUBLESHOOTING:** If one or more of these tables do not display in the ToC, reapply the Heading 1 style to them, and update the ToC again. Also, remove any extra page breaks that might occur when you refresh the table—you do not want blank pages in between reference pages.

b. Click **Zoom level** on the status bar. Click the **Many pages icon** and drag to display **2 × 2 Pages**. Click **OK**.

You view several pages of the document, as seen in Figure 3.28.

c. Save and close the *w03h3plan_LastnameFirstname* file, and submit based on your instructor's directions.

After reading this chapter, you have accomplished the following objectives:

1. **Insert comments in a document.** When you work as part of a team, you can use the Comment feature to collaborate. Comments enable you to ask a question or provide a suggestion to another person within a document, without modifying the content of the document. Comments are inserted using colored markup balloons, and a different color is assigned to each reviewer. Comments appear in the Print Layout, Web Layout, and Full Screen Reading views. You can display comments in the margins of a document or in a reading pane.

2. **Track changes in a document.** You use this feature to monitor all additions, deletions, and formatting changes made to a document. When active, the Track Changes feature applies revision marks to indicate where a change occurs. When you move your mouse over a revision mark, it will display the name of the person who made the change as well as the date and time of the change. You can use markup tools to accept or reject changes that have been tracked. These tools are especially helpful when several people make changes to the same document. If comments and tracked changes do not display initially, you can turn on the Show Markup feature to view them. You also can view the document as a final copy if all tracked changes are accepted or as the original before any changes were made and tracked. You can modify the Track Changes options to change settings such as fonts, colors, location, and size of markup balloons.

3. **Acknowledge a source.** It is common practice to use a variety of sources to supplement your own thoughts when authoring a paper, report, legal brief, or many other types of document. Failure to acknowledge the source of information you use in a document is a form of plagiarism. Word provides the citation feature to track, compile, and display your research sources for inclusion in several types of supplemental references such as a bibliography. A bibliography is a list of works cited or consulted by an author and should be included with the document when published. Any sources added with the citation feature and used in the current document will display in the appropriate format as a bibliography. When research papers are prepared, the author often must conform to a particular writing style. The Style list on the References tab includes the most commonly used international styles. When you select the style the citations that appear in the bibliography will be formatted exactly as required by that style.

4. **Create and modify footnotes and endnotes.** A footnote is a citation that appears at the bottom of a page, and an endnote is a citation that appears at the end of a document. You use footnotes or endnotes to credit the sources you quote or cite in your document. If you click the Footnotes Dialog Box Launcher, the Footnotes and Endnotes dialog box opens, and you can modify the location of the notes and the format of the numbers.

5. **Insert a table of contents and index.** A table of contents lists headings in the order they appear in a document with their respective page numbers. Word can create it automatically, provided the built-in heading styles were applied previously to the items for inclusion. Word also will create an index automatically, provided that the entries for the index have been marked previously. This result, in turn, requires you to go through a document, select the appropriate text, and mark the entries accordingly.

6. **Add other reference tables.** If your document includes pictures, charts, or graphs you can create captions for them. Using captions, you can create a table of figures, or list of the captions, for a point of reference. A table of figures is commonly placed after the table of contents for a document. A table of authorities is used in legal documents to reference cases, rules, treaties, and other documents referred to in a legal brief. Word's Table of Authorities feature enables you to mark, track, compile, and display citations, or references to specific legal cases and other legal documents, to be included in the table of authorities.

7. **Create cross-references.** A cross-reference is a note that refers the reader to another location in the document for more information about a topic. You can create cross-references to headings, bookmarks, footnotes, endnotes, captions, and tables.

KEY TERMS

Bibliography *p. 231*
Caption *p. 241*
Changed line *p. 221*
Citation *p. 229*
Comment *p. 218*
Cross-reference *p. 243*
Current List *p. 230*
Endnote *p. 232*

Final: Show Markup *p. 222*
Footnote *p. 232*
Index *p. 239*
Markup balloon *p. 218*
Master List *p. 230*
Original: Show Markup *p. 222*
Plagiarism *p. 229*
Reviewing Pane *p. 219*

Revision mark *p. 221*
Show Markup *p. 220*
Table of authorities *p. 242*
Table of contents *p. 237*
Table of figures *p. 241*
Track Changes *p. 221*

MULTIPLE CHOICE

1. Which of the following statements about comments is false?

   (a) Comment balloons appear on the right side in Print Layout view by default.
   (b) You cannot edit a comment that was created by another person.
   (c) You cannot print comments with the rest of the document.
   (d) You can use the Show Markup feature on the Review tab to filter markup balloons so only comments display on the page.

2. What option enables you to preview how a document will look if you accept all tracked changes?

   (a) Final: Show Markup
   (b) Final
   (c) Original: Show Markup
   (d) Original

3. How do you view and edit footnote text?

   (a) Position the mouse pointer over the footnote reference mark and click inside the ScreenTip that appears.
   (b) Open the Footnote and Endnote dialog box.
   (c) Double-click the footnote reference mark and type in the footnote.
   (d) Click Citation on the References tab.

4. Which option is not true about plagiarism?

   (a) It is the act of using another person's work and claiming it as your own.
   (b) It is considered academic dishonesty in academic communities.
   (c) It only applies to written works; ideas, spoken words, or graphics are not included.
   (d) It has serious moral and ethical implications.

5. What document item directs a reader to another location in a document by mentioning its location?

   (a) Cross-reference
   (b) Bookmark
   (c) Endnote
   (d) Thumbnail

6. A table of figures is generated from what type of entries?

   (a) Index
   (b) Bookmarks
   (c) Comments
   (d) Captions

7. What does a table of authorities display?

   (a) A list of pictures, tables, and figures in a document
   (b) A list of cases, rules, treaties, and other documents cited in a legal document
   (c) A list of key words and phrases in the document
   (d) A sequential list of section headings and their page numbers

8. Select the sequence of events to include a bibliography in your document.

   (a) Select writing style, insert bibliography, and then insert citations.
   (b) Type footnotes into document, insert bibliography, and then select writing style.
   (c) Select writing style, mark legal references, and then insert bibliography.
   (d) Insert a citation, select writing style, and then insert bibliography.

9. After you create and insert a table of contents into a document:

   (a) Any subsequent page changes arising from the insertion or deletion of text to existing paragraphs must be entered manually.
   (b) Any additions to the entries in the table arising due to the insertion of new paragraphs defined by a heading style must be entered manually.
   (c) An index cannot be added to the document.
   (d) You can right-click, then select Update Field to update the table of contents.

10. You are participating in a group project in which each member makes changes to the same document. Which feature in Word should you suggest the members use so each can see the edits made by fellow group members?

    (a) Mark index entries.
    (b) Track changes.
    (c) Mark citations.
    (d) Create cross-references.

1 Odom Law Firm

You work as a clerk in the Odom Law Firm and are responsible for preparing documentation used in all phases of the judicial process. A senior partner in the firm asks you to work on a document by inserting a table of authorities based on the cases cited in the document. As you work you notice it also needs another footnote and a caption on a graphic. So that the partner can double-check your work, you track the changes you make to the document. This exercise follows the same set of skills as used in Hands-On Exercises 1, 2, and 3 in the chapter. Refer to Figure 3.29 as you complete this exercise.

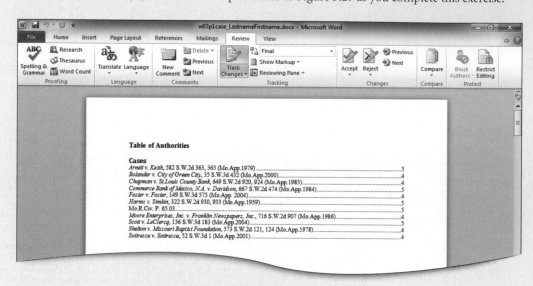

FIGURE 3.29 Table of Authorities ➤

a. Open *w03p1case* and save it as **w03p1case_LastnameFirstname**.

b. Press **Ctrl+Home** to move the insertion point to the beginning of the document.

c. Click the **Review tab**, click the **Track Changes arrow** in the Tracking group, and click **Change User Name**. Verify that your name displays as the *User Name* on this PC, and that your initials display in the Initials box; if necessary, type your name and initials in the appropriate text box, and then click **OK** to close the Word Options dialog box.

d. Click **Track Changes** in the Tracking group so the feature displays in orange and your edits are marked as you work.

e. Click **New Comment** in the Comments group, and then type **Second edit by *your name* on *date***.

f. Click **Next** in the Comments group two times to select the balloon containing the comment about a change you need to make to the footer. Read the comment.

g. Place the insertion point at the end of the footer on the bottom of the first page. Replace the year *2008* with **2012**.

h. Click **Previous** in the Comments group to select the comment balloon you previously read. Move the insertion point to the end of the comment inside the balloon, and then type the sentence **Completed by *your name*** after the existing text. Remember to use your name.

i. Scroll to the bottom of page 2. Position your cursor at the end of the last sentence in the first paragraph under the heading *Attorney Blanchard's withdrawal*. When your cursor is on the right side of the period after the words *anything on the case*, click the **References tab**, and then click **Insert Footnote** in the Footnotes group. Type **See Exhibit 9, attached** in the **footnote area** where your cursor is blinking at the bottom of the page.

j. Press **Ctrl+End** to move to the end of the document. Select the picture of the bicycle, and then click **Insert Caption** in the Captions group. If necessary, click the **Label arrow**, and then select **Figure** so that *Figure 1* displays as the caption. Place the insertion point at the end of the caption, press **colon (:)**, press **Spacebar** one time, and then type **Assembled Bicycle**. Click **OK** to close the Caption dialog box.

k. Go to page 3 in the document. Locate the *Shelton v. Missouri Baptist Foundation* case, and then select the case information from *Shelton* through and including the date *(1978)*. Select the closing parenthesis but not the comma after it. Click **Mark Citation** in the Table of Authorities group. Click **Mark All**, and then click **Close**.

l. Scan the remainder of that page, and then mark all citations for the following cases: *Foster, Sotirescu, Moore Enterprises, Scott, Chapman, Bolander,* and *Arnett.* After you mark the final citation on that page, click **Cancel** to close the dialog box. Click the **Home tab**, and then click **Show/Hide** (¶) in the Paragraph group to turn off display of formatting marks.

m. Press **Ctrl+Home** to position the insertion point at the beginning of the document, and then press **Ctrl+Enter** to add a blank page. Press **Ctrl+Home** to place the insertion point at the top of the new page, type **Table of Authorities**, and then press **Enter** one time. Click the **References tab**, and then click **Insert Table of Authorities** in the Table of Authorities group. Click **OK**.

n. Right-click the comment by William Kincaid on page 2 that says *Please add the Table of Authorities to this document,* and then click **Delete Comment**.

o. Press **Ctrl+F**, and then type **bike** in the **text box**. Place the insertion point after the first occurrence of the word *bike* that displays in the first sentence of the *Background* paragraph. Press **Spacebar** one time, and then type (**See picture on page** . Be sure to add a blank space after you type the word *page.* Click the **References Tab**, and then click **Cross-reference** in the Captions group.

p. Click the **Reference type arrow**, and then select **Figure**. Click **Figure 1 Assembled Bicycle** in the **For which caption list**, click the **Insert reference to arrow**, select **Page Number**, and then click **Insert** to complete the cross-reference. Click **Close** to close the Cross-reference dialog box. Type) to complete the parentheses that hold the cross-reference.

q. Click the **Review tab**, click the **Display for Review arrow**, and then click **Final** to display the document without markup. Press **Ctrl+Home** to view the table of authorities, and then compare to Figure 3.29.

r. Save and close the file, and submit based on your instructor's directions.

2 The Great Depression

Dr. Jared Dockery, your history professor, has assigned a short research paper project. You decide to write about the Great Depression, which started in 1929. In addition to writing an interesting overview of the financial struggles in the United States during that time, you intend to impress Dr. Dockery with your technical skills—submitting a paper that includes proper citations, reference tables, and even an index. This exercise follows the same set of skills as used in Hands-On Exercises 1, 2, and 3 in the chapter. Refer to Figure 3.30 as you complete this exercise.

Endnote displays at the end of the last page

FIGURE 3.30 Report About the Great Depression ➤

a. Open *w03p2gd* and save it as **w03p2gd_LastnameFirstname**.

b. Click the **Insert tab**, and then click **Cover Page** in the Pages group. Choose the **Alphabet style**, and then type **1929-1933** as the document subtitle. Click the date, click the date arrow, and then choose **Today**. Replace the current author, *Exploring Series,* with your name.

c. Press **Ctrl+Home** to move the insertion point to the beginning of the document. Click the **Review Tab**, and then click **Next** in the Changes group. Click **Reject** to prevent the insertion of the lines that are now included in the title page. Click the **Accept arrow**, and then click **Accept All Changes in Document**.

d. Place the insertion point on the left side of the heading *Introduction* at the top of this page. Press **Ctrl+Enter** to create a hard page break. At the top of page 3, select the **Introduction heading**, click the **Home tab**, and then apply the **Heading 1 style** from the Styles gallery. Apply the **Heading 1 style** to the remaining boldfaced paragraph headings in the document using the Format Painter.

e. Scroll to the top of page 2, which is the blank page you created in the last step, and place the insertion point on the first line. Click the **References tab**, click **Table of Contents**, and then click **Automatic Table 2**.

f. Scroll down to the third page, and then select the picture. Click **Insert Caption** in the Captions group. Press **Spacebar** two times, and then type **Families in Dismay**. Click the **Position arrow**, and then click **Below selected item**. Click **OK** to close the Caption dialog box.

g. Use the instructions from step f to apply the following captions to the remaining pictures in the document:
  • **Struggling Main Street**
  • **Recovery in Sight**

h. Place the insertion point at the end of the Table of Contents. Press **Ctrl+Enter** to insert a page break. Scroll to the top of the blank page you just created, if necessary, and then place the insertion point on the first line. Type **Table of Figures** and press **Enter** two times. Click **Insert Table of Figures** in the Captions group, and then click **OK**. Select the **Table of Figures heading**, click the **Home tab**, and then click **Heading 1** from the Styles gallery.

i. Click the **References tab**, and then click **Manage Sources** in the Citations & Bibliography group. Click **New**, and then select **Document from Web site**, if necessary, from the Type of Source menu. Use the following table to enter information for the two sources used in this paper. After both sources are created, click **Close** to close the Source Manager dialog box.

Field in Create Source Dialog box	Source #1
Name of Web Page	"Great Depression." The Columbia Encyclopedia, Sixth Edition
Name of Web Site	Encyclopedia.com
Year	2008
Year Accessed	2012
Month Accessed	June
Day Accessed	09
URL	http://www.encyclopedia.com/doc/1E1-GreatDep.html

Field in Create Source Dialog box	Source #2
Name of Web Page	West's Encyclopedia of American Law
Name of Web Site	Encyclopedia.com
Year	2005
Year Accessed	2012
Month Accessed	June
Day Accessed	09
URL	http://www.encyclopedia.com/doc/1G2-3437703075.html

j. Press **Ctrl+End** to move the insertion point to the end of the document, and then press **Ctrl+Enter** to insert a hard page break. Click the **Style arrow** in the Citations & Bibliography group, and then click **APA Fifth Edition**, if necessary. Click **Bibliography**, and then click **Works Cited**.

k. Place your cursor at the end of the first sentence (after the period) in the first paragraph under *The New Deal* paragraph heading. Click **Insert Endnote** in the Footnotes group. Type the following: "New Deal." West's Encyclopedia of American Law. **2005. Encyclopedia.com. 9 June 2009 http:// www.encyclopedia.com**. Compare your work to Figure 3.30.

l. Scroll to the page that contains the Table of Contents. Click one time anywhere in the table of contents, and then press **F9**. Click **Update Entire Table**, and then click **OK**.

m. Save and close the file, and submit based on your instructor's directions.

MID-LEVEL EXERCISES

1 WWW Web Services Agency

You work as a Web designer at WWW Web Services Agency and have been asked to provide some basic information to be used in a senior citizens workshop. You want to provide the basic elements of good Web design and format the document professionally. Use the basic information you have already, in a Word document, and revise it to include elements appropriate for a research-oriented paper.

a. Open *w03m1web* and save it as **w03m1web_LastnameFirstname**.

b. Insert your name at the bottom of the cover page.

c. Place the insertion point at the end of the *Proximity and Balance* paragraph on the second page of the document. Insert the following text into an endnote: **Max Rebaza, Effective Web Sites, Chicago: Windy City Publishing, Inc. (2004): 44.**

 DISCOVER

d. Change all endnotes into footnotes.

e. Insert a table of contents after the cover page. Use a style of your choice.

f. In preparation for adding a bibliography to your document, create a citation source using the source from step c. (Hint: It is a book section.) Use the **Source Manager** to create the source and prevent the citation from displaying in the document. Also create citation sources for the two additional sources identified in the document footnotes.

g. Insert a bibliography at the end of the document using the Chicago style. Use the default format and settings for the bibliography. Apply **Heading 2 style** to the *Bibliography* heading.

h. Add captions to each graphic that displays in the paper. Use the default caption for each; you do not have to create a description. Display the caption below the graphic. Add a caption to the table on page 6 and display the caption below the table.

i. Create a table of figures at the beginning of the document on a separate page after the table of contents. The table should provide a list of figures only. Give the page an appropriate heading and format the heading using the **Heading 2 style**.

j. Insert a cross-reference at the end of the *Font Size and Attributes* paragraph on the seventh page. Type **See also** and insert a cross-reference that uses the **Heading reference type** and the *Contrast and Focus* heading. End the sentence with a period.

k. Update the entire table of contents and the table of figures. Remove any unnecessary blank pages in the document.

l. Save and close the file, and submit based on your instructor's directions.

2 Tips for Healthy Living

 CREATIVE CASE

As a student in the Physician Assistant program at a local university, you create a document containing tips for healthier living. The facts have been entered into a Word document but are thus far unformatted. You will modify it to incorporate styles, and then you will create a comprehensive document by including a table of contents and index.

a. Open *w03m2healthy* and save it as **w03m2healthy_LastnameFirstname**.

b. Scroll through the document and view the changes that are currently marked in the document, and then accept each change. Turn on **Track Changes** so your changes will also be flagged. Change the Track Changes Options to display all formatting changes in color only.

c. Apply the **Heading 1** and **Body Text styles** throughout the document. It has been completed on the first and last paragraphs already.

d. Create a title page for the document consisting of the title, **Tips for Healthy Living**, and the subtitle, **Prepared by your name**. Replace *your name* with your name.

e. Create a footer for the document consisting of the title, **Tips for Healthy Living**, and a page number—use the page number style of your choice. The footer should not appear on the title page; that is, page 1 is actually the second page of the document.

f. Create a page specifically for the table of contents, and then give the page a title and generate a table of contents using the Healthy Living tip headings. Use a dashed leader to connect the headings to the page numbers in the table.

g. Mark the following text for inclusion in the index: *diet, exercise, metabolism, vegetables, fat.* At the end of your document, create the index and take necessary steps so the index heading displays in the table of contents.

h. Change the Display for Review setting to show the document as a final copy.

DISCOVER

i. Print only a **List of markup**, if allowed by your instructor.

j. Save and close the file, and submit based on your instructor's directions.

3 Table of Authorities

As the junior partner in a growing law firm, you must proofread and update all legal briefs before they are submitted to the courts. You are in the final stage of completing a medical malpractice case, but the brief cannot be filed without a table of authorities.

a. Open *w03m3legal* and save it as **w03m3legal_LastnameFirstname**.

b. Mark all references to legal cases throughout the document.

c. Insert a table of authorities at the beginning of the document. Insert an appropriate heading at the top of the page, and format it using **Heading 1 style**.

d. Insert a comment at the beginning of the document, and then type **Ready to include in court records**.

e. Save and close the file, and submit based on your instructor's directions.

CAPSTONE EXERCISE

You are a member of the Horticulture Society and have been asked to assist in the development of information packets about a variety of flowers and plants. A report about tulips has been started, and you are responsible for completing the document so that it is ready for the fall meeting. You know of many features in Word that you can use to finish and present an easy-to-follow report.

Track Revisions

The document you receive has a few comments and shows the last few changes by the author. You will accept or reject the changes, and then make a few of your own. You will turn on track changes to differentiate between your changes and the author's.

a. Open *w03c1tulip* and save it as **w03c1tulip_Lastname Firstname**.

b. Scroll through the document and review the comment. Return to the third page and reject the insertion of a sentence about squirrels.

c. Accept all other tracked changes in the document. Keep all comments.

d. Change all headings that use Heading 3 style so they use **Heading 1 style**, as per the comment left by the author

e. Click inside the author's comment, and then insert a new comment. In the new comment, type a message indicating you have made the style replacement. This new comment will display *R1* after your name in the balloon to indicate it is a response to the previous comment.

Credit Sources

You are now ready to add the citations for resources that the author used when assembling this report. The author sent some source citations as an external file, and she typed some of the source information at the end of the document. She did not format it appropriately for use as a citation, nor did she insert citations in the appropriate places in the document as a footnote or endnote.

a. Use the **Source Manager tool** to open the file *tulips.xml*, and then copy the citations into the current list for this document.

b. Scroll to the end of the document to view a list of sources. Use the **Source Manager tool** to create new citations for each source. After you create the citations, delete the *Sources* paragraph heading and each source below it.

c. Modify the source from the Gardenersnet Web site to indicate the information was retrieved on June 7, 2012. Modify the source only in your current list.

d. Create a bibliography using MLA style on a separate page at the end of the document.

e. Insert an endnote on page 3, at the end of the third paragraph in the *Planting* section, which ends with *made by the planter*. Type the following for the endnote:

Swezey, Lauren Bonar, A Westerner's Guide to Tulips (Sunset, October 1999). Change the number format for endnotes to **1, 2, 3** in the Footnotes dialog box launcher.

Figure References

The graphics in the document are quite informative, and you want to add descriptive captions to them and to list them on a reference page.

a. Select the tulip picture on the left side of the first row, and then assign the following caption below the photo: **Figure 1. Angelique**.

b. Assign captions to the remaining tulip photos on that page using information in the comments fields. Delete the comments after you create the captions.

c. Assign the caption **Planting Depth Guide** to the graphic titled *Planting Guide at a Glance*.

d. Create a blank page following the cover page, and then insert a table of figures, using the **Distinctive format**. Type **Table of Figures** at the top, and then format with the **Heading 1 style**.

Finish with Table of Contents and Index

To put the finishing touches on your document, you add a table of contents and an index. The document is short, but you decide to include both because they demonstrate a higher level of professionalism in your work.

a. Automatically generate a table of contents and display it on a page between the cover page and the table of figures.

b. Mark the following words as index entries: *Holland, perennials, deadheading, soil, store*. Create an index cross-reference entry using the word *storage* in the index to indicate where the word *store* is used in the document.

c. Add an index to the end of the document. Use the **Classic index format**. Format the Index title using the **Heading 1 style**.

d. Find the sentence *See the depth chart in Figure 6*, which displays in the third paragraph in the *Planting* section. Before the period and following the number 6, add the following text: **on page** . Then insert a cross reference to Figure 6. If correct, it informs the reader that the graphic is found on page 5.

e. Display a page number in the footer of the document using **Accent Bar 4 format**. Start numbering on the page that contains the Table of Contents. Also, in the left side of the footer, display the text **Compiled by *your name***, but use your first and last name.

f. Update all tables to reflect any changes made throughout this project.

g. Save and close the file, and submit based on your instructor's directions.

Group Collaboration

GENERAL CASE

This case requires collaboration between members of a group. Create groups of two or three people; the first person will open *w03b1_collaborate* and save it as **w03b1collaborate_LastnameFirstname**. The first person will turn on track changes and make at least two corrections, add comments to the document, and type his or her name in the footer. The first person will then save and send the document to the next group member, who also will turn on track changes, make additional corrections and suggestions, and add his or her name to the footer. It is acceptable to correct the previous member's corrections, but do not accept or reject changes at this time. Each member can also customize the track changes options. After each member adds corrections and comments to the document, and adds his or her name to the footer, the last person should save the document, and then print one copy of the document that shows markup and a second copy that shows final without markup. Save and close the file, and submit based on your instructor's directions.

Learn to Use Writing Styles

RESEARCH CASE

Do you know someone who has been the victim of identity theft? It occurs every day. But what exactly is involved in this growing crime? Use your research skills to locate information about identity theft. You should find at least one source from the Internet, at least one source from a book, and at least one source from a journal. Use your school's library or online library resources to help locate the information sources. After you find your sources, write a two-page report, double-spaced, describing identity theft. Include information about the crime, statistics, government policies, laws that have been passed because of this crime, and the crime's effects on victims. Cite the sources in your paper, use footnotes where appropriate, and develop a bibliography for your paper based on the APA writing style. Save the report as **w03b2idtheft_LastnameFirstname**. Save and close the file, and submit based on your instructor's directions.

Repairing Tables

DISASTER RECOVERY

You work in the city's Planning and Zoning department as an analyst. You begin to prepare the *Guide to Planned Developments* document for posting on the city's intranet. The administrative clerk who typed the document attempted to insert a table of contents and a table of figures, but he was not successful in displaying either table accurately. Open his file, *w03b3table*, and save your revised document as **w03b3table_LastnameFirstname**. He also attempted to insert cross-references, but they do not work correctly either. Before this document can be posted, you must repair both tables at the beginning of the document and the erroneous cross-references. The cross-references are highlighted in the document so you can locate them easily; the highlights should be removed when you have corrected the references. When you have corrected the problems, save and close the file, and submit based on your instructor's directions.

4 DOCUMENT PRODUCTIVITY

Working with Tables and Mail Merge

Watch the
Set-up Video
for this
Case Study!

CASE STUDY | Community Disaster Relief Center

Wacey Rivale is the Director of Fundraising at the local Community Disaster Relief Center (CDRC). She spends many hours giving speeches to local companies, organizations, and civic groups so they will be familiar with the efforts and activities of the Relief Center. Because the CDRC is a nonprofit organization, Wacey and other CDRC staffers must demonstrate the need, the benefits, and the success of the service they provide.

Wacey always sends a letter of appreciation to the people who donate and support the CDRC, but her latest marketing efforts have increased the response of the community. Typically, she sends one or two per week, but now she is in a position where she needs to send several dozen letters. She asks you, her co-worker, to start a list of donors, their addresses, and their contribution amounts so no donor is overlooked when it comes time to send the letters. You decide to document donor information in a table in Word. Then it will be part of a mail merge to create thank-you letters quickly and efficiently.

OBJECTIVES   AFTER YOU READ THIS CHAPTER, YOU WILL BE ABLE TO:

1. Insert a table *p.262*
2. Format a table *p.264*
3. Sort and apply formulas to table data *p.273*
4. Convert text to a table *p.275*

5. Select a main document *p.282*
6. Select or create recipients *p.283*
7. Insert merge fields *p.287*
8. Merge a main document and a data source *p.288*

Tables

A **table** is a series of columns and rows that organizes data effectively. The columns and rows in a table intersect to form **cells**. The table feature is one of the most powerful in Word and is an easy way to organize a series of data in a columnar list format. For example, you can create tables to organize data such as employee lists with phone numbers and e-mail addresses. The donor registry in Figure 4.1, for example, is actually an 8 × 13 table (8 columns and 13 rows). The completed table looks impressive, but it is very easy to create once you understand how a table works. In addition to the organizational benefits, tables make an excellent alignment tool. Although you can align text with tabs, you have more format control when you create a table. (See the Practice Exercises at the end of the chapter for other examples.)

> The table feature is one of the most powerful in Word and is an easy way to organize a series of data.... In addition to the organizational benefits, tables make an excellent alignment tool.

FIGURE 4.1 Table Containing Names of Donors ➤

After you create a basic table, you want to enhance the appearance to create interest for the reader and improve readability. Word includes many tools to assist with these efforts, and you will use several of them to complete the table used for the Donor Registry. In this section, you will insert a table in a document. After inserting the table, you can insert or delete columns and rows if you need to change the structure. Furthermore, you will learn how to merge and split cells within the table and how to change the row height and column width to accommodate data in the table. You also will learn how to format a table using borders, shading, and the styles provided by Word. Finally, you will modify table alignment and position.

Inserting a Table

You create a table from the Insert tab. Click Table in the Tables group on the Insert tab to see a gallery of cells on which you drag to select the number of columns and rows you require in the table, or you can choose the Insert Table command below the gallery to display the Insert Table dialog box and enter the table composition you prefer. When you select the table dimension from the gallery or from the Insert Table dialog box, Word creates a table structure with the number of columns and rows you specify. After you create a table, you can enter text, numbers, or graphics in individual cells. The text wraps as it is entered within a cell, so that you can add or delete text without affecting the entries in other cells.

You format the contents of an individual cell the same way you format an ordinary paragraph; that is, you change the font, apply boldface or italic, change the text alignment, or apply any other formatting commands. You can select multiple cells, rows, or columns and apply formatting to the selection all at once, or you can format a cell independently of every other cell.

After you insert a table in your document, use commands in the Table Tools Design and Layout tabs to modify and enhance it. Place the insertion point anywhere in the table, and

Click the **Table Move handle** to select a whole table at one time.

then click either the Design or Layout tab to view the commands. In either tab just point to a command and a ScreenTip describes its function. When you hover the mouse over any cell of a table the ***Table Move handle*** displays (see Figure 4.1). You can click this handle once to select the whole table at one time, which is useful when working with design and layout features.

> **TIP** Using Tabs to Move Within Tables
>
> The Tab key on your keyboard functions differently in a table than in a regular document. Press Tab to move to the next cell in the current row, or to the first cell in the next row if you are at the end of a row. Press Tab when you are in the last cell of a table to add a new blank row to the bottom of the table. Press Shift+Tab to move to the previous cell in the current row (or to the last cell in the previous row). You must press Ctrl+Tab to insert a regular tab character within a cell.

Insert and Delete Rows and Columns

You can change the structure of a table after it has been created. If you need more rows or columns to accommodate additional data in your table, it is easy to add or insert them using the Rows & Columns group on the Table Tools Layout tab. The Insert and Delete commands enable you to add new or delete existing rows or columns. When you add a column, you can specify if you want to insert it to the right or left of the current column. Likewise, you can specify where to place a new row—either above or below the currently selected row.

You can delete complete rows and columns using the commands mentioned previously, or you can delete only the data in those rows and columns using the Delete key on your keyboard. Keep in mind that when you insert or delete a complete row or a column, the remaining rows and columns will adjust to the positioning. For example, if you delete the third row of a 5 × 5 table, the data in the fourth and fifth rows move up and become the third and fourth rows. If you delete only the data in the third row, the cells would be blank and the fourth and fifth rows would not change at all.

> **TIP** Inserting Multiple Rows (or Columns) Simultaneously
>
> If you need to insert more than one row (or column) at a time, simply select multiple rows (or columns), right-click, and select the Insert command, and the same number of blank rows (or columns) you selected will display. For example, if you select three rows before you click the Insert row command, three blank rows will appear.

Merge and Split Cells

You can use the Merge Cells command in the Merge group on the Table Tools Layout tab to join individual cells together (merge) to form a larger cell, as was done in the first row of Figure 4.1. People often merge cells to enter a main title at the top of a table. Conversely, you can use the Split Cells command in the Merge group to split a single cell into multiple cells if you require more cells to hold data.

Change Row Height and Column Width

Row height is the vertical space from the top to the bottom of a row.

Column width is the horizontal space or length of a column.

When you create a table, Word builds evenly spaced columns. Frequently you need to change the row height or column width to fit your data. ***Row height*** is the vertical distance from the top to the bottom of a row. ***Column width*** is the horizontal space or width of a column. You might increase the column width to display a wide string of text, such as first and last name, to prevent it from wrapping in the cell. You might increase row height to better fit a header that has been enlarged for emphasis.

The Table command is easy to master, and as you might have guessed, you will benefit from reviewing the available commands listed in the Design and Layout tabs. Features in the Layout tab are described in Table 4.1. You will use many of these commands as you create a table in the Hands-On Exercises.

TABLE 4.1 Table Tools Layout Tab

Group	Commands	Enables You to
Table	Select, View Gridlines, Properties — Table	• Select particular parts of a table (cell, column, row, or entire table). • Show or hide the gridlines around the table. • Display the Table Properties dialog box to format the table.
Rows & Columns	Delete, Insert Above, Insert Below, Insert Left, Insert Right — Rows & Columns	• Delete cells, columns, rows, or the entire table. • Insert rows and columns. • Display the Insert Cells dialog box.
Merge	Merge Cells, Split Cells, Split Table — Merge	• Merge (join) selected cells together. • Split cells into separate cells. • Split the table into two tables.
Cell Size	6.65", 0.25", AutoFit — Cell Size	• Adjust the row height and column width. • Adjust the column width automatically based on the data in the column. • Display the Table Properties dialog box.
Alignment	Text Direction, Cell Margins — Alignment	• Specify the combined horizontal and vertical alignment of text within a cell. • Change the text direction. • Set margins within a cell.
Data	Sort, Repeat Header Rows, Convert to Text, Formula — Data	• Sort data within a table. • Repeat header rows when tables span multiple pages. • Convert tabulated text to table format. • Insert a formula in a table.

Formatting a Table

Shading affects the background color within a cell.

Border refers to the line style around each cell.

You can use basic formatting options to enhance the appearance of your table. The Borders and Shading commands, for example, offer a wide variety of choices for formatting the table structure. *Shading* affects the background color within a cell or group of cells. Table shading is similar to the Highlight feature that places a color behind the contents in a cell. You often apply shading to the header row of a table to make it stand out from the data. *Border* refers to the line style around each cell in the table. The default is a single line, but you can choose from many styles to outline a table such as a double, triple, or a wavy line. You can even choose invisible borders if you want only data to display in your document without the outline of a table. Borders and Shading commands are located on both the Home tab and the Table Tools Design tab, but you will probably find it more convenient to access the command from the Table Tools Design tab while you work with tables. The Design tab features are described in Table 4.2.

> **TIP Right-Click for Table Formatting Options**
>
> As an alternative to using the Layout tab, you can find many table options in the context-sensitive menu that displays when you right-click the mouse. The insertion point can be anywhere in the table, and after you right-click you see several table options including Insert, Delete Cells, and Split Cells. You also can change format and alignment of table cells using the Borders and Shading, Cell Alignment, and Text Direction commands in this menu. The Table Properties option is available in the menu if you need to access features such as table alignment and cell spacing.

TABLE 4.2 Table Tools Design Tab

Group	Commands	Enables You to
Table Style Options	☑ Header Row ☑ First Column ☐ Total Row ☐ Last Column ☑ Banded Rows ☐ Banded Columns *Table Style Options*	• Turn Header Row on or off. • Turn Total Row on or off. • Display banded rows; formats even- and odd-numbered rows differently. • Display special formatting for first column. • Display special formatting for last column. • Display banded columns; formats even- and odd-numbered columns differently.
Table Styles	*Table Styles* gallery with Shading and Borders	• Select predefined style from gallery. • Apply color behind the selected cell(s) or table. • Customize borders of selected cell(s) or table.
Draw Borders	½ pt, Pen Color, Draw Table, Eraser *Draw Borders*	• Alter style of line used around border of cell or table. • Alter size of line used for borders. • Change Pen Color feature; use with Draw Table feature. • Manually draw borders of cell(s) or table. • Erase borders of cell(s) or table. • Display the Borders and Shading dialog box.

Apply Table Styles

A **table style** contains borders, shading, and other attributes to enhance a table.

Word provides many predefined *table styles* that contain borders, shading, font sizes, and other attributes that enhance the readability of a table. The Table Styles feature is helpful in situations where you want to apply a professional-looking format to a table; when you are coordinating the design of a table with other features in Word, Excel, or PowerPoint; or when you do not have time to apply custom borders and shading. The styles are available in the Table Styles group on the Design tab. To use a predefined table style, click anywhere in your table, and then click a style from the Table Styles gallery. A few styles from the gallery display, but you can select from many others by clicking the More button on the right side of the gallery, as shown in Figure 4.2. The Live Preview of a style displays on your table when you hover your mouse over it in the gallery. To apply a style, click it one time.

Style gallery

Click the More button to view additional styles

Live Preview of style if applied to table

FIGURE 4.2 Table Styles Command ➤

You can modify a predefined style if you wish to make changes to features such as color or alignment. You also can create your own table style and save it for use in the current document, or add it to a document template for use in other Word documents. Click the More button in the Table Styles group to access the Modify Table Style and New Table Style commands.

Select the Table Position and Alignment

Table alignment is the position of a table between the left and right margins.

Table alignment refers to the position of a table between the left and right document margins. When you insert a table, Word aligns it at the left margin by default. However, you can click Properties in the Table group on the Layout tab to display the Table Properties dialog box, as seen in Figure 4.3. The *Alignment* section of the dialog box offers four choices for table alignment—Left, Center, Right, or a custom setting in which you specify an amount that the table is indented from the left margin. For example, you might want to use the custom setting to indent the table exactly two inches from the left margin so it aligns with other indented text.

Click to view Table Properties dialog box

Click to center table between margins

Enter a custom setting for indention

FIGURE 4.3 Table Properties Dialog Box ➤

You can also choose from two text wrapping options in the Table Properties dialog box. The option to wrap text Around will enable you to display text on the side of the table. This is useful if you have a small table so you will not waste a great deal of space on the page by displaying the table and text close together. The option for None prevents text from displaying beside the table, and will force text to display above or below it. If your table is small, this will enable a large amount of white space to display beside it.

You also can change alignment of the data in a table separately from the table itself using commands on the Layout tab. The Alignment group contains many options to quickly format table data. Table data can be formatted to align in many different horizontal and vertical combinations. We often apply horizontal settings, such as Center, to our data, but using vertical settings also increases readability. For example, when you want your data to be centered both horizontally and vertically within a cell so it is easy to read and does not appear to be elevated on the top or too close to the bottom, click Align Center in the Alignment group.

Text direction refers to the degree of rotation in which text displays.

The default *text direction* places text in a horizontal position. However, you can rotate text so it displays sideways. To change text direction, click Text Direction in the Alignment group. Each time you click Text Direction, the text rotates. This is a useful tool for aligning text that is in the header row of a narrow column.

A **cell margin** is the amount of space between data and the cell border in a table.

The *Cell Margins* command in the Alignment group on the Layout tab enables you to adjust the amount of white space inside a cell as well as spacing between cells. Use this setting to improve readability of cell contents by adjusting white space around your data or between cells if they contain large amounts of text or data. If you increase cell margins, it prevents data from looking squeezed together.

1 Tables

Since you will be tracking information about the donors and donations that Wacey Rivale receives for the Community Disaster Relief Center (CDRC), you quickly determine that a table is the logical choice for a professional and easy-to-read document. It also gives you flexibility in adding more information because you expect the donations to keep pouring in.

Skills covered: Create a Table • Insert Data, Rows, and Columns • Change Row Height and Column Width • Merge Cells to Create a Title Row • Apply a Table Style and Align Data

STEP 1 ▶ CREATE A TABLE

After a discussion with Wacey, you now know the donor information that should be documented. You determine the size of the table you will use is based on the fact that it must display the donor's name, address, date, and amount of donation. Refer to Figure 4.4 as you complete Step 1.

FIGURE 4.4 Inserting a Table ➤

a. Open a new blank document and save it as **w04h1donations_LastnameFirstname**.

b. Press **Enter** twice in the blank document, and then click the **Insert tab**.

You will find it easier to work with a table if it does not begin on the very first line of the document. The Insert tab contains the Table command.

c. Click **Table** in the Tables group, and then drag your mouse over the cells until you select seven columns and three rows; you will see the table size, 7 × 3, displayed above the cells, as shown in Figure 4.4. Click the bottom-right cell (where the seventh column and the third row intersect) to insert the table into your document.

Word creates an empty table that contains seven columns and three rows. The default columns have identical widths, and the table spans from the left to the right margin.

d. Practice selecting various elements from the table, something that you will have to do in subsequent steps:

- Select a single cell by pointing inside the left grid line. The pointer changes to a black slanted arrow when you are in the proper position, and then you can click to select the cell.

- Select a row by clicking in the left margin of the first cell in that row (the pointer changes to a right slanting white arrow).
- Select a column by pointing just above the top of the column (the pointer changes to a small black downward pointing arrow) and click.
- Select adjacent cells by clicking a cell and dragging the mouse over the adjacent cells.
- Select the entire table by dragging the mouse over the table or by clicking the Table Move handle that appears at the top-left corner of the table.

e. Save the document.

STEP 2 ▶ INSERT DATA, ROWS, AND COLUMNS

With the table in place, you can now begin entering the headings for each column, and then you can add the donor information later. When you realize you need one more column, you relax because Word makes it easy to add one just where you need it. Refer to Figure 4.5 as you complete Step 2.

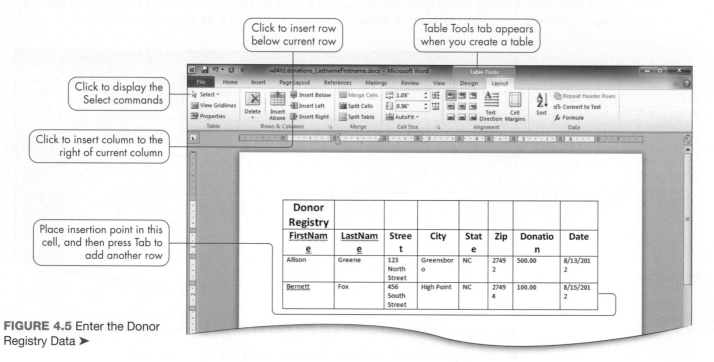

FIGURE 4.5 Enter the Donor Registry Data ➤

a. Enter data into the table by completing the following steps:
- Click in the first cell of the first row, and then type **Donor Registry**.
- Press ↓ to move to the first cell in the second row, and then type **FirstName** (this displays directly below *Donor Registry*).

    You do not insert spaces in the First Name column heading because this format is used in documents we later use to associate with this information.
- Press **Tab** (or →) to move to the next cell, and then type **LastName**.
- Press **Tab** to move to the next cell, and then type **Street**.
- Enter the following labels in the next four cells: **City**, **State**, **Zip**, and **Donation**.

    You realize you need one more column for the date of the donation.

b. Add another column by completing the following steps:
- Click anywhere in the last column of your table, and then click the **Layout tab**, if necessary. Click **Insert Right** in the Rows & Columns group to add a new column to your table.
- Click in the second row of the new column, and then type **Date**.

  You added a new column on the right side of the table. Notice that the column widths decrease to make room for the new column you just added.

> **TROUBLESHOOTING:** If the column you insert is not in the correct location within the table, click Undo on the Quick Access Toolbar, confirm your insertion point is in the last column, and then click the appropriate Insert command.

 FYI

c. Select the text *Donor Registry* in the first row. On the Mini toolbar, click the **Font Size arrow**, select **18**, click **Bold**, and then click **Center** to center the heading within the cell.

The table title stands out with the larger font size, bold, and center horizontal alignment.

d. Click in the left margin to select the entire second row. On the Mini toolbar, click the **Font Size arrow**, select **16**, and then click **Bold** and **Center**.

Now the labels in the second row stand out as well. They are not quite as large as the first row because they should not overpower the title.

e. Insert the donor information into your new table using data in the table below. When you get to the last column and find you need another row to hold the next row of data, press **Tab** to add a row to the end of your table, and then enter the next item and amounts. Compare your results to Figure 4.5.

FirstName	LastName	Street	City	State	Zip	Donation	Date
Allison	Greene	123 North Street	Greensboro	NC	27492	500.00	8/13/2012
Bernett	Fox	456 South Street	High Point	NC	27494	100.00	8/15/2012

f. Save the document.

 TIP Other Ways to Select a Table

You can click Select in the Table group on the Layout tab to display commands for selecting a cell, a column, a row, or the entire table. Figure 4.5 shows the location of the Select command.

STEP 3 ▶ CHANGE ROW HEIGHT AND COLUMN WIDTH

Now that you have donor information in the table, you decide to adjust the way it displays so it is easier to read. Adjusting the orientation of the page enables you to increase column widths so text does not need to wrap as much. This is especially useful for addresses, which are easier to read if they do not wrap. Refer to Figure 4.6 as you complete Step 3.

FIGURE 4.6 Adjust Cell Height and Width ➤

a. Click the **Page Layout tab**, click **Orientation**, and then click **Landscape**.

You have more room to display the donor information without wrapping the text if your page orientation is in landscape mode.

b. Hold your mouse above the top cell in the third column of data until the small black arrow appears, and then click to select the column that displays the street address.

c. Click the **Layout tab**, and then click the **Width arrow** in the Cell Size group until **1.5″** displays.

You changed the width of the column so that the whole address displays without wrapping. Other column widths did not change, even though the table stretches to the right of the page.

d. Change the height of the row by completing the following steps:

- Place the insertion point anywhere in the cell that contains the text *Allison*, and then click **Select** in the Table group.
- Click **Select Row**, and then hold down **Shift** and press ↓ on your keyboard to select the remaining row in the table.
- Click the **Height arrow** in the Cell Size group until **.3″** displays, as shown in Figure 4.6.

  You changed the height of the last two rows in the table to 0.3″ tall, which makes the data easier to read.

e. Save the document.

> **TIP** Adjusting Column Width and Row Height
>
> If you are not certain of the exact measurements needed for row height or column width, you can use the mouse to increase or decrease the size. Position the mouse pointer on the gridline that separates the rows (or columns) until the pointer changes to a two-headed arrow. The two-headed arrow indicates you can adjust the height (or width) by dragging the gridline up or down (right or left) to resize the cell.

STEP 4 ▶ **MERGE CELLS TO CREATE A TITLE ROW**

Any table that displays important information should have a title to explain the contents, and it should be easy to read and look professional. You recognize this table fits that description, so you merge the cells in the first row and center the text. Refer to Figure 4.7 as you complete Step 4.

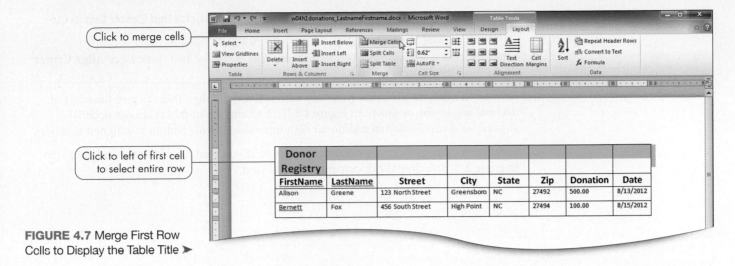

Click to merge cells

Click to left of first cell to select entire row

FIGURE 4.7 Merge First Row Cells to Display the Table Title ➤

a. Click outside the table to the left of the first cell in the first row to select the entire first row.

b. Click **Merge Cells** in the Merge group, as shown in Figure 4.7.

You merged the selected cells. The first row now contains a single cell.

c. Right-click the row to display the Mini toolbar, and then click **Center**.

d. Save the document.

STEP 5 ▶ APPLY A TABLE STYLE AND ALIGN DATA

The table is sufficient for holding information, but you want to format it using Table Styles in Word so that the information is easy to read when it displays. Using alternating colors across the rows prevents the data from being blurred together or mixed up when you read it. It is also a good practice to apply proper alignment to the columns that contain monetary values. Refer to Figure 4.8 as you complete Step 5.

Click to right align cell contents

Click to left align cell contents

Medium Shading 1 - Accent 6 style applied to table

Decimals line up

FIGURE 4.8 Style Applied to Donor Registry Table ➤

a. Apply a style to your table by completing the following steps:

• Click the **Design tab**, and then click the **More button** in the Table Styles group.

• Hover your mouse over several styles and notice how the table changes to preview that style.

• Click **Medium Shading 1 - Accent 6** (last column, fourth row) to apply it to your table.

Previous formatting such as alignment and cell shading, if it exists, may be replaced by the formatting attributes for a style when applied to a table.

b. Select rows three and four. Click the **Layout tab**, and then click **Align Center Left** in the Alignment group.

c. Select the cells which display the donation amount in the last two rows. Click **Align Center Right** from the Alignment group.

Because this column contains monetary values, you right align them to give the effect of decimal alignment, as shown in Figure 4.8. Technically, the numbers are not decimal aligned, so if you display an additional digit in a value, it will result in misaligned numbers.

d. Save the document. Keep the document onscreen if you plan to continue with Hands-On Exercise 2. If not, close the document and exit Word.

Advanced Table Features

You now have a good understanding of table features and realize there are many uses for them in your Word documents. But did you know you can use tables to perform simple tasks that are typically performed in a spreadsheet? Word includes features that enable the user to sort and perform simple mathematical calculations to data in a table. You can also convert plain text into a table.

> Word includes features that enable the user to sort and perform simple mathematical calculations to data in a table.

In this section, you will learn how to sort data within a table and insert formulas to perform calculations. Finally, you convert text to a table format.

Sorting and Applying Formulas to Table Data

Because tables provide an easy way to arrange numbers within a document, it is important to know how to use table calculations. This feature gives a Word document the power of a simple spreadsheet. Additional organization of table data is possible by *sorting*, or rearranging, data based on certain criteria. Figure 4.9 displays the donor list you created previously, but this table illustrates two additional capabilities of the table feature—sorting and calculating.

Sorting is the process of arranging data in a specific order.

Entries are sorted by date

Formula calculates total

FIGURE 4.9 Donor List Table with Enhancements ➤

Calculate Using Table Formulas

You know that the intersection of a row and column forms a cell, and the rows and columns are identified by numbers and letters, respectively. Word uses the column letter and row number of that intersection to identify the cell and to give it an address. Thus, the rows in the Donor Registry table are numbered top to bottom from 1 to 13 while the columns are labeled left to right from A to H. The row and column labels do not appear in the table, but are used in the formula for reference. The last entry in the Donation column in the table in Figure 4.9 is actually a formula entered into the table to perform a calculation. The entry is similar to that in a spreadsheet because it is adding the values in all the cells above it.

The formula is not entered (typed) into the cell explicitly, but is created using the Formula command in the Data group on the Layout tab. You often do not need to know the formula *syntax*, or rules for constructing the formula, because Word provides a dialog box that supplies basic formulas such as sum and average. But sometimes you construct a unique formula from your table entries. Once you use the table formula feature to create a formula,

Syntax refers to the rules for constructing an equation.

you will find it easy to understand because it uses field codes to identify the data and formats you use in the formula. You could, of course, use a calculator and type in the total in the cell. However, it is better to use the Formula command to calculate totals than to type the result because if you add data or change data already in the table, you can use formula tools to recalculate the total for you.

Figure 4.10 is a slight variation of Figure 4.9 in which the field codes have been toggled on to display formulas, as opposed to the calculated values. The cells are shaded to emphasize that these cells contain formulas (also called *fields*), as opposed to numerical values. The field codes are toggled on and off by selecting the formula and pressing Shift+F9 or by right-clicking the entry and selecting the Toggle Field Codes command.

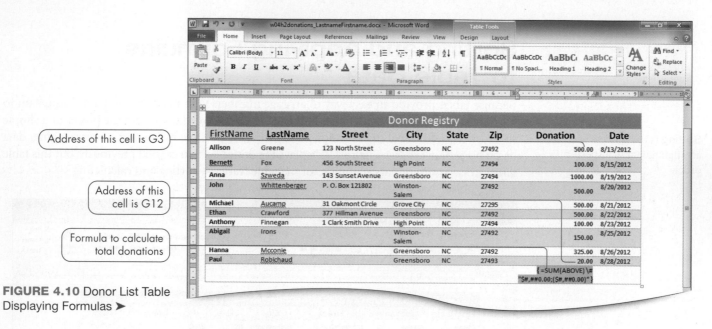

Address of this cell is G3

Address of this cell is G12

Formula to calculate total donations

FIGURE 4.10 Donor List Table Displaying Formulas ➤

Sort Data in a Table

At times, you might need to sort data in a table to enhance the order or understand the data. For example, when a list of employees is reviewed, a manager might prefer to view the names in alphabetical order by last name, or perhaps by department. You can sort data according to the entries in a specific column or row of the table. Sort orders include *ascending order*, which arranges text in alphabetical or sequential order starting with the lowest letter or number and continuing to the highest (A–Z or 0–9). Or you can sort in *descending order*, where data is arranged from highest to lowest (Z–A or 9–0).

Ascending order arranges data from lowest to highest.

Descending order arranges data from highest to lowest.

You can sort the rows in a table to display data in different sequences, as shown in Figure 4.11, where the donor list items are sorted by date. You also could sort the data in descending (high to low) sequence according to the donation amount or alphabetically by last name. In descending order the largest amount displays at the top of the list, and the smallest amount appears last. The first row of the table contains the title and the second row contains the field names for each column, so they are not included in the sort. The next 11 rows contain the sorted data; the last row is not included in the sort because it displays the total amount donated.

Second row is header row

Data sorted by date, oldest to newest

First, second, and last rows are not included in sort

FIGURE 4.11 Sort the Table Data ➤

To perform a sort of data in a table you select the rows that are to be sorted, rows 2 through 12 in this example, and then you click Sort in the Data group on the Layout tab. The Sort dialog box displays, as shown in Figure 4.12, which enables you to select the direction and sort criteria. In this case, you include the second row, which contains field names, and then select the option on the Sort dialog box that indicates your data includes a Header row. When you include the header row and then identify it to the sort program, it displays the header row names in the Sort by list so you can identify your sort criteria easily. Identifying the header row also removes it from the sort.

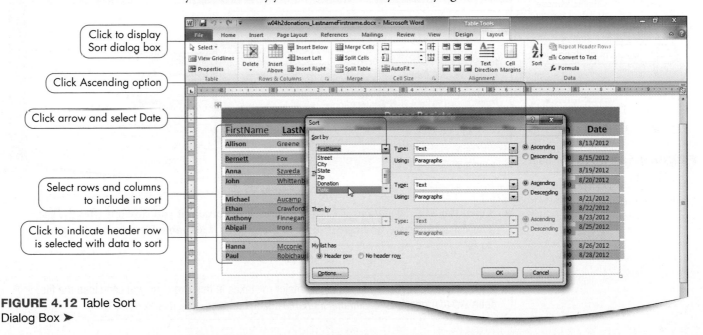

Click to display Sort dialog box

Click Ascending option

Click arrow and select Date

Select rows and columns to include in sort

Click to indicate header row is selected with data to sort

FIGURE 4.12 Table Sort Dialog Box ➤

Converting Text to a Table

The table feature is outstanding, but what if you are given a lengthy list of items that should have been formatted as a table but is currently just text? For example, you have a document containing a list of two items per line separated by a tab, and the list needs to be sorted. The Table command on the Insert tab includes the Convert Text to Table command, and it can aid you in this transformation. After you select the text and choose this command, the Convert Text to Table dialog box displays and offers several options to assist in a quick conversion of text into a table. The command also works in reverse; you can convert a table to text. You will perform a table conversion in the next Hands-On Exercise.

2 Advanced Table Features

The information you track for Wacey Rivale and the CDRC can be useful in a variety of ways. To prepare the information for reports and letters, you enhance the table in Word so it sorts the information and includes a row to display the total amount of donations. You also combine this table with another table of donor information that Wacey found on her flash drive.

Skills covered: Enter a Formula to Calculate Total Donations • Convert Text to a Table • Combine Two Tables into One • Sort Data in a Table

---

STEP 1 ▸ ENTER A FORMULA TO CALCULATE TOTAL DONATIONS

It is good to have an estimate of the amount of donations made to the CDRC over a period of time. Wacey would like you to include a row in the table that adds the donations together, and you agree that it can be done quickly and easily using the formula tool for tables. Refer to Figure 4.13 as you complete Step 1.

FIGURE 4.13 Insert a Formula in a Table ▸

a. Open the *w04h1donations_LastnameFirstname* document if you closed it after the last Hands-On Exercise, and save it as **w04h2donations_Lastname Firstname**, changing *h1* to *h2*.

> **TROUBLESHOOTING:** If you make any major mistakes in this exercise, you can close the file, open *w04h1donations_LastnameFirstname* again, and then start this exercise over.

b. Click in the last row of the table. Click the **Layout tab**, if necessary, and then click **Insert Below** in the Rows & Columns group.

You add a new row where you can sum the total amount of donations.

c. Click in **cell G5**, the cell in the seventh column and fifth row. Click **Formula** in the Data group to display the formula box.

Notice the formula *=SUM(ABOVE)* is entered by default. We can use the default formula because it will add the contents of cells directly above this one. The formula is not case sensitive; you can type formula references in lowercase or capital letters.

d. Click the **Number format arrow**, select **$#,##0.00;($#,##0.00)**, as shown in Figure 4.13, and then click **OK**.

The result of *$600.00* displays in a number format with a dollar sign and two decimal places because these numbers represent a monetary value.

e. Save the document and leave it open.

> **TIP** Updating Formula Results
>
> If you add or remove cells that affect the results of a formula in a table, the formula result will not change automatically. Right-click the formula, and then select Update Field to display the new results.

STEP 2 ▶ CONVERT TEXT TO A TABLE

Wacey remembered that she previously saved some raw data about donations received and asks you to put it in a table like the other information. You agree, knowing Word includes a feature for conversions of text to a table. Refer to Figure 4.14 as you complete Step 2.

FIGURE 4.14 Convert Text to Table Dialog Box ▶

a. Open *w04h2address* and save it as **w04h2address_LastnameFirstname**.

b. Press **Ctrl+A** to select all text in this document, and then click the **Insert tab**.

c. Click **Table** in the Tables group, and then click **Convert Text to Table**. View the options in the Convert Text to Table dialog box, as shown in Figure 4.14, but do not make any changes at this time. Click **OK**.

The listing of donors and their related information now displays in a table and the commas that separated the data are removed.

d. Press **Ctrl+C** to copy the table to the clipboard.

> **TROUBLESHOOTING:** If you deselect the table after step C, click the Table Move handle to select the entire table, and then perform step D.

e. Save the document.

Now that you have converted the additional data into a table, you want to combine it with the first table so you can manipulate all the data together. It is not always possible to combine two tables easily, but in this case, you can use Copy and Paste to merge the two tables that contain similar information into one. Refer to Figure 4.15 as you complete Step 3.

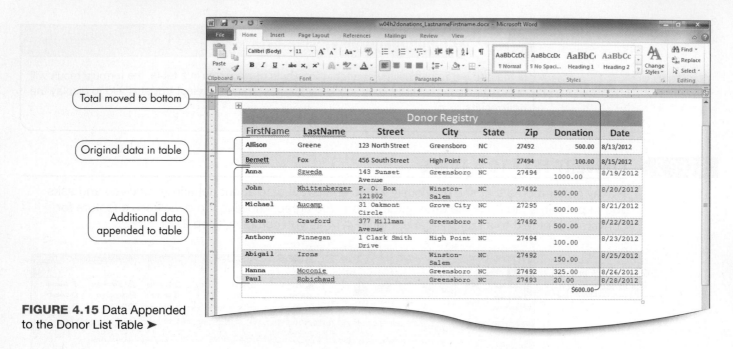

Total moved to bottom

Original data in table

Additional data appended to table

FIGURE 4.15 Data Appended to the Donor List Table ➤

a. Make *w04h2donations_LastnameFirstname* the active document.

b. Place the insertion point on the line immediately below the table.

> **TROUBLESHOOTING:** If you have trouble placing the insertion point on the line below the table, position the insertion point in the last cell of the table and click ⊟ two times.

c. Press **Ctrl+V** to paste the rows from the table in the clipboard into this document.

> **TROUBLESHOOTING:** If necessary, click Paste Options and select Merge Table.

Because both tables contained the same number of columns, the copied table appends directly to the existing table, displaying a table with many more rows of donor information. Unfortunately, there is an extra header row which needs to be removed, and the row containing the total line is no longer at the bottom, so you must move it.

d. Select the entire sixth row, which is a repeat of the column headings. Right-click and select **Delete Rows**.

e. Select the entire fifth row, which displays the formula to total the donations. Press **Ctrl+X** to cut the row. Place the insertion point on the line directly below the last row of the table, and then press **Ctrl+V**.

The row now displays at the bottom of the table, but the formula results are the same (as seen in Figure 4.15). Next, you update the formula to reflect the additional donations that now display in the table.

f. Right-click the formula that displays on the last row of the table, and then select **Update Field**.

The new total of *$3,695.00* now displays.

g. Save the document but leave it open for the next step. Close *w04h2address_LastnameFirstname*.

SORT DATA IN A TABLE

The data are combined and you are almost ready to turn the document over to Wacey for review. You know that it will be helpful to display the information sorted by date so she can try to remember the people she visited with on certain occasions. You complete the sort and then make a few last adjustments so the information displays nicely on paper. Refer to Figure 4.16 as you complete Step 4.

Ascending option is default

Click arrow and select Date

Click option for Header row

FIGURE 4.16 Sort Data in the Donor List Table ➤

a. Drag to select rows 2 through 12 in the table. That is, select all table rows *except* the first and last row. Click the **Layout tab**, and then click **Sort** in the Data group.

b. Click **Header row** in the *My list has* section, at the bottom of the dialog box.

c. Click the **Sort by arrow**, and then select **Date** (the column heading for the last column). Click **Ascending**, if necessary, and compare your settings to Figure 4.16. Click **OK**.

The entries in the table are rearranged chronologically from the oldest to most recent date of donation.

> **TROUBLESHOOTING:** If you do not first click Header row, the headings for each column will not display in the Sort by list; instead you will see the column numbers listed. You can sort by column number (1, 2, 3, or 4), but it is important to click the Header row option before you leave this dialog box so the header row is not included in the sort.

d. Select **cells G5 through G12** (the donation data from the added table), and then click **Align Center Right** in the Alignment group.

Now the donation amounts for the data appended to this table are aligned with the other amounts that you typed in earlier.

e. Change the font of the newly inserted donors to match the first two donors by completing the following steps:

- Select the rows that contain the data appended to the table, and then right-click to display the Mini toolbar.
- Click the **Font arrow** on the Mini toolbar, and then click **Calibri**.
- Right-click the selected rows again to display the Mini toolbar, if necessary, click the **Font Size arrow**, and then click **11**.

f. Click **Properties** in the Table group.

g. Click the **Table tab**, if necessary, and then click **Center** in the *Alignment* section. Click **OK**. Click anywhere to deselect the table.

Your table is now centered between the left and right margins. This alignment alters the location of the table, but not the data inside the table. It also creates an attractively styled and easy-to-read document.

h. Save the document.

i. Modify the document in preparation for an upcoming exercise by making the following changes:

- Press **Ctrl+Home**, and then delete the two empty lines at the top of the document.
- Place the insertion point on the first row of the table, if necessary. Right-click, and then select **Delete Rows**.

  This deletes the title of the table. Because the table uses a style, the row containing column headers now becomes row one and assumes the formatting of the previous title.

- Click **Properties** in the Table group. Click **Left** in the *Alignment* section. Click **OK**.
- Save this document as **w04h2donortable_LastnameFirstname**.

  To use this table of information in the next Hands-On Exericse, it is necessary to strip out some of the formatting. Whereas the formatting is beneficial if the table is distributed in print or strictly for viewing, it is unnecessary when the table is used in other activities where only the data are important, such as the one you will perform next.

j. Close the document.

Mail Merge

At some point in your personal or professional life, you will need to send the same message to a number of different people. For example, you will send a graduation announcement to all your family and friends, you might send a cover letter with a résumé to several organizations, or you might need to send a letter to a group of customers informing them of an upcoming sale. In each case, you will need to personalize either the letter or the recipient's address on the letter or an envelope. You can use Word's Mail Merge feature to generate these types of documents easily and efficiently. *Mail merge* is a process that combines content from a main document and a data source, with the option of creating a new document.

Mail merge is a process that combines content from a main document and a data source.

A form letter is a letter you will print or e-mail many times, personalizing each one for the recipient.

Mail merge is used most frequently to create a set of *form letters*, which are letters you might print or e-mail many times, personalizing or modifying each one for the recipient. When you apply for a job after graduation, you might send the same cover letter to many different companies. You could spend hours personalizing and resaving individual letters, but when you use mail merge, you can update several letters simultaneously and quickly. An example of a mail merge is illustrated in Figures 4.17, 4.18, and 4.19, in which Wacey Rivale

> ... you might send the same cover letter to many different companies. You could spend hours personalizing and resaving individual letters, but when you use mail merge, you can update several letters simultaneously and quickly.

has written a letter of appreciation to each person who donated to the CDRC, then merges that letter with her log that contains addresses, donation amount, and dates. When complete, she produces letters addressed to each donor individually.

In this section, you will learn about the mail merge process by creating a main document and selecting a recipient list. You then will create form letters by combining the information from both sources.

FIGURE 4.17 Main Document Showing Merge Fields ➤

FirstName	LastName	Street	City	State	Zip	Donation	Date
John	Whittenberger	P. O. Box 121802	Winston-Salem	NC	27492	500.00	8/20/2012
Anna	Szweda	143 Sunset Avenue	Greensboro	NC	27494	1000.00	8/19/2012
Paul	Robichaud		Greensboro	NC	27493	20.00	8/28/2012
Hanna	Mcconie		Greensboro	NC	27492	325.00	8/26/2012
Abigail	Irons		Winston-Salem	NC	27492	150.00	8/25/2012
Allison	Greene	123 North Street	Greensboro	NC	27492	500.00	8/13/2012
Bernett	Fox	456 South Street	High Point	NC	27494	100.00	8/15/2012
Anthony	Finnegan	1 Clark Smith Drive	High Point	NC	27494	100.00	8/23/2012
Ethan	Crawford	377 Hillman Avenue	Greensboro	NC	27492	500.00	8/22/2012
Michael	Aucamp	31 Oakmont Circle	Grove City	NC	27295	500.00	8/21/2012

FIGURE 4.18 List of Names, Addresses, and Donations ➤

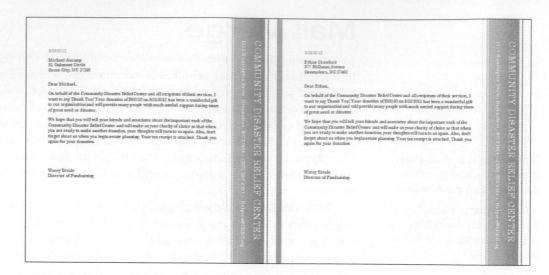

FIGURE 4.19 Merged Form Letters ➤

Selecting a Main Document

The mail merge process uses two files as input, a main document and a data source; by merging these two files you can create a set of individualized letters, envelopes, e-mails, or other documents. The *main document*, also known as a source or starting document, contains the information that stays the same for all recipients. The main document also includes one or more *merge fields* that serve as placeholders for the variable data that will be inserted into the individual letters, as shown in Figure 4.17.

You can use an existing document as a main document, or you can create one from a blank document. When you click *Start Mail Merge* in the Start Mail Merge group of the Mailings tab, you can choose from several categories to use as your main document. Table 4.3 describes the document types and how they are typically used in a mail merge.

The **main document** contains the information that stays the same for all recipients.

A **merge field** serves as a placeholder for data that will be inserted into the main document during the mail merge.

TABLE 4.3	Main Document Types
Document Type	**How It Is Typically Used in a Mail Merge**
Letters	To send letters to a group after personalizing each letter.
E-Mail Messages	To send e-mail messages to a group of people after personalizing each message.
Envelopes	To print an address on an envelope for each person in the group.
Labels	To print address labels for each person in the group, which can then be attached to an envelope for mailing.
Directory	To create a single document that contains a list of addresses.

A **wizard** makes a process easier by asking a series of questions, then creating a document structure based on your answers.

The last option displayed when you click *Start Mail Merge* is the Step by Step Mail Merge Wizard. A *wizard* makes a process easier by asking a series of questions, then creating a customized document structure based on your answers. In this case, the wizard simplifies the process of creating form letters and other types of merge documents through step-by-step directions that appear automatically on the Mail Merge pane. The options for the current step appear in the top portion of the pane and are self-explanatory. Click the link to the next step at the bottom of the pane to move forward in the process, or click the link to the previous step to correct any mistakes you might have made. This is a very easy-to-follow process and helps you work through the mail merge procedure without knowing exactly what you need to click in the Mailings tab.

Selecting or Creating Recipients

After you choose the type of document you will use in a merge, the next step is to create or select a list of recipients. Typically, this is the information you need to insert in an address block, or specific information, such as a company name. A recipient list, sometimes called a *data source*, contains individual pieces of data and each is known as a *field*. Common fields in a data source include first name, last name, address, city, state, ZIP code, phone number, and e-mail address. A group of fields for a particular person or thing is called a *record*. Figure 4.18 demonstrates a sample data source. Your data source might come from:

A **data source** is a listing of information.

A **field** is a single piece of data used in a source document, such as last name.

A **record** is a group of related fields.

- A Word document that contains information stored in a table
- An Access database
- An Excel worksheet
- Your Outlook Contacts

The **header row** is the first row in a data source.

The first row in the data source is called the *header row* and identifies the fields in the remaining rows. Each additional row contains a record, and every record contains the same fields in the same order—for example, Title, FirstName, LastName, and so on.

If you do not have a preexisting list to use as a data source, you can create one in Word. Click Select Recipients in the Start Mail Merge group of the Mailings tab, and then click Type New List. A New Address List dialog box displays with the most commonly used fields for a mail merge, as shown in Figure 4.20. You can enter data immediately or click Customize Columns to add, delete, or rename the fields to meet your particular needs. When you save, the list is saved as a database file with the .mdb extension.

FIGURE 4.20 Create a New Data Source ➤

If you want to add new records to a source file you created in Word, you can click Edit Recipient List in the Start Mail Merge group of the Mailings tab. Note that you can only edit the list after it has been selected as a recipient list for the mail merge. When the Mail Merge Recipients dialog box displays, click the name of the data source, and then click Edit. The Edit Data Source dialog box displays. Click Add New and a blank form displays as the last record, and you can immediately populate the fields with your data (see Figure 4.21).

FIGURE 4.21 Edit a Data Source in Word ➤

Using Excel Worksheets as a Data Source

Even though you can create and use data sources in Word, there is a very good probability you will also need to perform a mail merge with a data source that was created and saved in a different Office application such as Access or Excel. The database and spreadsheet applications are designed to organize large amounts of information, so they are perfect candidates to hold the source data you want to use in a mail merge.

> The database and spreadsheet applications are designed to organize large amounts of information, so they are perfect candidates to hold the source data you want to use in a mail merge.

An Excel worksheet is comparable to a giant table in Word; it can contain hundreds of rows and columns of data. A manager who must keep track of large amounts of information probably stores it in a spreadsheet, which makes a good candidate for a data source in a mail merge and prevents you from having to retype any data you might want to use in a merge. As long as the worksheet data has a header row, you can use it as a data source in a mail merge. Look at Figure 4.22 and notice how the worksheet displays data suitable for use in a mail merge.

Header row

Excel data suitable for use in a mail merge

FIGURE 4.22 Use an Excel Worksheet as a Data Source ➤

To merge a Word document with data stored in Excel, click Select Recipients in the Start Mail Merge group on the Mailings tab, and then click Use Existing List. When the Select Data Source dialog box opens, browse to the location where the Excel worksheet is stored, click the file name, and then click Open. Excel worksheets have the extension .xlsx (or .xls if an older version), so you might need to change the type of file in the *Files of type* box at the bottom of the window.

Using Access Databases as a Data Source

A **database table** is a collection of related records that contain fields to organize data.

Access is a database program, and databases are designed to store large amounts of data. Information in a database is stored in tables. A ***database table*** is a collection of related records that contain fields to organize data. Access also includes features that enable you to query the database tables so you can extract and view only data that meet your search criteria. Figure 4.23 provides a look at a database file. Because database files can contain so much data, it is advisable to use the query feature to narrow down the data to only that which will be needed in the mail merge. Filtering the data from the database is much more efficient and easier than sorting and deleting unwanted pages in a Word document after a mail merge.

Field names

Access data suitable for use in a mail merge

FIGURE 4.23 Use an Access Database as a Data Source ➤

The process of selecting recipients from a database for use in a mail merge is the same as in Excel. However, when you merge a Word document with an Access database, you can select to use a table or a query as the source of your data. If a database includes queries, the query names will display in the Select Table dialog box along with any tables it contains, as shown in Figure 4.24. When you select to use the query as a data source, only records that meet the query criteria will be available for your mail merge. This can be beneficial if you are certain all the data you need is extracted by that query, but it can limit your data and omit necessary records if the query is too restrictive.

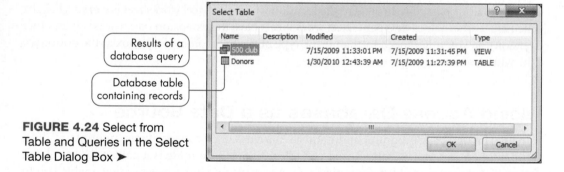

Results of a database query

Database table containing records

FIGURE 4.24 Select from Table and Queries in the Select Table Dialog Box ➤

Access database files have the extension .accdb (or .mdb if an older version). A database uses field names to classify the data it contains, which makes it very compatible for a mail merge. However, the Access file you use as a data source might not use the same field names as Word expects; for example, a database may use LNAME as a field name instead of LastName. In this situation, you can use the Match Fields command to create a link between the Word document fields and the Access database fields. After you select the recipient list for your mail merge, click Match Fields to display a list of fields that Word often uses and a list of the fields found in the data source. You can then select a database field that matches the required fields in Word.

Sorting and Filtering Records in a Data Source

Before merging the data source with the main document, you might want to rearrange the records in the data source. For example, you might want to sort the data source in alphabetical order by last name, or in descending order by sales, if included. If you have a large number of form letters to send, you can receive a discount at the post office if you follow certain procedures. One procedure is to sort the letters by ZIP code. You can save a lot of work hours if you sort the data source before merging instead of after merging and printing. When you click Edit Recipient List in the Start Mail Merge group on the Mailings tab to display the Mail

Merge Recipients dialog box, several options offer a variety of methods to sort the source data, as shown in Figure 4.25.

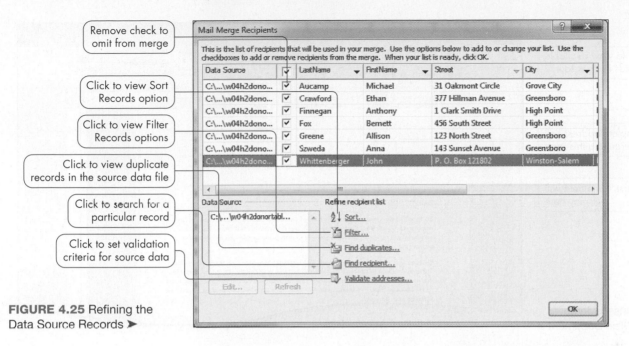

- Remove check to omit from merge
- Click to view Sort Records option
- Click to view Filter Records options
- Click to view duplicate records in the source data file
- Click to search for a particular record
- Click to set validation criteria for source data

FIGURE 4.25 Refining the Data Source Records ➤

A **filter** specifies criteria for including records that meet certain conditions.

When you click Sort or Filter, the Filter and Sort dialog box displays and enables you to perform more complex sorts. The Filter Records tab enables you to *filter*, or specify criteria for including records that meet certain conditions during the merge process. For example, you may want to filter the source data by state so only companies in the state of California are included in the mail merge.

The Sort Records tab enables you to specify up to three levels for sorting records. For example, you can first sort by state, further sort by city within state, and finally sort by last name within city (see Figure 4.26).

- Select from list of fields
- Data sorts by state first
- Within the state, data sorts by city
- After sorting by state and then city, data sorts by last name
- Choose Ascending or Descending order for each sort criteria

FIGURE 4.26 Sort Source Data ➤

Inserting Merge Fields

When you write a letter or set up your e-mail in preparation for a mail merge, you insert a merge field in the main document. The merge field is a placeholder that specifies where information from the data source will display in the main document. Because it corresponds with a field in the data source, matching the two fields guarantees that the right data will be inserted into the main document when you complete the merge. View Figure 4.17 again to view the merge fields that correspond to the fields in the source document in Figure 4.18.

The merge fields display in the main document within angle brackets, for example <<AddressBlock>>, <<FirstName>>, or <<Donation>>. These entries are not typed explicitly but are entered automatically when you select one of the source data fields that display when you click Insert Merge Field from the Write & Insert Fields group of the Mailings tab. (See Figure 4.27.)

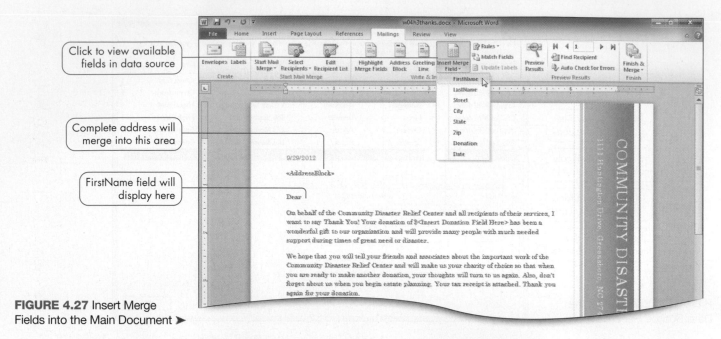

Click to view available fields in data source

Complete address will merge into this area

FirstName field will display here

FIGURE 4.27 Insert Merge Fields into the Main Document ➤

Merging a Main Document and a Data Source

After you create the main document and identify the source data, you are ready to begin the merge process. The merge process examines each record in the data source, and when a match is found, it replaces the merge field in the main document with the information from the data source. A copy of the main document is created for each record in the data source, thus creating individual form letters, for example. Figure 4.19 displays two of the personalized letters after a mail merge.

To complete the merge, click Finish & Merge in the Finish group on the Mailings tab. Three options display when you click Finish & Merge: *Edit Individual Documents*, *Print Documents*, and *Send E-mail Messages*. To create a new document that contains the results of the merge, you should select Edit Individual Documents. This enables you to preview each page of the merged documents prior to saving or printing. If you select Print Documents, you will have the opportunity to specify which pages to print; however, you cannot preview the document prior to printing. To conserve paper, you should choose *Edit Individual Documents* and use Print Preview before you print. The last option, *Send E-mail Messages*, enables you to make selections and complete the e-mail information prior to sending, as shown in Figure 4.28. To use this option, you must have an e-mail field where addresses display for the recipients in your data source.

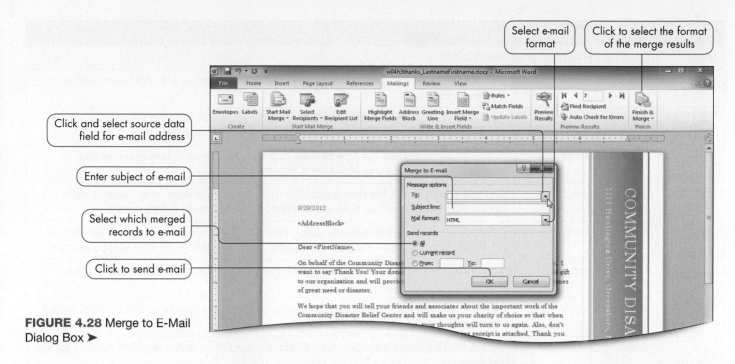

Select e-mail format

Click to select the format of the merge results

Click and select source data field for e-mail address

Enter subject of e-mail

Select which merged records to e-mail

Click to send e-mail

FIGURE 4.28 Merge to E-Mail Dialog Box ➤

The same data source can be used to create multiple sets of form documents. You could, for example, create a marketing campaign in which you send an initial letter to the entire list, and then send follow-up letters at periodic intervals to the same mailing list. Alternatively, you could filter the original mailing list to include only a subset of names, such as the individuals who responded to the initial letter. You could also create a different set of documents, such as envelopes or e-mail messages.

If you want to generate a list from the source data, you can use a Directory mail merge. Select Directory as your source document type and Word will merge all the source data onto the same page instead of merging each record onto a separate page.

The Mail Merge feature is exciting, yet a bit complex. Use Table 4.4 to acquaint yourself with the commands on the Mailings tab. Once you successfully complete a mail merge, you will enjoy finding ways to use it over and over!

TABLE 4.4　Mail Merge Commands

Icon	Command Name	Description
	Envelopes	Opens the Envelopes and Labels dialog box. Enables you to insert recipient and return address information.
	Labels	Opens the Envelopes and Labels dialog box. Enables you to insert an address for labels and select to print a full page of the same label or a single label.
	Start Mail Merge	Enables you to choose the type of main document, such as letters or envelopes, to create. Enables you to use Mail Merge Wizard.
	Select Recipients	Enables you to select the data source file that you want to open and use with the main document or opens a New Address List dialog box to create a data source.
	Edit Recipient List	Opens the Mail Merge Recipients dialog box. Enables you to sort or select records to include in a merge. Also enables you to add, edit, and delete the data source records.
	Highlight Merge Fields	Shades the fields in the main document so you can quickly see where the merged information will display.
	Address Block	Opens the Insert Address Block dialog box. Enables you to choose the formats for the inside address.
	Greeting Line	Opens the Greeting Line dialog box. Enables you to choose the level of formality for the salutation.
	Insert Merge Field	Opens the Insert Merge Field dialog box. Enables you to select and insert fields in the main document.
	Rules	Displays decision-making criteria to increase your options for filtering records.
	Match Fields	Opens the Match Fields dialog box. Enables you to select fields from another data source, such as an Access database table, to match with required fields in Word.
	Update Labels	Copies the merge fields from the first label to the other labels.
	Preview Results	Displays the data from the data source in the respective fields in the main document so that you can verify correct placement.
	First Record	Displays the first merged record. Works with Preview Results.
	Previous Record	Displays the previous merged record. Works with Preview Results.
	Go to Record	Enables you to enter the number of a specific record to go to.
	Next Record	Displays the next merged record. Works with Preview Results.
	Last Record	Displays the last merged record. Works with Preview Results.
	Find Recipient	Opens the Find Entry dialog box. Enables you to find data in a specific field or in all fields.
	Auto Check for Errors	Enables you to check for errors and report those errors during the merge process.
	Finish & Merge	Enables you to choose how to display or process the results of the mail merge.

3 Mail Merge

Wacey Rivale always sends a letter of gratitude to the people who have donated to the CDRC. You will use an existing letter as the main document and use the table you recently created as a recipient list in a mail merge process, which makes sending letters quick and easy. Wacey later finds more donor information, created in Excel and Access, which you also use to generate letters. Lastly, you create mailing labels for the letters.

Skills covered: Start the Mail Merge Process and Select a Recipient List • Complete the Main Document • Complete the Mail Merge and View Results • Use an Excel Spreadsheet Recipient List • Use an Access Database Recipient List • Use Mail Merge Wizard to Create Mailing Labels

---

STEP 1 ▷ START THE MAIL MERGE PROCESS AND SELECT A RECIPIENT LIST

You open the letter of gratitude to use as a source document in the mail merge process. Then you must select recipient information, which includes address and amount received from each donor. The document that contains the table of donor information you created recently will work perfectly in this process. Refer to Figure 4.29 as you complete Step 1.

Omit records without a street address

FIGURE 4.29 Sort Data in the Donor List Table ➤

a. Open *w04h3thanks*, and then save it as **w04h3thanks_LastnameFirstname**.

The document contains a letter that you will mail to the people who have donated to the CDRC.

b. Click the **Mailings tab**, click **Start Mail Merge** in the Start Mail Merge group, and then click **Letters**.

You are telling Word that this document onscreen is the main document you are using for the mail merge operation.

c. Click **Select Recipients** in the Start Mail Merge group, and then click **Use Existing List**. Navigate to the location where you store your documents, and then select *w04h2donortable_LastnameFirstname*.

This is the last document you created in Hands-On Exercise 2, which contains the donor information in a table with no title row.

d. Click **Edit Recipient List** in the Start Mail Merge group.

The Mail Merge Recipients dialog box opens and displays information about donors. It also provides features you use later, such as sort and filter.

e. Filter and sort the data used in the mail merge by completing the following steps:

- Scroll to the right to view more columns.
- Click the **Street arrow**, and then click (**Nonblanks**), as shown in Figure 4.29.
- Click **Sort**.
- Click the **Sort by arrow**, and then select **LastName**. Click **OK** to close the Query Options dialog box.
- Click **OK** to close the Mail Merge Recipients dialog box.

When the process is complete, letters will only be generated to people for whom Wacey has an address. When printed, the letters will be sorted by the donor's last name. This simplifies the process of matching letters with tax receipts before mailing.

f. Save the document.

STEP 2 ▶ **COMPLETE THE MAIN DOCUMENT**

Now you need to update the source of your mail merge, the letter of gratitude, to include placeholders for the information that it pulls in from the recipient list. You want to include the donor address, name, amount of donation, and date of donation. Refer to Figure 4.30 as you complete Step 2.

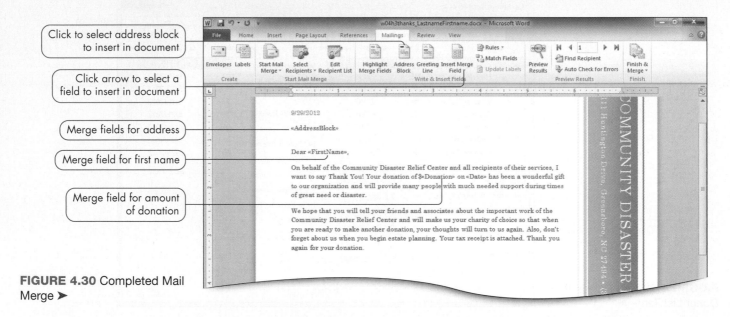

Click to select address block to insert in document

Click arrow to select a field to insert in document

Merge fields for address

Merge field for first name

Merge field for amount of donation

FIGURE 4.30 Completed Mail Merge ➤

a. Click **Pick the Date**, click the arrow, and then click **Today**.

b. Insert the address by completing the following steps:

- Place the insertion point on the left side of the text *Insert Name and*.
- Click **Address Block** in the Write & Insert Fields group. Look at the address in the Preview panel.

  Notice the first and last name display on the first line and the city, state, and ZIP display on the second line. The street address does not display, which is not correct. This is a problem with matching the names of the fields in the main letter and the source document which holds the recipient information.

- Click **Match Fields** in the bottom-right corner of the Insert Address Block dialog box.
- Locate *Address 1* in the column that displays fields in the Required for Address Block column.
- Click the **Address 1 arrow**, and then click **Street**.

- Click **OK** to close the Match Fields dialog box.

  In the Preview window, the address displays for the first recipient, *Michael Aucamp*.

- Click **Next** (an arrow pointing right) in the *Preview* section of the Insert Address Block dialog box.

  The entry for *Ethan Crawford* displays in the *Preview* section of the dialog box.

- Click **OK** to close the Address Block dialog box.

  The AddressBlock field displays in the document.

c. Select and delete the three lines that display *Insert Name and*, *Street and*, *City, ST, ZIP fields Here*.

d. Insert a salutation by completing the following steps:

- Click one time to position the cursor on the left side of *Insert Greeting Line here*. Type **Dear** and press the **spacebar**.
- Click the **Insert Merge Field arrow** in the Write & Insert group.
- Click **FirstName**. Press **,** to display a comma after the name.
- Delete the text *Insert Greeting Line here* from that line.

  The merge fields show the recipient's first name in the salutation line.

e. Insert the donation date and amount in the letter for each person by completing the following steps:

- Select the text *<Insert Donation Field Here>* in the second line of the first paragraph.

> **TROUBLESHOOTING:** If you find it difficult to drag to select the exact text and symbols to remove from this paragraph, position the insertion point at the left edge of the text, hold down Shift, and then press and hold → until all text is selected.

- Click **Insert Merge Field**.
- Click **Donation**, click **Insert**, and then click **Close**.
- Press **Spacebar**, type **on**, and then press **Spacebar**.
- Click the **Insert Merge Field arrow**.
- Click **Date**.

  The placeholder for donation and date displays in the paragraph, as shown in Figure 4.30. You now know two different ways to insert the individual fields into the main document.

f. Save the document.

STEP 3 ▶ COMPLETE THE MAIL MERGE AND VIEW RESULTS

You preview the final product before completing the mail merge, just to be sure you inserted the information correctly and included spaces where needed so words do not run together. Then you complete the merge and display the letters in a new document in which you can make individual edits if needed. Refer to Figure 4.31 as you complete Step 3.

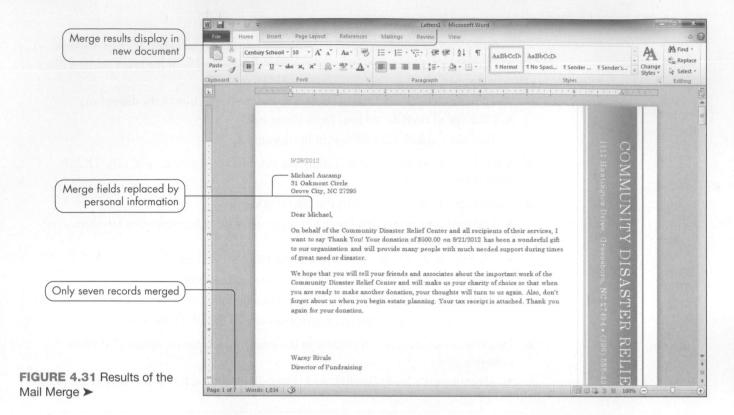

Merge results display in new document

Merge fields replaced by personal information

Only seven records merged

FIGURE 4.31 Results of the Mail Merge ➤

a. Click **Preview Results** in the Preview Results group. Click **Last Record** to preview the letter addressed to *John Whittenberger*.

You can navigate from record to record or specify a record to preview using the First Record, Previous Record, Go To Record, Next Record, and Last Record navigational commands in the Preview Results group on the Mailings tab.

b. Click **Preview Results** to return to the letter and view the mail merge fields.

The Preview Results command is a toggle that alternates between the original source document and a preview of the final documents.

c. Click **Finish & Merge** in the Finish group, and then click **Edit Individual Documents**. Click **OK** to merge all records with the letter.

The letter merges with the recipients and displays in a completely new document, as shown in Figure 4.31. Scroll through the new document and view the seven pages, one for each letter.

d. Press **Ctrl+S** to display the Save As dialog box, and then save the merged letters as **w04h3letters_LastnameFirstname**.

e. Save and close all documents.

STEP 4 ▶ USE AN EXCEL SPREADSHEET RECIPIENT LIST

Wacey has found another list of donor information which was stored in an Excel spreadsheet. You tell her you can print another set of letters with this information because the letter you use in the mail merge can be modified to use information from a different source or recipient list, such as a spreadsheet, just as easily as a Word table. Refer to Figure 4.32 as you complete Step 4.

Enter first record number here

Enter last record number here

Click to merge these letters into a new document

FIGURE 4.32 Filter Recipients After Merging with Recipients from an Excel Spreadsheet ➤

a. Open *w04h3thanks_LastnameFirstname*, and then click **Yes** if a screen displays the message *Opening this document will run the following SQL command.*

b. Click the **Mailings tab**, click **Select Recipients**, and then click **Use Existing List**.

The Select Data Source dialog box displays.

c. Navigate to the location of your data files, select *w04h3donorsheet.xlsx*, and then click **Open**. When the Select Table dialog box displays, click **OK**.

d. Click **Preview Results** to view the first merged letter. Click **Last Record** to view the last letter.

The last letter is number 20. Notice that there is no street address for that record. You do not want to print letters to people for whom addresses are unknown. You can do a manual filter when you complete the final merge step.

e. Click **Previous Record** again until you determine which letter has the last complete address.

You find that the 11th letter has a complete address displaying.

f. Click **Finish & Merge**, and then click **Edit Individual Documents**. Click **From**, type **1** in the first box, and then type **11** in the second box, as shown in Figure 4.32. Click **OK**.

You create a new document that contains letters for only the first 11 individuals in the recipient list.

g. Save the new file as **w04h3exletters_LastnameFirstname** and close the document. Leave *w04h3thanks_LastnameFirstname* open for the next step.

STEP 5 ▶ USE AN ACCESS DATABASE RECIPIENT LIST

Just as you finish the second mail merge, Wacey runs in to tell you she found another file that contains donor information. However, this list is in an Access database. You assure her that Word accepts Access tables and queries as source data too, so with one more round of mail merge, more letters will be ready today. Refer to Figure 4.33 as you complete Step 5.

Click to display Match Fields dialog box

Click to display fields from recipient list

Select field name that matches Address 1 field

FIGURE 4.33 Matching Fields from an Access Database ➤

a. Click **Select Recipients** in the Start Mail Merge group, and then click **Use Existing List**.

b. Navigate to the location of your data files, select *w04h3donordb.accdb*, and then click **Open**. When the Select Table dialog box displays, click **OK** to select the data in a query named *500 club*.

   The Access database file contains a table of data, but it also includes a query created to extract specific information from the table. In this case, the query displays only patrons who donated more than $500.

> **TROUBLESHOOTING:** If you click the Donors table in the Select Table dialog box by mistake, you can repeat steps a and b to select the 500 Club query. You can use the Donors table for the merge, but you will have more fields to select from than you have in the 500 Club query.

c. Click **Remove Field** in the Invalid Merge Field dialog box.

   An Invalid Merge Field dialog box displays because your letter includes a merge field for date (of donation) and the data in the query does not have a match for the field. Since that information is not available, you will remove the merge field in the source document (the letter).

d. Click **Preview Results**, if necessary, to view the first merged letter.

   Notice you are viewing the letter to Charles Reinthaler but the address block does not include a street address. Next, you check for unmatched fields between the query and the letter.

e. Click **Match Fields** in the Write & Insert Fields group. Click the **Address 1 arrow**, select **Street** (shown in Figure 4.33), and then click **OK**.

f. Click **Next Record**, and then click **Previous Record** in the Preview Results group.

   Now the complete address for Charles Reinthaler displays.

g. Delete the word *on* and the space that follows it from the second sentence in the first paragraph.

   Since you are no longer displaying the date of the donation, the sentence must be corrected.

h. Ensure the letter is only mailed to people for whom we have a complete mailing address by completing the following steps:

- Click **Edit Recipient List** in the Start Mail Merge group.
- Click **Filter** to display the Filter and Sort dialog box.
- Click the **Filter Records tab**, if necessary.
- Click the **Field arrow**, and then select **Street**.
- Click the **Comparison arrow**, and then select **Not equal to**.
- Click **OK** to close the dialog box. Click **OK** to close the Mail Merge Recipients dialog box.

  You have set a filter so any record containing blanks in the address field will not be used in the mail merge. Only two records meet all criteria.

i. Click **Finish & Merge** in the Finish group, click **Edit Individual Documents**, click **All**, and then click **OK**.

In a new document, two letters display.

j. Save the new document as **w04h3acletter_LastnameFirstname**, and then close it. Close *w04h3thanks_LastnameFirstname* without saving, but do not exit Word.

> ## TIP) Saving Merged Letters
>
> Typically, you only save the original documents and recipient lists used in a mail merge. The document that contains the individual letters as a result of the mail merge is usually printed and mailed. You save the merged documents in this exercise so you can submit them to your instructor, if necessary.

STEP 6) USE MAIL MERGE WIZARD TO CREATE MAILING LABELS

Wacey is hoping you can help with one last request—she needs to send out the first set of letters today. If you can create mailing labels to put on the envelopes, it will prevent another assistant from having to address envelopes manually. You agree to do it because creating labels is as easy as generating a letter. Refer to Figure 4.34 as you complete Step 6.

FIGURE 4.34 Labels Displaying the Address Block ➤

a. Press **Ctrl+N** to display a new document. Save the document as **w04h3labels_LastnameFirstname**.

b. Click the **Mailings tab**, click **Start Mail Merge**, and then click **Step by Step Mail Merge Wizard**.

   The Mail Merge pane displays.

c. Click **Labels** in the *Select document type* section of the Mail Merge pane, and then click **Next: Starting document** at the bottom of the pane.

d. Click **Label options** in the *Change document layout* section of the pane.

   The Label Options dialog box displays.

e. Click the **Label vendors arrow**, and then click **Avery A4/A5**. Click **C2651** from the Product number list. Click **OK**. Click **Next: Select recipients** at the bottom of the pane.

> **TROUBLESHOOTING:** If you do not have the Avery A4/A5 label, consult with your instructor for an alternative product.

Most packages of labels will display a product number on the package that will also display in this list. This product number helps Word to set up a template that matches the layout of the labels, which then ensures the labels print correctly.

f. Click **Browse** in the *Use an existing list* section of the pane, and then navigate to the location where you saved the recipient list, *w04h2donortable_LastnameFirstname*. Select the file, and then click **Open**.

   The Mail Merge Recipients dialog box displays.

g. Click the **Last Name arrow**. Click **Sort Ascending**.

h. Click the **Street arrow**, and then click (**Nonblanks**).

i. Click **OK** to select the remaining recipients, and then close the dialog box.

   The document displays the Next Record code throughout the document to indicate the labels are ready.

j. Click **Next: Arrange your labels** in the bottom of the Mail Merge pane. Click **Address block** in the *Arrange your labels* section of the pane.

   The Insert Address Block dialog box displays.

k. Click **Match Fields**, click the **Address 1 arrow**, click **Street**, and then click **OK**.

l. Click **OK** to close the Insert Address Block dialog box. Click **Update all labels** in the *Replicate labels* section of the pane.

   The Address Block field displays on each label, as shown in Figure 4.34. The default font size for the document is so large the addresses will not display correctly on the labels. You will reduce the size of the font to enable the address information to fit.

m. Press **Ctrl+A** to select all the label fields. Click the **Home tab**, click the **Font Size arrow**, and then select **9**. Click the **Paragraph dialog box launcher**, and then reduce the **Spacing Before** in the *Spacing* section to **0 pt**. Click **OK** to close the Paragraph dialog box.

n. Click **Next: Preview your labels** in Step 4 of 6 of the Mail Merge pane. In Step 5 of 6, click **Next: Complete the merge**.

o. Click **Edit individual labels** in the *Merge* section of the Mail Merge pane. Click **OK** in the Merge to New Document dialog box.

   A new document displays with seven labels at the top of the page.

p. Save the document as **w04h3mergelabels_LastnameFirstname**, and then close it. Close the original document without saving. Submit based on your instructor's directions.

After reading this chapter, you have accomplished the following objectives:

1. **Insert a table.** Tables represent a very powerful capability within Word and are used to organize a variety of data in documents. Tables are made up of rows and columns; the intersection of a row and column is called a *cell*. You can insert additional rows and columns if you need to add more data to a table, or you can delete a row or column if you no longer need data in the respective row or column. Individual cells can be merged to create a larger cell. Conversely, you can split a single cell into multiple cells. The rows in a table can be different heights and/or each column can be a different width.

2. **Format a table.** Each cell in a table is formatted independently and may contain text, numbers, and/or graphics. To enhance readability of table data, you can apply a predefined style, which Word provides, or use Borders and Shading tools to add color and enhance it. Furthermore, you can align table data—at the left margin, at the right margin, or centered between the margins. You also can change the text direction within a cell.

3. **Sort and apply formulas to table data.** You can sort the rows in a table to display the data in ascending or descending sequence, according to the values in one or more columns in the table. Sorting is accomplished by selecting the rows within the table that are to be sorted, and then executing the Sort command on the Layout tab. Calculations can be performed within a table using the Formula command in the same tab.

4. **Convert text to a table.** If you have a list of tabulated items that would be easier to manipulate in a table, you can use the Convert Text to Table command. The command also works in reverse, enabling you to remove data from a table and format it as tabulated text.

5. **Select a main document.** The mail merge process uses two files as input, a main document and a data source; by merging these two files, you can create a set of individualized letters, envelopes, e-mails, or other documents. The main document, also known as a *source* or *starting document*, contains the information that stays the same for all recipients. A wizard makes a process easier by asking a series of questions, and then creating a template based on your answers. If you want to create individual envelopes or a sheet of mailing labels, which are not part of a mail merge process, the Create group on the Mailings tab includes commands that you use to select the correct settings.

6. **Select or create recipients.** A recipient list, sometimes called a *data source*, contains individual pieces of data known as *fields*. Common fields in a data source include first name, last name, street, city, state, ZIP code, phone number, and e-mail address. You can sort or filter the recipient list to specify criteria for including records that meet certain conditions during the merge process. The Sort Records tab enables you to specify up to three levels for sorting records. You can also use Excel spreadsheets or Access databases or queries as source data for a mail merge.

7. **Insert merge fields.** When you write your letter or set up your e-mail in preparation for a mail merge, you insert a merge field in the main document. The merge field is a placeholder that specifies where information from the data source will display in the main document. The merge fields display in the main document within angle brackets. Because it corresponds with a field in the data source, matching the two fields guarantees that the right data will be inserted into the main document when you complete the merge.

8. **Merge a main document and a data source.** The merge process examines each record in the data source, and when a match is found, it replaces the merge field in the main document with the information from the data source. A copy of the main document is created for each record in the data source, thus creating individual form letters.

KEY TERMS

Ascending order *p.274*
Border *p.264*
Cell *p.262*
Cell margin *p.266*
Column width *p.263*
Data source *p.283*
Database table *p.285*
Descending order *p.274*
Field *p.283*

Filter *p.287*
Form letter *p.281*
Header row *p.283*
Mail merge *p.281*
Main document *p.282*
Merge field *p.282*
Record *p.283*
Row height *p.263*
Shading *p.264*

Sorting *p.273*
Syntax *p.273*
Table *p.262*
Table alignment *p.266*
Table Move handle *p.263*
Table style *p.265*
Text direction *p.266*
Wizard *p.282*

1. You have created a table containing numerical values and have entered the SUM(ABOVE) function at the bottom of a column. You then delete one of the rows included in the sum. Which of the following is true?

   (a) The row cannot be deleted because it contains a cell that is included in the sum function.

   (b) The sum is updated automatically.

   (c) The sum cannot be updated.

   (d) The sum will be updated after you right-click the cell and click the Update Field command.

2. What happens when you press Tab from within the last cell of a table?

   (a) A Tab character is inserted just as it would be for ordinary text.

   (b) Word inserts a new row below the current row.

   (c) Word inserts a new column to the right of the current column.

   (d) The insertion point appears in the paragraph below the table.

3. What happens when you type more than one line of text into a cell?

   (a) The cell gets wider to accommodate the extra text.

   (b) The row gets taller as word wrapping occurs to display the additional text.

   (c) The first line is hidden by default.

   (d) A new column is inserted automatically.

4. Assume you created a table with the names of the months in the first column. Each row lists data for that particular month. The insertion point is in the first cell on the third row, which lists goals for April. You realize that you left out the goals for March. What should you do?

   (a) Display the Insert tab, and then click the Table command.

   (b) Display the Table Tools Design tab, and then click the Insert Cell command.

   (c) Display the Table Tools Layout tab, and then click the Insert Left command.

   (d) Display the Table Tools Layout tab, and then click the Insert Above command.

5. You have a Word document that contains a list of people who were sent an invitation to a wedding. You are responsible for monitoring their responses to the invitation, whether they will attend or not, and to determine the grand total of those attending. Using skills learned in the chapter, what would be a good way to track this information?

   (a) Copy the names into an Excel spreadsheet, and then use mail merge to populate a table in Word.

   (b) Convert the list of names to a table; add columns that enable you to mark their response, including the number who will attend, and use a formula to add up the numbers when all responses are received.

   (c) Type the list of names into a Word table; add columns to mark a response, and a formula to add up responses.

   (d) Insert a two-column table beside the names and mark the responses as declined or attending.

6. When you generate a new data source during the mail merge process, what type of file do you create when it saves?

   (a) Document (.docx)

   (b) Worksheet (.xlsx)

   (c) Database (.mdb))

   (d) Rich text (.rtf)

7. During a mail merge process, what operation can you perform on a data source so only data that meet specific criteria, such as a particular city, are included in the merge?

   (a) Sort

   (b) Propagate

   (c) Delete

   (d) Filter

8. When you click Edit Individual Documents on the Mail Merge pane, and then click OK, the merged document _____.

   (a) overwrites the main document

   (b) is automatically printed

   (c) is saved to a new document file

   (d) appears in a new document window

9. When you use mail merge to create address labels, what option do you click to copy the address field from the first label to the rest of the labels before performing the merge?

   (a) Copy and paste

   (b) Update all labels

   (c) Edit recipient list

   (d) Sort and filter

10. Which of the following is not a good use for mail merge?

    (a) To print mailing labels for Christmas cards from a list of addresses in an Excel spreadsheet

    (b) To send the same personalized letter to all your business clients

    (c) To create return address labels that display your home address

    (d) To e-mail a meeting announcement to every member of your professional organization

1 Jacksonville City Theatre

You are the manager of the Jacksonville City Theatre and each month you mail tickets to patrons who have placed orders over the phone or online. You know that it is time-consuming to copy and paste the patrons' names and addresses from your Excel worksheet into the cover letter you send with the tickets, so you decide to create a mail merge document that you can quickly update and send each month. Later, you decide to use a filter so you print only letters to patrons attending the January performance. This exercise follows the same set of skills as used in Hands-On Exercise 3 in the chapter. Refer to Figure 4.35 as you complete this exercise.

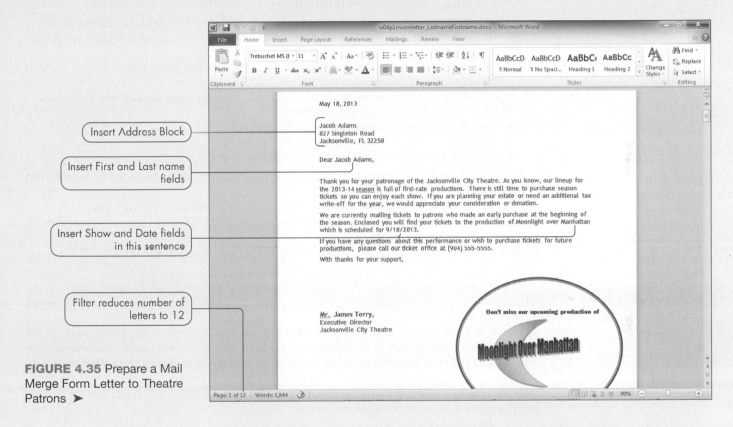

FIGURE 4.35 Prepare a Mail Merge Form Letter to Theatre Patrons ➤

a. Open *w04p1theatre* and save it as **w04p1theatre_LastnameFirstname**.

b. Click the **Mailings tab**, click **Start Mail Merge** in the Start Mail Merge group, and then click **Letters**.

c. Select a recipient by completing the following steps:
   - Click **Select Recipients**, and then click **Use Existing List**.
   - Navigate to the location where data files are stored, click **w04p1patrons.xlsx**, and then click **Open**.
   - Make sure *Sheet1* is selected, and then click **OK** when the Select Table dialog box displays.

d. Insert merge fields by completing the following steps:
   - Move the insertion point two lines below the date. Click **Address Block**, and then click **OK** to insert the patron's address at the top of the letter.
   - Move the insertion point to the left side of the comma in the salutation line *Dear*, and then click the **Insert Merge Field arrow**. Click **Fname**, press **Spacebar**, click **Insert Merge Field**, and then click **Lname**.
   - Place the insertion point between the two spaces on the right side of the word *of* in the last sentence of the second paragraph. Click **Insert Merge Field arrow**, and then click **Show**.

> **TROUBLESHOOTING:** If you find it difficult to determine where to place the cursor, click Show/Hide (¶) on the Home tab to display formatting marks such as spaces.

- Move the insertion point to the end of the last sentence of the second paragraph, just before the ending period. Click **Insert Merge Field arrow**, and then click **Date**.

e. Click **Preview Results**. To correct the extra spacing around the address block, complete these steps:
   - Select the three lines that make up the address block.
   - Click the **Page Layout tab**.
   - Click the **Spacing After arrow** in the Paragraph group until **0 pt** displays.

f. Finish the merge by completing these steps:
   - Click the **Mailings tab**, click **Finish & Merge**, and then click **Edit Individual Documents**.
   - Click **From**, type **1** in the first box, type **34** in the second box, and then click **OK**. There were four records at the end of the list that did not contain addresses. You do not want to print those letters.
   - Save the new document as **w04p1ticketletter_LastnameFirstname**. Close the file.

g. Select *w04p1theatre_LastnameFirstname*, and then save it as **w04p1theatre2_LastnameFirstname**.

h. Filter the recipient list in preparation for creating letters to patrons attending the January production by completing the following steps:
   - Click the **Mailings tab**, if necessary, and then click **Edit Recipient List** to display the Mail Merge Recipients dialog box.
   - Click **Filter** to display the Filter and Sort dialog box. Click the **Filter Records tab**, if necessary.
   - Click the **Field arrow**, and then click **Show**.
   - Click the **Comparison arrow**, and then click **Contains**.
   - Type **Moon** in the **Compare to box**, and then click **OK**.
   - Click **OK** again to close the Mail Merge Recipients dialog box.

i. Click **Last Record** to determine how many pages your merge will create. If the filter is set correctly, your merge will create 12 letters.

j. Click **Finish & Merge**, click **Edit Individual Documents**, click **All**, and then click **OK**.

k. Save the new document as **w04p1moonletter_LastnameFirstname**. Compare your letter to Figure 4.35, and then close the document.

l. Save and close all documents, and submit based on your instructor's directions.

2 Marti Appraisal Company

You work as a real estate assessor and must bill for services each month. Traditionally, you type the total amount of your services in the document, but after a discussion with another assessor you discover how to use table formulas and begin to use them to calculate your total fees on the invoice. In this exercise, you develop a professional-looking invoice and use formulas to calculate totals within the table. This exercise follows the same set of skills as used in Hands-On Exercises 1 and 2 in the chapter. Refer to Figure 4.36 as you complete this exercise.

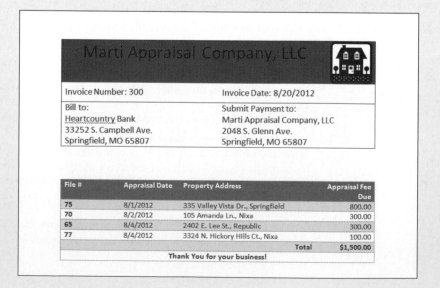

FIGURE 4.36 Completed Invoice ➤

a. Open a blank document and save it as **w04p2invoice_LastnameFirstname**.

b. Click the **Insert tab**, and then click **Table**. Drag to select one column and three rows (1 × 3 table).

c. Add information in the first row by completing the following steps:
    *   Type **Marti Appraisal Company, LLC**.
    *   Right-click to display the Mini toolbar, and then click **Center**.
    *   Select the text, click the **Font size arrow** on the Mini toolbar, and then select **28**.
    *   Click the **Page Layout tab**, and then click the **Spacing After arrow** until **12 pt** displays.
    *   Press ➡ to move the insertion point to the right side of the text.
    *   Click the **Insert tab**. Click **Clip Art**.
    *   Search for **House** and insert a graphic in the first row next to the Company name. Close the Clip Art pane.
    *   Click the **Format tab**, if necessary, click **Position** in the Arrange group, and then click **Position in Middle Right with Square Text Wrapping**.
    *   Reduce the height of the Clip Art so it is no more than 1″ high; the width can adjust proportionally to the height.

d. Select the second and third rows. Click the **Layout tab**, click **Split Cells** in the Merge group, and then click **OK** to accept the new size of 2 columns by 2 rows.

e. Fill in the last two rows of the table with the following information:

Invoice Number: 300	Invoice Date: 8/20/2012
Bill to: Heartcountry Bank 33252 S. Campbell Ave. Springfield, MO 65807	Submit Payment to: Marti Appraisal Company, LLC 2048 S. Glenn Ave. Springfield, MO 65807

f. Select the text you just typed and use the Mini toolbar to increase the font size to **14**. Press **Ctrl+L** to left justify, if necessary.

g. Select the second row of the table, click the **Page Layout tab**, and increase both **Spacing before** and **Spacing after** to **6 pt**.

h. Format the table borders by completing the following steps:
    *   Click the **Table Move handle** to select the whole table.
    *   Click the **Design tab**, click the **Borders arrow** in the Table Styles group, and then click **Borders and Shading**.
    *   Click the **Borders tab** in the Borders and Shading dialog box, if necessary.
    *   Click **Box** in the Setting area on the left side. Click **OK**.
    *   Select the second row of the table.
    *   Click the **Borders arrow** in the Table Styles group, and then click **Bottom Border**.
    *   Select the first row of the table.
    *   Click the **Borders arrow**, click **Borders and Shading**, and then click the **Shading tab**.
    *   Click the **Fill arrow**, select **Red, Accent 2, Darker 25%**, and then click **OK**.

i. Add a second table for invoice details by completing the following steps:
    *   Press **Ctrl+End** to move your cursor to the end of the document.
    *   Press **Enter** two times.
    *   Click the **Insert tab**.
    *   Click **Table**.
    *   Drag to select a four column by five row table (4 × 5).

j. Type the following column headings in the first row:

File #	Appraisal Date	Property Address	Appraisal Fee Due

k. Modify the size of the columns in this table by completing the following steps:
    *   Click the **Table Move handle** to select the whole table.
    *   Click the **Layout tab**, if necessary.
    *   Click the **Width arrow** until **1″** displays.
    *   Place the insertion point in the third column.
    *   Click the **Width arrow** until **2.5″** displays.

l. Type the following appraisal information in rows 2 through 4.

65	8/4/2012	2402 E. Lee St., Republic	300.00
70	8/2/2012	105 Amanda Ln., Nixa	300.00
75	8/1/2012	335 Valley Vista Dr., Springfield	800.00

m. Add the total amount due in row five by completing the following steps:
- Drag to select the first three cells in row five. Click **Merge Cells** in the Merge group on the Layout tab.
- Type **Total** in this new larger cell, and then press **Ctrl+R**.
- Place the insertion point in the last column of this row (**cell D5**), and then click **Formula** in the Data group.
- Make sure *=SUM(ABOVE)* displays in the Formula box. Click the **Number format arrow**, select **$#,##0.00;($#,##0.00)**, and then click **OK**.

n. Press **Tab** to add one more row to the table. In that row, complete the following steps:
- Drag your mouse across each cell in the last row to select the whole row.
- Click **Merge Cells** in the Merge group.
- Type **Thank you for your business!**
- Press **Ctrl +E** to center the sentence in the row.

o. Place the insertion point in the first cell of the fourth row, and then click **Insert Below** in the Rows & Columns group. In the new blank row, type the following:

| 77 | 8/4/2012 | 3324 N. Hickory Hills Ct., Nixa | 100.00 |

p. Sort the information in the table by date by completing the following steps:
- Select rows one through five.
- Click **Sort** in the Data group.
- Click **Header row** under *My list has.*
- Click the **Sort by arrow**, and then select **Appraisal Date**.
- Click **OK**.

q. Click in **cell D6**, which holds the formula. Right-click, and then select **Update Field**.

r. Format the table for readability by completing the following steps:
- Click the **Design tab**.
- Click anywhere in the second table, and then click the **More button** in the Table Styles group.
- Select **Medium Shading 1 - Accent 2** (third column, fourth row) from the gallery.
- Select **cells D1 through D6** (the first six rows of the last column), and then press **Ctrl+R** to right align.
- Click the **Layout tab**, click **AutoFit**, and then click **AutoFit Window** to expand the size of the table to the right margin.
- Select the total amount due in **cell D6**, and then click **Bold** on the Mini toolbar.
- Click the **Table Move handle** to select the whole table, and then increase the font size to **12 pt** using the Mini toolbar.
- Select the *Thank you* sentence in the last row, and then select **Bold** from the Mini toolbar, if necessary. Compare your results to Figure 4.36.

s. Save and close the document, and then submit based on your instructor's directions.

MID-LEVEL EXERCISES

1 Regional Science Fair

The Regional Science Fair will occur on the campus of Missouri State University in the spring, and students from schools across the southwest portion of the state compete in areas such as physics, chemistry, environment, meteorology, and astronomy. As the volunteer coordinator, you must maintain a list of people who will donate their time to the event. You decide to send a reminder to each volunteer so they will be sure to arrive at their designated time.

a. Open *w04m1reminder* and save it as **w04m1reminder_LastnameFirstname**.
b. Use the reminder as the main document in a mail merge.
c. Use *w04m1times.xlsx* as your data source. Insert fields for first and last name, time in (start time), and time out (end time) in the appropriate locations in the reminder document. Center the start and end time fields in the table.
d. Preview the merge results, and then edit the recipient list. Sort the source data so that it sorts the Time In field in ascending order.
e. Filter the source data so that any record containing a Time Out of *9:00:00 PM* will not be included in the merge.
f. Merge the documents, and then display the results in a new file. Save the merged reminders as **w04m1mergedreminder_LastnameFirstname**.
g. Save and close all documents, and then submit based on your instructor's directions.

2 Building Materials

You are the executive assistant to a general contractor, and your duties include listing the materials that will be used on a home remodeling project. Due to the large number of people who work on the project, from plumbers to electricians to carpenters, it is necessary to keep detailed records of the materials and supplies to use during the remodel. After the first job, you decide to provide the crew with a table of materials that includes pictures. This also might be helpful for any crew member who does not speak English. Refer to Figure 4.37 as you complete this exercise.

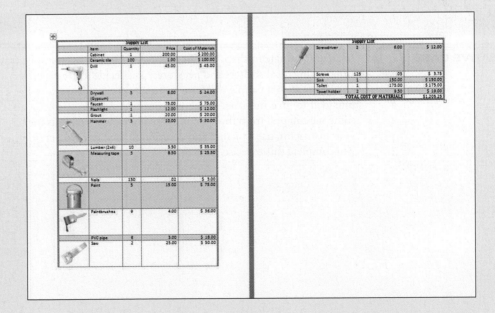

FIGURE 4.37 Supply List ➤

a. Open *w04m2construction* and save it as **w04m2construction_LastnameFirstname**.

b. Convert this list to a three-column table so you can organize the list of materials and add more data.

c. Insert two rows at the top to use for a heading and item descriptions.
- Create a title row on the table by merging cells in the first row.
- Insert the text **Supply List** as the title.
- Use the second row as a header for the columns.
- Enter the following labels for each column: **Item**, **Quantity**, **Price**.

d. Align the prices of each item in the third column. The prices should appear to align on the decimal point.

e. Center the data in the second column, which displays the quantity of each item you will use in the project.

f. Sort the data in ascending order by Item.

g. Use the **Split cell option** to split the third column in two. The label for the fourth column is **Total Cost**.

h. Insert a column to the left of the first column. Insert a picture of the supplies in the first column.
- Use symbols, clip art, or pictures to visually describe the following materials in your table: drill, hammer, paint, paintbrushes, saw, and screwdriver. You might not be able to locate a graphic for each item, but you should be able to find at least five to use in the table.
- Include Office.com content in your search, if needed.
- Resize the graphics as necessary so they do not exceed 1″ in height or width.
- Align each graphic in the center of the cell.

 i. Use a formula to calculate the total cost of each item and display it in the fifth column. To calculate the cost of materials, multiply the cell that contains the quantity by the cell that contains the price. For example, the formula for the cabinet is =C3*D3. You might also explore the Product function to calculate the cost of items. If you use a function, you can copy the formula from cell to cell, but must update each one to reflect the different data they calculate.

j. Add a row at the bottom of the table. Merge the first four columns of this row into one cell, and then type **TOTAL COST OF MATERIALS**. Insert a formula in the last column to calculate the total cost of materials used in this project.

k. Apply the **Light Grid - Accent 1** (sixth column, nineth row) style to the table. Use the Borders (and Shading) feature on the Design tab to add a double-line outside border to the table. (Hint: Use the Custom setting.) Center the table horizontally on the page.

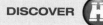 l. Use Help if needed to indicate the first row will repeat as a header row at the top of each page if your table spans more than one page. Merge cells in the first row to enlarge the cell containing the title.

m. Save and close the document, and then submit based on your instructor's directions.

3 Finding Dakota

  In an unfortunate mishap, your five-year-old dog, Dakota, escaped from your yard and is now missing. After calling local shelters and pet stores, you decide to create a flyer to post around the neighborhood and shops so that people will know whom to contact if they see her. Figure 4.38 displays a flyer that is intended to give information about your dog and also provide a tag with contact information that someone can pull from the flyer and take home. Use a table as the basis of this document. If allowed by your instructor, use a picture and description of your own pet or other animals. Refer to Figure 4.38 as you complete this exercise.

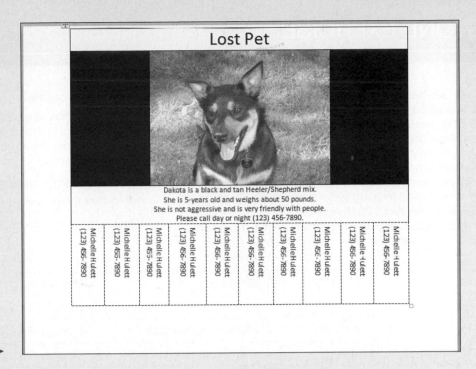

FIGURE 4.38 Lost Pet Flyer ➤

a. Open a new document and save it as **w04m3lostpet_LastnameFirstname**.

b. Create a table with five columns and four rows (5 × 4 table).

c. Merge all the cells in the first row, and then enter the text **Lost Pet**. Select the text, and then change the font size to **26 pt**. The row height will increase automatically to accommodate the larger text. Center the text in the cell.

d. Merge the cells in row 2. Use shading to place a black background in the cell. Locate pictures of your pet or pets; we have provided a picture of Dakota, *dakota.jpg*, in the Exploring Word folder. When you locate the file, insert the picture. The row height will expand automatically to accommodate the picture. Center the picture in the cell. You should use the Size features in Word to reduce the size of the photo if it displays too large for the page.

e. Merge cells in the third row, and then enter text to describe your pet or pets. Feel free to duplicate the information provided in Figure 4.38. Change the font size to **14 pt**, and then center the text in the cell.

 DISCOVER

f. Use the Draw Table tool to double the number of columns in the last row from 5 to 10. Use Help if needed to learn about this tool.

g. Type your name and phone number in the first cell of the fourth row. Use the Text Direction feature to rotate the text, as shown in Figure 4.38. Center and align the text at the top of the cell and increase the height of the cell, if necessary, to display the contents on two lines.

h. Use Copy and Paste to populate the remaining cells with the owner information.

i. Change the formatting of the fourth row to display a dashed line around each of the cells.

j. Save and close the document, and then submit based on your instructor's directions.

You work as the business manager for the local Sports Medicine Clinic and are responsible for many forms of correspondence. This week, you want to send a letter of welcome to three physical therapists recently hired at the clinic. Additionally, you need to send your weekly reminders to patients who are scheduled for upcoming treatment or consultations. In the past, the letters were generated manually and names were typed in each letter separately. However, because you now use Word 2010, you decide to create and use source data documents and implement a mail merge so you can produce the letters quickly and accurately.

Name	Credentials	Street	Days working	Salary
Mike Salat	M.S., ATC	2342 W. Cardinal Street	Monday–Thursday	$60,000
Justin Ebert	M.S., ATC	34234 S. Callie Place	Monday–Friday	$65,000
Karen Rakowski	ATC, PT	98234 E. Shepherd Lane	Monday–Friday	$65,000

c. Separate the name into two columns because it will be easier to use in form letters using mail merge features. Make necessary changes to the table to display the therapists' first and last names in two separate columns. (Hint: Uncheck the option *Merge cells before split* in the Split Cells dialog box.)

d. Create three new columns for the City, State, and ZIP Code information, and then populate each one with **Conway, AR 72032.**

e. Create a new row, and then use a formula to total the Salary column. This amount is referenced in the letter, although you do not use it in the mail merge. Use Currency formatting, which will cause total salary amount to display with two decimal places, unlike the salary entries in the cells above.

f. Sort the data in the table by Last Name.

g. Save the document.

Merge Therapist Information into a Welcome Letter

Now that you have documented information about the new Physical Therapists, you can use it as a source for the welcome letter.

a. Open *w04c1welcome* and save it as **w04c1welcome_LastnameFirstname**.

b. Start a mail merge using the welcome letter as the source document. The recipient information will come from *w04c1therapists_LastnameFirstname*.

c. Replace the starred placeholders in the letter with the fields from the recipient table. Insert today's date in the appropriate place.

Create a Table Containing Therapist Information

You will create a new document that includes a table of information about the new physical therapists. Then you personalize the welcome letter created for the therapists and use information from the table to create a personal letter for each person.

a. Open a new, blank document and save it as **w04c1therapists_LastnameFirstname**.

b. Create a table with the following information:

d. Preview the results before merging. Filter the recipients so the fourth record does not generate a letter.

e. Complete the mail merge, displaying the results in a new document. Save the merged letters as **w04c1ptwelcome_LastnameFirstname**. Close all files.

Produce a Reminder Letter for Patients

Your second project for the day is the generation of a letter to remind patients of their appointment with the therapists. For this project, you use an Access database as the source because that is how your office stores patient information.

a. Open a new document and save it as **w04c1reminder_LastnameFirstname**. Start a mail merge letter and pull your recipients from *w04c1patients.accdb*. When you select the database file, use the Patients table.

b. Insert today's date in the top-right corner of the letter. Insert an address block in the return address area of the letter. Add an appropriate salutation of greeting to the patient.

c. Type the following for the body of the reminder letter: **Please remember that you have an appointment at the Sports Medicine Clinic of Conway on *date*, at *time*. If you have paperwork to fill out, please arrive at our office 15 minutes prior to your appointment time stated above. Thank you!**

d. Insert the fields for date and time in the first sentence and remove the markers.

e. Finish the letter by typing the closing salutation:

Sincerely,
The Sports Medicine Clinic of Conway
(501) 555-5555

f. Edit the recipient list and add your name, address, and a date for an appointment. If file or network security does not enable you to modify the source data file, copy the file to your own disk and redirect the mail merge to use the file from the new location. If you cannot copy the file, omit this step.

g. Sort the recipient list by appointment date, and then appointment time. Do not print letters for people who do not have a scheduled appointment.

h. Change the formatting of the document so the letter is single spaced with no spacing before or after any paragraph.

i. Merge the documents into a new document, and then save it as **w04c1appointments_LastnameFirstname**. If a Mail Merge dialog box displays indicating Word found locked fields during the update, click **OK** to clear the dialog box.

j. Save and close all documents, and submit based on your instructor's directions.

Employee Directory

GENERAL CASE

The management of your company requires you to keep a current list of employee contact information in case you need to contact someone for an emergency situation. You have a worksheet that contains the contact information, but you do not yet know how to use Excel and you need to create and format a list very quickly. You are mastering the Mail Merge feature of Word and remember you have the option of creating a directory, which lists the source data on one page instead of printing each one on a separate page. This would be a good tool to use in generating the master list. Open a new document and prepare the contact information list using a mail merge operation. Use the file *w04b1personnel.xlsx* as your data source. Save the main document as **w04b1directory_LastnameFirstname**, and save the result of your mail merge as **w04b1directorylist_LastnameFirstname**. Use the Microsoft Help feature, if necessary. It might be helpful to format your data in a table so it is easier to read. Close all documents and submit based on your instructor's directions.

Great Plains Travel Agency

RESEARCH CASE

You are a travel agent at the Great Plains Travel Agency and your boss wants you to develop a travel itinerary to a popular destination. Choose a location, and then use the Internet to help you determine the expenses that a customer will incur if he or she chooses that location. Create a table in Word that details costs associated with transportation, lodging, activities, and food. Create multiple columns that enable you to break down costs by category and by day (such as seven nights in a hotel that costs $200 per night) and add formulas to show subtotals and the total cost of the trip. Save your work as **w04b2travel_LastnameFirstname**. Close the document and submit based on your instructor's directions.

Wedding Invitations

DISASTER RECOVERY

Your friend is experiencing high levels of anxiety because she cannot complete a mail merge operation to create labels for her wedding invitations. She has used the Mail Merge feature previously; however, when you open the labels, a dialog box appears and indicates there is no link from that main document to the data source (address list). You decide to troubleshoot the operation by first opening the file *w04b3labels*, to see how it was set up to use the addresses in *w04b3labeladdresses.accdb*, and then determine if you can find the reason why it does not work. If you can solve the problem, create mailing labels for the wedding and save the new file as **w04b3weddinglabels_LastnameFirstname**. Rename and save the original file you fix as **w04b3labels_LastnameFirstname**. Close all documents and submit based on your instructor's directions.

1 INTRODUCTION TO EXCEL

What Is a Spreadsheet?

CASE STUDY | OK Office Systems

Watch the
Set-up
Video
for this
Case Study!

You are an assistant manager at OK Office Systems (OKOS) in Oklahoma City. OKOS sells a wide range of computer systems, peripherals, and furniture for small- and medium-sized organizations in the metropolitan area. To compete against large, global big-box office supply stores, OKOS provides competitive pricing by ordering directly from local manufacturers rather than dealing with distributors.

The manager asked you to help prepare a markup, discount, and profit analysis for selected items on sale. The manager has been keeping these data in a ledger, but you will develop a spreadsheet to perform the necessary calculations. Although your experience with Microsoft Office Excel 2010 may be limited, you are excited to apply your knowledge and skills to your newly assigned responsibility.

When you get to the Hands-On Exercises, you will create and format the analytical spreadsheet to practice the skills you learn in this chapter.

OBJECTIVES AFTER YOU READ THIS CHAPTER, YOU WILL BE ABLE TO:

1. Plan for effective workbook and worksheet design *p.312*
2. Explore the Excel window *p.313*
3. Enter and edit cell data *p.316*
4. Use symbols and the order of precedence *p.321*
5. Use Auto Fill *p.323*
6. Display cell formulas *p.324*
7. Manage worksheets *p.330*
8. Manage columns and rows *p.333*
9. Select, move, copy, and paste *p.337*
10. Apply alignment and font options *p.346*
11. Apply number formats *p.348*
12. Select page setup options *p.354*
13. Print a worksheet *p.357*

Introduction to Spreadsheets

The ability to organize, calculate, and evaluate quantitative data is one of the most important skills needed today for personal, as well as managerial, decision making. In your personal life, you track expenses for your household budget, maintain a savings plan, and determine what amount you can afford for a house or car payment. Retail managers create and analyze their organizations' annual budgets, sales projections, and inventory records. Charitable organizations track the donations they receive, the distribution of those donations, and overhead expenditures. Scientists track the results of their experiments and perform statistical analysis to draw conclusions and recommendations.

> The ability to organize, calculate, and evaluate quantitative data is one of the most important skills needed today.

Regardless of what type of quantitative analysis you need to do, you can use a spreadsheet to help you maintain data and perform calculations. A *spreadsheet* is an electronic file that contains a grid of columns and rows used to organize related data and to display results of calculations, enabling interpretation of quantitative data for decision making. A *spreadsheet program* is a computer application, such as Microsoft Excel, that you use to create and modify electronic spreadsheets.

Performing calculations using a calculator and then entering the results into a ledger can lead to inaccurate values. If an input value is incorrect or needs to be updated, you have to recalculate the results manually, which is time-consuming and can lead to inaccuracies. An electronic spreadsheet makes data-entry changes easy. If the formulas are correctly constructed, the results recalculate automatically and accurately, saving time and reducing room for error. The left side of Figure 1.1 shows the original spreadsheet with the $450 cost, 75% markup rate, and calculated retail price. The right side shows the updated spreadsheet with a $500 cost, 65.5% markup, and automatically updated retail price.

> A **spreadsheet** is an electronic file that contains a grid of columns and rows containing related data.
>
> A **spreadsheet program** is a computer application used to create and modify spreadsheets.

Changed values • **Automatically updated retail price**

Original calculated retail price • **Original values**

Original Spreadsheet Values and Results			
Product	Cost	Markup Rate	Retail Price
Electronics:			
Computer System	$400.00	50.00%	$ 600.00
28" Monitor	$195.00	83.50%	$ 357.83
Color Laser Printer	$450.00	75.00%	$ 787.50

Modified Spreadsheet Values and Results			
Product	Cost	Markup Rate	Retail Price
Electronics:			
Computer System	$400.00	50.00%	$ 600.00
28" Monitor	$195.00	83.50%	$ 357.83
Color Laser Printer	$500.00	65.50%	$ 827.50

FIGURE 1.1 Original and Modified Values ➤

In this section, you will learn how to design workbooks and worksheets. In addition, you will explore the Excel window and learn the name of each window element. Then, you will enter text, values, dates, and formulas in a worksheet.

Planning for Effective Workbook and Worksheet Design

> A **worksheet** is a spreadsheet that contains formulas, functions, values, text, and visual aids.
>
> A **workbook** is a file containing related worksheets.

Microsoft Excel is the most popular spreadsheet program used today. In Excel, a *worksheet* is a single spreadsheet that typically contains descriptive labels, numeric values, formulas, functions, and graphical representations of data. A *workbook* is a collection of one or more related worksheets contained within a single file. By default, new workbooks contain three worksheets. Storing multiple worksheets within one workbook helps organize related data together in one file and enables you to perform calculations among the worksheets within the workbook. For example, you can create a budget workbook of 13 worksheets, one for each month to store your personal income and expenses and a final worksheet to calculate totals across the entire year.

You should plan the structure before you start entering data into a worksheet. Using the OKOS case study as an example, the steps to design the workbook and a worksheet include the following:

1. **State the purpose of the worksheet.** The purpose of the OKOS worksheet is to provide data, including a profit margin, on selected products on sale.

An **input area** is a range of cells containing values for variables used in formulas.

An **output area** is a range of cells containing results based on manipulating the variables.

2. **Decide what input values are needed.** Create an ***input area***, a range of cells to enter values for your variables or assumptions. Clearly label an input area so that users know where to change values. For the OKOS worksheet, list the product names, the costs OKOS pays the manufacturers, the markup rates, and the proposed discount rates for the sale. Enter these data in individual cells to enable changes if needed.

3. **Decide what outputs are needed to achieve the purpose of the worksheet.** Create an ***output area***, a range of cells that contains the results of manipulating values in the input area. As the OKOS assistant manager, you need to calculate the retail price (i.e., the selling price to your customers), the sale price, and the profit margin. As you plan your formulas, avoid constants (raw numbers); instead, use references to cells containing numbers.

4. **Assign the worksheet inputs and results into columns and rows, and consider labeling.** Typically, descriptive labels appear in the first column to represent each row of data. For the OKOS worksheet, enter the product names in the first column. Labels at the top of each column represent individual columns of data, such as cost, markup rate, and selling price.

5. **Enter the labels, values, and formulas in Excel.** Change the input values to test that your formulas produce correct results. If necessary, correct any errors in the formulas to produce correct results regardless of the input values. For the OKOS worksheet, change some of the original costs and markup rates to ensure the calculated retail price, selling price, and profit margin percentage results update correctly.

6. **Format the numerical values in the worksheet.** Align decimal points in columns of numbers. In the OKOS worksheet, use Accounting Number Format and the Percent Style to format the numerical data. Adjust the number of decimal places as needed.

7. **Format the descriptive titles and labels attractively but so as not to distract your audience from the purpose of the worksheet.** Include a descriptive title and label for each column. Add bold to headings, increase the font size for readability, and use color to draw attention to important values or trends. In the OKOS worksheet, you will center the main title over all the columns and apply a larger font size to it.

8. **Document the worksheet as thoroughly as possible.** Include the current date, your name as the author of the worksheet, assumptions, and purpose of the worksheet.

9. **Save the completed workbook.** Preview and prepare printouts for distribution in meetings, or send an electronic copy of the workbook to those who need it.

Figure 1.2 shows the completed worksheet in Excel.

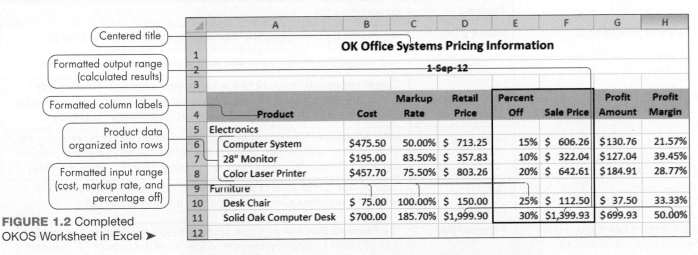

FIGURE 1.2 Completed OKOS Worksheet in Excel ➤

Callouts: Centered title / Formatted output range (calculated results) / Formatted column labels / Product data organized into rows / Formatted input range (cost, markup rate, and percentage off)

	A	B	C	D	E	F	G	H
1	OK Office Systems Pricing Information							
2	1-Sep-12							
3								
4	Product	Cost	Markup Rate	Retail Price	Percent Off	Sale Price	Profit Amount	Profit Margin
5	Electronics							
6	Computer System	$475.50	50.00%	$ 713.25	15%	$ 606.26	$130.76	21.57%
7	28" Monitor	$195.00	83.50%	$ 357.83	10%	$ 322.04	$127.04	39.45%
8	Color Laser Printer	$457.70	75.50%	$ 803.26	20%	$ 642.61	$184.91	28.77%
9	Furniture							
10	Desk Chair	$ 75.00	100.00%	$ 150.00	25%	$ 112.50	$ 37.50	33.33%
11	Solid Oak Computer Desk	$700.00	185.70%	$1,999.90	30%	$1,399.93	$699.93	50.00%
12								

Exploring the Excel Window

By now, you should be familiar with the standard interface of Microsoft Office applications: the Quick Access Toolbar, title bar, control buttons, Ribbon, Home tab, the Backstage view, and scroll bars. The Excel window includes screen elements that are similar to other Office applications and items that are unique to Excel. Figure 1.3 identifies elements specific to the Excel window, and Table 1.1 lists and describes the Excel window elements.

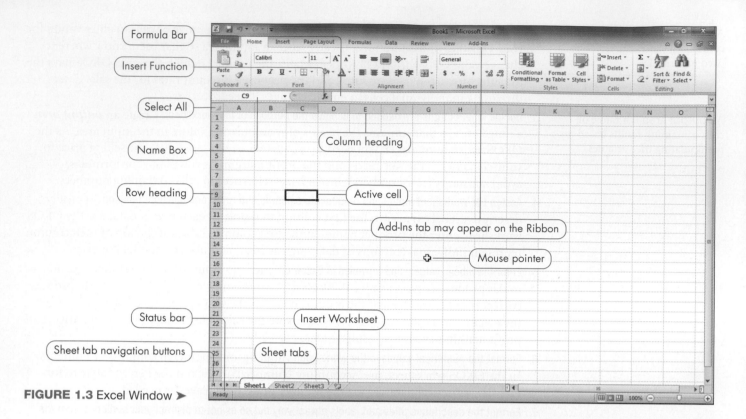

Formula Bar

Insert Function

Select All

Name Box

Row heading

Status bar

Sheet tab navigation buttons

Column heading

Active cell

Add-Ins tab may appear on the Ribbon

Mouse pointer

Insert Worksheet

Sheet tabs

FIGURE 1.3 Excel Window ➤

TIP Add-Ins Tab

You may see an Add-Ins tab on the Ribbon. This tab indicates that additional functionality, such as an updated Office feature or an Office-compatible program, has been added to your system. Add-Ins are designed to increase your productivity.

The **Name Box** identifies the address of the current cell.

The **Formula Bar** displays the content (text, value, date, or formula) in the active cell.

TABLE 1.1 Excel Elements

Element	Description
Name Box	The *Name Box* is an identifier that displays the address of the cell currently used in the worksheet. You can use the Name Box to go to a cell, assign a name to one or more cells, or select a function.
☒ Cancel	Cancel appears to the right of the Name Box when you enter or edit data. Click Cancel to cancel the data entry or edit and revert back to the previous data in the cell, if any. Cancel disappears after you click it.
☑ Enter	Enter appears to the right of the Name Box when you enter or edit data. Click Enter to accept data typed in the active cell and keep the current cell active. The Enter check mark disappears after you enter the data.
f_x Insert Function	Click to display the Insert Function dialog box, which enables you to search for and select a function to insert into the active cell.
Formula Bar	The *Formula Bar*, the area that appears below the Ribbon and to the right of Insert Function, shows the contents of the active cell. You can enter or edit cell contents here or directly in the active cell. Drag the bottom border of the Formula Bar down to increase the space of the Formula Bar to display large amounts of data or a long formula contained in the active cell.
Select All	The square at the intersection of the row and column headings in the top-left corner of the worksheet. Click it to select everything contained in the active worksheet.

TABLE 1.1   (Continued)

Element	Description
Column headings	The letters above the columns, such as A, B, C, and so on.
Row headings	The numbers to the left of the rows are row headings, such as 1, 2, 3, and so on.
Sheet tabs	*Sheet tabs*, located at the bottom-left corner of the Excel window, show the names of the worksheets contained in the workbook. Three sheet tabs, initially named Sheet1, Sheet2, and Sheet3, are included when you start a new Excel workbook. You can rename sheets with more meaningful names. To display the contents of a particular worksheet, click its sheet tab.
Sheet Tab Navigation buttons	If your workbook contains several worksheets, Excel may not show all the sheet tabs at the same time. Use the buttons to display the first, previous, next, or last worksheet.
Status bar	Located at the bottom of the Excel window, below the sheet tabs and above the Windows taskbar, the status bar displays information about a selected command or operation in progress. For example, it displays *Select destination and press ENTER or choose Paste* after you use the Copy command.

A **sheet tab** displays the name of a worksheet within a workbook.

Identify Columns, Rows, and Cells

A worksheet contains columns and rows, with each column and row assigned a heading. Columns are assigned alphabetic headings from columns A to Z, continuing from AA to AZ, and then from BA to BZ until XFD, which is the last of the possible 16,384 columns. Rows have numeric headings ranging from 1 to 1,048,576 (the maximum number of rows available).

A **cell** is the intersection of a column and row.

A **cell address** identifies a cell by a column letter and a row number.

The intersection of a column and row is a *cell*; a total of over 17 billion cells are available in a worksheet. Each cell has a unique *cell address*, identified by first its column letter and then its row number. For example, the cell at the intersection of column A and row 9 is cell A9. Cell references are useful when referencing data in formulas, or in navigation.

Navigate In and Among Worksheets

The **active cell** is the current cell, indicated by a dark border.

The *active cell* is the current cell. Excel displays a dark border around the active cell in the worksheet window, and the cell address of the active cell appears in the Name Box. The contents of the active cell, or the formula used to calculate the results of the active cell, appear in the Formula Bar. You can change the active cell by using the mouse to click in a different cell. If you work in a large worksheet, you may not be able to see the entire contents in one screen; use the vertical and horizontal scroll bars to display another area of the worksheet, and then click in the desired cell to make it the active cell.

To navigate to a new cell, click it, or use the arrow keys on the keyboard. When you press Enter, the next cell down in the same column becomes the active cell. Table 1.2 lists the keyboard methods for navigating within a worksheet. The Go To command is helpful for navigating to a cell that is not visible onscreen.

TABLE 1.2 Keystrokes and Actions	
Keystroke	**Used to**
↑	Move up one cell in the same column.
↓	Move down one cell in the same column.
←	Move left one cell in the same row.
→	Move right one cell in the same row.
Tab	Move right one cell in the same row.

(Continued)

TABLE 1.2 (Continued)

Keystroke	Used to
Page Up	Move the active cell up one screen.
Page Down	Move the active cell down one screen.
Home	Move the active cell to column A of current row.
Ctrl+Home	Make cell A1 the active cell.
Ctrl+End	Make the rightmost, lowermost active corner of the worksheet—the intersection of the last column and row that contains data—the active cell. Does not move to cell XFD1048576 unless that cell contains data.
F5 or Ctrl+G	Display the Go To dialog box to enter any cell address.

To display the contents of another worksheet within the workbook, click the sheet tab at the bottom of the workbook window. The active sheet tab has a white background color. After you click a sheet tab, you can then navigate within that worksheet.

Entering and Editing Cell Data

The four types of data that you can enter in a cell in an Excel worksheet are text; values; dates; and formulas, including functions. Figure 1.4 shows examples of text, values, dates, and formula results.

FIGURE 1.4 Data Entered in Cells ➤

Enter Text

Text includes letters, numbers, symbols, and spaces.

Text is any combination of letters, numbers, symbols, and spaces not used in calculations. Excel treats phone numbers, such as 555-1234, and social security numbers, such as 123-45-6789, as text entries. You enter text for a worksheet title to describe the contents of the worksheet, as row and column labels to describe data, and as cell data. Text aligns at the left cell margin by default. To enter text in a cell, do the following:

- Make sure the cell is active where you want to enter text.
- Enter the text.
- ☑ Press Enter, press an arrow key on the keyboard, or click Enter—the check mark between the Name Box and the Formula Bar. If you want to enter data without making another cell the active cell, click Enter instead of pressing Enter.

> **TIP** Line Break in a Cell
>
> If you have a long text label that does not fit well in a cell, you can insert a line break to display the text label on multiple lines within the cell. To insert a line break while you are typing a label, press Alt+Enter where you want to start the next line of text within the cell.

Enter Values

A **value** is a number that represents a quantity or an amount.

Values are numbers that represent a quantity or a measurable amount. Excel usually distinguishes between text and value data based on what you enter. The primary difference between text and value entries is that value entries can be the basis of calculations, whereas text cannot. Values align at the right cell margin by default. After entering values, you can align decimal places and add identifying characters, such as $ or %.

Enter Dates

You can enter dates and times in a variety of formats in cells, such as 9/15/2012; 9/15/12; September 15, 2012; or 15-Sep-12. You can also enter times, such as 1:30 PM or 13:30. You should enter a static date to document when you create or modify a workbook or to document the specific point in time when the data were accurate, such as on a balance sheet or income statement. Dates are values, so they align at the right cell margin.

Excel displays dates differently from the way it stores dates. For example, the displayed date 9/15/2012 represents the fifteenth day in September in the year 2012. Excel stores dates as serial numbers starting at 1 with January 1, 1900, so 9/15/2012 is stored as 41167 so that you can create formulas to calculate how many days exist between two dates.

Enter Formulas

A **formula** is a combination of cell references, operators, values, and/or functions used to perform a calculation.

Formulas are the combination of cell references, arithmetic operations, values, and/or functions used in a calculation. For Excel to recognize a formula, you must start the formula with an equal sign (=). Because Excel requires that formulas start with =, it treats phone numbers, such as (405) 555-1234, as text, not values. In Figure 1.4, cell E5 contains the formula =C5*D5+C5. The result of the formula (600) displays in the cell.

Edit and Clear Cell Contents

You can edit a cell's contents by doing one of the following:

- Click the cell, click in the Formula Bar, make the changes, and then click Enter on the left side of the Formula Bar.
- Double-click the cell, make changes in the cell, and then press Enter.
- Click the cell, press F2, make changes in the cell, and then press Enter.

You can clear a cell's contents by doing one of the following:

- Click the cell, and then press Delete.
- Click the cell, click Clear in the Editing group on the Home tab, and then select Clear Contents.

1 Introduction to Spreadsheets

As the assistant manager of OKOS, you need to create a worksheet that shows the cost (the amount OKOS pays its suppliers), the markup percentage (the amount by which the cost is increased), and the retail selling price. In addition, you need to list the discount percentage (such as 25% off) for each product, the sale price, and the profit margin percentage. Most of the cells in the worksheet will contain formulas. You have already planned the design as indicated in the steps listed earlier in this chapter.

Skills covered: Enter Text • Enter Unformatted Values • Enter a Date and Clear Cell Contents

---

STEP 1 ▶ ENTER TEXT

Now that you have planned your worksheet, you are ready to enter labels for the title, row labels, and column labels. Refer to Figure 1.5 as you complete Step 1.

	A	B	C	D	E	F	G	H
1	OK Office Systems Pricing Information							
2	1-Sep-12							
3								
4	Product	Cost		Markup Ra	Retail Pric	Percent O	Sale Price	Profit Margin
5	Computer System							
6	Color Laser Printer							
7	Filing Cabinet							
8	Desk Chair							
9	Solid Oak Computer Desk							
10	28" Monitor							
11								
12								

FIGURE 1.5 Text Entries ➤

FYI

a. Start Excel. Save the new workbook as **e01h1markup_LastnameFirstname**.

When you save files, use your last and first names. For example, as the Excel author, I would save my workbook as e01h1markup_MulberyKeith.

b. Type **OK Office Systems Pricing Information** in **cell A1**, and then press **Enter**.

When you press Enter, the next cell down—cell A2 in this case—becomes the active cell. The text does not completely fit in cell A1, and some of the text appears in cells B1, C1, and D1. If you make cell B1, C1, or D1 the active cell, the Formula Bar is empty, indicating that nothing is stored in those cells. If you were to type data in cell B1, that text would appear in cell B1, and although the contents of cell A1 would appear cut off, cell A1 still would contain the entire text.

c. Click **cell A4**, type **Product**, and then press **Enter**.

d. Continue typing the rest of the text in **cells A5** through **A10** as shown in Figure 1.5. Note that text appears to flow into column B.

When you start typing *Co* in cell A6, AutoComplete displays a ScreenTip suggesting a previous text entry starting with *Co—Computer System*—but keep typing to enter *Color Laser Printer* instead. You just entered the product labels to describe the data on each row.

e. Click **cell B4** to make it the active cell. Type **Cost** and press **Tab**.

Instead of pressing Enter to move down column B, you pressed Tab to make the cell to the right the active cell.

f. Type the following text in the respective cells, pressing **Tab** after typing each column heading:

- **Markup Rate** in **cell C4**
- **Retail Price** in **cell D4**
- **Percent Off** in **cell E4**
- **Sale Price** in **cell F4**
- **Profit Margin** in **cell G4**

Notice that the text looks cut off when you enter data in the cell to the right. Do not worry about this now. You will adjust column widths and formatting later in this chapter.

> **TROUBLESHOOTING:** If you notice a typographical error, click in the cell containing the error, and then retype the label. Or press F2 to edit the cell contents, move the insertion point using the arrow keys, press Backspace or Delete to delete the incorrect characters, type the correct characters, and then press Enter. If you type a label in an incorrect cell, click the cell, and then press Delete.

 FYI

g. Save the changes you made to the workbook.

You should develop a habit of saving periodically. That way if your system unexpectedly shuts down, you won't lose everything you worked on.

STEP 2 > **ENTER UNFORMATTED VALUES**

Now that you have entered the descriptive labels, you need to enter the cost, markup rate, and percent off for each product. Refer to Figure 1.6 as you complete Step 2.

	A	B	C	D	E	F	G	H
1	OK Office Systems Pricing Information							
2	1-Sep-12							
3								
4	Product	Cost	Markup Ra	Retail Pric	Percent O	Sale Price	Profit Margin	
5	Computer	400	0.5		0.15			
6	Color Lase	457.7	0.75		0.2			
7	Filing Cab	68.75	0.905		0.1			
8	Desk Chai	75	1		0.25			
9	Solid Oak	700	1.857		0.3			
10	28" Monit	195	0.835		0.1			
11								
12								

FIGURE 1.6 Unformatted Values ➤

a. Click **cell B5** to make it the active cell.

You are ready to enter the amount each product cost your company.

b. Type **400** and press **Enter**.

c. Type the remaining costs in **cells B6** through **B10** as shown in Figure 1.6.

> **TIP** Numeric Keypad
>
> To improve your productivity, you should use the numeric keypad on the right side of your keyboard if your keyboard contains a numeric keypad. If you use a laptop, you can purchase a separate numeric keypad device to use. It is much faster to type values and use Enter on the number keypad rather than using the numbers on the keyboard. Make sure Num Lock is active before using the keypad to enter values.

☑ d. Click **cell C5**, type **0.5**, and then press **Enter**.

You entered the markup rate as a decimal instead of a percentage. You will apply Percent Style later, but now you can concentrate on data entry. When you enter decimal values less than zero, you can type the period and value without typing the zero first, such as .5. Excel will automatically add the zero. You can also enter percentages as 50%, but the approach this textbook takes is to enter raw data without typing formatting such as % and then to use number formatting options through Excel to display formatting symbols.

e. Type the remaining markup rates in **cells C6** through **C10** as shown in Figure 1.6.

f. Click **cell E5**, type **0.15**, and then press **Enter**.

You entered the markdown or percent off sale value as a decimal.

g. Type the remaining markdown rates in **cells E6** through **E10** as shown in Figure 1.6, and then save the changes to the workbook.

STEP 3 ▶ ENTER A DATE AND CLEAR CELL CONTENTS

As you review the worksheet, you realize you need to provide a date to indicate when the sale starts. Refer to Figure 1.7 as you complete Step 3.

FIGURE 1.7 Date Entered ➤

a. Click **cell A2**, type **9/1/12**, and then press **Enter**.

The date aligns on the right cell margin by default. Note that Excel displays *9/1/2012* instead of *9/1/12* as you entered.

b. Click **cell A2**. Click **Clear** in the Editing group on the Home tab, and then select **Clear All**.

The Clear All command clears both cell contents and formatting in the selected cell(s).

c. Type **September 1, 2012** in **cell A2**, and then press **Enter**.

When you enter a date in the format *September 1, 2012*, Excel displays the date in the customer number format: *1-Sep-12*. However, you can select a date number format in the Format Cells dialog box.

d. Save the workbook. Keep the workbook onscreen if you plan to continue with Hands-On Exercise 2. If not, close the workbook and exit Excel.

Mathematics and Formulas

Formulas transform otherwise static numbers into meaningful results that can update as values change. For example, a payroll manager can build formulas to calculate the gross pay, deduc-

> Formulas transform otherwise static numbers into meaningful results.

tions, and net pay for an organization's employees, or a doctoral student can create formulas to perform various statistical calculations to interpret his or her research data.

You can use formulas to help you analyze how results will change as the input data change. You can change the value of your assumptions or inputs and explore the results quickly and accurately. For example, if the interest rate changes from 4% to 5%, how would that affect your monthly payment? Analyzing different input values in Excel is easy after you build formulas. Simply change an input value and observe the change in the formula results.

In this section, you will learn how to use mathematical operations in Excel formulas. You will refresh your memory of mathematical order of precedence and how to construct formulas using cell addresses so that when a value of an input cell changes, the result of the formula changes without you having to modify the formula.

Using Symbols and the Order of Precedence

The four mathematical operations—addition, subtraction, multiplication, and division—are the basis of mathematical calculations. Table 1.3 lists the common arithmetic operators and their symbols.

TABLE 1.3 Arithmetic Operators and Symbols

Operation	Common Symbol	Symbol in Excel
Addition	+	+
Subtraction	-	-
Multiplication	X	*
Division	÷	/
Exponentiation	^	^

Enter Cell References in Formulas

Start a formula by typing the equal sign (=), followed by the arithmetic expression. Do not include a space before or after the arithmetic operator. To add the contents of cells A2 and A3, enter =A2+A3 or =A3+A2. Excel uses the value stored in cell A2 (10) and adds it to the value stored in cell A3 (2). The result—12—appears in the cell instead of the formula itself. You can see the formula of the active cell by looking at the Formula Bar. Figure 1.8 shows a worksheet containing data and results of formulas. The figure also displays the actual formulas used to generate the calculated results.

◢	A	B	C	D
1	Contents		Description	Results
2	10		First input value	10
3	2		Second input value	2
4	=A2+A3		Sum of 10 and 2	12
5	=A2-A3		Difference between 10 and 2	8
6	=A2*A3		Product of 10 and 2	20
7	=A2/A3		Results of dividing 10 by 2	5
8	=A2^A3		Results of 10 to the 2nd power	100

Input values

Output (formula results)

FIGURE 1.8 Formula Results ➤

If you type A2+A3 without the equal sign, Excel does not recognize that you entered a formula and stores the data as text.

You should use cell addresses instead of values as references in formulas where possible. You may include values in an input area—such as dates, salary, or costs—that you will need to reference in formulas. Referencing these cells in your formulas, instead of typing the value of the cell to which you are referring, keeps your formulas accurate if the values change. If you change the value of cell A2 to 5, the result of =A2+A3 displays 7 in cell A4. If you had typed actual values in the formula, =10+2, you would have to edit the formula each time a value changes. Always design worksheets in such a way as to be able to change input values without having to modify your formulas if an input value changes later.

> ### TIP Constants in Formulas
>
> Use cell references instead of actual values in formulas, unless the value is a constant. For example, to calculate the reciprocal of a percentage stored in cell B4, type =1-B4. The constant, 1, represents 100%, a value that never changes, although the percentage in cell B4 might change.

Control the Results with the Order of Precedence

Recall the basic rules of performing calculations from a high school or college math class. What is calculated first in the expression =A1+A2*A3? Remember that multiplication is performed before addition, so the value in cell A2 is multiplied by the value in cell A3. Excel then adds the product to the value in cell A1.

The **order of precedence** controls the sequence in which Excel performs arithmetic operations.

The *order of precedence* (also called order of operations) is a rule that controls the sequence in which arithmetic operations are performed, which affects the results of the calculation. Excel performs mathematical calculations left to right in this order: **P**arentheses, **E**xponentiation, **M**ultiplication or **D**ivision, and finally **A**ddition or **S**ubtraction. Some people remember the order of precedence with the phrase **P**lease **E**xcuse **M**y **D**ear **A**unt **S**ally. Therefore, if you want to add the values in A1 and A2 and *then* multiply the sum by the value in cell A3, you need to enclose the addition operation in parentheses =(A1+A2)*A3 since anything in parentheses is calculated first. Without parentheses, multiplication has a higher order of precedence than addition and will be calculated first. Figure 1.9 shows formulas, formula explanations, and formula results based on the order of precedence. The result in cell A12 displays only five digits to the right of the decimal point.

	A	B	C	D
1	10			
2	5			
3	2			
4	4			
5				
6	Result		Formula	Explanation
7	20		=A1+A2*A3	5 x 2 = 10. The product 10 is then added to 10 stored in cell A1.
8	30		=(A1+A2)*A3	10 + 5 = 15. The sum of 15 is then multiplied by 2 stored in cell A3.
9	24		=A1+A2*A3+A4	5 x 2 = 10. 10 + 10 + 4 = 24.
10	90		=(A1+A2)*(A3+A4)	10 + 5 = 15; 2+4 = 6. 15 x 6 = 90.
11	10		=A1/A2+A3*A4	10 / 5 = 2; 2 x 4 = 8; 2 + 8 = 10.
12	5.71429		=A1/(A2+A3)*A4	5 + 2 = 7. 10 / 7 = 1.428571429. 1.42857149 * 4 = 5.714285714

FIGURE 1.9 Formula Results Based on Order of Precedence ➤

Using Auto Fill

Auto Fill enables you to copy the contents of a cell or cell range or to continue a sequence by dragging the fill handle over an adjacent cell or range of cells.

The **fill handle** is a small black square at the bottom-right corner of a cell.

Auto Fill enables you to copy the contents of a cell or a range of cells by dragging the *fill handle* (a small black square appearing in the bottom-right corner of a cell) over an adjacent cell or range of cells. To use Auto Fill, do the following:

1. Click the cell with the content you want to copy to make it the active cell.
2. Position the pointer over the bottom-right corner of the cell until it changes to the fill pointer (a thin black plus sign).
3. Drag the fill handle to repeat the content in other cells.

Copying Formulas with Auto Fill. After you enter a formula in a cell, you can duplicate the formula down a column or across a row without retyping it by using Auto Fill. Excel adapts each copied formula based on the type of cell references in the original formula.

Completing Sequences with Auto Fill. You can also use Auto Fill to complete a sequence. For example, if you enter *January* in a cell, you can use Auto Fill to enter the rest of the months in adjacent cells. Other sequences you can complete are quarters (Qtr 1, etc.), weekdays, and weekday abbreviations, by typing the first item and using Auto Fill to complete the other entries. For numeric values, however, you must specify the first two values in sequence. For example, if you want to fill in 5, 10, 15, and so on, you must enter the first two values in two cells, select the two cells, and then use Auto Fill so that Excel knows to increment by 5. Figure 1.10 shows the results of filling in months, abbreviated months, quarters, weekdays, abbreviated weekdays, and increments of 5.

Incremented values filled in

Click to see Auto Fill Options

FIGURE 1.10 Auto Fill Examples ➤

Immediately after you use Auto Fill, Excel displays the Auto Fill Options button in the bottom-right corner of the filled data (see Figure 1.10). Click the button to display four options: Copy Cells, Fill Series, Fill Formatting Only, or Fill Without Formatting.

 Fill Handle

To copy a formula down a column, double-click the fill handle. Excel will copy the formula in the active cell for each row of data to calculate in your worksheet. Cell addresses change automatically during the Auto Fill process. For example, if the original formula is =A1+B1 and you copy the formula down one cell, the copied formula is =A2+B2.

Displaying Cell Formulas

When you enter a formula, Excel shows the result of the formula in the cell (see the top half of Figure 1.11); however, you might want to display the formulas instead of the calculated results in the cells (see the bottom half of Figure 1.11). The quickest way to display cell formulas is to press Ctrl and the grave accent (`) key, sometimes referred to as the tilde key, in the top-left corner of the keyboard, below Esc. You can also click Show Formulas in the Formula Auditing group on the Formulas tab to show and hide formulas. This is a toggle feature; do the same step to redisplay formula results.

FIGURE 1.11 Formulas and Formula Results ➤

HANDS-ON EXERCISES

myitlab
HOE2 Training

2 Mathematics and Formulas

In Hands-On Exercise 1, you created the basic worksheet for OKOS by entering text, values, and a date for items on sale this week. Now you need to insert formulas to calculate the missing results—specifically, the retail (before sale) value, sale price, and profit margin. You will use cell addresses in your formulas, so when you change a referenced value, the formula results will update automatically.

Skills covered: Enter the Retail Price Formula • Enter the Sale Price Formula • Enter the Profit Margin Formula • Copy Formulas with Auto Fill • Change Values and Display Formulas

---

STEP 1 ▶ ENTER THE RETAIL PRICE FORMULA

The first formula you need to create is one to calculate the retail price. The retail price is the price you originally charge. It is based on a percentage of the original cost so that you earn a profit. Refer to Figure 1.12 as you complete Step 1.

Formula displayed in Formula Bar

| SUM | ▾ | X ✓ f_x | =B5*(1+C5) |

Blue border and blue cell reference

Green border and green cell reference

	A	B	C	D	E	F	G	H
1	OK Office Systems Pricing Information							
2	1-Sep-12							
3								
4	Product	Cost	Markup Ra	Retail Pric	Percent O	Sale Price	Profit Margin	
5	Computer	400	0.5	=B5*(1+C5)				
6	Color Lase	457.7	0.75		0.2			
7	Filing Cab	68.75	0.905		0.1			
8	Desk Chai	75	1		0.25			
9	Solid Oak	700	1.857		0.3			
10	28" Monit	195	0.835		0.1			
11								
12								

FIGURE 1.12 Retail Formula ➤

a. Open the *e01h1markup_LastnameFirstname* workbook if you closed it after the last Hands-On Exercise, and then save it as **e01h2markup_LastnameFirstname**, changing *h1* to *h2*.

> **TROUBLESHOOTING:** If you make any major mistakes in this exercise, you can close the file, open *e01h1markup_LastnameFirstname* again, and then start this exercise over.

b. Click **cell D5**, the cell where you will enter the formula to calculate the retail selling price of the first item.

c. Type **=B5*(1+C5)** and view the formula and the colored cell borders on the screen.

   As you type or edit a formula, each cell address in the formula displays in a specific color, and while you type or edit the formula, the cells referenced in the formula have a temporarily colored border. For example, in the formula =B5*(1+C5), B5 appears in blue, and C5 appears in green. Cell B5 has a temporarily blue border and cell C5 has a temporarily green border to help you identify cells as you construct your formulas (see Figure 1.12).

d. Click **Enter** to the left of the Formula Bar and view the formula.

The result of the formula, 600, appears in cell D5, and the formula displays in the Formula Bar. This formula first adds 1 (the decimal equivalent of 100%) to 0.5 (the value stored in cell C5). Excel multiplies that sum of 1.5 by 400 (the value stored in cell B5). The theory behind this formula is that the retail price is 150% of the original cost.

> **TIP** Alternative Formula
>
> An alternative formula also calculates the correct retail price: =B5*C5+B5 or =B5+B5*C5. In this formula, 400 (cell B5) is multiplied by 0.5 (cell C5); that result (200) represents the dollar value of the markup. Excel adds the value 200 to the original cost of 400 to obtain 600, the retail price. You were instructed to enter =B5*(1+C5) to demonstrate the order of precedence.

> **TROUBLESHOOTING:** If the result is not correct, click the cell and look at the formula in the Formula Bar. Click in the Formula Bar, edit the formula to match the formula shown in step 1c, and then click Enter. Make sure you start the formula with an equal sign.

e. Save the workbook with the new formula.

STEP 2 ▶ ENTER THE SALE PRICE FORMULA

Now that you calculated the retail price, you want to calculate a sale price. This week, the computer is on sale for 15% off the retail price. Refer to Figure 1.13 as you complete Step 2.

	F5			f_x	=D5-D5*E5			
	A	B	C	D	E	F	G	H
1	OK Office Systems Pricing Information							
2	1-Sep-12							
3								
4	Product	Cost	Markup Ra	Retail Pric	Percent O	Sale Price	Profit Margin	
5	Computer	400	0.5	600	0.15	510		
6	Color Lase	457.7	0.75		0.2			
7	Filing Cab	68.75	0.905		0.1			
8	Desk Chai	75	1		0.25			
9	Solid Oak	700	1.857		0.3			
10	28" Monit	195	0.835		0.1			
11								
12								

FIGURE 1.13 Sale Price Formula ➤

a. Click **cell F5**, the cell where you will enter the formula to calculate the sale price.

b. Type **=D5-D5*E5** and notice the color-coding in the cell addresses. Press **Ctrl+Enter** to keep the current cell the active cell.

The result is 510. Looking at the formula, you might think D5-D5 equals zero; remember that because of the order of precedence rules, multiplication is calculated before subtraction. The product of 600 (cell D5) and 0.15 (cell E5) equals 90, which is then subtracted from 600 (cell D5), so the sale price is 510. If it helps to understand the formula better, add parentheses: =D5-(D5*E5).

c. View the Formula Bar, and then save the workbook with the new formula.

The Formula Bar displays the formula you entered.

STEP 3 ▶ ENTER THE PROFIT MARGIN FORMULA

After calculating the sale price, you want to know the profit margin you earn. You paid $400 for the computer and will sell it for $510. The profit is $110, which gives you a profit margin of 21.57%. Refer to Figure 1.14 as you complete Step 3.

	G5					f_x	=(F5-B5)/F5		
	A	B	C	D	E	F	G	H
1	OK Office Systems Pricing Information							
2	1-Sep-12							
3								
4	Product	Cost	Markup R₂	Retail Pric	Percent O	Sale Price	Profit Margin	
5	Computer	400	0.5	600	0.15	510	0.215686	
6	Color Lase	457.7	0.75		0.2			
7	Filing Cab	68.75	0.905		0.1			
8	Desk Chai	75	1		0.25			
9	Solid Oak	700	1.857		0.3			
10	28" Monit	195	0.835		0.1			
11								
12								

FIGURE 1.14 Profit Margin Formula ➤

a. Click **cell G5**, the cell where you will enter the formula to calculate the profit margin.

The profit margin is the profit (difference in sales price and cost) percentage of the sale price. This amount represents the amount to cover operating expenses and tax, which are not covered in this analysis.

b. Type =**(F5-B5)/F5** and notice the color-coding in the cell addresses. Press **Ctrl+Enter**.

The formula must first calculate the profit, which is the difference between the sale price (510) and the original cost (400). The difference (110) is then divided by the sale price (510) to determine the profit margin of 0.215686 or 21.6%.

> **TROUBLESHOOTING:** If you type a backslash (\) instead of a forward slash (/), Excel will display an error message box. Make sure you type / as the division operator.

c. Look at the Formula Bar, and then save the workbook with the new formula.

The Formula Bar displays the formula you entered.

After double-checking the accuracy of your calculations for the first product, you are ready to copy the formulas down the columns to calculate the retail price, sale price, and profit margin for the other products. Refer to Figure 1.15 as you complete Step 4.

	G6	▼			f_x	=(F6-B6)/F6		
▲	A	B	C	D	E	F	G	H
1	OK Office Systems Pricing Information							
2	1-Sep-12							
3								
4	Product	Cost	Markup Ra	Retail Pric	Percent O	Sale Price	Profit Margin	
5	Computer	400	0.5	600	0.15	510	0.215686	
6	Color Lase	457.7	0.75	800.975	0.2	640.78	0.285714	
7	Filing Cab	68.75	0.905	130.9688	0.1	117.8719	0.41674	
8	Desk Chai	75	1	150	0.25	112.5	0.333333	
9	Solid Oak	700	1.857	1999.9	0.3	1399.93	0.499975	
10	28" Monit	195	0.835	357.825	0.1	322.0425	0.39449	
11								
12								

Cell references adjust in copied formula

Auto Fill Options

FIGURE 1.15 Auto Fill ➤

a. Click **cell D5**, the cell containing the formula to calculate the retail price for the first item.

b. Position the mouse pointer on the fill handle in the bottom-right corner of **cell D5**. When the pointer changes from a white plus sign to a thin black plus sign, double-click the **fill handle**.

Excel's Auto Fill feature copies the retail price formula for the remaining products in your worksheet. Excel detects when to stop copying the formula when it encounters a blank row, such as in row 11.

c. Click **cell D6**, the cell containing the first copied retail price formula, and look at the Formula Bar.

The original formula was =B5*(1+C5). The copied formula in cell D6 is =B6*(1+C6). Excel adjusts the cell addresses in the formula as it copies the formula down a column so that the results are based on each row's data rather than using the original formula's cell addresses for other products.

d. Select the **range F5:G5**. Double-click the **fill handle** in the bottom-right corner of **cell G5**.

Auto Fill copies the selected formulas down their respective columns. Notice Auto Fill Options down and to the right of the cell G10 fill handle, indicating you could select different fill options if you want.

e. Click **cell F6**, the cell containing the first copied sale price formula, and view the Formula Bar.

The original formula was =D5-D5*E5. The copied formula in cell F6 is =D6-D6*E6.

f. Click **cell G6**, the cell containing the first copied profit margin formula, and look at the Formula Bar. Save the changes to your workbook.

The original formula was =(F5-B5)/F5. The copied formula in cell G6 is =(F6-B6)/F6.

You want to see how the prices and profit margins are affected when you change some of the original values. For example, the supplier might notify you that the cost to you will increase. In addition, you want to see the formulas displayed in the cells temporarily. Refer to Figures 1.16 and 1.17 as you complete Step 5.

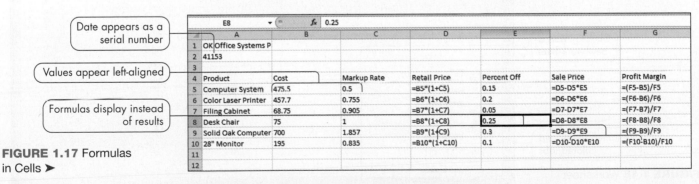

	E8			f_x	0.25		
	A	B	C	D	E	F	G	H
1	OK Office Systems Pricing Information							
2	1-Sep-12							
3								
4	Product	Cost	Markup Ra	Retail Pric	Percent O	Sale Price	Profit Margin	
5	Computer	475.5	0.5	713.25	0.15	606.2625	0.215686	
6	Color Lase	457.7	0.755	803.2635	0.2	642.6108	0.287749	
7	Filing Cab	68.75	0.905	130.9688	0.05	124.4203	0.447437	
8	Desk Chai	75	1	150	0.25	112.5	0.333333	
9	Solid Oak	700	1.857	1999.9	0.3	1399.93	0.499975	
10	28" Monit	195	0.835	357.825	0.1	322.0425	0.39449	
11								
12								

Updated formula results

Changed values

FIGURE 1.16 Results of Changed Values ➤

a. Click **cell B5**, type **475.5**, and then press **Enter**.

The results of the retail price, sale price, and profit margin formulas change based on the new cost.

b. Click **cell C6**, type **0.755**, and then press **Enter**.

The results of the retail price, sale price, and profit margin formulas change based on the new markup rate.

c. Click **cell E7**, type **0.05**, and then press **Enter**.

The results of the sale price and profit margin formulas change based on the new markdown rate. Note that the retail price did not change since that formula is not based on the markdown rate.

d. Press **Ctrl+`** (the grave accent mark).

The workbook now displays the formulas rather than the formula results (see Figure 1.17). This is helpful when you want to review several formulas at one time.

	E8			f_x	0.25		
	A	B	C	D	E	F	G
1	OK	Office Systems P					
2	41153						
3							
4	Product	Cost	Markup Rate	Retail Price	Percent Off	Sale Price	Profit Margin
5	Computer System	475.5	0.5	=B5*(1+C5)	0.15	=D5-D5*E5	=(F5-B5)/F5
6	Color Laser Printer	457.7	0.755	=B6*(1+C6)	0.2	=D6-D6*E6	=(F6-B6)/F6
7	Filing Cabinet	68.75	0.905	=B7*(1+C7)	0.05	=D7-D7*E7	=(F7-B7)/F7
8	Desk Chair	75	1	=B8*(1+C8)	0.25	=D8-D8*E8	=(F8-B8)/F8
9	Solid Oak Computer	700	1.857	=B9*(1+C9)	0.3	=D9-D9*E9	=(F9-B9)/F9
10	28" Monitor	195	0.835	=B10*(1+C10)	0.1	=D10-D10*E10	=(F10-B10)/F10
11							
12							

Date appears as a serial number

Values appear left-aligned

Formulas display instead of results

FIGURE 1.17 Formulas in Cells ➤

e. Press **Ctrl+`** (the grave accent mark).

The workbook now displays the formula results in the cells again.

f. Save the workbook. Keep the workbook onscreen if you plan to continue with Hands-On Exercise 3. If not, close the workbook and exit Excel.

Workbook and Worksheet Management

When you start a new blank workbook in Excel, the workbook contains three worksheets named Sheet1, Sheet2, and Sheet3. The text, values, dates, and formulas you enter into the individual sheets are saved under the one workbook file name. Having multiple worksheets in one workbook is helpful to keep related items together. For example, you might want one worksheet for each month to track your monthly income and expenses for one year. When tax time rolls around, you have all your data stored in one workbook file.

Although you should plan the worksheet and workbook before you start entering data, you might need to add, delete, or rename worksheets. Furthermore, within a worksheet you may want to insert a new row to accommodate new data, delete a column that you no longer need, adjust the size of columns and rows, or move or copy data to other locations.

In this section, you will learn how to manage workbooks by renaming, inserting, and deleting worksheets. You will also learn how to make changes to worksheet columns and rows, such as inserting, deleting, and adjusting sizes. Finally, you will learn how to move and copy data within a worksheet.

Managing Worksheets

Creating a multiple-worksheet workbook takes some planning and maintenance. Worksheet tab names should reflect the contents of the respective worksheets. In addition, you can insert, copy, move, and delete worksheets within the workbook. You can even apply background color to the worksheet tabs so that they stand out onscreen. Figure 1.18 shows a workbook in which the sheet tabs have been renamed, colors have been applied to worksheet tabs, and a worksheet tab has been right-clicked so that the shortcut menu appears.

FIGURE 1.18 Worksheet Tabs ➤

Rename Worksheets

The default worksheet names—Sheet1, Sheet2, and Sheet3—are vague; they do not describe the contents of each worksheet. You should rename the worksheet tabs to reflect the sheet contents so that you, and anyone with whom you share your workbook, will be able to find data. For example, if your budget workbook contains monthly worksheets, name the worksheets *September*, *October*, etc. A teacher who uses a workbook to store a grade book for several classes should name each worksheet by class name or number, such as *MIS 1000* and *MIS 3430*. Although you can have spaces in worksheet names, you should keep worksheet names relatively short. The longer the worksheet names, the fewer sheet tabs you will see at the bottom of the workbook window without scrolling.

To rename a worksheet, do one of the following:

- Double-click a sheet tab, type the new name, and then press Enter.
- Click Format in the Cells group on the Home tab (see Figure 1.18), select Rename Sheet (see Figure 1.19), type the new sheet name, and then press Enter.
- Right-click the sheet tab, select Rename from the shortcut menu (see Figure 1.18), type the new sheet name, and then press Enter.

FIGURE 1.19 Format Menu ➤

Change Worksheet Tab Color

The active worksheet tab is white, whereas the default color of the tabs depends on the Windows color scheme. When you use multiple worksheets, you might want to apply a different color to each worksheet tab to make the tab stand out or to emphasize the difference between sheets. For example, you might apply red to the September tab, green to the October tab, and dark blue to the November tab.

To change the color of a worksheet tab, do one of the following:

- Click Format in the Cells group on the Home tab (see Figure 1.18), point to Tab Color (see Figure 1.19), and then click a color on the Tab Color palette.
- Right-click the sheet tab, point to Tab Color on the shortcut menu (see Figure 1.18), and then click a color on the Tab Color palette.

Insert, Delete, Move, and Copy Worksheets

Sometimes you need more worksheets in the workbook than the three default sheets. For example, you might create a workbook that contains 12 worksheets—a worksheet for each month of the year. Each new worksheet you insert starts with a default name, such as Sheet4, numbered consecutively after the last Sheet#. After inserting worksheets, you can rename them to be more descriptive. You can delete extra worksheets from your workbook to keep it streamlined.

To insert a new worksheet, do one of the following:

- Click Insert Worksheet to the right of the last worksheet tab.
- Click the Insert arrow—either to the right or below Insert—in the Cells group on the Home tab, and then select Insert Sheet.
- Right-click any sheet tab, select Insert from the shortcut menu (see Figure 1.18), click Worksheet in the Insert dialog box, and then click OK.
- Press Shift+F11.

To delete a worksheet in a workbook, do one of the following:

- Click the Delete arrow—either to the right or below Delete—in the Cells group on the Home tab, and then select Delete Sheet.
- Right-click any sheet tab, and select Delete from the shortcut menu (see Figure 1.18).

> **TIP** Ribbon Commands with Arrows
>
> Some commands, such as Insert in the Cells group, contain two parts: the main command and an arrow. The arrow may be below or to the right of the command, depending on the command, window size, or screen resolution. Instructions in the Exploring Series use the command name to instruct you to click the main command to perform the default action, such as "Click Insert in the Cells group" or "Click Delete in the Cells group." Instructions include the word *arrow* when you need to select an additional option, such as "Click the Insert arrow in the Cells group" or "Click the Delete arrow in the Cells group."

After inserting and deleting worksheets, you can arrange the worksheet tabs in a different sequence, especially if the newly inserted worksheets do not fall within a logical sequence.

To move a worksheet, do one of the following:

- Drag a worksheet tab to the desired location. As you drag a sheet tab, the pointer resembles a piece of paper. A down-pointing triangle appears between sheet tabs to indicate where the sheet will be moved when you release the mouse button.
- Click Format in the Cells group on the Home tab (see Figure 1.18) or right-click the sheet tab you want to move, and select Move or Copy to see the Move or Copy dialog box (see Figure 1.20). Select the workbook if you want to move the sheet to another workbook. In the *Before sheet* list, select the worksheet on whose left side you want the moved worksheet to be located, and then click OK. For example, assume the October worksheet was selected before displaying the dialog box. You then select November so that the October sheet moves before (or to the left) of November.

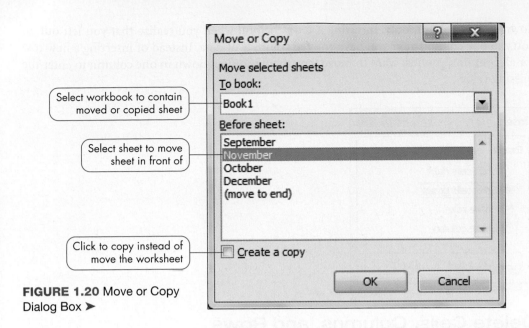

Select workbook to contain moved or copied sheet

Select sheet to move sheet in front of

Click to copy instead of move the worksheet

FIGURE 1.20 Move or Copy Dialog Box ➤

The process for copying a worksheet is similar to moving a sheet. To copy a worksheet, press and hold Ctrl as you drag the worksheet tab. Alternatively, display the Move or Copy dialog box, select the options (see Figure 1.20), click the *Create a copy* check box, and then click OK.

Managing Columns and Rows

As you enter and edit worksheet data, you can adjust the row and column structure. You can add rows and columns to accommodate new data, or you can delete data you no longer need. Adjusting the height and width of columns and rows can present the data better.

Insert Cells, Columns, and Rows

After you construct a worksheet, you might need to insert cells, columns, or rows to accommodate new data. For example, you might need to insert a new column to perform calculations or a new row to list a new product. When you insert cells, rows, and columns, cell addresses in formulas adjust automatically.

To insert a new column or row, do one of the following:

- Click in the column or row for which you want to insert a new column to the left or a new row above, respectively. Click the Insert arrow in the Cells group on the Home tab, and then select Insert Sheet Columns or Insert Sheet Rows.
- Right-click the column letter or row number for which you want to insert a new column to the left or a new row above, respectively, and select Insert from the shortcut menu.

Excel inserts new columns to the *left* of the current column and new rows *above* the current row. If the current column is column C and you insert a new column, the new column becomes column C, and the original column C data are now in column D. Likewise, if the current row is 5 and you insert a new row, the new row is row 5, and the original row 5 data are now in row 6.

You can insert a single cell in a particular row or column. To insert a cell, click in the cell where you want the new cell, click the Insert arrow in the Cells group on the Home tab, and then select Insert Cells. Select an option from the Insert dialog box (see Figure 1.21) to position the new cell, and then click OK. Alternatively, click Insert in the Cells group. The default action of clicking Insert is to insert a cell at the current location, which moves existing data down in that column only. Inserting a cell is helpful when you realize that you left out an entry in one column after you have entered columns of data. Instead of inserting a new row for all columns, you just want to move the existing content down in one column to enter the missing value.

FIGURE 1.21 Insert Dialog Box ➤

Delete Cells, Columns, and Rows

If you no longer need a cell, column, or row, you can delete it. In these situations, you are deleting the entire cell, column, or row, not just the contents of the cell to leave empty cells. As with inserting new cells, any affected formulas adjust the cell references automatically. To delete a column or row, do one of the following:

- Click the column or row heading for the column or row you want to delete. Click Delete in the Cells group on the Home tab.
- Click in any cell within the column or row you want to delete. Click the Delete arrow in the Cells group on the Home tab, and then select Delete Sheet Columns or Delete Sheet Rows, respectively.
- Right-click the column letter or row number for the column or row you want to delete, and then select Delete from the shortcut menu.

To delete a cell or cells, select the cell(s), click the Delete arrow in the Cells group, and then select Delete Cells to display the Delete dialog box (see Figure 1.22). Click the appropriate option to shift cells left or up, and then click OK. Alternatively, click Delete in the Cells group. The default action of clicking Delete is to delete the active cell, which moves existing data up in that column only.

FIGURE 1.22 Delete Dialog Box ➤

Adjust Column Width

Column width is the horizontal measurement of a column.

After you enter data in a column, you often need to adjust the *column width*—the number of characters that can fit horizontally using the default font or the number of horizontal pixels—to show the contents of cells. For example, in the worksheet you created in Hands-On Exercises 1 and 2, the labels in column A displayed into column B when those adjacent cells were empty. However, after you typed values in column B, the labels in column A appeared truncated, or cut off. You will need to widen column A to show the full name of all of your products. Numbers appear as a series of pound signs (######) when the cell is too narrow to display the complete value, and text appears to be truncated.

To widen a column to accommodate the longest label or value in a column, do one of the following:

- Position the pointer on the vertical border between the current column heading and the next column heading. When the pointer displays as a two-headed arrow, double-click the border. For example, if column B is too narrow to display the content in that column, double-click the border between the column B and C headings.
- Click Format in the Cells group on the Home tab (see Figure 1.18), and then select AutoFit Column Width (see Figure 1.19).

You can drag the vertical border to the left to decrease the column width or to the right to increase the column width. As you drag the vertical border, Excel displays a ScreenTip specifying the width (see Figure 1.23). Excel column widths range from 0 to 255 characters. The final way to change column width is to click Format in the Cells group on the Home tab (see Figure 1.18), select Column Width (see Figure 1.19), type a value in the Column width box in the Column Width dialog box, and then click OK.

ScreenTip displaying column width

Mouse pointer as you drag the border between column headings

Current column width

Column width when you release the mouse button

	E8	Width: 11.86 (88 pixels)	f_x	0.25			
	A	B	C	D	E	F	G	H
1	OK Office Systems Pricing Information						
2	1-Sep-12						
3							
4	Product	Cost	Markup Ra	Retail Pric	Percent O	Sale Price	Profit Margin
5	Computer	475.5	0.5	713.25	0.15	606.2625	0.215686
6	Color Lase	457.7	0.755	803.2635	0.2	642.6108	0.287749
7	Filing Cab	68.75	0.905	130.9688	0.05	124.4203	0.447437
8	Desk Chai	75	1	150	0.25	112.5	0.333333
9	Solid Oak	700	1.857	1999.9	0.3	1399.93	0.499975
10	28" Monit	195	0.835	357.825	0.1	322.0425	0.39449
11							
12							

FIGURE 1.23 Changing Column Width ➤

Adjust Row Height

Row height is the vertical measurement of a row.

When you increase the font size of cell contents, Excel automatically increases the *row height*—the vertical measurement of the row. However, if you insert a line break to create multiple lines of text in a cell, Excel might not increase the row height. You can adjust the row height in a way similar to how you change column width by double-clicking the border between row numbers or by selecting Row Height or AutoFit Row Height from the Format menu (see Figure 1.19). In Excel, row height is a value between 0 and 409 based on point size (abbreviated as *pt*). Whether you are measuring font sizes or row heights, one point size is equal to 1/72 of an inch. Your row height should be taller than your font size. For example, with an 11 pt font size, the default row height is 15.

> **TIP** Multiple Column Widths and Row Heights
>
> You can set the size for more than one column or row at a time to make the selected columns or rows the same size. Drag across the column or row headings for the area you want to format, and then set the size using any method.

Hide and Unhide Columns and Rows

If your worksheet contains confidential information, such as social security numbers or salary information, you might need to hide some columns and/or rows before you print a copy for public distribution. When you hide a column or a row, Excel prevents that column or row from displaying or printing. However, the column or row is not deleted. If you hide column B, you will see columns A and C side by side. If you hide row 9, you will see rows 8 and 10 together. Figure 1.24 shows that column B and row 9 are hidden. Excel displays a thicker border between column headings (such as between A and C), indicating one or more columns are hidden, and between row headings (such as between 8 and 10), indicating one or more rows are hidden.

Column B hidden (thicker border)

Row 9 hidden (thicker border)

	A	C	D	E	F	G	H	I	J	K	L
1	OK Office Systems Pricing Information										
2	1-Sep-12										
3											
4	Product	Markup R	Retail Pric	Percent O	Sale Price	Profit Margin					
5	Computer System	0.5	713.25	0.15	606.263	0.21569					
6	Color Laser Printer	0.755	803.264	0.2	642.611	0.28775					
7	Filing Cabinet	0.905	130.969	0.05	124.42	0.44744					
8	Desk Chair	1	150	0.25	112.5	0.33333					
10	28" Monitor	0.835	357.825	0.1	322.043	0.39449					
11											
12											

FIGURE 1.24 Hidden Column and Row ➤

To hide a column or row, do one of the following:

- Click in the column or row you want to hide, click Format in the Cells group on the Home tab (see Figure 1.18), point to Hide & Unhide (see Figure 1.19), and then select Hide Columns or Hide Rows, depending on what you want to hide.
- Right-click the column or row heading(s) you want to hide, and then select Hide.

You can hide multiple columns and rows at the same time. To select adjacent columns (such as columns B through E) or adjacent rows (such as rows 2 through 4), drag across the adjacent column or row headings. To hide nonadjacent columns or rows, press and hold down Ctrl while you click the column or row headings. After selecting multiple columns or rows, use any acceptable method to hide the selected columns or rows.

To unhide a column or row, select the columns or rows on both sides of the hidden column or row. For example, if column B is hidden, drag across column letters A and C. Then do one of the following:

- Click Format in the Cells group on the Home tab (see Figure 1.18), point to Hide & Unhide (see Figure 1.19), and then select Unhide Columns or Unhide Rows, depending on what you want to display again.
- Right-click the column(s) or row(s) you want to hide, and then select Unhide.

> **TIP** Unhiding Column A, Row 1, and All Hidden Rows/Columns
>
> Unhiding column A or row 1 is different because you cannot select the row or column on either side. To unhide column A or row 1, type A1 in the Name Box, and then press Enter. Click Format in the Cells group on the Home tab, point to Hide & Unhide, and then select Unhide Columns or Unhide Rows to display column A or row 1, respectively. If you want to unhide all columns and rows, click Select All, and then use the Hide & Unhide submenu.

Selecting, Moving, Copying, and Pasting

In the Office Fundamentals chapter, you learned the basics of selecting, cutting, copying, and pasting data. These tasks are somewhat different when working in Excel.

Select a Range

A **range** is a rectangular group of cells.

A **range** refers to a group of adjacent or contiguous cells. A range may be as small as a single cell or as large as the entire worksheet. It may consist of a row or part of a row, a column or part of a column, or multiple rows or columns, but will always be a rectangular shape, as you must select the same number of cells in each row or column for the entire range. A range is specified by indicating the top-left and bottom-right cells in the selection. For example, in Figure 1.25, the date is a single-cell range in cell A2, the Color Laser Printer data are stored in the range A6:G6, the cost values are stored in the range B5:B10, and the sales prices and profit margins are stored in range F5:G10. A **nonadjacent range** contains multiple ranges, such as C5:C10 and E5:E10. At times, you need to select nonadjacent ranges so that you can apply the same formatting at the same time, such as formatting the nonadjacent range C5:C10 and E5:E10 with Percent Style.

A **nonadjacent range** contains multiple ranges of cells.

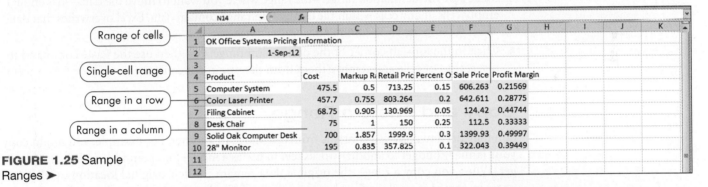

FIGURE 1.25 Sample Ranges ➤

Table 1.4 lists methods you can use to select ranges, including nonadjacent ranges.

TABLE 1.4 Selecting Ranges	
To Select:	**Do This:**
A Range	Click the first cell and drag until you select the entire range. Alternatively, click the first cell in the range, press and hold down Shift, and then click the last cell in the range.
An Entire Column	Click the column heading.
An Entire Row	Click the row heading.
Current Range Containing Data	Click in the range of data and then press Ctrl+A.
All Cells in a Worksheet	Click Select All, or press Ctrl+A twice.
Nonadjacent Range	Select the first range, press and hold down Ctrl, and then select additional range(s).

A border appears around a selected range. Any command you execute will affect the entire range. The range remains selected until you select another range or click in any cell in the worksheet.

Move a Range to Another Location

You can move cell contents from one range to another. For example, you might need to move an input area from the right side of the worksheet to above the output range. When you move a range containing text and values, the text and values do not change. However, any formulas that refer to cells in that range will update to reflect the new cell addresses. To move a range, do the following:

1. Select the range.
2. Use the Cut command to copy the range to the Clipboard. Excel outlines the range you cut with a moving dashed border. Unlike cutting data in other Office applications, the data you cut in Excel remain in their locations until you paste them elsewhere. After you use Cut, the status bar displays *Select destination and press ENTER or choose Paste*.
3. Make sure the destination range—the range where you want to move the data—has enough empty cells. If any cells within the destination range contain data, Excel overwrites that data when you use the Paste command.
4. Click in the top-left corner of the destination range, and then use the Paste command to insert the cut cells and remove them from the original location.

Copy and Paste a Range

You may need to copy cell contents from one range to another. For example, you might copy your January budget to another worksheet to use as a model for creating your February budget. When you copy a range, the original data remain in their original locations. Cell references in copied formulas adjust based on their relative locations to the original data. To copy a range, do the following:

1. Select the range.
2. Use the Copy command to copy the contents of the selected range to the Clipboard. Excel outlines the range you copied with a moving dashed border. After you use Copy, the status bar displays *Select destination and press ENTER or choose Paste*.
3. Make sure the destination range—the range where you want to copy the data—has enough empty cells. If any cells within the destination range contain data, Excel overwrites that data when you use the Paste command.
4. Click in the top-left corner of the destination range where you want the duplicate data, and then use the Paste command. The original selected range remains selected with a moving dashed border around it.
5. Press Esc to deselect the range. Figure 1.26 shows a selected range and a copy of the range.

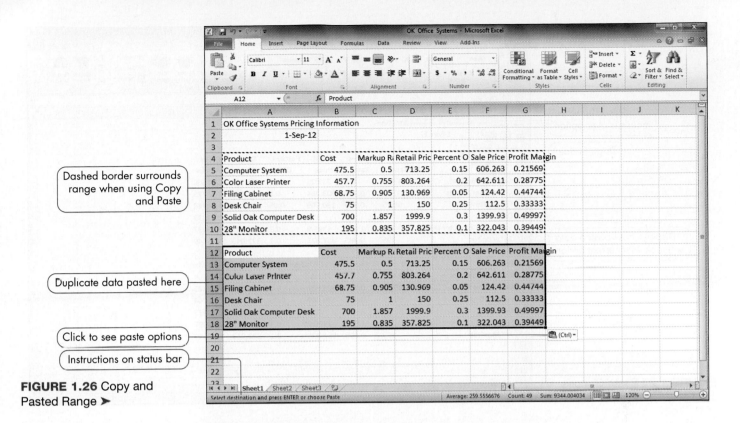

Dashed border surrounds range when using Copy and Paste

Duplicate data pasted here

Click to see paste options

Instructions on status bar

FIGURE 1.26 Copy and Pasted Range ➤

> ## TIP Copy as Picture
>
> Instead of clicking Copy, if you click the Copy arrow in the Clipboard group, you can select Copy (the default option) or Copy as Picture. When you select Copy as Picture, you copy an *image* of the selected data. You can then paste the image elsewhere in the workbook or in a Word document or PowerPoint presentation. However, when you copy the data as an image, you cannot edit individual cell data when you paste the image.

> ## TIP Paste Options Button
>
> When you copy or paste data, Excel displays Paste Options in the bottom-right corner of the pasted data (see Figure 1.26). Click Paste Options to see different results for the pasted data.

Use Paste Special

Sometimes you might want to paste data in a different format than they are in in the Clipboard. For example, you might want to copy a range containing formulas and cell references, and paste the range as values in another workbook that does not have the referenced cells. If you want to copy data from Excel and paste them into a Word document, you can paste the Excel data as a worksheet object, as unformatted text, or in another format. To paste data from the Clipboard into a different format, click the Paste arrow in the Clipboard group, and hover over a command to see a ScreenTip and a preview of how the pasted data will look. In Figure 1.27, the preview shows that a particular paste option will maintain formulas and number formatting; however, it will not maintain the text formatting, such as font color and centered text. After previewing different paste options, click the one you want in order to apply it.

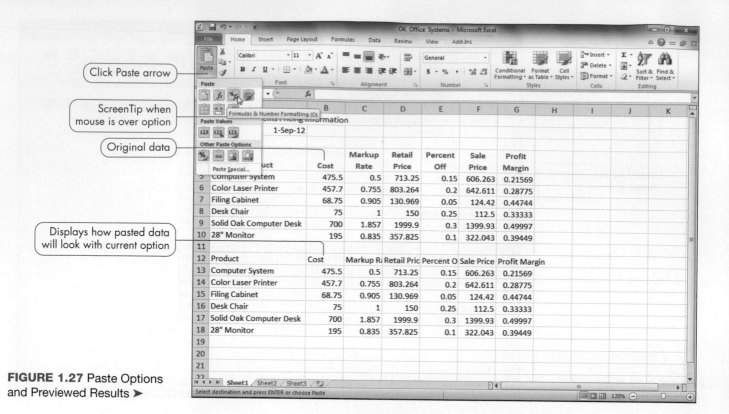

Click Paste arrow

ScreenTip when mouse is over option

Original data

Displays how pasted data will look with current option

FIGURE 1.27 Paste Options and Previewed Results ➤

For more specific paste options, click the Paste arrow, and then select Paste Special to display the Paste Special dialog box (see Figure 1.28). This dialog box contains more options than the Paste menu. Click the desired option, and then click OK.

FIGURE 1.28 Paste Special Dialog Box ➤

> **TIP** Transposing Columns and Rows
>
> After entering data into a worksheet, you might want to transpose the columns and rows so that the data in the first column appear as column labels across the first row, or the column labels in the first row appear in the first column. To transpose worksheet data, select and copy the original range, click the top-left corner of the destination range, click the Paste arrow, and then click Transpose.

HANDS-ON EXERCISES

3 Workbook and Worksheet Management

After reviewing the OKOS worksheet, you decide to rename the worksheet that contains the data and delete the other sheets. In addition, you decide to move the 28" Monitor data to display below the Computer System row and insert a column to calculate the amount of markup. You also need to adjust column widths to display data.

Skills covered: Manage Worksheets • Delete a Row • Insert a Column and Three Rows • Move a Row • Adjust Column Width and Row Height • Hide and Unhide Columns

STEP 1 ▶ MANAGE WORKSHEETS

You want to rename Sheet1 to describe the worksheet contents and add a color to the sheet tab. In addition, you want to delete the blank worksheets. Refer to Figure 1.29 as you complete Step 1.

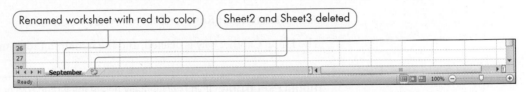

FIGURE 1.29 Worksheets Managed ➤

a. Open the *e01h2markup_LastnameFirstname* workbook if you closed it after the last Hands-On Exercise, and save it as **e01h3markup_LastnameFirstname**, changing *h2* to *h3*.

b. Double-click the **Sheet1 sheet tab**, type **September**, and then press **Enter**.

   You just renamed Sheet1 as September.

c. Right-click the **September sheet tab**, point to **Tab Color**, and then click **Red** in the Standard Colors section.

   The worksheet tab color is red.

d. Click the **Sheet2 sheet tab**, click the **Delete arrow** in the Cells group on the Home tab, and then select **Delete Sheet**.

   You deleted the Sheet2 worksheet from the workbook.

> **TROUBLESHOOTING:** Delete in the Cells group, like some other commands in Excel, contains two parts: the main command icon and an arrow. Click the main command icon when instructed to click Delete to perform the default action. Click the arrow when instructed to click the Delete arrow for additional command options.

> **TROUBLESHOOTING:** Notice that Undo is unavailable on the Quick Access Toolbar. You can't undo deleting a worksheet. It is deleted!

e. Right-click the **Sheet3 sheet tab**, and then select **Delete** to delete the sheet. Save the workbook.

STEP 2 ▶ DELETE A ROW

You just realized that you do not have enough filing cabinets in stock to offer on sale, so you need to delete the Filing Cabinet row. Refer to Figure 1.30 as you complete Step 2.

FIGURE 1.30 Row Deleted ➤

Delete menu

Filing Cabinet row deleted

a. Click **cell A7** (or any cell on row 7), the row that contains data for the Filing Cabinet.

b. Click the **Delete arrow** in the Cells group.

c. Select **Delete Sheet Rows**, and then save the workbook.

The Filing Cabinet row is deleted, and the remaining rows move up one row.

> **TROUBLESHOOTING:** If you accidentally delete the wrong row or accidentally select Delete Sheet Columns instead of Delete Sheet Rows, click Undo on the Quick Access Toolbar to restore the deleted row or column.

STEP 3 ▶ INSERT A COLUMN AND THREE ROWS

You decide that you need a column to display the amount of profit. Because profit is a dollar amount, you want to keep the profit column close to another column of dollar amounts. Therefore, you will insert the profit column before the profit margin (percentage) column. You also want to insert new rows for product information and category names. Refer to Figure 1.31 as you complete Step 3.

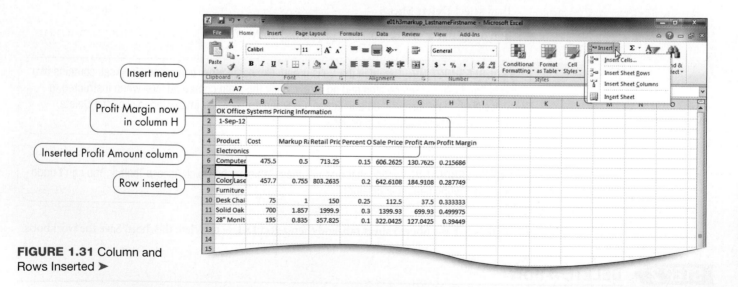

Insert menu

Profit Margin now in column H

Inserted Profit Amount column

Row inserted

FIGURE 1.31 Column and Rows Inserted ➤

a. Click **cell G5** (or any cell in column G), the column containing the Profit Margin.

You want to insert a column between the Sale Price and Profit Margin columns so that you can calculate the profit amount in dollars.

b. Click the **Insert arrow** in the Cells group, and then select **Insert Sheet Columns**.

You inserted a new, blank column G. The data in the original column G are now in column H.

c. Click **cell G4**, type **Profit Amount**, and then press **Enter**.

d. Make sure the active cell is **cell G5**. Type **=F5-B5** and then click **Enter** to the left of the Formula Bar. Double-click the **fill handle** to copy the formula down the column.

You calculated the profit amount by subtracting the original cost from the sale price. Although steps e and f below illustrate one way to insert a row, you can use other methods presented in this chapter.

e. Right-click the **row 5 heading**, the row containing the Computer System data.

Excel displays a shortcut menu consisting of commands you can perform.

f. Select **Insert** from the shortcut menu.

You inserted a new blank row 5, which is selected. The original rows of data move down a row each.

g. Click **cell A5**. Type **Electronics** and then press **Enter**.

You entered the category name Electronics above the list of electronic products.

h. Right-click the **row 8 heading**, the row containing the Desk Chair data, and then select **Insert** from the shortcut menu.

i. Click **cell A8**. Type **Furniture** and then press **Enter**.

You entered the category name Furniture above the list of furniture products. Now you want to insert a blank row after the Computer System row so that you can move the 28" Monitor data to the new row.

j. Insert a row between Computer System and Color Laser Printer. Click **cell A7**, and then save the workbook.

STEP 4 ▶ MOVE A ROW

You want to move the 28" Monitor product to be immediately after the Computer System product. You previously inserted a blank row. Now you need to move the monitor row to this empty row. Refer to Figure 1.32 as you complete Step 4.

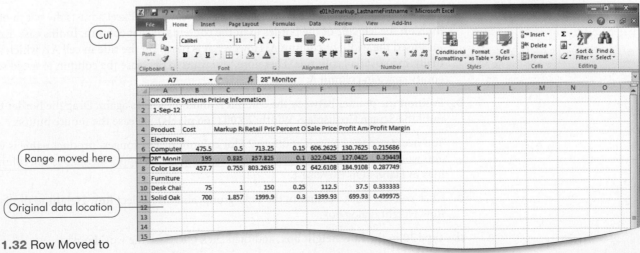

FIGURE 1.32 Row Moved to New Location ➤

a. Click **cell A12**, and then drag to select the **range A12:H12**.

You selected the range of cells containing the 28" Monitor data.

b. Cut the selected range.

A moving dashed border outlines the selected range. The status bar displays the message *Select destination and press ENTER or choose Paste.*

c. Click **cell A7**, the new blank row you inserted in step 3j.

This is the first cell in the destination range.

FYI

d. Paste the data that you cut, and then save the workbook.

The 28" Monitor data are now located on row 7.

> **TROUBLESHOOTING:** If you cut and paste a row without inserting a new row first, Excel will overwrite the original row of data, which is why you inserted a new row in step 3.

STEP 5 ▶ ADJUST COLUMN WIDTH AND ROW HEIGHT

As you review your worksheet, you notice that the labels in column A appear cut off. You need to increase the width of that column to display the entire product names. In addition, you want to make row 1 taller. Refer to Figure 1.33 as you complete Step 5.

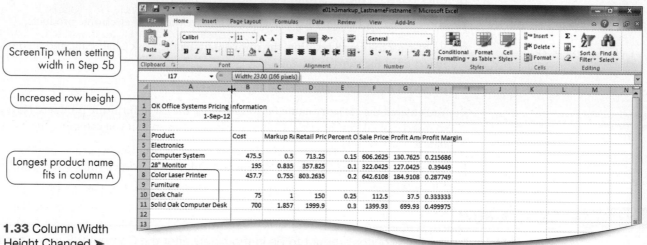

FIGURE 1.33 Column Width and Row Height Changed ➤

a. Position the pointer between the column A and B headings. When the pointer looks like a double-headed arrow, double-click the **border**.

When you double-click the border between two columns, Excel adjusts the width of the column on the left side of the border to fit the contents of that column. In this case, Excel increased the width of column A. However, it is based on the title in cell A1, which will eventually span over all columns. Therefore, you want to decrease the column to avoid so much empty space in column A.

b. Position the pointer between the column A and B headings again. Drag the border to the left until the ScreenTip displays **Width: 23.00 (166 pixels)**. Release the mouse button.

You decreased the column width to 23 for column A. The longest product name is visible. You won't adjust the other column widths until after you apply formats to the column headings in Hands-On Exercise 4.

c. Click **cell A1**. Click **Format** in the Cells group, and then select **Row Height** to display the Row Height dialog box.

d. Type **30** in the **Row height box**, and then click **OK**. Save the workbook.

You doubled the height of the first row.

To focus on the dollar amounts, you decide to hide the markup rate, discount rate, and profit margin columns. Refer to Figure 1.34 as you complete Step 6.

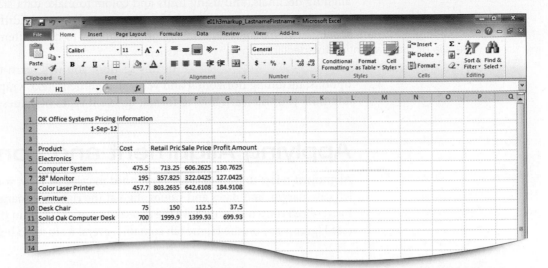

FIGURE 1.34 Hidden Columns ➤

a. Click the **column C heading**, the column containing the Markup Rate values.

b. Press and hold down **Ctrl** as you click the **column E heading** and the **column H heading**.

   Holding down Ctrl enables you to select nonadjacent ranges. You want to hide the rate columns temporarily.

c. Click **Format** in the Cells group, point to **Hide & Unhide**, and then select **Hide Columns**.

   Excel hides the selected columns. You see a gap in column heading letters, indicating columns are hidden (see Figure 1.34).

d. Drag to select the **column G and I headings**.

   You want to unhide column H, so you must select the columns on both sides of the hidden column.

e. Click **Format** in the Cells group, point to **Hide & Unhide**, and then select **Unhide Columns**.

   Column H, which contains the Profit Margin values, is no longer hidden. You will keep the other columns hidden to save the workbook as evidence that you know how to hide columns. You will unhide the remaining columns in the next Hands-On Exercise.

f. Save the workbook. Keep the workbook onscreen if you plan to continue with Hands-On Exercise 4. If not, close the workbook, and exit Excel.

Formatting

After entering data and formulas, you should format the worksheet to achieve a professional appearance. A professionally formatted worksheet—through adding appropriate symbols, aligning decimals, and using fonts and colors to make data stand out—makes finding and analyzing data easy. You apply different formats to accentuate meaningful details or to draw attention to specific ranges in the worksheet.

> Different formats accentuate meaningful details or draw attention to specific ranges.

In this section, you will learn to apply different alignment options, including horizontal and vertical alignment, text wrapping, and indent options. In addition, you will learn how to format different types of values.

Applying Alignment and Font Options

Alignment refers to how data are positioned in cells. By now, you know that text aligns at the left cell margin, and dates and values align at the right cell margin. You can change the alignment of cell contents to improve the appearance of data within the cells. The Alignment group (see Figure 1.35) on the Home tab contains several features to help you align and format data.

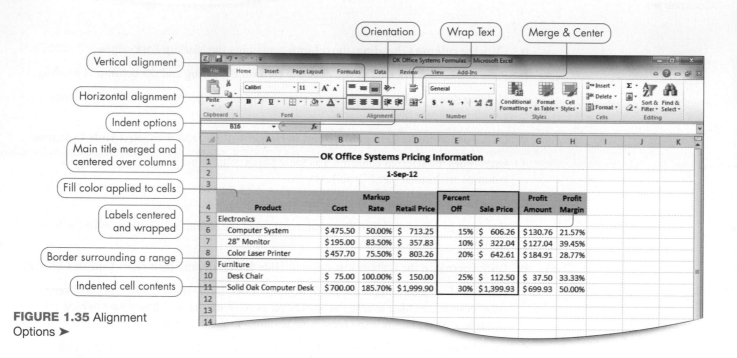

FIGURE 1.35 Alignment Options ➤

Change Horizontal and Vertical Cell Alignment

Horizontal alignment positions data between the left and right cell margins.

Vertical alignment positions data between the top and bottom cell margins.

You can align data horizontally or vertically. *Horizontal alignment* specifies the position of data between the left and right cell margins, and *vertical alignment* specifies the position of data between the top and bottom cell margins. Bottom Align is the default vertical alignment, as indicated by the orange background of Bottom Align on the Ribbon. After adjusting row height, you might need to change the vertical alignment to position data better in conjunction with data in adjacent cells. To change alignments, click the desired horizontal and/or vertical alignment setting in the Alignment group on the Home tab.

Merge and Center Labels

You may want to place a title at the top of a worksheet and center it over the columns of data in the worksheet. You can center main titles over all columns in the worksheet, and you can center category titles over groups of related columns. To create a title, enter the text in the far left cell of the range. Select the range of cells across which you want to center the title, and then click Merge & Center in the Alignment group on the Home tab. Any data in the merge area are lost, except what is in the far left cell in the range. Excel merges the selected cells together into one cell, and the merged cell address is that of the original cell on the left. The data are centered between the left and right sides of the merged cell. In Figure 1.35, the title *OK Office Systems Pricing Information* is merged and centered over the data columns.

If you merge too many cells and want to split the merged cell back into its original multiple cells, click the merged cell, and then click Merge & Center. Unmerging places the data in the top-left cell.

Increase and Decrease Indent

To offset labels, you can indent text within a cell. Accountants often indent the word Totals in financial statements so that it stands out from a list of items above the total row. Indenting helps others see the hierarchical structure of your spreadsheet data. To indent the contents of a cell, click Increase Indent in the Alignment group on the Home tab. The more you click Increase Indent, the more text is indented in the active cell. To decrease the indent, click Decrease Indent in the Alignment group. Figure 1.35 shows an example of an indented label.

Wrap Text

Wrap text enables a label to appear on multiple lines within the current cell.

Sometimes you have to maintain specific column widths, but the data do not fit entirely. You can use *wrap text* to make data appear on multiple lines by adjusting the row height to fit the cell contents within the column width. When you click Wrap Text in the Alignment group, Excel wraps the text on two or more lines within the cell. This alignment option is helpful when the column headings are wider than the values contained in the column. In the next Hands-On Exercise, you will apply the Wrap Text option for the column headings so that you can see the text without widening the columns. Figure 1.35 shows an example of wrapped text.

Apply Borders and Fill Color

A **border** is a line that surrounds a cell or a range.

You can apply a border or fill color to accentuate data in a worksheet. A **border** is a line that surrounds a cell or a range of cells. You can use borders to offset particular data from the rest of the data on the worksheet. To apply a border, select the cell or range that you want to have a border, click the Borders arrow in the Font group, and then select the desired border type. To remove a border, select No Border from the Borders menu.

Fill color is the background color appearing behind data in a cell.

To add some color to your worksheet to add emphasis to data or headers, you can apply a fill color. **Fill color** is a background color that displays behind the data. You should choose a fill color that contrasts with the font color. For example, if the font color is Black, you might want to choose Yellow fill color. If the font color is White, you might want to apply Blue or Dark Blue fill color. To apply a fill color, select the cell or range that you want to have a fill color, click the Fill Color arrow on the Home tab, and then select the color choice from the Fill Color palette. If you want to remove a fill color, select No Fill from the bottom of the palette.

For additional border and fill color options, display the Format Cells dialog box. Click the Border tab to select border options, including the border line style and color. Click the Fill tab to set the background color, fill effects, and patterns. Figure 1.35 shows examples of cells containing a border and fill color.

Applying Number Formats

Values appear in General format (i.e., no special formatting) when you enter data. You should apply number formats based on the type of values in a cell, such as applying either the Accounting or Currency number format to monetary values. Changing the number format changes the way the number displays in a cell, but the format does not change the number's value. If, for example, you entered 123.456 into a cell and format the cell with Currency number type, the value shows as $123.46 onscreen, but the actual value 123.456 is used for calculations. When you apply a number format, you can specify the number of decimal places to display onscreen.

Select an Appropriate Number Format

The default number format is General, which displays values as you originally enter them. General does not align decimal points in a column or include symbols, such as dollar signs, percent signs, or commas. Table 1.5 lists and describes the primary number formats in Excel.

TABLE 1.5 Number Formats

Format Style	Display
General	A number as it was originally entered. Numbers are shown as integers (e.g., 12345), decimal fractions (e.g., 1234.5), or in scientific notation (e.g., 1.23E+10) if the number exceeds 11 digits.
Number	A number with or without the 1000 separator (e.g., a comma) and with any number of decimal places. Negative numbers can be displayed with parentheses and/or red.
Currency	A number with the 1,000 separator and an optional dollar sign (which is placed immediately to the left of the number). Negative values are preceded by a minus sign or are displayed with parentheses or in red. Two decimal places display by default.
Accounting	A number with the 1,000 separator, an optional dollar sign (at the left border of the cell, vertically aligned within a column), negative values in parentheses, and zero values as hyphens. Two decimal places display by default.
Date	The date in different ways, such as March 14, 2012; 3/14/12; or 14-Mar-12.
Time	The time in different formats, such as 10:50 PM or 22:50 (24-hour time).

(Continued)

TABLE 1.5 (*Continued*)

Format Style	Display
Percentage	The value as it would be multiplied by 100 (for display purpose), with the percent sign. The default number of decimal places is zero if you click Percent Style in the Number group or two decimal places if you use the Format Cells dialog box. However, you should typically increase the number of decimal points to show greater accuracy.
Fraction	A number as a fraction; appropriate when no exact decimal equivalent exists. A fraction is entered into a cell as a formula such as =1/3. If the cell is not formatted as a fraction, you will see the results of the formula.
Scientific	A number as a decimal fraction followed by a whole number exponent of 10; for example, the number 12345 would appear as 1.23E+04. The exponent, +04 in the example, is the number of places the decimal point is moved to the left (or right if the exponent is negative). Very small numbers have negative exponents.
Text	The data left-aligned; is useful for numerical values that have leading zeros and should be treated as text, such as ZIP codes or phone numbers. Apply Text format before typing a leading zero so that the zero displays in the cell.
Special	A number with editing characters, such as hyphens in a Social Security number.
Custom	Predefined customized number formats or special symbols to create your own customized number format.

The Number group on the Home tab contains commands for applying Accounting Number Format, Percent Style, and Comma Style numbering formats. You can click the Accounting Number Format arrow and select other denominations, such as English pounds or euros. For other number formats, click the Number Format arrow and select the numbering format you want to use. For more specific numbering formats than those provided, select More Number Formats from the Number Format menu or click the Number Dialog Box Launcher to open the Format Cells dialog box with the Number tab options readily available. Figure 1.36 shows different number formats applied to values. The first six values are displayed with two decimal places.

◢	A	B	C
1	General	1234.56	
2	Number	1234.56	
3	Currency	$1,234.56	
4	Accounting	$ 1,234.56	
5	Comma	1,234.56	
6	Percent	12.34%	
7	Short Date	3/1/2012	
8	Long Date	Thursday, March 01, 2012	

FIGURE 1.36 Number Formats ➤

Increase and Decrease Decimal Places

After applying a number format, you may need to adjust the number of decimal places that display. For example, if you have an entire column of monetary values formatted in Accounting Number Format, Excel displays two decimal places by default. If the entire column of values contains whole dollar values and no cents, displaying .00 down the column looks cluttered. You can decrease the number of decimal places to show whole numbers only.

To change the number of decimal places displayed, click Increase Decimal in the Number group on the Home tab to display more decimal places for greater precision or Decrease Decimal to display fewer or no decimal places.

4 Formatting

In the first three Hands-On Exercises, you entered data about products on sale, created formulas to calculate markup and profit, and inserted new rows and columns to accommodate additional data. You are ready to format the worksheet. Specifically, you need to center the title, align text, format values, and apply other formatting to enhance the readability of the worksheet.

Skills covered: Merge and Center the Title • Wrap and Align Text • Apply Number Formats and Decimal Places • Apply Borders and Fill Color • Indent Cell Contents

STEP 1 MERGE AND CENTER THE TITLE

To make the title stand out, you want to center it over all the data columns. You will use the Merge & Center command to merge cells together and center the title at the same time. Refer to Figure 1.37 as you complete Step 1.

	A	B	C	D	E	F	G	H	I
1	OK Office Systems Pricing Information								
2	1-Sep-12								
3									
4	Product	Cost	Markup Ra	Retail Pric	Percent O	Sale Price	Profit Am	Profit Margin	
5	Electronics								
6	Computer System	475.5	0.5	713.25	0.15	606.2625	130.7625	0.215686	
7	28" Monitor	195	0.835	357.825	0.1	322.0425	127.0425	0.39449	
8	Color Laser Printer	457.7	0.755	803.2635	0.2	642.6108	184.9108	0.287749	
9	Furniture								
10	Desk Chair	75	1	150	0.25	112.5	37.5	0.333333	
11	Solid Oak Computer Desk	700	1.857	1999.9	0.3	1399.93	699.93	0.499975	
12									
13									

FIGURE 1.37 Formatted Title ➤

a. Open the *e01h3markup_LastnameFirstname* workbook if you closed it after the last Hands-On Exercise, and save it as **e01h4markup_LastnameFirstname**, changing *h3* to *h4*.

b. Select the **column B, D, and F headings**. Unhide columns C and E as you learned in Hands-On Exercise 3.

c. Select the **range A1:H1**.

   You want to center the title over all columns of data.

d. Click **Merge & Center** in the Alignment group.

   Excel merges cells in the range A1:H1 into one cell and centers the title horizontally within the merged cell, which is cell A1.

> **TROUBLESHOOTING:** If you merge too many or not enough cells, you can unmerge the cells and start again. To unmerge cells, click in the merged cell. The Merge & Center command has an orange border when the active cell is merged. Click Merge & Center to unmerge the cell. Then select the correct range to merge and use Merge & Center again.

 FYI

e. Bold the title, and then select **14 pt** size.

f. Select the **range A2:H2**. Merge and center the date, and then bold it.

g. Save the workbook.

WRAP AND ALIGN TEXT

You will wrap the text in the column headings to avoid columns that are too wide for the data, but which will display the entire text of the column headings. In addition, you will horizontally center column headings between the left and right cell margins. Refer to Figure 1.38 as you complete Step 2.

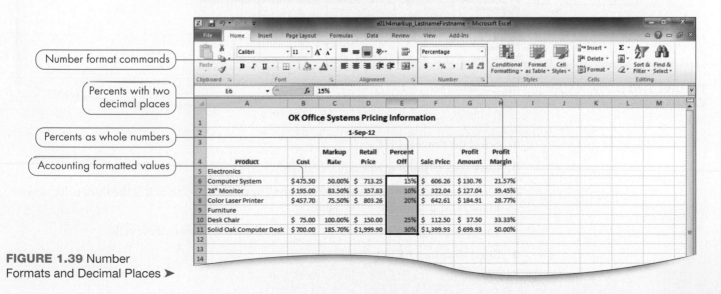

Middle Align applied

Text wrapped, centered, and bold

	A	B	C	D	E	F	G	H	I
1	OK Office Systems Pricing Information								
2	1-Sep-12								
3									
4	Product	Cost	Markup Rate	Retail Price	Percent Off	Sale Price	Profit Amount	Profit Margin	
5	Electronics								
6	Computer System	475.5	0.5	713.25	0.15	606.2625	130.7625	0.215686	
7	28" Monitor	195	0.835	357.825	0.1	322.0425	127.0425	0.39449	
8	Color Laser Printer	457.7	0.755	803.2635	0.2	642.6108	184.9108	0.287749	
9	Furniture								
10	Desk Chair	75	1	150	0.25	112.5	37.5	0.333333	
11	Solid Oak Computer Desk	700	1.857	1999.9	0.3	1399.93	699.93	0.499975	
12									

FIGURE 1.38 Formatted Column Headings ➤

a. Select the **range A4:H4**.

You selected the multiple-word column headings.

b. Click **Wrap Text** in the Alignment group.

The column headings are now visible on two lines within each cell.

c. Click **Center** in the Alignment group. Bold the selected column headings.

The column headings are centered horizontally between the left and right edges of each cell.

d. Click **cell A1**, which contains the title.

e. Click **Middle Align** in the Alignment group. Save the workbook.

Middle Align vertically centers data between the top and bottom edges of the cell.

APPLY NUMBER FORMATS AND DECIMAL PLACES

You need to format the values to increase readability and look more professional. You will apply number formats and adjust the number of decimal points displayed. Refer to Figure 1.39 as you complete Step 3.

Number format commands

Percents with two decimal places

Percents as whole numbers

Accounting formatted values

FIGURE 1.39 Number Formats and Decimal Places ➤

a. Select the **range B6:B11**, and then click **Accounting Number Format** in the Number group.

You formatted the selected range with Accounting Number Format. The dollar signs align on the left cell margins and the decimals align.

b. Select the **range D6:D11**. Press and hold down **Ctrl** as you select the **range F6:G11**.

Since you want to format nonadjacent ranges with the same formats, you hold down Ctrl.

c. Click **Accounting Number Format** in the Number group.

You formatted the selected nonadjacent ranges with the Accounting Number Format.

d. Select the **range C6:C11**, and then click **Percent Style** in the Number group.

You formatted the values in the selected ranges with Percent Style, showing whole numbers only.

e. Click **Increase Decimal** in the Number group twice.

You increased the decimal places to avoid misleading your readers by displaying the values as whole percentages.

FYI

f. Use Format Painter to copy the formats of the selected range to values in columns E and H.

g. Select the **range E6:E11**, and then click **Decrease Decimal** twice in the Number group. Save the workbook.

Since this range contained whole percentages, you do not need to show the decimal places.

STEP 4 ▶ **APPLY BORDERS AND FILL COLOR**

You want to apply a light purple fill color to highlight the column headings. In addition, you want to emphasize the percent off and sale prices. You will do this by applying a border around that range. Refer to Figure 1.40 as you complete Step 4.

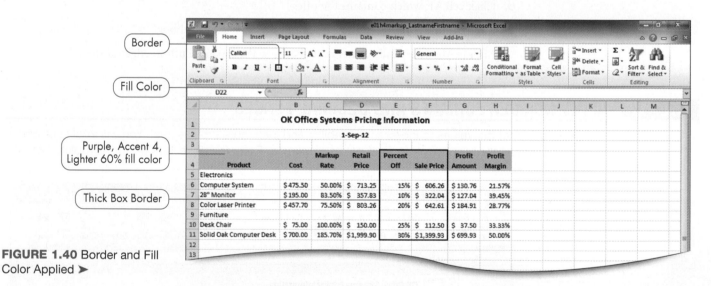

FIGURE 1.40 Border and Fill Color Applied ▶

a. Select the **range A4:H4**.

b. Click the **Fill Color arrow** in the Font group.

c. Click **Purple, Accent 4, Lighter 60%** in the *Theme Colors* section. It is the third color down in the third column from the right.

You applied a fill color to the selected cells to draw attention to these cells.

d. Select the **range E4:F11**.

e. Click the **Border arrow** in the Font group, and then select **Thick Box Border**.

You applied a border around the selected cells.

f. Click in an empty cell below the columns of data to deselect the cells. Save the workbook.

INDENT CELL CONTENTS

As you review the first column, you notice that the category names, Electronics and Furniture, don't stand out. You decide to indent the labels within each category to show which products are in each category. Refer to Figure 1.41 as you complete Step 5.

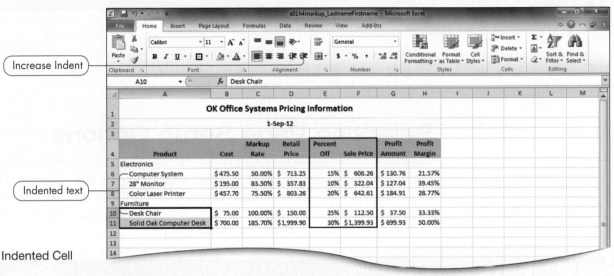

FIGURE 1.41 Indented Cell Contents ➤

a. Select the **range A6:A8**, the cells containing electronic products.

b. Click **Increase Indent** in the Alignment group twice.

The three selected product names are indented below the Electronics heading.

c. Select the **range A10:A11**, the cells containing furniture products, and then click **Increase Indent** twice.

The two selected product names are indented below the Furniture heading. Notice that the product names appear cut off.

d. Increase the **column A** width to **26.00**.

e. Save the workbook. Keep the workbook onscreen if you plan to continue with Hands-On Exercise 5. If not, close the workbook, and exit Excel.

Page Setup and Printing

Although you might distribute workbooks electronically as e-mail attachments or you might upload workbooks to a corporation server, you should prepare the worksheets in the workbook for printing. You should prepare worksheets in case you need to print them or in case others who receive an electronic copy of your workbook need to print the worksheets. The Page Layout tab provides options for controlling the printed worksheet (see Figure 1.42).

Page Setup Dialog Box Launcher

FIGURE 1.42 Page Layout Tab ➤

In this section, you will select options on the Page Layout tab. Specifically, you will use the Page Setup, Scale to Fit, and Sheet Options groups. After selecting page setup options, you are ready to print your worksheet.

Selecting Page Setup Options

The Page Setup group on the Page Layout tab contains options to set the margins, select orientation, specify page size, select the print area, and apply other options. The Scale to Fit group contains options for adjusting the scaling of the spreadsheet on the printed page. When possible, use the commands in these groups to apply page settings. Table 1.6 lists and describes the commands in the Page Setup group.

TABLE 1.6 Page Setup Commands

Command	Description
Margins	Displays a menu to select predefined margin settings. The default margins are 0.75" top and bottom and 0.7" left and right. You will often change these margin settings to balance the worksheet data better on the printed page. If you need different margins, select Custom Margins.
Orientation	Displays orientation options. The default page orientation is portrait, which is appropriate for worksheets that contain more rows than columns. Select landscape orientation when worksheets contain more columns than can fit in portrait orientation. For example, the OKOS worksheet might appear better balanced in landscape orientation because it has eight columns.
Size	Displays a list of standard paper sizes. The default size is 8.5" by 11". If you have a different paper size, such as legal paper, select it from the list.
Print Area	Displays a list to set or clear the print area. When you have very large worksheets, you might want to print only a portion of that worksheet. To do so, select the range you want to print, click Print Area in the Page Setup group, and select Set Print Area. When you use the Print commands, only the range you specified will be printed. To clear the print area, click Print Area, and select Clear Print Area.
Breaks	Displays a list to insert or remove page breaks.
Background	Enables you to select an image to appear as the background behind the worksheet data when viewed onscreen (backgrounds do not appear when the worksheet is printed).
Print Titles	Enables you to select column headings and row labels to repeat on multiple-page printouts.

Specify Page Options

To apply several page setup options at once or to access options not found on the Ribbon, click the Page Setup Dialog Box Launcher. The Page Setup dialog box organizes options into four tabs: Page, Margins, Header/Footer, and Sheet. All tabs contain Print and Print Preview buttons. Figure 1.43 shows the Page tab.

FIGURE 1.43 Page Setup Dialog Box Page Tab ➤

The Page tab contains options to select the orientation and paper size. In addition, it contains scaling options that are similar to the options in the Scale to Fit group on the Page Layout tab. You use scaling options to increase or decrease the size of characters on a printed page, similar to using a zoom setting on a photocopy machine. You can also use the Fit to option to force the data to print on a specified number of pages.

Specify Margins Options

The Margins tab (see Figure 1.44) contains options for setting the specific margins. In addition, it contains options to center the worksheet data horizontally or vertically on the page. To balance worksheet data equally between the left and right margins, Excel users often center the page horizontally.

FIGURE 1.44 Page Setup Dialog Box Margins Tab ➤

Create Headers and Footers

The Header/Footer tab (see Figure 1.45) lets you create a header and/or footer that appear at the top and/or bottom of every printed page. Click the arrows to choose from several preformatted entries, or alternatively, you can click Custom Header or Custom Footer, insert text and other objects, and then click the appropriate formatting button to customize your headers and footers. You can use headers and footers to provide additional information about the worksheet. You can include your name, the date the worksheet was prepared, and page numbers, for example.

Click to see list of preformatted headers

FIGURE 1.45 Page Setup Dialog Box Header/Footer Tab ➤

Instead of creating headers and footers using the Page Setup dialog box, you can click the Insert tab and click Header & Footer in the Text group. Excel displays the worksheet in Page Layout view with the insertion point in the center area of the header. If you click the View tab and then click Page Layout, you see an area that displays *Click to add header* at the top of the worksheet. You can click inside the left, center, or right section of a header or footer. When you do, Excel displays the Header & Footer Tools Design contextual tab (see Figure 1.46). You can enter text or insert data from the Header & Footer Elements group on the tab. To get back to Normal view, click any cell in the worksheet, and then click Normal in the Workbook Views group on the View tab.

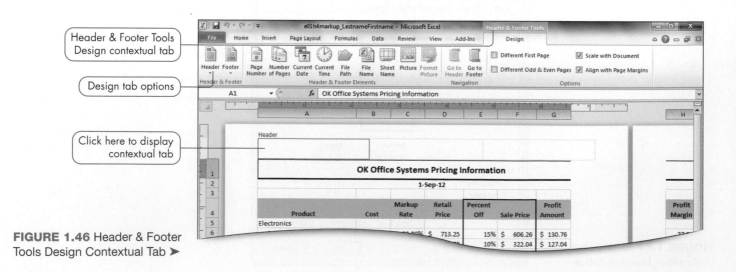

Header & Footer Tools Design contextual tab

Design tab options

Click here to display contextual tab

FIGURE 1.46 Header & Footer Tools Design Contextual Tab ➤

Select Sheet Options

The Sheet tab (see Figure 1.47) contains options for setting the print area, print titles, print options, and page order. Some of these options are also located in the Sheet Options group on the Page Layout tab on the Ribbon. By default, Excel displays gridlines onscreen to show you each cell's margins, but the gridlines do not print unless you specifically select the Gridlines check box in the Page Setup dialog box or the Print Gridlines check box in the Sheet Options group on the Page Layout tab. In addition, Excel displays row (1, 2, 3, etc.) and column (A, B, C, etc.) headings onscreen. However, these headings do not print unless you click the Row and column headings check box in the Page Setup dialog box or click the Print Headings check box in the Sheet Options group on the Page Layout tab.

FIGURE 1.47 Page Setup Dialog Box Sheet Tab ➤

> **TIP** Printing Gridlines and Headings
>
> For most worksheets, you do not need to print gridlines and row/column headings. However, when you want to display and print cell formulas instead of formula results, you might want to print the gridlines and row/column headings. Doing so will help you analyze your formulas. The gridlines help you see the cell boundaries, and the headings help you know what data are in each cell. At times, you might want to display gridlines to separate data on a regular printout to increase readability.

Printing a Worksheet

Before printing a worksheet, you should click the File tab and then select Print. The Backstage view displays print options and displays the worksheet in print preview mode. This mode helps you see in advance if the data are balanced on the page or if data will print on multiple pages. The bottom of the Backstage view indicates how many total pages will print. If the settings are correct, you can specify the print options. If you do not like how the worksheet will print, click the Page Layout tab so that you can adjust margins, scaling, column widths, and so on until the worksheet data appear the way you want them to print.

> The Backstage view helps you see in advance if the data are balanced on the page.

5 Page Setup and Printing

You are ready to complete the OKOS worksheet. Before printing the worksheet for your supervisor, you want to make sure the data will appear professional when printed. You will adjust some page setup options to put the finishing touches on the worksheet.

Skills covered: Set Page Orientation • Set Margin Options • Create a Header • Print Preview and Print • Adjust Scaling and Set Sheet Options

STEP 1 ▶ SET PAGE ORIENTATION

Because the worksheet has several columns, you decide to print it in landscape orientation.

a. Open the *e01h4markup_LastnameFirstname* workbook if you closed it after the last Hands-On Exercise, and save it as **e01h5markup_LastnameFirstname**, changing *h4* to *h5*.

b. Click the **Page Layout tab**.

c. Click **Orientation** in the Page Setup group.

d. Select **Landscape** from the list. Save the workbook.

If you print the worksheet, the data will print in landscape orientation.

STEP 2 ▶ SET MARGIN OPTIONS

You want to set a 1" top margin and center the data between the left and right margins.

a. Click **Margins** in the Page Setup group on the Page Layout tab.

As you review the list of options, you notice the list does not contain an option to center the worksheet data horizontally.

b. Select **Custom Margins**.

The Page Setup dialog box opens with the Margins tab options displayed.

c. Click the **Top spin box** to display *1*.

You set a 1" top margin. You don't need to change the left and right margins since you will center the worksheet data horizontally between the original margins.

d. Click the **Horizontally check box** in the *Center on page* section, and then click **OK**. Save the workbook.

The worksheet data will be centered between the left and right margins.

STEP 3 ▶ CREATE A HEADER

To document the worksheet, you want to include your name, the current date, and the worksheet tab name in a header. Refer to Figure 1.48 as you complete Step 3.

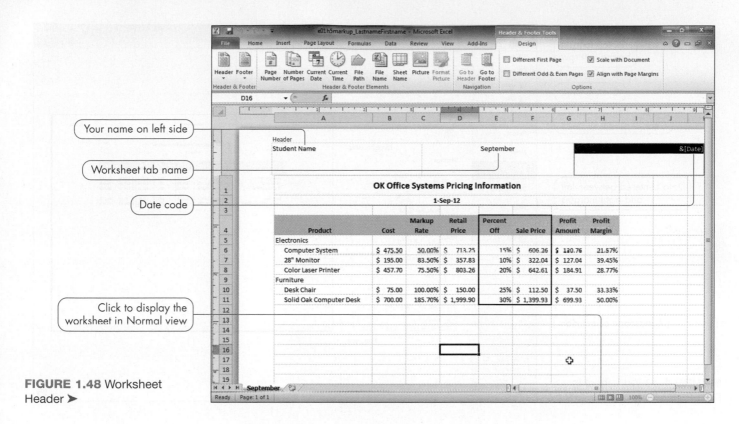

Your name on left side

Worksheet tab name

Date code

Click to display the
worksheet in Normal view

FIGURE 1.48 Worksheet
Header ➤

a. Click the **Insert tab**, and then click **Header & Footer** in the Text group.

Excel displays the Header & Footer Tools Design tab, and the worksheet displays in Page
Layout view. The insertion point blinks inside the center section of the Header.

b. Click in the left section of the header, and then type your name.

c. Click in the center section of the header, and then click **Sheet Name** in the Header & Footer
Elements group on the Design tab.

Excel inserts the code &[Tab]. This code displays the name of the worksheet. If you change
the worksheet tab name, the header will reflect the new sheet name.

d. Click in the right section of the header, and then click **Current Date** in the Header & Footer
Elements group on the Design tab.

Excel inserts the code &[Date]. This code displays the current date based on the computer
clock when you print the worksheet. If you want a specific date to appear regardless of the
date you open or print the worksheet, you would have to type that date manually. When you
click in a different header section, the codes, such as &[Tab], display the actual tab name
instead of the code.

e. Click in any cell in the worksheet, click **Normal** on the status bar, and then save the workbook.

STEP 4 ▶ PRINT PREVIEW AND PRINT

Before printing the worksheet, you should print preview it. Doing so helps you detect margin problems
and other issues, such as a single row or column of data flowing onto a new page. Refer to Figure 1.49
as you complete Step 4.

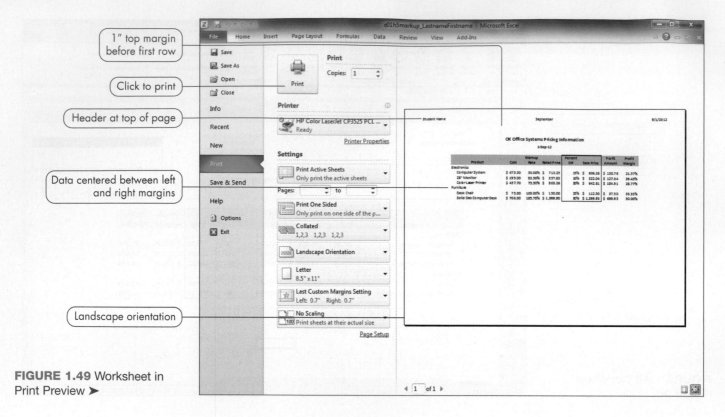

Click to print

Header at top of page

Data centered between left and right margins

Landscape orientation

FIGURE 1.49 Worksheet in Print Preview ➤

a. Click the **File tab**, and then click **Print**.

The Backstage view displays print options and a preview of the worksheet.

b. Verify the Printer name displays the printer that you want to use to print your worksheet.

c. Click **Print** to print the worksheet, and then save the workbook.

Check your printed worksheet to make sure the data are formatted correctly. After you click Print, the Home tab is displayed. If you decide not to print at this time, you need to click the Home tab yourself.

STEP 5 ▶ ADJUST SCALING AND SET SHEET OPTIONS

You want to print a copy of the worksheet formulas to check the logic of the formulas. You need to display the formulas, select options to print gridlines and headings, and then decrease the scaling so that the data print on one page. Refer to Figure 1.50 as you complete Step 5.

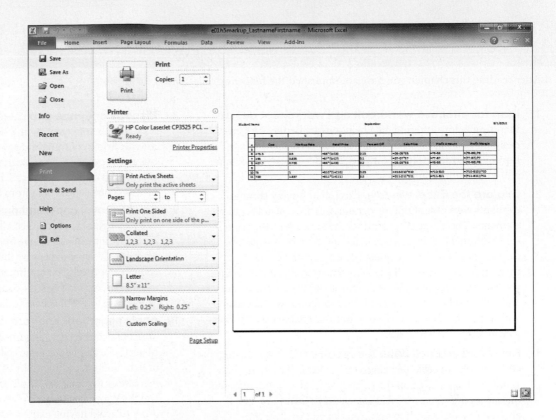

FIGURE 1.50 Worksheet in Print Preview ➤

a. Press **Ctrl+`** to display cell formulas.

b. Click the **Page Layout tab**. Click the **Print Gridlines check box**, and then click the **Print Headings check box** in the Sheet Options group.

   Since you want to print cell formulas, it is helpful to display the gridlines and row and column headings on that printout.

c. Click the **File tab**, and then click **Print**.

   The bottom of the Backstage view displays 1 of 2, indicating the worksheet no longer prints on one page.

d. Click **Next Page** (the right triangle at the bottom of the Backstage view), and then click the **Page Layout tab**.

e. Click **Margins** in the Page Setup group, and then select **Narrow**.

f. Select the **range B4:H11**, click **Print Area** in the Page Setup group, and then select **Set Print Area**.

g. Click the **Scale spin box** in the Scale to Fit group on the Page Layout tab until it displays **90%**.

   The dotted line indicating the page break now appears on the right side of the last column, indicating that the worksheet data will print on one page. If you want to verify that the worksheet will print on one page, display it in print preview.

h. Print the worksheet. Save and close the *e01h5markup_LastnameFirstname* workbook and submit the worksheet based on your instructor's directions.

   Check your printed worksheet to make sure the data are formatted correctly.

CHAPTER OBJECTIVES REVIEW

After reading this chapter, you have accomplished the following objectives:

1. **Plan for effective workbook and worksheet design.** Planning before entering data helps ensure better worksheet design. Planning involves stating the purpose, identifying input values, determining outputs, and deciding what data to add into columns and rows.

2. **Explore the Excel window.** Excel shares many common elements with other Office programs, but also includes unique elements. The Name Box identifies the location of the active cell, indicated first by column letter and then by row number, for example, A10. The Formula Bar displays the contents of the current cell. Select All enables users to select all items in the worksheet. Column and row headings identify column letters and row numbers. Sheet tabs provide different worksheets within the workbook. Navigation buttons enable users to navigate among worksheet tabs.

3. **Enter and edit cell data.** You can enter text, values, dates, and formulas in cells. Text aligns on the left cell margin, and values and dates align on the right cell margin. Values represent quantities that can be used in calculations. Dates may be entered in a variety of formats. You can edit or clear the contents of cells.

4. **Use symbols and order of precedence.** The basic arithmetic symbols are +, −, *, /, and ^ in Excel. The order of operations is the sequence in which mathematical operations is performed: parentheses, exponents, multiplication, division, addition, and subtraction. Formulas start with an equal sign, should include cell references containing values, and should not contain raw values except constants.

5. **Use Auto Fill.** To copy a formula down a column or across a row, double-click or drag the fill handle. You can use Auto Fill to copy formulas, number patterns, names of months, weekdays, etc.

6. **Display cell formulas.** By default, the results of formulas appear in cells instead of the actual formulas. You can display formulas within the cells to help troubleshoot formulas by pressing Ctrl+`.

7. **Manage worksheets.** The default worksheet tab names are Sheet1, Sheet2, and Sheet3. You can rename the worksheet tabs to be more meaningful, delete extra worksheets, insert new worksheets, and apply colors to worksheet tabs. In addition, you can move worksheets or copy worksheets.

8. **Manage columns and rows.** Although you should plan a worksheet before creating it, you can insert new columns and rows or delete columns and rows that you no longer need. You can also increase or decrease the height or width of rows and columns to display data better. Hiding rows and columns protects confidential data from being displayed or printed.

9. **Select, move, copy, and paste.** A range may be a single cell or a rectangular block of cells. After selecting a range, you can cut it to move it to another range or copy it to another location in the worksheet. You should ensure the designation range contains enough empty cells to accommodate the data you cut or copied to avoid overwriting existing data. The Paste Special option enables you to specify how the data are pasted into the worksheet.

10. **Apply alignment and font options.** You can apply horizontal and vertical alignment to format data in cells or use Merge & Center to combine cells and center titles over columns of data. To indicate hierarchy of data or to offset a label you can increase or decrease how much the data are indented in a cell. Use the Wrap Text option to present text on multiple lines in order to avoid having extra-wide columns. You can further improve readability of worksheets by adding appropriate borders around important ranges or applying fill colors to cells.

11. **Apply number formats.** The default number format is General, which does not apply any particular format to values. Apply appropriate formats to values to present the data with the correct symbols and decimal alignment. For example, Accounting is a common number format for monetary values. Other popular number formats include Percentage and Date. After applying a number format, you can increase or decrease the number of decimal points displayed.

12. **Select page setup options.** The Page Layout tab on the Ribbon contains options for setting margins, selecting orientation, specifying page size, selecting the print area, and applying other settings. In addition, you can display the Page Setup dialog box to specify these and other settings to control how data will print. You can insert a header or footer to display documentation, such as your name, date, time, and worksheet tab name.

13. **Print a worksheet.** Before printing a worksheet, you should display a preview in the Backstage view to ensure the data will print correctly. The Backstage view helps you see if margins are correct or if isolated rows or columns will print on separate pages. After making appropriate adjustments, you can print the worksheet.

KEY TERMS

Active cell *p.315*
Auto Fill *p.323*
Border *p.348*
Cell *p.315*
Cell address *p.315*
Column width *p.334*
Fill color *p.348*
Fill handle *p.323*
Formula *p.317*

Formula Bar *p.314*
Horizontal alignment *p.346*
Input area *p.313*
Name Box *p.314*
Nonadjacent range *p.337*
Order of precedence *p.322*
Output area *p.313*
Range *p.337*
Row height *p.335*

Sheet tab *p.315*
Spreadsheet *p.312*
Spreadsheet program *p.312*
Text *p.316*
Value *p.317*
Vertical alignment *p.346*
Workbook *p.312*
Worksheet *p.312*
Wrap text *p.347*

MULTIPLE CHOICE

1. What is the first step in planning an effective worksheet?
   (a) Enter labels, values, and formulas.
   (b) State the purpose of the worksheet.
   (c) Identify the input and output areas.
   (d) Decide how to format the worksheet data.

2. What Excel interface item is not displayed until you start typing or editing data in a cell?
   (a) Insert Function
   (b) Name Box
   (c) Formula Bar
   (d) Enter

3. Given the formula =B1*B2+B3/B4^2 where B1 contains 3, B2 contains 4, B3 contains 32, and B4 contains 4, what is the result?
   (a) 14
   (b) 121
   (c) 76
   (d) 9216

4. Why would you press Ctrl+` in Excel?
   (a) To display the print options
   (b) To undo a mistake you made
   (c) To display cell formulas
   (d) To enable the AutoComplete feature

5. Which of the following is a nonadjacent range?
   (a) C15:D30
   (b) L15:L65
   (c) A1:Z99
   (d) A1:A10, D1:D10

6. If you want to balance a title over several columns, what do you do?
   (a) Enter the data in the cell that is about midway across the spreadsheet.
   (b) Merge and center the data over all columns.
   (c) Use the Increase Indent command until the title looks balanced.
   (d) Click Center to center the title horizontally over several columns.

7. Which of the following characteristics is not applicable to the Accounting Number Format?
   (a) Dollar sign immediately on the left side of the value
   (b) Commas to separate thousands
   (c) Two decimal places
   (d) Zero values displayed as hyphens

8. If you want to see a preview of how a worksheet will appear on a hard copy, what do you do?
   (a) Change the Zoom to 100%.
   (b) Click the Page Layout tab, and then click the Print check box in the Sheet Options group.
   (c) Click the File tab, and then click Print.
   (d) Click the Page Setup Dialog Box Launcher.

9. Assume that the data on a worksheet consume a whole printed page and a couple of columns on a second page. You can do all of the following except what to force the data to print all on one page?
   (a) Decrease the Scale value.
   (b) Increase the left and right margins.
   (c) Decrease column widths if possible.
   (d) Select a smaller range as the print area.

10. What should you do if you see a column of pound signs (###) instead of values or results of formulas?
    (a) Increase the zoom percentage.
    (b) Delete the column.
    (c) Adjust the row height.
    (d) Increase the column width.

1 Mathematics Review

After a nice summer break, you want to brush up on your math skills. Since you are learning Excel, you decide to test your logic by creating formulas in Excel. Your first step is to plan the spreadsheet design. After having read Chapter 1, you realize that you should avoid values in formulas most of the time. Therefore, you will create an input area that contains values you will use in your formulas. To test your knowledge of formulas, you need to create an output area that will contain a variety of formulas using cell references from the input area. You need to include a formatted title, the date prepared, and your name. After creating and verifying formula results, you plan to change the input values and observe changes in the formula results. After verifying the results, you will copy the data to Sheet2, display cell formulas, and apply page layout options. This exercise follows the same set of skills as used in Hands-On Exercises 1, 2, 3, and 5 in the chapter. Refer to Figure 1.51 as you complete this exercise.

	A	B	C	D	E
1				Excel Formulas and Order of Precedence	
2	Date Created:	9/1/2012		Student Name	
3					
4	Input Area:			Output Area:	
5	First Value	1		Sum of 1st and 2nd values	3
6	Second Value	2		Difference between 4th and 1st values	3
7	Third Value	3		Product of 2nd and 3rd values	6
8	Fourth Value	4		Quotient of 3rd and 1st values	3
9				2nd value to the power of 3rd value	8
10				1st value added to product of 2nd and 4th values and difference between sum and 3rd value	6
11				Product of sum of 1st and 2nd and difference between 4th and 3rd values	3
12				Product of 1st and 2nd added to product of 3rd and 4th values	14
13					

FIGURE 1.51 Formula Practice ➤

a. Start Excel. If Excel is already open, click the **File tab**, select **New**, and then click **Create** to display a blank workbook. Save the workbook as **e01p1math_LastnameFirstname**.

b. Type **Excel Formulas and Order of Precedence** in **cell A1**, and then press **Enter**.

c. Type the labels in **cells A2** through **A8** as shown in Figure 1.51, type the current date in **cell B2** in the format shown, and then type the values shown in **cells B5:B8**. Column A labels will appear cut off after you enter values in column B, and the column B values will be right-aligned at this point.

d. Type your name in **cell D2**, and then type the labels in **cells D4:D12** as shown in Figure 1.51. Column D labels will overlap into columns E through L at this point.

e. Adjust the column widths by doing the following:
   - Click in any cell in column A, and then click **Format** in the Cells group.
   - Select **Column Width**, type **12.5** in the **Column width box**, and then click **OK**.
   - Use the instructions in the first two bullets above to set a **35.5** width for **column D**.
   - Use the instructions in the first two bullets above to set a **11.43** width for **column B**.

f. Format the title:
   - Select the **range A1:E1**.
   - Click **Merge & Center** in the Alignment group.
   - Bold the title and apply **14 pt** size.

g. Apply the following font and alignment formats:
- Bold **cells A4** and **D4**.
- Select the **range B5:B8**, and then click **Center** in the Alignment group.
- Select the **range D10:D12**, and then click **Wrap Text** in the Alignment group.

h. Enter the following formulas in **column E**:
- Click **cell E5**. Type **=B5+B6** and press **Enter**. Excel adds the value stored in cell B5 (1) to the value stored in cell B6 (2). The result (3) appears in cell E5, as described in cell D5. You can check your results with the results shown in Figure 1.51.
- Enter appropriate formulas in **cells E6:E8**, pressing **Enter** after entering each formula. Subtract to calculate a difference, multiply to calculate a product, and divide to calculate a quotient.
- Type **=B6^B7** in **cell E9**, and then press **Enter**. Estimate the answer: 2*2*2 = 8.
- Enter **=B5+B6*B8-B7** in **cell E10**, and then press **Enter**. Estimate the answer: 2*4=8; 1+8 = 9; 9-3 = 6. Multiplication occurs first, followed by addition, and finally subtraction.
- Enter **=(B5+B6)*(B8-B7)** in **cell E11**, and then press **Enter**. Estimate the answer: 1+2 = 3; 4-3 = 1; 3*1 = 3. Notice that this formula is almost identical to the previous formula; however, the parentheses affect the order of operations. Calculations in parentheses occur before the multiplication.
- Enter **=B5*B6+B7*B8** in **cell E12**, and then press **Enter**. Estimate the answer: 1*2 = 2; 3*4 = 12; 2+12 = 14.

i. Edit a formula and the input values:
- Click **cell E12**, and then click in the **Formula Bar** to edit the formula. Add parentheses as shown: **=(B5*B6)+(B7*B8)**, and then click **Enter** to the left side of the Formula Bar. The answer is still 14. The parentheses do not affect order of precedence since multiplication occurred before the addition. The parentheses help improve the readability of the formula.
- Click **cell B5**, type **2**, and then press **Enter**. Type **4**, press **Enter**, type **6**, press **Enter**, type **8**, and then press **Enter**.
- Double-check the results of the formulas using a calculator or your head. The new results in cells E5:E12 should be 6, 6, 24, 3, 4096, 28, 12, and 56, respectively.

j. Double-click the **Sheet1 tab**, type **Results**, and then press **Enter**. Right-click the **Results tab**, select **Move or Copy**, click (**move to end**) in the *Before sheet* section, click the **Create a copy check box**, and then click **OK**. Double-click the **Results (2) tab**, type **Formulas**, and then press **Enter**. Right-click the **Sheet2 tab**, and then select **Delete**. Delete the Sheet3 tab.

k. Make sure the Formulas worksheet tab is active, click the **Page Layout tab**, and then do the following:
- Click **Orientation** in the Page Setup group, and then select **Landscape**.
- Click the **Print Gridlines check box**, and then click the **Print Headings check box** in the Sheet Options group.

l. Click the **Formulas tab**, and then click **Show Formulas** in the Formula Auditing group. Double-click between the column A and column B headings to adjust the column A width. Double-click between the column B and column C headings to adjust the column B width. Set **24.0** width for **column D**.

m. Click the **File tab**, and then click **Print**. Verify that the worksheet will print on one page. Click the **File tab** again to close the Backstage view.

n. Save and close the workbook, and submit the worksheet based on your instructor's directions.

2 Calendar Formatting

You want to create a calendar for October. The calendar will enable you to practice alignment settings, including center, merge and center, and indents. In addition, you will need to adjust column widths and increase row height to create cells large enough to enter important information, such as birthdays, in your calendar. You will use Auto Fill to complete the days of the week and the days within each week. To improve the appearance of the calendar, you will add fill colors, font colors, borders, and clip art. This exercise follows the same set of skills as used in Hands-On Exercises 1–5 in the chapter. Refer to Figure 1.52 as you complete this exercise.

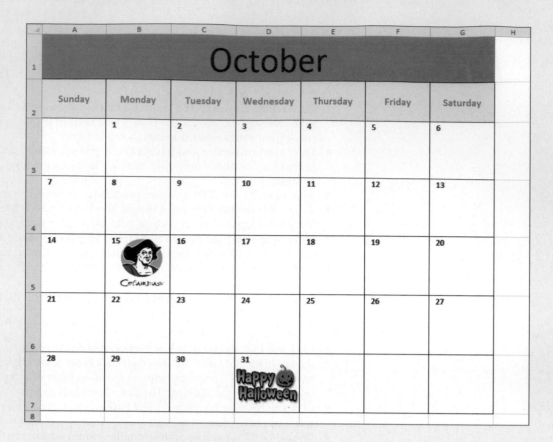

FIGURE 1.52 October Calendar Page ➤

a. Click the **File tab**, select **New**, and then click **Create** to display a blank workbook. Save the workbook as **e01p2october_LastnameFirstname**.

b. Type **October** in cell A1, and then click **Enter** on the left side of the Formula Bar.

c. Format the title:
   - Select the **range A1:G1**, and then click **Merge & Center** in the Alignment group.
   - Apply **48 pt** size.
   - Click the **Fill Color arrow**, and then click **Orange, Accent 6** on the top row of the *Theme Colors* section of the color palette.

d. Complete the days of the week:
   - Type **Sunday** in **cell A2**, and then click **Enter** on the left side of the Formula Bar.
   - Drag the fill handle in **cell A2** across the row through **cell G2** to use Auto Fill to complete the rest of the weekdays.
   - Click the **Fill Color arrow**, and then select **Orange, Accent 6, Lighter 80%**. Click the **Font Color arrow**, and then click **Orange, Accent 6**. Apply bold and **14 pt** size. Click **Middle Align**, and then click **Center** in the Alignment group.

e. Complete the days of the month:
   - Type **1** in **cell B3**, press **Tab**, type **2** in **cell C3**, and then click **Enter** on the left side of the Formula Bar.
   - Select the **range B3:C3**. Drag the fill handle in **cell C3** across the row through **cell G3** to use Auto Fill to complete the rest of the days for the first week.
   - Type **7** in **cell A4**, press **Tab**, type **8** in **cell B4**, and then click **Enter** on the left side of the Formula Bar. Use the fill handle to complete the days for the second week.
   - Type **14** in **cell A5**, press **Tab**, type **15** in **cell B5**, and then click **Enter** on the left side of the Formula Bar. Use the fill handle to complete the days for the third week.
   - Use the fill handle to complete the days of the month (up to 31).

f. Format the columns and rows:
   - Select **columns A:G**. Click **Format** in the Cells group, select **Column Width**, type **16** in the **Column width box**, and then click **OK**.
   - Select **row 2**. Click **Format** in the Cells group, select **Row Height**, type **54**, and then click **OK**.
   - Select **rows 3:7**. Set an **80** row height.
   - Select the **range A2:G7**. Click the **Borders arrow** in the Font group, and then select **All Borders**.
   - Select the **range A3:G7**. Click **Top Align** and **Align Text Left** in the Alignment group. Click **Increase Indent**. Bold the numbers and apply **12 pt** size.

g. Insert and size images:
  - Display the Clip Art task pane. Search for and insert the Halloween image in the **October 31 cell**. Size the image to fit within the cell.
  - Search for and insert an image of Columbus in the **October 15 cell**. Size the image to fit within the cell.

h. Double-click **Sheet1**, type **October**, and then press **Enter**. Right-click **Sheet2**, and then select **Delete**. Delete Sheet3.

i. Click the **Page Layout tab**. Click **Orientation** in the Page Setup group, and then select **Landscape**.

j. Click the **Insert tab**, and then click **Header & Footer** in the Text group. Click in the left side of the header, and then type your name. Click in the center of the header, and then click **Sheet Name** in the Header & Footer Elements group on the Design tab. Click in the right side of the header, and then click **File Name** in the Header & Footer Elements group on the Design tab. Click in any cell in the workbook, and then click **Normal** on the status bar.

k. Save and close the workbook, and submit based on your instructor's directions.

3 Elementary School Attendance

As the principal of Wellsville Elementary School, you have to prepare periodic reports about student attendance. You decided to create a spreadsheet in Excel to store data by each grade level for a particular day. You will complete your spreadsheet by entering formulas to calculate the percentages of students who were present and absent each day. You also want to format the spreadsheet to present the data effectively. This exercise follows the same set of skills as used in Hands-On Exercises 1–5 in the chapter. Refer to Figure 1.53 as you complete this exercise.

	A	B	C	D	E	F
1	**Wellsville Elementary**					
2	**Monday, April 30, 2012**					
3						
4	**Grade Level**	**Total Students**	**Number Present**	**Attendance Rate**	**Absence Rate**	
5	Pre-K	15	10	66.67%	33.33%	
6	Kindergarten	35	30	85.71%	14.29%	
7	First Grade	50	41	82.00%	18.00%	
8	Second Grade	45	44	97.78%	2.22%	
9	Third Grade	47	46	97.87%	2.13%	
10	Fourth Grade	38	38	100.00%	0.00%	
11	Fifth Grade	42	40	95.24%	4.76%	
12						

FIGURE 1.53 Attendance Report ➤

a. Open the *e01p3attend* workbook and save it as **e01p3attend_LastnameFirstname** so that you can return to the original workbook if necessary.

b. Adjust alignments by doing the following from the Alignment group on the Home tab:
  - Select the **range A1:F1**, and then click **Merge & Center** in the Alignment group to center the title over the data columns. Merge and center the date in the second row over the data columns.
  - Select the **range A4:F4**. Click **Wrap Text**, and then click **Center** in the Alignment group to center and word-wrap the column headings.

c. Click **cell D4**. Click the **Delete arrow** in the Cells group, and then select **Delete Sheet Columns** to delete the empty column D.

d. Move the Pre-K row above the Kindergarten row by doing the following:
- Right-click the **row 5 heading**, and then select **Insert** from the shortcut menu to insert a new row.
- Select the **range A12:E12**. Cut the selected range, click **cell A5**, and then paste.

e. Select the **range A5:E11**. Click **Format** in the Cells group, and then select **Row Height**. Type **24** and click **OK** to increase the row height.

f. Calculate the percentages of students who were present and absent today by doing the following:
- Click **cell D5**. Type **=C5/B5** and press **Tab** to enter the formula and make **cell E5** the active cell. This formula divides the number of students present by the total number of students in Pre-K.
- Type **=(B5-C5)/B5** and click **Enter** on the left side of the Formula Bar to enter the formula and keep **cell E5** as the active cell. This formula must first calculate the number of students who were absent by subtracting the number of students present from the total number of students in Pre-K. The difference is divided by the total number of students to determine the percentage of students absent.
- Select the **range D5:E5**. Click **Percent Style** in the Number group, and then click **Increase Decimal** twice in the Number group. With both cells still selected, double-click the fill handle in the bottom-right corner of **cell E5** to copy the formulas down the columns.
- Click the **Formulas tab**, and then click **Show Formulas** in the Formula Auditing group to display cell formulas. Review the formulas, and then click **Show Formulas** to display formula results again.

FYI

g. Press **Ctrl+Home** to make **cell A1** the active cell. Spell-check the worksheet and make necessary changes.

h. Click the **Page Layout tab**. Click **Margins** in the Page Setup group, select **Custom Margins**, click the **Horizontally check box**, and then click **OK**.

i. Click the **Insert tab**. Click **Header & Footer** in the Text group. Click in the left side of the header, and then type your name. Press **Tab**, and then click **Current Date** in the Header & Footer Elements group. Press **Tab**, and then click **File Name** in the Header & Footer Elements group. Click **cell A1**, and then click **Normal** on the status bar.

j. Save and close the workbook, and submit based on your instructor's directions.

MID-LEVEL EXERCISES

1 Fuel Efficiency

Your summer vacation involved traveling through several states to visit relatives and to view the scenic attractions. While traveling, you kept a travel log of mileage and gasoline purchases. Now that the vacation is over, you want to determine the fuel efficiency of your automobile. The partially completed worksheet includes the beginning mileage for the vacation trips and the amount of fuel purchased.

a. Open the *e01m1fuel* workbook and save the workbook as **e01m1fuel_LastnameFirstname** so that you can return to the original workbook if necessary.

b. Insert a new column between columns B and C, and then type **Miles Driven** as the column heading.

c. Select the range of beginning miles in **cells A5:A12**. Copy the selected range to duplicate the values in **cells B4:B11** to ensure that the ending mileage for one trip is identical to the beginning mileage for the next trip.

d. Create the formula to calculate the miles driven for the first trip. Copy the formula down the **Miles Driven column**.

e. Create the formula to calculate the miles per gallon for the first trip. Copy the formula down the **Miles Per Gallon column**.

f. Merge and center the title over the data columns. Apply bold, **16 pt** size, and **Blue, Accent 1** font color.

g. Format the column headings: bold, centered, wrap text, and **Blue, Accent 1, Lighter 80% fill color**.

h. Apply **Comma Style** to the values in the Beginning and Ending columns, and then display these values as whole numbers. Display the values in the Miles Per Gallon column with two decimal places.

i. Delete Sheet2 and Sheet3. Rename *Sheet1* as **Mileage**.

j. Set these page settings: **2"** top margin, centered horizontally, **125%** scaling.

k. Insert a header with your name on the left side, the sheet name code in the center, and the file name code on the right side.

l. Save and close the workbook, and submit based on your instructor's directions.

2 Guest House Rental Rates

You manage a beach guest house in Ft. Lauderdale. The guest house contains three types of rental units. You set prices based on peak and off-peak times of the year. You want to calculate the maximum daily revenue for each rental type, assuming all units of each type are rented. In addition, you want to calculate the discount rate for off-peak rental times. After calculating the revenue and discount rate, you want to improve the appearance of the worksheet by applying font, alignment, and number formats. Refer to Figure 1.54 as you complete this exercise.

	A	B	C	D	E	F	G
1	**Beachfront Guest House**						
2	Effective May 1, 2012						
3							
4			Peak Rentals		Off-Peak Rentals		
5	**Rental Type**	**No. Units**	**Per Day**	**Maximum Revenue**	**Per Day**	**Maximum Revenue**	**Discount Rate**
6	Studio Apartment	6	$ 149.95	$ 899.70	$ 112.50	$ 675.00	25.0%
7	1 Bedroom Suite	4	$ 250.45	$ 1,001.80	$ 174.00	$ 696.00	30.5%
8	2 Bedroom Suite	2	$ 450.00	$ 900.00	$ 247.55	$ 495.10	45.0%

FIGURE 1.54 Beachfront Guest House Rental Summary ➤

a. Open the *e01m2rentals* workbook and save the workbook as **e01m2rentals_LastnameFirstname** so that you can return to the original workbook if necessary.

b. Create and copy the following formulas:
- Calculate the Peak Rentals Maximum Revenue based on the number of units and the rental price per day.
- Calculate the Off-Peak Rentals Maximum Revenue based on the number of units and the rental price per day.
- Calculate the discount rate for the Off-Peak rental price per day. For example, using the peak and off-peak per day values, the studio apartment rents for 75% of its peak rental rate. However, you need to calculate and display the off-peak discount rate, which is 25%.

DISCOVER

c. Format the monetary values with **Accounting Number Format**. Format the discount rate in **Percent Style** with one decimal place.

d. Format the headings on row 4:
- Merge and center *Peak Rentals* over the two columns of peak rental data. Apply bold, **Dark Red fill color** and **White, Background 1 font color**.
- Merge and center *Off-Peak Rentals* over the three columns of off-peak rental data. Apply bold, **Blue fill color**, and **White, Background 1 font color**.

e. Center, bold, and wrap the headings on row 5.

f. Apply **Red, Accent 2, Lighter 80% fill color** to the **range C5:D8**. Apply **Blue, Accent 1, Lighter 80% fill color** to the **range E5:G8**.

g. Set **1″** top, bottom, left, and right margins. Center the data horizontally on the page.

h. Insert a header with your name on the left side, the sheet name code in the center, and the file name code on the right side.

i. Insert a new worksheet, and then name it **Formulas**. Copy the data from the Rental Rates worksheet to the Formulas worksheet. On the Formulas worksheet, select **landscape orientation** and the options to print gridlines and headings. Display cell formulas and adjust column widths so that the data will fit on one page. Insert a header with the same specifications that you did for the Rental Rates worksheet.

j. Save and close the workbook, and submit based on your instructor's directions.

3 Real Estate Sales Report

You own a small real estate company in Enid, Oklahoma. You want to analyze sales for selected properties. Your assistant prepared a spreadsheet with some of the data from the files. You need to calculate the number of days that the houses were on the market and their sales percentage of the list price. In one situation, the house was involved in a bidding war between two families that really wanted the house. Therefore, the sale price exceeded the list price.

a. Open the *e01m3sales* workbook and save the workbook as **e01m3sales_LastnameFirstname** so that you can return to the original workbook if necessary.

b. Delete the row that has incomplete sales data. The owners took their house off the market.

c. Calculate the number of days each house was on the market. Copy the formula down that column.

d. Calculate the sale price percentage of the list price. The second house was listed for $500,250, but it sold for only $400,125. Therefore, the sale percentage of the list price is 79.99%. Format the percentages with two decimal places.

e. Format prices with **Accounting Number Format** with zero decimal places.

f. Wrap the headings on row 4.

g. Insert a new column between the Date Sold and List Price columns. Move the Days on Market column to the new location. Then delete the empty column B.

h. Edit the list date of the 41 Chestnut Circle house to be **4/20/2012**. Edit the list price of the house on Amsterdam Drive to be **$355,000**.

i. Select the **property rows**, and then set a **20** row height. Adjust column widths as necessary.

j. Select **landscape orientation**, and then set the scaling to **130%**. Center the data horizontally and vertically on the page.

k. Insert a header with your name, the current date code, and the current time code.

l. Save and close the workbook, and submit based on your instructor's directions.

CAPSTONE EXERCISE

You manage a publishing company that publishes and sells books to bookstores in Austin. Your assistant prepared a standard six-month royalty statement for one author. You need to insert formulas, format the worksheets, and then prepare royalty statements for other authors.

Enter Data into the Worksheet

You need to enter and format a title, enter the date indicating the end of the statement period, and then delete a blank column. You also need to insert a row for the standard discount rate row, a percentage that you discount the books from the retail price to sell to the bookstores.

a. Open the *e01c1royal* workbook and save it as **e01c1royal_LastnameFirstname**.

b. Type **Royalty Statement** in **cell A1**. Merge and center the title over the four data columns. Select **16 pt** size, and apply **Purple font color**.

c. Type **6/30/2012** in **cell B3**, and then left-align the date.

d. Delete the blank column between the Hardback and Paperback columns.

e. Insert a new row between *Retail Price* and *Price to Bookstore*. Enter **Standard Discount Rate**, **0.55**, and **0.5**. Format the two values as **Percent Style**.

Calculate Values

You need to insert formulas to perform necessary calculations.

a. Enter the **Percent Returned formula** in the Hardback column. The percent returned indicates the percentage of books sold but returned to the publisher.

b. Enter the **Price to Bookstore formula**. This is the price at which you sell the books to the bookstore and is based on the retail price and the standard discount. For example, if a book has a $10 retail price and a 55% discount, you sell the book for $4.50.

c. Enter the **Net Retail Sales formula**. The net retail sales is the revenue from the net units sold at the retail price. Gross units sold minus the returned units equals net units sold.

d. Enter the **Royalty to Author formula**. Royalties are based on net retail sales and the applicable royalty rate.

e. Enter the **Royalty per Book formula**. This amount is the author's earnings on every book sold but not returned.

f. Copy the formulas to the Paperback column.

Format the Values

You are ready to format the values to improve the readability.

a. Apply **Comma Style** with zero decimal places to the quantities in the *Units Sold* section.

b. Apply **Percent Style** with one decimal place to the Units Sold values, **Percent Style** with zero decimal places to the Pricing values, and **Percent Style** with two decimal places to the Royalty Information values.

c. Apply **Accounting Number Format** to all monetary values.

Format the Worksheet

You want to improve the appearance of the rest of the worksheet.

a. Select the **Hardback** and **Paperback labels**. Apply bold, right-alignment, and **Purple font color**.

b. Select the **Units Sold section heading**. Apply bold and **Purple, Accent 4, Lighter 40% fill color**.

c. Use **Format Painter** to apply the formats from the Units Sold label to the Pricing and Royalty Information labels.

d. Select the individual labels within each section (e.g., *Gross Units Sold*) and indent the labels twice. Widen column A as needed.

e. Select the **range A7:C10** (the *Units Sold* section), and then apply the **Outside Borders border style**. Apply the same border style to the *Pricing* and *Royalty Information* sections.

Manage the Workbook

You want to duplicate the royalty statement worksheet to use as a model to prepare a royalty statement for another author. You will apply page setup options and insert a header on both worksheets.

a. Insert a new worksheet on the right side of the Jacobs worksheet. Rename the worksheet as **Lopez**.

b. Change the Jacobs sheet tab to **Red**. Change the Lopez sheet tab to **Dark Blue**.

c. Copy Jacobs' data to the Lopez worksheet.

d. Make these changes on the Lopez worksheet: **Lopez** (author), **5000** (hardback gross units), **15000** (paperback gross units), **400** (hardback returns), **175** (paperback returns), **19.95** (hardback retail price), and **7.95** (paperback retail price).

e. Click the **Jacobs sheet tab**, and then press and hold down **Ctrl** as you click the **Lopez sheet tab** to select both worksheets. Select the margin setting to center the data horizontally on the page. Insert a header with your name on the left side, the sheet name code in the center, and the file name code on the right side.

f. Change back to Normal view. Right-click the **Jacobs sheet name**, and then select **Ungroup Sheets**.

Display Formulas and Print the Workbook

You want to print the formatted Jacobs worksheet to display the calculated results. To provide evidence of the formulas, you want to display and print cell formulas in the Lopez worksheet.

a. Display the cell formulas for the Lopez worksheet.

b. Select options to print the gridlines and headings.

c. Adjust the column widths so that the formula printout will print on one page.

d. Submit either a hard copy of both worksheets or an electronic copy of the workbook to your professor as instructed. Close the workbook.

Server's Tip Distribution

GENERAL CASE

You are a server at a restaurant in Seattle. When you get tips, you calculate the percentage of the subtotal to determine your performance based on the tip. You must tip the bartender 15% of the drink amount and the server assistant 12% of your total tip amount. You started to design a spreadsheet to enter data for one shift. Open *e01b1tips* and save it as **e01b1tips_LastnameFirstname**. Now you need to insert columns for the bartender and assistant tip rates, perform calculations, and format the data. After entering the formulas, use Auto Fill to copy the formulas down the respective columns. Include a notes section that explains the tipping rates for the bartender and server assistant. Decide where to place this information. Add and format a descriptive title, date, and time of shift. To format the data, apply concepts learned in the chapter: font, borders, fill color, alignment, wrap text, and number formats. Select appropriate options on the Page Layout tab. Copy the data to Sheet2, display cell formulas, print gridlines, print headings, set the print area to the column headings and data, and adjust the column widths. Include a footer with appropriate data for the two worksheets. Manage the workbook by deleting extra worksheets, renaming the two worksheets that contain data, and adding worksheet tab colors to both sheets. Save and close the workbook, and submit based on your instructor's directions.

Credit Card Rebate

RESEARCH CASE

You recently found out the personal-use Costco TrueEarnings® American Express credit card earns annual rebates on all purchases, whether at Costco or other places. You want to see how much rebate you would have received had you used this credit card for purchases in the past year. Use the Internet to research the percentage rebates for different categories. Plan the design of the spreadsheet. Enter the categories, rebate percentages, amount of money you spent in each category, and a formula to calculate the amount of rebate. Use the Excel Help feature to learn how to add several cells using a function instead of adding cells individually and how to apply a Double Accounting underline. Then insert the appropriate function to total your categorical purchases and rebate amounts. Apply appropriate formatting and page setup options as discussed in this chapter for readability. Underline the last monetary values for the last data row, and apply the Double Accounting underline style to the totals. Insert a header with imperative documentation. Save the workbook as **e01b2rebate_LastnameFirstname**. Save and close the workbook, and submit based on your instructor's directions.

Housing Estimates

DISASTER RECOVERY

One of your friends is starting a house construction business. Your friend developed an Excel workbook to prepare a cost estimate for a potential client. However, the workbook contains several errors. You offer to review the workbook, identify the errors, and correct them. Open *e01b3house* and save it as **e01b3house_LastnameFirstname**. Research how to insert comments in cells. As you identify the errors, insert comments in the respective cells to explain the errors. Correct the errors. Insert your name on the left side of the header. The other header and page setup options are already set. Save and close the workbook, and submit based on your instructor's directions.

2 FORMULAS AND FUNCTIONS

Performing Quantitative Analysis

Watch the
Set-up
Video
for this
Case Study!

CASE STUDY | Denver Mortgage Company

You are an assistant to Erica Matheson, a mortgage broker at the Denver Mortgage Company. Erica spends her days reviewing mortgage rates and trends, meeting with potential clients, and preparing paperwork. She relies on your expertise in using Excel to help you analyze mortgage data.

Today, Erica provided you with a spreadsheet containing data for five mortgages. She asked you to perform some basic calculations so that she can check the output provided by her system. She needs you to calculate the amount financed, the periodic interest rate, the total number of payment periods, monthly payments, and other details for each mortgage. In addition, you will perform some basic statistics, such as totals and averages. After you complete these tasks, Erica wants you to create a separate worksheet with additional input data to automate calculations for future loans.

OBJECTIVES   AFTER YOU READ THIS CHAPTER, YOU WILL BE ABLE TO:

1. Use semi-selection to create a formula *p.374*

2. Use relative, absolute, and mixed cell references in formulas *p.374*

3. Avoid circular references *p.376*

4. Insert a function *p.382*

5. Total values with the SUM function *p.384*

6. Insert basic statistical functions *p.385*

7. Use date functions *p.387*

8. Determine results with the IF function *p.394*

9. Use lookup functions *p.396*

10. Calculate payments with the PMT function *p.398*

11. Create and maintain range names *p.403*

12. Use range names in formulas *p.405*

Formula Basics

By increasing your understanding of formulas, you can build robust spreadsheets that perform a variety of calculations for quantitative analysis. Your ability to build sophisticated spreadsheets and to interpret the results increases your value to any organization. By now, you should be able to build simple formulas using cell references and mathematical operators and using the order of precedence to control the sequence of calculations in formulas.

> Your ability to build sophisticated spreadsheets and to interpret the results increases your value to any organization.

In this section, you will use the semi-selection method to create formulas. In addition, you will create formulas in which cell addresses change or remain fixed when you copy them. Finally, you will learn how to identify and prevent circular references in formulas.

Using Semi-Selection to Create a Formula

You have learned how to create formulas by typing the cell references (for example, =A1+A2) to create a formula. To decrease typing time and ensure accuracy, you can use *semi-selection*, a process of selecting a cell or range of cells for entering cell references as you create formulas. Semi-selection is often called *pointing* because you use the mouse pointer to select cells as you build the formula. To use the semi-selection technique to create a formula, do the following:

Semi-selection (or **pointing**) is the process of using the mouse pointer to select cells while building a formula.

1. Click the cell where you want to create the formula.
2. Type an equal sign (=) to start a formula.
3. Click the cell or drag to select the cell range that contains the value(s) to use in the formula. A moving marquee appears around the cell or range you select, and Excel displays the cell or range reference in the formula.
4. Type a mathematical operator.
5. Continue clicking cells, selecting ranges, and typing operators to finish the formula. Use the scroll bars if the cell is in a remote location in the worksheet, or click a worksheet tab to see a cell in another worksheet.
6. Press Enter to complete the formula.

Using Relative, Absolute, and Mixed Cell References in Formulas

When you copy a formula, Excel either adjusts or preserves the cell references in the copied formulas based on how the cell references appear in the original formula. Excel uses three different ways to reference a cell in a formula: relative, absolute, and mixed. Figure 2.1 shows a worksheet containing various cell references in formulas. When you create an original formula that you will copy to other cells, ask yourself the following: Do the cell references need to adjust for the copied formulas, or should the cell references always refer to the same cell location, regardless where the copied formula is located?

Formula in cell B8 contains an absolute cell reference

Input cell; formulas referring to this cell should contain an absolute reference

B8		fx	=A8*$B$5	
	A	B	C	D
1	**Input Area**			
2	Today's Date	5/7/2012		
3	# Pmts Per Year	12		
4	PMI Rate:	0.5%		
5	Down Pmt. Rate	20.0%		
6				
7	House Cost	Down Payment	Amount Financed	
8	$400,000	$80,000	$320,000	
9	$350,000	$70,000	$280,000	
10	$175,500	$35,100	$140,400	
11	$265,950	$53,190	$212,760	
12	$329,750	$65,950	$263,800	

Formula contains relative cell references: =A8-B8

FIGURE 2.1 Relative, Absolute, and Mixed Cell References ➤

Use a Relative Cell Reference

A **relative cell reference** indicates a cell's relative location from the cell containing the formula; the cell reference changes when the formula is copied.

A *relative cell reference* indicates a cell's relative location, such as two rows up and one column to the left, from the cell containing the formula. When you copy a formula containing a relative cell reference, the cell references in the copied formula change relative to the position of the copied formula. Regardless of where you copy the formula, the cell references in the copied formula maintain the same relative distance from the copied formula cell, as the cell references relative location to the original formula cell.

In Figure 2.1, the formulas in column C contain relative cell references. When you copy the original formula =A8-B8 from cell C8 down to cell C9, the copied formula changes to =A9-B9. Because you copy the formula down the column to cell C12, the column letters in the formula stay the same, but the row numbers change, down one row number at a time. Relative references are indicated by using the cell address. Using relative cell addresses to calculate the amount financed ensures that each borrower's down payment is subtracted from his or her respective house cost.

Use an Absolute Cell Reference

An **absolute cell reference** indicates a cell's specific location; the cell reference does not change when you copy the formula.

An *absolute cell reference* provides a permanent reference to a specific cell. When you copy a formula containing an absolute cell reference, the cell reference in the copied formula does not change, regardless of where you copy the formula. An absolute cell reference appears with a dollar sign before both the column letter and row number, such as $B$5.

Figure 2.1 illustrates an effective use of an input area, a range in a worksheet that contains values that you can change. You build formulas using absolute references to the cells in the input area. By using cell references from an input area, you can change the value in the input area and the formulas that refer to those cells update automatically. If an input value changes (e.g., the down payment rate changes from 20% to 25%), enter the new input value in only one cell (e.g., B5), and Excel recalculates the amount of recommended down payment for all the formulas.

In Figure 2.1, the formulas in column B calculate down payments based on the house costs in column A and on the required down payment percentage, which is stored in cell B5. The formula uses an absolute cell reference to cell B5, which currently contains the value 20%. Cell B8 contains the formula to calculate the first borrower's down payment: =A8*$B$5. A8 is a relative address that changes as you copy the formula down the column so that the down payment is based on each borrower's respective house cost (A8 becomes A9 on the 9th row, A10 on the 10th row, etc.). $B$5 is an absolute cell reference to the cell B5, which currently contains 20%. The absolute cell reference $B$5 prevents the cell reference to B5 from changing when you copy the formula to calculate the recommended down payment for the other borrowers.

Use a Mixed Cell Reference

A **mixed cell reference** contains both an absolute and a relative cell reference in a formula; the absolute part does not change but the relative part does when you copy the formula.

A *mixed cell reference* combines an absolute cell reference with a relative cell reference. When you copy a formula containing a mixed cell reference, either the column letter or the row number that has the absolute reference remains fixed while the other part of the cell reference that is relative changes in the copied formula. $B5 and B$5 are examples of mixed cell references. In the reference $B5, the column B is absolute, and the row number is relative; when you copy the formula, the column letter, B, does not change, but the row number will change. In the reference B$5, the column letter, B, changes, but the row number, 5, does not change. To create a mixed reference, type the dollar sign to the left of the part of the cell reference you want to be absolute.

In the example shown in Figure 2.1, you could change the formula in cell B8 to be =A8*B$5. Because you are copying down the same column, only the row reference 5 must be absolute; the column letter stays the same. In situations where you can use either absolute or mixed references, consider using mixed references to shorten the length of the formula.

> ### TIP The F4 Key
>
> The F4 key toggles through relative, absolute, and mixed references. Click a cell reference within a formula on the Formula Bar, and then press F4 to change it. For example, click in B5 in the formula =A8*B5. Press F4, and the relative cell reference (B5) changes to an absolute cell reference ($B$5). Press F4 again, and $B$5 becomes a mixed reference (B$5); press F4 again, and it becomes another mixed reference ($B5). Press F4 a fourth time, and the cell reference returns to the original relative reference (B5).

Avoiding Circular References

A **circular reference** occurs when a formula directly or indirectly refers to itself.

If a formula contains a direct or an indirect reference to the cell containing the formula, a *circular reference* exists. For example, assume you enter the formula =A8-C8 in cell C8. Because the formula is in cell C8, using the cell address C8 within the formula creates a circular reference. Circular references usually cause inaccurate results, and Excel displays a warning message when you enter a formula containing a circular reference or when you open an Excel workbook that contains an existing circular reference (see Figure 2.2). Click Help to display the *Remove or allow a circular reference* Help topic, or click OK to accept the circular reference. The status bar indicates the location of a circular reference until it has been resolved.

FIGURE 2.2 Circular Reference Warning ➤

If the circular reference warning appears when creating a formula, use Help to activate formula auditing tools to help you identify what is causing the circular reference.

> ### TIP Green Triangles
>
> Excel displays a green triangle in the top-left corner of a cell if it detects a potential error in a formula. Click the cell to see the Trace Error button (yellow diamond with exclamation mark). When you click Trace Error, Excel displays information about the potential error and how to correct it. In some cases, Excel may anticipate an inconsistent formula or the omission of adjacent cells in a formula. For example, if you add a column of values for the year 2012, the error message indicates that you did not include the year itself. However, the year is merely a label and should not be included; therefore, you would ignore that error message.

1 Formula Basics

Erica prepared a workbook containing data for five mortgages financed with the Denver Mortgage Company. The data include house cost, down payment, mortgage rate, number of years to pay off the mortgage, and the financing date for each mortgage.

Skills covered: Use Semi-Selection to Create a Formula • Copy a Formula with a Relative Cell Reference • Enter a Formula with an Absolute Cell Reference • Enter a Formula with a Mixed Cell Reference • Create and Correct a Circular Reference

---

STEP 1 ► **USE SEMI-SELECTION TO CREATE A FORMULA**

Your first step is to calculate the amount financed by each borrower by creating a formula that calculates the difference between the cost of the house and the down payment. You decide to use the semi-selection technique. Refer to Figure 2.3 as you complete Step 1.

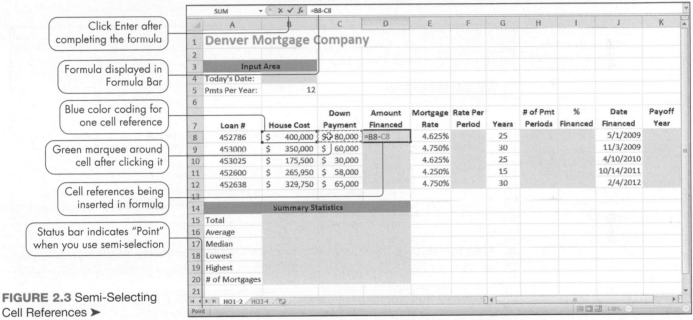

FIGURE 2.3 Semi-Selecting Cell References ➤

a. Open *e02h1loans* and save it as **e02h1loans_LastnameFirstname**.

TROUBLESHOOTING: If you make any major mistakes in this exercise, you can close the file, open *e02h1loans* again, and then start this exercise over.

The workbook contains two worksheets: HO1-2 (for Hands-On Exercises 1 and 2) and HO3-4 (for Hands-On Exercises 3 and 4). You will enter formulas in the shaded cells.

b. Click the **HO1-2 worksheet tab**, and then click **cell D8**.

This is where you will create a formula to calculate the first borrower's amount financed.

c. Type = and click **cell B8**, the cell containing the first borrower's house cost.

You type an equal sign to start the formula, and then you click the first cell containing a value you want to use in the formula. A blue marquee appears around cell B8, and the B8 cell reference appears to the right of the equal sign in the formula.

d. Type - and click **cell C8**, the cell containing the down payment by the first borrower.

A green marquee appears around cell C8, and the C8 cell reference appears to the right of the subtraction sign in the formula (see Figure 2.3).

> **TROUBLESHOOTING:** If you click the wrong cell, click the correct cell to change the cell reference in the formula. If you realize the mistake after typing an arithmetic operator or after entering the formula, you must edit the formula to change the cell reference.

e. Click **Enter** to the left of the Formula Bar to complete the formula. Save the workbook.

The first borrower financed (i.e., borrowed) $320,000, the difference between the cost ($400,000) and the down payment ($80,000).

STEP 2 ▶ COPY A FORMULA WITH A RELATIVE CELL REFERENCE

After verifying the results of the amount financed by the first borrower, you are ready to copy the formula. Before copying the formula, determine if the cell references should be relative or absolute. For this formula, you want cell references to change for each row. For each borrower, you want to base the amount financed on his or her own data, so you decide to keep the relative cell references in the formula. Refer to Figure 2.4 as you complete Step 2.

Cell references in the first copied formula

Cell containing the first copied formula

Auto Fill Options

FIGURE 2.4 Formula Containing Relative Cell References Copied ➤

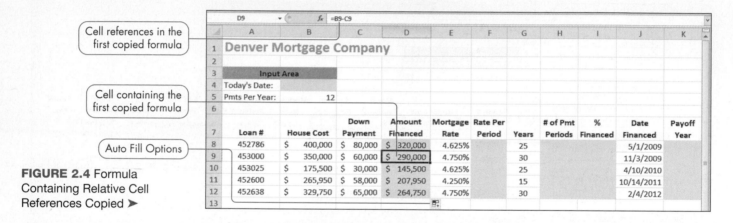

a. Make sure that **cell D8** is the active cell but does not have a blinking insertion point.

b. Double-click the **cell D8 fill handle**.

You copied the formula down the Amount Financed column for each mortgage row.

> **TIP Auto Fill Options**
>
> The Auto Fill Options button appears in the bottom-right corner of the copied formulas. If you click it, you can see that the default is Copy Cells. If you want to copy only formatting, click Fill Formatting Only. If you want to copy data only, click Fill Without Formatting.

c. Click **cell D9**, and then view the formula in the Formula Bar.

The formula in cell D8 is =B8-C8. The formula pasted in cell D9 is =B9-C9. Because the original formula contained relative cell references, when you copy the formula down a column, the row numbers for the cell references change. Each result represents the amount financed for that particular borrower.

d. Press ⬇ and look at the cell references in the Formula Bar to see how the references change for each formula you copied. Save the workbook with the new formula you created.

ENTER A FORMULA WITH AN ABSOLUTE CELL REFERENCE

Column E contains the annual percentage rate (APR) for each mortgage. Because the borrowers will make monthly payments, you need to calculate the monthly interest rate by dividing the APR by 12 (the number of payments in one year) for each borrower. Refer to Figure 2.5 as you complete Step 3.

	A	B	C	D	E	F	G	H	I	J	K
	F9		f_x =E9/B6								
1	Denver Mortgage Company										
2											
3	Input Area										
4	Today's Date:										
5	Pmts Per Year:	12									
6											
7	Loan #	House Cost	Down Payment	Amount Financed	Mortgage Rate	Rate Per Period	Years	# of Pmt Periods	% Financed	Date Financed	Payoff Year
8	452786	$ 400,000	$ 80,000	$ 320,000	4.625%	0.385%	25			5/1/2009	
9	453000	$ 350,000	$ 60,000	$ 290,000	4.7%	#DIV/0!	30			11/3/2009	
10	453025	$ 175,500	$ 30,000	$ 145,500	4.625%	#VALUE!	25			4/10/2010	
11	452600	$ 265,950	$ 58,000	$ 207,950	4.250%	0.000%	15			10/14/2011	
12	452638	$ 329,750	$ 65,000	$ 264,750	4.750%	0.000%	30			2/4/2012	
13											

Copied formula

Error results

FIGURE 2.5 Error Based on Not Having Absolute Reference ➤

a. Click **cell F8**.

   You need to create a formula to calculate the monthly interest rate for the first borrower.

b. Type = and click **cell E8**, the cell containing the first fixed mortgage rate.

c. Type / and click **cell B5**, the cell containing the value 12.

   Typically, you should avoid typing values directly in formulas. Although the number of months in one year will always be 12, you use a cell reference so that the company could change the payment period to bimonthly (24 payments per year) or quarterly (four payments per year) without adjusting the formula.

d. Click **Enter** to the left of the Formula Bar, double-click the **cell F8 fill handle**, click **cell F9**, and then view the results (see Figure 2.5).

   An error icon displays to the left of cell F9, cell F9 displays #DIV/0!, and cell F10 displays #VALUE!. The original formula was =E8/B5. Because you copied the formula =E8/B5 down the column, the first copied formula is =E9/B6, and the second copied formula is =E10/B7. Although you want the mortgage rate cell reference (E8) to change (E9, E10, etc.) from row to row, you do not want the divisor to change. You need all formulas to divide by the value stored in cell B5, so you will edit the formula to make B5 an absolute reference.

TIP Error Icons

You can position the mouse pointer over the error icon to see a tip indicating what is wrong, such as *The formula or function used is dividing by zero or empty cells*. You can click the icon to see a menu of options to learn more about the error and how to correct it.

FYI

e. Undo the Auto Fill process. Click within or to the right of **B5** in the Formula Bar.

f. Press **F4**, and then click **Enter** to the left of the Formula Bar.

   Excel changes the cell reference from B5 to $B$5, making it absolute.

g. Copy the formula down the Rate Per Period column. Click **cell F9**, and then view the formula in the Formula Bar. Save the workbook with the new formula you created.

   The formula in cell F9 is =E9/$B$5. The reference to E9 is relative and B5 is absolute.

ENTER A FORMULA WITH A MIXED CELL REFERENCE

The next formula you need to enter will calculate the total number of payment periods for each loan. Refer to Figure 2.6 as you complete Step 4.

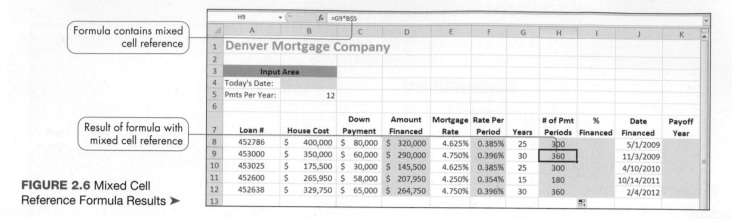

Formula contains mixed cell reference

Result of formula with mixed cell reference

FIGURE 2.6 Mixed Cell Reference Formula Results ➤

a. Click **cell H8**.

b. Type = and click **cell G8**, the cell containing *25*, the number of years to pay off the loan for the first borrower.

   You need to multiply the number of years (25) by the number of payment periods in one year (12) using cell references.

c. Type * and click **cell B5**.

   You want B5 to be absolute so that the cell reference remains B5 when you copy the formula.

d. Press **F4** to make the cell reference absolute, and then click **Enter** to the left of the Formula Bar.

   The product of 25 years and 12 months is 300.

e. Copy the formula down the # of Pmt Periods column.

   The first copied formula is =G9*$B$5, and the result is 360. You want to see what happens if you change the absolute reference to a mixed reference and then copy the formula again. Because you are copying down a column, the column letter B can be relative since it will not change either way, but the row number 5 must be absolute.

f. Undo the copied formulas. Click **cell H8**, and then click within the **$B$5 cell reference** in the Formula Bar. Press **F4** to change the cell reference to a mixed cell reference, B$5. Press **Ctrl+Enter**, and then copy the formula down the # of Pmt Periods column. Click **cell H9**. Save the workbook with the new formula you created.

   The first copied formula is =G9*B$5, and the result is still 360. In this situation, using either an absolute reference or a mixed reference provides the same results.

CREATE AND CORRECT A CIRCULAR REFERENCE

Erica wants to know what percentage of the house cost each borrower will finance. As you create the formula, you enter a circular reference. After studying the results, you correct the circular error and plan future formulas that avoid this problem. Refer to Figure 2.7 as you complete Step 5.

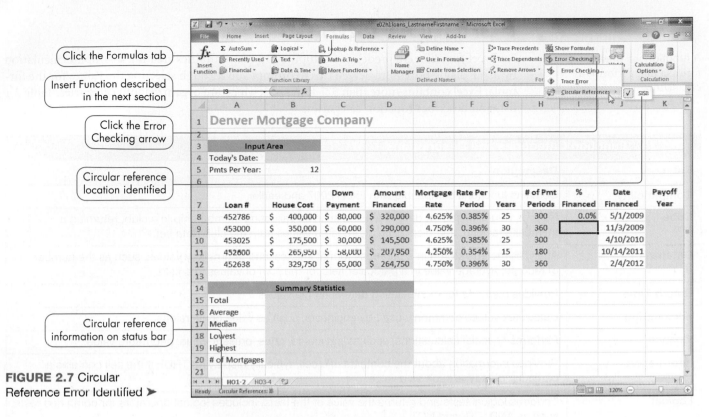

Click the Formulas tab

Insert Function described in the next section

Click the Error Checking arrow

Circular reference location identified

Circular reference information on status bar

FIGURE 2.7 Circular Reference Error Identified ➤

a. Click **cell I8**, type **=I8/B8**, and then press **Enter**.

The Circular Reference Warning message box appears.

b. Read the description of the error, and then click **Help**.

A Help window opens, displaying information about circular references.

c. Read the Help topic information, and then close the Help window.

Notice that the left side of the status bar displays *Circular References: I8.* You will follow the advice given in the Help window to fix it.

d. Click the **Formulas tab**, click the **Error Checking arrow** in the Formula Auditing group, and then point to **Circular References**.

The Circular References menu displays a list of cells containing circular references.

e. Select **$I$8** from the list to make it the active cell.

Because the formula is stored in cell I8, the formula cannot refer to the cell itself. You need to divide the value in the Amount Financed column by the value in the House Cost column.

f. Edit the formula to be **=D8/B8**. Copy the formula down the % Financed column.

The first borrower financed 80% of the cost of the house: $320,000 financed divided by $400,000 cost.

g. Save the workbook. Keep the workbook onscreen if you plan to continue with Hands-On Exercise 2. If not, close the workbook and exit Excel.

Function Basics

A **function** is a predefined formula that performs a calculation.

An Excel ***function*** is a predefined computation that simplifies creating a complex calculation by using dialog boxes and ScreenTips to prompt you through selecting the values for the formula. Excel contains more than 325 functions, which are organized into categories. Table 2.1 lists and describes function categories.

TABLE 2.1 Function Categories and Descriptions	
Category	**Description**
Compatibility	Contains functions compatible with Excel 2007 and earlier.
Cube	Returns values based on data in a cube, such as validating membership in a club, returning a member's ranking, and displaying aggregated values from the club data set.
Database	Analyzes records stored in a database format in Excel and returns key values, such as the number of records, average value in a particular field, or the sum of values in a field.
Date & Time	Provides methods for manipulating date and time values.
Engineering	Calculates values commonly used by engineers, such as value conversions.
Financial	Performs financial calculations, such as payments, rates, present value, and future value.
Information	Provides information about the contents of a cell, typically displaying TRUE if the cell contains a particular data type such as a value.
Logical	Performs logical tests and returns the value of the tests. Includes logical operators for combined tests, such as AND, OR, and NOT.
Lookup & Reference	Looks up values, creates links to cells, or provides references to cells in a worksheet.
Math & Trig	Performs standard math and trigonometry calculations.
Statistical	Performs common statistical calculations, such as averages and standard deviations.
Text	Manipulates text strings, such as combining text or converting text to lowercase.

Syntax is a set of rules that govern the structure and components for properly entering a function.

An **argument** is an input, such as a cell reference or value, needed to complete a function.

When using functions, you must adhere to correct ***syntax***, the rules that dictate the structure and components required to perform the necessary calculations. The basic syntax of a function requires a function to start with an equal sign, to contain the function name, and to specify its arguments. The function name describes the purpose of the function. For example, the function name SUM indicates that the function sums or adds values. A function's ***arguments*** specify the inputs—such as cells or values—that are required to complete the operation. Arguments are enclosed in parentheses, with the opening parenthesis immediately following the function name. Some functions, such as TODAY, do not require arguments; however, you must include the parentheses with nothing inside them. In some cases, a function requires multiple arguments separated by commas.

In this section, you will learn how to insert common functions using the keyboard and the Insert Function and Function Arguments dialog boxes.

Inserting a Function

Formula AutoComplete displays a list of functions and defined names as you enter a function.

To insert a function by typing, first type an equal sign, and then begin typing the function name. ***Formula AutoComplete*** displays a list of functions and defined names that match letters as you type a formula. For example, if you type =SU, Formula AutoComplete displays a list of functions and names that start with *SU* (see Figure 2.8). You can double-click the function name from the list or continue typing the function name. You can even scroll through the list to see the ScreenTip describing the function.

Start typing function name

List of functions

ScreenTip describing selected function name

FIGURE 2.8 Formula AutoComplete ➤

A **function ScreenTip** is a small pop-up description that displays the arguments for a function as you enter it.

After you type the function name and opening parenthesis, Excel displays the *function ScreenTip*, a small pop-up description that displays the function's arguments. The argument you are currently entering is bold in the function ScreenTip (see Figure 2.9). Square brackets indicate optional arguments. For example, the SUM function requires the number1 argument, but the number2 argument is optional. Click the argument name in the function ScreenTip to select the actual argument in the cell.

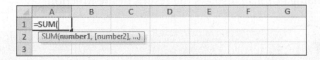

FIGURE 2.9 Function ScreenTip ➤

You can also use the Insert Function dialog box to search for a function, select a function category, and select a function from the list (see Figure 2.10). The dialog box is helpful if you want to browse a list of functions, especially if you are not sure of the function you need and want to see descriptions. To display the Insert Function dialog box, click Insert Function, which looks like *fx*, between the Name Box and the Formula Bar, or click Insert Function in the Function Library group on the Formulas tab. From within the dialog box, select a function category, such as Most Recently Used, and then select a function to display the syntax and a brief description of that function. Click *Help on this function* to display specific information about the selected function.

Specify type of functions to display

Selected function

Syntax and description of selected function

Click to see Help on selected function

FIGURE 2.10 Insert Function Dialog Box ➤

When you find the function you want, click OK. The Function Arguments dialog box opens so that you can enter the arguments for that specific function (see Figure 2.11). Bold arguments are required; argument names that are not bold are optional. The function can operate without the optional argument, which is used when you need additional specifications to calculate a result. Type the cell references in the argument boxes, or click a collapse button to the right side of an argument box to select the cell or range of cells in the worksheet to designate as that argument. The value or results of a formula contained in the argument cell displays on the right side of the argument box. If the argument is not valid, Excel displays an error description on the right side of the argument box.

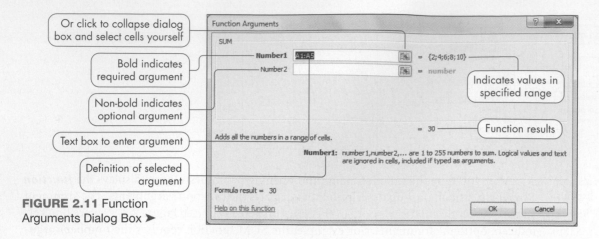

Or click to collapse dialog box and select cells yourself

Bold indicates required argument

Non-bold indicates optional argument

Text box to enter argument

Definition of selected argument

Indicates values in specified range

Function results

FIGURE 2.11 Function Arguments Dialog Box ➤

The bottom of the Function Arguments dialog box displays a description of the function and a description of the argument containing the insertion point. As you enter arguments, the dialog box also displays the results of the function.

> **TIP** #NAME?
>
> If you enter a function, and #NAME? appears in the cell, you might have mistyped the function name. To avoid this problem, select the function name from the Formula AutoComplete list as you type the function name, or use the Insert Function dialog box. You can also type the function name in all lowercase letters. If you enter a function name correctly, Excel converts the name to all capital letters when you press Enter, indicating that you spelled the function name correctly.

Totaling Values with the SUM Function

The **SUM function** calculates the total of values contained in two or more cells.

One of the most commonly used functions is the *SUM function*, which totals values in two or more cells and then displays the result in the cell containing the function. This function is more efficient to create when you need to add the values contained in three or more cells. For example, to add the contents of cells A2 through A14, you could enter =A2+A3+A4+A5+A6+A7+A8+A9+A10+A11+A12+A13+A14, which is time-consuming and increases the probability of entering an inaccurate cell reference, such as entering a cell reference twice or accidentally leaving out a cell reference. Instead, you could use the SUM function:

=SUM(number 1, [number 2], . . .)

> **TIP** Function Syntax
>
> In this book, the function syntax lines are highlighted. Arguments enclosed by brackets [ ] are optional. However, you do not actually type the brackets in the functions. The other arguments are required.

The SUM function contains one required argument—number1—that represents a range of cells to add. The number2 optional argument is used when you want to sum non-adjacent cells or ranges, such as =SUM(A2:A14,F2:F14).

To insert the SUM function, type =SUM(A2:A14). A2:A14 represents the range containing the values to sum. You can also use semi-selection to select the range of cells. Because the SUM function is the most commonly used function, it is available on the Ribbon: Click Sum in the Editing group on the Home tab, or click AutoSum in the Function Library group on the Formulas tab. Figure 2.12 shows the result of using the SUM function to total scores (898).

Selected range

Selection statistics on the status bar

FIGURE 2.12 Function Results ➤

	A	B	C	D	E	F
1	Scores		Measure	Statistic	Formula	
2	98		Total of All Scores	898	=SUM(A2:A14)	
3	94		Average Score	81.63636	=AVERAGE(A2:A14)	
4	92		Median Score	86	=MEDIAN(A2:A14)	
5	92		Low Score	50	=MIN(A2:A14)	
6	N/A		High Score	98	=MAX(A2:A14)	
7	90		No. of Numeric Cells	11	=COUNT(A2:A14)	
8	86		No. of Empty Cells	1	=COUNTBLANK(A2:A14)	
9			No. of Non-Empty Cells	12	=COUNTA(A2:A14)	
10	84					
11	82					
12	80					
13	50					
14	50					
15						

Sheet1 / Sheet2 / Sheet3

Ready   Average: 81.63636364   Count: 12   Sum: 898   100%

> ## TIP — Avoiding Functions for Basic Formulas
>
> Do not use a function for a basic mathematical expression. For example, although =SUM(B4/C4) produces the same result as =B4/C4, the SUM function is not needed to perform the basic arithmetic division. Use the most appropriate, clear-cut formula, =B4/C4.

Inserting Basic Statistical Functions

Excel includes commonly used statistical functions that you can use to calculate how much you spend on average per month on DVD rentals, what your highest electric bill is to control spending, and what your lowest test score is so you know what score you need to earn on your final exam to achieve the grade you desire. You can also use statistical functions to create or monitor your budget.

If you click AutoSum, Excel inserts the SUM function. However, if you click the AutoSum arrow in the Editing group on the Home tab, Excel displays a list of basic functions to select: Sum, Average, Count Numbers, Max, and Min. If you want to insert another function, select More Functions from the list.

Find Central Tendency with the AVERAGE and MEDIAN Functions

The **AVERAGE function** calculates the arithmetic mean, or average, of values in a range.

People often describe data based on central tendency, which means that values tend to cluster around a central value. Excel provides two functions to calculate central tendency: AVERAGE and MEDIAN. The *AVERAGE function* calculates the arithmetic mean, or average, for the values in a range of cells. You can use this function to calculate the class average on a biology test, or the average number of points scored per game by a basketball player. In Figure 2.12, =AVERAGE(A2:A14) returns 81.63636 as the average test score.

=AVERAGE(number 1,[number2], ...)

The **MEDIAN function** identifies the midpoint value in a set of values.

The *MEDIAN function* finds the midpoint value, which is the value that one half of the population is above or below. The median is particularly useful because extreme values often influence arithmetic mean calculated by the AVERAGE function. In Figure 2.12, the two extreme test scores of 50 distort the average. The rest of the test scores range from 80 to 98. The median for test scores is 86, which indicates that half the test scores are above 86 and half the test scores are below 86. This statistic is more reflective of the data set than the average is.

=MEDIAN(number 1,[number 2], ...)

Identify Low and High Values with MIN and MAX

The **MIN function** displays the lowest value in a range.

The **MIN function** analyzes an argument list to determine the lowest value, such as the lowest score on a test. Manually inspecting a range of values to identify the lowest value is inefficient, especially in large spreadsheets. If you change values in the range, the MIN function will identify the new lowest value and display it in the cell containing the MIN function. In Figure 2.12, =MIN(A2:A14) identifies that 50 is the lowest test score.

=MIN(number 1,[number 2],...)

The **MAX function** identifies the highest value in a range.

The **MAX function** analyzes an argument list to determine the highest value, such as the highest score on a test. Like the MIN function, when the values in the range change, the MAX function will display the new highest value within the range of cells. In Figure 2.12, =MAX(A2:A14) identifies 98 as the highest test score.

=MAX(number 1,[number 2],...)

 TIP Nonadjacent Ranges

You can use multiple ranges as arguments, such as finding the largest number within two nonadjacent (nonconsecutive) ranges. For example, you can find the highest test score where some scores are stored in cells A2:A14, and others are stored in cells K2:K14. Separate each range with a comma in the argument list, so that the formula is =MAX(A2:A14,K2:K14).

Identify the Total Number with COUNT Functions

The **COUNT function** tallies the number of cells in a range that contain values.

Excel provides three basic count functions: COUNT, COUNTBLANK and COUNTA to count the cells in a range that meet a particular criterion. The **COUNT function** tallies the number of cells in a range that contain values you can use in calculations, such as numerical and date data, but excludes blank cells or text entries from the tally. In Figure 2.12, the selected range spans 13 cells; however, the COUNT function returns 11, the number of cells that contain numerical data. It does not count the cell containing the text *N/A* or the blank cell.

The **COUNTBLANK function** tallies the number of blank cells in a range.

The **COUNTA function** tallies the number of cells in a range that are not empty.

The **COUNTBLANK function** tallies the number of cells in a range that are blank. In Figure 2.12, the COUNTBLANK function identifies that one cell in the range A2:A14 is blank. The **COUNTA function** tallies the number of cells in a range that are not blank, that is, cells that contain data whether a value, text, or a formula. In Figure 2.12, =COUNTA(A2:A14) returns 12, indicating the range A2:A14 contains 12 cells that contain some form of data. It does not count the blank cell.

=COUNT(number 1,[number 2],...)

=COUNTBLANK(number 1,[number 2],...)

=COUNTA(number 1,[number 2],...)

 TIP Average, Count, and Sum

When you select a range of cells containing values, by default Excel displays the average, count, and sum of those values on the status bar (see Figure 2.12). You can customize the status bar to show other selection statistics, such as the minimum and maximum values for a selected range. To display or hide particular selection statistics, right-click the status bar, and then select the statistic.

Use Other Math and Statistical Functions

In addition to the functions you have learned in this chapter, Excel provides over 100 other math and statistical functions. Table 2.2 lists and describes some of these functions that you might find helpful in your business, education, and general statistics courses.

TABLE 2.2 Math and Statistical Functions

Function Syntax	Description
=ABS(number)	Displays the absolute (i.e., positive) value of a number.
=FREQUENCY(data_array,bins_array)	Counts how often values appear in a given range.
=INT(number)	Rounds a value number down to the nearest whole number.
=MODE.SNGL(number1,[number2],...)	Displays the most frequently occurring value in a list.
=PI()	Returns the value of *pi* that is accurate up to 15 digits.
=PRODUCT(number1,[number2],...)	Multiplies all values within the argument list.
=RANDBETWEEN(bottom,top)	Generates a random number between two numbers you specify.
=RANK.AVG(number,ref,[order])	Identifies a value's rank within a list of values; returns an average rank for identical values.
=RANK.EQ(number,ref,[order])	Identifies a value's rank within a list of values; the top rank is identified for all identical values.
=ROUND(number,num_digits)	Rounds a value to a specific number of digits. Rounds numbers of 5 and greater up and those less than 5 down.
=SUMPRODUCT(array1,[array2],[array3],...)	Finds the result of multiplying values in one range by the related values in another column and then adding those products.
=TRIMMEAN(array,percent)	Returns the arithmetic average of the internal values in a range by excluding a specified percentage of values at the upper and lower values in the data set. This function helps reduce the effect outliers (i.e., extreme values) have on the arithmetic mean.
=TRUNC(number,[num_digits])	Returns the integer equivalent of a number by truncating or removing the decimal or fractional part of the number. For example, =TRUNC(45.5) returns 45.

 TIP ROUND vs. Decrease Decimal Points

When you click Decrease Decimal in the Number group to display fewer or no digits after a decimal point, Excel still stores the original value's decimal places so that those digits can be used in calculations. The ROUND function changes the stored value to its rounded state.

Using Date Functions

Because Excel treats dates as serial numbers, you can perform calculations using dates. For example, assume today is January 1, 2012, and you graduate on May 12, 2012. To determine how many days until graduation, subtract today's date from the graduation date. Excel uses the serial numbers for these dates (40909 and 41041) to calculate the difference of 132 days.

You can use date and time functions to calculate when employees are eligible for certain benefits, how many days it takes to complete a project, or if an account is 30, 60, or more days past due. The Reference table on the next page lists several popular date/time functions.

Insert the TODAY Function

The **TODAY function** displays the current date.

The ***TODAY function*** displays the current date in a cell. Excel updates the function results when you open or print the workbook. The function is expressed as =TODAY(). The TODAY() function does not require arguments, but you must include the parentheses for the function to work. If you omit the parentheses, Excel displays #NAME? in the cell with a green triangle in the top-left corner of the cell. When you click the cell, an error icon appears that you can click for more information.

Insert the NOW Function

The **NOW function** displays the current date and time.

The *NOW function* uses the computer's clock to display the current date and time you last opened the workbook, so the value will change every time the workbook is opened. Like the TODAY function, the NOW function does not require arguments, but you must include the parentheses. Omitting the parentheses creates a #NAME? error.

> **TIP** Update the Date and Time
>
> Both the TODAY and NOW functions display the date/time the workbook was last opened or last calculated. These functions do not continuously update the date and time while the workbook is open. To update the date and time, press F9 or click the Formulas tab, and then click Calculate now in the Calculation group.

REFERENCE Date/Time Functions

Function Syntax	Description	Example	Example Results
=TODAY()	Displays today's date: month, day, year.	=TODAY()	5/12/2012
=NOW()	Displays today's date and current military time.	=NOW()	5/12/2012 14:32
=DATE(year,month,day)	Returns the serial number for a date.	=DATE(2012,1,1)	40909 or 1/1/2012
=EDATE(start_date,months)	Displays the serial number of a date a specified number of months in the future or past.	=EDATE(DATE(2012, 1,1),6)	41091
=DAY(serial_number)	Displays the day within a month for a serial number (e.g., 41196 represents 10/14/2012). Entering 41196 as the DAY function argument returns 14 as the 14th day of the month.	=DAY(41196)	14
=EOMONTH(start_date, months)	Identifies the last day of a month a specified number of months from a serial number representing a date (e.g., 40915 represents 1/7/2012, 3 months is 4/7/2012, the last day of April is April 30, which is serial number 41029).	=EOMONTH(40915,3)	41029
=MONTH(serial_number)	Returns the month (1 to 12) for a serial number.	=MONTH(40945)	2
=NETWORKDAYS(start_date,end_date,[holidays])	Calculates the number of work days (excluding weekends and specified holidays) between two dates.	=NETWORKDAYS(40 915,41091,F9:F10)	124
=WEEKDAY(serial_number, [return_type])	Identifies the weekday (1 to 7) for a serial number.	=WEEKDAY(40915,1)	7
=WORKDAY(start_date, days,[holidays])	Calculates a serial number of a date a specified number of days before or after a particular date, excluding specified holidays.	=WORKDAY(41029, 25,E9:E11)	41065
=YEAR(serial_number)	Identifies the year for a serial number.	=YEAR(41029)	2012
=YEARFRAC(start_date, end_date,[basis])	Calculates the fraction of a year between two dates based on the number of whole days.	=YEARFRAC(40915, 41091)	0.483333333

2 Function Basics

The Denver Mortgage Company's worksheet contains an area in which you must enter summary statistics. In addition, you need to include today's date and identify what year each mortgage will be paid off.

Skills covered: Use the SUM Function • Use the AVERAGE Function • Use the MEDIAN Function • Use the MIN, MAX, and COUNT Functions • Use the TODAY and YEAR Functions

---

STEP 1 ▶ USE THE SUM FUNCTION

The first summary statistic you need to calculate is the total value of the houses bought by the borrowers. You will use the SUM function. Refer to Figure 2.13 as you complete Step 1.

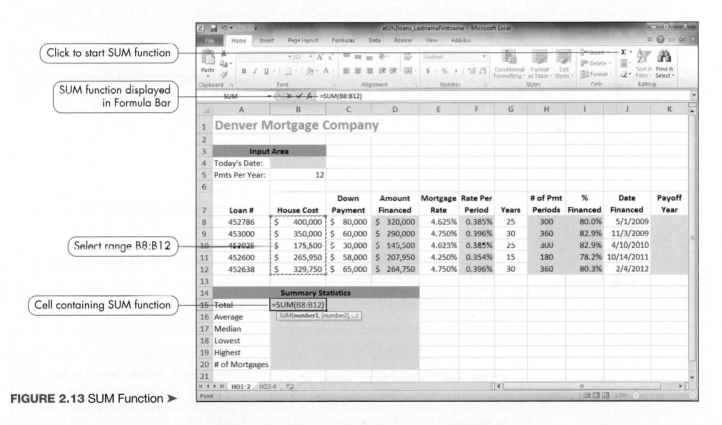

FIGURE 2.13 SUM Function ➤

a. Open *e02h1loans_LastnameFirstname* if you closed it at the end of Hands-On Exercise 1. Save the workbook with the new name **e02h2loans_LastnameFirstname**, changing *h1* to *h2*.

b. Click the **Home tab**, if needed, and then click **cell B15**, the cell where you will enter a formula for the total house cost.

c. Click **AutoSum** in the Editing group.

> **TROUBLESHOOTING:** Click the main part of the AutoSum command. If you click the AutoSum arrow, then select Sum.

Excel anticipates the range of cells containing values you want to sum based on where you enter the formula—in this case, A8:D14. This is not the correct range, so you must enter the correct range.

d. Select the **range B8:B12**, the cells containing house costs.

   As you use the semi-selection process, Excel enters the range in the SUM function.

> **TROUBLESHOOTING:** If you accidentally entered the function without changing the arguments, you can repeat steps b–d, or you can edit the arguments in the Formula Bar by deleting the default range, typing B8:B12 between the parentheses, and then pressing Enter.

e. Click **Enter** to the left of the Formula Bar, and then save the workbook.

   Cell B15 contains the function = SUM(B8:B12), and the result is $1,521,200.

STEP 2 USE THE AVERAGE FUNCTION

Before copying the functions to calculate the total down payments and amounts financed, you want to calculate the average value of houses bought by the borrowers. Refer to Figure 2.14 as you complete Step 2.

FIGURE 2.14 Select AVERAGE Function ➤

a. Click the **Formulas tab**, and then click **cell B16**, the cell where you will display the average cost of the houses.

b. Click the **AutoSum arrow** in the Function Library group, and then select **Average**.

   Excel anticipates cell B15, which is the total cost of the houses. You need to change the range.

> **TROUBLESHOOTING:** AutoSum, like some other commands in Excel, contains two parts: the main command icon and an arrow. Click the main command icon when instructed to click AutoSum to perform the default action. Click the arrow when instructed to click AutoSum arrow for additional options. If you accidentally clicked AutoSum instead of the arrow, press Esc to cancel the SUM function from being completed, and then try step b again.

c. Select the **range B8:B12**, the cells containing the house costs.

   The function is =AVERAGE(B8:B12).

d. Press **Enter** to complete the function and make **cell B17** the active cell, and then save the workbook.

   The average house cost is $304,240.

You realize that extreme values may distort the average. Therefore, you decide to identify the median value of houses bought to compare it to the average. Refer to Figure 2.15 as you complete Step 3.

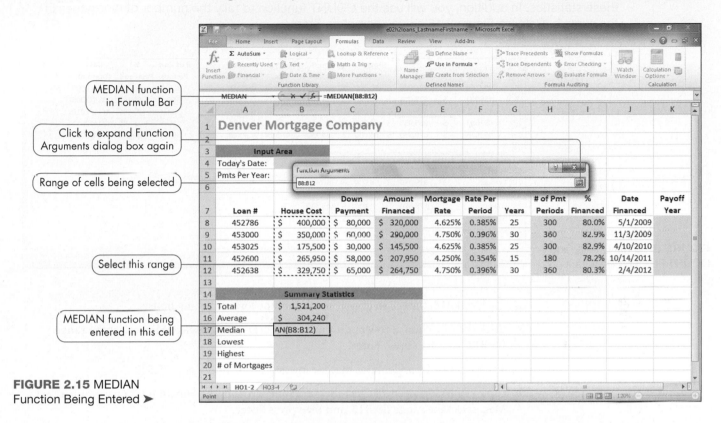

MEDIAN function in Formula Bar

Click to expand Function Arguments dialog box again

Range of cells being selected

Select this range

MEDIAN function being entered in this cell

FIGURE 2.15 MEDIAN Function Being Entered ➤

a. Make sure **cell B17** is the active cell. Click **Insert Function** to the left of the Formula Bar or in the Function Library group.

The Insert Function dialog box opens. Use this dialog box to select the MEDIAN function since it is not available on the Ribbon.

b. Type **median** in the **Search for a function box**, and then click **Go**.

Excel displays a list of possible functions in the *Select a function* list. The MEDIAN function is selected at the top of the list; the bottom of the dialog box displays the syntax and the description.

c. Read the MEDIAN function's description, and then click **OK**.

The Function Arguments dialog box opens. It contains one required argument, Number1, representing a range of cells containing values. It has an optional argument, Number2, which you can use if you have nonadjacent ranges that contain values.

d. Click the **collapse button** to the right of the Number1 box.

You collapsed the Function Arguments dialog box so that you can select the range.

e. Select the **range B8:B12**, and then click the **expand button** in the Function Arguments dialog box.

The Function Arguments dialog box expands again.

f. Click **OK** to accept the function arguments and close the dialog box. Save the workbook.

Half of the houses purchased cost over the median, $329,750, and half of the houses cost less than this value. Notice the difference between the median and the average: The average is lower because it is affected by the lowest-costing house, $175,500.

Erica wants to know the least and most expensive houses so that she can analyze typical customers of the Denver Mortgage Company. You will use the MIN and MAX functions to obtain these statistics. In addition, you will use the COUNT function to tally the number of mortgages in the sample. Refer to Figure 2.16 as you complete Step 4.

	Loan #	House Cost	Down Payment	Amount Financed	Mortgage Rate	Rate Per Period	Years	# of Pmt Periods	% Financed	Date Financed	Payoff Year
7											
8	452786	$ 400,000	$ 80,000	$ 320,000	4.625%	0.385%	25	300	80.0%	5/1/2009	
9	453000	$ 425,000	$ 60,000	$ 365,000	4.750%	0.396%	30	360	85.9%	11/3/2009	
10	453025	$ 175,500	$ 30,000	$ 145,500	4.625%	0.385%	25	300	82.9%	4/10/2010	
11	452600	$ 265,950	$ 58,000	$ 207,950	4.250%	0.354%	15	180	78.2%	10/14/2011	
12	452638	$ 329,750	$ 65,000	$ 264,750	4.750%	0.396%	30	360	80.3%	2/4/2012	
13											
14		Summary Statistics									
15	Total	$ 1,596,200	$ 293,000	$1,303,200							
16	Average	$ 319,240	$ 58,600	$ 260,640							
17	Median	$ 329,750	$ 60,000	$ 264,750							
18	Lowest	$ 175,500	$ 30,000	$ 145,500							
19	Highest	$ 425,000	$ 80,000	$ 365,000							
20	# of Mortgages	5	5	5							
21											

FIGURE 2.16 MIN, MAX, and COUNT Function Results ▶

a. Click **cell B18**, the cell to display the cost of the lowest-costing house.

b. Click the **AutoSum arrow** in the Function Library group, select **Min**, select the **range B8:B12**, and then press **Enter**.

The MIN function identifies that the lowest-costing house is $175,500.

c. Click **cell B19**, if needed. Click the **AutoSum arrow** in the Function Library group, select **Max**, select the **range B8:B12**, and then press **Enter**.

The MAX function identifies that the highest-costing house is $400,000.

d. Click **cell B20**, if needed. Type **=COUNT(B8:B12)** and press **Enter**.

As you type the letter *C*, Formula AutoComplete suggests functions starting with *C*. As you continue typing, the list of functions narrows. After you type the beginning parenthesis, Excel displays the function ScreenTip, indicating the arguments for the function. The range B8:B12 contains five cells.

e. Select the **range B15:B20**.

You want to select the range of original statistics to copy the cells all at one time to the next two columns.

f. Drag the fill handle to the right by two columns to copy the functions. Click **cell D20**.

Because you used relative cell references in the functions, the range changes from =COUNT(B8:B12) to =COUNT(D8:D12).

g. Change the value in **cell B9** to **425000**. Save the workbook.

The results of several formulas and functions change, including the total, average, and max house costs.

You have two date functions to enter to complete the first worksheet. Refer to Figure 2.17 as you complete Step 5.

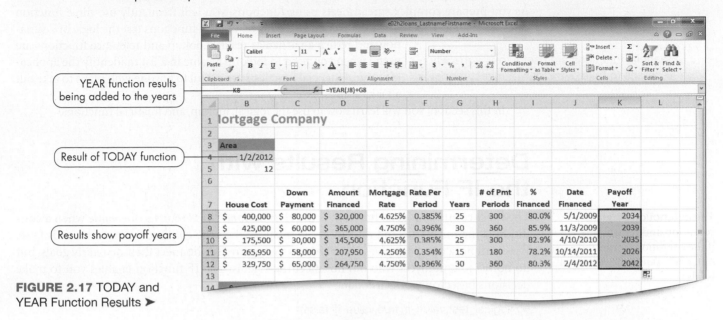

YEAR function results being added to the years

Result of TODAY function

Results show payoff years

FIGURE 2.17 TODAY and YEAR Function Results ➤

a. Click **cell B4**, the cell to contain the current date.

b. Click **Date & Time** in the Function Library group, select **TODAY** to display the Function Arguments dialog box, and then click **OK** to close the dialog box.

Excel inserts the current date in Short Date format, such as 1/2/2012, based on the computer system's date. The Function Arguments dialog box opens, although no arguments are necessary for this function.

c. Click **cell K8**, click **Date & Time** in the Function Library group, scroll through the list, and then select **YEAR**.

The Function Arguments dialog box opens so that you can enter the argument, a serial number for a date.

d. Click **cell J8** to enter it in the **Serial_number box**. Click **OK**.

The function returns 2009, the year the first mortgage was taken out. However, you want the year the mortgage will be paid off. The YEAR function returns the year from a date. You need to add the years to the result of the function to calculate the year that the borrower will pay off the mortgage.

e. Press **F2** to edit the formula stored in cell K8. With the insertion point on the right side of the closing parenthesis, type **+G8**, and then press **Ctrl+Enter**.

Pressing Ctrl+Enter is the alternative to clicking Enter by the Formula Bar. It keeps the current cell as the active cell. The results show a date: 7/26/1905. You need to apply the Number format to display the year.

f. Click the **Home tab**, click the **Number Format arrow** in the Number group, and then select **Number**. Decrease the number of decimal points to show the value as a whole number.

You applied the Number format instead of the Comma format because although the Comma format is correct for quantities, such as 2,034 units, it is not appropriate for the year 2034.

g. Copy the formula down the column.

h. Save the workbook. Keep the workbook onscreen if you plan to continue with Hands-On Exercise 3. If not, close the workbook and exit Excel.

Logical, Lookup, and Financial Functions

As you prepare complex spreadsheets using functions, you will frequently use three function categories: logical, lookup and reference, and finance. Logical functions test the logic of a situation and return a particular result. Lookup and reference functions are useful when you need to look up a value in a list to identify the applicable value. Financial functions are useful to anyone who plans to take out a loan or invest money.

> Financial functions are useful to anyone who plans to take out a loan or invest money.

In this section, you will learn how to use the logical, lookup, and financial functions.

Determining Results with the IF Function

> The **IF function** evaluates a condition and returns one value if the condition is true and a different value if the condition is false.

The most common logical function is the **IF function**, which returns one value when a condition is met or is true and returns another value when the condition is not met or is false. For example, a company gives a $500 bonus to employees who meet their quarterly goals, but no bonus to employees who did not meet their goals. The IF function enables you to make decisions based on worksheet data.

=IF(logical_test,value_if_true,value_if_false)

The IF function has three arguments: (1) a condition that is tested to determine if it is either true or false, (2) the resulting value if the condition is true, and (3) the resulting value if the condition is false.

Figure 2.18 lists several sample IF functions, how they are evaluated, and their results.

	A	B	C
1	Input Values		
2	$1,000		
3	$2,000		
4	10%		
5	5%		
6	$250		
7			
8			
9	**IF Function**	**Evaluation**	**Result**
10	=IF(A2=A3,A4,A5)	1000 is equal to 2000: FALSE	5%
11	=IF(A2<A3,A4,A5)	1000 is less than 2000: TRUE	10%
12	=IF(A2<A3,A5*A2,MAX(A3*A4,A6))	1000 is less than 2000: TRUE	$50
13	=IF(A2<>A3,"Not Equal","Equal")	1000 and 2000 are not equal: TRUE	Not Equal
14	=IF(A2*A4=A3*A5,A6,0)	100 (A2*A4) is equal to 100 (A3*A5): TRUE	$250

FIGURE 2.18 Sample IF Functions ➤

Design the Logical Test

> The **logical test** is an expression that evaluates to true or false.

The first argument for the IF function is the logical test. The **logical test** is a formula that contains either a value or an expression that evaluates to true or false. The logical expression is typically a binary expression, meaning that it requires a comparison between at least two variables, such as the values stored in cells A2 and A3. Table 2.3 lists and describes the logical operators to make the comparison in the logical test.

In Figure 2.18, the first logical test in cell A10 is A2=A3. The logical test compares the values in cells A2 and A3 to see if they are equal. The logical test in cell A14 is A2*A4=A3*A5. The value stored in cell A2 (1,000) is multiplied by the value in cell A4 (10%). The result (100) is then compared to the product of cell A3 (2,000) and cell A5 (5%), which is also 100. Note that the logical test can compare two cell references, or it can perform calculations and then compare the results of those calculations.

TABLE 2.3	Logical Operators
Operator	**Description**
=	Equal to
<>	Not equal to
<	Less than
>	Greater than
<=	Less than or equal to
>=	Greater than or equal to

 TIP Using Text in Formulas

You can use text within a formula. For example, to perform a logical test to see if the contents of a cell match text, the logical test would be: B5="Yes". When you compare text, you must surround the text with quotation marks.

Design the Value_If_True and Value_If_False Arguments

The second and third arguments of an IF function are value_if_true and value_if_false. When Excel evaluates the logical test, the result is either true or false. If the logical test evaluates to true, the value_if_true argument executes. If the logical test evaluates to false, the value_if_false argument executes. Only one of the last two arguments is executed; both arguments cannot be executed, since the logical test is either true or false but not both.

The value_if_true and value_if_false arguments can contain text, cell references, formulas, or constants (not recommended). In Figure 2.18, the value_if_true argument in cell A10 is A4, and the value_if_false argument is A5. Since the logical test (A2=A3) is false, the value_if_false argument is executed, and the result displays the same value that is stored in cell A5, which is 5%. In cell A13, the value_if_true argument is "Not Equal", and the value_if_false argument is "Equal". Since the logical test (A2<>A3) is true, the value_if_true argument is executed, and the result displays the text *Not Equal* in the cell containing the function. If you want the result of the function to be blank if a condition is met or not met, type "" (beginning and ending quotation marks).

Nest Basic Functions as Arguments

A **nested function** is a function that contains another function embedded inside one or more of its arguments.

A ***nested function*** occurs when one function is embedded as an argument within another function. For example, within the function in cell A12 in Figure 2.18, the MAX function is nested in the value_if_false argument of the IF function. Nesting functions enables you to create more complex formulas to handle a variety of situations. In this situation, if the logical test evaluates to false, the value_if_false argument of MAX(A3*A4,A6) would execute. Excel would find the product of A3 and A4 and return the higher of that value (200) or the contents of cell A6 (250). You can even nest functions as part of the logical test or value_if_true argument.

In addition to nesting functions within the IF function, you can nest functions within other functions, such as =SUM(MIN(A1:A5),D10:D15). The nested MIN function identifies the lowest value in the range A1:A5 and adds that value to those stored in the range D10:D15.

Using Lookup Functions

You can use lookup and reference functions to look up values to perform calculations or display results. For example, when you order merchandise on a Web site, the Web server looks up the shipping costs based on weight and distance, or at the end of a semester, your professor uses your numerical average, such as 88%, to look up the letter grade to assign, such as B+.

Create the Lookup Table

A **lookup table** is a range that contains data for the basis of the lookup and data to be retrieved.

Before you insert lookup functions, you need to create a lookup table. A *lookup table* is a range containing a table of values or text that can be retrieved. The table should contain at least two rows and two columns, not including headings. It is important to plan the table so that it conforms to the way in which Excel can utilize the data in it.

Excel cannot interpret the structure of Table 2.4. To look up a value in a range (such as the range 80–89), you must arrange data from the lowest to the highest value and include only the lowest value in the range (such as 80) instead of the complete range. If the values you look up are *exact* values, you can arrange the first column in any logical order. The lowest value for a category or in a series is the *breakpoint*. The first column contains the breakpoints—such as 60, 70, 80, and 90—or the lowest values to achieve a particular grade. The lookup table contains one or more additional columns of related data to retrieve. Table 2.5 shows how to construct the lookup table in Excel.

The **breakpoint** is the lowest value for a specific category or series in a lookup table.

TABLE 2.4 Grading Scale	
Range	Grade
90–100	A
80–89	B
70–79	C
60–69	D
Below 60	F

TABLE 2.5 Grades Lookup Table	
Range	Grade
0	F
60	D
70	C
80	B
90	A

Understand the VLOOKUP Function Syntax

The **VLOOKUP function** looks up a value in a vertical lookup table and returns a related result from the lookup table.

The *VLOOKUP function* accepts a value, looks the value up in a vertical lookup table, and returns a result. Use VLOOKUP to search for exact matches or for the nearest value that is less than or equal to the search value, such as assigning a B grade for an 87% class average. The VLOOKUP function has the following three required arguments and one optional argument: (1) lookup_value, (2) table_array, (3) col_index_number, and (4) range_lookup.

=VLOOKUP(lookup_value,table_array,col_index_number,[range_lookup])

Figure 2.19 shows a partial grade book that contains a vertical lookup table, as well as the final scores and letter grades. The function in cell F3 is =VLOOKUP(E3,$A$3:$B$7,2).

F3			f_x =VLOOKUP(E3,$A$3:$B$7,2)			
	A	B	C	D	E	F	G
1	Grading Scale			Partial Gradebook			
2	Breakpoint	Grade		Names	Final Score	Letter Grade	
3	0	F		Abbott	85	B	
4	60	D		Carter	69	D	
5	70	C		Hon	90	A	
6	80	B		Jackson	74	C	
7	90	A		Miller	80	B	
8				Nelsen	78	C	

FIGURE 2.19 VLOOKUP Function for Grade Book ➤

The **lookup value** is a reference to a cell containing a value to look up.

The **table array** is a range containing a lookup table.

The **column index number** is the argument in a VLOOKUP function that identifies which lookup table column from which to return a value.

The *lookup value* is the cell reference of the cell that contains the value to look up. The lookup value for the first student is cell E3, which contains 85. The *table array* is the range that contains the lookup table: $A$3:$B$7. The table array range must be absolute and cannot include column labels for the lookup table. The *column index number* is the column number in the lookup table that contains the return values. In this example, the column index number is 2.

> **TIP** Using Values in Formulas
>
> You know to avoid values in formulas because values might change. However, notice that the value 2 is the col_index_number argument of the VLOOKUP function. The value 2 refers to a particular column within the lookup table and is an acceptable use of a number within a formula.

Understand How Excel Processes the Lookup

The VLOOKUP function identifies the value stored in the lookup value argument and then searches the first column of the lookup table until it finds an exact match (if possible). If Excel finds an exact match, it returns the value stored in the column designated by the column index number on that same row. If the table contains breakpoints for ranges rather than exact matches, Excel identifies the correct range based on comparing the lookup value to the breakpoints in the first column. If the lookup value is larger than the breakpoint, it looks to the next breakpoint to see if the lookup value is larger than that breakpoint also. When Excel detects that the lookup value is not greater than the next breakpoint, it stays on that row. It then uses the column index number to identify the column containing the value to return for the lookup value. Because Excel goes sequentially through the breakpoints, it is mandatory that the breakpoints are arranged from the lowest value to the highest value for ranges.

For example, the VLOOKUP function to assign letter grades works like this: Excel identifies the lookup value (85 stored in cell E3) and compares it to the values in the first column of the lookup table (stored in cells A3:B7). It tries to find an exact match for the value 85; however, the table contains breakpoints rather than every conceivable numeric average. Because the lookup table is arranged from the lowest to the highest breakpoints, Excel detects that 85 is greater than the 80 breakpoint but is not greater than the 90 breakpoint. Therefore, it stays on the 80 row. Excel then looks at the column index number of 2 and returns the letter grade of B, which is located in the second column of the lookup table. The returned grade of B is then stored in cell F3, which contains the VLOOKUP function.

Instead of looking up values in a range, you can look up a value for an exact match using the optional range_lookup argument in the VLOOKUP function. By default, the range_lookup is set implicitly to TRUE, which is appropriate to look up values in a range. However, to look up an exact match, you must specify FALSE in the range_lookup argument. For example, if you are looking up product numbers, you must find an exact match to display the price. The function would look like this: =VLOOKUP(D15,$A$1:$B$50,2,FALSE). The VLOOKUP function returns a value for the first lookup value that matches the first column of the lookup table. If no exact match is found, the function returns #N/A.

Use the HLOOKUP Function

The **HLOOKUP function** looks up a value in a horizontal lookup table where the first row contains the values to compare with the lookup value.

You can design your lookup table horizontally, so that the first row contains the values for the basis of the lookup or the breakpoints, and additional rows contain data to be retrieved. With a horizontal lookup table, you must use the *HLOOKUP function*. Table 2.6 shows how the grading scale would look as a horizontal lookup table.

TABLE 2.6	Horizontal Lookup Table			
0	60	70	80	90
F	D	C	B	A

The syntax is almost the same as the syntax for the VLOOKUP function, except the third argument is row_index_number instead of col_index_number.

=HLOOKUP(lookup_value,table_array,row_index_number,[range_lookup])

Calculating Payments with the PMT Function

Excel contains several financial functions to help you perform calculations with monetary values. If you take out a loan to purchase a car, you need to know the monthly payment, which depends on the price of the car, the down payment, and the terms of the loan, in order to determine if you can afford the car. The decision is made easier by developing the worksheet in Figure 2.20 and then by changing the various input values as indicated.

	B9		f_x	=PMT(B6,B8,-B3)	
	A	B	C	D
1	Purchase Price	$25,999.00		
2	Down Payment	$ 5,000.00		
3	Amount to Finance	$20,999.00		
4	Payments per Year	12		
5	Interest Rate (APR)	5.250%		
6	Periodic Rate (Monthly)	0.438%		
7	Term (Years)	5		
8	No. of Payment Periods	60		
9	Monthly Payment	$ 398.69		
10				

FIGURE 2.20 Car Loan Worksheet ➤

Creating a loan model helps you evaluate your options. You realize that the purchase of a $25,999 car is prohibitive because the monthly payment is almost $398.69. Purchasing a less expensive car, coming up with a substantial down payment, taking out a longer term loan, or finding a better interest rate can decrease your monthly payments.

The **PMT function** calculates the periodic payment for a loan with a fixed interest rate and fixed term.

The ***PMT function*** calculates payments for a loan with a fixed amount at a fixed periodic rate for a fixed time period. The PMT function uses up to five arguments, three of which are required and two of which are optional: (1) rate, (2) nper, (3) pv, (4) fv, and (5) type.

=PMT(rate,nper,pv,[fv],[type])

The **rate** is the periodic interest rate, such as a monthly interest rate.

The ***rate*** is the periodic interest rate, the interest rate per payment period. If the annual percentage rate (APR) is 12% and you make monthly payments, the periodic rate is 1% (12%/12 months). With the same APR and quarterly payments, the periodic rate is 3% (12%/4 quarters). Divide the APR by the number of payment periods in one year. However, instead of dividing the APR by 12 within the PMT function, calculate the periodic interest rate in cell B6 in Figure 2.20 and use that calculated rate in the PMT function.

The **nper** is the number of total payment periods.

The ***nper*** is the total number of payment periods. The term of a loan is usually stated in years; however, you make several payments per year. For monthly payments, you make 12 payments per year. To calculate the nper, multiply the number of years by the number of payments in one year. Instead of calculating the number of payment periods in the PMT function, calculate the number of payment periods in cell B8 and use that calculated value in the PMT function.

The **pv** is the present value of the loan.

The ***pv*** is the present value of the loan. The result of the PMT function is a negative value because it represents your debt. However, you can display the result as a positive value by typing a minus sign in front of the present value cell reference in the PMT function.

3 Logical, Lookup, and Financial Functions

Erica wants you to complete a similar model that she might use for future mortgage data analysis. As you study the model, you realize you need to incorporate logical, lookup, and financial functions.

Skills covered: Use the VLOOKUP Function • Use the PMT Function • Use the IF Function

---

STEP 1 ▷ USE THE VLOOKUP FUNCTION

Rates vary based on the number of years to pay off the loan. Erica created a lookup table for three common mortgage years, and she entered the current APR. The lookup table will provide efficiency later when the rates change. You will use the VLOOKUP function to display the correct rate for each customer based on the number of years of the respective loans. Refer to Figure 2.21 as you complete Step 1.

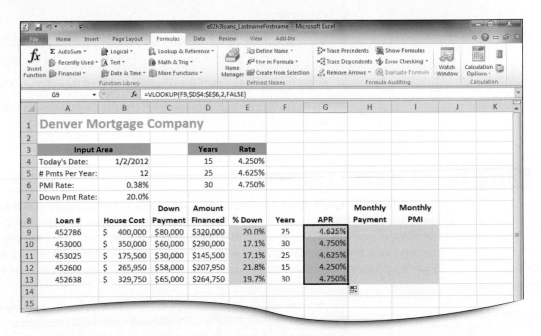

FIGURE 2.21 VLOOKUP Function ▶

a. Open *e02h2loans_LastnameFirstname* if you closed it at the end of Hands-On Exercise 2. Save the workbook with the new name **e02h3loans_LastnameFirstname**, changing *h2* to *h3*.

b. Click the **HO3-4 worksheet tab** to display the worksheet containing the data to complete. Click **cell G9**, the cell that will store the APR for the first customer.

c. Click the **Formulas tab**, click **Lookup & Reference** in the Function Library group, and then select **VLOOKUP**.

   The Function Arguments dialog box opens. You need to enter the three required and one optional argument.

d. Click **F9** to enter F9 in the **Lookup_value box**.

   Cell F9 contains the value you need to look up from the table: 25 years.

> **TROUBLESHOOTING:** If you cannot see the cell you need to use in an argument, click the Function Arguments dialog box title bar, and drag the dialog box on the screen until you can see and click the cell you need for the argument.

e. Press **Tab**, and then select the **range D4:E6** in the **Table_array box**.

This is the range that contains that data for the lookup table. The Years values in the table are arranged in ascending order (from lowest to highest). Do not select the column headings for the range. Anticipate what will happen if you copy the formula down the column. What do you need to do to ensure that the cell references always point to the exact location of the table? If your answer is to make the table array cell references absolute, then you answered correctly.

f. Press **F4** to make the range references absolute.

The Table_array box now contains $D$4:$E$6.

g. Press **Tab**, and then type **2** in the **Col_index_num box**.

The second column of the lookup table contains the APRs that you want to return and display in the cells containing the formulas.

h. Press **Tab**, and then type **False** in the **Range_lookup box**.

You want the formula to display an error if an incorrect number of years has been entered. To ensure an exact match to look up in the table, you enter *False* in the optional argument.

i. Click **OK**.

The VLOOKUP function looks up the first person's years (25), finds an exact match in the first column of the lookup table, and then returns the corresponding APR, which is 4.625%.

j. Copy the formula down the column, and then save the workbook.

Spot check the results to make sure the function returned the correct APR based on the number of years.

STEP 2 ▸ **USE THE PMT FUNCTION**

The worksheet now has all the necessary data for you to calculate the monthly payment for each loan: the APR, the number of years for the loan, the number of payment periods in one year, and the initial loan amount. You will use the PMT function to calculate the monthly payment, which includes paying back the principal amount with interest. This calculation does not include escrow amounts, such as property taxes or insurance. Refer to Figure 2.22 as you complete Step 2.

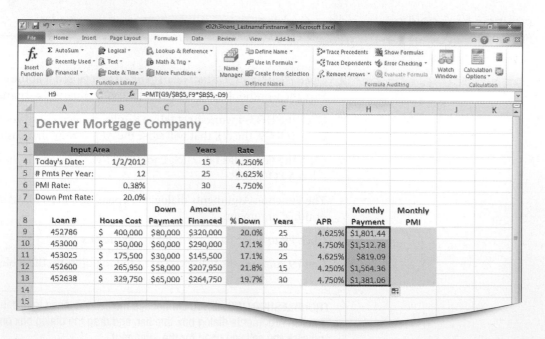

FIGURE 2.22 PMT Function ➤

a. Click **cell H9**, the cell that will store the payment for the first customer.

b. Click **Financial** in the Function Library group, scroll through the list, and then select **PMT**.

> **TROUBLESHOOTING:** Make sure you select PMT, not PPMT. The PPMT function calculates the principal portion of a particular monthly payment, not the total monthly payment itself.

The Function Arguments dialog box opens. You need to enter the three required arguments.

c. Type **G9/B5** in the **Rate box**.

Before going on to the next argument, think about what will happen if you copy the formula. The argument will be G10/B6 for the next customer. Are those cell references correct? G10 does contain the APR for the next customer, but B6 does not contain the correct number of payments in one year. Therefore, you need to make B5 an absolute cell reference because the number of payments per year does not vary.

d. Press **F4** to make the reference absolute.

e. Press **Tab**, and then type **F9*$B$5** in the **Nper box**.

You calculate the nper by multiplying the number of years by the number of payments in one year. Again, you must make B5 an absolute cell reference so that it does not change when you copy the formula down the column.

f. Press **Tab**, and then type **-D9** in the **Pv box**.

The bottom of the dialog box indicates that the monthly payment is 1801.444075 or $1,801.44.

> **TROUBLESHOOTING:** If the payment displays as a negative value, you probably forgot to type the minus sign in front of the D9 reference in the Pv box. Edit the function, and type the minus sign in the correct place.

g. Click **OK**. Copy the formula down the column, and then save the workbook.

STEP 3 ▶ USE THE IF FUNCTION

Lenders often want borrowers to have a 20% down payment. If borrowers do not put in 20% of the cost of the house as a down payment, they pay a private mortgage insurance (PMI) fee. PMI serves to protect lenders from absorbing loss if the borrower defaults on the loan, and it enables borrowers with less cash to secure a loan. The PMI fee is about 0.38% of the amount financed. Some borrowers have to pay PMI for a few months or years until the balance owed is less than 80% of the appraised value. The worksheet contains the necessary values input area. You need to use the IF function to determine which borrowers must pay PMI and how much they will pay. Refer to Figure 2.23 as you complete Step 3.

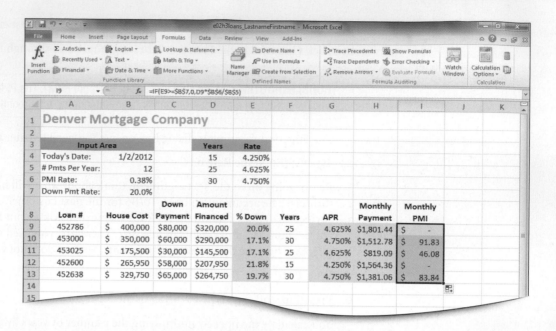

FIGURE 2.23 IF Function ➤

a. Click **cell I9**, the cell that will store the PMI, if any, for the first customer.

b. Click **Logical** in the Function Library group, and then select **IF**.

The Function Arguments dialog box opens. You need to enter the three arguments.

c. Type **E9>=$B$7** in the **Logical_test box**.

The logical test compares the down payment percentage to see if the customer's down payment is at least 20%, the threshold stored in B7, of the amount financed. The customer's percentage cell reference needs to be relative so that it will change when you copy it down the column; however, cell B7 must be absolute because it contains the threshold value.

d. Press **Tab**, and then type **0** in the **Value_if_true box**.

If the customer makes a down payment that is at least 20% of the purchase price, the customer does not pay PMI. The first customer paid 20% of the purchase price, so he or she does not have to pay PMI.

e. Press **Tab**, and then type **D9*$B$6/$B$5** in the **Value_if_false box**.

If the logical test is false, the customer must pay PMI, which is calculated by dividing the yearly PMI (0.38%) by 12 and multiplying the result by the amount financed.

f. Click **OK**, and then copy the formula down the column.

The second, third, and fifth customers must pay PMI because their respective down payments were less than 20% of the purchase price.

> **TROUBLESHOOTING:** If the results are not as you expected, check the logical operators. People often mistype < and > or forget to type = for >= situations. Correct any errors in the original formula, and then copy the formula again.

g. Save the workbook. Keep the workbook onscreen if you plan to continue with Hands-On Exercise 4. If not, close the workbook and exit Excel.

Range Names

A **range name** is a word or string of characters that represents one or more cells.

To simplify entering ranges in formulas, you can use range names. A ***range name*** is a word or string of characters assigned to one or more cells. Think of range names in this way: Your college identifies you by your student ID; however, your professors call you by an easy-to-remember name, such as Micah or Kristin. Similarly, instead of using cell addresses, you can use descriptive range names in formulas. Going back to the VLOOKUP example shown in Figure 2.19, you can assign the range name *Grades* to cells A3:B7 and then modify the VLOOKUP function to be =VLOOKUP(E3,Grades,2), using the range name *Grades* in the formula. Another benefit of using range names is that they are absolute references, which helps ensure accuracy in your calculations.

In this section, you will work with range names. First, you will learn how to create and maintain range names. Then you will learn how to use a range name in a formula.

Creating and Maintaining Range Names

Before you can use a range name in a formula, you must first create the name. Each range name within a workbook must be unique. For example, you can't assign the name *COST* to ranges on several worksheets or on the same sheet.

After you create a range name, you might need to change its name or change the range of cells. If you no longer need a range name, you can delete it. You can also insert a list of range names and their respective cell ranges for reference.

Create a Range Name

A range name can contain up to 255 characters, but it must begin with a letter or an underscore. You can use a combination of upper- or lowercase letters, numbers, periods, and underscores throughout the range name. A range name cannot include spaces or special characters. You should create range names that describe the range of cells being named, but names cannot be identical to the cell contents. Keep the range names relatively short to make them easier to use in formulas. Table 2.7 lists acceptable and unacceptable range names.

TABLE 2.7 Range Names	
Name	**Description**
Grades	Acceptable range name
COL	Acceptable abbreviation for cost-of-living
Tax_Rate	Acceptable name with underscore
Commission Rate	Unacceptable name; can't use spaces in names
Discount Rate %	Unacceptable name; can't use special symbols and spaces
2009_Rate	Unacceptable name; can't start with a number
Rate_2012	Acceptable name with underscore and numbers

To create a range name, select the range of cells you want to name, and do one of the following:

- Click in the Name Box, type the range name, and then press Enter.
- Click the Formulas tab, click Define Name in the Defined Names group to open the New Name dialog box (see Figure 2.24), type the range name in the Name box, and then click OK.
- Click the Formulas tab, click Name Manager in the Defined Names group to open the Name Manager dialog box, click New, type the range name in the Name box, click OK, and then click Close.

FIGURE 2.24 New Name
Dialog Box ➤

You can create several range names at the same time if your worksheet already includes ranges with values and descriptive labels. To do this, select the range of cells containing the labels that you want to become names and the cells that contain the values to name, click Create from Selection in the Defined Named group on the Formulas tab, and then select an option in the Create Names from Selection dialog box (see Figure 2.25).

FIGURE 2.25 Create Names
from Selection Dialog Box ➤

Edit or Delete a Range Name

You can use the Name Manager dialog box to edit existing range names, delete range names, and create new range names. To open the Name Manager dialog box shown in Figure 2.26, click Name Manager in the Defined Names group on the Formulas tab. To edit a range or range name, click the range name in the list, and then click Edit. In the Edit Name dialog box, make your edits, and then click OK.

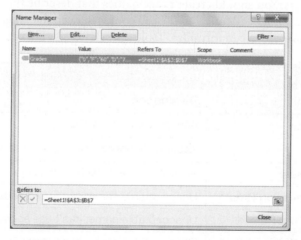

FIGURE 2.26 Name Manager
Dialog Box ➤

To delete a range name, open the Name Manager dialog box, select the name you want to delete, click Delete, and then click OK in the confirmation message box.

If you change a range name, any formulas that use the range name reflect the new name automatically. For example, if a formula contains =cost*rate and you change the name rate to tax_rate, Excel updates the formula to be =cost*tax_rate. If you delete a range name and a formula depends on that range name, Excel displays #NAME?—indicating an Invalid Name Error.

Insert a Table of Range Names

Documentation is an important part of good spreadsheet design. People often document workbooks with date or time stamps that indicate the last date of revision, notes describing how to use a workbook, and so on. One way to document a workbook is to insert a list of range names in a worksheet. To insert a list of range names, click *Use in Formula* in the Defined Names group on the Formulas tab, and then select Paste Names. The Paste Name dialog box opens (see Figure 2.27), listing all range names in the current workbook. Click Paste List to insert a list of range names in alphabetical order. The first column contains a list of range names, and the second column contains the worksheet names and range locations.

FIGURE 2.27 Paste Name Dialog Box and List of Range Names ➤

> **TIP** List of Range Names
>
> When you paste range names, the list will overwrite any existing data in a worksheet, so consider pasting the list in a separate worksheet. If you add, edit, or delete range names, the list does not update automatically. To keep the list current, you would need to paste the list again.

Using Range Names in Formulas

You can use range names in formulas instead of cell references. For example, if cell C15 contains a purchase amount, and cell C5 contains the sales tax rate, instead of typing =C15*C5, you can type the range names in the formula, such as =purchase*tax_rate. When you type a formula, Formula AutoComplete displays a list of range names, as well as functions, that start with the letters as you type (see Figure 2.28). Double-click the range name to insert it in the formula.

Indicates range name

Part of range name being entered

Indicates function

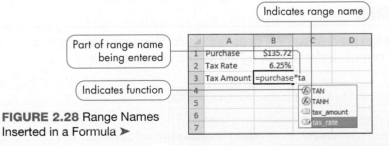

FIGURE 2.28 Range Names Inserted in a Formula ➤

Another benefit of using range names is that if you have to copy the formula, you do not have to make the cell reference absolute in the formula. Furthermore, if you share your workbook with others, range names in formulas help others understand what values are used in the calculations.

> **TIP** Go to a Range Name
>
> Use the Go To dialog box to go to the top-left cell in a range specified by a range name.

HANDS-ON EXERCISES

4 Range Names

You decide to simplify the VLOOKUP function by using a range name for the lookup table instead of the actual cell references. After creating a range name, you will modify some range names Erica created, and then create a list of range names.

Skills covered: Create a Range Name • Edit and Delete Range Names • Use a Range Name in a Formula • Insert a List of Range Names

STEP 1 ▶ CREATE A RANGE NAME

You want to assign a range name to the lookup table of years and APRs. Refer to Figure 2.29 as you complete Step 1.

FIGURE 2.29 Range Name ➤

a. Open *e02h3loans_LastnameFirstname* if you closed it at the end of Hands-On Exercise 3. Save the workbook with the new name **e02h4loans_LastnameFirstname**, changing *h3* to *h4*.

b. Make sure the **HO3-4 worksheet tab** is active. Select **range D4:E6** (the lookup table).

c. Type **Rates** in the **Name Box**, and then press **Enter**. Save the workbook.

STEP 2 ▶ EDIT AND DELETE RANGE NAMES

You noticed that Erica added some range names. You will open the Name Manager dialog box to view and make changes to the range names. Refer to Figure 2.30 as you complete Step 2.

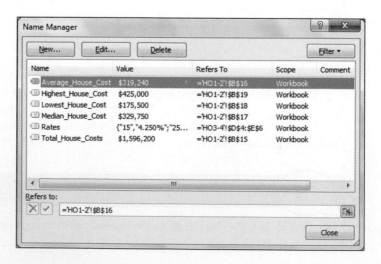

FIGURE 2.30 Updated Range Names ➤

a. Click **Name Manager** in the Defined Names group.

The Name Manager dialog box opens. The first name is *Avg_Cost*. You want to rename it to have a naming structure consistent with the other Cost names, such as Total_House_Costs.

b. Select **Avg_Cost**, and then click **Edit** to open the Edit Name dialog box.

c. Type **Average_House_Cost** in the **Name box**, and then click **OK**.

d. Select **Title** in the Name Manager dialog box.

This range name applies to a cell containing text, which does not need a name as it cannot be used in calculations. You decide to delete the range name.

e. Click **Delete**, read the warning message box, and then click **OK** to confirm the deletion of the Title range name.

f. Click **Close**, and then save the workbook.

STEP 3 ▶ USE A RANGE NAME IN A FORMULA

You will modify the VLOOKUP function by replacing the existing Table_array argument with the range name. This will help Erica interpret the VLOOKUP function. Refer to Figure 2.31 as you complete Step 3.

FIGURE 2.31 Range Name in Formula ➤

a. Click **cell G9**, the cell containing the VLOOKUP function.

b. Click **Insert Function** between the Name Box and the Formula Bar to open the Function Arguments dialog box.

The Table_array argument contains $D$4:$E$6, the absolute reference to the lookup table.

c. Select **$D$4:$E$6** in the **Table_array box**, type **Rates**, and then click **OK**.

The new function is =VLOOKUP(F9,Rates,2,FALSE).

d. Copy the updated formula down the column, and then save the workbook.

The results are the same as they were when you used the absolute cell references. However, the formulas are shorter and easier to read with the range names.

Before submitting the completed workbook to Erica, you want to create a documentation worksheet that lists all of the range names in the workbook. Refer to Figure 2.32 as you complete Step 4.

List of range names

Select this option

FIGURE 2.32 List of Range Names ➤

a. Click **Insert Worksheet** to the right of the worksheet tabs, and then double-click the default sheet name, **Sheet1**. Type **Range Names** and press **Enter**.

You inserted and renamed the new worksheet to reflect the data you will add to it.

b. Type **Range Names** in **cell A1**, and then type **Location** in **cell B1**. Bold these headings.

These column headings will appear above the list of range names.

c. Click **cell A2**, click **Use in Formula** in the Defined Names group on the Formulas tab, and then select **Paste Names**.

The Paste Name dialog box opens, displaying all of the range names in the workbook.

d. Click **Paste List**.

Excel pastes an alphabetical list of range names starting in cell A2. The second column displays the locations of the range names.

e. Increase the widths of columns A and B to fit the data.

f. Save and close the workbook, and submit based on your instructor's directions.

CHAPTER OBJECTIVES REVIEW

After reading this chapter, you have accomplished the following objectives:

1. **Use semi-selection to create a formula.** Semi-selection is a pointing process where you click or drag to select cells to add cell references to a formula.

2. **Use relative, absolute, and mixed cell references in formulas.** Cell references within formulas are relative, absolute, or mixed. A relative reference indicates a cell's location relative to the formula cell. When you copy the formula, the relative cell reference changes. An absolute reference is a permanent pointer to a particular cell, indicated with dollar signs before the column letter and row number, such as $B$5. When you copy the formula, the absolute cell reference does not change. A mixed reference contains part absolute and part relative reference, such as $B5 or B$5. Depending on the type of relative reference, either the column or row reference changes while the other remains constant when you copy the formula.

3. **Avoid circular references.** A circular reference occurs when a formula refers to the cell containing the formula. The status bar indicates the location of a circular reference. You should correct circular references to prevent inaccurate results.

4. **Insert a function.** A function is a predefined formula that performs a calculation. It contains the function name and arguments. Formula AutoComplete, function ScreenTips, and the Insert Function dialog box help you select and create functions. The Function Arguments dialog box guides you through entering requirements for each argument.

5. **Total values with the SUM function.** The SUM function calculates the total of a range of values. The syntax is =SUM(number1,[number2],...) where the arguments are cell references to one or more ranges.

6. **Insert basic statistical functions.** The AVERAGE function calculates the arithmetic mean of values in a range. The MEDIAN function identifies the midpoint value in a set of values. The MIN function identifies the lowest value in a range, whereas the MAX function identifies the highest value in a range. The COUNT function tallies the number of cells in a range, whereas the COUNTBLANK function tallies the number of blank cells in a range. Excel contains other math and statistical functions, such as FREQUENCY and MODE.

7. **Use date functions.** The TODAY function displays the current date, and the NOW function displays the current date and time. Other date functions identify a particular day of the week, identify the number of net working days between two dates, and display a serial number representing a date.

8. **Determine results with the IF function.** The IF function is a logical function that evaluates a logical test using logical operators, such as <, >, and =, and returns one value if the condition is true and another value if the condition is false. The value_if_true and value_if_false arguments can contain cell references, text, or calculations. You can nest or embed other functions inside one or more of the arguments of an IF function to create more complex formulas.

9. **Use lookup functions.** The VLOOKUP function looks up a value for a particular record, compares it to a lookup table, and returns a result in another column of the lookup table. Design the lookup table using exact values or the breakpoints for ranges. If an exact match is required, the optional fourth argument should be FALSE; otherwise, the fourth argument can remain empty. The HLOOKUP function looks up values by row (horizontally) rather than by column (vertically).

10. **Calculate payments with the PMT function.** The PMT function calculates periodic payments for a loan with a fixed interest rate and a fixed term. The PMT function requires the periodic interest rate, the total number of payment periods, and the original value of the loan. You can use the PMT function to calculate monthly car or mortgage payments.

11. **Create and maintain range names.** A range name is a descriptive name that corresponds with one or more cells. A range name may contain letters, numbers, and underscores, but must start with either a letter or an underscore. The quick way to create a range name is to select the range, type the name in the Name Box, and then press Enter. Use the Name Manager dialog box to edit, create, or delete range names. You can insert a list of range names on a worksheet.

12. **Use range names in formulas.** You can use range names in formulas instead of cell references. Range names are absolute and can make your formula easier to interpret by using a descriptive name for the value(s) contained in a cell or range.

KEY TERMS

Absolute cell reference *p.375*	Formula AutoComplete *p.382*	MEDIAN function *p.385*	Range name *p.403*
Argument *p.382*	Function *p.382*	MIN function *p.386*	Rate *p.398*
AVERAGE function *p.385*	Function ScreenTip *p.383*	Mixed cell reference *p.375*	Relative cell reference *p.375*
Breakpoint *p.396*	HLOOKUP function *p.397*	Nested function *p.395*	Semi-selection *p.374*
Circular reference *p.376*	IF function *p.394*	NOW function *p.388*	SUM function *p.384*
Column index number *p.397*	Logical test *p.394*	Nper *p.398*	Syntax *p.382*
COUNT function *p.386*	Lookup table *p.396*	PMT function *p.398*	Table array *p.397*
COUNTA function *p.386*	Lookup value *p.397*	Pointing *p.374*	TODAY function *p.387*
COUNTBLANK function *p.386*	MAX function *p.386*	Pv *p.398*	VLOOKUP function *p.396*

1. If cell D15 contains the formula =$C$5*D15, what is the D15 in the formula?

   (a) Mixed reference

   (b) Absolute reference

   (c) Circular reference

   (d) Range name

2. What function would most appropriately accomplish the same thing as =(B5+C5+D5+E5+F5)/5?

   (a) =SUM(B5:F5)/5

   (b) =AVERAGE(B5:F5)

   (c) =MEDIAN(B5:F5)

   (d) =COUNT(B5:F5)

3. When you type a function, what appears after you type the opening parenthesis?

   (a) Function ScreenTip

   (b) Formula AutoComplete

   (c) Insert Function dialog box

   (d) Function Arguments dialog box

4. A formula containing the entry =$B3 is copied to a cell one column to the right and two rows down. How will the entry appear in its new location?

   (a) =$B3

   (b) =B3

   (c) =$C5

   (d) =$B5

5. Cell B10 contains a date, such as 1/1/2012. Which formula will determine how many days are between that date and the current date, given that the cell containing the formula is formatted with Number Format?

   (a) =TODAY()

   (b) =CURRENT()-B10

   (c) =TODAY()-B10

   (d) =TODAY()+NOW()

6. Given that cells A1, A2, and A3 contain values 2, 3, and 10, respectively, and B6, C6, and D6 contain values 10, 20, and 30, respectively, what value will be returned by the function =IF(B6>A3,C6*A1,D6*A2)?

   (a) 10

   (b) 40

   (c) 60

   (d) 90

7. Given the function =VLOOKUP(C6,D12:F18,3), the entries in:

   (a) Range D12:D18 are in ascending order.

   (b) Range D12:D18 are in descending order.

   (c) The third column of the lookup table must be text only.

   (d) Range D12:D18 contain multiple values in each cell.

8. The function =PMT(C5,C7,-C3) is stored in cell C15. What must be stored in cell C7?

   (a) APR

   (b) Periodic interest rate

   (c) Loan amount

   (d) Number of payment periods

9. Which of the following is not an appropriate use of the SUM function?

   (a) =SUM(D15-C15)

   (b) =SUM(F1:G10)

   (c) =SUM(A8:A15,D8:D15)

   (d) =SUM(B3:B45)

10. Which of the following is not an acceptable range name?

    (a) FICA

    (b) Test_Weight

    (c) Goal for 2012

    (d) Target_2012

1 Blue Skies Airlines

You are an analyst for Blue Skies Airlines, a regional airline headquartered in Kansas City. Blue Skies has up to 10 departures a day from the Kansas City Airport. Your assistant developed a template for you to store daily flight data about the number of passengers per flight. Each regional aircraft can hold up to 70 passengers. You need to calculate the occupancy rate, which is the percent of each flight that is occupied. In addition, you need daily statistics, such as total number of passengers, averages, least full flights, and so forth, so that decisions can be made for future flight departures out of Kansas City. You also want to calculate weekly statistics per flight number. This exercise follows the same set of skills as used in Hands-On Exercises 1 and 2 in the chapter. Refer to Figure 2.33 as you complete this exercise.

FIGURE 2.33 Blue Skies Airlines ➤

a. Open *e02p1flights* and save it as **e02p1flights_LastnameFirstname**.

b. Click **cell D6**, the cell to display the occupancy percent for Flight 4520 on Sunday, and do the following:
   - Type = and click **cell C6**. Type / and click **cell C2**.
   - Press **F4** to make cell C2 absolute.
   - Click **Enter** to the left of the Formula Bar. The occupancy rate of Flight 4520 is 85.7%.
   - Double-click the **cell D6 fill handle** to copy the formula down the column.

c. Click **cell D7** and notice that the bottom border disappears from cell D15. When you copy a formula, Excel also copies the original cell's format. The cell containing the original formula did not have a bottom border, so when you copied the formula down the column, Excel formatted it to match the original cell with no border. To reapply the border, click **cell D15**, click the **Border arrow** in the Font group on the Home tab, and then select **Bottom Border**.

d. Select the **range D6:D15**, copy it to the Clipboard, and paste it starting in **cell F6**. Notice the formula in cell F6 changes to = E6/$C$2. The first cell reference changes from C6 to E6, maintaining its relative location from the pasted formula. $C$2 remains absolute so that the number of passengers per flight is always divided by the value stored in cell C2. The copied range is still in the Clipboard. Paste the formula into the remaining % Full columns (columns H, J, L, N, and P). Press **Esc** to turn off the marquee around the original copied range.

e. Clean up the data by deleting *0.0%* in cells, such as H7. The 0.0% is misleading as it implies the flight was empty; however, some flights do not operate on all days. Check your worksheet against the *Daily Flight Information* section in Figure 2.33.

f. Calculate the total number of passengers per day by doing the following:
- Click **cell C18**.
- Click **AutoSum** in the Editing group.
- Select the **range C6:C15**, and then press **Enter**.

g. Calculate the average number of passengers per day by doing the following:
- Click **cell C19**.
- Click the **AutoSum arrow** in the Editing group, and then select **Average**.
- Select the **range C6:C15**, and then click **Enter** to the left of the Formula Bar.

h. Calculate the median number of passengers per day by doing the following:
- Click **cell C20**.
- Click **Insert Function** to the left of the Formula Bar, type **median** in the **Search for a function box**, and then click **Go**.
- Click **MEDIAN** in the **Select a function box**, and then click **OK**.
- Select the **range C6:C15** to enter it in the **Number1 box**, and then click **OK**.

i. Calculate the least number of passengers on a daily flight by doing the following:
- Click **cell C21**.
- Click the **AutoSum arrow** in the Editing group, and then select **Min**.
- Select the **range C6:C15**, and then press **Enter**.

j. Calculate the most passengers on a daily flight by doing the following:
- Click **cell C22**.
- Click the **AutoSum arrow** in the Editing group, and then select **Max**.
- Select the **range C6:C15**, and then press **Enter**.

k. Calculate the number of flights for Sunday by doing the following:
- Click **cell C23**.
- Click the **AutoSum arrow** in the Editing group, and then select **Count Numbers**.
- Select the **range C6:C15**, and then press **Enter**.

l. Calculate the average, median, least, and full percentages in **cells D19:D22**. Format the values with Percent Style with zero decimal places. Do not copy the formulas from column C to column D, as that will change the borders. You won't insert a SUM function in cell D18 because it does not make sense to total the occupancy rate percentage column. Select **cells C18:D23**, copy the range, and then paste in these cells: **E18, G18, I18, K18, M18**, and **O18**. Press **Esc** after pasting.

m. Create a footer with your name on the left side, the date code in the center, and the file name code on the right side.

n. Save and close the workbook, and submit based on your instructor's directions.

2 Central Nevada College Salaries

You work in the Human Resources Department at Central Nevada College. You are preparing a spreadsheet model to calculate bonuses based on performance ratings, where ratings between 1 and 1.9 do not receive bonuses, ratings between 2 and 2.9 earn $100 bonuses, ratings between 3 and 3.9 earn $250 bonuses, ratings between 4 and 4.9 earn $500 bonuses, and ratings of 5 or higher earn $1,000 bonuses. In addition, you need to calculate annual raises based on years employed. Employees who have worked five or more years earn a 3.25% raise; employees who have not worked at least five years earn a 2% raise. The partially completed worksheet does not yet contain range names. This exercise follows the same set of skills as used in Hands-On Exercises 1, 2, 3, and 4 in the chapter. Refer to Figure 2.34 as you complete this exercise.

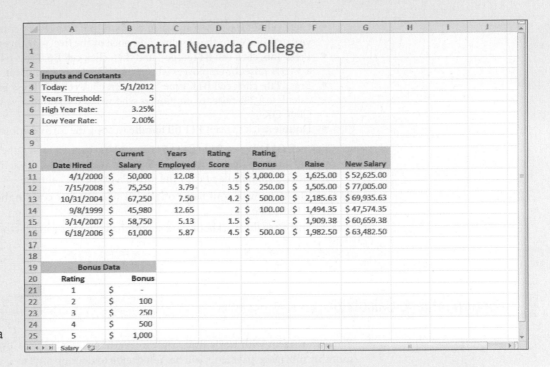

FIGURE 2.34 Central Nevada College Salaries ➤

The spreadsheet shown in the figure contains the following data:

Central Nevada College

Inputs and Constants	
Today:	5/1/2012
Years Threshold:	5
High Year Rate:	3.25%
Low Year Rate:	2.00%

Date Hired	Current Salary	Years Employed	Rating Score	Rating Bonus	Raise	New Salary
4/1/2000	$ 50,000	12.08	5	$ 1,000.00	$ 1,625.00	$ 52,625.00
7/15/2008	$ 75,250	3.79	3.5	$ 250.00	$ 1,505.00	$ 77,005.00
10/31/2004	$ 67,250	7.50	4.2	$ 500.00	$ 2,185.63	$ 69,935.63
9/8/1999	$ 45,980	12.65	2	$ 100.00	$ 1,494.35	$ 47,574.35
3/14/2007	$ 58,750	5.13	1.5	$ -	$ 1,909.38	$ 60,659.38
6/18/2006	$ 61,000	5.87	4.5	$ 500.00	$ 1,982.50	$ 63,482.50

Bonus Data

Rating	Bonus
1	$ -
2	$ 100
3	$ 250
4	$ 500
5	$ 1,000

a. Open *e02p2salary* and save it as **e02p2salary_LastnameFirstname**.

b. Click **cell B4**, click the **Formulas tab**, click **Date & Time** in the Function Library, select **TODAY**, and then click **OK** to enter today's date in the cell.

c. Enter a formula to calculate the number of years employed by doing the following:
   - Click **cell C11**.
   - Click **Date & Time** in the Function Library group, scroll through the list, and then select **YEARFRAC**.
   - Click **cell A11** to enter the cell reference in the **Start_date box**.
   - Press **Tab**, and then click **cell B4** to enter the cell reference in the **End_date box**.
   - Ask yourself if the cell references should be relative or absolute. You should answer *relative* for **cell A11** so that it will change as you copy it for the other employees. You should answer *absolute* or *mixed* for **cell B4** so that it always refers to the cell containing the TODAY function as you copy the formula.
   - Press **F4** to make **cell B4** absolute, and then click **OK**. (Although you could have used the formula =($B$4-A11)/365 to calculate the number of years, the YEARFRAC function provides better accuracy since it accounts for leap years and the divisor 365 does not.
   - Double-click the **cell C11 fill handle** to copy the YEARFRAC function down the Years Employed column. Your results will differ based on the date contained in cell B4.

d. Enter the breakpoint and bonus data for the lookup table by doing the following:
   - Click **cell A21**, type **1**, and then press **Ctrl+Enter**.
   - Click the **Home tab**, click **Fill** in the Editing group, and then select **Series**. Click **Columns** in the *Series in* section, leave the Step value at **1**, type **5** in the **Stop value box**, and then click **OK**.
   - Click **cell B21**. Enter **0, 100, 250, 500,** and **1000** down the column. The cells have been previously formatted with Accounting Number Format with zero decimal places.
   - Select **range A21:B25**, click in the **Name Box**, type **Bonus**, and then press **Enter** to name the range.

e. Enter the bonus based on rating by doing the following:
   - Click **cell E11**, and then click the **Formulas tab**.
   - Click **Lookup & Reference** in the Function Library group, and then select **VLOOKUP**.
   - Click **cell D11** to enter the cell reference in the **Lookup_value box**.
   - Press **Tab**, and then type **Bonus** to enter the range name for the lookup table in the **Table_array box**.
   - Press **Tab**, type **2** to represent the second column in the lookup table, and then click **OK**.
   - Double-click the **cell E11 fill handle** to copy the formula down the Rating Bonus column.

f. Enter the raise based on years employed by doing the following:
   - Click **cell F11**.
   - Click **Logical** in the Function Library group, and then select **IF**.

- Click **cell C11**, type >= and then click **cell B5**. Press **F4** to enter C11>=$B$5 to compare the years employed to the absolute reference of the five-year threshold in the **Logical_test box**.
- Press **Tab**, click **cell B11**, type * and then click **cell B6**. Press **F4** to enter B11*$B$6 to calculate a 3.25% raise for employees who worked five years or more in the **Value_if_true box**.
- Press **Tab**, click **cell B11**, type * and then click **cell B7**. Press **F4** to enter B11*$B$7 to calculate a 2% raise for employees who worked less than five years in the **Value_if_false box**. Click **OK**.
- Double-click the **cell F11 fill handle** to copy the formula down the Raise column.

g. Click **cell G11**. Type =B11+E11+F11 to add the current salary, the bonus, and the raise to calculate the new salary. Press **Ctrl+Enter** to keep **cell G11** the active cell, and then double-click the **cell G11 fill handle** to copy the formula down the column.

h. Create a footer with your name on the left side, the date code in the center, and the file name code on the right side.

i. Save and close the workbook, and submit based on your instructor's directions.

3 Client Mortgage Calculator

You are an agent with Koyle Real Estate in Bowling Green, Ohio. Customers often ask you what their monthly mortgage payments will be. You decide to develop an Excel template you can use to enter the house cost, current APR, yearly property tax, and estimated yearly property insurance. Borrowers who want the lowest interest rates make a 20% down payment. You will assign range names and use them in the formulas. This exercise follows the same set of skills as used in Hands-On Exercises 2, 3, and 4 in the chapter. Refer to Figure 2.35 as you complete this exercise.

FIGURE 2.35 Client Mortgage Calculator ➤

a. Open *e02p3client* and save it as **e02p3client_LastnameFirstname**.

b. Create a range name for the down payment requirement by doing the following: Click **cell B4**, click in the **Name Box**, type **DownRequired**, and then press **Enter**. The number of payments per year value has already been assigned the range name PmtsPerYear.

 DISCOVER

c. Name the input values by doing the following:
- Select **range A8:B12**.
- Click the **Formulas tab**, and then click **Create from Selection** in the Defined Names group.
- Make sure *Left column* is selected, and then click **OK**.
- Click each input value cell in **range B8:B12** and look at the newly created names in the Name Box.

d. Edit the range names by doing the following:
- Click **Name Manager** in the Defined Names group.
- Click **Cost_of_House**, click **Edit**, type **Cost**, and then click **OK**.
- Change *Property_Tax* to **PropertyTax**.
- Click **CONSTANTS** in the list, click **Delete**, and then click **OK** to delete it.
- Close the Name Manager.

e. Name the output values using the Create from Selection method you used in step c. Then edit the range names using the same approach you used in step d.
- Change *Down_Payment* to **Down**.
- Change *Monthly_Payment__P_I* to **MPmtPI**.
- Change *Monthly_Property_Tax_Escrow* to **MPropTax**.
- Change *Monthly_Insurance_Escrow* to **MInsurance**.
- Change *Total_Monthly_Payment* to **TotalPayment**.

f. Enter the first two formulas with range names in the Outputs area by doing the following:
- Click **cell B15**. Type **=Cost*down** and double-click **DownRequired** from the **Formula AutoComplete list**. If the list does not appear, type the entire name **DownRequired**. Then press **Enter** to enter the formula =Cost*DownRequired.
- Click **cell B16**. Type **=cost-down** and press **Enter**.

g. Enter the PMT function to calculate the monthly payment of principal and interest by doing the following:
- Click **cell B17**. Click **Financial** in the Function Library group, scroll down, and then select **PMT**.
- Click **cell B9**, type / and then click **cell B5** to enter APR/PmtsPerYear in the **Rate box**.
- Press **Tab**, click **cell B10**, type * and then click **cell B5** to enter Years*PmtsPerYear in the **Nper box**.
- Press **Tab**, type **-loan** in the **Pv box**, and then click **OK**.

DISCOVER

h. Enter the monthly property tax formula by doing the following:
- Click **cell B18**. Type = to start the formula.
- Click **Use in Formula** in the Defined Names group, and select **PropertyTax**.
- Type / and click **Use in Formula** in the Defined Names group. Select **PmtsPerYear**, and then press **Enter**.

i. Adapt step h to enter the formula =Insurance/PmtsPerYear in **cell B19**.

j. Enter **=SUM(B17:B19)** in **cell B20**.

k. Select **range B15:B20**, and then apply **Accounting Number Format**.

l. Click the **Range Names worksheet tab**, click **cell A2**, click the **Formulas tab**, click **Use in Formula** in the Defined Names group, select **Paste Names**, and then click **Paste List** to paste an alphabetical list of range names in the worksheet. Adjust the column widths.

m. Create a footer with your name on the left side, the date code in the center, and the file name code on the right side for both worksheets.

n. Save and close the workbook, and submit based on your instructor's directions.

1 Sunrise Credit Union Weekly Payroll

As manager of the Sunrise Credit Union, you are responsible for managing the weekly payroll. Your assistant developed a partial worksheet, but you need to enter the formulas to calculate the regular pay, overtime pay, gross pay, taxable pay, withholding tax, FICA, and net pay. In addition, you want to total pay columns and calculate some basic statistics. As you construct formulas, make sure you use absolute and relative cell references correctly in formulas and avoid circular references.

a. Open the *e02m1payroll* workbook and save it as **e02m1payroll_LastnameFirstname**.

b. Study the worksheet structure, and then read the business rules in the Notes section.

c. Use IF functions to calculate the regular pay and overtime pay based on a regular 40-hour workweek. Pay overtime only for overtime hours. Calculate the gross pay based on the regular and overtime pay. Abram's regular pay is $398. With eight overtime hours, Abram's overtime pay is $119.40.

d. Create a formula to calculate the taxable pay. With two dependents, Abram's taxable pay is $417.40.

e. Use the appropriate function to identify and calculate the federal withholding tax. With a taxable pay of $417.40, Abram's tax rate is 25%, and the withholding tax is $104.35.

f. Calculate FICA based on gross pay and the FICA rate, and then calculate the net pay.

g. Calculate the total regular pay, overtime pay, gross pay, taxable pay, withholding tax, FICA, and net pay.

h. Copy all formulas down their respective columns.

i. Apply **Accounting Number Format** to the **range C5:C16**. Apply **Accounting Number Format** to the first row of monetary data and to the total row. Apply **Comma Style** to the monetary values for the other employees. Underline the last employee's monetary values, and then use the Format Cells dialog box to apply **Double Accounting Underline** for the totals.

j. Insert appropriate functions to calculate the average, highest, and lowest values in the Summary Statistics area of the worksheet.

k. At your instructor's discretion, use Help to learn about the FREQUENCY function. The Help feature contains sample data for you to copy and practice in a new worksheet to learn about this function. You can close the practice worksheet containing the Help data without saving it. You want to determine the number (frequency) of employees who worked less than 20 hours, between 20 and 29 hours, between 30 and 40 hours, and over 40 hours. **Cells J28:J31** list the ranges. You need to translate this range into correct values for the Bin column in **cells I28:I30** and then enter the FREQUENCY function in **cells K28:K31**. The function should identify one employee who worked between 0 and 19 hours and six employees who worked more than 40 hours.

l. Apply other page setup formats as needed.

m. Insert a footer with your name on the left side, the date code in the center, and the file name code on the right side.

n. Save and close the workbook, and submit based on your instructor's directions.

2 First Bank of Missouri

As a loan officer at First Bank of Missouri, you track house loans. You started a spreadsheet that contains client names, the selling price of houses, and the term of the loans. You are ready to calculate the interest rate, which is based on the term. In addition, you need to calculate the required down payment, the amount to be financed, and the monthly payment for each customer. To keep your formulas easy to read, you will create and use range names. Finally, you need to calculate some basic statistics.

a. Open the *e02m2bank* workbook and save it as **e02m2bank_LastnameFirstname**.

b. Enter a function to display the current date in **cell G3**.

c. Assign appropriate range names to the number of payments per year value and to the lookup table.

d. Use range names when possible in formulas, and avoid creating circular references.

e. Use an appropriate function to display the interest rate for the first customer.

f. Use an appropriate lookup function to calculate the amount of the down payment for the first customer. The down payment is based on the term and the selling price. The first customer's amount is $68,975.

g. Calculate the amount to be financed for the first customer.

h. Calculate the monthly payment for the first customer using range names and cell references. The first customer's monthly payment is $1,142.65.

i. Copy the formulas down their respective columns. Format interest rates with **Percent Style** with two decimal places. Format monetary values with **Accounting Number Format** with two decimal places.

j. Calculate the number of loans and other summary statistics. Format the statistics as needed.

k. Create a section, complete with column headings, for the range names. Place this area below the lookup table.

l. Insert a footer with your name on the left side, the sheet name code in the center, and the file name code on the right side.

m. Save and close the workbook, and submit based on your instructor's directions.

3 Professor's Grade Book

You are a teaching assistant for Dr. Denise Gerber, who teaches an introductory C# programming class at your college. One of your routine tasks is to enter assignment and test grades into the grade book. Now that the semester is almost over, you need to create formulas to calculate category averages, the overall weighted average, and the letter grade for each student. In addition, Dr. Gerber wants to see general statistics, such as average, median, low, and high for each graded assignment and test, as well as category averages and total averages. Furthermore, you need to create the grading scale on the documentation worksheet and use it to display the appropriate letter grade for each student.

a. Open the *e02m3grades* workbook and save it as **e02m3grades_LastnameFirstname**.

b. Use breakpoints to enter the grading scale in the correct structure on the Documentation worksheet, and then name the grading scale range **Grades**. The grading scale is as follows:

95+	A
90–94.9	A–
87–89.9	B+
83–86.9	B
80–82.9	B–
77–79.9	C+
73–76.9	C
70–72.9	C–
67–69.9	D+
63–66.9	D
60–62.9	D–
0–59.9	F

c. Calculate the total lab points earned for the first student in **cell T8** in the Grades worksheet. The first student earned 93 lab points.

d. Calculate the average of the two midterm tests for the first student in **cell W8**. The student's midterm test average is 87.

e. Calculate the assignment average for the first student in cell I8. The formula should drop the lowest score before calculating the average. Hint: You need to use a combination of three functions: SUM, MIN, and COUNT. The first student's assignment average is 94.2 after dropping the lowest assignment score.

f. Calculate the weighted total points based on the four category points (assignment average, lab points, midterm average, and final exam) and their respective weights (stored in the range B40:B43) in cell Y8. Use relative and absolute cell references as needed in the formula. The first student's total weighted score is 90.

g. Use the appropriate function to calculate the letter grade equivalent in **cell Z8**. Use the range name in the function. The first student's letter grade is A–.

h. Copy the formulas down their respective columns for the other students.

i. Name the passing score threshold in **cell B5** with the range name **Passing**. Display a message in the last grade book column based on the student's semester performance. If a student earned a final score of 70 or higher, display *Enroll in CS 202*. Otherwise, display *RETAKE CS 101*.

j. Calculate the average, median, low, and high scores for each assignment, lab, test, category average, and total score. Display individual averages with no decimal places; display category and final score averages with one decimal place. Display other statistics with no decimal places.

k. Insert a list of range names in the designated area in the Documentation worksheet. Complete the documentation by inserting your name, today's date, and a purpose statement in the designated areas.

DISCOVER

l. At your instructor's discretion, add a column to display each student's rank in the class. Use Help to learn how to insert the RANK function.

m. Select page setup options as needed to print the Grades worksheet on one page.

n. Insert a footer with your name on the left side, the sheet name code in the center, and the file name code on the right side of each worksheet.

o. Save and close the workbook, and submit based on your instructor's directions.

CAPSTONE EXERCISE

You are a sales representative at the local fitness center, Buff and Tuff Gym. Your manager expects each representative to track weekly new membership data, so you created a spreadsheet to store data. Membership costs are based on membership type. Clients can rent a locker for an additional annual fee. You are required to collect a down payment based on membership type, determine the balance, and then calculate the monthly payment based on a standard interest rate. In addition, you need to calculate general statistics to summarize for your manager. Spot-check results to make sure you created formulas and functions correctly.

Perform Preliminary Work

You need to open the starting workbook you created, acknowledge the existing circular reference error, and assign a range name to the membership lookup table. You will correct the circular reference error later.

a. Open the *e02c1gym* workbook, click **Help**, read about circular references, close the Help window that appears, and save the workbook as **e02c1gym_LastnameFirstname**.

b. Assign the name **Membership** to the **range A18:C20**.

c. Insert a function to display the current date in **cell B2**.

Calculate Cost, Annual Total, and Total Due

You are ready to calculate the basic annual membership cost and the total annual cost. The basic annual membership is determined based on each client's membership type, using the lookup table.

a. Insert a function in **cell C5** to display the basic annual membership cost for the first client.

b. Use a function to calculate the annual total amount, which is the sum of the basic cost and locker fees for those who rent a locker. The Locker column displays *Yes* for clients who rent a locker and *No* for those who don't.

c. Calculate the total amount due for the first client based on the annual total and the number of years in the contract.

d. Copy the three formulas down their respective columns.

Determine the Down Payment and Balance

You need to collect a down payment based on the type of membership for each new client. Then you must determine how much each client owes.

a. Insert the function to display the amount of down payment for the first client.

b. Find and correct the circular reference for the balance. The balance is the difference between the total due and the down payment.

c. Copy the two formulas for the rest of the clients.

Calculate the Monthly Payment

Clients pay the remainder by making monthly payments. Monthly payments are based on the number of years specified in the client's contract and a standard interest rate.

a. Insert the function to calculate the first client's monthly payment, using appropriate relative and absolute cell references.

b. Copy the formula down the column.

c. Edit the formula by changing the appropriate cell reference to a mixed cell reference. Copy the formula down.

Finalize the Workbook

You need to perform some basic statistical calculations and finalize the workbook with formatting and page setup options.

a. Calculate totals on row 14.

b. Insert the appropriate functions in the *Summary Statistics* section of the worksheet: **cells H18:H22**. Format the payments with **Accounting Number Format**, and format the number of new members appropriately.

c. Format the other column headings on rows 4 and 17 to match the fill color in the **range E17:H17**. Wrap text for the column headings.

d. Format the monetary values for Andrews and the total row with **Accounting Number Format**. Use zero decimal places for whole amounts, and display two decimal places for the monthly payment. Apply **Comma Style** to the internal monetary values. Underline the values before the totals, and then apply **Double Accounting Underline** (found in the Format Cells dialog box) for the totals.

e. Set **0.3"** left and right margins, and then ensure the page prints on only one page.

f. Insert a footer with your name on the left side, the date code in the center, and the file name code on the right side.

g. Save and close the workbook, and submit based on your instructor's directions.

BEYOND THE CLASSROOM

Blue Skies Airlines GENERAL CASE	In Practice Exercise 1, you worked with the Blue Skies Airlines' daily flight statistics. If you did not complete that exercise, review the introductory paragraph, steps, and Figure 2.33. Open *e02b1blue* and save it as **e02b1blue_LastnameFirstName**. It is inefficient to delete 0.0% when a flight does not exist for a particular day, so you will create a formula that enters an empty text string if the number column contains a hyphen (-) using the IF function to evaluate if the # Pass column does not contain a hyphen. The value_if_true argument should calculate the occupancy percentage. The value_if_false argument should enter an empty text string, indicated by "". Copy the function to other days' % Full columns. Calculate the average daily percentage full for Flight 4520 in the Weekly Statistics area of the worksheet. Note that you need to use nonadjacent cell addresses in the function. Include empty % Full cells so that you can copy the formula down for the other flights. The empty cells do not affect the results. The average daily occupancy rate for Flight 4520 is 85.0%. Calculate the low and high daily occupancy rates. For Flight 4520, the lowest occupancy rate is 71.4%, and the highest occupancy rate is 92.9%. Insert a function to count the number of days each flight was made. Reapply the bottom border to the statistics area, if needed. Change the scaling so that the worksheet fits on one page. Include a footer with your name on the left side, the date code in the center, and the file name code on the right side. Save and close the workbook, and submit based on your instructor's directions.
Mall Lease Rates RESEARCH CASE	As general manager of a shopping mall, you developed a spreadsheet to list current tenant data. Open *e02b2mall*, and save it as **e02b2mall_LastnameFirstname**. You need to calculate the expiration date, price per square foot, annual rent, and monthly rent for each tenant. Use Help to research how you can construct a nested DATE function that will display the expiration date. The function should add the number of years for the lease but should subtract one day. For example, a five-year lease that started on January 1, 2010, expires on December 31, 2014, not on January 1, 2015. Assign three range names: the lookup table and the two constants. The price per square foot is based on two things: length of the lease and the number of square feet. If a tenant's space is less than the threshold, the tenant's price per square footage is based on the regular price. If a tenant's space is at least 3,000 square feet, the tenant's price is based on the adjusted square footage price. Use Help or search the Internet to learn how to nest the VLOOKUP within the IF function. You will need two nested functions. Use range names in the functions. Calculate the annual rent, which is the product of the square footage and price per square footage per tenant. Then calculate the monthly rent. Avoid circular references in your formulas. Format values appropriately. Include a footer with your name on the left side, the date code in the center, and the file name code on the right side. Save and close the workbook, and submit based on your instructor's directions.
Park City Condo Rental DISASTER RECOVERY	You and some friends are planning a Labor Day vacation to Park City, Utah. You have secured a four-day condominium that costs $1,200. Some people will stay all four days; others will stay part of the weekend. One of your friends constructed a worksheet to help calculate each person's cost of the rental. The people who stay Thursday night will split the nightly cost evenly. To keep the costs down, everyone agreed to pay $30 per night per person for Friday, Saturday, and/or Sunday nights. Depending on the number of people who stay each night, the group may owe more money. Kyle, Ian, Isaac, and Daryl agreed to split the difference in the total rental cost and the amount the group members paid. Open *e02b3parkcity*, address the circular reference error message that appears, and save the workbook as **e02b3parkcity_LastnameFirstname**. Review the worksheet structure, including the assumptions and calculation notes at the bottom of the worksheet. Check the formulas and functions, making necessary corrections. With the existing data, the number of people staying each night is 5, 7, 10, and 10, respectively. The total paid given the above assumptions is $1,110, giving a difference of $90 to be divided evenly among the first four people. Kyle's share should be $172.50. In the cells containing errors, insert comments to describe the error, and then fix the formulas. Verify the accuracy of formulas by entering an IF function in cell I1 to ensure the totals match. Nick, James, and Body inform you they can't stay Sunday night, and Rob wants to stay Friday night. Change the input accordingly. The updated total paid is now $1,200, and the difference is $150. Include a footer with your name on the left side, the date code in the center, and the file name code on the right side. Save and close the workbook, and submit based on your instructor's directions.

3 CHARTS

Depicting Data Visually

Watch the
Set-up
Video
for this
Case Study!

CASE STUDY | Hort University Majors

You are an assistant in the Institutional Research Department for Hort University, a prestigious university on the East Coast. You help conduct research using the university's information systems to provide statistics on the student population, alumni, and more. Your department stores an abundance of data to provide needed results upon request.

Dr. Alisha Musto, your boss, asked that you analyze the number of majors by the six colleges: Arts, Business, Education, Humanities & Social Science, Science & Health, and Technology & Computing. In addition, Dr. Musto wants you to include the undeclared majors in your analysis. You created an Excel worksheet with the data, but you want to create a series of charts that will help Dr. Musto analyze the enrollment data.

OBJECTIVES   AFTER YOU READ THIS CHAPTER, YOU WILL BE ABLE TO:

1. Decide which chart type to create *p.422*
2. Create a chart *p.432*
3. Change the chart type *p.441*
4. Change the data source and structure *p.442*
5. Apply a chart layout and a chart style *p.442*
6. Move a chart *p.443*

7. Print charts *p.444*
8. Insert and customize a sparkline *p.444*
9. Select and format chart elements *p.451*
10. Customize chart labels *p.453*
11. Format the axes and gridlines *p.455*
12. Add a trendline *p.456*

Chart Basics

The expression "a picture is worth a thousand words" means that a visual can be a more effective way to communicate or interpret data than words or numbers. Storing, organizing, and performing calculations on quantitative data, such as in the spreadsheets you have created, are important, but you must also be able to analyze the data to determine what they mean. A *chart* is a visual representation of numerical data that compares data and helps reveal trends or patterns to help people make informed decisions. An effective chart depicts data in a clear, easy-to-interpret manner and contains enough data to be useful but not too much that the data overwhelm people.

> An effective chart depicts data in a clear, easy-to-interpret manner....

A **chart** is a visual representation of numerical data.

In this section, you will learn chart terminology and how to choose the best chart type, such as pie or line, to fit your needs. You will select the range of cells containing the numerical values and labels from which to create the chart, choose the chart type, insert the chart, and designate the chart's location.

Deciding Which Chart Type to Create

Before creating a chart, study the data you want to represent visually. Look at the structure of the worksheet—the column labels, the row labels, the quantitative data, and the calculated values. Decide what you want to convey to your audience: Does the worksheet hold a single set of data, such as average snowfall at one ski resort, or multiple sets of data, such as average snowfall at several ski resorts? Do you want to depict data for one specific time period or over several time periods, such as several years or decades? Based on the data on which you want to focus, you decide which type of chart best represents that data. With Excel, you can create a variety of types of charts. The four most common chart types are column, bar, line, and pie.

You should organize the worksheet data before creating a chart by ensuring that the values in columns and rows are on the same value system (such as dollars or units) in order to make comparisons, that labels are descriptive, and that no blank rows or columns exist in the primary dataset. Figure 3.1 shows a worksheet containing the number of students who have declared a major within each college at Hort University. These data will be used to illustrate several chart types. Each cell containing a value is a *data point*. For example, the value 1,330 is a data point for the Arts data in the 2012 column. A group of related data points that appear in row(s) or column(s) in the worksheet create a *data series*. For example, the values 950, 1,000, 1,325, and 1,330 comprise the Arts data series. Textual information, such as column and row labels (college names, months, years, product names, etc.), is used to create *category labels* in charts.

A **data point** is a numeric value that describes a single value on a chart.

A **data series** is a group of related data points.

A **category label** is text that describes a collection of data points in a chart.

	A	B	C	D	E	F
1	**Hort University**					
2	Number of Majors by College					
3						
4		2009	2010	2011	2012	Average
5	Arts	950	1,000	1,325	1,330	1,151
6	Business	3,975	3,650	3,775	4,000	3,850
7	Education	1,500	1,425	1,435	1,400	1,440
8	Humanities & Social Science	2,300	2,250	2,500	3,500	2,638
9	Science & Health	1,895	1,650	1,700	1,800	1,761
10	Technology & Computing	4,500	4,325	4,400	4,800	4,506
11	Undeclared	5,200	5,500	5,000	4,700	5,100
12	Totals by Year	20,320	19,800	20,135	21,530	20,446
13						

FIGURE 3.1 Sample Dataset ➤

Create a Column Chart

A **column chart** displays data comparisons vertically in columns.

The **chart area** contains the entire chart and all of its elements.

The **plot area** contains a graphical representation of values in a data series.

The **X-axis** is a horizontal line that borders the plot area to provide a frame of reference for measurement.

The **Y-axis** is a vertical line that borders the plot area to provide a frame of reference for measurement.

The **category axis** provides descriptive group names for subdividing the data series.

The **value axis** displays incremental values to identify the values of the data series.

A *column chart* displays data vertically in columns. You use column charts to compare values across different categories, such as comparing revenue among different cities or comparing quarterly revenue in one year. Column charts are most effective when they are limited to small numbers of categories—generally seven or fewer. If more categories exist, the columns appear too close together, making it difficult to read the labels.

Before you create a chart, you need to know the names of the different chart elements. The *chart area* contains the entire chart and all of its elements, including the plot area, titles, legend, and labels. The *plot area* is the region containing the graphical representation of the values in the data series. Two axes form a border around the plot area. The *X-axis* is a horizontal border that provides a frame of reference for measuring data horizontally. The *Y-axis* is a vertical border that provides a frame of reference for measuring data vertically. Excel refers to the axes as the category axis and value axis. The *category axis* displays descriptive group names or labels, such as college names or cities, to identify data. The *value axis* displays incremental numbers to identify approximate values, such as dollars or units, of data points in the chart. In a column chart, the category axis is the X-axis, and the value axis is the Y-axis.

The column chart in Figure 3.2 compares the number of majors by college for only one year using the data from the worksheet in Figure 3.1. In Figure 3.2, the college labels stored in the first column—the range A5:A11—form the horizontal category axis, and the data points representing the number of majors in 2012 in the range E5:E11 form the vertical value axis. The height of each column represents the value of the individual data points: The larger the value, the taller the column. For example, Business has a taller column than the Arts and Education columns, indicating that more students major in Business than Arts or Education.

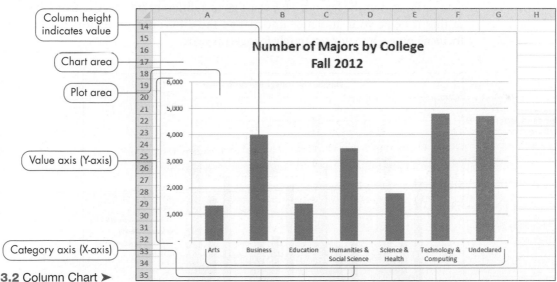

FIGURE 3.2 Column Chart ➤

A **single data series** compares values for one set of data.

A **multiple data series** compares two or more sets of data in one chart.

A **clustered column chart** groups or clusters similar data in columns to compare values across categories.

Figure 3.2 shows a column chart representing a *single data series*—data for only Fall 2012. However, you might want to create a column chart that contains multiple data series. A *multiple data series* chart compares two or more sets of data, such as the number of majors by college for four years. After you select the chart category, such as Column or Line, select a chart subtype. Within each chart category, Excel provides many variations or subtypes, such as clustered, stacked, and 100% stacked.

A *clustered column chart* compares groups or clusters of columns set side-by-side for easy comparison. The clustered column chart facilitates quick comparisons across data series, and it is effective for comparing several data points among categories. Figure 3.3 shows a clustered column chart created from the data in Figure 3.1. By default, the row titles appear on the category axis, and the yearly data series appear as columns with the value axis showing incremental numbers. Excel assigns a different color to each yearly data series and includes a legend. A ***legend*** is a key that identifies the color, gradient, picture, texture, or pattern assigned to each data series in a chart. For example, the 2012 data appear in purple. This chart clusters yearly data series for each college, enabling you to compare yearly trends for each major.

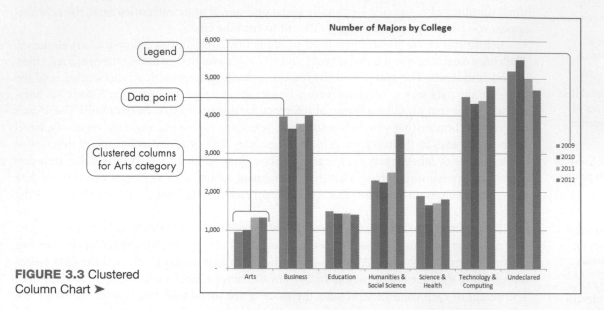

FIGURE 3.3 Clustered Column Chart ➤

Figure 3.4 shows another clustered column chart in which the categories and data series are reversed. The years appear on the category axis, and the colleges appear as color-coded data series and in the legend. This chart gives a different perspective from that in Figure 3.3 in that it helps your audience understand the differences in majors per year rather than focusing on each major separately for several years.

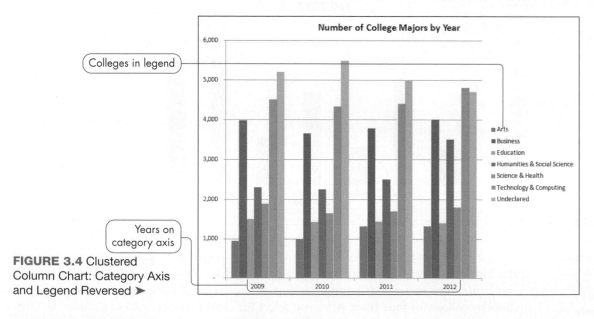

FIGURE 3.4 Clustered Column Chart: Category Axis and Legend Reversed ➤

A ***stacked column chart*** shows the relationship of individual data points to the whole category. Unlike a clustered column chart that displays several columns (one for each data series) for a category (such as Arts), a stacked column chart displays only one column for each category. Each category within the stacked column is color-coded for one data series. Use the stacked column chart when you want to compare total values across categories, as well as to display the individual category values. Figure 3.5 shows a stacked column chart in which a single column represents each categorical year, and each column stacks color-coded data-point segments representing the different colleges. The stacked column chart enables you to determine the total number of majors for each year. The height of each color-coded data point enables you to identify the relative contribution of each college to the total number of yearly majors. A disadvantage of the stacked column chart is that the segments within each column do not start at the same point, making it more difficult to compare individual segment values across categories.

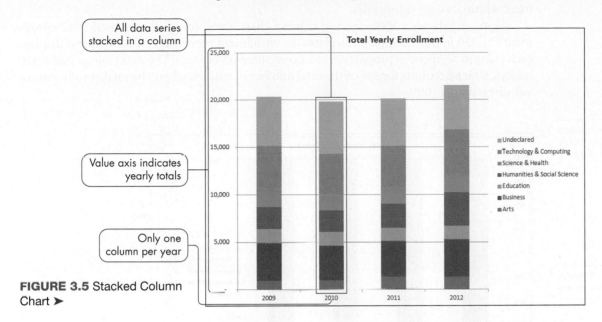

All data series stacked in a column

Value axis indicates yearly totals

Only one column per year

FIGURE 3.5 Stacked Column Chart ➤

When you create a stacked column chart, you must ensure data are *additive*, meaning that each column represents a sum of the data for each segment. Figure 3.5 correctly uses years as the category axis and the colleges as data series. Within each year, Excel adds the number of majors by college, and the columns display the sum of the majors. For example, the total number of majors in 2012 is over 20,000. Figure 3.6 shows an incorrectly constructed stacked column chart because the yearly number of majors by college is *not* additive. It is incorrect to state that the university has 15,000 total business majors for four years. Be careful when constructing stacked column charts to ensure that they lead to logical interpretation of data.

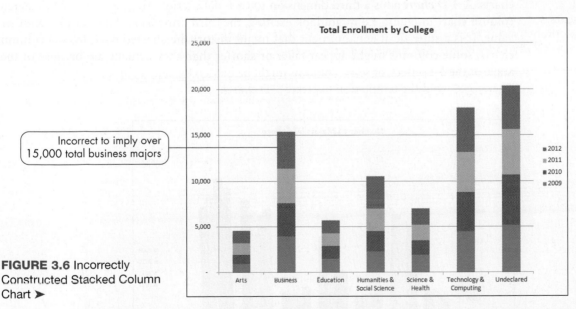

Incorrect to imply over 15,000 total business majors

FIGURE 3.6 Incorrectly Constructed Stacked Column Chart ➤

A **100% stacked column chart** places (stacks) data in one column per category, with each column having the same height of 100%.

A **100% stacked column chart** compares the percentage each data point contributes to the total for each category. Similar to the stacked column chart, the 100% stacked column chart displays only one column per category. The value axis displays percentages rather than values, and all columns are the same height: 100%. Excel converts each data point value into a percentage of the total for each category. Use this type of chart when you are more interested in comparing relative percentage contributions across categories rather than actual values across categories. For example, a regional manager for a department store realizes that not every store is the same size and that the different stores have different sales volumes. Instead of comparing sales by department for each store, you might want to display percentage of sales by department to facilitate comparisons of percentage contributions for each department within its own store's sales.

Figure 3.7 shows a 100% stacked column chart. Excel computes the total 2012 enrollment (21,530 in our example), calculates the enrollment percentage by college, and displays each column segment in proportion to its computed percentage. The Arts College had 1,330 majors, which accounts for 6% of the total number of majors, where the total enrollment for any given year is 100%.

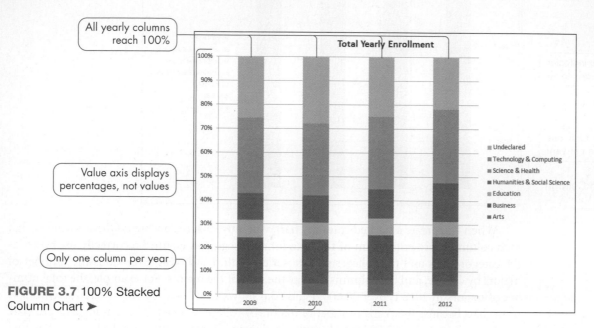

FIGURE 3.7 100% Stacked Column Chart ➤

Excel enables you to create special-effects charts, such as 3-D, cylinder, pyramid, or cone charts. A **3-D chart** adds a third dimension to each data series. Although the 3-D clustered column chart in Figure 3.8 might look exciting, the third dimension does not plot another value. It is a superficial enhancement that might distort the charted data. In 3-D column charts, some columns might appear taller or shorter than they actually are because of the angle of the 3-D effect, or some columns might be hidden by taller columns in front of them. Therefore, avoid the temptation to create 3-D charts.

A **3-D chart** adds a third dimension to each data series, creating a distorted perspective of the data.

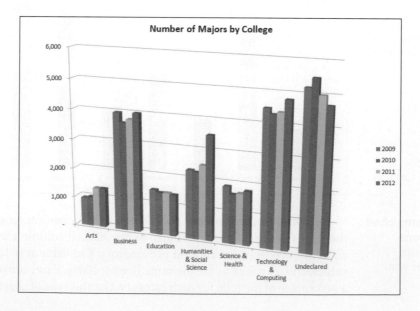

FIGURE 3.8 3-D Clustered Column Chart ➤

Create a Bar Chart

A **bar chart** compares values across categories using horizontal bars.

A **bar chart** compares values across categories using horizontal bars. In a bar chart, the horizontal axis displays values, and the vertical axis displays categories (see Figure 3.9). A bar chart conveys the same type of information as a column chart; however, a bar chart is preferable when category names are long, such as *Humanities & Social Science*. A bar chart enables category names to appear in an easy-to-read format, whereas a column chart might display category names at an awkward angle or smaller font size. Like column charts, bar charts have several subtypes, such as clustered, stacked, 100% stacked, 3-D, cylinder, cone, or pyramid subtypes.

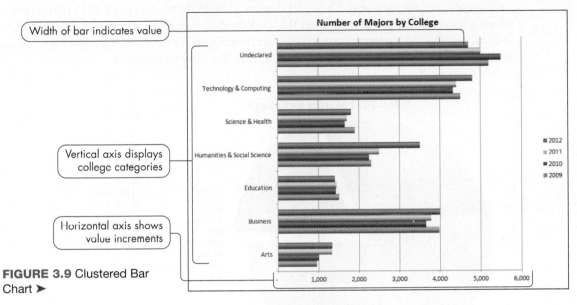

- Width of bar indicates value
- Vertical axis displays college categories
- Horizontal axis shows value increments

FIGURE 3.9 Clustered Bar Chart ➤

Create a Line Chart

A **line chart** uses a line to connect data points in order to show trends over a period of time.

A **line chart** displays lines connecting data points to show trends over equal time periods, such as months, quarters, years, or decades. With multiple data series, Excel displays each data series with a different line color. The category axis (X-axis) represents time, such as ten-year increments, whereas the value axis (Y-axis) represents the value, such as a monetary value or quantity. A line chart enables a user to easily spot trends in the data since the line continues to the next data point. The line, stacked, and 100% stacked line charts do not have specific indicators for each data point. To show each data point, select Line with Markers, Stacked Line with Markers, or 100% Stacked Line with Markers. Figure 3.10 shows a line chart indicating the number of majors by college over time, making it easy to see the enrollment trends. For example, the Arts enrollment spiked in 2010 while enrollments in other colleges decreased that year.

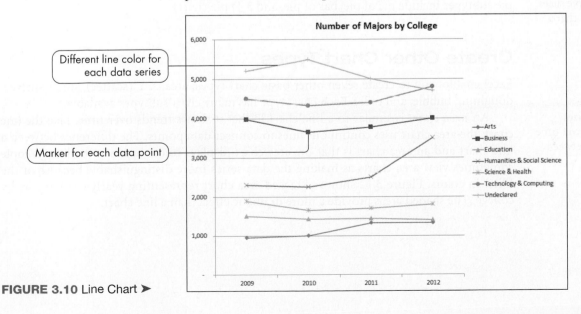

- Different line color for each data series
- Marker for each data point

FIGURE 3.10 Line Chart ➤

Create a Pie Chart

A **pie chart** shows each data point in proportion to the whole data series as a slice in a circular pie.

A *pie chart* shows each data point as a proportion to the whole data series. The pie chart displays as a circle or "pie," where the entire pie represents the total value of the data series. Each slice represents a single data point. The larger the slice, the larger percentage that data point contributes to the whole. Use a pie chart when you want to convey percentage or market share. Unlike column, bar, and line charts, pie charts represent a single data series only.

The pie chart in Figure 3.11 divides the pie representing total Fall 2012 enrollment into seven slices, one for each college. The size of each slice is proportional to the percentage of total enrollment for that year. The chart depicts a single data series (Fall 2012 enrollment), which appears in the range E5:E11 on the worksheet in Figure 3.1. Excel creates a legend to indicate which color represents which pie slice. When you create a pie chart, limit it to about seven slices. Pie charts with too many slices appear too busy to interpret.

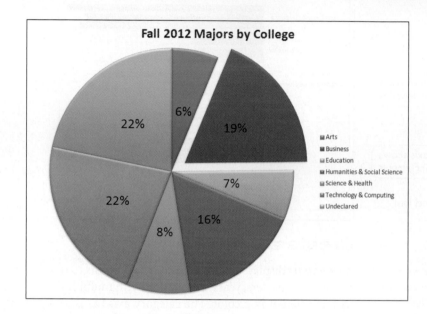

FIGURE 3.11 Pie Chart ➤

Similar to the way it creates a 100% stacked column chart, Excel creates a pie chart by computing the total 2012 enrollment (21,530 in our example), calculating the enrollment percentage by college and drawing each slice of the pie in proportion to its computed percentage. The Business College had 4,000 majors, which accounts for 19% of the total number of majors. You can focus a person's attention on a particular slice by separating one or more slices from the rest of the chart in an *exploded pie chart*, as shown in Figure 3.11. Additional pie subtypes include pie of pie, bar of pie, and 3-D pie charts.

An **exploded pie chart** separates one or more pie slices from the rest of the pie chart.

Create Other Chart Types

Excel enables you to create seven other basic chart types: area, X Y (scatter), stock, surface, doughnut, bubble, and radar. Each chart type has many chart subtypes available.

An **area chart** emphasizes magnitude of changes over time by filling in the space between lines with a color.

An *area chart* is similar to a line chart in that it shows trends over time. Like the line chart, the area chart uses continuous lines to connect data points. The difference between a line chart and an area chart is that the area chart displays colors between the lines. People sometimes view area charts as making the data series more distinguishable because of the filled-in colors. Figure 3.12 shows a stacked area chart representing yearly enrollments by college. The shaded areas provide a more dramatic effect than a line chart.

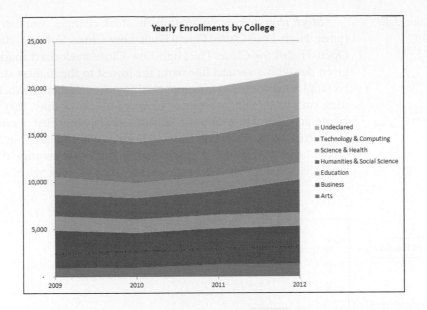

FIGURE 3.12 Stacked Area
Chart ➤

TIP Hidden Data

When creating an area chart, be careful which subtype you select. For some subtypes such as a 3-D area chart, the chart might hide smaller data values behind data series with larger values. If this happens, you can change subtypes or apply a transparency fill to see any hidden data values.

An **X Y (scatter) chart** shows a relationship between two variables.

An **X Y (scatter) chart** shows a relationship between two variables using their X and Y coordinates. Excel plots one variable on the horizontal X-axis and the other variable on the vertical Y-axis. Scatter charts are often used to represent data in educational, scientific, and medical experiments. A scatter chart is essentially the plotted values without any connecting line. A scatter chart helps you determine if a relationship exists between two different sets of numerical data. For example, you can plot the number of minutes students view a computer-based training (CBT) module and their test scores to see if a relationship exists between the two variables (see Figure 3.13).

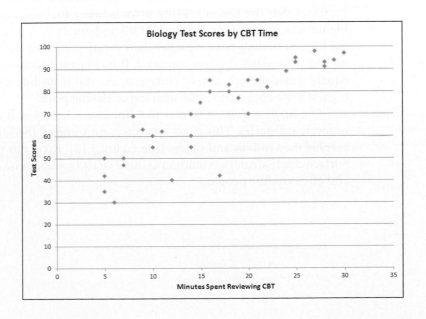

FIGURE 3.13 Scatter (X Y)
Chart ➤

A **stock chart** shows the high, low, and close prices for individual stocks over time.

Stock charts show fluctuations in stock changes. You can select one of four stock sub-types: High-Low-Close, Open-High-Low-Close, Volume-High-Low-Close, and Volume-Open-High-Low-Close. The High-Low-Close stock chart marks a stock's trading range on a given day with a vertical line from the lowest to the highest stock prices. Horizontal bars or rectangles mark the opening and closing prices. Although stock charts may have some other uses, such as showing a range of temperatures over time, they usually show stock prices. To create an Open-High-Low-Close stock chart, you must arrange data with Opening Price, High Price, Low Price, and Closing Price as column labels in that sequence. If you want to create other variations of stock charts, you must arrange data in a structured sequence required by Excel. Figure 3.14 shows three days of stock prices for a particular stock.

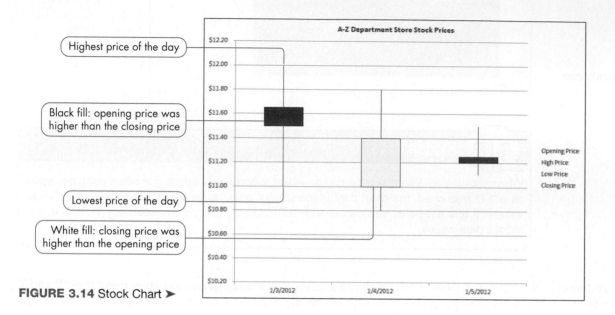

FIGURE 3.14 Stock Chart ➤

The stock chart legend may not explain the chart clearly. However, you can still identify prices. The rectangle represents the difference in the opening and closing prices. If the rectangle has a white fill, the closing price is higher than the opening price. If the rectangle has a black fill, the opening price is higher than the closing price. In Figure 3.14, the opening price was $11.65, and the closing price was $11.50 on January 3. A line below the rectangle indicates that the lowest trading price is lower than the opening and closing prices. In Figure 3.14, the lowest price was $11.00 on January 3. A line above the rectangle indicates the highest trading price is higher than the opening and closing prices. In Figure 3.14, the highest price was $12.00 on January 3. If no line exists below the rectangle, the lowest price equals either the opening or closing price, and if no line exists above the rectangle, the highest price equals either the opening or closing price.

A **surface chart** displays trends using two dimensions on a continuous curve.

The *surface chart* is similar to a line chart; however, it represents numeric data and numeric categories. This chart type takes on some of the same characteristics as a topographic map of hills and valleys (see Figure 3.15). Excel fills in all data points with colors. Surface charts are not as common as other chart types because they require more data points and often confuse people.

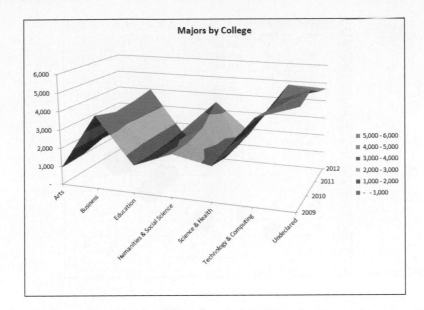

FIGURE 3.15 Surface
Chart ➤

A **doughnut chart** displays values as percentages of the whole but may contain more than one data series.

The ***doughnut chart*** is similar to a pie chart in that it shows the relationship of parts to a whole, but the doughnut chart can display more than one series of data, and it has a hole in the middle. Like a clustered or stacked column chart, a doughnut chart plots multiple data series. Each ring represents a data series, with the outer ring receiving the most emphasis. Although the doughnut chart is able to display multiple data series, people often have difficulty interpreting it. Figure 3.16 illustrates the 2011 and 2012 data series, with the 2012 data series on the outer ring. The chart shows each college as a segment of each ring of the doughnut. The larger the segment, the larger the value.

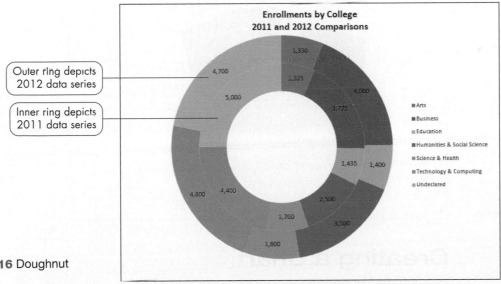

FIGURE 3.16 Doughnut
Chart ➤

A **bubble chart** shows relationships among three values by using bubbles.

The ***bubble chart*** is similar to a scatter chart, but it uses round bubbles instead of data points to represent a third dimension. Similar to the scatter chart, the bubble chart does not contain a category axis. The horizontal and vertical axes are both value axes. The third value determines the size of the bubble where the larger the value, the larger the bubble. People often use bubble charts to depict financial data. In Figure 3.17, age, years at the company, and salaries are compared. When creating a bubble chart, do not select the column headings, as they might distort the data.

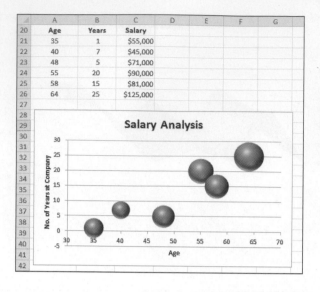

FIGURE 3.17 Bubble Chart ➤

A **radar chart** compares aggregate values of three or more variables represented on axes starting from the same point.

The final chart type is the ***radar chart***, which uses each category as a spoke radiating from the center point to the outer edges of the chart. Each spoke represents each data series, and lines connect the data points between spokes, similar to a spider web. You can create a radar chart to compare aggregate values for several data series. Figure 3.18 shows a radar chart comparing monthly house sales by house type (rambler, split level, 2 story). The house type categories appear in different colors, while the months appear on the outer edges of the chart.

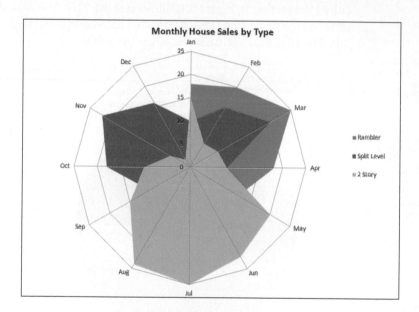

FIGURE 3.18 Radar Chart ➤

Creating a Chart

Creating a chart involves selecting the data source and choosing the chart type. After you insert a chart, you will position and size it.

Select the Data Source

Identify the chart data range by selecting the data series, any descriptive labels you need to construct the category labels, and the series labels you need to create the legend. Edit the row and column labels if they are not clear and concise. Table 3.1 describes what you should select for various charts. If the labels and data series are not stored in adjacent cells, press and hold Ctrl while selecting the nonadjacent ranges. Using Figure 3.1 as a guide, you would select the range A4:E11 to create a clustered column chart with multiple data series. To create the pie chart in Figure 3.11, select the range A5:A11, and then press and hold Ctrl while you select the range E5:E11. If your worksheet has titles and subtitles, you should not select them. Doing so would add unnecessary text to the legend.

TABLE 3.1 Data Selection for Charts

Chart Type	What to Select	Figure 3.1 Example
Column, Bar, Line, Area, Doughnut	Row labels (such as colleges), column labels (such as years), and one or more data series	A4:E11
Pie	Row labels (such as colleges) and only one data series (such as 2012), but not column headings	A5:A11,E5:E11
Bubble	Three different data series (such as age, years, and salary)	A21:C26 (in Figure 3.17)
X Y (Scatter)	Two related numeric datasets (such as minutes studying and test scores)	*

*Figure 3.1 does not contain data conducive to an X Y (scatter) chart.

TIP Total Rows and Columns

Make sure that each data series uses the same scale. For example, don't include aggregates, such as totals or averages, along with individual data points. Doing so would distort the plotted data. Compare the clustered column chart in Figure 3.3 to Figure 3.19. In Figure 3.19, the chart's design is incorrect because it mixes individual data points with the totals and yearly averages.

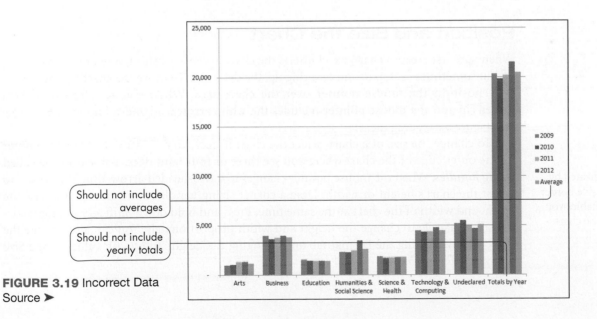

FIGURE 3.19 Incorrect Data Source ➤

Select the Chart Type

After you select the range of cells that you want to be the source for the chart, you need to select the chart type. To insert a chart for the selected range, click the Insert tab, and then do one of the following:

- Click the chart type (such as Column) in the Charts group, and then click a chart subtype (such as Clustered Column) from the chart gallery.

- Click the Charts Dialog Box Launcher to display the Insert Chart dialog box (see Figure 3.20), select a chart type on the left side, select a chart subtype, and then click OK.

FIGURE 3.20 Insert Chart Dialog Box ➤

A **chart sheet** contains a single chart and no spreadsheet data.

Excel inserts the chart as an embedded object on the current worksheet. You can leave the chart on the same worksheet as the worksheet data used to create the chart, or you can place the chart in a separate worksheet, called a **chart sheet**. A chart sheet contains a single chart only; you cannot enter data and formulas on a chart sheet. If you leave the chart in the same worksheet (see Figure 3.17), you can print the data and chart on the same page. If you want to print or view a full-sized chart, you can move the chart to its own chart sheet.

Position and Size the Chart

When you first create a chart, Excel inserts the chart in the worksheet, often to the right side of, but sometimes on top of and covering up, the data area. To move the chart to a new location, position the mouse pointer over the chart area. When you see the Chart Area ScreenTip and the mouse pointer includes the white arrowhead and a four-headed arrow (see Figure 3.21), drag the chart to the desired location.

A **sizing handle**, indicated by faint dots on the outside border of a selected chart, enables you to adjust the size of the chart.

To change the size of a chart, select the chart if necessary. Position the mouse pointer on the outer edge of the chart where you see three or four faint dots. These dots are called *sizing handles*. When the mouse pointer changes to a two-headed arrow, drag the border to adjust the chart's height or width. Drag a corner sizing handle to increase or decrease the height and width of the chart at the same time. Press and hold down Shift as you drag a corner sizing handle to change the height and width proportionately. You can also change the chart size by clicking the Format tab and changing the height and width values in the Size group (see Figure 3.21).

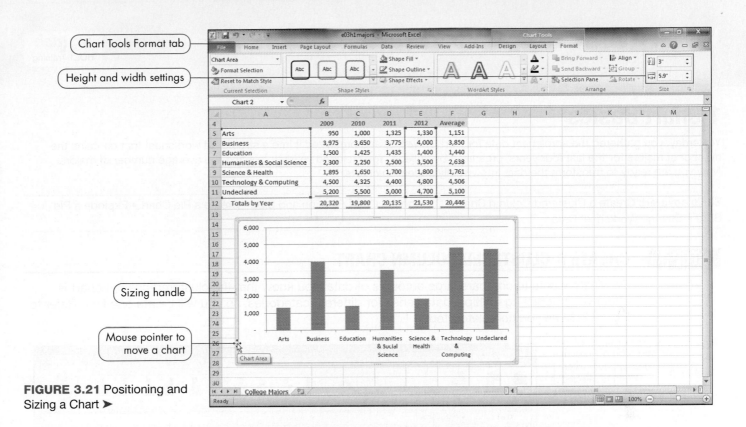

Chart Tools Format tab

Height and width settings

Sizing handle

Mouse pointer to move a chart

FIGURE 3.21 Positioning and Sizing a Chart ➤

TIP Chart Tools Contextual Tab

When you select a chart, Excel displays the Chart Tools contextual tab, containing the Design, Layout, and Format tabs. You can use the commands on these tabs to modify the chart.

1 Chart Basics

Yesterday, you gathered the enrollment data for Hort University and organized it into a structured worksheet that contains the number of majors for the last four years, organized by college. You included yearly totals and the average number of majors. Now you are ready to transform the data into visually appealing charts.

Skills covered: Create a Clustered Column Chart • Change the Chart Position and Size • Create a Pie Chart • Explode a Pie Slice • Change Worksheet Data

---

STEP 1 ▶ CREATE A CLUSTERED COLUMN CHART

Dr. Musto wants to compare large amounts of data. You know that the clustered column chart is effective at depicting multiple data series for different categories, so you will create one first. Refer to Figure 3.22 as you complete Step 1.

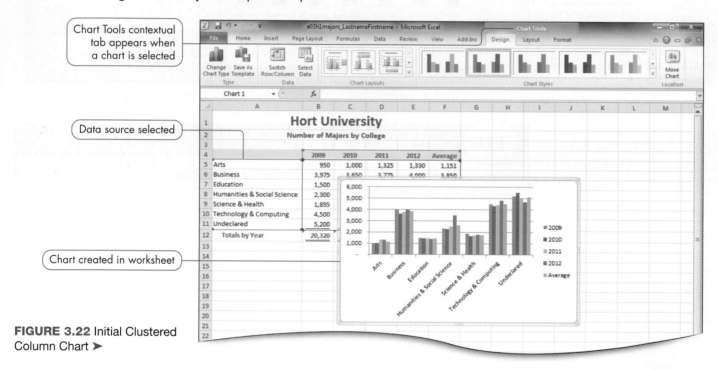

FIGURE 3.22 Initial Clustered Column Chart ▶

a. Open *e03h1majors* and save it as **e03h1majors_LastnameFirstname**.

> **TROUBLESHOOTING:** If you make any major mistakes in this exercise, you can close the file, open *e03h1majors* again, and then start this exercise over.

b. Select the **range A4:F11**.

   You included the average column in your selection. Although you should not mix individual values and aggregates such as averages in the same chart, we will do this now and later show you how you can modify the data source after you create the chart.

c. Click the **Insert tab**, and then click **Column** in the Charts group.

   The Column gallery opens, displaying the different column subtypes you can create.

d. Click **Clustered Column** in the *2-D Column* section of the gallery. Save the workbook.

   Excel inserts the clustered column chart in the worksheet.

Excel inserts the chart next to the worksheet data. You want to reposition the chart and then adjust the size so that the college category labels do not display at an angle to make the chart readable for Dr. Musto. Refer to Figure 3.23 as you complete Step 2.

FIGURE 3.23 Repositioned and Resized Chart ▶

a. Position the mouse pointer over the empty area of the chart area.

The mouse pointer includes a four-headed arrow with the regular white arrowhead, and the Chart Area ScreenTip displays.

> **TROUBLESHOOTING:** Make sure you see the Chart Area ScreenTip as you perform step b. If you move the mouse pointer to another chart element—such as the legend—you will move or size that element instead of moving the entire chart.

b. Drag the chart so that the top-left corner of the chart appears in **cell A14**.

You positioned the chart below the worksheet data.

c. Drag the bottom-right sizing handle down and to the right to **cell H29**. Save the workbook.

You increased both the height and the width at the same time. The college labels on the category axis no longer appear at an angle. You will leave the clustered column chart in its current state for the moment while you create another chart.

> **TIP** The F11 Key
>
> Pressing F11 is a fast way to create a column chart in a new chart sheet. Select the worksheet data source, and then press F11 to create the chart.

Dr. Musto has also asked you to create a chart showing the percentage of majors for the current year. You know that pie charts are excellent for illustrating percentages and proportions. Refer to Figure 3.24 as you complete Step 3.

FIGURE 3.24 Pie Chart ➤

a. Select the **range A5:A11**, which contains the college category labels.

b. Press and hold **Ctrl** as you select the **range E5:E11**, which contains the 2012 values.

   Remember that you have to press and hold Ctrl to select nonadjacent ranges.

> **TIP** Parallel Ranges
>
> Nonadjacent ranges should be parallel so that the legend will correctly reflect the data series. This means that each range should contain the same number of related cells. For example, A5:A11 and E5:E11 are parallel ranges in which E5:E11 contains values that relate to range A5:A11.

c. Click the **Insert tab**, click **Pie** in the Charts group, and then select **Pie** in the 2-D Pie group on the gallery.

   Excel inserts a pie chart in the worksheet. The pie chart may overlap part of the worksheet data and the clustered column chart.

d. Drag the chart so that the top-left corner appears in **cell J14**.

> **TROUBLESHOOTING:** Make sure that you see the Chart Area ScreenTip before you start dragging. Otherwise, you might accidentally drag a chart element, such as the legend or plot area. If you accidentally move the legend or plot area, press Ctrl+Z to undo the move.

e. Click the **Format tab**.

f. Type **3.25** in the **Shape Height box** in the Size group, and then press **Enter**.

   You increased the chart height to 3.25".

g. Type **4.5** in the **Shape Width box** in the Size group, and then press **Enter**. Save the workbook.

   Compare the size of your pie chart to the one shown in Figure 3.24. The zoom in the figure was decreased to display a broader view of the two charts together.

STEP 4 EXPLODE A PIE SLICE

Dr. Musto is concerned about the number of undeclared majors. You decide to explode the Undeclared pie slice to draw attention to it. Refer to Figure 3.25 as you complete Step 4.

Undeclared slice exploded

ScreenTip identifying Undeclared data point

FIGURE 3.25 Exploded Pie Slice ➤

a. Make sure the pie chart is still selected.

b. Click any slice of the chart.

   Excel selects all pie slices, as indicated by circular selection handles at the corner of each slice and in the center of the pie.

c. Click the **Undeclared slice**, the light blue slice in the top-left corner of the chart.

   The Undeclared slice is the only selected slice.

> **TROUBLESHOOTING:** If you double-click the chart instead of clicking a single data point, the Format Data Point dialog box appears. If this happens, click Close in the dialog box, and then click the individual pie slice to select that slice only.

d. Drag the **Undeclared slice** away from the pie a little bit. Save the workbook.

   You exploded the pie slice by separating it from the rest of the pie.

STEP 5 CHANGE WORKSHEET DATA

While you have been preparing two charts, some updated data came into the Institutional Research Department office. You need to update the worksheet data to update the charts. Refer to Figure 3.26 as you complete Step 5.

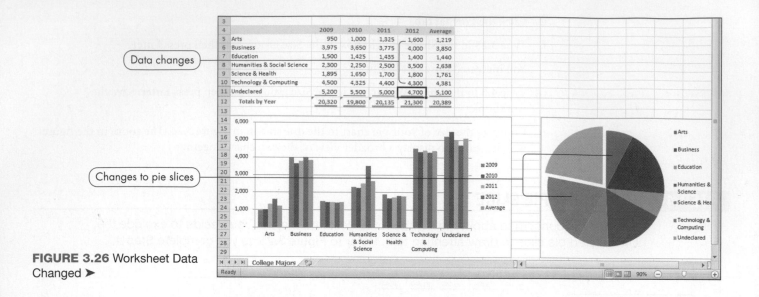

Data changes

Changes to pie slices

FIGURE 3.26 Worksheet Data Changed ➤

a. Click **cell E5**, the cell containing *1,330*—the number of students majoring in the College of Arts in 2012.

b. Type **1600** and press **Enter**.

Notice that the total changes in cell E12, the average yearly number of Arts majors changes in cell F5, the total average students changes in cell F12, and the two charts are adjusted to reflect the new value.

c. Click **cell E10**, the cell containing *4,800*—the number of students majoring in the College of Technology and Computing.

d. Type **4300** and press **Enter**.

Compare the updated charts to those shown in Figures 3.25 and 3.26. Notice the changes in the worksheet and the chart. With a smaller value, the Technology & Computing slice is smaller, while the other slices represent proportionally higher percentages of the total majors for 2012.

e. Save the workbook. Keep the workbook onscreen if you plan to continue with Hands-On Exercise 2. If not, close the workbook and exit Excel.

Chart Design

When you select a chart, Excel displays the Chart Tools contextual tab. That tab contains three specific tabs: Design, Layout, and Format. You used the Format tab to set the chart height and width in the first Hands-On Exercise. The Chart Tools Design contextual tab contains options to modify the overall chart design. You can change the chart type, modify the data source, select a chart layout, select a chart style, and move the chart. Figure 3.27 shows the Design tab.

FIGURE 3.27 Design Tab ➤

The Design tab provides commands for specifying the structure of a chart. Specifically, you can change the chart type and change the data source to build the chart. In addition, you can specify a chart layout that controls which chart elements display and where, select a chart style, and move the chart to a different location.

In this section, you will learn about the Design tab options and how to make changes to a chart's design. In addition, you will learn how to insert and format sparkline charts.

Changing the Chart Type

After you create a chart, you might want to change how the data are depicted by using other chart types. For example, you might want to change a line chart to a surface chart to see the dramatic effect of the fill colors or change a stacked column chart to a 100% stacked column chart to compare the segment percentages within their respective categories. To change the chart type, do the following:

1. Select the chart.
2. Click the Design tab.
3. Click Change Chart Type in the Type group to open the Change Chart Type dialog box.
4. Select the desired chart type, and then click OK.

> **TIP** Saving a Chart as a Template
>
> Companies often require a similar look for charts used in presentations. After you spend time customizing a chart to your company's specifications, you can save it as a template to create additional charts. To save a chart as a template, select the chart, click the Design tab, and then click Save as Template in the Type group. The Save Chart Template dialog box opens, in which you can select the template location and type a template name. Click Save in the dialog box to save the template. To use a chart template that you have created, click Templates in the Insert Chart dialog box, select the desired chart template, and then click OK.

Changing the Data Source and Structure

By default, Excel displays the row labels in the first column (such as the college names in Figure 3.1) on the category axis and the column labels (such as years) as the data series and in the legend. You can reverse how the chart presents the data—for example, place the column labels (e.g., years) on the category axis and the row labels (e.g., colleges) as data series and in the legend. To reverse the data series, click Switch Row/Column in the Data group. Figure 3.28 shows two chart versions of the same data. The chart on the left shows the row labels (months) on the category axis and the housing types as data series and in the legend. The chart on the right reverses the category axis and data series. The first chart compares house types for each month, and the second chart compares the number of sales of each house type throughout the year.

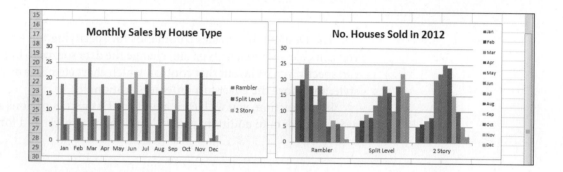

FIGURE 3.28 Original Chart and Reversed Row/Column Chart ➤

After creating a chart, you might notice extraneous data caused by selecting too many cells for the data source, or you might want to add to or delete data from the chart by clicking Select Data in the Data group to open the Select Data Source dialog box (see Figure 3.29). Select the desired range in the worksheet to modify the data source, or adjust the legend and horizontal axis within the dialog box.

FIGURE 3.29 Select Data Source Dialog Box ➤

Applying a Chart Layout and a Chart Style

The Chart Layouts group enables you to apply predefined layouts to a chart. A chart layout determines which chart elements appear in the chart area and how they are positioned within the chart area. Chart layouts are useful when you are first learning about charts and chart elements or to create consistently laid out charts. As you learn more about charting, you may want to customize your charts by using the commands on the Layout tab.

The Chart Styles group contains predefined styles that control the color of the chart area, plot area, and data series. Styles also affect the look of the data series, such as flat, 3-D, or beveled. Figure 3.30 shows the Chart Styles gallery. When choosing a chart style, make sure the style complements the chart data and is easy to read. Also, consider whether you will display the chart onscreen in a presentation or print the chart. If you will display the chart in a presentation, select a style with a black background. If you plan to print the chart, select a chart style with a white background to avoid wasting toner printing a background. If you print with a black and white printer, use the first column of black and gray styles.

FIGURE 3.30 Chart Styles Gallery ➤

Moving a Chart

By default, Excel creates charts on the same worksheet as the original dataset, but you can move the chart to its own chart sheet in the workbook. To move a chart to another sheet or a new sheet, do the following:

1. Select the chart to display the Chart Tools contextual tab.
2. Click the Design tab.
3. Click Move Chart in the Location group to open the Move Chart dialog box (see Figure 3.31).
4. Click *New sheet* to move the chart to its own sheet, or click *Object in*, click the *Object in* arrow, select the worksheet to which you want to move the chart, and then click OK.

FIGURE 3.31 Move Chart Dialog Box ➤

TIP Chart Sheet Name

The default chart sheet name is Chart1, Chart2, etc. You can rename the sheet before you click OK in the Move Chart dialog box or by double-clicking the chart sheet tab, typing a new name, and then pressing Enter.

Printing Charts

Just like for printing any worksheet data, preview the chart in the Backstage view before you print to check margins, spacing, and page breaks to ensure a balanced printout.

Print an Embedded Chart

If you embedded a chart on the same sheet as the data source, you need to decide if you want to print the data only, the data *and* the chart, or the chart only. To print the data only, select the data, click the File tab, click Print, click the first arrow in the Settings section and select Print Selection, and then click Print. To print only the chart, select the chart, and then display the Backstage view. The default setting is Print Selected Chart, and clicking Print will print the chart as a full-page chart. If the data and chart are on the same worksheet, print the worksheet contents to print both, but do not select either the chart or the data before displaying the Backstage view. The preview shows you what will print. Make sure it displays what you want to print before clicking Print.

Print a Chart Sheet

If you moved the chart to a chart sheet, the chart is the only item on that worksheet. When you display the print options, the default is Print Active Sheets, and the chart will print as a full-page chart. You can change the setting to Print Entire Workbook.

Inserting and Customizing a Sparkline

A **sparkline** is a miniature chart contained in a single cell.

Excel 2010 enables you to create miniature charts called sparklines. A ***sparkline*** is a small line, column, or win/loss chart contained in a single cell. The purpose of a sparkline is to present a condensed, simple, succinct visual illustration of data. Unlike a regular chart, a sparkline does not include a chart title or axes labels. Inserting sparklines next to data helps your audience understand data quickly without having to look at a full-scale chart.

A sparkline presents a condensed, simple, succinct visual illustration of data.

Create a Sparkline

Before creating a sparkline, identify what data you want to depict and where you want to place it. To create a sparkline, do the following:

1. Click the Insert tab.
2. Click Line, Column, or Win/Loss in the Sparklines group. The Create Sparklines dialog box opens (see Figure 3.32).
3. Type the cell references in the Data Range box, or click the collapse button (if necessary), select the range, and then click the expand button.
4. Enter or select the range where you want the sparkline to appear in the Location Range box, and then click OK. The default cell location is the active cell unless you change it.

Collapse/Expand button

FIGURE 3.32 Create Sparklines Dialog Box ➤

Apply Design Characteristics to a Sparkline

After you insert a sparkline, the Sparkline Tools Design contextual tab displays, with options to customize the sparkline. Click Edit Data in the Sparkline group to change the data source or sparkline location and indicate how empty cells appear, such as gaps or zeros. You can also change the sparkline type to Line, Column, or Win/Loss in the Type group.

The Show group enables you to display points within the sparkline. For example, click the Markers check box to display markers for all data points on the sparkline, or click High Point to display a marker for the high point, such as for the highest sales or highest price per gallon of gasoline for a time period. The Style group enables you to change the sparkline style, similar to how you can apply different chart styles to charts. Click Sparkline Color to change the color of the sparkline. Click Marker Color, point to a marker type—such as High Point—and then click the color for that marker. Make sure the marker color contrasts with the sparkline color. Figure 3.33 shows a blue sparkline to indicate trends for the yearly students. The High Point marker is red.

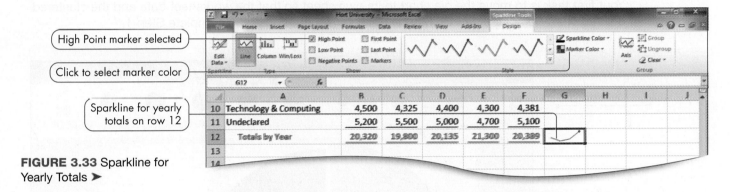

High Point marker selected

Click to select marker color

Sparkline for yearly totals on row 12

FIGURE 3.33 Sparkline for Yearly Totals ➤

TIP Clear Sparklines

To clear the sparklines, select the cells containing sparklines, click the Clear arrow in the Group group on the Sparkline Tools Design tab, and then select either Clear Selected Sparklines or Clear Selected Sparkline Groups.

2 Chart Design

You have studied the Design tab and decide to change some design elements on your two charts. You will move the pie chart to a chart sheet so that Dr. Musto can focus on the chart. You will use other options on the Design tab to modify the charts.

Skills covered: Move a Chart • Apply a Chart Style and Chart Layout • Change the Data • Change the Chart Type • Insert a Sparkline • Print a Chart

---

STEP 1 ▶ MOVE A CHART

Your first task is to move the pie chart to its own sheet so that the worksheet data and the clustered column chart do not distract Dr. Musto. Refer to Figure 3.34 as you complete Step 1.

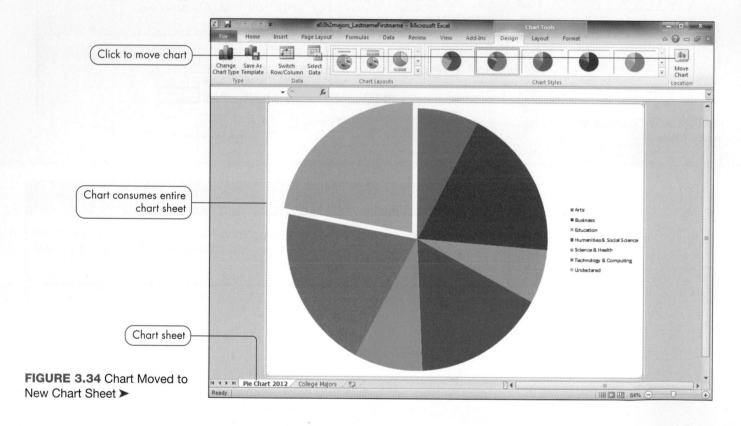

FIGURE 3.34 Chart Moved to New Chart Sheet ➤

a. Open *e03h1majors_LastnameFirstname* if you closed it at the end of Hands-On Exercise 1. Save the workbook with the new name **e03h2majors_LastnameFirstname**, changing *h1* to *h2*.

b. Click the outside border of the pie chart to select it.

c. Click the **Design tab**, and then click **Move Chart** in the Location group.

   The Move Chart dialog box opens so that you can specify a new or existing sheet to which to move the chart.

d. Click **New sheet**, type **Pie Chart 2012**, and then click **OK**. Save the workbook.

   Excel moves the pie chart out of the original worksheet, creates a new sheet named Pie Chart 2012, and inserts the chart on that sheet.

The pie chart looks a little flat, but you know that changing it to a 3-D pie chart could distort the data. A better solution is to apply an interesting chart style. In addition, you apply a layout to change the location of chart elements. Refer to Figure 3.35 as you complete Step 2.

FIGURE 3.35 Chart Style Applied ➤

a. Click the **More button** in the Chart Styles group.

TROUBLESHOOTING: More looks like a horizontal line with a down-pointing triangle.

Excel displays the Chart Styles gallery.

b. Click **Style 42**, the second style from the left on the last row of the gallery.

When you position the mouse pointer over a gallery option, Excel displays a ScreenTip with the style name. When you click Style 42, Excel closes the Chart Styles gallery and applies Style 42 to the chart.

c. Click **Layout 1** in the Chart Layouts group. Save the workbook.

Excel adds a Chart Title placeholder, removes the legend, and inserts the category labels and the respective percentages within the pie slices.

 TIP Pie Chart Labels

The Layout 1 chart layout displays the category names and related percentages on the respective pie slices and removes the legend. This layout is helpful when a pie chart has more than four slices so that you do not have to match pie slice colors with the legend.

d. Click the **Chart Title placeholder**, type **2012 College Majors**, and then press **Enter**. Save the workbook.

> **TROUBLESHOOTING:** If you click inside the Chart Title placeholder instead of just the outer boundary of the placeholder, you may have to delete the placeholder text before typing the new title. Also, the text you type appears only in the Formula Bar until you press Enter. Then it appears in the chart title.

STEP 3 **CHANGE THE DATA**

You realize that the clustered column chart contains aggregated data (averages) along with the other data series. You need to remove the extra data before showing the chart to Dr. Musto. In addition, you notice that Excel placed the years in the legend and the colleges on the X-axis. Dr. Musto wants to be able to compare all majors for each year (that is, all majors for 2009, then all majors for 2010, and so on) instead of the change in Arts majors throughout the years. Refer to Figure 3.36 as you complete Step 3.

FIGURE 3.36 Adjusted Data for Chart ➤

a. Click the **College Majors worksheet tab** to display the worksheet data and clustered column chart.

b. Click the clustered column chart to select it, and then click the **Design tab**, if necessary.

c. Click **Select Data** in the Data group.

The Select Data Source dialog box opens, and Excel selects the original data source in the worksheet.

d. Click **Average** in the **Legend Entries (Series) list**.

You need to remove the aggregated data.

e. Click **Remove**, and then click **OK**.

f. Click **Switch Row/Column** in the Data group.

Excel reverses the data series and category labels so that the years are category labels and the college data are data series and in the legend.

g. Drag the middle-right sizing handle to the right to the end of column J to widen the chart area. Save the workbook.

After reversing the rows and columns, the columns look tall and thin. You widened the chart area to make the columns appear better proportioned.

STEP 4 ▶ CHANGE THE CHART TYPE

Dr. Musto likes what you have done so far, but she would like the column chart to indicate total number of majors per year. You will change the chart to a stacked column chart. Refer to Figure 3.37 as you complete Step 4.

FIGURE 3.37 Stacked Column Chart ▶

a. Click the **Design tab**, if necessary, and then click **Change Chart Type** in the Type group.

   The Change Chart Type dialog box opens. The left side displays the main chart types, and the right side contains a gallery of subtypes for each main type.

b. Click **Stacked Column** in the *Column subtype* section, and then click **OK**.

   You converted the chart from a clustered column chart to a stacked column chart. The stacked column chart displays the total number of majors per year. Each yearly column contains segments representing each college. Now that you changed the chart to a stacked column chart, the columns look too short and wide.

c. Decrease the chart width so that the right edge ends at the end of column I. Save the workbook.

STEP 5 ▶ INSERT A SPARKLINE

You want to insert sparklines to show the enrollment trends for majors in each college at Hort University. After inserting the sparklines, you will display high points to stand out for Dr. Musto and other administrators who want a quick visual of the trends. Refer to Figure 3.38 as you complete Step 5.

FIGURE 3.38 Sparklines Inserted to Show Trends ▶

a. Type **Trends** in **cell G4**, use **Format Painter** to apply the styles from **cell F4** to **cell G4**, and then click **cell G5**.

You entered a heading in the column above where you will insert the sparklines.

b. Click the **Insert tab**, and then click **Line** in the Sparklines group.

c. Select the **range B5:E12** to enter it in the **Data Range box**.

d. Press **Tab**, select the **range G5:G12** to enter it in the **Location Range box**, and then click **OK**.

Excel inserts sparklines in range G5:G12. Each sparkline depicts data for its row. The sparklines are still selected, and the Sparkline Tools Design contextual tab displays.

e. Click the **More button** in the Style group, and then click **Sparkline Style Colorful #4**, the fourth style on the last row of the gallery.

f. Click **High Point** in the Show group.

A marker appears for the high point of each data series for each Trendline. You want to change the marker color to stand out.

g. Click **Marker Color** in the Style group, point to **High Point**, and then click **Red** in the *Standard Colors* section. Save the workbook.

STEP 6 ▶ PRINT A CHART

Dr. Musto wants you to print the stacked column chart and the worksheet data for her as a reference for a meeting this afternoon. You want to preview the pie chart to see how it would look when printed as a full page.

a. Click **cell A4** to deselect the sparklines.

To print both the chart and the worksheet data, you must deselect the chart.

b. Click the **File tab**, and then click **Print**.

The Backstage view shows a preview that the worksheet data and the chart will print on one page.

c. Click **Print** if you or your instructor wants a printout.

d. Click the **Pie Chart 2012 worksheet tab**, click the **File tab**, click **Print** to preview the printout to ensure it would print on one page, and then click the **Home tab** to go back to the chart window.

e. Save the workbook. Keep the workbook onscreen if you plan to continue with Hands-On Exercise 3. If not, close the workbook and exit Excel.

Chart Layout

The Chart Tools Layout tab (see Figure 3.39) enables you to enhance your charts by selecting specific chart elements, inserting objects, displaying or removing chart elements, customizing the axes, formatting the background, and including analysis. When adding visual elements to a chart, make sure these elements enhance the effectiveness of the chart instead of overpowering it.

> When adding visual elements to a chart, make sure these elements enhance the effectiveness of the chart instead of overpowering it.

FIGURE 3.39 Chart Tools Layout Tab ➤

In this section, you will learn how to modify a chart by adjusting individual chart elements, such as the chart title and data labels. In addition, you will learn how to format chart elements, including applying fill colors to a data series.

Selecting and Formatting Chart Elements

A chart includes several elements—the chart area, the plot area, data series, the horizontal axis, the vertical axis, and the legend—each of which you can customize. When you position the mouse pointer over the chart, Excel displays a ScreenTip with the name of that chart element. To select a chart element, click it when you see the ScreenTip, or click the Chart Elements arrow in the Current Selection group, and then select the element from the list.

After you select a chart element, you can format it and change its settings. You can apply font settings, such as increasing the font size, from the Font group on the Home tab. You can format the values by applying a number style or by changing the number of decimal places on the value axis using the options in the Number group on the Home tab.

You can apply multiple settings at once using a Format dialog box, such as Format Data Series. To format the selected chart element, click Format Selection in the Current Selection group, or right-click the chart element, and then select Format *element* to display the appropriate dialog box (see Figure 3.40).

FIGURE 3.40 Format Data Series Dialog Box ➤

The left side of the dialog box lists major categories, such as Fill and Border Color. When you click a category, the right side of the dialog box displays specific options to customize the chart element. For example, when you select the Fill category, the right side displays fill options. When you click a specific option in the right side, such as *Picture or texture fill*, the dialog box displays additional fill options. You can use the Fill options to change the fill color of one or more data series. Avoid making a chart look busy with too many different colors. If you are changing the fill color of a chart area or plot area, make sure the color you select provides enough contrast with the other chart elements.

To format the plot area, click Plot Area in the Background group. Select None to remove any current plot area colors, select Show Plot Area to display the plot area, or select More Plot Area Options to open the Format Plot Area dialog box so that you can apply a fill color to the plot area, similar to selecting fill colors in the Format Data Series dialog box shown in Figure 3.40.

> **TIP** | **Use Images or Textures**
>
> For less formal presentations, you might want to use images or a texture to fill the data series, chart area, or plot area instead of a solid fill color. To use an image or a texture, click *Picture or texture fill* in the Format Data Series dialog box. Click File or Clip Art in the *Insert from* section, and then insert an image file or search the Microsoft Web site to insert an image. Use the Stack option to avoid distorting the image. To add a texture, click Texture, and then select a textured background. Figure 3.41 shows a stacked image as the first data series fill, a texture fill for the second data series, and a gradient fill for the plot area. Generally, do not mix images and textures; in addition to illustrating different fill options, this figure also shows how adding too many features creates a distracting chart.

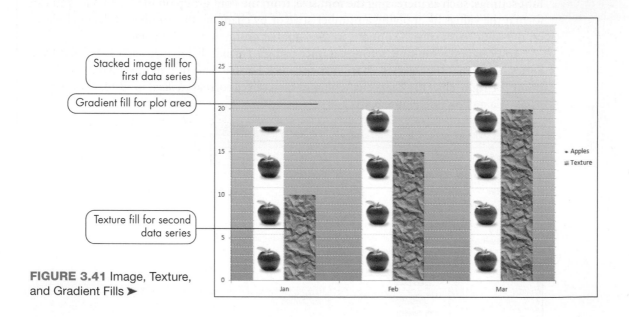

Stacked image fill for first data series

Gradient fill for plot area

Texture fill for second data series

FIGURE 3.41 Image, Texture, and Gradient Fills ➤

Customizing Chart Labels

You should include appropriate labels to describe chart elements. Figure 3.42 identifies basic chart labels.

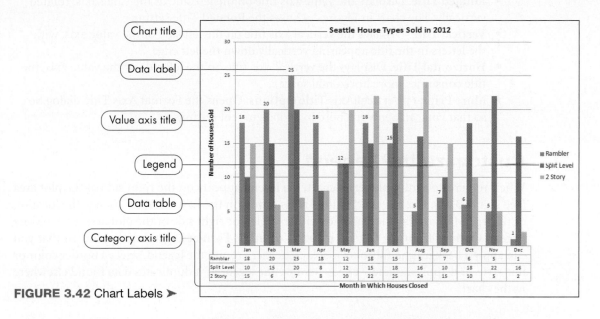

FIGURE 3.42 Chart Labels ➤

Insert and Format the Chart Title

A **chart title** is a label that describes the chart.

A *chart title* is the label that describes the entire chart. Chart titles should reflect the purpose of the chart. For example, *Houses Sold* would be too generic for the chart in Figure 3.42. *Seattle House Types Sold in 2012* indicates the where (Seattle), the what (House Types Sold), and the when (2012).

Excel does not include a chart title by default. Some chart layouts in the Chart Layouts group on the Design tab include a placeholder so that you can enter a title for the current chart. To add, remove, or change the position of a chart title, click Chart Title in the Labels group on the Layout tab, and then select one of the following options:

- **None.** Removes a chart title from the current chart.
- **Centered Overlay Title.** Centers the chart title horizontally without resizing the chart; the title appears over the top of the chart.
- **Above Chart.** Centers the title above the chart (see Figure 3.42), decreasing the chart size to make room for the chart title.
- **More Title Options.** Opens the Format Chart Title dialog box so that you can apply fill, border, and alignment settings.

Position and Format the Axis Titles

An **axis title** is a label that describes either the category axis or the value axis.

Axis titles are labels that describe the category and value axes. If the names on the category axis are not self-explanatory, you can add a label to describe it. The value axis often needs further explanation, such as *In Millions of Dollars* to describe the unit of measurement. To display category axis title options, click Axis Titles in the Labels group, point to Primary Horizontal Axis Title, and then select one of the following:

- **None.** Removes the horizontal axis title from the current chart.
- **Title Below Axis.** Displays the horizontal axis title below the category axis.
- **More Primary Horizontal Axis Title Options.** Opens the Format Axis Title dialog box so that you can apply fill, border, and alignment settings.

To display the value axis title options, click Axis Titles in the Labels group, point to Primary Vertical Axis Title, and then select one of the following:

- **None.** Removes the value axis title from the current chart.
- **Rotated Title.** Displays the value axis title on the left side of the value axis, rotated vertically. The chart in Figure 3.42 uses the Rotated Title setting.
- **Vertical Title.** Displays the vertical axis title on the left side of the value axis, with the letters in the title appearing vertically down the left edge.
- **Horizontal Title.** Displays the vertical axis title on the left side of the value axis; the title consumes more horizontal space.
- **More Primary Vertical Axis Title Options.** Opens the Format Axis Title dialog box so that you can apply fill, border, and alignment settings.

Customize the Legend

When you create a multiple series chart, the legend appears on the right side of the plot area (see Figure 3.42). Click Legend in the Labels group on the Layout tab to change the location of the legend or overlay the legend on either the left or right side of the plot area. Select More Legend Options from the Legend menu to open the Format Legend dialog box so that you can apply a background fill color, display a border around the legend, select a border color or line style, and apply a shadow effect. Remove the legend if it duplicates data found elsewhere in the chart.

Insert and Format Data Labels

A **data label** is the value or name of a data point.

Data labels are descriptive labels that show the exact value of the data points on the value axis. The chart in Figure 3.42 displays data labels for the Rambler data series. Only add data labels when they are necessary for a specific data series; adding data labels for every data point will clutter the chart.

When you select a data label, Excel selects all data labels in that data series. To format the labels, click Format Selection in the Current Selection group, or right-click and select Format Data Labels to open the Format Data Labels dialog box (see Figure 3.43).

FIGURE 3.43 Format Data Labels Dialog Box ➤

The Format Data Labels dialog box enables you to specify what to display as the label. The default Label Contains setting displays values, but you can display additional data such as the category name. Displaying additional data can clutter the chart. You can also specify the position of the label, such as Center or Outside End. If the numeric data labels are not formatted, click Number on the left side of the dialog box, and then apply number formats.

> **TIP** Pie Chart Data Labels
>
> When you first create a pie chart, Excel generates a legend to identify the category labels for the different slice colors, but it does not display data labels. You can display values, percentages, and even category labels on or next to each slice. Pie charts often include percentage data labels. If you also include category labels, hide the legend to avoid duplicating elements.

Include and Format a Data Table

A data table is a grid that contains the data source values and labels. If you embed a chart on the same worksheet as the data source, you do not need to include a data table. Only add a data table with a chart to a chart sheet if you need the audience to know the exact values.

To display a data table, click Data Table in the Labels group, and then select Show Data Table. Figure 3.42 shows a data table at the bottom of the chart area. To see the color-coding along with the category labels, select Show Data Table with Legend Keys, which enables you to omit the legend.

Formatting the Axes and Gridlines

Based on the data source values and structure, Excel determines the starting, incremental, and stopping values that display on the value axis when you create the chart. You might want to adjust the value axis. For example, when working with large values such as 4,567,890, the value axis displays increments, such as 4,000,000 and 5,000,000. You can simplify the value axis by displaying values in millions, so that the values on the axis are 4 and 5 with the word *Millions* placed by the value axis to indicate the units. Figure 3.44 shows two charts—one with original intervals and one in millions.

FIGURE 3.44 Value Axis Scaling ➤

To change the number representation, click Axes in the Axes group, and then point to Primary Vertical Axis. Next, select how you want to represent the value axis: Show Default Axis, Show Axis in Thousands, Show Axis in Millions, Show Axis in Billions, or Show Axis in Log Scale. Select More Primary Vertical Axis Options to open the Format Axis dialog box so that you can customize the value axis values.

Although less commonly used, the Primary Horizontal Axis menu enables you to display the axis from left to right (the default), right to left with the value axis on the right side of the chart and the categories in reverse order on the category axis, or without a category axis. Select More Primary Horizontal Axis Options to customize the horizontal axis.

A **gridline** is a horizontal or vertical line that extends from the horizontal or vertical axis through the plot area.

Gridlines are horizontal or vertical lines that span across the chart to help people identify the values plotted by the visual elements, such as a column. Excel displays horizontal gridlines for column, line, scatter, stock, surface, and bubble charts and vertical gridlines for bar charts. If you do not want to display gridlines in a chart, click Gridlines in the Axes group, point to either Primary Horizontal Gridlines or Primary Vertical Gridlines, and then select None. To add more gridlines, select Minor Gridlines or Major & Minor Gridlines.

Adding a Trendline

A **trendline** is a line used to depict trends and forecast future data.

Charts help reveal trends, patterns, and other tendencies that are difficult to identify by looking at values in a worksheet. A *trendline* is a line that depicts trends or helps forecast future data. Trendlines are commonly used in prediction, such as to determine the future trends of sales, or the success rate of a new prescription drug. You can use trendlines in unstacked column, bar, line, stock, scatter, and bubble charts. To add a trendline, click Trendline in the Analysis group, and then select the type you want: Linear Trendline, Exponential Trendline, Linear Forecast Trendline, or Two Period Moving Average. Figure 3.45 shows two linear forecast trendlines, one applied to the Business data series and one applied to the Undeclared data series. Notice that this trendline provides a forecast (prediction) for two additional time periods—2013 and 2014—although the years are not depicted on the X-axis. Excel analyzes the plotted data to forecast values for the next two time periods when you select the Linear Forecast Trendline. If you apply Linear Trendline only, Excel displays the trendline for the data but does not forecast data points for the future.

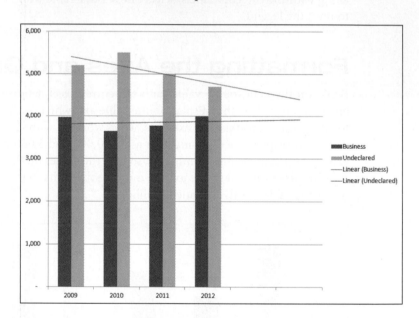

FIGURE 3.45 Trendlines ➤

HANDS-ON EXERCISES

myitlab
HOE3 Training

3 Chart Layout

You want to enhance the column chart by using some options on the Layout tab to add the final touches needed before you give the charts to Dr. Musto to review.

Skills covered: Add a Chart Title • Add and Format Axis Titles • Add Data Labels • Apply Fill Colors • Insert a Trendline

STEP 1 ▶ ADD A CHART TITLE

When you applied a chart layout to the pie chart, Excel displayed a placeholder for the chart title. However, you need to add a chart title for the column chart. You also want to copy the chart and modify it so that you can provide two different perspectives for Dr. Musto. Refer to Figure 3.46 as you complete Step 1.

FIGURE 3.46 Charts with Titles ➤

a. Open *e03h2majors_LastnameFirstname* if you closed it at the end of Hands-On Exercise 2. Save the workbook with the new name **e03h3majors_LastnameFirstname**, changing *h2* to *h3*.

b. Click the stacked column chart to select it.

c. Click the **Layout tab**, click **Chart Title** in the Labels group, and then select **Above Chart**.

Excel displays the Chart Title placeholder, and the plot area decreases to make room for the chart title.

d. Type **Hort University Majors by College** and press **Enter**.

e. Click the **Chart Elements arrow** in the Current Selection group, and then select **Chart Area**.

You selected the entire chart area so that you can copy it.

f. Press **Ctrl+C**, click **cell A33**, and then press **Ctrl+V** to paste the top-left corner of the chart here. Change the second chart to a **Clustered Column chart**. Save the workbook.

You decide to add an axis title to the value axis to clarify the values in the clustered column chart. For the stacked column chart, you want to change the value axis increments. Refer to Figure 3.47 as you complete Step 2.

FIGURE 3.47 Axis Titles and Values Changed ▶

a. Make sure the clustered column chart is selected, and then use the scroll bars if necessary to view the entire chart.

b. Click the **Layout tab**, click **Axis Titles** in the Labels group, point to **Primary Vertical Axis Title**, and then select **Rotated Title**.

   Excel inserts the Axis Title placeholder on the left side of the value axis.

c. Type **Number of Students** and press **Enter**.

   The text you typed replaces the placeholder text after you press Enter.

d. Select the stacked column chart, click the **Layout tab** (if necessary), click **Axes** in the Axes group, point to **Primary Vertical Axis**, and then select **Show Axis in Thousands**.

   Excel changes the value axis values to thousands and includes the label *Thousands* to the left side of the value axis.

e. Click **Thousands** to select it, type **Thousands of Students**, and then press **Enter**.

f. Drag the **Thousands of Students label** down to appear vertically centered with the value axis increments. Save the workbook.

Dr. Musto wants you to emphasize the Undeclared majors data series by adding data labels for that data series. You will have to be careful to add data labels for only the Undeclared data series, as adding data labels for all data series would clutter the chart. Refer to Figure 3.48 as you complete Step 3.

FIGURE 3.48 Data Labels for One Data Series ➤

a. Select the clustered column chart, click the **Chart Elements arrow** in the Current Selection group, and then select **Series "Undeclared"**.

Excel selects all of the Undeclared (light blue) columns in the chart.

b. Click **Data Labels** in the Labels group, and then select **Outside End**.

You added data labels to the selected Undeclared data series.

> **TROUBLESHOOTING:** If data labels appear for all columns, use the Undo feature. Make sure you select only the Undeclared data series columns, and then add data labels again.

c. Look at the data labels to see if they are on gridlines.

The 4,700 and 5,500 data labels are on gridlines.

d. Click the **4,700 data label** twice, pausing between clicks.

Only the 4,700 data label should be selected.

> **TROUBLESHOOTING:** If you double-click a data label instead of pausing between individual clicks, the Format Data Labels dialog box appears. If this happens, click Close in the dialog box, and then repeat step d, pausing longer between clicks.

e. Click the outer edge of the **4,700 data label border**, and then drag the label up a little so that it is off the gridline.

f. Select the **5,500 data label**, and then drag it below the top gridline. Save the workbook.

STEP 4 ▶ **APPLY FILL COLORS**

Dr. Musto wants the Business data series color to stand out, so you will apply a brighter red fill to that series. In addition, you want to apply a gradient color to the plot area so that the chart stands out from the rest of the page. Refer to Figure 3.49 as you complete Step 4.

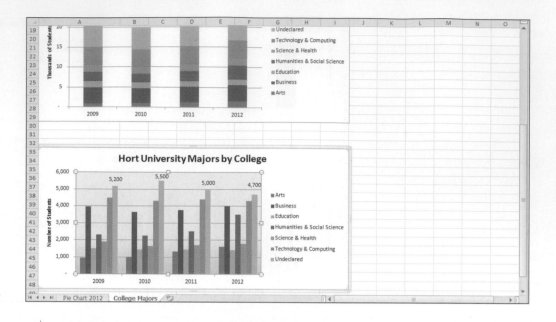

FIGURE 3.49 Chart with Different Fill Colors ➤

a. Make sure the clustered column chart is still selected, click the **Chart Elements arrow** in the Current Selection group, and then select **Series "Business"** or click one of the **Business columns**.

The Business data series columns are selected.

b. Click **Format Selection** in the Current Selection group.

The Format Data Series dialog box opens so that you can format the Business data series.

c. Click **Fill** on the left side of the dialog box, and then click **Solid fill**.

The dialog box displays additional fill options.

d. Click **Color**, click **Red** in the *Standard Colors* section of the gallery, and then click **Close**.

The Business data series appears in red.

e. Click **Plot Area** in the Background group, and then select **More Plot Area Options**.

The Format Plot Area dialog box opens.

f. Click **Gradient fill**, click **Preset colors**, click **Parchment** (using the ScreenTips to help you find the correct preset color), and then click **Close**.

Be careful when selecting plot area colors to ensure that the data series columns, bars, or lines still stand out. Print a sample on a color printer to help make the decision.

STEP 5 ▶ INSERT A TRENDLINE

Identifying trends is important when planning college budgets. Colleges with growing enrollments need additional funding to support more students. It looks like the numbers of humanities and social science majors are increasing, but you want to add a trendline to verify your analysis. Refer to Figure 3.50 as you complete Step 5.

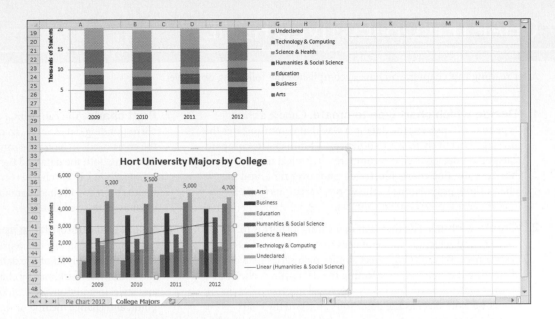

FIGURE 3.50 Trendline ➤

a. Make sure the clustered column chart is still selected.

b. Click **Trendline** in the Analysis group, and then select **Linear Trendlinc**.

The Add Trendline dialog box opens so that you can select which data series you want to use for the trendline.

c. Click **Humanities & Social Science**, and then click **OK**.

Excel adds a trendline based on the data series you specified. The trend is a steady increase in the number of majors in this discipline.

d. Save and close the workbook, and submit based on your instructor's directions.

After reading this chapter, you have accomplished the following objectives:

1. **Decide which chart type to create.** Choose a chart type that will present the data in a way that communicates the message effectively to your audience. Column charts compare categorical data, bar charts compare categorical data horizontally, line charts illustrate trends over time, and pie charts show proportions to the whole. Variations of each major chart type are called *subtypes*.

2. **Create a chart.** The first step in creating a chart is to identify and select the range of cells that will be used as the data source. Be careful to select similar data series to avoid distorting the chart. After selecting the data source, click the desired chart type on the Insert tab. Excel inserts charts on the same worksheet as the data. You can move the chart and adjust the size of the chart area. When you create a chart or select an existing chart, Excel displays the Chart Tools contextual tab with three tabs: Design, Layout, and Format.

3. **Change the chart type.** You can change a chart to a different chart type if you believe a different chart type will represent the data better.

4. **Change the data source and structure.** You can add or remove data from the data source to change the data in the chart. The Select Data Source dialog box enables you to modify the ranges used for the data series. Excel usually places the first column of data as the category axis and the first row of data as the legend, but you can switch the row and column layout. The Design tab contains options for changing the data source and structure.

5. **Apply a chart layout and a chart style.** You can apply a chart layout to control what chart elements are included and where they are positioned within the chart area. You can apply a chart style, which determines formatting, such as the background color and the data series color. The Design tab contains options for selecting the chart layout and chart style.

6. **Move a chart.** You can position a chart on the same worksheet as the data source, or you can move the chart to its own sheet. The Move Chart dialog box enables you to select a new sheet and name the new chart sheet at the same time. The chart sheet will then contain a full-sized chart and no data. You can also move a chart to an existing worksheet. When you do this, the chart is an embedded object on that sheet, and the sheet may contain other data.

7. **Print charts.** You can print a chart with or without its corresponding data source. To print a chart with its data series, the chart needs to be on the same worksheet as the data source. To ensure both the data and the chart print, make sure the chart is not selected. If the chart is on its own sheet or if you select the chart on a worksheet containing other data, the chart will print as a full-sized chart.

8. **Insert and customize a sparkline.** A sparkline is a miniature chart in one cell representing a single data series. It gives a quick visual of the data to aid in comprehension. You can customize sparklines by changing the data source, location, and style. In addition, you can display markers, such as High Point, and change the line or marker color.

9. **Select and format chart elements.** Because each chart element is an individual object in the chart area, you can select and format each element separately. The Format dialog boxes enable you to apply fill colors, select border colors, and apply other settings. For the value axis, you can format values and specify the number of decimal places to display. For basic formatting, such as font color, use the options in the Font group on the Home tab.

10. **Customize chart labels.** The Labels group on the Layout tab enables you to add or remove chart elements: chart title, axis titles, legend, data labels, and a data table. The chart title should clearly describe the data and purpose of the chart. Include axis titles when you need to clarify the values on the value axis or the categories on the category axis. Customize the legend when you want to change its position within the chart area or hide the legend. Display data labels to provide exact values for data points in one or more data series; however, be careful the data labels do not overlap. If a chart is contained on a chart sheet, you might want to show the data table that contains the values used from the data source.

11. **Format the axes and gridlines.** The Axes group on the Layout tab enables you to control the horizontal and vertical axes. You can select the minimum, maximum, and increments on the value axis, and you can display both major and minor gridlines to help your audience read across the plot area.

12. **Add a trendline.** A trendline is a line that depicts trends. Trendlines are used to help make predictions or forecasts based on the current dataset. Excel enables you to select different types of trendlines based on the type of statistical analysis you want to perform.

KEY TERMS

100% stacked column chart *p.425*

3-D chart *p.426*

Area chart *p.428*

Axis title *p.453*

Bar chart *p.427*

Bubble chart *p.431*

Category axis *p.423*

Category label *p.422*

Chart *p.422*

Chart area *p.423*

Chart sheet *p.434*

Chart title *p.453*

Clustered column chart *p.423*

Column chart *p.423*

Data label *p.454*

Data point *p.422*

Data series *p.422*

Doughnut chart *p.431*

Exploded pie chart *p.428*

Gridline *p.456*

Legend *p.424*

Line chart *p.427*

Multiple data series *p.423*

Pie chart *p.428*

Plot area *p.423*

Radar chart *p.432*

Single data series *p.423*

Sizing handle *p.434*

Sparkline *p.444*

Stacked column chart *p.424*

Stock chart *p.430*

Surface chart *p.430*

Trendline *p.456*

Value axis *p.423*

X Y (scatter) chart *p.429*

X-axis *p.423*

Y-axis *p.423*

1. Which type of chart is the **least** appropriate for depicting yearly rainfall totals for five cities for four years?

   (a) Pie chart

   (b) Line chart

   (c) Column chart

   (d) Bar chart

2. What is the typical sequence for creating a chart?

   (a) Select the chart type, select the data source, and then size and position the chart.

   (b) Select the data source, size the chart, select the chart type, and then position the chart.

   (c) Select the data source, select the chart type, and then size and position the chart.

   (d) Click the cell to contain the chart, select the chart type, and then select the data source.

3. Which of the following applies to a sparkline?

   (a) Chart title

   (b) Single-cell chart

   (c) Legend

   (d) Multiple data series

4. If you want to show exact values for a data series in a bar chart, what chart element should you display?

   (a) Chart title

   (b) Legend

   (c) Value axis title

   (d) Data labels

5. The value axis currently shows increments such as 50,000 and 100,000. What do you select to display increments of 50 and 100?

   (a) More Primary Vertical Axis Title Options

   (b) Show Axis in Thousands

   (c) Show Axis in Millions

   (d) Show Right to Left Axis

6. You want to create a single chart that shows each of five divisions' proportion of yearly sales for each year for five years. Which type of chart can accommodate your needs?

   (a) Pie chart

   (b) Surface chart

   (c) Clustered bar chart

   (d) 100% stacked column chart

7. Currently, a column chart shows values on the value axis, years on the category axis, and state names in the legend. What should you do if you want to organize data with the states on the category axis and the years shown in the legend?

   (a) Change the chart type to a clustered column chart.

   (b) Click Switch Row/Column in the Data group on the Design tab.

   (c) Click Layout 2 in the Chart Layouts group on the Design tab, and then apply a different chart style.

   (d) Click Legend in the Labels group on the Layout tab, and then select Show Legend at Bottom.

8. Which tab contains commands to apply a predefined chart layout that controls what elements are included, where, and their color scheme?

   (a) Design

   (b) Layout

   (c) Format

   (d) Page Layout

9. A chart and its related data source are located on the same worksheet. What is the default Print option if the chart is selected prior to displaying the Backstage view?

   (a) Print Entire Workbook

   (b) Print Selection

   (c) Print Selected Chart

   (d) Print Active Sheets

10. Which of the following is *not* a way to display the Format Data Series dialog box for the Arts data series in a column chart?

    (a) Press and hold Shift as you click each Arts column.

    (b) Click an Arts column, and then click Format Selection in the Current Selection group on the Layout tab.

    (c) Right-click an Arts column, and then select Format Data Series.

    (d) Click the Chart Elements arrow in the Current Selection group, select the Arts data series, and then click Format Selection in the Current Selection group on the Layout tab.

1 Family Utility Expenses

Your cousin, Rita Dansie, wants to analyze her family's utility expenses for 2012. She wants to save money during months when utility expenses are lower so that her family will have money budgeted for months when the total utility expenses are higher. She gave you her files for the electric, gas, and water bills for the year 2012. You created a worksheet that lists the individual expenses per month, along with yearly totals per utility type and monthly totals. You will create some charts to depict the data. This exercise follows the same set of skills as used in Hands-On Exercises 1 and 2 in the chapter. Refer to Figure 3.51 as you complete this exercise.

FIGURE 3.51 Dansie Family Utility Expenses ➤

a. Open *e03p1utilities* and save it as **e03p1utilities_LastnameFirstname**.

b. Select the **range A4:E17**, and then click the **Insert tab**.

c. Click **Column** in the Charts group, and then select **Clustered Column**. After creating the chart, you realize you need to adjust the data source because you included the monthly and yearly totals.

d. Click the **Design tab**, if necessary. Click **Select Data** in the Data group to open the Select Data Source dialog box, and then do the following:
   - Click **Monthly Totals** in the **Legend Entries (Series) list**, and then click **Remove**.
   - Click in the **Chart data range box**, and then change *17* to **16** at the end of the range.
   - Click **OK** to finalize removing the monthly and yearly totals from the chart.

e. Position the mouse pointer over the chart area. When you see the Chart Area ScreenTip, drag the chart so that the top-left edge of the chart is in **cell A19**.

f. Click the **Format tab**. Click in the **Shape Width box** in the Size group, type **6**, and then press **Enter**.

g. Click the **Design tab**, and then click **Layout 3** in the Chart Layouts group.

h. Click the **Chart Title placeholder**, type **Monthly Utility Expenses for 2012**, and then press **Enter**.

i. Click the **More button** in the Chart Styles group, and then click **Style 26** (second style, fourth row).

j. Click the clustered column chart, use the **Copy command**, and then paste a copy of the chart in **cell A36**. With the second chart selected, do the following:
   - Click the **Design tab**, click **Change Chart Type** in the Type group, select **Line with Markers** in the *Line* section, and then click **OK**.
   - Click the **More button** in the Chart Styles group, and then click **Style 2** (second style, first row).
   - Copy the selected chart, and then paste it in **cell A52**.

k. Make sure the third chart is selected, and then do the following:
   - Click the **Design tab**, if necessary, click **Change Chart Type** in the Type group, select **Area** on the left side, click **Stacked Area**, and then click **OK**.
   - Click **Move Chart** in the Location group, click **New sheet**, type **Area Chart**, and then click **OK**.

l. Click the **Expenses worksheet tab**, scroll up to see the line chart, and then select the line chart. Click the **Design tab**, if necessary, click **Move Chart** in the Location group, click **New sheet**, type **Line Chart**, and then click **OK**.

m. Create a footer with your name on the left side, the sheet name code in the center, and the file name code on the right side on the worksheet and on the two chart sheets.

n. Click the **File tab**, and then click **Print**. Look at the preview window for each worksheet. Print all three worksheets for your reference, based on your instructor's directions.

o. Save and close the workbook, and submit based on your instructor's directions.

2 U.S. Population Estimates

You work for a major corporation headquartered in Chicago. One of your responsibilities is to analyze population statistics to identify geographic regions in which you can increase your market presence. You often visit the U.S. Census Bureau's Web site to download and analyze the data. You need to create a chart to present at a meeting tomorrow morning. This exercise follows the same set of skills as used in Hands-On Exercises 1, 2, and 3 in the chapter. Refer to Figure 3.52 as you complete this exercise.

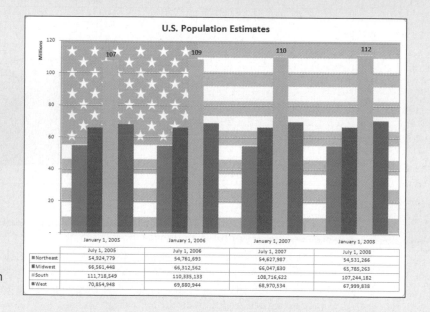

FIGURE 3.52 U.S. Population Estimates ➤

a. Open *e03p2uspop* and save it as **e03p2uspop_LastnameFirstname**.

b. Select the **range A3:E7**, click the **Insert tab**, click **Column** in the Charts group, and then click **Clustered Column** in the *2-D Column* section.

c. Click **Move Chart** in the Location group on the Design tab. Click **New sheet**, type **Column Chart**, and then click **OK**.

d. Click the **Layout tab**, and then add a chart title by doing the following:
   • Click **Chart Title** in the Labels group, and then select **Above Chart**.
   • Type **U.S. Population Estimates** and press **Enter**.

e. Add data labels by doing the following:
   • Click the **Chart Elements arrow** in the Current Selection group, and then select **Series "South"**.
   • Click **Data Labels** in the Labels group, and then select **Outside End**.
   • Click the data labels to select them, apply **bold**, and then apply a **12-pt font** size.

f. Click the **Layout tab**, if necessary, click **Data Table** in the Labels group, and then select **Show Data Table with Legend Keys**.

g. Click **Legend** in the Labels group, and then select **None**.

h. Click **Axes** in the Axes group, point to **Primary Vertical Axis**, and then select **Show Axis in Millions**.

i. Click **Plot Area** in the Background group, and then select **More Plot Area Options**. Do the following in the Format Plot Area dialog box:
   • Click **Picture or texture fill**.
   • Click **Clip Art**, then in the Select Picture dialog box, search for and insert a picture of the **U.S. flag**.

- Select the image, and then click **OK**.
- Drag the **Transparency slider** to **70%**, and then click **Close**.

j. Click the **Population worksheet tab**, click **cell B9**, and create sparklines by doing the following:
- Click the **Insert tab**, and click **Column** in the Sparklines group.
- Select the **range B4:B7** to enter the range in the **Data Range box**.
- Ensure **$B$9** appears in the **Location Range box**, and then click **OK**.
- Increase the row height of row 9 to **42.00**.

k. Adapt step j to create sparklines in the **range C9:E9**.

l. Create a footer with your name on the left side, the sheet name code in the center, and the file name code on the right side of both worksheets.

m. Save and close the workbook, and submit based on your instructor's directions.

3 Gas Prices in Boston

You are interested in moving to Boston, but you want to know about the city's gasoline prices. You downloaded data from a government site, but it is overwhelming to detect trends when you have over 200 weekly data points. You create a chart to help you interpret the data. This exercise follows the same set of skills as used in Hands-On Exercises 1, 2, and 3 in the chapter. Refer to Figure 3.53 as you complete this exercise.

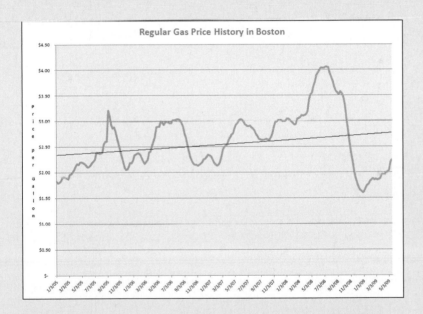

FIGURE 3.53 Boston Gas Prices ➤

a. Open *e03p3boston* and save it as **e03p3boston_LastnameFirstname**.

b. Select **cells A6:B235**, click the **Insert tab**, click **Line** in the Charts group, and then click **Line** in the *2-D Line* section. Excel creates the chart and displays the Chart Tools Design tab.

c. Click **Move Chart** in the Location group, click **New sheet**, type **Line Chart**, and then click **OK**.

d. Click the **Layout tab**, click **Legend** in the Labels group, and then select **None** to remove the legend.

e. Click the chart title to select it, type **Regular Gas Price History in Boston**, and then press **Enter**.

f. Click **Axis Titles** in the Labels group, point to **Primary Vertical Axis Title**, select **Vertical Title**, type **Price per Gallon**, and then press **Enter**.

g. Click **Axes** in the Axes group, point to **Primary Vertical Axis**, and then select **More Primary Vertical Axis Options**. Do the following in the Format Axis dialog box:
- Make sure that **Axis Options** is selected on the left side of the Format Axis dialog box, click the **Display units arrow**, and then select **Hundreds**.
- Click **Number** on the left side of the dialog box, click **Accounting** in the **Category list**, and then click **Close**.

h. Click the **Hundreds label**, and then press **Delete**. You converted the cents per gallon to dollars and cents per gallon.

i. Click **Axes** in the Axes group, point to **Primary Horizontal Axis**, and then select **More Primary Horizontal Axis Options**. Click **Number** on the left side of the Format Axis dialog box, click **Date** in the **Category list** if necessary, select **3/14/01** in the **Type list**, and then click **Close**.

j. Use the Home tab to change the category axis, value axis, and value axis labels to **9-pt** size. Apply the **Orange, Accent 6, Darker 25% font color** to the chart title.

k. Click the **Design tab**, click the **More button** in the Chart styles group, and then click **Style 40** (first style on the right side of the fifth row).

l. Click the **Layout tab**, click **Trendline**, and then select **Exponential Trendline**.

m. Create a footer with your name on the left side, the sheet name code in the center, and the file name code on the right side.

n. Click the **File tab**, click **Print**, and then look at the preview. Print the chart sheet if instructed.

o. Save and close the workbook, and submit based on your instructor's directions.

1 Car Ratings

You work for an independent automobile rating company that provides statistics to consumers. A group of testers recently evaluated four 2012 mid-sized passenger car models and provided the data to you in a worksheet. You need to transform the data into meaningful charts that you will include on your company's Web site. Refer to Figure 3.54 as you complete this exercise.

FIGURE 3.54 Automobile Ratings Chart ➤

DISCOVER

a. Open *e03m1autos* and save it as **e03m1autos_LastnameFirstname**.

b. Insert a column sparkline individually for each car model and for the overall category ratings in column H. Include all ratings, including the average. Apply a different style to each sparkline. Change the row height to **20** for rows containing sparklines.

c. Select the **range A3:F8**, and then create a stacked column chart. You realize that the data in this chart is not cumulative and that you included the overall ratings by category. You also notice that the chart is located to the side of the data. Make the following changes:
   - Change the chart to a clustered column chart.
   - Remove the overall category from the data source.
   - Position the chart starting in **cell A11**, and then increase the chart width through **cell G27**.

d. Make the following design changes:
   - Select **Layout 1** as the chart layout style.
   - Edit the chart title to be **2012 Mid-Sized Car Ratings by Category**.
   - Apply the **Red, Accent 2, Darker 25% font color** to the chart title.
   - Apply the **Style 12 chart style**.

e. Create another chart on a new chart sheet:
   - Select the **range A4:A7**, press and hold **Ctrl**, and then select the **range G4:G7**—the models and the overall ratings.
   - Create a clustered bar chart.
   - Move the chart to its own sheet named **Overall Ratings**.

f. Make the following changes to the bar chart (see Figure 3.54):
   - Remove the legend.
   - Add the title **2012 Mid-Sized Car Overall Ratings** above the chart.
   - Apply the **Style 2 chart style**, if necessary.
   - Add data labels in the Outside End position, and then bold the data labels. Apply the **Fog gradient fill color** to the data labels.
   - Select the data series, and then apply a picture fill, searching for clip art of a blue automobile. Select the option to stack the images instead of stretching one image per data marker.

g. Insert a footer with your name on the left side, the sheet name code in the center, and the file name code on the right side on all worksheets.

h. Adjust the page setup option to fit the worksheet to one page with 0.5" left and right margins. Print the worksheet that contains the data and the clustered column chart per your instructor's directions.

i. Save and close the workbook, and submit based on your instructor's directions.

2 Grade Analysis

You are a teaching assistant for Dr. Monica Unice's introductory psychology class. You have maintained her grade book all semester, entering three test scores for each student and calculating the final average. Dr. Unice wants to see a chart that shows the percentage of students who earn each letter grade. You decide to create a pie chart. She wants to see if a correlation exists between attendance and students' final grades, so you will create a scatter chart.

a. Open *e03m2psych* and save it as **e03m2psych_LastnameFirstname**.

b. Create a pie chart from the Final Grade Distribution data located below the student data, and then move the pie chart to its own sheet named **Grades Pie**.

c. Customize the pie chart with these specifications:
  • **Layout 1 chart layout** with the title **PSY 2030 Final Grade Distribution - Fall 2012**
  • F grade slice exploded
  • **20-pt** size for the data labels, with a center label position, and gradient fill
  • Border: no line

d. Apply these standard fill colors to the respective data points:
  • A: Blue
  • B: Green
  • C: Orange
  • D: Purple
  • F: Red

e. Create a Scatter with only Markers chart using the attendance record and final averages from the Grades worksheet, and then move the scatter chart to its own sheet. Name the sheet **Attend Grades**.

f. Apply these label settings to the scatter chart:
  • Legend: none
  • Chart title above chart: **Attendance - Final Average Relationship**
  • X-axis title: **Percentage of Attendance**
  • Y-axis rotated title: **Student Final Averages**

g. Use Help to learn how to apply the following axis settings:
  • Y-axis: 40 starting point, 100 maximum score, 10 point increments, and a number format with zero decimal places
  • X-axis: 40 starting point, automatic increments, automatic maximum

h. Add the **Parchment gradient fill** to the plot area.

i. Insert a linear trendline.

j. Center the worksheet horizontally between the left and right margins on the Grades worksheet.

k. Insert a footer with your name on the left side, the sheet name code in the center, and the file name code on the right side for all three worksheets.

l. Save and close the workbook, and submit based on your instructor's directions.

You are an assistant manager at Premiere Movie Source, an online company that enables customers to download movies for a fee. You are required to track movie download sales by genre. You gathered the data for September 2012 and organized it in an Excel workbook. You are ready to create charts to help represent the data so that you can make a presentation to your manager later this week.

Change Data Source, Position, and Size

You already created a clustered column chart, but you selected too many cells for the data source. You need to open the workbook and adjust the data source for the chart. In addition, you want to position and size the chart.

   a. Open the *e03c1movies* workbook and save it as **e03c1movies_LastnameFirstname**.

   b. Remove the Category Totals from the legend, and then adjust the data range to exclude the weekly totals.

   c. Position and size the chart to fill the **range A18:L37**.

   d. Change the row and column orientation so that the weeks appear in the category axis and the genres appear in the legend.

Add Chart Labels

You want to add a chart title and a value axis title and change the legend's position.

   a. Add a chart title above the chart.

   b. Enter the text **September 2012 Downloads by Genre**.

   c. Add a rotated value axis title.

   d. Enter the text **Number of Downloads**.

   e. Move the legend to the top of the chart, and then drag the bottom of the chart area down to cover row 40.

Format Chart Elements

You are ready to apply the finishing touches to the clustered column chart. You will adjust the font size of the category axis and display additional gridlines to make it easier to identify values for the data series. You will add and adjust data labels to the Drama data series. Finally, you will add a linear trendline to the chart to visualize trends.

   a. Format the category axis with **12-pt size**.

   b. Display major and minor horizontal gridlines.

   c. Select the **Drama data series**, and then add data labels in the Outside End position.

   d. Add a **Yellow fill color** to the data labels.

   e. Add a linear trendline to the Drama data series.

Insert and Format Sparklines

You want to show weekly trends for each genre by inserting sparklines in the column to the right of Category Totals.

   a. Insert a **Line sparkline** for the weekly (but not category totals) data for Action & Adventure in **cell G5**.

   b. Copy the sparkline down the column.

   c. Format the sparklines by applying **Sparkline Style Dark #6**, display the high point, and format the high point marker in **Red**.

Create Another Chart

You want to create a chart that will show the monthly volume of downloads by genre. You decide to create a bar chart with genre labels along the left side of the chart.

   a. Select the genres and weekly totals. Create a clustered bar chart.

   b. Move the chart to its own sheet, and then name the sheet **Bar Chart**.

   c. Change the chart type to a stacked bar chart.

   d. Add a chart title above the chart, and then enter **Sept 2012 Total Monthly Downloads by Genre**.

Format the Bar Chart

You want to enhance the appearance of the chart by applying a chart style and adjusting the axis values.

   a. Apply the **Style 31 chart style** to the bar chart.

   b. Display the value axis in units of thousands.

   c. Display the category axis names in reverse order using the Format Axis dialog box.

   d. Apply the **Layout 3 layout style** to the chart.

Printing the Charts

You want to print the bar chart on its own page, but you want to print the clustered column chart with the original data. To ensure the worksheet data and chart print on the same page, you need to adjust the page setup options.

   a. Create a footer on each worksheet with your name, the sheet name code, and the file name code.

   b. Apply landscape orientation for the original worksheet.

   c. Set 0.2" left, right, top, and bottom margins for the original worksheet.

   d. Select the option that makes the worksheet print on only one page.

   e. Print both worksheets.

   f. Save and close the workbook, and submit based on your instructor's directions.

Widget Company Stock Prices

GENERAL CASE

You want to track your investment in Widget Company. Open *e03b1stock* and save it as **e03b1stock_LastnameFirstname**. Create the appropriate stock chart based on the existing sequence of data, keeping in mind that data must be in a specific structure to create the chart. Move the chart to a new chart sheet, and name the sheet **Stock Chart**. Apply the Style 37 chart style, remove the legend, and display the data table. Add a centered overlay title that describes the chart. Select the chart title; apply a solid fill using Olive Green, Accent 3, Darker 50%; and apply White, Background 1 font color. Add a linear trendline for the closing price. Create a footer with your name, the sheet name code, and file name code. Save and close the workbook, and submit based on your instructor's directions.

Box Office Movie Data

RESEARCH CASE

As a contributing writer for an entertainment magazine, you have been asked to gather data on box office opening revenue for movies released in the theaters this month. Conduct some online research to identify six newly released movies, their release dates, and the revenue generated. Start a new workbook. Organize the data from the lowest-grossing movie to the highest-grossing movie. Apply appropriate formatting, and include a main and secondary title for the worksheet. Save the workbook as **e03b2boxoffice_LastnameFirstname**. Use the data to create a bar chart on a separate worksheet, showing the movie names on the vertical axis and revenue on the horizontal axis. Assign names to the worksheet tabs, and delete the extra worksheets. Format the value axis in millions, and apply Accounting or Currency format, if needed. Insert a chart title that describes the data. Apply a different chart style. Use Help to research how to insert text boxes. Insert a text box for the first bar containing the release date. Position the text box on top of the bar, and select a contrasting font color. Copy the text box for the remaining movie bars, and edit each text box to display the respective release dates. Create a footer with your name, the sheet name code, and the file name code. Print a copy of the chart for your records. Save and close the workbook, and submit based on your instructor's directions.

Harper County Houses Sold

DISASTER RECOVERY

You want to analyze the number of houses sold by type (e.g., rambler, two-story, etc.) in each quarter during 2012. Your intern created an initial chart, but it contains a lot of problems. Open *e03b3houses* and save it as **e03b3houses_LastnameFirstname**. Identify the errors and poor design. List the errors and your corrections in a two-column format below the chart. Then correct problems in the chart. Create a footer with your name, the sheet name code, and the file name code. Adjust the margins and scaling to print the worksheet data, including the error list, and chart on one page. Save and close the workbook, and submit based on your instructor's directions.

EXCEL

4 DATASETS AND TABLES

Managing Large Volumes of Data

Watch the
**Set-up
Video**
for this
Case Study!

CASE STUDY | The Spa Experts

Shortly after graduating from college, you and your best friend, Ryan Paap, started a business selling spas and hot tubs. Business has been good, and your expansive showroom and wide selection appeal to a variety of customers. You and Ryan maintain a large inventory to attract the impulse buyer and currently have agreements with three manufacturers: Serenity Spas, The Original Hot Tub, and Port-a-Spa. Each manufacturer offers spas and hot tubs that appeal to different segments of the market, from affordable to exorbitant.

The business has grown rapidly, and you need to analyze the sales data in order to increase future profits. For example, which vendor generates the most sales? Who is the leading salesperson? Do most customers purchase or finance? Are sales promotions necessary to promote business, or will customers pay the full price?

You created a worksheet that has sales data for the current month. Each transaction appears on a separate row and contains the transaction number, date, sales representatives' first and last names, the spa manufacturer, payment type (financed or paid in full), transaction (standard or promotion), and the amount of the sale. You are ready to start analyzing the data in Excel.

OBJECTIVES AFTER YOU READ THIS CHAPTER, YOU WILL BE ABLE TO:

1. Freeze rows and columns *p.475*

2. Print large datasets *p.476*

3. Understand table design *p.484*

4. Create a table *p.485*

5. Apply a table style *p.487*

6. Sort data *p.493*

7. Filter data *p.495*

8. Use structured references and a total row *p.498*

9. Apply conditional formatting *p.509*

10. Create a new rule *p.512*

11. Sort and filter using conditional formatting *p.514*

Large Datasets

So far you have worked with worksheets that contain small datasets, a collection of structured, related data in columns and rows. In reality, you will probably work with large datasets consisting of hundreds or thousands of rows and columns of data. When you work with small datasets, you can usually view most or all of the data without scrolling. When you work with large datasets, column and row labels scroll offscreen when you scroll through the worksheet. Large, widescreen monitors set at high resolutions display more data onscreen; however, you may not be able to view the entire dataset. You might want to keep some data always in view, even as you scroll throughout the dataset. Figure 4.1 shows the Spa Experts' January sales transactions. Because it contains a lot of transactions, the entire dataset is not visible. You could decrease the zoom level; however, doing so decreases the text size onscreen, making it hard to read the data.

> Working with large datasets is challenging because column and row labels scroll offscreen....

FIGURE 4.1 Large Dataset ➤

In order to view other columns, use the horizontal scroll bar to view one or more columns to the right. When the active cell is in the last visible column (cell J1, for example), pressing ➡ displays one or two more columns on the right. Clicking the down arrow in the vertical scroll bar or pressing ⬇ when the active cell is in the bottom visible row moves the screen down one row. As you scroll down and to the right, the rows and columns that were originally visible are no longer visible.

In this section, you will learn how to freeze panes and print large worksheets. In particular, you will learn how to keep labels onscreen as you scroll and how to adjust settings that control how large worksheets print.

TIP Go to a Specific Cell

You can navigate through a large worksheet by using the Go To command. Click Find & Select in the Editing group on the Home tab and select Go To (or press F5 or Ctrl+G) to display the Go To dialog box, enter the cell address in the Reference box, and then press Enter to go to the cell. You can also click in the Name Box, type the cell reference, and then press Enter.

Freezing Rows and Columns

When you scroll to parts of a dataset not initially visible, some rows and columns disappear from view. When the row and column labels scroll off the screen, you may not remember what each column represents. You can keep labels onscreen by freezing them. *Freezing* is the process of keeping rows and/or columns visible onscreen at all times even when you scroll through a large dataset. To freeze labels from scrolling offscreen, click the View tab, click Freeze Panes in the Window group, and then select a freeze option. Table 4.1 describes the three freeze options.

Freezing keeps rows and/or columns visible as you scroll through a worksheet.

TABLE 4.1	Freeze Options
Option	**Description**
Freeze Panes	Keeps both rows and columns above and to the left of the active cell visible as you scroll through a worksheet.
Freeze Top Row	Keeps only the top row visible as you scroll through a worksheet.
Freeze First Column	Keeps only the first column visible as you scroll through a worksheet.

To freeze one or more rows and columns, use the Freeze Panes option. Before selecting this option, make the active cell one row below and one column to the right of the rows and columns you want to freeze. For example, to freeze the first five rows and the first two columns, make cell C6 the active cell before clicking a Freeze Panes option. As Figure 4.2 shows, Excel displays a horizontal line below the last frozen row (row 5) and a vertical line to the right of the last frozen column (column B). As you scroll down, the unfrozen rows, such as rows 6–14, disappear. As you scroll to the right, the unfrozen columns, such as columns C and D, disappear.

- Rows 1–5 frozen
- Columns A and B frozen
- Horizontal line below last frozen row
- Vertical line to the right of the last frozen column

FIGURE 4.2 Freeze Panes Set ➤

To unlock the rows and columns from remaining onscreen as you scroll, click Freeze Panes in the Window group, and then select Unfreeze Panes, which only appears on the menu when you have frozen rows and/or columns. After you unfreeze the panes, the Unfreeze Panes option disappears, and the Freeze Panes option appears on the menu again.

> **TIP** Edit Data in Frozen Range
>
> When you freeze panes and press Ctrl+Home, the first unfrozen cell is the active cell instead of cell A1. For example, with columns A and B and rows 1–5 frozen in Figure 4.2, pressing Ctrl+Home makes cell C6 the active cell. If you need to edit a cell in the frozen area, click the particular cell to make it active, and then edit the data.

Printing Large Datasets

Printing all or parts of a large dataset presents special challenges. For a large dataset, some columns and rows may print on several pages. Analyzing the data for individual printed pages is difficult when each page does not contain column and row labels. To prevent wasting paper, always preview large datasets in the Backstage view before printing data. Doing so enables you to adjust page settings until you are satisfied with how the data will print.

The Page Layout tab (see Figure 4.3) contains many options to help you prepare large datasets to print. Previously, you changed the page orientation, set different margins, and adjusted the scaling. In addition, you can manage page breaks, set the print area, and print titles.

Click to insert a page break

Click to print titles (labels) on each printed page

Click to set the print area

FIGURE 4.3 Page Setup Options ➤

Manage Page Breaks

*A **page break** indicates where data starts on a new printed page.*

Based on the paper size, orientation, margins, and other settings, Excel identifies how much data can print on a page. Then it displays a ***page break***, indicating where data will start on another printed page. To identify where these automatic page breaks will occur, click Page Break Preview on the status bar or in the Workbook Views group on the Views tab. If the Welcome to Page Break Preview message box appears, click OK. Excel displays watermarks, such as *Page 1*, indicating the area that will print on a specific page. Blue dashed lines indicate where the automatic page breaks occur, and solid blue lines indicate manual page breaks.

If the automatic page breaks occur in undesirable locations, you can adjust the page breaks. For example, if you have a worksheet listing sales data by date, the automatic page break might occur within a group of rows for one date, such as between two rows of data for 1/21/2012. To make all rows for that date appear together, insert a page break above the first data row for that date. To do this, drag a page break line to the desired location. You can also set a manual break at a specific location by doing the following:

1. Click the cell that you want to be the first row and column on a new printed page. If you want cell A50 to start a new page, click cell A50. If you click cell D50, you create a page for columns A through C, and then column D starts a new page.
2. Click the Page Layout tab.
3. Click Breaks in the Page Setup group, and then select Insert Page Break. Excel displays a solid blue line in Page Break Preview or a dashed line in Normal view to indicate the manual page breaks you set in the worksheet. Figure 4.4 shows a worksheet with both automatic and manual page breaks.

Indicates active view

Watermark indicating page number

Dashed blue line indicates automatic page break

Solid blue line indicates manual page break

FIGURE 4.4 Page Breaks in Page Break Preview ➤

To remove a manual page break, click the cell below a horizontal page break or the cell to the right of a vertical page break, click Breaks in the Page Setup group, and then select Remove Page Break. To reset all page breaks back to the automatic page breaks, click Breaks in the Page Setup group, and then select Reset All Page Breaks.

Set and Clear a Print Area

The default settings send an entire dataset on the active worksheet to the printer. However, you might want to print only part of the worksheet data. For example, you might want to print an input area only or transactions that occurred on a particular date. You can set the *print area*, which is the range of cells that will print. To print part of a worksheet, do the following:

A **print area** defines the range of data to print.

1. Select the range you want to print.
2. Click the Page Layout tab, and then click Print Area in the Page Setup group.
3. Select Set Print Area. Excel displays solid blue lines in Page Break Preview or thin black dashed lines around the print area in Normal view or Page Layout view (see Figure 4.5).

Click to set print area

Dotted lines indicate boundaries of print area

FIGURE 4.5 Print Area ➤

When you use the Print command, only the print area will print. In Page Break Preview, the print area has a white background and solid blue border; the rest of the worksheet has a gray background. You can add ranges to the print area. To add print areas, select the range of cells you want to print, click Print Area, and then select Add to Print Area. When you add more print areas, each print area will print on a separate page. To clear the print area, click Print Area in the Page Setup group, and then select Clear Print Area.

> **TIP** Print a Selection
>
> Another way to print part of a worksheet is to select the range you want to print. Click the File tab, and then click Print to see the print options and the worksheet in print preview. Click the first arrow in the *Settings* section, and then select Print Selection. Selecting the Print Selection option is a quick way to print a selected range. If you want to always print the same range, select the range in the worksheet, and set it as a print area.

Print Titles

When you print large worksheets, make sure every column and row contains descriptive labels on each page. Having the column and row labels print on only the first page does not help your audience identify data on subsequent pages. When you click Print Titles in the Page Setup group on the Page Layout tab, Excel opens the Page Setup dialog box. The Sheet tab within the dialog box is active so that you can select which row(s) and/or column(s) to repeat on each printout (see Figure 4.6).

FIGURE 4.6 Sheet Tab Options ➤

In the Spa Experts dataset, not all of the rows will print on the same page as the column labels. To print the column labels at the top of each printout, select the range in the *Rows to repeat at top* box. For example, row 5 contains column labels, such as Manufacturer. If your worksheet has more columns that can print on a page, you might want to display the row labels. To print the row headings on the left side of each printout, select the range in the *Columns to repeat at left* box. For example, columns A and B contain the transaction numbers and dates.

Control Print Page Order

Print order is the sequence in which pages print.

Print order is the sequence in which the pages are printed. By default, the pages print in this order: top-left section, bottom-left section, top-right section, and bottom-right section. However, you might want to print the entire top portion of the worksheet before printing the bottom portion.

To change the print order, click the Page Setup Dialog Box Launcher in the Page Setup group, click the Sheet tab, and then click either *Down, then over* or *Over, then down* (see Figure 4.6).

HANDS-ON EXERCISES

1 Large Datasets

You want to review the large dataset you created that shows the January transactions for your business, Spa Experts. You want to view the data and adjust some page setup options so that you can print necessary headings on each printed page.

Skills covered: Freeze and Unfreeze Panes • Display and Change Page Breaks • Set and Clear a Print Area • Print Worksheet Titles • Change the Page Order

STEP 1 FREEZE AND UNFREEZE PANES

Before setting up the dataset to print, you want to view the data onscreen. The dataset contains more rows than will display onscreen at the same time. You decide to freeze the headings to stay onscreen as you scroll through the transactions. Refer to Figure 4.7 as you complete Step 1.

FIGURE 4.7 Freeze Panes Activated ➤

a. Open *e04h1spa* and save it as **e04h1spa_LastnameFirstname**.

> **TROUBLESHOOTING:** If you make any major mistakes in this exercise, you can close the file, open *e04h1spa* again, and then start this exercise over.

The workbook contains three worksheets: January Data (to complete tasks in Hands-On Exercises 1, 2, and 3), January Totals (to complete tasks in Hands-On Exercise 3), and January Range (to complete tasks in Hands-On Exercise 4).

b. Click the **View tab**, click **Freeze Panes** in the Window group, and then select **Freeze Top Row**.

A black horizontal line appears between rows 1 and 2.

Hands-On Exercises • Excel 2010   **479**

c. Press **Page Down** to scroll down through the worksheet.

As rows scroll off the top of the Excel window, the first row remains frozen onscreen. The title by itself is not helpful; you need to freeze the column headings as well.

d. Click **Freeze Panes** in the Window group.

Notice that the first option is now Unfreeze Panes.

e. Select **Unfreeze Panes**.

The top row is no longer frozen.

f. Click **cell B6**, the cell below the row and one column to the right of what you want to freeze. Click **Freeze Panes** in the Window group, and then select **Freeze Panes**.

Excel displays a vertical line between columns A and B, indicating that column A is frozen, and a horizontal line between rows 5 and 6, indicating the first five rows are frozen.

g. Press **Ctrl+G**, type **M40** in the **Reference box** of the Go To dialog box, and then click **OK** to make **cell M40** the active cell. Save the workbook.

Notice that rows 6 through 17 are not visible, and columns B and C are not visible since they scrolled off the screen.

> **TROUBLESHOOTING:** Your screen may differ from what Figure 4.7 shows due to different Windows resolution settings. If necessary, continue scrolling right and down until you see columns and rows scrolling offscreen while column A and the first five rows remain onscreen.

STEP 2 ▶ DISPLAY AND CHANGE PAGE BREAKS

You plan to print the dataset so that you and your business partner Ryan can discuss the transactions in your weekly meeting. You know that large datasets do not fit on one printed page, so you want to see where the automatic page breaks will be. Refer to Figure 4.8 as you complete Step 2.

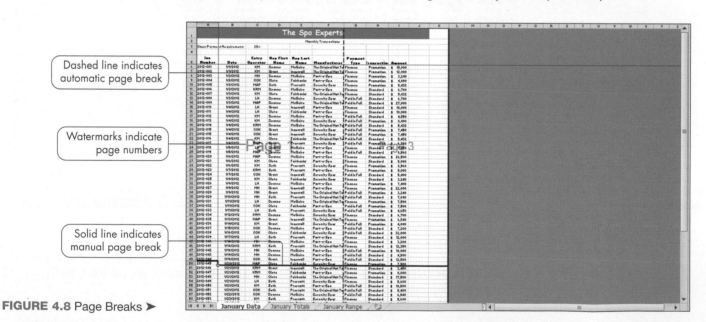

Dashed line indicates automatic page break

Watermarks indicate page numbers

Solid line indicates manual page break

FIGURE 4.8 Page Breaks ➤

a. Press **Ctrl+Home** to jump to **cell B6**, the first cell in the unfrozen area. Click the **View tab** if necessary, and then click **Page Break Preview** in the Workbook Views group or on the status bar.

> **TROUBLESHOOTING:** If the Welcome to Page Break Preview message box opens instructing you how to adjust page breaks, click OK.

b. Drag the **Zoom slider** to the left until the zoom is **50%**.

Excel displays blue dashed lines to indicate the page breaks. The horizontal page break is between rows 51 and 52. You want to make sure all transactions for a particular day do not span between printed pages, so you need to move the page break up to keep all 1/21/2012 transactions together.

c. Click **cell A51**, the cell to start the top of the second page.

d. Click the **Page Layout tab**, click **Breaks** in the Page Setup group, and then select **Insert Page Break**. Save the workbook.

You inserted a page break between rows 50 and 51 so that the 1/21/2012 transactions will be on one page.

> **TROUBLESHOOTING:** If Excel displays a solid line between columns and removes the automatic vertical page break, you selected the wrong cell before inserting a page break. Excel inserts page breaks above and to the left of the active cell. If the page breaks are in the wrong place, click Undo on the Quick Access Toolbar and complete steps c and d again.

> **TIP** Using the Pointer to Move Page Breaks
>
> Instead of clicking Breaks in the Page Setup group, you can use the mouse pointer to adjust a page break. Position the pointer on the page break line to see the two-headed arrow. Drag the page break line to move it where you want the page break to occur.

STEP 3 ▶ **SET AND CLEAR A PRINT AREA**

You want to focus on the first five days of transactions. To avoid printing more data than you need, you can set the print area to only that data. Refer to Figure 4.9 as you complete Step 3.

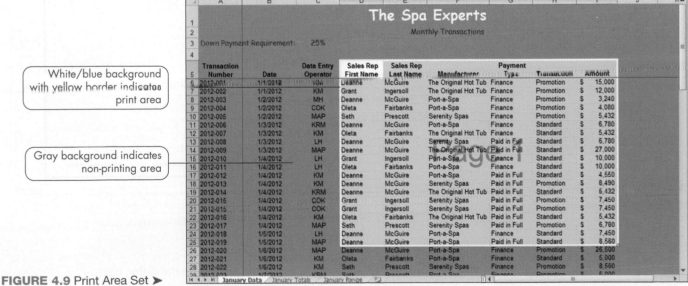

FIGURE 4.9 Print Area Set ➤

a. Change the zoom back to **100%**. Scroll up to see the first row of January data. Select the **range D5:I25**, the range of data for the first five days of the month.

b. Click the **Page Layout tab**, if necessary, click **Print Area** in the Page Setup group, and then select **Set Print Area**.

Excel displays the print area with a solid yellow border. The rest of the worksheet displays with a gray background, as shown in Figure 4.9.

c. Click the **Page Setup Dialog Box Launcher** in the Page Setup group. Use the dialog box to create a footer with your name on the left side, the sheet name code in the center, and the file name code on the right side.

d. Click the **File tab**, and then click **Print** to verify that only the print area will print. Click the **File tab** to close the Backstage view.

e. Click **Print Area** in the Page Setup group, and then select **Clear Print Area**. Save the workbook.

STEP 4 ▶ PRINT WORKSHEET TITLES

When you looked at the entire dataset in Page Break Preview, you noticed it would print on four pages. Only the first page will print both row and column headings. Page 2 will print the remaining row headings, page 3 will print the remaining column headings, and page 4 will not print either heading. You want to make sure the column and row headings print on all pages. To do this, you will print titles. Refer to Figure 4.10 as you complete Step 4.

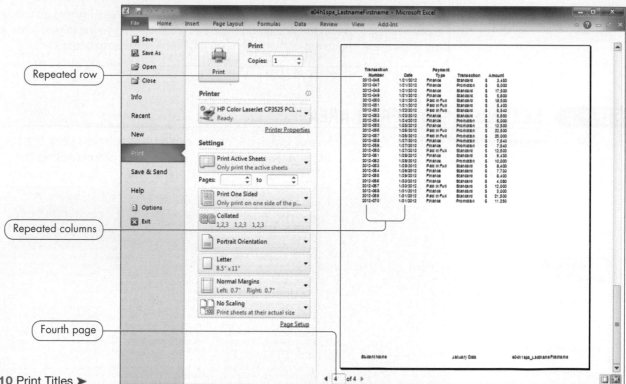

FIGURE 4.10 Print Titles ➤

a. Click **Print Titles** in the Page Setup group.

The Page Setup dialog box opens, displaying the Sheet tab.

b. Click the **Rows to repeat at top collapse button** to collapse the dialog box.

c. Click the **row 5 heading**, and then click the **expand button** to expand the Page Setup dialog box again.

You selected the fifth row, which contains the headings that identify content in the columns.

d. Click in the **Columns to repeat at left box**, type **A:B**, and then click **Print Preview**.

You should verify the page breaks and titles in Print Preview.

e. Click **Next Page** at the bottom of the Backstage view. Look at the second page to see the column headings for the last 11 days of transactions. Click **Next Page** twice to see the third and fourth pages.

Figure 4.10 shows a preview of the fourth page. The fifth row—the descriptive column headings—appears at the top of the page, and the first two columns of row headings (Transaction Number and Date) appear on all pages now.

f. Click the **Page Layout tab** to close the Backstage view. Save the workbook.

CHANGE THE PAGE ORDER

Although all four pages will print with titles, you want to print all columns for the first half of the monthly transactions rather than printing the first few columns of all transactions and then printing the last columns for all transactions. Refer to Figure 4.11 as you complete Step 5.

Page 2 instead of page 3 now

FIGURE 4.11 Different Page Order ➤

a. Click the **Page Layout tab**, if necessary, and then click the **Page Setup Dialog Box Launcher** in the Page Setup group.

b. Click the **Sheet tab** in the Page Setup dialog box.

c. Click **Over, then down**.

The preview shows that the pages print left to right and then back down left to right, in a Z manner.

d. Click **OK**.

Notice the Page 2 watermark appears on the right side of Page 1 rather than below it.

e. Save the workbook. Keep the workbook onscreen if you plan to continue with Hands-On Exercise 2. If not, close the workbook and exit Excel.

Excel Tables

All organizations maintain lists of data. Businesses maintain inventory lists, educational institutions maintain lists of students and faculty, and governmental entities maintain lists of

contracts. Although more complicated related data should be stored in a database management program, such as Access, you can maintain structured lists in Excel tables. A *table* is a structured range that contains related data organized in such a way as to facilitate data management and analysis. Although you can manage and analyze a range of data, a table provides many advantages over a range of data:

A **table** is an area in the worksheet that contains rows and columns of related data formatted to enable data management and analysis.

- Column headings that remain onscreen during scrolling without having to use Freeze Panes
- Filter lists for efficient sorting and filtering
- Predefined table styles to format table rows and columns with complementary fill colors
- Ability to create and edit calculated columns where the formulas copy down the columns automatically
- Calculated total row enabling the user to choose from a variety of functions
- Use of structured references instead of cell references in formulas
- Ability to export the table data to a SharePoint list

In this section, you will learn table terminology and rules for structuring data. You will create a table from existing data, manage records and fields, and remove duplicates. Then, you will apply a table style to format the table.

Understanding Table Design

An Excel table is like a database table: it provides a structured organization of data in columns and rows. Each column represents a *field*, which is an individual piece of data, such as last names or quantities sold. You should create fields with the least amount of data. For example, instead of a Name field, separate data into First Name and Last Name fields. Instead of one large address field, separate addresses into Street Address, City, State, and ZIP Code fields. Storing data into the smallest units possible enables you to manipulate the data in a variety of ways for output.

A **field** is an individual piece of data, such as a last name.

Each row in an Excel table represents a *record*, which is a collection of data about one entity, such as data for one person. For example, your record in your professor's grade book contains specific data about you, such as your name, ID, test scores, etc. The professor maintains a record of similar data for each student in the class. In an Excel table, each cell represents one piece of data (in the respective field columns) for a particular record.

A **record** is a complete set of data for an entity.

Often, people create tables from existing worksheet data. For example, a data-entry operator for the Spa Experts might enter data in a worksheet instead of creating a table first. Just as you spend time planning a worksheet, you should plan the structure for a table. Think about who will use the table, what types of reports you need to produce, and what types of searches might be done. The more thorough your planning process, the fewer changes you will have to make to the table after you create it. To help plan your table, follow these guidelines:

- Enter field names on the top row.
- Keep field names relatively short, descriptive, and unique. No two field names should be identical.
- Format the field names so that they stand out from the data.
- Enter data for each record on a row below the field names.
- Do not leave blank rows between records or between the field names and the first record.
- Delete any blank columns between fields in the dataset.

- Make sure each record has something unique about it, such as a transaction number or ID.
- Insert at least one blank row and one blank column between the table and other data, such as the main titles, input area, or other tables. When possible, place separate tables on separate worksheets.

Creating a Table

When your worksheet data are structured correctly, you can easily create a table. To create a table from existing data, do the following:

1. Click within the existing range of data.
2. Click the Insert tab, and then click Table in the Tables group. As Figure 4.12 shows, the Create Table dialog box opens, prompting you to enter the range of data. If Excel does not correctly predict the range, select the range for the *Where is the data for your table?* box. If the existing range contains column headings, select the *My table has headers* check box.
3. Click OK to create the table.

FIGURE 4.12 Create Table Dialog Box ➤

The Table Tools Design tab appears. Excel applies the default Table Style Medium 9 banded rows to your table, and each cell in the header row has filter arrows (see Figure 4.13). Excel assigns a name to each table, such as Table1. You can change the table name by clicking in the Table Name box in the Properties group, typing a new name using the same rules you applied when assigning range names, and then pressing Enter.

FIGURE 4.13 Excel Table in Default Format ➤

If you do not have existing data, you can create a table structure, and then add data to it later. Select an empty range, and then follow the above steps to create the range for the table. The default table style is Table Style Medium 2, and the default column headings are Column1, Column2, and so on. Click the column heading and type a descriptive label to replace the temporary heading. Excel applies table formatting to the empty rows. You are then ready to add data for each row in the empty table.

> **TIP** Converting a Table to a Range
>
> Tables provide an abundance of advantages to regular ranges. You might want to convert a table back to a range of data to accomplish other tasks. To convert a table back to a range, click within the table range, click the Table Tools Design tab, click Convert to Range in the Tools group, and then click Yes in the message box asking, *Do you want to convert the table to a normal range?*

Add, Edit, and Delete Records

After you create a table, you will need to maintain it, such as by adding new records. For example, you might need to add a new client or employee record, or add a new item to an inventory table or transaction table. To add a record to your table, do the following:

1. Click a cell in the record below where you want the new record inserted. If you want to add a new record below the last record, click the row containing the last record.
2. Click the Home tab, and then click the Insert arrow in the Cells group.
3. Select Insert Table Rows Above to insert a row above the current row, or select Insert Table Row Below if the current row is the last one and you want a row below it.

Sometimes, you need to change data for a record. For example, when a client moves, you need to change the client's address and phone number. You edit data in a table the same way you edit data in a regular worksheet cell.

Finally, you can delete records. For example, if you maintain an inventory of artwork in your house and sell a piece of art, delete that record from the table. To delete a record from the table:

1. Click a cell in the record that you want to delete.
2. Click the Home tab, and then click the Delete arrow in the Cells group.
3. Select Delete Table Rows.

Add and Delete Fields

Even if you carefully plan the fields for a table, you might decide to add new fields. For example, you might want to add a field for the customer names to the Spa Experts transaction table. To insert a field:

1. Click in any data cell (but not the cell containing the field name) in a field that will be to the right of the new field. For example, to insert a new field between the fields in columns A and B, click any cell in column B.
2. Click the Home tab, and then click the Insert arrow in the Cells group.
3. Select Insert Table Columns to the Left.

You can also delete a field if you no longer need any data for that particular field. Although deleting records and fields is easy, you must make sure not to delete data erroneously. If you accidentally delete data, click Undo immediately. To delete a field, do the following:

1. Click a cell in the field that you want to delete.
2. Click the Delete arrow in the Cells group on the Home tab.
3. Select Delete Table Columns.

Remove Duplicate Rows

You might accidentally enter duplicate records in a table, which can give false results when totaling or performing other calculations on the dataset. For a small table, you might be able to detect duplicate records by scanning the data. For large tables, it is more difficult to identify duplicate records by simply scanning the table with the eye. To remove duplicate records, do the following:

1. Click within the table, and then click the Design tab.
2. Click Remove Duplicates in the Tools group to display the Remove Duplicates dialog box (see Figure 4.14).
3. Click Select All to set the criteria to find a duplicate for every field in the record, and then click OK. If you select individual columns, Excel looks for duplicates in that one column only, and deletes all but one record that contains that data. For example, if you delete duplicate records where the manufacturer is Serenity Spas, only one transaction would remain. The other customers' transactions that contain Serenity Spas would be deleted. Excel will display a message box informing you how many duplicate rows it removed.

FIGURE 4.14 Remove Duplicates Dialog Box ➤

Applying a Table Style

A **table style** controls the fill color of the header row, columns, and records in a table.

Formatting tables can make them more attractive and easier to read, and can emphasize data. The Design tab provides a variety of formatting options for tables. Excel applies a table style when you create a table. *Table styles* control the fill color of the header row (the row containing field names) and rows of records. In addition, table styles specify bold and border lines. You can change the table style to a color scheme that complements your organization's color scheme or to emphasize data in the table. Click the More button to see the Table Styles gallery (see Figure 4.15). To see how a table style will format your table using Live Preview, position the pointer over a style in the Table Styles gallery. After you identify a style you want, click it to apply it to the table.

FIGURE 4.15 Table Styles Gallery ➤

After you select a table style, you can control what the style formats. The Table Style Options group contains check boxes to select specific format actions in a table. Table 4.2 lists the options and the effect of each check box. Whatever formatting and formatting effects you choose to use, avoid overformatting the table. It is not good to apply so many formatting effects that the message you want to present with the data is obscured or lost.

TABLE 4.2 Table Style Options

Check Box	Action
Header Row	Displays the header row (field names) when checked; removes field names when not checked. Header Row formatting takes priority over column formats.
Total Row	Displays a total row when selected. Total Row formatting takes priority over column formats.
First Column	Applies a different format to the first column so that the row headings stand out. First Column formatting takes priority over Banded Rows formatting.
Last Column	Applies a different format to the last column so that the last column of data stands out; effective for aggregated data, such as grand totals, per row. Last Column formatting takes priority over Banded Rows formatting.
Banded Rows	Displays alternate fill colors for even and odd rows to help distinguish records.
Banded Columns	Displays alternate fill colors for even and odd columns to help distinguish fields.

2 Excel Tables

Now that you understand Excel tables, you need to convert the January transactions data from basic worksheet data to a table. As you review the table, you will adjust its structure by deleting an unnecessary field and adding two missing fields. Then, you will focus on the transaction records by adding a missing record and removing a duplicate record. Finally, you will enhance the table appearance by selecting a table style.

Skills covered: Create a Table • Delete and Add Fields • Add a Record • Remove Duplicate Rows • Apply a Table Style

STEP 1 ▶ CREATE A TABLE

Although the Spa Experts' January transaction data are organized in an Excel worksheet, you know that you will have additional functionality if you convert the range to a table. Refer to Figure 4.16 as you complete Step 1.

FIGURE 4.16 Range Converted to a Table ➤

Table column headings replace lettered column headings

	Transaction	Date	Data Entry	Sales Rep F	Sales Rep L	Manufacturer	Payment Ty	Transaction	Amount	J
10	2012-005	1/2/2012	MAP	Seth	Prescott	Serenity Spas	Finance	Promotion	$ 5,432	
11	2012-006	1/3/2012	KRM	Deanne	McGuire	Port-a-Spa	Finance	Standard	$ 6,780	
12	2012-007	1/3/2012	KM	Oleta	Fairbanks	The Original Hot Tub	Finance	Standard	$ 5,432	
13	2012-008	1/3/2012	LH	Deanne	McGuire	Serenity Spas	Paid in Full	Standard	$ 6,780	
14	2012-009	1/3/2012	MAP	Deanne	McGuire	The Original Hot Tub	Paid in Full	Standard	$ 27,000	
15	2012-010	1/4/2012	LH	Grant	Ingersoll	Port-a-Spa	Finance	Standard	$ 10,000	
16	2012-011	1/4/2012	LH	Oleta	Fairbanks	Port-a-Spa	Finance	Standard	$ 10,000	
17	2012-012	1/4/2012	KM	Deanne	McGuire	Port-a-Spa	Paid in Full	Standard	$ 4,550	
18	2012-013	1/4/2012	KM	Deanne	McGuire	Serenity Spas	Paid in Full	Promotion	$ 8,490	
19	2012-014	1/4/2012	KRM	Deanne	McGuire	The Original Hot Tub	Paid in Full	Standard	$ 5,432	
20	2012-015	1/4/2012	COK	Grant	Ingersoll	Serenity Spas	Paid in Full	Promotion	$ 7,450	
21	2012-015	1/4/2012	COK	Grant	Ingersoll	Serenity Spas	Paid in Full	Promotion	$ 7,450	
22	2012-016	1/4/2012	KM	Oleta	Fairbanks	The Original Hot Tub	Paid in Full	Standard	$ 5,432	
23	2012-017	1/4/2012	MAP	Seth	Prescott	Serenity Spas	Paid in Full	Promotion	$ 6,780	
24	2012-018	1/5/2012	LH	Deanne	McGuire	Port-a-Spa	Finance	Standard	$ 7,450	
25	2012-019	1/5/2012	MAP	Deanne	McGuire	Port-a-Spa	Paid in Full	Standard	$ 8,560	
26	2012-020	1/6/2012	MAP	Deanne	McGuire	Port-a-Spa	Finance	Promotion	$ 26,500	
27	2012-021	1/6/2012	KM	Oleta	Fairbanks	Port-a-Spa	Finance	Standard	$ 5,000	
28	2012-022					Serenity Spas	Finance	Promotion	$ 8,560	
						Spa	Finance	Promotion	$	

a. Open *e04h1spa_LastnameFirstname* if you closed it at the end of Hands-On Exercise 1, and then save it as **e04h2spa_LastnameFirstname**, changing *h1* to *h2*.

b. Click **Normal** on the status bar, and then click the **Insert tab**.

c. Click in any cell within the transactional data. Click **Table** in the Tables group.

The Create Table dialog box opens. The Where is the data for your table? box displays =$A$5:$I$75. You need to keep the *My table has headers* check box selected so that the headings on the fifth row become the field names for the table.

d. Click **OK**, and then click **cell A5**.

Excel creates a table from the specified range and displays the Table Tools Design tab, filter arrows, and alternating fill colors for every other record. The columns widen to fit the field names, although the wrap text option is still applied to those cells.

e. Set **12.00 column widths** to these fields: Transaction Number, Data Entry Operator, Sales Rep First Name, Sales Rep Last Name, and Payment Type.

f. Unfreeze the panes, and then scroll through the table. Save the workbook.

With a regular range of data, column headings scroll off the top of the screen if you don't freeze panes. When you scroll within a table, the table column headings remain onscreen by moving up to where the Excel column (letter) headings usually display (see Figure 4.16).

The original range included the Data Entry Operator's initials. You decide that you no longer need this column, so you will delete it. In addition, you want to add a field to display down payment amounts in the future. Refer to Figure 4.17 as you complete Step 2.

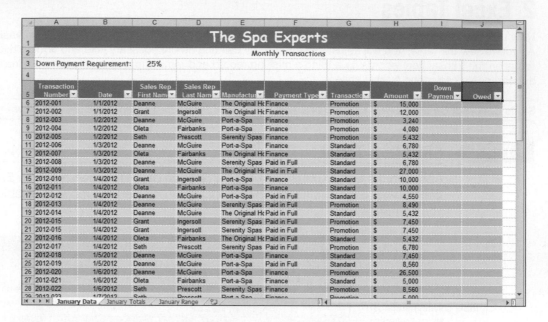

FIGURE 4.17 Field Name Changes ➤

a. Click **cell C6** or any cell containing a value in the Data Entry Operator column.

You need to make a cell active in the field that you want to remove.

b. Click the **Home tab**, click the **Delete arrow** in the Cells group, and then select **Delete Table Columns**.

Excel deletes the Data Entry Operator column. Notice that the 25% remains in cell C3.

> **TROUBLESHOOTING:** If the 25% is deleted in cell C3, you probably selected Delete Sheet Columns instead of Delete Table Columns. Undo the deletion, and then repeat step b.

c. Click **cell I5**, the first blank cell on the right side of the field names.

d. Type **Down Payment** and press **Ctrl+Enter**.

Excel extends the table formatting to column I automatically. A filter arrow appears for the newly created field name, and alternating fill colors appear in the rows below the field name.

e. Click **Wrap Text** in the Alignment group.

f. Click **cell J5**, type **Owed**, and then press **Ctrl+Enter** to keep cell J5 active. Click **Center** in the Alignment group. Save the workbook.

STEP 3 ▶ **ADD A RECORD**

As you review the January transaction table, you notice that transaction 2012-030 is missing. After finding the paper invoice, you are ready to add a record with the missing transaction data. Refer to Figure 4.18 as you complete Step 3.

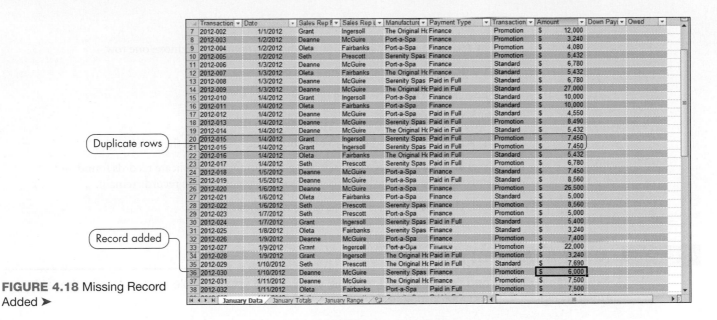

Transaction	Date	Sales Rep F	Sales Rep L	Manufacture	Payment Type	Transaction	Amount	Down Pay	Owed
7 2012-002	1/1/2012	Grant	Ingersoll	The Original H	Finance	Promotion	$ 12,000		
8 2012-003	1/2/2012	Deanne	McGuire	Port-a-Spa	Finance	Promotion	$ 3,240		
9 2012-004	1/2/2012	Oleta	Fairbanks	Port-a-Spa	Finance	Promotion	$ 4,080		
10 2012-005	1/2/2012	Seth	Prescott	Serenity Spas	Finance	Promotion	$ 5,432		
11 2012-006	1/3/2012	Deanne	McGuire	Port-a-Spa	Finance	Standard	$ 6,780		
12 2012-007	1/3/2012	Oleta	Fairbanks	The Original H	Finance	Standard	$ 5,432		
13 2012-008	1/3/2012	Deanne	McGuire	Serenity Spas	Paid in Full	Standard	$ 6,780		
14 2012-009	1/3/2012	Deanne	McGuire	The Original H	Paid in Full	Standard	$ 27,000		
15 2012-010	1/4/2012	Grant	Ingersoll	Port-a-Spa	Finance	Standard	$ 10,000		
16 2012-011	1/4/2012	Oleta	Fairbanks	Port-a-Spa	Finance	Standard	$ 10,000		
17 2012-012	1/4/2012	Deanne	McGuire	Port-a-Spa	Paid in Full	Standard	$ 4,550		
18 2012-013	1/4/2012	Deanne	McGuire	Serenity Spas	Paid in Full	Promotion	$ 8,490		
19 2012-014	1/4/2012	Deanne	McGuire	The Original H	Paid in Full	Standard	$ 5,432		
20 2012-015	1/4/2012	Grant	Ingersoll	Serenity Spas	Paid in Full	Promotion	$ 7,450		
21 2012-015	1/4/2012	Grant	Ingersoll	Serenity Spas	Paid in Full	Promotion	$ 7,450		
22 2012-016	1/4/2012	Oleta	Fairbanks	The Original H	Paid in Full	Standard	$ 5,432		
23 2012-017	1/4/2012	Seth	Prescott	Serenity Spas	Paid in Full	Promotion	$ 6,780		
24 2012-018	1/5/2012	Deanne	McGuire	Port-a-Spa	Finance	Standard	$ 7,450		
25 2012-019	1/5/2012	Deanne	McGuire	Port-a-Spa	Paid in Full	Standard	$ 8,560		
26 2012-020	1/6/2012	Deanne	McGuire	Port-a-Spa	Finance	Promotion	$ 26,500		
27 2012-021	1/6/2012	Oleta	Fairbanks	Port-a-Spa	Finance	Standard	$ 5,000		
28 2012-022	1/6/2012	Seth	Prescott	Serenity Spas	Finance	Promotion	$ 8,560		
29 2012-023	1/7/2012	Seth	Prescott	Port-a-Spa	Finance	Promotion	$ 5,000		
30 2012-024	1/7/2012	Grant	Ingersoll	Serenity Spas	Paid in Full	Standard	$ 5,400		
31 2012-025	1/8/2012	Oleta	Fairbanks	Serenity Spas	Finance	Standard	$ 3,240		
32 2012-026	1/9/2012	Deanne	McGuire	Port-a-Spa	Finance	Promotion	$ 7,400		
33 2012-027	1/9/2012	Grant	Ingersoll	Port-a-Spa	Finance	Promotion	$ 22,000		
34 2012-028	1/9/2012	Grant	Ingersoll	The Original H	Paid in Full	Promotion	$ 3,240		
35 2012-029	1/10/2012	Seth	Prescott	The Original H	Paid in Full	Standard	$ 7,690		
36 2012-030	1/10/2012	Deanne	McGuire	Serenity Spas	Finance	Promotion	$ 6,000		
37 2012-031	1/11/2012	Deanne	McGuire	The Original H	Finance	Promotion	$ 7,500		
38 2012-032	1/11/2012	Oleta	Fairbanks	Port-a-Spa	Paid in Full	Promotion	$ 7,500		

Duplicate rows → (rows 20, 21)

Record added → (row 36)

FIGURE 4.18 Missing Record Added ➤

a. Click **cell A36** or any cell within the table range on row 36.

You need to make a cell active on the row in which you want to insert the new table row.

b. Click the **Home tab**, click the **Insert arrow** in the Cells group, and then select **Insert Table Rows Above**.

Excel inserts a new table row on row 36. The rest of the records move down by one row.

c. Enter the following data in the respective fields on the newly created row. AutoComplete will help you enter the names, manufacturer, payment type, and transaction text. Then save the workbook.

- Transaction Number: **2012-030**
- Date: **1/10/2012**
- Sales Rep First Name: **Deanne**
- Sales Rep Last Name: **McGuire**
- Manufacturer: **Serenity Spas**
- Payment Type: **Finance**
- Transaction: **Promotion**
- Amount: **6000**

STEP 4 ▶ REMOVE DUPLICATE ROWS

As you continue checking the transaction records, you think the table contains some duplicate records. To avoid having to look at the entire table row-by-row, you want to have Excel find and remove the duplicate rows for you. Refer to Figure 4.19 as you complete Step 4.

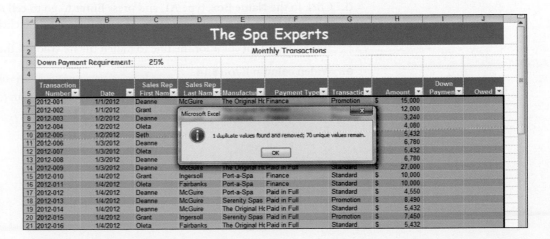

FIGURE 4.19 Duplicate Record Removed ➤

a. Scroll to see rows 20 and 21. Click the **Design tab**.

The records on rows 20 and 21 are identical. You need to remove one row.

b. Click **Remove Duplicates** in the Tools group.

The Remove Duplicates dialog box opens.

c. Click **Select All**, if necessary, to select all table columns.

d. Click the **My data has headers check box**, if necessary, and then click **OK**.

Excel displays a message box indicating the number of duplicate records found and removed. The message box also specifies how many unique records remain.

e. Click **OK** in the message box. Save the workbook.

STEP 5 **APPLY A TABLE STYLE**

Now that you have modified fields and records, you want to apply a table style to format the table. Refer to Figure 4.20 as you complete Step 5.

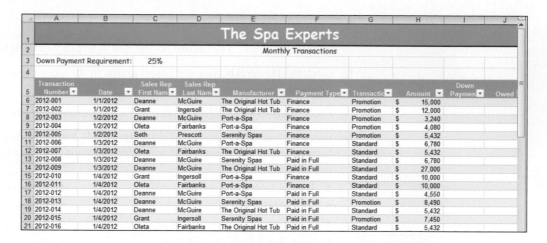

FIGURE 4.20 Table Style Applied ➤

a. Click the **More button** in the Table Styles group to display the Table Styles gallery.

b. Position the mouse pointer over the fourth style on the second row in the *Light* section.

Live Preview shows the table with the Table Style Light 10 style but does not apply it.

c. Click **Table Style Medium 6**, the sixth style on the first row in the *Medium* section.

Excel formats the table with the Table Style Medium 6 format.

d. Click in the **Name Box**, type **A1**, and press **Enter** to go to **cell A1**, the title. Click the **Home tab**, click the **Fill Color arrow** in the Font group, and then click **Aqua, Accent 5**.

You applied a fill color for the title to match the fill color of the field names.

e. Widen column E to **18.14**.

f. Save the workbook. Keep the workbook onscreen if you plan to continue with Hands-On Exercise 3. If not, close the workbook and exit Excel.

Table Manipulation and Aggregation

When you convert data to a table, you have a variety of options to manipulate that data, in addition to managing fields and records and applying predefined table styles. You can arrange data in different sequences, display only particular records instead of the entire dataset, and aggregate data. Although Excel provides many advantages for using tables over a range, you might need to convert a table back to a range to perform a few tasks that are not available for tables.

> You can add more meaning to tables by aggregating data.

In this section, you will learn how to sort records by text, numbers, and dates in a table. In addition, you will learn how to filter data based on conditions you set. You will create structured formulas to perform calculations, and add a total row.

Sorting Data

Table data are easier to understand and work with if you organize the data. In Figure 4.1, the data are arranged by transaction number. You might want to organize the table by showing sales by sales associate, or to display all financed spas together, followed by all paid-in-full spas. *Sorting* arranges records by the value of one or more fields within a table.

> **Sorting** arranges records in a table by the value in field(s) within a table.

Sort One Column

You can sort data by one or more columns. To sort by only one column, you can use any of the following methods for either a range of data or a table:

- Click Sort & Filter in the Editing group on the Home tab.
- Click Sort A to Z, Sort Z to A, or Sort in the Sort & Filter group on the Data tab.
- Right-click the field to sort, point to Sort from the shortcut menu, and select the type of sort you want.

When you format data as a table, the field names appear in a header row, which contains sort and filter arrows. Click the arrow for the column you want to sort and select the type of sort you want. Table 4.3 lists sort options by data type.

TABLE 4.3	Sort Options	
Data Type	**Options**	**Explanation**
Text	Sort A to Z	Arranges data in alphabetical order.
	Sort Z to A	Arranges data in reverse alphabetical order.
Dates	Sort Oldest to Newest	Displays data in chronological order, from oldest to newest.
	Sort Newest to Oldest	Displays data in reverse chronological order, from newest to oldest.
Values	Sort Smallest to Largest	Arranges values from the smallest value to the largest value.
	Sort Largest to Smallest	Arranges values from the largest value to the smallest value.

Use the Sort Dialog Box to Sort Multiple Columns

At times sorting by only one field yields several records that have the same information—for example the same last name or the same manufacturer. Sales representative names and manufacturer names appear several times. A single sort field does not uniquely identify a record. You might need both last name and first name to identify an individual. Using multiple level sorts allows differentiation among records with the same data in the first (primary) sort level. For example, you might want to sort by sales rep names, manufacturer, and then by price. Excel enables you to sort data on 64 different levels. To perform a multiple level sort:

1. Click in any cell in the table.
2. Click Sort in the Sort & Filter group on the Data tab to display the Sort dialog box.
3. Select the primary sort level by clicking the *Sort by* arrow and selecting the column to sort by, and then clicking the Order arrow and selecting the sort order from the list.
4. Click Add Level, select the second sort level by clicking the *Then by* arrow and selecting the column to sort by, clicking the Order arrow, and then selecting the sort order from the list.
5. Continue to click Add Level and add sort levels until you have entered all sort levels. See Figure 4.21. Click OK.

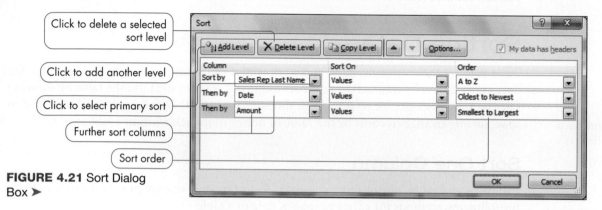

FIGURE 4.21 Sort Dialog Box ➤

Create a Custom Sort

Excel arranges data in defined sequences, such as alphabetical order. For example, weekdays are sorted alphabetically: Friday, Monday, Saturday, Sunday, Thursday, Tuesday, and Wednesday. However, you might want to create a custom sort sequence. For example, you can create a custom sort to arrange weekdays in order from Sunday to Saturday.

To create a custom sort sequence, click Sort in the Sort & Filter group on the Data tab. Click the Order arrow, and then select Custom List to display the Custom Lists dialog box (see Figure 4.22). Select an existing sort sequence in the *Custom lists* box, or select NEW LIST, click Add, and then type the entries in the desired sort sequence in the *List entries* box, pressing Enter between entries. Click Add, and then click OK.

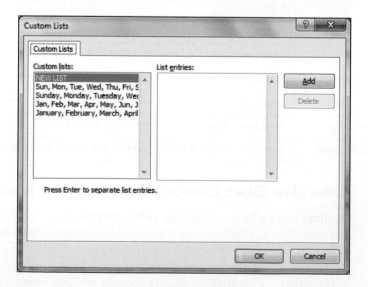

FIGURE 4.22 Custom Lists Dialog Box ➤

Filtering Data

You might want to show only particular records. **Filtering** is the process of specifying conditions to display only those records that meet certain conditions. For example, you might want to filter the data to show transactions for only Oleta Fairbanks. To filter records by a particular field, click the column's filter arrow. The list displays each unique label, value, or date contained in the column. Deselect the (Select All) check box, and then click the check box for each value you want to include in the filtered results.

Often you will need to apply more than one filter to display the needed records. You can filter more than one column. Each additional filter is based on the current filtered data and further reduces a data subset. To apply multiple filters, click each column's filter arrow, and select the values to include in the filtered data results.

> **TIP** Copying Before Filtering Data
>
> Often, you need to show different filters applied to the same dataset. You can copy the data to another worksheet, and then filter the copied data to preserve the original dataset.

Apply Text Filters

When you apply a filter to a text column, the filter menu displays each unique text item. You can select one or more text items from the list. For example, select Fairbanks to show only records for this salesperson. To display records for both Fairbanks and Prescott, deselect the (Select All) check mark, and then click the Fairbanks and Prescott check boxes. You can also select Text Filters to see a submenu of additional options, such as *Begins With*, to select all records where the name begins with the letter G, for example.

Figure 4.23 shows the Last Name filter menu with two names selected. Excel displays records for these two reps only. The records for the other sales reps are hidden but not deleted. The filter arrow displays a filter icon, indicating which column is filtered. Excel displays the row numbers in blue, indicating that you applied a filter. The missing row numbers indicate hidden rows of data. When you remove the filter, all the records display again.

- Filter icon indicates filtered column
- Blue row numbers indicate filtered data
- Only two names selected
- Submenu for additional options
- Status bar indicates number of records meeting the filtered conditions

FIGURE 4.23 Filtered Text ➤

Apply Number Filters

When you filter a column of numbers, you can select specific numbers. You might want to filter numbers by a range, such as numbers greater than $5,000 or numbers between $4,000 and $5,000. The submenu enables you to set a variety of number filters. In Figure 4.24, the amounts are filtered to show only those that are above the average amount. In this situation, Excel calculates the average amount as $9,577. Only records above that amount display.

If the field contains a large number of unique entries, you can click in the Search box, and then type a value, text label, or date. Doing so narrows the visible list so that you do not have to scroll through the entire list. For example, if you enter $7, the list will display only values that start with $7.

Selected number filter

Enter data here to narrow the list

FIGURE 4.24 Filtered Numbers ➤

The Top 10 option enables you to specify the top records. Although the option name is Top 10, you can specify the number or percentage of records to display. For example, you can filter the list to display only the top five or the bottom 7%. Figure 4.25 shows the Top 10 AutoFilter dialog box. Click the first arrow to select either Top or Bottom, click the spin arrows to indicate a value, and then click the last arrow to select either Items or Percent.

FIGURE 4.25 Top 10 AutoFilter Dialog Box ➤

Apply Date Filters

When you filter a column of dates, you can select specific dates or a date range, such as dates after 1/15/2012 or dates between 1/1/2012 and 1/7/2012. The submenu enables you to set a variety of date filters. In Figure 4.26, the dates are filtered to show only those that are after 1/15/2012. For more specific date options, point to Date Filters, point to All Dates in the Period, and then select a period, such as Quarter 2 or October.

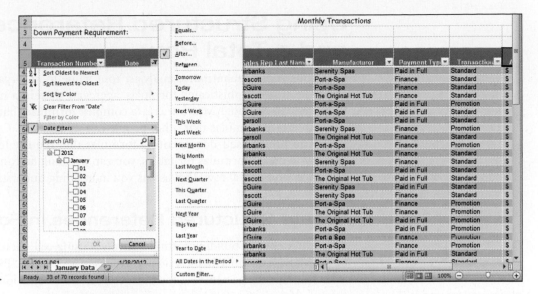

FIGURE 4.26 Filtered Dates ➤

Apply a Custom Filter

If you select options such as *Greater Than* or *Before*, Excel displays the Custom AutoFilter dialog box (see Figure 4.27). You can also select Custom Filter from the menu to display this dialog box, which is designed for more complex filtering requirements.

Date is the column being filtered

FIGURE 4.27 Custom AutoFilter Dialog Box ➤

The dialog box indicates the column being filtered, such as Date. To set the filters, click the arrows to select the comparison type, such as equals or contains. Click the arrow on the right to select a specific text, value, or date entry, or type the data yourself. For ranges of dates or values, click And, and then specify the comparison operator and value or date for the next condition row. For text, click Or. For example, if you want both Kansas and Kentucky, you must select Or because one data entry contains either Kansas or Kentucky but not both at the same time.

You can use wildcards to represent characters. For example, to select all states starting with New, type New * in the second box. The asterisk (*) represents any number of characters. If you want a wildcard for only a single character, type the question mark (?).

Clear Filters

After reviewing the filtered data, you can remove the filters to see the entire dataset again. To remove only one filter and keep the other filters, click the filter arrow for the column from which you wish to clear the filter, and then select Clear Filter From. Excel then removes that column's filter and displays records previously hidden by that filter. To remove all filters, click Filter in the Sort & Filter group on the Data tab, or click Sort & Filter in the Editing group on the Home tab and select Filter. Excel clears all filters and displays all records in the dataset.

Using Structured References and a Total Row

Excel aids you in quantitative analysis. Your value to an organization increases with your ability to create sophisticated formulas, aggregate data in a meaningful way, and interpret those results. Although you can create complex formulas that you understand, you should strive to create formulas that other people can understand. Creating easy-to-read formulas helps you present self-documenting formulas that require less explanation on your part. When you create formulas for tables, you can use built-in functionality (such as structured references and a total row) that assists you in building understandable formulas.

Create Structured References in Formulas

Your experience in building formulas involves using cell references, such as =SUM(B1:B15) or =H6*$B$3, or range names, such as grades in =VLOOKUP(E5,grades,2). You can use cell references and range names in formulas to perform calculations in a table, as well as another type of reference for formulas in tables: structured references. A ***structured reference*** is a tag or use of a table element, such as a column heading, as a reference in a formula. Structured references in formulas clearly indicate what type of data is used in the calculations.

> A **structured reference** is a tag or use of a table element as a reference in a formula.

A structured reference requires brackets around column headings or field names, such as =[Amount]-[Down Payment]. The use of column headings without row references in a structured formula is called an *unqualified reference*. While creating a formula by typing, Formula AutoComplete displays a list of column headings after you type the equal sign and the opening bracket (see Figure 4.28). Type or double-click the name from the list, and then type the closing bracket. Excel displays a colored border around the column being referenced. When you enter a formula using structured references, Excel copies the formula down the rest of the column in the table automatically, compared to typing references in formulas and copying the formula down a column.

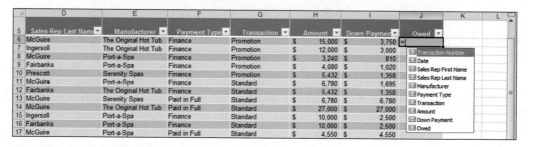

FIGURE 4.28 Structured Reference Creation ➤

You can still use the semi-selection process to create a formula. If you use the pointing process to enter a formula in a table, Excel builds a formula like this: =[@Amount]-[@Down Payment], where the @ indicates the current row. If you use the semi-selection process to create a formula outside the table, the formula includes the table name and row as well, such as =Table1[@Amount]-Table1[@Down Payment]. Table1 is the name of the table, and Amount and Down Payment are column headings. This structured formula that includes references, such as table numbers, is called a *fully qualified reference*. When you build formulas *within* a table, you can use either unqualified or fully qualified structured references. If you need to use table data in a formula *outside* the table boundaries, you must use fully qualified structured references.

TIP Complex Structured References

You can create structured reference tags to other elements, such as headers and totals. The more you know how to incorporate structured references, the more powerful your tables are to you. Look up *structured references* in Help for detailed explanations and examples of more complex use of structured references.

Create a Total Row

Aggregating data provides more meaningful quantitative interpretation than individual values at times. For regular ranges of data, you use basic statistical functions, such as SUM, AVERAGE, MIN, and MAX, to provide meaning for a dataset. An Excel table provides the advantage of being able to display a total row automatically without creating the aggregate function yourself. A *total row* appears below the last row of records in an Excel table and enables you to display summary statistics, such as a sum of values displayed in a column. To display and use the total row:

A **total row** appears as the last row of a table to display summary statistics, such as a sum.

1. Click the Design tab.
2. Click Total Row in the Table Style Options group. Excel displays the total row below the last record in the table. Excel displays *Total* in the first column of the total row. Excel either sums or counts data for the last column, depending on the type of data stored in that column. If the last column consists of values, Excel sums the values. If the last column is text, Excel counts the number of records.
3. Click a cell in the total row, and then click that cell's total row arrow and select the function results, such as Average, that you desire. To add a total to another column, click in the empty cell for that column in the total row, and then click the arrow to select the desired function. Select None to remove the function.

Figure 4.29 shows the active total row with totals applied to the Amount and Down Payment columns. A list of functions displays to change the function for the last column.

Total Row check box selected

SUBTOTAL formula in Formula Bar

Total row displayed

Menu of functions for total row

FIGURE 4.29 Total Row ➤

=SUBTOTAL(function_num,ref1,...)

The **SUBTOTAL function** calculates an aggregate for values in a range or database.

The SUBTOTAL function calculates results on the total row. The **SUBTOTAL function** calculates an aggregate value, such as totals, for values in a range or database. The function for the total row looks like this: =SUBTOTAL(109,[Owed]). The function_num argument is a number that represents a function (see Table 4.4). The number 109 represents the SUM function. The ref1 argument indicates the range of values to calculate. In this case, [Owed] represents the Owed field. A benefit of the SUBTOTAL function is that it subtotals data for filtered records, so you have an accurate total for the visible records.

TABLE 4.4 SUBTOTAL Function Numbers

Function	Database Number	Table Number
AVERAGE	1	101
COUNT	2	102
COUNTA	3	103
MAX	4	104
MIN	5	105
PRODUCT	6	106
STDEV	7	107
STDEVP	8	108
SUM	9	109
VAR	10	110
VARP	11	111

TIP Filtering Data and Subtotals

If you filter the data and display the total row, the SUBTOTAL function's 109 argument ensures that only the displayed data are summed; data for hidden rows are not calculated in the aggregate function.

3 Table Manipulation and Aggregation

You want to start analyzing the January transactions for Spa Experts by sorting and filtering data in a variety of ways to help you understand the transactions better. In addition, you need to calculate the required down payment amount and how much customers owe for their spas. Finally, you will convert the table back to a range.

Skills covered: Sort Individual Columns • Use the Sort Dialog Box • Apply Text Filters • Apply a Number Filter • Apply a Date Filter • Create Structured References • Add a Total Row • Convert a Table to a Range

---

STEP 1 ▸ SORT INDIVIDUAL COLUMNS

First, you want to compare the number of transactions by sales rep, so you will sort the data by the Last Name field. After reviewing the transactions by sales reps, you want to see what manufacturer's spas are sold most often. Refer to Figure 4.30 as you complete Step 1.

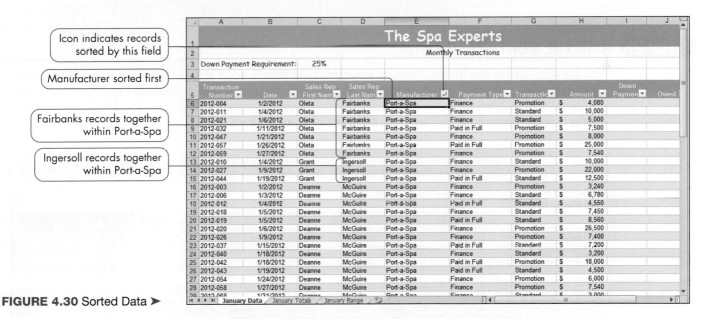

FIGURE 4.30 Sorted Data ➤

a. Open *e04h2spa_LastnameFirstname* if you closed it at the end of Hands-On Exercise 2. Save the workbook with the new name **e04h3spa_LastnameFirstname**, changing *h2* to *h3*.

b. Click the **Sales Rep Last Name filter arrow**, and then select **Sort A to Z**.

Excel arranges the records in alphabetical order by last name. All transactions completed by Fairbanks display first. Within each sales rep, records appear in their original sequence by transaction number. Without actually counting the records, which sales rep appears to have the most sales? According to the sorted list, McGuire sold the most spas in January. The up arrow icon on the Last Name filter arrow indicates records are sorted in alphabetical order by that column.

TIP Name Sorts

Always check the table to determine how many levels of sorting you need to apply. If your table contains several people with the same last name but different first names, you would first sort by the Last Name field, and then sort by First Name field individually. All the people with the last name Fairbanks would be grouped together and then further sorted by first name, such as Amanda and then Bradley. To ensure that Excel sorts in the sequence you desire, use the Sort dialog box instead of sorting columns individually.

c. Click the **Manufacturer filter arrow**, and then select **Sort A to Z**.

Excel arranges the records in alphabetical order by manufacturer. Port-a-Spa displays first. Within the Port-a-Spa group, the records are further sorted by the previous sort: last name. Fairbanks appears before Ingersoll. The up arrow icon within the Manufacturer filter arrow indicates that records are sorted in alphabetical order by this column (see Figure 4.30).

d. Click the **Transaction Number filter arrow**, and then select **Sort A to Z**. Save the workbook.

Excel arranges the records back in their original sequence—by transaction number.

STEP 2 ▶ USE THE SORT DIALOG BOX

You want to review the transactions by payment type (financed or paid in full). Within each payment type, you want to further compare the transaction type (promotion or standard). Finally, you want to compare costs within the sorted records by displaying the highest costs first. You will use the Sort dialog box to perform a three-level sort. Refer to Figure 4.31 as you complete Step 2.

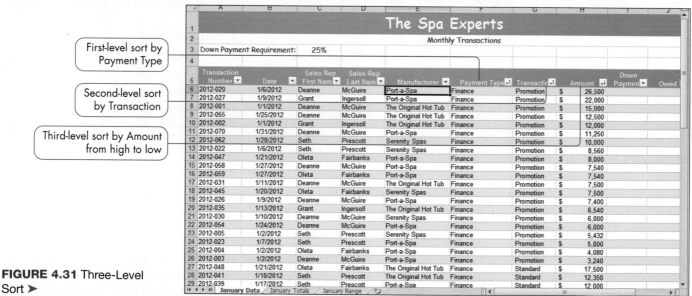

FIGURE 4.31 Three-Level Sort ▶

a. Click inside the table. Click the **Data tab**.

Both the Data and Home tabs contain commands to open the Sort dialog box.

b. Click **Sort** in the Sort & Filter group.

The Sort dialog box opens. You start by specifying the column for the primary sort. In this case, you want to sort the records first by the Payment Type column.

c. Click the **Sort by arrow**, and then select **Payment Type**.

The default Sort On is Values, and the default Order is A to Z.

d. Click **Add Level.**

The Sort dialog box adds the *Then by* row, which adds a secondary sort.

e. Click the **Then by arrow,** and then select **Transaction.**

Excel will first sort the records by the Payment Type. Within each Payment Type, Excel will further sort records by Transaction.

f. Click **Add Level** to add another *Then by* row. Click the second **Then by arrow,** and then select **Amount.**

g. Click the **Order arrow** for the Amount sort, and then select **Largest to Smallest.**

Within the Payment Type and Transaction sorts, this will arrange the records with the largest amount first in descending order to the smallest amount.

h. Click **OK** and scroll through the records. Save the workbook.

Figure 4.31 shows the sorted records. Most customers finance their spas instead of paying for their spas in full. For the financed spas, about half were promotional sales and half were standard sales. For those spas paid in full, a majority of the transactions were standard sales, indicating that people with money don't necessarily wait for a promotional sale to buy their spas.

STEP 3 ▶ APPLY TEXT FILTERS

Now that you know McGuire had the most transactions, you want to focus on her sales for January. In particular, you want to filter the table to show only her records. You notice that she sells more Port-a-Spas and The Original Hot Tub than the Serenity Spas, so you will filter out the Serenity Spa sales. Refer to Figure 4.32 as you complete Step 3.

FIGURE 4.32 McGuire Sales for Two Manufacturers ➤

a. Click the **Sales Rep Last Name filter arrow.**

The (Select All) check box is selected.

b. Click the **(Select All) check box** to deselect all last names.

c. Click the **McGuire check box,** and then click **OK.**

The status bar indicates that 27 out of 70 records meet the filtering condition. The Last Name filter arrow includes a funnel icon, indicating that this column is filtered.

d. Click the **Manufacturer filter arrow.**

e. Click the **Serenity Spas check box** to deselect this manufacturer, and then click **OK**. Save the workbook.

You filtered out the Serenity Spas brand that McGuire sold. The remaining 22 records show McGuire's sales for the Port-a-Spas and The Original Hot Tub brands sold. The Manufacturer filter arrow includes a funnel icon, indicating that this column is also filtered.

You now want to focus on the amount of sales for McGuire. In particular, you are interested in how much gross revenue she generated for spas that cost at least $10,000 or more. Refer to Figure 4.33 as you complete Step 4.

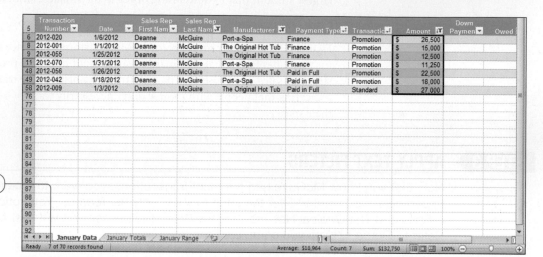

Number of filtered records

FIGURE 4.33 Filtered to Amounts Greater Than or Equal To $10,000 ➤

a. Select the **range H6:H75** of the filtered list, and then view the status bar.

The average transaction amount is $10,159 with 22 transactions (i.e., 22 filtered records). McGuire's total January sales are $223,502. You will use this total to see how much of the $223,502 sales generated are for higher-priced models she sold.

b. Click the **Amount filter arrow**.

c. Point to **Number Filters**, and then select **Greater Than Or Equal To**.

The Custom AutoFilter dialog box opens. The default comparison is *is greater than or equal to*, although you could change it if needed.

d. Type **10000** in the box to the right of *is greater than or equal to*, and then click **OK**. Save the workbook.

When typing numbers, you can type raw numbers such as 10000 or formatted numbers such as $10,000. Out of the original 27 spas McGuire sold, she sold only 7 of the Port-a-Spas and The Original Hot Tub brands that cost $10,000 or more. Out of the $223,502 total sales for those two brands, McGuire sold $132,750 in the higher-priced models costing $10,000 or more.

> **TROUBLESHOOTING:** If no records display or if too many records display, you might have entered 100000 or 1000. Repeat steps b–d.

Finally, you want to study McGuire's sales records for the week of January 22. You will add a date filter to identify those sales records. Refer to Figure 4.34 as you complete Step 5.

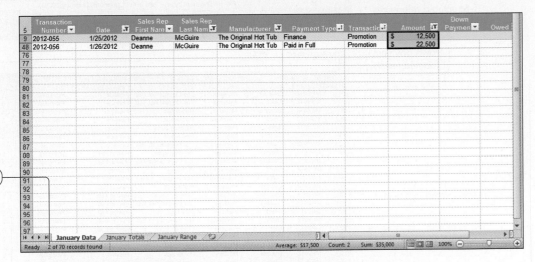

Number of filtered records

FIGURE 4.34 Filtered by Dates Between 1/22/2012 and 1/28/2012 ➤

a. Click the **Date filter arrow**.

b. Point to **Date Filters**, and then select **Between**.

The Custom AutoFilter dialog box opens. The default comparisons are *is after or equal to* and *is before or equal to*, ready for you to enter the date specifications.

c. Type **1/22/2012** in the box on the right side of *is after or equal to*.

You specified the starting date of the range of dates to include. You will keep the *And* option selected.

d. Type **1/28/2012** in the box on the right side of *is before or equal to*. Click **OK**. Save the workbook.

McGuire had only two sales during that week, totaling $35,000.

To continue reviewing the January transactions, you need to calculate the required down payment for customers who financed their spas. The required down payment is located above the table data so that you can change that value if needed later. In addition, you need to calculate how much customers owe on their spas if they did not pay in full. You will use structured formulas to perform these calculations. Refer to Figure 4.35 as you complete Step 6.

Structured references in formula

Down payment formula results

Formulas copied down their respective table columns

I6 — fx =IF([Payment Type]="Paid in Full",[Amount],[Amount]*$C$3)

The Spa Experts

Monthly Transactions

Requirement: 25%

Date	Sales Rep First Name	Sales Rep Last Name	Manufacturer	Payment Type	Transaction	Amount	Down Payment	Owed
1/1/2012	Deanne	McGuire	The Original Hot Tub	Finance	Promotion	$ 15,000	$ 3,750.00	$ 11,250.00
1/1/2012	Grant	Ingersoll	The Original Hot Tub	Finance	Promotion	$ 12,000	$ 3,000.00	$ 9,000.00
1/2/2012	Deanne	McGuire	Port-a-Spa	Finance	Promotion	$ 3,240	$ 810.00	$ 2,430.00
1/2/2012	Oleta	Fairbanks	Port-a-Spa	Finance	Promotion	$ 4,080	$ 1,020.00	$ 3,060.00
1/2/2012	Seth	Prescott	Serenity Spas	Finance	Promotion	$ 5,432	$ 1,358.00	$ 4,074.00
1/3/2012	Deanne	McGuire	Port-a-Spa	Finance	Standard	$ 6,780	$ 1,695.00	$ 5,085.00
1/3/2012	Oleta	Fairbanks	The Original Hot Tub	Finance	Standard	$ 5,432	$ 1,358.00	$ 4,074.00
1/3/2012	Deanne	McGuire	Serenity Spas	Paid in Full	Standard	$ 6,780	$ 6,780.00	$ -
1/3/2012	Deanne	McGuire	The Original Hot Tub	Paid in Full	Standard	$ 27,000	$ 27,000.00	$ -
1/4/2012	Grant	Ingersoll	Port-a-Spa	Finance	Standard	$ 10,000	$ 2,500.00	$ 7,500.00
1/4/2012	Oleta	Fairbanks	Port-a-Spa	Finance	Standard	$ 10,000	$ 2,500.00	$ 7,500.00
1/4/2012	Deanne	McGuire	Port-a-Spa	Paid in Full	Standard	$ 4,550	$ 4,550.00	$ -
1/4/2012	Deanne	McGuire	Serenity Spas	Paid in Full	Promotion	$ 8,490	$ 8,490.00	$ -
1/4/2012	Deanne	McGuire	The Original Hot Tub	Paid in Full	Standard	$ 5,432	$ 5,432.00	$ -
1/4/2012	Grant	Ingersoll	Serenity Spas	Paid in Full	Promotion	$ 7,450	$ 7,450.00	$ -
1/4/2012	Oleta	Fairbanks	The Original Hot Tub	Paid in Full	Standard	$ 5,432	$ 5,432.00	$ -
1/4/2012	Seth	Prescott	Serenity Spas	Paid in Full	Promotion	$ 6,780	$ 6,780.00	$ -
1/5/2012	Deanne	McGuire	Port-a-Spa	Finance	Standard	$ 7,450	$ 1,862.50	$ 5,587.50
1/5/2012	Deanne	McGuire	Port-a-Spa	Paid in Full	Standard	$ 8,560	$ 8,560.00	$ -
1/6/2012	Deanne	McGuire	Port-a-Spa	Finance	Promotion	$ 26,500	$ 6,625.00	$ 19,875.00
1/6/2012	Oleta	Fairbanks	Port-a-Spa	Finance	Standard	$ 5,000	$ 1,250.00	$ 3,750.00
1/6/2012	Seth	Prescott	Serenity Spas	Finance	Promotion	$ 8,560	$ 2,140.00	$ 6,420.00
1/7/2012	Seth	Prescott	Port-a-Spa	Finance	Promotion	$ 5,000	$ 1,250.00	$ 3,750.00
1/7/2012	Grant	Ingersoll	Serenity Spas	Paid in Full	Standard	$ 5,400	$ 5,400.00	$ -

January Data | **January Totals** | January Range

Ready 100%

FIGURE 4.35 Structured References in Formulas ➤

a. Click the **January Totals worksheet tab**.

   To preserve the integrity of the sorting and filtering in case your instructor wants to verify your work, you will continue with an identical table on another worksheet.

b. Click in the **Name Box**, type **I6**, and then press **Enter** to go to **cell I6**. Click **Insert Function** on the Formula Bar to open the Insert Function dialog box, select **IF** in the **Select a function list**, and then click **OK**.

c. Type [**Payment Type**]=**"Paid in Full"** in the **Logical_test box**.

   The logical test evaluates whether a customer paid in full, indicated in the Payment Type column. Remember to type the brackets around the column heading.

d. Type [**Amount**] in the **Value_if_true box**.

   If a customer pays in full, their down payment is the full amount.

e. Type [**Amount**]*$C$3 in the **Value_if_false box**.

   If a customer does not pay in full, they must pay a required down payment. You use [Amount] to refer to the Amount column in the table. You must enclose the column heading in brackets. The amount of the spa is multiplied by the absolute reference to C3, the cell containing the required down payment percentage. You make this cell reference absolute so that it does not change when Excel copies the formula down the Down Payment column. Figure 4.35 shows the formula in the formula bar.

f. Click **OK** to enter the formula (see Figure 4.35).

   Because you are entering formulas in a table, Excel copies the formula down the column automatically. The first customer must finance $3,750 (25% of $15,000). The columns in the current worksheet have been formatted as Accounting Number Format for you.

> **TROUBLESHOOTING:** If the results seem incorrect, check your function. Errors will result if you do not enclose the field names in brackets, if you have misspelled a field name, if you omit the quotation marks around *Paid in Full*, and so on. Correct any errors.

g. Click **cell J6**. Type the formula =[**Amount**]-[**Down Payment**] and press **Enter**. Save the workbook.

The formula calculates how much customers owe if they finance their hot tubs. Excel copies the formula down the column.

STEP 7 **ADD A TOTAL ROW**

The table is almost complete, but you want to see the monthly totals for the Amount, Down Payment, and Owed columns. Instead of entering SUM functions yourself, you will add a total row. Refer to Figure 4.36 as you complete Step 7.

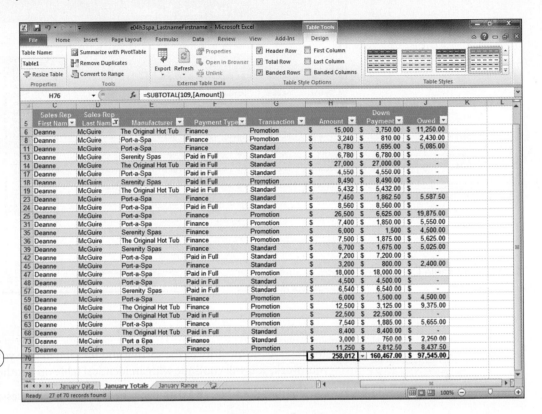

Totals added

FIGURE 4.36 Totals for Filtered Table ➤

a. Click the **Design tab**, and then click **Total Row** in the Table Style Options group.

Excel displays the total row after the last record. It sums the last column of values automatically. The total amount customers owe is $259,893.00.

b. Click the **Down Payment cell** in row 76, click the **total arrow**, and then select **Sum**. Increase the Down Payment column width as needed.

You added a total to the Down Payment column. The total amount of down payment collected is $406,925.00. The formula appears as =SUBTOTAL(109,[Down Payment]) in the Formula Bar.

c. Click the **Amount cell** in row 76, click the **total arrow**, and then select **Sum**.

You added a total to the Amount column. The total amount of spa sales is $666,818. The formula appears as =SUBTOTAL(109,[Amount]) in the Formula Bar.

d. Filter by McGuire again. Save the workbook.

Notice that the total row values change to display the totals for only the filtered records.

Your last task for now is to convert a copy of the table to a range again so that you can apply other formats. Refer to Figure 4.37 as you complete Step 8.

FIGURE 4.37 Table Converted to a Range ➤

a. Click the **January Range worksheet tab**.

To preserve the integrity of the sorting and filtering in case your instructor wants to verify your work, you will continue with an identical table on another worksheet.

b. Click within the table, and then click the **Design tab**, if necessary.

c. Click **Convert to Range** in the Tools group.

Excel displays a message box asking if you want to convert the table to a range.

d. Click **Yes**.

Excel converts the table to a range. The filter arrows disappear, and the Table Tools no longer display. The range is still formatted using the table style you applied. The structured formula =[Amount]-[Down Payment] changes (see Figure 4.37).

e. Double-click the border between the column I and J headers to increase the width of column I so that the down payment total displays on the last row.

f. Save the workbook. Keep the workbook onscreen if you plan to continue with Hands-On Exercise 4. If not, close the workbook and exit Excel.

Conditional Formatting

Conditional formatting highlights or emphasizes cells that meet certain conditions.

You use table styles, or a variety of font, alignment, and number formats on the Home tab, to format a worksheet. You can also apply special formatting to cells that contain particular values or text using conditional formatting. **Conditional formatting** applies special formatting to highlight or emphasize cells that meet specific conditions. For example, a sales manager might want to highlight cells containing the top 10 sales amounts, or a professor might want to highlight test scores that fall below the average. You can also apply conditional formatting to point out data for a specific date or duplicate values in a range.

In this section, you will learn about the five conditional formatting categories and how to apply conditional formatting to a range of values based on a condition you set.

Applying Conditional Formatting

Conditional formatting helps you and your audience understand a dataset better because it adds a visual element to the cells. The term is called *conditional* because the formatting occurs when a condition is met. This is similar logic to the IF function you have used. Remember with an IF function, you create a logical test that is evaluated. If the logical or conditional test is true, the function produces one result. If the logical or conditional test is false, the function produces another result. With conditional formatting, if the condition is true, Excel formats the cell automatically based on that condition. If the condition is false, Excel does not format the cell. If you change a value in a conditionally formatted cell, Excel examines the new value to see if it should apply the conditional format. Table 4.5 lists and describes a number of different conditional formats that you can apply.

> Conditional formatting helps you and your audience understand a dataset better because it adds a visual element to the cells.

TABLE 4.5 Conditional Formatting Options	
Conditional Formatting	**Description**
Highlight Cells Rules	Highlights cells with a fill color, font color, or border (such as Light Red Fill with Dark Red Text) if values are greater than, less than, between two values, equal to a value, or duplicate values; text that contains particular characters; or dates when a date meets a particular condition, such as *In the last 7 days*.
Top/Bottom Rules	Formats cells with values in the top 10 items, top 10%, bottom 10 items, bottom 10%, values, above average, or below average. You can change the exact values to format the top or bottom items or percentages, such as top 5 or bottom 15%.
Data Bars	Applies a gradient or solid fill bar in which the width of the bar represents the current cell's value compared to other cells' values.
Color Scales	Formats different cells with different colors, assigning one color to the lowest group of values and another color to the highest group of values, with gradient colors to other values.
Icon Sets	Inserts an icon from an icon palette in each cell to indicate values compared to each other.

To apply a conditional format, select the cells for which you want to apply a conditional format, click the Home tab, click Conditional Formatting in the Styles group, and select the conditional formatting category you want to apply.

Apply the Highlight Cells Rules

The Highlight Cells Rules category enables you to apply a highlight to cells that meet a condition, such as a value greater than a particular value. This option contains predefined combinations of fill colors, font colors, and/or borders. This category is useful because it helps you identify and format automatically values of interest. For example, a weather tracker who developed a worksheet containing the temperatures for each day of a month might want to apply a conditional format to cells that contain temperatures between 70 and 75 degrees. To apply this conditional formatting, she would select Highlight Cells Rules, and then select Between. In the Between dialog box (see Figure 4.38), the weather tracker would type 70 in the *Format cells that are BETWEEN* box and 75 in the *and* box, select the type of conditional formatting, such as *Light Red Fill with Dark Red Text*, and then click OK to apply the formats.

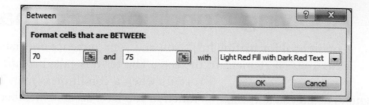

FIGURE 4.38 Between Dialog Box ➤

Figure 4.39 shows two columns of data that contain conditional formats. The Manufacturer column contains a conditional format to highlight text with a Light Red Fill with Dark Red Text for cells that contain *Serenity Spas*, and the Amount column contains a conditional format to highlight with Red Border values between $10,000 and $20,000.

FIGURE 4.39 Highlight Cells Rules Conditional Formatting ➤

Specify Top/Bottom Rules

You may not know the exact values to format conditionally. You might be interested in identifying the top five sales to reward the sales associates, or want to identify the bottom 15% of automobile dealers so that you can close underperforming locations. The Top/Bottom Rules category enables you to specify the top or bottom number or percentage in a selected range. In addition, the Top/Bottom Rules category enables you to identify values that are above or below the average value in that range. In Figure 4.40, the selected range is conditionally formatted to highlight the top three amounts. Although the menu option is Top 10 Items, you can specify the exact number of items to highlight.

Click to select format

Enter number of cells here

Conditional formatting applied to top three items

FIGURE 4.40 Top 10 Items Dialog Box ➤

Display Data Bars, Color Scales, and Icon Sets

A **data bar** is a horizontal gradient or solid fill indicating the cell's relative value compared to other selected cells.

Data bars help you visualize the value of a cell relative to other cells, as shown in Figure 4.41. The width of the gradient or solid data bar represents the value in a cell, with a wider bar representing a higher value and a shorter bar a lower value. Use data bar conditional formatting when identifying high and low values. Excel locates the largest value and displays the widest data bar in that cell. Excel then finds the smallest value and displays the smallest data bar in that cell. Excel sizes the data bars for the remaining cells based on their relative values. If you change the values in your worksheet, Excel automatically updates the widths of the data bars. Data bars are more effective with wider columns than narrow columns. Figure 4.41 shows data bar conditional formatting applied to the Amount column. The widest data bar displays in the cell containing the largest amount of $27,000, and the smallest data bar appears in the cells containing the smallest value of $3,240. The data bar widths of other cells help you see the value differences. Excel uses the same color for each data bar, but each bar differs in size based on the value in the respective cells.

Data bars applied to Amount column

Icon set applied to Owed column

Color scales applied to Down Payment column

FIGURE 4.41 Data Bars, Color Scales, and Icon Sets ➤

A **color scale** is a conditional format that displays a particular color based on the relative value of the cell contents to other selected cells.

Color scales format cells with different colors based on the relative value of a cell compared to other selected cells. You can apply a two- or three-color scale. This scale assists in comparing a range of cells using gradations of those colors. The shade of the color represents higher or lower values. In Figure 4.41, for example, the red color scales display for the lowest values, the green color displays for the highest values, and gradients of yellow and orange represent the middle range of values in the Down Payment column. Use color scales to understand variation in the data to identify trends, for example to view good stock returns and weak stock returns.

An **icon set** is a conditional format that displays an icon representing a value in the top third, quarter, or fifth based on values in the selected range.

Icon sets are little symbols or signs that display in cells to classify data into three, four, or five categories, based on the values in the selected range. Excel determines categories of value ranges and assigns an icon to each range. In Figure 4.41, a three-icon set was applied to the Owed column. Excel divided the range of values between the lowest value $0 and the highest value of $19,875 into thirds. The red diamond icon displays for the cells containing values in the lowest third ($0 to $6,625), the yellow triangle icon displays for cells containing the values in the middle third ($6,626 to $12,150), and the green circle icon displays for cells containing values in the top third ($13,251 to $19,875). This helps you identify the spas with the most financing. Most spa purchases fall into the lowest third.

> **TIP** Don't Overdo It!
>
> Although conditional formatting helps identify trends, you should use this feature wisely. Apply conditional formatting when you want to emphasize important data. When you decide to apply conditional formatting, think about which category is best to highlight the data. Sometimes simple highlighting will suffice when you want to point out data meeting a particular condition; other times, you might want to apply data bars to point out relative differences among values. Finally, don't apply conditional formatting to too many columns.

Clear Rules

To clear conditional formatting from the entire worksheet, click Conditional Formatting in the Styles group on the Home tab, point to Clear Rules, and select Clear Rules from Entire Sheet. To remove conditional formatting from a range of cells, select cells. Then click Conditional Formatting, point to Clear Rules, and then select Clear Rules from Selected Cells.

Creating a New Rule

The default conditional formatting categories provide a variety of options. Excel also enables you to create your own rules to specify different fill colors, borders, or other formatting if you don't want the default settings. Excel provides three ways to create a new rule:

- Click Conditional Formatting in the Cell Styles group, and then select New Rule.
- Click Conditional Formatting in the Cell Styles group, select Manage Rules to open the Conditional Formatting Rules Manager dialog box, and then click New Rule.
- Click Conditional Formatting in the Cell Styles group, select a rule category such as Highlight Cells Rules, and then select More Rules.

The New Formatting Rule dialog box opens (see Figure 4.42) so that you can define your new conditional formatting rule. First, select a rule type, such as *Format all cells based on their values*. The *Edit the Rule Description* section changes, based on the rule type you select. With the default rule type selected, you can specify the format style (2-Color Scale, 3-Color Scale, Data Bar, or Icon Sets). You can then specify the minimum and maximum values, the fill colors for color sets or data bars or the icons for icon sets. After you edit the rule description, click OK to save your new conditional format.

FIGURE 4.42 New Formatting Rule Dialog Box ➤

If you select any rule type except the *Format all cells based on their values* rule, the dialog box contains a Format button. When you click Format, the Format Cells dialog box opens so that you can specify number, font, border, and fill formats to apply to your rule.

> **TIP** Format Only Cells That Contain
>
> This option provides a wide array of things you can format: values, text, dates, blanks, no blanks, errors, or no errors. Formatting blanks is helpful to see where you are missing data, and formatting cells containing errors helps you find those errors quickly.

Use Formulas in Conditional Formatting

Excel provides a vast number of conditional formatting options. If you need to create a complex conditional formatting rule, you can select a rule that uses a formula to format cells. For example, you might want to format amounts of financed spas *and* amounts that are $10,000 or more. Figure 4.43 shows the Edit Formatting Rule dialog box and the corresponding conditional formatting applied to cells.

Formula to control formatting

Formatting applied

FIGURE 4.43 Formula Rule Created and Applied ➤

To create a formula-based conditional formatting rule, select the data and create a new rule. In the New Formatting Rule dialog box, select *Use a formula to determine which cells to format*, and then type the formula in the *Format values where this formula is true* box. You write the formula for the first data row, such as F6 and H6. Excel then applies the general formula to the selected range, substituting the appropriate cell reference as it makes the comparisons. In this example, =AND(F6="Finance",H6>=10000) requires that the text in the Payment Type column (column F) contain Finance and the Amount column (column H) contain a value that is greater than or equal to $10,000. The AND function requires that both logical tests be met to apply the conditional formatting. Two logical tests are required; however, you can include additional logical tests. Note that *all* logical tests must be true to apply the conditional formatting.

= AND(logical1,logical2,...)

Manage Rules

To edit or delete conditional formatting rules you create, click Conditional Formatting in the Styles group, and then select Manage Rules. The Conditional Formatting Rules Manager dialog box opens (see Figure 4.44). Click the *Show formatting rules for* arrow and select from current selection, the entire worksheet, or a specific table. Then select the rule, and then click Edit Rule or Delete Rule.

FIGURE 4.44 Conditional Formatting Rules Manager Dialog Box ➤

Sorting and Filtering Using Conditional Formatting

Earlier in this chapter, you learned how to sort and filter to change the order of fields or the records displayed. Now that you know how to apply conditional formatting, you can sort and filter by conditional formatting as well.

For example, if you applied the Highlight Cells Rules, Top/Bottom Rules, or Color Scales conditional formatting, you can sort the column by color so that all cells containing the highlight appear first or last. To do this, display the filter arrows, click the arrow for the conditionally formatted column you wish to sort, point to Sort by Color, and then click the fill color or No Fill in the Sort by Cell Color area. If you applied the Data Bars conditional format, you can't sort by data bars, but you can sort by values, which will arrange the data bars in ascending or descending order. If you applied the Icon Sets conditional formatting, you can filter by icon.

4 Conditional Formatting

Your business partner, Ryan, wants to review the transactions with you. He is interested in Fairbanks' sales record and the five highest spa amounts. In addition, he wants to compare the down payment amounts visually. Finally, he wants to analyze the amounts owed for sales completed by Prescott.

Skills covered: Highlight Cells Rules • Specify Top/Bottom Rules • Display Data Bars • Create a New Rule • Filter by Rule

STEP 1 HIGHLIGHT CELLS RULES

You want to identify Fairbanks' spa sales for January without filtering the data. You will apply a conditional format to apply a fill and font color so that cells containing her last name stand out. Refer to Figure 4.45 as you complete Step 1.

FIGURE 4.45 Text Formatted with Highlight Text Rules ➤

a. Open *e04h3spa_LastnameFirstname* if you closed it at the end of Hands-On Exercise 3. Save the workbook with the new name **e04h4spa_LastnameFirstname**, changing *h3* to *h4*.

b. Select **row headings 6 through 75** in the January Range worksheet. Click the **Home tab**, if necessary, click the **Fill Color arrow**, and then select **No Fill**.

   You removed the previous table style with banded rows. This will avoid having too many fill colors when you apply conditional formatting rules.

c. Select the **range D6:D75**, which is the column containing the sales representatives' last names.

d. Click **Conditional Formatting** in the Styles group, point to **Highlight Cells Rules**, and then select **Text that Contains**.

   The Text That Contains dialog box opens.

e. Type **Fairbanks** in the box, click the **with arrow**, and then select **Green Fill with Dark Green Text**. Click **OK**. Deselect the range, and then save the workbook.

   Excel formats only cells that contain Fairbanks with the fill and font color.

While the range is selected, you can apply another conditional format, such as Light Yellow with Dark Yellow text for another last name.

STEP 2 ▶ SPECIFY TOP/BOTTOM RULES

Ryan is now interested in identifying the highest five spa sales in January. Instead of sorting the records, you will use the Top/Bottom Rules conditional formatting. Refer to Figure 4.46 as you complete Step 2.

	B	C	D	E	F	G	H	I	J
14	1/3/2012	Deanne	McGuire	The Original Hot Tub	Paid in Full	Standard	$ 27,000	$ 27,000.00	$ -
15	1/4/2012	Grant	Ingersoll	Port-a-Spa	Finance	Standard	$ 10,000	$ 2,500.00	$ 7,500.00
16	1/4/2012	Oleta	Fairbanks	Port-a-Spa	Finance	Standard	$ 10,000	$ 2,500.00	$ 7,500.00
17	1/4/2012	Deanne	McGuire	Port-a-Spa	Paid in Full	Standard	$ 4,550	$ 4,550.00	$ -
18	1/4/2012	Deanne	McGuire	Serenity Spas	Paid in Full	Promotion	$ 8,490	$ 8,490.00	$ -
19	1/4/2012	Deanne	McGuire	The Original Hot Tub	Paid in Full	Standard	$ 5,432	$ 5,432.00	$ -
20	1/4/2012	Grant	Ingersoll	Serenity Spas	Paid in Full	Promotion	$ 7,450	$ 7,450.00	$ -
21	1/4/2012	Oleta	Fairbanks	The Original Hot Tub	Paid in Full	Standard	$ 5,432	$ 5,432.00	$ -
22	1/4/2012	Seth	Prescott	Serenity Spas	Paid in Full	Promotion	$ 6,780	$ 6,780.00	$ -
23	1/5/2012	Deanne	McGuire	Port-a-Spa	Finance	Standard	$ 7,450	$ 1,862.50	$ 5,587.50
24	1/5/2012	Deanne	McGuire	Port-a-Spa	Paid in Full	Standard	$ 8,560	$ 8,560.00	$ -
25	1/6/2012	Deanne	McGuire	Port-a-Spa	Finance	Promotion	$ 26,500	$ 6,625.00	$ 19,875.00
26	1/6/2012	Oleta	Fairbanks	Port-a-Spa	Finance	Standard	$ 5,000	$ 1,250.00	$ 3,750.00
27	1/6/2012	Seth	Prescott	Serenity Spas	Finance	Promotion	$ 8,560	$ 2,140.00	$ 6,420.00
28	1/7/2012	Seth	Prescott	Port-a-Spa	Finance	Promotion	$ 5,000	$ 1,250.00	$ 3,750.00
29	1/7/2012	Grant	Ingersoll	Serenity Spas	Paid in Full	Standard	$ 5,400	$ 5,400.00	$ -
30	1/8/2012	Oleta	Fairbanks	Serenity Spas	Finance	Standard	$ 3,240	$ 810.00	$ 2,430.00
31	1/9/2012	Deanne	McGuire	Port-a-Spa	Finance	Promotion	$ 7,400	$ 1,850.00	$ 5,550.00
32	1/9/2012	Grant	Ingersoll	Port-a-Spa	Finance	Promotion	$ 22,000	$ 5,500.00	$ 16,500.00
33	1/9/2012	Grant	Ingersoll	The Original Hot Tub	Paid in Full	Promotion	$ 3,240	$ 3,240.00	$ -
34	1/10/2012	Seth	Prescott	The Original Hot Tub	Paid in Full	Standard	$ 7,690	$ 7,690.00	$ -
35	1/10/2012	Deanne	McGuire	Serenity Spas	Finance	Promotion	$ 6,000	$ 1,500.00	$ 4,500.00
36	1/11/2012	Deanne	McGuire	The Original Hot Tub	Finance	Promotion	$ 7,500	$ 1,875.00	$ 5,625.00
37	1/11/2012	Oleta	Fairbanks	Port-a-Spa	Paid in Full	Promotion	$ 7,500	$ 7,500.00	$ -
38	1/11/2012	Seth	Prescott	Serenity Spas	Paid in Full	Promotion	$ 4,650	$ 4,650.00	$ -
39	1/12/2012	Deanne	McGuire	Serenity Spas	Finance	Standard	$ 6,700	$ 1,675.00	$ 5,025.00
40	1/13/2012	Grant	Ingersoll	The Original Hot Tub	Finance	Promotion	$ 6,540	$ 1,635.00	$ 4,905.00
41	1/14/2012	Grant	Ingersoll	Serenity Spas	Paid in Full	Promotion	$ 4,800	$ 4,800.00	$ -
42	1/15/2012	Deanne	McGuire	Port-a-Spa	Paid in Full	Standard	$ 7,200	$ 7,200.00	$ -
43	1/16/2012	Oleta	Fairbanks	Serenity Spas	Paid in Full	Standard	$ 32,000	$ 32,000.00	$ -
44	1/17/2012	Seth	Prescott	Port-a-Spa	Finance	Standard	$ 12,000	$ 3,000.00	$ 9,000.00
45	1/18/2012	Deanne	McGuire	Port-a-Spa	Finance	Standard	$ 3,200	$ 800.00	$ 2,400.00

January Data | January Totals | **January Range**

FIGURE 4.46 Top 5 Amounts Conditionally Formatted ➤

a. Select the **range H6:H75**, the range containing the amounts.

b. Click **Conditional Formatting** in the Styles group, point to **Top/Bottom Rules**, and then select **Top 10 Items**.

The Top 10 Items dialog box opens.

c. Click the **spin arrow** to display 5, click the **with arrow**, and then select **Light Red Fill**. Click **OK**.

d. Scroll through the worksheet to see the top five amounts (three of which are shown in Figure 4.46). Save the workbook.

STEP 3 ▶ DISPLAY DATA BARS

Now Ryan wants to compare all of the down payments. Data bars would add a nice visual element as Ryan compares down payment amounts. Refer to Figure 4.47 as you complete Step 3.

Figure 4.47 table (rows 44–75):

	B	C	D	E	F	G	H	I	J
44	1/17/2012	Seth	Prescott	Port-a-Spa	Finance	Standard	$ 12,000	$ 3,000.00	$ 9,000.00
45	1/18/2012	Deanne	McGuire	Port-a-Spa	Finance	Standard	$ 3,200	$ 800.00	$ 2,400.00
46	1/18/2012	Seth	Prescott	The Original Hot Tub	Finance	Standard	$ 12,350	$ 3,087.50	$ 9,262.50
47	1/18/2012	Deanne	McGuire	Port-a-Spa	Paid in Full	Promotion	$ 18,000	$ 18,000.00	$ -
48	1/19/2012	Deanne	McGuire	Port-a-Spa	Paid in Full	Standard	$ 4,500	$ 4,500.00	$ -
49	1/19/2012	Grant	Ingersoll	Port-a-Spa	Paid in Full	Standard	$ 12,500	$ 12,500.00	$ -
50	1/20/2012	Oleta	Fairbanks	Serenity Spas	Finance	Promotion	$ 7,500	$ 1,875.00	$ 5,625.00
51	1/21/2012	Grant	Ingersoll	The Original Hot Tub	Finance	Standard	$ 3,450	$ 862.50	$ 2,587.50
52	1/21/2012	Oleta	Fairbanks	Port-a-Spa	Finance	Promotion	$ 8,000	$ 2,000.00	$ 6,000.00
53	1/21/2012	Oleta	Fairbanks	The Original Hot Tub	Finance	Standard	$ 17,500	$ 4,375.00	$ 13,125.00
54	1/21/2012	Seth	Prescott	Serenity Spas	Finance	Standard	$ 5,600	$ 1,400.00	$ 4,200.00
55	1/21/2012	Seth	Prescott	Port-a-Spa	Paid in Full	Standard	$ 18,500	$ 18,500.00	$ -
56	1/21/2012	Seth	Prescott	The Original Hot Tub	Paid in Full	Standard	$ 5,400	$ 5,400.00	$ -
57	1/22/2012	Deanne	McGuire	Serenity Spas	Paid in Full	Standard	$ 6,540	$ 6,540.00	$ -
58	1/23/2012	Seth	Prescott	Serenity Spas	Finance	Standard	$ 5,600	$ 1,400.00	$ 4,200.00
59	1/24/2012	Deanne	McGuire	Port-a-Spa	Finance	Promotion	$ 6,000	$ 1,500.00	$ 4,500.00
60	1/25/2012	Deanne	McGuire	The Original Hot Tub	Finance	Promotion	$ 12,500	$ 3,125.00	$ 9,375.00
61	1/26/2012	Deanne	McGuire	The Original Hot Tub	Paid in Full	Promotion	$ 22,500	$ 22,500.00	$ -
62	1/26/2012	Oleta	Fairbanks	Port-a-Spa	Paid in Full	Promotion	$ 25,000	$ 25,000.00	$ -
63	1/27/2012	Deanne	McGuire	Port-a-Spa	Finance	Promotion	$ 7,540	$ 1,885.00	$ 5,655.00
64	1/27/2012	Oleta	Fairbanks	Port-a-Spa	Finance	Promotion	$ 7,540	$ 1,885.00	$ 5,655.00
65	1/27/2012	Oleta	Fairbanks	The Original Hot Tub	Paid in Full	Standard	$ 12,500	$ 12,500.00	$ -
66	1/28/2012	Seth	Prescott	Port-a-Spa	Finance	Standard	$ 9,430	$ 2,357.50	$ 7,072.50
67	1/28/2012	Seth	Prescott	Serenity Spas	Finance	Promotion	$ 10,000	$ 2,500.00	$ 7,500.00
68	1/28/2012	Deanne	McGuire	The Original Hot Tub	Paid in Full	Standard	$ 8,400	$ 8,400.00	$ -
69	1/29/2012	Grant	Ingersoll	Serenity Spas	Finance	Standard	$ 7,730	$ 1,932.50	$ 5,797.50
70	1/29/2012	Grant	Ingersoll	The Original Hot Tub	Finance	Standard	$ 8,400	$ 2,100.00	$ 6,300.00
71	1/30/2012	Oleta	Fairbanks	The Original Hot Tub	Finance	Standard	$ 4,080	$ 1,020.00	$ 3,060.00
72	1/30/2012	Seth	Prescott	Port-a-Spa	Finance	Standard	$ 12,000	$ 12,000.00	$ -
73	1/31/2012	Deanne	McGuire	Port-a-Spa	Finance	Standard	$ 3,000	$ 750.00	$ 2,250.00
74	1/31/2012	Seth	Prescott	The Original Hot Tub	Paid in Full	Standard	$ 21,500	$ 21,500.00	$ -
75	1/31/2012	Deanne	McGuire	Port-a-Spa	Finance	Promotion	$ 11,250	$ 2,812.50	$ 8,437.50

January Data / January Totals / **January Range**

FIGURE 4.47 Data Bars Conditional Formatting ➤

a. Select the **range I6:I75**, which contains the down payment amounts.

b. Click **Conditional Formatting** in the Styles group, point to **Data Bars**, and then select **Purple Data Bar** in the *Gradient Fill* section. Scroll through the list, and then save the workbook.

Excel displays data bars in each cell. The larger bar widths help Ryan identify quickly the largest down payments. However, the largest down payments are identical to the original amounts when the customers pay in full. This result illustrates that you should not accept the results at face value. Doing so would provide you with an inaccurate analysis.

STEP 4 CREATE A NEW RULE

Ryan's next request is to analyze the amounts owed by Prescott's customers. In particular, he wants to know how many customers owe more than $5,000. To do this, you realize you need to create a custom rule that evaluates both the Sales Rep Last Name column and the Owed column. Refer to Figure 4.48 as you complete Step 4.

FIGURE 4.48 Custom Rule Created ➤

a. Select the **range J6:J75**, which contains the amounts owed.

b. Click **Conditional Formatting** in the Styles group, and then select **New Rule**.

The New Formatting Rule dialog box opens.

c. Select **Use a formula to determine which cells to format**.

d. Type **=AND(D6="Prescott",J6>=5000)** in the **Format values where this formula is true box**.

Because you are comparing the contents of cell D6 to text, you must enclose the text within quotation marks.

e. Click **Format** to open the Format Cells dialog box.

f. Click the **Font tab**, if necessary, and then click **Bold** in the **Font style list**. Click the **Border tab**, click the **Color arrow**, select **Purple**, and then click **Outline**. Click the **Fill tab**, click the **lightest purple background color** (the eighth color on the first row below the first horizontal line), and then click **OK**. Look at Figure 4.48 to compare your new rule.

The figure shows the Edit Formatting Rule dialog box, but the options are similar to the New Formatting Rule dialog box.

g. Click **OK** in New Formatting Rule dialog box, and then scroll through the list to see which amounts owed are greater than $5,000 for Prescott only. Save the workbook.

STEP 5 **FILTER BY RULE**

Ryan commented that it is difficult to see which of Prescott's transactions were greater than $5,000 without scrolling. To help Ryan review the Owed column where you applied a formula-based conditional format, you will filter that column by the fill color. Refer to Figure 4.49 as you complete Step 5.

FIGURE 4.49 Owed Column
Filtered by Fill Color ➤

a. Deselect the range by clicking inside the dataset. Click **Sort & Filter** in the Editing group, and then select **Filter**.

Filter arrows display for the column headings.

b. Click the **Owed filter arrow**, point to **Filter by Color**, and then select the **light purple fill color**.

Excel filters the range to display records where the fill color is lavender. Now it is easy to see that Prescott sold five spas where the customers owe more than $5,000.

c. Save and close the workbook, and submit based on your instructor's directions.

After reading this chapter, you have accomplished the following objectives:

1. **Freeze rows and columns.** To prevent labels from scrolling offscreen, freeze rows or columns. The Freeze Panes setting freezes the row(s) above and the column(s) to the left of the active cell. When you scroll, those rows and columns remain onscreen so that you know what type of data is in each row or column. You can use Unfreeze Panes to clear the frozen rows and columns.

2. **Print large datasets.** Display the data in Page Break Preview to see the automatic page breaks. Dashed blue lines indicate automatic page breaks. You can insert manual page breaks, indicated by solid blue lines. If you do not want to print an entire worksheet, select a range and set a print area. Dotted lines surround the print area onscreen. When a dataset will print on several pages, you can control the sequence in which the pages will print.

3. **Understand table design.** A table is a structured range that contains related data. Tables have several benefits over regular ranges, such as keeping headings onscreen as you scroll. Each table column is a field. The column headings, called *field names*, appear on the first row of a table. Each row is a complete set of data for one record. You should plan a table. For example, create unique field names on the first row of the table, and enter data immediately below the field names, avoiding blank rows.

4. **Create a table.** You can create a table from existing structured data. Excel applies the Table Style Medium 9 format and assigns a default name, such as Table1, to the table. When the active cell is within a table, the Table Tools display with the Design tab. You can insert and delete table rows and columns and remove duplicate records in your table.

5. **Apply a table style.** Table styles control the fill color of the header row and records within the table. To further customize the formatting, click options, such as First Column or Total Row in the Table Style Options group.

6. **Sort data.** The data in a table are often easier to understand and work with if they are in some meaningful order. Sorting arranges records in a table by the value of one or more fields within the table. You can sort text in alphabetical or reverse alphabetical order, values from smallest to largest or largest to smallest, and dates from oldest to newest or newest to oldest. To sort a single field, click the filter arrow and select the sort method from the list. To sort multiple fields, open the Sort

dialog box and add column levels and sort orders. You can create a custom sort for unique data.

7. **Filter data.** Filtering is the process of specifying conditions for displaying records in a table. Only records that meet those conditions display; the other records are hidden until you clear the filters. You can apply text, value, and date filters based on the data in a particular field.

8. **Use structured references and a total row.** A structured reference uses field names instead of cell references, such as =[Amount]-[Down Payment]. Field names must appear in brackets within the formula. When you press Enter, Excel copies the formula down the column. You can display a total row after the last record. Excel sums the values in the last column automatically or counts the number of text entries. You can add totals to other columns, and you can select a different function, such as Average.

9. **Apply conditional formatting.** Conditional formatting applies special formatting to cells that contain values that meet set conditions. The five major conditional formatting categories are Highlight Cells Rules, Top/Bottom Rules, Data Bars, Color Scales, and Icon Sets. Data bars display horizontal bars that compare values within the selected range. The larger the value, the wider the horizontal bar. Color scales indicate values that occur within particular ranges. Icon sets display icons representing a number's relative value compared to other numbers in the range. When you no longer need conditional formatting, you can clear it for the selected range or entire worksheet.

10. **Create a new rule.** You can create conditional format rules. The New Formatting Rule dialog box enables you to select a rule type. Based on the type you select, the *Edit the Rule Description* section changes to provide specific options for defining your rule. You can create rules based on formulas to set conditions based on content in multiple columns. Use the Conditional Formatting Rules Manager dialog box to edit and delete rules.

11. **Sort and filter using conditional formatting.** After you apply conditional formatting, you can sort or filter a column based on its formats. Use Sort by Color to select a sort sequence, or select Filter by Color to filter out records that do not meet the color condition you specify.

KEY TERMS

Color scale *p.512*
Conditional formatting *p.509*
Data bar *p.511*
Field *p.484*
Filtering *p.495*
Freezing *p.475*

Icon set *p.512*
Page break *p.476*
Print area *p.477*
Print order *p.478*
Record *p.484*
Sorting *p.493*

Structured reference *p.498*
SUBTOTAL function *p.499*
Table *p.484*
Table style *p.487*
Total row *p.499*

1. You have a large dataset that will print on several pages. You want to ensure that related records print on the same page with column and row labels visible and that confidential information is not printed. You should apply all of the following page setup options except which one to accomplish this?

   (a) Set a print area.
   (b) Print titles.
   (c) Adjust page breaks.
   (d) Change the print page order.

2. You are working with a large worksheet. Your row headings are in column A. Which command(s) should be used to see the row headings and the distant information in columns X, Y, and Z?

   (a) Freeze Panes command
   (b) Hide Rows command
   (c) New Window command and cascade the windows
   (d) Split Rows command

3. Which statement is not a recommended guideline for planning a table in Excel?

   (a) Avoid naming two fields with the same name.
   (b) Ensure no blank columns separate data columns within the table.
   (c) Leave one blank row between records in the table.
   (d) Include field names on the first row of the table.

4. You have a list of all the employees in your organization. The list contains employee name, office, title, and salary. You want to list all employees in each office branch. The branches should be listed alphabetically, with the employee earning the highest salary listed first in each office. Which is true of your sort order?

   (a) Branch office is the primary sort and should be in A to Z order.
   (b) Salary is the primary sort and should be from highest to lowest.
   (c) Salary is the primary sort and should be from lowest to highest.
   (d) Branch office is the primary sort and should be in Z to A order.

5. You suspect a table has several identical records. What should you do?

   (a) Do nothing; a logical reason probably exists to keep identical records.
   (b) Use the Remove Duplicates command.

   (c) Look at each row yourself, and manually delete duplicate records.
   (d) Find the duplicate records and change some of the data to be different.

6. Which check box in the Table Style Options group enables you to apply different formatting to the records in a table?

   (a) Header Row
   (b) Banded Rows
   (c) Banded Columns
   (d) Total Row

7. Which date filter option enables you to specify criteria for selecting a range of dates, such as between 3/15/2012 and 7/15/2012?

   (a) Equals
   (b) Before
   (c) All Dates in the Period
   (d) Between

8. You want to display a total row that identifies the oldest date in a field in your table. What function do you select from the list?

   (a) Max
   (b) Sum
   (c) Min
   (d) Count

9. What type of conditional formatting displays horizontal colors in which the width of the bar indicates relative size compared to other values in the selected range?

   (a) Color Scales
   (b) Icon Sets
   (c) Data Bars
   (d) Sparklines

10. When you select the _____ rule type, the New Formatting Rule dialog box does not show the Format button.

    (a) Format all cells based on their values
    (b) Format only cells that contain
    (c) Use a formula to determine which cells to format
    (d) Format only unique or duplicate values

1 Fiesta® Collection

Your Aunt Laura has been collecting Fiesta dinnerware, a popular brand from The Homer Laughlin China Company, since it was reintroduced in 1986. Her collection has grown, and she enlisted you to help her maintain a list. So far, you and Aunt Laura have entered data by color, item number, and item. In addition, you researched current replacement costs from Homer Laughlin's Web site (www.fiestafactorydirect.com); Replacements, Ltd. (www.replacements.com); and eBay (www.ebay.com). Now you need to apply techniques to manage the list, convert it to a table, and then apply table features. This exercise follows the same set of skills as used in Hands-On Exercises 1, 2, and 3 in the chapter. Refer to Figure 4.50 as you complete this exercise.

FIGURE 4.50 Fiesta® Collection ➤

a. Open *e04p1fiesta* and save it as **e04p1fiesta_LastnameFirstname**.

b. Click **cell C2**, click the **View tab**, click **Freeze Panes** in the Window group, and then select **Freeze Panes**.

c. Press **Ctrl+End** to go to the last data cell. Note that the frozen rows and column headings remain onscreen. Press **Ctrl+Home** to go back to **cell C2**.

d. Click the **Insert tab**, click **Table** in the Tables group, and then click **OK** in the Create Table dialog box.

e. Click the **More button** in the Table Styles group, and then click **Table Style Medium 3**.

f. Click **Remove Duplicates** in the Tools group, click **Select All** to ensure all columns are selected, and then click **OK**. Click **OK** in the message box that informs you that 12 duplicate values were found and removed.

g. Click within the table. Click the **Data tab**, and then click **Sort** in the Sort & Filter group. Do the following in the Sort dialog box:
   • Click the **Sort by arrow**, and then select **Year Introduced**.
   • Click **Add Level**, click the **Then by arrow**, and then select **Color**.
   • Click **Add Level**, click the **Then by arrow**, select **Replacement Value**, click the **Order arrow**, and then select **Largest to Smallest**. Click **OK**.

h. Click the **Year Retired filter arrow**, deselect the **(Blanks) check box**, and then click **OK** to filter out current colors and display only retired colors.

i. Click the **Design tab**, and then click **Total Row** in the Table Style Options group. Scroll down to the total row on row 316, click the **Source total cell** (which contains a count), click the **Source total arrow**, and then select **None**. Click **cell G6**, the Replacement Value total cell, click the **Replacement Value total arrow**, and then select **Sum**.

j. Prepare the worksheet in case your Aunt Laura wants a printout by doing the following:
   - Click the **Page Layout tab**, click **Orientation** in the Page Setup group, and then select **Landscape**.
   - Click **Print Titles**, click the **Rows to repeat at top collapse button**, click the **row 1 header**, and then click the **expand button**. Click **OK**.
   - Select **cells A1:G316**. Click **Print Area**, and then select **Set Print Area**.
   - Click the **View tab**, and then click **Page Break Preview**. If the message box appears, click **OK**.

k. Click **cell A89**, click the **Page Layout tab**, click **Breaks** in the Page Setup group, and then select **Insert Page Break** to insert a page break so that the Periwinkle Blue item on row 89 appears after the page break, along with the other Periwinkle Blue items.

l. Adapt step k to insert a page break before **cell A120** to move Persimmon to the top of a page. Insert another page break before **cell A151** to move Juniper to the top of a page.

m. Create a footer with your name on the left side, the date code in the center, and the file name code on the right side.

n. Save and close the workbook, and submit based on your instructor's directions.

2 Salary Data

As the Human Resources Manager, you maintain employee salary data. You exported data from the corporate database into an Excel workbook. You want to convert the data to a table. You will use structured references to calculate raises and new salaries. Finally, you want to display a total row to show the total salaries. This exercise follows the same set of skills as used in Hands-On Exercises 1, 2, and 3 in the chapter. Refer to Figure 4.51 as you complete this exercise.

FIGURE 4.51 Salary Data ➤

a. Open *e04p2salary* and save it as **e04p2salary_LastnameFirstname**.

b. Click in the dataset. Click the **Insert tab**, click **Table** in the Tables group, and then click **OK**.

c. Click the **More button** in the Table Styles group, and then click **Table Style Light 10**.

d. Click the **Data tab**, click **Sort** in the Sort & Filter group, and then do the following in the Sort dialog box:
   - Click the **Sort by arrow**, and then select **Location**.
   - Click **Add Level**, click the **Then by arrow**, and then select **Title**.

- Click **Add Level**, click the **Then by arrow**, select **Salary**, click the **Order arrow**, and then select **Largest to Smallest**. Then click **OK**.

e. Click **cell I3**, type **Raise**, and then press **Tab**. Type **New Salary** in **cell J3**, and then press **Enter**.

f. Click **cell I4**, type –[and then double-click **Salary** from the list. Type]*$I$1 and press **Enter**.

g. Click **cell J4**, type =[Salary]+[Raise], and then press **Enter**.

h. Format the last two columns with **Accounting Number Format** with no decimal places.

i. Click the **Design tab**, and then click **Total Row** in the Table Style Options group. Scroll to the bottom of the table, click the **Raise total cell** on row 159, click the **Raise total row arrow**, and then select **Sum**. Click the **Salary total cell** on row 159, click the **Salary total row arrow**, and then select **Sum**.

j. Prepare the worksheet to be printed by doing the following:
   - Click the **Page Layout tab**, and then set **landscape orientation**. Adjust column widths so that the data fits on one page, wrap text, and center align field names.
   - Click **Print Titles**, click the **Rows to repeat at top collapse button**, click **row 3**, click the **expand button**, and then click **OK**.
   - Click the **View tab**, and then click **Page Break Preview**. If a message box appears, click **OK**.

k. Drag the second page break to be between rows 58 and 59. Move the third page break to be between rows 81 and 82. Move the fourth page break to be between rows 110 and 111. Move the last page break to be between rows 139 and 140.

l. Create a footer with your name on the left side, the date code in the center, and the file name code on the right side.

m. Save and close the workbook, and submit based on your instructor's directions.

3 Dentist Association Donation List

The Midwest Regional Dentist Association is planning its annual meeting in Lincoln, Nebraska, this spring. Several members donated items for door prizes at the closing general session. You need to organize the list of donations and format it to highlight particular data for your supervisor, who is on the conference board of directors. This exercise follows the same set of skills as used in Hands-On Exercises 2, 3, and 4 in the chapter. Refer to Figure 4.52 as you complete this exercise.

FIGURE 4.52 Donation List ➤

a. Open *e04p3donate* and save it as **e04p3donate_LastnameFirstname**.

b. Click the **Design tab**, click **Remove Duplicates** in the Tools group, and then click **OK**. Click **OK** in the message box that tells you that Excel removed three duplicate records.

c. Click **Convert to Range** in the Tools group, and then click **Yes** in the message box.

d. Select the **range A2:J35**, click the **Home tab**, click the **Fill Color arrow** in the Font group, and then select **No Fill** to remove the table fill colors.

e. Select the **range I2:I35**. Click **Conditional Formatting** in the Styles group, point to **Highlight Cells Rules**, and then select **Greater Than**. Type **99** in the **Format cells that are GREATER THAN box**, and then click **OK**.

f. Select **cells H2:H35**. Create a custom conditional format by doing the following:

- Click **Conditional Formatting** in the Styles group, and then select **New Rule**.
- Click **Use a formula to determine which cells to format**.
- Type =(**J2="Equipment"**) in the **Format values where this formula is true box**. The basic condition is testing to see if the contents of cell J2 equal the word *Equipment*. You type *Equipment* in quotation marks since you are comparing text instead of a value.
- Click **Format**, click the **Fill tab** if necessary, and then click **Red, Accent 2, Lighter 60%** (sixth background color on the second row below the first horizontal line).
- Click the **Border tab**, click the **Color arrow**, click **Dark Red**, and then click **Outline**.
- Click **OK** in each dialog box.

g. Click anywhere in the table to deselect the range. Click **Sort & Filter** in the Editing group, and then select **Custom Sort**. The dialog box may contain existing sort conditions for the State and City fields, which you will replace. Set the following sort conditions:

- Click the **Sort by arrow**, and then select **Item Donated**. Click the **Sort On arrow**, and then select **Cell Color**. Click the **Order arrow**, and then select the **RGB(242, 220, 219)** or **RGB(230, 184, 183) fill color**. The fill color displays for the Order.
- Click the **Then by arrow**, and then select **Value**. Click the **Order arrow**, and then select **Largest to Smallest**.
- Click **OK**.

h. Select **landscape orientation**, set appropriate margins, and adjust column widths so that all the data will print on one page. Do not decrease the scaling.

i. Create a footer with your name on the left side, the sheet name code in the center, and the file name code on the right side.

j. Save and close the workbook, and submit based on your instructor's directions.

1 University Band Member List

You are the assistant to the band director at Mountain State University. The secretary created a list of band members, which you need to prepare to print. In addition, you want to convert the data to a table, manipulate the data, and meet with the band director to discuss the roster and ensure you have ample coverage of all instruments, chair position, and classification. For example, if 75% of flute players are 2nd chair, you might want to reassign some flute players to 1st or 3rd chair. Or if all of your baritone players are seniors, you might need to recruit some freshmen baritone players.

a. Open *e04m1band* and save it as **e04m1band_LastnameFirstname**.
b. Freeze the panes so that the column headings and the student IDs, last names, and first names do not scroll offscreen.

c. Convert the data to a table, and then name the table **BandRoster**.
d. Apply **Table Style Medium 7** to the table. Use Format Painter to copy the heading formats to the Solo Rating heading, if needed.
e. Sort the table by Instrument, then Chair, and then Class. Create a custom sort order for Class so that it appears in this sequence: Senior, Junior, Sophomore, and Freshman.
f. Remove duplicate records from the table. Excel should find and remove two duplicate records.
g. Add a total row to determine the average scholarship amount per student. Remove any other totals that appear. Change the row heading in **cell A75** to **Average**.
h. Copy the Band Members worksheet, and then place the copied worksheet to the right of the original worksheet. Rename the duplicate worksheet **Filtered Seniors**.
i. Filter the copied table to show only seniors who are 1st or 2nd chair and were awarded a scholarship of at least $4,750 or more. The status bar indicates 10 of 73 records found.
j. Adjust orientation, column widths, margins, row height, and wrap text so that the filtered data will fit on one page.
k. Display the Band Members worksheet in Page Break Preview.
   - Select **landscape orientation**. Adjust the page breaks so that the Instrument column will print on the same pages as the Chair, Class, and Scholarship columns.
   - Repeat the column headings and student ID, last name, and first name on printouts. Adjust the widths of the last five columns as needed, and increase the height of the first row. Do not change the margins or orientation.
   - Set the print range to print all columns and rows except the Solo Rating column.
   - Change the print page order to print horizontally and then down.
l. Create a footer with your name on the left side, the sheet name code in the center, and the file name code on the right side of each worksheet.
m. Check the Band Members worksheet in Print Preview to ensure that it can print on six pages.
n. Save and close the workbook, and submit based on your instructor's directions.

2 Credit Card Expenses

You started recording every credit card transaction so that you can analyze your monthly expenses. You used an Excel worksheet to track dates, places, categories, and amounts. Because you are a consultant who travels periodically, you also have business expenses. You included a column to indicate the business-related transactions. You are now ready to analyze the data. Refer to Figure 4.53 as you complete this exercise.

DISCOVER

DISCOVER

FIGURE 4.53 Credit Card Analysis ➤

a. Open *e04m2credit* and save it as **e04m2credit_LastnameFirstname**.

b. Make sure the Dining Out worksheet is active. Convert the data to a table, and then apply **Table Style Light 11**.

c. Sort the table by the description in alphabetical order, sort the store in alphabetical order, and then sort by amount from smallest to largest in that sequence.

d. Filter the records to show personal (i.e., non-business) lunches and dinner expenses. Add a total row to sum the amounts but do not include other totals.

e. Click the **June Expenses worksheet tab**, and then apply the **Green Data Bar** in the *Gradient Fill* section setting to the Amount column.

f. Create a conditional formatting rule with these specifications:
- Applies to the **range A2:C47**.
- Uses a formula to determine which cells to format based on amounts of $100 or more *and* that are classified as business expenses. Because this conditional formatting applies to several columns (A, B, and C), you must use mixed cell references in the formula.
- Formats data with a **Medium Green fill color** and a **Green line border** using the **Outline preset border style**.

 DISCOVER

g. Create a conditional formatting rule with these specifications:
- Applies to the **range A2:C47**.
- Uses a formula to determine which cells to format based on amounts less than $100 *and* that are classified as business expenses. Because this conditional formatting applies to several columns (A, B, and C), you must use mixed cell references in the formula.
- Formats data with a **Light Green fill color** and a **Green line border** using the **Outline preset border style**.

DISCOVER

h. Create a custom color sort for the Description column with these specifications:
- Sorts on cell color.
- Displays the **Medium Green fill color** on Top as the primary sort.
- Displays the **Light Green fill color** on Top as the secondary sort.

 DISCOVER

i. Create a footer with your name on the left side, the sheet name code in the center, and the file name code on the right side on each worksheet.

j. Save and close the workbook, and submit based on your instructor's directions.

You work for a gallery that is an authorized Greenwich Workshop fine art dealer (www. greenwichworkshop.com). Customers in your area are especially fond of James C. Christensen's art. Although customers can visit the Web site to see images and details about his work, they have requested a list of all his artwork. Your assistant prepared a list of artwork: art, type, edition size, release date, and issue price. In addition, you included a column to identify what pieces are sold out at the publisher, indicating the rare, hard-to-obtain artwork that is available on the secondary market. You now want to convert the data to a table so that you can provide information to your customers.

a. Open *e04m3fineart* and save it as **e04m3fineart_LastnameFirstname**.

b. Convert the data to a table, and then apply **Table Style Medium 5**.

c. Add a row (below the The Yellow Rose record) for this missing piece of art: **The Yellow Rose**, **Masterwork Canvas Edition**, **50** edition size, **May 2009** release date, **$895** issue price. Enter **Yes** to indicate the piece is sold out.

d. Sort the table by type in alphabetical order and then by release date from newest to oldest.

e. Add a total row that shows the largest edition size and the most expensive issue price. Delete the Total label in **cell A173**. Add a descriptive label in **cell C173** to reflect the content on the total row.

f. Create a custom conditional format for the Issue Price column with these specifications:
   - 4 Traffic Lights icon set (Black, Red, Yellow, Green)
   - Red icon when the number is greater than 1000
   - Yellow icon when the number is less than or equal to 1000 and greater than 500
   - Green icon when the number is less than or equal to 500 and greater than 250
   - Black icon when the number is less than or equal to 250.

g. Filter the table by the Green Traffic Light conditional formatting icon.

h. Set the print area to print the **range C1:H173**, select the **first row to repeat at the top of each printout**, set **1"** top and bottom margins, set **0.3"** left and right margins, and then select **landscape orientation**.

i. Wrap text and horizontally center column labels, and then adjust column widths and row heights as needed.

j. Adjust the page break so that at least five Limited Edition Canvas records print on the second page.

k. Create a footer with your name on the left side, the sheet name code in the center, and the file name code on the right side.

l. Save and close the workbook, and submit based on your instructor's directions.

You just got an internship at Mountain View Realty, a real estate firm that focuses on the North Utah County area. The previous intern developed a spreadsheet listing houses listed and sold during the past several months. She included addresses, location, list price, selling price, listing date, and date sold. You need to convert the data to a table and manipulate the table. You will manage the large worksheet, prepare the worksheet for printing, sort and filter the table, include calculations, and format the table.

Prepare the Large Worksheet as a Table

You need to freeze the panes so that labels remain onscreen. You also want to convert the data to a table so that you can apply table options.

a. Open the *e04c1houses* workbook and save it as **e04c1houses_LastnameFirstname**.

b. Freeze the first row on the Sales Data worksheet.

c. Convert the data to a table, and then apply the **Table Style Medium 17**.

d. Remove duplicate records.

Add Calculated Fields and a Total Row

The office manager asked you to insert a column to display the percent of list price. The formula finds the sale price percentage of the list price. For example, if a house was listed at $100,000 and sells for $75,000, the percentage of list price is 75%. In some cases, the percentage is more than 100%. This happens when a bidding war occurs, and buyers increase their offers, which results in the seller getting more than the list price.

a. Insert a new field to the right of the Selling Price field. Name the new field **Percent of List Price**.

b. Create a formula with structured references to calculate the percent of the list price.

c. Format the column with **Percent Style** with one decimal place.

d. Insert a new field to the right of the Sale Date field. Name the new field **Days on Market**.

e. Create a formula with structured references to calculate the number of days on the market. If the result displays in a date format, apply the **General number format** to the average.

f. Add a total row to display the average percent of list price and average number of days on market. Format the average number of days on market as a whole number. Use an appropriate label for the total row.

Sort and Print the Table

To help the office manager compare house sales by city, you will sort the data. Then, you will prepare the large table to print.

a. Sort the table by city in alphabetical order, and add a second level to sort by days on market with the houses on the market the longest at the top within each city.

b. Adjust column widths so that the data is one page across (three pages total), and then wrap the column headings as needed.

c. Repeat the column headings on all pages.

d. Display the table in Page Break Preview.

e. Change page breaks so that city data does not span between pages, and then change back to Normal view.

f. Add a footer with your name on the left side, the sheet name code in the center, and the file name code on the right side.

Copy and Filter the Data

The office manager needs to focus on houses that took longer than 30 days to sell within 3 cities. To keep the original data intact for the agents, you will copy the table data to a new sheet and use that sheet to display the filtered data.

a. Copy the Sales Data worksheet, and then place the duplicate worksheet to the right of the original worksheet tab. Convert the table to a range of data, and delete the average row.

b. Rename the duplicate worksheet **Filtered Data**.

c. Display the filter arrows for the data.

d. Filter the data to display the cities of *Alpine, Cedar Hills,* and *Eagle Mountain.*

e. Filter the data to display records for houses that were on the market 30 days or more.

Apply Conditional Formatting

To highlight housing sales to illustrate trends, you will apply conditional formatting. Since data are sorted by city, you will use an icon set to color-code the number of days on market. You will also apply a data bar conditional formatting to the sale prices to help the office manager visualize the difference among the sales.

a. Apply the **3 Arrows (Colored) icon set** to the days on market values.

b. Apply the **Light Blue Data Bar conditional formatting** in the *Gradient Fill* section to the selling prices.

c. Create a new conditional format that applies **Yellow fill** and **bold font** to values that contain 95% or higher for the Percent of List Price column.

d. Edit the conditional format you created so that it formats values 98% or higher.

Finalize the Workbook

You are ready to finalize the workbook by adding a footer to the new worksheet and saving the final workbook.

a. Add a footer with your name on the left side, the sheet name code in the center, and the file name code on the right side.

b. Remove all page breaks in the Filtered Data worksheet.

c. Select **landscape orientation**, and then set appropriate margins so that the data will print on one page.

d. Save and close the workbook, and submit based on your instructor's directions.

Doctor Search

GENERAL CASE

You just moved to Florida with your family and are searching for doctors who can meet your family's medical needs. You obtained a list of more than 150 board-certified physicians from the state licensing agency. Open *e04b1doctors* and save it as **e04b1doctors_LastnameFirstname**. Freeze the panes to keep the column labels and IDs from scrolling offscreen. Convert the data to a table, and apply an appropriate table style. Filter the table to show only those who practice Cardiology, Pediatrics, and Internal Medicine and who are accepting new patients in Fort Lauderdale. Sort the filtered records by specialty, last name, and then first name. Set a print area to include all columns except the ID and New Patient columns. Apply a conditional format for dates after 1/1/2008 with a custom format of an Orange fill and a White font. Create a footer with your name, the sheet name code, and the file name code. Save and close the workbook, and submit based on your instructor's directions.

Automobile Car Comparisons

RESEARCH CASE

You want to research various car models. Choose a category, such as sedan. Use the Internet to research at least 40 new vehicles. Start a new workbook and save it as **e04b2cars_LastnameFirstname**. Create an input area for a down payment of $5,000, APR, number of payment periods, and number of payments per year (12). Create a source area to list the URL of the Web site you used and the date you retrieved the information. Design the worksheet to list the make, model, year, transmission (automatic or manual), cylinders, liters, horsepower (HP), city miles per gallon (MPG), highway MPG, and manufacturer's suggested retail price. If you can't find the mpg for a particular vehicle, leave those cells blank. Format columns appropriately. Find information for at least five different makes. Include a few similar models, such as a Nissan Altima 2.5 and a Nissan Altima 3.5. Use the base prices. Freeze panes as necessary. Convert the data to a table and apply a table style of your choice. Sort by transmission, then by HP with the largest first, then by make, and finally by model. Add a new calculated column and use structured references to calculate the estimated monthly payment given the input cells. Add a total row to calculate the average HP, MPG, MSRP, and monthly payment. Apply a conditional format to apply a custom fill and font color for the five most expensive vehicles in the sorted list. Apply an icon set to the highway MPG values. On another worksheet, answer these questions: (1) What are the averages? (2) What are the averages for only automatic transmissions with V6 engines? (3) Which vehicle(s) had the highest highway MPG of all the vehicles? and (4) What is the mpg? Filter the Hwy MPG column by one icon color. Prepare both worksheets to print using appropriate page setup options. Create a footer with your name, the sheet name code, and the file name code. Save and close the workbook, and submit based on your instructor's directions.

U.S. Population

DISASTER RECOVERY

A colleague at an advertising firm downloaded U.S. population information from the government Web site. In the process of creating tables, he made some errors and needs your help. Open *e04b3populate* and save it as **e04b3populate_LastnameFirstname**. As you find the errors, document them on the Errors worksheet and make the corrections. Your documentation should include these columns: Error Number, Location, Problem, and Solution. Both tables in the U.S. Population worksheet should show grand total populations per year. The state table should be sorted by region and then by state. Your colleague wants to emphasize the top 15% state populations for the most recent year in the state table. The last column should show percentage changes from year to year, such as 0.6%. Your colleague wants to print only the state data. Select the sorted data population for one region at a time to compare to the regional totals in the first table to crosscheck the totals. For example, when you select the July 1, 2008, Midwest values in the second table, the status bar should display the same value as shown for the Midwest July 1, 2008, values in the first table. Create a footer with your name, the sheet name code, and the file name code. Save and close the workbook, and submit based on your instructor's directions.

1 INTRODUCTION TO ACCESS

Finding Your Way Through a Database

CASE STUDY | Managing a Business in the Global Economy

Watch the
Set-up
Video
for this
Case Study!

Northwind Traders* is an international gourmet food distributor that imports and exports specialty foods from around the world. Northwind's products include meats, seafood, dairy products, beverages, and produce. Keeping track of customers, vendors, orders, and inventory is no small task. The owners of Northwind have just purchased an order-processing database created with Microsoft Office Access 2010 to help manage their customers, suppliers, products, and orders.

Because the owners do not have time to operate the new database, you have been hired to learn, use, and manage the database. The Northwind owners are willing to provide training about their business and on Access. They expect the learning process to take about three months. After three months, your job will be to support the order-processing team as well as to provide detail and summary reports to the sales force as needed. Your new job at Northwind Traders will be a challenge! It is also an opportunity to make a great contribution to a global company. Are you up to the task?

*Northwind Traders was created by the Microsoft Access Team and is shipped with Access as a sample database you can use to learn about Access. The names of companies, products, people, characters, and/or data are fictitious. The practice database you will use is a modified version of Northwind Traders.

OBJECTIVES   AFTER YOU READ THIS CHAPTER, YOU WILL BE ABLE TO:

1. Navigate among the objects in an Access database *p.533*

2. Understand the difference between working in storage and memory *p.540*

3. Practice good database file management *p.541*

4. Back up, compact, and repair Access files *p.541*

5. Create filters *p.549*

6. Sort table data on one or more fields *p.552*

7. Know when to use Access or Excel to manage data *p.553*

8. Use the Relationships window *p.560*

9. Understand relational power *p.561*

Databases Are Everywhere!

If you use the Internet, you use databases often. When you shop online or check your bank statement, you are connecting to a database. Even when you type a search phrase into Google and click Search, you are using Google's massive database with all of its stored Web page references and keywords. Look for something on eBay, and you are searching eBay's database to find a product on which you might want to bid. Need a new pair of shoes? Log on to the Columbia Web site (see Figure 1.1), and find the right pair in your style, your size, and your price range. All this information is stored in its products database.

> If you use the Internet, you use databases often.

FIGURE 1.1 Columbia Web Site ➤

You are exposed to other databases on a regular basis outside of Internet shopping. For example, your community college or university uses a database to store the registration data. When you registered for this course, your data was entered into a database. The database probably told you the number of available seats but not the names of the other students who enrolled in the class. In addition, social networking Web sites such as Facebook and LinkedIn are storing data on large database servers.

Organizations rely on data to conduct daily operations, regardless of whether the organization exists as a profit or not-for-profit environment. Organizations maintain data about their customers, employees, orders, volunteers, activities, and facilities. Every keystroke and mouse click creates data about the organization that needs to be stored, organized, and available for analysis. Access is a valuable decision-making tool that many organizations are using or want to use.

In this section, you will explore Access database objects and work with table views. You will also learn the difference between working in storage and working in memory, and you will learn how changes to database objects are saved. Finally, you will practice good database maintenance techniques by backing up, compacting, and repairing databases.

Navigating Among the Objects in an Access Database

An **object** in an Access database is a main component that is created and used to make the database function.

A **field** is the smallest data element contained in a table. Examples of fields are first name, last name, address, and phone number.

A **record** is a complete set of all of the data elements (fields) about one person, place, event, or concept.

A **table**, the foundation of every database, is a collection of related records.

A **database** consists of one or more tables to store data, one or more forms to enter data into the tables, and one or more reports to output the table data as organized information.

The *objects* in an Access database are the main components that are created and used to make the database function. The four main object types are tables, queries, forms, and reports. Two other object types, macros and modules, are used less frequently. Throughout this chapter, you will learn how to use each type of object.

To understand how an Access database works and how to use Access effectively, you should first learn the terms of the key object—the table. A *field* is the smallest data element contained in a table. Fields define the type of data that is collected, for example, text, numeric, or date. Examples of fields are first name, last name, address, and phone number. A field may be required or optional. For example, a person's last name may be required, but a fax number may be optional. A *record* is a complete set of all of the data elements (fields) about one person, place, event, or concept. For example, your first name, last name, student ID, phone number, and e-mail address constitute your record in your instructor's class roster. A *table*, the foundation of every database, is a collection of related records. For example, all the students in your class would be entered into the Class Roster table during registration.

A *database* consists of one or more tables to store data, one or more forms to enter data into the tables, and one or more reports to output the table data as organized information. The main functions of a database are to collect data, to store data logically, to manipulate data to make it more useful, and to output the data to the screen and printed reports. Databases also export data to files so the files can be imported by other databases or other information-processing systems.

TIP Data Versus Information

Data and *information* are two terms that are often used interchangeably. However, when it comes to databases, the two terms mean different things. *Data* is what is entered into the tables of the database. *Information* is the finished product that is produced by the database in a query or in a printed report. Data is converted to information by selecting, calculating, sorting, or summarizing records. Decisions in an organization are usually based on information produced by a database, rather than raw data.

Examine the Access Interface

Figure 1.2 shows the Access Interface for the Northwind Traders database, which was introduced in the Case Study at the beginning of this chapter. The top section, known as the Ribbon, remains the same no matter which database is open. Below the Ribbon, you find all the objects that are needed to make the current database function; these objects are stored in the Navigation Pane (on the left). To the right of the Navigation Pane, the currently open objects are displayed and are delimited with tabs. The title bar at the top of the window contains the name of the application (Microsoft Access), the name of the currently loaded database (Northwind), and the file format (Access 2007) of the loaded database. Because Access 2010 does not have a new file format, you will see Access 2007 in the title bar throughout this textbook. The Minimize, Maximize (or Restore), and Close icons can be found on the right of the title bar. The tab below the Ribbon shows that the Employees table is currently open. When more than one object is open at a time, one tab will be shown for each open object. Click on a tab to view or modify that object independently of the other objects.

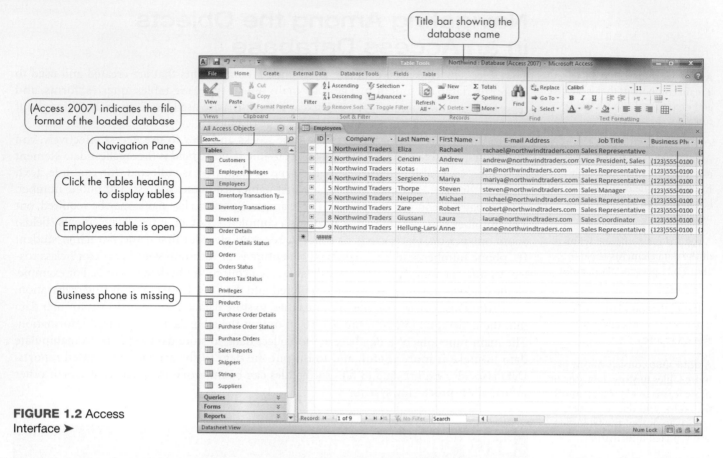

Callouts on the figure:

- Title bar showing the database name
- (Access 2007) indicates the file format of the loaded database
- Navigation Pane
- Click the Tables heading to display tables
- Employees table is open
- Business phone is missing

FIGURE 1.2 Access Interface ➤

Figure 1.2 shows that the Northwind database contains 20 tables: Customers, Employee Privileges, Employees, etc. Each table contains multiple records. The Employees table is currently open and shows nine records for the nine employees who work for the company. The Employees table contains 18 fields (or attributes) about each employee, including the employee's Last Name, First Name, E-Mail Address, Job Title, and so on. Occasionally, a field does not contain a value for a particular record. One of the employees, Rachael Eliza, did not provide a business phone. The value of that field is missing. Access shows a blank cell when data is missing.

The Suppliers table holds a record for each vendor from whom the firm purchases products; the Orders table holds one record for each order. The real power of Access is derived from a database with multiple tables and the relationships that connect the tables.

The ***Navigation Pane*** organizes and lists the database objects in an Access database. As stated earlier, six types of objects—tables, queries, forms, reports, macros, and modules—can exist in a database. Most databases contain multiple tables, queries, forms, and reports. Tables store the data, forms enable users to enter information into the tables, reports enable users to display data in an organized format, and queries enable users to ask questions about the data. In Figure 1.2, the Tables group shows all the table objects; the other objects are hidden until you click a group heading to expand the group and display the objects. Click a visible group name to hide the group. To change the way objects are displayed within a group, right-click the group, and select from a list of options. For example, you can right-click the Queries category, point to View By, and then click Details to see when each query was created.

The Access Ribbon contains the icons that help you perform the database functions to maintain a database. These commands are described in detail on the following Reference page. You do not need to memorize every icon, group, and tab; however, it will be helpful to refer to this page as you are learning Access.

The **Navigation Pane** organizes and lists the database objects in an Access database.

REFERENCE Access Ribbon

Tab and Groups	Description
File	The File tab leads to the Backstage view, which gives you access to a variety of database tools such as Compact and Repair, Back Up Database, and Print.
Home Views Clipboard Sort & Filter Records Find Text Formatting	The default Access tab. Contains basic editing functions, such as cut and paste, filtering, find and replace, and most formatting actions.
Create Templates Tables Queries Forms Reports Macros & Code	This tab contains all the create tools, such as create Tables, create Forms, create Reports, and create Queries.
External Data Import & Link Export Collect Data Web Linked Lists	This tab contains all of the operations to facilitate data import and export.
Database Tools Tools Macro Relationships Analyze Move Data Add-Ins	This tab enables you to use the more advanced features of Access. Set relationships between tables, analyze a table or query, and migrate your data to SQL Server or SharePoint.

Work with Table Views

The **Datasheet view** is where you add, edit, and delete the records of a table.

The **Design view** is where you create tables, add and delete fields, and modify field properties.

Access provides two different ways to view a table: the Datasheet view and the Design view. The *Datasheet view* is a grid containing columns (fields) and rows (records), similar to an Excel spreadsheet. You can view, add, edit, and delete records in the Datasheet view. The *Design view* is used to create and modify a table's design by specifying the fields it will contain, the fields' data types, and their associated properties. Data types define the type of data that will be stored in a field, such as currency, numeric, text, etc. For example, if you need to store the pay rate of an employee, you would enter the field name Pay Rate and select the data type currency. The field properties define the characteristics of the fields in more detail. For example, for the field Pay Rate, you could set a field property that requires Pay Rate to be less than $25 (a higher rate would trigger a manager's approval). To accomplish this, you would set the validation rule to <25 to prevent users from entering a pay rate higher than $25.

Figure 1.3 shows the Design view for the Customers table. In the top portion, each row contains the field names, the data type, and an optional description for each field in the table. In the bottom portion, the Field Properties pane contains the properties (details) for each field. Click on a field, and the field properties will be displayed in the bottom portion of the Design view window.

Figure 1.4 shows the Datasheet view for the Customers table. The top row in the table contains the field names. Each additional row contains a record (the data for a specific customer). Each column represents a field (one attribute about a customer). Every record in the table represents a different customer; all records contain the same fields.

Each field is assigned a data type

Customers table in Design view

First Name field is selected

Field Properties for the First Name field

FIGURE 1.3 Customers Table in Design View ➤

Customers table is open

ID field is the primary key (unique identifier) for the Customers table

Pencil in record selector indicates the record is being edited

Navigation bar indicates 29 customers in the table

FIGURE 1.4 Customers Table in Datasheet View ➤

The **primary key** is the field (or combination of fields) that uniquely identifies each record in a table.

The ***primary key*** is the field (or combination of fields) that uniquely identifies each record in a table. The ID field is the primary key in the Customers table; it ensures that each record in the table can be distinguished from every other record. It also helps prevent the occurrence of duplicate records. Primary key fields may be numbers, letters, or a combination of both. In this case, the primary key is an autonumber (a number that is generated by Access and is incremented each time a record is added). Another example of a primary key is Social Security Number, which is often used in an employee table.

The navigation bar at the bottom of Figure 1.4 shows that the Customers table has 29 records and that record number 10 is the current record. The vertical scroll bar on the right side of the window only appears when the table contains more records than can appear in the window at one time. Similarly, the horizontal scroll bar at the bottom of the window only appears when the table contains more fields than can appear in the window at one time.

The pencil symbol to the left of Record 10 indicates that the data in that record is being edited and that changes have not yet been saved. The pencil symbol disappears when you move to another record. It is important to understand that Access saves data automatically as soon as you move from one record to another. This may seem counter-intuitive at first, since Word and Excel do not save changes and additions automatically. With Word and Excel, you must click the Save icon in order to save your work (or set auto-save to save automatically in the background).

Figure 1.5 shows the navigation buttons that you use to move through the records in a table, query, or form. The buttons enable you to go to the first record, the previous record, the next record, or the last record. The button with the asterisk is used to add a new (blank) record. You can also type a number directly into the current record cell, and Access will take you to that record. Finally, the navigation bar enables you to locate a record based on a single word. Type a word in the search cell box, and Access will locate the first record that contains the word.

FIGURE 1.5 Navigation Buttons ➤

No system, no matter how sophisticated, can produce valid output from invalid input. Access database systems are built to anticipate data entry errors. These systems contain table validation rules created to prevent invalid data entry. Two types of validation rules exist: those built into Access and those a developer creates specifically for a database. For example, Access will automatically prevent you from adding a new record with the same primary key as an existing record. Access does not allow you to enter text or numeric data into a date field. A database developer can add validation rules, such as requiring a person's last name or requiring an employee's social security number. A developer can also limit the length of data, such as only enabling five digits for a zip code or two characters for a state abbreviation.

Use Forms, Queries, and Reports

As previously indicated, an Access database is made up of different types of objects together with the tables and the data they contain. The tables are the heart of any database because they contain the *actual* data. The other objects in a database—such as forms, queries, and reports—are based on one or more underlying tables. Figure 1.6 displays a form based on the Customers table shown earlier.

Customer Details form

Field names and data values match the Customers table

Navigation buttons are the same as in the table

FIGURE 1.6 Customer Details Form ➤

A **form** is an object that enables you to enter, modify, or delete table data.

A **query** is a question that you ask about the data in the tables of your database.

A **criterion** (**criteria**, pl) is a number, a text phrase, or an expression used to filter the records in a table.

A ***form*** is an object that enables you to enter, modify, or delete table data. A form enables you to manipulate data in the same manner that you would in a table's Datasheet view. The difference is that you can create a form that will limit the user to viewing only one record at a time. This helps the user to focus on the data being entered or modified and also provides more reliable data entry. A form may also contain command buttons that enable you to add a new record, print a record, or close the form. The status bar and navigation buttons at the bottom of the form are similar to those that appear at the bottom of a table. As an Access user, you will add, delete, and edit records in Form view. As the Access designer, you will create and edit the form structure in Design view.

A ***query*** is a question that you ask about the data in the tables of your database. The answer is shown in the query results. A query can be used to display only records that meet a certain criterion and only the fields that are required. Figure 1.7 shows the query design for the question "Which products does Northwind purchase from Supplier A?" The Products table contains records for many vendors, but the records shown in Figure 1.8 are only the products that were supplied by Supplier A. If you want to know the details about a specific supplier (such as Supplier A), you set the criterion in the query to specify which supplier you need to know about.

A ***criterion*** (***criteria***, pl) is a number, a text phrase, or an expression used to filter the records in a table. If you need the names of all the suppliers in New York, you can set the supplier's state criterion to *New York*. The results would yield only those suppliers from New York. Query results are in Datasheet view and are similar in appearance to the underlying table, except that the query contains selected records and/or selected fields for those records. The query also may list the records in a different sequence from that of the table.

You also can use a query to add new records and modify existing records. If you open a query and notice an error in an address field, you can edit the record directly in the query results. When you edit a value in a query, you are also updating the data in the underlying table. Editing in a query is efficient but should be used with caution to avoid inadvertently updating the tables. Queries may be opened in Datasheet view or Design view. You use the Datasheet view to examine the query output; you use the Design view to specify which fields to display and what criteria you want.

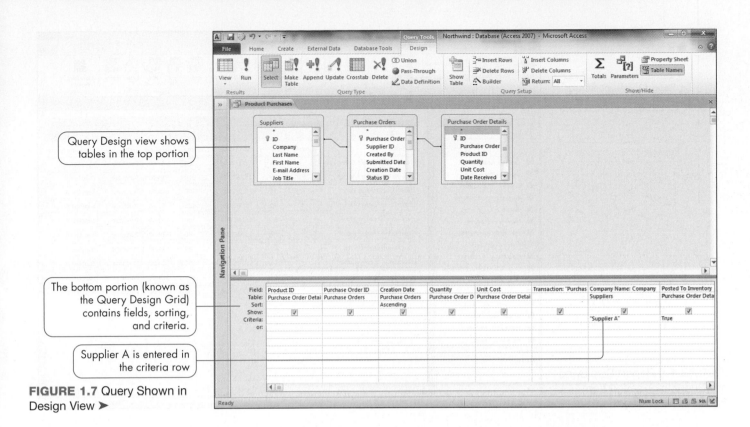

Query Design view shows tables in the top portion

The bottom portion (known as the Query Design Grid) contains fields, sorting, and criteria.

Supplier A is entered in the criteria row

FIGURE 1.7 Query Shown in Design View ➤

Query Datasheet view shows purchases from Supplier A

Queries group expanded

Navigation buttons are the same as in a table or form

FIGURE 1.8 Query Shown in Datasheet View ➤

A **report** contains professional-looking formatted information from underlying tables or queries.

A *report* contains professional-looking formatted information from underlying tables or queries. Figure 1.9 displays a report that contains the same information as the query in Figure 1.8. Because the report information contains a more professional look than a query or table, you normally present database information using a report. Access provides different views for designing, modifying, and running reports. Most Access users use only the Print Preview, Layout, and Report views of a report.

Report shows purchases from Supplier A

Reports group expanded

FIGURE 1.9 Report Displaying the Query Information from Figure 1.8 ➤

Understanding the Difference Between Working in Storage and Memory

Access is different from the other Microsoft Office applications. Word, Excel, and PowerPoint all work primarily from memory. In those applications, your work is not automatically saved to your hard drive unless you click the Save icon. This could be catastrophic if you are working on a large Word document and you forget to save it. If the power is lost, you may lose your document. Access, on the other hand, works primarily from storage. As you enter and update the data in an Access database, the changes are automatically saved to your hard drive. If a power failure occurs, you will only lose the changes from the record that you are currently editing. Another common characteristic among Word, Excel, and PowerPoint is that usually only one person uses a file at one time. Access is different. With an Access database file, several users can work in the same file at the same time.

When you make a change to a field's content in an Access table (for example, changing a customer's phone number), Access saves your changes as soon as you move the insertion point (or focus) to a different record. You do not need to click the Save icon. However, you are required to Save after you modify the design of a table, a query, a form, or a report. When you modify an object's design, such as the Customers form, and then close it, Access will prompt you with the message "Do you want to save changes to the design of form 'Customers'?" Click Yes to save your changes.

Also in Access, you can click Undo to reverse the most recent change (the phone number you just modified) to a single record immediately after making changes to that record. However, unlike other Office programs that enable multiple Undo steps, you cannot use Undo to reverse multiple edits in Access.

Multiple users, from different computers, can work on an Access database simultaneously. As long as two users do not attempt to change the same record at the same time, Access will enable two or more users to work on the same database file at the same time. One person can be adding records to the Customers table while another can be creating a query based on the Products table. Two users can even work on the same table as long as they are not working on the same record.

Practicing Good Database File Management

Database files are similar to other files (spreadsheets, documents, and images) on your computer. They must be filed in an organized manner using folders and subfolders, they must be named appropriately, and they must be backed up in case of a computer failure. Access files require additional understanding and maintenance to avoid data loss.

Every time you open a student file, you will be directed to copy the file and to rename the copied file. As you are learning about Access databases, you will probably make mistakes. Since you'll be working from the copy, you can easily recover from one of these mistakes by reverting back to the original and starting over.

Access runs best from a local disk drive or network disk drive because those drives have sufficient access speed to support the software. ***Access speed*** measures the time it takes for the storage device to make the file content available for use. If your school provides you with storage space on the school's network, store your student files there. The advantage to using the network is that the network administration staff back up files regularly. If you have no storage on the school network, your next best storage option is a thumb drive, also known as a USB jump drive, a flash drive, a pen drive, or a stick drive.

Access speed measures the time it takes for the storage device to make the file content available for use.

Backing Up, Compacting, and Repairing Access Files

Data is the lifeblood of any organization. Access provides two utilities to help protect the data within a database: ***Compact and Repair*** and ***backup***. These two functions both help protect your data, but they each serve a different purpose. Compact and Repair reduces the size of the database. Backup creates a duplicate copy of the database.

Compact and Repair reduces the size of the database.

Backup creates a duplicate copy of the database.

Compact and Repair a Database

All Access databases have a tendency to expand with everyday use. Entering data, creating queries, running reports, deleting objects, and adding indexes will all cause a database file to expand. This growth may increase storage requirements and may also impact database performance. In addition, databases that are compacted regularly are less likely to become corrupt—resulting in loss of data. Access provides a utility—Compact and Repair Database—in the Backstage view that addresses this issue. When you run the Compact and Repair utility, it creates a new database file behind the scenes and copies all the objects from the original database into the new one. As it copies the objects into the new file, Access will remove temporary objects and unclaimed space due to deleted objects, resulting in a smaller database file. Compact and Repair will also defragment a fragmented database file if needed. When the utility is finished copying the data, it deletes the original file and renames the new one with the same name as the original. This utility can also be used to repair a corrupt database. In most cases, only a small amount of data—the last record modified—will be lost during the repair process. You should compact your database every day.

Back Up a Database

Imagine what would happen to a firm that loses the orders placed but not shipped, a charity that loses the list of donor contributions, or a hospital that loses the digital records of its patients. Fortunately, Access recognizes how critical backup procedures are to organizations and makes backing up the database files easy. You back up an Access file (and all of the objects inside) with just a few mouse clicks. To back up files, click the File tab, and then click Save & Publish from the list of options. From the list of Save & Publish options, double-click Back Up Database, and the Save As dialog box opens. You can designate the folder location and the file name for the backup copy of the database. Access provides a default file name that is the original file name followed by the current date. The default database type is accdb.

In the next Hands-On Exercise, you will work with the Northwind Traders database you read about in the Case Study at the beginning of the chapter. Northwind purchases food items from suppliers around the world and sells them to restaurants and specialty food shops. Northwind depends on the data stored in its Access database to process orders and make daily decisions.

HANDS-ON EXERCISES

1 Databases Are Everywhere!

In your new position with Northwind Traders, you need to spend time getting familiar with its Access database. You will open its database and add, edit, and delete records using both tables and forms. Finally, you will perform management duties by compacting and backing up the database file.

Skills covered: Open an Access File, Save the File with a New Name, and Work with the New File • Edit a Record • Navigate an Access Form and Add Records • Recognize the Connection Between Table and Form, Delete a Record • Compact, Repair, and Back Up the Database

---

STEP 1 ▶ OPEN AN ACCESS FILE, SAVE THE FILE WITH A NEW NAME, AND WORK WITH THE NEW FILE

This exercise introduces you to the Northwind Traders database. You will use this database to practice working with database files. Refer to Figure 1.10 as you complete Step 1.

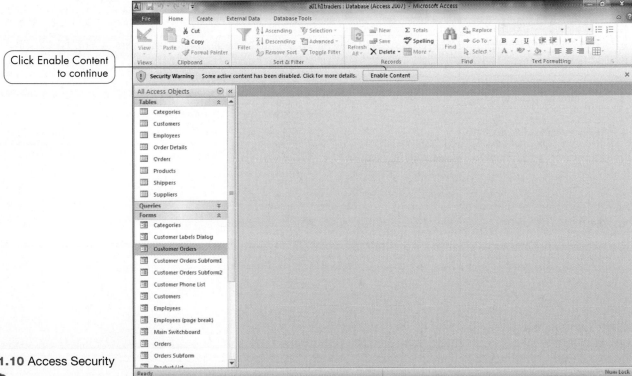

Click Enable Content to continue

FIGURE 1.10 Access Security Warning ➤

 FYI

a. Open the database named *a01h1traders* in the folder location designated by your instructor.

b. Click the **File tab**, click **Save Database As**, and then locate the folder location designated by your instructor.

When you name solution files, use your last and first names. For example, as the Access author, I would name my database a01h1traders_MastKeith.

> **TROUBLESHOOTING:** If you make any major mistakes in this exercise, you can close the file, make another copy of *a01h1traders*, and then start this exercise over.

c. Type **a01h1traders_LastnameFirstname** as the new file name, and then click **Save** to create the new database.

This step creates the new Access database file. The Security Warning message bar may appear below the Ribbon, indicating that some database content is disabled.

d. Click **Enable Content** on the Security Warning message bar.

When you open an Access file from this book, you will need to enable the content. Several viruses and worms may be transmitted via Access files. You may be confident of the trustworthiness of the files in this book. However, if an Access file arrives as an attachment from an unsolicited e-mail message, you should not open it. Microsoft warns all users of Access that a potential threat exists every time a file is opened. Keep the database open for the rest of the exercise.

STEP 2 ▶ EDIT A RECORD

You need to modify the data in the Northwind database since customers will change their address, phone numbers, and order data from time to time. Refer to Figure 1.11 as you complete Step 2.

FIGURE 1.11 Edit the Employees Table ➤

a. Click the **Tables group** in the Navigation Pane (if necessary) to expand the list of available tables.

The list of tables contained in the database file opens.

b. Double-click the **Employees table** to open it (see Figure 1.11).

c. Click on the **Last Name field** in the fourth row. Double-click **Peacock**; the entire name highlights. Type your last name to replace *Peacock*.

d. Press **Tab** to move to the next field in the fourth row. Replace *Margaret* with your first name, and then press **Tab**.

You have made changes to two fields in the same record (row); note the pencil symbol on the left side in the row selector box.

e. Click **Undo** in the Quick Access Toolbar.

Your first and last names reverts back to *Margaret Peacock* because you have not yet left the record.

f. Type your first and last names again to replace *Margaret Peacock*. Press **Tab**.

You should now be in the Title field and your title, *Sales Representative*, is selected. The pencil symbol still displays in the row selector.

g. Click anywhere in the third row where Janet Leverling's data is stored.

The pencil symbol disappears, indicating your changes have been saved.

h. Click the **Address field** in the first record, the one for Nancy Davolio. Select the entire address, and then type **4004 East Morningside Dr**. Click anywhere on Andrew Fuller's record.

i. Click **Undo**.

Nancy's address reverts back to *507 - 20th Ave. E*. However, the Undo command is now faded. You can no longer undo the change that you made replacing Margaret Peacock's name with your own.

j. Click the **Close button** (the X at the top of the table) to close the Employees table.

The Employees table closes. You are not prompted about saving your changes; they have already been saved for you because Access works in storage, not memory. If you reopen the Employees table, you will see your name in place of Margaret Peacock's name.

> **TROUBLESHOOTING:** If you click the Close (X) button on the title bar at the top right of the window and accidentally close the database, locate the file, and then double-click it to start again.

STEP 3 ▶ NAVIGATE AN ACCESS FORM AND ADD RECORDS

You need to add new products to the Northwind database since the company will be adding a new line of products to the database. Refer to Figure 1.12 as you complete Step 3.

FIGURE 1.12 Newly Created Record in the Products Form ➤

a. Click the **Tables group** in the Navigation Pane to collapse it.

The list of available tables collapses.

b. Click the **Forms group** in the Navigation Pane (if necessary) to expand the list of available forms.

c. Double-click the **Products form** to open it.

d. Use Figure 1.12 to locate the navigation buttons (arrows) at the bottom of the Access window. Practice moving from one record to the next. Click **Next record**, and then click **Last record**; click **Previous record**, and then **First record**.

e. Click **Find** in the Find group on the Home tab.

The Find command is an ideal way to search for specific records within a table, form, or query. You can search a single field or the entire record, match all or part of the selected field(s), move forward or back in a table, or specify a case-sensitive search. The Replace command can be used to substitute one value for another. Be careful when using the Replace All option for global replacement because unintended replacements are possible.

FYI

f. Type **Grandma** in the **Find What box**, click the **Match arrow**, and select **Any Part of Field**. Click **Find Next**.

You should see information about Grandma's Boysenberry Spread. Selecting the *any part of the field* option will return a match even if it is contained in the middle of a word.

g. Close the Find dialog box.

h. Click **New (blank) record** on the navigation bar.

i. Enter the following information for a new product. Press **Tab** to navigate through the form.

Field Name	Value to Type
Product Name	*your name* **Pecan Pie**
Supplier	**Grandma Kelly's Homestead** (Note: click the arrow to select from the list of Suppliers)
Category	**Confections** (Click the arrow to select from the list of Categories)
Quantity Per Unit	1
Unit Price	25.00
Units in Stock	18
Units on Order	50
Reorder Level	20
Discontinued	**No** (the checkbox remains unchecked)

As soon as you begin typing in the product name box, Access assigns a Product ID, in this case 78, to the record. The Product ID is used as the primary key in the Products table.

j. Click anywhere on the Pecan Pie record you just entered. Click the **File tab**, click **Print**, and then click **Print Preview**.

The first four records appear in the Print Preview.

k. Click **Last Page** in the navigation bar, and then click the previous page to show the new record you entered.

The beginning of the Pecan Pie record is now visible. The record continues on the next page.

l. Click **Close Print Preview** in the Close Preview group.

m. Close the Products form.

You need to understand how Access stores data. After you add the new products using a form, you verify that the products are also in the table. You also attempt to delete a record. Refer to Figure 1.13 as you complete Step 4.

Attempt to delete the fifth record

Row selector

Access error message

FIGURE 1.13 Deleting a Record with Related Records ▶

a. Click the **Forms group** in the Navigation Pane to collapse it.

The list of available forms collapses.

b. Click the **Tables group** in the Navigation Pane to expand it.

The list of available tables is shown. You need to prove that the change you made to the Products form will appear in the Products table.

c. Double-click the **Products table** to open it.

d. Click **Last record** in the navigation bar.

The Pecan Pie record you entered in the Products form is listed as the last record in the Products table. The Products form was created from the Products table. Your newly created record, Pecan Pie, is stored in the Products table even though you added it in the form.

e. Navigate to the fifth record in the table, *Chef Anton's Gumbo Mix*.

f. Use the horizontal scroll bar to scroll right until you see the Discontinued field.

The check mark in the Discontinued check box tells you that this product has been discontinued.

g. Click the **row selector box** to the left of the fifth record.

The row highlights with a gold-colored border.

h. Click **Delete** in the Records group. Read the error message.

An error message appears. It tells you that you cannot delete this record because the table Order Details has related records. (Customers ordered this product in the past.) Even though the product is now discontinued and none of it is in stock, it cannot be deleted from the Products table because related records exist in the Order Details table.

i. Click **OK**.

j. Navigate to the last record. Click the **row selector box** to highlight the entire row.

k. Click **Delete** in the Records group. Read the warning.

A warning box appears. It tells you that this action cannot be undone. Although this product can be deleted because it was just entered and no orders were created for it, you do not want to delete the record.

l. Click **No**. You do not want to delete this record. Close the Products table.

> **TROUBLESHOOTING:** If you clicked Yes and deleted the record, return to Step 3i. Reenter the information for this record. You will need it later in the lesson.

STEP 5 ▶ COMPACT, REPAIR, AND BACK UP THE DATABASE

You will protect the Northwind Traders database by using the two built-in Access utilities—Compact and Repair and Backup. Refer to Figure 1.14 as you complete Step 5.

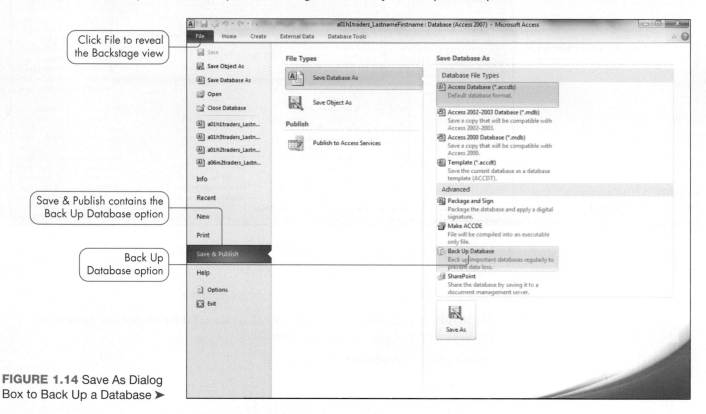

FIGURE 1.14 Save As Dialog Box to Back Up a Database ➤

a. Click the **File tab**.

The File tab reveals the Backstage view, which gives you access to a variety of database tools: Compact and Repair, Back Up Database, and Print, to name a few.

b. Click **Compact & Repair Database**.

Databases tend to get larger as you use them. This feature acts as a defragmenter and eliminates wasted space. Before running this feature, close any open objects in the database.

c. Click the **File tab**, click **Save & Publish**, and then double-click **Back Up Database**.

The Save As dialog box opens. Verify the Save in folder is correct before saving. The backup utility assigns a default name by adding a date to your file name.

d. Click **Save** to accept the default backup file name with today's date.

You just created a backup of the database after completing Hands-On Exercise 1. The original database *a01h1traders_LastnameFirstname* remains onscreen.

e. Keep the database onscreen if you plan to continue with Hands-On Exercise 2. If not, close the database and exit Access.

Filters, Sorts, and Access Versus Excel

Access provides you with many tools that you can use to identify and extract only the data needed at the moment. For example, you might need to know which suppliers are located in New Orleans or which customers have outstanding orders that were placed in the last seven days. You might use that information to identify possible disruptions to product deliveries or customers who may need a telephone call to let them know the status of their orders. Both Access and Excel contain powerful tools that enable you to extract the information you need and arrange it in a way that makes it easy to analyze. An important part of becoming a proficient Office user is learning how to use these tools to accomplish a task.

> Access provides you with many tools that you can use to identify and extract only the data needed at the moment.

In this section, you will learn how to isolate records in a table based on certain criteria. You will also examine the strengths of Access and Excel in more detail so you can better determine when to use which application to complete a given task.

Creating Filters

In the first Hands-On Exercise, you added Pecan Pie to the Products table with a category of *Confections*, but you also saw many other products. Suppose you wanted a list of all of the products in the Confections category. To do this, you could open the Products table in Datasheet view and create a filter. A *filter* displays a subset of records based on specified criteria. A filter works with either a table's datasheet or a query's datasheet. You can use filters to analyze data quickly. Applying a filter does not delete any records; filters only *hide* records that do not match the criteria. Two types of filters are discussed in this section: Filter by Selection and Filter by Form. Filter by Selection selects only the records that match preselected single criteria, whereas Filter by Form offers a more versatile way to select a subset of records, including the use of comparison operators.

Figure 1.15 displays the Customers table with 29 records. The records in the table are displayed in sequence according to the CustomerID, which is also the primary key (the field or combination of fields that uniquely identifies a record). The navigation bar at the bottom indicates that the active record is the first row in the table. Many times you will only want to see a subset of the customer records—you can accomplish this using a filter. For example, suppose you want a list of all customers whose Job Title is *Owner*.

A **filter** displays a subset of records based on specified criteria.

FIGURE 1.15 Unfiltered
Customers Table ➤

Figure 1.16 displays a filtered view of the Customers table, showing records with Job Title of *Owner*. The navigation bar shows that this is a filtered list containing 6 records matching the criteria. (The Customers table still contains the original 29 records, but only 6 records are visible with the filter applied.)

FIGURE 1.16 Filtered
Customers Table Shows
Owners ➤

Filter by Selection displays only the records that match the selected criteria.

Filter by Selection displays only the records that match the selected criteria. The easiest way to implement a Filter by Selection is as follows:

1. Click in any field that contains the criterion on which you want to filter.
2. Click Filter by Selection in the Sort & Filter group.
3. Select Equals "criterion" from the list of options.

Only the records that match the selected criterion will be displayed.

Figure 1.17 illustrates another, more versatile, way to apply a filter, using Filter by Form. *Filter by Form* displays table records based on multiple criteria. Filter by Form enables the user to apply the logical operators AND and OR. For the AND operator, a record is included in the results if all the criteria are true; for the OR operator, a record is included if at least one criterion is true. Another advantage of the Filter by Form function is that you can use a comparison operator. A *comparison operator* is used to evaluate the relationship between two quantities to determine if they are equal or not equal; and, if they are not equal, a comparison operator determines which one is greater than the other. Comparison operator symbols include: equal (=), not equal (<>), greater than (>), less than (<), greater than or equal to (>=), and less than or equal to (<=). For example, you can use a comparison operator to select products with an inventory level greater than 30 (>30). Filter by Selection, on the other hand, requires you to specify criteria equal to an existing value. Figure 1.17 shows a Filter by Form designed to select Products with a reorder level of more than 10 units.

Filter by Form displays table records based on multiple criteria. Filter by Form enables the user to apply the logical operators AND and OR.

A **comparison operator** is used to evaluate the relationship between two quantities to determine if they are equal or not equal; and, if they are not equal, a comparison operator determines which one is greater than the other.

Click Advanced to select Filter by Form

Enter an expression

Add criteria by clicking the Or tab

FIGURE 1.17 Filter by Form Design Grid ➤

To apply an OR comparison operator to a Filter by Form, click the Or tab at the bottom of the window. For example, you could add the criterion *Baked Goods & Mixes* to the category field, which would show all the Products with a reorder level of more than 10 units and all

Products in the Baked Goods & Mixes category. (This OR example is not shown in Figure 1.17.) Filters enable you to obtain information from a database quickly without creating a query or a report.

Sorting Table Data on One or More Fields

You can also change the order of the information by sorting by one or more fields. A *sort* lists records in a specific sequence, such as alphabetically by last name or by ascending EmployeeID.

To sort a table, do the following:

1. Click in the field that you want to use to sort the records.
2. Click Ascending or Descending in the Sort & Filter group.

Ascending sorts a list of text data in alphabetical order or a numeric list in lowest to highest order. *Descending* sorts a list of text data in reverse alphabetical order or a numeric list in highest to lowest order. Figure 1.18 shows the Customers table sorted in ascending order by state. You may apply both filters and sorts to tables or query results.

FIGURE 1.18 Customers Table Sorted by State ➤

The operations can be done in any order; that is, you can filter a table to show only selected records, and then sort the filtered table to display the records in a certain order. Conversely, you can sort a table first and then apply a filter. It does not matter which operation is performed first. You can also filter the table further by applying a second, third, or more criteria; for example, click in a Job Title cell containing *Owner*, and apply a Filter by Selection. Then click *WA* in the State column, and apply a second Filter by Selection to display all the customers from WA. You can also click Toggle Filter at any time to remove all filters and display all of the records in the table. Filters are a temporary method for examining table data. If you close the filtered table and then reopen it, the filter will be removed, and all of the records will be restored.

Knowing When to Use Access or Excel to Manage Data

You are probably familiar with working in an Excel spreadsheet. You type the column headings, then enter the data, perhaps add a formula or two, then add totals to the bottom. Once the data has been entered, you can apply a filter, or sort the data, or start all over—similar to what we learned to do in Access with filters. It is true that you can accomplish many of the same tasks using either Excel or Access. In this section, you will learn how to decide whether to use Access or Excel. Although the two programs have much in common, they each have distinct advantages. How do you choose whether to use Access or Excel? The choice you make may ultimately depend on how well you know Access. Users who only know Excel are more likely to use a spreadsheet even if a database would be better. When database features are used in Excel, they are generally used on data that is in one table. When the data is better suited to be on two or more tables, then using Access is preferable. Learning how to use Access will be beneficial to you since it will enable you to work more efficiently with large groups of data. Ideally, the type of data and the type of functionality you require should determine which program will work best.

Select the Software to Use

A contact list (e.g., name, address, phone number) created in Excel may serve your needs just fine at first. Each time you meet a new contact, you can add another row to the bottom of your worksheet, as shown in Figure 1.19. You can sort the list by last name for easier look-up of names. In Excel, you can easily move an entire column, insert a new column, or copy and paste data from one cell to another. This is the "ease of use" characteristic of Excel.

If you needed to expand the information in Excel, to keep track of each time you contacted someone on your contact list, for example, you may need an additional worksheet. This additional sheet would only list the contacts who you contacted and some information about the nature of the contact. Which contact was it? When was the contact made? Was it a phone contact or a face-to-face meeting? As you track these entries, your worksheet will contain a reference to the first worksheet using the Contact Name. As the quantity and complexity of the data increase, the need to organize your data logically also increases.

Access provides built-in tools to help organize data better than Excel. One tool that helps Access organize data is the ability to create relationships between tables. A ***relationship*** is a connection between two tables using a common field. The benefit of a relationship is to efficiently combine data from related tables for the purpose of creating queries, forms, and reports. Relationships are the reason why Access is referred to as a relational database. For example, assume you want to create a Contact Management Database. You would first create two tables to hold contact names and contact notes. You would then create a relationship between the Contact Name table and the Contact Notes table using ContactID as the common field. To create a Contacts Form or Query, you would take advantage of the two related tables.

A **relationship** is a connection between two tables using a common field.

Contact list created in Excel

Names can be sorted by last name as needed

Names are entered chronologically

FIGURE 1.19 Excel Contacts List ➤

Use Access

You should use Access to manage data when you:

- Require multiple related tables to store your data.
- Have a large amount of data.
- Need to connect to and retrieve data from external databases, such as Microsoft SQL Server.
- Need to group, sort, and total data based on various parameters.
- Have an application that requires multiple users to connect to one data source at the same time.

Use Excel

You should use Excel to manage data when you:

- Only need one worksheet to handle all of your data (i.e., you do not need multiple worksheets).
- Have mostly numeric data—for example, you need to maintain an expense statement.
- Require subtotals and totals in your worksheet.
- Want to primarily run a series of "what if" scenarios on your data.
- Need to create complex charts and/or graphs.

In the next Hands-On Exercise, you will create and apply filters, create comparison operator expressions using Filter by Form, and sort records in the Datasheet view of the Customers table.

HANDS-ON EXERCISES

myitlab
HOE2 Training

2 Filters, Sorts, and Access Versus Excel

The sales managers at Northwind Traders need quick answers to their questions about customer orders. You use the Access database to filter tables to answer most of these questions. Before printing your results, make sure you sort the records based on the managers' needs.

Skills covered: Use Filter by Selection with an Equal Condition • Use Filter by Selection with a Contains Condition • Use Filter by Form with a Comparison Operator • Sort a Table

STEP 1 ▶ USE FILTER BY SELECTION WITH AN EQUAL CONDITION

As you continue to learn about the Northwind Traders database, you are expected to provide answers to questions about the customers and products. In this exercise, you use filters to find customers who live in London. Refer to Figure 1.20 as you complete Step 1.

FIGURE 1.20 Customers Table Filtered for London Records ➤

a. Open *a01h1traders_LastnameFirstname* if you closed it at the end of Hands-On Exercise 1. Click the **File tab**, click **Save Database As**, and then type **a01h2traders_LastnameFirstname**, changing *h1* to *h2*. Click **Save**.

> **TROUBLESHOOTING:** If you make any major mistakes in this exercise, you can delete the *a01h2traders_LastnameFirstname* file, repeat step a above, and then start the exercise over.

b. Open the Customers table, navigate to record four, and then replace *Thomas Hardy* with your name in the Contact Name field.

c. Scroll right until the City field is visible. The fourth record has a value of *London* in the City field. Click on the field to select it.

The word *London* has a gold-colored border around it to let you know that it is active.

d. Click **Selection** in the Sort & Filter group.

e. Choose **Equals "London"** from the menu.

Six records should be displayed.

f. Click **Toggle Filter** in the Sort & Filter group to remove the filter.

g. Click **Toggle Filter** again to reset the filter. Leave the Customers table open for the next step.

STEP 2 USE FILTER BY SELECTION WITH A CONTAINS CONDITION

At times, you need to print information for the Northwind managers. In this exercise, you print your results. Refer to Figure 1.21 as you complete Step 2.

Click Selection and choose Contains "Sales Representative"

Select *Sales Representative*

Three customers match the criteria

FIGURE 1.21 Customers from London with Contact Title *Sales Representative* ➤

a. Click in any field in the Contact Title column that contains the value *Sales Representative*.

Sales Representative has a gold-colored border around it to let you know that it is activated.

b. Click **Selection** on the Sort & Filter group.

c. Click **Contains "Sales Representative"**.

You have applied a second layer of filtering to the customers in London. The second layer further restricts the display to only those customers who have the words *Sales Representative* contained in their titles.

d. Scroll left until you see your name. Compare your results to those shown in Figure 1.21.

e. Click **Toggle Filter** in the Sort & Filter group to remove the filters.

f. Close the Customers table. Click **No** if a dialog box asks if you want to save the design changes to the Customers table.

At Northwind Traders, you are asked to provide a list of records that do not match just one set of criteria. Use a Filter by Form to provide the information when two or more criteria are needed. Refer to Figure 1.22 as you complete Step 3.

Click Advanced to select Filter by Form

Select your first and last names

Open Order Details Extended query

Enter <50 for the ExtendedPrice criteria

FIGURE 1.22 Filter by Form Selection Criteria ➤

a. Click the **Tables group** in the Navigation Pane to collapse the listed tables.

b. Click the **Queries group** in the Navigation Pane to expand the lists of available queries.

c. Locate and double-click the **Order Details Extended query** to open it.

This query contains information about orders. It has fields containing information about the salesperson, the Order ID, the product name, the unit price, quantity ordered, the discount given, and an extended price. The extended price is a field used to total order information.

d. Click **Advanced** in the Sort & Filter group.

While you are applying a Filter by Form to a query, you can use the same process to apply a Filter by Form to a table.

e. Select **Filter by Form** from the list.

All of the records are now hidden, and you only see field names with an arrow in the first field. Click on the other fields, and an arrow appears.

f. Click in the first row under the First Name field.

An arrow appears at the right of the box.

g. Click the **First Name arrow**.

A list of all available first names appears. Your name should be on the list. Figure 1.22 shows Keith Mast, which replaced Margaret Peacock in Hands-On Exercise 1.

> **TROUBLESHOOTING:** If you do not see your name and you do see Margaret on the list, you probably skipped Steps 3c and 3d in Hands-On Exercise 1. Close the query without saving changes, turn back to the first Hands-On Exercise, and rework it, making sure not to omit any steps. Then you can return to this spot and work the remainder of this Hands-On Exercise.

h. Select your first name from the list.

i. Click in the first row under the Last Name field to reveal the arrow. Locate and select your last name by clicking it.

j. Scroll right until you see the Extended Price field. Click in the first row under the Extended Price field, and then type **<50**.

This will select all of the items that you ordered where the total was under $50. You ignore the arrow and type the expression needed.

k. Click **Toggle Filter** in the Sort & Filter group.

You have specified which records to include and have executed the filtering by clicking Toggle Filter. You should have 31 records that match the criteria you specified.

l. Click the **File tab**, click **Print**, and then click **Print Preview**.

You instructed Access to preview the filtered query results.

m. Click **Close Print Preview** in the Print Preview group.

n. Close the Order Details Extended query. Click **No** if a dialog box asks if you want to save your changes.

TIP Deleting Filter by Form Criterion

While working with Filter by Selection or Filter by Form, you may inadvertently save a filter. To view a saved filter, open the table or query that you suspect may have a saved filter. Click Advanced in the Sort & Filter group, and then click Filter by Form. If criteria appear in the form, then a filter has been saved. To delete a saved filter, click Advanced, and then click Clear All Filters. Close and save the table or query.

STEP 4 SORT A TABLE

Your boss at Northwind is happy with your work; however, he would like some of the information to appear in a different order. Sort the records in the Customers table using the boss's new criteria. Refer to Figure 1.23 as you complete Step 4.

FIGURE 1.23 Customers Table Sorted by Country and Then City ➤

a. Click the **Queries group** in the Navigation Pane to collapse the listed queries.

b. Click the **Tables group** in the Navigation Pane to expand the lists of available tables.

c. Locate and double-click the **Customers table** to open it.

This table contains information about customers. It is sorted in ascending order by the Customer ID field. Because this field contains text, the table is sorted in alphabetical order.

d. Click any value in the Customer ID field. Click **Descending** in the Sort & Filter group on the Home tab.

Sorting in descending order on a character field produces a reverse alphabetical order.

e. Scroll right until you can see both the Country and City fields.

If you close the Navigation Pane, locating the fields on the far right will be easier.

f. Click the **Country column heading**.

The entire column is selected.

g. Click the **Country column heading** again, and hold down the **left mouse button**.

A thick dark blue line displays on the left edge of the Country field column.

h. Check to make sure that you see the thick blue line. Drag the **Country field** to the left until the thick black line moves between the City and Region fields. Release the mouse and the Country field position moves to the right of the City field.

You moved the Country field next to the City field so you can easily sort the table based on both fields.

i. Click any city name in the City field, and then click **Ascending** in the Sort & Filter group.

j. Click any country name in the Country field, and then click **Ascending**.

The countries are sorted in alphabetical order. The cities within each country also are sorted alphabetically. For example, the customer in Graz, Austria, is listed before the customer in Salzburg, Austria.

k. Close the Customers table. Do not save the changes.

l. Click the **File tab**, and then click **Compact & Repair Database**.

m. Click the **File tab**, click **Save & Publish**, and then double-click **Back Up Database**. Accept *a01h2traders_LastnameFirstname_date* as the file name, and then click **Save**.

You just created a backup of the database after completing Hands-On Exercise 2. The *a01h2traders_LastnameFirstname* database remains onscreen.

n. Keep the database onscreen if you plan to continue with Hands-On Exercise 3. If not, close the database and exit Access.

Relational Database

In the previous section, we compared Excel worksheets to Access relational databases. Access has the ability to create relationships between two tables, whereas Excel does not. Access is known as a *relational database management system* (RDBMS); using an RDBMS, you can manage groups of data (tables) and then set rules (relationships) between tables. When relational databases are designed properly, users can easily combine data from multiple tables to create queries, forms, and reports.

Access is known as a **relational database management system** (RDBMS); using an RDBMS, you can manage groups of data (tables) and then set rules (relationships) between tables.

Good database design begins with grouping data into the correct tables. This practice, known as normalization, will take time to learn, but over time you will begin to understand the fundamentals. The design of a relational database management system is illustrated in Figure 1.24, which shows the table design of the Northwind Traders database. The tables have been created, the field names have been added, and the data types have been set. The diagram also shows the relationships that were created between tables using join lines. *Join lines* enable you to create a relationship between two tables using a common field. When relationships are established, three options are available to further dictate how Access will manage the relationship: Enforce referential integrity, Cascade update related fields, and Cascade delete related records. Later in this section, you will learn more about enforcing referential integrity. The other two options will be covered in another chapter. Using the enforce referential integrity option will help keep invalid data out of your database. Examples of invalid data include (1) entering an order for a customer that does not exist, (2) tagging a new product with a nonexistent category, and (3) entering a person's address with an invalid state abbreviation.

Join lines enable you to create a relationship between two tables using a common field.

Figure 1.24 shows the join lines between related tables as a series of lines connecting the common fields. For example, the Suppliers table is joined to the Products table using the common field SupplierID.

When the database is set up properly, the users of the data can be confident that searching through the Customers table will produce accurate results about their order history or their outstanding invoices.

In this section, you will explore relationships between tables and learn about the power of relational data.

Using the Relationships Window

The relationships in a database are represented by the lines between the tables, as shown in Figure 1.24. Relationships are set in the Relationships window by the database developer after the tables have been created but before any sample data is entered. The most common method of connecting two tables is to connect the primary key from one table to the foreign key of another. A *foreign key* is a field in one table that is also the primary key of another table. For example, the SupplierID (primary key) in the Suppliers table is joined to the SupplierID (foreign key) in the Products table. As you learned before, the primary key is a field that uniquely identifies each record in a table.

A **foreign key** is a field in one table that is also the primary key of another table.

To create a relationship between two tables, follow these guidelines:

1. Click Relationships in the Relationships group on the Database Tools tab.
2. Add the two tables that you want to join together to the Relationships window.
3. Drag the common field (e.g., SupplierID) from the primary table (e.g., Suppliers) onto the common field (e.g., SupplierID) of the related table (e.g., Products).
4. The data types of the common fields must be the same.
5. Check the Enforce Referential Integrity check box.
6. Close the Relationships window.

Enforce Referential Integrity

Enforce referential integrity ensures that data cannot be entered into a related table unless it first exists in the primary table.

Enforce referential integrity is one of the three options you can select when setting a table relationship. When *enforce referential integrity* is checked, Access ensures that data cannot be entered into a related table unless it first exists in the primary table. For example, in Figure 1.24, you cannot enter an order into the Order table for a Customer with CustomerID 9308 if Customer 9308 has not been entered in the Customer table. This rule ensures the integrity of the data in the database and improves overall data accuracy. Referential integrity also prohibits users from deleting a record in one table if it has records in related tables (i.e., you cannot delete Customer 8819 if Customer 8819 has any orders).

FIGURE 1.24 Relationships Window Displaying Table Connections ➤

Create Sample Data

When learning database skills, starting with a smaller set of sample data prior to entering all company records can be helpful. The same design principles apply regardless of the number of records. A small amount of data gives you the ability to check the tables and quickly see if your results are correct. Even though the data amounts are small, as you test the database tables and relationships, the results will prove useful as you work with larger data sets.

> When learning database skills, starting with a smaller set of sample data prior to entering all company records can be helpful.

Understanding Relational Power

In the previous section, you learned that you should use Access when you have relational data. Access derives power from multiple tables and the relationships between those tables. This type of database is illustrated in Figure 1.24. This diagram describes the database structure of the Northwind Traders company. If you examine some of the connections, you will see that the EmployeeID is a foreign key in the Orders table. That means you can produce a report displaying all orders for a customer and the employee name (from the Employees table) that entered the order. The Orders table is joined to the Order Details table where the OrderID is the common field. The Products table is joined to the Order Details table where ProductID is the common field. These table connections enable you to query (ask) the database for information stored in multiple tables. This feature gives the manager the ability to ask questions like "How many different beverages were shipped last week?" and "What was the total revenue generated from seafood orders last year?"

Suppose a customer called to complain that his orders were arriving late. Because the ShipperID is a foreign key field in the Orders table, you could query the database to find out which shipper delivered that customer's merchandise. Are the other orders also late? Does the firm need to reconsider its shipping options? The design of a relational database enables us to extract information from multiple tables in a single query or report.

In the next Hands-On Exercise, you will examine the Relationships window, create a filter in a query and a report, and remove a filter.

HANDS-ON EXERCISES

3 Relational Database

You continue to use the Access database to filter tables and provide answers to the Northwind employees' questions. When the same question is repeated by several employees, you look for a way to save your filter by form specifications.

Skills covered: Use the Relationships Window • Filter a Query • Use Filter by Form with a Comparison Operator and Reapply a Saved Filter • Filter a Report • Remove a Filter

---

STEP 1 ▶ USE THE RELATIONSHIPS WINDOW

In this exercise, you examine the relationships established in the Northwind Traders database to learn more about the overall design of the database. Refer to Figure 1.25 as you complete Step 1.

FIGURE 1.25 Relationships Window for the Northwind Database ➤

a. Open *a01h2traders_LastnameFirstname* if you closed it at the end of Hands-On Exercise 2. Click the **File tab**, click **Save Database As**, and then type **a01h3traders_LastnameFirstname**, changing *h2* to *h3*. Click **Save**.

> **TROUBLESHOOTING:** If you make any major mistakes in this exercise, you can delete the *a01h3traders_LastnameFirstname* file, repeat step a above, and then start the exercise over.

b. Click the **Database Tools tab**, and then click **Relationships** in the Relationships group.

Examine the relationships that connect the various tables. For example, the Products table is connected to the Suppliers, Categories, and Order Details tables.

c. Click **Show Table** in the Relationships group on the Relationship Tools Design tab.

The Show Table dialog box opens. It tells you that eight tables are available in the database. If you look in the Relationships window, you will see that all eight tables are in the relationships diagram.

d. Click the **Queries tab** in the Show Table dialog box.

You could add all of the queries to the Relationships window. Things might become cluttered, but you could tell at a glance where the queries get their information.

e. Close the Show Table dialog box.

f. Click **All Access Objects** on the Navigation Pane.

g. Select **Tables and Related Views**.

You now see each table and all the queries, forms, and reports that are based on each table. If a query is created using more than one table, it appears multiple times in the Navigation Pane.

h. Close the Relationships window. Click **All Tables** on the Navigation Pane, and then select **Object Type**.

STEP 2 FILTER A QUERY

You notice a connection between tables and queries. Whenever you make a change in the query, the table is updated as well. Run a few tests on the Northwind database to confirm your findings. Refer to Figure 1.26 as you complete Step 2.

FIGURE 1.26 Filtered Query Results ➤

a. Collapse the Tables group, and expand the Queries group, and then locate and double-click the **Order Details Extended query**.

b. Find an occurrence of your last name, and then click it to select it.

c. Click **Selection** in the Sort & Filter group. Select **Equals "YourName"** from the selection menu.

The query results are reduced to 420 records.

d. Click **Toggle Filter** in the Sort & Filter group to remove the filter.

Use Filter by Form to solve more complex questions about the Northwind data. After you retrieve the records, you save the Filter by Form specifications so you can reapply the filter later. Refer to Figure 1.27 as you complete Step 3.

FIGURE 1.27 Query Results with Your Name and Extended Prices > $2,000 ➤

a. Click **Advanced** in the Sort & Filter group.

b. Select **Filter By Form** from the list.

Because Access will save the last filter you created, the Filter by Form design sheet opens with one criterion already filled in. Your name displays in the selection box under the Last Name field.

c. Scroll right (or press **Tab**) until the Extended Price field is visible. Click the first row in the Extended Price field.

d. Type **>2000**.

The Extended Price field shows the purchased amount for each item ordered. If an item sold for $15 and a customer ordered 10, the Extended Price would display $150.

e. Click **Toggle Filter** in the Sort & Filter group. Examine the filtered results.

Your comparison operator instruction, >2000, identified 18 items ordered where the extended price exceeded $2,000.

f. Close the Order Details Extended query by clicking the **Close button**. Answer **Yes** when asked *Do you want to save changes?*.

g. Open the Order Details Extended query again.

The filter disengages when you close and reopen the object. However, the filter has been stored with the query. You may reapply the filter at any time by clicking the Toggle Filter command (until the next filter replaces the current one).

h. Click **Toggle Filter** in the Sort & Filter group.

i. Compare your results to Figure 1.27. If your results are correct, close and save the query.

You wonder if one report can serve several purposes. You discover that a report can be customized using the Filter by Selection feature. Refer to Figure 1.28 as you complete Step 4.

Close Print Preview

Click Print after previewing

Landscape layout is selected

Report filtered for Confections

FIGURE 1.28 Products by Category Report—Filtered by Confections ➤

a. Click the **Queries group** in the Navigation Pane to collapse the listed queries, and then click the **Reports group** in the Navigation Pane to expand the list of available reports.

b. Open the Products by Category report located in the Reports group on the Navigation Pane. You may need to scroll down to locate it.

The report should open in Print Preview with a gray title background highlighting the report title. The Print Preview displays the report exactly as it will print. This report was formatted to display in three columns.

> **TROUBLESHOOTING:** If you do not see the gray title background and three columns, you probably opened the wrong object. The database also contains a Product by Category query. It is the source for the Products by Category report. Make sure you open the report (shown with the green report icon) and not the query. Close the query and open the report.

c. Examine the Confections category products. You should see *Your Name Pecan Pie*.

You created this product by entering data in a form in Hands-On Exercise 1. You later discovered that changes made to a form affect the related table. Now you see that other related objects also change when the source data changes.

d. Right-click the **Products by Category tab**, and then select **Report View** from the shortcut menu.

The Report view displays the information a little differently. It no longer shows three columns. If you clicked the Print command while in Report view, the columns would print even though you do not see them. The Report view permits limited data interaction (for example, filtering).

e. Scroll down in the report until you see the title *Category: Confections*. Right-click the word *Confections* in the title. Select **Equals "Confections"** from the shortcut menu.

The report now displays only *Confections*.

f. Right-click the **Products by Category tab**, and then select **Print Preview** from the shortcut menu.

If you need to print a report, always view the report in Print Preview prior to printing.

g. Click **Close Print Preview** in the Close Preview group.

h. Save and close the report.

> The next time the report opens in Report view, it will not be filtered. However, since the filter was saved, the filter can be reapplied by clicking Toggle Filter in the Sort & Filter group.

STEP 5 REMOVE A FILTER

You notice that Access keeps asking you to save your changes when you close a table or query. You say "Yes" each time since you do not want to lose your data. Now you need to remove the filters that you saved. Refer to Figure 1.29 as you complete Step 5.

Click Advanced, and then click Clear All Filters

Order Details Extended query is filtered

18 records match the criteria

FIGURE 1.29 Query Results Before *Clear All Filters* Is Clicked ➤

a. Click the **Queries group** in the Navigation Pane to expand the list of available reports, then open the Order Details Extended query.

> All 2,155 records should display in the query. You have unfiltered the data. However, the filter from the previous step still exists.

b. Click **Toggle Filter** in the Sort & Filter group.

> You will see the same 18 filtered records that you created in Step 3.

c. Click **Advanced** in the Sort & Filter group, and then click **Clear All Filters**.

> All 2,155 records are shown again.

d. Close the query. A dialog box opens asking if you want to save changes. Click **Yes**.

e. Open the Order Details Extended query.

f. Click **Advanced** in the Sort & Filter group.

g. Check to ensure the Clear All Filters option is dim, indicating there are no saved filters. Save and close the query.

h. Click the **File tab**, and then click **Compact & Repair Database**.

i. Click the **File tab**, and then click **Exit** (to exit Access).

j. Submit based on your instructor's directions.

CHAPTER OBJECTIVES REVIEW

After reading this chapter, you have accomplished the following objectives:

1. **Navigate among the objects in an Access database.** An Access database has six types of objects: tables, forms, queries, reports, macros, and modules. The Navigation Pane displays these objects and enables you to open an existing object or create new objects. You may arrange these by Object Type or by Tables and Related Views. The Tables and Related Views provides a listing of each table and all other objects in the database that use that table as a source. Thus, one query or report may appear several times, listed once under each table from which it derives information. Each table in the database is composed of records, and each record is in turn composed of fields. Every record in a given table has the same fields in the same order. The primary key is the field (or combination of fields) that makes every record in a table unique.

2. **Understand the difference between working in storage and memory.** Access automatically saves any changes in the current record as soon as you move to the next record or when you close the table. The Undo Current Record command reverses the changes to the previously saved record.

3. **Practice good database file management.** Because organizations depend on the data stored in databases, you need to implement good file management practices. For example, you need to develop an organized folder structure so you can easily save and retrieve your database files. You also need to develop a naming convention so it is easy to determine which file contains which data. As you learn new Access skills, it is recommended that you make a copy of the original database file and practice on the copy. This practice provides a recovery point in the event you make a fatal error.

4. **Back up, compact, and repair Access files.** Because using a database tends to increase the size of the file, you should always close any database objects and compact and repair the database prior to closing the file. Compact & Repair will reduce the size of the database by removing temporary objects and unclaimed space due to deleted objects. Adequate backup is essential when working with an Access database (or any other Office application). For increased security, a duplicate copy of the database can be created at the end of every session and stored externally (on a flash drive or an external hard drive).

5. **Create filters.** A filter is a set of criteria that is applied to a table to display a subset of the records in that table. Access lets you Filter by Selection or Filter by Form. The application of a filter does not remove the records from the table, but simply hides them temporarily from view.

6. **Sort table data on one or more fields.** The records in a table can be displayed in ascending or descending order by first selecting the appropriate column and clicking Ascending or Descending on the Home tab. The sort order will hold only if you save the table; otherwise the table will return to the original sort order when you close the table.

7. **Know when to use Access or Excel to manage data.** You should use Access to manage data when you require multiple related tables to store your data; have a large amount of data; need to connect to and retrieve data from external databases, such as Microsoft SQL Server; need to group, sort, and total data based on various parameters; and/or have an application that requires multiple users to connect to one data source at the same time. You should use Excel to manage data when you only need one worksheet to handle all of your data (i.e., you do not need multiple worksheets); have mostly numeric data—for example, if you need to maintain an expense statement; require subtotals and totals in your worksheet; want to primarily run a series of "what if" scenarios on your data; and/or need to create complex charts and/or graphs.

8. **Use the Relationships window.** Access enables you to create relationships between tables using the Relationships window. A *relationship* is a connection between two tables using a common field. The benefit of a relationship is to efficiently combine data from related tables for the purpose of creating queries, forms, and reports. Relationships are the reason why Access is referred to as a relational database.

9. **Understand relational power.** A relational database contains multiple tables and enables you to extract information from those tables in a single query. The related tables must be consistent with one another, a concept known as referential integrity. Once referential integrity is set, Access enforces data validation to protect the integrity of a database. No system, no matter how sophisticated, can produce valid output from invalid input. Changes made in one object can affect other related objects. Relationships are based on joining the primary key from one table to the foreign key of another table.

KEY TERMS

Access speed *p.541*
Backup *p.541*
Compact and Repair *p.541*
Comparison operator *p.551*
Criterion *p.538*
Database *p.533*
Datasheet view *p.535*
Design view *p.535*
Enforce referential integrity *p.561*
Field *p.533*

Filter *p.549*
Filter by Form *p.551*
Filter by Selection *p.551*
Foreign key *p.560*
Form *p.538*
Join lines *p.560*
Navigation Pane *p.534*
Object *p.533*
Primary key *p.536*
Query *p.538*

Record *p.533*
Relational database management
    system *p.560*
Relationship *p.553*
Report *p.539*
Sort *p.552*
Sort Ascending *p.552*
Sort Descending *p.552*
Table *p.533*

1. Which sequence represents the hierarchy of terms, from smallest to largest?

   (a) Database, table, record, field

   (b) Field, record, table, database

   (c) Record, field, table, database

   (d) Field, record, database, table

2. You perform several edits in a table within an Access database. When should you execute the Save command?

   (a) Immediately after you add, edit, or delete a record

   (b) Each time you close a table or a query

   (c) Once at the end of a session

   (d) Records are saved automatically; the save command is not required.

3. You have opened an Access file. The left pane displays a table with forms, queries, and reports listed below a table name. Then another table and its objects display. You notice some of the object names are repeated under different tables. Why?

   (a) The Navigation Pane has been set to Object Type. The object names repeat because a query or report is frequently based on multiple tables.

   (b) The Navigation Pane has been set to Tables and Related Views. The object names repeat because a query or report is frequently based on multiple tables.

   (c) The Navigation Pane has been set to Most Recently Used View. The object names repeat because an object has been used frequently.

   (d) The database objects have been alphabetized.

4. Which of the following is not true of an Access database?

   (a) Every record in a table has the same fields as every other record.

   (b) Every table in a database contains the same number of records as every other table.

   (c) Text, Number, Autonumber, and Currency are valid data types.

   (d) Each table should contain a primary key; however, a primary key is not required.

5. Which of the following is true regarding the record selector box?

   (a) A pencil symbol indicates that the current record already has been saved.

   (b) An empty square indicates that the current record has not changed.

   (c) An asterisk indicates the first record in the table.

   (d) A gold border surrounds the active record.

6. You have finished an Access assignment and wish to turn it in to your instructor for evaluation. As you prepare to transfer the file, you discover that it has grown in size. It is now more than double the original size. You should:

   (a) Zip the database file prior to transmitting it to the instructor.

   (b) Turn it in; the size does not matter.

   (c) Compact and repair the database file prior to transmitting it to the instructor.

   (d) Delete extra tables or reports or fields to make the file smaller.

7. Which of the following will be accepted as valid during data entry?

   (a) Adding a record with a duplicate primary key

   (b) Entering text into a numeric field

   (c) Entering numbers into a text field

   (d) Omitting an entry in a required field

8. Which of the following conditions is available through Filter by Selection?

   (a) The AND condition

   (b) The OR condition

   (c) An Equals condition

   (d) A delete condition

9. You open an Access form and use it to update an address for customer Lee Fong. After closing the form, you later open a report that generates mailing labels. What will the address label for Lee Fong show?

   (a) The new address

   (b) The old address

   (c) The new address if you remembered to save the changes made to the form

   (d) The old address until you remember to update it in the report

10. You are looking at an Employees table in Datasheet view. You want the names sorted alphabetically by last name and then by first name—for example, Smith, Andrea is listed before Smith, William. To accomplish this, you must:

    (a) First sort ascending on first name and then on last name.

    (b) First sort descending on first name and then on last name.

    (c) First sort ascending on last name and then on first name.

    (d) First sort descending on last name and then on first name.

1 Member Rewards

The Prestige Hotel chain caters to upscale business travelers and provides state-of-the-art conference, meeting, and reception facilities. It prides itself on its international, four-star cuisine. Last year, it began a member rewards club to help the marketing department track the purchasing patterns of its most loyal customers. All of the hotel transactions are stored in the database. Your task is to update a customer record and identify the customers who had weddings in St. Paul. This exercise follows the same set of skills as used in Hands-On Exercise 1 in the chapter. Refer to Figure 1.30 as you complete this exercise.

FIGURE 1.30 Member Service by City—Filtered and Sorted ➤

a. Open the *a01p1rewards* file, and then save the database as **a01p1rewards_LastnameFirstname**.

b. Open the Members Form, and then click **New (blank) record** on the bottom navigation bar. (It has a yellow asterisk.)

c. Enter the information in the following table in the form. Press **Tab** to move to the next field.

Field Name	Value
MemNumber	4852
LastName	your last name
FirstName	your first name
JoinDate	7/30/2010
Address	124 West Elm, Apt 12

(Continued)

Field Name	Value
City	your hometown
State	your state
Zip	your zip
Phone	**9995551234**
Email	your e-mail
OrderID	**9325**
ServiceDate	**8/1/2012**
ServiceID	**3**
NoInParty	**2**
Location	**20**

d. Click the **Close (X) button** to close the form.

e. Double-click the **Members table** in the Navigation Pane. Use **Find** to verify your name is in the table.

f. In the Members table, find a record that displays *Charlotte* as the value in the City field. Click **Charlotte** to select that data value.

g. Click **Selection** in the Sort & Filter group on the Home tab. Select **Equals "Charlotte"**.

h. Find a record that displays *28217* as the value in the Zip field. Click **Zip** to select that data value.

i. Click **Selection** in the Sort & Filter Group, and then select **Equals "28217"**.

j. Right-click on any phone number field with a missing phone number, and then click **Does not Equal Blank**.

k. Click any value in the FirstName field. Click **Ascending** in the Sort & Filter group on the Home tab. Click any value in the LastName field. Click **Ascending** in the Sort & Filter group on the Home tab.

l. Click the **File tab**, click **Print**, and then click **Print Preview** to preview the sorted and filtered query.

m. Click **Close Print Preview** in the Close Preview group. Close the query (do not save when asked).

n. Click the **File tab**, and then click **Compact and Repair Database**.

o. Click the **File tab**, click **Save & Publish**, and then double-click **Back Up Database**.

p. Click **Save** to accept the default backup file name with today's date.

q. Click the **File tab**, and then click **Exit** (to exit Access).

r. Submit based on your instructor's directions.

2 Custom Coffee

The Custom Coffee Company provides coffee, tea, and snacks to offices in Miami. Custom Coffee also provides and maintains the equipment for brewing the beverages. The firm has a reputation for providing outstanding customer service. To improve customer service even further, the owner recently purchased an Access database to keep track of customers, orders, and products. This database will replace the Excel spreadsheets currently maintained by the office manager. The Excel spreadsheets are out of date and they do not allow for data validation while data is being entered. The company hired a temp to verify and enter all the Excel data into the Access database. This exercise follows the same set of skills as used in Hands-On Exercises 2 and 3 in the chapter. Refer to Figure 1.31 as you complete this exercise.

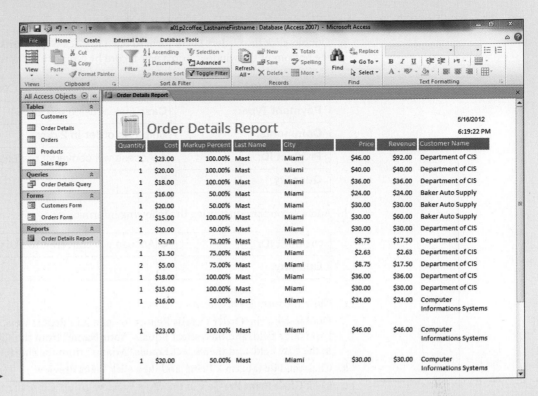

FIGURE 1.31 Order Details Report Filtered for *YourName* ➤

a. Open the *a01p2coffee* file, and then save the database as **a01p2coffee_LastnameFirstname**.

b. Click the **Database Tools tab**, and then click **Relationships** in the Relationships group. Review the table relationships. Take note of the join line between the Customers and Orders Tables.

c. Click **Close** in the Relationships group.

d. Double-click the **Sales Reps table** in the Navigation Pane to open it. Replace *YourName* with your name in both the LastName and FirstName fields. Close the table by clicking the **Close (X) button** on the right side of the Sales Reps window.

e. Double-click the **Customers Form form** to open it. Click **New (blank) record** in the navigation bar at the bottom of the window. Add a new record by typing the following information; press **Tab** after each field.

Customer Name:	*your name* **Company**
Contact:	your name
Email:	*your name***@yahoo.com**
Address1:	**123 Main St**
Address2:	**Skip**
City:	**Miami**
State:	**FL**
Zip Code:	**33133**
Phone:	**(305) 555-1234**
Fax:	**Skip**
Service Start Date:	**1/17/2012**
Credit Rating:	**A**
Sales Rep ID:	**2**

Notice the pencil in the top-left margin of the form window. This symbol indicates the new record has not been saved to storage. Press **Tab**. The pencil symbol disappears, and the new customer is automatically saved to the table.

f. Close the Customers Form form.

g. Double-click the **Orders Form form** to open it. Click **New (blank) record** in the navigation bar at the bottom of the window. Add a new record by typing the following information:

Customer ID:	**15** (Access will convert it to *C0015*)
Payment Type:	**Cash** (select using the arrow)
Comments:	**Ship this order in 2 days**
Product ID:	**4** (Access will convert it to *P0004*)
Quantity:	2

h. Add a second product using the following information:

Product ID:	**6** (Access will convert it to *P0006*)
Quantity:	1

i. Close the form (save changes if asked.)

j. Double-click the **Order Details Report** to open it in Report view. Right-click your name in the Last Name field, and then select **Equals "Your Name"** from the shortcut menu. Right-click **Miami** in the City field, and then select **Equals "Miami"** from the shortcut menu.

k. Click the **File tab**, click **Print**, and then click **Print Preview**.

l. Click **Close Print Preview** in the Close Preview group. Close the report.

m. Click the **File tab**, click **Info**, and then click **Compact and Repair Database**.

n. Click the **File tab**, click **Save & Publish**, and then double-click **Back Up Database**. Use the default backup file name.

o. Click the **File tab**, and then click **Exit** (to exit Access).

p. Submit based on your instructor's directions.

1 Real Estate

You are the senior partner in a large, independent real estate firm that specializes in home sales. Most of your time is spent supervising the agents who work for your firm. The firm has a database containing all of the information on the properties it has listed. You use the database to help evaluate the productivity of your team during weekly sales meetings you hold with each sales agent. Today, you are evaluating agent Angela Scott, who is responsible for the high-end properties at the firm. To prepare for your meeting, find all properties that are listed for over $1,000,000, and have four or more bedrooms. When you find these properties, sort the data by Subdivision then by list price in ascending order. Refer to Figure 1.32 as you complete this exercise.

FIGURE 1.32 Your Properties Listed for Over $1 Million ➤

a. Open the *a01m1property* file, and then save the database as **a01m1property_LastnameFirstname**.

b. Open the Agents table. Find and replace *YourName* with your name in the FirstName and LastName fields. Notice the pencil appears in the record selector box on the left while you type your name, then disappears once the record has been saved. Close the table.

c. Open the Over 1 Million query, and then create a filter by form on the data. Set the criteria to identify more than three bedrooms, a listing price over $1,000,000, and sales rep first and last names of your name.

d. Sort the filtered results by ascending **ListPrice** and by ascending **Subdivision**.

e. Save and close the query.

f. Compact and repair the database.

g. Back up the database. Use the default backup file name.

h. Exit Access.

i. Submit based on your instructor's directions.

The Association of Higher Education will host its National Conference on your campus next year. To facilitate the conference, the information technology department has replaced last year's Excel spreadsheets with an Access database containing information on the rooms, speakers, and sessions. Your assignment is to create a room itinerary that will list all of the sessions, dates, and times for each room. The list will be posted on the door of each room for the duration of the conference. Refer to Figure 1.33 as you complete this exercise.

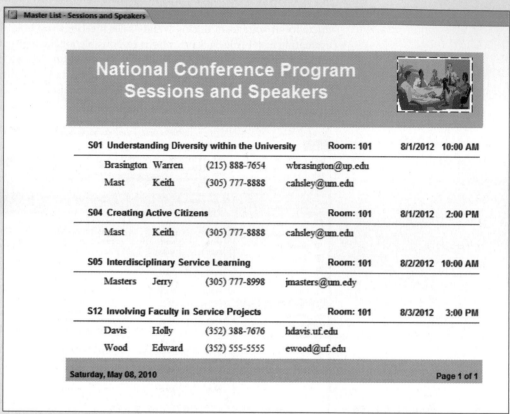

FIGURE 1.33 Sessions and Speakers Report— Room 101 ➤

 DISCOVER

a. Open the *a01m2natconf* file, and then save the database as **a01m2natconf_LastnameFirstname**.

b. Open the Relationships window.

c. Review the objects in the database to see if any of the existing objects will provide the room itinerary information described above.

d. Open the SessionSpeaker table. Scroll to the first blank record at the bottom of the table, and then enter a new record using SpeakerID: **99** and SessionID: **09**. (Note: speaker 99 does not exist.) How does Access respond? Press **Esc**. Close the SessionSpeaker table. In the Relationships window, right-click on the join line between the Speakers table and SessionSpeaker table, and then click **Delete**. Click **Yes**, and then close the Relationships window. Open the SessionSpeaker table, and then enter the same record again. How does Access respond this time? Close the SessionSpeaker table. Open the Speakers table. Find and replace *YourName* with your name. Close the Speakers table.

e. Open the Speaker - Session Query query, and then apply a filter to identify the sessions where you or Holly Davis are the speakers. Use **Filter by Form** and the **Or tab**.

f. Sort the filtered results in ascending order by the RoomID field.

g. Save and close the query.

h. Open the Master List – Sessions and Speakers report in Report view.

i. Apply a filter that limits the report to sessions in Room 101 only.

j. Click the **File tab**, click **Print**, and then click **Print Preview**.

k. Click **Close Print Preview** in the Close Preview group.

l. Close the report.

m. Compact and repair the database.

n. Back up the database. Use the default backup file name.

o. Exit Access (and save the relationships layout when asked).

p. Submit based on your instructor's directions.

Your boss expressed a concern about the accuracy of the inventory reports in the bookstore. He needs you to open the inventory database, make modifications to some records, and determine if the changes you make carry through to the other objects in the database. You will make changes to a form and then verify those changes in a table, a query, and a report. When you have verified that the changes update automatically, you will compact and repair the database and make a backup of it.

Database File Setup

You will open an original database file, and then save the database with a new name. Use the new database to replace an existing employee's name with your name, examine the table relationships, and then complete the remainder of this exercise.

a. Open the *a01c1books* file, and then save the database as **a01c1books_LastnameFirstname**.

b. Open the Maintain Authors form.

c. Navigate to Record 7, and then replace *YourName* with your name.

d. Add a new Title: **Technology in Action**. The ISBN is **0-13-148905-4**, the PubID is **PH**, the PublDate is **2006**, the Price is **$89.95** (just type 89.95, no $), and StockAmt is **95** units.

e. Move to any other record to save the new record. The pencil that appeared in the record selector box on the left while you were typing has now disappeared. Close the form.

f. Open the Maintain Authors form again, and then navigate to Record 7. The changes are there because Access works from storage, not memory. Close the form.

Sort a Query and Apply a Filter by Selection

You need to reorder a detail query so that the results are sorted alphabetically by the publisher name.

a. Open the Publishers, Books, and Authors query.

b. Click in any record in the PubName column, and then sort the field in ascending order.

c. Check to make sure that three books list you as the author.

d. Click your name in the Author's Last Name field, and then filter the records to show only your books.

e. Close the query and save the changes.

View a Report

You need to examine the *Publishers, Books, and Authors* report to determine if the changes you made in the Maintain Authors form appear in the report.

a. Open the Publishers, Books, and Authors report.

b. Check to make sure that the report shows three books listing you as the author.

c. Check the layout of the report in Print Preview.

d. Close the report.

Filter a Table

You need to examine the Books table to determine if the changes you made in the Maintain Authors form carried through to the related table. You also will filter the table to display books published after 2006 with fewer than 100 copies in inventory.

a. Open the Books table.

b. Create a filter that will identify all books published after 2006 with fewer than 100 items in stock.

c. Apply the filter.

d. Preview the filtered table.

e. Close the table and save the changes.

Compact and Repair a Database, Back Up a Database

Now that you are satisfied that any changes made to a form or query carry through to the table, you are ready to compact, repair, and back up your file.

a. Compact and repair your database.

b. Create a backup copy of your database, accept the default file name, and save it.

c. Exit Access.

d. Submit based on your instructor's directions.

Applying Filters, Printing, and File Management

GENERAL CASE

The *a01b1bank* file contains data from a small bank. Open the *a01b1bank* file, and then save the database as **a01b1bank_LastnameFirstname**. Check the table relationships by opening the Relationships window, and then close the window. Use the skills from this chapter to perform several tasks. Open the Customer table, and sort the data in ascending order by LastName. Open the Branch table and make yourself the manager of the Western branch. Remove the Field1 field from the table design. Close the Branch table. Open the Branch Customers query and filter it to show only the accounts at the Campus branch with balances less than $2,000.00. Display the filtered query results in print preview. Close and save the query. Compact, repair, and back up your database, and then exit Access.

Filtering a Report

RESEARCH CASE

Open the *a01b2nwind* file, and then save the database as **a01b2nwind_LastnameFirstname**. Open the Employees table and replace *YourName* with your first and last names. Before you can filter the Revenue report, you need to update the criterion in the underlying query to match the dates in the database. Right-click the Revenue query in the Navigation Pane, and then click Design View in the shortcut list. Scroll to the right until you see *Between #1/1/2007# And #3/31/2007#* in the OrderDate criteria row. Change the criterion to **Between #1/1/2012# And #3/31/2012#**. Save and close the query. Open the Revenue report. Use the tools that you have learned in this chapter to filter the report for only your sales of Confections. Close the report. Compact, repair, and back up your database, and then exit Access.

Coffee Revenue Queries

DISASTER RECOVERY

A coworker called you into his office, explained that he was having difficulty with Access 2010, and asked you to look at his work. Open the *a01b3recover* file, and then save the database as **a01b3recover_LastnameFirstname**. Open the Relationships window, review the table relationships, and then close the window. Your coworker explains that the 2012 Product Introduction Report report is incorrect. It shows that Sazcick is the sales representative for Coulter Office Supplies and the Little, Joiner, & Jones customers, when in fact they are your customers. First, replace *YourName* in the Sales Reps table. Next, find the source of the error and correct it. Preview the corrected report. Compact, repair, and back up your database, and then exit Access.

2 RELATIONAL DATABASES AND QUERIES

Designing Databases and Extracting Data

CASE STUDY | Bank Auditor Uncovers Mishandled Funds

Watch the
Set-up
Video
for this
Case Study!

During a year-end review, a bank auditor uncovers mishandled funds at Commonwealth Federal Bank, in Wilmington, Delaware. In order to analyze the data in more detail, the auditor asks you to create an Access database so he can enter the compromised accounts, the associated customers, and the involved employees. Once the new database is created and all the data is entered, you will help the auditor answer questions by creating and running queries.

As you begin, you realize that some of the data is contained in Excel spreadsheets. After discussing this with the auditor, you decide importing this data directly into the new database would be best. Importing from Excel into Access is commonplace and should work well. Importing will also help avoid errors that are associated with data entry. Once the Excel data has been imported, you will use queries to determine which data does not belong in the database. Unaffected records will be deleted.

This chapter introduces the Bank database case study to present the basic principles of table and query design. You will use tables and forms to input data, and you will create queries and reports to extract information from the database in a useful and organized way. The value of that information depends entirely on the quality of the underlying data—the tables.

OBJECTIVES AFTER YOU READ THIS CHAPTER, YOU WILL BE ABLE TO:

1. Design data **p.580**

2. Create tables **p.584**

3. Understand table relationships **p.596**

4. Share data with Excel **p.598**

5. Establish table relationships **p.602**

6. Create a single-table query **p.613**

7. Specify criteria for different data types **p.616**

8. Copy and run a query **p.619**

9. Use the Query Wizard **p.619**

10. Create a multi-table query **p.625**

11. Modify a multi-table query **p.626**

Table Design, Properties, Views, and Wizards

Good database design begins with the tables. Tables provide the framework for all of the activities you perform in a database. If the framework is poorly designed, the rest of the database will be poorly designed as well. Whether you are experienced in designing tables or just learning how, the process should not be done haphazardly. You should follow a systematic approach when creating tables for a database. This process will take practice; however, over time you will begin to see the patterns and eventually see the similarities among all databases.

In this section, you will learn the principles of table design and the other essential guidelines used when creating tables. After developing and testing the table design on paper, you will implement that design in Access. The first step is to list all the tables you need for the database and then list all the fields in each table. When you create the tables in Access, you will refine them further by changing the properties of various fields. You will also be introduced to the concept of data validation. You want to make sure the data entered into the database is valid for the field and valid for the organization. Allowing invalid data into the tables will only cause problems later.

Designing Data

> A **table** is a storage location in a database that holds related information. A table consists of records, and each record is made up of a number of fields.

Most likely you have a bank account and you know that your bank or credit union maintains data about you. Your bank has your name, address, phone number, and Social Security number. It also knows what accounts you have (checking, savings, money market), if you have a credit card with that bank, and what its balance is. Additionally, your bank keeps information about its branches. If you think about the data your bank maintains, you could make a list of the categories of data needed to store that information. These categories for the bank—customers, accounts, branches—become the tables in the bank's database. Previously, we defined a table as a collection of records. In this chapter, we expand on the definition—a *table* is a storage location in a database that holds related information. A table consists of records, and each record is made up of a number of fields. A bank's customer list is an example of a table: It contains a record for each bank customer, and each customer's details are contained in fields such as first and last name, street, city, state, and zip code. Figure 2.1 shows a customer table and two other tables found in a sample bank database.

During the design process, it will help if you consider the output required for the database. Looking at the output will help determine the tables and fields needed to produce that output. Think of the specific fields you need in each table; list the fields under the correct table and assign each field a data type (such as text, number, or date) as well as its size (length) or format. The order of the fields within the table and the specific field names are not significant. What is important is that the tables contain all necessary fields so that the system can produce the required information.

Customers Table
o CustomerID
o FirstName
o LastName
o Street
o City
o State
o Zip
o Phone

Accounts Table
o AccountID
o CustomerID
o BranchID
o OpenDate

Branch Table
o BranchID
o Manager
o Location
o StartDate

FIGURE 2.1 Tables and Fields in a Sample Bank Database ➤

Figure 2.1 shows the tables and fields needed in a sample bank database. After the tables have been identified, add the necessary fields using these six guidelines:

1. Include the necessary data.
2. Design for now and the future.
3. Store data in its smallest parts.
4. Add calculated fields to a table.
5. Design to accommodate date arithmetic.
6. Link tables using common fields.

Include the Necessary Data

...ask yourself what information will be expected from the database, and then determine the data required to produce that information.

A good way to determine what data is necessary in the tables is to create a rough draft of the reports you will need and then to design tables that contain the fields necessary to create those reports. In other words, ask yourself what information will be expected from the system, and then determine the data required to produce that information. Consider, for example, the tables and fields in Figure 2.1. Is there required information that could not be generated from those tables?

- You can determine which branch a customer uses.
- You cannot, however, generate the monthly bank statement. In order to generate a customer bank statement (showing all deposits and withdrawals for the month), you would need to add an additional table—the Account Activity table.
- You can determine who manages a particular branch and which accounts are located there.
- You can determine how long a customer has banked with the branch because the date he or she opened the account is stored in the Accounts table.

If you discover a missing field, you can insert a row anywhere in the appropriate table and add the missing field. The databases found in a real bank are more complex, with more tables and more fields; however, the concepts illustrated here apply to both our sample bank database and to real bank databases.

Design for Now and the Future

As the data requirements of an organization evolve over time, the information systems that hold the data must change as well. When designing a database, try to anticipate the future needs of the system, and then build in the flexibility to satisfy those demands. For example, when you add a text field, make sure that the number of characters allocated is sufficient to accommodate future expansion. On the other hand, if you include all the possible fields that anyone might ever need, you could drive up the cost of the database. Each additional field can increase the cost of the database, since it will require additional employee time to enter and maintain the data. The additional fields will also require more storage space, which you will need to calculate, especially when working with larger databases. Good database design must balance the data collection needs of the company with the cost associated with collection and storage.

> Good database design must balance the data collection needs of the company with the cost associated with collection and storage.

Suppose you are designing a database for a college. You would need to store each student's name, address, and phone number. You will need to store multiple phone numbers for most students—a cell phone number, a work number, and an emergency number. As a database designer, you will need to design the tables to accommodate multiple entries for similar data.

Store Data in Its Smallest Parts

The table design in Figure 2.1 divides a customer's name into two fields (Firstname and Lastname) to reference each field individually. You might think it easier to use a single field consisting of both the first and last name, but that approach is too limiting. Consider a list of customers stored as a single field:

- Sue Grater
- Rick Grater
- Nancy Gallagher
- Harry Weigner
- Barb Shank
- Pete Shank

The first problem in this approach is the lack of flexibility: You could not easily create a salutation for a letter of the form *Dear Sue* or *Dear Ms. Gallagher* because the first and last names are not accessible individually.

A second difficulty is that the list of customers cannot be easily displayed in alphabetical order by last name because the last name begins in the middle of the field. The names could easily be alphabetized by first name because the first name is at the beginning of the field. However, the most common way to sort names is by the last name, which can be done more efficiently if the last name is stored as a separate field.

Think of how an address might be used. The city, state, and postal code should always be stored as separate fields. Any type of mass mailing requires you to sort on postal codes to take advantage of bulk mail. Other applications may require you to select records from a particular state or postal code, which can be done more efficiently if you store the data as separate fields. Often database users enter the postal code, and the database automatically retrieves the city and state information. You may need to direct a mailing only to a neighborhood or to a single street. The guideline is simple: Store data in its smallest parts.

Add Calculated Fields to a Table

A **calculated field** produces a value from an expression or function that references one or more existing fields.

A *calculated field* produces a value from an expression or function that references one or more existing fields. Access 2010 enables you to store calculated fields in a table using the calculated data type. An example of a calculated field can be found in the bank database. Suppose the bank pays its customers 1.0% interest on the principal each month. A calculated field, such as Monthly Interest, could store the expression Principal x .01. The interest amount would then appear on the customer's monthly bank statement.

Previous versions of Access did not have the option of adding a calculated field to a table. Calculated fields were not available because they do not adhere to conventional database design principles. Database design principles avoid storing data that can be derived from other data. The Monthly Interest field mentioned above can be derived from the product of Principal x .01; therefore, you would not need to store the Monthly Interest value.

The new calculated field* can be very useful in certain circumstances, like a Monthly Interest field. Storing calculated data in a table enables you to add the data easily to queries, forms, and reports without the trouble of an additional calculation. Storing calculated data in a table may increase the size of the database slightly, but the benefits may outweigh this drawback. In the chapters ahead, you will examine calculations and calculated fields in greater detail. You will learn when to add calculated fields to a table and when to avoid them.

Design to Accommodate Date Arithmetic

Calculated fields are frequently created with numeric data, as the Monthly Interest field example above illustrates. You can also create calculated fields using date/time data. If you want to store the length of time a customer has been a customer, you would first create a field to hold the start date for each customer. Next, you would create a calculated field that contains an expression that subtracts the start date from today's date. The resulting calculation would store the number of days each customer has been a customer. Divide the results by 365 to convert days to years.

This same concept applies to bank accounts; a bank is likely to store the Open Date for each account in the Accounts table, as shown in Figure 2.1. Using this date, you can subtract the open date from today's date and calculate the number of days the account has been open. (Again, divide the results by 365 to convert to years.) If you open the Accounts table at least one day later, the results of the calculated field will be different.

A person's age is another example of a calculated field using date arithmetic—date of birth is subtracted from today's date and the results are divided by 365. It might seem easier to store a person's age rather than the birth date to avoid the calculation. But that would be a mistake because age changes over time and would need to be updated each time age changes. Storing the date of birth is much better since the data remains *constant*. You can use *date arithmetic* to subtract one date from another to find out the number of days, months, or years that have lapsed between them. You can also add or subtract a constant from a date.

A **constant** is an unchanging value, like a birth date.

Date arithmetic is the process of subtracting one date from another, or adding or subtracting a constant from a date.

Link Tables Using Common Fields

As you create the tables and fields for the database, keep in mind that the tables will be joined in relationships using common fields. Draw a line between common fields to indicate the joins, as shown in Figure 2.2. These join lines will be created in Access when you learn to create table relationships later in the chapter. For now, you should name the common fields the same and make sure they have the same data type. For example, CustomerID in the Customers table will join to the CustomerID field in the Accounts table. CustomerID must have the same data type (in this case number/long integer) in both tables; otherwise, the join line will not be allowed.

Avoid *data redundancy*, which is the unnecessary storing of duplicate data in two or more tables. You should avoid duplicate information in multiple tables in a database, because errors may result. Suppose the customer address data was stored in both the

Data redundancy is the unnecessary storing of duplicate data in two or more tables.

*If you add a calculated field to a table in Access 2010, you will not be able to open the table using Access 2007.

Customers and Accounts tables. If a customer moved to a new address, a possible outcome would be that the address would be updated in only one of the two tables. The result would be unreliable data. Depending on which table served as the source for the output, either the new or the old address might be given to the person requesting the information. Storing the address in only one table is more reliable.

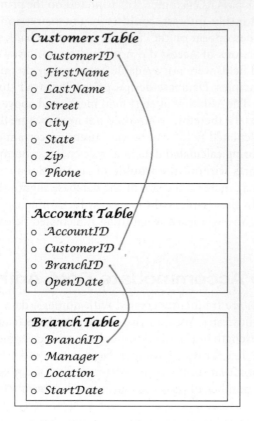

FIGURE 2.2 Create Relationships Using Common Fields ➤

Creating Tables

Before you can begin creating your tables, you must first create a new blank database and save it to a specific storage location. If you are creating tables in an existing database, you open the existing database and then create new tables or modify existing ones.

Access provides several ways to create a table. You can create a table by creating the fields in Design view (as shown in Figure 2.3) or by entering table data into a new row in Datasheet view, or you can import data from another database or application such as Excel. Regardless of how a table is first created, you can always modify it later to include a new field or to change an existing field.

Design view of Customers table

Field Names

Data Types

Field Properties

FIGURE 2.3 Creating a Table in Design View ➤

CamelCase notation uses no spaces in multi-word field names, but uses uppercase letters to distinguish the first letter of each new word.

The **data type** determines the type of data that can be entered and the operations that can be performed on that data.

The **AutoNumber** data type is a number that automatically increments each time a record is added.

Each field in a table has a field name to identify the data that it holds. The field name should be descriptive of the data and can be up to 64 characters in length, including letters, numbers, and spaces. Database developers use *CamelCase notation* for field names, object names, and filenames. Instead of spaces in multi-word field names, use uppercase letters to distinguish the first letter of each new word, for example, ProductCost or LastName. It is best to avoid spaces in field names, since spaces can cause problems when creating the other objects based on tables—such as queries, forms, and reports.

Every field also has a *data type* that determines the type of data that can be entered and the operations that can be performed on that data. Access recognizes 10 data types.

Establish a Primary Key

As you learned earlier, the primary key is the field (or combination of fields) that uniquely identifies each record in a table. Access does not require that each table have a primary key. However, good database design usually includes a primary key in each table. You should select unique and infrequently changing data for the primary key. For example, a complete address (street, city, state, and postal code) may be unique but would not make a good primary key because it is subject to change when someone moves.

You probably would not use a person's name as the primary key, because several people could have the same name. A customer's account number, on the other hand, is unique and is a frequent choice for the primary key, as in the Customers table in this chapter. The primary key can be easily identified in many tables; for example, a PartNumber in a parts table, the ISBN in the book database of a bookstore, or a Student ID that uniquely identifies a student. When no primary key occurs naturally, you can create a primary key field with the AutoNumber data type. The *AutoNumber* data type is a number that automatically increments each time a record is added.

REFERENCE Data Types and Uses

Data Type	Description	Example
Number	Contains a value that can be used in a calculation, such as the number of credits a course is worth. The contents are restricted to numbers, a decimal point, and a plus or minus sign.	Credits
Text	Stores alphanumeric data, such as a customer's name or address. It can contain alphabetic characters, numbers, and/or special characters (i.e., an apostrophe in O'Malley). Social Security Numbers, telephone numbers, and postal codes should be designated as text fields since they are not used in calculations. A text field can hold up to 255 characters.	Last name
Memo	Stores up to 65,536 characters; used to hold descriptive data (several sentences or paragraphs).	Notes or comments
Date/Time	Holds dates or times and enables the values to be used in date or time arithmetic.	10/31/2012
Currency	Used for fields that contain monetary values.	Account balance
Yes/No	Assumes one of two values, such as Yes or No, True or False, or On or Off (also known as a Boolean).	Dean's list
OLE	Contains an object created by another application. OLE objects include spreadsheets, pictures, sounds, or graphics.	One photo
AutoNumber	A special data type used to assign the next consecutive number each time you add a record. The value of an AutoNumber field is unique for each record in the file.	Customer ID
Hyperlink	Stores a Web address (URL) or the path to a folder or file. Hyperlink fields can be clicked to retrieve a Web page or to launch a file stored locally.	http://www.keithmast.com
Attachment	Used to store multiple images, spreadsheet files, Word documents, and other types of supported files.	An Excel workbook; a photo
Calculated	The results of an expression that references one or more existing fields.	[IntRate] + 0.25

In Figure 2.4, the book's ISBN is the natural primary key for the book table because no two book titles can have the same ISBN. This field uniquely identifies the records in the table. Figure 2.5 depicts the Speakers table, where no unique field can be identified from the data. When this happens, you can add the SpeakerID field with an AutoNumber data type. Access will automatically number each speaker record sequentially with a unique ID as each record is added.

AuthorCode	Title	ISBN	PubID	PublDate	Price	StockAmt
15	Chasing the Dime	0-316-15391-5	LBC	2002	$51.75	400
13	Blackhills Farm	0-275-41199-7	KN	2002	$18.87	528
13	Blood and Gold	0-679-45449-7	KN	2001	$18.87	640
11	Reaching for Glory	0-684-80408-5	SS	2001	$24.00	480
14	From a Buick 8	0-743-21137-5	SS	2002	$16.80	368
15	City of Bones	0-316-15405-9	LBC	2002	$20.76	394
16	Follow the Stars Home	0-553-58102-3	BB	2000	$6.99	496
14	Hearts in Atlantis	0-684-85351-5	SS	1999	$28.00	528
12	Personality Injuries	0-742095692-X	FSG	1999	$27.00	403
15	Darkness More than Midnight	0-316-15407-5	LBC	2001	$20.76	432
13	Interview with the Vampire	0-394-49821-6	KN	1976	$19.57	371
16	True Blue	0-553-38398-0	BB	2002	$7.50	492

ISBN provides a unique identifier

FIGURE 2.4 Books Table with a Natural Primary Key ➤

SpeakerID (AutoNumber data type) is the primary key

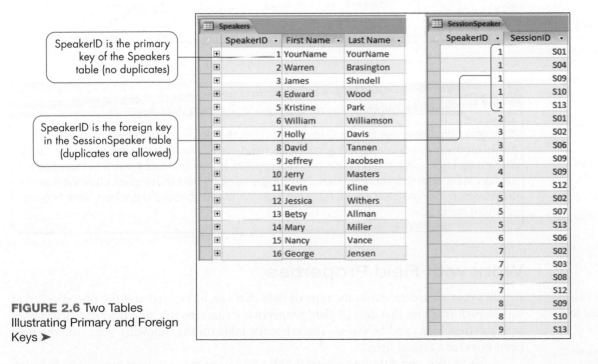

SpeakerID	First Name	Last Name	Address	City	Sta	Zip Co	Phone Number	Email
1	YourName	YourName	10000 SW 59 Court	Miami	FL	33146	(305) 777-8888	cahsley@um.edu
2	Warren	Brasington	9470 SW 25 Street	Philadelphia	PA	19104	(215) 888-7654	wbrasington@up.edu
3	James	Shindell	14088 Malaga Avenue	Miami	FL	33146	(305) 773-4343	jshindell@um.edu
4	Edward	Wood	400 Roderigo Avenue	Gainesville	FL	32611	(352) 555-5555	ewood@uf.edu
5	Kristine	Park	9290 NW 59 Steet	Athens	GA	30602	(706) 777-1111	kpark@ug.edu
6	William	Williamson	108 Los Pinos Place	Tuscaloosa	AL	35487	(205) 888-4554	wwilliamson@ua.edu
7	Holly	Davis	8009 Riviera Drive	Gainesville	FL	32611	(352) 388-7676	hdavis.uf.edu
8	David	Tannen	50 Main Street	Philadelphia	PA	19104	(215) 777-2211	dtannen@up.edu
9	Jeffrey	Jacobsen	490 Bell Drive	Athens	GA	30602	(706) 388-9999	jjacobsen@ug.edu
10	Jerry	Masters	2000 Main Highway	Miami	FL	33146	(305) 777-8998	jmasters@um.edy
11	Kevin	Kline	2980 SW 89 Street	Gainesville	FL	32611	(352) 877-8900	kkline@uf.edu
12	Jessica	Withers	110 Center Highway	Athens	GA	30602	(706) 893-8872	jwithers@ug.edu
13	Betsy	Allman	2987 SW 14 Avenue	Philadelphia	PA	19104	(215) 558-7748	ballman@up.edu
14	Mary	Miller	1008 West Marine Road	Miami	FL	33146	(305) 877-4993	mmiller@um.edu
15	Nancy	Vance	1878 W. 6 Street	Gainesville	FL	32611	(352) 885-4330	nvance@uf.edu
16	George	Jensen	42-15 81 Street	Elmhurst	NY	11373	(718) 555-6666	gjensen@school.edu
(New)								

Next record will be assigned SpeakerID 17

FIGURE 2.5 Speakers Table with an AutoNumber Primary Key ➤

Explore Foreign Key

A foreign key, as defined earlier, is a field in one table that is also the primary key of another table. The CustomerID is the primary key in the Customers table. It serves to uniquely identify each customer. It also appears as a foreign key in a related table. For example, the Accounts table contains the CustomerID field to establish which customer owns the account. A CustomerID can appear only once in the Customers table, but it may appear multiple times in the Accounts table (when viewed in Datasheet view) since one customer may own multiple accounts (checking, money market, home equity).

If you were asked to create an Access database for the speakers at a national conference, you would create a database with the tables Speakers and SessionSpeaker. You would add a primary key field to the Speakers table (SpeakerID) along with the speaker's First Name and Last Name; you would add two fields to the SessionSpeaker table (SpeakerID and SessionID). The SpeakerID in the SessionSpeaker table enables you to join the two tables in a relationship. The SpeakerID field in the SessionSpeaker table is an example of a foreign key. Figure 2.6 shows portions of the Speakers and SessionSpeaker tables.

SpeakerID is the primary key of the Speakers table (no duplicates)

SpeakerID is the foreign key in the SessionSpeaker table (duplicates are allowed)

Speakers

SpeakerID	First Name	Last Name
1	YourName	YourName
2	Warren	Brasington
3	James	Shindell
4	Edward	Wood
5	Kristine	Park
6	William	Williamson
7	Holly	Davis
8	David	Tannen
9	Jeffrey	Jacobsen
10	Jerry	Masters
11	Kevin	Kline
12	Jessica	Withers
13	Betsy	Allman
14	Mary	Miller
15	Nancy	Vance
16	George	Jensen

SessionSpeaker

SpeakerID	SessionID
1	S01
1	S04
1	S09
1	S10
1	S13
2	S01
3	S02
3	S06
3	S09
4	S09
4	S12
5	S02
5	S07
5	S13
6	S06
7	S02
7	S03
7	S08
7	S12
8	S09
8	S10
9	S13

FIGURE 2.6 Two Tables Illustrating Primary and Foreign Keys ➤

Use Table Views

As defined earlier, users can work in Datasheet view to add, edit, and delete records. The Datasheet view of an Access table resembles an Excel spreadsheet and displays data in a grid format—rows represent records, and columns represent fields. Datasheet view indicates the current record using a gold border; you can select a record by clicking the record selector on the left side of each record, as shown in Figure 2.7. Use the new blank record (marked with an asterisk) at the end of the table to add a new record. Design view is used to create and modify the table structure by adding and editing fields and by setting the field properties. PivotTable view and PivotChart view will be covered in a later chapter.

Datasheet view is used to add, edit, and delete records

Highlighting indicates the current record

Click the record selector (to select a record)

Asterisk indicates the next blank record

FIGURE 2.7 Customers Table in Datasheet View ➤

TIP Toggle Between Datasheet and Design Views

To toggle from Datasheet view to Design view, click the Home tab, and then click View in the Views group. If you click the view arrow by accident, select the view you want from the menu. Or you can right-click on the table tab that appears above the datasheet and then choose Design View from the shortcut menu. To toggle back to Datasheet view, click View in the Views group, or right-click on the table tab again, and then choose Datasheet View from the shortcut menu.

Work with Field Properties

A **field property** is a characteristic of a field that determines how the field looks and behaves.

A **text data type** can store either text or numerical characters.

A field's data type determines the type of data that can be entered and the operations that can be performed on that data. A **field property** is a characteristic of a field that determines how the field looks and behaves. (The reference table on the following page lists the field properties for a typical field.)

A field with a **text data type** can store either text or numerical characters. A text field can hold up to 255 characters; however, you can limit the characters by reducing the field size

A **number data type** can store only numerical data.

A **caption property** is used to create a more readable label that appears in the top row in Datasheet view and in forms and reports.

A **validation rule** prevents invalid data from being entered into the field.

property. For example, you would limit the State field to only two characters since all state abbreviations are two letters. A field with a ***number data type*** can store only numerical data. Set the Format field property to Integer to display the field contents as integers from –32768 to 32768. Set the Format field property to Long Integer for larger values.

You can use the ***caption property*** to create a more readable label that appears in the top row in Datasheet view and in forms and reports. For example, a field named ProductCostPerUnit could have the caption *Per Unit Product Cost*. The caption displays at the top of a table or query column in Datasheet view and when the field is used in a report or form. You must use the actual field name, ProductCostPerUnit, in any calculation.

Set the validation rule property to restrict data entry in a field to ensure the correct type of data is entered or that the data does not violate other enforced properties. The ***validation rule*** checks the data entered when the user exits the field. If the data entered violates the validation rule, an error message appears and prevents the invalid data from being entered into the field.

The field properties are set to default values according to the data type, but you can modify them if necessary. The property types are defined in the following Reference table.

In Hands-On Exercise 1, you will create a new database and enter data into a table. Then you will switch to the table's Design view to add additional fields and modify selected field properties of various fields within the table.

REFERENCE   Access Table Property Types and Descriptions

Property Type	Description
Field Size	Determines the maximum characters of a text field or the format of a number field.
Format	Changes the way a field is displayed or printed, but does not affect the stored value.
Input Mask	Simplifies data entry by providing literal characters that are typed for every entry, such as hyphens in a Social Security Number or slashes in a date. It also imposes data validation by ensuring that data entered conforms to the mask.
Caption	This enables an alternate name to be displayed other than the field name; alternate names appear in datasheets, forms, and reports.
Default Value	This option automatically enters a predetermined value for a field each time a new record is added to the table. For example, if most of your customers live in Los Angeles, you might consider setting the default value for the City to Los Angeles to save data entry time.
Validation Rule	Requires the data entered to conform to the specified rule.
Validation Text	Specifies the error message that is displayed when the validation rule is violated.
Required	Indicates that a value for this field must be entered.
Allow Zero Length	Enables text or memo strings of zero length.
Indexed	Increases the efficiency of a search on the designated field.
Expression	Used for calculated fields only. Enter the expression you want Access to evaluate and store.
Result Type	Used for calculated fields only. Enter the format for the calculated field results.

1 Table Design, Properties, Views, and Wizards

Assisting the bank auditor at Commonwealth Federal Bank as he investigates the mishandled funds will be a great opportunity for you to showcase your Access skills. Be sure to check your work each step of the way since your work will come under substantial scrutiny. Do a good job with this Access project and more opportunities might come your way, along with a promotion.

Skills covered: Create a New Database • Create a Table by Entering Data • Change the Primary Key, Modify Field Properties, and Delete a Field • Modify Table Fields in Design View • Create a New Field in Design View • Switch Between the Table Design and the Table Datasheet Views

---

STEP 1 ▶ **CREATE A NEW DATABASE**

To start a new Access database project, you first need to create a new database. Use the Access interface to create a new file for the mishandled funds database. Refer to Figure 2.8 as you complete Step 1.

FIGURE 2.8 Creating a New Microsoft Office Access Database ▶

a. Start Microsoft Access.

You will see the Backstage view with New selected by default.

b. Click **Blank database** in the Available Templates section of the Backstage view.

c. Type **a02h1bank_LastnameFirstname** into the **File Name box**.

d. Click **Browse**—the yellow folder icon—to find the folder location designated by your instructor, and then click **OK**.

e. Click **Create** to create the new database.

Access will create the new database named *a02h1bank_LastnameFirstname*, and a new table will automatically appear in Datasheet view.

> **TROUBLESHOOTING:** If you have a problem finding your file, use the Windows search tool to locate the file.

STEP 2 ▶ CREATE A TABLE BY ENTERING DATA

Create a new Branch table and enter the branch data as instructed. Only branches with suspicious data will be added. Refer to Figure 2.9 as you complete Step 2.

Save the table as Branch

Type the data directly into the datasheet

ID	Field1	Field2	Field3	Click to Add
1	B10	Mast	Uptown	
2	B20	Esposito	Eastern	
3	B30	Amoako	Western	
4	B40	Singh	Southern	
5	B50	YourLastName	Campus	
*	(New)			

FIGURE 2.9 Enter Data into the Branch Table in Datasheet View ▶

a. Type **B10** in the second column, and then click **Click to Add**.

   The column heading becomes Field1 and Click to Add now appears as the third column.

b. Type **Mast** in the third column, press **Tab**, and then type **Uptown** in the fourth column.

   You can advance to the next field by pressing Tab or move to the previous field by pressing Shift+Tab.

c. Press **Tab** three times. Type **B20**, press **Tab**, type **Esposito**, press **Tab**, and then type **Eastern**.

d. Enter the additional data for the new table as shown in Figure 2.9. Replace *YourLastName* with your last name.

e. Click **Save** on the Quick Access Toolbar. Type **Branch** in the **Save As dialog box**, and then click **OK**.

   Entering data provides an easy way to create the table initially. You can now modify the table in Design view as described in the next several steps.

STEP 3 ▶ CHANGE THE PRIMARY KEY, MODIFY FIELD PROPERTIES, AND DELETE A FIELD

It is common to modify tables even after data has been entered; however, pay attention to the messages from Access after you make a design change. In this example, you will be modifying the Branch table field names to match the auditor's requirements. Refer to Figure 2.10 as you complete Step 3.

BranchID is the primary key

Rename field names in Design view

Design view for the Branch table

Change Field Size property here

Change the Indexed property here

Field Name	Data Type	Description
BranchID	Text	
Manager	Text	
Location	Text	

Field Properties

General | Lookup

Field Size	255
Format	
Input Mask	
Caption	
Default Value	
Validation Rule	
Validation Text	
Required	No
Allow Zero Length	Yes
Indexed	Yes (No Duplicates)
Unicode Compression	Yes
IME Mode	No Control
IME Sentence Mode	None
Smart Tags	

A field name can be up to 64 characters long, including spaces. Press F1 for help on field names.

FIGURE 2.10 Branch Table in Design View ➤

a. Click **View** in the Views group to switch to the Design view of the Branch table.

The fields are named ID, Field1, Field2, and Field3, because they are the default names given to the fields when you create the table in Datasheet view. These field names are not descriptive of the data, so you need to change Field1, Field2, and Field3 to BranchID, Manager, and Location, respectively. You will also delete the ID field.

b. Click the **ID field** to select it. Click **Delete Rows** in the Tools group. Click **Yes** to both warning messages.

Access responds with a warning that you are about to permanently delete a field and a second warning that the field is the primary key. You delete the field since you will set a different field as the primary key.

c. Double-click the **Field1 field name** to select it, if necessary, and then type **BranchID**. Replace *Field2* with **Manager** and *Field3* with **Location**.

d. Click the **BranchID field**.

The cell field name now has an orange border as shown in Figure 2.10.

e. Click **Primary Key** in the Tools group.

You set BranchID as the primary key. The Indexed property in the *Field Properties* section at the bottom of the design window displays *Yes (No Duplicates)*.

f. Click **Save** to save the table.

TIP Shortcut Menu

You can right-click a row selector to display a shortcut menu to copy a field, set the primary key, and insert or delete rows. Use the shortcut menu to make these specific changes to the design of a table.

You need to modify the table design further to comply with the bank auditor's specifications. Be aware of messages from Access that indicate you may lose data. Refer to Figure 2.11 as you complete Step 4.

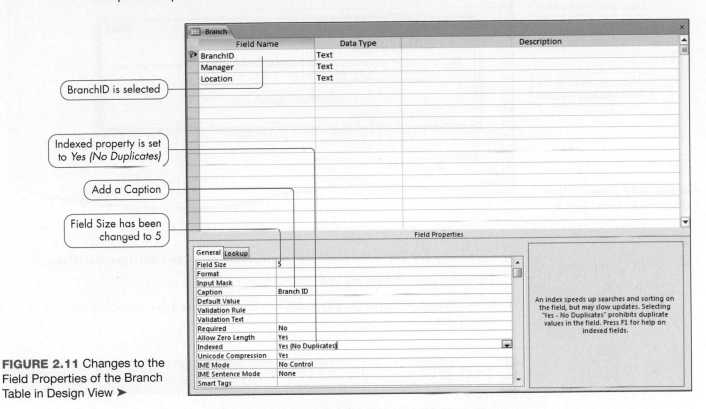

BranchID is selected

Indexed property is set to *Yes (No Duplicates)*

Add a Caption

Field Size has been changed to 5

FIGURE 2.11 Changes to the Field Properties of the Branch Table in Design View ➤

a. Click the **BranchID field name** in the top section of the design window; modify the BranchID field properties in the bottom of the design window:

- Click in the **Field Size property**, and then change *255* to **5**.
- Click in the **Caption property**, and then type **Branch ID**. Make sure *Branch* and *ID* have a space between them.

  A caption provides a more descriptive field name. It will appear as the column heading in Datasheet view.

- Check the Indexed property; confirm it is *Yes (No Duplicates)*.

b. Click the **Manager field name** at the top of the window; modify the following field properties:

- Change the **Field Size property** from *255* to **30**.
- Click in the **Caption property**, and then type **Manager's Name**.

c. Click the **Location field name**, and then modify the following field properties:

- Change the **Field Size property** from *255* to **30**.
- Click in the **Caption property**, and then type **Branch Location**.

You notify the auditor that a date field is missing in your new table. Modify the table and add the new field. The data can be entered at a later time. Refer to Figure 2.12 as you complete Step 5.

Date/Time data type

New field added

Description was added

Message indicates the
field size was reduced

FIGURE 2.12 Adding a New
Field to the Branch Table ➤

a. Click in the first blank row below the Location field name, and then type **StartDate**.

You added a new field to the table.

b. Press **Tab** to move to the Data Type column. Click the **Data Type arrow**, and then select
Date/Time.

> **TIP** Keyboard Shortcut for Data Types
>
> You also can type the first letter of the data type such as *d* for Date/Time, *t* for Text, or *n* for
> number. To use the keyboard shortcut, click on the field name, and then press Tab to advance
> to the Data Type column. Next, type the first letter of the data type.

c. Press **Tab** to move to the Description column, and then type **This is the date the manager
started working at this location.**

d. Click in the **Format property**, click the arrow, and then select **Short Date** from the list of
date formats.

e. Click in the **Caption property**, and then type **Manager's Start Date**.

f. Click **Save** on the Quick Access Toolbar to save the changes you made to the
a02h1bank_LastnameFirstname database.

A warning dialog box opens to indicate that "Some data may be lost" since the size of the
BranchID, Manager, and Location field properties were shortened. It asks if you want to
continue anyway. Always read the Access warnings! In this case, you can click Yes to continue.
You changed the size of the BranchID field from 255 to 5 in Step 4a.

g. Click **Yes** in the warning box.

As you work with the auditor, you will need to modify tables in the bank database from time to time. To modify the table, you will need to switch between Design view and Datasheet view. Refer to Figure 2.13 as you complete Step 6.

Right-click the Branch tab and use the shortcut menu to switch views

Start dates were entered for each manager

Pencil indicates the last record has not been saved

Branch ID	Manager's Name	Branch Local	Manager's Sta	Click to Add
B10	Mast	Uptown	12/3/2007	
B20	Esposito	Eastern	6/18/2008	
B30	Amoako	Western	3/13/2006	
B40	Singh	Southern	9/15/2009	
B50	YourLastName	Campus	10/11/2011	

FIGURE 2.13 Start Dates Added to the Branch Table ➤

a. Right-click the **Branch tab** shown in Figure 2.13, and then select **Datasheet View** from the shortcut menu. (To return to the Design view, right-click the tab again, and then select Design View.)

b. Click inside the **Manager's Start Date** in the first record, and then click the **Calendar**. Use the navigation arrows to find and select **December 3, 2007** from the calendar.

You can also enter the dates by typing them directly into the StartDate field.

c. Type directly in each field the Start Date for the rest of the managers as shown in Figure 2.13.

d. Click the **Close button** at the top-right corner of the datasheet, below the Ribbon.

> **TROUBLESHOOTING:** If you accidentally click the Close button on top of the Ribbon, you will exit out of Access completely. To start again, launch Access, click the File tab, click Recent, and then select the first database from the recent documents list.

e. Double-click the **Branch table** in the Navigation Pane to open the table. Check the start dates.

The start dates are still there even though you did not save your work in the previous step. Access saves the data to the hard drive as soon as you move off the current record (or close an object).

f. Click the **File tab**, click **Print**, and then click **Print Preview**.

Occasionally, users will print an Access table. However, database developers usually create reports to print table data.

g. Click **Close Print Preview**. Close the Branch table.

h. Click the **File tab**, and then click **Compact & Repair Database** (the top button).

i. Click the **File tab**, click **Save & Publish**, and then double-click **Back Up Database** in the right column. Accept *a02h1bank_LastnameFirstname_date* as the file name, and then click **Save**.

You created a backup of the database. The original database, *a02h1bank_LastnameFirstname*, remains open.

j. Keep the database onscreen if you plan to continue with Hands-On Exercise 2. If not, close the database and exit Access.

Multiple Table Databases

In Figure 2.1, the sample bank database contains three tables—Customers, Accounts, and Branch. You already created one table, the Branch table, in the previous section using the Datasheet view. The two remaining tables will be created using a different method—importing data from Excel. In this section, you will learn how to import data from Excel, modify tables, create indexes, create relationships between tables, and enforce referential integrity.

Understanding Table Relationships

The benefit of a relationship is to efficiently combine data from related tables.

Relationships between tables are set in the Relationships window. In this window, join lines are created to establish relationships between two tables. As discussed earlier, the benefit of a relationship is to efficiently combine data from related tables for the purpose of creating queries, forms, and reports. For example, the join line between the CustomerID in the Accounts table and the CustomerID in the Customers table (see Figure 2.14) enables you to combine data from the Accounts and the Customers tables.

CustomerID is the primary key in the Customers table

Join lines indicate a relationship between two tables

CustomerID is the foreign key in the Accounts table

FIGURE 2.14 Relationships in the Bank Database ➤

The primary key of a table plays a significant role when setting relationships. You cannot join two tables unless a primary key has been set in the primary table. In our Bank database, the CustomerID has been set as the primary key in the Customers table. Therefore, a relationship can be set between the Customers table and the Accounts table. Similarly, the Branch table can be joined to the Accounts table since BranchID has been set as the primary key in the Branch table.

Relationships between tables will almost always be set using primary and foreign keys.

The other side of the relationship join line is most often the foreign key of the related table. A foreign key is a field in one table that is also the primary key of another table. In the previous example, CustomerID in the Accounts table is a foreign key; BranchID in the Accounts table is a foreign key. Relationships between tables will almost always be set using primary and foreign keys.

Establish Referential Integrity

When you create a relationship in Access, the Edit Relationships dialog box appears, as shown in Figure 2.15. The first check box, Enforce Referential Integrity, should be checked in most cases. When *referential integrity* is enforced, you cannot enter a foreign key value in a related table unless the primary key value exists in the primary table. In the case of the Bank database, a customer's account information (which includes CustomerID) cannot be entered into the Accounts table unless the customer information is first entered into the Customers table. If you attempt to enter an account prior to entering the customer information, an error will appear, as shown in Figure 2.16. When referential integrity is enforced, you cannot delete a record in one table if it has related records in other tables.

> When **referential integrity** is enforced, you cannot enter a foreign key value in a related table unless the primary key value exists in the primary table.

Click Enforce Referential Integrity

FIGURE 2.15 Edit Relationships Dialog Box ➤

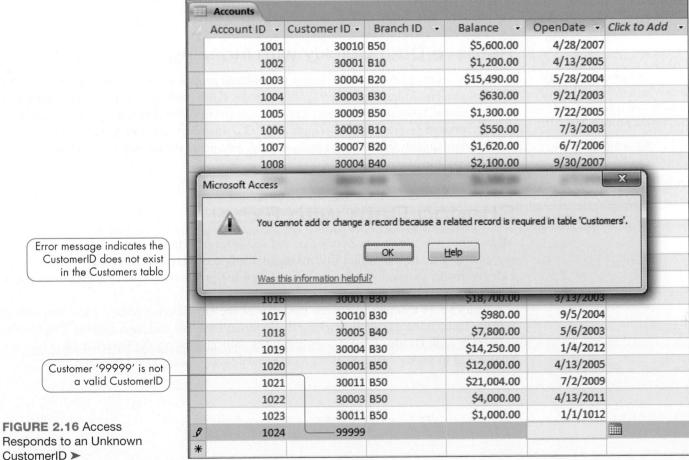

Error message indicates the CustomerID does not exist in the Customers table

Customer '99999' is not a valid CustomerID

FIGURE 2.16 Access Responds to an Unknown CustomerID ➤

Set Cascade Options

Cascade Update Related Fields is an option that directs Access to automatically update all foreign key values in a related table when the primary key value is modified in a primary table.

When you create a relationship in Access and click the Enforce Referential Integrity checkbox, Access gives you two additional options—Cascade Update Related Fields and Cascade Delete Related Records. Check the **Cascade Update Related Fields** option so that when the primary key is modified in a primary table, Access will automatically update all foreign key values in a related table (see Figure 2.17). If a CustomerID is updated for some reason, all the CustomerID references in the Accounts table will automatically be updated.

Cascade Delete Related Records is an option that directs Access to automatically delete all records in related tables that match the primary key that is deleted from a primary table.

Check the **Cascade Delete Related Records** option so that when the primary key is deleted in a primary table, Access will automatically delete all records in related tables that reference the primary key (see Figure 2.17). If one branch of a bank closes and its record is deleted from the Branch table, any account that was not transferred to a different branch would be deleted. Access will give a warning first and enable you to avoid the action. This may be a desired business rule, but it should be set with caution.

FIGURE 2.17 Cascade Options ➤

Retrieve Data Quickly with Indexing

The **indexed property** setting enables quick sorting in primary key order and quick retrieval based on the primary key.

When you set the primary key in Access, the **indexed property** is automatically set to *Yes (No Duplicates)*. The Indexed property setting enables quick sorting in primary key order and quick retrieval based on the primary key. For non-primary key fields, it may be beneficial to set the Indexed property to *Yes (Duplicates OK)*. Again, Access uses indexing to sort and retrieve data quickly based on the indexed field. As a general rule, indexed fields are usually foreign keys and are numeric.

Sharing Data with Excel

Most companies store some type of data in Excel spreadsheets. Often the data stored in those spreadsheets can be more efficiently managed in an Access database. Fortunately, Access provides you with a wizard that guides you through the process of importing data from Excel. Access can also export data to Excel easily.

Figures 2.18 through 2.24 show the steps of the *Get External Data - Excel Spreadsheet* feature. Launch the feature by clicking the External Data tab and then clicking Excel in the Import & Link Group. Table 2.1 describes the four groups on the External Data tab. See Figure 2.18 to see the first step of the *Get External Data - Excel Spreadsheet* feature.

TABLE 2.1	Options on the External Data Tab
Group	**When Used**
Import & Link	To bring data into an Access database. The data sources include Excel, Access (other Access files), ODBC Database, Text File, XML File, and More.
Export	To send a portion of a database to other applications. You might use this to create a Mail Merge letter and envelopes in Word. You could create an Excel file for a coworker who is not using Access, or you could share your data over the Internet via a SharePoint List.
Collect Data	You could create an e-mail mail merge to send e-mails to your clients and then use Access to manage the clients' responses.
Web Linked Lists	Use these commands to interact with SharePoint lists on the Internet. If an Internet connection is unavailable, you can work offline and synchronize with SharePoint later.

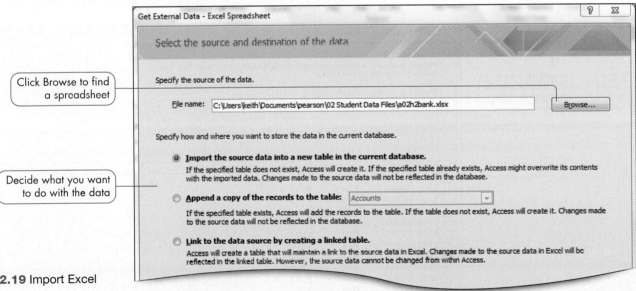

FIGURE 2.18 External Data Tab ➤

Figure 2.19 shows the *Get External Data - Excel Spreadsheet* dialog box. This step enables you to locate the Excel file you want to import by clicking Browse. It asks you to choose among three options for the incoming data: Place it in a new table, append the data to an existing table, or create a link to the Excel source.

FIGURE 2.19 Import Excel Data ➤

After you select an Excel workbook and accept the default option, import the source data into a new table in the current database, and then click OK. The Import Spreadsheet Wizard dialog box launches and displays a list of the worksheets in the specified workbook. The Customers worksheet is selected; click the Accounts worksheet, which will be imported first (see Figure 2.20). The bottom of the Import Spreadsheet Wizard dialog box displays a preview of the data stored in the specified worksheet.

Choose the worksheet to import

Preview of the worksheet data

Click Next to continue

FIGURE 2.20 Show Available Worksheets and Preview Data ➤

Although a well-designed spreadsheet may include descriptive column headings, not all spreadsheets are ready to import. You may have to revise the spreadsheet before importing it. The second window of the Import Spreadsheet Wizard dialog box contains a check box that enables you to convert the first row of column headings to field names in Access (see Figure 2.21). If a column heading row exists in the spreadsheet, check the box. If no column headings exist, leave the check box unchecked, and the data will import using Field1, Field2, Field3, etc.

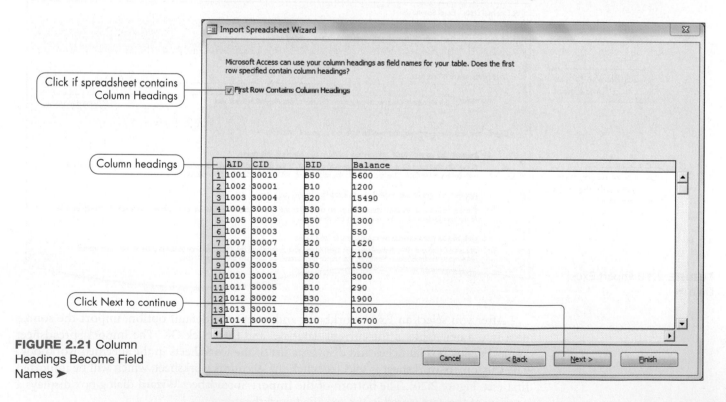

Click if spreadsheet contains Column Headings

Column headings

Click Next to continue

FIGURE 2.21 Column Headings Become Field Names ➤

The third window of the Import Spreadsheet Wizard dialog box enables you to specify field options (see Figure 2.22). The AID field is shown in this figure. Because it will become this table's primary key, you need to set the Indexed Property to *Yes (No Duplicates)*.

To modify the field options of the other fields, click the Field Name column heading, and then make the changes. Not all Access table properties are supported by the wizard. You will need to open the table in Design view after importing it to make additional field property changes.

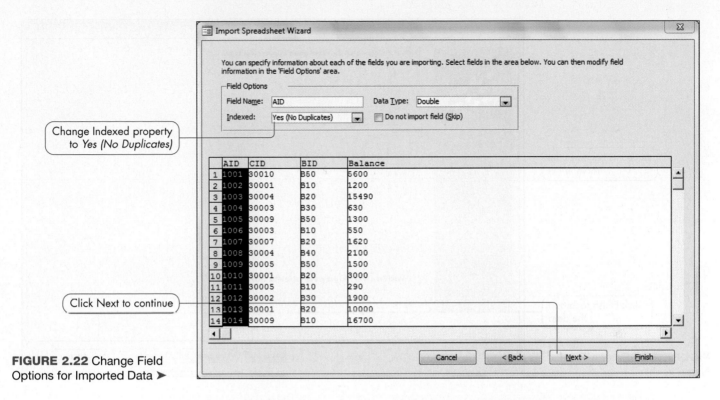

FIGURE 2.22 Change Field Options for Imported Data ➤

The fourth window of the Import Spreadsheet Wizard dialog box enables you to choose a primary key before the import takes place (see Figure 2.23). If the option *Let Access add primary key* is selected, Access will generate an AutoNumber field and designate it as the primary key. Otherwise, you can designate a field to be the primary key. In the import described in the figure, the Excel data has a unique identifier (AID) that will become the table's primary key.

FIGURE 2.23 Set the Primary Key ➤

Use the final window of the Import Spreadsheet Wizard to name the Access table. If the worksheet in the Excel workbook was named, Access uses the worksheet name as the table name (see Figure 2.24).

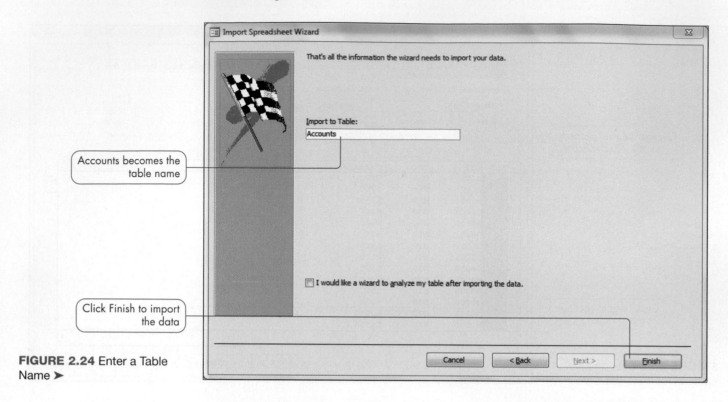

Accounts becomes the table name

Click Finish to import the data

FIGURE 2.24 Enter a Table Name ➤

Finally, the Wizard will ask if you wish to save the import steps. If the same worksheet is imported from Excel to Access on a recurring basis, you could save the parameters and use them again. To save the import steps such as the indexing option and any new field names, click Saved Imports in the Import group. Saving the import steps will help you import the data the next time it is needed.

Establishing Table Relationships

You should store like data items together in the same table. The customer data is stored in the Customers table. The Branch table stores data about the bank's branches, management, and location. The Accounts table stores data about account ownership and balances. You learned earlier that relationships enable you to combine data from related tables for the purpose of creating queries, forms, and reports. Access provides three different relationships for joining your data: one-to-one, one-to-many, and many-to-many. The most common type by far is the one-to-many relationship. A *one-to-many relationship* is established when the primary key value in the primary table can match many of the foreign key values in the related table. For example, a bank customer will be entered into the Customers table once and only once. The primary key value, which is also the customer's CustomerID number, might be 1585. That same customer could set up a checking, savings, and money market account. With each account, the CustomerID (1585) is required and therefore will occur three times in the Accounts table. The value appears once in the Customers table and three times in the Accounts table. Therefore, the relationship between Customers and Accounts would be described as one-to-many.

Table 2.2 lists and describes all three types of relationships you can create between Access tables.

A **one-to-many relationship** is established when the primary key value in the primary table can match many of the foreign key values in the related table.

TABLE 2.2   Relationship Types

Relationship Name	Definition
One-to-Many	This relationship is between a primary key in the first table and a foreign key in the second table. The first table must have only one occurrence of each value. For example, each customer must have a unique identification number in the Customers table, or each employee must have a unique EmployeeID in the Employee table. The foreign key field in the second table may have repeating values. For example, one customer may have many different account numbers, or one employee can perform many services.
One-to-One	Two different tables use the same primary key. Exactly one record exists in the second table for each record in the first table. Sometimes security reasons require a table to be split into two related tables. For example, anyone in the company can look in the Employee table and find the employee's office number, department assignment, or telephone extension. However, only a few people need to have access to the employee's salary, Social Security Number, performance review, or marital status. Both tables use the same unique identifier to identify each employee.
Many-to-Many	This is an artificially constructed relationship giving many matching records in each direction between tables. It requires construction of a third table called a junction table. For example, a database might have a table for employees and one for projects. Several employees might be assigned to one project, but one employee might also be assigned to many different projects. When Access connects to databases using Oracle or other software, you find this relationship type.

Establish a One-to-Many Relationship

Click the Database Tools tab, and then click Relationships in the Relationships group; the Relationships window opens (as shown in Figure 2.25). If this were an established database, this window would already contain tables and join lines indicating the relationships that were established in the database.

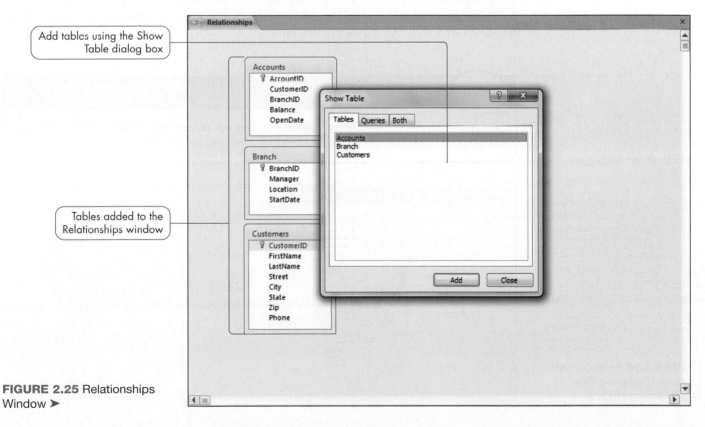

FIGURE 2.25 Relationships Window ➤

The first time you open the Relationships window, you will not see any established relationships; you must first use the Show Table dialog box to add the required tables to the Relationships window. Select the tables you want to use to set relationships, and then add them to the Relationships window by clicking Add (as shown in Figure 2.25).

> **TIP** Navigating Between the Relationships Window and a Table's Design
>
> When you right-click on a table's title bar in the Relationships window, the shortcut menu offers you a chance to open the table in Design view. This is a convenient feature because if you want to link **one** table to another table, the joined fields must have the same data type, and a table may contain a field with the wrong data type. This shortcut enables you to check the fields and revise them if necessary.

Where necessary, expand the table windows to display the complete list of field names shown in the table.

Establish the relationships by dragging the common field name from the primary table onto the common field name in the related table. (The common field name does not have to be an exact match, but the data type and field size must be the same.) When you release the mouse, the Edit Relationships dialog box opens (look back at Figure 2.15). Click Enforce Referential Integrity, and then click Create; Access checks the table data to ensure that the rules you are attempting to establish can be met. For example, in the bank database, if you attempt to enforce referential integrity between the Branch table and the Accounts table, Access will verify that one BranchID value exists in the Branch table for each BranchID value in the Accounts table. If one BranchID value (e.g., B80) in the Accounts table does not exist in the Branch table, Access cannot establish the relationship with referential integrity enforced. The data must be corrected prior to checking enforce referential integrity.

Figure 2.26 shows the Relationships window for the Bank database and all the relationships created using referential integrity. The join line between the CustomerID field in the Customers table and the CustomerID field in the Accounts table indicates that a one-to-many relationship has been set. You can rearrange the tables by dragging the tables by the title bar. You can switch the positions of the Branch and Accounts tables in the Relationships window without changing the relationship itself.

> **TIP** Editing a Relationship
>
> If the relationship has already been established and you need to edit it, right-click the join line. You can also right-click the join line to delete a relationship.

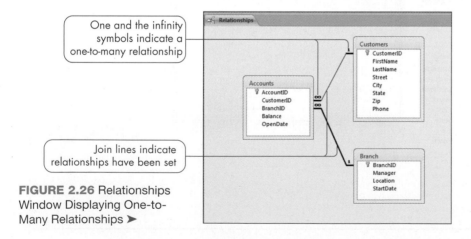

One and the infinity symbols indicate a one-to-many relationship

Join lines indicate relationships have been set

FIGURE 2.26 Relationships Window Displaying One-to-Many Relationships ➤

In the following Hands-On Exercise, you will create two additional tables by importing data from Excel spreadsheets into the Bank database. You will establish and modify field properties. Then you will connect the newly imported data to the Branch table by establishing relationships between the tables.

2 Multiple Table Databases

You created a new Bank database, and you created a new Branch table. Now you are ready to import Commonwealth Federal's customer and account data from Excel spreadsheets. Even though you believe the Excel data is formatted correctly, you decided to open the Excel spreadsheets before you import them into Access. Once you are satisfied the data is structured properly, you can begin the import process.

Skills covered: Import Excel Data into an Access Table • Import Additional Excel Data • Modify an Imported Table's Design • Add Data to an Imported Table • Establish Table Relationships • Test Referential Integrity

---

STEP 1 ▶ IMPORT EXCEL DATA INTO AN ACCESS TABLE

You and the auditor have discovered several of Commonwealth's Excel spreadsheets that contain customer data. These files need to be analyzed, so you decide to import the Excel data into Access. Refer to Figure 2.27 as well as Figures 2.19 through 2.24 as you complete Step 1.

Excel data imported into Access

FIGURE 2.27 Imported Accounts Table ▶

a. Open *a02h1bank_LastnameFirstname* if you closed it at the end of Hands-On Exercise 1. Click the **File tab**, click **Save Database As**, and then type **a02h2bank_LastnameFirstname**, changing *h1* to *h2*. Click **Save**.

b. Click the Enable Content button below the Ribbon to indicate you trust the contents of the database.

> **TROUBLESHOOTING:** Throughout the remainder of this chapter and textbook, click the Enable Content button whenever you are working with student files.

c. Click the **External Data tab**, and click **Excel** in the Import & Link group to launch the *Get External Data - Excel Spreadsheet* feature. Select the **Import the source data into a new table in the current database option**, if necessary, as shown in Figure 2.19.

d. Click **Browse**, and then go to the student data folder. Select the *a02h2bank* workbook. Click **Open**, and then click **OK** to open the Import Spreadsheet Wizard.

The top of the first window shows all of the worksheets in the workbook. This particular workbook contains only two worksheets: Customers and Accounts. The Customers worksheet is active, and a list of the data contained in the Customers worksheet displays in the Wizard.

e. Click **Accounts** (see Figure 2.20), and then click **Next**.

f. Ensure that the *First Row Contains Column Headings* check box is checked to tell Access that column headings exist in the Excel file (see Figure 2.21).

The field names, AID, CID, BID, and Balance, will import from Excel along with the data stored in the rows in the worksheet. The field names will be modified later in Access.

g. Click **Next**.

The AID (AccountID) will become the primary key in this table. It needs to be a unique identifier, so we must change the properties to no duplicates.

h. Ensure that *AID* is displayed in the Field Name box in Field Options. Then click the **Indexed arrow**, and then select **Yes (No Duplicates)**, as shown in Figure 2.22. Click **Next**.

i. Click the **Choose my own primary key option** (see Figure 2.23). Make sure that the *AID* field is selected. Click **Next**.

The final screen of the Import Spreadsheet Wizard asks you to name your table. The name of the Excel worksheet was Accounts, and Access defaults to the worksheet name. It is an acceptable name (see Figure 2.24).

j. Click **Finish** to accept the Accounts table name.

A dialog box opens asking if you wish to save the steps of this import to use again. If this were sales data that was collected in Excel and updated to the database on a weekly basis, saving the import steps would save time. You do not need to save this example.

k. Click the **Close button**.

The new table displays in the Navigation Pane and resides in the Bank database.

l. Open the imported Accounts table in Datasheet view, and then compare it to Figure 2.27. Close the table.

STEP 2 ▶ **IMPORT ADDITIONAL EXCEL DATA**

The first spreadsheet that you imported contained account information related to the mishandled funds. The auditor has asked you to import a second spreadsheet that contains customer account information. Follow the same process as you did in Step 1 as you answer each Import Wizard question. Refer to Figure 2.28 as well as Figures 2.19 through 2.24 as you complete Step 2.

FIGURE 2.28 Imported Customers Table ▶

a. Click the **External Data tab**, and then click **Excel** in the Import & Link group to launch the *Get External Data - Excel Spreadsheet* feature. Select the **Import the source data into a new table in the current database option**, if necessary.

b. Click **Browse**, and then go to the student data folder. Select the *a02h2bank* workbook. Click **Open**, and then click **OK** to open the Import Spreadsheet Wizard.

   The Customers worksheet is active; you will import this worksheet.

c. Click **Next**.

d. Ensure that the *First Row Contains Column Headings* check box is checked to tell Access that column headings exist in the Excel file. Click **Next**.

   The CID will become the primary key in this table. It needs to be a unique identifier, so you change the properties to no duplicates.

e. Ensure that *CID* is displayed in the Field Name box in Field Options. Click the **Indexed arrow**, and then select **Yes (No Duplicates)**. Click **Next**.

f. Click the **Choose my own primary key option**. Make sure that the *CID* field is selected. Click **Next**.

   Access defaults to the table name Customers.

g. Click **Finish** to accept the Customers table name.

h. Click **Close** on the Save Import Steps dialog box.

   The Navigation Pane contains three tables: Accounts, Branch, and Customers.

i. Open the imported Customers table in Datasheet view, and then compare it to Figure 2.28. Close the table.

STEP 3 ▶ MODIFY AN IMPORTED TABLE'S DESIGN

The Excel worksheets became Access tables when you imported them into the Bank database. However, in order to answer all the auditor's questions (using queries), you need to modify the tables so that each field has the correct data type and field size. Refer to Figure 2.29 as you complete Step 3.

FIGURE 2.29 Change the Balance Field to Currency ➤

a. Double-click the **Accounts table** in the Navigation Pane to open it in Datasheet view.

b. Click **View** in the Views group on the Home tab to switch to Design view.

c. Change the AID field name to **AccountID**.

d. Change the Field Size property to **Long Integer** in the Field Properties at the bottom of the design window.

Long Integer ensures that there will be enough numbers as the number of accounts grow over time. Importing data from Excel saves typing, but modifications will usually be required.

e. Type **Account ID** in the **Caption property box** for the AccountID field. The caption contains a space between *Account* and *ID*.

f. Change the CID field name to **CustomerID**.

g. Change the Field Size property to **Long Integer** in the Field Properties at the bottom of the design window.

You can select the Field Size option using the arrow, or you can type the first letter of the option you want. For example, type *l* for Long Integer or *s* for Single. Make sure the current option is completely selected before you type the letter.

h. Type **Customer ID** in the **Caption property box** for the CustomerID field. The caption contains a space between *Customer* and *ID*.

i. Click the **BID field**. Change the BID field name to **BranchID**.

j. Type **5** in the **Field Size property box** in the Field Properties.

k. Type **Branch ID** in the **Caption property box** for the Branch ID field.

l. Change the Data Type of the Balance field from *Number* to **Currency**.

m. Type a new field name, **OpenDate**, under the Balance field name. Assign data type **Date/Time**, and then add the **Short Date format** in the Field Properties.

n. Click **View** in the Views group to switch to Datasheet View. Read the messages, and then click **Yes** twice.

In this case, it is OK to click Yes because the size of three fields was shortened. The new OpenDate field will store the date that each account was opened.

o. Add the OpenDate values as shown below:

Account ID	OpenDate
1001	4/28/2007
1002	4/13/2005
1003	5/28/2004
1004	9/21/2003
1005	7/22/2005
1006	7/3/2003
1007	6/7/2006
1008	9/30/2007
1009	2/7/2006
1010	3/18/2010
1011	10/16/2012
1012	3/14/2007
1013	5/15/2009
1014	9/17/2007
1015	4/4/2003
1016	3/13/2003
1017	9/5/2004
1018	5/6/2003
1019	1/4/2012
1020	4/13/2005

p. Right-click the **Customers table** in the Navigation Pane, and then select **Design View** from the shortcut menu. Change the CID field name to **CustomerID**. Change the Field Size property of the CustomerID field to **Long Integer**, and then add a caption, **Customer ID**. Take note of the intentional space between *Customer* and *ID*.

The Accounts table and the Customers table will be joined using the CustomerID field. Both fields must have the same data type.

q. Change the Field Size property to **20** for the FirstName, LastName, Street, and City fields. Change the Field Size for State to **2**.

r. Change the data type for Zip and Phone to **Text**. Change the Field size property to **15** for both fields. Remove the @ symbol from the Format property where it exists for all fields in the Customers table.

s. Click the **Phone field name**, and then click **Input Mask** in Field Properties. Click **Build** on the right side to launch the Input Mask Wizard. Click **Yes** to save the table, and then click **Yes** to the *some data may be lost* warning. Click **Finish** to apply the default phone number Input Mask.

The phone number input mask will enable users to enter 6105551212 and Access to display (610) 555-1212.

t. Click **Save** to save the design changes to the Customers table. Read the Warning Box, and then click **Yes**.

STEP 4 ▶ ADD DATA TO AN IMPORTED TABLE

Now that you have created the Access tables, add data as directed by the auditor. You may also need to update and delete records if you and the auditor decide the information is no longer needed. Refer to Figure 2.30 as you complete Step 4.

Enter yourself as a new customer

FIGURE 2.30 Customers Table Showing Your Information ➤

a. Click **View** in the Views group to display the Customers table in Datasheet view.

The asterisk at the bottom of the table data in the row selector area is the indicator of a place to enter a new record.

b. Click the **Customer ID field** in the record after *30010*. Type **30011**. Fill in the rest of the data using your information as the customer. You may use a fictitious address and phone number.

c. Close the Customers table. Click the **Accounts table tab** if necessary.

d. Locate the new row indicator—the * in the row selector—and click in the **Account ID column**. Type **1021**. Type **30011** as the **Customer ID** and **B50** as the **Branch ID**. Type **21004** for the Balance field value. Type **7/2/2009** for the OpenDate.

e. Close the Accounts table; keep the database open.

STEP 5 ▶ ESTABLISH TABLE RELATIONSHIPS

The tables for the bank investigation have been designed. Now, you will need to establish connections between the tables. Look at the primary and foreign keys as a guide. Refer to Figure 2.31 as you complete Step 5.

One-to-many relationships

Edit Relationships dialog box

FIGURE 2.31 Relationships Between Tables ➤

a. Click the **Database Tools tab**, and then click **Relationships** in the Relationships group.

The Relationships window opens and the Show Table dialog box appears.

> **TROUBLESHOOTING:** If the Show Table dialog box does not open, click Show Table in the Relationships group on the Relationships Tools Design tab.

b. Double-click each of the three tables displayed in the Show Table dialog box to add them to the Relationships window. (Alternatively, click a table, and then click Add.) Click **Close** in the Show Table dialog box.

> **TROUBLESHOOTING:** If you have a duplicate table, click the title bar of the duplicated table, and then press Delete.

c. Resize the Customers table box so all the fields are visible. Arrange the tables as shown in Figure 2.31.

d. Drag the **BranchID field** in the Branch table onto the BranchID field in the Accounts table. The Edit Relationships dialog box opens. Click the **Enforce Referential Integrity** and **Cascade Update Related Fields check boxes**. Click **Create**.

A black line displays, joining the two tables. It has a 1 on the end near the Branch table and an infinity symbol on the end next to the Accounts table. You have established a one-to-many relationship between the Branch and Accounts tables.

e. Drag the **CustomerID field** in the Customers table onto the CustomerID field in the Accounts table. The Edit Relationships dialog box opens. Click the **Enforce Referential Integrity** and **Cascade Update Related Fields check boxes**. Click **Create**.

You have established a one-to-many relationship between the Customers and Accounts tables. A customer will have only a single CustomerID number. The same customer may have many different accounts: Savings, Checking, CDs, etc.

> **TROUBLESHOOTING:** If you get an error message when you click Create, verify the data types of the joined fields are the same. To check the data types from the Relationships window, right-click the title bar of a table, and then select Table Design from the shortcut menu. Modify the data type and field size of the join fields if necessary.

f. Click **Save** on the Quick Access Toolbar to save the changes to the Relationships. Close the Relationships window.

STEP 6 ▸ TEST REFERENTIAL INTEGRITY

The design of the bank database must be 100% correct; otherwise, data entry may be compromised. Even though you are confident that the table relationships are correct, you decide to test them by entering some invalid data. If the relationships are working, the invalid data will be rejected by Access. Refer to Figure 2.32 as you complete Step 6.

Access warns you that B60 is invalid

B60 is not a valid branch

FIGURE 2.32 Referential Integrity Works to Protect Data ➤

a. Double-click the **Accounts table** to open it in Datasheet view.

b. Add a new record, pressing **Tab** after each field: Account ID: **1022**, Customer ID: **30003**, Branch ID: **B60**, Balance: **4000**, OpenDate: **4/13/2011**.

   A warning message is telling you that a related record in the Branch table is required since the Accounts table and the Branch table are connected by a relationship with enforce referential integrity checked.

c. Click **OK**. Double-click the **Branch table** in the Navigation Pane, and then examine the data in the BranchID field. Notice the Branch table has no B60 record. Close the Branch table.

d. Replace *B60* with **B50** in the new Accounts record, and then press **Tab** three times. As soon as the focus moves to the next record, the pencil symbol disappears and your data is saved.

   You successfully identified a BranchID that Access recognizes. Because referential integrity between the Accounts and Branch tables has been enforced, Access looks at each data entry item in a foreign key and matches it to a corresponding value in the table where it is the primary key. In Step 6b, you attempted to enter a nonexistent BranchID and were not allowed to make that error. In Step 6d, you entered a valid BranchID. Access examined the index for the BranchID in the Branch table and found a corresponding value for B50.

e. Close the Accounts table. Reopen the Accounts table; you will find that the record you just entered for 1022 has been saved. Close the table.

f. Close all open tables, if necessary.

g. Click the **File tab**, and then click **Compact & Repair Database**.

h. Click the **File tab**, click **Save & Publish**, and then double-click **Back Up Database**. Accept *a02h2bank_LastnameFirstname_date* as the file name, and then click **Save**.

   You just created a backup of the database. The *a02h2bank_LastnameFirstname* database remains open.

i. Keep the database onscreen if you plan to continue with Hands-On Exercise 3. If not, close the database and exit Access.

Single-Table Queries

A **query** enables you to ask questions about the data stored in a database.

If you wanted to see which customers currently have an account with a balance over $5,000, you could find the answer by creating an Access query. A *query* enables you to ask questions about the data stored in a database. Since data is stored in tables in a database, you always begin a query by asking, "Which table holds the data I want?" For the question about account balances over $5,000, you would reference the Accounts table. In some cases, the data may be held in two or more tables. Multi-table queries will be covered later; for now, you will limit your study of queries to only one table.

If you want to invite customers in a certain zip code to the Grand Opening of a new branch, you could create a query based on the Customers table.

Query Design view enables you to create queries; the Design view is divided into two parts—the top portion displays the tables, and the bottom portion (known as the query design grid) displays the fields and the criteria.

You use the *Query Design view* to create queries; the Design view is divided into two parts—the top portion displays the tables, and the bottom portion (known as the query design grid) displays the fields and the criteria.

Using the Query Design view, you select only the fields you want arranged in the order that you want them. The design grid also enables you to sort the records based on one or more fields. You can also create calculated fields to display data based on expressions that use the fields in the underlying table. For example, you could calculate the monthly interest earned on each bank account.

In this section, you will use the Query Wizard and Query Design to create queries that display only data that you select.

Creating a Single-Table Query

The **Simple Query Wizard** provides dialog boxes to guide you through the query design process.

You can create a single-table query in two ways—by using the Simple Query Wizard or by using the Query Design tool in the Queries group. Like all of the Microsoft wizards, the *Simple Query Wizard* provides dialog boxes to guide you through the query design process. The wizard is helpful for users who are not experienced with Access or with queries. More advanced users will usually use the Query Design tool to create queries. This method provides the most flexibility when creating queries (but without the prompting of the wizard). You can add criteria to a query while in the Query Design view, as compared to the wizard where you cannot add criteria while the wizard is running. After the query is created, you can switch to Design view and add criteria manually.

After you design a query (using either method), you can display the results of the query by switching to Datasheet view. A query's datasheet looks and acts like a table's datasheet, except that it is usually a subset of the records found in the entire table. The subset only shows the records that match the criteria that were added in the query design. The subset will usually contain different sorting of the records than the sorting in the underlying table. Datasheet view allows you to enter a new record, modify an existing record, or delete a record. Any changes made in Datasheet view are reflected in the underlying table.

> **TIP** Caution: Changes Made to Query Results Overwrite Table Data
>
> Be aware that query results display the actual records that are stored in the underlying table(s). On the one hand, being able to correct an error immediately while it is displayed in query results is an advantage. You save time by not having to close the query, open the table, find the error, fix it, and run the query again. However, you should use caution when editing records in query results since you might not expect to change the table data.

Create a Single-Table Select Query

As stated above, more experienced users create queries using the Query Design tool. To begin click the Create tab, and then click Query Design in the Queries group. The Show Table dialog box appears automatically. Select the table that you need in your query, and then click Add to add the table to the top section of the query design, as shown in Figure 2.33. After the table has been added, close the Show Table dialog box and begin dragging the fields from the table to the query design grid. The grid holds the fields as well as the criteria (for filtering records) and the sorting options. Figure 2.34 shows the Design view of a sample query with four fields, with criteria set for one field, and sorting set on another field. After the query design is finished, click Run in the Results group to show the results in Datasheet view, as shown in Figure 2.35.

A **select query** displays only the records that match the criteria entered in Design view.

By default, when you create a query, you create a select query, which is the most common type of query. A *select query* displays only the records that match the criteria entered in Design view. A select query does not change the data. Other types of queries, known as action queries, can update, append, or delete records when they are run. Examples include Update Query, Append Query, and Make Table Query.

> **TIP** Examine the Records
>
> An experienced Access user always examines the records returned in the query results. Verify that the records in the query results match the criteria that you specified in Design view. As you add additional criteria, the number of records returned will usually decrease.

FIGURE 2.33 Query Design View ➤

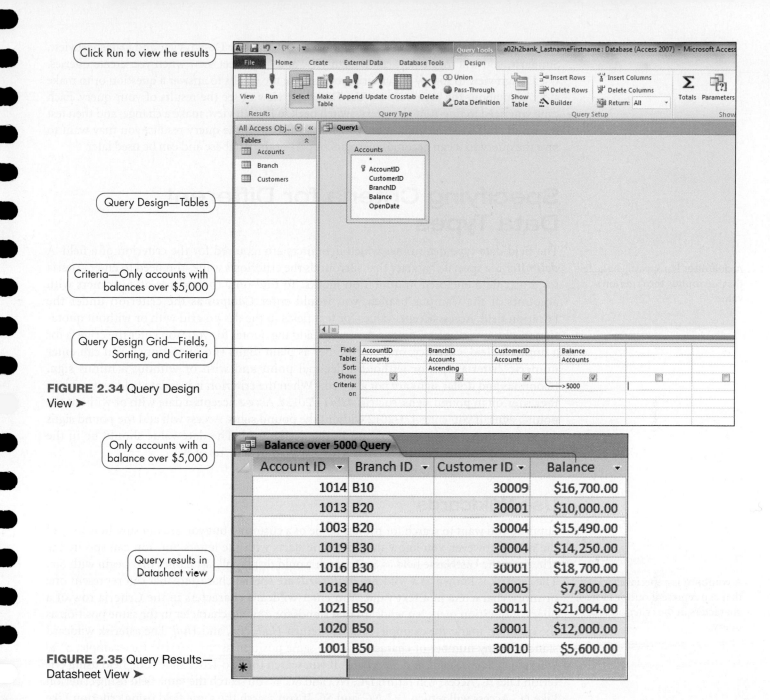

Click Run to view the results

Query Design—Tables

Criteria—Only accounts with balances over $5,000

Query Design Grid—Fields, Sorting, and Criteria

FIGURE 2.34 Query Design View ➤

Only accounts with a balance over $5,000

Query results in Datasheet view

FIGURE 2.35 Query Results—Datasheet View ➤

The **Field row** in the Query Design view displays the field name.

The **Table row** in the Query Design view displays the data source.

The **Sort row** in the Query Design view enables you to sort in ascending or descending order.

The **Show row** in the Query Design view controls whether the field will be displayed in the query results.

The **Criteria row** in the Query Design view determines which records will be selected.

Use Query Design View

The Query Design view consists of two parts. The top portion contains tables with their respective field names. If a query contains more than one table, the join lines between tables will be displayed as they were created in the Relationships window.

The bottom portion (known as the query design grid) contains columns and rows. Each field in the query has its own column and contains multiple rows. The rows permit you to control the query results.

- The *Field row* in the Query Design view displays the field name.
- The *Table row* in the Query Design view displays the data source.
- The *Sort row* in the Query Design view enables you to sort in ascending or descending order.
- The *Show row* in the Query Design view controls whether the field will be displayed in the query results.
- The *Criteria row* in the Query Design view is used to set the rules that determine which records will be selected, such as customers with accounts greater than $5,000.

When you developed the tables, you toggled between the Design view and Datasheet view. Similarly, you will toggle between Design view and Datasheet view when you create queries. Use Design view to specify the criteria; you can use the results to answer a question or to make a decision about the organization. Use Datasheet view to see the results of your query. Each time you need to fine-tune the query, switch back to Design view, make a change, and then test the results in Datasheet view. After you are satisfied with the query results, you may want to save the query so it can become a permanent part of the database and can be used later.

Specifying Criteria for Different Data Types

A **delimiter** is a special character that surrounds the criterion's value.

The field data type determines which delimiters are required for the criterion of a field. A **delimiter** is a special character that surrounds the criterion's value. You need to enter criteria for a text field enclosed in quotation marks. To find only the records of customers with accounts at the Campus branch, you would enter *Campus* as the criterion under the Location field. Access accepts values for text fields in the design grid with or without quotation marks; if you enter *Campus*, Access will add the quotes for you. You enter the criteria for a numeric field, currency, or AutoNumber as plain digits (no quotations). You can enter numeric criteria with or without a decimal point and with or without a minus sign. (Commas and dollar signs are not allowed.) When the criterion is in a date field, you enclose the criterion in pound signs, such as *#10/14/2012#*. Access accepts a date with or without the pound signs; if you enter 1/1/2012 without the pound signs, Access will add the pound signs when you move to another column in the design grid. The date value should be in the mm/dd/yyyy format. You enter criteria for a Yes/No field as *Yes* or *No*.

Use Wildcards

A **wildcard** is a special character that can represent one or more characters in the criterion of a query.

Suppose you want to search for the last name of a customer but you are not sure how to spell the name; however, you know that his name starts with the letters Sm. You can specify the criteria in the LastName field as *Sm**, which would display all last names that begin with *Sm*. The asterisk is known as a wildcard. **Wildcards** are special characters that can represent one or more characters in a text value. You enter wildcard characters in the Criteria row of a query. A question mark is a wildcard that stands for a single character in the same position as the question mark; for example, *H?ll* will return *Hall*, *Hill*, and *Hull*. The asterisk wildcard stands for any number of characters in the same position as the asterisk; for example, *S*nd* will return *Sand*, *Stand*, and *StoryLand*. If you search the two-letter state code field using criterion Like *?C*, Access will return *DC*, *NC*, and *SC*. If you search the same field using criterion Like **C*, Access will return *DC*, *NC*, and *SC*. If you search the same field using criterion Like *C**, Access will return *CA*, *CO*, and *CT*.

Use Comparison Operators in Queries

A **comparison operator**, such as equal (=), not equal (<>), greater than (>), less than (<), greater than or equal to (>=), and less than or equal to (<=), can be used in the criteria of a query.

A **comparison operator**, such as equal (=), not equal (<>), greater than (>), less than (<), greater than or equal to (>=), and less than or equal to (<=), can be used in the criteria of a query. Comparison operators enable you to limit the query results to only those records that meet the criteria. For example, if you only want to see accounts that have a balance greater than $5,000, you would type >5000 in the criteria row. Table 2.3 shows more comparison operator examples as well as other sample expressions.

TABLE 2.3 Sample Query Criteria

Expression	Example
>10	For a Price field, items with a price over $10.00.
<10	For a Price field, items with a price under $10.00.
>=10	For a Price field, items with a price of at least $10.00.
<=10	For a Price field, items with a price of $10.00 or less.
=10	For a Price field, items with a price of exactly $10.00.
<>10	For a Price field, items with a price not equal to $10.00.
#2/2/2012#	For a field with a Date/Time data type, such as a ShippedDate field, orders shipped on February 2, 2012.
"Harry"	For a Text field, find the name Harry.
Date()	For an OrderDate field, orders for today's date.
Between #1/1/2012# and #3/31/2012#	For a specified interval between a start and end date, including the start and end dates.

Work with Null and Zero-Length Strings

Sometimes finding what is missing is an important part of making a decision. For example, if you need to know which orders have been completed but not shipped, you would ask for the orders with a missing ShipDate. Are there missing phone numbers or addresses for some of your customers? Ask for customers with a missing PhoneNumber. The term that Access uses for a blank field is *null*. Table 2.4 gives two illustrations of when to use the null criterion in a query.

Null is the term Access uses to describe a blank field.

TABLE 2.4 Establishing Null Criteria Expressions

Expression	Example
Is Null	For an Employee field in the Customers table when the customer has not been assigned a sales representative.
Is Not Null	For the ShipDate field; a value inserted indicates the order was shipped to the customer.

Understand Query Sort Order

The **query sort order** determines the order of records in the query's Datasheet view.

The *query sort order* determines the order of records in a query's Datasheet view. You can change the order of records by specifying the sort order in the Design view. The sort order is determined from left to right. The order of columns should be considered when first creating the query. For example, a query sorted by Lastname and then by Firstname must have those two fields in the correct order in the design grid. Change the order of the query fields in the design grid to change the sort order of the query results. To change the order of fields, select the column you want to move by clicking the column selector. Release the mouse, then click again and drag the selected field to its new location. To insert additional columns in the design grid, first select a column, and then click Insert Columns in the Query Setup group. The inserted column will insert to the left of the selected column.

Establish AND, OR, and NOT Criteria

Recall the earlier question, "Which customers currently have an account with a balance over $5,000?" This question was answered by creating a query with a single criterion, as shown in Figure 2.34. At times, questions are more specific and require queries with multiple criteria. For example, you may need to know "Which customers from the Eastern branch currently have an account with a balance over $5,000?" To answer this question, you need to specify

The **AND logical operator** returns only records that meet all criteria.

The **OR logical operator** returns records meeting any of the specified criteria.

The **NOT logical operator** returns all records except the specified criteria.

criteria in multiple fields. When the criteria are in the same row of the query design grid, Access interprets the instructions using the **AND logical operator**. This means that the query results will display only records that match *all* criteria. When the criteria are positioned in different rows of the design grid, Access interprets the instructions using the **OR logical operator**. The query results will display records that match any of the specified criteria. The **NOT logical operator** returns all records except the specified criteria. For example, "Not Eastern" would return all accounts except those opened at the Eastern branch.

Figure 2.36a shows a query with an AND logical operator. It will return all of the B20 branch accounts with balances over $5,000. (Both conditions must be met for the record to be included.) Figure 2.36b shows a query with an OR logical operator. It will return all of the B20 branch accounts regardless of balance plus all accounts at any branch with a balance over $5,000. (One condition must be met for a record to be included.) Figure 2.36c shows a query that uses the NOT logical operator. It will return all of the accounts—excluding the B20 branch—with a balance over $5,000. Figure 2.36d shows a query that combines AND and OR logical operators. The top row will return B20 branch accounts with a balance over $5,000, and the second row will return B30 branch accounts with a balance over $15,000.

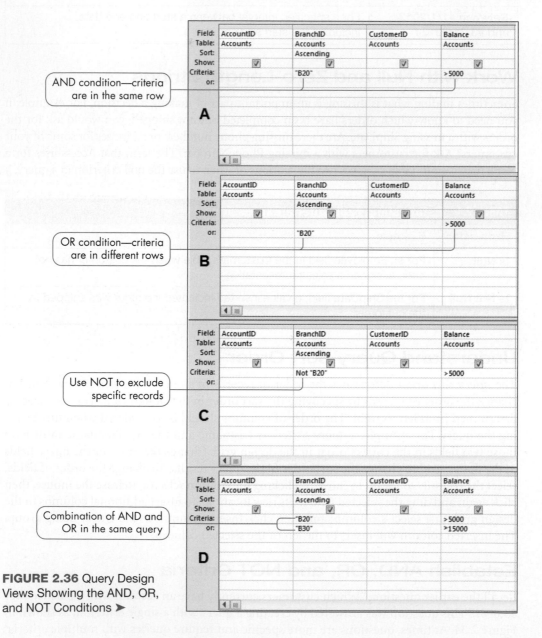

AND condition—criteria are in the same row

OR condition—criteria are in different rows

Use NOT to exclude specific records

Combination of AND and OR in the same query

FIGURE 2.36 Query Design Views Showing the AND, OR, and NOT Conditions ➤

Copying and Running a Query

After you create a query, you may want to create a duplicate copy to use as the basis for creating a similar query. Duplicating a query saves time when you need the same tables and fields but with slightly different criteria.

Several ways exist to run a query. One method is to locate the query in the Navigation Pane, and then double-click it. A similar method is to select the query, and then press Enter. Another way is to click Run in the Results group, when you are in Design view.

Copy a Query

Sometimes you have a one-of-a-kind question about your data. You would create a query to answer this question and then delete the query. However, sometimes you need a series of queries where each query is similar to the first. For example, you need "Sales for This Month" in Houston, in Dallas, and in Chicago. In cases like this, you create a query for the first city and then save the query. Click Save As to save a copy of the query and name it for the second city. Change the criteria to match the second city. Repeat the process for the third city.

Run a Query

The **Run command** (the red exclamation point) is used to produce the query results.

After you create a query and save it, you can run it directly from the Design view. You run a query by clicking ***Run command*** (the red exclamation point) in the Results group. In the sample databases, the queries run quickly. For larger databases, query results may take several minutes to display. When you design queries in larger databases, include all necessary fields and tables, but do not include fields or tables that are not necessary to answer the question. You can also run a query from the Navigation Pane. Locate the query you want to run, and then double-click the query. The results will appear as a tab in the main window. (Note: This method is only recommended for select queries. This method is not recommended for action queries, which will be covered later.)

Using the Query Wizard

You may create a query directly in Design view or by using the Query Wizard. Even if you initiate the query with a wizard, you will need to learn how to modify it in Design view. Often, copying an existing query and making slight modifications to its design is much faster than starting at the beginning with the wizard. You also will need to know how to add additional tables and fields to an existing query when conditions change. To launch the Query Wizard, click the Create tab, and then click Query Wizard in the Queries group (see Figure 2.37).

FIGURE 2.37 Launching the Query Wizard ➤

Select the Simple Query Wizard in the Query Wizard dialog box, as shown in Figure 2.38.

FIGURE 2.38 Select the Simple Query Wizard ➤

In the first step of the Simple Query Wizard dialog box, you specify the tables or queries and fields needed in your query. When you select a table from the Tables/Queries arrow, a list of the table's fields displays in the Available Fields list box. See Figures 2.39 and 2.40.

FIGURE 2.39 Specify Which Tables or Queries to Use ➤

Select the necessary fields, and then add them to the Selected Fields list box using the directional arrows shown in Figure 2.40.

FIGURE 2.40 Specify the Fields for the Query ➤

In the next screen (shown in Figure 2.41), you choose between a detail and a summary query. The detail query shows every field of every record in the result. The summary query enables you to group data and view only summary records. For example, if you were interested in the total funds deposited at each of the bank branches, you would set the query to Summary, click Summary Options, and then click sum on the balance field. Access would then sum the balances of all accounts for each branch.

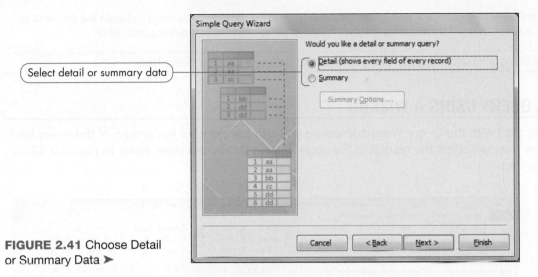

Select detail or summary data

FIGURE 2.41 Choose Detail or Summary Data ➤

The final dialog box of the Simple Query Wizard asks for the name of the query. Assign a descriptive name to your queries so that you know what each does by looking at the query name. See Figure 2.42.

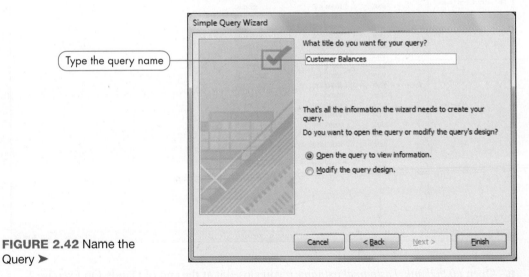

Type the query name

FIGURE 2.42 Name the Query ➤

The next Hands-On Exercise enables you to create and run queries in order to find answers to questions you have about your data. You will use the Query Wizard to create a basic query and then modify the query in Design view by adding an additional field and by adding query criteria.

3 Single-Table Queries

The tables and table relationships have been created, and some data has been entered. Now, you need to begin the process of analyzing the bank data for the auditor. You will do so using queries. You decide to begin with the Accounts table.

Skills covered: Create a Query Using a Wizard • Specify Query Criteria and Sorting • Change Query Data

---

STEP 1 ▶ CREATE A QUERY USING A WIZARD

You decide to start with the Query Wizard, knowing you can always alter the design of the query later in Design view. You will show the results to the auditor using Datasheet view. Refer to Figure 2.43 as you complete Step 1.

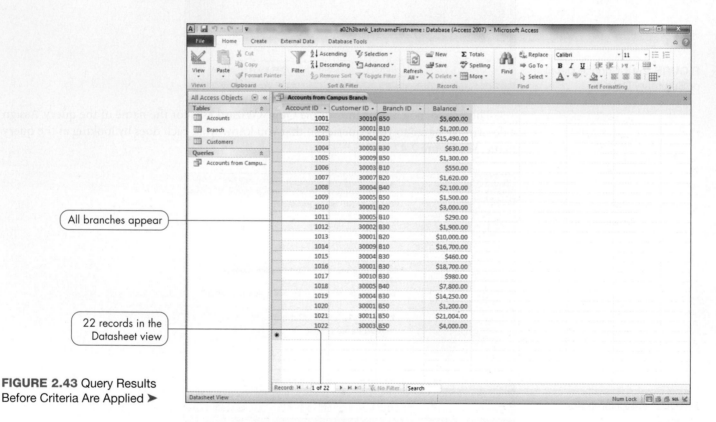

All branches appear

22 records in the
Datasheet view

FIGURE 2.43 Query Results
Before Criteria Are Applied ➤

a. Open *a02h2bank_LastnameFirstname* if you closed it at the end of Hands-On Exercise 2. Click the **File tab**, click **Save Database As**, and then type **a02h3bank_LastnameFirstname**, changing *h2* to *h3*. Click **Save**.

b. Click the **Create tab**, and then click **Query Wizard** in the Queries group to launch the New Query wizard.

The New Query Wizard dialog box opens. Simple Query Wizard is selected by default.

c. Click **OK**.

d. Verify that **Table: Accounts** is selected.

e. Select **AccountID** from the **Available Fields list**, and then click >. Repeat the process with **CustomerID, BranchID,** and **Balance**. The four fields should now appear in the Selected Fields list box. Click **Next**.

f. Confirm **Detail** is selected, and then click **Next**.

g. Name the query **Accounts from Campus Branch**. Click **Finish**.

   This query name describes the data in the query results. Your query should have four fields: AccountID, CustomerID, BranchID, and Balance.

STEP 2 ▶ SPECIFY QUERY CRITERIA AND SORTING

The auditor indicated that the problem seems to be confined to the Campus branch. You use this knowledge to revise the query accordingly. Refer to Figure 2.44 as you complete Step 2.

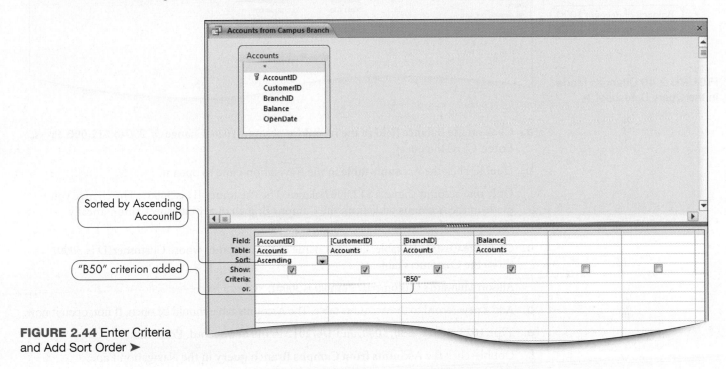

Sorted by Ascending AccountID

"B50" criterion added

FIGURE 2.44 Enter Criteria and Add Sort Order ➤

a. Click the **Home tab**, and then click **View** in the Views group to views the Accounts from Campus Branch query in Design view.

   You have created the Campus Branch Customers query to view only those accounts at the Campus branch. However, other branch's accounts also display. You need to limit the query results to only the records of interest.

b. Click in the **Criteria row** (fifth row) in the **BranchID column**, and then type **B50**.

   B50 is the BranchID for the Campus branch. Access queries are not case sensitive; therefore, b50 and B50 will produce the same results. Access adds quotation marks around text criteria.

c. Click in the **Sort row** (third row) in the **AccountID column**, and then choose **Ascending** from the list.

d. Click **Run** in the Results group.

   You should see six records, all from Branch B50, in the query results.

e. Save the query.

When the query results are on the screen, the auditor notices that some of the data is incorrect, and one of the accounts is missing. From your experience with Access, you explain to the auditor that the data can be changed directly in a query rather than switching back to the table. Refer to Figure 2.45 as you complete Step 3.

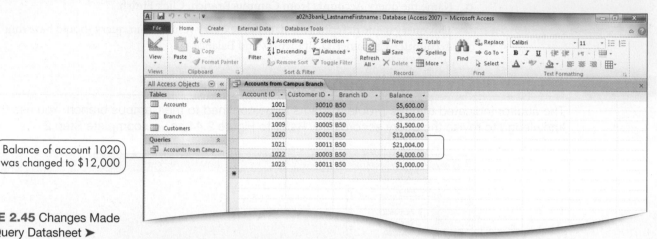

Balance of account 1020 was changed to $12,000

FIGURE 2.45 Changes Made in the Query Datasheet ➤

a. Click on the **Balance field** in the record for account *1020*. Change *$1,200* to **$12,000**. Press **Enter**. Close the query.

b. Double-click the **Accounts table** in the Navigation Pane to open it.

Only one account shows a $12,000 balance. The Customer ID is 30001. The change you made in the Accounts table from the Campus Branch query datasheet automatically changed the data stored in the underlying table.

c. Open the Customers table. Find the name of the customer whose CustomerID is *30001*. Close the Customers table.

Allison Millward's CustomerID number is 30001.

d. Add a new record to the Accounts table. The Accounts table should be open. If not, open it now.

e. Type **1023**, **30011**, **B50**, **1000**, and **1/4/2012** in the new record. Press **Tab**.

f. Double-click the **Accounts from Campus Branch query** in the Navigation Pane.

Customer 30011 now shows two accounts: one with a balance of $21,004 and one with a balance of $1,000.

g. Close the Accounts from Campus Branch query. Close the Accounts table.

h. Click the **File tab**, and then click **Compact & Repair Database**.

i. Click the **File tab**, click **Save & Publish**, and then double-click **Back Up Database**. Accept *a02h3bank_date* as the file name, and then click **Save**.

You just created a backup of the database. The *a02h3bank_LastnameFirstname* database remains open.

j. Keep the database onscreen if you plan to continue with Hands-On Exercise 4. If not, close the database and exit Access.

Multi-Table Queries

The sample bank database contains three tables: Customers, Accounts, and Branch. You learned how to connect the tables through relationships in order to store data efficiently and enforce consistent data entry. *Multi-table queries* contain two or more tables. They enable you to take advantage of the relationships that have been set in your database. When you need to extract information from a database with a query, most times you will need multiple tables to provide the answers you need.

A **multi-table query** contains two or more tables. It enables you to take advantage of the relationships that have been set in your database.

One table may contain the core information that you need. Another table may contain the related data that makes the query relevant to the users. For example, the Accounts table will list the balances of each account at the bank—the key financial information. However, the Accounts table does not list the contact information of the owner of the account. Therefore, the Customers table is needed to provide the additional information.

Creating a Multi-Table Query

Creating a multi-table query is similar to creating a single-table query; however, choosing the right tables and managing the table relationships will require some additional skills. First, you should only include related tables in a multi-table query. *Related tables* are tables that are joined in a relationship using a common field. As a rule, related tables should already be established when you create a multi-table query. Using Figure 2.46 as a guide, creating a query with the Accounts and Branch tables would be acceptable, as would using Accounts and Customers tables, or Accounts, Branch, and Customers tables. All three scenarios include related tables. Creating a query with the Branch and Customers tables would not be acceptable, since these tables are *not* directly related.

Related tables are tables that are joined in a relationship using a common field.

> **TIP** Print the Relationship Report to Help Create a Multi-Table Query
>
> When creating a multi-table query, you should only include related tables. As a guide, you can print the Relationship Report in the Tools group on the Relationship Tools Design tab when the Relationships window is open. This report will help you determine which tables are related in your database.

In the previous example, you answered the question "Which customers from the Campus branch have an account with a balance over $5,000?" Figure 2.35 displays the datasheet results of the query. To make this report more useful, we can add the Branch Location (in place of the BranchID) and the Customer LastName (in place of the CustomerID). To make these changes we would need to add the Branch table and the Customers table to the query design.

Add Additional Tables to a Query

As discussed earlier, you can modify a saved query using Design view for the query. If you wanted to change the Balance Over $5000 query, first open the query in Design view. To add additional tables to a query, open the Navigation Pane, and then drag tables directly into the top portion of the query design grid. For example, the Branch and Customers tables were added to the query as shown in Figure 2.46. The join lines between tables indicate that relationships were previously set in the Relationships window.

FIGURE 2.46 Add Additional Tables to a Query ➤

Get Answers Using a Multi-Table Query

You can get key information from your database using a multi-table query. For example, if you want to know how many orders each customer placed since the database was created, you would create a new query and add the Customers and Orders tables to the Query Design view. After you verify that the join lines are correct, add the CustomerID field from the Customers table and the OrderID field from the Order table to the query design grid. When you run the query, the results show duplicates in the CustomerID column because Customers place multiple orders.

To fix the duplicate CustomerID problem, return to the Query Design view, and then click Totals in the Show/Hide group. Both columns show the Group By option in the Total row. Change the total row of the OrderID field to Count, and then run the query again. This time the results show one row for each customer and the number of orders each customer placed since the database was created.

Modifying a Multi-Table Query

To modify multi-table queries, you use the same techniques you learned for single-table queries. Add tables using the Show Table dialog box; remove tables by clicking the unwanted table and then pressing Delete. Add fields by double-clicking the field you want; remove fields by clicking the column selector and then pressing Delete. Join lines between related tables should appear automatically in a query if the relationships were previously established, as shown in Figure 2.46.

> **TIP** Changes in Multi-Table Queries Do Not Affect Relationships
>
> When you add two or more tables to a query, join lines appear automatically. You can delete the join lines in a query with no impact on the relationships themselves. Deleting a join line only affects the relationships in the individual query. The next time you create a query with the same tables, the join lines will be restored. And, if you open the Relationships window, you will find the join lines in tact.

Add and Delete Fields in a Multi-Table Query

In Figure 2.46, three tables, as well as the join lines between the tables, now appear in the top pane of the Query Design view. All the fields from each of the tables are available to be used in the query design grid. Figure 2.47 shows that Location (from the Branch table) and LastName (from the Customers table) have been added to the design, and BranchID and CustomerID have been deleted. The BranchID was deleted from the query; therefore, the 'B50' criterion was removed as well. 'Campus' was added to the Location field's criteria row in order to extract the same results. Because criteria values are not case sensitive, typing 'campus' is the same as typing 'Campus', and both will return the same results. Run the query to see that the datasheet is more useful now that the Location and LastName fields have been added. The results are shown in Figure 2.48.

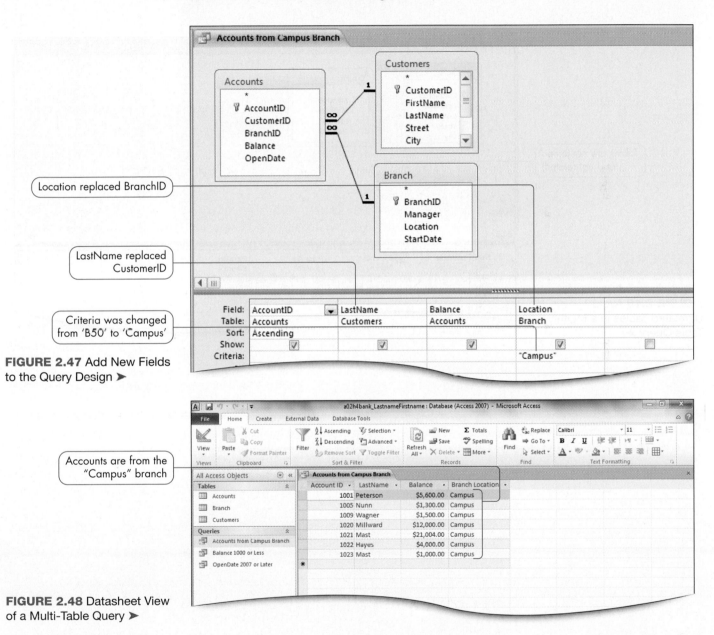

Location replaced BranchID

LastName replaced CustomerID

Criteria was changed from 'B50' to 'Campus'

FIGURE 2.47 Add New Fields to the Query Design ➤

Accounts are from the "Campus" branch

FIGURE 2.48 Datasheet View of a Multi-Table Query ➤

Fix a Common Problem in a Multi-Table Query

In Figure 2.49, two tables are added to the query design, but no join line connects them. The results of the query will be unpredictable and larger (i.e., more records) than expected. The Customers table contains 11 records, and the Branch table contains 5 records. Since Access does not know how to interpret the unrelated tables, the results will show 55 records—every possible combination of customer and branch (11 × 5). See Figure 2.50.

To fix this problem, you can create join lines using the existing tables if the tables facilitate this. Or you can add an additional table that will provide a join between all three tables. In the Branch query, you can add the Accounts table, which will facilitate a join between the two existing tables, Customers and Branch. As soon as the third table is added to the query design, the join lines appear automatically, as shown in Figure 2.47.

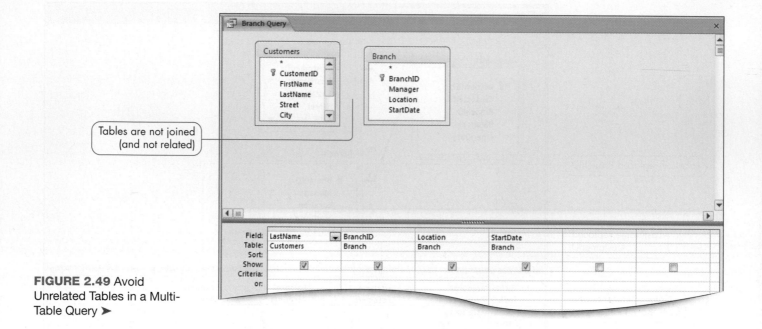

FIGURE 2.49 Avoid Unrelated Tables in a Multi-Table Query ➤

Access shows one record for every Branch for each Customer

Result shows 55 Records

FIGURE 2.50 Query Result with Unrelated Tables ➤

LastName	Branch ID	Branch Location	Manager's Start Date
Millward	B10	Uptown	12/1/2007
Millward	B20	Eastern	6/17/2008
Millward	B30	Western	3/11/2006
Millward	B40	Southern	9/15/2009
Millward	B50	Campus	10/11/2011
Fox	B10	Uptown	12/1/2007
Fox	B20	Eastern	6/17/2008
Fox	B30	Western	3/11/2006
Fox	B40	Southern	9/15/2009
Fox	B50	Campus	10/11/2011
Hayes	B10	Uptown	12/1/2007
Hayes	B20	Eastern	6/17/2008
Hayes	B30	Western	3/11/2006
Hayes	B40	Southern	9/15/2009
Hayes	B50	Campus	10/11/2011
Collins	B10	Uptown	12/1/2007
Collins	B20	Eastern	6/17/2008
Collins	B30	Western	3/11/2006
Collins	B40	Southern	9/15/2009
Collins	B50	Campus	10/11/2011
Wagner	B10	Uptown	12/1/2007
Wagner	B20	Eastern	6/17/2008
Wagner	B30	Western	3/11/2006
Wagner	B40	Southern	9/15/2009
Wagner	B50	Campus	10/11/2011
Williams	B10	Uptown	12/1/2007
Williams	B20	Eastern	6/17/2008

Record: 1 of 55   No Filter   Search

Add a Join Line in a Multi-Table Query

Over time, your database will grow, and additional tables will be added. Occasionally, new tables are added to the database but not added to the Relationships window. When queries are created with the new tables, join lines will not be established. When this happens, you can create temporary join lines in the query design. These join lines will provide a temporary relationship between two tables and enable Access to interpret the query properly.

The process of creating a multi-table query works the same as creating a single-table query (covered previously in this chapter). In the Query Design view, you will add fields to the bottom portion (the query design grid), set the sorting, decide whether to show the fields, and add criteria as needed. You should take some precautions when working with multiple tables; these precautions will be discussed later.

HANDS-ON EXERCISES

4 Multi-Table Queries

Based on the auditor's request, you will need to evaluate the data further. This requires creating queries that are based on multiple tables, rather than a single table. You decide to open an existing query, add additional tables, and then save the query with a new name.

Skills covered: Add Additional Tables to a Query • Create a Multi-Table Query • Modify a Multi-Table Query

---

STEP 1 ▶ ADD ADDITIONAL TABLES TO A QUERY

The previous query was based on the Accounts table, but now you need to add information to the query that is in the Branch table. You will need to add the Branch and Customers tables to the query. Refer to Figure 2.51 as you complete Step 1.

FIGURE 2.51 Add Tables to the Query Design Grid ➤

a. Open *a02h3bank_LastnameFirstname* if you closed it at the end of Hands-On Exercise 3. Click the **File tab**, click **Save Database As**, and then type **a02h4bank_LastnameFirstname**, changing *h3* to *h4*. Click **Save**.

b. Right-click the **Accounts from Campus Branch query** in the Navigation Pane, and then select **Design View** from the shortcut menu.

c. Drag the **Branch table** from the Navigation Pane to the top pane of the query design grid next to the Accounts table.

   A join line connects the Branch table to the Accounts table. The query inherits the join lines from the relationships created in the Relationships window.

d. Drag the **Location field** from the Branch table to the first empty column in the design grid.

   The Location field should be positioned to the right of the Balance column.

e. Click the **Show check box** under the BranchID field to clear the check box and hide this field in the results.

The BranchID field is no longer needed since the Location field provides the same information. Because you unchecked the BranchID show check box, the BranchID field will not appear the next time the query is opened.

f. Delete the **B50 criterion** in the BranchID field.

g. Type **Campus** as a criterion in the **Location field**, and then press **Enter**.

Access adds quotation marks around *Campus* for you; quotes are required for text criteria. You are substituting the Location criterion (*Campus*) in place of the BranchID criterion (B50).

h. Remove Ascending from the AccountID sort row. Click in the **Sort row** of the Balance field. Click the arrow, and then select **Descending** from the list.

The query will be sorted by descending balance order. The largest balance will be listed first, and the smallest will be last.

i. Click **Run** in the Results group.

Only Campus accounts should appear in the datasheet. Next, you will add the Customer LastName and criteria, and then delete CustomerID from the query.

j. Click **View** in the Views group to return to the Design view.

k. Drag the **Customers table** from the Navigation Pane to the top section of the query design grid.

The one-to-many relationship lines automatically connect the Customers table to the Accounts table (similar to step c above).

l. Drag the **LastName field** in the Customers table to the second column in the design grid.

The LastName field should be positioned to the right of the AccountID field.

m. Click the column selector in the CustomerID field to select it. Press **Delete**.

The CustomerID field is no longer needed in the results because we added the LastName field.

n. Click **Run** in the Results group.

o. Save and close the query.

STEP 2 ▸ CREATE A MULTI-TABLE QUERY

After discussing the query results with the auditor, you realize that another query is needed to show those customers with account balances of $1,000 or less. You create the query and view the results in Datasheet view. Refer to Figure 2.52 as you complete Step 2.

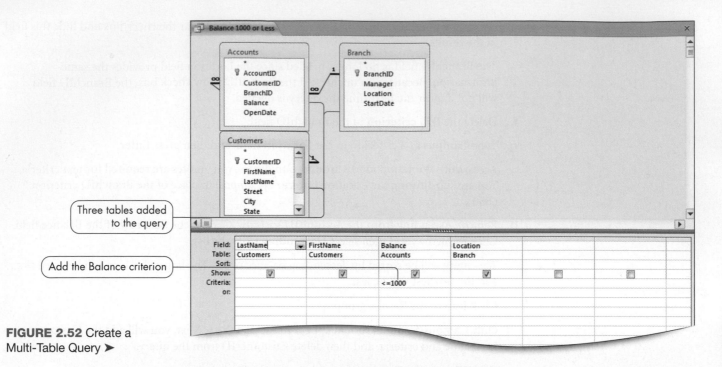

Three tables added to the query

Add the Balance criterion

FIGURE 2.52 Create a Multi-Table Query ➤

a. Click the **Create tab**, and click **Query Design** in the Queries group.

b. Double-click each table name in the Show Table dialog box to add each one to the Query Design view. Click **Close** in the Show Table dialog box.

c. Double-click the following fields to add them to the design grid: **LastName**, **FirstName**, **Balance**, and **Location**.

d. Type **<=1000** in the **Criteria row** of the Balance column.

e. Click **Run** in the Results group to see the query results.

Six records appear in the query results.

f. Click **Save** on the Quick Access Toolbar, and then type **Balance 1000 or Less** as the Query Name in the **Save As dialog box**. Click **OK**.

STEP 3 ▶ MODIFY A MULTI-TABLE QUERY

The auditor requests additional changes to the Balance 1000 or Less query you just created. You will modify the criteria to display the accounts that were opened after January 1, 2006, with balances of $2,000 or less. Refer to Figure 2.53 as you complete Step 3.

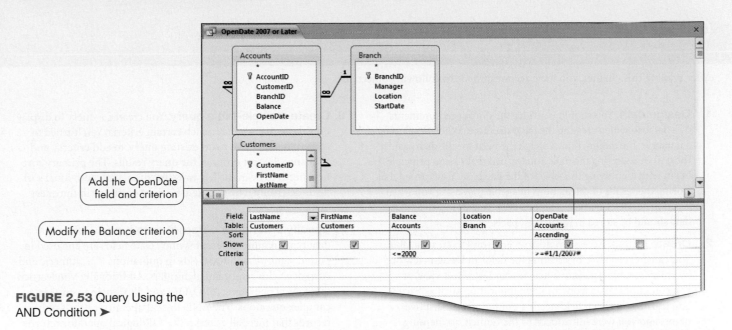

Add the OpenDate field and criterion

Modify the Balance criterion

FIGURE 2.53 Query Using the AND Condition ➤

a. Click **View** in the Views group to switch the *Balance 1000 or Less* query to Design view.

b. Type **<=2000** in place of *<=1000* in the **Criteria row** of the Balance field.

c. Double-click the **OpenDate field** in the Accounts table in the top section of the Query Design view to add it to the first blank column in the design grid.

d. Type **>=1/1/2007** in the **Criteria row** of the OpenDate field to extract only accounts that have been opened since January 2007.

   After you type the expression and then move to a different column, Access will add the # symbols automatically.

e. Click **Run** in the Results group to display the results of the query.

   Three records appear in the query results.

f. Click the **File tab**, click **Save Object As**, and type **OpenDate 2007 or Later** as the query name. Click **OK**.

g. Click the **File tab** again to return to the database.

h. Click **View** in the Views group to return to the Design view of the query.

i. Click in the **Sort row** of the OpenDate field, and then select **Ascending**.

j. Click **Run** in the Results group to display the results of the query.

k. Save and Close the query.

l. Click the **File tab**, and then click **Compact & Repair Database**.

m. Click the **File tab**, click **Save & Publish**, and then double-click **Back Up Database**. Accept *a02h4bank_LastnameFirstname_date* as the file name, and then click **Save**.

   You just created a backup of the database. The *a02h4bank_LastnameFirstname* database remains open.

n. Click the **File tab**, and then click **Exit** (to exit Access).

o. Submit based on your instructor's directions.

After reading this chapter, you have accomplished the following objectives:

1. **Design data.** You should consider the output requirements of a database when creating the table structure. When developing a database, the designer must weigh the need for the data against the cost of collecting the data. You learned that design principles begin with identifying the tables of the database. You learned that storing the results of calculations in a table may assist you when creating queries, forms, and reports later. You also learned that data should be stored in its smallest parts.

2. **Create tables.** Access employs several ways to create a table. You can create a table by creating the fields in Design view or by entering table data into a new row in Datasheet view, or you can import data from another application such as Excel. You learned that each field needs a unique and descriptive name, and you were introduced to the CamelCase naming convention. Access accommodates many different types of data, including Text, Number, Date/Time, Yes/No, Memo, and others.

3. **Understand table relationships.** Relationships between tables are set in the Relationships window. In this window, join lines are created, and three options can be set: Enforce Referential Integrity, Cascade Update Related Fields, and Cascade Delete Related Records. When referential integrity is enforced, data cannot be entered into the related table unless it first exists in the primary table. Frequently, the primary key (unique identifier) from one table is entered as a foreign key in a related table. These two fields often become the basis of creating relationships between tables.

4. **Share data with Excel.** Microsoft Access can easily import and export data to (and from) Excel. You used the Import Wizard to import an Excel worksheet into an Access database table. The settings of the Import Wizard may be saved and reused when the import is cyclical.

5. **Establish table relationships.** You created relationship links between tables in the database and attempted to enter an invalid branch number in a related table. You discovered that the enforcement of referential integrity prevented you from creating an account in a nonexistent branch. The Cascade Update Related Fields option ensures that if the primary key is modified in one table, Access will automatically update all fields in related tables. Similarly, the Cascade Delete Related Records option ensures that if the primary key is deleted in one table, Access will automatically delete all records in related tables.

6. **Create a single-table query.** You created a query to display only those records that match certain criteria. You learned to add additional fields to an existing query, to add criteria, and to change the sort order of the query results. The primary sort field needs to be in the left-most position, with additional sort fields determined by their left-to-right positions in the query design grid.

7. **Specify criteria for different data types.** Different data types require different syntax. Date fields are enclosed in pound signs (#) and text fields in quotations ("). Numeric and currency fields require no delimiters. Additionally, you learned that logical operators, AND, OR, and NOT, help to answer complex questions. The AND logical operator returns only records that meet all criteria. The OR logical operator returns records meeting any of the specified criteria. The NOT logical operator returns all records except the specified criteria.

8. **Copy and run a query.** After specifying tables, fields, and conditions for one query, you can copy the query, rename it, and then modify the fields and criteria in the second query. Copying queries saves time since you do not have to select tables and fields again for queries that have a similar structure. To run a query during the design process, click Run in the Results group. To run a saved query, double-click the query name in the Navigation Pane.

9. **Use the Query Wizard.** An alternative way to create a select query is to use the Query Wizard. The wizard enables you to select tables and fields from lists. The last step of the wizard prompts you to save the query.

10. **Create a multi-table query.** Creating a multi-table query is similar to creating a single-table query; however, choosing the right tables and managing the table relationships requires some additional skills. You should only include related tables in a multi-table query. To add additional tables to a query, open the Navigation Pane, and then drag tables directly into the top section of the Query Design view.

11. **Modify a multi-table query.** To modify multi-table queries, you use the same techniques you used for single-table queries. Join lines between related tables should appear automatically in a query if the relationships were previously established. If join lines do not appear, the results will not be correct when you run the query. You can add temporary join lines from inside the query or set the Relationships permanently in the Relationships window.

KEY TERMS

AND logical operator *p. 618*
AutoNumber *p. 585*
Calculated field *p. 583*
CamelCase notation *p. 585*
Caption property *p. 589*
Cascade Delete Related Records *p. 598*
Cascade Update Related Fields *p. 597*
Comparison operator *p. 616*
Constant *p. 583*
Criteria row *p. 615*
Data redundancy *p. 583*
Data type *p. 585*
Date arithmetic *p. 583*

Delimiter *p. 616*
Field property *p. 588*
Field row *p. 615*
Indexed property *p. 598*
Multi-table query *p. 625*
NOT logical operator *p. 618*
Null *p. 617*
Number data type *p. 589*
One-to-many relationship *p. 602*
OR logical operator *p. 618*
Query *p. 613*
Query Design view *p. 613*
Query sort order *p. 617*

Referential integrity *p. 597*
Related tables *p. 625*
Run command *p. 619*
Select query *p. 614*
Show row *p. 615*
Simple Query Wizard *p. 613*
Sort row *p. 615*
Table *p. 580*
Table row *p. 615*
Text data type *p. 588*
Validation rule *p. 589*
Wildcard *p. 616*

1. When entering, deleting, or editing table data:
   (a) The table must be in Design view.
   (b) The table must be in Datasheet view.
   (c) The table may be in either Datasheet or Design view.
   (d) Data may be entered only in a form.

2. Which of the following is true for the Query Wizard?
   (a) You can only select tables as the source.
   (b) No criteria can be added.
   (c) Fields from multiple tables are not allowed.
   (d) You do not need a summary.

3. Which of the following was not a suggested guideline for designing a table?
   (a) Include all necessary data.
   (b) Store data in its smallest parts.
   (c) Avoid calculated fields.
   (d) Link tables using common fields.

4. A query's specifications providing instructions about which records to include must be entered:
   (a) On the Show row of the query design grid.
   (b) On the Sort row of the query design grid.
   (c) On the Criteria row of the query design grid.
   (d) On the Table row of the query design grid.

5. An illustration of a one-to-many relationship would be:
   (a) A person changes his/her primary address.
   (b) A customer may have multiple orders.
   (c) A branch location has an internal BranchID code.
   (d) A balance field is totaled for all accounts for each person.

6. When adding criteria to the query design view:
   (a) The value you enter must be delimited by quotes (")(").
   (b) The value you enter must be delimited by pound signs (#).
   (c) The value you enter must be delimited by nothing ().
   (d) Access will add the correct delimiters for you ("),("), (#), or ().

7. Which of the following is true with respect to an individual's hire date and years of service?
   (a) Hire date should be a calculated field; years of service should be a stored field.
   (b) Hire date should be a stored field; years of service should be a calculated field.
   (c) Both should be stored fields.
   (d) Both should be calculated fields.

8. When importing data into Access, which of the following statements is true?
   (a) The Import Wizard only works for Excel files.
   (b) The wizard can be found on the Create tab.
   (c) You can assign a primary key while you are importing Excel data.
   (d) The wizard will import the data in one step after you select the file.

9. The main reason to enforce referential integrity in Access is to:
   (a) Limit the number of records in a table.
   (b) Keep invalid data from being entered into a table.
   (c) Make it possible to delete records.
   (d) Keep your database safe from unauthorized users.

10. It is more efficient to make a copy of an existing query, rather than create a new query, when which of the following is true?
    (a) The existing query contains only one table.
    (b) The existing query and the new query use the same tables and fields.
    (c) The existing query and the new query have the exact same criteria.
    (d) The original query is no longer being used.

1 Tom & Erin's Bookstore

Tom and Erin Mullaney own and operate a bookstore in Philadelphia, Pennsylvania. Erin asked you to help her create an Access database because of your experience in this class. You believe that you can help her by creating a database and then importing the Excel spreadsheets they use to store the publishers and the books that they sell. You determine that a third table—for authors—is also required. Your task is to design and populate the three tables, set the table relationships, and enforce referential integrity. If you have problems, reread the detailed directions presented in the chapter. This exercise follows the same set of skills as used in Hands-On Exercises 1 and 2 in the chapter. Refer to Figure 2.54 as you complete this exercise.

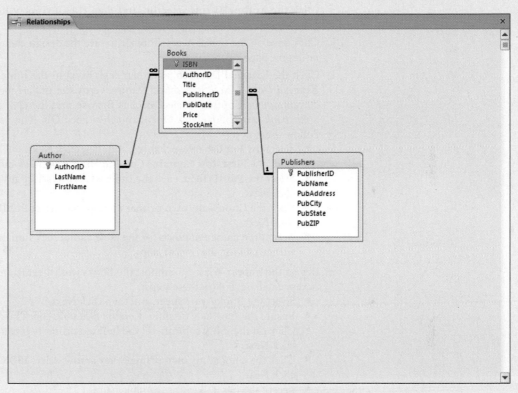

FIGURE 2.54 Access Relationships Window ➤

a. Start Access, and then click **Blank Database** in the Available Templates section of the Backstage view. Click **Browse** to choose a folder location to store the database, type **a02p1books_LastnameFirstname** as the file name, click **OK**, and then click **Create** to create the new database.

b. Type **11** in the **Click to Add column**, and then click **Click to Add**. The field name becomes *Field1*, and *Click to Add* now appears as the third column. Type **Wayne** and press **Tab**. The process repeats for the fourth column; type **John** and then press **Tab** twice.

c. The cursor returns to the first column where *(New)* is selected. Press **Tab**. Type the rest of the data using the following table. This data will become the records of the Author table.

ID	Field1	Field2	Field3
1	11	Wayne	John
(New)	12	Allen	Keith
	13	Scott	Michael
	14	Carl	Richard
	15	Keen	Clara
	16	Swartz	Millie
	17	Allen	John

d. Click **Save** on the Quick Access Toolbar. Type **Author** in the **Save As dialog box**, and then click **OK**.

e. Click **View** in the Views group to switch to the Design view of the Author table.

f. Select **Field1**—in the second row—in the top portion of the table design, and then type **AuthorID** to rename the field. In the *Field Properties* section in the lower portion of the table design, type **Author ID** in the **Caption property box**, and then verify that *Long Integer* appears for the Field Size property.

g. Select **Field2**, and then type **LastName** to rename the field. In the *Field Properties* section in the bottom portion of the table design, type **Author's Last Name** in the **Caption property box** and **20** as the field size.

h. Select **Field3**, and then type **FirstName** to rename the field. In the *Field Properties* section in the bottom portion of the table design, type **Author's First Name** as the caption, and then type **15** as the field size.

i. Click the **ID field row selector** (which shows the primary key) to select the row, and then click **Delete Rows** in the Tools group. Click **Yes** twice to confirm both messages.

j. Click the **AuthorID row selector**, and then click **Primary Key** in the Tools group to reset the primary key.

k. Click **Save** on the Quick Access Toolbar to save the design changes. Click **Yes** to the *Some data may be lost* message. Close the table.

l. Click the **External Data tab**, and then click **Excel** in the Import & Link group to launch the *Get External Data - Excel Spreadsheet* feature. Verify the *Import the source data into a new table in the current database* option is selected, click **Browse**, and then go to the student data folder. Select the *a02p1books* workbook, click **Open**, and then click **OK**. This workbook contains two worksheets. Follow these steps:
    *   Select the **Publishers worksheet**, and then click **Next**.
    *   Click the **First Row Contains Column Headings check box**, and then click **Next**.
    *   Select the **PubID field**, click the **Indexed arrow**, select **Yes (No Duplicates)**, and then click **Next**.
    *   Click the **Choose my own primary key arrow**, select **PubID**, if necessary, and then click **Next**.
    *   Accept the name *Publishers* for the table name, click **Finish**, and then click the **Close button** without saving the import steps.

m. Repeat the Import Wizard to import the Books worksheet from the *a02p1books* workbook into the Access database. Follow these steps:
    *   Select the **Books worksheet**, and then click **Next**.
    *   Ensure the *First Row Contains Column Headings* check box is checked, and then click **Next**.
    *   Click on the **ISBN column**, set the Indexed property box to **Yes (No Duplicates)**, and then click **Next**.
    *   Click the **Choose my own primary key arrow**, select **ISBN** as the primary key field, and then click **Next**.
    *   Accept the name *Books* as the table name. Click **Finish**, and then click the **Close button** without saving the import steps.

n. Right-click the **Books table** in the Navigation Pane, and then select **Design View**. Make the following changes:
    *   Change the PubID field name to **PublisherID**.
    *   Change the Caption property to **Publisher ID**.
    *   Change the PublisherID Field Size property to **2**.
    *   Click the **ISBN field** at the top, and then change the Field Size property to **13**.
    *   Click the **Price field**, and then change the Price field Data Type to **Currency**.
    *   Change the AuthorCode field name to **AuthorID**.
    *   Change the AuthorID Field Size property to **Long Integer**.
    *   Click the **ISBN field row selector** (which shows the primary key) to select the row, then release, press, and hold the mouse. Drag the row up to the first position.
    *   Click **Save** on the Quick Access Toolbar to save the design changes to the Books table. Click **Yes** to the *Some data may be lost* warning.
    *   Close the table.

o. Right-click the **Publishers table** in the Navigation Pane, and then select **Design View**. Make the following changes:
    *   Change the PubID field name to **PublisherID**.
    *   Change the PublisherID Field Size property to **2**.
    *   Change the Caption property to **Publisher's ID**.
    *   Change the Field Size property to **50** for the PubName and PubAddress fields.

- Change the Pub Address field name to **PubAddress** (remove the space).
- Change the PubCity Field Size property to **30**.
- Change the PubState Field Size property to **2**.
- Change the Pub ZIP field name to **PubZIP** (remove the space).
- Click **Save** on the Quick Access Toolbar to save the design changes to the Publishers table. Click **Yes** to the *Some data may be lost* warning. Close all open tables.

p. Click the **Database Tools tab**, and then click **Relationships** in the Relationships group. Click **Show Table** if necessary. Follow these steps:
- Double-click each table name in the Show Table dialog box to add it to the Relationships window, and then close the Show Table dialog box.
- Drag the **AuthorID field** from the Author table onto the AuthorID field in the Books table.
- Click the **Enforce Referential Integrity** and **Cascade Update Related Fields check boxes** in the Edit Relationships dialog box. Click **Create** to create a one-to-many relationship between the Author and Books tables.
- Drag the **PublisherID field** from the Publishers table onto the PublisherID field in the Books table.
- Click the **Enforce Referential Integrity** and **Cascade Update Related Fields check boxes** in the Edit Relationships dialog box. Click **Create** to create a one-to-many relationship between the Publishers and Books tables.
- Click **Save** on the Quick Access Toolbar to save the changes to the Relationships window.
- Click **Relationship Report** in the Tools group on the Design tab.
- Close the report; do not save it. Close the Relationships window.

q. Click the **File tab**, and then click **Compact & Repair Database**.

r. Click the **File tab**, click **Save & Publish**, and then double-click **Back Up Database**.

s. Click **Save** to accept the default backup file name with today's date.

t. Click the **File tab**, and then click **Exit** (to exit Access).

u. Submit based on your instructor's directions.

2 Davis Insurance Company

The Davis Insurance Company offers a full range of insurance services in four locations: Miami, Boston, Chicago, and Philadelphia. They store all of the firm's employee data in an Excel spreadsheet. This file contains employee name and address, job performance, salary, and title. The firm is converting from Excel to Access. A database file containing two of the tables already exists; your job is to import the employee data from Excel for the third table. Once imported, you will need to modify field properties and set new relationships. The owner of the company, Paul Davis, is concerned that some of the Philadelphia and Boston salaries may be below the guidelines published by the national office. He asks that you investigate the salaries of the two offices and create a separate query for each city. If you have problems, reread the detailed directions presented in the chapter. This exercise follows the same set of skills as used in Hands-On Exercises 2 and 3 in the chapter. Refer to Figure 2.55 as you complete this exercise.

FIGURE 2.55 Philadelphia Salaries Query ➤

a. Open *a02p2insurance*. Click the **File tab**, click **Save Database As**, and then type **a02p2insurance_LastnameFirstname**. Click **Save**. In the Navigation Pane, double-click to open the **Location** and **Titles tables**, and then look at the contents to become familiar with the field names and the type of information stored in each table. Note the number of Position titles. Close the tables.

b. Click the **External Data tab**, click **Excel** in the Import & Link group, and then follow these steps:
   - Click **Browse**, and then locate the *a02p2employees* workbook. Select it, click **Open**, and then click **OK**.
   - Select the **Employees worksheet**, and then click **Next**.
   - Click the **First Row Contains Column Headings check box**, and then click **Next**.
   - Click the **Indexed arrow** for the EmployeeID field, select **Yes (No Duplicates)**, and then click **Next**.
   - Click **Choose my own primary key arrow**, select the **EmployeeID** as the primary key, and click **Next**.
   - Accept the name *Employees* for the table name, click **Finish**, and then click **Close** without saving the import steps.

c. Double-click the **Employees table** in the Navigation Pane, click the **Home tab**, and then click **View** in the Views group to switch to the Design view of the Employees table. Make the following changes:
   - Click the **LocationID field**, and then change the Field Size property to **3**.
   - Change the Caption property to **Location ID**.
   - Click the **TitleID field**, and then change the Field Size property to **3**.
   - Change the Caption property to **Title ID**.
   - Change the Salary data type to **Currency**, select **General Number** in the Format property in field properties, and then press **Delete**.
   - Save the design changes. Click **Yes** to the *Some data may be lost* warning.

d. Click **View** in the Views group to view the Employees table in Datasheet view, and then examine the data. Click any record in the Title ID, and then click **Ascending** in the Sort & Filter group on the Home tab. Multiple employees are associated with the T01, T02, T03, and T04 titles.

e. Double-click the **Titles table** in the Navigation Pane to open it in Datasheet view. Notice the T04 title is not in the list.

f. Add a new record in the first blank record at the bottom of the Titles table. Using the following data:
- Type **T04** in the **TitleID field**.
- Type **Senior Account Rep** in the **Title field**.
- Type **A marketing position requiring a technical background and at least three years of experience** in the **Description field**.
- Type **Four year degree** in the **Education Requirements field**.
- Type **45000** in the **Minimum Salary field**.
- Type **75000** in the **Maximum Salary field**.

g. Close all tables. Click **No** if you are asked to save the table.

h. Click the **Database Tools tab**, and then click **Relationships** in the Relationships group. Click **Show Table** if necessary. Follow these steps:
- Double-click each table name in the Show Table dialog box to add them to the Relationships window, and then close the Show Table dialog box.
- Drag the **LocationID field** in the Location table onto the LocationID field in the Employees table.
- Click the **Enforce Referential Integrity** and **Cascade Update Related Fields check boxes** in the Edit Relationships dialog box. Click **Create** to create a one-to-many relationship between the Location and Employees tables.
- Drag the **TitleID field** in the Titles table onto the TitleID field in the Employees table.
- Click the **Enforce Referential Integrity** and **Cascade Update Related Fields check boxes** in the Edit Relationships dialog box. Click **Create** to create a one-to-many relationship between the Titles and Employees tables.
- Click **Save** on the Quick Access Toolbar to save the changes to the Relationships window.
- Close the Relationships window.

i. Click the **Create tab**, and then click the **Query Wizard** in the Queries group. Follow these steps:
- Select **Simple Query Wizard**, and then click **OK**.
- Select **Table: Location** in the Tables/Queries box.
- Double-click **Location** in the **Available Fields list** to move it to the Selected Fields list.
- Select **Table: Employees** in the **Tables/Queries list**.
- Double-click **LastName**, **FirstName**, and **Salary**.
- Select **Table: Titles** in the **Tables/Queries list**.
- Double-click **MinimumSalary** and **MaximumSalary**. Click **Next**.
- Select the **Detail (shows every field of every record) option**, and then click **Next**.
- Type **Philadelphia Salaries** as the query title, and then click **Finish**.

j. Click the **Home tab**, and then click **View** to switch to the Design view of the Philadelphia Salaries Query. In the **Criteria row** of the Location field, type **Philadelphia**. Click in the **Sort row** in the Salary field, and then select **Ascending**. Click **Run** in the Results group on the Design tab. Visually inspect the data to see if any of the Philadelphia employees have a salary less than the minimum or greater than the maximum when compared to the published salary range. These salaries will need to be updated later. Save and close the query.

k. Right-click on the **Philadelphia Salaries query** in the Navigation Pane, and then select **Copy**. Right-click a blank area in the Navigation Pane, and then select **Paste**. In the Paste As dialog box, type **Boston Salaries** for the query name. Click **OK**.

l. Right-click on the **Boston Salaries query** in the Navigation Pane, and then click **Design View**. In the Criteria row of the Location field, replace *Philadelphia* with **Boston**. Click **Run** in the Results group on the Design tab. Visually inspect the data to see if any of the Boston employees have a salary less than the minimum or greater than the maximum when compared to the published salary range. Save and close the query.

m. Click the **File tab**, and then click **Compact & Repair Database**.

n. Click the **File tab**, click **Save & Publish**, and then double-click **Back Up Database**.

o. Click **Save** to accept the default backup file name with today's date.

p. Click the **File tab**, and then click **Exit** (to exit Access).

q. Submit based on your instructor's directions.

1 Real Estate Firm

You are an intern in a large, independent real estate firm that specializes in home sales. A database contains all of the information on the properties marketed by your firm. Most real estate transactions involve two agents—one representing the seller (the listing agent) and the other the buyer (the selling agent). The firm owner has asked that you examine the records of recent listings (real estate is listed when the home owner signs a contract with an agent that offers the property for sale) and sort them by subdivision and the listing agent's name. The results need to include only the sold properties and be sorted by subdivision and the listing agent's last name. Refer to Figure 2.56 as you complete this exercise.

Subdivision	LastName	FirstName	DateListed	DateSold	ListPrice	SellingAgent
Eagle Valley	Lookabil	Steven	9/28/2012	11/6/2012	$449,000.00	5
Eagle Valley	Lookabil	Steven	9/24/2012	11/2/2012	$389,900.00	5
Eagle Valley	Lor	Pa	9/29/2012	11/7/2012	$449,900.00	3
Eagle Valley	Mast	Keith	9/26/2012	11/4/2012	$407,500.00	2
Eagle Valley	Rosario-Galarce	Juan	9/25/2012	11/3/2012	$399,000.00	1
Eagle Valley	Scott	Angela	9/30/2012	11/8/2012	$450,000.00	6
Eagle Valley	Yang	Ko-Yun	9/23/2012	11/1/2012	$389,000.00	4
Eagle Valley	Yang	Ko-Yun	9/27/2012	11/5/2012	$430,000.00	4
Seeley Lake	Lookabil	Steven	5/28/2012	11/14/2012	$725,000.00	5
Seeley Lake	Lor	Pa	10/2/2012	11/29/2012	$825,000.00	3
The Estates	Lookabil	Steven	7/26/2012	11/14/2012	$1,475,000.00	5
The Orchards	Lor	Pa	10/18/2012	11/29/2012	$326,000.00	3
The Orchards	Scott	Angela	10/13/2012	11/1/2012	$319,900.00	6
The Orchards	Yang	Ko-Yun	10/14/2012	11/2/2012	$319,900.00	4
Water Valley	Lookabil	Steven	10/2/2012	11/2/2012	$348,000.00	5
Water Valley	Scott	Angela	7/16/2012	11/1/2012	$345,900.00	6

Record: 1 of 16 — No Filter — Search

FIGURE 2.56 Sold Properties by Subdivision Query Results ►

a. Open *a02m1property*. Click the **File tab**, click **Save Database As**, and then type **a02m1property_ LastnameFirstname**. Click **Save**. Open the Agents table. Find and replace Kia Hart's name with your name. Close the Agents table.

b. Open the SubDivision table in Design view, and then add the field **AssociationFee** with data type **Currency** to indicate the monthly fee for each subdivision. Save the table, switch to Datasheet view, and then enter in the AssociationFee field **95** for each subdivision without a pool and **125** for subdivisions with a pool. Close the table.

c. Open the Query Wizard, and then create a detail query using the Agents and Properties tables. Add the following fields: **LastName**, **FirstName**, **DateListed**, **DateSold**, **ListPrice**, **SellingAgent**, and **SubdivisionID**. Name the query **Sold Properties by Subdivision**. Run the query, and then examine the number of records.

d. In Design view, enter the appropriate criteria to exclude all of the records that contain properties from the Red Canyon Subdivision (SubdivisionID #7). Run the query, and then examine the number of records. It should be a smaller number than in step c.

e. Add the SubDivision table to the query design, and then drag the **Subdivision field** to the first column in the query design grid. Modify the SubdivisionID field so that the field does not show in the query results. Run the query, and then examine the results. The number of records should be the same as in step d; the first column will be different.

f. Sort the records by ascending Subdivision first, then by ascending LastName.

g. Add criteria that will limit the results to the properties sold after October 31, 2012. Run the query.

h. Save and close the query.

i. Compact and repair the database.

j. Make a backup copy of the database.

k. Close Access.

l. Submit based on your instructor's directions.

2 The Prestige Hotel

The Prestige Hotel chain caters to upscale business travelers and provides state-of-the-art conference, meeting, and reception facilities. It prides itself on its international, four-star cuisine. Last year, it began a member reward club to help the marketing department track the purchasing patterns of its most loyal customers. All of the hotel transactions are stored in the database. Your task is to help the managers of the Prestige Hotel in Denver and Chicago identify their customers who stayed in a room last year and who had three persons in their party. Refer to Figure 2.57 as you complete this exercise.

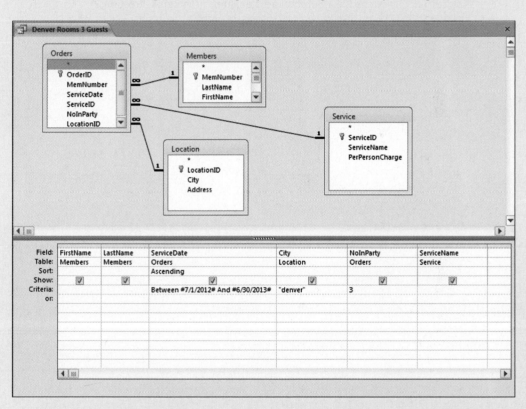

FIGURE 2.57 Denver Rooms 3 Guests Query ➤

a. Open *a02m2hotel*. Click the **File tab**. click **Save Database As**, and then type **a02m2hotel_ LastnameFirstname**. Click **Save**. Review the data contained in the three tables. Specifically, look for the tables and fields containing the information you need: dates of stays in Denver suites, the members' names, and the numbers in the parties.

b. Import the Location data from the Excel file *a02m2location* into your database as a new table. Set the LocationID Indexed property to **Yes (No Duplicates)**, and then set the data type to **Long Integer**. Select the **LocationID field** as the primary key. Name the table **Location**.

c. Open the Relationships window, and then create a relationship between the Location table and the Orders table using the LocationID field. Enforce referential integrity, and then select **Cascade Update Related Fields**. Set the other two relationships as shown in Figure 2.57. Save and close the Relationships window.

d. Open the Members table, and then find Bryan Gray's name. Replace his name with your own first and last name. Now find Nicole Lee's name, and then replace it with your name.

e. Create a query with fields ServiceDate, City, NoInParty, ServiceName, FirstName, and LastName. Set the criteria to limit the output to **denver**. Use the Between command to only show services from **7/1/2012** to **6/30/2013**. Set the Number in Party criterion to **3**. Sort the results in ascending order by the Service Date.

f. Run the query, and then examine the number of records in the status bar at the bottom of the query. It should display *154*. If your number of records is different, examine the criteria.

g. Change the order of the query fields so that they display as FirstName, LastName, ServiceDate, City, NoInParty, and ServiceName. Compare your results to Figure 2.57.

h. Save the query as **Denver Rooms 3 Guests**. Close the query, and then copy it and rename the new query **Chicago Rooms 3 Guests**. One of your colleagues in Chicago asked for your help in analyzing the guest data.

i. Open the Chicago Rooms 3 Guests query in Design view, and then change the criterion for denver to **chicago**. Run and save the changes.

DISCOVER

j. Combine the two previous queries into a third query named **Denver and Chicago Rooms 3 Guests**. Use the criteria from the two individual queries to create a combination AND – OR condition. The records in the combined query should equal the sum of the records in the two individual queries.

k. Compact, repair, and back up the database file. Close the database.

l. Submit based on your instructor's directions.

The Morris Arboretum in Chestnut Hill, Pennsylvania, tracks its donors in Excel. They also use Excel to store a list of plants in stock. As donors contribute funds to the Arboretum, they can elect to receive a plant gift from the Arboretum. These plants are both rare plants and hard-to-find old favorites, and they are part of the annual appeal and membership drive to benefit the Arboretum's programs. The organization has grown, and the files are too large and inefficient to handle in Excel. Your task will be to begin the conversion of the files from Excel to Access.

Create a New Database

You need to examine the data in the Excel worksheets to determine which fields will become the primary keys in each table and which fields will become the foreign keys. Primary and foreign keys are used to form the relationships between tables.

a. Locate the Excel workbook named *a02c1donors* and open it.

b. Locate the Excel workbook named *a02c1plants* and open it.

c. Examine the data in each worksheet and identify the column that will become the primary key in an Access table. Identify the foreign keys in each table.

d. Launch Access and create a new, blank database named **a02c1arbor_LastnameFirstname**.

Create a New Table

Use the new blank table created automatically by Access to hold the donations as they are received from the donors. Switch to Design view, and then save the table as **Donations**. Add the remaining field names in Design view. Note: The data for this table will be added later in this exercise.

a. Change *ID* to **DonationID** with an **AutoNumber Data Type**.

b. Add **DonorID** (a foreign key) as **Number (Long Integer) Data Type**.

c. Add **PlantID** (a foreign key) as **Number (Long Integer) Data Type**.

d. Enter two additional fields with an appropriate data type and field properties. Hint: You need the date of donation and the amount of donation.

e. Verify the primary key is *DonationID*.

f. Save the table. Close the table.

Import Data from Excel

You need to use the Import Spreadsheet Data Wizard twice to import a worksheet from each Excel workbook into Access. You need to select the worksheets, specify the primary keys, set the indexing option, and name the newly imported tables (see Figures 2.19 through 2.24).

a. Click the **Import Excel data command**.

b. Locate and select the *a02c1donors* workbook.

c. Set the DonorID field Indexed option to **Yes (No Duplicates)**.

d. Select **DonorID** as the primary key when prompted.

e. Accept the table name *Donors*.

f. Import the *a02c1plants* file, set the ID field as the primary key, and then change the indexing option to **Yes (No Duplicates)**.

g. Select the **ID** as the primary key when prompted.

h. Accept the table name *Plants*.

i. Open each table in Datasheet view to examine the data.

j. Change the ID field name in the Plants table to **PlantID**.

Create Relationships

You need to create the relationships between the tables using the Relationships window. Identify the primary key fields in each table and connect them with their foreign key counterparts in related tables. Enforce referential integrity, and check the Cascade Update Related Fields option.

a. Open the Donors table, and then change the Field Size property for DonorID to **Long Integer** so it matches the Field Size property of DonorID in the Donations table.

b. Open the Plants table, and then change the Field Size property for PlantID to **Long Integer** so it matches the Field Size property for PlantID in the Donations table.

c. Close the open tables, and then open the Relationships window.

d. Add the three tables to the Relationships window using the Show Table dialog box. Close the Show Tables dialog box.

e. Drag the **DonorID field** in the Donors table onto the DonorID field in the Donations table. Enforce referential integrity, and then check the **Cascade Update Related Fields option**. Drag the **PlantID field** from the Plants table onto the PlantID field of the Donations table. Enforce referential integrity, and then check the **Cascade Update Related Fields option**.

f. Close the Relationships window and save your changes.

Add Sample Data to the Donations Table

You need to add sample data to the Donations table. Add 20 records using the following guidelines:

a. Use any donor from the Donors table.

b. Enter the date of donation using dates from last month, this month, and next month.

c. Use any amount of donation.

d. Use any plant from the Plants table.

Use the Query Wizard

Use the Query Wizard to create a query of all donations greater than $100 in the Donations table. Use the following guidelines:

a. Include the DonorID and AmountOfDonation fields.

b. Name the query **Donations Over 100**.

c. Add criteria to include only donations of more than $100.

d. Sort by descending AmountOfDonation.

Create a Query in Design View

You need to create a query that identifies the people who have made a donation in the current month. The query should list the donor's full name, phone number, the amount of the donation, the date of the donation, and name of the plant they want. Sort the query by date of donation, then by donor last name and first name. This list will be given to the Arboretum staff so they can notify the donors that a plant is ready for pick up.

a. Click the **Create tab**, and then click **Query Design** in the Queries group.

b. Add the tables and fields necessary to produce the query as stated previously. Name the query **Plant Pickup List**.

c. Run and print the query from Datasheet view.

d. Compact, repair, and back up the file. Close the database.

e. Submit based on your instructor's directions.

Employee Performance Review

GENERAL CASE

The *a02b1perform* file contains employee performance data for a large insurance agency. Open *a02b1perform*. Click the **File tab**, click **Save Database As**, and then type **a02b1perform_ LastnameFirstname**. Click **Save**. Use the skills from this chapter to perform several tasks. Replace *yourname* in the Employees table with your name. The firm's employee policy states that an employee needs to maintain a performance rating of good or excellent to maintain employment. If an employee receives an average or poor performance rating, he or she receives a letter reminding him or her of this policy along with suggestions of how to improve. You are the manager of the Atlanta office. You need to identify the employees who need a letter of reprimand. You will prepare a query so that someone else can generate a form letter to the employees. You need to include fields in the query that contain the employees' first and last names, their position title, and their salary. You do not need to write the letter, only assemble the data that will later be merged into the letter. The query results need to be alphabetized by the employees' last names. As you work, consider the order that the fields will need to be used in the letter and order the query fields accordingly. Close the database. Check with your instructor and submit based on your instructor's directions.

Database Administrator Position

RESEARCH CASE

You arrive at Secure Systems, Inc., for a database administrator position interview. After meeting the Human Resources coordinator, you are given a test to demonstrate your skills in Access. You are asked to create a database from scratch to keep track of all the candidates for the positions currently open at Secure Systems. Use these requirements:

a. Name the database **a02b2admin_LastnameFirstname**.
b. Create three tables: Candidates, JobOpenings, and Interviews.
c. Include a field to rank each candidate on a scale of 1 to 5 (5 is highest).
d. Set the table relationships.
e. Add 10 candidates—yourself and 9 other students in your class.
f. Add the Database Administrator job and four other sample jobs.
g. Add eight sample Interviews—four for the Database Administrator position and four others.
h. Create a query that lists all the Database Administrator interviews with a ranking of 4 or 5.
i. Add the last name and first name of the candidate to the query design. Sort by last name and first name. Run the query.
j. Close the database. Submit based on your instructor's directions.

May Beverage Sales

DISASTER RECOVERY

A coworker called you into his office, explained that he was having difficulty with Access 2010, and asked you to look at his work. Open *a02b3traders*. Click the **File tab**, click **Save Database As**, and then type **a02b3traders_ LastnameFirstname**. Click **Save**. It contains two queries, *May 2012 Orders of Beverages and Confections* and *2012 Beverage Sales by Ship Country*. The May 2012 Orders of Beverages and Confections query is supposed to have only information from May 2012. You find other dates included in the results. Change the criteria of ShippedDate to exclude the other dates. The 2012 Beverage Sales by Ship Country query returns no results. Check the criteria in all fields. Once the criteria are fixed, the records need to be ordered by ShipCountry. After you find and correct the error(s), close the database. Submit based on your instructor's directions.

3 CUSTOMIZE, ANALYZE, AND SUMMARIZE QUERY DATA

Creating and Using Queries to Make Decisions

CASE STUDY | Housing Slump Means Opportunity for College Students

Watch the **Set-up Video** for this Case Study!

Two students from Montgomery County Community College decided they would take advantage of the declining housing market. After taking several business courses at MCCC and a weekend seminar in real estate investing, Jeff Bryan and Bill Ryder were ready to test their skills in the marketplace. Jeff and Bill had a simple strategy—buy distressed properties at a significant discount, then resell the properties for a profit one year later when the market rebounds.

As they drove through the surrounding neighborhoods, if they noticed a For Sale sign in the yard, they would call the listing agent and ask for the key information such as the asking price, the number of bedrooms, square feet, and days on the market. Since they were just starting out, they decided to target houses that were priced at $100,000 or below and only houses that were on the market at least six months.

For the first two months, they gathered lots of information and began to get a feel for the houses and prices in the area. Some neighborhoods were definitely more distressed than others! But they still had not made any offers. The two MCCC investors realized they needed a more scientific approach to finding an investment property. Based on a tip from the real estate seminar, they decide to gather free lists of homes for sale and use that information to prequalify houses that meet their criteria. They have asked you to help them import the lists into Access. Once the data is in Access, Jeff, Bill, and you will be able to easily identify the qualifying properties.

This new database approach should help them become more successful and hopefully help them acquire their first investment property. And who knows, you might even become one of the partners.

OBJECTIVES AFTER YOU READ THIS CHAPTER, YOU WILL BE ABLE TO:

1. Understand the order of operations *p.650*

2. Create a calculated field in a query *p.651*

3. Create expressions with the Expression Builder *p.660*

4. Use built-in functions in Access *p.662*

5. Perform date arithmetic *p.665*

6. Add aggregate functions to datasheets and queries *p.675*

Calculations, Expressions, and Functions

Previously, you learned that Access now allows calculated fields to be added to tables. In previous versions of Access, you could not add calculated fields to tables; you could only add calculated fields to queries, forms, and reports. In Access 2010, many situations exist where you will still need to add arithmetic calculations—using expressions and functions—to queries, forms, and reports.

In Access 2010, many situations exist where you will still need to add arithmetic calculations ... to queries, forms, and reports.

For example, many Access developers prefer to create calculated fields in queries. Queries with calculated fields can then become the data source (or record source) for forms and reports. Calculated fields on a form cannot be edited the same way fields from a table can be edited. Calculated fields can only be displayed on a form. For example, if you store information about credit cards in a table, you would enter the bank (Chase), the credit card type (Visa), and the interest rate (9%). You would not enter the current amount due. That amount would be calculated and displayed on the form. You will recognize this restriction later when you create a form containing calculated fields.

In this section, you will learn about the order of operations and how to create a calculated field in a query.

Understanding the Order of Operations

The **order of operations** determines the sequence by which operations are calculated in an expression.

The **order of operations** determines the sequence by which operations are calculated in an expression. Evaluate expressions in parentheses first, then exponents, then multiplication and division, and, finally, addition and subtraction. Operations of equal value will be calculated from left to right. Table 3.1 shows some examples of the order of operations. You must have a solid understanding of these rules in order to create calculated fields in Access. Access, like Excel, uses the following symbols:

- Parentheses ( )
- Exponentiation ^
- Multiplication *
- Division /
- Addition +
- Subtraction –

TABLE 3.1	Examples of Order of Operations	
Expression	**Order to Perform Calculations**	**Output**
=2+3*3	Multiply first, and then add.	11
=(2+3)*3	Add the values inside the parentheses first, and then multiply.	15
=2+2^3	Evaluate the exponent first, $2^3=2*2*2$ or 8. Then add.	10
=(2+2)^3	Add the parenthetical values first (2+2=4), and then raise the result to the 3rd power. $4^3=4*4*4$.	64
=10/2+3	Divide first, and then add.	8
=10/(2+3)	Add first to simplify the parenthetical expression, and then divide.	2
=10*2–3*2	Multiply first, and then subtract.	14

Creating a Calculated Field in a Query

When creating a query, in addition to using fields from tables, you may also need to create a calculation based on the fields from one or more tables. For example, a table might contain the times when employees clock in and out of work. You could create a calculated field to calculate how many hours each employee worked by subtracting the ClockIn field from the ClockOut field. You create calculated fields in the Design view of a query. A formula used to calculate new fields from the values in existing fields is known as an *expression*. An expression can consist of a number of different elements to produce the desired output. The elements used in an expression may include the following:

An **expression** is a formula used to calculate new fields from the values in existing fields.

- Identifiers (the names of fields, controls, or properties)
- Arithmetic operators (e.g., * , / , + , or −)
- Functions (built-in functions like Date() or IIf())
- *Constants* (numbers such as 30 or .5)

A **constant** refers to a value that does not change.

You can use calculations to create a new value based on an existing field, verify data entered, set grouping levels in reports, or to help set query criteria.

Build Expressions with Correct Syntax

Expressions are entered in the first row of the query design grid. You must follow the correct *syntax*—the set of rules that Access follows when evaluating expressions. You can create expressions to perform calculations using field names, constants, and functions. If you use a field name, such as Balance, in an expression, you must spell the field name correctly or Access will display an error. You should assign descriptive field names to the calculated fields. Access ignores spaces in calculations. An example of an expression with correct syntax is:

Syntax is the set of rules that Access follows when evaluating expressions.

MonthlyInterest: [Balance] * .035 / 12

In the above expression, if you omit the brackets [ ] around Balance, Access will add them for you. The arithmetic operators, the * symbol (multiply) and the / symbol (divide), first multiply the operands, [Balance] and .035, and then divide the result by 12. In calculated fields, the operands are usually a constant, a field name, or another calculated field. Figure 3.1 shows the NewBalance field which adds the [Balance] and the calculated field [MonthlyInterest]. This calculation will show the total amount owed.

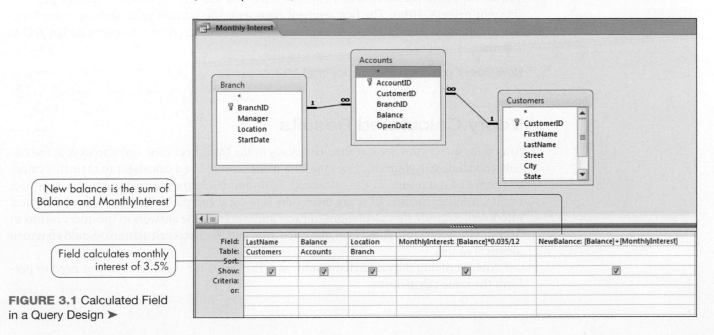

New balance is the sum of Balance and MonthlyInterest

Field calculates monthly interest of 3.5%

FIGURE 3.1 Calculated Field in a Query Design ➤

The query contains a second calculated field named NewBalance. Its value is derived from the sum of the original balance plus the monthly interest amount. The query results, as shown in Figure 3.2, display a decimal number in the Interest column. The NewBalance column appears to be rounded to two decimal places since the output is in currency format. However, when you click in the NewBalance field, Access displays the extra digits that are stored behind the scenes.

Monthly Interest				
LastName	Balance	Branch Locat	MonthlyInterest	NewBalance
Peterson	$5,600.00	Campus	16.3333333333333	$5,616.3333
Millward	$1,200.00	Uptown	3.5	$1,203.50
Collins	$15,490.00	Eastern	45.1791666666667	$15,535.18
Hayes	$630.00	Western	1.8375	$631.84
Nunn	$1,300.00	Campus	3.79166666666667	$1,303.79
Hayes	$550.00	Uptown	1.60416666666667	$551.60
Simpson	$1,620.00	Eastern	4.725	$1,624.73
Collins	$2,100.00	Southern	6.125	$2,106.13
Wagner	$1,500.00	Campus	4.375	$1,504.38
Millward	$3,000.00	Eastern	8.75	$3,008.75
Wagner	$290.00	Uptown	0.845833333333333	$290.85
Fox	$1,900.00	Western	5.54166666666667	$1,905.54
Millward	$10,000.00	Eastern	29.1666666666667	$10,029.17
Nunn	$16,700.00	Uptown	48.7083333333333	$16,748.71
Collins	$460.00	Western	1.34166666666667	$461.34
Millward	$18,700.00	Western	54.5416666666667	$18,754.54
Peterson	$980.00	Western	2.85833333333333	$982.86
Wagner	$7,800.00	Southern	22.75	$7,822.75
Collins	$14,250.00	Western	41.5625	$14,291.56
Millward	$12,000.00	Campus	35	$12,035.00
YourName	$21,004.00	Campus	61.2616666666667	$21,065.26
Hayes	$4,000.00	Campus	11.6666666666667	$4,011.67
YourName	$1,000.00	Campus	2.91666666666667	$1,002.92
*				

NewBalance appears to be rounded to two digits (currency format)

MonthlyInterest field shows a decimal number with many digits

Click in the NewBalance field to reveal a decimal number with four digits

Record: 14 ◄ 1 of 23 ► ►I ►⊡ No Filter Search

FIGURE 3.2 Results of Calculated Fields in a Query ➤

Another example of when to use a calculated field is calculating a price increase for a product or service. Suppose you need to calculate a 10% price increase on certain products you sell. You could name the calculated field NewPrice and use the expression (current price) + (current price × 10%). The first segment represents the current price and the second segment adds an additional 10%. The expression would be entered into the query design grid as follows:

NewPrice: [CurrentPrice] + [CurrentPrice] * .10

Verify Calculated Results

After your query runs, look at the field values in the Datasheet view and also look at the calculated values. Ask yourself, "Does the data make sense?" Use a calculator to manually calculate some of the results in the calculated fields and compare the answers to the datasheet results. Another method to verify the results is to copy and paste all or part of the datasheet into Excel. Recreate the calculations in Excel and compare the answers to the query results in Access. The Access calculated field, the calculator, and the Excel calculations should all return identical results.

After verifying the calculated results, save the query for the next time you need to perform the same calculations.

Save a Query Containing Calculated Fields

As you already know, saving a query only saves the design of the query; saving does not save the data displayed in Datasheet view. While viewing the results of a query in Datasheet view, you can edit the data (and consequently update the data in the underlying table) providing the query is updatable. Calculated fields are the exception to this rule—calculated fields cannot be updated in Datasheet view. However, when the components of a calculated field are updated, the calculated field value will update automatically.

You can use a calculated field as input for other calculated fields. For example, calculate a 10% discount on an item (Calculation #1) and then calculate the sales tax on the discount price (Calculation #2).

In the first Hands-On Exercise, you will create calculated expressions, practice verification techniques, and recover from a common error.

1 Calculations, Expressions, and Functions

Using the data from the homes for sale lists that Jeff and Bill acquired, you are able to help them target properties that meet their criteria. As you examine the data, you discover other ways to analyze the properties. You create several queries and present your results to the two investors for their comments.

Skills covered: Create and Save a Query • Create a Calculated Field and Run the Query • Verify the Calculated Results • Recover from a Common Error

STEP 1 › CREATE AND SAVE A QUERY

You begin your analysis by creating a query using the Properties and Agents tables. The Properties table contains all the properties the investors will evaluate; the Agents table contains a list of real estate agents who represent the properties' sellers. In this exercise, add the fields you need and only show properties that have not been sold. Refer to Figure 3.3 as you complete Step 1.

FIGURE 3.3 Query Results for Properties NOT Sold ➤

a. Open *a03h1property*. Click the **File tab**, click **Save Database As**, and then type **a03h1property_LastnameFirstname**. Click **Save**.

> **TROUBLESHOOTING:** Throughout the remainder of this chapter and textbook, click Enable Content whenever you are working with student files.

> **TROUBLESHOOTING:** If you make any major mistakes while completing this Hands-On Exercise, you can delete the *a03h1property_LastnameFirstname* file, repeat step a above, and then start over.

b. Open the Agents table, and then replace *Angela Scott* with your name. Close the table.

c. Click the **Create tab**, and then click **Query Design** in the Queries group to start a new query.

The Show Table dialog box opens so you can specify the table(s) and/or queries to include in the query design.

d. Select the **Agents table**, and then click **Add**. Select the **Properties table**, and then click **Add**. Close the Show Table dialog box.

e. Double-click the **FirstName** and **LastName fields** in the Agents table to add them to the design grid.

f. Double-click the **DateListed**, **ListPrice**, **SqFeet**, and **Sold fields** in the Properties table to add them to the query design grid.

g. Click **Run** in the Results group to display the results in Datasheet view.

You should see 303 properties in the results.

h. Click **View** in the Views group to switch to Design view. Type **No** in the **Criteria row** of the Sold field.

i. Select **Ascending** from the Sort row of the ListPrice field.

j. Click **Run** to see the results.

You only want to see properties that were not sold. There should now be only 213 properties in the datasheet. Compare your results to those shown in Figure 3.3.

k. Save the query as **TargetHouses**.

STEP 2 ▶ CREATE A CALCULATED FIELD AND RUN THE QUERY

You need to create a calculated field to evaluate the relative value of all unsold properties on the market. To do this, you create a calculated field to analyze the sale price compared to the square footage of each property. Refer to Figure 3.4 as you complete Step 2.

FIGURE 3.4 Syntax for a Calculated Field ➤

a. Click **View** in the Views group to switch to Design view.

> **TROUBLESHOOTING:** If you accidentally click the View arrow, Access displays a list of options. Select the Design View option.

The TargetHouses query is based on two tables. The top portion of Query Design view displays the two tables, Agents and Properties, and the bottom portion (query design grid) displays the fields currently in the query.

b. Click the **File tab**, and then select **Save Object As**. Type **PricePerSqFt** in the **Save As dialog box**, and then click **OK**.

You made a copy of the TargetHouses query so you can add a calculated field to the new query but still preserve the original query.

c. Click the **File tab** to return to the query.

d. Scroll to the right until you see the first blank column in the query design grid.

e. Click in the top row of the first blank column, type **PricePerSqFt: ListPrice/SqFeet**, and then press **Enter**. Widen the PricePerSqFt column in order to see the entire expression.

Access inserts square brackets around the fields for you. The new field divides the values in the ListPrice field by the values in the SqFeet field. The *:* after *PricePerSqFt* is required.

f. Click **Run** in the Results group to view the results.

The new calculated field, PricePerSqFt, is displayed. Widen the PricePerSqFt column, if necessary, to see all the values.

g. Click **View** to switch back to Design view. Use Figure 3.4 to check your syntax. Click in the **PricePerSqFt calculated field cell**, and then click **Property Sheet** in the Show/Hide group.

The Property Sheet controls how the results of the calculated field will display in Datasheet view when you run the query.

h. Click the **Format property arrow**, and then select **Currency** from the list. Click in the **Caption box**, and then type **Price Per Sq Ft**. Close the Property Sheet.

i. Click **Run** to view your changes.

The calculated field values are formatted with Currency, and the column heading displays *Price Per Sq Ft* instead of *PricePerSqFt*.

STEP 3 ▶ VERIFY THE CALCULATED RESULTS

Because you are in charge of the Access Database, you decide to verify your data prior to showing it to the investors. You use two methods to check your calculations: estimation and checking your results using Excel. Refer to Figure 3.5 as you complete Step 3.

	A	B	C	D	E	F	G	H	I
1	First Name	Last Name	Date Listed	List Price	Square Feet	Sold	Price Per Sq Ft		
2	Your Name	Your Name	1/24/2012	$30,080.00	4834	FALSE	$6.22	$6.22	
3	Keith	Mast	2/10/2012	$31,596.00	6179	FALSE	$5.11	$5.11	
4	Karean	Eissler	1/24/2012	$31,780.00	4362	FALSE	$7.29	$7.29	
5	Keith	Mast	2/25/2012	$31,800.00	4712	FALSE	$6.75	$6.75	
6	Keith	Mast	4/1/2012	$31,996.00	3832	FALSE	$8.35	$8.35	
7	Keith	Mast	1/25/2012	$31,996.00	4768	FALSE	$6.71	$6.71	
8	Bill	Sabey	2/10/2012	$33,800.00	4949	FALSE	$6.83	$6.83	
9	Bill	Sabey	2/10/2012	$33,960.00	3405	FALSE	$9.97	$9.97	
10	Bill	Sabey	1/24/2012	$34,000.00	5180	FALSE	$6.56	$6.56	
11	Bill	Sabey	1/6/2012	$35,200.00	4447	FALSE	$7.92	$7.92	
12									
13									
14									

Verified results in Excel

Calculated results from Access

First 10 rows of the Access query

FIGURE 3.5 Verify Calculated Results in Excel ▶

a. Examine the Price Per Sq Ft column in the current query.

One of the ways to verify the accuracy of the calculated data is to ask yourself if the numbers make sense.

b. Locate the eighth record with *Bill Sabey* as the listing agent, an asking price of *$33,960*, and square footage of *3405*. Ask yourself if the calculated value of *$9.97* makes sense.

The sale price is $33,960 and the square footage is 3405. You can verify the calculated field easily by rounding the two numbers (to 34,000 and 3400) and then dividing the values in your head (34,000 div by 3400 = 10) to verify that the calculated value, $9.97 per sq ft, makes sense.

c. Launch Excel, and then switch to Access. Click the first row selector, and then drag through the first 10 records (the tenth record has a list price of *$35,200*). Click **Copy** in the Clipboard group on the **Home tab**.

You will also verify the calculation in the first 10 records by pasting the results in Excel.

d. Switch to Excel, and then click **cell A1** of the blank workbook. Click **Paste** in the Clipboard group on the Home tab.

The field captions appear in the first row, and the 10 records appear in the next 10 rows. The fields are located in columns A–G. The calculated field results are pasted in column G as values rather than as a formula.

> **TROUBLESHOOTING:** If you see pound signs (#####) in an Excel column, use the vertical lines between columns to increase the width.

e. Type **=D2/E2** in **cell H2**, and then press **Enter**. Copy the formula from **cell H2** and paste it into **cells H3 to H11**.

The formula divides the list price by the square feet. Compare the results in columns G and H. The numbers should be the same. If the values differ, look at both the Excel and Access formulas. Determine which is correct, and then find and fix the error in the incorrect formula.

f. Close Excel without saving the workbook. Return to the Access database, and then click **Save** on the Quick Access Toolbar to save the design modifications made to the PricePerSqFt query.

TIP Use Zoom (Shift+F2) to View Long Expressions

To see the entire calculated field expression, click the field in Query Design view, and then press Shift+F2. A new window will appear to enable you to easily see and edit the entire contents of the cell. Access refers to this window as the Zoom dialog box, as shown in Figure 3.6.

FIGURE 3.6 Use Zoom to See the Entire Calculated Field ➤

A few errors pop up as you test the new calculated fields. You check the spelling of the field names in the calculated field since that is a common mistake. Refer to Figure 3.7 as you complete Step 4.

Results are the same ($100) for every record

FIGURE 3.7 Results of a Misspelled Field Name ➤

a. Click **View** in the Views group to switch to Design view. Scroll to the first blank column, and then click in the top row.

b. Type **WrongPricePerSqFt: xListPrice/xSqFeet**, and then press **Enter**. Widen the column to see the entire expression.

Be sure that you added the extra *x's* to the field names. You are intentionally misspelling the field names to see how Access will respond. Access inserts square brackets around the fields for you.

c. Click **Run** in the Results group.

You should see the Enter Parameter Value dialog box. The dialog box indicates that Access does not recognize xListPrice in the tables defined for this query in the first record. When Access does not recognize a field name, it will ask you to supply a value.

d. Type **100000** in the **first parameter box**. Press **Enter** or click **OK**.

Another Enter Parameter Value dialog box displays, asking that you supply a value for xSqFeet. Again, this error occurs because the tables defined for this query do not contain an xSqFeet field.

e. Type **1000** in the **second parameter box**, and then press **Enter**.

The query has the necessary information to run and returns the results in Datasheet view.

f. Scroll right and examine the results of the calculation for *WrongPricePerSqFt*.

All of the records show 100 because you entered the values 100000 and 1000, respectively, into the parameter boxes. The two values are treated as constants and give the same results for all the records.

g. Return to Design view and correct the errors in the WrongPricePerSqFt field by changing the formula to **WrongPricePerSqFt: [ListPrice]/[SqFeet]**.

Press Shift+F2 to view the calculated field and remove the *x* from the two field names.

h. Click in the **WrongPricePerSqFt calculated field**, click **Property Sheet**, and then change the Format property to **Currency**. Add the caption **Wrong Price Per Sq Ft**. Close the Property Sheet.

i. Run and save the query.

The calculated values in the last two columns should be the same.

j. Close the query.

k. Click the **File tab**, and then click **Compact & Repair Database**.

l. Click the **File tab**, click **Save & Publish**, and then double-click **Back Up Database**. Accept *a03h1property_LastnameFirstname_date* as the file name, and then click **Save**.

You just created a backup of the database you used to complete the first Hands-On Exercise. The *a03h1property_LastnameFirstname* database remains open.

m. Keep the database onscreen if you plan to continue with Hands-On Exercise 2. If not, close the database and exit Access.

TIP Learning from Your Mistakes

Following step-by-step instructions is a good way to begin learning about Access. If you want to become proficient, however, you must learn how to recover from errors. As you work through the rest of the Hands-On Exercises in this book, follow the instructions as presented and save your work along the way. Then go back a few steps and make an intentional error just to see how Access responds. Read the error messages (if any) and learn from your mistakes.

Expression Builder, Functions, and Date Arithmetic

In the last Hands-On Exercise, you calculated the price per square foot for real estate properties. That simple calculation helped you to evaluate all the properties on the investment list. You were able to type the expression manually.

When you encounter more complex expressions, you can use the *Expression Builder* tool to help you create more complicated expressions. When you create an expression in the field cell, you must increase the column width to see the entire expression. The Expression Builder's size enables you to easily see complex formulas and functions in their entirety.

In this section, you will learn how to create expressions using the Expression Builder. You also will learn how to use built-in functions. Finally, you will perform date arithmetic using the Expression Builder.

> The **Expression Builder** is a tool to help you create more complicated expressions.

Creating Expressions with the Expression Builder

Launch the Expression Builder while in the query design grid to assist you with creating a calculated field (or other expression). The Expression Builder helps you create expressions by supplying you with the fields, operators, and functions you need to create them. When you use the expression builder to help you create expressions, you can eliminate spelling errors in field names. Another advantage is with functions; functions require specific arguments in a specific order. When you insert a function using the Expression Builder, the builder gives you placeholders that tell you where each argument belongs.

> Launch the Expression Builder while in the query design grid to assist you with creating a calculated field.

After you create an expression in the Expression Builder, click OK to close the Expression Builder window. The expression is then entered into the current cell in the query design grid. From the query design, click Run in the Results group to view the results (in Datasheet view). If the results are incorrect, return to Design view and click the cell that contains the calculated field. Next, launch the Expression Builder again and make any corrections to the expression.

You can also use the Expression Builder when working with controls in forms and reports. For example, if you need a calculated field in a form, you can launch the Expression Builder by clicking Build on the right side of the control source box in the Property Sheet. You will learn more about this in later chapters. You can also use the Expression Builder to select a built-in function—for example, to calculate a payment on a loan. It will take some practice to master the Expression Builder; however, the effort will be well worth it as you learn to create more complication expressions.

Launch the Expression Builder

To launch the Expression Builder, open a query in Design view and verify the Design tab is selected on the Ribbon. Click Builder in the Query Setup group and the Expression Builder launches, as shown in Figure 3.8. (You can also launch the Expression Builder by right-clicking the cell where you want the expression and selecting Build from the shortcut menu.) The top section of the Expression Builder dialog box contains a rectangular area (known as the *expression box*) where you create an expression. You can type your expression in the box manually, or you can use the Expression Elements, Expression Categories, and Expression Values in the bottom portion of the Expression Builder. Double-click an item in the *Expression Categories* or *Expression Values* section and it will automatically be added to the expression box.

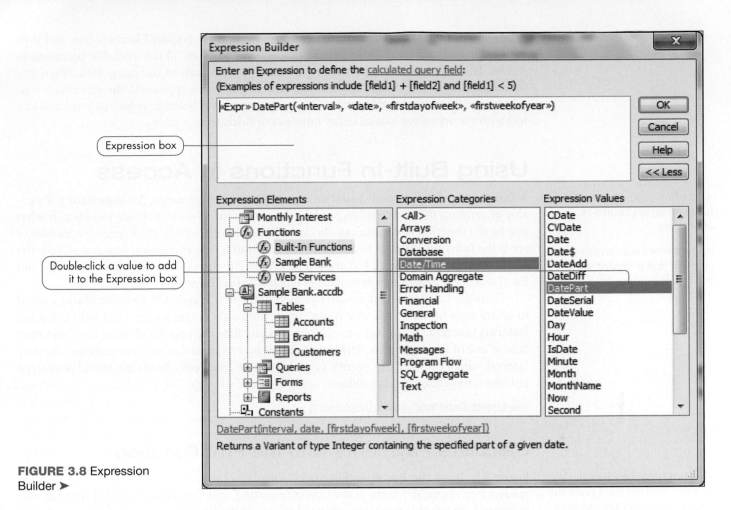

FIGURE 3.8 Expression Builder ➤

Create an Expression

The left column of the Expression Builder dialog box contains Expression Elements, which include the built-in functions, the tables and other objects from the current database, and common expressions. Select an item in this column; the middle column will show the list of options. For example, click a table in the left column and the fields from that table will appear in the middle column.

The middle column displays the Expression Categories based on the item selected in the Expression Elements box. For example, when the Built-in Functions item is selected in the Expression Elements box, the available built-in function categories are displayed in the Expression Categories box, such as the Date/Time category.

The right column displays the Expression Values, if any, for the categories that you selected in the Expression Categories box. For example, if you click Built-In Functions in the Expression Elements box, and then click Date/Time in the Expression Categories box, the Expression Values box lists all of the built-in functions in the Date/Time category, including DatePart.

You can create an expression by manually typing text in the expression box or by double-clicking the elements from the bottom section in the Expression Builder dialog box. For example, to create a calculated field using the fields in the tables, type the calculated field name, and then type a colon. Next, click the desired table listed in the *Expression Elements* section, and then double-click the field you want. Click the Operators item in the *Expression Elements* section, and then choose an operator (such as + or *) from the *Expression Categories* section (or just type the operator). The Expression Builder is flexible and will enable you to find what you need while still enabling you to modify the expression manually.

Calculated fields are relatively simple to create and most Access developers can create them without the Expression Builder. The main reason to use the builder for a calculated field is to eliminate spelling errors in field names. Using functions in Access almost always requires the Expression Builder since the syntax of functions can be difficult to remember.

When you double-click the Functions command in the Expression Elements box, and then click Built-In Functions, the Expression Categories box lists all the available functions in Access. The Expression Values box lists the functions in each of the categories. When you find the function you need, double-click it and the function appears in the expression box. You can see the <<placeholder text>> where the arguments belong; replace each placeholder text with the argument values, either numbers or fields from a table.

Using Built-In Functions in Access

A **function** produces a result based on inputs known as arguments.

An **argument** is a variable or constant that is needed to produce the output for a function.

A *function* produces a result based on inputs known as arguments. An *argument* is a variable or constant that is needed to produce the output for a function. Once you identify what you need a function to do, you can check the Built-in Functions in the Expression Builder to see if the function exists. If it does, add the function to the expression box and replace the <<placeholder text>> with the argument values. Functions work the same in Access and Excel and other programming languages (such as Visual Basic).

Consider the Property database you used in the first Hands-On Exercise. If you wanted to group each home by the year it was listed, you could create a year listed field using the DatePart function. This function will help you calculate the year listed using the DateListed field as one of the arguments. The DatePart function requires one other argument—the date interval, which could be day, month, or year. The year listed calculated field would be entered into the query design grid as follows:

YearListed: DatePart("yyyy", [DateListed])

Calculate Payments with the Pmt Function

The **Pmt function** calculates the monthly loan payment given the interest rate (monthly), term of the loan (in months), and the original value of the loan (the principal).

Figure 3.9 shows the *Pmt function*, which calculates the monthly loan payment given the interest rate (monthly), term of the loan (in months), and the original value of the loan (the principal). To use this function, you need to supply the five arguments as field names from underlying tables or as constants.

The first argument is the interest rate per period. Interest rates are usually stated as annual rates, so you will need to convert them to monthly rates by dividing by 12. The second argument is the number of periods. Because loan terms are usually stated in years, you will need to convert the period to months by multiplying by 12. The next argument is the present value—or principal—of the loan. It tells you how much each customer has borrowed. The last two arguments, future value and type (both optional), are usually 0 or blank. The future value shows the amount the borrower will owe after the last payment has been made. The type argument tells Access whether the payment is made at the beginning or the end of the period.

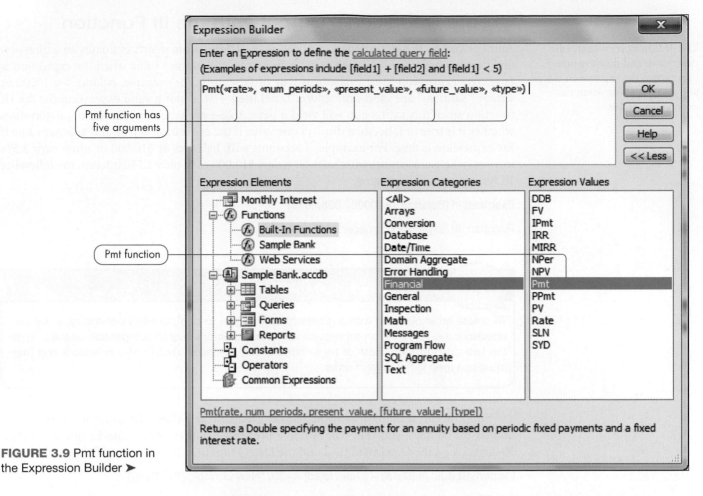

FIGURE 3.9 Pmt function in the Expression Builder ➤

The following example shows how to use the Pmt function to calculate the monthly payment on a $12,500 loan, at a 6.0% interest rate, with a four-year payback term. Table 3.2 describes the arguments for the Pmt function in more detail.

Function: Pmt(*rate, num_periods, present value, future value, type*)

Example: Pmt(0.06/12, 4*12, 12500)

TABLE 3.2	Arguments of the Pmt Function
Part	**Description**
()	Items inside the parentheses are arguments for the function. The arguments are separated by commas. Some arguments are optional; some arguments have a default value; in the Pmt function, the first three arguments are required and the last two are optional.
rate	Required. Expression or value specifying interest rate per period, usually monthly. A mortgage with an annual percentage rate of **6.0%** with monthly payments would have a rate entered as **0.06/12**. *The interest rate must match the period.*
num_periods	Required. Expression or integer value specifying total number of payment periods in the loan. For example, monthly payments on a four-year car loan give a total of 4 * 12 (or 48) payment periods.
present_value	Required. Expression or value specifying the present value of the money you borrow. If you borrow $12,500 for a car, the value would be 12500.
future_value	Optional. Expression or value specifying the future value after you've made the final payment. Most consumer loans have a future value of $0 after the final payment. However, if you want to save $50,000 over 18 years for your child's education, then 50000 is the future value. Zero is assumed if left blank.
type	Optional. Value (0 or 1) identifying when payments are due. Use 0 if payments are due at the end of the payment period (the default), or 1 if payments are due at the beginning of the period. Zero is assumed if left blank.

Create Conditional Output with the IIf Function

The **IIf function** evaluates an expression and displays one value when the expression is true and another value when the expression is false.

Another common function used in Access is the *IIf function*, which evaluates an expression and displays one value when the expression is true and another value when the expression is false. The expression must evaluate as true or false only. For example, *balance >= 10000* or *City = "Sarasota"* are valid expressions. DateListed + *90* is not a valid expression for the IIf function since this expression will yield a date. Access evaluates the expression, determines whether it is true or false, then displays one value if the expression is true and another value if the expression is false. For example, if accounts with balances of $10,000 or more earn 3.5% interest, whereas accounts with balances below $10,000 earn only 1.5% interest, the following IIf function could be created:

Example: IIf (Balance>=10000, .035, .015)

Function: IIf (expression, truepart, falsepart)

> **TIP** Using Comparison Operators
>
> To create an expression with a *greater than or equal to* comparison operator, type the two operators >=. To create an expression with a *less than or equal to* comparison operator, type the two operators <=. Both of these comparison operators require two operators and they must be typed in the correct order.

Suppose you want to display the phrase "New Listing" when a property has been on the market for 30 days, and "For Sale" when a property has been on the market for more than 30 days. Using the DateListed field and the Date() function, the calculated field would be:

PropertyStatus: IIf (Date() – [DateListed] <=30, "New Listing", "For Sale")

The expression Date() – [DateListed]<=30 evaluates each property and determines if the number of days on market is less than or equal to 30. When the expression is true, the function displays "New Listing." When the expression is false, the function displays "For Sale."

The IIf function can also evaluate text values. For example, to classify a list of customers based on whether they are in or out of the state of California, you could create the IIf function:
IIf([State]="CA", "CA", "Out of State")

> **TIP** Use a Nested IIf
>
> Experienced Access users sometimes need to create nested IIf functions. This happens when two conditions are not sufficient to evaluate an expression. For example, in the earlier example where a property was classified based on days on market, the function PropertyStatus: IIf(Date() – [DateListed]<=30,"New Listing","For Sale") was used. If a third status were needed for properties that were on the market for six months, the nested PropertyStatus: IIf(Date() – [DateListed]<=30,"New Listing", IIf(Date() – [DateListed]>=180,"Stagnant","For Sale")) would be used.

When you finish the expression, click OK to close the Expression Builder dialog box. If you are working in a query, nothing will happen until you run the query. Your newly calculated field displays in the Datasheet view of the query. If you are working in a form, switch to Form view to see the results of your expression. And if you are working in a report, click Print Preview to see the results.

1. Open the query in Design view.
2. Click in the top row of the first blank column.
3. Verify the Design tab is displayed.
4. Click Builder in the Query Setup group to launch the Expression Builder (or right-click in the blank column and select Build from the list).
5. Type the name of the calculated field followed by a colon (:).
6. If the expression requires a field from a table, select a table from the Expression Elements box, and then double-click field names as needed to add them to the expression.
7. Type an arithmetic operator (such as + or *), or click Operators in the Expression Elements box, and then double-click a symbol in the Expression Values box.
8. If the expression requires a function, double-click the Functions folder, click Built-In Functions to see the function categories displayed in the Expression Categories box, and then select the function category. From the Expression Values box, double-click the specific function needed, and then fill in the correct arguments.
9. Click OK to exit the Builder box and place the expression in the field cell.
10. Run the query.
11. Examine and verify the output.
12. Return to the Design view.
13. Modify the new expression if necessary.
14. Run the query.
15. Save the query.

Performing Date Arithmetic

Working with dates in Access can be challenging, especially when performing date arithmetic. This can be even more problematic if your output will contain multiple formats for the United States, Europe, and Asia. Each has their own method of formatting dates. Fortunately, Access has some built-in functions to help work with dates and date arithmetic.

Date formatting affects the date's display without changing the actual underlying value in the table. All dates and times in Access are stored as the number of days that have elapsed since December 31, 1899. For example, January 1, 1900, is stored as 1, indicating one day after December 31, 1899. If the time were 9:00 PM on November 20, 2010, no matter how the date or time is formatted, Access stores it as 40502.875. The 40502 represents the number of days elapsed since December 31, 1899, and the .875 reflects the fraction of the 24-hour day that has passed at 9:00 PM. Because dates are stored by Access as sequential numbers, you can calculate the total numbers of hours worked in a week if you record the starting and ending times for each day. Using **date arithmetic** you can create expressions to calculate lapsed time, such as a person's age based on birth date or the number of days past due an invoice is based on the invoice date.

Date formatting affects the date's display without changing the actual underlying value in the table.

> All dates and times in Access are stored as the number of days that have elapsed since December 31, 1899.

Using **date arithmetic** you can create expressions to calculate lapsed time.

Identify Partial Dates with the DatePart Function

Using a date function, you can isolate a portion of the date that is of interest to you. If your company increases the number of weeks of annual vacation from two weeks to three weeks after an employee has worked for five or more years, then the only part of the date of interest is the time lapsed in years. Access has a function, the **DatePart function**, to facilitate this. Table 3.3 shows the DatePart function parameters.

The **DatePart function** enables you to isolate a specific part of a date, such as the year.

Example: DatePart("yyyy", [Employees]![HireDate])

Function: DatePart(interval, date), firstdayofweek, firstweekofyear

Useful date functions are:

- Date—Inserts the current date into an expression.
- DatePart—Evaluates a date and returns only the portion of the date that is designated.
- DateDiff—Measures the amount of time elapsed between two dates. This is most often today's date as determined by the date function and a date stored in a field. For example, you might calculate the number of days a payment is past due by comparing today's date with the payment DueDate.

TABLE 3.3   Using the DatePart Function

Function Portion	Explanation
DatePart	An Access function that examines a date and returns a portion of the date.
≪interval≫	The first argument, the interval, describes the portion of the date that you wish to return. Use "yyyy" for years, "m" for month, or "d" for day.
≪date≫	The second argument, the date, tells Access where to find the Date/Time information. In this case, it is stored in the Employee table in a field named HireDate.
≪firstdayofweek≫	Optional. A constant that specifies the first day of the week. If not specified, Sunday is assumed.
≪firstweekofyear≫	Optional. A constant that specifies the first week of the year. If not specified, the first week is assumed to be the week in which January 1 occurs.

After you practice using the DatePart function, the syntax for all date functions will become easier to understand. In the next Hands-On Exercise, you will copy and paste a query, use the Expression builder, and use functions.

2 Expression Builder, Functions, and Date Arithmetic

As you learn more about Access, you find it easier to answer Jeff and Bill's questions about the properties using queries. When they ask you to calculate the price per bedroom and the price per room for each property, you use the Expression Builder to make the task easier. You also add two additional fields that calculate the days on market and the estimated commission for each property.

Skills covered: Copy and Paste a Query Using a New Name • Use the Expression Builder to Modify a Field • Use the Expression Builder to Add a Field • Use Functions • Work with Date Arithmetic and Add Criteria

---

STEP 1 ▶ COPY AND PASTE A QUERY USING A NEW NAME

You create a copy of the PricePerSqFt query from the previous Hands-On Exercise and paste it using a new name. You will add a few more calculated fields to the new query. Refer to Figure 3.10 as you complete Step 1.

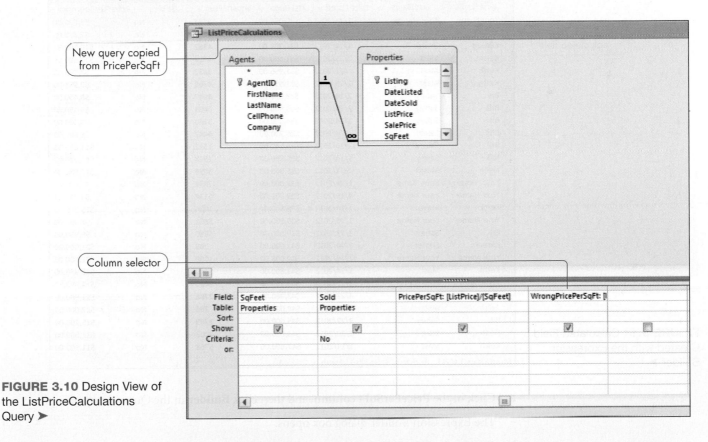

FIGURE 3.10 Design View of the ListPriceCalculations Query ▶

a. Open *a03h1property_LastnameFirstname* if you closed it at the end of Hands-On Exercise 1. Click the **File tab**, click **Save Database As**, and then type **a03h2property_LastnameFirstname**, changing *h1* to *h2*. Click **Save**.

b. Select the **PricePerSqFt query**, and then click **Copy** in the Clipboard group to copy the query.

c. Click **Paste**, and then type **ListPriceCalculations** as the query name. Click **OK**.

The new query is displayed in the Navigation Pane. The name of the query indicates that it contains calculations based on each property's list price.

d. Right-click **ListPriceCalculations**, and then choose **Design View** from the shortcut menu.

e. Delete the WrongPricePerSqFt field by clicking the column selector at the top of the column (as shown in Figure 3.10), and then pressing **Delete**.

The WrongPricePerSqFt field is not needed for this query.

f. Click **Run** to see the query results.

g. Click **View** to return to Design view. Save the query.

STEP 2 ▶ USE THE EXPRESSION BUILDER TO MODIFY A FIELD

You need another calculation to help Jeff and Bill determine which houses to purchase. You will use the Expression Builder to modify an existing field. Refer to Figure 3.11 as you complete Step 2.

Price Per Bedroom calculated field

First Name	Last Name	Date Listed	List Price	Square Feet	Sold	Price Per Bedroom
Your Name	Your Name	1/24/2012	$30,080.00	4834	No	$7,520.00
Keith	Mast	2/10/2012	$31,596.00	6179	No	$7,899.00
Karean	Eissler	1/24/2012	$31,780.00	4362	No	$10,593.33
Keith	Mast	2/25/2012	$31,800.00	4712	No	$10,600.00
Keith	Mast	4/1/2012	$31,996.00	3832	No	$7,999.00
Keith	Mast	1/25/2012	$31,996.00	4768	No	$7,999.00
Bill	Sabey	2/10/2012	$33,800.00	4949	No	$8,450.00
Bill	Sabey	2/10/2012	$33,960.00	3405	No	$8,490.00
Bill	Sabey	1/24/2012	$34,000.00	5180	No	$8,500.00
Bill	Sabey	1/6/2012	$35,200.00	4447	No	$8,800.00
Bill	Sabey	12/20/2012	$35,560.00	1512	No	$11,853.33
Bill	Sabey	1/14/2012	$35,960.00	1568	No	$11,986.67
Keith	Mast	4/1/2012	$35,960.00	3096	No	$17,980.00
Your Name	Your Name	1/24/2012	$38,000.00	7033	No	$7,600.00
Your Name	Your Name	4/19/2012	$39,000.00	5134	No	$9,750.00
Keith	Mast	1/14/2012	$39,800.00	1056	No	$19,900.00
Your Name	Your Name	1/20/2012	$39,800.00	5861	No	$7,960.00
Bill	Sabey	3/23/2012	$39,800.00	5690	No	$9,950.00
Karean	Eissler	2/20/2012	$42,000.00	768	No	$21,000.00
Your Name	Your Name	12/26/2012	$42,000.00	1000	No	$21,000.00
Keith	Mast	1/24/2012	$43,800.00	5440	No	$10,950.00
Your Name	Your Name	11/22/2012	$43,960.00	1497	No	$14,653.33
Karean	Eissler	4/23/2012	$43,960.00	2788	No	$21,980.00
Keith	Mast	1/22/2012	$44,000.00	766	No	$22,000.00
Bill	Sabey	2/22/2012	$45,600.00	1749	No	$15,200.00
Keith	Mast	1/20/2012	$46,000.00	4003	No	$11,500.00
Keith	Mast	1/14/2012	$47,600.00	5768	No	$11,900.00

Record: I◄ ◄ 1 of 213 ▶ ▶I ▶⧸ No Filter Search

FIGURE 3.11 Calculated Field Created with the Expression Builder ➤

a. Click in the **PricePerSqFt column**, and then click **Builder** in the Query Setup group.

The Expression Builder dialog box opens.

b. Change the PricePerSqFt field name to **PricePerBR**.

c. Double-click the **[SqFeet] field** in the expression, and then press **Delete**.

d. Under Expression Elements, click the **plus sign** (+) next to the *a03h2property_ LastnameFirstname* database in the Expression Elements box to expand the list. Click the (+) next to *Tables*, and then click the **Properties table**.

The fields from the Properties table are now listed in the middle column (Expression Categories).

e. Double-click the **Beds field** to add it to the expression box.

The expression now reads *PricePerBR: [ListPrice]/[Properties]![Beds]*.

f. Select the [**Properties**]! **prefix** in front of *Beds*, and then press **Delete**.

The expression now reads *PricePerBR: [ListPrice]/[Beds]*.

g. Click **OK**, and then click **Run** to view the query results.

h. Click **View** to switch to Design view, and then click the **PricePerBR field**. Click **Property Sheet** in the Show/Hide group, change the Format property to **Currency**, and then type **Price Per Bedroom** in the **Caption box**. Close the Property Sheet. Run the query and examine the changes.

i. Click **View** in the Views group to switch back to Design view. Save the query.

TIP Switching Between Object Views

You can switch between object views quickly by clicking View or you can click the View arrow and select the desired view from the list. Another way to switch between views is to right-click the object tab, and then select the view from the shortcut menu. See Figure 3.12.

Right-click the tab to display the shortcut menu

Select the desired view

FIGURE 3.12 Use the Shortcut Menu to Switch Views ➤

TIP Expression Builder and Property Sheet

You can launch the Expression Builder by either clicking Builder in the Query Setup group on the Design tab or by right-clicking in the top row of the query design grid and selecting Build. Similarly, you can display the Property Sheet by clicking Property Sheet in the Show/Hide group on the Design tab or by right-clicking the top row of the query design grid and selecting Properties from the shortcut menu.

STEP 3 USE THE EXPRESSION BUILDER TO ADD A FIELD

The MCCC investors ask you for another calculation—the list price per room. For this calculation, you will assume that each property has a kitchen, a living room, a dining room, and the listed bedrooms and bathrooms. Refer to Figure 3.13 as you complete Step 3.

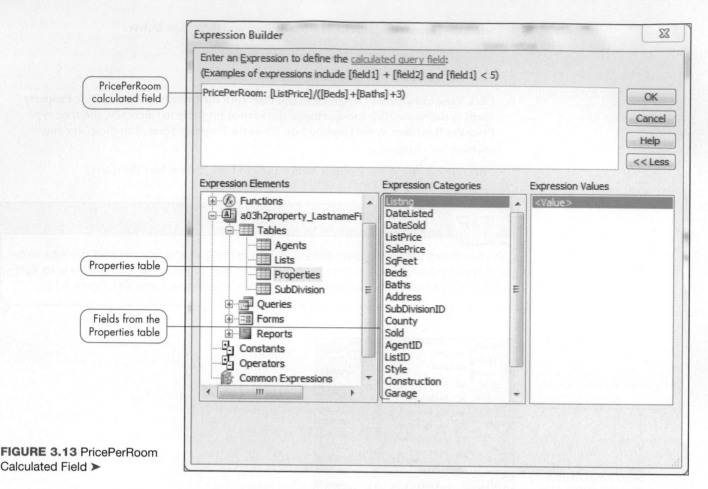

Expression Builder

Enter an Expression to define the calculated query field:
(Examples of expressions include [field1] + [field2] and [field1] < 5)

PricePerRoom: [ListPrice]/([Beds]+[Baths]+3)

OK

Cancel

Help

<< Less

Expression Elements

Expression Categories

Expression Values

- Functions
  - a03h2property_LastnameFi
    - Tables
      - Agents
      - Lists
      - Properties
      - SubDivision
    - Queries
    - Forms
    - Reports
  - Constants
  - Operators
  - Common Expressions

Listing
DateListed
DateSold
ListPrice
SalePrice
SqFeet
Beds
Baths
Address
SubDivisionID
County
Sold
AgentID
ListID
Style
Construction
Garage

<Value>

FIGURE 3.13 PricePerRoom
Calculated Field ➤

a. Select the entire **PricePerBR expression**, right-click the selected expression, and then select **Copy**.

b. Right-click in the next blank column, and then click **Paste**.

   You will edit the copy so that it reflects the price per room.

c. Click the new field, and then click **Builder** in the Query Setup group.

d. Add **parentheses** around the [Beds] portion of the formula. Type a **plus sign** (+) after *[Beds]*, inside the parentheses.

   The expression box should read *PricePerBR: [ListPrice]/([Beds]+)*.

e. Click the **plus sign** (+) next to the *a03h2property_LastnameFirstname* database in the Expression Elements box to expand the list. Click the **plus sign** (+) next to *Tables*, and then click the **Properties table**.

   The fields from the Properties table are now listed in the Expression Categories box.

f. Double-click the **Baths field** to add it to the expression box.

   The expression now reads *PricePerBR: [ListPrice]/([Beds]+[Properties]![Baths])*.

g. Type another plus sign after *[Baths]*, and then type **3**.

   The expression now reads *PricePerBR: [ListPrice]/([Beds]+[Properties]![Baths]+3)*.

h. Delete the [Properties]! portion of the expression.

i. Change the PricePerBR field name to **PricePerRoom**.

   The expression now reads *PricePerRoom: [ListPrice]/([Beds]+[Baths]+3)*.

j. Click **OK** to close the Expression Builder. Run the query. Widen the PricePerRoom column in order to see all the values.

k. Switch to **Design view**, click the **PricePerRoom field**, and then click **Property Sheet**.

l. Change the Format property to **Currency**, and then type **Price Per Room** in the **Caption box**. Close the Property Sheet.

m. Run the query and examine the query results.

n. Save the query, and then close the query.

STEP 4 ▶ USE FUNCTIONS

Jeff and Bill feel like they are close to making an offer on a house. They would like to calculate the estimated mortgage payment for each house. You create this calculation using the Pmt function. Refer to Figures 3.14 and 3.15 as you complete Step 4.

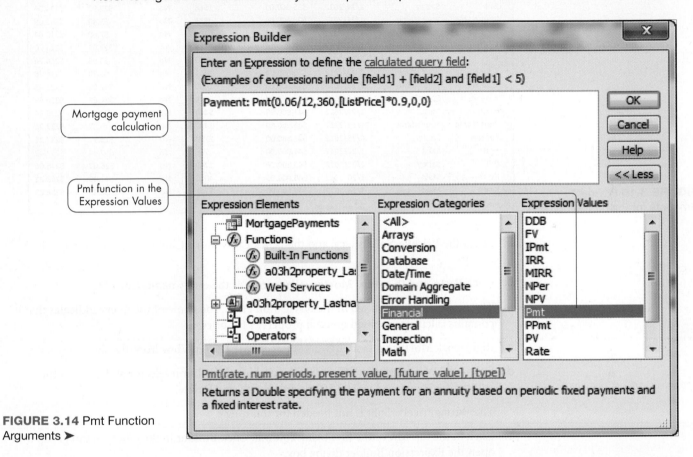

Mortgage payment calculation

Pmt function in the Expression Values

FIGURE 3.14 Pmt Function Arguments ➤

Mortgage payment calculation

First Name	Last Name	Date Listed	List Price	Square Feet	Sold	Price Per Sq Ft	Payment
Your Name	Your Name	1/24/2012	$30,080.00	4834	No	$6.22	$162.31
Keith	Mast	2/10/2012	$31,596.00	6179	No	$5.11	$170.49
Karean	Eissler	1/24/2012	$31,780.00	4362	No	$7.29	$171.48
Keith	Mast	2/25/2012	$31,800.00	4712	No	$6.75	$171.59
Keith	Mast	4/1/2012	$31,996.00	3832	No	$8.35	$172.65
Keith	Mast	1/25/2012	$31,996.00	4768	No	$6.71	$172.65
Bill	Sabey	2/10/2012	$33,800.00	4949	No	$6.83	$182.38
Bill	Sabey	2/10/2012	$33,960.00	3405	No	$9.97	$183.25
Bill	Sabey	1/24/2012	$34,000.00	5180	No	$6.56	$183.46
Bill	Sabey	1/6/2012	$35,200.00	4447	No	$7.92	$189.94
Bill	Sabey	12/20/2012	$35,560.00	1512	No	$23.52	$191.88
Keith	Mast	4/1/2012	$35,960.00	3096	No	$11.61	$194.04
Bill	Sabey	1/14/2012	$35,960.00	1568	No	$22.93	$194.04
Your Name	Your Name	1/24/2012	$38,000.00	7033	No	$5.40	$205.05
Your Name	Your Name	4/19/2012	$39,000.00	5134	No	$7.60	$210.44
Keith	Mast	1/14/2012	$39,800.00	1056	No	$37.69	$214.76
Bill	Sabey	3/23/2012	$39,800.00	5690	No	$6.99	$214.76
Your Name	Your Name	1/20/2012	$39,800.00	5861	No	$6.79	$214.76
Your Name	Your Name	12/26/2012	$42,000.00	1000	No	$42.00	$226.63
Karean	Eissler	2/20/2012	$42,000.00	768	No	$54.69	$226.63
Keith	Mast	1/24/2012	$43,800.00	5440	No	$8.05	$236.34
Your Name	Your Name	11/22/2012	$43,960.00	1497	No	$29.37	$237.21
Karean	Eissler	4/23/2012	$43,960.00	2788	No	$15.77	$237.21
Keith	Mast	1/22/2012	$44,000.00	766	No	$57.44	$237.42
Bill	Sabey	2/22/2012	$45,600.00	1749	No	$26.07	$246.06
Keith	Mast	1/20/2012	$46,000.00	4003	No	$11.49	$248.21
Keith	Mast	1/14/2012	$47,600.00	5768	No	$8.25	$256.85

Record: 14 ◀ 1 of 84 ▶ ▶I ▶▣ No Filter Search

FIGURE 3.15 Payment Amounts for Each Property ➤

a. Select the **PricePerSqFt query**, and then click **Copy** in the Clipboard group to copy the query.

b. Click **Paste**, and then type **MortgagePayments** as the query name. Click **OK**.

   The new query is displayed in the Navigation Pane. The name of the query indicates that it contains calculations based on each property's list price.

c. Right-click **MortgagePayments**, and then choose **Design View** from the shortcut menu.

d. Delete the WrongPricePerSqFeet field by clicking the column selector at the top of the column (as shown in Figure 3.10), and then pressing **Delete**.

   The WrongPricePerSqFt is not needed for this query.

e. Click in the top row of the first blank column. Click **Builder** in the Query Setup group to open the Expression Builder dialog box.

   You will use the Pmt function to calculate an estimated house payment for each of the sold properties. You make the following assumptions: 90% of the sale price will be financed, a 30-year term, monthly payments, and a fixed 6.0% annual interest rate.

f. Double-click **Functions** in the Expression Elements box, and then click **Built-In Functions**.

g. Click the **Financial category** in the Expression Categories box.

h. Double-click the **Pmt function** in the Expression Values box. The expression box displays:

   Pmt(«rate», «num_periods», «present_value», «future_value», «type»)

i. Type **Payment:** to the left of the Pmt function. The expression box now displays:

   Payment: Pmt(«rate», «num_periods», «present_value», «future_value», «type»)

TROUBLESHOOTING: If you forget to add the calculated field name to the left of the expression, Access will add *Expr1* to the front of your expression for you. You can edit the Expr1 name later, after the Expression Builder is closed.

j. Click each argument to select it, and then substitute the appropriate information. Make sure there is a comma between each argument.

Argument	Replacement Value
<<rate>>	0.06/12
<<num_periods>>	360
<<present_value>>	[ListPrice] * 0.9 *(this represents 90% of the list price)*
<<future_value>>	0
<<due>>	0

k. Examine Figure 3.14 to make sure that you have entered the correct arguments. Click **OK**. Run the query.

The Payment column shows ########. Widen the column and notice the payment amounts are negative numbers. You will edit the formula to change the negative payment values to positive.

l. Right-click the **MortgagePayments tab**, and then choose **Design View** from the shortcut menu. Right-click the **Payment field**, and then select **Build**. Add a **minus sign** (−) to the left of *[ListPrice]*.

The expression now reads *Payment: Pmt(0.06/12,360,−[ListPrice]*0.9,0,0).*

m. Click **OK**. Open the **Property Sheet** for *Payment*, and then change the format to **Currency**. Close the Property Sheet.

The calculated field values should now appear as positive values formatted as currency, as shown in Figure 3.15.

n. Run and save the query.

STEP 5 ▶ **WORK WITH DATE ARITHMETIC AND ADD CRITERIA**

You need to limit the query results to only houses on the market at least six months. The investors also want you to add the commission fee to the query since they are getting ready to make a purchase and this information will help them figure out their commission cost. Refer to Figure 3.16 as you complete Step 5.

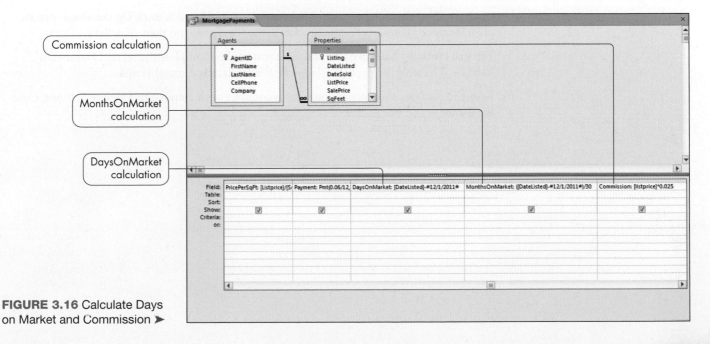

FIGURE 3.16 Calculate Days on Market and Commission ▶

a. Click **View** to return to the Design view of the MortgagePayments query. Click in the top row of the first blank column. Press **Shift+F2** to open the Zoom dialog box.

You need to enter an expression to calculate the number of days that each property has been on the market.

b. Type **DaysOnMarket: [DateListed] – #12/1/2011#.**

This will display the number of days a house has been on the market since 12/1/2011.

c. Click **OK** to close the Zoom dialog box. Open the **Property Sheet**, and then add the Caption to **Days on Market**. Close the Property sheet.

d. Type **<=100000** in the **Criteria row** of the **ListPrice column**. Run the query. Save the query.

This expression will limit the query results to only houses with a list price of $100,000 or less. There should be 84 records.

e. Click **View** to switch to Design view. Click in the top row of the first blank column. Press **Shift+F2** to open the Zoom dialog box.

f. Type the formula **MonthsOnMarket: ([DateListed] – #12/1/2011#) / 30.**

The formula for MonthsOnMarket requires placing parentheses around *[DateListed] – #12/1/2011#* and then dividing the result by 30. This is an example of how to control the order of operations.

g. Click **OK** to close the Zoom dialog box. Open the Property Sheet, and then change the Format to **Fixed**, and the Caption to **Months on Market**. Close the Property Sheet dialog box. Run the query. Save the query.

h. Switch to Design view. Click in the top row of the first blank column to create another calculated field. Open the Zoom dialog box, and then type the formula **Commission: ListPrice * .025**. Click **OK** to close the Zoom dialog box.

The Commission field displays the projected commission for each house. The agent earns 2.5% of the sale price.

i. Right-click the **Commission field**, and then select **Properties**. Change the format to **Currency**, and then close the Property Sheet.

j. Run the query, examine the results, and then save the query. Close the query.

The values in the Commission field now display in Currency format.

k. Click the **File tab**, and then click **Compact & Repair Database**.

l. Click the **File tab**, click **Save & Publish**, and then double-click **Back Up Database**. Accept *a03h2property_LastnameFirstname_date* as the file name, and then click **Save**.

You just created a backup of the database you used to complete the second Hands-On Exercise. The *a03h2property_LastnameFirstname* database remains open.

m. Keep the database onscreen if you plan to continue with Hands-On Exercise 3. If not, close the database and exit Access.

Aggregate Functions

Aggregate functions—such as Sum, Average, and Minimum—are used when you need to evaluate a group of record values rather than the individual records in a table or query.

Aggregate functions perform calculations on an entire column of data and return a single value. Aggregate functions—such as Sum, Average, and Minimum—are used when you need to evaluate a group of record values rather than the individual records in a table or query.

Access refers to aggregate functions as Totals. In the Datasheet view of a query or table, click Totals in the Records group on the Home tab to add a Total row to the bottom of the datasheet. Each column can have its own aggregate function. Numeric fields are eligible for all of the functions, whereas text fields are only eligible for the count function.

When you create a query in Design view, click Totals in the Show/Hide group to change it to a totals query. The Total row now appears and you can select from the list of aggregate functions (e.g., Sum, Avg, Min).

The Datasheet view of a query or table displays individual records; users can edit these records, enter a new record, or delete a record in Datasheet view. However, when you work within a totals query in Datasheet view, no updates are allowed. A user cannot add, update, or delete records that have been totaled.

A car dealer's monthly inventory report is a good example of a report that might contain aggregate information. The cars would be grouped by model, and then by options package and color. At the end of the report, a summary page would list the count of cars in each model for quick reference by the sales reps. In the property database, aggregate information could be grouped by county or by subdivision. For example, the average home price per county could be presented

Almost every company or organization that uses a database will require some type of aggregate data.

in a query or a report. This would give prospective buyers a good idea of home prices in their target counties. Almost every company or organization that uses a database will require some type of aggregate data.

A list of common aggregate functions is shown in Table 3.4.

TABLE 3.4	**Aggregate Functions**	
Function	**Description**	**Use with Data Type(s)**
Average	Calculates the average value for a column. The function ignores null values.	Number, Currency, Date/Time
Count	Counts the number of items in a column. The function ignores null values.	All data types except a column of multivalued lists.
Maximum	Returns the item with the highest value. For text data, the highest value is 'Z.' The function ignores null values.	Number, Currency, Date/Time, Text
Minimum	Returns the item with the lowest value. For text data, the lowest value is 'a.' The function ignores null values.	Number, Currency, Date/Time, Text
Standard Deviation	Measures how widely values are dispersed from an average value.	Number, Currency
Sum	Adds the items in a column. Works only on numeric and currency data.	Number, Currency
Variance	Measures the statistical variance of all values in the column.	Number

In this section, you will learn how to create and work with aggregate functions. Specifically, you will learn how to use the Total row and create a totals query.

Adding Aggregate Functions to Datasheets and Queries

Aggregate functions are most commonly used in tables, queries, and reports. Occasionally, aggregate functions are also added to the form footer section of forms. Aggregate data helps users evaluate the values in a single record as compared to the average of all the records.

If you are considering buying a property in Bucks county for $150,000 and the average price of a property in Bucks county is $450,000, you know you are getting a good deal (or buying a bad property).

A **Total row** displays as the last row in the Datasheet view of a table or query and provides a number of aggregate functions.

Access provides two methods of adding aggregate functions to a query—a ***Total row*** displayed as the last row in the Datasheet view of a table or query and a totals query created in query Design view.

The first method enables you to add a Total row to the Datasheet view. This method is quick and easy and has the advantage of showing the total information while still showing the individual records. Adding a Total row to a query or table can be accomplished by most users (even those who are not familiar with designing a query).

The second method requires you to add a Total row in the Query Design view. This method has the advantage of enabling you to group your data by categories. For example, you can use the Count function to show the number of houses sold in each county in each subdivision. You could also use the Average function to show the average sale price for houses sold in each subdivision.

Once the totals data are assembled, you can use them to make decisions. Who is the leading salesperson? Which subdivisions are selling the most houses? This method requires the user to understand how to alter the design of a query.

Access also permits aggregates in reports. The Report Wizard gives users a choice to show all detail records or summary-only statistics. Select summary only to see aggregate data. You will learn to use both methods of creating aggregate data.

Add a Total Row in a Query or Table

Figure 3.17 shows the Total row added to the Datasheet view of a query. Using the balance column as illustrated, you can choose any of the aggregate functions that apply to numeric fields. To begin, click Totals in the Records group on the Home tab. The Total row is added at the bottom of the datasheet, below the new record row of the query or table. In the Total row, you can select one of the aggregate functions by clicking in the cell and then clicking the arrow. The list of aggregate functions includes Sum, Average, Count, and others.

Click Totals to add the Totals row

Click the Total row arrow to show aggregate functions

FIGURE 3.17 Adding a Total Row to a Query in Datasheet View ➤

Create a Totals Query

A **totals query** contains an additional row in the design grid and is used to display only aggregate data when the query is run.

A *totals query* contains an additional row in the query design grid and is used to display only aggregate data when the query is run. This is in contrast to using the Total row in a datasheet which shows both the detail records and the summary (as described in the previous section). The first column of a totals query will usually be a grouping field; the Total row will contain the Group function. The second and subsequent columns will usually contain the Count, Sum, or Avg function. Problems can arise when too many columns are included in a totals query; a typical totals query contains only two to five columns. Figure 3.18 shows the Design view of a totals query with three columns.

FIGURE 3.18 Totals Query in Design View ➤

Figure 3.18 groups the properties by county and then shows the count of houses and the average price in each county. You could add the Subdivision field to the second column of this query—to create a group within a group. The data will now be grouped by county and then by subdivision within each county. In order to show the subdivision field, you must add the Subdivision table to the query design. Figure 3.19 shows the results of the Housing Info by County by Subdivision totals query.

FIGURE 3.19 Totals Query in Datasheet View ➤

If you were asked to evaluate a database that contains home sales information, you could quickly determine which agents sold houses by creating a totals query with two tables and three fields. From the Properties and Agents tables, you would add the LastName field, the Listing field, and the Sold field. Click Totals in the Show/Hide group. Accept Group By in column one; change column two to Count, and change column three to Where. Add Yes to the Criteria row of column three. The results of this query would show which agents sold homes, as shown in Figure 3.20.

Reps who sold homes

Number of homes sold

FIGURE 3.20 Totals Query Shows Agents Who Sold Houses ➤

3 Aggregate Functions

The investors decide it would be helpful to analyze the property lists they purchased. Some of the lists do not have homes that match their target criteria. The investors will either need to purchase new lists or alter their criteria. You create several totals queries to evaluate the property lists.

Skills covered: Add a Total Row to Datasheet View • Create a Totals Query Based on a Select Query • Add a Calculated Field to a Totals Query

STEP 1 ▷ ADD A TOTAL ROW TO DATASHEET VIEW

You begin your property list analysis by creating a Total row in the Datasheet view of the MortgagePayments query. This will give you a variety of aggregate information for each column. Refer to Figure 3.21 as you complete Step 1.

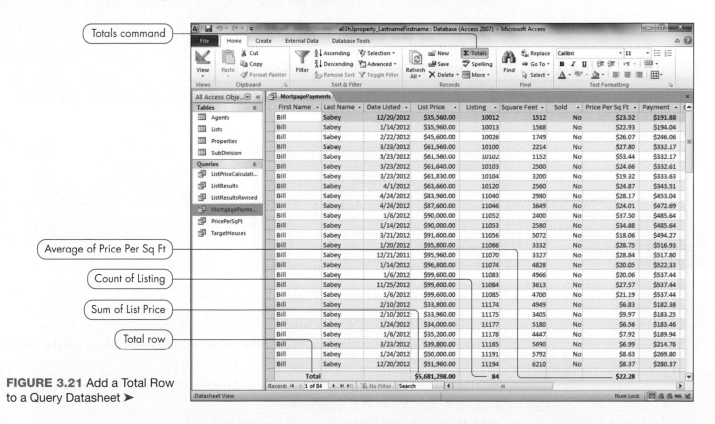

FIGURE 3.21 Add a Total Row to a Query Datasheet ➤

a. Open *a03h2property_LastnameFirstname* if you closed it at the end of Hands-On Exercise 2. Click the **File tab**, click **Save Database As**, and then type **a03h3property_LastnameFirstname**, changing *h2* to *h3*. Click **Save**.

b. Right-click the **MortgagePayments query** in the Navigation Pane, and then select **Design View** from the shortcut menu. Drag the **Listing field** from the Properties table to the fifth column.

The Listing field is now in the fifth column and the other columns shift to the right.

c. Click **View** to switch to Datasheet view. Click **Totals** in the Records group on the Home tab to show the Total row.

The Total row is now displayed as the last row of the query results. Click Totals again to hide the Total row, then one more time to show it.

d. Click in the cell that intersects the Total row and the List Price column.

e. Click the arrow, and then select **Sum** to display the total of all the properties that have not sold. Widen the List Price column if you can't see the entire total value.

The total list price of all properties is $5,681,298.00.

f. Click the arrow in the Total row in the Listing column, and then select **Count** from the list.

The count of properties in this datasheet is 84.

g. Click in the Total row in the Price Per Sq Ft column. Click the arrow, and then select **Average** to display the average price per square foot.

h. Save and close the query.

STEP 2 ▶ CREATE A TOTALS QUERY BASED ON A SELECT QUERY

You create a totals query to help Jeff and Bill evaluate the properties in groups. Refer to Figure 3.22 as you complete Step 2.

Source of the data ⟶

Average sale price ⟶

Number of homes sold ⟶

ListResults		
NameOfList ▾	AvgOfSalePrice ▾	Number Sold ▾
MLS	$89,750.00	8
PhillyHousesForSale	$170,250.00	24
Reading Eagle	$242,450.00	8
Realtor.com	$130,422.73	11
Trulia	$145,781.82	18
Wholesaler	$223,316.67	16
ZIP	$322,000.00	5

FIGURE 3.22 Results of a Totals Query ▶

a. Click the **Create tab**, and then click **Query Design** in the Queries group.

You create a new query in Query Design; the Show Table dialog box opens.

b. Add the Properties table and the Lists table from the Show Table dialog box. Close the Show Table dialog box.

c. Add the NameOfList field from the Lists table and the SalePrice and Sold fields from the Properties table to the query design grid.

d. Click **Totals** in the Show/Hide Group to show the Total row.

e. Change the Total row to **Avg** in the SalePrice column.

f. Change the Total row to **Where** in the Sold column. Type **Yes** in the **Criteria row**.

This criterion will limit the results to sold houses only.

g. Click in the **SalePrice field**, and then click **Property Sheet** in the Show/Hide group. Change the SalePrice format to **Currency**. Close the Property Sheet. Run the query.

The query results indicate that the MLS list is the only source that is under the investor's target of $100,000 or less. They decide to continue using Realtor.com and Trulia even though the average price is over $100,000. The other sources will no longer be used.

h. Click **View** to switch to Design View. Add the Listing field from the Properties table to the fourth column in the design grid. Change the Total row for *Listing* to **Count**. Run the query.

The query results now show the number of properties sold in each source, in addition to the average sale price. This will help determine which sources have been more effective.

i. Click **View** to return to the Design view of the query. Change the caption of the Listing column to **Number Sold**. Run the query, and then widen the columns as shown in Figure 3.22.

j. Save the query as **ListResults**. Keep the query open for the next step.

STEP 3 ## ADD A CALCULATED FIELD TO A TOTALS QUERY

The totals query helped group the houses into categories. However, the groups contain all the properties, even the ones that do not match the investor's criteria. You need to create a new query with the investor's criteria included. Refer to Figure 3.23 as you complete Step 3.

FIGURE 3.23 Add Criteria to a Totals Query ➤

a. Click the **File tab**, and then click **Save Object As**. Save the query as **ListResultsRevised**. Click the **File tab** to return to the query.

b. Click **Totals** in the Records group, and then add **Sum** to the Number Sold column.

The total number of houses sold is 90.

c. Click **View** in the Views group to switch to Design view. In the first blank column, type **DaysOnMarket: [DateListed] – #12/1/2011#** to create a new calculated field. Change the Total row to **Avg**.

d. Right-click the **DaysOnMarket field**, and then select **Properties** from the shortcut menu. Change the Format property to **Fixed**. Close the Property Sheet.

e. Run the ListResultsRevised query, and then examine the DaysOnMarket.

f. Save and close the query.

g. Click the **File tab**, and then click **Compact & Repair Database**.

h. Click the **File tab**, click **Save & Publish**, and then double-click **Back Up Database**. Accept *a03h3property_LastnameFirstname_date* as the file name, and then click **Save**.

You just created a backup of the database you used to complete the third Hands-On Exercise. The *a03h3property_LastnameFirstname* database remains open.

i. Click the **File tab**, and then click **Exit** (to exit Access).

j. Submit based on your instructor's directions.

After reading this chapter, you have accomplished the following objectives:

1. **Understand the order of operations.** The order of operations determines the sequence by which operations are calculated in an expression. Evaluate expressions in parentheses first, then exponents, then multiplication and division, and, finally, addition and subtraction. Operations of equal value will be calculated from left to right. A solid understanding of these rules will enable you to easily create calculated fields in Access.

2. **Create a calculated field in a query.** When creating a query, you may need to create a calculation based on the fields from one or more tables. Add a calculated field in the Design view of a query to the first blank column or by inserting a blank column where needed. A formula used to calculate new fields from the values in existing fields is known as an *expression*. An expression can consist of a number of fields, operators (such as *, /, +, or −), functions (such as IIf), and constants (numbers). When creating a calculated field, you must follow proper syntax—the set of rules that Access follows when evaluating an expression.

3. **Create expressions with the Expression Builder.** Launch the Expression Builder while in the query design grid to assist you with creating a calculated field (or other expression). The Expression Builder helps you create expressions by supplying you with the fields, operators, and functions you need to create them. When you use the Expression Builder to help you create expressions, you can eliminate spelling errors in field names. Another advantage is with functions; functions require specific arguments in a specific order. When you insert

a function using the Expression Builder, the builder gives you placeholders that tell you where each argument belongs.

4. **Use built-in functions in Access.** A function produces a result based on variable inputs known as *arguments*. Once you identify what you need a function to do, you can open the Built-In Functions folder in the Expression Builder to see if the function exists. If it does, add the function to the expression box and supply the required arguments. Functions work the same in Access and Excel.

5. **Perform date arithmetic.** All dates and times in Access are stored as the number of days that have elapsed since December 31, 1899. Working with dates in Access can be challenging, especially when performing date arithmetic. Fortunately, Access has some built-in functions to help work with dates and date arithmetic. Sample functions include DateDiff (), DateAdd(), Date(), and Now(). These functions help perform arithmetic on date fields.

6. **Add aggregate functions to datasheets and queries.** Aggregate functions perform calculations on an entire column of data and return a single value. Aggregate functions—such as Sum, Average, and Minimum—are used when you need to evaluate a group of records rather than the individual records in a table or query. Access refers to aggregate functions as Totals. In the Datasheet view of a query or table, click Totals to add a Total row to the bottom of the datasheet. When you create a query in Design view, click Totals to show the Total row.

KEY TERMS

Aggregate function *p.675*
Argument *p.662*
Constant *p.651*
Date arithmetic *p.665*
Date formatting *p.665*

DatePart function *p.665*
Expression *p.651*
Expression Builder *p.660*
Function *p.662*
IIf function *p.664*

Order of operations *p.650*
Pmt function *p.662*
Syntax *p.651*
Total row *p.676*
Totals query *p.677*

1. Which of the following correctly identifies the rules for the order of operations?

   (a) Exponentiation, parentheses, addition, subtraction, multiplication, division

   (b) Parentheses, exponentiation, addition, subtraction, multiplication, division

   (c) Parentheses, exponentiation, multiplication, division, addition, subtraction

   (d) Addition, subtraction, multiplication, division, exponentiation, parentheses

2. What is the result of the following expression?

   $(3 * 5) + 7 - 2 - 6 * 2$

   (a) 12

   (b) 7

   (c) 28

   (d) 8

3. The Builder command that opens the Expression Builder is found in the:

   (a) Manage group on the Databases Tools tab.

   (b) Query Setup group on the Design tab.

   (c) Database Management group on the Design tab.

   (d) Design group on the Query Setup tab.

4. Which function enables you to insert today's date into an expression?

   (a) Date()

   (b) DatePart()

   (c) Now()

   (d) DateDiff()

5. You correctly calculated a value for the OrderAmount using an expression. Now you need to use the newly calculated value in another expression calculating sales tax. The most efficient method is to:

   (a) Run and save the query to make OrderAmount available as input to subsequent expressions.

   (b) Create a new query based on the query containing the calculated Order amount, and then calculate the sales tax in the new query.

   (c) Close the Access file, saving the changes when asked; reopen the file and reopen the query; calculate the sales tax.

   (d) Create a backup of the database, open the backup and the query, then calculate the sales tax.

6. If state law requires that a restaurant's wait staff be at least 21 to serve alcohol and you have a database that stores each employee's birth date in the Employee table, which of the following is the proper syntax to identify the employees' year of birth?

   (a) Age:DatePart("yyyy",[Employee]![BirthDate])

   (b) Age=DatePart("yyyy",[Employee]![BirthDate])

   (c) Age:DatePart("yyyy",[BirthDate]![Employee])

   (d) Age=DatePart("yyyy",[BirthDate]![Employee])

7. Which statement about a totals query is true?

   (a) A totals query is created in Datasheet view.

   (b) A totals query may contain several grouping fields but only one aggregate field.

   (c) A totals query is limited to only two fields, one grouping field, and one aggregate field.

   (d) A totals query may contain several grouping fields and several aggregate fields.

8. After creating a calculated field, you run the query and a parameter dialog box appears on your screen. How do you respond to the Parameter dialog box?

   (a) Click OK to make the parameter box go away.

   (b) Read the field name specified in the parameter box, and then look for a possible typing error in the calculated expression.

   (c) Type numbers in the parameter box, and then click OK.

   (d) Close the query without saving changes. Re-open it and try running the query again.

9. An updatable query contains student names. You run the query and while in Datasheet view, you notice a spelling error on one of the student's names. You correct the error in Datasheet view. Which statement is true?

   (a) The name is correctly spelled in this query but will be misspelled in the table and all other queries based on the table.

   (b) The name is correctly spelled in the table and in all queries based on the table.

   (c) The name is correctly spelled in this query and any other queries, but will remain misspelled in the table.

   (d) You cannot edit data in a query.

10. Which of the following is not true about the Total row in the query design grid?

    (a) The Total row enables you to apply aggregate functions to the fields.

    (b) The Total row can apply to fields stored in different tables.

    (c) The Total row is located between the Table and Sort rows.

    (d) The Total row can only be applied to numeric fields.

PRACTICE EXERCISES

1 Comfort Insurance

The Comfort Insurance Agency is a mid-sized company with offices located across the country. Each employee receives a performance review annually. The review determines employee eligibility for salary increases and the annual performance bonus. The employee data are stored in an Access database, which is used by the human resources department to monitor and maintain employee records. Your task is to calculate the salary increase for each employee; you will also calculate each employee's performance bonus for employees who have been employed at least one year. This exercise follows the same set of skills as used in Hands-On Exercises 1 and 2 in the chapter. Refer to Figure 3.24 as you complete this exercise.

FIGURE 3.24 Raises and Bonuses ➤

a. Open *a03p1insurance*. Click the **File tab**, click **Save Database As**, and then type **a03p1insurance_LastnameFirstname**. Click **Save**.

b. Click the **Database Tools tab**, and then click **Relationships** in the Relationships group. Examine the table structure, relationships, and fields. Once you are familiar with the database, close the Relationships window.

c. Click the **Create tab**, and then click **Query Design** in the Queries group to start a new query. The Show Table dialog box opens. Add the Employees and Titles tables. Close the Show Table dialog box.

d. Add the **LastName**, **FirstName**, **Performance**, and **Salary fields** to the query. From the Titles table, add the **2012Increase field** to the query.

e. Click the top row of the first blank column in the query design grid, and then type **NewSalary:[Salary]*[2012Increase]+[Salary]** to create a calculated field.

f. Click **Run** in the Results group to run the query. (If you receive the Enter Parameter Value dialog box, check your expression carefully for spelling errors.) Look at the output in the Datasheet view. Verify that your answers are correct. Notice that the fourth column heading displays *2012 Increase*. This is the caption for the 2012Increase field in the Titles table that was carried over to the query. When a caption exists for a field in the table Design view, the caption also displays in the Query Datasheet view instead of the field name in the query.

g. Click **View** in the Views group to switch back to Design view. Open the Property Sheet, click in the **NewSalary calculated field**, and then change the format to **Currency**. Type **New Salary** in the **Caption box**. Close the Property Sheet.

h. Save the query as **Raises and Bonuses**.

i. Click the top row of the first blank column, and then click **Builder** in the Query Setup group. In the Expression Elements box, double-click the folder for **Functions**. Select the **Built-In Functions folder**. Scroll down the Expression Values box to locate the IIf function. Double-click **IIf** to insert the function.

j. Click <<**expression**>>, and then replace it with **Performance = "Excellent"**. Click <<**truepart**>>, and then replace it with **1000**. Click <<**falsepart**>>, and then replace it with **50**.

k. Type **Bonus:** to the left of *IIf*, as the calculated field name. Click **OK**.

l. Change the format of the Bonus field to **Currency** in the Property Sheet.

m. Run the query. Save and close the query.

n. Click the **File tab**, and then click **Compact and Repair Database**.

o. Click the **File tab**, click **Save & Publish**, and then double-click **Back Up Database**. Click **Save** to accept the default backup file name.

p. Click the **File tab**, and then click **Exit** (to exit Access).

q. Submit based on your instructor's directions.

---

2 Northwind Traders

Northwind Traders maintains a database to store all of its product and inventory information, customer information, and sales information. You are the marketing manager of Northwind Traders and use this database to monitor sales trends. You need to determine the revenue from each order filled in the last year, and to summarize the revenue figures by product category. This exercise follows the same set of skills as used in Hands-On Exercises 2 and 3 in the chapter. Refer to Figure 3.25 as you complete this exercise.

Revenue by Category

Category Name	Total Revenue	Average Discount
Beverages	$25,109.20	5.74%
Condiments	$11,148.23	6.96%
Confections	$18,018.21	4.00%
Dairy Products	$24,288.60	6.62%
Grains/Cereals	$9,539.75	3.46%
Meat/Poultry	$11,474.25	5.63%
Produce	$10,637.46	2.69%
Seafood	$11,302.55	5.74%

FIGURE 3.25 Revenue by Category ➤

a. Open *a03p2traders*. Click the **File tab**, click **Save Database As**, and then type **a03p2traders_LastnameFirstname**. Click **Save**.

b. Click the **Database Tools tab**, and then click **Relationships** in the Relationships group. Examine the tables, fields, and relationships. After you are familiar with the database, close the Relationships window.

c. Click the **Create tab**, and then click **Query Design** in the Queries group to start a new query. The Show Table dialog box opens.

d. Add the Orders, Order Details, Products, and Categories tables. Close the Show Table dialog box.

e. Add the following fields to the query design grid:
   - OrderDate from the Orders table
   - Quantity and Discount from the Order Details table
   - UnitPrice and ProductCost from the Products table
   - CategoryName from the Categories table

f. Save the query as **Revenue**.

g. Type **>=1/1/2012 and <=3/31/2012** into the **Criteria row** of the OrderDate column (to limit the results to orders placed in the first Qtr of 2012).

h. Click the top row of the first blank column, and then click **Builder** in the Query Setup group. Type **Revenue:UnitPrice * (1-Discount) * Quantity**. Click **OK**.

i. Click **Property Sheet** in the Show/Hide group, and then change the format of the Revenue field to **Currency**. Close the Property Sheet dialog box.

j. Click **Run** to run the query. Use a calculator to check several records to verify the revenue calculation is correct. Save the query, and then close it.

k. Click the **Create tab**, and then click **Query Design** in the Queries group. Click the **Queries tab** in the Show Table dialog box. Double-click the **Revenue query** to add it to the design grid. Click **Close** in the Show Table dialog box.

l. Double-click the **CategoryName**, **Revenue**, and **Discount fields** in the Revenue query to add them to the design grid. Run the query.

m. Switch to Design View, and then click **Totals** in the Show/Hide group on the Design tab. The Total row will display. Change the Revenue Total row to **Sum**, and then change the Discount Total row to **Avg**.

n. Click **Property Sheet** in the Show/Hide group. Change the Revenue format to **Currency** and the Discount format to **Percent**.

o. Run the query. Verify the results. Notice that the second and third column headings are *SumOfRevenue* and *AvgOfDiscount*, respectively, to indicate the functions used on those fields. Save the query as **Revenue by Category**.

p. Click **View** in the Views group to switch to Design view. Change the Revenue field caption to **Total Revenue** and the Discount field caption to **Average Discount**. Save the query, and then run the query to see the captions. Close the query.

q. Click the **File tab**, and then click **Compact & Repair Database**.

r. Click the **File tab**, click **Save & Publish**, and then double-click **Back Up Database**. Use the default backup file name.

s. Click the **File tab**, and then click **Exit** (to exit Access).

t. Submit based on your instructor's directions.

1 The National Bank

You are the manager of the loan department of the National Bank. You need to monitor the total indebtedness of each customer to help them manage their debt load. Several customers may have multiple loans—a mortgage, a car loan, and a home equity loan. Your task is to use the Pmt function to calculate the loan payments for each loan and then to summarize the loans by customer. Refer to Figure 3.26 as you complete this exercise.

Payment Summary	
Last Name ▾	Total Payment ▾
Collins	$3,318.36
Fox	$7,274.63
Greene	$3,798.04
Hayes	$717.03
Jones	$4,403.31
Peterson	$956.21
Simpson	$1,122.13
Wagner	$2,529.52
Williams	$3,462.30
Your name	$4,152.81
Total	$31,734.32

FIGURE 3.26 Payment Summary ➤

a. Open *a03m1bank*. Click the **File tab**, click **Save Database As**, and then type **a03m1bank_LastnameFirstname**. Click **Save.**

b. Open the Customers table. Replace *Megan Royes* with your name. Close the table.

c. Create a query that will calculate the payments for each loan. Add the following fields: LastName, Amount, InterestRate, Term, and Type from the Customers and Loans tables. Save the query as **Loan Payments**.

d. Create a calculated field for the loan payment of each loan. Remember to divide the annual interest rate by 12 and multiply the loan's term by 12. Include a **minus sign** (–) in front of the loan amount in the expression so the result returns a positive value.

e. Run the query. In the Datasheet view, add a Total row. Use it to calculate the average interest rate and the sum for the payment. Save and close the query.

f. Create a totals query based on the Loan Payments query. Add the LastName and Payment fields to the design grid. Group by the LastName field, and then sum the Payment field.

g. Format the Payment field as **Currency**, and then add the caption **Total Payment**.

h. Run the query. Add a Total row to the Datasheet view that will sum the Total Payments. Save this query as **Payment Summary**.

i. Compact the database. Back up the database. Exit Access.

j. Submit based on your instructor's directions.

2 Investment Properties

You are in charge of LGS Investment's database, which contains all of the information on the properties your firm has listed and sold. Your task is to determine the length of time each property was on the market before it sold. You also need to calculate the sales commission from each property sold. Two agents will receive commission on each transaction: the listing agent and the selling agent. You also need to summarize the sales data by employee and calculate the average number of days each employee's sales were on the market prior to selling and the total commission earned by the employees. Refer to Figure 3.27 as you complete this exercise.

FIGURE 3.27 Sales Summary ➤

Sales Summary				
Subdivision	Avg Days On Mkt	Sale Price	Listing Comm	Sell Comm
The Orchards	22.8	$1,288,000.00	$45,080.00	$32,200.00
Fair Brook	24.8	$1,053,900.00	$36,886.50	$26,347.50
Eagle Valley	39.0	$4,012,000.00	$140,420.00	$100,300.00
Wood	47.9	$1,428,650.00	$50,002.75	$35,716.25
Red Canyon	52.0	$3,790,000.00	$132,650.00	$94,750.00
Total		$11,572,550.00	$405,039.25	$289,313.75

a. Open *a03m2homes*. Click the **File tab**, click **Save Database As**, and then type **a03m2homes_LastnameFirstname**. Click **Save**.

b. Open the Agents table, and then replace *David Royes* with your name. Close the table.

c. Create a new query, add the necessary tables, and then add the following fields: LastName, DateListed, DateSold, SalePrice, SellingAgent, ListingAgent, and Subdivision. Type **Is Not Null** into the criterion row of the DateSold field. Save the query as **Sales Report**. Format the SalePrice field as **Currency**.

d. Using the Expression Builder, create the DaysOnMarket calculated field by subtracting DateListed from DateSold. This will calculate the number of days each sold property was on the market when it sold. Add an appropriate caption.

e. Calculate the commissions for the selling and listing agents using two calculated fields. The listing commission rate is **3.5%** and the selling commission rate is **2.5%**. Name the newly created fields **ListComm** and **SellComm**. These fields contain similar expressions. They need to be named differently so that the proper agent—the listing agent or the selling agent—gets paid. Add captions and format the fields as **Currency**.

f. Save the query after you verify that your calculations are correct. In Datasheet view, add the Total row. Calculate the Average number of days on the market and the sum for the SalePrice and the two commission fields. Save and close the query.

g. Create a totals query based on the Sales Report query. Group by LastName, and then show the average of the DaysOnMarket. Show the sum of SalePrice, ListComm, and SellComm. Format the fields as **Currency**, and then add appropriate captions. Run the query. Adjust column widths.

h. Add a Total row to the Datasheet view that will sum the sale price and commission fields. Save the query as **Sales Summary**.

i. Format the average of the Days on Market fields as fixed, one decimal place. (Note: if you do not see the Decimal Places property in the Property Sheet, switch to Datasheet view, then switch back to Design view.) Format the remaining numeric fields as **Currency**. Run the query.

DISCOVER

j. Modify the query so the grouping is based on Subdivision, not LastName. Sort the query results so the fewest Days on Market is first and the most Days on Market is last. Limit the results to the top five rows.

k. Compact the database. Back up the database. Exit Access.

l. Submit based on your instructor's directions.

Northwind Traders, an international gourmet food distributor, is concerned about shipping delays over the last six months. Review the orders over the past six months and identify any order that was not shipped within 30 days. Each customer that falls within that time frame will be called to inquire about any problems the delay may have caused. In addition, an order summary and an order summary by country will be created.

Database File Setup

Open the food database, use Save As to make a copy of the database, and then use the new database to complete this capstone exercise. You will replace an existing employee's name with your name.

a. Locate and open *a03c1food*.

b. Click the **File tab**, click **Save Database As**, and then type **a03c1food_LastnameFirstname**.

c. Click **Save**.

d. Open the Employees table.

e. Replace *Rachael Eliza* with your name. Close the table.

DaysToShip Query

You need to create a query to calculate the number of days between the date an order was placed and the date the order was shipped for each order. As you create the query, run the query at several intervals so you can verify that the data looks correct. The result of your work will be a list of orders that took more than three weeks to ship. The salespeople will be calling each customer to see if there was any problem with their order.

a. Create a query using Query Design. Include the fields CompanyName, ContactName, ContactTitle, Phone, OrderID, LastName, OrderDate, and ShippedDate. Use the Relationships window to determine which tables you need before you begin.

b. Run the query, and then examine the records. Save the query as **Shipping Efficiency**.

c. Add a calculated field named **DaysToShip** to calculate the number of days taken to fill each order. (*Hint*: The expression will include the OrderDate and the ShippedDate; the results will not contain negative numbers.)

d. Run the query, and then examine the results. Does the data in the DaysToShip field look accurate? Save the query.

e. Add criteria to limit the query results to include any order that took more than 30 days to ship.

f. Add the ProductID and Quantity fields to the Shipping Efficiency query. Sort the query by ascending OrderID. When the sales reps contact these customers, these two fields will provide useful information about the orders.

g. Switch to Datasheet view to view the final results. This list will be distributed to the sales reps so they can contact the customers. In Design view, add the **Sales Rep caption** to the LastName field.

h. Save and close the query.

Order Summary Query

You need to create an Order Summary that will show the total amount of each order in one column and the total discount amount in another column. This query will require four tables: Orders, Order Details, Products, and Customers. Query to determine if employees are following the employee discount policy. You will group the data by employee name, count the orders, show the total dollars, and show the total discount amount. You will then determine which employees are following the company guidelines.

a. Create a query using Query Design and add the four tables above plus the Products table. Add the fields OrderID and OrderDate. Click **Totals** in the Show/Hide Group; the Total row for both fields should be Group By.

b. In the third column, add a calculated field: **ExtendedAmount: Quantity*UnitPrice**. Format the calculated field as Currency. This calculation will calculate the total amount for each order. Change the Total row to **Sum**.

c. In the fourth column, add a calculated field: **DiscountAmount: Quantity*UnitPrice*Discount**. Format the calculated field as **Currency**. This will calculate the total discount for each order. Change the Total row to **Sum**.

d. Run the query. Save the query as **Order Summary**. Return to Design view.

e. Enter the expression **Between 1/1/2012 And 12/31/2012** in the criteria of OrderDate. Change the Total row to **Where**. This expression will display only orders that were created in 2012.

f. Run the query and view the results. Save the query.

g. Add the **Total Dollars caption** to the ExtendedAmount field and add the **Discount Amt caption** to the DiscountAmount field.

h. Run the query. Save and close the query.

Order Summary by Country Query

You need to create one additional query based on the Order Summary query you created in the previous step. This new query will enable you to analyze the orders by country.

a. Select the **Order Summary query**, and then use **Save Object As** to create a new query named **Order Summary by Country**.

b. In Design view of the new query, replace the OrderID field with the Country field.

c. Run the query, and then examine the summary records; there should be 21 countries listed.

d. In Design view, change the sort order so that the country with the highest Total Dollars is first, and the country with the lowest Total Dollars is last.

e. Run the query and verify the results.

f. Save and close the query, and then close the database and exit Access.

g. Submit based on your instructor's directions.

Vacation Time for Bank Employees

GENERAL CASE

The *a03b1vacation* file contains data from a local bank. Open *a03b1vacation*. Click the File tab, click Save Database As, and then type **a03b1vacation_LastnameFirstname**. Click Save. Replace *Your Name* in the Customers table and the Branch table with your name. Use the skills from this chapter to perform several tasks. The bank's employee handbook states that a manager can take two weeks of vacation each year for the first three years of service, and three weeks of vacation after three years of employment. The Branch table stores the start date of each manager.

Create a query to determine how many years each manager has worked for the bank.

- Add a new field to calculate the number of weeks of vacation each manager is eligible to take.
- Use a nested IIf function to change the weeks of vacation to zero for any employee with a start date later than today.
- Change the format of each field to the appropriate type, and then add appropriate captions for the calculated fields.
- Save the query as **Vacation**.

Create another query to summarize each customer's account balances.

- List the customer's last name, first name, and a total of all account balances.
- Format the query results, and then add appropriate captions.
- Add the grand total of all accounts to the Datasheet view.
- Save the query as **Customer Balances**.

Close the query, and then close the database. Submit based on your instructor's directions.

Combining Name Fields

RESEARCH CASE

This chapter introduced you to expressions. Use a search engine to search for information using the phrase *Combine text values by using an expression*. Open *a03b2combine*. Click the File tab, click Save Database As, and then type **a03b2combine_LastnameFirstname**. Click Save. Using the information from the Internet, create an expression to combine the last and first name fields into one field that displays "last name, first name." (Make sure you include a comma and a space after the last name.) You will use the Customers table in your query with LastName and FirstName. Once you successfully combine the fields in the query, alphabetize the list by last name, first name. Save the query as **Combined Names**. Close the query, and then close the database. Submit your work based on your instructor's directions.

Coffee Revenue Queries

DISASTER RECOVERY

A co-worker called you into his office, explained that he was having difficulty with Access 2010, and then asked you to look at his work. Open *a03b3coffee*. Click the File tab, click Save Database As, and then type **a03b3coffee_LastnameFirstname**. Click Save. Replace *Your Name* in the Sales Reps table with your name. It contains two queries: Revenue and Revenue by City. The Revenue query calculates ProductRetailPrice (Cost + Cost * MarkupPercent) and NetRevenue ((ProductRetailPrice − Cost) * Quantity). You manually calculate the first row and discover both the ProductRetailPrice and NetRevenue fields are incorrect. Diagnose the error(s) in the two fields and correct them. After correcting the Revenue query, correct the Revenue by City query. Run both queries, and then add appropriate captions. Save and close both queries. Close the database and exit Access. Submit based on your instructor's directions.

4 CREATING AND USING PROFESSIONAL FORMS AND REPORTS

Moving Beyond Tables and Queries

Watch the
Set-up Video
for this
Case Study!

CASE STUDY | Coffee Shop Starts New Business

For over 10 years, the Santiago Coffee Shop was an ordinary coffee shop selling retail coffee, tea, and pastries to its loyal customers in Bucks County. Then, in 2005, owner Alex Santiago decided to use his knowledge of the coffee industry to sell coffee products to businesses in his area. This new venture grew quickly and soon became 25% of his annual revenue. Realizing that this new business would need more of his time each day, he decided to create an Access database to help track his customer, product, and order information.

With the help of a student from Bucks County Community College, he created tables for customers, products, sales reps, and orders. He is currently using these tables as his primary method of entering and retrieving information.

Alex wants to have one of his employees, Tonya, manage the database. But he does not want her to work in the tables; he wants her to work with forms. Alex heard that forms have an advantage over tables because they can be designed to show one record at a time—this will reduce data entry errors. Alex would also like to create several reports for his own benefit so he can stay on top of the business by reviewing the reports each week.

You have been hired to help Alex create the new forms and reports that he needs for his business. He will describe the forms and reports to you in detail and also provide written instructions. You will be expected to work independently to create the forms and reports. Remember to identify the data source for each new form and report.

OBJECTIVES   AFTER YOU READ THIS CHAPTER, YOU WILL BE ABLE TO:

1. Create forms using the form tools *p.694*
2. Modify a form *p.699*
3. Sort records in a form *p.700*
4. Identify form sections *p.709*
5. Revise forms using form views *p.710*
6. Identify control types in forms *p.712*
7. Create reports using report tools *p.721*
8. Modify a report *p.728*
9. Sort records in a report *p.730*
10. Identify report sections *p.737*
11. Revise reports using report views *p.741*
12. Identify control types in reports *p.742*

Form Basics

A **form** is a database object that is used to add data into or edit data in a table.

A *form* is a database object that is used to add data into or edit data in a table. Most Access database applications use forms rather than tables for data entry and for looking up information. Three main reasons exist for using forms rather than tables for adding, updating, and deleting data. They are:

You are less likely to edit the wrong record by mistake.
You can create a form that shows data from more than one table simultaneously.
You can create Access forms to match paper forms.

> You are less likely to edit the wrong record by mistake ... You can create a form that shows data from more than one table simultaneously ... You can create Access forms to match paper forms.

If you are adding data using a table with many columns, you could jump to the wrong record in the middle of a record accidentally. For example, you could enter the data for one record correctly for the first 10 fields but then jump to the row above and overwrite existing data for the remaining field values unintentionally. In this case, two records have incorrect or incomplete data. A form will not allow this type of error since most forms restrict entry to one record at a time.

Many forms require two tables as their record source. For example, you may want to view a customer's details (name, address, e-mail, phone, etc.) as well as all of the orders he or she has placed. This would require using data from both the Customers and the Orders tables in one form. Similarly, you may want to view the header information for an order while also viewing the detail line items for the order. This would require data from both the Orders and Order Details tables. Both of these examples enable a user to view two record sources at the same time and make changes—additions, edits, or deletions—to one or both sources of data.

Finally, when paper forms are used to collect information, it is a good idea to design the electronic forms to match the paper forms. This will make data entry more efficient and reliable. Access forms can be designed to emulate the paper documents already in use in an organization. This facilitates the simultaneous use of both paper forms and electronic data. Databases do not necessarily eliminate paper forms; they supplement and coexist with them.

In this section, you will learn the basics of form design. You will discover multiple methods to create and modify Access forms. And you will learn how to create calculated controls.

Creating Forms Using the Form Tools

Access provides a variety of options for creating forms. One size does not fit all—some developers may prefer a stacked layout form, whereas others prefer the multiple items form. The multiple items form can be styled to match a company's standards, whereas the datasheet form is simple and requires very little maintenance. And let's not forget the users; they will have their opinions about the type of forms they want to use.

Access provides 16 different tools for creating forms. The Forms group, located on the Create tab, contains four of the most common form tools (Form, Form Design, Blank Form, and Form Wizard), a list of Navigation forms, and a list of More Forms, as shown in Figure 4.1. Navigation forms provides a list of six templates to create a user interface for a database; the More Forms command lists six additional form tools (Multiple Items, Datasheet, Split Form, and more). Select a table or query, click one of the tools, and Access will create an automatic form using the selected table or query. The most common of these tools, the *Form tool*, is used to create data entry forms for customers, employees, products, and other primary tables. A primary table, introduced in a previous chapter has a single field as its primary key and represents the "one" side of a one-to-many relationship. Once the form is created, as shown in Figure 4.2, you can customize the form using the Layout or Design views. After the form is created, it should be tested by both the database designer and the end users.

The **Form tool** is used to create data entry forms for customers, employees, products, and other primary tables.

FIGURE 4.1 Forms Group ➤

A complete list of all the Form tools available in Access is found in the Form Tools Reference at the end of this section. Many of the tools will be covered in this chapter. Some will not be covered since they are not commonly used or because they are beyond the scope of this chapter (e.g., Form Design, Blank Form, Navigation forms, and Modal Dialog form). Use Microsoft Access Help to find more information about Form tools not covered in this chapter.

FIGURE 4.2 Employees Form
Created with the Form Tool ➤

Ideally, a form should simplify data entry. Creating a form is a collaborative process between the form designer and the form users. This process continues throughout the life of the form, because the data needs of an organization may change. Forms designed long ago to collect information for a new customer account may not have an e-mail field; the form would have to be modified to include an e-mail field. The form designer needs to strike a balance between collecting the information users need to do their jobs and cluttering the form with extraneous fields. The users of the data know what they need and usually offer good feedback about which fields should be on a form. By listening to their suggestions, your forms will function more effectively, the users' work will be easier, and your data will contain fewer data entry errors.

> Ideally, a form should simplify data entry.

Identify a Record Source

> A **record source** is the table or query that supplies the records for a form or report.

Before you create a form, you must identify the record source. A **record source** is the table or query that supplies the records for a form or report. Use a table if you want to include all the records from a single table. Use a query if you need to filter the records in a table, or if you need to combine records from two or more related tables.

> **TIP** Record Source vs. Data Source
>
> The term *record source* can be interchanged with the term *data source*. Both terms refer to the source of data for a form or a report. In this chapter, the term *record source* will be used exclusively. As stated earlier, a record source can refer to either a table or a query.

For example, if a sales rep wants to create a form that only displays customers from a single state—where his customers reside—he should base the form on a query. Or, if a parts manager needs to review only parts with a zero on-hand quantity, he could create a form based on a query that only includes records with on-hand equal to zero.

Sketch the Form

It will help you to create the form in Access if you sketch the form first. A sketch may look similar to the form in Figure 4.2. After sketching the form, you will have a better idea of which form tool to use to create the form. After the form is created, use the sketch to determine which fields are required and what the order of fields should be.

Use the Form Tool

A **stacked layout form** displays fields in a vertical column, and displays one record at a time.

A **tabular layout form** displays records horizontally, with label controls across the top and the data values in rows under the labels.

Layout view is used to modify the design of a form.

As noted earlier, the Form tool is the most common tool for creating forms. Select a table or query from the Navigation Pane, and then click Form in the Forms Group on the Create tab, and Access creates a new form. You may need to modify the form slightly, but you can create a stacked layout form in a just one click. A *stacked layout form* displays fields in a vertical column, and displays one record at a time, as shown in Figure 4.3. Multiple Items and Datasheet forms, in contrast to stacked layout forms, are examples of tabular layout forms. A *tabular layout form* displays records horizontally, with label controls across the top and the data values in rows under the labels. When a new form is created using the Form tool, Access opens the form in Layout view ready for customizing. You can generate forms for your database using the Form tool, and then use *Layout view* to modify the design of a form. Figure 4.3 shows the Employees form in Layout view.

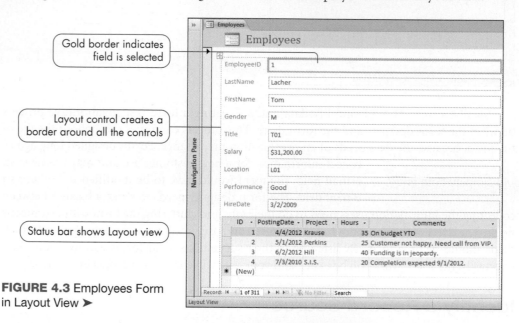

Gold border indicates field is selected

Layout control creates a border around all the controls

Status bar shows Layout view

FIGURE 4.3 Employees Form in Layout View ➤

Work with a Subform

When you use the Form tool to create a form, Access will analyze the table relationships you created in the database and automatically add a subform to the main form. A subform displays records with foreign key values that match the primary key value in the main form. For example, assume you have a database that contains the tables Employees and Project Time, and a relationship exists between the two tables based on the EmployeeID field. If you create a new form based on Employees, using the Form tool, Access will add a Project Time subform to the bottom of the main form (see Figure 4.3).

At times, you may want the subform as part of your form; other times, you may want to remove it. To remove a subform control from a form, switch to Design view, click the subform control, and then press Delete. The subform is deleted!

Create a Split Form

A **split form** combines two views of the same record source—one section is displayed in a stacked layout and the other section is displayed in a tabular layout.

A *split form* combines two views of the same record source—one section is displayed in a stacked layout and the other section is displayed in a tabular layout. By default, the form view is positioned on the top and the datasheet view is displayed on the bottom; however, the orientation can be changed from horizontal to vertical in Layout view. If you select a record in the top half of the form, the same record will be selected in the bottom half of the form, and vice versa. For example, if you create a split form based on the Employees table, you can select an employee in the datasheet section and then see the employee's information in the *Form view* section (see Figure 4.4). If the selected employee is incorrect, click another employee in the datasheet section. The top and bottom halves are synchronized at all times.

The **splitter bar** divides the form into two halves.

To create a split form, first select a table or query in the Navigation Pane. Next, click the Create tab, click More Forms in the Forms group, and then select Split Form from the list of options. A new split form now appears. You can add, edit, or delete records in either section. The *splitter bar* divides the form into two halves. Users can adjust the splitter bar up or down unless the form designer disables this option.

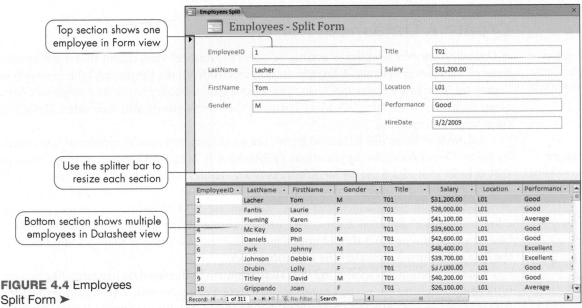

Top section shows one employee in Form view

Use the splitter bar to resize each section

Bottom section shows multiple employees in Datasheet view

FIGURE 4.4 Employees Split Form ➤

Create a Multiple Items Form

A **Multiple Items form** displays multiple records in a tabular layout similar to a table's Datasheet view.

A *Multiple Items form* displays multiple records in a tabular layout similar to a table's Datasheet view. However, a Multiple Items form gives you more customization options than a datasheet, such as the ability to add graphical elements, buttons, and other controls. Figure 4.5 shows a Multiple Items form created from the Employees table. Compare this Multiple Items form to the Employees Datasheet form shown in Figure 4.6. The color scheme applied to the Multiple Items form could not be applied to the Datasheet form since the Datasheet form is much more limited in design and control options. To create a Multiple Items form, first select a table or query from the Navigation Pane. Next, click the Create tab, click More Forms in the Forms group, and then select Multiple Items from the list of options.

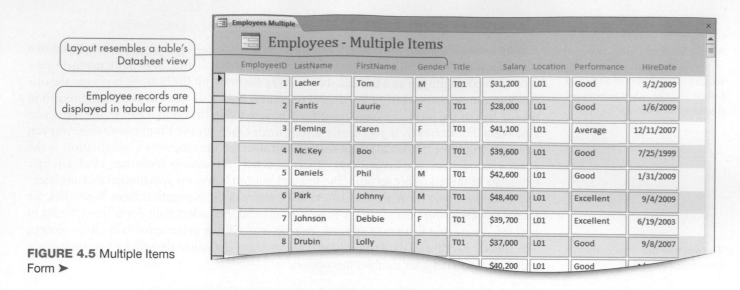

FIGURE 4.5 Multiple Items Form ➤

- Layout resembles a table's Datasheet view
- Employee records are displayed in tabular format

Create a Datasheet Form

A **Datasheet form** is a replica of a table or query's Datasheet view except that it still retains some of the form properties.

Visual Basic for Applications (VBA) is Microsoft's programming language that is built into all of the Office products.

A *Datasheet form* is a replica of a table or query's Datasheet view except that it still retains some of the form properties. A Datasheet form created from the Employees table is shown in Figure 4.6. To create a Datasheet form, first select a table or query from the Navigation Pane. Next, click the Create tab, click More Forms in the Forms group, and then select Datasheet from the list of options.

A datasheet form, like all Access forms, can be customized to add additional functionality using *Visual Basic for Applications (VBA)*. VBA is Microsoft's programming language that is built into all of the Office products. VBA enables an advanced Access user to customize forms and reports. Although a field's data type and field properties help prevent invalid data from being added to a table, you can use VBA to enforce more complex data entry rules. For example, if a data entry person were entering new products into the database, the cost of a product should not be more than the sale price. If that condition existed, the data entry form could alert the user using VBA.

Database designers can also use the Datasheet form to display data in a table-like format, but change the form properties to not allow a record to be deleted. This would protect the data from accidental damage while still providing the users with the familiar Datasheet view.

Employees Datasheet

EmployeeID	LastName	FirstName	Gender	Title	Salary	Location	Performance
1	Lacher	Tom	M	T01	$31,200.00	L01	Good
2	Fantis	Laurie	F	T01	$28,000.00	L01	Good
3	Fleming	Karen	F	T01	$41,100.00	L01	Average
4	Mc Key	Boo	F	T01	$39,600.00	L01	Good
5	Daniels	Phil	M	T01	$42,600.00	L01	Good
6	Park	Johnny	M	T01	$48,400.00	L01	Excellent
7	Johnson	Debbie	F	T01	$39,700.00	L01	Excellent
8	Drubin	Lolly	F	T01	$37,000.00	L01	Good
9	Titley	David	M	T01	$40,200.00	L01	Good
10	Grippando	Joan	F	T01	$26,100.00	L01	Average
11	Block	Leonard	M	T01	$26,200.00	L01	Excellent
12	Mills	Jack	M	T01	$44,600.00	L01	Average
13	Nagel	Mimi	F	T01	$46,200.00	L01	Average
14	Rammos	Mitzi	F	T01	$32,500.00	L01	Excellent
15	Vieth	Paula	F	T01	$40,400.00	L01	Good
16	Novicheck	Deborah	F	T01	$46,800.00	L01	Good
17	Brumbaugh	Paige	F	T01	$49,300.00	L01	Average
18	Abrams	Wendy	F	T01	$47,500.00	L01	Good
19	Harrison	Jenifer	F	T01	$44,800.00	L01	Excellent
20	Gander	John	M	T01	$38,400.00	L01	Average
21	Sell	Mike	M	T01	$43,500.00	L01	Excellent
22	Smith	Denise	F	T01	$45,200.00	L01	Average
				T01	$42,700.00	L01	Excell

- Layout is a replica of a table's Datasheet view

FIGURE 4.6 Datasheet Form ➤

Create Forms Using the Other Form Tools

The Form Design tool and the Blank Form tools can be used to create a form manually. Click one of these tools and Access will open a completely blank form. Click Add Existing Fields, on the Design tab, in the Tools group and add the necessary fields.

The Navigation option in the Forms group enables you to create user interface forms that have the look and feel of a Web-based form, and enable users to open and close the objects of a database. These forms are also useful for setting up an Access database on the Internet. For more information about Navigation forms, visit www.microsoft.com.

PivotTables and PivotCharts, discussed in a later chapter, can also be converted to forms by selecting PivotChart or PivotTable in the More Forms option in the Forms group. After you create a PivotTable form or a PivotChart form, use the Layout view and Design view to customize the form.

The Modal Dialog Form tool can be used to create a dialog box. This feature is useful when you need to gather information from the user before working with another object. Dialog boxes are common in all Microsoft Office applications; creating a custom dialog box in Access can be useful when you need to collect information from the user.

REFERENCE Form Tools

Form Tool	Location	Use
Form	Create tab, Forms group	Creates a form with a stacked layout displaying all of the fields in the record source.
Form Design	Create tab, Forms group	Create a new blank form in Design view.
Blank Form	Create tab, Forms group	Create a new blank form in Layout view.
Form Wizard	Create tab, Forms group	Answer a series of questions and Access will create a custom form for you.
Navigation	Create tab, Forms group, Navigation button	Create user interface forms that can also be used on the Internet.
Split Form	Create tab, Forms group, More Forms button	Creates a two-part form with a stacked layout in one section and a tabular layout in the other.
Multiple Items	Create tab, Forms group, More Forms button	Creates a tabular layout form that includes all of the fields from the record source.
Datasheet	Create tab, Forms group, More Forms button	Creates a form that resembles the datasheet of a table or query.
PivotTable	Create tab, Forms group, More Forms button	The PivotTable form tool enables you to present data from a table or query using a multi-dimensional table format.
PivotChart	Create tab, Forms group, More Forms button	The PivotChart form tool enables you to present data from a table or query using a multi-dimensional chart format.
Modal Dialog	Create tab, Forms group, More Forms button	Creates a custom dialog box that forces the user to respond before working with another object.

Modifying a Form

After a form is generated by a Form tool, you will usually need to modify it. The most common form changes are add a field, remove a field, change the order of fields, change the width of a field, and modify label text. These changes, as well as adding a theme, can be made in a form's Layout view. Advanced changes, such as adding a calculated field or adding VBA code, can be made in a form's Design view.

Add a Field to a Form

To add a field to a form with a stacked layout, open the form in Layout view. Click Add Existing Fields in the Tools group on the Design tab to reveal the available fields from the form's record source. Drag the new field to the precise location on the form, using the orange line as a guide for the position of the new field. The other fields will automatically adjust to make room for the new field.

To add a field to a form with a tabular layout, follow the same steps for adding a field to a stacked layout form. The only difference is the orange line will appear vertically to help determine the insertion point of the new field.

Work with a Form Layout Control

A **layout control** provides guides to help keep controls aligned horizontally and vertically, and give your form a uniform appearance.

Whenever you use one of the form tools to create a new form, Access will add a layout control to help align the fields. In general, form layout controls can help you create and modify forms. A *layout control* provides guides to help keep controls aligned horizontally and vertically, and give your form a uniform appearance. However, there are times when a layout control is too restrictive and will keep you from positioning controls where you want them. In this case, you can remove the layout control and position the controls manually on the grid.

To remove a form layout control, switch to Design view, and then click anywhere inside the control you want to remove. On the Arrange tab, click Select Layout in the Rows & Columns group. (You can also click the Layout Selector, the small square with a cross inside, to select the layout.) Click Remove Layout in the Table group and the layout control is gone. All of the other controls are still on the form, but the rectangle binding them together is gone.

You can add a layout control to a form by first selecting all the controls you want to keep together. Then, click Stacked or Tabular in the Table group and the layout control appears.

Delete a Field from a Form

To delete a field in Layout view, click the text box control of the field to be deleted and note the orange border around the control. With the orange border showing, press Delete. The field's text box and label are both removed from the form and a space remains where the field used to be. Click the space, and then press Delete again, and the other fields will automatically adjust to close the gap around the deleted field.

Adjust Column Widths in a Form

When column widths are adjusted in a form with a stacked layout, all columns will increase and decrease together. Therefore, it is best to make sure that field columns are wide enough to accommodate the widest value in the table. For example, if a form contains first name, last name, address, city, state, ZIP, phone, and e-mail address, you will need to make sure the longest address and the longest e-mail address are completely visible (since those fields are likely to contain the longest data values).

To decrease column widths in a form with a stacked layout, open the form in Layout view. Click the text box control of the first field—usually on the right—to select it. Move the mouse over the right border of the field until the mouse pointer turns into a double arrow, then drag the right edge to the left until you arrive at the desired width. All the fields change as you change the width of the first field. Drag the same edge to the right to increase the width.

Add a Theme to a Form

An **Office Theme** is a defined set of colors, fonts, and graphics that can be applied to a form.

You can apply an Office Theme to a form in order to give the form a more professional finish. An *Office Theme* is a defined set of colors, fonts, and graphics that can be applied to a form. Click the Themes picker in the Themes group on the Design tab, select a theme from the Themes Gallery, and Access will apply the theme to your form. You can apply a theme to a single form or to all the forms in your database that share a common theme. Applying the same theme to all forms will provide a consistent look to your database; most users prefer a consistent theme when using Access forms. The same Office Themes found in Access are also available in Excel, Word, and PowerPoint. Therefore, you can achieve a uniformed look across all Office applications.

Sorting Records in a Form

When a form is created using a Form tool, the sort order of the records in the form is dependent on the sort order of the record source—a table or a query. Tables are usually sorted by the primary key, whereas queries can be sorted in a variety of ways.

Change the Sorting in a Form

To modify the sort order of a form, open the form in Form view, and then select the field you want to use for sorting. Next, click Ascending in the Sort & Filter group on the Home tab and the records will immediately be reordered based on the selected field.

You can also modify the sort order of a form by modifying the underlying query's sort order. The method enables you to create a more advanced sort order, based on multiple fields. To begin, switch to Design view, and then open the Property Sheet. Select the form by clicking the arrow under Selection type at the top of the Property Sheet, and then clicking Form. Next, locate the Record Source property on the Data tab, click in the property box, and then click Build to the right of the property box. Answer Yes to the message that appears. Access opens the underlying query in Design view. Add the sorting you want, close the query, and save the query when prompted. You will also need to save the form.

Remove Sorting in a Form

To remove the sort order in a form, switch to Form view, and then click Remove Sort in the Sort & Filter group on the Home tab. If the form's sort order was modified, clicking this command will reset the form to the original order.

1 Form Basics

It is your first day on the job at Santiago Coffee Shop. After talking with Alex about his data entry needs, you decide to create several sample forms with different formats. You will show each form to Alex to get his feedback and see if he has a preference. Remember to select the correct record source prior to creating each new form.

Skills covered: Use the Form Tool and Adjust Column Widths in a Form • Create a Split Form • Create a Multiple Items Form • Create a Datasheet Form and Delete a Field from a Form • Add a Field to a Form • Change the Sorting in a Form and Remove Sorting in a Form

---

STEP 1 ▶ USE THE FORM TOOL AND ADJUST COLUMN WIDTHS IN A FORM

Use the Form tool to create an Access form to help Alex manage his customers. This form will enable Tonya to add, edit, and delete records more efficiently than working with tables. Refer to Figure 4.7 as you complete Step 1.

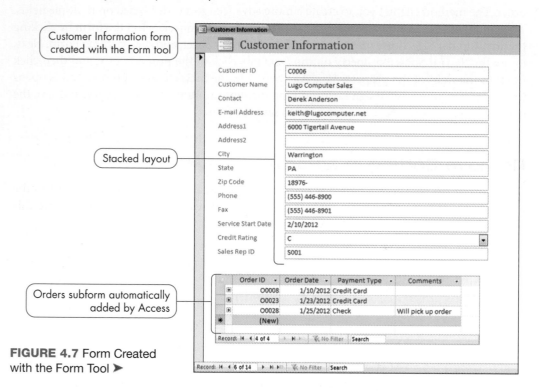

Customer Information form created with the Form tool

Stacked layout

Orders subform automatically added by Access

FIGURE 4.7 Form Created with the Form Tool ▶

a. Open *a04h1coffee*. Click the **File tab**, click **Save Database As**, and then type **a04h1coffee_LastnameFirstname**. Click Save.

> **TROUBLESHOOTING:** Throughout the remainder of this chapter and textbook, click Enable Content whenever you are working with student files.

> **TROUBLESHOOTING:** If you make any major mistakes in this exercise, you can close the file, repeat step a above, and then start over.

b. Click the **Customers table** in the Navigation Pane. Click the **Create tab**, and then click **Form** in the Forms group.

Access creates a new form with two record sources—Customers (with stacked layout, on top) and Orders (with tabular layout, below). Access found a one-to-many relationship between the Customers and Orders tables. The form opens in Layout view.

c. Click the top text box containing *C0001*. The text box is outlined with an orange border. Move the mouse to the right edge of the orange border until the mouse pointer changes to a double-headed arrow. Drag the right edge to the left until the text box is approximately 50% of its original size.

All the text boxes and the subform at the bottom adjust in size when you adjust the top text box. This is a characteristic of Layout view—enabling you to easily modify all controls at once.

> **TROUBLESHOOTING:** You may need to maximize the Access window, or close the Navigation Pane, if the right edge of the text box is not visible.

d. Click the Arrange tab, and then click **Select Layout** in the Rows & Columns group.

All the controls are now selected.

> **TROUBLESHOOTING:** Click any control in the top part of the form before you click Select layout.

e. On the Arrange tab, click **Control Padding** in the Position group. Select **Narrow** from the list of choices.

The space between the controls is reduced.

f. Click **Save** in the Quick Access Toolbar, and then type **Customer Information** as the form name in the **Save As dialog box**. Click **OK**.

g. Click the **Home tab**, and then click **View** in the Views group to switch to Form view, the view that most users will see. Advance to the sixth customer, *Lugo Computer Sales*, using the **Navigation bar** at the bottom of the form.

> **TROUBLESHOOTING:** Two Navigation bars exist, one for the main form and one for the subform. Make sure you use the bottom one that shows 14 records.

h. Double-click the **Customers table** in the Navigation Pane.

Two tabs now appear in the main window. You will compare the table data and the form data while you make changes to both.

i. Verify the sixth record of the Customers table is *Lugo Computer Sales*, which corresponds to the sixth record in the Customer Information form. Click the tabs to switch between the table and the form.

j. Click the **Customer Information tab**, and then replace *Derek Anderson*, the contact for Lugo Computer Sales, with your name. Advance to the next record to save the changes. Click the **Customers tab** to see that the contact name changed in the table as well.

The contact field and the other fields on the Customer Information form are bound controls. Changing the data in the form automatically changes the data in the underlying table.

> **TROUBLESHOOTING:** If the change to Derek Anderson does not appear in the Customers table, check the Customer Information form to see if the pencil appears in the left margin. If it does, save the record by advancing to the next customer, and then recheck to see if the name has changed.

k. Replace your name with **Derek Anderson**. Save the record by clicking on the record below *Lugo Computer Sales*. Click the **Customer Information tab**, and then find the sixth record. You should see the change you just made—Derek is back!

l. Switch to Layout view. Click the **Customers title** at the top of the form to select it, and then click again and change the title to **Customer Information**.

The Customer Information title, a label control, is an example of an unbound control; an unbound control does not have a connection to an underlying table.

m. Click **Save** in the Quick Access Toolbar to save the changes to the form's title. Close the form and the table.

> **TROUBLESHOOTING:** If you make a mistake that you cannot easily recover from, consider deleting the form and starting over. The Form tool makes it easy to start over again.

STEP 2 ▶ CREATE A SPLIT FORM

Use the Split Form tool to create a different form to show to Tonya. She may prefer to use a split form to add, edit, and delete records rather than the Customer Information form that you created in the previous step. Refer to Figure 4.8 as you complete Step 2.

FIGURE 4.8 Form Created with the Split Form Tool ▶

a. Verify the Customers table is selected in the Navigation Pane. Click the **Create tab**, click **More Forms** in the Forms group, and then select **Split Form** from the list.

   Access creates a new form with a split view, one view in stacked layout and one view in tabular layout.

b. Switch to Form view. In the bottom portion of the split form, click **Lugo Computer Sales**, the sixth record. Notice the top portion now displays the information for Lugo Computer Sales.

c. Change *service@lugocomputer.net* to **yourname@lugocomputer.net** in the top portion of the form.

   The bottom portion reflects your change when you move to another field or advance to another record.

d. Click another record, and then click back on **Lugo Computer Sales**.

   The pencil disappears from the record selector box and the changes are saved to the table.

e. Click anywhere on the Coulter Office Supplies customer in the bottom portion of the form (record 14).

   The top portion shows all the information for this customer.

f. Modify the Contact, E-mail Address, and Address1 information in the top portion of the form, by typing **xyz** at the end of each cell. Save your changes by clicking anywhere in the bottom portion of the window.

Notice the xyz characters appear in the bottom portion of the form.

g. Remove the xyz's from the Coulter Office Supplies record in the top section.

h. Switch to Layout view. Click the **Customers title** at the top of the form to select it, and then click **Customers** again and change the title to **Customers - Split View**.

i. Click **Save** on the Quick Access Toolbar, and then type **Customers - Split View** in the **Form Name box**. Click **OK**.

j. Move your mouse over the splitter bar, the border between the top and bottom portions of the window. When the pointer shape changes to a double-headed arrow, drag the splitter bar up until it almost touches the Sales Rep ID field.

k. Close the form and save the changes when prompted.

STEP 3 ▶ **CREATE A MULTIPLE ITEMS FORM**

You decide to use the Multiple Items tool to create a form for Alex to manage his products. Because of its tabular format, it will enable Alex and Tonya to view multiple records at one time. Refer to Figure 4.9 as you complete Step 3.

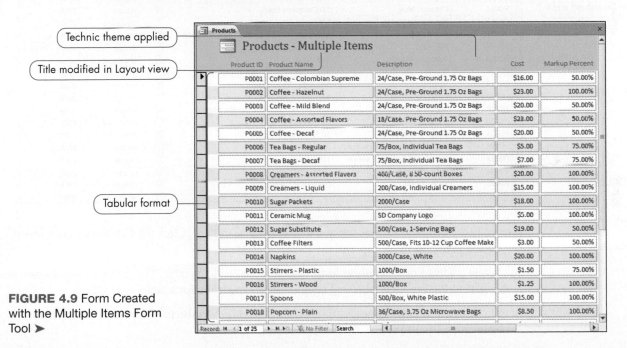

FIGURE 4.9 Form Created with the Multiple Items Form Tool ▶

a. Click the **Products table** in the Navigation Pane. Click the **Create tab**, click **More Forms** in the Forms group, and then select **Multiple Items** from the list.

Access creates a new multiple items form based on the Products table. The form resembles the datasheet of a table—both have a tabular layout.

b. Click **cell P0001**. Move the mouse over the bottom edge of cell P0001 until the pointer shape changes to a two-headed arrow. Drag the bottom edge up to reduce the height of the rows by 50%.

Changing the height of one row affects the height of all the rows.

c. Click the **Products title** at the top of the form to select it, and then click again on **Products** and change the title to **Products - Multiple Items**.

d. Click the **Themes arrow** in the Themes group on the Design tab. Right-click the **Technic Theme** (near the bottom of the gallery), and then choose **Apply Theme to This Object Only**.

Hover over a theme and its name will display as a ScreenTip. The Technic theme is applied to the Products - Multiple Items form.

e. Close and save the form as **Products - Multiple Items**.

STEP 4 ▶ CREATE A DATASHEET FORM AND DELETE A FIELD FROM A FORM

You decide to use the Datasheet tool to create another form for Alex to manage his products. The Datasheet form is in tabular format and is similar to the Multiple Items form, but requires little or no maintenance, which Alex may like. Refer to Figure 4.10 as you complete Step 4.

Datasheet form based on the Products table

Field name modified

Datasheet form looks similar to Datasheet view

Product ID ▾	Product Name ▾	Description ▾	Refrig? ▾	Brand ▾	Year Introduce
P0001	Coffee - Colombian Supreme	24/Case, Pre-Ground 1.75 Oz Bags	☐	Discount	2008
P0002	Coffee - Hazelnut	24/Case, Pre-Ground 1.75 Oz Bags	☐	Premium	2008
P0003	Coffee - Mild Blend	24/Case, Pre-Ground 1.75 Oz Bags	☐	House	2008
P0004	Coffee - Assorted Flavors	18/Case. Pre-Ground 1.75 Oz Bags	☐	House	2008
P0005	Coffee - Decaf	24/Case, Pre-Ground 1.75 Oz Bags	☐	Discount	2008
P0006	Tea Bags - Regular	75/Box, Individual Tea Bags	☐	House	2008
P0007	Tea Bags - Decaf	75/Box, Individual Tea Bags	☐	House	2008
P0008	Creamers - Assorted Flavors	400/Case, 8 50-count Boxes	☐	Discount	2008
P0009	Creamers - Liquid	200/Case, Individual Creamers	☑	Premium	2008
P0010	Sugar Packets	2000/Case	☐	House	2008
P0011	Ceramic Mug	SD Company Logo	☐	House	2008
P0012	Sugar Substitute	500/Case, 1-Serving Bags	☐	Discount	2008
P0013	Coffee Filters	500/Case, Fits 10-12 Cup Coffee Maker	☐	House	2008
P0014	Napkins	3000/Case, White	☐	House	2008
P0015	Stirrers - Plastic	1000/Box	☐	Discount	2008
P0016	Stirrers - Wood	1000/Box	☐	Discount	2008
P0017	Spoons	500/Box, White Plastic	☐	House	2008
P0018	Popcorn - Plain	36/Case, 3.75 Oz Microwave Bags	☐	House	2008
P0019	Popcorn - Buttered	36/Case, 3.75 Oz Microwave Bags	☐	House	2008
P0020	Soup - Chicken	50 Envelopes	☐	Premium	2008
P0021	Soup - Variety Pak	50 Envelopes	☐	Premium	2008
P0022	Styrofoam Cups - 10 ounce	1000/Case	☐	House	2008
P0023	Styrofoam Cups - 12 ounce	1000/Case	☐	House	2008
P0024	Milk - 1 quart	Delivered Daily	☑	House	2008
P0025	Milk - 1 pint	Delivered Daily	☑	House	2008
*(New)			☐	House	2010

FIGURE 4.10 Datasheet Form ▶

a. Verify the Products table is selected in the Navigation Pane. Click the **Create tab**, click **More Forms** in the Forms group, and then select **Datasheet**.

Access creates a new datasheet form based on the Products table. The Tabular form looks similar to the Products table and could be easily mistaken for a table.

b. Click **Save** in the Quick Access Toolbar, and then type **Products - Datasheet** in the **Form Name box**. Click **OK**.

c. Widen the Navigation Pane so all object names are visible. Right-click the **Products - Datasheet form** in the Navigation Pane, and then choose **Layout View** from the list of options.

> **TROUBLESHOOTING:** The View arrow does not contain the Layout view options.

d. Click anywhere in an empty area to deselect the controls.

e. Click the **Cost box**, the control on the right, to select it (you will see the orange border), and then press **Delete**. Click the blank space, and then press **Delete** to remove the blank space. Repeat the process to delete *MarkupPercent*.

You removed fields from the Products form and the other fields adjust to maintain an even distribution (after you remove the blank space).

f. Click the **Refrigeration Needed label** to select it. Change the label to the abbreviation **Refrig?**. Save the form, and then switch to Datasheet view.

g. Double-click the **Products table** in the Navigation Pane to open it.

    The Products - Datasheet form and the Products table now appear different because the Cost and MarkupPercent fields were deleted from the form.

h. Close the Products Datasheet form and the Products table.

STEP 5 ADD A FIELD TO A FORM

The form tools made it easy to create forms for Alex's company. But Alex decided he needs a Website field, so you need to modify the form. Refer to Figure 4.11 as you complete Step 5.

Customer information form in Layout view

Website field added to customers table

Orange line indicates the position of the new field

FIGURE 4.11 Add a New Field to a Form ➤

a. Right-click the **Customers table** in the Navigation Pane, and then click **Design View**.

    You will add the Website field to the Customers table.

b. Click the **Address1 field**, and then click **Insert Rows** in the Tools group.

    A new row is inserted above the Address1 field.

c. Type **Website** in the blank **Field Name box**, and then choose **Hyperlink** as the Data Type.

d. Close and save the Customers table.

e. Right-click the **Customer Information form** in the Navigation Pane, and then click **Layout View**.

    You will add the Website field to the Customer Information form.

f. Click **Add Existing Fields** in the Tools group to display the Field List pane (if necessary).

g. Drag the **Website field** from the Field List pane to the form, below the E-mail Address field, until an orange line displays between E-mail Address and Address1 and release the mouse.

    Access shows an orange line to help you place the field in the correct location.

h. Switch to Form view. Press **Tab** until you reach the **Website field**, and then type **www.microsoft.com** into the field.

i. Press **Tab** until the focus reaches the Orders subform to verify the tab order is correct.

j. Close and save the Customer Information form.

STEP 6 ➤ **CHANGE THE SORTING IN A FORM AND REMOVE SORTING IN A FORM**

Alex tested the Customer Information form and likes the way it is working. He asks you to change the sorting to make it easier to find customers with a similar Customer Name. Refer to Figure 4.12 as you complete Step 6.

FIGURE 4.12 Datasheet Form ➤

a. Open the Customer Information form. Click **Next record** in the Navigation bar at the bottom several times to advance through the records.

Take note that the customers are in Customer ID order.

b. Click **First record** in the Navigation bar to return to customer Abel & Young.

c. Click the **Customer Name field**, and then click **Ascending** in the Sort & Filter group.

d. Click **Next record** in the Navigation bar at the bottom to advance through the records.

The records are now in Customer Name order.

e. Close the Customer Information form.

f. Click the **File tab**, and then click **Compact & Repair Database**.

g. Keep the database onscreen if you plan to continue with Hands-On Exercise 2. If not, close the database and exit Access.

Form Sections, Views, and Controls

As you work with the form tools to create and modify forms, you will often need to switch between the three form views in Access—Layout view, Form view, and Design view. Most of your design work will be done in Layout view; occasionally, you will switch to Design view to add a more advanced feature, such as a calculated field. Users of the form will only work in Form view. There should be no reason for a user to switch to Layout or Design view. Modifications to the form should be done by the designated form designer.

> ... you will often need to switch between the three form views in Access—Layout view, Form view, and Design view.

In this section, you will examine the different form sections. As you learn how to create forms, placing fields and labels in the right section will become second nature. You may have to use trial and error at first, switching between Form view and Layout view until the form is working correctly.

Controls are also covered in this section. You will learn the difference between bound and unbound controls. You will also learn how to add a calculated control. Because calculated fields were covered in the queries in a previous chapter, you should be familiar with the syntax found in calculated controls on forms.

Identifying Form Sections

Access forms, by default, are divided into three sections that can be viewed when you display a form in Design view. Each section can be collapsed or expanded as needed, but only in Design view.

Identify the Default Form Sections

Each form by default contains three main sections—*Form Header, Detail,* and *Form Footer.* These sections can vary depending on what type of form you create. Stacked layout forms will have different requirements than a tabular layout form. Form designers also have the option of removing certain sections from a form. Two additional sections—*Page Header* and *Page Footer*—are optional and can be added to a form as needed. These sections are visible in Design view and also during Print Preview and printing; however, page headers and footers are not visible in Form view or Layout view. Because these sections are less common in forms, they will not be explored further in this chapter. Use Microsoft Help for more information about the *Page Header* and *Page Footer* sections.

The **Form Header section** displays at the top of each form. This section will usually contain the form title, a logo or other graphic, and the current date and time. Column headings (labels) will also be located in this section for Multiple Item forms.

The **Detail section** displays the records in the form's record source. Stacked forms will display one label and one text box for each field placed in the *Detail* section. Navigation controls enable the user to advance to the next, last, previous, and first record. Multiple Item forms will display multiple records (text boxes) in the *Detail* section, as many as can fit onto one screen.

The **Form Footer section** displays at the bottom of the form. The Form Footer is commonly used to add totals for field values. For example, an invoice form would display the invoice subtotal, the shipping charges, the taxes, and the invoice total in the *Form Footer* section.

The **Form Header section** displays at the top of each form.

The **Detail section** displays the records in the form's record source.

The **Form Footer section** displays at the bottom of the form.

Modify the Default Form Sections

In Figure 4.13, three light grey section bars mark the top boundary of each form section. The top bar denotes the top boundary of the Form Header; the middle bar designates the top of the *Detail* section; and the bottom bar shows the top boundary of the Form Footer. The grid-like area under the bars shows the amount of space allotted to each section. If you decide that the allotted space for a particular section is not needed, you can collapse that section fully so that the section bars are touching. In Figure 4.13, the form has no space allocated to the Form Footer. The section remains in the form's design but will not take up space in Form view. If you want to remove the *Form Footer* section from the form, right-click the Form Footer bar, and then click Form Header/Footer from the list. When you remove the Form Footer, the *Form Header* section will also be removed. This may cause a problem since the title of the form usually resides in the Form Header.

To expand or collapse the space between sections, move your mouse over the bottom bar, and when the mouse pointer changes to a double-headed arrow, click and drag to expand or collapse the section. If you expand or collapse the space allotment for one section, the overall height of the form will be affected.

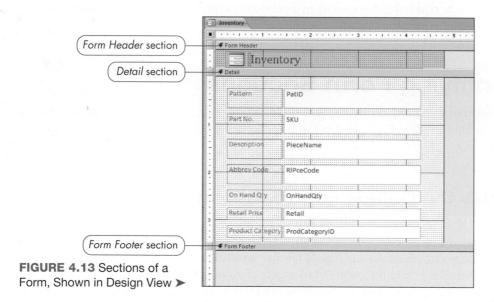

FIGURE 4.13 Sections of a Form, Shown in Design View ➤

Revising Forms Using Form Views

Access provides different views for a form, similar to the different views in tables and queries. Tables and queries have Design view and Datasheet view. Most forms have Layout view, Form view, and Design view. A Datasheet form has one additional view, the Datasheet view, but it does not have the Form view.

Switch Between Form Views

A variety of methods for switching between form views exist: click View in the Views group, click the View arrow, right-click a form in the Navigation Pane, right-click the form tab, or click one of the small view icons in the status bar at the bottom right of the form. Perhaps the quickest method for switching between views is clicking View. This will toggle the form between Layout view and Form view. Click the View arrow or right-click the form tab to switch to Design view. Each view is described in the sections below.

Edit Data in Form View

Use **Form view** to add, edit, and delete data in a form; the layout and design of the form cannot be changed in this view.

Use **Form view** to add, edit, and delete data in a form; the layout and design of the form cannot be changed in this view. Most users will only see Form view; if a form needs modification, the user will notify the database designer, who will make a change on the fly or during the next scheduled maintenance interval. Figure 4.14 shows a form in Form view. Users can print from this view by clicking the File tab and then selecting the Print option. However, printing from a form should be done with caution. A form with a stacked layout of 810 records could print as many as 810 pages (depending on how many records fit onto one page) unless you choose the Selected Record(s) option in the Print dialog box. The Selected Record(s) option will only print the current record or the number of records you selected.

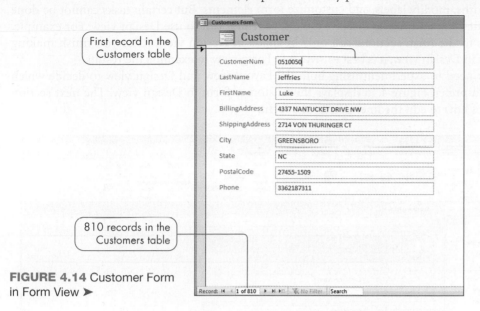

FIGURE 4.14 Customer Form in Form View ➤

Alter a Form in Layout View

Use Layout view to alter the form design while still viewing the data. You use Layout view to add or delete fields in a form, modify field properties, change the column widths, and enhance a form by adding a color scheme or styling. While you are working in Layout view, you can see the data as it would appear in Form view, but you cannot edit the data in Layout view. Seeing the data in Layout view makes it easier to size controls, for example, to ensure the data is visible (see Figure 4.15). It is good practice to test a form in Form view after making changes in Layout view.

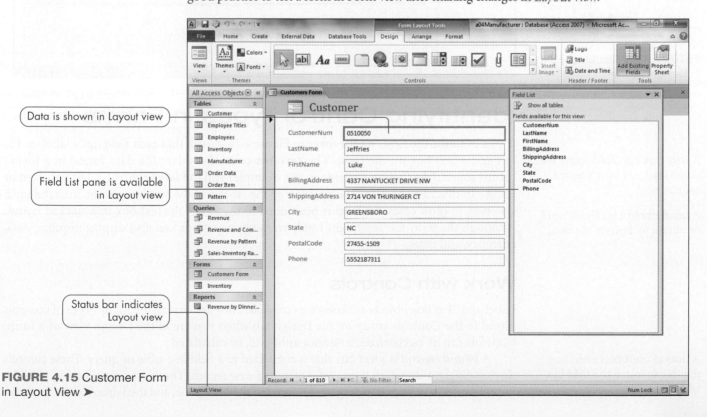

FIGURE 4.15 Customer Form in Layout View ➤

Perform Advanced Changes to a Form in Design View

Use **Design view** to perform advanced changes to a form's design.

Use **Design view** to perform advanced changes to a form's design. It provides you the most advanced method of editing an Access form. You can perform many of the same tasks in Design view as you can in Layout view—add and delete fields, change the field order, adjust field widths, modify labels, and customize form elements. But certain tasks cannot be done in Layout view, and Access displays a message telling you to use Design view. For example, changes to the form sections can only be made in Design view. After you finish making changes in Design view, it is best to switch to Form view to examine the results.

You need to experiment using both the Layout view and Design view to decide which view you prefer. Figure 4.16 displays the Customer form in Design view. The next section describes how to edit the finer details of a form.

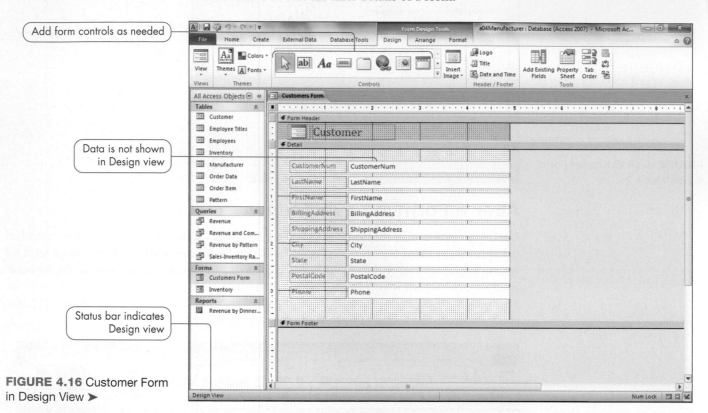

Add form controls as needed

Data is not shown in Design view

Status bar indicates Design view

FIGURE 4.16 Customer Form in Design View ➤

Identifying Control Types in Forms

A **text box control** displays the data found in a form's record source.

A **label control** is a literal word or phrase to describe the data.

If you examine the fields on the form in Figure 4.16, notice that each field has a label on the left and a text box on the right. The **text box control** displays the data found in a form's record source (the Customers table in this example) and the **label control** is a literal word or phrase to describe the data. The position of the label and the text box can be interchanged; however, in most cases, the label is positioned to the left of the text box in a stacked layout. Although the term *text box* might imply *text only*, a text box can also display numeric data, currency, and dates.

Work with Controls

A **bound control** is a text box that is connected to a field in a table or query.

Label and Text Box objects are known as *controls*. They are among the many types of controls found in the Controls group on the Design tab when you are in the Design view of a form. Controls can be categorized as bound, unbound, or calculated.

A **bound control** is a text box that is connected to a field in a table or query. These controls display different data each time you switch to a new record. The most common way to add a bound control to a form is to drag a field from the Field List pane, and then drop it onto the form.

An **unbound control** is a label or other decorative design element, and is not connected to a source of data.

A **calculated control** contains an expression that generates a calculated result when displayed in Form view.

An ***unbound control*** is a label or other decorative design element, and is not connected to a source of data. These controls usually describe and decorate the data rather than display the data, and remain the same each time you switch to a new record. Unbound controls include labels, lines, borders, and images; they can be added to a form using the Controls group on the Design tab while in Design view. For example, a label that displays the title of the form is an unbound control.

A ***calculated control*** contains an expression that generates a calculated result when displayed in Form view. The expression can contain field names from the form's record source, constants, and functions. Use a text box, found in the Controls group, to create a calculated control.

Most forms include an unbound control (label) to describe each bound control (text box) on the form. In the form in Figure 4.17, each text box has a label describing it. As you add or delete fields from a form, be aware that many bound controls are connected to an unbound label. If you move the bound control, the label moves, too. Likewise, if you move the label, the bound control moves along with it. You can ungroup the controls and move them separately, but the default is that they are joined together.

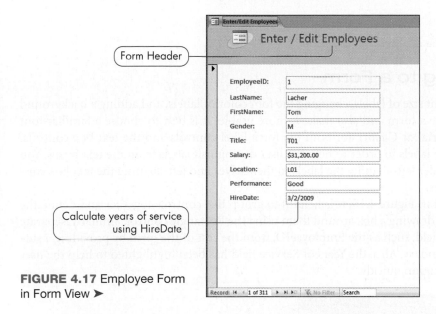

FIGURE 4.17 Employee Form in Form View ➤

Add a Calculated Control to a Form

Review the Enter/Edit Customers form in Figure 4.17 above. Users must manually calculate an employee's years of service using the HireDate field at the bottom of the form. Based on your knowledge of date arithmetic from a previous chapter, you could calculate each employee's years of service using the expression:

= (Date( ) – HireDate) / 365

To add this expression to the form, you add a calculated field using a text box. Open the form in Design view, and then click Text Box in the Controls group on the Design tab. Place a text box at the desired location, and then enter the expression =(Date() – HireDate)/365 into the control source property of the new text box. Format the control as needed. Figure 4.18 shows the Years of Service text box formatted as fixed with one decimal.

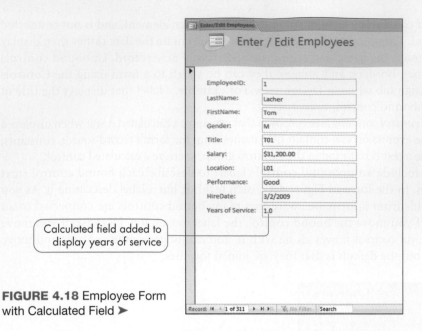

Calculated field added to
display years of service

FIGURE 4.18 Employee Form
with Calculated Field ➤

Add Styling to a Form

Modifying the font size of labels, changing the font color of labels, and adding a background color can enhance a form and also make it more usable. It is best to choose a familiar font family, such as Arial or Calibri, for both the form label controls and the text box controls. Apply bold to the labels in order to help the user distinguish labels from the text boxes. You should also consider left-aligning the labels to themselves and left-aligning the text box controls to themselves.

As illustrated in Figure 4.19, it is helpful to group like controls together and define the group visually by drawing a box around them using the Rectangle control. Similarly, separate the primary key field, such as the EmployeeID, from the rest of the form by providing a sufficient visual boundary. Also, the Years of Service field has been highlighted to help the user locate this information quickly.

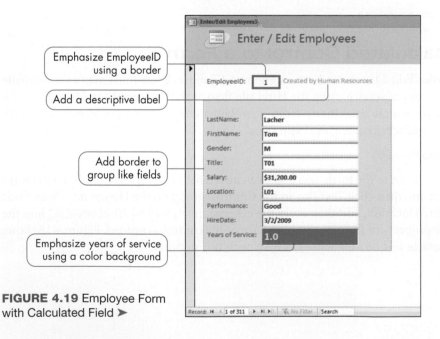

Emphasize EmployeeID
using a border

Add a descriptive label

Add border to
group like fields

Emphasize years of service
using a color background

FIGURE 4.19 Employee Form
with Calculated Field ➤

HANDS-ON EXERCISES

2 Form Sections, Views, and Controls

You already created several forms for the Santiago Coffee Shop; however, Alex would like some additional forms. After the new forms are created, you use the different views to make changes and test the forms.

Skills covered: Understand the Main Form Sections and Alter a Form in Design View • Edit Data in Form View • Work with Controls • Add a Calculated Control to a Form • Add Styling to a Form

---

STEP 1 ▶ UNDERSTAND THE MAIN FORM SECTIONS AND ALTER A FORM IN DESIGN VIEW

You have decided to use the Form tool to create a Revenue form. This form will enable Alex to track revenue for his company. You will use Design view to modify this form. Refer to Figure 4.20 as you complete Step 1.

FIGURE 4.20 Revenue Form with Modified Header and Footer ➤

a. Open *a04h1coffee_LastnameFirstname* if you closed it at the end of Hands-On Exercise 1. Click the **File tab**, click **Save Database As**, and then type **a04h2coffee_LastnameFirstname**, changing *h1* to *h2*. Click **Save**.

b. Select **Revenue query** in the Navigation Pane. Click the **Create tab**, and then click **Form** in the Forms group.

   Access creates a new form based on the Revenue query. The form opens in Layout view, ready to edit.

c. Place the mouse on the right edge of the Last Name control so the mouse pointer changes to a double-headed arrow. Drag to the left to size the control section to 50% of its original size.

   Access simultaneously reduces the size of all the controls.

d. Switch to Design view.

   Notice the three sections of the form—*Form Header*, *Detail*, and *Form Footer*.

e. Place the mouse on the bottom edge of the Form Footer bar so the mouse pointer changes to a double-headed arrow. Drag the bar down until the size of the *Form Footer* section is **1"**, using the vertical ruler.

f. Switch to Form view.

With a white background, it is difficult to tell where the *Form Footer* section begins and ends.

g. Switch to Design view. Click **Property Sheet** in the Tools group. Click the **Selection type arrow**, and select **FormFooter**.

h. In the Property Sheet, click the **Format tab**, click the **Back Color arrow**, and then select **Background Light Header** from the list. Close the Property Sheet, and then switch to Form view.

With the new background color, the Form Footer is now evident. You will add content to the footer in a later step.

i. Switch to Design view.

j. Place the mouse on the top edge of the Detail bar so the mouse pointer changes to a double-headed arrow. Drag the bar down until the *Form Header* section is 3/4".

k. Click **Save** in the Quick Access Toolbar and save the form as **Revenue**. Close the form.

STEP 2 ▶ EDIT DATA IN FORM VIEW

You will use the Form tool to create an Access form to help Alex manage his products. This form will enable Tonya to make changes easily when product information changes. Refer to Figure 4.21 as you complete Step 2.

Form is based on the Products table

Modify data in Form view

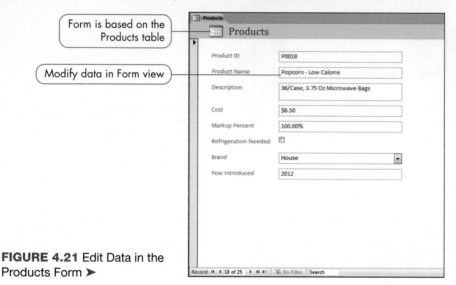

FIGURE 4.21 Edit Data in the Products Form ➤

a. Select the **Products table** in the Navigation Pane. Click the **Create tab**, and then click **Form** in the Forms group.

Access creates a new form based on the Products table.

b. Click anywhere in the subform at the bottom of the window, click the Layout Selector, and then press **Delete** to delete the subform. Click **View** in the Views group to switch to Form view.

c. Click **Next Record** in the Navigation bar to advance to the third record in the Products form.

Use Next Record to advance through the records.

d. Click in the **Product Name box**, and then change *Coffee - Mild Blend* to **Coffee - Light**.

e. Click **Last Record** in the Navigation bar to advance to the last record in the Products form. Click **Previous Record** to locate record 23.

Use Last Record to advance to the last record.

f. Click in the **Product Name box**, and change *Styrofoam Cups - 12 ounce* to **Heavy Paper Cups - 12 ounce**.

g. Click in the **Current Record box** in the Navigation bar, type **12**, and then press **Enter** to go to the 12th record in the Products form.

Use the Current Record box to advance to a specific record.

h. Click in the **Product Name box**, and then change *Sugar Substitute* to **Splenda**.

i. Click in the **Search box** in the Navigation bar, and then type **pop** to locate any records with *pop* in any data value, in this case, record 18.

Use the Search box to find a record with a value you type.

j. Click in the **Product Name box**, and then change *Popcorn - Plain* to **Popcorn - Low Calorie**.

k. Click **Save** in the Quick Access Toolbar and save the form as **Products**. Close the form.

STEP 3 ▶ WORK WITH CONTROLS

You make some enhancements to the Revenue form to increase its usability. Afterwards, Tonya and Alex test the form to determine if the changes are an improvement to the form. Refer to Figure 4.22 as you complete Step 3.

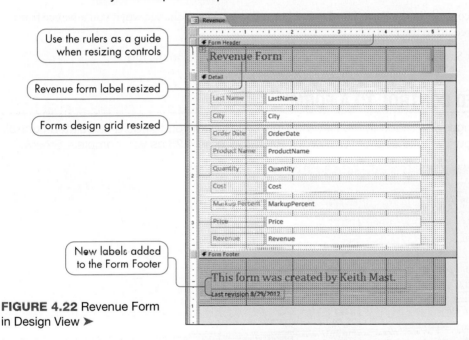

Use the rulers as a guide when resizing controls

Revenue form label resized

Forms design grid resized

New labels added to the Form Footer

FIGURE 4.22 Revenue Form in Design View ▶

a. Right-click the **Revenue form** in the Navigation Pane, and then click **Design View**.

b. Click the **Revenue label** in the Form Header, and then click it again to edit it. Change the label to **Revenue Form**.

c. Click the **Form Logo** to the left of the Revenue Form label, and then press **Delete** to delete the image.

d. Click **Label** in the Controls group, and then click in the **Form Footer** at the 1/4" mark from both the horizontal and vertical rulers to insert a text box. Type **This form was created by** *your name*.

e. Click the **Revenue Form label** in the Form Header, and then click **Format Painter** in the Clipboard group on the Home tab. Click the new label in the Form Footer to apply the same format. Click the label, and then drag the bottom-right sizing handle down and to the right so the entire text is visible.

f. Click **Label** in the Controls group on the Design tab, and then add a second label under the first label in the Form Footer at the 1/4" mark on the horizontal ruler. Type **Last revision** *today's date*. Accept the default font.

g. Click the **Form Header bar**, and then open the Property Sheet if necessary. Change the Height property to **.65**.

You can change the height of the Form Header by dragging it with the mouse or by modifying the Height property.

h. Click the **Revenue Form label** in the Form Header. Modify the following properties:
- Change the Height property to **.5**.
- Change the Width property to **4.75**. Close the Property Sheet.

i. Place the mouse on the right edge of the form's design grid so the mouse pointer changes to a double-headed arrow. Drag the grid to the left to change the form's width to **5.25"**.

Use the horizontal ruler to locate the 5.25" mark.

> **TROUBLESHOOTING:** If other Text box controls are too wide, reduce their width first, and then reduce the grid to 5.25".

j. Switch to Form view. Advance through the records using the Navigation bar at the bottom.

The controls in the Form Header and Form Footer do not change when you advance from one record to the next.

k. Click **Save** in the Quick Access Toolbar to save the changes to the form.

STEP 4 ▶ ADD A CALCULATED CONTROL TO A FORM

After reviewing the changes you made to the Revenue form, Alex asks you to add a calculated control. The new control will show the total cost of each order. Refer to Figure 4.23 as you complete Step 4.

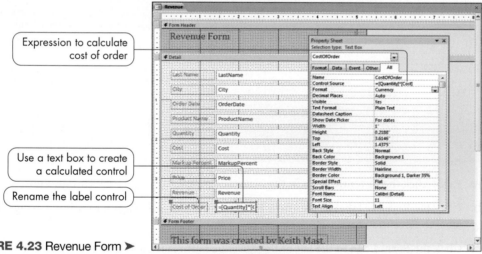

FIGURE 4.23 Revenue Form ➤

a. Switch to Design view.

b. Position the mouse on the top edge of the Form Footer bar until the mouse pointer changes to the double-arrow resizing shape. Drag the **Form Footer bar** down to increase the *Detail* section to **4"**.

c. Click **Text Box** in the Controls group, and then click just below the **Revenue text box** (the white rectangle) at the bottom of the *Detail* section.

d. Click in the **text box**, and then type =[**Quantity**]*[**Cost**] in place of *Unbound*. Press **Enter**.

The expression you typed creates a calculated control that shows the total value of the current product.

e. Open the Property Sheet if necessary. Click the **All tab** in the Property Sheet, click in the **Name property box**, and then replace the existing text with **CostOfOrder**. Click the **Format property**, and then use the arrow to select **Currency** from the list of options.

f. Switch to Form view. Advance through the records using the Navigation bar at the bottom.

As you advance from one record to the next, the cost of each order is displayed in the calculated control.

> **TROUBLESHOOTING:** If you see *#Name* in the calculated control, you have typed the expression incorrectly. Be sure you begin the expression with =.

g. Switch to Design view.

h. Click the label control for the new calculated control, and then replace the existing label caption with **Cost of Order**. Resize label control to fit new text, if necessary.

i. Click the calculated control, and then click the **Other tab** on the Property Sheet. Locate the Tab Stop property and change it to **No**.

j. Click **View** in the Views Group to switch to Form view. Press **Tab** to advance through the fields to test the tab stop change.

A calculated control does not require data entry. It is now skipped when Tab is pressed.

k. Save the form.

STEP 5 ▶ ADD STYLING TO A FORM

The users of the Santiago Coffee Shop database have asked you to add some styling to the new form. You discuss their ideas with Alex, and then decide to apply the suggested styles. Refer to Figure 4.24 as you complete Step 5.

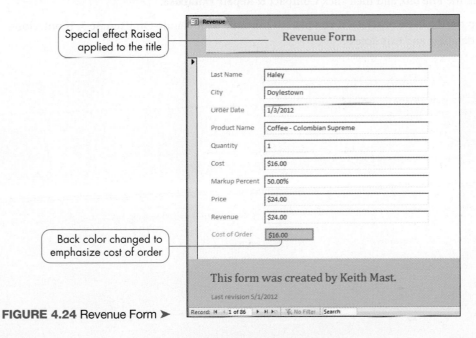

FIGURE 4.24 Revenue Form ➤

a. Switch to Design view.

b. Open the Property Sheet (if necessary), and then click the **Revenue Form label**.

c. Click the **Back Color arrow** on the Property Sheet Format tab, and then choose **Access Theme 2**.

The background color of the title changes to a light blue.

d. Click the **Special Effect arrow** on the Property Sheet Format tab, and then choose **Raised**.

The title now appears raised.

e. Click **Center** in the Font group on the Format tab on the Ribbon.

The form title is now centered within the control box.

f. Click just above the LastName box on the blank grid space, and then drag the mouse through all the fields, except Cost of Order.

All the text box fields are now selected as indicated with an orange border, except the Cost of Order field.

g. Click the **Special Effect arrow** on the Property Sheet Format tab, and then choose **Sunken**.

The fields now appear sunken.

h. Click the **Cost of Order box control**, click the **Border Width arrow** in the Property Sheet Format tab, and then click **2 pt**. Close the Property Sheet.

The border of the calculated control increases.

i. Click **Background Color arrow** in the Font group on the Format tab, and then select **Light Gray 2** (Standard Colors, first column, third row).

The background color of the calculated control is now gray to set it apart from the bound data entry fields.

j. Click the **Cost of Order label control**, click the **Font Color arrow** in the Font group, and then select **Light Gray 4** (Standard Colors, first column, fifth row).

The font color of the calculated control is now gray to set it apart from the bound data entry fields.

k. Switch to Form view. Compare your results to Figure 4.24, and then close and save the form.

l. Click the **File tab**, and then click **Compact & Repair Database**.

m. Keep the database onscreen if you plan to continue with Hands-On Exercise 3. If not, close the database and exit Access.

Report Basics

By now, you know how to plan a database, create a table, establish relationships between tables, enter data into tables, and extract data using queries. You generated output by printing table and query datasheets. You also learned how to create several types of data entry forms. These forms can also be used for inquiries about the data in a database. In this section, you will learn how to create professional reports using the report-writing tools in Access. A ***report*** is a printed document that displays information from a database in a format that provides meaningful information to its readers.

> A **report** is a printed document that displays information from a database in a format that provides meaningful information to its readers.

Although you can print information from tables, queries, and forms, information printed from these database objects may not be in the best format. Most of the printed documents generated by Access will come from reports. Reports can be enhanced to help the reader understand and analyze the data. For example, if you print the Datasheet view from the Customers table, you will be able to locate the key information about each customer. However, using report tools, you can group the customers by sales rep, and then highlight the customers who have not placed an order in six months. This is an example of converting a list of customers into an effective business tool. To increase business, each sales rep could contact their customers who have not ordered in six months, and then review his or her findings with the sales manager. A sales report could be run each month to see if the strategy has helped produce any new business.

> Most of the printed documents generated by Access will come from reports.

In this section, you will create reports in Access by first identifying a record source, then sketching the report, and finally choosing a Report tool. You will learn how to modify a report by adding and deleting fields, by resizing columns, and by adding a color scheme. You will also learn about the report sections, the report views, and controls on reports. After having worked through forms in the section above, you will discover that there are many similarities between forms and reports.

Creating Reports Using Report Tools

Access provides five different report tools for creating reports. The report tools are found in the Reports group, as shown in Figure 4.25. Click one of these tools and Access will create an automatic report (or launch a wizard to guide you) using the table or query that is currently selected. The most common of the tools, the ***Report tool***, is used to instantly create a tabular report based on the table or query currently selected. The Blank Report tool is used to create a new blank report so that you can insert fields and controls manually and design the report. The Report Design tool is used to create a new blank report in Design view. In Design view, you can make advanced design changes to reports, such as adding custom control types and working with report sections. The Report Wizard tool will ask a series of questions and help you create a report based on your answers. The Labels tool is used to create a page of labels using one of the preformatted templates provided by Access. After you create a report using one of the report tools, you can perform modifications in Layout view or Design view.

> The **Report tool** is used to instantly create a tabular report based on the table or query currently selected.

FIGURE 4.25 Report Tools in the Reports Group ➤

Before you create a report in Access, you should ask these questions:

- What is the purpose of the report?
- Who will use the report?
- Which tables are needed for the report?
- What fields, labels, and calculations need to be included?
- How will the report be distributed? Will users pull the information directly from Access or will they receive it through e-mail, fax, or the Internet?
- Will the results be converted to Word, Excel, HTML, or another format?

Sample reports include a telephone directory sorted by last name, a customer list grouped by sales rep, an employee list sorted by most years of service, a financial statement, a bar chart showing sales over the past 12 months, a shipping label, and a letter to customers reminding them about a past due payment.

Identify the Record Source

The first step in planning your report is to identify the record source. You may use one or more tables, queries, or a combination of tables and queries as the report's record source. Sometimes, a single table contains all of the records you need for the report. Other times, you will need to incorporate several tables. When multiple tables are needed to create a report, you can add all the necessary tables into a single query, and then base the report on that query. (As stated earlier, multiple tables in a query must be related, as indicated with join lines. Tables with no join lines usually indicate an incorrect record source.)

Reports can also contain graphics as well as text and numeric data. For example, you can add a company logo, or a watermark to indicate the information is confidential or just a draft. After you identify the record source, you also need to specify which graphic images are needed (and the location of the images).

Sketch the Report

In the *Forms* section, you learned that it is helpful to sketch an Access form before you launch Access. The same holds true for creating an Access report. Design the report and indicate the record source (table names or query name), the title, the format of the report (stacked or tabular), the fields, and the order of fields. It would also be helpful to indicate the grouping and totals needed for the report. Sketch the report first and you will be happier with the results. A sample sketch is shown in Figure 4.26.

Physicians Report - Draft

First Name	Last Name	Address	City	State	Zip Code	Phone Number	Specialization
Bonnie	Clinton	10000 SW 59 Court	Coral Springs	FL	33071	(954) 777-8889	Obstetrics
Warren	Brasington	9470 SW 25 Street	Coral Springs	FL	33071	(954) 888-7654	Hematology
James	Shindell	Avenue	Coral Springs	FL	33070	(954) 773-4343	General Medicine
Edward	Wood	Avenue	Coral Springs	FL	33072	(954) 555-5555	Cardiology
Michelle	Quintana	3990 NW 3 Street	Coral Springs	FL	33071	(954) 888-1221	Internal Medicine
Kristine	Park	9290 NW 59 Steet	Coral Springs	FL	33072	(954) 777-1111	Exercise Physiology
William	Williamson	108 Los Pinos Place	Coral Springs	FL	33071	(954) 888-4554	General Medicine
Holly	Davis	8009 Riviera Drive	Coral Springs	FL	33072	(954) 388-7676	Cardiology
Steven	Fisher	444 SW 190 Street	Coral Springs	FL	33070	(954) 777-3333	Internal Medicine
David	Tannen	50 Main Street	Coral Springs	FL	33171	(954) 777-2211	Hematology
Jeffrey	Jacobsen	490 Bell Drive	Coral Springs	FL	33070	(954) 388-9999	Internal Medicine
Patsy	Clark	200 Harding Blvd	Coral Springs	FL	33070	(954) 777-1087	Cardiology
Keith	Mast	102 SCC	E. Norriton	PA	19401	(610) 555-1212	General Medicine

FIGURE 4.26 Sketch of the Physicians Report ➤

Use the Report Tool

After you sketch the report, you can decide which report tool is appropriate to produce the desired report. Access provides several tools that you can use to create a report, as shown in Figure 4.27. Which one you select depends on the layout of the report, the record source, and the complexity of the report design.

The easiest way to create a report is with the Report tool. Select a table or query in the Navigation Pane, then click Report in the Reports group on the Create tab, and Access creates a tabular layout report instantly. A **tabular layout report** displays data horizontally across the page in a landscape view, as shown in Figure 4.27.

A **tabular layout report** displays data horizontally across the page in a landscape view.

A **stacked layout report** displays fields in a vertical column.

You can also create a *stacked layout report* in Access, although this type of report is less common. A stacked layout report displays fields in a vertical column. The number of records on one page depends on the number of fields in the record source. You can also force a new page at the start of each record.

Report created with the Report tool

Information is presented in tabular format

Physicians report could be grouped by specialization

		Physicians				January 2012		
First Name	Last Name	Address	City	State	Zip Cod	Phone Number	Specialization
Bonnie	Clinton	10000 SW 59 Court	Coral Springs	FL	33071	(954) 777-8889	Obstetrics
Warren	Brasington	9470 SW 25 Street	Coral Springs	FL	33071	(954) 888-7654	Hematology
James	Shindell	14088 Malaga Avenue	Coral Springs	FL	33070	(954) 773-4343	General Medicine
Edward	Wood	400 Roderigo Avenue	Coral Springs	FL	33072	(954) 555-5555	Cardiology
Michelle	Quintana	3990 NW 3 Street	Coral Springs	FL	33071	(954) 888-1221	Internal Medicine
Kristine	Park	9290 NW 59 Steet	Coral Springs	FL	33072	(954) 777-1111	Exercise Physiology
William	Williamson	108 Los Pinos Place	Coral Springs	FL	33071	(954) 888-4554	General Medicine
Holly	Davis	8009 Riviera Drive	Coral Springs	FL	33072	(954) 388-7676	Cardiology
Steven	Fisher	444 SW 190 Street	Coral Springs	FL	33070	(954) 777-3333	Internal Medicine
David	Tannen	50 Main Street	Coral Springs	FL	33171	(954) 777-2211	Hematology
Jeffrey	Jacobsen	490 Bell Drive	Coral Springs	FL	33070	(954) 388-9999	Internal Medicine
Patsy	Clark	200 Harding Blvd	Coral Springs	FL	33070	(954) 777-1087	Cardiology
Keith	Mast	102 SCC	E. Norriton	PA	19401	(610) 555-1212	General Medicine

FIGURE 4.27 Tabular Report ➤

Use the Report Wizard

The Report Wizard.... uses six dialog boxes to collect information about your report.

The **Report Wizard** asks you questions and then uses your answers to generate a report.

You can also create a professional report with the Report Wizard. The **Report Wizard** asks you questions and then uses your answers to generate a report. The wizard uses six dialog boxes to collect information about your report.

Start the Report Wizard

After thinking through the structure, the layout, and the record source, you are ready to launch the Report Wizard. First, select the report's record source in the Navigation Pane, and then click Report Wizard in the Reports group on the Create tab. The wizard opens with the table or query (the record source) displayed in the first dialog box. Although you chose the record source before you started, the first dialog box enables you to select fields from additional tables or queries.

To demonstrate the Report Wizard, an Access database was created to track several health studies being conducted by a local physicians group. The studies are tracked using a StudyID code, S01, S02, S03, etc. The report that you need to create will list each volunteer alphabetically, grouped by study. See Figure 4.28 to review the fields in the Volunteers table—a key table in the Physicians database.

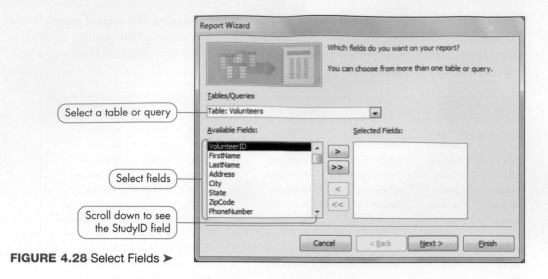

Select a table or query

Select fields

Scroll down to see
the StudyID field

FIGURE 4.28 Select Fields ➤

Add Grouping

The next dialog box asks, "Do you want to add any grouping levels?" As we learned earlier in this chapter, grouping lets you organize and summarize your data. You can also add totals (sum, count, average) at the end of a group. In the sample report, Access correctly predicts that you want the data grouped by the study field (as shown in Figure 4.29). If you did not want to group the report by the StudyID field, you could click the < button to remove the group in step two of the Report Wizard. After you remove the unwanted grouping, select the field you want to group by, and then click the > button to add the new group. If you need a second or third grouping level, add those field names in order. The order in which you select the groups dictates the order of display in the report.

Access adds StudyID
automatically

Add a group

Select a field to group by

Remove a group

FIGURE 4.29 Grouping
Options ➤

Add Sorting and Summary Options

The next dialog box asks, "What sort order and summary information do you want for detail records?" The summary information option will only appear if there is a numeric field in the selected fields (see Figure 4.30). Click Summary Options if you want to add aggregate functions (e.g., sum, average, minimum, and maximum) and to specify whether you want to see detail records on the report or only the aggregate results. Click OK or Cancel to return to the Report Wizard (see Figure 4.31). For the sort options, specify which field you want to sort by first, then second, third, and fourth. For each field, choose ascending order and/or descending order.

Choose the sort fields

Choose Ascending or Descending order

Click Summary Options to add aggregate functions

FIGURE 4.30 Specify Sort Order ➤

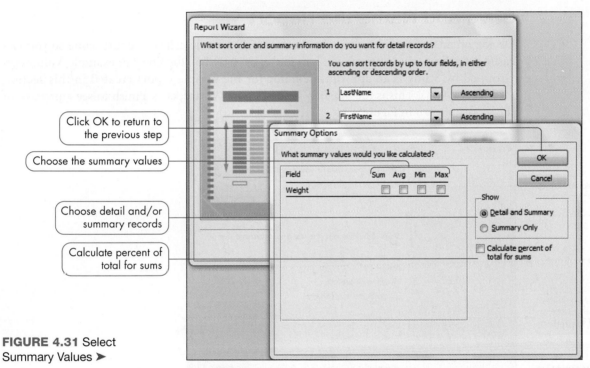

Click OK to return to the previous step

Choose the summary values

Choose detail and/or summary records

Calculate percent of total for sums

FIGURE 4.31 Select Summary Values ➤

Choose the Layout for the Report

The next dialog box will determine the report's appearance. First, you select the layout from three options—Stepped, Block, or Outline. Clicking an option will give you a general preview in the preview area. You can also select the orientation for the report, either Portrait or Landscape (see Figure 4.32). Select an appropriate format for the report.

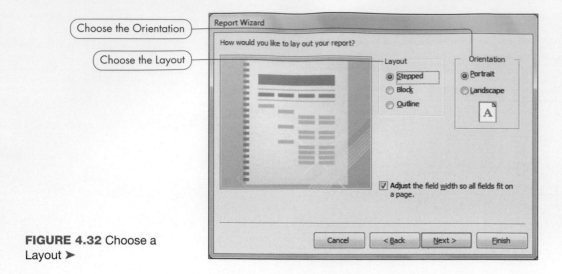

FIGURE 4.32 Choose a
Layout ➤

Save and Name the Report

Decide on an appropriate name for the report. Type a descriptive report name so you can easily determine what information is in the report based on the title. For example, Volunteers Grouped by Study is an appropriate name for the sample report created in this section (see Figure 4.33). This is the last step in the Report Wizard; click Finish to see a preview of the report, shown in Figure 4.34.

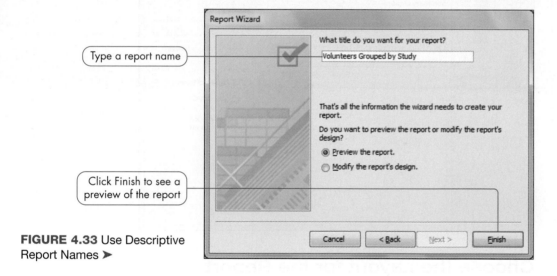

FIGURE 4.33 Use Descriptive
Report Names ➤

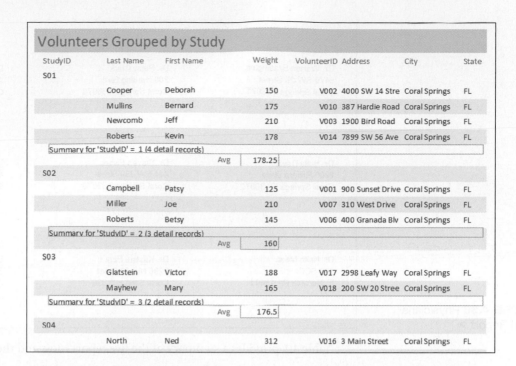

Volunteers Grouped by Study							
StudyID	Last Name	First Name	Weight	VolunteerID	Address	City	State
S01							
	Cooper	Deborah	150	V002	4000 SW 14 Stre	Coral Springs	FL
	Mullins	Bernard	175	V010	387 Hardie Road	Coral Springs	FL
	Newcomb	Jeff	210	V003	1900 Bird Road	Coral Springs	FL
	Roberts	Kevin	178	V014	7899 SW 56 Ave	Coral Springs	FL
Summary for 'StudyID' = 1 (4 detail records)							
		Avg	178.25				
S02							
	Campbell	Patsy	125	V001	900 Sunset Drive	Coral Springs	FL
	Miller	Joe	210	V007	310 West Drive	Coral Springs	FL
	Roberts	Betsy	145	V006	400 Granada Blv	Coral Springs	FL
Summary for 'StudyID' = 2 (3 detail records)							
		Avg	160				
S03							
	Glatstein	Victor	188	V017	2998 Leafy Way	Coral Springs	FL
	Mayhew	Mary	165	V018	200 SW 20 Stree	Coral Springs	FL
Summary for 'StudyID' = 3 (2 detail records)							
		Avg	176.5				
S04							
	North	Ned	312	V016	3 Main Street	Coral Springs	FL

FIGURE 4.34 Volunteers Grouped by Study Report ➤

Use the Label Wizard

The **Label Wizard** enables you to easily create mailing labels, name tags, and other specialized tags.

A **mailing label** is a specialized report that comes preformatted to coordinate with name-brand labels, such as Avery.

The ***Label Wizard*** enables you to easily create mailing labels, name tags, and other specialized tags. A ***mailing label*** is a specialized report that comes preformatted to coordinate with name-brand labels, such as Avery. You then use the Label Wizard to create a label that fits the 5660 template. To begin, click Labels in the Reports group on the Create tab, and then select the manufacturer, the product number, and the label type. Next, choose the font type and size, and then add the fields to the label template, as shown in Figure 4.35. The Physicians Labels report is shown in Figure 4.36.

FIGURE 4.35 Create a Mailing Label ➤

FIGURE 4.36 Physicians Label Report ➤

Table 4.1 provides a summary of the five report tools and their usage.

TABLE 4.1   Report Tools and Their Usage

Report Tool	Usage
Report	Create a tabular report showing all of the fields in the record source.
Report Design	Create a new blank report in Design view. Add fields and controls manually.
Blank Report	Create a new blank report in Layout view. Add fields and controls manually.
Report Wizard	Answer a series of questions and Access will design a custom report for you.
Labels	Choose a preformatted label template and create a sheet of labels.

Modifying a Report

After a report is generated by one of the report tools, you will usually need to modify it. Similar to forms, the common changes to a report are add a field, remove a field, change the order of fields, change the width of a field, and modify the title. These changes, as well as adding a grouping level, are made in Layout view. Advanced changes, such as adding a calculated field or adding VBA code, can only be made in Design view.

Add a Field to a Report

Adding a field to a report with a tabular layout is similar to adding a field to a form with a tabular layout. Right-click a report in the Navigation Pane, and then click Layout view. Next, click Add Existing Fields in the Tools group on the Design tab to reveal the available fields in the report's record source. Drag the new field to a precise location on the report, using the vertical orange line as a guide for the position of the new field, and release the mouse. The other fields will automatically adjust to make room for the new field.

The process of adding a field to a report with a stacked layout is the same as a tabular layout. The only difference is the orange line will appear horizontally.

Delete a Field from a Report

To delete a field from the *Detail* section of a tabular report, first switch to the Layout view or Design view of the report. Next, click the text box of the field to be deleted and note the orange border around the field. With the orange border visible, press Delete. Repeat the process to delete the associated label from the Page Header. After the controls are deleted, click in the blank space, and then press Delete again. After the text box and label are removed from the report, the other fields automatically adjust to close the gap around the deleted field.

Work with a Report Layout Control

Whenever you use one of the report tools to create a new report, Access will add a layout control to help align the fields. Layout controls in reports work the same as layout controls in forms. As discussed earlier in this chapter, the layout control provides guides to help keep controls aligned horizontally and vertically, and give your report a uniform appearance.

There are times when you may want to remove the layout control from a report in order to position the fields without aligning them to each other. If you want to remove the layout control from a report, switch to Design view, and then click anywhere inside the control you want to remove. On the Arrange tab, click Select Layout in the Rows & Columns group. Click Remove Layout in the Table group and the layout control is gone. All of the other controls are still on the report, but the rectangle binding them together is gone.

You can add a layout control to a report by first selecting all the controls you want to keep together. Then, click Stacked or Tabular in the Table group and the layout control appears.

Adjust Column Widths in a Report

You can adjust the width of each column in a tabular report individually so that each column is wide enough to accommodate the widest value. For example, if a report contains first name, last name, address and city, and e-mail address, you will need to make sure the longest value in each field is completely visible. Scroll through the records to make sure this is the case.

To modify column widths in a tabular report, first switch to the Layout view or Design view of the report. Click the text box of the field you want to adjust. The field will have an orange border around it, indicating it is selected. Move the mouse to the right border of the selected field; when the mouse pointer turns to a double arrow, drag the edge to the right (to increase) or the left (to decrease) until you arrive at the desired width.

Add a Theme to the Report

You can enhance the report's appearance by applying one of the themes provided by Access. To apply a theme, switch to Layout view, and then click Themes in the Themes group on the Design tab. Scroll through the themes until you find a theme you like; hover over one of the options to see a quick preview of the current report using the current theme. Right-click a theme, and then choose Apply Theme to This Object Only (as shown in Figure 4.37). You can also apply the theme to all matching objects.

Click Themes

Select a theme from
the Built-In options

FIGURE 4.37 Apply a Theme
to a Report ➤

Sorting Records in a Report

When a report is created using the Report tool, the sort order of the records in the report is initially dependent on the sort order of the record source—similar to the way records are sorted in a form. The primary key of the record source usually dictates the sort order. However, a report has an additional feature for sorting. While in Layout view or Design view, click Group & Sort in the Grouping & Totals group on the Design tab. The Group, Sort, and Total pane now appears at the bottom of the report. This section enables you to set the sort order for the report and override the sorting in the report's record source.

Change the Sorting in a Report

While working in the Layout view of a report, click Group & Sort to display the *Group, Sort, and Total* section, as shown in Figure 4.38. To sort the records in a report by last name, click Add a sort and select LastName from the list. The report records will instantly sort by LastName in ascending order. Next, you can set a second sort by clicking Add a Sort again. For example, you could add the FirstName sort after the LastName sort, as shown in Figure 4.38.

Select FirstName for
the second sort

LastName is the first sort

FIGURE 4.38 Group, Sort,
and Total Pane in a Report ➤

3 Report Basics

You create a Products report using the Access Report tool to help Alex stay on top of the key data for his business. After Access creates the report, you modify the column widths so the entire report fits on one page (portrait or landscape, depending on the report). You also use the Report Wizard tool to create other reports for Alex.

Skills covered: Use the Report Tool • Add a Field to a Report • Delete a Field from a Report and Adjust Column Widths in a Report • Apply a Theme to the Report • Change the Sorting in a Report • Use the Report Wizard

---

STEP 1 ▶ USE THE REPORT TOOL

You use the Report tool to create an Access report to help Alex manage his product information. This report is especially useful for determining which products he needs to order to fill upcoming orders. Refer to Figure 4.39 as you complete Step 1.

FIGURE 4.39 Products Report in Landscape ➤

a. Open *a04h2coffee_LastnameFirstname* if you closed it at the end of Hands-On Exercise 2. Click the **File tab**, click **Save Database As**, and then type **a04h3coffee_LastnameFirstname**, changing *h2* to *h3*. Click **Save**.

b. Select the **Products table** in the Navigation Pane. Click the **Create tab**, and then click **Report** in the Reports group.

Access creates a new tabular layout report based on the Products table. The report opens in Layout view ready to edit.

c. Click the **Products title** at the top of the report to select it, and then click again on **Products** and change the title to **Products Report**.

d. Display the report in Print Preview.

The report is too wide for the page; you will change the orientation to Landscape.

e. Click **Close Print Preview**.

f. Click the **Page Setup tab**, and then click **Landscape** in the Page Layout group.

The report changes to Landscape orientation. Most of the columns now fit onto one page. You will make further revisions to the report later on so that it fits on one page.

g. Display the report in Print Preview.

h. Close and save the report as **Products**.

STEP 2 ## ADD A FIELD TO A REPORT

The Products report you created for Santiago Coffee looks very good (according to Alex). However, Alex asks you to add a new field to the Products table and incorporate that into the Products report. Refer to Figure 4.40 as you complete Step 2.

Navigation Pane Open/Close button

Another field is bumped to page two

OnHand field added

FIGURE 4.40 OnHand Field Added to the Report ➤

a. Open the Products table, and then click **View** in the Views group to switch to Design view.

You need to add the OnHand field to the Products table.

b. Click the **MarkupPercent field**, and then click **Insert Rows** in the Tools group.

A new blank row appears above the MarkupPercent field.

c. Type **OnHand** in the **Field Name box**, and then select **Number** as the Data Type. In the Field Properties at the bottom, change the Field Size to **Integer**.

d. Save the table. Click **View** to change to Datasheet view.

The new OnHand column appears empty in each row. Next you will add sample data to the new field.

e. Type the following OnHand values starting at the top and continuing through the last row: **10, 10, 10, 10, 10, 10, 10, 25, 25, 55, 40, 55, 125, 75, 200, 200, 200, 75, 75, 42, 42, 175, 175, 22, 37.**

f. Close the Products table.

g. Open the Products report in Layout view.

h. Click the **Open/Close button** on the Navigation Pane to collapse the Navigation Pane so more of the report is visible. Close the Property sheet, if necessary.

i. Click **Add Existing Fields** in the Tools group on the Design tab. Drag the **OnHand field** from the Field List pane onto the Products report between the Cost and MarkupPercent fields. Close the Field List pane.

Because of the tabular layout control, Access adjusts all the columns to make room for the new OnHand field.

j. Insert a space in the OnHand label control in the Report Header so that it reads *On Hand*.

A space was added to make the heading more readable.

k. Display the report in Print Preview.

The report is still too wide for a single page. Next, you will modify the column widths.

l. Save the report.

STEP 3 ▶ **DELETE A FIELD FROM A REPORT AND ADJUST COLUMN WIDTHS IN A REPORT**

The Products report now contains the new OnHand value that Alex requested, but the report is too wide to print on one page. In this step, you delete unnecessary fields and read just the remaining column widths. Refer to Figure 4.41 as you complete Step 3.

All fields fit on page one

Refrigeration Needed label shortened

FIGURE 4.41 All Fields Fit on the Products Report ▶

a. Click **Close Print Preview**.

b. Scroll to the right, right-click anywhere on the **Year Introduced column**, and then click **Select Entire Column** from the shortcut menu. Press **Delete** to remove the column.

The Year Introduced column is removed from the report.

c. Click the **ProductID column heading**, and then drag the right border to the left until the Product ID heading still fits, but any extra white space is removed.

d. Click the **Refrigeration Needed column heading**, and then rename the column **Refrig?**. Adjust the column width of the Refrig? column.

e. Adjust the width of the remaining columns until all fields fit on one page.

f. Display the report in Print Preview.

This report now fits nicely onto one landscape page.

g. Click **Close Print Preview**, and then save the report.

STEP 4 **APPLY A THEME TO THE REPORT**

The Products report now contains the new OnHand value and the report fits nicely onto one landscape page. You create two color schemes for Alex and ask him to select one of them. Refer to Figure 4.42 as you complete Step 4.

FIGURE 4.42 Products Report with Solstice Theme ➤

a. Switch to Layout view, if necessary.

b. Click **Themes** in the Themes group on the Design tab.

The available predefined themes display.

c. Right-click a **Solstice theme** (second column, second row from bottom), and then choose **Apply Theme to This Object Only**. Display the report in Print Preview.

Access reformats the report using the Solstice theme.

d. Click **Close Print Preview**. Click the **File tab**, and then click **Save Object As**. Type **Products Solstice** as the report name, and then click **OK**. Click the **File tab** to return to the report.

You saved the report with one theme. Now, you will apply a second theme to the report and save it with a different name.

e. Switch to Layout view, and then click **Themes** in the Themes group to apply a different theme.

f. Right-click a **Module theme** (first column, seventh row), and then choose **Apply Theme to This Object Only**. Display the report in Print Preview.

    Compare the Solstice theme to the Module theme.

g. Click **Close Print Preview**. Click the **File tab**, and then click **Save Object As**. Type **Products Module** as the report name, and then click **OK**. Click the **File tab** to return to the report.

STEP 5 CHANGE THE SORTING IN A REPORT

Alex would like the Products Module report to be sorted by Product Name order (rather than ProductID order). You change the sort order and preview again to see the results. Refer to Figure 4.43 as you complete Step 5.

FIGURE 4.43 Products Report Sorted by Product Name ➤

Report sorted by Product Name

a. Verify the Products Module report is in Layout view.

b. Click **Group & Sort** in the Grouping & Totals group.

    The Add a group and Add a sort options appear at the bottom of the report.

c. Click **Add a sort**.

    A new Sort bar appears at the bottom of the report.

d. Select **ProductName** from the list.

    The report is now sorted by ProductName.

e. Display the report in Print Preview.

f. Close Print Preview, and then save and close the report.

STEP 6 USE THE REPORT WIZARD

You decide to create the Sales by City report for Santiago Coffee. After discussing the report parameters with Alex, you decide to use the Report Wizard. Refer to Figure 4.44 as you complete Step 6.

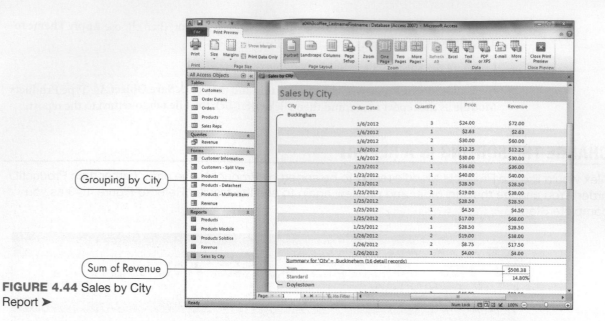

Grouping by City

Sum of Revenue

FIGURE 4.44 Sales by City Report ➤

a. Open the Navigation Pane, and then select the **Revenue query** in the Navigation Pane. Click the **Create tab**, and then click **Report Wizard** in the Reports group.

The Report Wizard launches.

b. Click the >> **button** to add all the fields to the selected Fields box. Click **Cost**, and then click the < **button** to remove the Cost field. Also remove the MarkupPercent, Lastname, and ProductName fields. Click **Next**.

c. Select **City**, and then click the > **button** to add grouping by city. Click **Next**.

d. Select **OrderDate** for the sort order. Click **Summary Options**.

e. Click **Sum** to summarize the Revenue field. Click the **Calculate percent of total for sums check box** to show the relationship between each group and the whole. Click **OK**.

f. Click **Next**. Click **Next** again to accept the default layout.

g. Type **Sales by City** for the title of the report. Click **Finish**.

The report is displayed in Print Preview mode. Some of the data values and labels cannot be seen. Next, you will adjust the controls.

h. Click **Close Print Preview**. In Layout view, adjust the controls so all the field values are visible, as shown in Figure 4.44. Widen the totals controls under the Revenue column. Click in the **Revenue total field**, open the Property Sheet, and then select the **Currency format**.

i. Display the report in Print Preview to verify your changes.

j. Close and save the report.

k. Click the **File tab**, and then click **Compact & Repair Database**.

l. Keep the database onscreen if you plan to continue with Hands-On Exercise 4. If not, close the database and exit Access.

Report Sections, Views, and Controls

You just created and modified reports in the previous section. In this section, you will learn about the various views you accessed while creating and modifying the reports. As you work with the report tools to create and modify reports, you will find the need to frequently switch between the four report views in Access—Layout view, Print Preview, Design view, and Report view. Most of your design work will be done in Layout view, but occasionally, you will need to switch to Design view to apply a more advanced feature, such as a calculated field. Users of the report will use Print Preview, Print, and occasionally Layout view. There should be no reason for a user to switch to Layout view or Design view. Modifications to the report should be done by the designated report designer.

To switch between the four views, click the View arrow in the Views group and select the desired view. Layout view and Print Preview are the most common views; Report view is useful for filtering a report based on a field value. You can also switch between views by right-clicking on the report tab or by right-clicking a report in the Navigation Pane. You can also click one of the small view icons in the bottom right of the Access window.

In this section, you will learn how to identify report sections. You learned about the form sections earlier in this chapter; you can apply that knowledge as you learn about the report sections. Even though reports have more default sections than forms, working with report sections will be similar to working with form sections.

> Even though reports have more default sections than forms, working with report sections will be similar to working with form sections.

Controls are also covered in this section. Again, the overlap between forms and reports will become evident (and be helpful).

Identifying Report Sections

Access reports are divided into five main sections that can be viewed when you display a report in Design view. You need to become familiar with each section so you can manipulate reports to meet your needs.

Identify the Default Report Sections

In the forms section, you learned that Access divides forms into three main sections. For reports, Access creates five main sections—*Report Header*, *Page Header*, *Detail*, *Page Footer*, and *Report Footer* as shown in Figure 4.45. When in Design view, you can collapse or expand each section as needed, and delete any header or footer section.

The Report Header section prints at the beginning of each report.

The ***Report Header section*** prints at the beginning of each report. This section will usually contain the report title, a logo or other graphic, and the date and time when the report was printed. You can remove this section by right-clicking on a section bar, and then clicking the Report Header/Footer option. Follow the same process to add the Report Header/Footer to a report. When you remove the Report Header, the Report Footer is also removed automatically.

The Page Header section appears once at the top of each page.

The ***Page Header section*** appears at the top of each page. Use this section to add or edit column headings on the top of each page. The Page Header will usually contain a horizontal line to separate the column headings from the data values. You can remove this section by right-clicking on a section bar, and then clicking the Page Header/Footer option. Follow the same process to add the Report Header/Footer to a report. If you remove the Page Header, the Page Footer is also removed automatically.

The *Detail* section prints one line for each record in the report's record source. Fields that are connected to the report's record source are known as *bound controls*. The *Detail* section can be hidden, if necessary, by clicking Hide Details in the Grouping & Totals group on the Design tab. For reports that only require summarized data, you will want to hide the details. Access makes it easy for you to show or hide detail levels. Click Hide Details again to redisplay hidden details.

Although the *Detail* section cannot be removed from a report, you can hide it from Print Preview, Layout view, and Design view to show only the headers and footers. This is relevant when the output only requires the totals of each category and not the details that make up the category.

The **Page Footer section** appears at the bottom of each page. Use this section to show page numbers at the bottom of each page. Totals should not be added to this section since the results will produce an error. You can remove this section by right-clicking on a section bar, and then clicking the Page Header/Footer option. Follow the same process to add the Report Header/Footer to a report. If you remove the Page Footer, the Page Header is also removed automatically.

The **Report Footer section** prints one time at the bottom of the report. The Report Footer is commonly used for displaying the grand total of certain columns. You can also display the count of all records in the *Report Footer* section. You can remove this section by right-clicking on a section bar, and then clicking the Report Header/Footer option. Follow the same process to add the Report Header/Footer to a report. If you remove the Report Footer, the Report Header is also removed automatically.

In Figure 4.45, each gray section bar marks the top boundary of a report section. The top bar denotes the top boundary of the Report Header. The bottom bar displays the top boundary of the Report Footer. The grid-like area under the bars shows the space allotted to that section. Notice that the report has no space allocated to the Report Footer. If you decide that the allotted space for a particular section is not needed, you can collapse that section fully so that the section bars are touching. The section remains in the report's design but will not be visible on the Print Preview or the printed page.

Similar to form sections, you can expand or collapse the space between report sections by moving your mouse over the section bar. When the mouse pointer shape changes to a double-headed arrow, drag to expand or collapse the section. A grid-like area appears as your mouse drags down. If you expand or collapse the space allotment for one section, the other sections may also be affected.

The Page Footer section appears once at the bottom of each page.

The Report Footer section prints once at the bottom of the report.

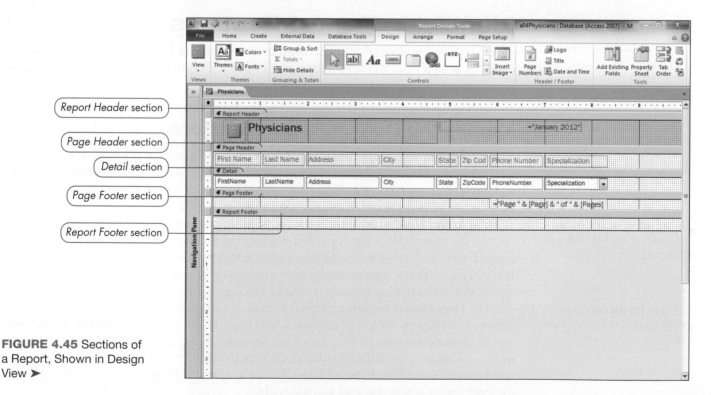

Report Header section
Page Header section
Detail section
Page Footer section
Report Footer section

FIGURE 4.45 Sections of a Report, Shown in Design View ➤

Add a Group Header/Footer

In addition to the five main sections listed above, you can also add a custom *group header/footer* section to a report. For example, if you use the Report tool to create a report based on the Physicians table (as shown in Figure 4.46), you may want this report to be grouped by Specialization. It will be easier for users to locate a physician within a given specialization. Otherwise, you would have to search through the entire list to locate a doctor within a certain specialization.

To add a custom group to a report, open the report in Layout view, and then click Group & Sort in the Grouping & Totals group on the Design tab. The Group, Sort, and Total pane appears below the report. This section enables you to add a custom group. Click Add a Group, and then select the field that you want to group by. For a field to be a candidate for grouping, field values must repeat in the *Detail* section. For example, since specialization repeats in the *Detail* section, it could be used for grouping.

A **Group Header section**, when activated, will appear just above the *Detail* section in Design view, with the name of the field you are grouping.

Once you establish the custom group, a ***Group Header section*** will appear just above the *Detail* section in Design view, along with the name of the field you are grouping. If you select the Specialization field as a custom group, the section will be named *Specialization Header*, as shown in Figure 4.46. Click Print Preview in the Views group to view the data in the report; each time the grouping field value changes, the group header will print with the new value. For example, in a physicians report with five specializations, grouped by Specialization, the group header will print five times, once for each specialization, with the physicians printed under each specialization.

The **Group Footer section**, when activated, will appear just below the *Detail* section in Design view, but only when you select this option in the Group, Sort, and Total pane.

A ***Group Footer section*** appears just below the *Detail* section in Design view, but only when you select this option in the Group, Sort, and Total pane. Locate the group header in question, and then click the More option on that group header bar; then click the *without a footer* arrow and select the *with a footer* option. The group footer is useful for totaling the data at the end of each group. If a group of physicians is part of a major practice, it would be good to know how many physicians are assigned to each specialization. The group footer could display the count of physicians for each specialization.

Click Group & Sort to add grouping

Specialization Group Header section

Specialization Group Footer section

Modify the grouping and sorting

FIGURE 4.46 Add a Header to the Physicians Report ➤

Add Totals to a Group Footer/Report Footer

Often, reports require totals at the group level and/or at the grand total level. For example, the Physicians Report might contain a count of physicians in each Specialization group, and again at the end of the report. Figure 4.47 shows a report with a total number of customers for each sales rep and the total number of customers at the end of the report.

To add totals to a report, first create the group section required for the totals. For example, add the Sales Rep group to a Customers report. Next, in Layout view, click the field that contains the data you want to total, click Totals in the Grouping & Totals group on the

Design tab, and then select the appropriate option. Access will add a total after each group and again at the end of the report.

You remove a total from a report in the same way you add a total. First, select the field that contains the total, click Totals in the Grouping & Totals group, and then uncheck the option you want to remove.

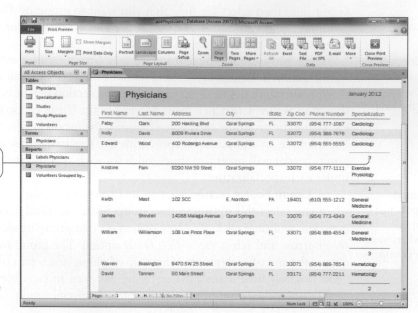

Count is shown at the bottom of each Specialization

FIGURE 4.47 Totals Added to a Report ➤

See the reference table below for a summary of each report section.

REFERENCE Report Sections

Section	Location	Frequency	Usage	Default
Report Header	Top of the report	Once	Holds the report title, the organization's name, the company logo, and the run date & time.	On
Page Header	Top of each page	Once per page	Page Headers generally contain the column headings. In a multi-page report, the labels repeat at the top of each page to provide continuity.	On
Group Header	At the start of each new group	At the start of each group	Prints the value of each unique instance for a grouped field. A report grouped by state would print up to 50 unique state names.	Off
Detail	Middle	Once per record in the record source	Repeats for each record in the record source. If there were 500 records in the record source, the report would have 500 detail lines.	On
Group Footer	At the end of each group	At the end of each group	This section generally mirrors the group header. For a report grouped by state, group footer could be used to show a count of the records in each state.	Off
Page Footer	Bottom of each page	Once per page	The Page Footer is generally used to print page numbers on the report.	On
Report Footer	End of the report	Once	Use the Report Footer to print grand totals or other aggregate information for the records.	On

Revising Reports Using Report Views

Access provides different views for a report similar to the different views in tables, queries, and forms. Tables and queries have Design view and Datasheet view. Forms have Layout view, Form view, and Design view. Reports have Layout view, Print Preview, Design view, and Report view. To switch between certain views, click View in the Views group, or click the View arrow, and then select a view from the list. Each view is described in the sections below.

Layout View

Use Layout view to alter the report design while still viewing the data. You should use Layout view to add or delete fields in the report, modify field properties, change the column widths, add grouping and sorting levels to a report, and to filter data by excluding certain records. Although Layout view appears similar to Print Preview, you will find sufficient variations between the two views, so that you will always need to verify the report in Print Preview to evaluate all the changes made in Layout view.

Print Preview

Print Preview enables you to see exactly what the report will look like when it is printed.

Print Preview enables you to see exactly what the report will look like when it is printed. Most users prefer to use Print Preview prior to printing the report. This enables you to intercept errors in reports before you send the report to the printer. You cannot modify the design in this view; switch to Layout view or Design view to modify the design. By default, Print Preview will display all the pages in the report. Figure 4.47 shows an Access report in Print Preview.

Design View

Design view displays the report's design without displaying the data. You can perform many of the same tasks in Design view as you can in Layout view—add and delete fields, add and remove sorting and grouping layers, rearrange columns, adjust column widths, and modify report elements. When a report is very long, Design view is useful because you can alter the design without needing to scroll through pages of data. However, after you make a change in Design view, it is best to switch to Layout view or Print Preview to examine the final output. You need to experiment using both the Layout view and Design view to decide which view you prefer. As with forms, some changes to reports can only be done in Design view. Figure 4.46 displays the Physicians report in Design view.

Report View

Report view enables you to see what the printed report will look like in a continuous page layout.

Report view enables you to see what a printed report will look like in a continuous page layout. Because Report view is similar to Layout view, but not used as frequently, this view will not be discussed further in this chapter.

Identifying Control Types in Reports

If you examine the fields in a report, such as the one in Figure 4.47, you will notice that each field has a label (heading) at the top with a column of data values under the heading. As you learned in the forms section earlier in this chapter, a text box displays the data found in the record source and a label is a literal word or phrase to describe the data. The heading in Figure 4.47 is a label, and the data values are displayed using a text box.

The label and text box controls are among the many types of controls found on the Controls group on the Design tab when you are in the Design view of a report. As discussed earlier in the forms section, controls can be categorized as bound, unbound, or calculated.

Work with Controls

Bound controls are text boxes that are connected to a field in a table or a query. These controls display different data for each new record that is printed. To add a bound control to a report, switch to Layout view, and then drag a field from the Field List pane onto the report.

Unbound controls are labels and other decorative design elements. These controls usually describe and decorate the data rather than display the data. These controls remain the same each time a new record is printed. Unbound controls include labels, lines, borders, and images. Add an unbound control to a report using the Controls group on the Design tab in the Design view of a report.

Calculated controls contain an expression that generates a calculated result when displayed in Print Preview. The expression can contain field names from the report's record source, constants, or functions. Use a text box, found in the Controls group on the Design tab, while in Design view to create a calculated control.

Add a Calculated Control to a Report

To add a calculated control to the report, switch to Design view, and then click Text Box in the Controls group on the Design tab. Place a text box at the desired location, then enter the expression to create the calculation. Format the control as needed.

In Hands-On Exercise 4, you will create a report, add sorting and grouping to refine the content, work with data aggregates, and add a new field to the report.

HANDS-ON EXERCISES

4 Report Sections, Views, and Controls

The reports you created for Alex are working nicely. Alex would like you to modify the layout of the new reports to make them more attractive. You suggest he add grouping to one of the reports.

Skills covered: Identify the Default Report Sections and Add a Group Header/Footer in Layout View • Add Totals to a Group Footer/Report Footer in Layout View • Work with Controls in Design View • Add a Calculated Control to a Report in Design View

---

STEP 1 ▶ **IDENTIFY THE DEFAULT REPORT SECTIONS AND ADD A GROUP HEADER/FOOTER IN LAYOUT VIEW**

Alex asks you to make several changes to the Monthly Revenue by Salesperson report. First, you update the Sales Rep table with the latest information. Refer to Figure 4.48 as you complete Step 1.

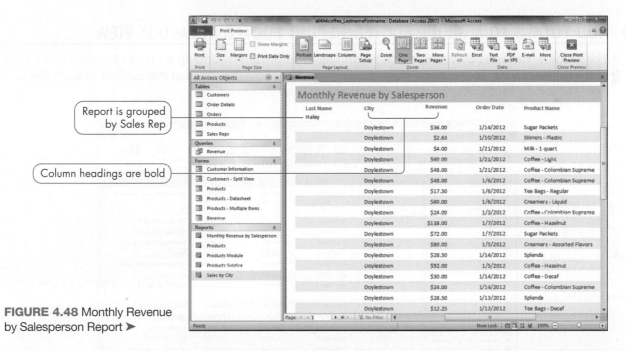

FIGURE 4.48 Monthly Revenue by Salesperson Report ➤

a. Open *a04h3coffee_LastnameFirstname* if you closed it at the end of Hands-On Exercise 3. Click the **File tab**, click **Save Database As**, and then type **a04h4coffee_LastnameFirstname**, changing *h3* to *h4*. Click **Save**.

b. Open the Sales Reps table. Add your first name and last name to sales rep S0002. Leave the other fields as they are. Close the table.

c. Open the Customers table. For all the customers in the city of Buckingham, change the Sales Rep ID to **003**. The leading *S* appears automatically due to the Format property. Close the table.

d. Select the **Revenue query** in the Navigation Pane, click the **Create tab**, and then click **Report Wizard** in the Reports group.

e. Add the **LastName, City, Revenue, OrderDate**, and **ProductName fields** to the Selected Fields list. Click **Next** four times to accept the default settings. The wizard now asks "What title do you want for your report?" Type **Monthly Revenue by Salesperson**.

The completed report is displayed in Print Preview.

f. Close Print Preview, and then switch to Layout view.

Next, you will add the Last Name group.

g. Click **Group & Sort** in the Grouping and Sorting group. Click **Add a group**, and then select **LastName**. Close Group & Sort.

The report now contains the LastName group.

h. Select the **Last Name column heading**, and then click **Bold** in the Font group on the Format tab. Apply bold to the rest of the column headings.

i. Select the **Last Name column heading**, and then type **Sales Rep**.

j. Modify the report column widths so the column spacing is uniform (as shown in Figure 4.48).

k. Switch to Print Preview.

The report is now divided into Sales Rep groups.

l. Click **Close Print Preview**, and then save the report.

STEP 2 ▶ **ADD TOTALS TO A GROUP FOOTER/REPORT FOOTER IN LAYOUT VIEW**

The Monthly Revenue by Salesperson report can be improved by adding a count of orders and a total of the revenue field. You suggest to Alex that the report show the totals at the bottom of each *Sales Rep* section. Refer to Figure 4.49 as you complete Step 2.

FIGURE 4.49 Revenue by Salesperson Report with Totals ▶

a. Verify the Monthly Revenue by Salesperson report is open in Layout view. Click the **Revenue field**, click **Totals** in the Grouping & Totals group, and then select **Sum** from the list.

A sum of revenue is now added to the group footer of each Sales Rep group.

b. Click the **View arrow** in the Views group, and then select **Print Preview**.

c. Advance to the next page to view the order count for each Sales Rep.

d. Click **Close Print Preview**, and then click the **City field**. Click **Totals** in the Grouping & Totals group, and then select **Count Records**.

e. Scroll down until the first totals control in the Revenue column is visible. Select the **totals calculated control box**, and then click **Property Sheet** in the Tools group. Click the **Format arrow** on the Format tab, and then choose **Currency** from the list.

The totals are now formatted for currency.

f. Scroll down to the bottom of the report, and then click the **grand total calculated control box** under the Revenue column. Click the **Format arrow** on the Format tab, and then choose **Currency** from the list. Close the Property Sheet.

The grand total is now formatted for currency.

g. Display the report in Print Preview. Advance through all the pages.

The total revenue is now added to the group footer of each Sales Rep group.

h. Click **Close Print Preview**, and then scroll to the bottom of the report.

The count of orders and the total revenue were automatically added to the Report Footer.

i. Switch to Design View.

In Design view, you can see the seven sections of the Monthly Revenue by Salesperson report. The data is no longer visible.

j. Save the report.

STEP 3 ▶ WORK WITH CONTROLS IN DESIGN VIEW

Alex asks you to add Santiago Coffee Shop at the top of the Monthly Revenue by Salesperson report. You add a new label to the report section and make a few other formatting enhancements. Refer to Figure 4.50 as you complete Step 3.

FIGURE 4.50 Revenue by Salesperson Report with Enhancements ▶

a. Click the **Monthly Revenue by Salesperson label** in the Report Header. Press ⬇ to move the label down 1/4" to make room for another label.

When you move the title down using ⬇, the *Report Header* section grows automatically.

b. Click **Label** in the Controls group on the Design tab, and then click just above the *M* in the Monthly Revenue title.

The label control is ready for you to type a phrase.

c. Type **Santiago Coffee Shop** into the new label, and then press **Enter**.

An orange border indicates the label control is still selected.

d. Click the **Format tab**, and then use the **Font group commands** to modify the new label:

Font Size: **14**
Font Color: **Dark Blue, Text 2, Darker 25%** (fifth row, fourth column)
Style: **Italic**

e. Resize the new label using the bottom-right corner of the control box. Widen the box so the entire phrase is visible.

f. Click the **LastName text box** in the *LastName Header* section, and then modify the properties as follows:

Font Size: **12**
Font Color: **Dark Blue, Text 2** (first row, fourth column)
Style: **Bold**
Align: **Center**
Background Color: **Yellow**

g. Resize the **LastName text box** using the bottom-right corner of the control box. Widen the field so the entire last name is visible when you switch to Layout view.

h. Click the **Count control** in the LastName Footer, and then click **Center** in the Font group. Hold down **Shift**, and then click the **Revenue Sum control** in the LastName Footer.

Both controls are now selected.

i. Click **Bold** in the Font group.

j. Click the **Count control** in the Report Footer, hold down **Shift**, and then click the **Sum control** in the Report Footer.

Both controls are now selected.

k. Click **Bold** in the Font group. Click the **Background Color arrow**, and then select **Blue, Accent 1, Lighter 80%** (second row, fifth column in Theme Colors).

l. Display the report in Print Preview. Advance through all the pages to review your changes.

m. Click **Close Print Preview**, and then save the report.

STEP 4 ▶ **ADD A CALCULATED CONTROL TO A REPORT IN DESIGN VIEW**

Alex asks you to add a comment to the report for all orders that are less than $10. You add a new expression using a text box control to display the word *minimum* if the order is under $10. Refer to Figure 4.51 as you complete Step 4.

Minimum control identifies orders <$10

FIGURE 4.51 Revenue by Salesperson Report with Minimum Flag ➤

a. Switch to Design View if necessary. Click the **OrderDate box**, press **Delete**, and then delete the Order Date label. Drag the **Product Name box and label** to the **4 1/2"** mark on the horizontal ruler, moving the other labels and boxes, if necessary.

b. Click **Text Box** in the Controls group on the Design tab. Click in the **Detail section** to the right of the ProductName control.

A new text box is created along with a label. The label overlaps the ProductName text box.

c. Click the new **Label control**, and then press **Delete**.

The label control is deleted.

> **TROUBLESHOOTING:** If you delete the text box control, click Undo to restore the deleted control and delete only the Label control.

d. Click **Property Sheet** in the Tools group. Click the new text box, labeled *Unbound*, to select it.

e. Click the **All tab** in the Property Sheet pane. Type **MinimumOrder** in the **Name property box** and **="minimum"** in the **Control Source property box**. Change the Border Style property to **Transparent**.

f. Display the report in Print Preview.

Minimum shows on all orders. You will now add an expression so that only orders less than $10 will show.

g. Click **Close Print Preview**. Verify the MinimumOrder control is selected.

h. Click the **Control Source**, and then press **Shift+F2** to expand the cell. Change the expression in the Control Source property to **=IIf(Revenue < 10, "minimum", "")**. Click **OK**.

The second set of quote marks is an empty text string.

i. Display the report in Print Preview. Advance through all the pages to examine the minimum orders. Click **Close Print Preview**.

j. Click the **MinimumOrder control** in the *Detail* section, click **Bold** in the Font group on the Format tab, click the **Font Color arrow**, and then select **Red** under Standard Colors.

k. Display the report in Print Preview. Review the changes to the report, and then close and save the report.

l. Click the **File tab,** and then click **Compact & Repair Database**.

m. Exit Access.

n. Submit based on your instructor's directions.

After reading this chapter, you have accomplished the following objectives:

1. **Create forms using the form tools.** Access provides 16 different tools for creating forms. The form tools are found in the Forms group located on the Create tab, as shown in Figure 4.1. Click one of these tools and Access will create an automatic form using the table or query that is currently selected. The most common of these tools, the Form tool, is used to create stacked layout forms for customers, employees, products, and other primary tables. Once a form is created, you can customize the form using Layout and Design views.

2. **Modify a form.** After a form is generated by one of the form tools, you often need to modify it. Some common form changes are to add a field, remove a field, change the order of fields, change the width of a field, and modify label text. These changes, as well as adding a theme, can be made in a form's Layout view. Advanced changes, such as adding a calculated field or adding VBA code, can be made in a form's Design view.

3. **Sort records in a form.** When a form is created using a form tool, the sort order of the records in the form is dependent on the sort order of the record source. To modify the sort order of a form, open the form in Form view, and then select the field you want to use for sorting and click Ascending in the Sort & Filter group on the Home tab.

4. **Identify form sections.** Access forms, by default, are divided into three sections—Form Header, Detail, and Form Footer. These sections can vary depending on what type of form you create. Form designers also have the option of removing certain sections from a form. The *Form Header* section is displayed at the top of each form. This section will usually contain the form title, a logo or other graphic, and the date and time the report was printed. The *Detail* section displays the records in the form's record source. The *Form Footer* section is displayed at the bottom of the form. The Form Footer is commonly used to display totals for relevant field values.

5. **Revise forms using form views.** Access provides different views for a form, similar to the different views in tables and queries. Forms can be displayed in Layout view, Form view, and Design view. Use Layout view to alter the form design while still viewing the data. Use Design view to add or delete fields in a form, modify field properties, change the column widths, and enhance a form by adding a color scheme or styling.

   Most users will only see Form view; if a form needs modification, the user should notify the database designer. Use Design view to perform advanced changes to a form's design. It provides you the most advanced method of editing an Access form. You can perform many of the same tasks in Design view as you can in Layout view—add and delete fields, change the field order, adjust field widths, modify labels, and customize form elements.

6. **Identify control types in forms.** If you examine the elements on a form, you will notice that each field has a Label control box on the left and a Text Box control on the right. The text box displays the data found in the form's record source and the label is a literal word or phrase to describe the data. Although text box might imply text only, numeric data, currency, and dates can also be displayed with a text box.

   These two types of objects—Label and Text Box—are known as controls. They are among the many types of controls found in the Controls group on the Design tab when you are in Design view. Controls can be categorized as bound, unbound, or calculated. Bound controls are text boxes that are connected to a table or a query. Unbound controls are labels and other decorative design elements. These controls usually describe and decorate the data rather than display the data. Calculated controls contain an expression that generates a calculated result when displayed in Form view.

7. **Create reports using report tools**. Access provides five different report tools for creating reports. The report tools are found in the Reports group located on the Create tab, as shown in Figure 4.25. Click one of these tools and Access will create an automatic report using the table or query that is currently selected. The most common of the tools, the Report tool, is used to instantly create a tabular layout report based on the table or query currently selected. The Report Wizard will ask a series of questions and help you create the most appropriate report based on your answers. Use the Labels tool to create a page of labels using one of the preformatted templates provided by Access. After you create a report, you can perform modifications in Layout view and Design view.

8. **Modify a report**. After a report is generated by one of the report tools, you will usually need to modify it. The most common changes are to add a field, remove a field, change the order of fields, change the width of a field, and modify the title. These changes, as well as adding a grouping level, adding a sort order, and adding a theme, can be made in a report's Layout view or Design view. Advanced changes, such as adding a calculated field or adding VBA code, can be made in a report's Design view.

9. **Sort records in a report.** When a report is created using the Report tool, the sort order of the records in the report is initially dependent on the sort order of the record source. A report can be sorted while in Layout view or Design view by clicking Group & Sort in the Grouping & Totals group on the Design tab. The Group, Sort, and Total pane will appear at the bottom of the report. This section enables you to set the sort order for the report and override the sorting in the report's record source.

10. **Identify report sections.** Access reports are divided into five main sections, as shown in Figure 4.45. Each section can be collapsed or expanded as needed, but only in Design view. You can also remove any of the sections, except the *Detail* section, by right-clicking any section bar, and then clicking the *Header/Footer* section you wish to remove. The *Report Header* section prints once at the beginning of each report. The *Page Header* section appears once at the top of each page. The *Detail* section prints one line for each record in the report's record

source. The *Page Footer* section appears once at the bottom of each page. The *Report Footer* section prints once at the bottom of the report.

11. **Revise reports using report views.** Access provides different views for a report similar to the different views in tables, queries, and forms. Reports have Layout view, Print Preview, Design view, and Report view. To switch between views, click the View arrow in the Views group and select the Layout view or Design view. Use Layout view to alter the report design while still viewing the data. Print Preview enables you to see the closest approximation of what the report will look like when it is printed. Design view displays the report's layout without displaying the data. Report view enables you to see what the printed report will look like in a continuous page layout.

12. **Identify control types in reports.** If you examine the fields on a report, such as the one in Figure 4.47, you will notice that each field has a label (heading) at the top with a column of data values under the heading. A text box displays the data found in the record source and a label is a literal word or phrase to describe the data. The Label and Text Box controls are among the many types of controls found in the Controls group when you are in the Layout view or the Design view of a report. As discussed earlier, controls can be categorized as bound, unbound, or calculated. Bound controls are text boxes that are connected to a table or a query. Unbound controls are labels and other decorative design elements. Calculated controls contain an expression that generates a calculated result when displayed in Print Preview.

KEY TERMS

Bound control *p.712*
Calculated control *p.713*
Datasheet form *p.698*
Design view *p.712*
Detail section *p.709*
Form *p.694*
Form Footer section *p.709*
Form Header section *p.709*
Form tool *p.694*
Form view *p.710*
Group Footer section *p.739*
Group Header section *p.739*
Label control *p.712*

Label Wizard *p.727*
Layout control *p.700*
Layout view *p.696*
Mailing label *p.727*
Multiple Items form *p.697*
Page Footer section *p.738*
Page Header section *p.737*
Print Preview *p.741*
Record source *p.695*
Report *p.721*
Report Footer section *p.738*
Report Header section *p.737*
Report tool *p.721*

Report view *p.741*
Report Wizard *p.723*
Split form *p.697*
Splitter bar *p.697*
Stacked layout form *p.696*
Stacked layout report *p.723*
Tabular layout form *p.696*
Tabular layout report *p.722*
Text box control *p.712*
Unbound control *p.713*
Visual Basic for Applications
  (VBA) *p.698*

1. Which form tool does not place controls onto a form automatically?

   (a) Form Wizard

   (b) Form tool

   (c) Form Design tool

   (d) Datasheet tool

2. The Design view for a form enables you to do all of the following except:

   (a) Modify the form.

   (b) Add a new group.

   (c) View the data as it will be presented in the form.

   (d) Add a background color.

3. Which of the following guides you as you create a new report?

   (a) Report tool

   (b) Report Wizard

   (c) Blank Report tool

   (d) Report Design tool

4. Use the _____ to see exactly what the printed report will look like before printing.

   (a) Report tool

   (b) Report Wizard

   (c) Report view

   (d) Print Preview

5. The easiest way to modify control widths in a form is in:

   (a) Layout view.

   (b) Form view.

   (c) Design view.

   (d) Report view.

6. What happens if you click a text box control in Layout view, and then press Delete?

   (a) The control is deleted from the report, but the other controls do not adjust to the empty space.

   (b) Nothing; you cannot change fields in Layout view.

   (c) The record is deleted from the report and from the database.

   (d) An error message appears stating that you should not attempt to delete records in a report.

7. The mouse pointer shape changes to a _____ when you widen or narrow a column in Layout view.

   (a) single arrow

   (b) hand

   (c) two-headed arrow

   (d) four-headed arrow

8. Which of these is not a section in an Access form?

   (a) *Detail* section

   (b) *Group* section

   (c) *Form Header* section

   (d) *Form Footer* section

9. Which statement is true about controls?

   (a) Unbound controls are not used in reports.

   (b) Unbound controls are not used in the *Detail* section.

   (c) A calculated field is created with a text box control.

   (d) A form's title is usually created with the title control.

10. To organize your data in categories, you would use:

    (a) Sorting.

    (b) Grouping.

    (c) Queries.

    (d) Calculated fields.

1 National Conference

You are working on a database that will track speakers for a national conference. The data entry person entered information in the Speakers table incorrectly. He entered the first half of a new record correctly, but then jumped to a different record and overwrote the existing information with incorrect data. When you discovered the error, it took you a long time to find the correct information and correct both records. You decide that a form would help your co-workers enter data more accurately and help eliminate these types of errors. You create a form that will help the office staff add new speakers and sessions to the database as plans are finalized. After creating the form, you will customize it to be more user-friendly. If you have problems, reread the detailed directions presented in the chapter. This exercise follows the same set of skills as used in Hands-On Exercises 1 and 2 in the chapter. Refer to Figure 4.52 as you complete this exercise.

FIGURE 4.52 Sessions and Speakers Form in Form View ➤

a. Open *a04p1natconf*. Click the **File tab**, click **Save Database As**, and then type **a04p1natconf_LastnameFirstname**. Click **Save**.

b. Open the Speakers table, and then replace *Your_Name* with your name in the First Name and Last Name fields. Close the Speakers table.

c. Open the Sessions and Speakers query in Datasheet view, and then review the data.

d. Close the query; make sure it remains selected.

e. Click the **Create tab**, and then click **Form** in the Forms group to create a new form that opens in Layout view.

f. Click the **SpeakerID box**. Drag the right border of the first field to the left to shrink the column by 50%.

g. Right-click the **SessionID box**, and then select **Select Entire Row** from the list. Drag the **SessionID control** up to the first position.

h. Right-click the **SessionTitle box**, and then select **Select Entire Row** from the list. Drag the **SessionTitle** up to the second position.

i. Remove the stacked layout of the form as follows:
   • Switch to Design view.
   • Click the **SessionID label**.
   • Click **Select Layout** in the Rows & Columns group on the Arrange tab.
   • Click **Remove Layout** in the Table group.

j. Modify and reposition the controls as follows:
- Switch to Layout view.
- Click the **SessionID box**.
- Drag the right border of the SessionID text box to the left to shrink the control to about 1/2" wide.
- Click the **SessionTitle box**.
- Drag the left border of the Understanding Diversity text box to the right to reduce the size of the control by 1/2".
- Drag the **SessionTitle box** up and position it even with the SessionID control, as shown in Figure 4.52.
- Rename the *SessionID* label as **Session:**
- Delete the SessionTitle label.

k. Switch to Form view.

l. Click the **SessionID box**. Click **Ascending** in the Sort & Filter group. Click **Next Record** in the Navigation bar several times to verify the records are now ordered by SessionID.

m. Switch to Design view.

n. Add a message to the bottom of the form as follows:
- Place the mouse on the bottom edge of the Form Footer bar so the mouse pointer changes to the double-arrow resizing shape. Drag the **Form Footer section** down to **2"**.
- Click **Label** in the Controls group.
- Click in the **Form Footer** on the 1" horizontal line, approximately 1/4" from the left edge.
- Type **To register for a session, contact Steve Jones at sjones@yahoo.com**.
- Compare the position of the new label to Figure 4.52.

o. Click **View** in the Views group to switch to Form view. Click **Next Record** in the Navigation bar to verify the new message appears on every record.

p. Save the form as **Sessions and Speakers**. Close the form and any other open objects.

q. Click the **File tab**, and then click **Compact & Repair Database**.

r. Close the database. Exit Access.

s. Submit based on your instructor's directions.

2 Comfort Insurance

The Human Resources department of the Comfort Insurance Agency has initiated its annual employee performance reviews. The reviews affect employee salary increases and bonuses. The employee data, along with forms and reports, are stored in an Access database. You need to prepare a report showing employee raises and bonuses by city. This exercise follows the same set of skills as used in Hands-On Exercises 1, 3, and 4 in the chapter. Refer to Figure 4.53 as you complete this exercise.

FIGURE 4.53 Employee Compensation Report with Totals ➤

a. Open *a04p2insurance*. Click the **File tab**, click **Save Database As**, and then type **a04p2insurance_LastnameFirstname**. Click **Save**.

b. Select the **Locations table**. Click the **Create tab**, and then click **Form** in the Forms group to create a new form that opens in Layout view.

c. Click the **LocationID text box** containing *L01*. Move the mouse to the right edge of the orange border until the mouse pointer changes to a double-headed arrow. Drag the right edge to the left to reduce the size of the text box to approximately 50% of its original size.

d. Click the subform at the bottom of the form, and then click the **Layout Selector** (the small square with a four-headed arrow inside). Press **Delete** to delete the subform.

e. Click **Themes** in the Themes group on the Design tab. Right-click a **Solstice theme** (second column, second row from bottom), and then choose **Apply Theme to This Object Only**.

f. Save the form as **Locations**. Close the form.

g. Select the **Locations table**. Click the **Create tab**, and then click **Report** in the Reports group to create a new tabular layout report in Layout view.

h. Click the **Locations label**, and then drag the right border of the label to the left to reduce the size of the control to **50%**.

i. Repeat the sizing process with the Zipcode label and the OfficePhone label. Adjust the other columns if necessary until there are no controls on the right side of the vertical dashed line.

j. Display the report in Print Preview. Verify that the report is only one page wide. Close and save the report using the name **Locations**.

k. Select the **Employee Query**. Click the **Create tab**, and then click **Report Wizard** in the Reports group to launch the Report Wizard. Respond to the questions as follows:
   - Click (>>) to add all the fields to the Selected Fields box. Click **Next**.
   - Accept grouping by Location. Click **Next**.
   - Select **LastName** for the first sort order and **FirstName** for the second. Click **Summary Options**.
   - Click **Sum** for Salary, **Avg** for 2012Increase, and **Avg** for YearsWorked. Click **OK**. Click **Next**.
   - Accept the Stepped layout. Change Orientation to **Landscape**. Click **Next**.
   - Type **Employee Compensation** for the title of the report. Click **Finish**.
   - The Report is displayed in Print Preview mode. Some of the columns are too narrow. Next, you will adjust the columns and summary controls.

l. Click **Close Print Preview**. Switch to Layout view.

m. Adjust the column widths so that all the data values are showing. Some of the columns will need to be reduced and some will need to be widened. Change the YearsWorked label to **Years**. Use Figure 4.53 as a guide.

n. Adjust the Summary controls at the bottom of the first Location (L01) so all the values are visible. Adjust the Summary controls in the Report Footer so all the values are visible. Align all the Summary controls with their associated detail columns.

o. Open the Property Sheet. Click the **Avg Of YearsWorked control**, and then select **Fixed** for the Format property and **0** for the Decimal Places property.

p. Click **Themes** in the Themes group. Right-click the **Module theme** (first column, fourth row from bottom), and then choose **Apply Theme to This Object Only**.

q. Display the report in Print Preview. Close the Navigation Pane, and then verify that the report is still one page wide. Compare your report to Figure 4.53. Adjust column widths if necessary.

r. Save and close the Employee Compensation report.

s. Click the **File tab**, and then click **Compact & Repair Database**.

t. Close the database. Exit Access.

u. Submit based on your instructor's directions.

1 Hotel Chain

You are the general manager of a large hotel chain. You track revenue by categories: hotel rooms, conference rooms, and weddings. You need to create a report that shows which locations are earning the most revenue in each category. You also need to create a form that will enable you to enter and maintain member data for those guests who pay an annual fee in exchange for discounts and hotel privileges. Refer to Figure 4.54 as you complete this exercise.

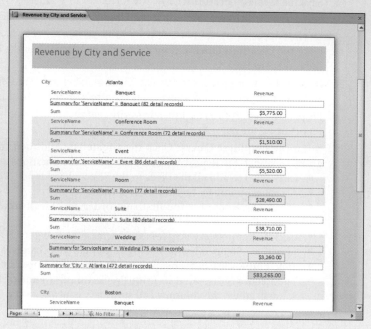

FIGURE 4.54 Revenue by City and Service, Summary Only ➤

a. Open *a04m1rewards*. Click the **File tab**, click **Save Database As**, and then type **a04m1rewards_ LastnameFirstname**. Click **Save**.

b. Select the **Members table**, and then create a Multiple Items form. Save the form as **Maintain Members**.

c. Modify the form in Layout view as follows:
   - Reduce the row height by 50%.
   - Change the MemNumber label to **MemID**, and then reduce the MemNumber column width.
   - Adjust the column widths to eliminate extra white space.
   - Delete the form icon in the Form Header.

d. Switch to Design view, and then modify the form as follows:
   - Open the Property sheet, and then click the **Members title control** to change the Width property to **2.5"**.
   - Add the special effect **Raised** to the **Members title control**.
   - Increase the Form Footer to **1/2"**.
   - Add a new label control to the left side of the Form Footer.
   - Type **Form created by** *your name*.
   - Reduce the width of the form to **12"** (reduce the e-mail column width, if necessary).
   - Add today's date to the right side of the Form Header using the **Date and Time command** in the Header/Footer group.

e. Switch to Form view. Verify that the controls in the *Header* and *Footer* sections remain constant as you advance through the records. Close and save the form.

f. Select the **Revenue query**, and then create a report using the Report Wizard. Answer the wizard prompts as follows:
   - Include all fields.
   - Add grouping by City and by ServiceName.
   - Add a Sum to the Revenue field.
   - Check the **Summary Only option**.

- Choose **Outline Layout**.
- Name the report **Revenue by City and Service**.

g. Scroll through all the pages to check the layout of the report while in Print Preview mode.

h. Switch to Design view, and then delete the NoInParty and PerPersonCharge controls in the *Detail* and *ServiceName Header* sections. Drag the remaining controls in the *ServiceName Header* section to the top of the section. Reduce the height of the *ServiceName Header* section as shown in Figure 4.54.

i. Open the Property Sheet, and then use the Width property to change the width of the Revenue control in the *Detail* section to **1.0"**, the width of the Sum of Revenue control in the ServiceName Footer to **1.0"**, the width of the Sum of Revenue1control in the City Footer to **1.0"**, and the width of the Revenue Grand Total Sum control in the Report Footer to **1.0"**.

j. Click each of the revenue controls while holding down **Shift**, and then set the Format property of all the selected controls to **Currency**.

k. Change the font size, font color, and background color of the Sum of Revenue1 control in the City Footer so the control stands out from the other controls.

l. Apply a different style to the Grand Total Sum control in the Report Footer.

m. Close and save the report.

n. Compact and repair the database.

o. Close the database. Exit Access.

p. Submit based on your instructor's directions.

---

2 Philadelphia National Bank

You are the manager of the loan department at Philadelphia National Bank (PNB). PNB issues mortgages, car loans, and personal loans to its customers. The bank's database contains the records of all of the customer loans. You need to create a form to manage the customer list. You also need to create a report that summarizes the loan payments by month. Refer to Figure 4.55 as you complete this exercise.

FIGURE 4.55 Payments Received Report ➤

a. Open *a04m2bank*. Click the **File tab**, click **Save Database As**, and then type **a04m2bank_LastnameFirstname**. Click **Save**.

b. Create a form based on the Customers table. Access automatically adds the Loans subform to the bottom of the Customers form.

c. Close the form, but do not save it.

DISCOVER ⓗ

d. Open the Relationships window, and then find the relationship between Customers and Loans (this relationship caused the subform to appear in step b). Double-click the join line, and then make a note of which check boxes are checked in the Edit Relationships dialog box. Close the dialog box. Right-click the join line, select **Delete**, and then click **Yes** to confirm deletion. Save the relationship changes. Create the Customers form again and notice the subform is not there. Save the form as **Customers**, and then close it. Restore the relationships.

e. Open the Customers form in Layout view. Reduce the size of the text box controls by 50%, and then close and save the form.

f. Select the **Payments Received query**, and then create a report using the Report Wizard. Include all fields, view data by Payments, add grouping by PaymentDate, skip the sorting step, accept the default layout, and name the report **Payments Received**.

g. Switch to Design view, and then add a label to the right side of the Report Header that says **Created by** *your name*. Switch to Layout view.

h. Click the **AmountReceived field**, and then click **Totals** in the Grouping & Totals group. Select **Sum** from the list of options.

i. Add a different style to the AccessTotalsAmountReceived control so it stands out from the other controls. Add a light gray box around the AccessTotalsAmountReceived1 control.

j. Close the Navigation Pane, preview the report, and then adjust column widths as needed. Close and save the report.

k. Compact and repair the database.

l. Close the database. Exit Access.

m. Submit based on your instructor's directions.

Your boss asked you to prepare a schedule for each speaker for the national conference being hosted next year on your campus. She wants to mail the schedules to the speakers so that they can provide feedback on the schedule prior to its publication. You assure her that you can accomplish this task with Access.

Database File Setup

You need to copy an original database file, rename the copied file, and then open the copied database to complete this capstone exercise. After you open the copied database, you replace an existing employee's name with your name.

a. Open *a04c1natconf*.

b. Click the **File tab**, click **Save Database As**, and then type **a04c1natconf_LastnameFirstname**. Click **Save**.

c. Open the Speakers table.

d. Find and replace *Your_Name* with your name. Close the table.

Create a Form

You need to create a form to add and update Speakers. Use the Form tool to create the form, and then modify the form as explained.

a. Select the **Speakers table** as the record source for the form.

b. Use the **Form tool** to create a new stacked form.

c. Change the title to **Enter/Edit Speakers**.

d. Reduce the width of the text box controls to **50%**.

e. Delete the Sessions subform.

f. Add a new label control in the Form Footer that says **Contact Elaine Carey if you have questions about Speakers**.

g. View the form and data in Form view. Sort the records by LastName. Locate your record.

h. Save the form as **Edit Speakers**. Close the form.

Create a Report

You need to create a report based on the Speaker and Room Schedule query. You decide to use the Report Wizard to accomplish this task.

a. Select the **Speaker and Room Schedule query** as the record source for the report.

b. Activate the **Report Wizard** and use the following options as you go through the Wizard:
   • Select all of the available fields for the report.
   • View the data by Speakers.
   • Verify that LastName and FirstName will provide grouping levels.
   • Use **Date** as the primary sort field.
   • Accept the **Stepped** and **Portrait options**.
   • Name the report **Speaker Schedule**.
   • Switch to Layout view, and apply the **Module theme** to only this report.

c. Preview the report, and then adjust the column widths if necessary.

d. Close and save the report.

Add an Additional Field

You realize the session times were not included in the query. You add the field to the query and then start over with the Report Wizard.

a. Open the Speaker and Room Schedule query in Design view.

b. Add the **StartingTime field** in the Sessions table to the design grid. Run the query.

c. Close and save the query.

d. Start the Report Wizard again and use the following options:
   • Select the **Speaker and Room Schedule query**.
   • Select all of the available fields for the report.
   • View the data by Speakers.
   • Use the **LastName, FirstName fields** as the primary grouping level.
   • Use **Date** as the primary sort field.
   • Use **StartingTime** as the secondary sort field.
   • Select the **Stepped** and **Portrait options**.
   • Name the report **Speaker Schedule Revised**.
   • Switch to Layout view, and then apply the **Trek theme** to only this report.

e. Adjust the column widths in Layout View so that all the data is visible.

f. Increase the width of the StartingTime label control in the *Page Header* section in Design view, so that the entire phrase is visible. Add a space to the column heading labels as needed.

g. Close and save the report. Compact the database.

h. Close the database. Exit Access.

i. Submit based on your instructor's directions.

Inventory Value

GENERAL CASE

The owner of a bookstore asked for your help with her database. Her insurance company asked her to provide an inventory report listing the values of the books she has in stock. Open *a04b1books*. Click the File tab, click Save Database As, and then type **a04b1books_LastnameFirstname**. Click Save. Use the skills you learned in this chapter to create three stacked layout forms for Authors, Publishers, and Books. Delete any attached subforms. Next, create the inventory report that shows the inventory values for the books on hand. The database contains a query that you can use to create the report. Group the records by publisher name; alphabetize authors by last name and first name within groups. Name the report **Bookstore Inventory Value**. In Layout view, create a total value control for each publisher and create a grand total. Resize and reposition the total controls so they are visible and aligned with the correct column. Add Currency formatting where applicable, and then modify column headings as needed. Preview the report and verify that all the columns are correct, and then save and close the report. Compact and repair the database, and then close the database and close Access. Submit based on your instructor's directions.

Create Mailing Labels

RESEARCH CASE

This chapter introduced you to Access reports. Use Access Help to search for mailing labels. Then put your new knowledge to the test. Open *a04b2arbor*. Click the File tab, click Save Database As, and then type **a04b2arbor_LastnameFirstname**. Click Save. It contains a query identifying volunteers who will be invited to this year's gala. Your challenge is to print the names and addresses as mailing labels in the format shown below. You already purchased Avery 5260 labels. Sort the labels by lastname, firstname. Name the report **Volunteer Invitation Labels**. After you create the labels, preview them and verify everything will fit onto the 5260 label template. Save and close the label report. Compact and repair the database, and then close the database and close Access. Submit based on your instructor's directions.

Label format:
Mr. (Dr., Ms., Mrs.,) John Doe, Jr.
Street Address
City, State Postal Code

Real Estate Development Report

DISASTER RECOVERY

A co-worker is having difficulty with an Access report and asked you for your assistance. Open *a04b3property*. Click the File tab, click Save Database As, and then type **a04b3property_LastnameFirstname**. Click Save. The database contains the Sales Report query that was used to create the Sales by Agent report. The report is supposed to show each agent's total sales grouped by Subdivision. There should be totals for the sale price, the sales commissions, and the list price columns for each subdivision and each agent. The Percent of List should be averaged for each subdivision and each agent. Find and correct the errors. If you are unable to correct the errors, try creating the report again using the Report Wizard. Compact and repair the database, close the database, and then close Access. Submit based on your instructor's directions.

1 INTRODUCTION TO POWERPOINT

Presentations Made Easy

Watch the
Set-up
Video
for this
Case Study!

CASE STUDY | Be a Trainer

You teach employee training courses for the Training and Development department of your State Department of Personnel. You begin each course by delivering a presentation using an electronic slide show. The slide show presents your objectives for the course, organizes your content, and aids your audience's retention. You prepare the presentation using Microsoft Office PowerPoint 2010.

Because of the exceptional quality of your presentations, the director of the State Department of Personnel has asked you to prepare a new course on presentation skills. In the Hands-On Exercises for this chapter, you will work with two presentations for this course. One presentation will focus on the benefits of using PowerPoint, and the other will focus on the preparation for a slide show, including planning, organizing, and delivering.

OBJECTIVES   AFTER YOU READ THIS CHAPTER, YOU WILL BE ABLE TO:

1. Use PowerPoint views *p.761*

2. Save as a slide show *p.765*

3. Plan a presentation *p.769*

4. Assess presentation content *p.772*

5. Use slide layouts *p.772*

6. Apply themes *p.773*

7. Review the presentation *p.774*

8. Insert media objects *p.780*

9. Add a table *p.781*

10. Use animations and transitions *p.781*

11. Insert a header or footer *p.784*

12. Run and navigate a slide show *p.791*

13. Print in PowerPoint *p.793*

Introduction to PowerPoint

A **slide** is the most basic element of PowerPoint.

A **slide show** is a collection of slides that can be used in a presentation.

A **PowerPoint presentation** is an electronic slide show that can be edited or displayed.

You can use Microsoft PowerPoint 2010 to create an electronic slide show or other materials for use in a professional presentation. A ***slide*** is the most basic element of PowerPoint (similar to a page being the most basic element of Microsoft Word). Multiple slides may be arranged to create an electronic ***slide show*** that can be used to deliver your message in a variety of ways: you can project the electronic slideshow on a screen as part of a presentation, run it automatically at a kiosk or from a DVD, display it on the World Wide Web, or create printed handouts. A ***PowerPoint presentation*** is an electronic slide show saved with a .pptx extension after the file name.

Figure 1.1 shows a PowerPoint presentation with slides containing content, such as text, clip art images, and SmartArt. The presentation has a consistent design and color scheme. It is easy to create presentations with consistent and attractive designs using PowerPoint templates and slide layouts, which allow you to focus on the text, images, and other objects you will add to your slides.

> It is easy to create presentations with consistent and attractive designs using PowerPoint templates and slide layouts.

FIGURE 1.1 Various PowerPoint Slide Layouts ➤

In this section, you will start your exploration of PowerPoint by viewing a previously completed presentation so that you can appreciate the benefits of using PowerPoint. You will modify the presentation and add identifying information, examine PowerPoint views to discover the advantages of each view, and save the presentation. Finally, you will use Help to obtain assistance within PowerPoint.

TIP Polish Your Delivery

The speaker is the most important part of any presentation. Poor delivery will ruin even the best presentation. Speak slowly and clearly, maintain eye contact with your audience, and use the information on the slides to guide you. Do not just read the information on the screen, but expand on each bullet, paragraph, or image to give your audience the intended message.

Using PowerPoint Views

Normal view is the three-pane default PowerPoint view.

A **thumbnail** is a miniature of a slide that appears in the Slides tab.

Figure 1.2 shows the default PowerPoint view, *Normal view*, with three panes that provide maximum flexibility in working with the presentation. The pane on the left side of the screen has two tabs: the Slides tab, which shows *thumbnails* (slide miniatures), and the Outline tab, which displays an outline of the presentation. The Slide pane on the right displays the current slide, and is where you make edits to slide content. The Notes pane, located at the bottom of the screen, is where you enter notes pertaining to the slide or the presentation. You can change the size of these panes by dragging the splitter bar that separates one pane from another.

FIGURE 1.2 Normal View (Default PowerPoint View) ➤

The PowerPoint **status bar** contains the slide number, the design theme name, and View buttons.

Figure 1.3 shows PowerPoint's *status bar*, which contains the slide number, the theme name, and options that control the view of your presentation: View buttons, the Zoom level button, a Zoom slider, and the Fit slide to current window button. The status bar is located at the bottom of your screen and can be customized. To customize the status bar, right-click it, and then click the options you want displayed from the Customize Status Bar list.

> **TIP** Add-Ins Tab
>
> You may see an Add-Ins tab on the Ribbon. This tab indicates that additional functionality, such as an updated Office feature or an Office-compatible program, has been added to your system. Add-Ins are designed to increase your productivity.

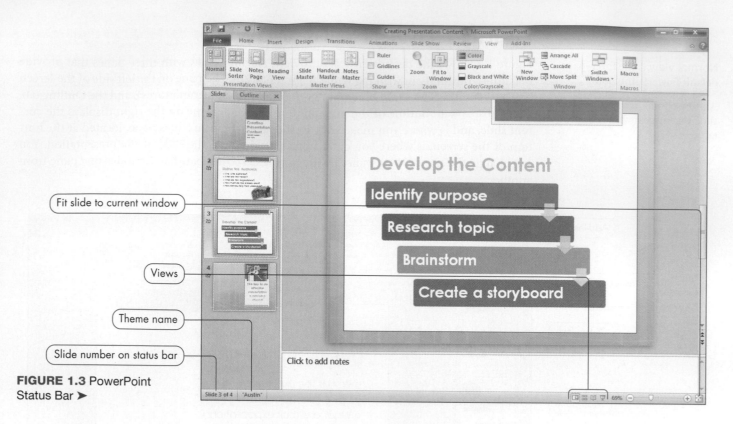

Fit slide to current window

Views

Theme name

Slide number on status bar

FIGURE 1.3 PowerPoint Status Bar ➤

While in Normal view, you can completely close the left pane—which includes the Slides and Outline tabs but is often just referred to as the Slides tab—to expand the Slide pane so that you can see more detail while editing slide content. When you close the Slides tab, the Notes pane at the bottom of the PowerPoint window also closes. Figure 1.4 shows an individual slide in Normal view with the Slides tab and the Notes pane closed. You can restore the default view by clicking the View tab, and then clicking Normal in the Presentation Views group.

Click to restore Normal (three-pane) view

FIGURE 1.4 Individual Slide View ➤

PowerPoint offers views in addition to Normal view, including Slide Sorter, Notes Page, Reading View, and Slide Show views. Access Slide Sorter, Notes Page, and Reading View views from the Presentation Views group on the View tab. Access options for the Slide Show view from the Start Slide Show group on the Slide Show tab. For quick access, all of these views, except Notes Page, are available on the status bar.

Notes Page view is used for entering and editing large amounts of text to which the speaker can refer when presenting.

Notes Page view is used when you need to enter and edit large amounts of text to which the speaker can refer when presenting. If you have a large amount of technical detail in the speaker notes, you can use Notes Page view to print audience handouts that include the slide and associated notes. Notes do not appear when the presentation is shown, but are intended to help the speaker remember the key points or additional information about each slide. Figure 1.5 shows an example of the Notes Page view.

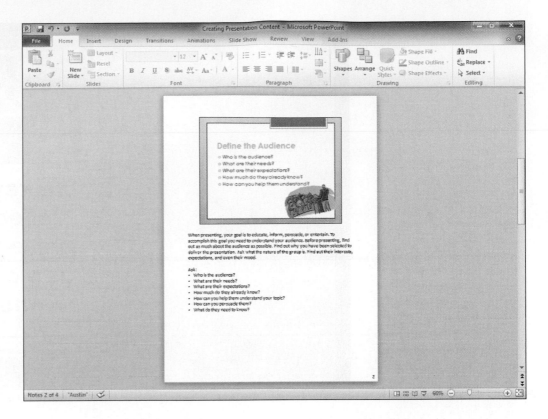

FIGURE 1.5 Notes
Page View ➤

Slide Sorter view displays
thumbnails of slides.

Slide Sorter view displays thumbnails of your presentation slides, which allow you to view multiple slides simultaneously (see Figure 1.6). This view is helpful when you wish to change the order of the slides or to delete one or more slides. You can set transition effects for multiple slides in Slide Sorter view. If you are in Slide Sorter view and double-click a slide thumbnail, PowerPoint returns the selected slide to Normal view.

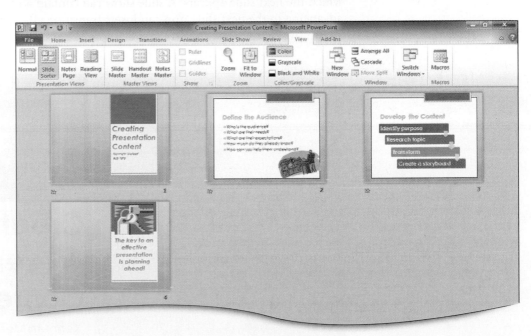

FIGURE 1.6 Slide
Sorter View ➤

Reading View displays a
full-screen view of a presentation
that includes bars and buttons
for additional functionality.

Reading View, a new view in PowerPoint 2010, is used to view the slide show full screen, one slide at a time. A Title bar including the Minimize, Maximize/Restore (which changes its name and appearance depending on whether the window is maximized or at a smaller size), and Close buttons is visible, as well as a modified status bar (see Figure 1.7). In addition to View buttons, the status bar includes navigation buttons for moving to the next or previous slide, as well as a menu for accomplishing common tasks such as printing.

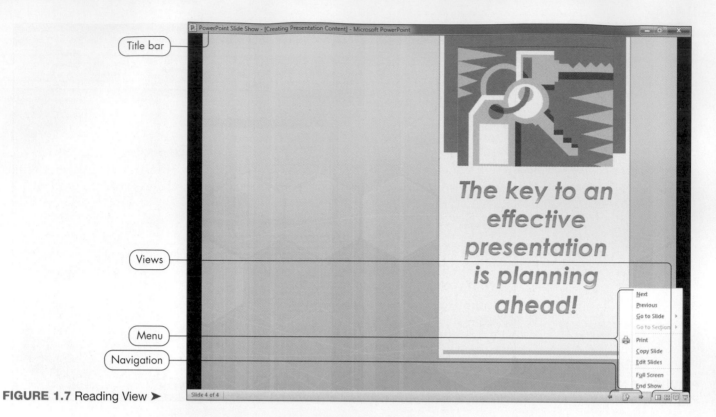

Title bar

Views

Menu

Navigation

Next
Previous
Go to Slide
Go to Section
Print
Copy Slide
Edit Slides
Full Screen
End Show

Slide 4 of 4

FIGURE 1.7 Reading View ➤

Slide Show view displays a full-screen view of a presentation to an audience.

Slide Show view is used to deliver the completed presentation full screen to an audience, one slide at a time, as an electronic presentation (see Figure 1.8). The slide show can be presented manually, where the speaker clicks the mouse to move from one slide to the next, or automatically, where each slide stays on the screen for a predetermined amount of time, after which the next slide appears. A slide show can contain a combination of both methods for advancing to the next slide. You can insert transition effects to impact the look of how one slide moves to the next. To end the slide show, you press Esc.

FIGURE 1.8 Slide Show View ➤

TIP Start the Slide Show

To start a slide show, click the Slide Show tab, and then click either From Beginning or From Current Slide in the Start Slide Show group.

Presenter view delivers a presentation on two monitors simultaneously.

Presenter view is a specialty view that delivers a presentation on two monitors simultaneously. Typically, one monitor is a projector that delivers the full screen presentation to the audience; the other monitor is a laptop or computer so that the presenter can see the slide, speaker notes, and slide thumbnails. This enables the presenter to jump between slides as needed, navigate using arrows that navigate to the previous or next slide, or write on the slide with a marker. A timer displays the time elapsed since the presentation began so that you can keep track of the presentation length. Figure 1.9 shows the audience view on the left side of the figure and the Presenter view on the right side. To use Presenter view, you must use a computer that has multiple monitor support activated.

- Speaker notes
- Presenter view of slide
- Audience view of slide
- Pointer options
- Presenter view screen
- Slide thumbnails
- Timer

FIGURE 1.9 Presenter view ➤

Saving as a Slide Show

A **PowerPoint show** (.ppsx) is an electronic slide show format used for distribution.

PowerPoint presentations are saved with a .pptx file extension and opened in Normal view so that you can make changes to the presentation. You can save your presentation as a *PowerPoint show* with a .ppsx extension by using the Save As command. This file type will open the presentation in Slide Show view and is best for distributing an unchangeable version of a completed slide show to others for viewing. While the .ppsx file cannot be changed while viewing, you can open the file in PowerPoint and edit it. This file type is primarily used for distribution of a finished product.

1 Introduction to PowerPoint

You have been asked to create a presentation on the benefits of PowerPoint for the Training and Development department. You decide to view an existing presentation to determine if it contains material you can adapt for your presentation. You view the presentation, add a speaker note, and then save the presentation as a PowerPoint show.

Skills covered: View the Presentation • Type a Speaker Note • Save as a PowerPoint Show

STEP 1 ▶ VIEW THE PRESENTATION

In this step, you view the slide show created by your colleague. As you read the contents, you use various methods of advancing to the next slide and then return to Normal view. As you experiment with the various methods of advancing to the next slide, find the one that is most comfortable to you and then use that method as you view slide shows in the future. An audio clip of audience applause will play when you view Slide 4, The Essence of PowerPoint. You will want to wear a headset if you are in a classroom lab so that you do not disturb classmates.

FYI

a. Start PowerPoint. Open *p01h1intro* and save it as **p01h1intro_LastnameFirstname**.

> **TROUBLESHOOTING:** If you make any major mistakes in this exercise, close the file, open *p01h1intro* again, and start this exercise over.

When you save files, use your last and first names. For example, as the PowerPoint author, I would name my presentation p01h1intro_KrebsCynthia.

b. Click the **Slide Show tab**, and then click **From Beginning** in the Start Slide Show group.

The presentation begins with the title slide, the first slide in all slide shows. The title has an animation assigned, so it comes in automatically.

c. Press **Spacebar** to advance to the second slide, and read the slide.

The title on the second slide automatically wipes down, and the arrow wipes to the right.

d. Position the pointer in the bottom-left corner side of the slide, and note the navigation bar that appears. Click the **right arrow** in the navigation bar to advance to the next slide. Read the slide content.

The text on the third slide, and all following slides, has the same animation applied to create consistency in the presentation.

e. Click the **left mouse button** to advance to the fourth slide, which has a sound icon displayed on the slide.

The sound icon on the slide indicates sound has been added. The sound has been set to come in automatically so you do not need to click anything for the sound to play. You can hide sound icons if desired.

> **TROUBLESHOOTING:** If you do not hear the sound, your computer may not have a sound card.

f. Continue to navigate through the slides until you come to the end of the presentation.

g. Press **Esc** to return to Normal view.

TYPE A SPEAKER NOTE

In this step, you add a speaker note to a slide to help you remember to mention some of the many objects that can be added to a slide. You also view the note in Notes view to see how it will print. Refer to Figure 1.10 as you complete Step 2.

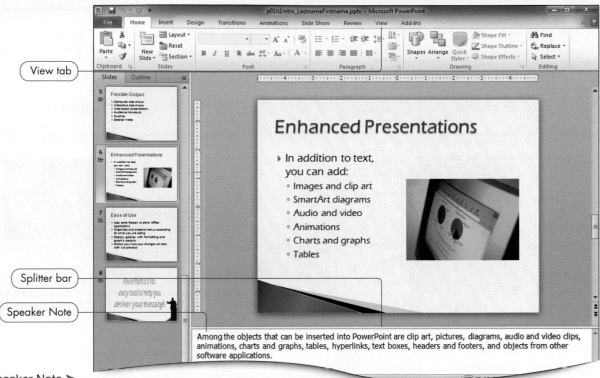

FIGURE 1.10 Speaker Note ➤

a. Scroll down in the **Slides tab**, if necessary, and then click the **Slide 6 thumbnail**.

   Slide 6 is selected, and the slide appears in the Slide pane.

b. Drag the splitter bar between the Slide pane and the Notes pane up to expand the Notes pane.

c. Type the following in the Notes pane: **Among the objects that can be inserted into PowerPoint are clip art, pictures, diagrams, audio and video clips, animations, charts and graphs, tables, hyperlinks, text boxes, headers and footers, and objects from other software applications.**

d. Click the **View tab**, and then click **Notes Page** in the Presentation Views group.

   The slide is shown at a reduced size, and the speaker note is shown below the slide. Drag the vertical scroll bar up to view the speaker note on the first slide.

e. Click **Normal** in the Presentation Views group on the View tab.

f. Save the presentation.

SAVE AS A POWERPOINT SHOW

You want to save the slide show as a PowerPoint show so that it opens in Slide Show view rather than Normal view. Refer to Figure 1.11 as you complete Step 3.

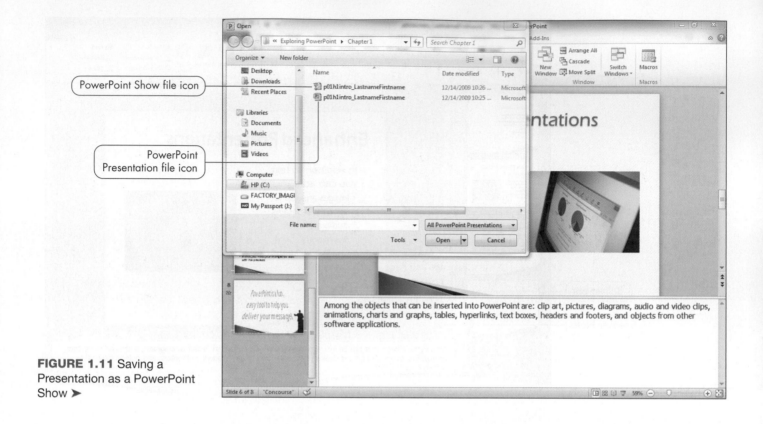

PowerPoint Show file icon

PowerPoint Presentation file icon

FIGURE 1.11 Saving a Presentation as a PowerPoint Show ➤

a. Click the **File tab**, click **Save As**, click the **Save as type arrow**, and then click **PowerPoint Show**.

b. Leave the file name *p01h1intro_LastnameFirstname* for the PowerPoint show.

   Although you are saving this file with the same file name as the presentation, it will not overwrite the file, as it is a different file type.

c. Click **Save**.

d. Click the **File tab**, and then click **Open**.

   The Open dialog box displays all of the presentations in the folder. Note two *p01h1intro_LastnameFirstname* files are listed. The gray icon is used to indicate the PowerPoint Show file that opens in Slide Show view. The orange icon listed is used to indicate the PowerPoint Presentation file. See Figure 1.11 to view these icons.

e. Click **Cancel**.

f. Save and close the *p01h1intro_LastnameFirstname* presentation, and submit based on your instructor's directions. Keep the presentation open if you plan to continue with Hands-On Exercise 2. If not, save and close the presentation, and exit PowerPoint.

Presentation Creation

You are ready to create your own presentation by adding content and applying formatting. You should create the presentation by adding the content first and then applying formatting so that you can concentrate on your message and its structure without getting distracted by the formatting and design of the presentation.

Planning a Presentation

Creating an effective presentation requires advance planning. First, determine the goal of your presentation. An informative presentation could notify the audience about a change in policy or procedure. An educational presentation could teach an audience about a subject or a skill. Sales presentations are often persuasive calls to action to encourage the purchase of a product, but they can also be used to sell an idea or process. A goodwill presentation could be used to recognize an employee or acknowledge an organization. You could even create a certificate of appreciation using PowerPoint.

> Creating an effective presentation requires advance planning.

Next, research your audience—determine their level of knowledge about your topic. Find out what needs the audience has, what their expectations are, and what their level of interest is.

After determining your purpose and researching your audience, brainstorm how to deliver your message. Sketch out your thoughts on paper to help you organize them. After organizing your thoughts, add them as content to the slide show, and then format the presentation.

In this section, you will create a visual plan called a storyboard. You also learn to polish your presentation by using layouts, applying design themes, and reviewing your presentation for errors.

Prepare a Storyboard

A *storyboard* is a visual plan that displays the content of each slide in the slide show.

A *storyboard* is a visual plan for your presentation that helps you plan the direction of your presentation. It can be a very rough draft you sketch out while brainstorming, or it can be an elaborate plan that includes the text and objects drawn as they would appear on a slide.

A simple PowerPoint storyboard is divided into sections representing individual slides. The first block in the storyboard is used for the title slide. Subsequent blocks are used to introduce the topics, develop the topics, and then summarize the information. Figure 1.12 shows a working copy of a storyboard for planning presentation content. The storyboard is in rough-draft form and shows changes made during the review process. The PowerPoint presentation shown in Figure 1.13 incorporates the changes.

Storyboard

Purpose: [ ] Informative [X] Educational [ ] Persuasive [ ] Goodwill [ ] Other _____

Audience: IAAP membership
Location: Marriott Hotel
Date and Time: 9/20/12 7 p.m.

Content	Layout	Visual Element(s)
Title Slide Planning ~~Before~~ Creating Presentation Content	Title Slide	○ Shapes ○ Chart ○ Table ○ WordArt ○ Picture ○ Movie ○ Clip Art ○ Sound ○ SmartArt ○ _____ *Description:*
Introduction (Key Points, Quote, Image, Other) "If you don't know where you are going, you might end up someplace else." Casey Stengel	Section Header	○ Shapes ○ Chart ○ Table ○ WordArt ○ Picture ○ Movie ⊗ Clip Art ○ Sound ○ SmartArt ○ _____ *Description:* Stengel ~~Content Image~~ pic
Key Point #1 Identify Purpose ~~Selling~~ (E-Commercial) Persuading Informing Advertising Building Good Will Entertaining Educating Motivating	Two Content	○ Shapes ○ Chart ○ Table ○ WordArt ○ Picture ○ Movie ○ Clip Art ○ Sound ○ SmartArt ○ _____ *Description:*
Key Point #2 Define Audience Who is going to be in the audience? What are the audience's expectations? How much does the audience already know?	Title and Content	○ Shapes ○ Chart ○ Table ○ WordArt ⊗ Picture ○ Movie ○ Clip Art ○ Sound ○ SmartArt ○ _____ *Description:* Audience Pic
Key Point #3 Develop the Content Brainstorm and write ideas down Research the topic and take notes Storyboard a rough draft and then refine	Title and Content	○ Shapes ○ Chart ○ Table ○ WordArt ○ Picture ○ Movie ○ Clip Art ○ Sound ○ SmartArt ○ _____ *Description:* Smart Art
Key Point #4 Edit the Content Shorten the text from sentences, phrases + make if concise. Make bullets parallel + use action verbs	Title and Content	○ Shapes ○ Chart ○ Table ○ WordArt ○ Picture ○ Movie ○ Clip Art ○ Sound ○ SmartArt ○ _____ *Description:*
Summary (Restatement of Key Points, Quote, Other) The key to an effective presentation is planning ahead.	Title	○ Shapes ○ Chart ○ Table ○ WordArt ○ Picture ○ Movie ⊗ Clip Art ○ Sound ○ SmartArt ○ _____ *Description:* Key

Callout labels: Title slide · Introduction · Key topics with main points · Summary

FIGURE 1.12 Rough Draft Storyboard ➤

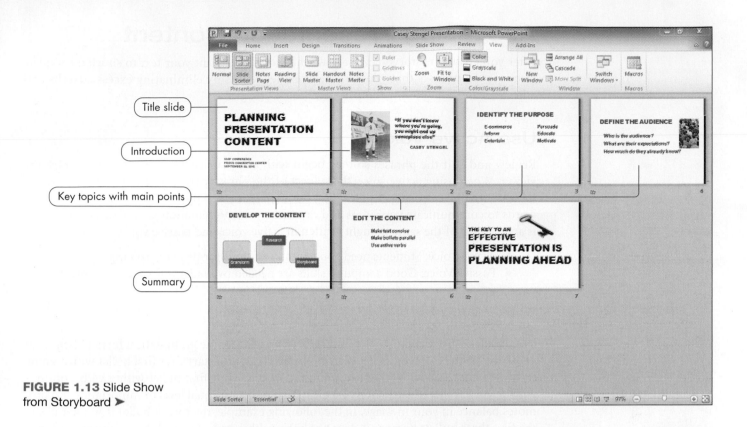

FIGURE 1.13 Slide Show from Storyboard ➤

Create a Title Slide and Introduction

The title slide should have a short title that indicates the purpose of the presentation. Try to capture the title in two to five words. The title slide should also contain information such as the speaker's name and title, the speaker's organization, the organization's logo, and the date of the presentation. This information is typically included as subtitles.

After the title slide, you may want to include an introduction slide that will get the audience's attention. The introduction could be a list of topics covered in the presentation, a thought-provoking quotation or question, or an image that relates to the topic. Introduction slides can also be used to distinguish between topics or sections of the presentation.

Create the Main Body of Slides

The content of your presentation follows the title slide and the introduction. Each key thought should be a separate slide with the details needed to support that thought. Present the details as bullets or a short paragraph that relates to the content. When determining the content, ask yourself what you want your audience to learn and remember. Support the content with facts, examples, charts or graphs, illustrations, images, or video clips.

Create the Conclusion

End your presentation with a summary or conclusion that reviews the main points, restates the purpose of the presentation, or invokes a call to action. You may also want to repeat your contact information at the end of the presentation so the audience knows how to follow up with any questions or needs.

Assessing Presentation Content

After you create the storyboard, review what you wrote. Edit your text to shorten complete sentences to phrases that you can use as bullet points by eliminating excess adverbs and adjectives and using only a few prepositions.

Use Active Voice

Review and edit the phrases so they begin with active voice when possible to involve the viewer. When using active voice, the subject of the phrase performs the action expressed in the verb. In phrases using passive voice, the subject is acted upon. Passive voice needs more words to communicate your ideas and can make your presentation seem flat. The following is an example of the same thought written in active voice and passive voice.

- Active Voice: Students need good computer skills for problem solving.
- Passive Voice: Good computer skills are needed by students for problem solving.

Use Parallel Construction

Use parallel construction so that your bullets are in the same grammatical form to help your audience see the connection between your phrases. If you start your first bullet with a noun, start each successive bullet with a noun; if you start your first bullet with a verb, continue with verbs. Parallel construction also gives each bullet an equal level of importance and promotes balance in your message. In the following example, the fourth bullet is not parallel to the first three bullets because it does not begin with a verb. The fifth bullet shows the bullet in parallel construction.

- Find a good place to study.
- Organize your study time.
- Study for tests with a partner.
- Terminology is important so learn how to use it properly. (Incorrect)
- Learn and use terminology properly. (Correct)

Follow the 7 × 7 Guideline

Keep the information on your slide concise. You will expand on the slide content when delivering your presentation with the use of notes. Follow the 7 × 7 guideline, which suggests that you use no more than seven words per line and seven lines per slide. Although you may be forced to exceed this guideline on occasion, follow it as often as possible.

After you complete the planning and review process, you are ready to prepare the PowerPoint slide show to use with your presentation.

Using Slide Layouts

A slide **layout** determines the position of objects containing content on the slide.

A **placeholder** is a container that holds content.

PowerPoint provides a set of predefined slide *layouts* that determine the position of the objects or content on a slide. Slide layouts contain any number and combination of placeholders. When you click the New Slide arrow on the Home tab, a gallery is displayed from which you can choose a layout. All of the layouts except the Blank layout include placeholders. *Placeholders* are objects that hold content, such as titles, subtitles, or images. Placeholders determine the position of the objects on the slide.

After you select a layout, click a placeholder to add your content. When you click a placeholder you can edit it. The border of the placeholder becomes a dashed line and you are able to enter content. If you click the dashed line placeholder border, the placeholder and its content are selected. The border changes to a solid line. Once selected, you can drag the placeholder to a new position or delete the placeholder. Any change you make impacts all content in the placeholder. Unused placeholders in a layout do not show when you display a slide show.

A new, blank presentation includes a title slide layout with a placeholder for the presentation title and subtitle. Add new slides using the layout from the layout gallery. By default, text on slides following the title slide appears as bullets. You can change the layout of an existing slide by dragging placeholders to a new location or by adding new placeholders and objects.

> **TIP** New Slide Button
>
> Click the New Slide arrow when you want to choose a layout from the gallery. Click New Slide, which appears above the New Slide arrow, to quickly insert a new slide. If you click New Slide when the Title slide is selected, the new slide uses the Title and Content layout. If the current slide uses any layout other than Title slide, the new slide uses the same layout.

Applying Themes

PowerPoint enables you to concentrate on the content of a presentation without concern for its appearance. You focus on what you are going to say, and then use PowerPoint features to format the presentation attractively. The easiest method to format a slide show is to select a design by choosing a theme. A ***theme*** is a collection of formatting choices that includes colors, fonts, and special effects such as shadowing or glows. A theme is automatically applied to all slides, giving a consistent look to the presentation.

A **theme** is a collection of design choices that includes colors, fonts, and special theme effects.

To choose a theme, click the Design tab, and then click the More button in the Themes group to display the Themes gallery. Position the pointer over each theme to display a Live Preview of the theme on the current slide, and then click a theme to apply it. The themes are listed alphabetically in the gallery. After applying a theme, be sure to review each slide to make sure the content still fits on the slide. As you gain experience with PowerPoint, you can use other formatting tools to create custom presentation designs. Figure 1.14 shows an image of four title slides, each with a different theme applied. Note the color, font, and text alignment in each theme.

FIGURE 1.14 Example of PowerPoint Themes ➤

Reviewing the Presentation

After you create the presentation, check for spelling errors and incorrect word usage. Nothing is more embarrassing and can make you appear unprofessional than a misspelled word enlarged on a big screen.

Use a four-step method for checking spelling in PowerPoint. First, read the slide content after you enter it. Second, use the Spelling feature located in the Review tab to check the entire presentation. Third, ask a friend or colleague to review the presentation. Finally, display the presentation in Slide Show view and read each word on each slide out loud. Although proofreading four times may seem excessive, it will help ensure your presentation is professional.

> **TIP** Proofing Options
>
> The Spelling feature, by default, does not catch contextual errors like *to*, *too*, and *two*, but you can set the Proofing options to help you find and fix this type of error. To modify the proofing options, click File, and then click Options. Click Proofing in the PowerPoint Options window, and then click Use contextual spelling. With this option selected, the spelling checker will flag contextual mistakes with a red wavy underline. To correct the error, right-click the flagged word, and then select the proper word choice.

Use the Thesaurus

As you create and edit your presentation, you may notice that you are using one word too often, especially at the beginning of bullets. Use the Thesaurus so your bullet lists do not constantly begin with the same word and so you make varied word choices.

HANDS-ON EXERCISES

2 Presentation Creation

To help state employees learn the process for presentation creation, you decide to give them guidelines for determining content, structuring a slide show, and assessing content. You create a slide show to deliver these guidelines.

Skills covered: Create a New Presentation • Add New Slides • Modify Text and Layout • Reorder Slides • Apply a Theme

---

STEP 1 ▶ CREATE A NEW PRESENTATION

You begin creating the presentation for employees using the default slide layout. You start by entering the text of your presentation, knowing that you can format the presentation later.

a. Press **Ctrl+N** to create a new blank presentation.

PowerPoint opens a new blank presentation using the default template with the Office theme. The slides have a white background, and the font for the placeholder text is Calibri.

> **TROUBLESHOOTING:** Open PowerPoint if you closed it after completing Hands-On Exercise 1.

b. Save the presentation with the name **p01h2content_LastnameFirstname**.

c. Click inside the **title placeholder** containing the *Click to add title* prompt, and then type **Creating Presentation Content**.

d. Click inside the **subtitle placeholder**, and then type your name.

e. Click in the **Notes pane**, and then type today's date and the name of the course for which you are creating this slide show.

f. Save the presentation.

STEP 2 ▶ ADD NEW SLIDES

You continue creating your presentation by adding a second slide with the Title and Content layout. After adding a title to the slide, you create a bulleted list to develop your topic. After adding the presentation content, you proofread the presentation to ensure no errors exist. Refer to Figure 1.15 as you complete Step 2.

FIGURE 1.15 New Slides with Text Content ➤

a. Click **New Slide** in the Slides group on the Home tab.

The new Slide 2 contains two placeholders: one for the title and one for body content. You can insert an object, such as a table or image, by clicking a button in the center of the content placeholder. To enter text in a bulleted list, type the text in the content placeholder.

b. Type **Simplify the Content** in the **title placeholder**.

c. Click in the **content placeholder**, type **Use one main concept per slide**, and then press **Enter**.

By default, the list level is the same as the previous level.

d. Type **Use the 7 × 7 guideline** and press **Enter**.

e. Click **Increase List Level** in the Paragraph group.

The list level indents, and the bullet changes from a solid round bullet to a hyphen indicating this is a subset of the main level.

f. Type **Limit slide to seven or fewer lines** and press **Enter**.

g. Type **Limit lines to seven or fewer words**.

By default, the list level is the same as the previous level.

h. Click **New Slide** four times to create four more slides with the Title and Content layout.

i. Type the following text in the appropriate slide. Use Increase List Level and Decrease List Level to change levels.

Slide	Slide Title	Bullet Data
3	Define the Audience	Who is the audience?
		What are their needs?
		What are their expectations?
		How much do they already know?
		How can you help them understand?
4	Develop the Content	Identify purpose
		Research topic
		Brainstorm
		Create the storyboard
		Title slide
		Introduction
		Key points
		Conclusion
5	Edit the Content	Make text concise
		Use consistent verb tense
		Eliminate excess adverbs and adjectives
		Use few prepositions
		Use strong active verbs
		Keep bullets parallel
6		The key to an effective presentation is planning ahead!

j. Click **Spelling** in the Proofing group on the Review tab, and correct any errors. Carefully proofread each slide.

The result of the spelling check depends on how accurately you entered the text of the presentation.

k. Click the **Slide 2 thumbnail** in the Slides tab pane. Use the Thesaurus to change *main* in the first bullet point to **key**, and then click the **Close button** on the Thesaurus.

l. Save the presentation.

STEP 3 ▶ MODIFY TEXT AND LAYOUT

You want to end the slide show with a statement emphasizing the importance of planning and decide to modify the text and layout of the slide to give it more emphasis. You also leave space on the slide so that later you can add an animated clip. Refer to Figure 1.16 as you complete Step 3.

The key to an effective presentation is planning ahead!

FIGURE 1.16 Slide with Modified Text and Layout ➤

a. Click the **Slide 6 thumbnail** in the Slides tab.

b. Click the **Home tab**, and then click **Layout** in the Slides group.

c. Click **Title Slide** from the Layout gallery.

The layout for Slide 6 changes to the Title Slide layout. The Title Slide layout can be used on any slide in a slide show if its format meets your needs.

d. Click the border of the title placeholder, and then press **Delete**.

The dotted line border becomes a solid line, which indicates the placeholder is selected. Pressing Delete removes the placeholder and the content of that placeholder.

e. Click in the subtitle text.

Clicking inside a placeholder shows the dashed line border, which indicates the placeholder is in edit mode.

f. Click the placeholder border to change it to a solid line, which selects the entire object, and then drag the border of the subtitle placeholder containing your text downward until it is near the bottom of your slide.

The layout of Slide 6 has now been modified.

g. Select the text in the subtitle placeholder if necessary, and then apply **Bold** and **Italic**.

h. Save the presentation.

STEP 4 ▶ REORDER SLIDES

You notice that the slides do not follow a logical order. You change the slide positions in Slide Sorter view. Refer to Figure 1.17 as you complete Step 4.

Slide 2 moved to the Slide 5 position

FIGURE 1.17 Reordered Slide Show ➤

a. Click the **View tab**, and then click **Slide Sorter** in the Presentation Views group.

The view changes to thumbnail views of the slides in the slide show with the current slide surrounded by a thick border to indicate it is selected. Your view may differ from Figure 1.17 depending on your zoom level and screen resolution settings. Notice that the slides do not follow a logical order.

b. Select **Slide 2**, and then drag it before the summary (last) slide so that it becomes Slide 5.

As you drag Slide 2, the pointer becomes the move pointer, and a vertical bar appears to indicate the position of the slide when you drop it. After you drop the slide, all slides renumber.

c. Double-click **Slide 6**.

Your presentation returns to Normal view.

d. Save the presentation.

STEP 5 ▶ APPLY A THEME

To create a more consistent and business-like look for your presentation, you decide to apply a theme. After applying the theme, you reposition a placeholder to create a more attractive appearance. Refer to Figure 1.18 as you complete Step 5.

FIGURE 1.18 Slide 6 with Urban Theme and Repositioned Placeholder ➤

The key to an effective presentation is planning ahead!

a. Click the **Design tab**, and then click the **More button** in the Themes group.

   Point to each of the themes that appear in the gallery to display the ScreenTip with the name of each theme and a Live Preview of the theme on the current slide.

b. Click **Urban** to apply the theme to the presentation.

   The Urban theme has a clean, simple background with a business-like color scheme, making it a good choice for this presentation.

c. Click to select the placeholder at the bottom of the screen, and then drag a sizing handle to resize the placeholder so that it contains three lines.

d. Drag the placeholder to the left side of the slide and position it slightly under the double green lines.

e. Keep the presentation open if you plan to continue with Hands-On Exercise 3. If not, save and close the presentation, and exit PowerPoint.

Presentation Development

You can strengthen your slide show by adding objects that relate to the message and support the text. PowerPoint enables you to include a variety of visual objects to add impact to your presentation. You can add clip art, images, WordArt, sound, animated clips, and video clips to increase your presentation's impact. You can add tables, charts and graphs, and SmartArt diagrams created in PowerPoint, or you can insert objects that were created in other applications, such as a chart from Microsoft Excel or a table from Microsoft Word. You can add animations and transitions to catch audience attention. You can also add identifying information on slides or audience handouts by adding headers and footers.

> Clip art, images, WordArt, sound, animated clips, and video clips increase your presentation's impact.

In this section, you will add a table to organize data in columns and rows. You will insert clip art objects that relate to your topics and will move and resize the clip art. You will apply transitions to control how one slide changes to another and animations to text and clip art to help maintain your audience's attention. You will finish by adding identifying information in a header and footer.

Inserting Media Objects

Adding media objects such as pictures, clip art, audio, and/or video is especially important in PowerPoint, as PowerPoint is a visual medium. In addition to using the Insert tab to insert media objects in any layout, the following layouts include specific buttons to quickly insert objects:

- Title and Content
- Two Content
- Comparison
- Content with Caption

Clicking Insert Picture from File or Insert Media Clip on the Insert tab opens an Insert dialog box you use to browse for files on your hard drive or a removable storage device. Clicking Clip Art opens the Clip Art pane. Figure 1.19 displays the layout buttons.

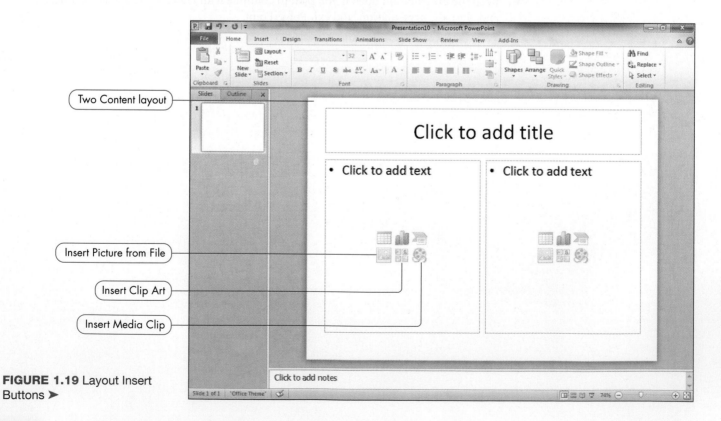

FIGURE 1.19 Layout Insert Buttons ➤

Adding a Table

A **table** organizes information in columns and rows.

A *table* organizes information in columns and rows. Tables can be simple and include just a few words or images, or they can be more complex and include structured numerical data.

To create a table on a new slide, you can select any layout, click the Insert tab, and then click Table in the Tables group. You can also click Insert Table on any slide layout that includes it. These two options create a table with a slightly different size, however. Figure 1.20 shows the same data entered into tables created in each of these ways. Once the table is created, you can resize a column or a row by positioning the pointer over the border you wish to resize and then dragging.

Table created using Insert Table on slide

Table created using the Insert tab

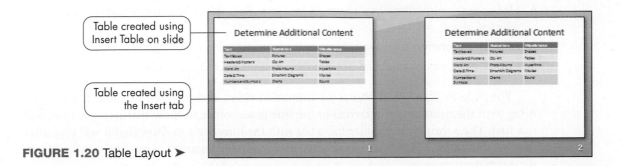

FIGURE 1.20 Table Layout ➤

> **TIP** Movement Within a Table
>
> The insertion point will show you where the text you type will appear in the table. Use the arrow keys or click anywhere in the table to move the insertion point to a new cell. You can also use the Tab key to move the insertion point. Press Tab to move to the next cell or press Shift+Tab to move to the previous cell. Pressing Ctrl+Tab inserts an indent within the cell. Pressing Tab in the last cell of a table creates a new blank row at the end of the table.

Using Animations and Transitions

An **animation** is movement applied to an object in a slide show.

A **transition** is an animation that is applied as a previous slide is replaced by a new slide.

An *animation* is a movement that controls the entrance, emphasis, exit, and/or path of objects in a slide show. A *transition* is a specific animation that is applied as a previous slide is replaced by a new slide while displayed in Slide Show view or Reading view. Animating objects can help focus the audience's attention on an important point, can control the flow of information on a slide, and can help you keep the audience's attention. Transitions provide visual interest as the slides change.

> **TIP** Animation Painter
>
> PowerPoint's new Animation Painter feature lets you copy an animation from one object to another. To use the Painter, select an object with an animation applied, click Animation Painter in the Advanced Animation group on the Animations tab, and then click the text or object to which you want to apply the animation.

Animate Objects

You can animate objects using a variety of animations, and each animation can be modified by changing its effect options. Keep animations consistent for a professional presentation. The options available for animations are determined by the animation type. For example, if you choose a Wipe animation, you can determine the direction of the wipe. If you choose an Object Color animation, you can determine the color to be added to the object.

To apply an animation to text or other objects, do the following:

1. Select the object you want to animate.
2. Click the Animations tab.
3. Click the More button in the Animation group to display the Animation gallery.
4. Mouse over animation types to see a Live Preview of the animation applied to the selected object.
5. Click an animation type to apply.
6. Click Effect Options to display any available options related to the selected animation type.

The slide in Figure 1.21 shows an animation effect added to the title and the subtitle. A tag with the number 1 is attached to the title placeholder to show that its animation will run first. The subtitle placeholder has a tag with the number 2 to show that it will play after the first animation. The picture is selected and ready for an animation to be attached from the Animation gallery.

FIGURE 1.21 Animation Gallery ➤

The slide in Figure 1.22 shows a Fly In animation effect added to the picture. A tag with the number 3 is attached and is shaded orange to show that it is selected. The Fly In Effect Options gallery is open so that a direction for the image to fly in from can be selected. Click Preview in the Preview group to see all animations on the slide play. You can also see the animations in Reading View and in Slide Show view. Slides that include an animation display a star icon beneath the slide when viewing the slides in Slide Sorter view.

FIGURE 1.22 Fly In Animation
Effect Options ➤

- Preview
- Fly In animation applied
- Active animation
- Effect Options gallery

Apply Transitions

Transitions are selected from the Transitions to This Slide group on the Transitions tab. You can select from the basic transitions displayed or from the Transitions gallery. To display the Transition gallery, click the More button in the Transition to This Slide group on the Transitions tab. The gallery in Figure 1.23 displays the available transitions in the following groups: Subtle, Exciting, and Dynamic Content. Click Effect Options in the Transition to This Slide group to see any effects that can be applied to the transition. Figure 1.23 shows the Transition gallery.

FIGURE 1.23 Transition
Gallery ➤

> ## TIP Slide Sorter View and Transitions
>
> Transition effects also can be applied from the Slide Sorter view, where you can apply the same transition to multiple slides by selecting the slides prior to applying the effect. Once a transition is applied to a slide, a star icon appears beneath the slide when viewing the slides in Slide Sorter view.

After you choose a transition effect, you can select a sound to play when the transition takes effect. You can choose the duration of the transition in seconds, which controls how quickly the transition takes place. You can also control whether the transition applies to all the slides or just the current slide.

Another determination you must make is how you want to start the transition process. Use the Advance Slide options in the Timing group to determine whether you want to manually click or press a key to advance to the next slide or if you want the slide to automatically advance after a specified number of seconds. You can set the number of seconds for the slide to display in the same area.

To delete a transition attached to a slide, click the Transitions tab, and then click None in the Transitions to This Slide group. If you wish to remove all transitions, click the Transitions tab, click None in the Transitions to This Slide group, and then click Apply To All in the Timing group.

> **TIP** Effectively Adding Transitions, Animations, and Sound
>
> When you select your transitions, sounds, and animations, remember that too many transition and animation styles can be distracting. The audience will be wondering what is coming next rather than paying attention to your message. On the other hand, very slow transitions will lose the interest of your audience. Too many sound clips can be annoying. Consider whether you need to have the sound of applause with the transition of every slide. Is a typewriter sound necessary to keep your audience's attention, or will it grate on their nerves if it is used on every word? Ask someone to review your presentation and let you know of any annoying or jarring elements.

Inserting a Header or Footer

The date of the presentation, the presentation audience, a logo, a company name, and other identifying information are very valuable, and you may want such information to appear on every slide, handout, or notes page. Use the Header and Footer feature to do this. A *header* contains information that generally appears at the top of pages in a handout or on a notes page. A *footer* contains information that generally appears at the bottom of slides in a presentation or at the bottom of pages in a handout or of a notes page. Because the template determines the position of a header or footer, however, you may find them in various locations on the slide.

To insert text in a header or footer, do the following:

1. Click the Insert tab.
2. Click Header & Footer in the Text group.
3. Click the Slide tab or the Notes and Handouts tab.
4. Click desired options, and enter desired text, if necessary.
5. Click Apply to All to add the information to all slides or pages, or if you are adding the header or footer to a single slide, click Apply.

Figure 1.24 shows the Slide tab of the Header and Footer dialog box.

A **header** is information that generally appears at the top of pages in a handout or notes page.

A **footer** is information that generally appears at the bottom of slides in a presentation or at the bottom of pages in a handout or of a notes page.

Click to insert Header and/or Footer

Choose location

Active Slide number option

Slide number field

Date field in footer

FIGURE 1.24 Header and Footer Dialog Box ➤

Click the Date and time check box to insert the current date and time signature. Click Update automatically if you wish the date to always be current. Once you select Update automatically, you can select the date format you prefer. Alternatively, you can choose the option to enter a fixed date to preserve the original date, which can help you keep track of versions.

Click in the Footer box to enter information. The Preview window allows you to see the position of these fields. Always note the position of the fields, as PowerPoint layouts vary considerably in Header and Footer field positions. If you do not want the footer to appear on the title slide, select *Don't show on title slide*. Click Apply All to apply the footer to every slide in the presentation, or click Apply to apply to the current slide only.

The Notes and Handouts tab gives you an extra field box for the Header field. Since this feature is used for printouts, the slides are not numbered, but the pages in the handout are. As you activate the fields, the preview window shows the location of the fields. The date and time are located on the top right of the printout. The Header field is located on the top left. The page number is located on the bottom right, and the footer field is on the bottom left.

HANDS-ON EXERCISES

myitlab
HOE3 Training

3 Presentation Development

You decide to strengthen the slide show by adding objects. You know that adding clip art and additional information in a table will help state employees stay interested and retain information. You insert a table, add and resize clip art, apply a transition, and animate the objects you have included. Finally, you enter a slide footer and a Notes and Handouts header and footer.

Skills covered: Add a Table • Insert, Move, and Resize Clip Art • Apply a Transition • Animate Objects • Create a Handout Header and Footer

---

STEP 1 ▶ ADD A TABLE

To organize the list of objects that can be added to a PowerPoint slide, you create a table on a new slide. Listing these objects as bullets would take far more space than a table takes. Refer to Figure 1.25 as you complete Step 1.

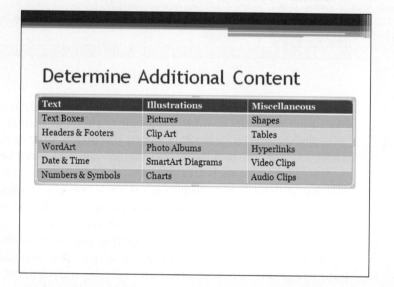

FIGURE 1.25 PowerPoint Table ➤

a. Open *p01h2content_LastnameFirstname* if you closed it at the end of Hands-On Exercise 2. Save the presentation as **p01h3content_LastnameFirstname**, changing *h2* to *h3*.

> **TROUBLESHOOTING:** If you make any major mistakes in this exercise, you can close the file, open *p01h2content_LastnameFirstname* again, and start this exercise over.

b. On Slide 5, click the **Home tab**, and then click **New Slide** in the Slides group.

   A new slide with the Title and Content layout is inserted after Slide 5.

c. Click in the **title placeholder**, and then type **Determine Additional Content**.

d. Click **Insert Table** in the center of the slide.

   The Insert Table dialog box opens.

e. Type **3** in the **Number of columns box**, press **Tab**, type **6** in the **Number of rows box**, and then click **OK**.

   PowerPoint creates the table and positions it on the slide. The first row of the table is formatted differently than the other rows so that it can be used for column headings.

f. Type **Text** in the **top-left cell** of the table. Press **Tab** to move to the next cell, and then type **Illustrations**. Press **Tab**, type **Miscellaneous**, and then press **Tab** to move to the next row.

g. Type the following text in the remaining table cells, pressing **Tab** after each entry.

Text Boxes	Pictures	Shapes
Headers & Footers	Clip Art	Tables
WordArt	Photo Albums	Hyperlinks
Date & Time	SmartArt Diagrams	Video Clips
Numbers & Symbols	Charts	Audio Clips

h. Save the presentation.

STEP 2 ▶ INSERT, MOVE, AND RESIZE CLIP ART

In this step, you insert clip art and resize it to better fit the slide. The clip art you insert relates to the topic and adds visual interest. You also add a Microsoft video clip to add movement to a slide. Refer to Figure 1.26 as you complete Step 2.

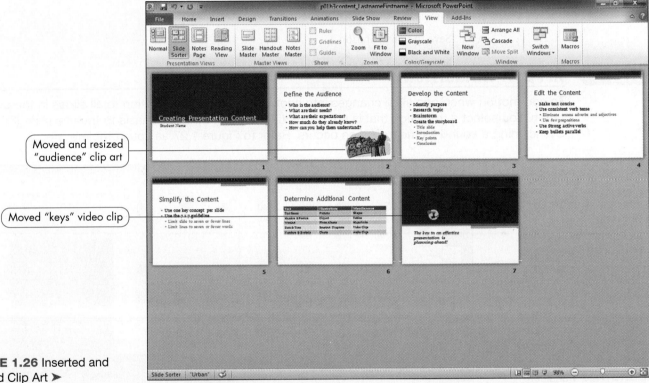

Moved and resized "audience" clip art

Moved "keys" video clip

FIGURE 1.26 Inserted and Resized Clip Art ➤

a. On Slide 2, click the **Insert tab**, and then click **Clip Art** in the Images group.

The Clip Art pane displays on the right side of your screen.

b. Type **audience** in the **Search for box** in the Clip art pane.

c. Click the **Results should be arrow**, deselect all options except *Illustrations*, and then click **Go**.

d. Click the image shown in Figure 1.26 to insert it on Slide 2.

> **TROUBLESHOOTING:** If you cannot locate the image in Figure 1.26, select another clip art image that looks like an audience. Expand your search terms to include other result types if necessary.

e. Position the pointer in the center of the image, and then, with the mouse pointer showing as a four-headed arrow, drag the image to the bottom-right corner of the slide.

The clip art is too small. It is overwhelmed by the amount of text on the slide.

f. Position the pointer over the top-left sizing handle of the image, and then drag to increase the size of the clip art.

When you drag a corner sizing handle, the image retains its proportions.

g. Move the clip art image, if necessary, so that it is positioned attractively on the slide.

h. On Slide 7, change the *Search for* keyword in the Clip Art pane to **keys**, change the results to show **Videos**, and then click **Go**.

The videos in the Clip Art pane are animated clip art images that can be inserted in a slide.

i. Refer to Figure 1.26 to determine the keys movie clip to select, and then click the movie to insert it on Slide 7. Close the Clip Art pane.

> **TROUBLESHOOTING:** If you cannot locate the video in Figure 1.26, select another video clip of keys.

j. Reposition the clip so that it is centered above the placeholder containing the text. Do not resize the clip art.

Since this clip is an animated movie clip, if it is enlarged, the image will become distorted.

k. Press **F5** to play the presentation to view the animation.

l. Save the presentation.

STEP 3 ▶ APPLY A TRANSITION

To add motion when one slide changes into another, you apply a transition to all slides in the presentation. You select a transition that is not distracting but that adds emphasis to the title slide (Slide 1) by including a sound as the transition occurs. Refer to Figure 1.27 as you complete Step 3.

FIGURE 1.27 Transition Gallery ➤

a. Click the **Transitions tab**, and then click the **More button** in the Transition to This Slide group.

b. Click **Doors**.

c. Click **Apply To All** in the Timing group.

The transition effect will apply to all slides in the slide show.

d. On Slide 1, click the **Sound arrow** in the Timing group, and then select **Push**.

The Push sound will play as Slide 1 enters.

e. Click **Preview** in the Preview group.

Because Slide 1 is active, you hear the Push sound as the Doors transition occurs.

f. Click the **View tab**, and then click **Slide Sorter** in the Presentation Views group.

The small star beneath each slide indicates a transition has been applied to the slide.

g. Click any of the stars to see a preview of the transition applied to that slide.

h. Save the presentation.

STEP 4 ▶ ANIMATE OBJECTS

You add animation to your slide show by controlling how individual objects such as lines of text or images enter or exit the slides. Refer to Figure 1.28 as you complete Step 4.

FIGURE 1.28 Slide with Animation and Timing Settings ➤

a. Double-click **Slide 1** to open it in Normal view, and then select the title placeholder.

b. Click the **Animations tab**, and then click the **More button** in the Animation group.

c. Click **Float In**.

The Float In animation is applied to the title placeholder.

d. On Slide 1, select the subtitle placeholder, and then select **Fly In** in the Animation group.

e. Click the **Start arrow** in the Timing group, and then select **After Previous**.

f. On Slide 2, select the clip art image.

You decide to apply and modify the Zoom animation and change the animation speed.

g. Click the **More button** in the Animation group, and then click **Zoom**.

h. Click **Effect Options** in the Animation group, and then select **Slide Center**.

The clip art now grows and zooms from the center of the slide to the bottom right of the slide.

i. Click the **Start arrow**, and then select **With Previous**.

The clip art animation will now start automatically when the bullets enter.

j. Click the **Duration down arrow** once.

The duration changes from *00.50* to *00.25*, so the animation is faster.

k. Save the presentation.

STEP 5 ▶ CREATE A HANDOUT HEADER AND FOOTER

Because you are creating this presentation to the Training and Development department, you include this identifying information in a slide footer. You also decide to include your personal information in a Notes and Handouts Header and Footer. Refer to Figure 1.29 as you complete Step 5.

FIGURE 1.29 Slide Footer ➤

a. Click the **Insert tab**, and then click **Header & Footer** in the Text group.

The Header and Footer dialog box opens, with the Slide tab active.

b. Click **Slide number**.

The slide number will now appear on each slide. Note the position of the slide number in the Preview window: top right of the slide. The template determined the position of the slide number.

c. Click the **Footer check box**, and then type **Training and Development**.

Training and Development will appear on each slide. Note the position of the footer in the Preview window: top right of the slide.

d. Click **Don't show on title slide**, and then click **Apply to All**.

The slide footer appears at the top right on all slides except the title slide. The template positioned the footer at the top of the slide instead of the bottom.

e. Click **Header & Footer**, and then click the **Notes and Handouts tab**.

The Notes and Handouts header and footer options become available.

f. Click the **Date and time check box**, click **Fixed**, and then type the current date in the **Fixed box**, if necessary.

Using this option lets you use the date of the presentation on the handout rather than the date you edited the presentation.

g. Click the **Header check box**, and then enter your name in the **Header box**.

h. Click the **Footer check box**, and then type your instructor's name and your class in the **Footer box**.

i. Click **Apply to All**.

j. Switch to Notes Page view to see the header and footer. Return to Normal view, and then save the presentation.

k. Keep the presentation open if you plan to continue with Hands-On Exercise 4. If not, save and close the presentation, and exit PowerPoint.

Navigation and Printing

In the beginning of this chapter, you opened a slide show and advanced one by one through the slides by clicking the mouse button. Audiences may ask questions that can be answered by going to another slide in the presentation. As you respond to the questions, you may find yourself needing to jump back to a previous slide or needing to move to a future slide. PowerPoint's navigation options enable you to maneuver through a presentation easily.

> Various options are available for audience handouts. Be aware of the options, and choose the one that best suits your audience's needs.

To help your audience follow your presentation, you can choose to provide them with a handout. Various options are available for audience handouts. Be aware of the options, and choose the one that best suits your audience's needs. You may distribute handouts at the beginning of your presentation for note taking, or provide your audience with the notes afterward.

In this section, you will run a slide show and navigate within the show. You will practice a variety of methods for advancing to new slides or returning to previously viewed slides. You will annotate slides during a presentation and will change from screen view to black-screen view. Finally, you will print handouts of the slide show.

Running and Navigating a Slide Show

PowerPoint provides multiple methods to advance through the slide show. You can also go backward to a previous slide, if desired. Use Table 1.1 to identify the navigation options, and then experiment with each method for advancing and going backward. Find the method that you are most comfortable using and stay with that method.

TABLE 1.1 Navigation Options

Navigation Option	Navigation Method
Advance Through the Slide Show	Press the Spacebar.
	Press Page Down.
	Press N for next.
	Press → or ↓.
	Press Enter.
Return to a Previous Slide or Animation	Right-click, and then choose Previous from the shortcut menu.
	Press Page Up.
	Press P for previous.
	Press ← or ↑.
	Press Backspace.
End the Slide Show	Press Esc.
	Press - (the hyphen).
Go to a Specific Slide	Type the slide number, and then press Enter.
	Right-click, point to Go to Slide, and then click the slide desired.

Slide Show Controls

You can press F1 at any time during your presentation to see a list of slide show controls. Familiarize yourself with these controls before you present to a group.

When an audience member asks a question that is answered in another slide on your slide show, you can go to that specific slide by using the Go to Slide command. The Go to Slide command is found on the shortcut menu, which displays when you right-click anywhere on the active slide during your presentation. Pointing to the Go to Slide command displays a list of your slide titles so you can easily identify and select the slide to which you want to go. This shortcut menu also lets you end the slide show as well as access other features.

After the last slide in your slide show displays, the audience sees a black slide. This slide has two purposes: It enables you to end your show without having your audience see the PowerPoint design screen, and it cues the audience to expect the room lights to brighten. If you need to blacken the screen at any time during your presentation, you can type B. If you blacken the screen in a darkened room, you must be prepared to quickly brighten some lights. When you are ready to start your slide show again, simply type B again.

If you prefer bringing up a white screen, type W. White is much harsher on your audience's eyes, however. Only use white if you are in an extremely bright room. Whether using black or white, you are enabling the audience to concentrate on you, the speaker, without the slide show interfering.

REFERENCE   Delivery Tips

Practice the following delivery tips to gain confidence and polish your delivery.

Before the presentation:

- Practice or rehearse your presentation with your PowerPoint at home until you are comfortable with the material and its corresponding slides.
- Do not read from a prepared script or your PowerPoint Notes. Presenting is not karaoke. Know your material thoroughly. Glance at your notes infrequently. Never post a screen full of small text and then torture your audience by saying, "I know you can't read this, so I will …"
- Arrive early to set up so you do not keep the audience waiting while you manage equipment.
- Have a backup in case the equipment does not work: Overhead transparencies or handouts work well.
- Prepare handouts for your audience so they can relax and participate in your presentation rather than scramble taking notes.
- Make sure your handouts acknowledge and document quotes, data, and sources.

During the presentation:

- Speak to the person farthest away from you to be sure the people in the last row can hear you. Speak slowly and clearly.
- Vary your delivery. Show emotion or enthusiasm for your topic. If you do not care about your topic, why should the audience?
- Pause to emphasize key points when speaking.
- Look at the audience, not at the screen, as you speak and you will open communication and gain credibility.
- Use the three-second guide: Look into the eyes of a member of the audience for three seconds and then scan the entire audience. Continue doing this throughout your presentation. Use your eye contact to keep members of the audience involved.
- Blank the screen by typing B or W at any time during your presentation when you want to solicit questions, comments, or discussion.
- Do not overwhelm your audience with your PowerPoint animations, sounds, and special effects. These features should not overpower you and your message, but should enhance your message.

After the presentation:

- Thank the audience for their attention and participation. Leave on a positive note.

Annotate the Slide Show

An **annotation** is a written note or drawing on a slide for additional commentary or explanation.

You may find it helpful to add *annotations* (notes or drawings) to your slides during a presentation. To add written notes or drawings, do the following:

1. Right-click on a slide in Slide Show view.
2. Point to Pointer Options.
3. Click Pen or Highlighter.
4. Hold down the left mouse button and write or draw on the screen.

If you want to change the ink color for the Pen or Highlighter, right-click to bring up the shortcut menu, and then point to Pointer Options to select your pen type and ink color. To erase what you have drawn, press E. Your drawings or added text will be clumsy efforts at best, unless you use a tablet computer that includes a stylus and drawing screen. The annotations you create are not permanent unless you save the annotations when exiting the slide show and then save the changes upon exiting the file. You may want to save the annotated file with a different file name from the original presentation.

> **TIP Annotating Shortcuts**
>
> Press Ctrl+P to change the pointer to a drawing pointer while presenting, and then click and drag on the slide, much the same way your favorite football announcer diagrams a play. With each slide, you must press Ctrl+P again to activate the drawing pointer, in order to avoid accidentally drawing on your slides. Use Page Down and Page Up to move forward and backward in the presentation while the annotation is in effect. Press Ctrl+A to return the mouse pointer to an arrow.

Printing in PowerPoint

A printed copy of a PowerPoint slide show can be used to display speaker notes for reference during the presentation, for audience handouts or a study guide, or as a means to deliver the presentation if there were an equipment failure. A printout of a single slide with text on it can be used as a poster or banner. Figure 1.30 shows the print options in the Backstage view. Depending on your printer and printer settings, your button names may vary. To print a copy of the slide show using the default PowerPoint settings, do the following:

1. Click the File tab to display the Backstage view.
2. Click Print.
3. Click Printer to choose the print device you want to use.
4. Click Print All Slides to select print area and range.
5. Click Full Page Slides to select the layout of the printout.
6. Click Collated to change to uncollated.
7. Click Grayscale to select color, grayscale, or pure black and white.
8. Click Print.

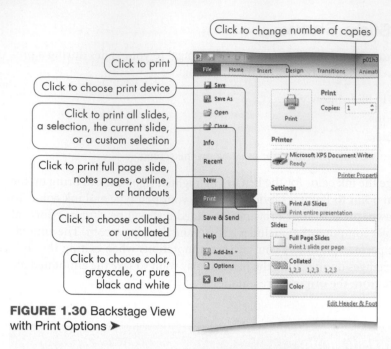

Click to change number of copies

Click to print

Click to choose print device

Click to print all slides, a selection, the current slide, or a custom selection

Click to print full page slide, notes pages, outline, or handouts

Click to choose collated or uncollated

Click to choose color, grayscale, or pure black and white

FIGURE 1.30 Backstage View with Print Options ➤

Print Full Page Slides

Use the Print Full Slides option to print the slides for use as a backup or when the slides contain a great deal of detail the audience needs to examine. You can also print the full slides on overhead transparencies to use with an overhead projector during a presentation. You will be extremely grateful for the backup if your projector bulb blows out or if your computer quits working during a presentation.

If you are printing the slides on transparencies or on paper smaller than the standard size, be sure to change the slide size and orientation before you print. By default, PowerPoint sets the slides for landscape orientation for printing so that the width is greater than the height ($11'' \times 8.5''$). If you are going to print a flyer or overhead transparency, however, you need to set PowerPoint to portrait orientation, to print so that the height is greater than the width ($8.5'' \times 11''$).

To change your slide orientation, click the Design tab, click Slide Orientation in the Page Setup group, and then click Portrait or Landscape. If you are going to change the size of the slide as well as the orientation, click Page Setup, and then change the settings in the Page Setup dialog box. If you want to create a custom size of paper to print, enter the height and width. Figure 1.31 displays the Page Setup options. Note that in the figure, the slide show has been sized to print on overhead transparencies.

Click Design tab

Click to open Page Setup dialog box

Click to set handouts orientation

Click to set slide orientation

Click to select slide size

Click to set custom width

Click to set custom height

FIGURE 1.31 Page Setup Options ➤

After you click the File tab, then click Print, you can determine the color option with which to print. Selecting Color prints your presentation in color if you have a color printer or grayscale if you are printing on a black-and-white printer. Selecting Grayscale prints in shades of gray, but be aware that backgrounds do not print when using the Grayscale option. By not printing the background, you make the text in the printout easier to read and you save a lot of ink or toner. Printing with the Pure Black and White option prints with no gray fills.

When you click Full Page Slides in the Print Backstage view, additional options become available. The Frame Slides option puts a black border around the slides in the printout, giving the printout a more polished appearance. The Scale to Fit Paper option ensures that each slide prints on one page even if you have selected a custom size for your slide show, or if you have set up the slide show so that is it larger than the paper on which you are printing. If you have applied shadows to text or objects, click High Quality so that the shadows print. The final option, Print Comments and Ink Markup, is only active if you have used this feature.

Print Handouts

The principal purpose for printing handouts is to give your audience something they can use to follow and take notes on during the presentation. With your handout and their notes, the audience has an excellent resource for the future. Handouts can be printed with one, two, three, four, six, or nine slides per page. Printing three handouts per page is a popular option because it places thumbnails of the slides on the left side of the printout and lines on which the audience can write on the right side of the printout. Figure 1.32 shows the option set to Handouts and the Slides per page option set to 6.

FIGURE 1.32 Setting Print Options ➤

Print Notes Pages

If you include charts, technical information, or references in a speaker note, you will want to print a Notes Page if you want the audience to have a copy. To print a specific Notes Page, change the print layout to Notes Pages, and then click the Print All Slides arrow. Click Custom Range, and then enter the specific slides to print.

Print Outlines

You may print your presentation as an outline made up of the slide titles and main text from each of your slides if you only want to deal with a few pages. The outline generally gives you enough detail to keep you on track with your presentation, but does not display speaker notes.

HANDS-ON EXERCISES

myitlab
HOE4 Training

4 Navigation and Printing

To prepare for your presentation to Training and Development department employees, you practice displaying the slide show and navigating to specific slides. You also annotate a slide and print audience handouts.

Skills covered: Start a Slide Show • Annotate a Slide • Print Audience Handouts

---

STEP 1 ▶ START A SLIDE SHOW

In this step, you practice various slide navigation techniques to become comfortable with their use. You also review the Slide Show Help feature to become familiar with navigation shortcuts.

a. Open the *p01h3content_LastnameFirstname* presentation if you closed it after the last Hands-On Exercise and save it as **p01h4content_LastnameFirstname**, changing *h3* to *h4*.

b. On Slide 1, type your class title under your name in the **subtitle placeholder**.

c. Click the **Slide Show tab**, and then click **From Beginning** in the Start Slide Show group.

Note the transition effect and sound you applied in Hands-On Exercise 3.

d. Press **Spacebar** to display the first animation, and then press **Spacebar** again to display the second animation.

e. Click the **left mouse button** to advance to Slide 2.

Note that the clip art animation plays automatically.

f. Press **Page Down** to advance to Slide 3.

g. Press **Page Up** to return to Slide 2.

h. Press **Enter** to advance to Slide 3.

i. Press **N** to advance to Slide 4.

j. Press **Backspace** to return to Slide 3.

k. Right-click, point to **Go to Slide**, and then select **5 Simplify the Content**.

Slide 5 displays.

l. Press the number **3**, and then press **Enter**.

Slide 3 displays.

m. Press **F1**, and then read the Slide Show Help window showing the shortcut tips that are available during the display of a slide show. Practice moving between slides using the shortcuts shown in Help.

n. Close the Help window.

STEP 2 ▶ ANNOTATE A SLIDE

You practice annotating a slide using a pen, and then you remove the annotations. You practice darkening the screen and returning to the presentation from the dark screen.

a. Press **Ctrl+P**.

The mouse pointer becomes a pen.

b. Circle and underline several words on the slide.

c. Press **E**.

The annotations erase.

d. Press **B**.

The screen blackens.

e. Press **B** again.

The slide show displays again.

f. Press **Esc** to end annotations.

g. Press **Esc** to end the slide show.

STEP 3 ▶ PRINT AUDIENCE HANDOUTS

To enable your audience to follow along during your presentation, you print handouts of your presentation. You know that many of the audience members will also keep your handouts for future reference.

a. Click the **File tab** to display the Backstage view, and then click **Print**.

b. Click **Full Page Slides**, and then select **4 Slides Horizontal** in the *Handouts* section.

> **TROUBLESHOOTING:** If you have previously selected a different print layout, Full Page Slides will be changed to that layout. Click the arrow next to the displayed layout option.

c. Click **Print** to print the presentation if your instructor asks you to print.

d. Save and close the file, and submit based on your instructor's directions.

After reading this chapter, you have accomplished the following objectives:

1. **Use PowerPoint views.** Slide shows are electronic presentations that enable you to advance through slides containing content that will help your audience understand your message. Normal view displays either thumbnail images or an outline in one pane, the slide in one pane, and a Notes pane. Slide Sorter view displays thumbnails of slides to enable you to organize slides. Notes Page view displays a thumbnail of the slide and speaker notes. Slide Show view displays the slide show in full-screen view for an audience. If a presenter has multiple monitors, Presenter view gives the presenter options such as a timer and notes, whereas the audience views the full-screen presentation.

2. **Save as a slide show.** You can save a presentation as a slide show, so that when the file opens it is in Slide Show mode. Slide shows cannot be edited and are saved with the file extension .ppsx.

3. **Plan a presentation.** Before creating your slide show, analyze your audience and research your message. Organize your ideas on a storyboard, and then create your presentation in PowerPoint. After completing the slide show, practice it so that you are comfortable with your slide content and the technology with which you will present it.

4. **Assess presentation content.** After creating presentation content, review what you wrote. Check bullet structure, word usage, and spelling.

5. **Use slide layouts.** When you add a slide, you can choose from a set of predefined slide layouts that determine the position of the objects or content on a slide. Placeholders hold content and determine the position of the objects on the slide.

6. **Apply themes.** PowerPoint design themes give the presentation a consistent look. The theme controls the font, background, layout, and colors.

7. **Review the presentation.** Use the Spelling and Thesaurus features, and review the presentation in Normal and Slide Show views to ensure no errors exist in the presentation.

8. **Insert media objects.** Media objects such as clip art, images, movies, and sound can be added to enhance the message of your slides and to add visual interest.

9. **Add a table.** Tables organize information in rows and columns.

10. **Use animations and transitions.** Animations control the movement of an object on the slide. Transitions control the movement of slides as one slide changes to another. Both features can aid in keeping the attention of the audience, but animations are especially valuable in directing attention to specific elements you wish to emphasize.

11. **Insert a header and footer.** Headers and footers are used for identifying information on the slide or on handouts and note pages. Header and footer locations vary depending on the theme applied.

12. **Run and navigate a slide show.** Various navigation methods advance the slide show, return to previously viewed slides, or go to specific slides. Slides can be annotated during a presentation to add emphases or comments to slides.

13. **Print in PowerPoint.** PowerPoint has four ways to print the slideshow. The Full Page Slide method prints each slide on a separate page. Handouts print miniatures of the slides using 1, 2, 3, 4, 6, or 9 slide thumbnails per page. Notes Page method prints a single thumbnail of a slide with its associated notes per page. Outline View prints the titles and main points of the presentation in outline format.

KEY TERMS

Animation *p.781*
Annotation *p.793*
Footer *p.784*
Header *p.784*
Layout *p.772*
Normal view *p.761*
Notes Page view *p.762*
Placeholder *p.772*

PowerPoint presentation *p.760*
PowerPoint show *p.765*
Presenter view *p.765*
Reading view *p.763*
Slide *p.760*
Slide show *p.760*
Slide Show view *p.764*
Slide Sorter view *p.763*

Status bar *p.761*
Storyboard *p.769*
Table *p.781*
Theme *p.773*
Thumbnail *p.761*
Transition *p.781*

1. Which of the following print methods would you use for a large detailed table in your presentation?

   (a) Handout, 6 Slides Horizontal
   (b) Outline
   (c) Notes Pages
   (d) Full Page Slide

2. While displaying a slide show, which of the following will display a list of shortcuts for navigating?

   (a) F1
   (b) F11
   (c) Ctrl+Enter
   (d) Esc

3. PowerPoint's predefined slide arrangements are:

   (a) Placeholder views.
   (b) Slide layouts.
   (c) Slide guides.
   (d) Slide displays.

4. To add an object such as clip art to a slide, use the _____ tab.

   (a) Add-Ins
   (b) Design
   (c) Slide
   (d) Insert

5. Which of the following is a true statement regarding themes?

   (a) A theme must be applied before slides are created.
   (b) The theme can be changed after all of the slides have been created.
   (c) Themes control fonts and backgrounds but not placeholder location.
   (d) Placeholders positioned by a theme cannot be moved.

6. Which of the following views is best for reordering the slides in a presentation?

   (a) Presenter view
   (b) Reading view
   (c) Slide Sorter view
   (d) Slide Show view

7. Normal view contains which of the following components?

   (a) Slide Sorter pane, Slides and Outline tabs pane, and Reading pane
   (b) Slides and Outline tabs pane, Slide pane, and Reading pane
   (c) Slides and Outline tabs pane, Slide pane, and Notes pane
   (d) Slide pane, Notes pane, and Slide Sorter pane

8. Which of the following is the animation effect that controls how one slide changes to another slide?

   (a) Transition
   (b) Timing
   (c) Animation
   (d) Advance

9. Which of the following cannot be used to focus audience attention on a specific object on a slide during a slide show?

   (a) Put nothing on the slide but the object.
   (b) Apply an animation to the object.
   (c) Use the pen tool to circle the object.
   (d) Apply a transition to the object.

10. Which of the following bullet points concerning content development is not in active voice and is not parallel to the other bullets?

    (a) Identify the purpose of the presentation.
    (b) Storyboards are used to sketch out thoughts.
    (c) Brainstorm your thoughts.
    (d) Research your topic.

PRACTICE EXERCISES

1 Student Success

The slide show you modify in this practice exercise covers concepts and skills that will help you be successful in college. You edit an existing presentation structure by changing a layout and by creating an introduction slide. You review the presentation and then edit a slide so that the title is in active voice and the bullets are parallel. You create a summary of what you learn and enter it as a note for the conclusion slide. Finally, you print a cover and notes pages to staple together as a reference. This exercise follows the same set of skills as used in Hands-On Exercises 1, 2, 3, and 4 in the chapter. Refer to Figure 1.33 as you complete this exercise.

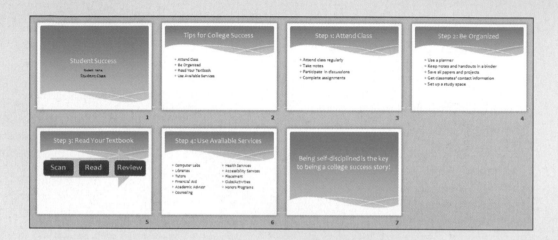

FIGURE 1.33 Student Success Strategies ➤

a. Open *p01p1success* and save it as **p01p1success_LastnameFirstname**.

b. Click the **Insert tab**, click **Header & Footer**, and then click the **Notes and Handouts tab**.

c. Click the **Date and time check box**, and then click **Update automatically**.

d. Click the **Header check box**, and then type your name in the **Header box**.

e. Click the **Footer check box**, and then type your instructor's name and your class in the **Footer box**. Click **Apply to All**.

f. Click the **Slide Show tab**, and then click **From Beginning** in the Start Slide Show group. Read each of the slides by pressing **Spacebar** to advance through the slides. Press **Esc** to exit Slide Show view.

g. Click the **View tab**, and then click **Notes Page** in the Presentation Views group.

h. Click **Zoom** in the Zoom group, click **100%**, and then click **OK**. Read each of the notes by dragging the scroll bar to advance through the slides.

i. Click **Slide Sorter** in the Presentation Views group. Reposition the slides so the slide titles display the steps in the correct order. Return to Normal view.

j. On Slide 1, click in the **subtitle placeholder**, and then replace the words *Student Name* with your name. Replace *Student Class* with the name of the class you are taking.

k. Click **New Slide** in the Slides group on the Home tab to create a new slide for the introduction.

l. Click in the **title placeholder**, and then type **Tips for College Success**.

m. Click in the **content placeholder**, and then type the following bullet items:
   - **Attend Class**
   - **Be Organized**
   - **Read Your Textbook**
   - **Use Available Services**

n. On Slide 6, click **Layout** in the Slides group, and then click **Two Content**.

o. Click in the **new content placeholder**, and then type the following bullet items:
   - **Health Services**
   - **Accessibility Services**

- Placement
- Clubs/Activities
- Honors Programs

p. On Slide 3, select **Class Attendance** in the title, and type **Attend Class**.

q. Select the third bullet, and then type **Participate in discussions**.

r. On Slide 7, click the border of the subtitle placeholder, and then press **Delete**.

s. Click in the **Notes pane**, select the **existing text**, and then type a short note about what you learned regarding student success strategies by reviewing this slide show.

t. Click the **Design tab**, click the **More button** in the Themes group, and then click **Waveform**.

u. On Slide 2, click **File**, click **Print**, click **Print All Slides**, and then click **Print Current Slide**.

v. Click **Full Page Slides**, click **Frame Slides** to activate it, and then click **Print**. Slide 1 will print as a cover page.

w. Open Print again, click **Print Current Slide**, and then click **Custom Range**. Type **2–7** as the slide range.

x. Click **Full Page Slides**, and then select **Notes Pages**.

y. Click **Full Page Slides**, click **Frame Slides**, and then click **Print**. Staple the cover page to the Notes Pages.

z. Press **Ctrl+S** to save the presentation. Click **File**, click **Save As**, change the Save as type to **PowerPoint Show**, and then click **Save**. Close the presentation. Submit based on your instructor's directions.

2 Tips for a Successful Presentation

Your employer is a successful author who has been asked by the local International Association of Administrative Professionals (IAAP) to give tips for presenting successfully using PowerPoint. He created a storyboard of his presentation and has asked you to create the presentation from the storyboard. This exercise follows the same set of skills as used in Hands-On Exercises 2 and 3 in the chapter. Refer to Figure 1.34 as you complete this exercise.

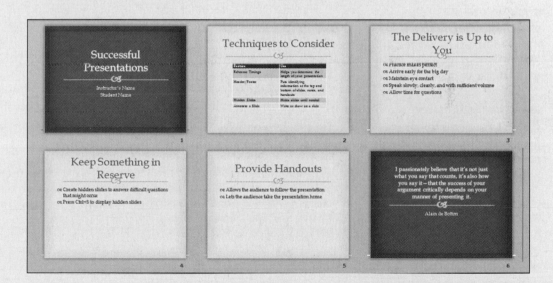

FIGURE 1.34 Successful Presentations ➤

a. Open a new blank presentation and save it as **p01p2tips_LastnameFirstname**.

b. Click the **Insert tab**, click **Header & Footer**, and then click the **Notes and Handouts tab**.

c. Click the **Date and time check box**, and then click **Update automatically**, if necessary.

d. Click the **Header check box**, and then type your name in the **Header box**.

e. Click the **Footer check box**, and then type your instructor's name and your class. Click **Apply to All**.

f. On Slide 1, click in the **title placeholder**, and then type **Successful Presentations**. Click in the **subtitle placeholder**, and then type your instructor's name. On the next line of the subtitle placeholder, type your name.

g. Click the **Home tab**, click the **New Slide arrow** in the Slides group, and then click **Title Only**.

h. Click in the **title placeholder**, and then type **Techniques to Consider**.

i. Click the **Insert tab**, click **Table** in the Tables group, and then use the grid to select two columns and five rows.

j. Type the following information in the table cells, pressing **Tab** to move from cell to cell. Position the table attractively on the slide.

Feature	Use
Rehearse Timings	Helps you determine the length of your presentation
Header/Footer	Puts identifying information on the top and bottom of slides, notes, and handouts
Hidden Slides	Hides slides until needed
Annotate a Slide	Write or draw on a slide

k. Click the **Home tab**, click the **New Slide arrow** in the Slides group, and then click **Title and Content**. Type **The Delivery is Up to You** in the **title placeholder**.

l. Click in the **content placeholder**, and then type the following bullet text:
   - **Practice makes perfect**
   - **Arrive early on the big day**
   - **Maintain eye contact**
   - **Speak slowly, clearly, and with sufficient volume**
   - **Allow time for questions**

m. Click **New Slide**, and then type **Keep Something in Reserve** in the **title placeholder**.

n. Click in the **content placeholder**, and then type the following bullet text:
   - **Create hidden slides to answer difficult questions that might occur**
   - **Press Ctrl+S while in Slide Show view to display hidden slides**

o. Click **New Slide**, and then type **Provide Handouts** in the **title placeholder**.

p. Click in the **content placeholder**, and then type the following bullet text:
   - **Allows the audience to follow the presentation**
   - **Lets the audience take the presentation home**

q. Click the **New Slide arrow**, and then click **Title Slide**.

r. Type **I passionately believe that it's not just what you say that counts, it's also how you say it—that the success of your argument critically depends on your manner of presenting it.** in the **title placeholder**, and then click the placeholder border. Change the font size to **28**.

s. Type **Alain de Botton** in the **subtitle placeholder**.

t. Check **Spelling**. Accept *Lets* in Slide 5, if necessary. Review the presentation in Slide Show view to fix any spelling or grammatical errors.

u. Click the **Design tab**, click the **More button** in the Themes group, and then click **Hardcover**.

v. Click the **Slide Show tab**, and then click **From Beginning** in the Start Slide Show group. Press **Page Down** to advance through the slides. When you reach the last slide of the slide show, press the number **3**, and then press **Enter** to return to Slide 3.

w. Right-click, point to **Pointer Options**, and then click **Highlighter**. Highlight **Speak slowly, clearly, and with sufficient volume**.

x. Press **Esc** when you reach the black slide at the end of the slide show, and then click **Keep** to keep your slide annotations.

y. Press **Ctrl+S** to save the presentation. Close the file and submit based on your instructor's directions.

3 Copyright and the Law

The ethics and values class you are taking this semester requires a final presentation to the class. You create a presentation to review basic copyright law and software licensing. You add clip art, a transition, and an animation. This exercise follows the same set of skills as used in Hands-On Exercises 2, 3, and 4 in the chapter. Refer to Figure 1.35 as you complete this exercise.

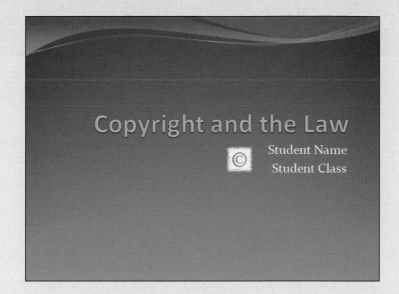

FIGURE 1.35 Copyright and the Law Presentation ➤

a. Open *p01p3copyright* and save it as **p01p3copyright_LastnameFirstname**.

b. Click the **Insert tab**, click **Header & Footer**, and then click the **Notes and Handouts tab**.

c. Click the **Date and time check box**, and then click **Update automatically**, if necessary.

d. Click the **Header check box**, and then type your name in the **Header box**.

e. Click the **Footer check box**, and then type your instructor's name and your class in the **Footer box**. Click **Apply to All**.

f. Click the **Slide Show tab**, and then click **From Beginning** in the Start Slide Show group. Read each of the slides' bullet items. Press **Esc** to return to Normal view.

g. Click the **Design tab**, click the **More button** in the Themes group, and then select the **Flow theme**.

h. On Slide 1, click in the **subtitle placeholder**, and then replace the words *Student Name* with your name. Replace *Student Class* with the name of the class you are taking.

i. Click the **Insert tab**, and then click **Clip Art** in the Images group. Type **copyright** in the **Search for box**. Click the **Results should be arrow**, and remove the check mark from all categories except *Videos*. Include results from Office.com. Select the **animated copyright symbol**, and then drag it to the title slide next to your name. Close the Clip Art pane.

> **TROUBLESHOOTING:** If the animated copyright clip does not appear when you search for the copyright keyword, change the keyword to *law*, and then select an image that relates to the presentation content and that uses the same colors.

j. Click the **Transitions tab**, and then click the **More button** in the Transition to This Slide group. Click **Rotate**, and then click **Apply To All**.

k. On Slide 6, select the **blue box** at the bottom of the slide.

l. Click the **Animations tab**, and then click **Fly In** in the Animation group.

m. Click **Effect Options**, and then click **From Bottom-Left**.

n. Click the **Start arrow** in the Timing group, and then click **After Previous**.

o. Click **Preview** in the Preview group to see the result of your custom animation.

p. On Slide 9, click the **Home tab**, and then click the **New Slide arrow** in the Slides group.

q. Click **Section Header** from the list of layouts.

r. Click in the **title placeholder**, and then type **Individuals who violate copyright law and/or software licensing agreements may be subject to criminal or civil action by the copyright or license owners**.

s. Click the placeholder border, change the font size to **40 pt**, and then click **Center** in the Paragraph group.

t. Click the border of the content placeholder, and then press **Delete**.

u. Resize the title placeholder until all of the text is visible and is centered vertically on the slide.

v. Save and close the file, and submit based on your instructor's directions.

FYI

1 Presentation Structure and Speaker Notes

CREATIVE CASE PowerPoint will help you create an attractive presentation, but the delivery is still up to you. It is easier than you think, and you should not be intimidated at the prospect of facing an audience. You can gain confidence and become an effective speaker by following the basic tenets of good public speaking.

a. Open the *p01m1public* presentation and save it as **p01m1public_LastnameFirstname**.

b. Add your name and e-mail address to the title slide. Add your e-mail address to the summary slide as well.

c. Print the notes for the presentation, and then view the slide show while looking at the appropriate notes for each slide. Note the presentation plan. Does it have an introduction? Which slides contain the main body of the information? Is the summary slide adequate?

d. Which slides have notes attached? Are the notes redundant, or do they add something extra? Would the notes help a speaker deliver an effective presentation?

e. Which slide contains the phrase *Common sense is not common practice*? In what context is the phrase used within the presentation?

f. Which personality said, "You can observe a lot just by watching?" In what context is the phrase used during the presentation?

g. Join a group of three or four students, and then have each person in the group deliver the presentation to his or her group. Were they able to follow the tenets of good public speaking? Share constructive criticism with each of the presenters. Constructive criticism means you identify both positive aspects of the presentations and aspects that could be improved with practice. The goal of constructive criticism is to help one another improve.

h. Summarize your thoughts about this exercise as a note in Slide 1. Submit your thoughts to your instructor as directed.

i. Save the presentation and close the file.

2 University Housing Office Presentation

You are a work-study student employed by the housing office. Your boss has been asked to present to university officials about the purpose and goals of the housing office. You have been asked to take the administrator's notes and prepare a presentation.

a. Open the *p01m2university* presentation and save it as **p01m2university_LastnameFirstname**.

b. Add **University Housing Office** as a footer on all slides except the title slide. Also include an automatically updated date and time and a slide number.

c. Create a Notes and Handouts header with your name and a footer with your instructor's name and your class. Include the current date.

d. Apply the **Equity design theme**.

e. Add your name and the name of the class to the title slide.

f. Insert a new slide using the **Title and Content layout** as the second slide in the presentation. Type **Mission** as the title.

g. Type **The mission of the University Housing Office is to provide an environment that will enrich the educational experience of its residents. The office seeks to promote increased interaction between faculty and students through resident masters, special programs, and intramural activities.** in the **content placeholder.**

h. Move to the end of the presentation, and then insert a new slide with the **Blank layout**. Insert and position two photograph clips related to college life from the Clip Art pane. Resize the photos if necessary. Close the Clip Art pane.

i. On Slide 4, create a table using the following information:

Dorm Name	Room Revenue	Meal Revenue	Total Revenue
Ashe Hall	$2,206,010	$1,616,640	$3,822,650
Memorial	$1,282,365	$934,620	$2,216,985
Ungar Hall	$2,235,040	$1,643,584	$3,878,624
Merrick Hall	$1,941,822	$1,494,456	$3,436,278
Fort Towers	$1,360,183	$981,772	$2,341,955
Totals	$9,025,420	$6,671,072	$15,696,492

j. Select the cells containing numbers, and then right-align the numbers. Select the cells containing the column titles, and then center-align the text. Position the table attractively on the page.

k. Apply the **Cut transition** from the Subtle category to all slides in the slide show.

l. Add the **Bounce animation** from the Entrance category to each of the images on Slide 6. Set the animations so that they start automatically after the previous event.

DISCOVER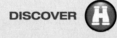

m. Add an additional animation, **Float Out**, to the images on Slide 6. Set the animations so they float out at the same time.

n. Review the presentation and correct any errors you find.

o. Print the handouts, three per page, framed.

p. Save and close the file, and submit based on your instructor's directions.

The Entertainment Lair is a successful retail store. The Lair sells traditional board games, role-playing games, puzzles, and models, and is renowned for hosting game nights. The Lair is a place where gamers can find gaming resources, supplies, gaming news, and a good challenge. The store has been in operation for three years and has increased its revenue and profit each year. The partners are looking to expand their operation and need to prepare a presentation for an important meeting with financiers.

Entertainment Lair Mission Statement

You add your name to the title slide, apply a theme, and create a slide for the Entertainment Lair mission statement.

a. Open *p01c1capital* and save it as **p01c1capital_ LastnameFirstname**.

b. Create a Notes and Handouts header with your name, and a footer with your instructor's name and your class. Include the current date. Apply to all.

c. On Slide 1, replace *Your Name* in the **subtitle placeholder** with your name.

d. Apply the **Thatch design theme**.

e. Insert a new slide using the **Title Only layout** after Slide 1. Type the following in the **title placeholder: The Entertainment Lair provides a friendly setting in which our friends and customers can purchase game equipment and resources as well as participate in a variety of challenging gaming activities.**

f. Change the font size to **40 pt**, apply **Italic**, and then resize the placeholder so all text fits on the slide.

Tables Displaying Sales Data

You create tables to show the increase in sales from last year to this year, the sales increase by category, and the sales increase by quarters.

a. On Slide 5, create a table of six columns and three rows. Type the following data in your table:

b. Format the table text font to **16 pt**. Center-align the column headings, and then right-align all numbers. Position the table on the slide so it is approximately centered.

c. On Slide 6, create a table of five columns and three rows. Type the following data in your table, and then apply the same formatting to this table that you applied in step b.

Year	Qtr 1	Qtr 2	Qtr 3	Qtr 4
Last Year	$37,761	$51,710	$52,292	$58,101
This Year	$61,594	$64,497	$67,057	$112,551

d. Check the spelling in the presentation, and review the presentation for any other errors. Fix anything you think is necessary.

e. View the presentation, and as you navigate through the slides, note that the presentation plan included the mission statement as the introduction slide, included supporting data in the body of the presentation, and included a plan for the future as the conclusion (summary) slide.

Year	Board Games	Role-Playing Games	Puzzles	Models	Events
Last Year	$75,915	$47,404	$31,590	$19,200	$25,755
This Year	$115,856	$77,038	$38,540	$28,200	$46,065

Clip Art and Animation

FIGURE 1.36 Dice Clip Art as Identifying Element ▲

The Entertainment Lair uses dice in its logo. You use dice on the title slide to continue this identifying image.

a. On Slide 1, open the Clip Art pane. Use **dice** as your search keyword and locate the image of dice. Refer to Figure 1.36 to position and resize the image.

> **TROUBLESHOOTING:** If you cannot find the image of the dice, select an image that relates to games and that matches the color scheme.

b. Use the same clip art of dice on the last slide of your slide show. Position the clip in the bottom-right portion of your slide, and reduce its size.

c. On Slide 4, select the **Our first year was profitable box**, and then apply a **Fly In entrance animation**. Change the duration to **01.00**.

d. Select the **Our second year was significantly better box**, and then apply the **Fly In entrance animation**. Change the duration to **00.75**, and then change the Start option to **After Previous**.

Presentation View and Printout

You proofread the presentation in Slide Show view and check the transitions and animations. You print a handout with 4 slides per page.

a. Start the slide show and navigate through the presentation.

b. Annotate the conclusion slide, *The Next Steps*, by under-lining *detailed financial proposal* and circling *two* and *ten* with a red pen.

c. Exit the presentation and keep the annotations.

d. Print handouts in Grayscale, four slides per page, horizontal, framed.

e. Save and close the file, and submit based on your instructor's directions.

Yard Care

You decide to create a presentation for the yard care service you operate. The company name is Green Scene and the company offers the following services:

- Lawn mowing, trimming, and edging
- Aeration, fertilization, and weed control
- Spring and Fall clean-up
- Tree and shrub service

Create a storyboard on paper or in Microsoft Word using the following plan for the presentation. The title slide should give the name of the company and your name. Slide 2 should be an introduction slide listing your services. Details for each service should be provided in additional slides. Create a summary slide asking the potential customer to **Call today for a free estimate!** and include your name and telephone number as the contact information.

Select and apply a theme. Insert, size, and position several images throughout the presentation. Reposition placeholders and modify text as desired. Apply a transition to all slides. Add a minimum of two animations. Create a handout header with your name and the current date. Include a handout footer with your instructor's name and your class. Review the presentation to ensure no errors exist by viewing each slide in Slide Show view. Save your file as both a PowerPoint presentation and as a PowerPoint show using the file name **p01b1green_LastnameFirstname**.

Save and close the file, and submit based on your instructor's directions.

The National Debt

The national debt is staggering—more than \$11 trillion as of March 2009, or approximately \$35,000 for every man, woman, and child in the United States. The annual budget is approximately \$3.7 trillion. Use the Internet to obtain exact figures for the current year, and then use this information to plan a storyboard. Create a presentation about the national debt using your storyboard and the theme of your choice. A good place to start your research is the Web site for the United States Department of the Treasury (http://www.treas.gov), where entering National Debt in the FAQ (Frequently Asked Questions) search box brings up several interesting hyperlinks to information that you can use to develop your presentation.

Do some additional research and obtain the national debt for the years 1945 and 1967. How does the debt for the current year compare to the debt in 1945 (at the end of World War II)? To the debt in 1967 (at the height of the Vietnam War)? Create a table displaying the historical data on national debt. Include your references on a Resources slide at the end of your presentation. Add a transition and add animation to two objects. Create a handout header with your name and the current date. Include a handout footer with your instructor's name and your class. Review the presentation to ensure no errors exist by viewing each slide in Slide Show view as well as by checking spelling. Print as directed by your instructor. Save the presentation as **p01b2debt_LastnameFirstname**. Save and close the file, and submit based on your instructor's directions.

Disaster Recovery

Do you have a backup strategy? Do you know what a backup strategy is? Sooner or later you will need to recover a file that you accidentally erased or are unable to read from a storage device like a flash drive. Backups can restore your files if you have a hardware failure in which you are unable to access the hard drive or if your computer is stolen.

Use the Internet to research ideas for backup strategies. Create a storyboard on paper or using Microsoft Word. Include a title slide and at least four slides related to a backup strategy or ways to protect files. Include a summary on what you plan to implement. Choose a theme, transitions, and animations. Insert an appropriate clip art image. Create a handout header with your name and the current date. Include a handout footer with your instructor's name and your class. Review the presentation to ensure no errors exist by viewing each slide in Slide Show view. Print as directed by your instructor. Save the presentation as **p01b3disaster_LastnameFirstname**. Save and close the file, and submit based on your instructor's directions.

2 PRESENTATION DEVELOPMENT

Planning and Preparing a Presentation

Watch the Set-up Video for this Case Study!

CASE STUDY | The Wellness Education Center

The Wellness Education Center at your school promotes overall good health to students and employees. The director of the Center has asked you to create two slide shows that she can use to deliver presentations to the campus community.

You create a presentation to inform campus groups about the center by downloading a template with a wellness theme from Microsoft Office Online. You modify several of the layouts the template provides to customize the template to your needs. To concentrate on the content of the slides, you use the Outline view to enter slide text and edit the presentation outline.

You create a second presentation for the center using an outline the director created in a word processor. You import the outline, supplement it with slides you reuse from another presentation, and divide the presentation into sections. Using standard slide show design guidelines, polish the presentation by editing the content and the theme.

OBJECTIVES   AFTER YOU READ THIS CHAPTER, YOU WILL BE ABLE TO:

1. Create a presentation using a template *p.810*
2. Modify a template *p.812*
3. Create a presentation in Outline view *p.817*
4. Modify an outline structure *p.818*
5. Print an outline *p.819*

6. Import an outline *p.825*
7. Add existing content to a presentation *p.825*
8. Use sections *p.830*
9. Examine slide show design principles *p.831*
10. Modify a theme *p.833*

Templates

One of the hardest things about creating a presentation is getting started. You may have a general idea of what you want to say but not how to organize your thoughts. Or you may know what you want to say but need help designing the look for the slides. PowerPoint's templates enable you to create professional-looking presentations and may even include content to help you decide what to say. In this section, you will learn how to create a presentation using a template that you modify to fit your needs.

Creating a Presentation Using a Template

A **template** is a file that incorporates a theme, a layout, and content that can be modified.

A *template* is a file that includes the formatting elements like a background, a theme with a color scheme and font selections for titles and text boxes, and slide layouts that position content placeholders. Some templates include suggestions for how to modify the template, whereas others include ideas about what you could say to inform your audience about your topic. These suggestions can help you learn to use many of the features in PowerPoint.

PowerPoint offers installed templates for you to use, or you can visit Microsoft Office Online to quickly and easily download additional professional templates in a variety of categories. These templates were created by Microsoft, a Microsoft partner, or a member of the Microsoft community. For example, you can select Presentations in the Browse Templates section of Office.com. Then you can select Business to download a template for a Renewable energy presentation created by a Microsoft partner, an Active Listening Presentation created by a Microsoft community member, or a Business financial report created by Microsoft. Figure 2.1 shows four PowerPoint templates.

> Visit Microsoft Office Online to quickly and easily download professional templates in a variety of categories.

Project Status Report Sample template

Contemporary Photo Album Sample template

Product/Service Evaluation Business Plan template

Food pyramid presentation template from Office.com

FIGURE 2.1 PowerPoint Templates ➤

> **TIP** Submitting a Template to Microsoft Office Online
>
> You can share a template you have created at Office.com/templates. Click the Submit a Template link in the Community group, and then follow Microsoft's instructions for uploading a template.

When you create a new blank presentation, PowerPoint uses the default template with the Office Theme. To begin a presentation using a different template or theme, do the following:

1. Click the File tab.
2. Click New.
3. Click a category in Home or Office.com Templates.
4. Click a template or theme to view it in the Preview pane.
5. Click Create or Download.

In the Home category, you can select from templates you have recently used, sample templates that were installed with the software, themes, templates you have created, or an existing template on the basis of which you created a new presentation. Click a folder in the Office.com Templates category to locate a specific type of presentation online, or enter the presentation type in the Office.com search box and click the Start search arrow.

> **TIP** Downloading Templates in a Lab
>
> Check with your instructor to find out if you are able to download and save Microsoft Office Online templates in your lab. If not, use an installed Sample template when completing assignments that ask you to download a template.

Figure 2.2 displays the Backstage view of Available Templates and Themes. Your view may show different template options, as Microsoft frequently updates the available templates.

FIGURE 2.2 Template and Theme Options ➤

When you select the Sample templates option, templates installed with PowerPoint 2010 display. In Figure 2.3, the Classic Photo Album template is selected. The title slide for the template displays in the Preview pane.

Preview pane for selected template

Sample templates selected

Classic Photo Album selected

Click to create a presentation based on the selected template

FIGURE 2.3 PowerPoint Sample Templates ➤

Modifying a Template

The templates you download may have custom layouts unique to that particular template. After you download a template you can modify it, perhaps by changing a font style or size, moving or deleting a placeholder, or moving an object on the slide. After you modify the template, you can save it and use it repeatedly. The ability to save changes to a template can save you a tremendous amount of time, since you will not have to redo your modifications the next time you use the template.

HANDS-ON EXERCISES

1 Templates

To promote the Wellness Education Center at your school, you decide to create a presentation that can be shown to campus groups and other organizations to inform them about the center and its mission.

Skills covered: Create a New Presentation Based on an Installed Template • Modify a Template Placeholder • Modify a Template Layout • Add Pictures and Modify a Caption

STEP 1 ▶ CREATE A NEW PRESENTATION BASED ON AN INSTALLED TEMPLATE

You begin the Wellness Education Center presentation by looking for a template that is upbeat and that will represent the idea that being healthy makes you feel good. You locate the perfect template (a photo album with warm sunflowers on the cover) from the Sample templates category. You open a new presentation based on the template and save the presentation. Refer to Figure 2.4 as you complete Step 1.

FIGURE 2.4 New Presentation Dialog Box ➤

a. Start PowerPoint, click the **File tab**, and then click **New**.

b. Click **Sample templates** in the Home category.

  Thumbnails of sample templates installed on your computer display.

c. Click **Contemporary Photo Album**, and then click **Create** in the Preview pane.

d. View the slide show, and then read each of the instructions included in the template.

  Templates may include instructions for their use or tips on the content that may be added to create a specific presentation. For example, Slide 2 includes instructions to follow for adding your own pages to the album.

e. Click the **Insert tab**, and then click **Header & Footer** in the Text group. Click the **Notes and Handouts tab** in the Header and Footer dialog box. Create a handout header with your name, and a handout footer with your instructor's name and your class. Include the current date.

f. Save the presentation as **p02h1center_LastnameFirstname**.

MODIFY A TEMPLATE PLACEHOLDER

The template you selected and downloaded consists of a Title Slide layout you like, but the text in the placeholders needs to be changed to the Wellness Clinic information. You edit the title slide to include the clinic name and slogan. You also modify the title placeholder to make the clinic name stand out. Refer to Figure 2.5 as you complete Step 2.

Modified subtitle placeholder text

Dedicated to Promoting Healthy Lifestyles

Modified title placeholder text

Wellness Education Center

FIGURE 2.5 Edited Title Slide ➤

a. On Slide 1, select the text *Contemporary Photo Album* in the **title placeholder**, and then type **Wellness Education Center**.

> **TROUBLESHOOTING:** If you make any major mistakes in this exercise, close the file, open *p02h1center_LastnameFirstname* again, and then start this exercise over.

b. Select the subtitle text *Click to add date or details*, and then type **Dedicated to Promoting Healthy Lifestyles!**.

When you click in the subtitle placeholder, the text disappears. Begin typing the new subtitle text, and the text reappears as right-aligned text.

 FYI

c. Select the title text, and then click **Italic** and **Text Shadow** in the Font group.

The template's title placeholder is modified to make the title text stand out.

d. Save the presentation.

STEP 3 **MODIFY A TEMPLATE LAYOUT**

The Contemporary Photo Album template includes many layouts designed to create an interesting photo album. Although the layout you selected conveys the warm feeling you desire, the layouts need to be modified to fit your needs. You modify a section layout and add a new slide with the layout of your choice. You also delete unnecessary slides. Refer to Figure 2.6 as you complete Step 3.

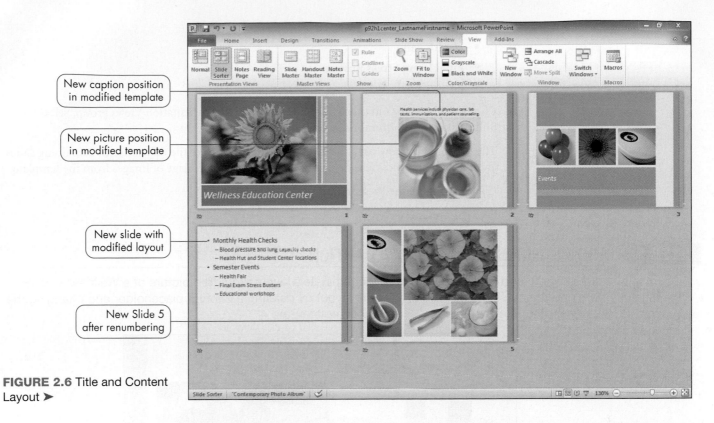

New caption position
in modified template

New picture position
in modified template

New slide with
modified layout

New Slide 5
after renumbering

FIGURE 2.6 Title and Content
Layout ➤

a. On Slide 2, replace the sample text with **Health services include physician care, lab tests, immunizations, and patient counseling.**

b. Click **Slide Layout** in the Slides group, and then click the **Square with Caption layout**.

Note that the Contemporary Photo Album template has many more layouts than the default Office Theme template. The number of layouts provided with a template varies, so always check to see your options.

c. Click the caption, hold **Shift**, and then drag the caption to the top of the picture (not above it).

Shift constrains the movement of the caption as you drag so that the new position of the caption is aligned left with its original position.

d. Select the picture, hold **Shift**, and then drag the picture below the caption.

The template layout is modified to show the caption above the picture.

e. On Slide 3, select the placeholder text that reads *Choose a layout...*, and then type **Events**. Delete the subtitle text.

When you delete existing text in a new template placeholder, it is replaced with instructional text such as *Click to add subtitle*. It is not necessary to delete this text, as it will not display when the slide show is viewed.

f. Click the **New Slide arrow**, and then click the **Title and Content layout**.

> **TROUBLESHOOTING:** Clicking the New Slide arrow opens the layout gallery for you to select a layout. Clicking New Slide directly above the New Slide arrow creates a new slide using the layout of the current slide.

g. Delete the title placeholder in the new slide, and then drag the content placeholder to the top of the slide. Enter the following information:
   - **Monthly Health Checks**
     - **Blood pressure and lung capacity checks**
     - **Health Hut and Student Center locations**

- Semester Events
  - Health Fair
  - Final Exam Stress Busters
  - Educational workshops

h. Click the **View tab**, and then click **Slide Sorter** in the Presentation Views group. Select the **Slide 5** and **Slide 6 thumbnails**, and then press **Delete**.

The presentation now contains five slides. After you make the deletions, the remaining slides are renumbered, and the slide that becomes Slide 5 is a collage of images from the template.

i. Click **Normal** in the Presentation Views group.

j. Save the presentation.

STEP 4 ▶ ADD PICTURES AND MODIFY A CAPTION

You decide to add a slide using one of the template's layouts to add a picture of a Wellness Center room and the nursing staff. You modify the layout by deleting a caption placeholder and changing the size of another. Refer to Figure 2.7 as you complete Step 4.

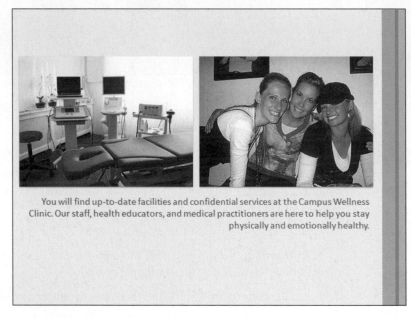

FIGURE 2.7 Title and Content Layout ➤

a. On Slide 4, click the **New Slide arrow** on the Home tab, and then click **2-Up Landscape with Captions**.

A new slide is created. The layout includes two picture placeholders and two caption placeholders.

b. Click the picture icon in the left picture placeholder, navigate to your student files, click *p02h1center*, and then click **Insert**.

The image is sized to fit in the placeholder.

c. Click the picture icon in the right picture placeholder, navigate to your student files, click *p02h1nurses*, and then click **Insert**.

d. Delete one of the caption placeholders, and then drag a sizing handle on the remaining caption placeholder to stretch it to the width of the two pictures.

e. Type the following in the **caption placeholder: You will find up-to-date facilities and confidential services at the Campus Wellness Clinic. Our staff, health educators, and medical practitioners are here to help you stay physically and emotionally healthy.**

f. Keep the presentation open if you plan to continue with Hands-On Exercise 2. If not, save and close the presentation, and then exit PowerPoint.

Outlines

An **outline** is a method of organizing text in a hierarchy to depict relationships.

A **hierarchy** indicates levels of importance in a structure.

An *outline* organizes text using a *hierarchy* with main points and subpoints to indicate the levels of importance of the text. When you use a storyboard to determine your content, you create a basic outline. An outline is the fastest way to enter or edit text for a presentation. Think of an outline as the road map you use to create your presentation. Rather than having to enter the text in each placeholder on each slide separately, you can type the text directly into an outline.

In this section, you will add content to a presentation in Outline view. After creating the presentation, you will modify the outline structure. Finally, you will print the outline.

Creating a Presentation in Outline View

Outline view shows the presentation in an outline format displayed in levels according to the points and any subpoints on each slide.

To create an outline for your presentation you must be in Normal view; then you click the Outline tab to switch to *Outline view*. In Outline view, the presentation is displayed as a list of all slides that illustrates the hierarchy of the titles and text in each individual slide. Beside each slide is a slide number, next to which is a slide icon, followed by the slide title if the slide contains a title placeholder. The slide title is bolded. Slide text is indented under the slide title.

One benefit of working in Outline view is that you get a good overview of your presentation without the distraction of design elements, and you can move easily from one slide to the next. You can copy text or bullets from one slide to another and rearrange the order of the slides or bullets. Outline view makes it easy to see relationships between points and to determine where information belongs. Figure 2.8 shows a portion of a presentation in Outline view.

FIGURE 2.8 Outline View ➤

PowerPoint accommodates nine levels of indentation, although you will likely only use two or three per slide. Levels make it possible to show hierarchy or relationships between the information on your slides. The main points appear on Level 1; subsidiary items are indented below the main point to which they apply, and their font size is decreased.

You can promote any item to a higher level or demote it to a lower level, either before or after the text is entered, by clicking Increase List Level or Decrease List Level in the Paragraph group on the Home tab. When designing your slides, consider the number of subsidiary or lower-level items you add to a main point—too many levels within a single slide make the slide difficult to read or understand since the text size becomes smaller with each additional level. The level of an item in an outline indicates its importance: Level 1 items are main points, whereas level 9 items are less significant in comparison.

Level 1 items are main points, whereas level 9 items are less significant in comparison.

> **TIP** Changing List Levels in an Outline
>
> As a quick alternative to using Increase and Decrease List Level commands on the Home tab, press Tab to demote an item, or press Shift+Tab to promote an item.

On Slide 4 in Figure 2.8, the title of the slide, *Develop the Content*, appears immediately after the slide number and icon. The first-level bullet, *Create a storyboard outline*, is indented under the title. The next first-level bullet, *Input the outline*, has two subsidiary, or second-level, bullets. The following bullet, *Review the flow of ideas*, is moved back to Level 1, and it also has two subsidiary bullets.

Outline view can be an efficient way to create and edit a presentation. Press Enter to create a new slide or bullet at the same level. Demote or promote items as you type to create a hierarchy of information on each slide. Editing is accomplished through the same techniques used in other Office applications. Use the Cut, Copy, and Paste commands in the Clipboard group on the Home tab to move and copy selected text. Or you can simply drag and drop text from one place to another. To locate text you want to edit, click Find or Replace in the Editing group on the Home tab.

Modifying an Outline Structure

Because Outline view shows the overall structure of your presentation, you can use it to move bullets or slides until your outline's organization is refined. You can collapse or expand your view of the outline contents to see slide contents or just slide titles. A ***collapsed outline*** view displays only slide icons and the titles of the slides, whereas the ***expanded outline*** view displays the slide icon, the title, and the content of the slides. You can collapse or expand the content in individual slides or in all slides.

A **collapsed outline** displays only the slide number, icon, and title of each slide in Outline view.

An **expanded outline** displays the slide number, icon, title, and content of each slide in Outline view.

Figure 2.9 displays a collapsed view of the outline displaying only the icon and title of each slide. When a slide is collapsed, a wavy line appears below the slide title letting you know additional levels exist but are not displayed. The collapsed view makes it easy to move slides. To move a slide, position the pointer over a slide icon until the pointer changes to a four-headed arrow, and then drag the icon to the desired position.

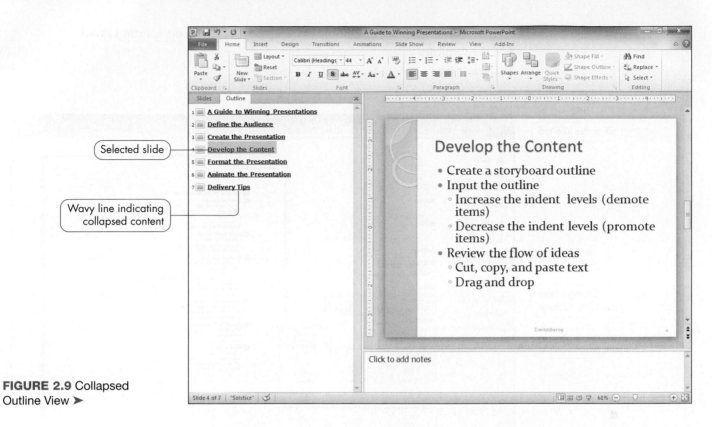

FIGURE 2.9 Collapsed
Outline View ➤

Selected slide

Wavy line indicating
collapsed content

To collapse or expand a slide, double-click the slide icon. Right-click the text following an icon to display a shortcut menu with options for collapsing or expanding the selected slides or all slides. Figure 2.10 shows the shortcut menu options.

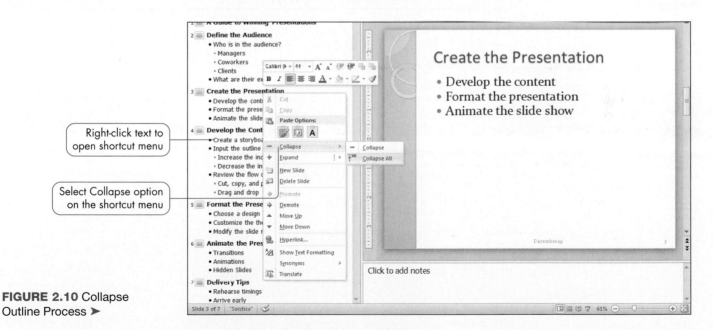

Right-click text to
open shortcut menu

Select Collapse option
on the shortcut menu

FIGURE 2.10 Collapse
Outline Process ➤

Printing an Outline

You can print an outline in either expanded or collapsed view. Figure 2.11 displays a preview of an expanded view of the outline ready to print. The slide icon and slide number will print with the outline. To print the outline, do the following:

1. Click the File tab.
2. Click Print.

3. Click Full Page Slides or Outline (whichever displays) to open Print Layout.
4. Click Outline.
5. Click Print.

FIGURE 2.11 Outline Printing ➤

HANDS-ON EXERCISES

my**it**lab
HOE2 Training

2 Outlines

The Wellness Center sponsors a Walking Wellness group to help campus members increase their physical activity and cardiovascular fitness. The director of the Wellness Center believes that joining a group increases a member's level of commitment and provides an incentive for the member to stay active. She asks you to edit the slide show you created in Hands-On Exercise 1 to include information about the walking group.

Skills covered: Use Outline View • Edit the Outline • Modify the Outline Structure and Print

---

STEP 1 ▶ USE OUTLINE VIEW

Because you want to concentrate on the information in the presentation rather than the design elements, you use Outline view. You add the information about the walking group as requested by the director. Refer to Figure 2.12 as you complete Step 1.

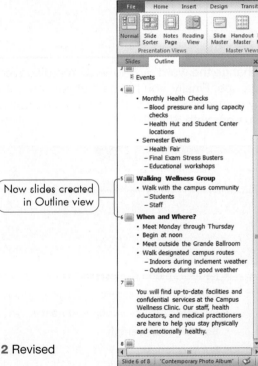

FIGURE 2.12 Revised Outline ➤

a. Open *p01h1center_LastnameFirstname*, if necessary, and save the presentation as **p02h2center_LastnameFirstname**, changing *h1* to *h2*.

b. Click the **Outline tab**.

Note that each slide in the presentation is numbered and has a slide icon. Slides 1 through 5 include text on the slides. Slide 6 contains images only, so no text is displayed in the outline.

c. Click at the end of the last bullet on Slide 4, and then press **Enter**.

The text in the outline is also displayed on the slide in the Preview pane. The insertion point is now positioned to enter text at the same level as the previous bullet point. To create a new slide at a higher level, you must decrease the indent level.

d. Click **Decrease List Level** in the Paragraph group on the Home tab twice.

A new Slide 5 is created, the previous Slide 5 is renumbered as Slide 6, Slide 6 is renumbered as Slide 7, etc.

e. Type **Walking Wellness Group** and press **Enter**.

Pressing Enter moves the insertion point to the next line and creates a new slide, Slide 6.

f. Press **Tab** to move to the next level.

The insertion point is now positioned to enter bulleted text.

g. Type **Walk with the campus community** and press **Enter**.

h. Press **Tab** to move to the next level and type **Students**.

Students becomes Level 2 text.

i. Press **Enter**, and then type **Staff**.

j. Press **Enter**, and then press **Shift+Tab** twice.

Pressing Shift+Tab decreases the indent level and creates a new Slide 6.

k. Refer to Figure 2.12 to enter the information for Slide 6.

l. Save the presentation.

STEP 2 ▸ **EDIT THE OUTLINE**

While proofreading your outline, you decide to change the word *meet* to *walk*. You discover that you did not identify one of the campus community groups. Finally, you notice that you left out one of the most important slides in your presentation—why someone should walk. You edit the outline and make these changes. Refer to Figure 2.13 as you complete Step 2.

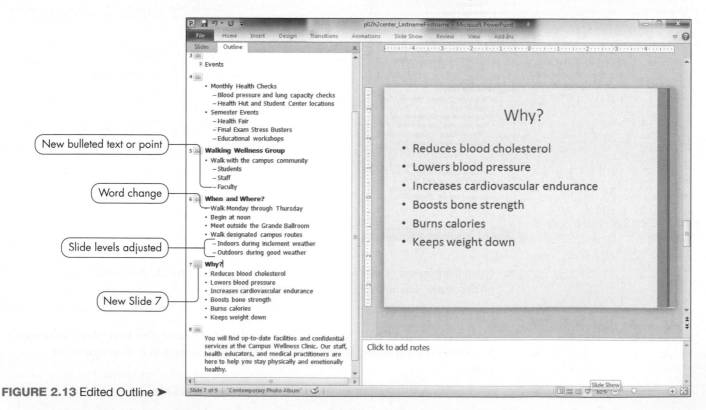

FIGURE 2.13 Edited Outline ➤

a. Select the word *Meet* in the first bullet on Slide 6. Type **Walk**.

b. Click at the end of the word *Staff* on Slide 5 of the outline.

c. Press **Enter**, and then type **Faculty**.

d. Click at the beginning of the fifth bullet point, *Indoors during inclement weather*, on Slide 6, and then press **Tab**.

e. Click at the beginning of the sixth bullet point, *Outdoors during good weather*, and then press **Tab**.

   Slide 6 now contains two levels of bullets.

f. Click at the end of the sixth bullet point, press **Enter**, and then press **Shift+Tab** twice.

   A new slide is created.

g. Type **Why?** as the title on Slide 7, and then press **Enter**.

h. Press **Tab**, and then enter the following bullet points:
   - **Keeps weight down**
   - **Reduces blood cholesterol**
   - **Lowers blood pressure**
   - **Increases cardiovascular endurance**
   - **Boosts bone strength**
   - **Burns calories**

i. Save the presentation.

STEP 3 ▶ MODIFY THE OUTLINE STRUCTURE AND PRINT

The director of the Wellness Clinic has reviewed the slide show and made several suggestions about its structure. She feels that keeping weight down belongs at the bottom of the list of reasons for walking and asks you to reposition it. She requests that the "Why?" slide be moved before the "When and Where?" slide so people are motivated to find out when and where the group walks. To easily move the bullet point and the slide, you collapse the outline, position the slide, and then expand the outline. Refer to Figure 2.14 as you complete Step 3.

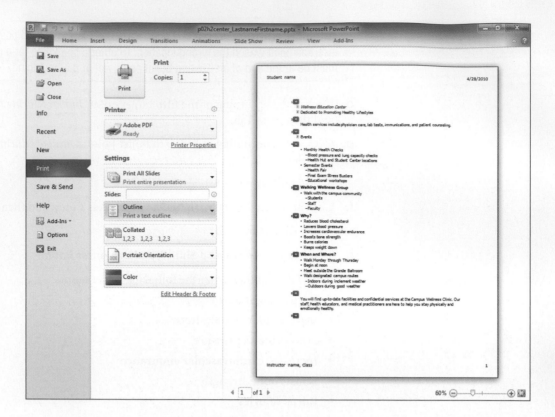

FIGURE 2.14 Expanded Outline in Print Preview ➤

a. Position the pointer over the first bullet, *Keeps weight down*, on Slide 7. When the mouse pointer looks like a four-headed arrow, drag the text until it becomes the last bullet on the slide.

b. Right-click the Slide 7 text, point to **Collapse**, and then click **Collapse All**.

c. Click the **Slide 6 icon** to select the collapsed slide, and then drag the **Slide 6 icon** below the Slide 7 icon.

> **TROUBLESHOOTING:** If you are unable to drag, check to make sure you are pointing at the icon, not the bullet text. Point directly at the icon until your mouse pointer looks like a four-headed arrow, and then drag.

d. Click the **File tab**, click **Print**, and then click the **Full Page Slides arrow**, if necessary. Click **Outline**.

   A preview of the collapsed outline shows in the Preview pane. Because so few slides contain titles, the collapsed outline is not helpful.

e. Click the **Home tab**.

   The Outline tab is once again visible.

f. Right-click any text visible in the Outline tab, point to **Expand**, and then select **Expand All**.

g. Click the **File tab**, and then click **Print**.

   The Outline Print Layout is retained from step d, and the expanded outline shows in the Preview pane.

h. Save and close the *p01h2center_LastnameFirstname* presentation, and submit based on your instructor's directions. Keep PowerPoint open if you plan to continue with Hands-On Exercise 3.

Data Imports

You can add slides to a presentation in several ways if the content exists in other formats, such as an outline in Word or slides from other presentations. PowerPoint can create slides based on Microsoft Word outlines (.docx or .doc formats) or outlines saved in another word processing format that PowerPoint recognizes. You can import data into a slide show to add existing slides from a previously created presentation. This is a very efficient way to add content to a slide show.

In this section, you will learn how to import an outline into a PowerPoint presentation and how to add slides from another presentation into the current presentation.

Importing an Outline

Rich Text Format (.rtf) is a file format that retains structure and most text formatting when transferring documents between applications or platforms.

PowerPoint recognizes outlines created and saved in a ***Rich Text Format (.rtf)***, a file format you can use to transfer formatted text documents between applications such as word processing programs and PowerPoint. You can even transfer documents between different platforms such as Macintosh and Windows. The outline structure and most of the text formatting is retained when you import the outline into PowerPoint.

Plain Text format (.txt) is a file format that retains only text, but no formatting, when you transfer documents between applications or platforms.

PowerPoint also recognizes outlines created and saved in a ***Plain Text format*** (which uses the file extension ***.txt***), a file format that retains text without any formatting. Because .txt outlines have no saved hierarchical structure, each line of the outline becomes a slide. Another alternative is to import a Web document (.htm), but in this case all the text from the file appears in one placeholder on one slide. Avoid saving outlines you create in these formats, but if you receive an outline in a .txt or .htm format, you can create a hierarchy in PowerPoint without having to retype the text.

To create a new presentation from an outline created in another format, do the following:

1. Click the File tab.
2. Click Open.
3. Click the All PowerPoint Presentations arrow.
4. Select All Outlines. (Any files in a format PowerPoint recognizes will be listed.)
5. Double-click the document you wish to use as the basis for your presentation.

> **TIP** Problems Importing a Word Outline
>
> If you import a Word document that appears to be an outline and after importing each line of the Word document becomes a title for a new slide, the Word document is actually a bulleted list rather than an outline. These two features are separate and distinct in Word and do not import into PowerPoint in the same manner. Open the bulleted list in Word, apply outline formatting, save, and then re-import it to PowerPoint. Or work on the bulleted list in Outline view and promote and demote text as necessary to create an outline format.

Adding Existing Content to a Presentation

You can also use an outline to add slides to a presentation that is currently open. The new slides that are created when you insert an outline appear after the current slide. To add slides to an existing presentation using an outline, do the following:

1. Click the New Slide arrow in the Slides group on the Home tab.
2. Click Slides from Outline.

3. Browse to navigate to the folder containing the outline.
4. Click Open.

You can reuse slides from a different file when creating PowerPoint presentations. To import existing slides without having to open the other file, do the following:

1. Click the New Slide arrow in the Slides group on the Home tab.
2. Click Reuse Slides.
3. Type the address of the presentation or Slide Library from which you want to use slides, or click Browse to navigate to the folder containing the presentation that has the slides you want to use.
4. Click Browse Slide Library or Browse File depending on whether the presentation is stored in a shared Slide Library or in your personal files.
5. Navigate to the presentation's saved location, and then click Open.
6. Point to a slide to view an enlarged thumbnail.
7. Click a slide to add it to the presentation, or right-click any slide and select Insert All Slides to add all of the slides to the presentation.

By default, when you insert a slide into the presentation it takes on the formatting of the open presentation. If the new slides do not take on the formatting of the open presentation, select the imported text in Outline view, and then click Clear all Formatting in the Font group of the Home tab. It will format the slides using the active theme. If you wish to retain the formatting of the original presentation, click the *Keep source formatting* check box at the bottom of the Reuse Slides pane, shown in Figure 2.15.

FIGURE 2.15 Reuse Slides Pane ➤

3 Data Imports

The director of the Wellness Clinic is impressed with the clinic overview presentation you created. She gives you an electronic copy of an outline she created in a word-processing software package and asks if you can convert it into a slide show. You create a slide show from the outline and then supplement it with content from another slide show.

Skills covered: Import a Rich Text Format Outline • Reuse Slides from Another Presentation

---

STEP 1 ▶ **IMPORT A RICH TEXT FORMAT OUTLINE**

The director of the Wellness Clinic saves an outline for a presentation in Rich Text Format. You import the outline into PowerPoint to use as the basis for a presentation about the clinic, its mission, and the services it provides to students, staff, and faculty. Refer to Figure 2.16 as you complete Step 1.

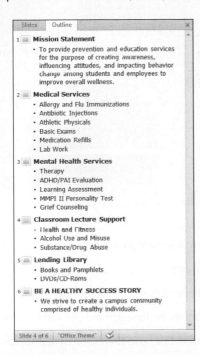

FIGURE 2.16 New Presentation Based on a Rich Text Format (.rtf) Outline ➤

a. Click the **File tab**, click **Open**, and then navigate to the location of your Chapter 2 student data files.

b. Click the **All PowerPoint Presentations arrow**, and then select **All Outlines**.

c. Open *p02h3medoutline*.

The Rich Text Format outline is opened in PowerPoint, and a new presentation based on the imported document is created. Notice that the font is Cambria and the font color is blue, based on the outline imported into the presentation rather than the default template theme of a Calibri font with a black font color.

d. Click the **Outline tab**, and then review the outline.

The Rich Text Format outline retains its hierarchy. Each slide has a title and bulleted text.

e. Create a handout header with your name, and a handout footer with your instructor's name, and your class. Include the current date.

f. Save the presentation as **p02h3mission_LastnameFirstname**.

While reviewing the Wellness Center presentation, you realize you do not have a title slide or a final slide inviting students to contact the center. You reuse slides from another slide show created for the center that has slides that would fit well with this presentation. Refer to Figure 2.17 as you complete Step 2.

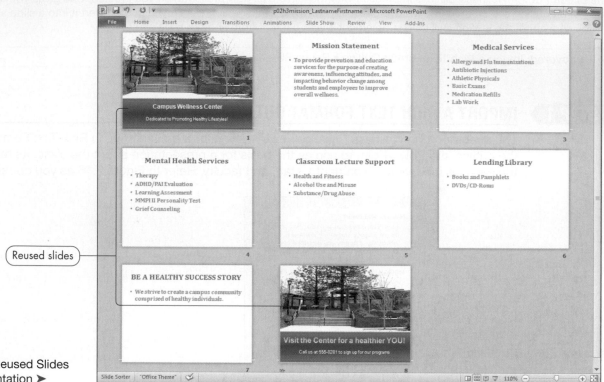

FIGURE 2.17 Reused Slides Added to Presentation ➤

a. On Slide 1, click the **New Slide arrow** in the Slides group on the Home tab.

The New Slide gallery opens.

b. Click **Reuse Slides** at the bottom of the New Slides gallery.

The Reuse Slides pane opens on the right side of your screen.

c. Click **Browse**, click **Browse File**, and then locate your student data files.

d. Select *p02h3health.pptx*, and then click **Open**.

> **TROUBLESHOOTING:** If you do not see the *p02h3health* file, click Files of type, and then select All PowerPoint Presentations.

e. Click the **Keep source formatting check box** at the bottom of the Reuse Slides pane.

With Keep source formatting selected, the images and design of the slides you reuse will transfer with the slide.

f. Click the first slide (*Campus Wellness...*) in the Reuse Slides pane.

The slide is added to your presentation after the current slide, Slide 1. The new slide needs to be in the Slide 1 position to serve as the title slide of your presentation.

g. Click the slide icon next to the *Mission Statement* slide on the Outline tab, and then drag it so it becomes the second slide.

h. Click the **Slide 7 icon** (*BE A HEALTHY SUCCESS STORY*).

i. Click **Slide 7** in the Reuse Slides pane, and then close the Reuse Slides pane.

> The slide show now contains 8 slides. The last slide contains contact information for the Wellness Center.

j. Keep the presentation open if you plan to continue with Hands-On Exercise 4. If not, save and close the presentation, and then exit PowerPoint.

Design

When working with the content of a presentation, it can be helpful to work with the blank Office Theme template. Working in the blank template lets you concentrate on what you want to say. After you are satisfied with the content, then you can consider the visual aspects of the presentation. You should evaluate many aspects when considering the visual design of your presentation. Those aspects include dividing the content into sections, layout, background, typography, color, and animation.

Because the majority of people using PowerPoint are not graphic artists and do not have a strong design background, Microsoft designers created a variety of methods to help users deal with design issues. Using these features, you can create a slide show using a professional design and then modify it to reflect your own preferences. Before doing so, however, you need to consider some basic visual design principles for PowerPoint.

Using Sections

Content organization is an effective design element. Content divided into sections can help you group slides meaningfully. When you create a section, it is given the name *Untitled Section*. You can change the section name to give it a meaningful name, which enables you to jump to a section quickly. For example, you may be creating a slide show for a presentation on Geothermal Energy. You could create sections for Earth, Plate Boundaries, Plate Tectonics, and Thermal Features.

Slide sections can be collapsed or expanded. Use either Normal view or Slide Sorter view to create sections. Figure 2.18 shows a section added to a presentation in Normal view. To create a section, do the following:

1. Select the first slide of the new section.
2. Click Section in the Slides group on the Home tab.
3. Click Add Section.
4. Right-click Untitled Section, and then select Rename Section.
5. Type a new name for the section.

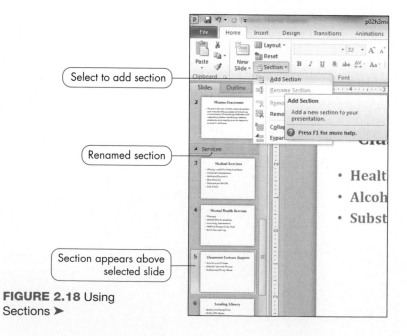

FIGURE 2.18 Using Sections ➤

Examining Slide Show Design Principles

When applied to a project, universally accepted design principles can increase its appeal and professionalism. Some design aspects may be applied in specific ways to the various types of modern communications: communicating through print media such as flyers or brochures, through audio media such as narrations or music, or through a visual medium such as a slide show. The following reference table focuses on principles that apply to slide shows and examines examples of slides that illustrate these principles.

REFERENCE Slide Show Design Principles

Example	Design Tip
FIGURE 2.19 Examples of Templates Appropriate for Different Audiences ▲	• **Choose design elements appropriate for the audience.** Consider the audience's background. A presentation to elementary students might use bright, primary colors and cartoon-like clip art. Fonts should be large and easy to read. For an adult audience, choose muted earth tones and use photographs rather than clip art to give the slide show a more professional appearance. Figure 2.19 shows design examples suitable for grade school and business audiences, respectively.
FIGURE 2.20 Examples of a Cluttered Design (left) and a Clean Design (right) ▲	• **Keep the design neat and clean.** This principle is often referred to as KISS: Keep it sweet and simple! Figure 2.20 shows an example of a cluttered and a clean design. Avoid using multiple fonts and font colors on a slide. Do not use more than three fonts on a slide. Avoid using multiple clip art images. Use white space (empty space) to open up your design.
FIGURE 2.21 Examples of an Ineffective Focal Point (left) and an Effective Focal Point (right) ▲	• **Create a focal point that leads the viewer's eyes to the critical information on the slide.** The focal point should be the main area of interest. Pictures should always lead the viewer's eyes to the focal point, not away from it. Images should not be so large that they detract from the focal point, unless your goal is to make the image the focal point. Figure 2.21 illustrates examples of ineffective and effective focal points.

(Continued)

Example

FIGURE 2.22 Examples of Disjointed (left) and Unified (right) Design Elements ▲

Sans Serif   Serif

FIGURE 2.23 Sans Serif (left) and Serif (right) Fonts ▲

Text Guidelines

• <u>Do not underline text.</u>

• DO NOT USE ALL CAPS.

• Use **bold** and *italics* sparingly.

• Avoid text that leaves one word on a line on its own.

• Avoid using multiple spaces after punctuation.

Space once after punctuation in a text block. Spacing more can create rivers of white. The white "river" can be very distracting. The white space draws the eye from the message. It can throb when projected.

FIGURE 2.24 Appropriate and Inappropriate Text Examples ▲

Design Tip

• **Use unified design elements for a professional look.**
  Visual unity creates a harmony between the elements of the slide and between the slides in the slide show. Unity gives the viewer a sense of order and peace. Create unity by repeating colors and shapes. Use clip art in only one style. Figure 2.22 shows a disjointed and a unified design.

• **Choose fonts appropriate for the output of your presentation.**
  If a presentation is to be delivered through a projection device, consider using sans serif fonts with short text blocks. If your presentation will be delivered as a printout, consider using serif fonts. Serif fonts help guide the reader's eyes across the page. You may use longer text blocks in printed presentations. Figure 2.23 displays an example of a sans serif font—a font that does not have serifs, or small lines, at the ends of letters. It also shows an example of a serif font with the serifs on the letter *S* circled. Decorative fonts are also available but should be used sparingly. When choosing a font, remember that readability is critical in a presentation.

• **Do not underline text.**
  Underlined text is harder to read, and it is generally assumed that underlined text is a hyperlink.

• **Avoid using all capital letters.**
  In addition to being difficult to read, words or phrases in all caps are considered to be "yelling" at the audience.

• **Use italics and bold sparingly.**
  Too much emphasis through the use of italics and bold is confusing and makes it difficult to determine what is important.

• **Avoid creating lines of text that leave a single word hanging on a line of its own.**
  Modify the placeholder size so that more than one word is on a subsequent line.

• **Use just one space after punctuation in text blocks.**
  Using more than one space can create distracting white space in the text block.
  Figure 2.24 illustrates these principles.

(Continued)

Example

Title Text and Bullet Text

- Title text should be in title case and 36 pt or more
- Bulleted text should be in sentence case and 28 pt or more

FIGURE 2.25 Readable Text Guidelines ▲

Design Tip

- **Make text readable.**
  Title text should use title case and be 36 pt or higher.
  Bulleted text should be in sentence case and be 28 pt or higher.
  Figure 2.25 illustrates readable text.

Remember that these design principles are guidelines. You may choose to avoid applying one or more of the principles, but you should be aware of the principles and carefully consider why you are not following them. If you are in doubt about your design, ask a classmate or colleague to review the design and make suggestions. Fresh eyes can see things you might miss.

Modifying a Theme

Themes can be modified once they have been applied. You can change the colors, the fonts, and the effects used in the theme. You can even change the background styles. Each of these options is on the Design tab, and each has its own gallery. Figure 2.26 shows the locations for accessing the galleries.

FIGURE 2.26 Design Galleries ➤

The **Colors gallery** provides a set of colors for every available theme.

Each PowerPoint theme includes a *Colors gallery*, a gallery that provides a set of colors with each color assigned to a different element in the theme design. Once the theme is selected, you can click Colors to display the built-in gallery. Click one of the Theme Colors to apply it. You can even create your own color theme set by clicking Create New Theme Colors at the bottom of the gallery.

Selecting a font for the title and another for the bullets or body text of your presentation can be difficult. Without a background in typography, determining which fonts go together well is difficult. The *Fonts gallery* is a gallery that pairs a title font and a body font. Click any of the samples in the Fonts gallery, and the font pair is applied to your theme. You do not need to select the slides because the change applies to all slides.

The **Fonts gallery** contains font sets for title text and bulleted text.

The **Effects gallery** includes a range of effects for shapes used in the presentation.

The *Effects gallery* displays a full range of special effects that can be applied to all shapes in the presentation. Using effects aids you in maintaining a consistency to the appearance of your presentation. The gallery includes effects such as a soft glow, soft edges, shadows, or three-dimensional (3-D) look.

The **Background Styles gallery** provides both solid color and background styles for application to a theme.

You can change the background style of the theme by accessing the *Background Styles gallery*, a gallery containing backgrounds consistent with the selected Theme Colors. The backgrounds fall into one of three areas: subtle, moderate, or intense. Subtle backgrounds are a solid color, whereas intense backgrounds are designed with patterns such as checks, stripes, blocks, or dots. Simply changing your background style can liven up a presentation and give it your individual style.

Some of the themes, like Angles, include background shapes to create the design. If the background designs interfere with other objects on the slide, such as tables, images, or charts, you can select Hide Background Graphics in the Backgrounds group, and the background shapes will not display for that slide. Figure 2.27 displays a Title slide with background graphics displayed and a slide with background graphics hidden.

Click to hide or display background graphics

Title Slide using Angles theme with background graphics displayed

Title Slide using Angles theme with background graphics hidden

FIGURE 2.27 Background Styles ➤

4 Design

The director of the Wellness Clinic plans to add more content to the Campus Wellness Center mission presentation. To help her organize the content, you create sections in the slide show. You apply your knowledge of design principles to make the text more professional and readable. Finally, you change the theme and make modifications.

Skills covered: Create Sections • Apply Design Principles • Modify a Theme

STEP 1 ▶ CREATE SECTIONS

After reviewing the Campus Wellness Center mission slide show, you decide to create four sections organizing the content. Refer to Figure 2.28 as you complete Step 1.

FIGURE 2.28 Content Divided into Sections ➤

a. Open *p02h3mission_LastnameFirstname*, if necessary, and save the presentation as **p02h4mission_LastnameFirstname**, changing *h3* to *h4*.

b. Click the **Slides tab**, and then click the **Slide 2 icon**.

c. Click **Section** in the Slides group on the Home tab, and then click **Add Section**.

   A section divider is positioned between Slide 1 and Slide 2 in the Slides tab. It is labeled *Untitled Section*.

d. Right-click the **Untitled Section divider**, and then click **Rename Section**.

   The Rename Section dialog box opens.

e. Type **Mission** in the **Section name box**, and then click **Rename**.

   The section divider name changes and displays in the Slides tab.

f. Create a new section between Slides 2 and 3.

g. Right-click **Untitled Section**, click **Rename**, and name the section **Services**.

h. Right-click between **Slide 4** and **Slide 5**, click **Add Section**, and then rename the section **Support**.

i. Right-click between **Slide 6** and **Slide 7**, and then create a section named **Closing**.

   The slide show content is divided into logical sections.

j. Right-click any section divider, and then click **Collapse All**.

The Slides tab shows the four sections you created: *Mission, Services, Support,* and *Closing,* as well as the *Default* Section. Each section divider displays the section name and the number of slides in the section.

k. Right-click the **Support section**, and then click **Move Section Up**.

The *Support* section and all its associated slides moved above the *Services* section.

l. Right-click any section divider, and then click **Expand All**.

m. Click the **View tab**, and then click **Slide Sorter**.

Slide Sorter view displays the slides in each section.

n. Save the presentation.

STEP 2 ▶ APPLY DESIGN PRINCIPLES

You note that several of the slides in the presentation do not use slide show text design principles. You edit these slides so they are more readable. Refer to Figure 2.29 as you complete Step 2.

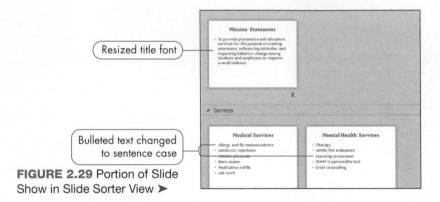

FIGURE 2.29 Portion of Slide Show in Slide Sorter View ➤

a. On Slide 1, select the title, and then change the font size to **44 pt**.

The title font now meets the guideline that title text should be 36 pt or greater.

b. On Slide 3, select the bulleted text, and then change the case to **sentence case**.

The bulleted text now meets the guideline and is more readable.

c. Change the bulleted text in Slides 4, 5, and 6 to **sentence case**.

d. On Slide 4, change the second bullet point to **DVDs/CD-ROMs**.

Always proofread to ensure that the case feature accurately reflects proper capitalization.

e. On Slide 7, select the title text, click **Change Case** in the Font group, and then click **Capitalize Each Word**.

Each word in the title begins with a capital letter.

f. Change the uppercase *A* in the title to a lowercase **a**.

Title case capitalization guidelines state that only significant parts of speech of four or more letters should be capitalized. Minor parts of speech including articles and words shorter than four letters should not be capitalized.

g. Click the **View tab**, and then click **Slide Sorter** in the Presentation Views group.

Note the sentence case in the *Services* section.

h. Save the presentation.

Although you are satisfied with the opening and closing slides, you think the main body of slides should be enhanced. You decide to change the theme and then modify the new theme to customize it. Refer to Figure 2.30 as you complete Step 3.

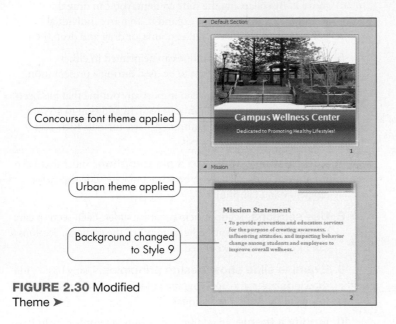

Concourse font theme applied

Urban theme applied

Background changed to Style 9

FIGURE 2.30 Modified Theme ➤

a. Click the **Design tab**, and then click the **More button** in the Themes group.

The Themes gallery opens.

b. Click **Urban** in the Built-In category.

The Urban theme, which provides a new background, is applied to the slide show.

c. Click **Background Styles** in the Background group, and then click **Style 9** (third row, first column).

d. On Slide 1, click **Fonts** in the Themes group, and then point to several Theme Fonts in the gallery to see how the different Theme Fonts impact the title and subtitle text.

e. Click the **Concourse Theme Font**.

The title and subtitle text fonts are modified.

> **TROUBLESHOOTING:** If you are on another slide, you will not see a font change. Slides created from outlines retain the original font. You can select individual placeholders and change the font, however.

f. Save and close the file, and submit based on your instructor's directions.

CHAPTER OBJECTIVES REVIEW

After reading this chapter, you have accomplished the following objectives:

1. **Create a presentation using a template.** Using a template saves time and enables you to create a more professional presentation. Templates incorporate a theme, a layout, and content that you can modify. You can use templates that are installed with Microsoft Office, or you can download templates from Microsoft Office Online.

2. **Modify a template.** You can modify the structure of a template. The structure is modified by changing the layout of a slide. To change the layout, drag placeholders to new locations or resize placeholders. You can even add placeholders so that elements such as logos can be included.

3. **Create a presentation in Outline view.** When you use a storyboard to determine your content, you create a basic outline. Entering your presentation in Outline view enables you to concentrate on the content of the presentation and saves time because you can enter information efficiently without moving from placeholder to placeholder.

4. **Modify an outline structure.** Because Outline view helps you see the structure of the presentation, you are able to see where content needs to be strengthened or where the flow of information needs to be revised. If you decide a slide contains content that would be presented better in another location in the slide show, use the Collapse and Expand features to easily

move it. By collapsing the slide content, you can drag the slide to a new location and then expand it. To move individual bullet points, cut and paste the bullet points, or drag and drop them.

5. **Print an outline.** An outline can be printed in either collapsed or expanded form to be used during a presentation.

6. **Import an outline.** You can import any outline that has been saved in a format PowerPoint can read. In addition to a Word outline, you can use the common generic formats Rich Text Format and Plain Text format.

7. **Add existing content to a presentation.** Slides that have been previously created can be reused in new slide shows for efficiency and continuity.

8. **Use sections.** Sections help organize slides. Each section can be named to help identify the contents of the sections. Sections can be collapsed or expanded.

9. **Examine slide show design principles.** Using basic slide show principles and applying the guidelines make presentations more polished and professional.

10. **Modify a theme.** In addition to layouts, a template includes themes that define its font attributes, colors, and backgrounds. Themes can be changed to customize a slide show.

KEY TERMS

Background Styles gallery *p.834*
Collapsed outline *p.818*
Colors gallery *p.834*
Effects gallery *p.834*

Expanded outline *p.818*
Fonts gallery *p.834*
Hierarchy *p.817*
Outline *p.817*

Outline view *p.817*
Plain Text format (.txt) *p.825*
Rich Text Format (.rtf) *p.825*
Template *p.810*

1. A format that incorporates a theme, a layout, and content that can be modified is a(n):

   (a) Theme.
   (b) Outline.
   (c) Background.
   (d) Template.

2. To create a presentation based on an installed template, click the:

   (a) File tab, and then click New.
   (b) File tab, and then click Open.
   (c) Insert tab, and then select Add Template.
   (d) Design tab, and then select New.

3. What is the advantage to collapsing the outline so only the slide titles are visible?

   (a) More slide titles are displayed at one time, making it easier to rearrange the slides in the presentation.
   (b) Transitions and animations can be added.
   (c) Graphical objects become visible.
   (d) All of the above

4. Which of the following is true?

   (a) Slides cannot be added to a presentation after a template has been chosen.
   (b) Themes applied to a template will not be saved with the slide show.
   (c) Placeholders downloaded with a template cannot be modified.
   (d) The slide layout can be changed after the template has been chosen.

5. Which of the following is the fastest and most efficient method for reusing a slide layout you have customized in another presentation?

   (a) Open the slide with the customized layout, delete the content, and enter the new information.
   (b) Open the slide with the customized layout, and cut and paste the placeholders to a new slide.
   (c) Save the custom slide layout, and reuse it in the new presentation.
   (d) Drag the placeholders from one slide to the next.

6. Which of the following is not an efficient method for adding existing content to a presentation?

   (a) Reuse Slides
   (b) Slides from Outline
   (c) Copy and paste slides from an existing slide show into a new slide show.
   (d) Retype the content from an existing slide show into a new slide show.

7. Which of the following demotes a bullet point from the first level to the second level in Outline view?

   (a) Shift+Tab
   (b) Tab
   (c) Decrease List Level
   (d) Ctrl+Tab

8. Which of the following is not true of sections?

   (a) A slide show can be divided into only six logical sections.
   (b) Sections can be created in Normal view or Slide Sorter view.
   (c) Sections can be collapsed.
   (d) Sections can be renamed.

9. Which of the following formats cannot be imported to use as an outline for a presentation?

   (a) .docx
   (b) .jpg
   (c) .txt
   (d) .rtf

10. You own a small business and decide to institute an Employee of the Month award program. Which of the following would be the fastest way to create the award certificate with a professional look?

    (a) Enter the text in the title placeholder of a slide, change the font for each line, and drag several clip art images of awards onto the slide.
    (b) Access Microsoft Office Online and download an Award certificate template.
    (c) Create a table, enter the award text in the table, and then add clip art.
    (d) Select a Theme, modify the placeholders, and then enter the award text information.

1 Certificate of Excellence

Figure 2.31 displays a Certificate of Excellence, created from a template downloaded from Microsoft Office Online for K&H Design, a small concrete design shop. You are the owner of K&H Design, and you want to present your employee, Jennifer Reed Hulse, with the Certificate of Excellence. This exercise follows the same set of skills as used in Hands-On Exercises 1 and 4 in the chapter. Refer to Figure 2.31 as you complete this exercise.

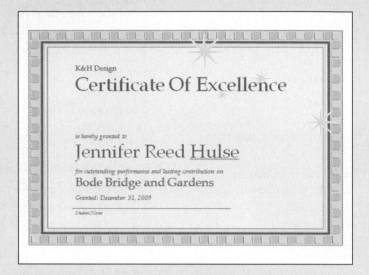

FIGURE 2.31 Downloaded and Modified Template ➤

a. Click the **File tab**, and then click **New**.

b. Click **Award certificates** in the Office.com Templates category, and then open the Business folder.

c. Click **Certificate of employee excellence**, and then click **Download**.

d. Save the file as **p02p1award_LastnameFirstname**.

e. Create a Notes and Handouts header with your name, and a footer with your instructor's name and your class. Include the current date set to update automatically.

f. Select the text *Company Name*, including the brackets, and then type **K&H Design**.

g. Select the text *CERTIFICATE OF EXCELLENCE*, change the case to **Capitalize Each Word**, and then change the font size to **42 pt**.

h. Select the text *Name Here*, including the brackets, and then type **Jennifer Reed Hulse**.

i. Select the text *Project Name*, including the brackets, and then type **Bode Bridge and Gardens**.

j. Select the text placeholder for *Name, title*, including the brackets, and then type your first name and last name.

k. Click the **Design tab**, and then click **Fonts** in the Themes group.

l. Click **Hardcover**.

m. Save and close the file, and submit based on your instructor's directions.

2 Classic Photo Album

You enjoy using your digital camera to record nature shots during trips you take on weekends. You decide to store these pictures in an electronic slide show that you can display for your family. You use the Classic Photo Album template. This exercise follows the same set of skills as used in Hands-On Exercises 1 and 4 in the chapter. Refer to Figure 2.32 as you complete this exercise.

Theme Fonts changed to Austin

Modified title

Theme Colors changed to Slipstream

Background style changed to Style 7

Modified template layout

FIGURE 2.32 Classic Photo Album in Slide Sorter View ➤

a. Click the **File tab**, and then select **New**.

b. Click **Sample templates** in the Home category.

c. Select **Classic Photo Album**, if necessary, and then click **Create**.

d. Save the presentation file as **p02p2album_LastnameFirstname**.

e. Create a Notes and Handouts header with your name, and a footer with your instructor's name and your class. Include the current date set to update automatically.

f. Select the word *CLASSIC* in the **title placeholder** of the first slide, and then type **Nature**.

g. Change the case of the title to **Capitalize Each Word**.

h. Replace the text in the **subtitle placeholder**, *Click to add date and other details*, with **Favorite Pictures in 2011**.

i. Click the **New Slide arrow** to display the layout gallery.

j. Click the **Portrait with Caption layout** to add a new Slide 2.

k. Click the picture icon, locate the image *p02p2tinman* from your student data files, and then click **Insert**.

l. Click in the **caption placeholder**, and then type **The most beautiful things in the world cannot be seen or even touched. They must be felt with the heart.** Press **Enter** twice, and then type **Helen Keller**.

m. On Slide 3, read the text in the placeholder, and then click anywhere in the text.

n. Click the border of the caption placeholder, and then press **Delete** to remove the content. Select the placeholder again, and then press **Delete** to remove the placeholder. Modify the layout of the slide by dragging the picture placeholder to the right side of the slide.

o. Select the **Slide 4 thumbnail**, click **Layout** in the Slides group, and then click the **2-Up Landscape with Captions layout** to apply it to the slide.

p. Select the extra photograph (the smaller one), and then press **Delete**. Select a border surrounding one of the caption placeholders, and then press **Delete**. Repeat selecting and deleting until all caption placeholders have been deleted. Delete the CHOOSE A LAYOUT placeholder.

q. Select the **Slide 5** and **Slide 6 thumbnails** in the Slides tab, and then press **Delete**.

r. Click the **Design tab**, and then click **Colors** in the Themes group.

s. Click **Slipstream** to change the Theme Colors.

t. Click **Background Styles** in the Background group, and then click **Style 7** (second row, third column).

u. On Slide 1, click **Fonts** in the Themes group, and then select **Austin**.

v. Click the **Slide Show tab**, and then click **From Beginning** in the Start Slide Show group to view your presentation. Note the variety of layouts. Press **Esc** when you are done viewing the presentation.

w. Save and close the file, and submit based on your instructor's directions.

3 A Guide to Successful Presentations

Your community's Small Business Development Center (SBDC) asks you to provide training to local small business owners on preparing and delivering presentations. You create an outline and then supplement it by reusing slides from another presentation and by adding slides from an outline. Because the slides come from different sources, they have different fonts, and you change the fonts to match, one of the design principles discussed in the chapter. You create sections to organize the presentation and then polish the presentation by adding and modifying a theme. This exercise follows the same set of skills as used in Hands-On Exercises 2, 3, and 4 in the chapter. Refer to Figure 2.33 as you complete this exercise.

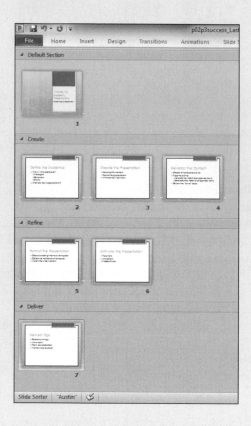

FIGURE 2.33 A Guide to Successful Presentations ➤

a. Click the **Outline tab** in a new blank presentation. Click next to the Slide 1 icon, and then type **A Guide to Winning Presentations**. Press **Enter**, and then press **Tab**. Type your name, and then add the title **Consultant**.

b. Save the new presentation as **p02p3success_LastnameFirstname**.

c. Create a Notes and Handouts header with your name, and a footer with your instructor's name and your class. Include the current date set to update automatically.

d. Click the **New Slide arrow** in the Slides group, click **Slides from Outline**, locate *p02p3tipsoutline* in your student data files, and then click **Insert**.

e. In Outline view, select the word *Winning* on Slide 1, and then type **Successful**.

f. Click at the end of the last bulleted text on Slide 3, press **Enter**, and then press **Shift+Tab** to create a new Slide 4. Type **Develop the Content**, and then press **Enter**.

g. Press **Tab**, type **Create a storyboard outline**, and then press **Enter**.

h. Type **Type the outline** and press **Enter**.

i. Press **Tab** to create a subpoint, and then type **Increase the indent levels (demote items)**. Press **Enter**.

j. Type **Decrease the indent levels (promote items)** and press **Enter**.

k. Press **Shift+Tab** to return to the previous level, and then type **Review the flow of ideas**.

l. Click at the end of the last bulleted text on Slide 5, and then click the **New Slide arrow** in the Slides group.

m. Click **Reuse Slides** at the bottom of the gallery to open the Reuse Slides pane. Click **Browse**, click **Browse File**, select *p02p3reuse*, and then click **Open**.

> **TROUBLESHOOTING:** If you do not see the *p02p3reuse* file, change the Files of type option to All PowerPoint Presentations.

n. Double-click each of the slides in the Reuse Slides pane to insert the slides into the slide show. Close the Reuse Slides pane.

o. Press **Ctrl+A** to select all text in the outline, change the font to **Calibri (Body)**, and then deselect the text.

p. Right-click any bullet point to collapse, point to **Collapse**, and then select **Collapse All**.

q. Drag the **Slide 5 icon** below the Slide 7 icon.

r. Right-click one of the slide titles, point to **Expand**, and then click **Expand All**.

s. Click the **Slides tab** to switch from Outline view to Slides view, and then click the **Design tab**.

t. Click the **More button** in the Themes group, and then click **Austin**.

u. On Slide 2, click the **Home tab**, click **Section**, and then select **Add Section**.

v. Right-click **Untitled Section**, select **Rename Section**, select **Untitled Section** (if necessary), and then type **Create**. Click **Rename**.

w. Repeat steps u and v to create a section named **Refine** before Slide 5 and a section named **Deliver** before Slide 7.

x. Click the **File tab**, click **Print**, click **Full Page Slides**, and select **Outline**. View the outline in the Preview pane, and then press **Cancel** to close the Print dialog box.

y. Save and close the file, and submit based on your instructor's directions.

1 USDA Food Pyramid

You have been asked to help in a local elementary school. The teacher would like you to teach the children about nutrition and healthy eating. You decide to create a presentation about the U.S. Department of Agriculture (USDA)'s recommended food pyramid. (Visit www.mypyramid.gov.) You locate a Microsoft Office Online template based on the food pyramid. After reading the content tips on the template slides, you think they would make excellent speaker notes for you to refer to during your presentation. You move the tips to the Notes pane. Figure 2.34 displays the downloaded template applied to the conclusion slide of your presentation. Refer to Figure 2.34 as you complete this exercise.

FIGURE 2.34 Food Pyramid Revised Slide 2 ➤

a. Download the Food pyramid presentation located in the Available Templates and Themes, Office.com Templates section, Presentations category, Healthcare folder. Save it as **p02m1food_LastnameFirstname**.

b. Create a Notes and Handouts header with your name, and a footer with your instructor's name and your class. Include the current date.

c. Click the **Slide 2 icon**, and then cut the text from the content placeholder on the slide. Click in the notes area, and then paste the cut text into the notes area. As you create each new slide in the rest of the exercise, cut the information on the slide and paste it to the notes as you did in this step.

d. Type the following bullet points on Slide 2:
   • **Choosing the right foods helps you feel better**
   • **Eating a good diet keeps you healthier**

e. Replace the text on the remaining slides with the information in the following table.

Slide	Bulleted Text

4	• Great Grains!
	  • Whole-wheat flour
	  • Cracked wheat
	  • Oatmeal
	  • Whole cornmeal
	  • Brown rice

5	• Very Cool Veggies!
	  • Broccoli
	  • Spinach
	  • Carrots
	  • Cauliflower
	  • Mushrooms
	  • Green beans

6	• Fresh Fruit!
	  • Apples
	  • Bananas
	  • Grapes
	  • Peaches
	  • Oranges

7	• Only a Little Oil!
	  • Olive oil
	  • Canola oil
	  • Sunflower oil
	  • Margarine
	  • Butter
	  • Mayonnaise (food containing oil)

8	• Magnificent Milk!
	  • Milk
	  • Cheese
	  • Yogurt
	  • Pudding

9	• Mighty Meats and Beans!
	  • Chicken
	  • Turkey
	  • Beef
	  • Pork
	  • Fish
	  • Beans and nuts

10	• Provide bonus calories to give you energy
	• Use for:
	  • Eating more of the foods on the list
	  • Eating higher calorie food
	• Eat more than advised, and you will gain weight

11	Delete slide
12	• Use the MyPyramid Worksheet provided by the USDA
13	• Follow the Food Pyramid Steps for a healthier you!

f. Change the layout for Slide 12, the conclusion, to a **Title Slide layout**.

g. Delete the graphic box with the white background that was left over when you changed the layout.

h. Check the spelling of your presentation and ignore any references to *MyPyramid*, the USDA worksheet name.

i. Save and close the file, and submit based on your instructor's directions.

The local senior citizens' center has asked you to speak on photography. The center has many residents interested in learning about digital photography. You decide to create a presentation with sections on learning the advantages of a digital camera, choosing a camera, taking pictures with a digital camera, and printing and sharing photos. In this exercise, you begin the presentation by creating the sections and completing the content for the first section. Figure 2.35 shows the four slides in the Advantages section in Slide Sorter view. Refer to Figure 2.35 as you complete this exercise.

FIGURE 2.35 Go Digital Presentation ➤

DISCOVER

a. Open Microsoft Word, click the **View tab**, and then click **Outline** in the Document Views group.

b. Create the following outline using **Tab** and **Shift+Tab** to promote and demote bullets the same way you do in PowerPoint.

> **Go Digital, Get Creative!**
> - **Your name in First name Last name format**
>
> **Why Go Digital?**
> - **Inexpensive**
> - **Improved pictures**
> - **Instant feedback**
> - **Image sharing**
>
> **Inexpensive**
> - **No film cost**
> - **Free experimentation**
> - **Cameras in all price ranges**
>
> **Improved Pictures**
> - **Image editing with software**
>   - **Remove red eye**
>   - **Improve exposure**
>   - **Crop the pictures**
> - **Free experimentation**
>   - **Take extra pictures for practice**
>   - **Try new camera settings**

Instant Feedback
- Viewing screen

Image Sharing
- Traditional
- Web pages/Online photo albums
- E-mail

c. Save the outline as **p02m2word_LastnameFirstname**, and then close Microsoft Word.

d. Open PowerPoint, click **New Slide** in the Slides group, and then create slides from the *p02m2word_LastnameFirstname* outline. Save the slide show as **p02m2digital_LastnameFirstname**.

e. Delete the blank Slide 1, and then change the layout of the new Slide 1 to **Title Slide**.

f. Review the presentation in PowerPoint's Outline view and note that *Free experimentation* appears in two locations, that the *Instant Feedback* slide does not have enough information to be a slide on its own, and that the presentation does not contain a conclusion slide.

g. Cut the two bulleted items under *Free experimentation* on Slide 4, and then paste the two bulleted items as subpoints under *Free experimentation* on Slide 3.

h. Delete the Free experimentation bullet on Slide 5.

i. Cut the information on Slide 5, and then paste it as the first bullet point on Slide 4.

j. Use the spelling checker to check your presentation, and then save and close the presentation.

k. Create a new presentation by downloading a template from Office.com in the Design slides category. Open the Hobbies folder, and then download the **Photo journal design template**.

l. Open the Reuse Slides pane, and then browse to locate and open the *p02m2digital_LastnameFirstname* presentation you created in the previous steps. Right-click any slide, and then click **Insert All Slides**.

m. Delete the empty Slide 1.

n. Select all text in Outline view, and then click **Clear All Formatting** in the Font group on the Home tab.

o. Apply the **Flow Theme Colors** and the **Essential Theme Fonts**.

p. Create a section between Slide 1 and 2 named **Advantages**.

q. Create three sections after Slide 5 named **Choosing a Camera**, **Taking Pictures**, and **Printing and Sharing Photos**.

r. Create a Notes and Handouts header with your name, and a footer with your instructor's name and your class. Include the current date.

s. Save the file as **p02m2camera_LastnameFirstname**, close the file, and submit based on your instructor's directions.

3 The Impressionists

CREATIVE CASE

The paintings of the Impressionists are some of the most loved paintings in the world. Their paintings may be viewed by going to the Web page of the WebMuseum, Paris (www.ibiblio.org/wm), navigating to the Famous Artworks collections page and then to the Impressionism page. The museum is maintained by Nicolas Pioch and is not part of any official or supported project. Figure 2.36 shows a sample of the completed presentation using the Flow theme and the Metro color theme. Refer to Figure 2.36 as you complete this exercise.

FIGURE 2.36 Impressionist Presentation in Slide Sorter View ➤

a. In PowerPoint, open the *p02m3artists* file, a Microsoft Word outline. Save the presentation as **p02m3art_LastnameFirstname**.

b. Create a Notes and Handouts header with your name, and a footer with your instructor's name and your class. Include the current date.

c. Change the layout of Slide 1 to the **Title Slide layout**, and enter your name in the **subtitle placeholder**.

d. Change the layout of Slide 7 to the **Blank layout**. Move and resize the placeholder so all text is able to be seen. Change font size as necessary—remember the design guidelines discussed in the white pages regarding white space.

e. Use Outline tab view to create a new Slide 2 with the following information:

- **Impressionist Paintings**
  - **Characterized by small brush strokes**
  - **Reproduced the artist's visual impression**
  - **Studied**
    - **Light**
    - **Atmosphere**
    - **Reflections**
    - **Color**

f. Apply the design and color themes of your choice, but make sure that all text is clearly visible. Change fonts as necessary to maintain a professional appearance.

g. Save and close the file, and submit based on your instructor's directions.

Your neighbors in your small southwestern subdivision are concerned about drought, fire danger, and water conservation. You volunteer to gather information about possible solutions and share the information with them in a PowerPoint presentation at the next neighborhood association meeting. In this capstone project, you concentrate on developing the content of the presentation.

Design Template

You download an Office.com template to create the basic design and structure for your presentation, save the presentation, and create the title slide.

a. Create a new presentation using one of the Available Templates and Themes in the Office.com Templates category. Open **Design slides**, open **Seasons**, and then download the **Sunny days design template**.

b. Save the presentation as **p02c1wise_LastnameFirstname**.

c. Type **Conserve** as the title on the title slide.

d. Type the subtitle **Waterwise Landscaping**.

e. Create a handout header with your name, and a handout footer with your instructor's name and your class. Include the current date.

Outline and Modifications

Based on the storyboard you created after researching water conservation on the Internet, you type the outline of your presentation. As you create the outline, you also modify the outline structure.

a. Click the **Outline tab**.

b. Type **Waterwise Options** as the title for Slide 2.

c. Enter each of the following as Level 1 bullets for Slide 2: **Zeroscaping, Xeriscaping**.

d. Type **Purpose of Landscaping** as the title for Slide 3.

e. Type each of the following as Level 1 bullets for Slide 3: **Beauty, Utility, Conservation**.

f. Add this speaker note to Slide 3: **With water becoming a limited resource, conservation has become a third purpose of landscaping.**

g. Modify the outline structure by reversing Slides 2 and 3.

Imported Outline

You have an outline on zeroscaping that was created in Microsoft Word and a slide show on xeriscaping. You reuse this content to build your slide show.

a. Position the insertion point at the end of the outline.

b. Use the **Slides from Outline option** to insert the *p02c1zero* outline.

c. Change the layout of Slide 4 from Title and Text to **Picture with Caption**.

d. Insert *p02c1zeropic* in the picture placeholder.

e. Position the point of insertion at the end of the outline.

f. Reuse all of the slides from *p02c1xeri* to add four slides to the end of the presentation.

g. Insert *p02cxeripic* in the picture placeholder on Slide 8.

Design

You know that the room in which you will be displaying the slide show is very light. You decide to change the color theme to darken the slides, which will increase the slide visibility. You also adjust the font size of two captions to increase their readability.

a. Change the Theme Colors to **Solstice**.

b. Change the background style to **Style 3** (first row, third column).

c. Increase the font size of the title and caption text two levels on Slides 4 and 8.

d. Use the spelling checker and proofread the presentation.

e. Apply the **Fade transition** to all slides.

Sections

To facilitate moving between the slides concerning zeroscaping and the slides concerning xeriscaping, you create sections.

a. Add a section before Slide 4, and rename it **Zeroscaping**.

b. Add a section before Slide 8, and rename it **Xeriscaping**.

c. Print the outline as directed by your instructor.

d. Save and close the file, and submit based on your instructor's directions.

Identity Theft

GENERAL CASE

Import the *p02b1identity* outline and save the presentation as **p02b1identity_LastnameFirstname**. This partially completed presentation is intended to aid you in recognizing the global value of the Outline tab view and how it can be used to modify the structure of a presentation. A combination of slides containing only titles and slides containing content are randomly entered as if they were created from brainstorming. Organize the presentation so that each topic has content under it and so that the content matches the topic in the Title Slide. Create sections reflecting this organization. Create an appropriate conclusion. You may add additional slides, if desired. Good resources for your presentation include the Federal Trade Commission Web site (www.ftc.gov/idtheft) and the Identity Theft is a Crime: Resources from the Government Web site (www.idtheft.gov). Be sure to check the spelling and proofread the content of the presentation.

When you have completed the outline, save and close the presentation. Locate a template to use for the design, and reuse the *p02b1identity_LastnameFirstname* slides to create a new presentation. Apply a theme and modify the Theme Fonts, Theme Colors, and Background Style as desired. Keeping in mind good slide show design principles, you also may modify layouts and add appropriate clip art, transitions, and animations as desired. Create a handout header with your name, and a handout footer with your instructor's name and your class. Include the current date. Print the outline as directed by your instructor. Save the presentation and submit as directed by your instructor.

Digital Film

RESEARCH CASE

You have a bright, creative, and energetic personality, and you are using these talents in college as a senior majoring in Digital Film. You hope to become a producer for a major film company. The Administration of Studio Operations course you are taking this semester requires every student to create his or her own fictional feature film company and to present an overview of the company to the class. This presentation should include the company purpose, the company's history, and past and present projects—all of which you are to "creatively invent." Include a final slide giving the resources you used to create your presentation.

Search Office.com for an appropriate template to use in creating your presentation. Research what a feature film company does, and use what you learn to add your own content to comply with the case requirements. Add clip art, transitions, and animations as desired. Organize using sections. Create a handout header with your name, and a handout footer with your instructor's name and your class. Include the current date. Save the presentation as **p02b2film_LastnameFirstname**, and submit as directed by your instructor.

Florida, My State

DISASTER RECOVERY

Your sister spent a lot of time researching and creating a presentation on the state of Florida for a youth organization merit badge to present the information to her leader and team members. She does not like the presentation's design and has asked for your help. You show her how to download the state history report presentation template from Office.com, Presentations category, Academic subcategory. Save the new presentation as **p02b3state_LastnameFirstname**. Reuse her slides, which are saved as *p02b3florida*. Cut and paste the images she gathered into the correct placeholders, and then move bulleted text to the correct slide. Resize placeholders as needed. You tell your sister that mixing clip art with pictures is contributing to the cluttered look. Choose one format based on your preference. Create new slides with appropriate layouts as needed. You remind her that although federal government organizations allow use of their images in an educational setting, your sister should give proper credit if she is going to use their data. Give credit to the State of Florida's Web site for the information obtained from MyFlorida.com (http://dhr.dos.state.fl.us/facts/symbols). Give credit to the U.S. Census Bureau (www.census.gov) for the Quick Facts. Finalize the presentation by deleting unneeded slides, adding appropriate sections, modifying themes, proofreading, and applying transitions. Create a handout header with your name, and a handout footer with your instructor's name and your class. Include the current date. Print the outline as directed by your instructor. Save the presentation and submit as directed by your instructor.

3 PRESENTATION DESIGN
Illustrations and Infographics

CASE STUDY | Illustrations and Infographics
Mini-Camp

Watch the
Set-up
Video
for this
Case Study!

Your city sponsors youth programs including art, sports, academics, and computers. As one of the youth program coordinators, you are responsible for scheduling the activities held in the high school's computer lab. You receive a request for a mini-camp to introduce students to drawing using computer-based drawing tools, creating infographics, and working with clip art. You decide to teach the mini-camp yourself because you want to introduce the young participants to PowerPoint's many tools for creating and modifying illustrations.

You begin the camp by teaching the participants how to create and modify lines and shapes, how to use shapes to create flow charts, how to use SmartArt diagrams, and how to modify clip art to meet their needs. You also teach participants WordArt manipulation because it is a creative way to enhance text used in illustrations and infographics.

OBJECTIVES | AFTER YOU READ THIS CHAPTER, YOU WILL BE ABLE TO:

1. Create shapes *p.852*
2. Apply Quick Styles and customize shapes *p.857*
3. Create SmartArt *p.873*
4. Modify SmartArt *p.877*
5. Create WordArt *p.881*
6. Modify WordArt *p.881*
7. Modify objects *p.887*
8. Arrange objects *p.892*

Shapes

In addition to text, you can use a variety of visual elements to add impact to a presentation. One type of visual element is a *shape*, a geometric or non-geometric object used to create an illustration or to highlight information. For example, on a slide containing a list of items, you could include a quote related to the items and create the quote inside a shape to call attention to it. You can combine shapes to create complex images. Figure 3.1 shows three PowerPoint themes utilizing shapes in each of these ways. The Apothecary theme uses a rectangular shape to draw attention to the information in the title placeholder. The Oriel theme utilizes circles and lines to create an interesting design. The ListDiagram theme from Office.com uses rectangles to emphasize each concept.

A **shape** is a geometric or non-geometric object, such as a rectangle or an arrow.

FIGURE 3.1 Using Shapes in Themes ➤

An **Infographic** is a visual representation of data or knowledge.

Infographics, a shortened term for information graphics, are visual representations of data or knowledge. Infographics typically use shapes to present complex data or knowledge in an easily understood visual representation. PowerPoint includes powerful drawing tools you can use to create lines and shapes, which are the basis for infographics. Because clip art is created with shapes, you learn to modify the shapes used for clip art to meet your needs. In addition to using the drawing tools, you can enhance shapes by warping or adding effects such as 3-D, shadow, glow, warp, bevel, and others. These effects are accessible through style galleries. Utilizing these visual effects makes it easy for you to create professional-looking infographics to enhance your presentation.

> Utilizing … visual effects makes it easy for you to create professional looking infographics to enhance your presentation.

In this section, you will create and modify various shapes and lines. You will also customize shapes and apply special effects to objects. Finally, you will learn how to apply and change outline effects.

Creating Shapes

PowerPoint provides tools for creating shapes. You can insert a multitude of standard geometric shapes like circles or squares and hearts or stars. You can insert equation shapes, such as + and ÷, and a variety of banners. After you create a shape, you can modify it and apply fills and special effects.

To create a shape:

1. Click the Insert tab.
2. Click Shapes in the Illustrations group.
3. Click the shape you desire from the Shapes gallery.
4. Click the slide where you wish to place the shape, or drag the cross-hair pointer from the starting position of the shape until the shape is approximately the size you want.
5. Release the mouse button.

To resize the shape, drag any of the sizing handles that surround the shape after it is created. Figure 3.2 shows the Shapes gallery and the many shapes from which you can choose. Notice that the most recently used shapes are at the top of the list so you can conveniently reuse them.

Insert tab

Shapes

Recently Used Shapes

Click the Right Arrow
shape to insert on slide

FIGURE 3.2 Shapes Gallery ➤

TIP Using the Drawing Group

You can also access the Shapes gallery from the Drawing group on the Home tab. This group allows you to choose a shape, arrange its order and position, apply a Quick Style, and change properties of the shape. If you have a widescreen monitor or if your monitor is set for a higher resolution, the Drawing group displays individual shapes instead of one Shapes command. If this is the case, click the More button to open Shapes gallery.

Lock Drawing Mode enables the creation of multiple shapes of the same type.

The Shapes command deactivates the selected shape after you draw it once, forcing you to reselect the shape each time you want to use it. By activating the *Lock Drawing Mode* feature, you can add several shapes of the same type on your slide without selecting the shape each time. To activate Lock Drawing Mode, right-click the shape you want to use in the Shapes gallery, and then select Lock Drawing Mode. Next, click anywhere on the slide, and then drag to create the first shape. Drag repeatedly to create additional shapes of the same type. To release the Lock Drawing Mode, press Esc.

A **callout** is a shape that includes a text box you can use to add notes.

An **adjustment handle** is a yellow diamond that enables you to modify a shape.

Figure 3.3 shows a series of squares created with the Lock Drawing Mode activated, a cloud created using the Cloud shape located in the Basic Shapes category, an explosion created using the Explosion 2 shape located in the Stars and Banners category, a Smiley Face located in the Basic Shapes category, and a *callout* created using the Oval Callout located in the Callouts category. A callout is a shape that includes a line with a text box that can be used to add notes, often used in cartooning. Notice that the Smiley Face shape is selected. The sizing handles display around the shape, and a yellow diamond appears at the curved line of the mouth. This yellow diamond is an *adjustment handle* that you can drag to change the shape. If you drag the adjustment handle downward, the smile becomes a frown. Some shapes have an adjustment handle, and some do not.

Multiple Rectangle shapes created with Lock Drawing Mode activated

Right-click shape to access Lock Drawing Mode

Cloud shape

Explosion shape

Drag adjustment handle to change shape

Oval callout

FIGURE 3.3 Basic Shapes ➤

Draw Lines and Connectors

Lines are shapes that can be used to point to information, to connect shapes on a slide, or to divide a slide into sections. Lines also are often used in slide design. Draw a straight line by selecting the line in the Lines category, positioning the pointer on the slide where you want the line to begin, and then dragging to create the line.

To create a curved line:

1. Click the Curve shape in the Lines category of the Shapes gallery.
2. Click the slide at the location where you want to start the curve.
3. Continue to click and move the mouse to shape the curve in the desired pattern.
4. Double-click to end the curve.

As you click while creating the curve, you set a point for the curve to bend around. To draw a shape that looks like it was drawn with a pen, select the Scribble shape.

A **connector** is a Lines shape that is attached to and moves with other shapes.

In addition to drawing simple lines to create dividing lines and waves, you may need *connectors* or lines that attach to the shapes you create. Connector lines move with shapes when the shapes are moved. The three types of connectors are straight, elbow (to create angled lines), and curved. To determine which line shapes are connectors, point to the line in the gallery and a ScreenTip will appear with the shape name.

The first step in working with connectors is to create the shapes you want to connect with lines. After you create the shapes, select a connector line from the Shape gallery. After you select the connector, red squares appear around the shapes when you move your pointer over them. These are the locations where you can attach the connector. Click one of the red squares and drag the line until it connects with the red circle that will appear on the next shape. The two shapes are now connected. You can also connect placeholders with a connector line.

If you move a shape that is joined to another shape with a connector line, the connecting line moves with it, extending or shortening as necessary to maintain the connection. Sometimes when you rearrange the shapes, the connectors may no longer extend to the shape that was not moved, or the connectors may cross shapes and be confusing. If that happens, you can use the yellow adjustment handle located on the connector line to reshape the connectors. Select the connector lines and drag the handles to obtain a clearer path.

A **flow chart** is an illustration showing the sequence of a project or plan.

A *flow chart* is an illustration that shows a sequence to be followed or a plan containing steps. For example, you could use a flow chart to illustrate the sequence to follow when taking a multiple-choice test. Connector lines join the shapes in a flow chart.

The typical flow chart sequence includes start and end points shown in oval shapes, steps shown in rectangular shapes, and decisions to be made shown in diamond shapes. Connectors with arrows demonstrate the order in which the sequence should be followed to accomplish the goal. Each shape has a label to which you can add text, indicating what the shape represents. When you select a shape and then type or paste text into it, the text becomes part of the shape.

A **text box** is an object that enables you to place text anywhere on a slide.

If you need to add text to a slide, create a text box. For example, use a text box to add a quote to a slide that you do not want in the slide content placeholder. A *text box* is an extremely useful object because it gives you the freedom to create and position text outside the slide content placeholders. Text inside a text box can be formatted just as text in placeholders is formatted. You can even add a border, fill, shadow, or 3-D effect to the text in a text box. Figure 3.4 shows a basic flow chart created with shapes, connectors, and text boxes.

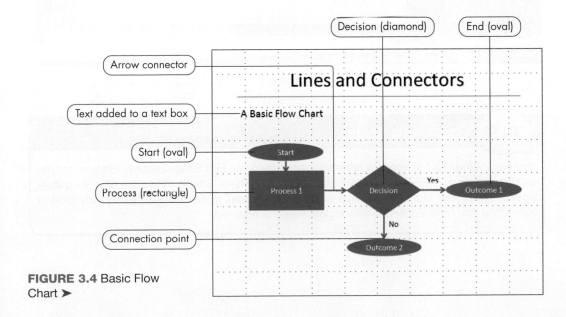

FIGURE 3.4 Basic Flow Chart ➤

Create and Modify Freeform Shapes

A **freeform shape** is a shape that combines both curved and straight lines to create a shape.

A **vertex** is the point where a curve ends or the point where two line segments meet in a freeform shape.

A *freeform shape* is a shape that can be used to create customized shapes using both curved and straight-line segments. Select the freeform shape in the Lines category of the Shapes gallery, and then click the slide. Drag to create curves; move the mouse and click to draw straight lines. Double-click to end the freeform shape. If you click the starting point of the shape, you create a closed shape just as you do with lines.

To modify a freeform shape, select the shape, and the Drawing Tools tab containing the Format tab displays. Click the Format tab, click Edit Shape in the Insert Shapes group, and then select Edit Points. *Vertexes*, or black squares that indicate where a curve ends or the point where two line segments meet, will appear and can be moved if you click a point and drag it. A vertex can be deleted if you right-click the point, and then click Delete Point. Either moving a vertex or deleting it will redefine the object's shape. Figure 3.5 shows a freeform shape with its vertexes displayed. Figure 3.6 shows a selected vertex dragged to a new position. When you release the left mouse button, the freeform will take the new shape.

FIGURE 3.5 Modifying a Freeform Shape ➤

TIP Changing a Shape

You can change any shape to a different shape using the Edit Shape feature. First, select the existing shape, click Edit Shape, and then point to Change Shape. When the Shapes gallery opens, click a new shape. The shape on the slide updates to the new shape, and any style or formatting you have applied to the original shape is retained.

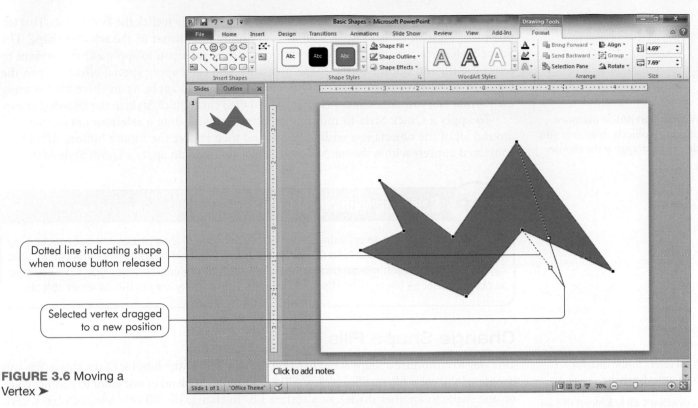

Dotted line indicating shape when mouse button released

Selected vertex dragged to a new position

FIGURE 3.6 Moving a Vertex ➤

Applying Quick Styles and Customizing Shapes

A **Quick Style** is a combination of formatting options that can be applied to a shape or graphic.

A *Quick Style* is a combination of different formats that can be selected from the Quick Style gallery and applied to a shape or other objects. To see how a Quick Style would look when applied, position your pointer over the Quick Style thumbnail. When you identify the style you want, click to apply the style to a selected object. Options in the gallery include edges, shadows, line styles, gradients, and 3-D effects. Figure 3.7 shows the Quick Style gallery and several shapes with a variety of Quick Styles applied to them.

Drawing Tools contextual tab

Quick Style gallery

Light 1 Outline, Colored Fill - Purple, Accent 4

Intense Effect - Red, Accent 2

Subtle Effect - Blue, Accent 1

Light 1 Outline, Colored Fill - Orange, Accent 6

Colored Outline - Black, Dark 1

FIGURE 3.7 Using Quick Styles ➤

To apply a Quick Style to a shape, select the shape, and then click the Format tab. This tab provides you with tools to work with as you modify the format of the selected shape. The Shape Styles group includes the More button, which enables you to apply a Quick Style or to select the fill and outline of the shape manually, and then apply special effects. When the Quick Style gallery is open, click the Quick Style you wish to apply. As an alternative to using the Format tab, you can click the Home tab, and then click Quick Style in the Drawing group.

To apply a Quick Style to multiple objects, click and drag a *selection net* or marquee around all of the objects you wish to select, and then release the mouse button. All objects contained entirely within the net will be selected, and you can apply a Quick Style to them.

A **selection net** or marquee selects all objects in an area you define by dragging the mouse.

> **TIP** Selecting Multiple Objects
>
> If objects are difficult to select with a selection net because of their placement or because they are non-adjacent, press and hold Ctrl or Shift as you click each object. While the Ctrl or Shift keys are pressed, each mouse click adds an object to the selection. When you have selected all objects, choose the style or effect you want and it will apply only to the selected objects.

Change Shape Fills

A **fill** refers to the interior contents of a shape.

A **gradient fill** is a blend of two or more colors or shades.

One way to customize a shape is by changing the shape *fill* or the interior of the shape. You can choose a solid color fill, no fill, a picture fill, a *gradient fill* (a blend of one color to another color or one shade to another shade), or a texture fill. To change the fill of a selected object, click Shape Fill in the Shape Styles group on the Format tab. The Shape Fill gallery provides color choices that match the theme colors or color choices based on Standard Colors. Figure 3.8 shows the Shape Fill options and a shape filled with the Yellow Standard Color.

FIGURE 3.8 Shape Fill Options ➤

If these color choices do not meet your needs, select More Fill Colors to open the Colors dialog box where you can mix colors based on an RGB color model (Red Green Blue) or an HSL color model (Hue Saturation Luminosity). The default RGB color model gives each of the colors red, green, and blue a numeric value that ranges from 0 to 255. The combination of these values creates the fill color assigned to your shape. When all three RGB values are 0, you get black. When all three RGB values are 255, you get white. By using different combinations of numbers between 0 and 255, you can create over 16 million shades of color.

The Color dialog box also enables you to determine the amount of *transparency* or visibility of the fill. At 0% transparency, the fill is *opaque* or solid, while at 100% transparency, the fill is clear. The Color dialog box enables you to drag a slider to specify the percentage of transparency. Figure 3.9 shows the Color dialog box with the RGB color mode selected, Red assigned a value of 236, Green assigned a value of 32, Blue assigned a value of 148, and a transparency set at 80%.

Transparency refers to how much you can see through a fill.

Opaque refers to a solid fill, one with no transparency.

FIGURE 3.9 Color Dialog Box ➤

A **picture fill** inserts an image from a file into a shape.

You can fill shapes with images using the *picture fill* option. This option enables you to create unusual frames for your pictures and can be a fun way to vary the images in your presentation or create interesting frames for scrapbook images. To insert a picture as a fill, select Picture in the Shape Fill gallery, which is accessible from the Drawing Tools Format tab. Browse to locate the picture that you want to add, and then double-click the picture to insert it. Figure 3.10 shows the plaque shape filled with a casual snapshot taken with a digital camera.

FIGURE 3.10 Shape Filled with a Picture ➤

As discussed earlier in the chapter, you can fill shapes with gradient fills, a blend of two or more colors. When you select Gradient from the Shape Fill gallery, another gallery of options opens, enabling you to select Light and Dark Variations that blend the current color with white or black in linear or radial gradients. Figure 3.11 shows the gradient options for a selected object.

Light Variations or blends of current object color and white

Select to remove gradient

Point to Gradient to open Gradient gallery

Dark Variation From Center applied to object

Dark Variations or blends of current object color and black

FIGURE 3.11 Gradient Light and Dark Variations ➤

When you select More Gradients at the bottom of the Gradients gallery, the Format Shape dialog box displays. The Gradient fill option provides access to the Preset colors gallery. This gallery gives you a variety of gradients using a multitude of colors to create truly beautiful impressions. Figure 3.12 shows the Preset colors gallery.

Click to select Gradient fill options

Click to open Preset colors gallery

Click to apply Rainbow Preset

FIGURE 3.12 PowerPoint's Preset Color Gradients ➤

You can create a custom gradient in the Format Shape dialog box. You can select the colors to blend for the gradient, the direction and angle of the gradient, the brightness of the colors, and the amount of transparency to apply. Figure 3.13 shows a custom gradient created for a sunburst.

Click to add an additional gradient stop

Click to remove a gradient stop

Click to select the last color for the gradient

Gradient stop is added

Click to select the first color for the gradient

Drag to adjust gradient brightness

Drag to adjust transparency of gradient

FIGURE 3.13 Custom Gradient ➤

To create a custom gradient:

1. Select the shape you want to contain the gradient.
2. Click the Format tab.
3. Click Shape Fill in the Shape Styles group.
4. Point to Gradient, and then select More Gradients.
5. Click Gradient fill if necessary.
6. Click the first Gradient stop to select it.
7. Click the Color arrow and select the color from Theme Colors, Standard Colors, or More Colors.
8. Click the last Gradient stop to select it.
9. Click the Color arrow and select the color from one of the three color categories.
10. Click *Add gradient stop* to add an additional color if desired.
11. Drag the new gradient stop until you create the desired blend.
12. Click a gradient stop, and then click *Remove gradient stop* to remove a color.
13. Click Close.

A **texture fill** inserts a texture such as marble into a shape.

Selecting Texture from the Shape Fill gallery gives you access to common *texture fills*, such as canvas, denim, marble, and cork, which you can use to fill your object. Selecting More Textures at the bottom of the Texture gallery opens the Format Shape dialog box that has a multitude of options, including a tiling option. A picture can be stretched to fit the shape or tiled so the texture is repeated to fill the shape. Tiled textures have seamless edges so that you cannot tell where one tile ends and another begins. Figure 3.14 shows the Texture gallery and a rectangle used as a background that contains the woven mat fill.

Click to apply
Woven mat texture

Select to open
Texture gallery

Woven mat texture
applied to shape

Select to see additional
choices in the Format
Picture dialog box

FIGURE 3.14 Texture Fills ➤

Change Shape Outlines

By default, shapes have outlines forming a border around the shape. You can modify a shape's outline by changing its color, style, or *line weight* (thickness). You can modify outlines using the Shape Styles feature accessible in the Shape Styles group. You can customize outlines using the Shape Outline options available in the Shape Styles group on the Drawing Tools Format tab. First, select the line or object, and then open the Shape Outline gallery by clicking Shape Outline. The same color options used to change the color of fills are available to change the color of outlines. If you wish to remove an outline, select the No Outline option. In Figure 3.15, the outline surrounding the shape with the picture fill has been removed so that it does not detract from the image.

The width or thickness of a line is measured in *points* (pt), the smallest unit of measurement in typography. One vertical inch contains 72 points. To set the line width, click Shape Outline in the Shape Styles group on the Drawing Tools Format tab, and then point to Weight to display line weight choices from 1/4 pt to 6 pt. To access additional line weight options, select More Lines to open the Format Shape dialog box with the Line Style options displayed. This dialog box enables you to change the line weight using the spin arrows in the Width box or by typing the weight directly into the Width box. You can also use the Format Shape dialog box to create Compound type outlines, which combine thick and thin lines. Figure 3.15 displays lines and an outline for a shape in various weights.

Line weight is the width or thickness of a line.

A **point** is the smallest unit of measurement in typography.

FIGURE 3.15 Outline Weight
Options ➤

For variety, you can change a solid line to a dashed line. Dashed lines make interesting boxes or borders for shapes and placeholders by using round dots, square dots, and combinations of short dashes, long dashes, and dots. To make a line or object outline dashed, select it, and then on the Drawing Tools Format tab, click Shape Outline. Point to the Dashes option, and then click the desired line style. Figure 3.16 illustrates a variety of dash styles applied to 4 1/2-pt lines.

You can add an arrowhead to the beginning or end of a line to create an arrow that points to critical information on the slide. The Shape Outline feature enables you to create many different styles of arrows using points, circles, and diamonds. Figure 3.16 shows the arrow options as well as 4 1/2-pt lines with arrow styles applied.

FIGURE 3.16 Dash and Arrow
Outline Styles ➤

Change Shape Effects

You do not need an expensive, high-powered graphics editor for special effects because PowerPoint enables you to apply many stunning effects to shapes: preset three-dimensional effects, shadow effects, reflections, glows, soft edge effects, bevels, and 3-D rotations. One of the greatest strengths of PowerPoint is its ability to immediately update any shape effects if you choose a new theme. Figure 3.17 shows an example of some of the shape effects available.

> ... PowerPoint enables you to apply many stunning effects to shapes....

FIGURE 3.17 Shape Effects ➤

To apply effects to a selected shape, click Shape Effects in the Shape Styles group on the Drawing Tools Format tab. Point to Preset effects and select a built-in combination, or select one of the options listed below Preset to set individual effects. To customize an effect, click 3-D Options at the bottom of the Preset gallery to open the Format Shape dialog box, where you can define the bevel, depth, contour, and surface of the effect. Figure 3.18 displays the Format Shape dialog box and the Material options for the surface of a shape.

FIGURE 3.18 3-D Surface Options ➤

HANDS-ON EXERCISES

1 Shapes

You begin your mini-camp by having the participants create basic shapes using PowerPoint's drawing tools. You then ask the group to customize the shapes by adding styles and effects.

Skills covered: Create Basic Shapes • Draw and Format Connector Lines • Create and Modify Freeform Shapes • Apply a Quick Style and Customize Shapes • Change Shape Outlines • Change Outline Dash and Arrow Styles • Use Shape Effects

---

STEP 1 ▷ CREATE BASIC SHAPES

To teach participants how to create multiple shapes using the Lock Drawing Mode, you have them create several rectangles. You teach them to constrain the rectangles so they become squares. You have them create a cloud, an explosion, and a callout. Refer to Figure 3.19 as you complete Step 1.

FIGURE 3.19 Basic Shapes ➤

a.   Start PowerPoint, open *p03h1shapes*, and then save it as **p03h1shapes_LastnameFirstname**.

> **TROUBLESHOOTING:** If you make any major mistakes in this exercise, you can close the file, open *p03h1shapes*, and then start this exercise over.

b.   On Slide 1, replace *First Name Last Name* with your name. Create a handout header with your name, and a handout footer with your instructor's name and your class. Include the current date.

c.   On Slide 2, click **Rectangle** in the Drawing group on the Home tab. Position your pointer on the top-left side of the slide below the title, and then drag to create a rectangle.

Do not worry about the exact placement or size of the shapes you create at this time. You will learn how to precisely place and size shapes later in the chapter.

d. Click the **Insert tab**, and then click **Shapes** in the Illustrations group. Right-click **Rectangle** in the Rectangles category, and then select **Lock Drawing Mode**.

You activate Lock Drawing Mode so that you can create multiple shapes of the same kind.

e. Press and hold **Shift**, position the pointer to the right of the previously created rectangle, and then drag to create a square. Repeat this process so that you have one rectangle and two squares on the slide.

You create two squares by constraining the rectangle shapes.

f. Click **Shapes** in the Illustrations group, select **Cloud** from the Basic Shapes category, and then drag to create a cloud shape beneath the rectangle.

g. Click **Shapes** in the Illustrations group, select **Explosion 2** from the Stars and Banners category, and then drag to create an explosion shape on the right side of the cloud.

h. Click **Shapes** in the Illustrations group, select **Oval Callout** from the Callouts category, and then drag to create a callout on the right side of the explosion.

i. Save the presentation.

STEP 2 ▶ DRAW AND FORMAT CONNECTOR LINES

Knowing how to use a flow chart to diagram the processes or steps needed to complete a project or task is a valuable skill. Because the mini-camp has practiced creating shapes, you decide to concentrate on creating connecting lines between shapes to complete the flow chart. You also teach the group how to add a text box to a slide so they can add text when no placeholder exists. Refer to Figure 3.20 as you complete Step 2.

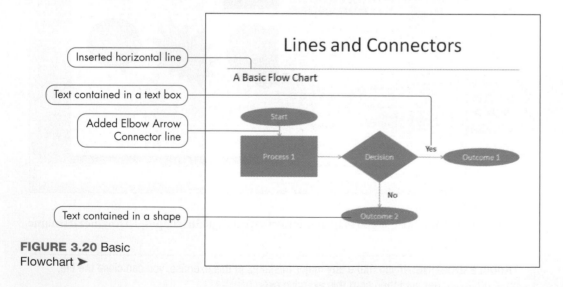

FIGURE 3.20 Basic Flowchart ➤

a. On Slide 3, click **Shapes** in the Illustrations group.

b. Click **Line** in the Line category, hold **Shift**, and then drag a horizontal line between the slide title, *Lines and Connectors*, and the words *A Basic Flow Chart*.

You create a line to separate the title from the flow chart. Because this line is not used to connect shapes, you do not need to use a connector line.

c. Click **Shapes** in the Illustrations group, click **Arrow** in the Lines category, move the cross-hair pointer over the oval on the left side of the slide, and then position the pointer on the bottom-center red handle.

The shape's connector handles appear when a connector line is selected and the cross-hair pointer is moved onto the shape.

d. Drag a connecting line that attaches the bottom-center red connecting handle of the oval to the top red connecting handle of the rectangle below it.

The default line weight is very thin at 1/2 pt.

e. Create connecting arrows that attach the rectangle to the diamond and the diamond to each of the remaining ovals, as shown in Figure 3.20.

f. Select the oval on the top-left of the slide, and then type **Start**.

The text you typed becomes part of the oval shape.

g. Select each of the remaining shapes, and then type the text shown in Figure 3.20.

h. Click **Text Box** in the Text group on the Insert tab.

Clicking Text Box enables you to create text that is not contained in a shape or in a placeholder on the slide.

i. Position the pointer above the connector between the *Decision* diamond and the *Outcome 1* oval, click, and then type **Yes**.

> **TROUBLESHOOTING:** If the text box is not positioned above the connector line between the *Decision* diamond and the *Outcome 1* oval, click the border (not the sizing handle) of the text box, and then drag it into position.

j. Click **Text Box** in the Text group, position the pointer to the right side of the connector between the *Decision* diamond and the *Outcome 2* oval, click, and then type **No**. Reposition the text box if necessary.

k. Save the presentation.

STEP 3 ▶ CREATE AND MODIFY FREEFORM SHAPES

Knowing how to manipulate the vertexes of a freeform shape gives you the ability to change drawings and clip art—a powerful skill! You introduce this concept to your mini-camp participants by having them draw some freeform shapes and then manipulate the vertexes of a previously created shape. Refer to Figure 3.21 as you complete Step 3 (your shapes may vary from the figure).

Repositioned vertex

Repositioned vertex

Shape created using
Freeform tool

Student first name created
using Scribble tool

Shape created using
Curve tool

FIGURE 3.21 Modified
Freeform Shape ➤

a. On Slide 4, click the **Insert tab**, if necessary, click **Shapes** in the Illustrations group, and then click **Freeform** in the Lines category.

b. To create the shape, click to the left of the existing freeform shape. Move your insertion point to a new location, and then click. Continue moving to new locations and clicking to set four new points, and then click the starting point to end your shape.

> **TROUBLESHOOTING:** Do not drag to create your lines, or they will not be straight.

The freeform shape you created consists of vertexes connected by straight lines.

c. Click **Shapes** in the Illustrations group, and then click **Curve** in the Lines category. Click anywhere on the bottom-right side of the slide to begin your shape. Position your insertion point in a new location, and then click. Continue moving to new positions and clicking to set new points, and then click the starting point to end your shape.

The curve shape you created consists of vertexes connected by lines curving around vertexes.

d. Click **Shapes** in the Illustrations group, and then click **Scribble** in the Lines category. Position your insertion point at the bottom of the slide, hold down the left mouse button, and then drag as you would a pencil. Continue dragging to create your name in cursive.

> **TROUBLESHOOTING:** If you release the mouse button, the line ends. If you end the line before completing your name, reselect the Scribble tool and continue.

e. Select the freeform shape in the top right of the slide. Click the **Format tab**, and then click **Edit Shape** in the Insert Shapes group.

f. Select **Edit Points**.

The freeform shape is selected—a red line surrounds its border, and the vertexes appear as black squares.

g. Select the vertex on the farthest right side of the slide, and then drag it down and to the left.

h. Select the vertex on the farthest top-left side of the shape, and then drag it toward the left of the slide title.

i. Modify the vertex locations on the forms you created as desired.

j. Save the presentation.

STEP 4 ## APPLY A QUICK STYLE AND CUSTOMIZE SHAPES

You encourage participants of the mini-camp to experiment with Quick Styles and to modify shape fills and outlines so that they are able to customize shapes. Then they set the shapes to styles of your choice to show they can meet specifications when asked. Refer to Figure 3.22 as you complete Step 4.

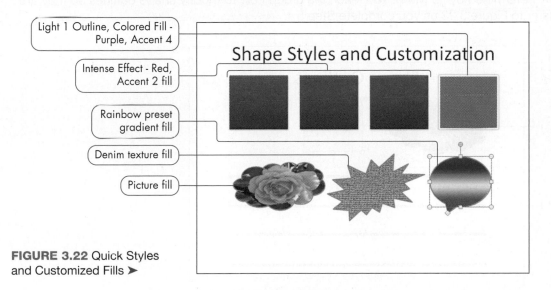

FIGURE 3.22 Quick Styles and Customized Fills ➤

a. On Slide 5, select the far-right square.

b. Click the **Format tab**, and then click the **More button** in the Shape Styles group.

   The Quick Style gallery opens.

c. Move your pointer over the Quick Styles and note the changes in fill, outline, and effects to the shape as you do so. After you are through experimenting, click **Light 1 Outline, Colored Fill - Purple, Accent 4** (third row, fifth column). Deselect the square.

   Live Preview shows the effects on your object as you move the pointer over the Quick Style options.

d. Press and hold **Ctrl**, click the remaining three squares to select them, and then click the **More button** in the Shape Styles group. Click **Intense Effect - Red, Accent 2** (sixth row, third column).

   You apply a Quick Style to more than one shape at a time.

e. Click the cloud shape, click **Shape Fill** in the Shape Styles group, and then select **Picture**.

   The Insert Picture dialog box opens.

f. Locate the file *p03h1rose.jpg* in your class files, and then double-click to insert the picture into the shape.

   The rose picture fills the cloud shape.

g. Click the explosion shape, click **Shape Fill** in the Shape Styles group, point to **Texture**, and then select **Denim**.

h. Click the callout shape, click **Shape Fill** in the Shapes Styles group, point to **Gradient**, and then select **More Gradients** at the bottom of the gallery.

The Format Shape dialog box opens with options for customizing the fill of the shape.

i. Click **Gradient fill**, click the **Preset colors arrow**, and then click the preset gradient of your choice. Make other selections to see different effects, and finally select **Rainbow**. Click **Close**.

Live Preview does not work while in the Preset gallery, so you must apply selections to see the effect of the applied gradient.

j. Save the presentation.

STEP 5 ▶ CHANGE SHAPE OUTLINES

The line surrounding a shape can enhance or detract from the shape and its fill. The visibility of the line is mostly determined by its width. You teach the group how to modify shape outlines so they are effective. Refer to Figure 3.23 as you complete Step 5.

FIGURE 3.23 Outline Colors and Weights ➤

a. On Slide 6, click the cloud shape with the picture fill.

b. Click the **Drawing Tools Format tab** if necessary.

> **TROUBLESHOOTING:** If you see two Format tabs (one under Drawing Tools and one under Picture Tools), be sure to select the Drawing Tools Format tab. Picture Tools opens next to the Drawing Tools because of the picture fill.

c. Click **Shape Outline** in the Shape Styles group, and then select **No Outline**.

The outline surrounding the shape is removed.

d. Select the square with the orange tint fill, click **Shape Outline**, and then select **Orange, Accent 6** (first row, last column) in the Theme Colors gallery.

e. Select the square on the far right that has no fill, click **Shape Outline**, and then select **More Outline Colors**. Click the **Custom tab**, if necessary.

f. Type **255** in the **Red box**, and then type **0** in each of the **Green** and **Blue boxes**. Click **OK**.

This selection creates a pure red outline.

g. Beginning above and to the left of the top horizontal line, drag a selection net around the four horizontal lines.

All four lines have open circle handles at each end indicating you have selected them.

h. Click the **Format tab**, if necessary, click **Shape Outline** in the Shape Styles group, select **Weight**, and then click **6 pt**. Click to deselect the lines.

i. On Slide 3, press and hold **Ctrl**, and then click each of the connecting lines in the flow chart.

The endpoints of each connecting line turn red, indicating you have added the line to the selection.

j. Click the **Format tab**, click **Shape Outline** in the Drawing group, select **Weight**, and then select **2 1/4 pt**. Click to deselect the lines.

All of the connecting line weights are increased.

k. Save the presentation.

STEP 6 ▶ CHANGE OUTLINE DASH AND ARROW STYLES

For additional experience in modifying outlines, you ask the mini-camp participants to modify the dash and arrow styles of lines. Dashed lines are effective in calling attention to a shape, and arrows are effective in directing attention. Refer to Figure 3.24 as you complete Step 6.

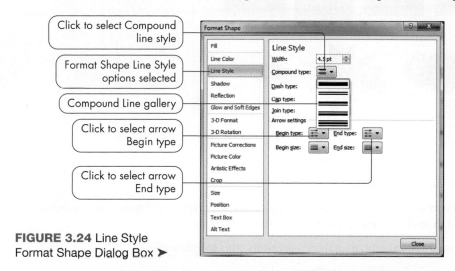

FIGURE 3.24 Line Style Format Shape Dialog Box ➤

a. On Slide 7, click the first horizontal line.

b. Click the **Format tab**, click **Shape Outline** in the Shape Styles group, point to **Dashes**, and then select **Long Dash Dot Dot**.

The line style changes from the default solid line to a long dash dot dot style.

c. Click the second horizontal line, click **Shape Outline**, point to **Dashes**, and then select **Long Dash**.

d. Select the third horizontal line, click **Shape Outline**, point to **Dashes**, and then select **More Lines**.

The Format Shape dialog box opens, providing you with options for creating custom lines, including compound line types.

e. Click the **Compound type arrow**, and then select **Triple** (last option).

This selection creates a compound line composed of three lines of different weights: one thin line, one thick line, and then one thin line.

f. Click the **Width spin arrow**, and then change the width to **8 pt**. Click **Close**.

g. Select the fourth horizontal line, click **Shape Outline**, point to **Arrows**, and then select **Arrow Style 3**.

h. Select the fifth horizontal line, click **Shape Outline**, point to **Arrows**, and then select **Arrow Style 9**.

i. Select the last horizontal line, click **Shape Outline**, point to **Arrows**, and then select **More Arrows**.

j. Click the **Begin type arrow**, and then select **Stealth Arrow** (second row, first column).

k. Click the **End type arrow**, select **Oval Arrow** (second row, third column), and then click **Close**.

l. Save the presentation.

STEP 7 ▶ **USE SHAPE EFFECTS**

PowerPoint provides many shape effects that you can use for emphasis. You ask the participants to apply effects to shapes so they become familiar with the options available. Refer to Figure 3.25 as you complete Step 7.

FIGURE 3.25 Shape Effects ➤

a. On Slide 8, click **Rectangle 1**.

b. Click the **Format tab**, if necessary, click **Shape Effects** in the Shape Styles group, point to **Preset**, and then click **Preset 7** (second row, third column).

   Preset 7 combines a bevel type, a depth, contours, and a surface effect.

c. Select the number **1**, and then type **Preset** to label the shape with the shape effect you applied.

d. Select **Rectangle 2**, click **Shape Effects** in the Shape Styles group, point to **Shadow**, and then click **Offset Diagonal Top Right** (third row, first column in the Outer category). Replace *2* with the word **Shadow**.

   The Offset Diagonal option applies a 4 pt soft shadow to the top right of the rectangle.

e. Select **Rectangle 3**, click **Shape Effects**, point to **Reflection**, and then click **Tight Reflection, touching** (first row, first column in the Reflection Variations group). Replace *3* with the word **Reflection**.

f. Select **Rectangle 4**, click **Shape Effects**, point to **Glow**, and then click **Red, 11 pt glow, Accent color 2** (third row, second column). Replace *4* with the word **Glow**.

g. Continue to use the Shape Effects options to apply effects to the remaining shapes, as indicated in the following table:

Shape	Effect and Name	Style
Cloud	Soft Edges	10 Point
Explosion	Bevel	Soft Round
Callout	3-D Rotation	Off Axis 1 Top (Parallel category)

h. Save the presentation, close the file, and exit PowerPoint if you do not want to continue with the next exercise at this time.

SmartArt and WordArt

Diagrams are infographics used to illustrate concepts and processes. PowerPoint includes a feature to create eye-catching diagrams: SmartArt. Attention is drawn to an infographic using text created by another eye-catching PowerPoint feature: WordArt. In this section, you will create and modify SmartArt diagrams and WordArt text.

Creating SmartArt

A **SmartArt** diagram presents information visually to effectively communicate a message.

The *SmartArt* feature enables you to create a diagram and to enter the text of your message in one of many existing layouts. The resulting illustration is professional looking and complements the theme you selected. You can also convert existing text to SmartArt, creating a visual representation of your information. Figure 3.26 compares a text-based slide in the common bullet format to a second slide showing the same information converted to a SmartArt diagram. The arrows and colors in the SmartArt diagram make it easy for the viewer to understand the message and remember the cycle. It is especially effective when you add animation to each step.

> The arrows and colors in the SmartArt diagram make it easy for the viewer to understand the message....

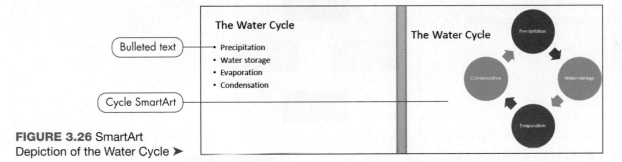

FIGURE 3.26 SmartArt Depiction of the Water Cycle ➤

A SmartArt diagram creates a layout for your information, provides a pane for quickly entering information, automatically sizes shapes and text, and gives you the ability to switch between layouts, making it easy to choose the most effective layout. Some layouts can be used for any type of information and are designed to be visually attractive, while other layouts are created specifically for a certain type of information. SmartArt types include options for presenting lists of information in ordered (steps to complete a task) or unordered (features of a product) formats.

To create a SmartArt diagram, choose a diagram type that fits your message. The SmartArt gallery has nine different categories of diagrams: List, Process, Cycle, Hierarchy, Relationship, Matrix, Pyramid, Picture, and Office.com. At the top of the list of categories is All, which you can click to display the choices from all categories. Each category includes a description of the type of information appropriate for the layouts in that category. The following Reference table shows the SmartArt categories and their purposes.

REFERENCE   SmartArt Diagram

Type	Purpose	Sample SmartArt
List	Use to show nonsequential information. For example: a list of items to be checked on a roof each year.	Flashing Shingles Soffits
Process	Use to show steps in a process or a timeline. For example: the steps to take to wash a car.	Hose › Sponge › Rinse
Cycle	Use to show a continual process. For example: the recurring business cycle.	Expansion / Downturn / Recession / Recovery
Hierarchy	Use to show a decision tree, organization chart, or pedigree. For example: a pedigree chart showing the parents of an individual.	Reed J. Olsen — Ivan Olsen / Gladys Jones
Relationship	Use to illustrate connections. For example: the connections among outdoor activities.	Camping / Hiking / Fishing

(Continued)

Type	Purpose	Sample SmartArt
Matrix	Use to show how parts relate to a whole. For example: the Keirsey Temperament Theory of four groups describing human behavior.	
Pyramid	Use to show proportional relationships with the largest component on the top or bottom. For example: an ecology chart.	
Picture	Use to show nonsequential or grouped blocks of information. Maximizes both horizontal and vertical display space for shapes.	
Office.com	Miscellaneous shapes for showing blocks of information.	

Figure 3.27 shows the Choose a SmartArt Graphic dialog box. The pane on the left side shows the types of SmartArt diagrams available. Each type of diagram includes subtypes that are displayed in the center pane. Clicking one of the subtypes enlarges the selected graphic and displays it in the preview pane on the right side. The preview pane describes purposes for which the SmartArt subtype can be used effectively. Some of the descriptions include tips for the type of text to enter.

Basic Cycle subtype selected

Cycle SmartArt graphic selected

Preview Pane displaying description

FIGURE 3.27 SmartArt Gallery ➤

To create a SmartArt diagram:

1. Click the Insert tab.
2. Click SmartArt in the Illustrations group.
3. Click the type of SmartArt diagram you want in the left pane.
4. Click the SmartArt subtype you want in the center pane.
5. Preview the selected SmartArt and subtype in the right pane.
6. Click OK.

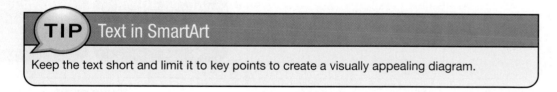

TIP Text in SmartArt

Keep the text short and limit it to key points to create a visually appealing diagram.

A **Text pane** is a pane for text entry that opens when you select a SmartArt diagram.

Once you select the SmartArt diagram type and the subtype, a **Text pane** opens in which you can enter text. If the Text pane does not open, click Text Pane in the Create Graphic group on the SmartArt Tools Design tab. The Text pane works like an outline—enter a line of text, press Enter, and then press Tab or Shift+Tab to increase or decrease the indent level. The font size will decrease to fit text inside the shape, or the shape may grow to fit the text, depending on the size and number of shapes in your SmartArt diagram. The layout accommodates additional shapes as you enter text unless the type of shape is designed for a specific number of shapes, such as the Relationship Counterbalance Arrows layout, which is designed to show two opposing ideas. If you choose a diagram with more shapes than you need, you may need to delete the extra shapes; then PowerPoint will automatically rearrange the shapes to eliminate any blank space. Figure 3.28 shows text entered into the Text pane for a Basic Cycle SmartArt diagram. Because five lines of text were entered, five shapes were created.

Text pane

Bullet point

Shape created for bullet point

FIGURE 3.28 SmartArt Text Pane ➤

Modifying SmartArt

You can modify SmartArt diagrams with the same tools used for other shapes and text boxes. You can reposition or resize a SmartArt diagram by dragging its borders. You also can modify SmartArt text in the Text pane just as if it is in a placeholder, or you can modify the text in the shape itself. If you need an additional shape, click an existing shape in the diagram, position your insertion point in the Text pane at the beginning of the text where you want to add a shape, type the text, and then press Enter.

An alternative method for adding shapes is to use the Add Shape command. To use the Add Shape command, do the following:

1. Click an existing shape in the SmartArt diagram.
2. Click the SmartArt Tools Design tab.
3. Click the Add Shape arrow in the Create Graphic group.
4. Select Add Shape After, Add Shape Before, Add Shape Above, or Add Shape Below.

SmartArt diagrams have two galleries used to enhance the appearance of the diagram, both of which are located under the SmartArt Tools Design tab in the SmartArt Styles group. One gallery changes colors, and the other gallery applies a combination of special effects.

Change SmartArt Theme Colors

To change the color scheme of your SmartArt diagram, click Change Colors to display the Colors gallery (see Figure 3.29). The gallery contains Primary Theme Colors, Colorful, and Accent color schemes. Click a color variation to apply it to the SmartArt diagram.

FIGURE 3.29 SmartArt Theme Color Options ➤

Use Quick Styles with SmartArt

After creating the diagram, you can use Quick Styles to adjust the style to match other styles you have used in your presentation or to make the diagram easier to understand. To apply a Quick Style to a SmartArt diagram, click the diagram, and then click the Quick Style from the SmartArt Styles gallery. To see the complete gallery, click the More button in the SmartArt Styles group on the SmartArt Tools Design tab. The gallery opens and displays simple combinations of special effects, such as shadows, gradients, and 3-D effects that combine perspectives and surface styles. Figure 3.30 displays the SmartArt Quick Styles gallery.

FIGURE 3.30 SmartArt Quick Styles Gallery ➤

Change the Layout

After creating a SmartArt diagram, you may find the layout needs adjusting. For example, as you enter text, PowerPoint reduces the size of the font. If you enter too much text, the font size becomes too small. Figure 3.31 shows a Hierarchy diagram displaying the relationship between the Mesozoic Era and its periods, along with the types of mammals and dinosaurs that lived during the period. To allow the text to fit in the shapes of the diagram, PowerPoint reduced the font size to 10 pt. Even projected on a screen, this text would be unreadable for most audience members.

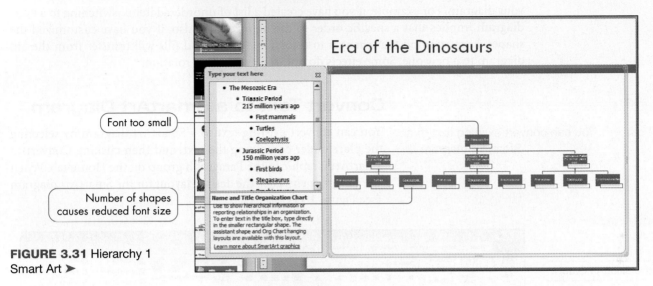

FIGURE 3.31 Hierarchy 1 Smart Art ➤

By adjusting the layout, you can make the Mesozoic Era diagram easier to read. First, select the SmartArt diagram, and then click the SmartArt Tools Design tab. Click the More button in the Layouts group to display the Layouts gallery. Layouts use combinations of effects such as shadowing, fills, box shapes and borders, and orientation, whether the layout is horizontally or vertically placed on the slide. Figure 3.32 shows the Mesozoic information in a Hierarchy List diagram that uses a vertical orientation.

FIGURE 3.32 Hierarchy List Smart Art ➤

Change SmartArt Type

You can change the SmartArt diagram type if you decide a different layout would be better. The process is the same as changing the SmartArt layout. To change the SmartArt diagram type, click to select the SmartArt diagram. Click the More button in the Layouts group on the SmartArt Tools Design tab, and then click More Layouts. The Choose a SmartArt Graphic gallery opens, displaying all the layouts grouped by category. Click the type and layout you desire.

Changing diagram types alters the layout, which may affect the audience's perception of your diagram. For example, if you have created a list of unordered items, switching to a cycle diagram implies that a specific order to the items exists. Also, if you have customized the shapes, keep in mind that changes to colors, line styles, and fills will transfer from the old diagram to a new one. Some effects do not transfer, such as rotation.

Convert Text to a SmartArt Diagram

You can convert existing text to a SmartArt diagram....

You can convert existing text to a SmartArt diagram by selecting the placeholder containing the text, and then clicking Convert to SmartArt Graphic in the Paragraph group on the Home tab. When the gallery opens, click the desired layout for the SmartArt diagram (see Figure 3.33).

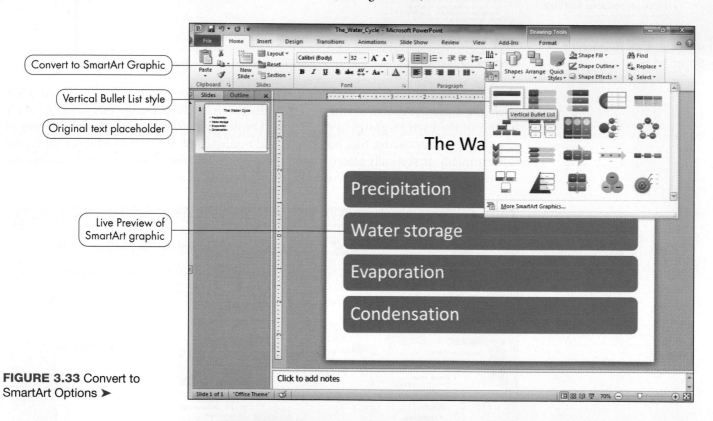

Convert to SmartArt Graphic

Vertical Bullet List style

Original text placeholder

Live Preview of SmartArt graphic

FIGURE 3.33 Convert to SmartArt Options ➤

TIP Converting Text to SmartArt Using a Shortcut

To quickly convert text to a SmartArt graphic, select the text, right-click, and then select Convert to SmartArt. The Convert to SmartArt gallery opens so you can select a SmartArt style.

Creating WordArt

WordArt is text that has a decorative effect applied.

WordArt is text that uses special effects based on styles in the WordArt gallery to call attention to the text. In WordArt, special effects apply to the text itself, not to the shape surrounding the text. For example, in a WordArt graphic the text would have a 3-D reflection rather than the box surrounding the text. By applying special effects, such as curves or waves, directly to the text, you can create text that emphasizes the information for your audience.

The WordArt gallery has a variety of text styles to choose from, as well as the option to change individual settings or elements to modify the style. You can convert existing text to WordArt text, or you can create a WordArt object and then enter text.

To create WordArt:

1. Click the Insert tab.
2. Click WordArt in the Text group.
3. Click the WordArt style of your choice.
4. Enter your text in the WordArt placeholder.

To convert existing text to a WordArt graphic:

1. Select the text to convert to WordArt text.
2. Click the More button in the WordArt Styles group on the Format tab.
3. Click the WordArt style of your choice.

Modifying WordArt

You can change the style of a WordArt object by clicking a Quick Style located in the WordArt Styles group on the Format tab. Alternatively, you can modify the individual elements of the WordArt by clicking Text Fill, Text Outline, or Text Effects in the WordArt Styles group. WordArt Text Effects includes a unique Transform option. Transform can rotate the WordArt text around a path or add a warp to stretch, angle, or bloat letters. Figure 3.34 shows the WordArt gallery options and Figure 3.35 shows the warp options available in the WordArt Transform category.

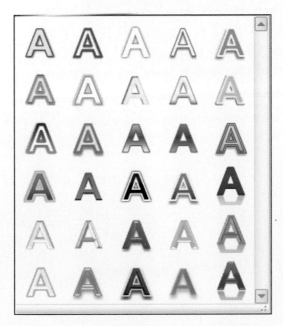

FIGURE 3.34 WordArt Quick Styles Gallery ➤

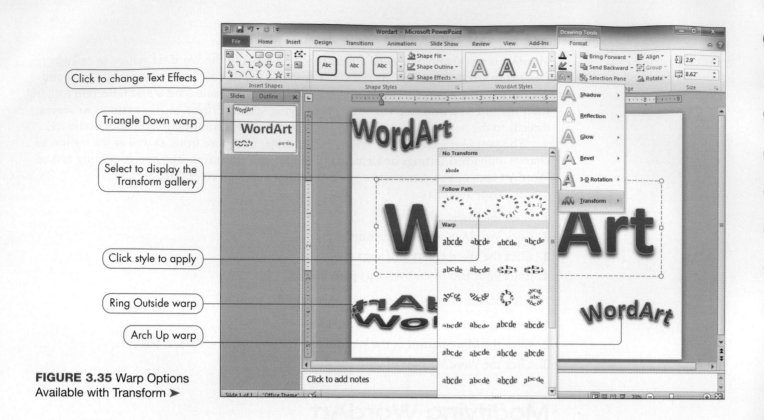

Click to change Text Effects

Triangle Down warp

Select to display the Transform gallery

Click style to apply

Ring Outside warp

Arch Up warp

FIGURE 3.35 Warp Options Available with Transform ➤

HANDS-ON EXERCISES

my**it**lab
HOE2 Training

2 SmartArt and WordArt

To teach your mini-camp participants how to work with SmartArt and WordArt, you choose to have the group work with a presentation about a process—the water cycle. To make the slide show interesting, you have included fun, interesting water facts.

Skills covered: Create SmartArt • Modify a SmartArt Diagram • Change SmartArt Layout • Create and Modify WordArt

---

STEP 1 ▸ CREATE SMARTART

A SmartArt diagram is perfect for introducing the concept of the water cycle and is an example of a simple infographic explaining a complex concept. You teach your students to diagram using PowerPoint's SmartArt feature. Refer to Figure 3.36 as you complete Step 1.

FIGURE 3.36 Basic Cycle SmartArt ➤

a. Open the *p03h2water* presentation and save it as **p03h2water_LastnameFirstname**.

b. On Slide 1, replace *First Name Last Name* with your name. Create a handout header with your name, and a handout footer with your instructor's name and your class. Include the current date.

c. On Slide 3, click the **Insert tab**, and then click **SmartArt** in the Illustrations group.

   The Choose a SmartArt Graphic dialog box opens.

d. Click **Cycle**, click the subtype **Basic Cycle**, and then click **OK**.

   The Text pane opens with the insertion point in the first bullet location so that you can enter the text for the first cycle shape.

> **TROUBLESHOOTING:** If the Text pane is not displayed, click Text Pane in the Create Graphic group, or click the arrows on the left side of the SmartArt boundary.

e. Type **Precipitation**.

As you type, the font size for the text gets smaller so the text fits in the shape.

f. Press ↓ to move to the second bullet, and then type **Water Storage**. Add two more bullet points: **Evaporation** and **Condensation**.

g. Press ↓ to move to the blank bullet point, and then press **Backspace**.

The extra shape in the Basic Cycle SmartArt is removed.

h. Click the **Close button** on the top right of the Text pane to close it.

i. Drag the SmartArt object down so that it does not sit on the blue border.

j. Save the presentation.

STEP 2 ▶ MODIFY A SMARTART DIAGRAM

You need to modify the structure of the SmartArt diagram because a step in the cycle was omitted. The diagram could be enhanced with a color style change. You teach your participants these skills. Refer to Figure 3.37 as you complete Step 2.

FIGURE 3.37 Modified SmartArt ➤

a. Click the **Precipitation shape**, and then click the **SmartArt Tools Design tab**, if necessary.

b. Click the **Add Shape arrow** in the Create Graphic group, and then select **Add Shape After**.

You have added a new shape after *Precipitation* and before *Water Storage*.

> **TROUBLESHOOTING:** If you had clicked Add Shape, you would have automatically added a shape after the selected shape. Using the Add Shape arrow gives you a choice of adding before or after.

c. Type **Surface Runoff** in the new shape.

d. Click the SmartArt border to select all the shapes in the SmartArt diagram, click **Change Colors** in the SmartArt Styles group, and then click **Dark 2 Fill** in the Primary Theme Colors category.

e. Click the **More button** in the SmartArt Styles group, and then move the pointer over the styles.

Live Preview shows the impact each style has on the text in the SmartArt diagram.

f. Click **Cartoon** in the 3-D category (first row, third column).

This choice makes the text readable and enhances the appearance of the SmartArt diagram.

g. Save the presentation.

STEP 3 ▶ ## CHANGE SMARTART LAYOUT

Many different layouts are available for SmartArt diagrams, and you teach the mini-camp group that for an infographic to be effective, it must be understood quickly. You ask the group to note the reduced font size on the hierarchy SmartArt showing the Era of the Dinosaurs, The Mesozoic Era. You teach them to change the layout of the SmartArt to make it more effective. Refer to Figure 3.38 as you complete Step 3.

Era of the Dinosaurs

The Mesozoic Era	**Triassic Period** 215 million years ago	First mammals
		Turtles
		Coelophysis
	Jurassic Period 150 million years ago	First birds
		Stegosaurus
		Brachiosaurus
	Cretaceous Period 70 million years ago	First snakes
		Pteranodon
		Tyrannosaurus Rex

FIGURE 3.38 Line List Hierarchy SmartArt ➤

a. On Slide 5, select the **SmartArt Hierarchy shape** by clicking any shape.

b. Click the **SmartArt Tools Design tab**, click the **More button** in the Layouts group, select **More Layouts** at the bottom of the Layouts gallery, and then click **Lined List** under the *Hierarchy* section. Click **OK**.

c. Deselect the SmartArt diagram.

d. Save the presentation.

STEP 4 ▶ ## CREATE AND MODIFY WORDART

You teach the participants how to use WordArt to call attention to text and how to modify the Text effects applied to the WordArt. You also have them insert text in a text box so they can compare the options available with each method for adding text to a slide. Refer to Figure 3.39 as you complete Step 4.

Modified WordArt shape

Fun Fact

Text inserted in a text box

The water you drink today could have been consumed by a dinosaur or other ancient animal in the past.

FIGURE 3.39 Modified WordArt ➤

a. On Slide 4, click the **Insert tab**, and then click **WordArt** in the Text group.

b. Click **Fill - Turquoise, Accent 3, Outline - Text 2** (first row, fifth column).

A WordArt placeholder is centered on the slide.

c. Type **Fun Fact** in the **WordArt placeholder**.

d. Click the **Format tab**, if necessary, click **Text Effects** in the WordArt Styles group, and then point to **Transform**.

The Transform gallery opens, showing No Transform, Follow Path, and Warp options.

e. Click **Cascade Up** (last row, third column).

> **TROUBLESHOOTING:** If you do not see the Cascade Up option, scroll down until it becomes available.

f. Type **1.5** in the **Shape Height box**, and then press **Enter**.

The height of the WordArt shape adjusts to 1.5″.

g. Drag the WordArt shape to the top-left corner of the slide, and then deselect the shape.

h. Click the **Insert tab**, and then click **Text Box** in the Text group.

i. Click to the right of the WordArt shape, and then type **The water you drink today could have been consumed by a dinosaur or other ancient animal in the past.**

The text box expands to fit the text with the result that the text is contained in one long line that flows off the slide.

j. Click the **Format tab**, type **5.75″** in the **Shape Width box** in the Size group, and then press **Enter**.

⊛ **FYI**

k. Click the **Size Dialog Box Launcher**, select **Text Box**, and then click the **Wrap text in shape checkbox**.

l. Change the font size of the text to **28 pt**, and then drag the text box until the top edge is aligned with the WordArt shape.

m. Save the presentation. Keep the presentation onscreen if you plan to continue with Hands-On Exercise 3. If not, close the presentation and exit PowerPoint.

Object Manipulation

As you add objects to your slides, you may need to manipulate them. Perhaps you have several shapes created, and you want them to align at their left edges, or you want to arrange them by their center points, and then determine the order of the shapes. You may have inserted a clip art image, and the colors used in the clip art do not match the color of the SmartArt on a slide. You may have added a clip art image that includes something you do not want.

In this section, you will learn to modify objects. You will isolate objects, flip and rotate objects, group and ungroup objects, and recolor clip art. You will also learn to determine the order of objects and align objects to one another and to the slide.

Modifying Objects

Clip art images are made from a series of combined shapes. You can modify existing clip art by breaking it into individual shapes and removing pieces you do not need, changing or recoloring shapes, rotating shapes, and combining shapes from several clip art objects to create a new clip art object. Figure 3.40 shows a picnic clip art image available from Microsoft Office Online. The clip art was broken apart; the fireworks, flag, fries, and tablecloth removed; the hamburger, hotdogs, and milkshake flipped and resized; and the chocolate milkshake recolored.

FIGURE 3.40 Modified Clip Art ➤

Resizing objects is the most common modification procedure. You have learned to resize an object by dragging a sizing handle; however, you may need a more precise resizing method. For example, you use PowerPoint to create an advertisement for an automobile trader magazine, and the magazine specifies that the ad must fit in a 2″ by 2″ space. You can specify the exact height and width measurement of an object or adjust to a specific proportion of its original size.

To enter an exact measurement, select the object, and then click the Format tab, which is located under any of the Tools contextual tabs (such as Drawing Tools, SmartArt Tools, Picture Tools, and Chart Tools). The Size group contains boxes to change the Shape Height and Shape Width of an object quickly. It also contains a Size Dialog Box Launcher that opens the Format Shape dialog box with more options.

The Size section in the Format Shape dialog box contains boxes for entering exact measurements for shape height and width. The Size section also allows you to use a precise rotation angle and to scale an object based on its original size (note that not all clip art entered from the Clip Art task pane is added at its full size).

To keep the original height and width proportions of a clip art object, make sure the *Lock aspect ratio* check box is selected. ***Aspect ratio*** is the ratio of an object's width to its height. The clip art image in Figure 3.41 was proportionally sized to 50% of its original size.

Aspect ratio refers to the ratio of an object's width to its height.

The callouts in the figure, from top to bottom, read:

- Size Dialog Box Launcher
- Enter exact width
- Enter exact height
- Enter rotation angle
- Enter scale height
- Check Lock aspect ratio to keep height and width in proportion
- Click to reset size
- Enter scale width

FIGURE 3.41 Sizing Options ➤

Flip and Rotate

To **flip** an object is to reverse the direction it faces.

To **rotate** an object is to move it around its axis.

Sometimes you will find that an object is facing the wrong way and you need to reverse the direction it faces or *flip* it. You can flip an object vertically or horizontally to get a mirror image of the object. You may find that you need to *rotate* or move the object around its axis. Perhaps you took a photograph with your digital camera sideways to get a full-length view, but when you download the image, it is sideways. You can quickly rotate an object left or right 90°, flip it horizontally or vertically, or freely rotate it any number of degrees.

You can rotate a selected object by dragging the green rotation handle located at the top of the object in the direction you want it to rotate. To constrain the rotation to 15° angles, press and hold Shift while dragging. To rotate exactly 90° to the left or the right, click Rotate in the Arrange group on the Format tab. If you need a mirror image, click Rotate, and then select Flip Vertical or Flip Horizontal. You can also drag one of the side sizing handles over the opposite side and flip it. If you do not drag far enough, you will distort the image. Figure 3.42 shows rotate options and a clip art image that has been flipped.

Click Rotate for rotate and flip options

Drag rotation handle to change angle of rotation

Drag handle over opposite handle to flip object

FIGURE 3.42 Rotating and Flipping Options ➤

Ungrouping is breaking a combined object into individual objects.

Grouping is combining two or more objects.

A **vector graphic** is an object-oriented graphic based on geometric formulas.

Group and Ungroup Objects

A clip art object is usually created in pieces, layered, and then grouped to create the final image. Clip art can be *ungrouped* or broken apart, so you can modify or delete the individual pieces. *Grouping* enables multiple objects to act or move as though they were a single object, while ungrouping separates an object into individual shapes.

In order for a clip art image to be ungrouped and grouped, you must create and save it as a vector graphic. *Vector graphics* are created using geometrical formulas to represent images and are created in drawing programs such as Adobe Illustrator and CorelDRAW. The advantage of vector files is that they are easily edited and layered, and they use a small amount of storage space. Many of the clip art images available from the Clip Art pane are vector graphics.

> **TIP** Clip Art That Will Not Ungroup
>
> If your selected clip art image will not ungroup for editing, it is not in a vector format. The Clip Art task pane also contains clips in bitmap, .jpg, .gif, and .png formats, which are not vector-based images and cannot be ungrouped.

Some non-vector graphics can be converted into drawing objects. Right-click the clip art image on the slide, and then select Edit Picture if the option is available. If the option is not available, the graphic cannot be converted into a drawing object. After you select Edit Picture, a message opens asking if you want to convert the picture into a drawing object. Click Yes. This action converts the object into a vector graphic.

After you convert the object into a drawing object, right-click the clip art image again, point to Group, and then select Ungroup. The clip art object ungroups and the individual pieces are selected. Complex clip art images may have more than one grouping. The artist may create an image from individual shapes, group it, layer it on other images, and then group it again. Figure 3.43 is an example of a complex Microsoft Windows Metafile that has multiple groups.

Group 1

Group 2

FIGURE 3.43 Complex Clip
Art with Multiple Groups ➤

To continue ungrouping, select the clip, right-click, click Group, and then click Ungroup as many times as necessary to break the image down to all shapes. You can also select the clip, and then click the Drawing Tools Format tab. Click Group in the Arrange group, and if the clip art image can be broken down further, the Ungroup option will be active with Group and Regroup grayed out. Select Ungroup, and each individual shape is surrounded by adjustment handles. Click outside of the clip art borders to deselect the shapes, and then click the individual shape you wish to change. Figure 3.44 shows a clip art graphic that has been repeatedly ungrouped until only individual objects are left.

Click to Group, Regroup,
or Ungroup clip art

Individual shapes
with adjustment handles

Click outside of clip
borders to deselect shapes

FIGURE 3.44 Ungrouped
Complex Clip Art ➤

When working with the individual shapes of a clip art image, it is helpful to zoom in on the clip art. Zooming helps you make sure you have the correct shape before you make modifications. Figure 3.45 shows a selected shape that has had its fill changed to a theme color. Once you have made all of your needed changes, drag a selection net around all the shapes of the image and Group or Regroup the image. If you do not group the image, you risk moving the individual pieces inadvertently.

- Theme Colors fill options
- Original color of shape
- Selected shape with Theme color applied
- Drag Zoom slider to enlarge image

FIGURE 3.45 Modifying Ungrouped Shapes ➤

Recolor Pictures

You can quickly change the colors in a clip art image using the Recolor Picture option, which enables you to match your image to the color scheme of your presentation without ungrouping the image and changing the color of each shape. You can select either a dark or a light variation of your color scheme.

You also can change the color mode of your picture to Grayscale, Sepia, Washout, or Black and White. Grayscale changes your picture to up to 256 shades of gray. Sepia gives you that popular golden tone often used for an old-fashioned photo look. Washout is used to create watermarks, whereas Black and White is a way to reduce image color to black and white. Figure 3.46 shows a clip art image and three variations of color.

- Blue, Accent color 1 light
- Black and White: 75%
- Original clip from Clip Art pane
- Washout

FIGURE 3.46 Recoloring Images ➤

To change the colors in your clip art image:

1. Select the clip art image you want to change.
2. Click the Format tab.
3. Click Color in the Adjust group.
4. Click the color variation of your choice, or select More Variations to open the Theme Colors options and select a theme color.

The Recolor gallery includes a Set Transparent Color option that is extremely valuable for creating a transparent area in many pictures. When you click Set Transparent Color, the pointer changes shape and includes an arrowhead for pointing. Move the pointer until the arrowhead is pointing directly at the color you wish to make transparent, and then click. The color becomes transparent so that anything underneath shows through. In Figure 3.47, the girl's shirt color is transparent so the white background shows.

Pointer changes to this shape

Click to select a color to make transparent

Original shirt color

Shirt color set to transparent

FIGURE 3.47 Set Transparent Color ➤

> **TIP** Changing the Color of Multiple Shapes Easily
>
> Press Ctrl as you click several shapes, and then apply a shape fill to all the selected shapes at the same time. You do not have to keep opening the Shape Fill gallery to apply the color to your shapes. The fill bucket immediately to the left of the Shape Fill command now reflects your color choice. Simply click it to apply the color to selected shapes.
>
> Another method is to use Format Painter in the Home tab to select the color of an object, and then "paint" it over the other objects. For further information, see the Fundamentals chapter.

Arranging Objects

When you have multiple objects such as shapes, clip art, SmartArt, and WordArt on the page, it can become challenging and time consuming to arrange them. PowerPoint has several features to control the order and position of the objects, how the objects align to one another, and how they align to the slide. Before using any of these features, you must select the object(s). You can select the object(s) by using the *Selection Pane*. The Selection Pane contains a list of all objects on the slide. Click any object on the list to select it, and then make changes to it. Click Selection Pane in the Arrange group on the Format tab to open the Selection Pane if an object is selected. If an object is not selected, click the Home tab, click Select in the Editing group, and then select Selection Pane. The object you selected is highlighted in the Selection Pane.

The **Selection Pane** is a pane designed to help select objects.

Order Objects

The **stacking order** is the order of objects placed on top of one another.

You can layer shapes by placing them under or on top of one another. The order of the layers is called the *stacking order*. PowerPoint adds shapes or other objects in a stacking order as you add them to the slide. The last shape you place on the slide is on top and is the highest in the stacking order. Clip art images are comprised of shapes that have been stacked. Once you ungroup a clip art image and modify it, you may need to change the stacking order. You can open the Selection Pane to see the order in which objects are placed. The topmost object on the list is at the top of the stacking order.

To change the order of a stack of shapes, select a shape, and then click the Drawing Tools Format tab. The Arrange group on the Format tab includes the Arrange arrow to open a submenu that includes the Bring to Front option, which lets you move the shape all the way to the top of the stacking order, and Bring Forward, which lets you move the shape up one layer. The Send to Back option enables you to move the shape all the way to the bottom of the stacking order, and Send Backward lets you move the shape back one layer. Figure 3.48 shows the results of changing a square at the bottom of a stacking order to the top of a stacking order.

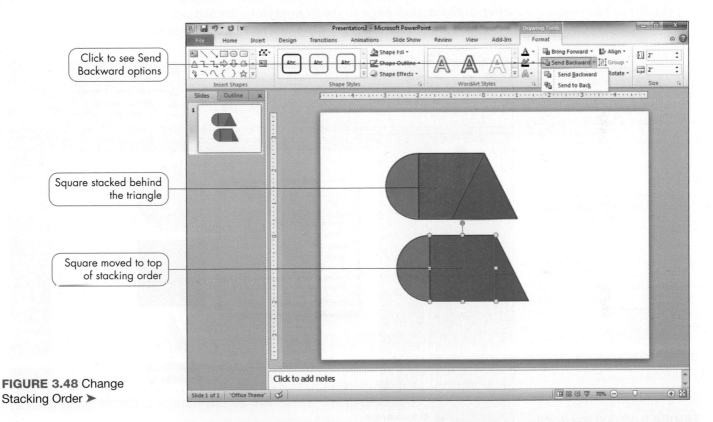

FIGURE 3.48 Change Stacking Order ➤

TIP Ordering Shortcuts

You can right-click a shape and select Bring to Front or Send to Back. Using this method, you can still choose whether to move one layer or all layers. You also can open the Selection Pane, select the object, and click the Re-order Bring Forward arrow or the Send Backward arrow to move the object up the list or down the list.

Align Objects

You can position objects precisely on the slide. For example, you can align a series of boxes at their tops or adjust the amount of space between the boxes so that they are evenly spaced. PowerPoint has rulers, a grid, and drawing guides that enable you to complete the aligning process quickly.

A grid is a set of intersecting lines used to align objects.

Each slide can display a **grid** containing intersecting lines, similar to traditional graph paper. Grids are hidden and are nonprinting, but you can display the grid to align your objects and to keep them evenly spaced. When you activate the grid, you will not see it in Slide Show view and it will not print. Rulers can also help keep your objects aligned by enabling you to see the exact size of an object, or the distance between shapes.

To view the grid and the ruler, click the View tab and click the check boxes for Gridlines and Ruler. To change the grid settings:

1. Click the Home tab.
2. Click Arrange in the Drawing group.
3. Point to Align, and then select Grid Settings.

By default, objects snap to the gridlines and measurement lines on the rulers. The *Snap to* feature forces an object to align with the grid by either the center point or the edge of the object, whichever is closer to the gridline. You can turn off the *Snap to* feature or change the setting so that objects snap to other objects and/or to the grid. To change the grid settings, select an object, click Align on the Drawing Tools Format tab, and then select Grid Settings. Figure 3.49 displays the Grid and Guides dialog box options.

Click to access Grid and Guide settings

Horizontal ruler

Click to change spacing between grid dots

Click to display grid onscreen

Click to display drawing guides onscreen

Vertical ruler

FIGURE 3.49 Grid and Guide Settings ➤

TIP Overriding Snap-to

To override the *Snap object to grid* feature temporarily so that you can freely move an object to any position, press Alt as you drag the object.

A guide is a straight horizontal or vertical line used to align objects.

Guides are nonprinting vertical or horizontal lines that you can place on a page to help you align objects or determine regions of the slide. For example, you can use guides to mark margins on a slide.

To activate guides:

1. Click the Home tab.
2. Click Arrange in the Drawing group.
3. Point to Align, and then select Grid Settings.
4. Click Display drawing guides onscreen.
5. Click OK.

When you first display the guides, you see two guides that intersect at the center of the slide (the zero setting on both the horizontal and vertical rulers). To move a guide, position your cursor over it and drag. A directional arrow will appear as well as a measurement telling you the distance from the center point you are moving the guide. To create additional guides, press Ctrl+Shift while dragging. To remove guides, drag them off the slide. Figure 3.50 displays the default guides and a new guide in the process of being created.

Newly added horizontal guide at 2″ below 0 on vertical ruler

Horizontal guide at 0″ on vertical ruler

Vertical guide at 0″ on horizontal ruler

FIGURE 3.50 Creating a Guide ➤

To **align** is to arrange in a line to be parallel.

The *Align* feature makes it simple to line up shapes and objects in several ways. You can align with other objects by lining up the sides, middles, or top/bottom edges of objects. Or, if you have only one object or group selected, you can align in relation to the slide—for example, the top or left side of the slide. To align selected objects, click Align on the Format tab. When the alignment options display, select Align to Slide or Align Selected Objects. After you have determined whether you want to align to the slide or align objects to one another, determine which specific align option you want to use: Align Left, Align Center, Align Right, Align Top, Align Middle, or Align Bottom.

To **distribute** is to divide or evenly spread over a given area.

The Align feature also includes options to *distribute* selected shapes evenly over a given area. Perhaps you have shapes on the page but one is too close to another, and another is too far away. You want to have an equal amount of space between all the shapes. After selecting the shapes, click Align in the Arrange group on the Format tab. Then select Distribute Horizontally or Distribute Vertically. Figure 3.51 shows three shapes that are aligned at their middles, aligned to the middle of the slide, and distributed horizontally so that the space between them is equidistant.

Select to align selected objects

Select to distribute the horizontal space evenly between selected objects

FIGURE 3.51 Alignment Options ➤

3 Object Manipulation

While you could teach your mini-camp participants how to size, position, align, ungroup, and use other object manipulation techniques using shapes, you have them use clip art. The ability to manipulate clip art by grouping and ungrouping, recoloring, combining, and using other techniques turns the thousands of clip art images available from Microsoft Office Online into millions of possibilities. You want your group to have these skills.

Skills covered: Size and Position Clip Art • Flip Clip Art • Ungroup, Modify, and Regroup Clip Art • Recolor a Picture • Create and Reorder Shapes • Align and Distribute Clip Art

STEP 1 ▶ SIZE AND POSITION CLIP ART

You teach your mini-camp participants to use the Size Dialog Box Launcher. You want them to be able to precisely size and position objects on the slide. Refer to Figure 3.52 as you complete Step 1.

FIGURE 3.52 Alignment Options ➤

a. Open the *p03h2water_LastnameFirstname* presentation if you closed it after the previous exercise. Save the presentation as **p03h3water_LastnameFirstname**, changing *h2* to **h3**.

b. On Slide 4, click the **Insert tab**, and then click **Clip Art** in the Illustrations group.

   The Clip Art pane opens.

c. Select any text in the **Search for box**, type **dinosaurs**, check the **Include Office.com content checkbox**, and then click **Go**.

   Entering the keyword *dinosaurs* narrowed your search more than if you had entered the generic keyword *extinct*.

d. Insert the clip art image of the dinosaur as shown in Figure 3.52, and then close the Clip Art pane.

You have inserted the clip art image in the center of Slide 4.

> **TROUBLESHOOTING:** If you cannot locate the image in Figure 3.52, select another clip art image of a dinosaur. Expand your search terms to include other result types if necessary.

e. Click the **Size Dialog Box Launcher** in the Size group on the Format tab.

f. Type **3.45** in the **Height box**, and then click in the **Width box**.

Because Lock aspect ratio is selected, the width of the image changes to 6.78, keeping the image in proportion.

g. Click **Position** in the left pane, type **3.2** in the **Horizontal box**, type **3.34** in the **Vertical box**, and then click **Close**.

h. Save the presentation.

STEP 2 ▶ **FLIP CLIP ART**

Rotating and flipping are both ways to angle an object on the slide. You can rotate using precise measurements, or for an imprecise method of rotation, you can rotate the object using the Rotation handle. You ask your participants to use these methods so that they are familiar with the benefits of each. Refer to Figure 3.53 as you complete Step 2.

FIGURE 3.53 Flipping and Rotating ▶

a. Click the dinosaur clip art, and then click **Rotate** in the Arrange group on the Format tab.

The rotate and flip options appear.

b. Select **Flip Horizontal**.

c. Click **Rotate** in the Arrange group, and then select **More Rotation Options**.

d. Type **180** in the **Rotation box**, and then click **Close**.

The picture is rotated upside down.

e. Click **Rotate**, and then select **Flip Vertical**.

The clip art picture appears to be in its original position, but the rotation angle is still set at 180°.

> **TROUBLESHOOTING:** If the rotation causes your clip art image to cover the text box, move the clip art toward the bottom of the slide. See Figure 3.53.

f. Select the text box in the top right of the slide, and then drag it down and to the left to the approximate center of the slide. Position the insertion point over the green rotation handle, and then drag the rotation handle to the left until the text box is rotated to approximately match the slant in the *Fun Fact* WordArt.

> **TROUBLESHOOTING:** As you change the angle of rotation for the text box, you will need to reposition it on the slide. An easy way to make small position adjustments is to press the arrow keys on the keyboard.

g. Save the presentation.

STEP 3 ▸ **UNGROUP, MODIFY, AND REGROUP CLIP ART**

Being able to change colors, remove shapes, add shapes, and group and regroup clip art images are important skills you want your participants to master. You ask the participants to change the color of plants, move the dinosaur shape, and regroup the dinosaur clip art image. Refer to Figure 3.54 as you complete Step 3.

Clip art image reset to original rotation and moved

Plant fills changed to theme color

FIGURE 3.54 Modified Clip Art ➤

a. On Slide 4, right-click the dinosaur clip art, select **Edit Picture**, and then click **Yes** when the Microsoft Office PowerPoint message box opens.

The image has been converted to a drawing object and flips back to its original rotation angle.

b. Click the **Format tab**, click **Group** in the Arrange group, select **Ungroup**, and then click outside the clip art border.

When you ungroup the clip art, each shape comprising the image is selected and surrounded with adjustment handles. Clicking outside the border deselects the shapes so that you can select just the one you wish to modify.

c. Drag the **Zoom slider** until the image is at a level with which you are comfortable, and then drag the scroll bars to locate the plant in the left side of the clip art.

Zooming in makes selecting the individual shape you wish to modify easier.

d. Select the dull green shape of the plant, click the **Format tab** if necessary, click **Shape Fill** in the Shape Styles group, and then click **Turquoise, Accent 3, Darker 50%** (last row, seventh column).

You change the dull green in the original clip art to a color that matches your theme color.

e. Change the fill color of the other dull green plants to **Turquoise, Accent 3, Darker 50%**.

f. Click the **View tab**, and then click **Fit to Window** in the Zoom group.

g. Drag a selection net around all the shapes used to make the dinosaur clip art image.

All the shapes are selected. Pressing Ctrl and clicking the shapes would be time consuming because of the many shapes involved.

h. Click the **Format tab**, select **Group** in the Arrange group, and then select **Regroup**. Drag the new group to the bottom right of the slide.

Because the WordArt and the text box were not part of the original group, they do not become part of the group.

i. Save the presentation.

STEP 4 ▶ RECOLOR A PICTURE

You teach your mini-camp participants to recolor a clip art image so that it matches the color scheme of the presentation. Refer to Figure 3.55 as you complete Step 4.

FIGURE 3.55 Recolored Picture ➤

a. On Slide 5, click the **Insert tab**, and then click **Clip Art** in the Images group.

b. Type **tyrannosaurus** in the **Search for box**, and then click **Go**.

c. Refer to Figure 3.55 to determine which tyrannosaurus to insert on the bottom left of your slide, drag the clip art object into position, and then close the Clip Art task pane.

d. Click the **Format tab**.

Because the clip art has not been converted to a drawing object, you can use the picture tools to modify it. Recoloring an image does not require clip art to be ungrouped.

e. Click **Color** in the Adjust group, and then click **Blue, Accent color 1 Light** (third row, second column).

The color of the clip art image now matches the colors in the theme.

f. Save the presentation.

STEP 5 ▶ **CREATE AND REORDER SHAPES**

Being able to create and reorder shapes allows you to be creative, enabling you to create backgrounds, borders, and corners. You ask your group to create a background for three clip art images, which unifies the images. Refer to Figure 3.56 as you complete Step 5.

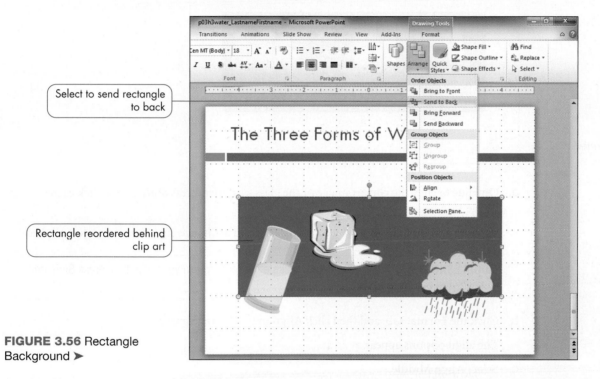

FIGURE 3.56 Rectangle Background ➤

a. On Slide 6, click the **View tab**, and then click the **Ruler check box** in the Show group (if necessary).

The horizontal and vertical rulers appear.

b. Click the **Home tab**, and then click **Rectangle** in the Drawing group.

> **TROUBLESHOOTING:** Depending on your screen resolution, you may need to select Shapes first.

c. Position the cross-hair pointer on the slide so that the indicator on the ruler is at the 4″ mark to the left of the zero point on the horizontal ruler and the 1″ mark above the zero point on the vertical ruler.

This is the beginning point for the rectangle.

d. Drag to the 4″ mark to the right of the zero point on the horizontal ruler and the 2″ mark below the zero point on the vertical ruler, and then release.

A large rectangle shape in the theme color is created on top of the clip art on the slide. You will use the rectangle as a background for the clip art. Currently, it is hiding a portion of the clip art and must be reordered.

e. Click **Arrange** in the Drawing group, and then select **Send to Back**.

f. Save the presentation.

STEP 6 ▶ ALIGN AND DISTRIBUTE CLIP ART

Dragging objects into position on a slide can be a time consuming and frustrating process. You teach your group to align objects quickly and efficiently using the Drawing Tools Arrange feature. Refer to Figure 3.57 as you complete Step 6.

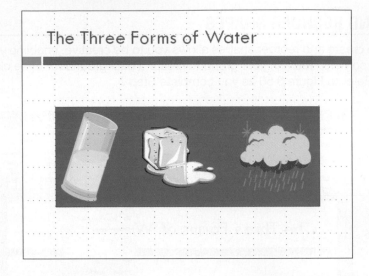

FIGURE 3.57 Arranged Objects ➤

a. On Slide 6, click the clip art image of the glass, and then press **Shift** as you click each clip art image.

Pressing and holding Shift while clicking each clip art image enables you to select all three.

> **TROUBLESHOOTING:** If you accidentally include the rectangle in your selection, press Shift, and then click the rectangle to deselect it.

b. Click the **Format tab**, and then click **Align** in the Arrange group.

The align options appear.

c. Select **Align Middle**.

You align the clip art images by their middles.

d. Click **Align**, and then select **Distribute Horizontally**.

The objects are distributed evenly.

e. Click **Group** in the Arrange group, and then select **Group**.

The three clip art images are grouped.

f. Press **Shift**, and then click the **blue rectangle**.

The rectangle and the clip art group are now both selected.

g. Click **Align** in the Arrange group, and then select **Align Middle**.

The rectangle and grouped clip art images are aligned by the horizontal middle. This ensures the blue rectangle is behind all of the images.

h. Deselect the objects.

i. Save and close the presentation.

After reading this chapter, you have accomplished the following objectives:

1. **Create shapes.** You can use shapes to highlight information, as a design element, as the basis for creating clip art illustrations, or to contain information in infographics. PowerPoint provides tools for creating, sizing, and positioning shapes.

2. **Apply Quick Styles and customize shapes.** A shape can be customized by changing its default fill to another color, to a picture, to a gradient, to a texture, or to no fill. The shape outline color, weight, or dash style can be modified. Special effects such as shadows, reflections, and glows may be added. Applying a Quick Style enables you to apply preset options. The vertexes of shapes can be edited.

3. **Create SmartArt.** SmartArt graphics are diagrams that present information visually to effectively communicate your message. SmartArt can be used to create effective infographics. You can convert text to a SmartArt diagram.

4. **Modify SmartArt.** SmartArt can be modified to include additional shapes, to delete shapes, to apply a SmartArt style, to revise the color scheme, or to add special effects. The direction of the SmartArt can be changed. SmartArt can be resized and repositioned.

5. **Create WordArt.** WordArt is text with decorative effects applied to draw attention to the text. Select a WordArt style, and then type the text you desire.

6. **Modify WordArt.** WordArt can be modified by transforming the shape of the text and by applying special effects and colors. The shape of the WordArt can be warped along a path. Text created as WordArt can be edited. Among the many special effects available are 3-D presets and rotations.

7. **Modify objects.** An object may be flipped horizontally or vertically, or rotated by dragging its green rotation handle. Vector clip art can be ungrouped so basic shapes can be customized, and then objects can be regrouped so they can be moved as one object. Pictures can be recolored by changing their color mode or by applying dark or light variations of a theme color or custom color.

8. **Arrange objects.** Objects are stacked in layers. The object at the top of the layer is the one that fully displays, while other objects in the stack may have some portions blocked. The stacking order of shapes can be reordered so that objects can be seen as desired. Features such as rulers, grids, guides, align, and distribute can be used to arrange objects on a slide and arrange objects in relation to one another.

KEY TERMS

Adjustment handle *p. 853*
Align *p. 895*
Aspect ratio *p. 887*
Callout *p. 853*
Connector *p. 855*
Distribute *p. 895*
Fill *p. 858*
Flip *p. 888*
Flow chart *p. 855*
Freeform shape *p. 856*
Gradient fill *p. 858*
Grid *p. 894*

Grouping *p. 889*
Guide *p. 894*
Infographic *p. 852*
Line weight *p. 862*
Lock Drawing Mode *p. 853*
Opaque *p. 859*
Picture fill *p. 859*
Point *p. 862*
Quick Style *p. 857*
Rotate *p. 888*
Selection net *p. 858*
Selection Pane *p. 892*

Shape *p. 852*
SmartArt *p. 873*
Stacking order *p. 893*
Text box *p. 855*
Text pane *p. 876*
Texture fill *p. 861*
Transparency *p. 859*
Ungrouping *p. 889*
Vector graphic *p. 889*
Vertex *p. 856*
WordArt *p. 881*

MULTIPLE CHOICE

1. Shapes are:

   (a) Images that you search for in the Shape Clip Organizer.
   (b) Graphics such as lines, arrows, and squares, which you add using the Shapes gallery.
   (c) A category of SmartArt.
   (d) Graphics that you create by clicking in the Shape group on the Design tab.

2. To rotate a shape on your slide:

   (a) Drag the green handle at the top of the image.
   (b) Drag one of the corner adjustment handles.
   (c) Double-click the lightning bolt, and then enter the number of degrees to rotate.
   (d) Do nothing because shapes cannot be rotated.

3. Which of the following is a reason for grouping shapes?

   (a) To be able to change each shape individually
   (b) To move or modify the objects as one
   (c) To connect the shapes with connectors
   (d) To create a relationship diagram

4. Which of the following is a reason for ungrouping a clip art object?

   (a) To resize the group as one piece
   (b) To move the objects as one
   (c) To add text on top of the group
   (d) To be able to individually change shapes used to create the composite image

5. You have inserted a clip art image of the ocean with a palm tree on the right side of the beach. If you flip the image vertically, what would the resulting image look like?

   (a) The image would show right side up, but the palm tree would be on the left side.
   (b) The image would be rotated 270°, and the palm tree would be at the top.
   (c) The image would be upside down with the palm tree pointing down.
   (d) The image would be rotated 90°, and the palm tree would be on the bottom.

6. Which of the following might be a reason for changing the stacking order of shapes?

   (a) To show a relationship by placing shapes in front of or behind each other
   (b) To hide something on a shape
   (c) To uncover something hidden by another shape
   (d) All of the above

7. Which of the following is not available from the SmartArt gallery?

   (a) Data table
   (b) Pyramid diagram
   (c) Process graphic
   (d) Matrix block

8. You have items needed for a camping trip in a bullet placeholder. Which of the following SmartArt diagrams would you use to display the data as an infographic?

   (a) Hierarchy
   (b) Cycle
   (c) List
   (d) Relationship

9. You are trying to align a shape directly on top of another, but it always jumps above or below where you need to place it. What feature should you deactivate?

   (a) Align to
   (b) Snap to
   (c) AutoAlign
   (d) Line Snap

10. Which of the following may be used to add emphasis to text on a slide?

    (a) Apply a WordArt Quick Style to the selected text.
    (b) Apply a Text Effect to the selected text.
    (c) Create the text using the WordArt feature.
    (d) All of the above

1 Greeting Card Template

Because you give a lot of greeting cards, you decide to create your own PowerPoint pattern that you can use to quickly create cards. You use guides and text boxes to create the card, and then you use PowerPoint's alignment and rotate features to help you position the text boxes on the slide. This exercise follows the same set of skills as used in Hands-On Exercises 1 and 3 in the chapter. Refer to Figure 3.58 as you complete this exercise.

FIGURE 3.58 Greeting Card Template ➤

a. Open a blank presentation file and save it as **p03p1card_LastnameFirstname**.

b. Create a Notes and Handouts header with your name, and a footer with your instructor's name and your class. Include the current date.

c. Click the **Design tab**, click **Slide Orientation** in the Page Setup group, and then select **Portrait**.

d. Click the **Home tab**, and then click **Layout** in the Slides group. Select the **Blank layout**.

e. Click **Arrange** in the Drawing group, point to **Align**, and then select **Grid Settings**. Click the **Display drawing guides on screen check box**, and then click **OK**.

f. Click the **Insert tab**, and then click **Text Box** in the Text group. Click the approximate middle of the slide, and type **Front of Card** in the **text box**.

g. Click the **Format tab**, click the **Rotate arrow**, and then select **Flip Vertical**. Drag the selected text box to the top-left quadrant of the card.

   • This location will serve as a reminder that when the card is folded after printing, the top of the page becomes the bottom.

h. With the text box still selected, press **Ctrl+D**.

   • This is a shortcut for duplicating. A duplicate of the first text box is created.

i. Drag the duplicate text box to the top-right quadrant of the card, and edit the text to read **Back of Card**.

   • You will be editing upside-down text. You edit upside-down text several times in this exercise, but when the card is folded, the text will be in the right position.

j. Drag a selection net around both text boxes, click the **Format tab**, click **Align**, and then select **Align Top**.

k. With both text boxes selected, press **Ctrl+D** to make a duplicate of the boxes. Drag the duplicates to the middle of the bottom quadrants of the card. Edit the text on the bottom-left quadrant to read **Left Inside of Card** and the text on the bottom-right quadrant to read **Right Inside of Card**.

l. Select the two text boxes at the bottom of the card, click the **Format tab**, click **Rotate**, and then select **Flip Vertical**.

m. Select the text boxes on the left side of the card (*Front of Card* and *Left Inside of Card*), click the **Format tab**, click **Align**, and then select **Align Center**. Select the text boxes on the right side of the card (*Back of Card* and *Right Inside of Card*), click the **Format tab**, click **Align**, and then click **Align Center**. Deselect the text boxes.

n. Save and close the file, and submit based on your instructor's directions.

2 Greeting Card Template

You use a greeting card pattern to make a birthday card for your roommate's 21st birthday. You customize the card to include modified clip art, a freeform shape, WordArt, and lines. This exercise follows the same set of skills as used in Hands-On Exercises 1, 2, and 3 in the chapter. Refer to Figure 3.59 as you complete this exercise.

FIGURE 3.59 Greeting Card ➤

a. Open *p03p2bday* and save the file again as **p03p2bday_LastnameFirstname**.

b. Click the **Insert tab**, and then click **Clip Art** in the Images group. Search for **birthday border** and include Office.com content. Click the image of the birthday border (see Figure 3.59) to insert it on your slide, and then close the Clip Art pane.

c. With the image selected, click the **Format tab**, and then click the **Size Dialog Box Launcher**.

d. Deselect the *Lock aspect ratio* check box in the scale area. Click in the **Scale Height box**, and then type **76**. Leave the width setting at **100%**.

e. Click **Position** in the left pane, and then type **0** in the **Horizontal box**. Type **0** in the **Vertical box**. Click **Close**.

f. Right-click the selected image, and then select **Edit Picture**. Click **Yes** to convert the picture to a drawing object.

g. Click the **Format tab**, click **Group** in the Arrange group, and then select **Ungroup**.

h. Click the turquoise border to select it, click **Shape Fill** in the Shape Styles group, and then click **Blue** in the Standard category.

i. Click the **Format tab**, click the **Send Backward arrow**, and then select **Send to Back**. Deselect the borders by clicking somewhere else on the slide.

j. Right-click any shape in the border clip art, point to **Group**, and then select **Regroup**.

k. Click **Rotate** in the Arrange group, and then select **Flip Vertical**.

l. Delete the text box that reads *Front of Card*.

m. Click the **Insert tab**, and then click **WordArt** in the Text group. Click **Fill - Red, Accent 2, Warm Matte Bevel** (fifth row, third column). Type **Happy**, press **Enter**, type **21st**, press **Enter**, and then type **Birthday**.

n. With the WordArt object selected, click the **Format tab**, click **Text Effects** in the WordArt Styles group, point to **Transform**, and then click **Button** (third row, fourth column in Warp).

o. Click in the **Shape Height box** in the Size group, and then type **2**. Type **2** in the **Shape Width box**.

p. Click **Rotate** in the Arrange group. Select **Flip Vertical**. Click **Rotate** again, and then select **Flip Horizontal**. Drag the WordArt object into the *Front of Card* quadrant.

q. Click the **Back of Card box**, select the **existing text**, and then type **Created by** *your first name*. If the text is too long to fit in the quadrant, press **Enter** before your first name. Drag the text box into the approximate center of the back of the card.

r. Select the **Right Inside of Card text**, type **You are a STAR!**, and then drag the text box to the top of the *Right Inside of Card* quadrant.

s. Click the **Insert tab**, click **Shapes** in the Illustrations group, and then click **5-Point Star** in the *Stars and Banners* section. Press **Shift**, and then drag to create a star below the text box on the right side of the card quadrant.

t. Click the **Format tab**, and then click **Shape Fill** in the Shape Styles group. Click **Yellow** in the *Standard Colors* section. Click **Shape Outline**, and then select **No Outline**.

u. Click **Shape Effects** in the Shape Styles group, point to **Glow**, and then click **Blue, 18 pt glow, Accent color 1** (fourth row, first column in Glow).

v. Press and hold **Ctrl**, and then click the text box above the star to add it to the selection. Click the **Format tab**, click **Align**, and then select **Align Center**.

w. Delete the *Left Inside of Card* box.

x. If directed to do so by your instructor, print the card and fold it to check the text rotations. Save and close the file, and submit based on your instructor's directions.

3 Principles of Judo

You have created a slide show on Judo for your *sensei* (teacher) to show prospective students. You use infographics, shapes, and clip art to share his message. This exercise follows the same set of skills as used in Hands-On Exercises 1, 2, and 3 in the chapter. Refer to Figure 3.60 as you complete this exercise.

FIGURE 3.60 Judo, the Gentle Way ➤

a. Open *p03p3judo* and save it as **p03p3judo_LastnameFirstname**.

b. Create a handout header with your name, and a handout footer with your instructor's name and your class. Include the current date.

c. On Slide 2, click the placeholder containing the bullet points, and then click the **Home tab**.

d. Click **Convert to SmartArt Graphic** in the Paragraph group, and then select **Basic Venn**.

e. Click **Change Colors** in the SmartArt Styles group. Click **Colorful Range - Accent Colors 5 to 6** in the *Colorful* section.

f. On Slide 3, click the **Insert tab**, click **Shapes** in the Illustrations group, and then select **Double Arrow** in the *Lines* section. Drag an arrow from the right-center connecting point on the *Maximum Efficiency* shape to the left-center connecting point on the *Mutual Welfare and Benefit* shape.

g. On Slide 5, select the **Hierarchy SmartArt**, and then click the **SmartArt Tools Design tab**.

h. Select the **Striking (Atemi) shape**, and then click **Add Shape arrow** in the Create Graphic group. Select **Add Shape Below**, and then type **Leg (Ashi Ate)**.

i. Click **Simple Fill** in the SmartArt Styles group.

j. Click the **More button** in the Layouts group on the SmartArt Tools Design tab, and then select **More Layouts**. Click **Horizontal Hierarchy** in the *Hierarchy* section.

k. On Slide 1, select the image, click the **Format tab**, and then click **Color** in the Adjust group. Click **Grayscale** in the Recolor variations category (first row, second column).

l. On Slide 4, right-click the image, and then select **Edit Picture**. Click **Yes** to convert the picture into a drawing object. Select the image again.

m. Click the **Format tab**, and then click **Group** in the Arrange group. Select **Ungroup**.

n. Click the **View tab**, and then click **Zoom** in the Zoom group. Select **200%**, and then click **OK**. Deselect the shapes, and then scroll until you see the faces.

o. Press and hold **Ctrl**, and then click each of the lines and shapes that were used to create the eyebrows, eyes, and mouths on the two fighters. Press **Delete**.

p. Click **Fit to Window** in the Zoom group.

q. Drag a selection net around all the shapes composing the clip art image, click the **Format tab**, click **Group** in the Arrange group, and select **Regroup**.

r. Click the **Insert tab**, and then click **Shapes** in the Illustrations group. Click **Freeform** in the *Line* section.

s. Click approximately **1″** from the left knee of the fighter on the left to create the first point of a freeform shape you create to resemble a mat (see Figure 3.60).

t. Click approximately **1″** from the right foot of the fighter on the left to create the second point of the freeform shape.

u. Click approximately **1/2″** vertically and horizontally from the bottom right of the slide.

v. Click approximately **1/2″** vertically and horizontally from the bottom left of the slide.

w. Click the starting point of the freeform shape to complete the shape.

x. Click the **Format tab**, click the **Send Backward arrow**, and then select **Send to Back**.

y. View the slide show. Save and close the file, and submit based on your instructor's directions.

1 Project Management Life Cycle

CREATIVE CASE

You have been asked to train the employees of a family-owned company about the life cycle of a project. You begin a slide show by creating an infographic, and then you apply Quick Styles and make customizations to create a professional look. Refer to Figure 3.61 as you complete this exercise.

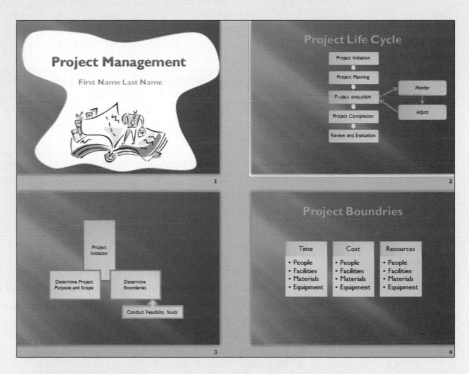

FIGURE 3.61 Project Management ➤

a. Open *p03m1projmgt* and save it as **p03m1projmgt_LastnameFirstname**. On Slide 1, replace *First Name Last Name* with your name.

b. Create a handout header with your name, and a handout footer with your instructor's name and your class. Include the current date.

c. On Slide 2, insert a **Process SmartArt diagram** using the **Vertical Process style**.

d. Type the following points in the **Text pane**, and then close the Text pane.
   - **Project Initiation**
   - **Project Planning**
   - **Project Execution**
   - **Project Completion**
   - **Review and Evaluation**

e. Apply the **Subtle Effect** from the SmartArt styles group.

f. Create two rounded rectangle shapes to the right of the SmartArt. Type **Monitor** in the top rounded rectangle shape, and then type **Adjust** in the bottom rounded rectangle shape.

g. Change the font style in the two new shapes to **Italic**.

h. Apply the Shape Style **Subtle Effect - Brown, Accent 2** (fourth row, third column) to the new shapes.

i. Apply the Shape Outline Theme Color **Brown, Accent 2, Darker 50%** to the new shapes.

j. Change the Shape Fill color of the Project Execution shape to **Subtle Effect -Brown, Accent 2**, and then change the Shape Outline Theme Color to **Brown, Accent 2, Darker 50%** (sixth row, sixth column).

k. Create arrows between the *Project execution, Monitor,* and *Adjust* rectangles to indicate the cycle. Change the Shape Outline weight to **3 pt**.

l. On Slide 3, create four shapes with the following specifications:

Shape	Fill	Position	Dimensions	Text
Rectangle 1	Subtle Effect - Brown, Accent 2	From Top Left Corner: Horizontal: 3.25" Vertical: 1.33"	Height: 3" Width: 2.17"	Project Initiation
Rectangle 2	Subtle Effect - Brown, Accent 5	From Top Left Corner: Horizontal: 1.61" Vertical: 3.75"	Height: 1.42" Width: 2.5"	Determine Project Purpose and Scope
Rectangle 3	Subtle Effect - Brown, Accent 5	From Top Left Corner: Horizontal: 4.58" Vertical: 3.83"	Height: 1.42" Width: 2.5"	Determine Boundaries
Up Arrow Callout (*Block Arrows* section)	Subtle Effect - Orange, Accent 1	From Top Left Corner: Horizontal: 5.17" Vertical: 5.25"	Height: .92" Width: 3"	Conduct Feasibility Study

m. Change the outline weight for all shapes to **4 1/2 pt**.

n. On Slide 4, create a SmartArt List diagram using the **Horizontal Bullet List style**.

o. Type the following as the first and second level bullets in the **Text pane**:

- **Time**
  - **People**
  - **Facilities**
  - **Materials**
  - **Equipment**

p. Copy the text you entered, and then paste it into the Text pane two times. Edit the second and third first level bullets so they read **Cost** and **Resources**, as shown in Figure 3.61.

q. Apply the **Subtle Effect** from SmartArt styles.

r. On Slide 1, insert your choice of *project* clip art. Ungroup the clip art image, and then change the fill color of several shapes to theme colors.

s. Use the Freeform tool or Curve tool to create a shape that covers the title, your name, and the clip art image. Move the shape you created to the back so all other objects on the slide are visible. Edit the shape fill and outline, and then move the objects on the slide until you are satisfied with your title slide.

t. Modify the WordArt Style used on the title in the title slide by changing the fill, outline, and shape effects. Apply a WordArt Style to your name in the subtitle placeholder.

u. View the slide show. Save and close the file, and submit based on your instructor's directions.

2 SmartArt and Clip Art Ideas

To help you become familiar with the SmartArt Graphic gallery and the types of information appropriate for each type of diagram, you create a slide show of "SmartArt ideas." You also manipulate clip art. In this activity, you work extensively with sizing, placement, and fills. Refer to Figure 3.62 as you complete this exercise.

FIGURE 3.62 SmartArt and Clip Art ➤

a. Open *p03m2smart* and save it as **p03m2smart_LastnameFirstname**. On Slide 1, replace *First Name Last Name* with your name.

b. Create a handout header with your name, and a handout footer with your instructor's name and your class. Include the current date.

c. View the gridlines.

d. On Slide 2, insert a **Vertical Box List SmartArt diagram** (second row, second column in the List category), and then make the following modifications:
   - Apply the **Subtle Effect** from SmartArt Styles.
   - Change the text font size to **24 pt**.
   - Type the following list items into the **Text Pane**:
     - **List**
     - **Process**
     - **Cycle**
     - **Hierarchy**
     - **Relationship**
     - **Matrix**
     - **Pyramid**
     - **Picture**
   - Size the SmartArt diagram to **7″** wide, and then drag it so that it is at the horizontal center of the page using the grid to help you determine placement.
   - Align the bottom border of the SmartArt diagram with the last row of the gridline.

e. On Slide 3, insert an **Upward Arrow Process SmartArt diagram** (ninth row, third column in the Process category), and then make the following modifications:
   - Apply the **Simple Fill SmartArt Style**.
   - Type the following process steps in the **Text Pane**:
     - **Initiation and Development**
     - **Institutional Review**
     - **Campus Community Review**
     - **Preparation for Trustees**
     - **Trustees Approval**
   - Change the height of the SmartArt diagram to **6.17″** and the width to **10″**.
   - **Align Center** the diagram.
   - Align the top border of the SmartArt with the green border of the title placeholder.

f. On Slide 4, insert a **Basic Radial SmartArt diagram** (third row, second column in the Cycle category), and then make the following modifications:
   - Apply the **Polished SmartArt Style**.
   - Change the SmartArt colors to **Transparent Gradient Range - Accent 2** (first row, fifth column, Accent 2 variation).

- Type **Residential College** as the center hub, and then type **Build Community**, **Promote Personal Growth**, and **Support Academic Success** as the spokes around the hub. Remove the extra shapes.
- Set the height of the SmartArt to **5.5"** and the width to **6.67"**.
- Change the text fill to **Light Green, Accent 3, Lighter 80%**.

g. On Slide 5, insert a **Horizontal Hierarchy SmartArt diagram** (third row, fourth column in the Hierarchy category), and then make the following modifications:
- Apply the **Metallic Scene SmartArt Style** (third row, first column 1, 3-D variation).
- Leave the first- and second-level bullets blank in the Text pane, and then type the following in the third-level bullets: **Jones Paint & Glass**, **Quality Cleaners**, **Ames Automotive**, and **Smith Real Estate**.
- Use the Right to Left option in the Create Graphic group to change the orientation of the diagram.
- Drag the borders of the SmartArt graphic until it fits the page and the text is large enough to read.
- Change the text fill to **Light Green, Accent 3, Lighter 80%**.

h. On Slide 6, insert a **Basic Venn SmartArt diagram** (tenth row, fourth column in the Relationship category), and then make the following modifications:

DISCOVER

- Type the following as three bullets in the Text pane: **Anesthesiology**, **Nurses**, and **Surgeon**.
  - Insert a picture fill in the *Anesthesiology* shape using *p03m2anesth*.
  - Insert a picture fill in the *Nurses* shape using *p03m2nurses*.
  - Insert a picture fill in the *Surgeon* shape using *p03m2surgeon*.
- Recolor all images using the **Grayscale variation**.
- Format the SmartArt text with the **Gradient Fill - Dark Green, Accent 4, Reflection WordArt Style**.
- Use the grid to center the Venn diagram in the available space.

i. On Slide 7, insert a **Basic Matrix SmartArt diagram** (first row, first column in the Matrix category), and then make the following modifications:
- Apply the **Subtle Effect SmartArt Style**.
- Change the colors to **Colorful - Accent Colors**.
- Type the following text in the **Text pane**:
  - **Urgent & Important**
  - **Not Urgent & Important**
  - **Urgent & Not Important**
  - **Not Urgent & Not Important**

j. On Slide 8, insert a **Basic Pyramid SmartArt diagram** (first row, first column in the Pyramid category), and then make the following modifications:
- Apply the **Subtle Effect SmartArt Style**.
- Enter a blank space at the top pyramid level, and then add the following text to the remaining levels. You will add the text for the top pyramid level in a text box in a later step so that the font in the SmartArt is not reduced to a difficult-to-read font size.
  - **Esteem**
  - **Belonging and Love**
  - **Safety**
  - **Biological Needs**
- Drag the border of the SmartArt diagram until it fills the available white space on the slide. Deselect the pyramid.
- Create a text box on the top left of the slide, and then type **Self-Actualization** in the **text box**. Change the font size to **39 pt**. Drag the text box so it is centered over the top of the empty pyramid top.

k. On Slide 9, ungroup the complex clip art image until all grouping is undone. Make the following changes:
- Use a selection net to select all the shapes that make up the bottom-right balloon, and then drag the balloon up into the white cloud area.
- Click one of the bright red stripes in the balloon on the bottom left to select it. Shift-click, and then click the remaining two bright red stripes to add them to the selection. Change their fill color to **Yellow** in the Standard category.
- Use a selection net to select all the shapes that make up the balloon on the left, and then apply a **Dark Blue outline** from the Standard category.
- Click anywhere on the clip art image, click **Group** in the Arrange group, and then click **Regroup**.

l. View the slide show. Save and close the file, and submit based on your instructor's directions.

You began a presentation on Waterwise landscaping and concentrated on the content of the presentation. You decide to use the SmartArt feature to create infographics to demonstrate a process and to incorporate shapes to demonstrate concepts.

Create a "Fire Aware" Landscape

You decide to create shapes to explain the concept of creating zones to protect a home from fire and indicate the depth of the zones on the landscape. You stack three oval shapes to create the zones, and then you use a combination of text boxes and clip art to create the landscape. Refer to Figure 3.63 as you complete this exercise.

FIGURE 3.63 Fire Aware Landscaping ➤

a. Open *p03c1xeri* and save it as **p03c1xeri_Lastname Firstname**. Create a handout header with your name, and a handout footer with your instructor's name and your class. Include the current date.

b. On Slide 12, insert an oval shape in the approximate center of the blank area of the slide. This will be the center oval in a stack of ovals used to define the zones. Apply the following modifications to the shape:
   - Change the Shape Fill to a custom RGB color: **Red:51, Green:102, and Blue:0**, and a **Transparency** of **50%**.
   - Remove the outline from the shape.
   - Change the oval size to a height of **1.67"** and width of **6"**.

c. Make a copy of the oval you created in step b. Change the second oval size to a height of **2.92"** and width of **8.08"**.

d. Make a third copy of the oval, and then change the third oval size to a height of **4"** and width of **10"**.

e. Select all three ovals, and then **Align Center** and **Align Middle**. Group the three ovals so they will move as one, and then position the group at horizontal position: **0"**

from the top-left corner and vertical position: **1"** from the top-left corner.

f. Insert a text box, type **Zone 1**, and then drag it to the bottom center of the small oval. Apply the **Fill - White, Outline - Accent 1 WordArt Quick Style** (use the **More button**) to the text. Make two copies of the text box, and then edit them to read *Zone 2* and *Zone 3*. Drag **Zone 2** to the bottom center of the medium-sized oval, and then drag **Zone 3** to the bottom center of the large oval.

g. **Align Center** the text boxes.

h. Locate and insert a clip art image of a house, and position it in the center of Zone 1. Size it appropriately.

i. Create an arrow that begins near the left edge of the house image and points left to the edge of the Zone 1 oval (see Figure 3.63). Create another arrow that begins near the end of the first arrow and ends at the edge of the Zone 2 oval, and a similar arrow for Zone 3. Set the weight for the arrows at **1 pt**. Set the arrow color to **White, Background 1**.

j. Create three text boxes and center one above each arrow. Label the Zone 1 text box **30'**, and then label the Zone 2 and 3 text boxes **10'**. Format the text color to **white**.

k. Locate and insert a clip art image of a tree. Duplicate it multiple times, and then position a few trees in Zone 2 and more trees in Zone 3. Size trees toward the top of the slide smaller than trees nearer the bottom of the zones. Refer to Figure 3.63, but your tree and tree placement can vary.

Convert Text to SmartArt

To add visual interest to slides, you go through the slide show and convert some of the bulleted lists to SmartArt graphics. Refer to Figure 3.64 as you complete this exercise.

FIGURE 3.64 Text Converted to SmartArt ➤

a. On Slide 2, convert the bulleted text to a **Basic Venn SmartArt graphic**.

b. On Slide 3, select the **Waterwise Options bulleted text**, and then convert it to a **Converging Arrow SmartArt graphic**. Apply the following modifications to the graphic:
  - Resize the graphic so that the arrows almost touch in the middle to show the convergence of the methods around the theme of conserving water.
  - Align the SmartArt diagram in the middle of the horizontal space for *Waterwise Options*.
  - Apply the **Polished SmartArt Style**.

c. Select the **Wildfire Aware Options bulleted text**, and convert it to a **Continuous Arrow Process SmartArt graphic** to indicate that the creation of defensible landscaping leads to zones. Apply the **Polished SmartArt Style**, and then change the text color for each text block in the arrow to **White, Background 1**.

d. Check the spelling in the slide show, and then accept all spellings on the slide.

Create SmartArt

You have a list of waterwise landscaping principles that you decide would present well as a SmartArt list. Refer to Figure 3.65 as you complete this exercise.

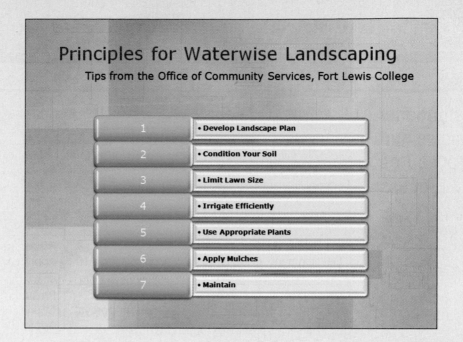

FIGURE 3.65 SmartArt Showing a Work-Flow Process ➤

a. Add a new slide after Slide 12 using a **Title Only layout**.

b. Type **Principles for Waterwise Landscaping** in the **title placeholder**. Change the title font size to **32 pt**, and then resize the placeholder so the title displays on one line.

c. Insert a text box, and then type **Tips from the Office of Community Services, Fort Lewis College** inside. Center the text under the title.

d. Insert a Vertical Block List SmartArt to show the steps, or work flow, in the Waterwise Landscaping process. Type the text in the following table in the **Text pane**. The number should be at Level 1, and the process text should be at Level 2.

Number	Process Text
1	Develop Landscape Plan
2	Condition Your Soil
3	Limit Lawn Size
4	Irrigate Efficiently
5	Use Appropriate Plants
6	Apply Mulches
7	Maintain

Convert Text to WordArt

The last graphic you want to insert is a WordArt object. After inserting the WordArt, you will apply an animation scheme.

a. On Slide 1, select the title.

b. Apply the **Gradient Fill - Indigo, Accent 6, Inner Shadow WordArt Style** (fourth row, second column) to the title.

c. Apply a **Transform Text Effect** to the title using the **Chevron Up Warp style** (second row, first column in the Warp category).

d. Apply the **Fill - White, Drop Shadow WordArt Style** (first row, third column) to the subtitle.

e. Apply the **Fly In animation** to the title, and then apply the **Fade animation** to the subtitle.

f. View the slide show. Save and close the file, and submit based on your instructor's directions.

Institutional Policies and Procedures Approval Process

GENERAL CASE

The president of your college has asked you to create a one-page document that shows the process that a policy or procedure must go through to be adopted. Create the flow chart using grids and guides to place the necessary shapes. Refer to Figure 3.66 for the text to be placed in the shapes. Because your output will be printed, you can use smaller fonts than you would use for a presentation. Create a handout header with your name, and a handout footer with your instructor's name and your class. Include the current date. Save your file as **p03b1flow_LastnameFirstname**. Save and close the file, and submit based on your instructor's directions.

Stage 1	Stage 2	Stage 3	Stage 4	Stage 5
Initiation and Development	Institutional Entity Review	Campus Community Review	Procedures Approval	Policy Approval
Origination	Steward	President's Council Approval for Review	President's Council Final Approval	Board of Trustees Reviews Policy
President's Council Sponsorship	Dean's Council	Posted on Intranet for Review	Procedures Approved	Policies Approved
Policy Steward Assigned	Faculty Senate		Web Manager Notifies Campus Community	Web Manager Notifies Campus Community
Policy/ Procedure Development	PACE			Forward Policy to Board of Regents When Required
	Student Council			
	Others as Needed			

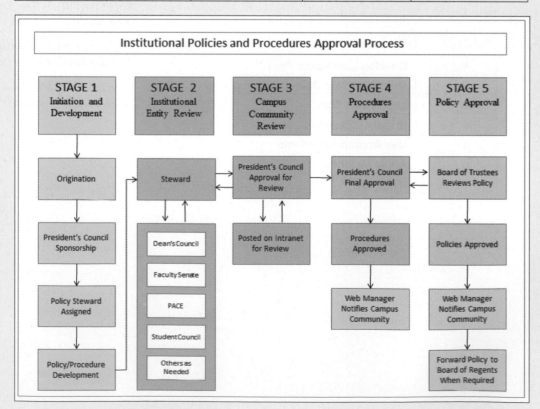

FIGURE 3.66 Policies and Procedures Approval Process Flow Chart ➤

Learning from the Professionals

RESEARCH CASE

Referring to professional Web sites can provide you with a wealth of tips and ideas for creating slide shows and presenting effectively. Search the Internet for articles relating to PowerPoint tips and tricks. Visit the sites listed in the table below, and read the articles. If a Web site is no longer active, move to another article. Create a slide show with a minimum of four slides summarizing what you learn. One of the slides should be a slide with Tips and Tricks. Create a slide illustrating a tip you learned. Insert SmartArt, Word Art, and clip art, and then modify the objects so they have an attractive and professional format. Create a handout header with your name, and a handout footer with your instructor's name and your class. Include the current date. Save the presentation as **p03b2ppt_LastnameFirstname**. Save and close the file, and submit based on your instructor's directions.

Professional Web Sites to Visit		
Web/Article Title	**Author**	**Web Site**
Presentation Zen	Garr Reynolds	http://presentationzen.blogs.com
Beyond Bullet Points	Cliff Atkinson	http://www.beyondbullets.com
Better Presenting	Rick Altman	http://www.betterppt.com
The Gettysburg Power-Point Presentation	Peter Norvig	http://www.norvig.com/Gettysburg
Ask the PowerPoint Experts	Microsoft Office Online	http://blogs.msdn.com/powerpoint
Microsoft PowerPoint	Indezine, compiled by Geetesh Balaj	http://www.indezine.com

Kelso Performing Arts Center

DISASTER RECOVERY

The chair of a local volunteer group has asked you to review and make changes to a presentation about the Kelso Performing Arts Center. Open *p03b3arts* and save it as **p03b3arts_LastnameFirstname**. Improve the presentation by converting the title to WordArt and applying WordArt transformations, recoloring images to match the theme, creating SmartArt to match the theme, and converting bullet content into SmartArt. Create a hierarchy SmartArt clarifying the organization structure of the Executive Committee. The committee has the following subcommittees: Finance Committee (Investments, Financial Oversight), Program Committee (Grants, Distribution), and Marketing (Public Relations, Fundraising). Create a handout header with your name, and a handout footer with your instructor's name and your class. Include the current date. Save and close the file, and submit based on your instructor's directions.

4 POWERPOINT RICH MEDIA TOOLS

Enhancing with Multimedia

Watch the
Set-up Video
for this
Case Study!

CASE STUDY | Wedding Albums

Your sister was recently married. As a gift to the couple, you decide to create two memory slide shows to celebrate. The first slide show will feature images of the couple in high school at their first formal dance, a few engagement photos, and two wedding photos. The second slide show will display photos taken during family vacations.

As you prepare the first slide show, you edit the images using PowerPoint's Picture Tools. Each slide in the first slide show is created individually, and each image is manipulated individually. You download an image from the Internet representing the couple's honeymoon and insert a video of fireworks recorded by the groom during the honeymoon. You insert a fireworks sound clip and also narrate a portion of the bride's vows. Finally, you create the second slide show of family vacations using PowerPoint's Photo Album feature. You utilize the Photo Album options for image manipulation.

OBJECTIVES AFTER YOU READ THIS CHAPTER, YOU WILL BE ABLE TO:

1. Insert a picture *p.920*
2. Transform a picture *p.922*
3. Use the Internet as a resource *p.933*
4. Add video *p.943*
5. Use Video Tools *p.946*

6. Add audio *p.953*
7. Change audio settings *p.955*
8. Create a Photo Album *p.961*
9. Set Photo Album options *p.962*

Pictures

Multimedia is multiple forms of media used to entertain or inform an audience.

Multimedia is multiple forms of media such as text, graphics, sound, animation, and video that are used to entertain or inform an audience. You can utilize any of these types of media in PowerPoint by placing the multimedia object on a slide. You already have placed text and graphics in presentations, and you have applied animations to objects and transitions to slides. In this chapter, you will expand your experience with multimedia by inserting pictures, sound, and video in slides.

Inserting a Picture

Multimedia graphics include clip art, objects created using drawing programs, diagrams and illustrations, pictures or photographs, scanned images, and more. You have worked extensively with clip art, diagrams, and illustrations using the Clip Organizer. In this section, you will concentrate on pictures.

A **bitmap image** is an image created by bits or pixels placed on a grid to form a picture.

Pictures are bitmap images that computers can read and interpret to create a photorealistic image. Unlike clip art vector images that are created by mathematical statements, *bitmap images* are created by bits or pixels placed on a grid or map. In a bitmap image, each pixel contains information about the color to be displayed. A bitmap image is required to have the realism necessary for a photograph. Think of vector images as connect-the-dots and bitmap images as paint-by-number, and you begin to see the difference in the methods of representation.

Each type of image has its own advantages and disadvantages. Vector graphics can be sized easily and still retain their clarity but are not photorealistic. Bitmap images represent a much more complex range of colors and shades but can become pixelated (individual pixels are visible and display square edges for a "jaggies" effect) when they are enlarged. A bitmap image can also be a large file, so *compression*, a method applied to data to reduce the amount of space required for file storage, may be applied. The compression may be lossy (some data may be lost when decompressed) or lossless (no data is lost when decompressed).

Compression is a method applied to data to reduce the amount of space required for file storage.

Figure 4.1 displays a pumpkin created as a vector image and one created as a bitmap image. Note the differences in realism. The boxes show a portion of the images enlarged. Note the pixelation in the enlarged portion of the bitmap image.

Enlarged vector graphic
Enlarged bitmap image
Bitmap image
Vector graphic

FIGURE 4.1 Types of Graphics ➤

To display a photograph in a slide, you must save it in a computer bitmap format. You can accomplish this task by scanning and saving a photograph or piece of artwork, by downloading images from a digital camera, by downloading a previously created bitmap image from the Microsoft Clip Organizer or the Internet, or by creating an image in a graphics-editing software package like Photoshop. Table 4.1 displays the types of graphic file formats that you can add to a PowerPoint slide in alphabetical order by file extension.

TABLE 4.1 Types of Graphic File Formats Supported by PowerPoint

File Format	Extension	Description
Windows Bitmap (Device Independent Bitmap)	.bmp, dib	A representation consisting of rows and columns of dots. The value of each dot is stored in one or more bits of data. Uncompressed and creates large file size.
Windows Enhanced Metafile	.emf, .wmf	A Windows 32-bit file format.
Microsoft Windows Metafile	.wmf	A Windows 16-bit file format.
Graphics Interchange Format	.gif	Limited to 256 colors. Effective for scanned images such as illustrations rather than for color photographs. Good for line drawings and black-and-white images. Supports transparent backgrounds.
Joint Photographic Experts Group	.jpg, .jpeg	Supports 16 million colors and is optimized for photographs and complex graphics. Format of choice for most photographs on the Web. Uses compression, but it is lossy.
Macintosh PICT	.pict, pic, pct	Holds both vector and bitmap images. PICT supports 8 colors; PICT2 supports 16 million colors.
Portable Network Graphics	.png	Supports 16 million colors. Approved as a standard by the World Wide Web Consortium (W3C). Intended to replace .gif format. Uses compression, but it is lossy.
Tagged Image File Format	.tif, .tiff	Best file format for storing bitmapped images on personal computers. Can be any resolution. Lossless image storage creates large file sizes. Not widely supported by browsers.

 Scanning Images

You can scan and download images directly to Microsoft's Clip Organizer. Put your image on the scanner glass, and then open the Clip Organizer. To open the Clip Organizer in Windows 7, click the Start button, click All Programs, click Microsoft Office, click Microsoft Office 2010 Tools, and then click Microsoft Clip Organizer. In Microsoft Clip Organizer, click File, point to Add Clips to Organizer, and then click From Scanner or Camera. When the Insert Picture from Scanner or Camera dialog box opens, select your scanner from the Device box, and then click Insert. The clip you scanned appears in My Collections, not on your slide. You would then need to insert the scanned image as you do any other image from the Clip Organizer. If you are in a lab setting, do this only if you have permission to add to the Clip Organizer and have permission for the photo rights.

To add a picture using a placeholder, do the following:

1. Select a layout with a placeholder that includes an Insert Picture from File button.
2. Click Insert Picture from File to open the Insert Picture dialog box.
3. Navigate to the location of your picture files, and then click the picture you want to use.
4. Click Insert.

Figure 4.2 shows two examples of placeholders with Insert Picture buttons. When you insert a picture in this manner, the picture is centered within the placeholder frame and is sometimes cropped to fit within the placeholder. This effect can cause unwanted results, such as the tops of heads cropped off. If this situation occurs, undo the insertion, enlarge the placeholder, and then repeat the steps for inserting an image.

Content placeholder

Picture placeholder

Insert Picture from File button

Click to add title

Click icon to add picture

• Click to add text

FIGURE 4.2 Insert Picture Using Placeholders ➤

Another way to insert an image is to click Picture on the Insert tab. The advantage of this method is that your image comes in at full size rather than centered and cropped in a placeholder, and you do not need a picture placeholder. You can then resize the image to fit the desired area. The disadvantage is you spend time resizing and positioning the image.

To add a picture using the Insert tab, do the following:

1. Click the Insert tab.
2. Click Picture in the Images group.
3. Navigate to the location of your picture files, and then click the picture you want to use.
4. Click Insert.
5. Adjust the size and position of the picture as necessary.

> **TIP** Adding Images Using Windows Explorer
>
> If you are adding multiple images to a slide show, you can speed up the process by inserting images directly from Windows Explorer. Open Windows Explorer and navigate to the folder where the images are located. Position the Windows Explorer window on top of the PowerPoint window, and then drag the images from the Explorer window onto the slides of your choice.

Transforming a Picture

Once you insert a picture onto a slide, PowerPoint provides powerful tools that you can use to adjust the image. Picture Tools are designed to adjust an image background, correct image problems, manipulate image color, or add artistic or stylized effects. You can also arrange, crop, or resize an image using Picture Tools. The Picture Tools are available when you select the picture in the slide and click the Picture Tools Format tab (see Figure 4.3).

Picture Tools tab

FIGURE 4.3 Picture Tools ➤

Remove a Picture Background

PowerPoint 2010's new feature, the Remove Background tool, enables you to remove portions of a picture you do not want to keep. Rather than have a rectangle-shaped picture on your slide, you can have an image that flows into the slide. When you select a picture and click the Remove Background tool in the Adjust group on the Format tab, PowerPoint creates an automatic marquee selection area in the picture that determines the *background*, or area to be removed, and the *foreground*, or area to be kept. PowerPoint identifies the background selection with magenta coloring. You can then adjust PowerPoint's automatic selection by marking areas you want to keep, marking areas you want to remove, and deleting any markings you do not want. You can discard any changes you have made or keep your changes. Figure 4.4 shows a picture in which the Remove Background tool has created a marquee identifying the foreground and background.

The **background** of a picture is the portion of a picture to be removed.

The **foreground** of a picture is the portion of the picture to be kept.

Remove Background marquee handle

Magenta-colored background showing areas to remove

Normally colored foreground showing areas to keep

FIGURE 4.4 Remove Background Marquee, Foreground, and Background ➤

Once the background has been identified by the marquee, you can refine the marquee size and shape so that it contains everything you want to keep without extra areas. Resize the marquee by dragging a marquee handle, the same process you use to resize clip art. Refine the picture further by using the tools available in the Background Removal tab (see Figure 4.5).

Click to mark areas to remove

Click to delete an unwanted mark

Click to discard all changes made to the picture

Click to keep all changes made to the picture

Background Removal tab

Click to mark areas to keep

FIGURE 4.5 Background Removal Tools ➤

Use the Mark Areas to Keep tool to add to the foreground, which keeps the area. Use the Mark Areas to Remove tool to add to the background, which eliminates the area. To use both tools, click and drag a line to indicate what should be added or removed. At any time in the process, you can press Esc or click away from the selection to see what the picture looks like. Then you can return to Background Removal and continue working with your picture. Figure 4.6 shows a resized marquee with enlarged areas marked to show areas to keep and to remove. Figure 4.7 shows the flower picture with the background removed.

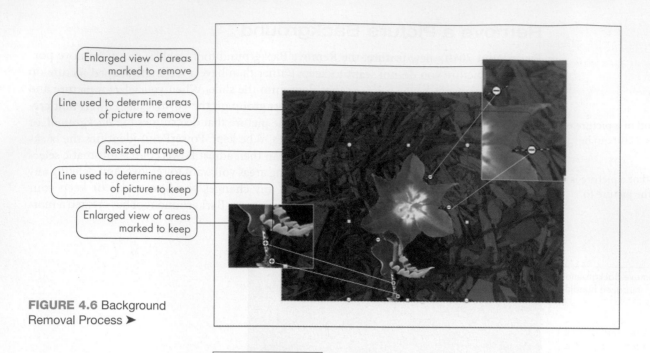

Enlarged view of areas
marked to remove

Line used to determine areas
of picture to remove

Resized marquee

Line used to determine areas
of picture to keep

Enlarged view of areas
marked to keep

FIGURE 4.6 Background
Removal Process ➤

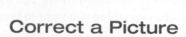

FIGURE 4.7 Background
Removed from Flower ➤

Correct a Picture

PowerPoint 2010 includes Corrections, a new set of tools in the Adjust group. As well as being able to adjust brightness and contrast as in previous versions, you can now soften or sharpen a picture. You can see what a correction will look like by previewing it in Live Preview.

You can enhance a picture by **sharpening** it or bringing out the detail by making the boundaries of the content more prominent. Or, you may want to **soften** the content or blur the edges so the boundaries are less prominent. Sharpening a picture can make it clearer, but oversharpening can make the picture look grainy. Softening is a technique often used for a more romantic image or to make skin appear softer, but applying too much blur can make the picture difficult to see.

To sharpen or soften a picture, do the following:

1. Select the picture.
2. Click the Picture Tools Format tab.
3. Click Corrections in the Adjust group.
4. Point to the thumbnails in the *Sharpen and Soften* section to view the corrections in Live Preview.
5. Click the thumbnail to apply the degree of correction you want.

You can make fine adjustments to the amount of brightness and contrast you apply to a picture. To make adjustments, follow Steps 1–3 above, and then click Picture Corrections Options at the bottom of the gallery. The Format Picture dialog box opens. Drag the Sharpen and Soften slider, or enter a percentage in the box next to the slider. Figure 4.8 shows the Corrections gallery, a picture that has been softened, and a picture that has been sharpened.

Sharpening enhances the edges of the content in a picture to make the boundaries more prominent.

Softening blurs the edges of the content in a picture to make the boundaries less prominent.

Click to open Corrections gallery

Sharpen and Soften options

Picture with 50% sharpening applied

Picture with 10% softening applied

FIGURE 4.8 Corrections Gallery and Softened and Sharpened Pictures ➤

Brightness refers to the lightness or darkness of a picture.

Contrast refers to the difference between the darkest and lightest areas of a picture.

The *brightness* (lightness or darkness) of a picture is often a matter of individual preference. You might need to change the brightness of your picture for reasons other than preference, however. For example, sometimes printing a picture requires a different brightness than is needed when projecting an image. This situation occurs because during printing, the ink may spread when placed on the page, making the picture darker. Or, you might want a picture as a background and need to reduce the brightness so that text will show on the background.

Contrast refers to the difference between the darkest area (black level) and lightest area (white level). If the contrast is not set correctly, your picture can look washed out or muddy; too much contrast, and the light portion of your image will appear to explode off the screen or page. Your setting may vary depending on whether you are going to project the image or print it. Projecting impacts an image because of the light in the room. In a very light room the image may seem to need a greater contrast than in a darker room, and you may need to adjust the contrast accordingly. Try to set your control for the lighting that will appear when you display the presentation.

To adjust the brightness and contrast of a picture, do the following:

1. Select the picture.
2. Click the Picture Tools Format tab.
3. Click Corrections in the Adjust group.
4. Point to the thumbnails in the *Brightness and Contrast* section to view the corrections in Live Preview.
5. Click the thumbnail to apply the degree of correction you want.

You can make fine adjustments to the amount of sharpening or softening you apply. To make adjustments, follow Steps 1–3 above, and then click Picture Corrections Options at the bottom of the gallery. The Format Picture dialog box opens. Drag the Brightness and Contrast sliders until you get the result you want, or enter percentages in the boxes next to the sliders. Figure 4.9 shows the Format Picture gallery displaying an adjustment for Brightness, an adjustment for Contrast, the original picture, and the adjusted picture.

Click to open Corrections gallery

Original picture

Darkened picture with more contrast

Reduced brightness setting (Brightness: −20%)

Click to open Format Picture dialog box

Increased contrast setting (Contrast: 30%)

FIGURE 4.9 Format Picture Dialog Box and Adjusted Picture ➤

Change Picture Color

You can change the colors in your picture by using PowerPoint's color tools. To access the color tools, do the following:

1. Select the picture.
2. Click the Picture Tools Format tab.
3. Click Color in the Adjust group.
4. Point to the thumbnails in the gallery to view the corrections in Live Preview.
5. Click the thumbnail to apply the color effect you want.

Saturation refers to the intensity of a color.

You can change a picture's *saturation*, or the intensity of the colors in an image. A high saturation level makes the colors more vivid, whereas 0% saturation converts the picture to grayscale. Figure 4.10 shows a picture at its original (100%) intensity and with various levels of intensity.

FIGURE 4.10 Picture Saturation ➤

- Click to access Color gallery
- Click thumbnail to select Saturation level
- Original picture at Saturation: 100%
- Picture with Saturation: 0%
- Picture with Saturation: 33%
- Picture with Saturation: 400%

Tone is the temperature of a color.

Kelvin is the unit of measurement for absolute temperature.

The *tone* or temperature of a color is a characteristic of lighting in pictures. It is measured in *kelvin (K)* units of absolute temperature. Higher color temperatures are cool colors and appear blueish white, whereas lower color temperatures are warm colors and appear yellowish to red. PowerPoint enables you to increase or decrease a picture's temperature to enhance its details. Point to a thumbnail to see the amount of temperature in Kelvin units that would be applied. Figure 4.11 shows a picture with its original cooler tone and a copy of the picture at a higher temperature with a warmer tone.

- Click thumbnail to select Color Tone
- Original image, Temperature: 6500 K
- Image with Temperature: 11200 K

FIGURE 4.11 Picture Color Tone ➤

Recolor is the process of changing picture colors to a duotone style.

Previously you *recolored* clip art illustrations by changing multiple colors to two colors. You can use the same process to recolor pictures. You can click a preset thumbnail from the gallery, or you can click More Variations to pick from additional colors. To return a picture to its original color, click the No Recolor preset thumbnail under the *Recolor* section. Figure 4.12 shows a picture with the Sepia Recolor preset applied.

FIGURE 4.12 Sepia Recolor Preset ➤

Use Artistic Effects

PowerPoint's new artistic effects enable you to change the appearance of a picture so that it looks like it was created with a marker, as a pencil sketch or watercolor painting, or using other effects. Use Live Preview to see how an artistic effect changes your picture because you can only apply one effect at a time. Any artistic effects that you have previously applied are lost when you apply a new effect. Figure 4.13 shows a Pencil Sketch artistic effect applied to a picture.

Click to open Artistic Effects gallery

Original picture

Pencil Sketch Artistic Effect applied

FIGURE 4.13 Pencil Sketch Artistic Effect ➤

To use an artistic effect, do the following:

1. Select the picture.
2. Click the Picture Tools Format tab.
3. Click Artistic Effects in the Adjust group.
4. Point to the thumbnails in the gallery to view the artistic effects in Live Preview.
5. Click the thumbnail of the artistic effect you want to use.

Apply Picture Styles

With Picture Styles, you can surround your picture with attractive frames, soften the edges of pictures, add shadows to the edges of pictures, apply 3-D effects to pictures, and add glossy reflections below your pictures. Many other effects are possible with Picture Styles, and when you consider that each of these effects can be modified, your creative opportunities are endless! Figure 4.14 shows a few of the possibilities.

> Many ... effects are possible with Picture Styles, and when you consider that each of these effects can be modified, your creative opportunities are endless!

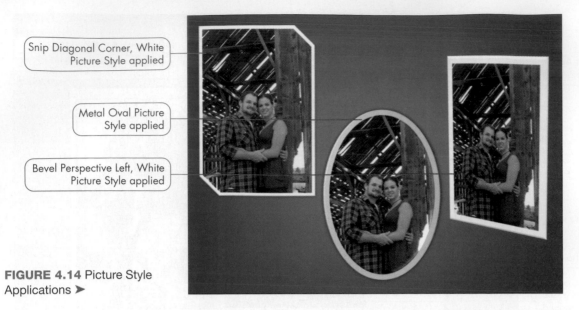

Snip Diagonal Corner, White Picture Style applied

Metal Oval Picture Style applied

Bevel Perspective Left, White Picture Style applied

FIGURE 4.14 Picture Style Applications ➤

To apply a picture style, select a picture and click a gallery image displayed in the Picture Style group on the Picture Tools Format tab. To see more styles, click the More button. Picture Border in the Picture Styles group enables you to select your border color, weight, or dash style. You can use the Picture Effects option to select from Preset, Shadow, Reflection, Glow, Soft Edges, Bevel, and 3-D Rotation effects. Use Picture Layout to apply your picture to a SmartArt diagram.

Crop a Picture

Cropping is the process of eliminating unwanted portions of an image from view.

Cropping a picture using the Crop tool lets you eliminate unwanted portions of an image from view, focusing the viewer's attention on what you want him or her to see. Remember that if you crop an image and try to enlarge the resulting picture, pixelation may occur that reduces the quality of the image. Figure 4.15 shows a picture with the areas to be cropped from view displayed in gray.

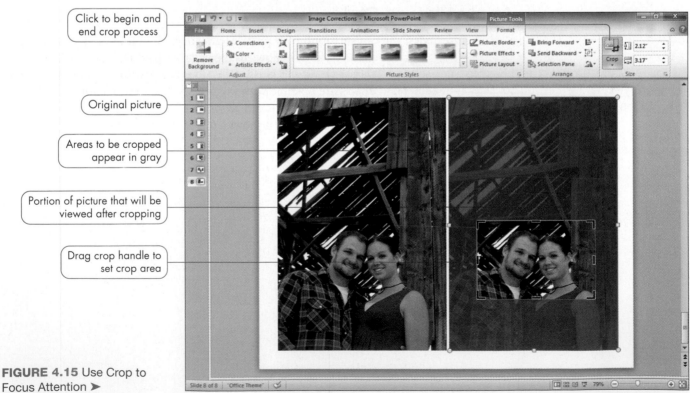

Click to begin and end crop process

Original picture

Areas to be cropped appear in gray

Portion of picture that will be viewed after cropping

Drag crop handle to set crop area

FIGURE 4.15 Use Crop to Focus Attention ➤

To crop a picture, do the following:

1. Select the picture.
2. Click the Picture Tools Format tab.
3. Click the Crop tool in the Size group.
4. Position the cropping tool over a cropping handle and drag inward to eliminate the portion of the image you do not want to view. Use a corner handle to crop in two directions at once.
5. Repeat Step 4 for the remaining sides of the picture.
6. Click the Crop tool.

When you crop a picture, the cropped part does not display on the slide, but it is not removed from the presentation file. This is helpful in case you decide later to reset the picture to its original state. When you crop an image, because the unwanted portions of the image are not deleted, the file size is not reduced. Use the Compress Pictures feature to reduce the file size of the image, or all images at once, to reduce the file size of the presentation.

Compress Pictures

When you add pictures to your PowerPoint presentation, especially high-resolution pictures downloaded from a digital camera, the presentation file size dramatically increases. It may increase to the point that the presentation becomes slow to load and sluggish to play. The increase in the file size depends on the resolution of the pictures you add. Use the Compress Pictures feature to eliminate a large part of this problem. The Compress Pictures feature is in the Adjust group in the Picture Tools Format tab.

The Compress Pictures option can help you manage large image files by changing the resolution of pictures and by permanently deleting any cropped areas of a selected picture. By default, you apply compression to only the selected image. If you remove the check, all pictures in the presentation are compressed. You select the amount of compression applied by determining your output. Select 220 pixels per inch (ppi) to ensure you will obtain a good quality printout. Select 150 ppi, however, if you will only be displaying the slide show onscreen or using it for a Web page. Select 96 ppi if you plan to e-mail the slide show. Figure 4.16 shows the Compress Pictures dialog box.

FIGURE 4.16 Picture Compression Options ➤

Create a Background from a Picture

Pictures can make appealing backgrounds if they are transparent enough that text on top of them can be easily read. Picture backgrounds personalize your presentation. To use a photograph as a background, use the Format Background command rather than the Insert Picture feature. Using Insert Picture involves more time because when the picture is inserted it must be resized and the order of the objects on the screen has to be changed to prevent the photograph from hiding placeholders. Figure 4.17 shows an image inserted using Insert Picture that must be resized if it is to be used as a background. It hides the placeholders, so it needs to be positioned at the back and its transparency must be adjusted. Figure 4.18 shows the same picture as Figure 4.17, but in this figure, it was inserted as a background. It is automatically placed behind placeholders and resized to fit the slide, and the transparency is adjusted.

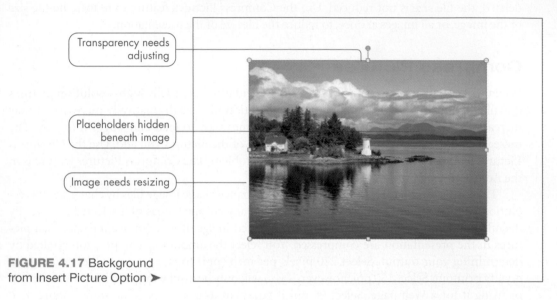

FIGURE 4.17 Background from Insert Picture Option ➤

FIGURE 4.18 Background from Background Styles Option ➤

To create a background from a picture using the Background command, do the following:

1. Click the Design tab.
2. Click Background Styles in the Background group.
3. Select Format Background, and then click the Fill category.
4. Click *Picture or texture fill.*
5. Click File, and then navigate to the location where your picture is stored.
6. Click the picture file, and then click Insert.
7. Click Close to apply the picture background to the current slide, or click Apply to All to apply it to all slides in the presentation.

The dialog box also includes options for moving the picture by offsetting it to the left or right or the top or bottom, and for adjusting the transparency amount.

Using the Internet as a Resource

PowerPoint interacts with the Internet in three important ways. First, you can download resources from any Web page for inclusion in a PowerPoint presentation. Second, you can insert hyperlinks into a PowerPoint presentation, and then click those links to display the associated Web page in your browser. Finally, you can convert any PowerPoint presentation into a Web page. Be sure to check for copyright permissions and to give credit to sources. In this chapter, you will use the Internet as a resource for pictures, video, and audio.

Regardless of how you choose to use a photograph, your first task is to access the Web and locate the required image. After you choose an image, right-click it to display a shortcut menu, and then select Save Picture As to download the file to your hard drive. When you right-click the photograph, you can also select Copy to copy the picture onto the Clipboard.

To insert a downloaded picture in PowerPoint, click the Insert tab, and then click Picture in the Images group. If you copied the picture, simply paste it onto the slide. You also can click Insert Hyperlink in the Links group on the Insert tab to insert a hyperlink to the resource Web site. You can click the hyperlink during the slide show, and provided you have an Internet connection, your browser will display the associated page.

Understand Copyright Protection

Copyright is the legal protection afforded to a written or artistic work.

A **copyright** provides legal protection to a written or artistic work, including literary, dramatic, musical, and artistic works such as poetry, novels, movies, songs, computer software, and architecture. It gives the author of a work the exclusive right to the use and duplication of that work. A copyright does not protect facts, ideas, systems, or methods of operation, although it may protect the way these things are expressed.

> Anything on the Internet should be considered copyrighted unless the site specifically says it is in the public domain....

The owner of the copyright may sell or give up a portion of his or her rights; for example, an author may give distribution rights to a publisher and/or grant movie rights to a studio. **Infringement of copyright** occurs anytime a right held by the copyright owner is violated without permission of the owner. Anything on the Internet should be considered copyrighted unless the site specifically says it is in the **public domain**, in which case the author is giving everyone the right to freely reproduce and distribute the material, thereby making the work owned by the public at large. A work also may enter the public domain when the copyright has expired. Facts themselves are not covered by copyright, so you can use statistical data without fear of infringement. Images are protected unless the owner gives his or her permission for downloading.

Infringement of copyright occurs when a right of the copyright owner is violated.

Public domain refers to rights to a literary work or property owned by the public at large.

The answer to what you can use from the Web depends on many things, including the amount of the information you reference, as well as the intended use of that information. It is considered fair use, and thus not an infringement of copyright, to use a portion of a work for educational or nonprofit purposes, or for critical review or commentary. In other words, you can use quotes, facts, or other information from the Web in an educational setting, but you should cite the original work in your footnotes, or list the resource on a bibliography page or slide. The Reference table below presents guidelines for students and teachers to help determine what multimedia can be used in an educational project based on the Proposal for Fair Use Guidelines for Educational Multimedia created in 1996. These guidelines were created by a group of publishers, authors, and educators who gathered to interpret the Copyright Act of 1976 as it applies to educational and scholarly uses of multimedia. You should note that although these guidelines are part of the Congressional Record, they are not law. They can, however, help you determine when you can use multimedia materials under Fair Use principles in a non-commercial, educational use.

REFERENCE Multimedia Copyright Guidelines for Students and Teachers

The following guidelines are based on Section 107 of the U.S. Copyright Act of 1976 and the Proposal for Fair Use Guidelines for Educational Multimedia (1996), which sets forth fair use factors for multimedia projects. These guidelines cover the use of multimedia based on Time, Portion, and Copying and Distribution Limitations. For the complete text of the guidelines, see www.uspto.gov/web/offices/dcom/olia/confu/confurep.pdf.

General Guidelines

- Student projects for specific courses may be displayed and kept in personal portfolios as examples of their academic work.
- Students in specific courses may use multimedia in projects with proper credit and citations. Full bibliographic information must be used when available.
- Students and teachers must display copyright notice if copyright ownership information is shown on the original source. Copyright may be shown in a sources or bibliographic section unless the presentation is being used for distance learning. In distance learning situations, copyright must appear on the screen when the image is viewed.
- Teachers may use media for face-to-face curriculum-based instruction, for directed self-study, in demonstrations on how to create multimedia productions, for presentations at conferences, and for distance learning. Teachers may also retain projects in their personal portfolios for personal use such as job interviews or tenure review.
- Teachers may use multimedia projects for educational purposes for up to two years, after which permission of the copyright holder is required.
- Students and teachers do not need to write for permission to use media if it falls under multimedia guidelines unless there is a possibility that the project could be broadly distributed at a later date.

(Continued)

Text Guidelines

- Up to 10 percent of a copyrighted work, or up to 1000 words, may be used, whichever is less.
- Up to 250 words of a poem, but no more than five poems (or excerpts) from different poets or an anthology. No more than three poems (or excerpts) from a single poet.

Illustrations

- A photograph or illustration may be used in its entirety.
- Up to 15 images, but no more than 15 images from a collection.
- No more than 5 images of an artist's or photographer's work.

Motion Media

- Up to 10 percent of a copyrighted work or 3 minutes, whichever is less.
- Clip cannot be altered in any way.

Music and Sound

- Up to 10 percent of a copyrighted musical composition, not to exceed 30 seconds.
- Up to 10 percent of a sound recording, not to exceed 30 seconds.
- Alterations cannot change the basic melody or fundamental character of the work.

Distribution Limitations

- Multimedia projects should not be posted to unsecured Web sites.
- No more than two copies of the original may be made, only one of which may be placed on reserve for instructional purposes.
- A copy of a project may be made for backup purposes, but may be used only when the original has been lost, damaged, or stolen.
- If more than one person created a project, each person may keep only one copy.

In the following Hands-On Exercise, you will insert pictures (bitmap images) into slides, both with and without using content placeholders. You will use Picture Tools to remove a background from an image, to soften and sharpen an image, and to adjust the brightness, contrast, saturation, and tone of a picture. You will apply a picture style and modify its effects. You will crop a picture and compress all the images in the slide show. You will also create a background for a slide from a picture. Finally, you will learn about using the Internet as a resource for images and review the Fair Use guidelines relating to student use of media downloaded from the Internet. You will download a picture from the Internet and insert the picture into a slide show.

1 Pictures

You decide to create a memories slide show for your sister and her husband, who were recently married. You include their high school Sweetheart Ball image, engagement and wedding pictures, and a picture to remind them of scuba diving on their honeymoon.

Skills covered: Insert Pictures and Remove a Background • Apply an Artistic Effect and a Picture Style • Correct a Picture and Change Picture Color • Crop and Compress Pictures • Create a Background from a Picture • Insert a Picture from the Internet

---

STEP 1 ▶ INSERT PICTURES AND REMOVE A BACKGROUND

You start the memory album with a picture from the couple's Sweetheart Ball. Because the Title Slide layout does not include a placeholder for content, you add a picture using the Insert Picture from File feature. You then insert images into content placeholders provided in the album layout. Refer to Figure 4.19 as you complete Step 1.

Resized and positioned image

Images inserted using content placeholders

Background removed

FIGURE 4.19 Inserted Pictures ➤

a. Open the *p04h1memory* presentation, and then save it as **p04h1memory_LastnameFirstname**. Use your last and first names. For example, as the PowerPoint author, I would name my workbook "p04h1memory_KrebsCynthia."

> **TROUBLESHOOTING:** If you make any major mistakes in this exercise, you can close the file, open *p04h1memory* again, and then start this exercise over.

b. Create a handout header with your name, and a handout footer with your instructor's name and your class. Include the current date.

c. On Slide 1, click the **Insert tab**, and then click **Picture** in the Images group.

   You add a picture using the Insert Picture from File command because the Title Slide layout does not include a placeholder for content. The Insert Picture dialog box opens.

d. Locate the *p04h1mem1.jpg* file in the *p04h1_3memory_media* folder, and then click **Insert**.

   The picture is inserted, sized to fit within the slide margins, and centered on the slide.

e. Click the **Size Dialog Box Launcher** in the Size group on the Picture Tools Format tab to open the Format Picture dialog box. Click in the **Height box** in the *Scale* section, select **100**, and then type **90**. Click in the **Width box** in the *Scale* section, and it will change to *90%* automatically.

   Typing 90 in the Height box automatically sets the scale for Width to 90% because the *Lock aspect ratio* check box is selected.

f. Click **Position** in the Format Picture dialog box, and then set the **Position on slide Horizontal option** to **4.5″** from the Top Left Corner. Set the **Position on slide Vertical option** to **.5″** from the Top Left Corner. Click **Close**.

g. Click the **Insert tab**, click **Picture** in the Images group, and then locate and insert *p04h1mem2.jpg*.

The picture fills the slide. It is selected, and the Picture Tools Format tab is active.

h. Click **Remove Background** in the Adjust group.

An automatic marquee appears around the image that includes most of the flower. Some petals are cut off and need to be added back in.

i. Drag the top-center sizing handle of the marquee to the top of the image.

The top petal is now included in the marquee.

j. Drag the left-center and bottom-center sizing handles of the marquee until all petals are included in the picture (see Figure 4.20).

FIGURE 4.20 Adjusted Marquee ➤

k. Click **Keep Changes**.

The background is removed from the flower.

l. Click the **Size Dialog Box Launcher** in the Size group to open the Format Picture dialog box, and then remove the check in the **Relative to original picture size checkbox** in the *Scale* section. Click in the **Height box**, and then type **40**. Click in the **Width box** in the *Scale* section, and it will change to *40%* automatically.

m. Click the **Position tab** in the Format Picture dialog box, and then set the **Position on slide Horizontal option** to **0.17″** from the Top Left Corner. Set the **Position on slide Vertical option** to **4.83″** from the Top Left Corner. Click **Close**.

n. On Slide 2, click **Insert Picture from File** in the large content placeholder on the left side of the slide. Click the *p04h1mem3.jpg* file to select it, and then click **Insert**.

o. Use the **Insert Picture from File buttons** in the two small content placeholders on the right side of the screen to insert *p04h1mem4.jpg* and *p04h1mem5.jpg* into your presentation.

Note that in all three cases the images were centered inside the placeholders. The picture of the hands is cropped because it was in portrait orientation but placed in a landscape placeholder.

p. Save the presentation.

The title slide includes a picture of the couple that you want to stand out. The Artistic Effects gallery includes many picture effects, and the Picture Styles gallery includes a variety of Picture Border effects. You decide to experiment with the options available in the galleries to see the impact they have on the title slide picture. You apply an artistic effect and a picture style. Refer to Figure 4.21 as you complete Step 2.

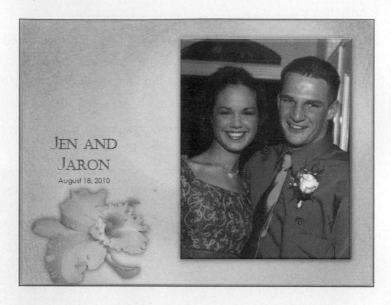

FIGURE 4.21 Applied Artistic Effect and Picture Styles ▶

a. On Slide 1, select the picture of the couple, and then click the **Picture Tools Format tab**.

b. Click **Artistic Effects** in the Adjust group.

   The Artistic Effects gallery opens. Point to the effects, and watch how each effect impacts the image.

> **TROUBLESHOOTING:** Some of the artistic effects involve extensive changes, so expect a slowdown as the preview is created.

c. Click **Texturizer** (fourth row, second column).

   A light texture is applied to the picture.

d. Click the **More button** in the Picture Styles group.

   The Picture Styles gallery opens. Point to the styles and watch how each style impacts the image.

e. Click **Center Shadow Rectangle** (third row, first column).

   A gray shadow appears evenly around the picture.

f. Click the **Home tab**, click **Format Painter**, and then click the flower picture.

   You copied the artistic effect and picture style and then applied it to the flower.

g. Select the picture of the couple again, and then click the **Picture Tools Format tab**.

h. Click **Picture Border** in the Picture Styles group, and then click **White, Accent 3, Darker 10%** (second row, seventh column) in the *Theme Colors* section.

i. Click **Picture Effects** in the Picture Styles group, point to **Bevel**, and then click **Cool Slant** (first row, fourth column of the *Bevel* section).

The Bevel effect is applied to the outer edges of the picture.

j. Save the presentation.

STEP 3 ## CORRECT A PICTURE AND CHANGE PICTURE COLOR

You want to include two pictures of the couple in the memory album, but the pictures were taken in different lighting conditions. You decide to use PowerPoint's correction tools to enhance the pictures. You also change the color of a picture to match the cool-toned blue theme of the presentation. Refer to Figure 4.22 as you complete Step 3.

FIGURE 4.22 Applied Artistic Effect and Picture Styles ➤

a. On Slide 3, use **Insert Picture from File** in the content placeholders to insert *p04h1mem6.jpg* into the left placeholder and *p04h1mem7.jpg* into the right placeholder.

b. Select the image on the left, and then click **Corrections** in the Adjust group on the Picture Tools Format tab. Click **Brightness: −20% Contrast: +20%** (fourth row, second column of the *Brightness and Contrast* section).

The image became slightly darker, and the increased contrast brings out the picture detail.

c. Select the image on the right, and then click **Corrections** in the Adjust group on the Picture Tools Format tab. Click **Brightness: +20% Contrast: −40%** (first row, fourth column of the *Brightness and Contrast* section).

The image became brighter, and the contrast is reduced.

d. On Slide 4, select the picture of the bride.

e. Click **Color** in the Adjust group, and then click **Temperature: 4700 K** in the Color Tone gallery.

The warm tones in the image are converted to cooler tones, which casts a blue hue over the picture.

f. Click the **More button** in the Picture Styles group, and then click **Soft Edge Oval** (fourth row, second column).

g. Save the presentation.

STEP 4 ## CROP AND COMPRESS PICTURES

You have included pictures of the groom dancing with the flower girl but decide to crop one image. You compress the image to delete the unwanted areas. You also compress all images in the slide show to reduce the file size of the slide show. Refer to Figure 4.23 as you complete Step 4.

FIGURE 4.23 Cropped and Compressed Pictures ➤

a. On Slide 6, examine the picture on the far right of the slide.

Because the picture was framed with a window in the background, the light is a bright, white distraction. You decide to crop a portion of the window from view.

b. Click the **View tab**, and then click **Ruler** in the Show group, if necessary.

Activating the ruler will make it easier for you to determine the area to crop.

> **TROUBLESHOOTING:** The rulers are a toggle feature, so if yours are already displayed, skip step b or repeat it to redisplay the rulers if you closed them.

c. Select the large picture on the far right, click the **Picture Tools Format tab**, and then click **Crop** in the Size group.

d. Position the Crop tool over the right center cropping handle, and then drag inward until the guiding line on the vertical ruler reaches the +4 1/4″ mark.

The resulting size of the image is 7.5″ high and 4.29″ wide.

e. Click **Crop** in the Size group again to crop the area from view and to turn off the Crop feature.

f. Select the top-left picture, and then click the **Home tab**. Click **Format Painter**, and then click the picture you just cropped on the far right of the slide.

The picture style is copied onto the cropped picture.

g. Select the cropped picture, and then click the **Picture Tools Format tab**.

h. Click **Compress Pictures** in the Adjust group.

The Compress Pictures dialog box opens.

i. Click **Screen** in the *Target output* section.

j. Click the **Apply only to this picture check box** to deselect it.

You need to compress all the pictures you have used in the presentation to reduce the presentation file size, not just the selected picture.

k. Click **OK**.

The portions of the image that were cropped from view are deleted, and all pictures in the slide show are compressed.

l. Save the presentation.

STEP 5 ▶ CREATE A BACKGROUND FROM A PICTURE

The bride chose orchids for her table decorations, and you want to include a picture of one of the orchids as the background setting of a picture of the bride and groom. Refer to Figure 4.24 as you complete Step 5.

FIGURE 4.24 Background from a Picture ➤

a. Click the **Design tab**.

b. On Slide 5, click **Background Styles** in the Background group, and then select **Format Background**.

c. Click the **Hide background graphics check box** in the Format Background dialog box.

d. Click **Picture or texture fill**, and then click **File** to open the Insert Picture dialog box.

e. Select *p04h1mem2.jpg*, click **Insert**, and then click **Close**.

> **TROUBLESHOOTING:** If the orchid is not displayed, it may be blocked by the background graphics. Click the Hide Background Graphics check box in the Background group on the Design tab.

f. Save the presentation.

STEP 6 ▶ INSERT A PICTURE FROM THE INTERNET

The couple went scuba diving in Cancun, Mexico, during their honeymoon so you want to insert a picture of an underwater scene to end the slide show. You insert an image from Image*After, a Web site that provides pictures free for personal or commercial use. Refer to Figure 4.25 as you complete Step 6.

FIGURE 4.25 Inserted Picture from the Internet ➤

a. On Slide 7, note the text *Image*After* (imageafter.com) is a hyperlink.

The hyperlink will display if you view the presentation in Slide Show view.

b. Right-click the link, and then select **Open Hyperlink** to launch the Web site in your default browser.

> **TROUBLESHOOTING:** If you are not connected to the Internet, the hyperlink will not work. Connect to the Internet, and then repeat step b.

The Image*After Web site displays the nature-underwater group and shows thumbnails of images pertaining to underwater views.

c. Point, without clicking, to each thumbnail to see a bigger image. Try to find the same image that is shown in Figure 4.25. If you do not see that image, find another image that is similar.

d. Click the thumbnail to display a larger image. Right-click the image, select **Copy**, and then close the browser.

e. On Slide 7, paste the image using the **Picture paste option**.

f. Adjust the image size, depending on the size of the image you insert. If you located the image shown in Figure 4.25, resize the picture with a height of **7.5″** and a width of **5.63″**.

g. Drag the picture to position it on the slide, leaving the Image*After text box visible.

The Image*After text box should be visible to give credit to the image source.

h. Save the presentation, close the file, and then exit PowerPoint if you do not want to continue with the next Hands-On Exercise at this time.

Video

With video added to your project, you can greatly enhance and reinforce your story, and your audience can retain more of what they see. For example, a video of water tumbling over a waterfall would stir the emotions of a viewer far more than a table listing the number of gallons of water falling within a designated period of time. Anytime you can engage a viewer's emotions, he or she will better remember your message.

In this section, you will learn the types of video file formats that PowerPoint supports, examine the options available when using video, and insert a video clip into the memories presentation.

> With video added to your project, you can greatly enhance and reinforce your story, and your audience can retain more of what they see.

Adding Video

Table 4.2 displays the common types of movie file formats you can add to a presentation listed in alphabetical order by file extension. Different file formats use different types of *codec* (coder/decoder) software, which use algorithms to compress or code movies, and then decompress or decode the movies for playback. Video playback places tremendous demand on your computer system in terms of processing speed and memory. Using a codec reduces that demand. In order for your video file to be viewed correctly, the video player must have the appropriate software installed. Even though your video file extension is the same as the one listed in Table 4.2 or in Help, the video may not play correctly if the correct version of the codec software is not installed.

A **codec** (coder/decoder) is a digital video compression scheme used to compress a video and decompress for playback.

TABLE 4.2 Types of Video File Formats Supported by PowerPoint		
File Format	**Extension**	**Description**
Windows Media File	.asf	**Advanced Streaming Format** Stores synchronized multimedia data. Used to stream audio and video content, images, and script commands over a network.
Windows Video File	.avi	**Audio Video Interleave** Stores sound and moving pictures in Microsoft Resource Interchange File Format (RIFF).
Movie File	.mpg or .mpeg	**Moving Picture Experts Group** Evolving set of standards for video and audio compression developed by the Moving Picture Experts Group. Designed specifically for use with Video-CD and CD-i media.
Adobe Flash Media	.swf	**Flash Video** File format generally used to deliver video over the Internet. Uses Adobe Flash Player.
Windows Media Video File	.wmv	**Windows Media Video** Compresses audio and video by using Windows Media Video compressed format. Requires minimal amount of storage space on your computer's hard drive.

To **embed** is to store an object from an external source within a presentation.

To **link** is to establish a connection from a presentation to another location.

When you add video to your presentation, you can *embed* the video or store the video within the presentation, or you can *link* the video, which creates a connection from the presentation to another location such as a storage device or Web site. The advantage of embedding video is that a copy of the video file is placed in the slide so moving or deleting the original video will not impact your presentation. The advantage of linking a video file is that your presentation file size is smaller. A linked video is stored in its own file. Another advantage of linking over embedding is that the presentation video is updated automatically if the original video object is changed. One caution for using a linked video—the video is not part of the presentation, and if you save the presentation file to a different location, such as a flash drive, you must make sure you save the video to the new location, too. If you change the location of the video, you must make sure to change the link to the movie file in the presentation.

To insert or link a video in a presentation, do the following:

1. Click the Insert tab
2. Click the Video arrow in the Media group.
3. Click Video from File.
4. Browse, locate, and select the video you want to use in the presentation.
5. Click Insert to insert the video in your presentation, or click the Insert arrow and select Link to File to link the video to your presentation.

You can also embed video from an online video site such as YouTube. When you embed video from the online site, you have to copy and paste the Embed code from the online site into the Video from Web Site dialog box. Figure 4.26 shows the Embed code for the video in Figure 4.27 inserted into PowerPoint's Video from Web Site dialog box. Figure 4.27 shows a Commoncraft Video stored on YouTube (used with permission) and the location of the Embed code. If you have embedded video from an online site, you must be connected to the Internet when you display the presentation.

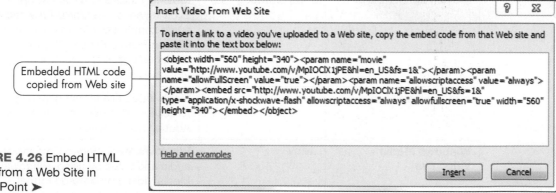

Embedded HTML code copied from Web site

FIGURE 4.26 Embed HTML Code from a Web Site in PowerPoint ➤

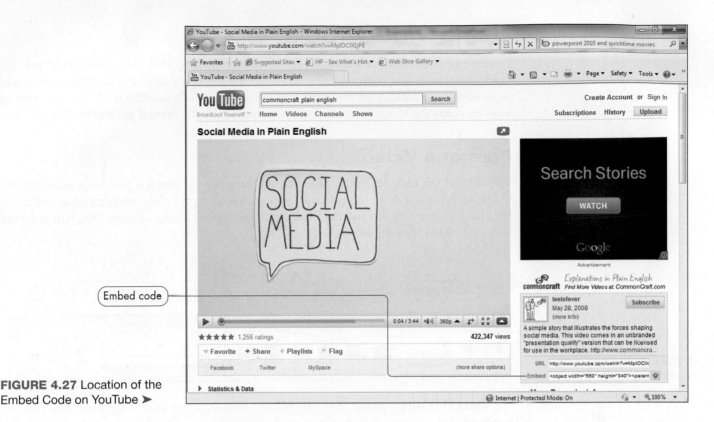

Embed code

FIGURE 4.27 Location of the Embed Code on YouTube ➤

To insert video from an online video site, do the following:

1. Locate video on an online video site.
2. Copy embedding code.
3. Click Insert tab in PowerPoint.
4. Click the Video arrow in the Media group.
5. Click Video from Web Site.
6. Paste the embedded HTML code into the box.
7. Click Insert.

Whether you have inserted your own video or video from a Web site, the video will include a Media Controls bar with a Play/Pause button, a Move Back 0.25 seconds button, a Move Forward 0.25 seconds button, a time notation, and a Mute/Unmute control slider. The Move Back and Move Forward 0.25 seconds buttons aid you when editing the video. The Media Controls bar is shown in Figure 4.20.

Play/Pause

Move Back and Move Forward 0.25 seconds

Mute/Unmute slider

FIGURE 4.28 Video Control Panel ➤

Using Video Tools

PowerPoint 2010 includes wonderful new tools for working with video. You can format the video's brightness and contrast, color, and style. You can apply most artistic image effects, add or remove bookmarks, trim the video, and set fade in or fade out effects. When you select an inserted video, the Video Tools tab displays with two tabs: the Format tab and the Playback tab.

Format a Video

The Format tab includes options for playing the video for preview purposes, adjusting the video, applying a style to the video, arranging a video on the slide, and cropping and sizing the video. Figure 4.29 displays the Video Tools Format tab. Some of these tools will not work with embedded Web site videos.

FIGURE 4.29 Video Tools Format Tab ➤

A **Poster Frame** is the frame that displays on a slide when a video is not playing.

Using the Adjust group, you can adjust video contrast and brightness, and you can recolor a video as you did when you worked with images. The Adjust group also includes the **Poster Frame** option, which enables you to choose a frame from within the embedded video or any image from your storage device to display on the PowerPoint slide when the video is not playing.

To create a poster frame from the video, do the following:

1. Click Play in the Preview group to display the video.
2. Pause the video when the frame you want to use as the poster frame appears.
3. Click Poster Frame in the Adjust group.
4. Click Current Frame.

To create a poster frame from an image stored in your storage device, do the following:

1. Click Poster Frame in the Adjust group.
2. Click Image from File.
3. Locate and select desired image.
4. Click Insert.

Figure 4.30 shows a video using the default first frame on the slide and a copy of the video with a poster frame set from the video.

FIGURE 4.30 Poster Frame Option ➤

The Style effects available for images are also available for videos. In addition to the styles in the Style gallery, you can edit the shape of a video, change the border of the video, and add style effects like Shadow, Reflection, Glow, Soft Edges, Bevel, and 3-D Rotation. Figure 4.31 shows a video formatted to fit a PowerPoint shape, with an olive green border and perspective shadow added.

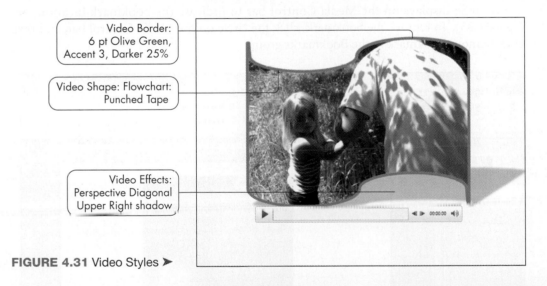

FIGURE 4.31 Video Styles ➤

TIP Resetting a Video

To discard all formatting changes from a selected video, click the Reset Design arrow in the Adjust group on the Video Tools Format tab, and then select Reset Design or Reset Design & Size.

Set Video Playback Options

The Video Tools Playback tab includes options used when viewing a video. You can preview the video, add or remove bookmarks, trim the video, fade the video in and out, control the volume, determine how to start the video, set the video to play full screen, hide the video while not playing, loop the video until stopped, and set the video to rewind after playing. Figure 4.32 displays the Video Tools Playback tab.

FIGURE 4.32 Video Tools Playback Tab ➤

You can use bookmarks to mark specific locations in a video, making it possible to quickly advance to the part of the video you want to display or to trigger an event in an animation.

To bookmark a video, do the following:

1. Select the video, and then click the Playback tab.
2. Click Play on the Media Control bar.
3. Click Add Bookmark in the Bookmarks group when the video reaches the location you want to quickly move to during your presentation.

A circle displays on the Media Control bar to indicate the bookmark location (see Figure 4.33). To remove the bookmark, click the circle on the Media Control bar, and then click Remove Bookmark in the Bookmarks group.

FIGURE 4.33 Bookmarks ➤

PowerPoint enables you to perform basic video editing by enabling you to determine the starting and ending of a video and setting a Fade In and Fade Out duration. In the Trim Video dialog box, which you access in the Editing group on the Playback tab, you can use the Trim option to specify the Start Time and End Time for a video, or you can drag the Start marker and the End marker on the Timing slide bar to select the time. The advantage to dragging the markers is that as you drag, you can view the video. Any bookmarks you set will also display in the Trim Video dialog box. Figure 4.34 shows the Trim Video dialog box.

FIGURE 4.34 Trim Video Dialog Box ➤

To set a Fade In or Fade Out duration, click the spin buttons or enter an exact time in the appropriate boxes in the Editing group on the Playback tab. If you have selected a poster frame for your video, the poster frame will fade into the first frame of your video.

The Video Options group of the Playback tab enables you to control a variety of display options. You can control the volume of the video by clicking the Volume arrow and selecting Low, Medium, or High. You can also mute any sound attached to the video.

The Video Options group also enables you to determine whether the video starts on the click of the mouse (the default setting) or automatically when the slide displays. You can choose to play the video at full screen, hide the video when it is not playing, loop continuously until you stop the playback, and rewind after playing.

HANDS-ON EXERCISES

2 Video

In Cancun, the couple recorded some fireworks displayed during a sports event. The groom gave you a copy of the fireworks because you think it would be an excellent finale to the slide show. You insert the video, add a photo frame, and set the video playback options.

Skills covered: Insert a Movie from a File • Format a Video • Set Video Playback Options

STEP 1 INSERT A MOVIE FROM A FILE

You create a blank slide at the end of the memories presentation, and then insert the fireworks video. Refer to Figure 4.35 as you complete Step 1.

FIGURE 4.35 Inserted Windows Media Video File ➤

a. Open *p04h1memory_LastnameFirstname*, if necessary, and then save as **p04h2memory_LastnameFirstname**, changing *h1* to *h2*.

b. On Slide 7, click the **New Slide arrow** in the Slides group on the Home tab, and then click the **Blank layout**.

A new slide (Slide 8) with the same presentation theme is created and should be positioned after Slide 7.

c. Click the **Insert tab**, and then click the **Video arrow** in the Media group.

d. Click **Video from File**, open the *p04h13memory_media* folder, select *p04h2fireworks.wmv*, and then click **Insert**.

e. Save the presentation.

STEP 2 FORMAT A VIDEO

The first image of the video shows the fireworks in the beginning stages. You decide to use a poster frame of the fireworks while they are fully bursting so the slide has an attractive image on display before the video begins. You also decide that a shape removing the edges of the video would be an improvement. Finally, you add a shadow video effect. Refer to Figure 4.36 as you complete Step 2.

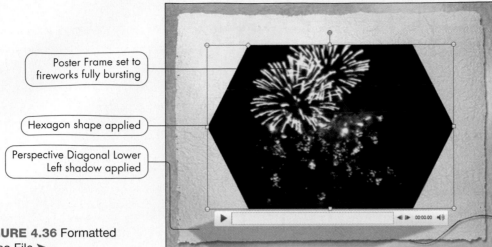

Poster Frame set to fireworks fully bursting

Hexagon shape applied

Perspective Diagonal Lower Left shadow applied

FIGURE 4.36 Formatted Video File ➤

a. Click **Move Forward 0.25 Seconds** on the Media Controls bar located beneath the video to advance the video to the frame at 2.00 seconds.

b. Click the **Video Tools Format tab**, if necessary, click **Poster Frame** in the Adjust group, and then click **Current Frame**.

The frame you selected becomes the poster frame and displays on the slide.

c. Click **Video Shape** in the Video Styles group, and then click **Hexagon** in the Basic Shapes category.

The video shape changes to a hexagon.

d. Click **Video Effects**, point to **Shadow**, and then click **Perspective Diagonal Lower Left** in the Perspective category.

The shadow displays in a hexagon shape with a perspective view.

e. Click the **Slide Show tab**, and then click **From Current Slide** in the Start Slide Show group.

Slide 7 opens with the video displayed on the slide. The poster frame shows the fireworks at full cascade with the video shadow.

f. Move the pointer to the bottom of the video to display the Media Controls bar, and then click **Play**.

g. Save the presentation.

STEP 3 ▶ SET VIDEO PLAYBACK OPTIONS

The last burst of fireworks does not finish its crescendo, so you decide to trim away this last portion of the video. Because you do not want the viewers of the presentation to have to click to begin the video, you change the start setting to start automatically. You decide to loop the video to play continuously until stopped because it is so short. Refer to Figure 4.37 as you complete Step 3.

Video End Time set at
6.644 seconds

Trim Video

p04h2fireworks.wmv   Duration: 00:06.644

00:00.000

Duration changed
to 00:06.644

00:00 ⇕   ◀| ▶ |▶   00:06.644 ⇕
Start Time   End Time

OK   Cancel

FIGURE 4.37 Video Duration
Change ➤

a. Select the movie object, if necessary, click the **Video Tools Playback tab**, and then click **Trim Video** in the Editing group.

   The Trim Video dialog box opens.

b. Drag the red **End Time marker** on the slider until **00:06.644** appears in the End Time box or type **00:06.644** in the **End Time box**, and then click **OK**.

   The duration of the video changes from 7.755 seconds to 6.644 seconds.

c. Click the **Start arrow** in the Video Options group, and then click **Automatically**.

d. Check the **Loop until Stopped check box** in the Video Options group.

   The fireworks video will continue to play until you advance to end the slide show.

e. Click the **Slide Show tab**, and then click **From Beginning** in the Start Slide Show group.

   Advance through the slide show. Note the movie plays in the Hexagon shape.

f. Save the presentation, close the file, and then exit PowerPoint if you do not want to continue with the next Hands-On Exercise at this time.

Audio

Audio can draw on common elements of any language or culture—screams, laughs, sobs, etc.—to add excitement, provide a pleasurable background, set the mood, or serve as a wake-up call for the audience. Harnessing the emotional impact of sound in your presentation can transform your presentation from good to extraordinary. On the other hand, use sound incorrectly, and you can destroy your presentation, leaving your audience confused and with a headache. Keep in mind the guideline emphasized throughout this book—any added object must enhance, not detract from, your message.

> Harnessing the emotional impact of sound in your presentation can transform your presentation from good to extraordinary.

In this section, you will review the methods for inserting sound and tips for each method. You insert sound from the Clip Organizer and learn how to determine the number of times a sound clip plays, the number of slides through which the sound plays, and the method for launching the sound. Finally, you record a short narration for a presentation.

Adding Audio

Your computer needs a sound card and speakers to play audio. In a classroom or computer laboratory, you will need a headset or headphones for playback so that you do not disturb other students. You can locate and play sounds and music from the Clip Art pane, or from a hard drive, flash drive, or any other storage device. You can also record your own sounds, music, or narration to play from PowerPoint.

Add Sounds from the Clip Art Pane

To insert sound from the Clip Art pane, click the Insert tab, and then click Clip Art in the Images group. When the task pane opens, enter a term in the *Search for* box, and then change the *Results should be* option to Audio. Point to a sound clip in the results pane to display a tip showing keywords, length of the sound track, file size, and the sound format of the clip. To hear a preview of the clip, click the bar that appears on the right side of the clip when your mouse points to it, and then select Preview/Properties. The Preview/Properties dialog box opens, playing the sound clip and providing you with information about the clip.

Insert Audio from a File

Table 4.3 lists the types of Audio file formats supported by PowerPoint in alphabetical order by extension.

TABLE 4.3 Types of Audio File Formats Supported by PowerPoint		
File Format	**Extension**	**Description**
AIFF Audio File	.aiff	**Audio Interchange File Format** Waveform files stored in 8-bit monaural (mono or one-channel) format. Not compressed. Can result in large files. Originally used on Apple and Silicon Graphics (SGI) computers.
AU Audio File	.au	**UNIX Audio** Typically used to create sound files for UNIX computers or the Web.
MIDI File	.mid or .midi	**Musical Instrument Digital Interface** Standard format for interchange of musical information between musical instruments, synthesizers, and computers.
MP3 Audio File	.mp3	**MPEG Audio Layer 3** Sound file that has been compressed by using the MPEG Audio Layer 3 codec (developed by the Fraunhofer Institute).
Windows Audio File	.wav	**Wave Form** Stores sounds as waveforms. Depending on various factors, one minute of sound can occupy as little as 644 kilobytes or as much as 27 megabytes of storage.
Windows Media Audio File	.wma	**Windows Media Audio** Sound format used to distribute recorded music, usually over the Internet. Compressed using the Microsoft Windows Media Audio codec.

To insert audio from a file, do the following:

1. Click the Insert tab.
2. Click the Audio arrow in the Media group.
3. Click Audio from File.
4. Browse, locate, and select the desired file.
5. Click Insert.

A gray speaker icon representing the file appears in the center of the slide with a Media Controls bar beneath it. The same controls are available when you select audio as when you select video except the volume control is a slider for audio files.

Record and Insert Audio

Narration is spoken commentary that is added to a presentation.

Sometimes you may find it helpful to add recorded audio to a slide show. Although you could record music, *narration* or spoken commentary is more common. One example of a need for recorded narration is when you want to create a self-running presentation, such as a presentation displaying in a kiosk at the mall. Other examples include creating an association between words and an image on the screen for a presentation to a group learning a new language and vocabulary building for young children. Rather than adding a narration prior to a presentation, you could create the narration during the presentation. For example, recording the discussion and decisions made during a meeting would create an archive of the meeting.

Before creating the narration, keep in mind the following:

- Your computer will need a sound card, speakers, and a microphone.
- Comments on selected slides may be recorded rather than narrating the entire presentation.
- Voice narration takes precedence over any other sounds during playback, making it possible for a voice to play over inserted audio files.
- PowerPoint records the amount of time it takes you to narrate each slide, and if you save the slide timings, you can use them to create an automatic slide show.
- You can pause and resume recording during the process.

To record audio, do the following:

1. Click the Insert tab.
2. Click the Audio arrow in the Media group.
3. Click Record Audio.
4. Click Record (see Figure 4.38).
5. Record your message.
6. Click Stop.
7. Click Play to check the recording.
8. Type a name for the recording, and then press OK.

FIGURE 4.38 Record Sound Dialog Box ➤

Changing Audio Settings

When an audio clip is selected, the Audio Tools tab appears with two tabs: Format and Playback. The Format tab is not relevant, as it provides options relating to images. The Playback tab provides options for playing and pausing the audio clip, adding a bookmark, trimming, fading in and out, adjusting volume, determining starting method, hiding the audio icon while playing, looping, and rewinding after playing. All of these features work similarly to the video features except that the Trim audio feature provides an audio time line rather than a video preview window.

Animate an Audio Sequence

Although the Audio Tools Playback tab gives you only two options for starting, On Click or Automatically, you have other options available through the Animation Timing group. You can choose whether the audio plays with a previous event or after a previous event; for example, you can have the audio play as a picture appears or after.

To set the audio to play with or after a previous event:

1. Select the sound icon.
2. Click the Animations tab.
3. Click the Start arrow in the Timing group.
4. Click With Previous or After Previous.

The Timing group on the Animations tab also includes a Delay spin box that you can use to delay the play of an audio clip (see Figure 4.39).

Click to select With Previous or After Previous

Click to set delay in seconds

Selected audio icon

FIGURE 4.39 Audio Sequencing Options ➤

Play a Sound over Multiple Slides

By default, audio plays until it ends or until the next mouse click. If you are playing background music, this means the music ends when you click to advance to the next slide.

To continue audio over multiple slides, do the following:

1. Click the Animations tab.
2. Click Animation Pane in the Advanced Animation group.
3. Select the sound you want to continue over multiple slides.
4. Click the arrow to the right of the sound.

5. Click Effect Options.
6. Click the After option in the Stop playing section of the Effect tab.
7. Enter the number of slides during which you want the sound to play (see Figure 4.40).

If the background music stops before you get to the last slide, use the Loop Until Stopped feature to keep the sound repeating. Click the Audio Tools Playback tab, and then click the Loop Until Stopped check box in the Audio Options group.

Click to open Animation Pane

Click to open Effect Options

Click to change number of slides during which audio should play

FIGURE 4.40 Audio Effects ➤

TIP Play Across Slides

You can set an audio clip to play across slides easily by clicking the Audio Tools Playback tab, clicking the Start arrow in the Audio Options group, and then clicking Play Across Slides. This option does not let you set the number of slides over which you wish the audio to play, however.

3 Audio

You decide to create a background mood for the memories presentation by inserting a favorite audio clip of the bride—Beethoven's Symphony No. 9. You also want to experience the full effect of the fireworks finale slide by adding the sounds of fireworks exploding.

Skills covered: Add Audio from a File • Change Audio Settings • Insert Sound from the Clip Art Pane • Add Narration

---

STEP 1 ▶ ADD AUDIO FROM A FILE

The bride is a classically trained pianist, so you decide to enhance the slide show with one of her favorite pieces. Refer to Figure 4.41 as you complete Step 1.

FIGURE 4.41 Slide 1 Audio Settings ➤

a. Open the *p04h2memory_LastnameFirstname* presentation if you closed it after the last exercise, and then save it as **p04h3memory_LastnameFirstname**, changing *h2* to *h3*.

> **TROUBLESHOOTING:** To complete this exercise, it is best that you have a sound card, a microphone, and speakers. Even if this equipment is not available, however, you can still perform these steps to gain the knowledge.

b. On Slide 1, click the **Insert tab**, click the **Audio arrow** in the Media group, and then select **Audio from File**.

The Insert Audio dialog box opens.

c. Locate the *p04h1_3memory_media* folder, select **Beethoven's Symphony No. 9**, and then click **Insert**.

The sound icon and Media Controls bar are displayed in the center of the slide.

d. Click the **Audio Tools Playback tab**, click the **Start arrow** in the Audio Options group, and then select **Automatically**.

e. Drag the sound icon to the top-left corner of the slide.

f. Click the **Hide During Show check box** in the Audio Options group.

g. Click **Play** in the Preview group.

h. Save the presentation.

STEP 2 ▶ CHANGE AUDIO SETTINGS

Because PowerPoint's default setting ends a sound file when a slide advances, the Beethoven file is abruptly cut off when you advance to the next slide. You adjust the sound settings so the file plays continuously through all slides in the slide show. Refer to Figure 4.42 as you complete Step 2.

FIGURE 4.42 Play Audio Dialog Box ➤

a. Click the **Slide Show tab**, and then click **From Beginning** in the Start Slide Show group. Advance through the slides, and then end the slide show.

Note that the sound clip on Slide 1 discontinues playing as soon as you click to advance to the next slide.

b. Select the sound icon on the top-left of Slide 1.

c. Click the **Animations tab**, and then click **Animation Pane** in the Advanced Animation group.

d. Click the **Beethoven's Symphony sound arrow** in the animation list, and then select **Effect Options**.

e. Click **After** in the *Stop playing* section, type **7** in the box, and then click **OK**. Close the Animation Pane.

f. Save the presentation.

g. Play the slide show and note the music plays through the seventh slide.

INSERT SOUND FROM THE CLIP ART PANE

The sound of fireworks exploding would make the finale slide more effective. You locate a fireworks audio clip in the Microsoft Clip Art pane, add it to the fireworks slide, set it to start automatically, and set it to loop until the presentation ends. After adding the audio clip, you modify its setting so it plays concurrently with the video. You move the audio icon so that it does not block the view of the fireworks. You also hide the audio icon during the presentation. Refer to Figure 4.43 as you complete Step 3.

Fireworks audio set to Start: Automatically

Fireworks audio set to Loop until Stopped

Fireworks audio icon set to Hide During Show

FIGURE 4.43 Audio Tools Tab ➤

a. On Slide 8, click the **Insert tab**, and then click **Clip Art** in the Images group.

b. Type the keyword **fireworks** in the **Search for box**, change Results to **Audio**, include Office.com content, and then click **Go**.

c. Point to the resulting sound clips to display the sound name, size, and file type. Locate and select the **Fireworks Loop, 5.00 sec, 29 KB, WAV clip**.

d. Click the arrow in the blue bar on the clip, and then click **Insert**. Close the Clip Art pane.

> **TROUBLESHOOTING:** If the sound clip speaker icon and Media Controls bar do not appear on the slide, you may be dragging the clip onto the slide instead of inserting the clip.

e. Select the sound icon if necessary, click the **Audio Tools Playback tab**, click the **Start arrow** in the Audio Options group, and then select **Automatically**.

f. Click the **Hide During Show check box** in the Audio Options group.

g. Click the **Loop until Stopped check box**.

h. Drag the sound icon down into the shadow of the video so that it will not block the fireworks on the slide.

i. Click the **Animations tab**, click the **Start arrow** in the Timing group, and then select **With Previous**.

j. Click the **Slide Show tab**, and then click **From Current Slide** in the Start Slide Show group.

k. Save the presentation.

ADD NARRATION

A small portion of the bride's vows is included on Slide 4. You narrate the vow and save it with the slide show so that it has a greater impact. Refer to Figure 4.44 as you complete Step 4.

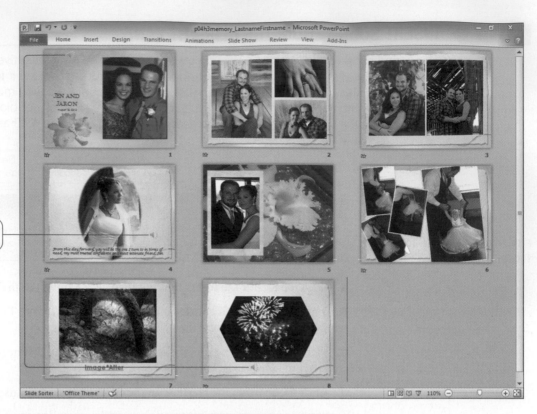

Audio icons showing location of audio clips

FIGURE 4.44 Completed Memories Presentation ➤

a. On Slide 4, click the **Insert tab**.

b. Click the **Audio arrow**, and then click **Record Audio**.

> **TROUBLESHOOTING:** You will not be able to complete this step without a microphone, speakers, and a sound card.

c. Click the red **Record button** in the Record Sound dialog box, and then read.

From this day forward, you will be the one I turn to in times of need, my most trusted confidante and most intimate friend.

d. Click the blue **Stop Recording button**, and then click **OK**.

e. Move the audio icon to the bottom-right of the slide.

f. Click the **Playback tab**, click the **Start arrow** in the Audio Options group, and then select **Automatically**.

g. Click the **Hide During Show check box** in the Audio Options group.

h. Click **From Beginning** in the Start Slide Show group so that you can hear the narration and sound clips you have added.

i. Save and close the slide show.

Photo Albums

PowerPoint has a Photo Album feature designed to speed up the album creation process. This feature takes the images you select and arranges them on album pages based on selections you make.

In this section, you will use the Photo Album feature to create an album and use the feature settings to customize your album.

Creating a Photo Album

A **Photo Album** is a presentation containing multiple pictures organized into album pages.

A PowerPoint *Photo Album* is a presentation that contains multiple pictures that are imported and formatted through the Photo Album feature. Because each picture does not have to be formatted individually, you save a considerable amount of time. The photo album in Figure 4.45 took less than two minutes to create and assign a theme. Because a four-per-page layout was selected, images were reduced to fit the size of the placeholder. This setting drastically reduced the size of some images, although it does create an interesting asymmetrical design on the page.

> Because each picture does not have to be formatted individually, you save a considerable amount of time using the Photo Album feature.

Album Title page automatically created

Slipstream theme

Album layout, four per page

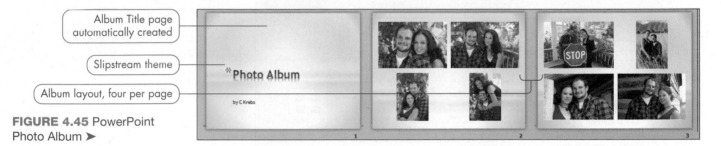

FIGURE 4.45 PowerPoint Photo Album ➤

To create a photo album, do the following:

1. Click the Insert tab.
2. Click Photo Album in the Images group.
3. Click File/Disk.
4. Navigate to your pictures, and then select the pictures to include in the album.
5. Click Insert.
6. Select the Photo Album options you want.
7. Click Create.

If you click the Photo Album arrow, you may choose between creating a new album and editing a previously created album. When you select the pictures you want to include in the album, do not worry about the order of the pictures. You can change the order later. Once an album has been created, you can edit the album settings by clicking the Photo Album arrow in the Images group on the Insert tab, and then selecting Edit Photo Album.

> **TIP** Creating Family Albums
>
> After creating an album, add transitions and you have a beautiful presentation for a family gathering or special event. Loop the presentation, and let it run so people can watch as they desire. Burn the presentation to a CD and send it as a holiday greeting.

Setting Photo Album Options

After selecting pictures, they will appear in a list in the dialog box. Click the name of a picture to display a preview to help you determine the order of pictures in the album. Use the Move up arrow and the Move down arrow to reposition a selected photograph. Use Ctrl or Shift to select more than one image. Delete any unwanted photographs by selecting them and clicking Remove.

If you have downloaded photographs from a digital camera, you may need to rotate some images. Rotate buttons are included in the *Album Content* section. Contrast and brightness controls enable you to fine-tune your pictures. This section also includes the New Text Box button so that you can insert a text placeholder in the album. The text placeholder is the same size as the placeholders for pictures. The *Captions below ALL pictures* option will not become available until you choose a layout. When this option is active, the file name of the picture appears as a caption below the picture in the album. Figure 4.46 shows the location of these tools.

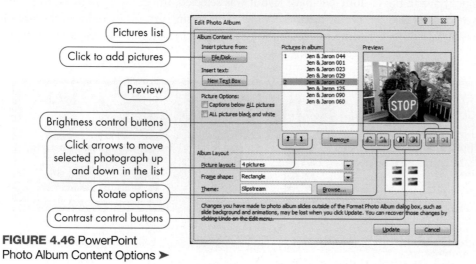

FIGURE 4.46 PowerPoint Photo Album Content Options ➤

The *Album Layout* section of the Photo Album dialog box gives many options for personalizing the album. First, you can select a layout: a single picture fitted to a full slide; one, two, or four pictures on a page; or one, two, or four pictures and a title placeholder per page. When you fit a single picture per page, the image is maximized on the page.

You can select from a variety of frame shapes in the *Album Layout* section. Options include rectangles, rounded rectangles, simple black or white frames, a compound black frame, a center shadow rectangle, or a soft edge rectangle.

You can apply a theme for the background of your album while in the Photo Album dialog box. If you are in a networked lab situation it may be difficult to navigate to the location where themes are stored. If this is the case, create the album, and then in the main PowerPoint window, click the Design tab, click the More button in the Themes group, and then select your theme from the gallery.

4 Photo Albums

The bride's mother is a professional photographer and traveled with the couple, extensively capturing images from around the world. You prepare an album to help them preserve their memories.

Skills covered: Select and Order Pictures • Adjust Contrast and Brightness • Set Picture Layout • Select Frame Shape • Edit Album Settings and Apply a Theme

STEP 1 ▶ SELECT AND ORDER PICTURES

You have a folder in which you have saved the images you wish to use for the vacation album. In this step, you add the images to the album and order the images by the year during which the trip was taken. Refer to Figure 4.47 as you complete Step 1.

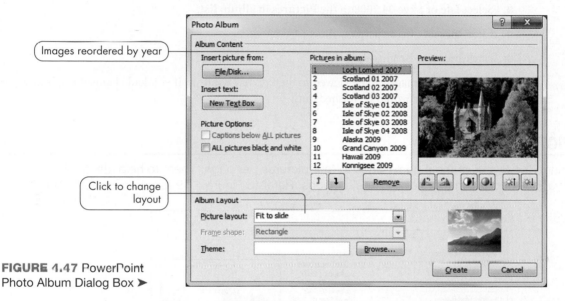

FIGURE 4.47 PowerPoint Photo Album Dialog Box ➤

a. In a new blank presentation, click the **Insert tab**, and then click **Photo Album** in the Images group.

   The Photo Album dialog box opens.

b. Click **File/Disk**. Open the *p04h4album_media* folder.

c. Press **Ctrl+A** to select all pictures in the folder, and then click **Insert**.

   The list of pictures displays in the *Pictures in album* box.

d. Use the **Move up arrow** to reposition *Loch Lomand 2007* so that it is the first picture in the list.

e. Continue using the **Move up arrow** and the **Move down arrow** to reposition each picture by the image number and by the year. Press and hold **Ctrl** to select multiple images to move them as a group. Refer to Figure 4.47 to ensure your images are in the correct order, and then click **Create**.

STEP 2 ▶ ADJUST CONTRAST AND BRIGHTNESS

The Photo Album feature includes buttons that enable you to adjust the contrast and brightness of images without having to access PowerPoint's Picture Tools. You use the Photo Album buttons to adjust the contrast in one of the Isle of Skye pictures. Refer to Figure 4.48 as you complete Step 2.

Contrast increased four levels and brightness increased two levels

Click to increase contrast

Click to increase brightness

FIGURE 4.48 PowerPoint Photo Album Picture Tools ➤

a. Select **Isle of Skye 04 2008** in the **Pictures in album list**.

b. Click **Increase Contrast** four times.

c. Click **Increase Brightness** twice.

The adjusted image can be viewed in the Preview window. If you had changed brightness only, the image would be washed out.

STEP 3 ▸ SET PICTURE LAYOUT

You change the layout of the album pages to four pictures per page. Then, to help identify the location and year of each trip, you include captions. Refer to Figure 4.49 as you complete Step 3.

Include captions below all pictures

Layout set to four pictures per page

FIGURE 4.49 Album Setup ➤

a. Click the **Picture layout arrow** in the *Album Layout* section of the Photo Album dialog box.

b. Click each of the layouts and view the layout in the Album Layout Preview window on the right (below the larger Album Content Preview window), and then select **4 pictures**.

Clicking 4 pictures will create an album of four pages—a title page and three pages with four pictures each.

c. Click the **Captions below ALL pictures check box** in the *Picture Options* section.

Captions below ALL pictures only becomes available after the layout is selected.

STEP 4 ▸ SELECT FRAME SHAPE

You decide to use a simple white frame to enhance the pictures taken during the trips. Refer to Figure 4.50 as you complete Step 4.

FIGURE 4.50 Frame Shape Selection ➤

a. Click the **Frame shape arrow** in the *Album Layout* section.

b. Select each of the frames, and then view the Preview window on the right.

c. Select **Simple Frame, White**, and then click **Create**.

The album is created, but because portrait and landscape pictures are included on the same page and portrait pictures are squeezed into small placeholders, the appearance of the album is not the best it can be. You will edit the appearance in the next step.

d. Create a handout header with your name, and a handout footer with your instructor's name and your class. Include the current date.

e. On Slide 1, enter your name in the subtitle placeholder.

f. Save the presentation as **p04h4album_LastnameFirstname**.

STEP 5 ▸ EDIT ALBUM SETTINGS AND APPLY A THEME

You decide to edit your album settings so that you include only one picture per page rather than four. This allows more space for the pictures so the bride and her mother can see more detail. You also change the frame shape. Finally, you apply a theme to the album. Refer to Figure 4.51 as you complete Step 5.

Frame changed to Center Shadow Rectangle

Paper theme applied

Layout changed to 1 per page

FIGURE 4.51 Slides 4–12 of the Revised Photo Album ➤

a. Click the **Insert tab**, click the **Photo Album arrow** in the Images group, and then select **Edit Photo Album**.

The Edit Photo Album dialog box opens displaying the current settings, which you may now change.

b. Click the **Picture layout arrow**, and then select **1 picture**.

c. Click the **Frame shape arrow**, and then select **Center Shadow Rectangle**.

d. Click **Browse**, and then navigate to the location where your Microsoft Document Themes are located. Click **Paper**, and then click **Select** to apply the theme to the presentation.

> **TROUBLESHOOTING:** It may be difficult to locate Themes and Themed Documents in a networked laboratory. If this is the case, close your album and apply a theme from the Design tab.

e. Click **Update**.

The pictures now appear one per page.

f. Save and close the file, and submit based on your instructor's directions.

CHAPTER OBJECTIVES REVIEW

After reading this chapter, you have accomplished the following objectives:

1. **Insert a picture.** Pictures are in a bitmap format and are photorealistic portrayals. They can be inserted using the Insert Picture option, which centers the image on the slide, or by using placeholders that might center and crop the image inside the placeholder.

2. **Transform a picture.** Pictures can be transformed in a variety of ways, including removing the background, applying corrections, changing colors, applying artistic effects and picture styles, and cropping. Pictures can be compressed to save file storage.

3. **Use the Internet as a resource.** The Internet can be extremely valuable when searching for information for a presentation. Although students and teachers have rights under the Fair Use Act, care should be taken to honor all copyrights. Before inserting any information or clips into your slide show, research the copyright ownership. To be safe, contact the Web site owner and request permission to use the material. Any information used should be credited and include hyperlinks when possible, although attribution does not relieve you of the requirement to honor copyrights.

4. **Add video.** You can insert video located on your hard drive or storage device or embed HTML coding from an online site.

5. **Use Video Tools.** PowerPoint includes video editing tools. You can adjust the brightness and contrast, recolor, set a poster frame, select a style, and arrange and size a video. You can also add a bookmark, trim, set a fade in and fade out effect, control

the volume, determine how to start the video, set the video to play full screen, hide the video when not playing, loop until stopped, rewind after playing, and show media controls.

6. **Add audio.** Audio catches audience attention and adds excitement to a presentation. Take care when adding sound that it enhances your message rather than detracts from it.

7. **Change audio settings.** You can also add a bookmark, trim, set a fade in and fade out effect, control the volume, and determine how to start audio. You can hide the speaker icon when not playing, loop until stopped, rewind after playing, and show media controls. By default audio plays during one slide and stops when you advance to a new slide, but it can be set to play over multiple slides.

8. **Create a Photo Album.** When you have multiple images to be inserted, using the Photo Album feature enables you to quickly insert the images into a slide show. After identifying the images you wish to use, you can rearrange the order of the pictures in the album. You also can choose among layouts for the best appearance.

9. **Set Photo Album options.** Album options for contrast and brightness enable you to make image changes without having to leave the Photo Album dialog box. In addition to adjusting contrast and brightness, you can change the pictures to black and white. File names can be turned into captions for the pictures. A frame shape can be selected and a theme applied to complete the album appearance.

KEY TERMS

Background *p.923*	Embed *p.944*	Poster Frame *p.946*
Bitmap image *p.920*	Foreground *p.923*	Public domain *p.933*
Brightness *p.925*	Infringement of copyright *p.933*	Recolor *p.928*
Codec *p.940*	Kelvin *p.927*	Saturation *p.926*
Compression *p.920*	Link *p.944*	Sharpening *p.924*
Contrast *p.925*	Multimedia *p.920*	Softening *p.924*
Copyright *p.933*	Narration *p.954*	Tone *p.927*
Cropping *p.930*	Photo Album *p.961*	

1. Which of the following file formats supports 16 million colors, is optimized for photographs and complex graphics, and is the format of choice for most photographs on the Web?

   (a) .bmp
   (b) .jpg
   (c) .gif
   (d) .tiff

2. To transform a picture from cool colors (lower K) to warm colors (higher K), which of the following should you do?

   (a) Sharpen the picture.
   (b) Adjust the contrast of the picture.
   (c) Increase the saturation of the picture.
   (d) Change the tone of the picture.

3. Which of the following Picture Tools would help you adjust a scanned photograph that appears muddy and does not show much difference between the light and dark areas of the image?

   (a) Brightness
   (b) Contrast
   (c) Recolor
   (d) Compress Pictures

4. Which of the following is not permitted for a student project containing copyrighted material?

   (a) The educational project is produced for a specific class and then retained in a personal portfolio for display in a job interview.
   (b) Only a portion of copyrighted material was used, and the portion was determined by the type of media used.
   (c) The student received permission to use copyrighted material to be distributed to classmates in the project.
   (d) The student markets the project on a personal Web site.

5. Which of the following can be obtained from the Clip Art pane?

   (a) Windows Video files (.avi)
   (b) Moving Picture Experts Group movies (.mpg or .mpeg)
   (c) Animated GIF files (.gif)
   (d) Windows Media Video files (.wmv)

6. All of the following can be used to play a selected sound clip for preview except:

   (a) Click Play in the Preview group on the Audio Tools Format tab.
   (b) Click Play/Pause on the Media Controls bar.
   (c) Click Play in the Preview group on the Audio Tools Playback tab.
   (d) Click the blue bar on the right side of the clip in the Clip Art pane, and then select Preview/Properties.

7. Which of the following is a true statement regarding recording a narration?

   (a) Narration cannot play at the same time as other audio clips.
   (b) Narration is embedded on the slide on which it is recorded.
   (c) Narration time cannot be recorded for use in a self-running presentation.
   (d) Narrations cannot be paused during recording.

8. The Photo Album dialog box enables you to make all but this edit to pictures:

   (a) Rotate.
   (b) Crop.
   (c) Brightness.
   (d) Contrast.

9. Which of the following formatting options is available for video?

   (a) Brightness adjustment
   (b) Sharpen adjustment
   (c) Artistic effect application
   (d) Background removal

10. Audio Playback tools enables you to do all of the following except:

    (a) Add a bookmark.
    (b) Fade the audio out.
    (c) Loop the audio.
    (d) Apply an artistic effect.

1 Geocaching Slide Show

The slide show in Figure 4.52 is designed to be used with a presentation introducing a group to the sport of geocaching. Geocaching became a new sport on May 2, 2000, when 24 satellites around the globe stopped the intentional degradation of GPS signals. On May 3, Dave Ulmer hid a bucket of trinkets in the woods outside Portland, Oregon, and the sport was born! It continues to grow at remarkable speed. Your Geocaching presentation is designed to teach the basics of taking something, leaving something, and signing the logbook. This exercise follows the same set of skills as used in Hands-On Exercises 1 and 3 in the chapter. Refer to Figure 4.52 as you complete this exercise.

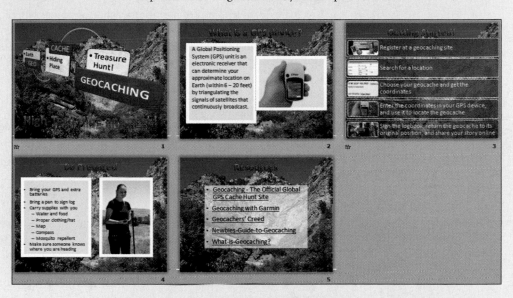

FIGURE 4.52 Geocaching Slide Show ➤

a. Open the *p04p1cache* slide show, and then save it as **p04p1cache_LastnameFirstname**.

b. Create a handout header with your name, and a handout footer with your instructor's name and your class. Include the current date.

c. Click the **Design tab** in any slide, click **Background Styles** in the Background group, and then select **Format Background**.

d. Click **Picture or texture fill**, select **File**, locate and open the *p04p1cache_media* folder, click **p04p1bkgd**, and then click **Insert**. Drag the **Transparency slider** to **10%**. Click **Apply to All**, and then click **Close**.

e. On Slide 2, click the **Insert Picture from File icon** on the toolbar in the right placeholder. In the *p04p1cache_media* folder, click and examine the **p04p1gps picture**. Click **Insert**, and then examine the image on Slide 2 and note the resizing of the placeholder to keep the image in proportion.

f. Click **Remove Background** in the Adjust group, and then drag the top, left, and bottom marquee handles to the edge of the picture. Click **Keep Changes**.

g. Click the border of the text box on the left side of the slide, click the **Home tab**, click **Format Painter** in the Clipboard group, and then click the gps picture.

h. Open your browser, and then type **garminuk.geocaching.com** in the **address bar** to open the Geocaching with Garmin Web site. Right-click **Geocaching with Garmin**, and then select **Save Background As**. Save the image as **p04p1garminlogo** (used with permission) to your student data folder for this chapter. Close your browser.

> **TROUBLESHOOTING:** The Save Background As option is available in Internet Explorer. If you are using Firefox, click View Background Image, and then right-click and save the image. If you are using another browser, right-click the image and select the appropriate option from the menu.

i. On Slide 3, click the first **Insert Picture from File icon** (next to *Register at a geocaching site*) in the top SmartArt diagram box, click the *p04p1garminlogo* image, and then click **Insert**.

j. Click the second **Insert Picture from File icon** in the SmartArt diagram, locate *p04p1seek*, and then click **Insert**.

k. Repeat Step j to enter *p04p1coordinates* in the third image location, *p04p1gps* in the fourth image location, and *p04p1locate* in the last image location.

l. On Slide 4, click the picture of the geocacher, and then click the **Format tab**. Click **Color** in the Adjust group, and then select **No Recolor** in the Recolor gallery.

m. Click **Corrections** in the Adjust group, and then click **Sharpen: 25%** in the Sharpen and Soften gallery.

n. On Slide 1, if you are able to record narration in your computer lab, click the **Insert tab**, click the **Audio arrow** in the Media group, and then select **Record Audio**. Click the red **Record Sound button**, and then read the Speaker Note at the bottom of Slide 1. When finished reading, click the blue **Stop button**, and then click **OK**.

o. If you are not able to record narration in your computer lab, click **Insert**, click the **Audio arrow** in the Media group, and then select **Audio from File**. Click *p04p1narration*, and then click **Insert**.

p. Click the **Audio Tools Playback tab**, and then click the **Hide During Show check box** in the Audio Options group. Drag the audio icon to the top right of the slide.

q. With the audio icon still selected, click the **Start arrow** in the Audio Options group. Select **Automatically**.

r. Click the **Animations tab**, and then click **Animation Pane** in the Advanced Animation group. The audio object displays on the Animation Pane. Click the **Re-Order up arrow** until the sound object moves to the top of the list.

s. Click the **Start arrow**, and then select **With Previous**. Close the Animation Pane.

t. View the slide show.

u. Save and close the file, and submit based on your instructor's directions.

2 Geocaching Album

Geocachers are asked to share their geocaching experience in the geocache logbook. The *Geocaching – The Official Global GPS Cache Hunt Site* includes some easy steps for logging a Geocache find and even enables you to upload a photo with your log entry. Often, geocachers also put their geocaching stories, photos, and videos online in the form of slide shows using a variety of software packages. In this exercise, you create a geocache slide show quickly and easily using the PowerPoint Album feature, and then add video and text to the slide show. This exercise follows the same set of skills as used in Hands-On Exercises 2 and 4 in the chapter. Refer to Figure 4.53 as you complete this exercise.

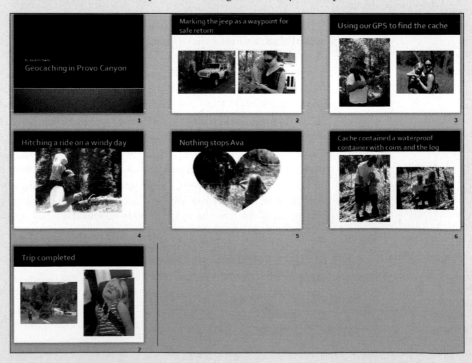

FIGURE 4.53 Geocaching Album ➤

a. In a new blank presentation, click the **Insert tab**, and then click **Photo Album** in the Images group.

b. Click **File/Disk**, open the *p04p2geo_media* folder, click one of the files, and then press **Ctrl+A** to select all pictures in the folder. Click **Insert**.

c. Click *p04p2img3* in the *Pictures in album* section, and then click **Rotate Right**. Repeat to rotate *p04p2img5* and *p04p2img8* to the right.

d. Click the **Picture layout arrow** in the *Album Layout* section, and then select **2 pictures with title**.

e. Click the **Frame shape arrow** in the *Album Layout* section, and then select **Center Shadow Rectangle**.

f. Click **Create**, and then save the album as **p04p2geo_LastnameFirstname**.

g. Create a handout header with your name, and a handout footer with your instructor's name and your class. Include the current date.

h. On Slide 1 of the resulting album, change the title to **Geocaching in Provo Canyon**. Change the subtitle to your name.

> **TROUBLESHOOTING:** If you get an error message that says "PowerPoint cannot insert a video from the selected file" while inserting *p04p2vid1*, it is because, currently, the Windows operating system does not have a 64-bit video or audio codec for the three QuickTime media formats: MPEG-4 video (*.mp4), MPEG-4 audio (*.m4a), or QuickTime Movie (*.mov). Substitute any of the videos provided in your data files or a video of your choice. Do the same whenever asked to insert a QuickTime video in this exercise.

i. Click the **Design tab**, click the **More button** in the Themes group, and then click the **Module theme**.

j. Enter the following slide titles.

Slide 2	Marking the jeep as a waypoint for safe return
Slide 3	Using our GPS to find the cache
Slide 4	Cache contained a waterproof container with coins and the log
Slide 5	Trip completed

k. On Slide 3, click the **Home tab**, click the **New Slide arrow**, and then select **Title Only**. Change the title of the slide to **Hitching a ride on a windy day**.

l. Click the **Insert tab**, click the **Video arrow** in the Media group, and then select **Video from File**. Click *p04p2vid1* from the *p04p2geo_media* folder, and then click **Insert**.

m. Click the **Video Tools Playback tab**, and then click **Trim Video**. Type **00:17.491** in the **Start Time box**, and then click **Play**. Type **00:22.337** in the **End Time box**, and then click **OK**.

n. Type **00.01** in the **Fade Out box** in the Editing group.

o. Click the **Start arrow** in the Video Options group, and then select **Automatically**.

p. Click the **Video Tools Format tab**, and then move to the video frame at 4.75 seconds. Click **Poster Frame**, and then click **Current Frame**.

q. Insert a new Title Only slide, change the title to **Nothing stops Ava**, and then insert *p04p2vid2* from the *p04p2geo_media* folder.

r. Click the **Video Tools Playback tab**, and then click **Move Forward 0.25 Seconds** on the Media Controls bar to advance the video to the frame at 14 seconds. Click **Add Bookmark** in the Bookmark group.

s. Click the **Video Tools Format tab**, click **Video Shape** in the Video Styles group, and then click **Heart** in the Basic Shapes gallery.

t. Click the **Insert tab**, click **Clip Art** in the Images group, type the keyword **supplies**, change Results to **Audio**, and then click **Go**.

u. Point to the resulting audio clips to display the audio name, size, and file type. Locate the *Pencil Scratch, 1.00 Seconds [6 KB] WAV* clip, and then click the clip to insert it into the slide show. Close the Clip Art pane.

v. Drag the audio icon to the bottom of the screen.

w. Select one of the images in your album, click the **Picture Tools Format tab**, click **Compress Pictures** in the Adjust group, and then click the **Apply only to this picture check box** to deselect it. Click **OK**.

x. View the slide show. On Slide 5, point to the Media Controls bar, click the bookmark, and then click **Play** to begin the video at the bookmark site.

y. Save and close the file, and submit based on your instructor's directions.

3 Accident Record

Your parents helped you buy a small car to drive while you are at school. While you are stopped at a streetlight, someone drives into the back of your car. You decide to use your digital camera to take pictures to keep a record of the damage. Your father wants to see the damage to the car, so you quickly create a Photo Album that is suitable for sending by e-mail. You then edit the Photo Album to include a text box so that you have a location in which to enter the accident details. This exercise follows the same set of skills as used in Hands-On Exercises 1 and 4 in the chapter. Refer to Figure 4.54 as you complete this exercise.

FIGURE 4.54 Accident Record Compressed for E-Mail ➤

a. In a blank presentation, click the **Insert tab**, and then click **Photo Album** in the Images group.

b. Click **File/Disk**, navigate to the *p04h3accdnt_media* folder, click one of the files, press **Ctrl+A**, and then click **Insert**.

c. Click **Create**, and then note that each picture fits the slide.

d. Click the **Insert tab**, click the **Photo Album arrow**, and then select **Edit Photo Album**.

e. Select *p04p3accidnt3* in the *Pictures in album* section, and then click **New Text Box**.

f. Select *p04p3accident7*, and then click **Remove**.

g. Select *p04p3accident5*, click **Increase Contrast** four times, and then click **Increase Brightness** two times.

h. Click the **Picture layout arrow** in the *Album Layout* section, and then click **4 pictures**.

i. Click the **Frame shape arrow** in the *Album Layout* section, and then click **Compound Frame, Black**.

j. Click **Update**, and then save the new photo album as **p04p3accdnt_LastnameFirstname**.

k. Create a handout header with your name, and a handout footer with your instructor's name and your class. Include the current date.

l. On Slide 1, change the Photo Album title to **Accident Record** on one line and **September 7, 2013** on the following line. Change the subtitle to your name.

m. On Slide 2, select the words **Text Box**, and then type the following information:
   - **September 7, 2013**
   - **5:10 p.m.**
   - **210 West & Bridger Dr.**

n. Select the top-right picture on Slide 2. Click the **Picture Tools Format tab**, and then click **Crop** in the Size group.

o. Drag the center left handle to remove the person from the image. Click **Crop** again to complete the cropping process.

p. With the image still selected, click **Compress Pictures** in the Adjust group on the Picture Tools Format tab, and deselect the *Apply only to this picture* check box so that all pictures will be compressed.

q. Click **E-mail** in the *Target output* section, and then click **OK**.

r. Save and close the file, and submit based on your instructor's directions.

1 Motorcycle for Sale

You have enjoyed a number of years as a motorcyclist but now decide that you would like to sell your first bike and purchase a car. Using PowerPoint, you create a flyer that you can reproduce advertising the motorcycle and hang on bulletin boards at the college. Refer to Figure 4.55 as you complete this exercise.

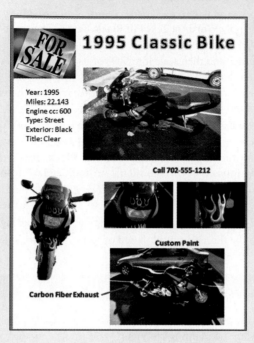

FIGURE 4.55 Motorcycle Sales Flyer ➤

a. Open a blank presentation and save it as **p04m1flyer_LastnameFirstname.**

b. Create a handout header with your name, and a handout footer with your instructor's name and your class. Include the current date.

c. Change the layout to a blank layout.

d. Change your slide orientation to **Portrait**, as you will be printing a single slide to use as a flyer.

e. Search the Clip Art pane for the *For Sale* sign shown in Figure 4.55. The results should be photographs. Insert the clip art, and then change the scale to 47% of its original size. Position the sign horizontally at **0"** from the Top Left Corner. Position it vertically at **.33"** from the Top Left Corner.

f. Create a WordArt using **Gradient Fill - Blue, Accent 1, Outline – White, Glow – Accent 2** (fourth row, first column), and then type **1995 Classic Bike.** Change the WordArt Text Fill to **Black, Text 1.** Change the WordArt Font Size to **44 pt.** Change the Height to **.84"** and the Width to **5.21".** Position the WordArt horizontally at **2.12"** from the Top Left Corner. Position it vertically at **.33"** from the Top Left Corner.

g. Create a text box, and type the following information inside it:

   Year: 1995

   Miles: 22,145

   Engine cc: 600

   Type: Street

   Exterior: Black

   Title: Clear

h. Position the text box horizontally at **.3"** from the Top Left Corner. Position it vertically at **2.17"** from the Top Left Corner.

i. Insert the *p04m1bike1* image located in your student files in the *p04m1flyer_media* folder. Scale the picture to 60% of its original size. Drag the image so that it is to the right of the text box and beneath the WordArt.

j. Insert *p04m1bike2*. Crop the image to the motorcycle. Size the Width to **2.75″**, and then position the image horizontally at **0″** from the Top Left Corner and vertically at **4.75″** from the Top Left Corner.

k. Create a text box, and then type **Call 702-555-1212**. Apply the WordArt Style to the text using **WordArt Gradient Fill Blue –Accent 1**, and then apply **WordArt Text Fill Black, Text 1**. Drag it so it is approximately centered under the photograph above.

l. Insert *p04m1bike3*, and then scale it to 30% of its original size. Position the photograph horizontally at **2.94″** from the Top Left Corner. Position it vertically at **5.25″** from the Top Left Corner.

m. Insert *p04m1bike4*, and then scale it to 30% of its original size. Position the photograph horizontally at **5.3″** from the Top Left Corner. Position it vertically at **5.25″** from the Top Left Corner.

n. Create a text box, and then type **Custom Paint**. Apply **WordArt Gradient Fill Blue –Accent 1** to the text, and then apply **WordArt Text Fill Black, Text 1**. Drag it so it is approximately centered under the two photographs above.

o. Insert *p04m1bike5*, and then scale it to 50% of its original size. Position the photograph horizontally at **3.12″** from the Top Left Corner. Position it vertically at **7.38″** from the Top Left Corner.

p. Adjust the brightness and contrast of *p04m1bike5* so that there is more contrast between the bike and the car behind it.

q. Use the **Remove Background tool** to remove the background from the *p04m1bike2* picture.

r. Create a text box, and then type **Carbon Fiber Exhaust**. Apply **WordArt Gradient Fill Blue - Accent 1** to the text, and then apply **WordArt Text Fill Black, Text 1**. Position the text box horizontally at **.42″** from the Top Left Corner. Position it vertically at **8.67″** from the Top Left Corner.

s. Insert an arrow that starts at *Carbon Fiber Exhaust* and points to the exhaust pipe of the motorcycle. Change the weight of the arrow to **3 pt**. Change the outline color to **Red, Accent 2**.

t. Compress the photographs on the flyer using the default setting.

u. Save and close the file, and submit based on your instructor's directions.

2 Impressionist Paintings

CREATIVE CASE

In this exercise, you will use the Internet to obtain images of paintings by some of the masters of the Impressionist style. The paintings in Figure 4.56 may be viewed at the Web Museum (**www.ibiblio. org/wm/paint**) that is maintained by Nicolas Pioch for academic and educational use. On the Famous Artworks exhibition page, click the Impressionism Theme (or search for Impressionist paintings or painters). Refer to Figure 4.56 as you complete this exercise.

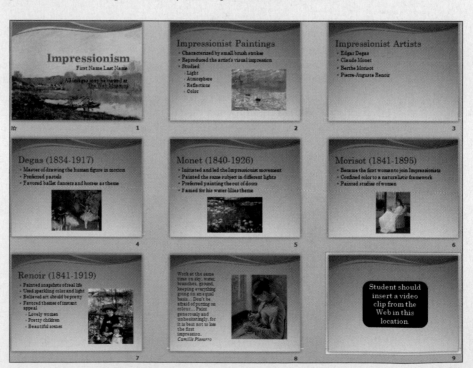

FIGURE 4.56 Impressionist Presentation ➤

a. Open the *p04m2painting* presentation and save it as **p04m2painting _LastnameFirstname.pptx**.

b. Create a handout header with your name, and a handout footer with your instructor's name and your class. Include the current date. On Slide 1, change the subtitle *First Name Last Name* to your name.

c. View the slide show, and then click the hyperlink to *The Web Museum* on Slide 1 to open the Famous Artworks exhibition. Locate the images you will copy and paste into the slide show.

d. When you locate a painting, click the thumbnail image to enlarge it, then right-click it and save the image to a new folder on your storage device named **Impressionist Paintings**. If necessary, change the name of the file to include the artist and the name of the painting. Repeat this process until you have saved each of the images of the paintings shown in the table below.

Slide #	Artist	Title
Slide 1	**Alfred Sisley**	***Autumn: Banks of the Seine near Bougival***
Slide 2	**Claude Monet**	***Impression: soleil levant***
Slide 4	**Edgar Degas**	***Ballet Rehearsal***
Slide 5	**Claude Monet**	***Waterlilies, Green Reflection, Left Part***
Slide 6	**Berthe Morisot**	***The Artist's Sister at a Window***
Slide 7	**Pierre-Auguste Renoir**	***On the Terrace***
Slide 8	**Camille Pissarro**	***Peasant Girl Drinking her Coffee***

e. Return to your slide show. Insert the picture for Slide 1 as a background, and then insert each of the remaining pictures on the appropriate artist's slide. Resize and postion the images as needed. Use picture styles. You do not need to compress the images, as they are already low resolution.

f. Insert an audio clip of your choice in Slide 1. As an alternative to providing your own audio clip, search for the keyword **classical** in the Clip Art pane. Find *Nocturne in ES-Dur* in the search results, and then insert it in Slide 1.

g. Position the audio icon on the slide, and then hide it during play. Loop the audio clip, and then set the song so it plays continuously across slides and does not stop with the next mouse click.

DISCOVER h. Insert a blank slide after Slide 8. Search the Web for a video clip on Impressionist art, copy the Embed code for the video, and then insert the Embed code in PowerPoint. Apply a **Video Style**, and then choose other video settings as desired.

i. Save and close the file, and submit based on your instructor's directions.

3 Red Butte Garden

You visited Red Butte Garden, a part of the University of Utah, and enjoyed the natural gardens and the botanical garden. You want to create a Photo Album of the pictures you took that day.

a. Create a new Photo Album, and then insert all of the pictures in the *p04m3garden_media* folder.

b. Remove the *p04m3img1* (Red Butte Garden & Arboretum) picture.

c. Locate *p04m3img2*, increase the brightness six times, and then increase the contrast twice.

d. Locate *p04m3img14*, increase the brightness twice, and then increase the contrast six times.

e. Apply a **2 pictures layout** and the **Simple Frame, White frame shape style**.

f. Create the album, and then save it as **p04m3garden_LastnameFirstname**.

g. Create a handout header with your name, and a handout footer with your instructor's name and your class. Include the current date.

h. Edit the album so only one picture per page displays, and then click **Update**.

i. Insert *p04m3img1* as the background for Slide 1, and then remove the title and subtitle placeholders.

j. Move Slide 2 to the end of the slide show, and then apply the **Paint Brush Artistic Effect**.

k. On Slide 14, apply a **Sharpen: 50% correction**.

l. On any slide, apply the **Reveal transition**, and set the advance to automatically advance after **00:02:00**. Apply to all slides.

m. Save and close the file, and submit based on your instructor's directions.

A friend and his wife recently had a new baby. You volunteer to create a slide show announcing the birth of the baby that your friend can e-mail to family and friends. You use a modified version of Microsoft's Contemporary Photo Album template. The album has been modified to use a Surfer theme. In this activity, you will create the content, insert the photos, modify the photos, add sound, and insert a video clip of the baby. All media for this activity are located in the *p04c1birth_media* folder.

Insert Pictures

Using template layouts and picture placeholders, you insert photos of the expectant couple taken by Shanna Michelle Photography and photos taken by the family at the baby's birth. You modify template placeholders for better fit. Refer to Figures 4.57 through 4.61 as you complete this section.

a. Open the file named *p04c1birth*, and then save it as **p04c1birth_LastnameFirstname**.

b. Create a handout header with your name, and a handout footer with your instructor's name and your class. Include the current date.

c. On Slide 1, click **Insert Picture from File** in the large content placeholder. Locate the *p04c1birth_media* folder, and then insert *p04c1baby1*. Apply the **Paint Brush artistic effect** (refer to Figure 4.57).

d. Change the title to **IT'S A BOY!**, and change the title font size to **72 pt**.

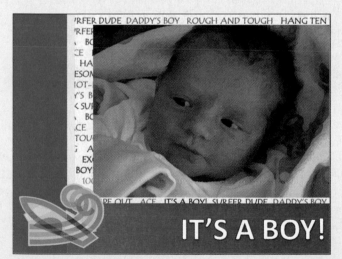

FIGURE 4.57 Slide 1 ▲

e. On Slide 2, insert *p04c1parents1*. Replace the text in the right placeholder with **A grand adventure is about to begin.** *Winnie the Pooh.*

f. Select the text placeholder, right-click, and then select **Format Shape**. Modify the Text Box settings to resize the shape to fit the text (refer to Figure 4.58).

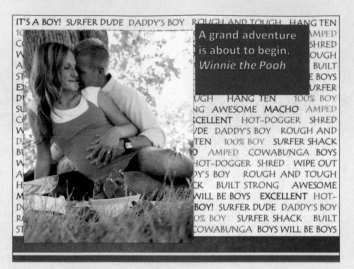

FIGURE 4.58 Slide 2 ▲

g. On Slide 3, change the slide layout to **Landscape with Caption**. Insert *p04c1family1*. Replace the caption text with **FIRST FAMILY PHOTO** (refer to Figure 4.59).

FIGURE 4.59 Slide 3 ▲

h. On Slide 4, replace the text in the blue placeholder with **Father**. Insert *p04c1dad1* in the left picture placeholder. Crop all but the father's head and shoulders. Resize the width of the picture to **2.83"**, let the height adjust automatically, and then drag the picture into a position above the caption (refer to Figure 4.60).

i. Replace the text in the green placeholder with **Mother**. Insert *p04c1mom1* in the right picture placeholder. Crop all but the mother's head and shoulders. Resize the width of the picture to **2.83″**. Drag the picture into a position above the caption (refer to Figure 4.60).

j. Replace the text in the red placeholder with **Baby Boy Jas**. Insert *p04c1baby2* in the center placeholder (refer to Figure 4.60).

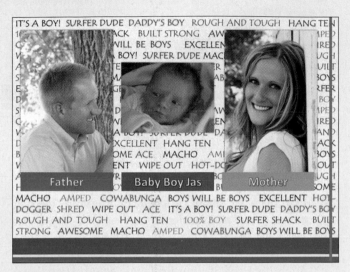

FIGURE 4.60 Slide 4 ▲

k. On Slide 5, insert *p04c1family2* in the large placeholder. Continue in a clockwise direction, and then insert *p04c1family3* through *p04c1family6* in the remaining placeholders (refer to Figure 4.61).

l. View and save the presentation.

Apply and Modify a Picture Style, Change Images

The pictures on Slide 4 would stand out better if they had a frame. You apply and modify a Picture Style. You replace the image of the parents (refer to Figure 4.62).

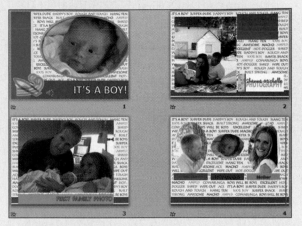

FIGURE 4.62 Picture Style Applied and Modified ▲

a. On Slide 4, select the picture of the father, and then apply the **Beveled Oval, Black picture style**.

b. Apply the **Preset 5 Picture Effect** (second row, first column).

c. Use the Format Painter to copy the effects applied to the center and right photographs.

d. Adjust the Text Box shapes to fit the text.

FIGURE 4.61 Slide 5 ➤

e. Correct the color tone of the baby picture so it is warmer by changing it to **Temperature 11200 K**.

f. On Slide 1, select the baby picture. Apply the **Metal Oval picture style**, and then change the color of the picture border to **Aqua, Accent 5** (first row, ninth column).

g. Select the image on Slide 2, and using the **Adjust tools group** on the Picture Tools Format tab, change the image to *p04c1parents2*.

h. Save the presentation.

Adjust and Compress Images

Some pictures on Slide 5 need the brightness, contrast, and color tones adjusted. You use Picture Tools to adjust the pictures, and then you apply an e-mail compression to all photographs (refer to Figure 4.63).

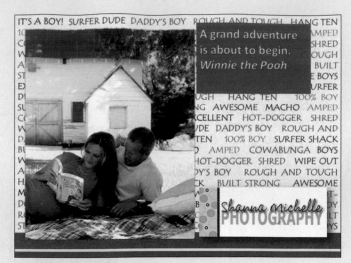

FIGURE 4.64 Image downloaded from Web site ▲

FIGURE 4.63 Image Adjustments ▲

a. Select the bottom-center picture on Slide 5, and then increase the image brightness **+20%**.

b. Select the bottom-left picture, set the saturation to **66%**, and then set the color tone to **4700 K**.

c. Select the large picture of the parents, and then set the color tone to **8800 K**.

d. Compress all images for e-mail output.

e. Save the presentation.

Use the Internet as a Resource

Shanna Michelle Photography has given you permission to include photos in your presentation. You copy the company logo from their Web site and paste it into your presentation (refer to Figure 4.64).

a. Connect to the Internet, and then go to **http://shannamichellephotography.blogspot.com/**.

b. Right-click the **Shanna Michelle photography logo**, and then save it as **p04c1smlogo**.

c. Insert the logo on Slide 2.

d. Apply the **Drop Shadow Rectangle picture style**.

e. Positioning and size the logo (refer to Figure 4.64).

f. Save the presentation.

Insert a Movie and Add Sound

You insert a video clip of the baby, and then modify the settings. Finally, you add a soft lullaby music clip that plays continuously through all slides using the Clip Art pane.

a. On Slide 6, insert *p04c1babyvid.avi*.

b. Set a Poster Frame at **00:00:75**.

c. Set the movie to play automatically.

d. Change the Video Options to **Hide While Not Playing** and to **Rewind after Playing**.

e. On Slide 1, search the Clip Organizer for an audio clip using **lullaby** as the keyword for your search.

f. Insert *Kinderscenen* on Slide 1, and then have it **Play across Slides**.

g. Hide the audio icon during the show.

h. Activate the **Loop until Stopped sound option**.

i. Save and close the file, and submit based on your instructor's directions.

Create a Photo Album

Your friend asks you for a printed copy of all of the images. You prepare a photo album, and then print it.

a. Create a New Photo Album using the images in the *p04c1birth_media* folder.

b. Rearrange the pictures so they appear in the following order: berries, dad1, mom1, parents 1 and 2, baby 1 and 2, and then the family pictures in numerical order.

c. Create the album using four pictures per slide and a **Simple Frame, White**.

d. Save the album as **p04c1baby_LastnameFirstname**.

e. Create a handout header with your name, and a handout footer with your instructor's name and your class. Include the current date.

f. Edit the album to remove the *p04c1berries* picture on the first slide and the text box on the last slide (if necessary).

g. Apply *p04c1berries* at 10% transparency as the background image for all slides.

h. Modify the title on the Title Slide to **Baby Jas Photo Album**, and then type your name in the subtitle.

i. Move the title and subtitle above the strawberries.

j. Save and close the file, and submit based on your instructor's directions.

BEYOND THE CLASSROOM

A Visit to the Zoo

GENERAL CASE

As a first-grade teacher, each year you take your students and parent helpers to the local zoo. The day your class visits, a zookeeper takes your students to specific animals and gives presentations on the animal, its habitat, its diet, and other fun facts. The keeper also teaches the children the difference between skin, fur, feathers, and scales. The keeper asks you to teach the students about animal facts before the visit. You prepare a presentation about the coverings of some of the animals you took pictures of during last year's visit to the zoo.

Create a new photo album with the file name **p04b1zoo_LastNameFirstName**. Include a handout header with your name, and a handout footer with your instructor's name and your class. Include the current date. The title of your slide show should be *OUR ZOO VISIT!*, and the subtitle should be *Animals and Their Coverings*. Use the pictures located in the *p04b1zoo_media* folder. Choose the layout and frame of your choice, but include a text box for each type of animal. Transform and crop images as desired. After creating the album, enter the type of covering for each animal in the text box (example: Crocodiles are covered with scales). Insert the movie *p04b1spray* on the Title slide. Create a Poster Frame and add a Bookmark. If it is possible to record narration in your classroom lab, read the text box on the first slide while recording. Add other narrations if desired. If you are unable to record the narration, insert sounds from the Clip Organizer in appropriate locations. Save and close the file, and submit based on your instructor's directions.

Zeroscaping vs. Xeriscaping

RESEARCH CASE

While on a trip through the Southwest, you took pictures of zeroscaping examples. You plan to use them in an existing slide show on Waterwise Landscaping. You want to know more about xeriscaping, however, so you research xeriscaping online. One site, XericUtah (xericutah.com), has beautiful images of xeriscaping, so you contact them and receive permission to use images from their Web site.

Open *p04b2landscape* and save it as **p04b2landscape_LastnameFirstname**. Add a handout header with your name, and a handout footer with your instructor's name and your class. Include the current date. Research zeroscaping and xeriscaping online, and include the Web sites on a Resources slide at the end of the slide show. Please remember that giving credit to your source does not mean you are released from copyright requirements. Create several speaker notes with information you find during your research. Use the zeroscaping images located in the *p04b2landscape_media* folder where appropriate, but visit xericutah.com to obtain images for the xeriscaping portion of the slide show. Use a xeriscaping picture for the background of the Title slide. You may change the template and add animations as desired. Add an audio clip, and set it to play across all slides. Save and close the file, and submit based on your instructor's directions.

ESL Tutor

DISASTER RECOVERY

As a tutor of ESL (English as a Second Language) students, you would like to introduce the students to the English names of common musical instruments. You asked a former student to help you by creating a slide presentation featuring one instrument per slide, with narration of the name of the instrument and a sound button that plays the instrument's sound. The student did not have a lot of time but began the presentation for you. You edit the existing presentation and add to it by creating the musical instruments introduction.

Open *p04b3esl* and save it as **p04b3esl_LastnameFirstname**. Add a handout header with your name, and a handout footer with your instructor's name and your class. Include the current date. View the slide show to determine the changes needed. When completed, each slide should have a photograph (not clip art) of a musical instrument, a narration of the name of the instrument, and a sound clip of the instrument's sound. The instrument sound icons should be clicked to play the sound of the instrument. Locate missing photographs and sounds of instruments on Office.com. Compress all images to Screen Target Output. When finished, view the slide show, and test each icon to ensure they work properly. Save and close the file, and submit based on your instructor's directions.

GLOSSARY

100% stacked column chart A chart type that places (stacks) data in one column per category, with each column having the same height of 100%.

3-D chart A chart that contains a third dimension to each data series, creating a distorted perspective of the data.

Absolute cell reference A designation that provides a permanent reference to a specific cell. When you copy a formula containing an absolute cell reference, the cell reference in the copied formula does not change, regardless of where you copy the formula. An absolute cell reference appears with a dollar sign before both the column letter and row number, such as $B$5.

Access A database program that is included in Microsoft Office.

Access speed Measures the time it takes for the storage device to make the file content available for use.

Action Center A Windows 7 component that monitors maintenance and security settings, alerting a user when necessary. It provides alerts in pop-ups from an icon in the notification area.

Active cell The current cell in a worksheet. It is indicated by a dark border onscreen.

Adjustment handle A yellow diamond that enables you to modify a shape.

Aero Flip 3D A Windows feature that shows open windows in a rotating 3D stack from which you can click to bring a window to view on the desktop.

Aero Peek A preview of an open window, shown when you place the mouse pointer over the taskbar icon without clicking. Aero Peek also enables you to minimize all open windows, showing the desktop temporarily.

Aggregate function A function that performs calculations on an entire column of data and returns a single value.

Align To arrange objects by lining up the sides, middles, or top/bottom edges of the objects.

AND logical operator Returns only records that meet all criteria.

Animation A movement that controls the entrance, emphasis, exit, and/or path of objects in a slide show.

Annotation A written note or drawing on a slide for additional commentary or explanation.

Area chart A chart type that emphasizes magnitude of changes over time by filling in the space between lines with a color.

Argument A variable or constant input, such as a cell reference or value, needed to complete a function. The entire group of arguments for a function is enclosed within parentheses.

Ascending order A feature that arranges data in alphabetical order or sequential order from lowest to highest.

Aspect ratio The ratio of an object's width to its height.

Auto fill A feature that enables you to copy the contents of a cell or a range of cells or to continue a sequence by dragging the fill handle over an adjacent cell or range of cells.

AutoNumber A data type that stores a unique number for each record as it is added to a table and increments automatically each time a record is entered.

AutoRecover Enables Word to recover a previous version of a document.

AVERAGE function A predefined formula that calculates the arithmetic mean, or average, of values in a range.

Axis title A label that describes either the category axis or the value axis.

Background (Word) A color, design, image, or watermark that appears behind text in a document or on a graphical image. (PPT) The portion of a picture to be removed during the Background Removal process.

Background Styles gallery Provides both solid color and background styles for application to a theme.

Backstage view Display that includes commands related to common file activities and that provides information on an open file.

Backup (Office Fundamentals) A copy of a file, usually on another storage medium. (Access) Creates a duplicate copy of the database.

Bar chart A chart type that compares values across categories using horizontal bars. In a bar chart, the horizontal axis displays values, and the vertical axis displays categories.

Bar tab Tab that inserts a vertical line at the location of a tab setting. Useful as a separator for text printed on the same line.

Bibliography A list of works cited or consulted by an author in his or her work and should be included with the published work.

Bitmap image An image created by bits or pixels containing color information and placed on a grid that forms a picture.

Border A line that surrounds a paragraph, a page, a table, or an image in a document, or that surrounds a cell or range of cells in a worksheet.

Bound control A text box that is connected to a field in a table or query.

Breakpoint The lowest value for a specific category or series in a lookup table.

Brightness The ratio between lightness and darkness of an image.

Bubble chart A chart type that shows relationships among three values by using bubbles to show a third dimension.

Bulleted list Itemizes and separates paragraph text to increase readability.

Calculated control A text box that contains an expression that generates a calculated result when displayed in Form view.

...duces a value from an expression or function ...e or more existing fields.

...7 accessory program that acts as a ...with four different views—standard, ...g, and statistical.

...es a text box you can use to add notes.

...t... A style of writing which uses no spaces ...-word field names, but uses uppercase letters to distinguish the first letter of each new word.

Caption A descriptive title for an image, an equation, a figure, or a table.

Caption property Used to create a more readable label instead of a field name, and displays in the top row in Datasheet view and in forms and reports.

Cascade Delete Related Records An option that directs Access to automatically remove all records that are deleted from a primary table from those related tables that match the primary key.

Cascade Update Related Fields An option that directs Access to automatically update all foreign key values in a related table when the primary key value is modified in a primary table.

Category axis The chart element that displays descriptive group names or labels, such as college names or cities, to identify data.

Category label Text that describes a collection of data points in a chart.

Cell The intersection of a column or row in a worksheet or table.

Cell address The unique identifier of a cell, starting with the column letter and then the row number, such as A9.

Cell margin The amount of space between data and the cell border in a table.

Center tab Sets the middle point of the text you type; whatever you type will be centered on that tab setting.

Change Case Feature that enables you to change capitalization of text to all capital letters, all lowercase letters, sentence case, or toggle case.

Changed line A vertical bar in the margin to pinpoint the area where changes are made in a document when the Track Changes feature is active.

Character spacing The horizontal space between characters.

Character style Stores character formatting (font, size, and style) and affects only selected text.

Chart A visual representation of numerical data that compares data and helps reveal trends or patterns to help people make informed decisions.

Chart area A boundary that contains the entire chart and all of its elements, including the plot area, titles, legends, and labels.

Chart sheet A sheet within a workbook that contains a single chart and no spreadsheet data.

Chart title The label that describes the entire chart.

Circular reference A situation that occurs when a formula contains a direct or an indirect reference to the cell containing the formula.

Citation A note recognizing a source of information or a quoted passage.

Clip art An electronic illustration that can be inserted into an Office project.

Clipboard An Office feature that temporarily holds selections that have been cut or copied.

Clustered column chart A type of chart that groups or clusters similar data into columns to compare values across categories.

Codec (coder/decoder) A digital video compression scheme used to compress a video and decompress for playback.

Collapsed outline Displays only the slide number, icon, and title of each slide in Outline view.

Color scale A conditional format that displays a particular color based on the relative value of the cell contents to other selected cells.

Colors gallery Provides a set of colors with each color assigned to a different element for every available theme.

Column A format that sections a document into side-by-side vertical blocks in which the text flows down the first vertical block and then continues at the top of the next vertical block.

Column chart A type of chart that displays data vertically in columns to compare values across different categories.

Column index number The number of the column in the lookup table that contains the return values.

Column width The horizontal measurement of a column in a table or a worksheet. In Excel, it is measured by the number of characters or pixels.

Command A button or area within a group that you click to perform tasks.

Comment A private note, annotation, or additional information to the author or another reader about the content of a document.

Compact and Repair Reduces the size of the database, and repairs any corruptions to the database.

Comparison operator Used to evaluate the relationship between two quantities to determine if they are equal or not equal; and, if they are not equal, a comparison operator determines which one is greater than the other.

Compatibility Checker Looks for features that are not supported by previous versions of Word.

Compress The process of reducing the file size of an object.

Compression A method applied to data to reduce the amount of space required for file storage.

Conditional formatting A set of rules that apply special formatting to highlight or emphasize cells that meet specific conditions.

Connector A Lines shape that is attached to and moves with other shapes.

Constant An unchanging value, such as a birth date.

Contextual tab A Ribbon tab that displays when an object, such as a picture or clip art, is selected.

Contrast The difference between the lightest and darkest areas of an image.

Copy Duplicates a selection from the original location and places the copy in the Office Clipboard.

Copyright The legal protection afforded to a written or artistic work.

COUNT function A predefined formula that tallies the number of cells in a range that contain values you can use in calculations, such as numerical and date data, but excludes blank cells or text entries from the tally.

COUNTA function A predefined formula that tallies the number of cells in a range that are not blank; that is, cells that contain data whether a value, text, or a formula.

COUNTBLANK function A predefined formula that tallies the number of cells in a range that are blank.

Criteria row A row in the Query Design view that determines which records will be selected.

Criterion (criteria, pl) An expression used to filter the records in a table.

Cropping (or to crop) The process of reducing an image size by eliminating unwanted portions of an image or other graphical object.

Cross-reference A note that refers the reader to another location for more information about a topic.

Current List Includes all citation sources you use in the current document.

Cut Removes a selection from the original location and places it in the Office Clipboard.

Data bar A conditional format that displays horizontal gradient or solid fill indicating the cell's relative value compared to other selected cells.

Data label A descriptive label that shows the exact value of the data points on the value axis.

Data point A numeric value that describes a single value on a chart.

Data redundancy The unnecessary storing of duplicate data in two or more tables.

Data series A group of related data points that appear in row(s) or column(s) in the worksheet.

Data source A listing of information.

Data type Determines the type of data that can be entered and the operations that can be performed on that data.

Database Consists of one or more tables to store data, one or more forms to enter data into the tables, and one or more reports to output the table data as organized information.

Database table A collection of related records that contain fields to organize data.

Datasheet form A replica of a table's or query's Datasheet view except that it still retains some of the form properties.

Datasheet view A view of a database object, which displays data in row and column format, and in which you can add, edit, and delete the records of a table, form, or query.

Date arithmetic The process of manipulating dates, or adding or subtracting a constant from a date.

Date formatting Formatting that affects a date's display without changing the actual underlying value in the table.

DatePart function Enables you to isolate a specific part of a date, such as the year.

Decimal tab Marks where numbers align on a decimal [...] you type.

Default A setting that is in place unless you specify otherwise.

Delimiter A special character that surrounds the criterion's value.

Descending order Arranges data in alphabetical or sequential order from highest to lowest.

Design view A view in which new database objects are created, and the design of existing objects is modified. Where you create tables, add and delete fields, and modify field properties.

Desktop The screen display that appears after you turn on a computer. It contains icons and a taskbar.

Detail section Displays the records in the form's record source and prints one line for each record in the report's record source.

Dialog box A window that opens when you are accomplishing a task that enables you to make selections or indicate settings beyond those provided on the Ribbon.

Dialog Box Launcher An icon in Ribbon groups that you can click to open a related dialog box.

Distribute To divide or evenly spread over a given area.

Document Inspector Checks for and removes different kinds of hidden and personal information from a document.

Document Panel Provides descriptive information about a document, such as a title, subject, author, keywords, and comments.

Doughnut chart A chart type that displays values as percentages of the whole but may contain more than one data series.

Draft view Shows a simplified work area, removing white space and other elements from view.

Effects gallery Includes a range of special effects that can be used on objects in the presentation.

Embed To store an object from an external source within a presentation.

Endnote A citation that appears at the end of a document.

Enforce referential integrity Ensures that data cannot be entered into a related table unless it first exists in the primary table.

Enhanced ScreenTip Provides a brief summary of a command when you place the mouse pointer on the command button.

Excel Software included in Microsoft Office that specializes in organizing data in worksheet form.

Expanded outline Displays the slide number, icon, title, and content of each slide in Outline view.

Exploded pie chart A chart type in which one or more pie slices are separated from the rest of the pie chart.

Expression A formula used to calculate new fields from the values in existing fields.

Expression Builder A tool in Access to help you create expressions.

Field The smallest data element contained in a table, such as first name, last name, address, and phone number.

...racteristic of a field that determines how the ...haves.

... Query Design view that displays the

... information that you create with ... you give a name.

...identifier, such as author or date created.

...The interior contents of a shape.

Fill color The background color that appears behind data in a cell.

Fill handle A small black square at the bottom-right corner of a cell used to copy cell contents or text or number patterns to adjacent cells.

Filter Specifies criteria for including records that meet certain conditions, and displays a subset of records based on specified criteria.

Filter by Form A filtering technique that displays table records based on multiple criteria, and allows the user to apply AND conditions and OR conditions.

Filter by Selection A filtering technique that displays only the records that match the selected criteria.

Filtering The process of specifying conditions to display only those records that meet the conditions.

Final: Show Markup A view that displays inserted text in the body of the document and shows deleted text in a markup balloon.

Find Locates a word or phrase that you indicate in a document.

Firewall Software or hardware that protects a computer from unauthorized access.

First line indent Marks the location to indent only the first line in a paragraph.

Flip To reverse the direction and object faces.

Flow chart An illustration showing the sequence of a project or plan containing steps.

Folder A named storage location where you can save files.

Font A complete set of characters—upper- and lowercase letters, numbers, punctuation marks, and special symbols with the same design that includes size, spacing, and shape.

Fonts gallery Contains font sets for title text and bulleted text.

Footer Information that displays at the bottom of each document page, presentation slide, handout, or notes page.

Footnote A citation that appears at the bottom of a page.

Foreground (Word) Appears in front of text or images in a document or on a graphical image. (PPT) The portion of the picture to be kept during the Background Removal process.

Foreign key A field in one table that is also the primary key of another table.

Form A database object that enables you to enter, modify, or delete table data.

Form Footer section A part of a form that displays at the bottom of the form in Display view.

Form Header section A part of a form that displays at the top of each form in Display view.

Form letter A letter with standard information that you personalize with recipient information. You might print or e-mail this to many people.

Form tool Used to create data entry forms for customers, employees, products, and other primary tables.

Form view Use to add, edit, and delete data in a form; the layout and design of the form cannot be changed in this view.

Format Painter A Clipboard group command that copies the formatting of text from one location to another.

Formula A combination of cell references, operators, values, and/or functions used to perform a calculation.

Formula AutoComplete A feature that displays a list of functions and defined names that match letters as you type a formula.

Formula Bar An element in Excel that appears below the Ribbon and to the right of the Insert command that shows the contents of the active cell so that you edit the text, value, date, formula, or function.

Freeform shape A shape that combines both curved and straight-line segments.

Freezing The process of keeping rows and/or columns visible onscreen at all times even when you scroll through a large dataset.

Full Screen Reading view A viewing format that eliminates tabs and makes it easier to read a document.

Function A predefined computation that simplifies creating a complex calculation and produces a result based on inputs known as arguments.

Function ScreenTip A small pop-up description that displays the arguments for a function as you enter it.

Gadget A desktop item that can represent things that change, such as the weather or a clock. Gadgets also include such things as puzzles and games.

Gallery A set of selections that appears when you click a More button, or in some cases when you click a command, in a Ribbon group.

Gradient fill A fill that contains a blend of two or more colors or shades.

Grid A set of intersecting lines used to align objects.

Gridline A horizontal or vertical line that extends from the horizontal or vertical axis through the plot area.

Group A subset of a tab that organizes similar tasks together.

Group Footer section When activated, will appear just below the *Detail* section in Design view, but only when you select this option in the Group, Sort, and Total pane. Provides aggregated information at the end of a group of records.

Group Header section When activated, will appear just above the *Detail* section in Design view; the name of the field you are grouping on provides information such as group name at the beginning of a group of records.

Grouping Combining two or more objects, which enables them to move or act as one object.

Guide A straight horizontal or vertical line used to align objects on a slide.

Hanging indent Aligns the first line of a paragraph at the left margin and indents the remaining lines.

Hard page break Forces the next part of a document to begin on a new page.

Hard return Created when you press Enter to move the insertion point to a new line.

Header Information that displays at the top of each document page, presentation slide, handout, or notes page.

Header row The first row in a data source that contains labels describing the data.

Help and Support A built-in library of help topics that is available from the Start menu. Using Help and Support, you can get assistance with specific questions or broad topics.

Hidden text Document text that does not appear onscreen.

Hierarchy Uses main points and subpoints to indicate levels of importance in a structure.

Highlighter Background color used to mark text that you want to stand out or locate easily.

HLOOKUP function A predefined formula that looks up a value in a horizontal lookup table where the first row contains the values to compare with the lookup value.

Horizontal alignment The placement of data or text between the left and right margins in a document, or cell margins in a spreadsheet.

Icon A small picture on the desktop that represents a program, file, or folder.

Icon set A conditional format that displays an icon representing a value in the top third, quarter, or fifth based on values in the selected range.

IF function (IIf in Access) A predefined logical formula that evaluates a condition and returns one value if the condition is true and a different value if the condition is false.

Index An alphabetical listing of topics covered in a document, along with the page numbers where the topic is discussed.

Indexed property A setting that allows quick sorting in primary key order and quick retrieval based on the primary key.

Infographic Information graphic that is a visual representation of data or knowledge.

Infringement of copyright Occurs when a right of the copyright owner is violated.

Input area A range of cells to enter values for variables or assumptions that will be used in formulas within a workbook.

Join lines Used to create a relationship between two tables using a common field.

Jump List A list of actions or resources associated with an *open window* button or a pinned icon on the taskbar.

Kelvin The unit of measurement for absolute temperature as a characteristic of lighting in pictures.

Kerning Automatically adjusts spacing between characters to achieve a more evenly spaced appearance.

Key Tip The letter or number that displays over features on the Ribbon and Quick Access Toolbar.

Label control A literal word or phrase to describe the data.

Label Wizard A guide that steps you through the process of easily creating mailing labels, name tags, and other specialized tags.

Landscape Page or worksheet that is wider than it is tall.

Layout Determines the position of objects containing content on the slide.

Layout control Provides guides to help keep controls aligned horizontally and vertically, and to give your form a uniform appearance.

Layout view A view that is used to modify the design of a form or report while still viewing the data.

Leader character Typically dots or hyphens that connect two items, to draw the reader's eye across the page.

Left tab Sets the start position on the left so as you type, text moves to the right of the tab setting.

Legend A key that identifies the color, gradient, picture, texture, or pattern assigned to each data series in a chart.

Library An organization method that collects files from different locations and displays them as one unit.

Line chart A chart type that displays lines connecting data points to show trends over equal time periods, such as months, quarters, years, or decades.

Line spacing The vertical space between the lines in a paragraph and between paragraphs.

Line weight The width or thickness of a line.

Link To establish a connection from a presentation to another location.

Live Preview An Office feature that provides a preview of the results of a selection when you point to an option in a list.

Lock Drawing Mode Enables the creation of multiple shapes of the same type.

Logical test An expression that evaluates to true or false.

Lookup table A range that contains data for the basis of the lookup and data to be retrieved.

Lookup value The cell reference of the cell that contains the value to look up within a lookup table.

Mail merge A process that combines content from a main document and a data source.

Mailing label Specialized report that comes preformatted to coordinate with name-brand labels such as Avery.

Main document Contains the information that stays the same for all recipients.

Margin The blank space around the sides, top, and bottom of a document or worksheet.

...lored circle that contains comments, ...tions in the margin with a line drawn to ...point was in the document prior to ...nt or editing the document.

...f all citation sources created in Word on

...ed formula that finds the highest value

MEDIAN function A predefined formula that finds the midpoint value, which is the value that one-half of the population is above or below.

Merge field Serves as a placeholder for the variable data that will be inserted into the main document during the mail merge.

Microsoft Office A productivity software suite that includes word processing, spreadsheet, presentation, and database software components.

MIN function A predefined formula that finds the lowest value in a range.

Mini toolbar An Office feature that provides access to common formatting commands when text is selected.

Mixed cell reference A designation that combines an absolute cell reference with a relative cell reference. When you copy a formula containing a mixed cell reference, either the column letter or the row number that has the absolute reference remains fixed, whereas the other part of the cell reference that is relative changes in the copied formula. A mixed cell reference appears with the $ symbol before either the column letter or row number, such as $B5 or B$5.

Monospaced typeface Uses the same amount of horizontal space for every character.

Multilevel list Extends a numbered list to several levels, and is updated automatically when topics are added or deleted.

Multimedia Multiple forms of media used to entertain or inform an audience.

Multiple data series Two or more sets of data, such as the values for Chicago, New York, and Los Angeles sales for 2010, 2011, and 2012.

Multiple Items form Displays multiple records in a tabular layout similar to a table's Datasheet view.

Multi-table query A query that contains two or more tables. It allows you to take advantage of the relationships that have been set in your database.

Name Box An element in Excel that identifies the address or range name of the active cell in a worksheet.

Narration Spoken commentary that is added to a presentation.

Navigation Pane (Office Fundamentals) Located on the left side of the Windows Explorer window, providing access to Favorites, Libraries, Homegroup, Computer, and Network areas. (Access) Organizes and lists the database objects in an Access database.

Nested function A function that contains another function embedded inside one or more of its arguments.

Nonadjacent range A collection of multiple ranges that are not positioned in a contiguous cluster in an Excel worksheet.

Nonbreaking hyphen Keeps text of a hyphenated word on both sides of the hyphen together, thus preventing the hyphenated word from becoming separated at the end of a line.

Nonbreaking space A special character that keeps two or more words together.

Normal view The three-pane default PowerPoint view used when working with a presentation.

NOT logical operator A logical operator that returns all records except the specified criteria.

Notepad A text-editing program built into Windows 7.

Notes Page view Used for entering and editing large amounts of text to which the speaker can refer when presenting.

Notification area An area located on the right side of the taskbar. It displays icons for background programs and system resources. It also provides status information in pop-up windows.

NOW function A predefined formula that uses the computer's clock to display the current date and time in a cell.

Nper The number of payment periods over the life of the loan.

Null Missing or unknown data in a field.

Number data type A data type that can store only numerical data.

Numbered list Sequences and prioritizes the items in a list and is automatically updated to accommodate additions or deletions.

Object A main component in an Access database that is created and used to make the database.

Office Theme A defined set of colors, fonts, and graphics that can be applied to a form.

One-to-many relationship A relationship in which it is established when the primary key value in the primary table can match many of the foreign key values in the related table.

Opaque A solid fill, one with no transparency.

OpenType A form of font designed for use on all platforms.

Operand The part of an expression that is being manipulated.

Operating system Software that directs computer activities, performing such tasks as recognizing keyboard input, sending output to a display, and keeping track of files and folders.

Operator A mathematical symbol, such as +, −, *, and /.

OR logical operator A logical operator that returns records that meet any of the specified criteria.

Order of operations Determines the sequence by which operations are calculated in an expression.

Order of precedence A rule that controls the sequence in which arithmetic operations are performed.

Original: Show Markup A view that shows deleted text within the body of the document (with a line through the deleted text) and displays inserted text in a markup balloon.

Orphan The first line of a paragraph appearing by itself at the bottom of a page.

Outline A method of organizing text in a hierarchy with main points and subpoints to indicate levels of importance.

Outline view Displays varying amount of detail; a structural view of the document or presentation that can be collapsed or expanded as necessary.

Output area A range of cells that contains the results of manipulating values in an input area.

Page break An indication where data will start on another printed page. The software inserts automatic page breaks based on data, margins, and paper size. Users can insert additional page breaks.

Page Footer section Appears once at the bottom of each page to display page summaries, dates, or page numbers at the bottom of every page in a form or report.

Page Header section Appears once at the top of each page to display page summaries, dates, or page numbers at the top of every page in a form or report.

Paint A graphics program built into Windows 7 that enables you to create drawings and open picture files.

Paragraph spacing The amount of space before or after a paragraph.

Paragraph style Stores paragraph formatting such as alignment, line spacing, and indents, as well as the font, size, and style of the text in the paragraph.

Paste Places a cut or copied item in another location.

Photo Album A presentation containing multiple pictures organized into album pages.

Picture A graphic file that is retrieved from the Internet, a disk, or CD and placed in an Office project.

Picture fill Inserts an image from a file into a shape.

Picture Styles A gallery that contains preformatted options that can be applied to a graphical object.

Pie chart A chart type that shows each data point in proportion to the whole data series as a slice in a circular pie.

Pin The process of placing icons of frequently used programs on the taskbar or on the Start menu.

Placeholder A container that holds content.

Plagiarism The act of using and documenting the works of another as one's own.

Plain Text format (.txt) A file format that retains only text, but no formatting, when you transfer documents between applications or platforms.

Plot area The region containing the graphical representation of the values in the data series.

PMT function A predefined formula that calculates the periodic payment for a loan with a fixed interest rate and fixed term.

Point The smallest unit of measurement in typography.

Pointing The process of using the mouse pointer to select cells while building a formula. Also known as *semi-selection*.

Portrait Page or worksheet that is taller than it is wide.

Position Raises or lowers text from the baseline without creating superscript or subscript size.

Poster Frame The frame that displays on a slide when a video is not playing.

PowerPoint A Microsoft Office software component that enables you to prepare slideshow presentations for audiences.

PowerPoint presentation An electronic slide show that can be edited or displayed.

PowerPoint show (.ppsx) An unchangeable electronic slide show format used for distribution.

Presenter view Specialty view that delivers a presentation on two monitors simultaneously.

Primary key The field (or combination of fields) that uniquely identifies each record in a table.

Print area The range of cells within a worksheet that will print.

Print Layout view The default view that closely resembles the printed document.

Print order The sequence in which the pages are printed.

Print Preview Allows you to see exactly what the report will look like when it is printed.

Proportional typeface Allocates horizontal space to the character.

Public domain Rights to a literary work or property owned by the public at large.

Pv The present value of the loan or an annuity.

Query A question that you ask about the data in the tables of your database.

Query Design view A view that allows you to create queries; the Design view is divided into two parts—the top portion displays the tables, and the bottom portion (known as the query design grid) displays the fields and the criteria.

Query sort order Determines the order of records in the query's Datasheet view.

Quick Access Toolbar Provides one-click access to commonly used commands.

Quick Style A combination of formatting options that can be applied to a shape or other objects.

Radar chart A chart type that compares aggregate values of three or more variables represented on axes starting from the same point.

Range A group of adjacent or contiguous cells in an Excel worksheet.

Range name A word or string of characters assigned to one or more cells. It can be up to 255 letters, characters, or numbers, starting with a letter.

Rate The periodic interest rate; the percentage of interest paid for each payment period.

Reading view Displays a full-screen view one slide at a time that includes bars and buttons for additional functionality.

Recolor The process of changing picture or illustration colors to a duotone style.

Record A group of related fields, representing one entity, such as data for one person, place, event, or concept.

Record source The table or query that supplies the records for a form or report.

Referential integrity Rules in a database that are used to preserve relationships between tables when records are changed.

Related tables Tables that are joined in a relationship using a common field.

Relational database management system (RDBMS) A database system in which you can manage groups of data (tables) and then set rules (relationships) between tables.

Relationship A connection between two tables using a common field.

Relative cell reference A designation that indicates a cell's relative location within the worksheet using the column letter and row number, such as B5. When a formula containing a relative cell reference is copied, the cell references in the copied formula change relative to the position of the copied formula.

Replace Finds text and replaces it with a word or phrase that you indicate.

Report An Access database object that displays professional-looking formatted information from underlying tables or queries.

Report Footer section A *report* section in Access that displays page numbers, dates, and/or aggregate totals once at the bottom of the report.

Report Header section A *report* section in Access that displays page numbers, dates, and/or aggregate totals and prints once at the beginning of each report.

Report tool A feature used to instantly create a tabular report based on the table or query currently selected.

Report view A view that allows you to see what the printed report will look like in a continuous page layout.

Report Wizard A guide that asks you questions and then uses your answers to generate a report.

Reviewing Pane A window that displays all comments and editorial changes made to the main document.

Revision mark Indicates where text is added, deleted, or formatted while the Track Changes feature is active.

Ribbon The long bar of tabs, groups, and commands located just beneath the Title bar.

Rich Text Format (.rtf) A file format that retains structure and most text formatting when transferring documents between applications or platforms.

Right tab Sets the start position on the right so as you type, text moves to the left of that tab setting and aligns on the right.

Rotate To move an object around its axis.

Row height The vertical measurement of a row in a table or a worksheet.

Run command Used to produce the query results (the red exclamation point).

Sans serif typeface A typeface that does not contain thin lines on characters.

Saturation The intensity of a color in an image.

Scaling (or to **scale**) Increases or decreases text or a graphic as a percentage of its original size.

Screen saver A series of images or a graphic display that continually moves over the screen when the computer has been idle for a specified period of time. Screen savers can be used for security purposes to keep others from viewing computer contents.

Section break A marker that divides a document into sections, thereby allowing different formatting in each section.

Select query A type of query that displays only the records that match criteria entered in Query Design view.

Selection net Selects all objects in an area you define by dragging the mouse.

Selection Pane A pane designed to help select objects from a listing of all objects on a slide.

Semi-selection The process of using the mouse pointer to select cells while building a formula. Also known as *pointing*.

Serif typeface A typeface that contains a thin line or extension at the top and bottom of the primary strokes on characters.

Shading A background color that appears behind text in a paragraph, a page, a table, or within a cell.

Shape A geometric or non-geometric object, such as a rectangle or an arrow, used to create an illustration or to highlight information.

Sharpen To enhance the edges of the content in a picture to make the boundaries more prominent.

Sheet tab A visual item in Excel that looks like a folder tab that displays the name of a worksheet, such as *Sheet1* or *June Sales*.

Shortcut A link, or pointer, to a program or computer resource.

Shortcut menu Provides choices related to the selection or area at which you right-click.

Show Markup Enables you to view document revisions by reviewer; it also allows you to choose which type of revisions you want to view such as comments, insertions and deletions, or formatting changes.

Show row A row in the Query Design view that controls whether the field will be displayed in the query results.

Show/Hide feature Reveals where formatting marks, such as spaces, tabs, and returns, are used in the document.

Simple Query Wizard A guide that walks you through the query design process to facilitate new query development.

Single data series A collection of data points for one set of data, such as the values for Chicago sales for 2010, 2011, and 2012.

Sizing handles (Word) The small circles and squares that appear around a selected object and enable you to adjust the height and width of an object. (Excel) A series of faint dots on the outside border of a selected chart; enables you to adjust the size of the chart.

Slide The most basic element of PowerPoint.

Slide show A collection of slides that can be used in a presentation.

Slide Show view Used to deliver the completed presentation full screen to an audience, one slide at a time, as an electronic presentation.

Slide Sorter view Displays thumbnails of your presentation slides, which allow you to view multiple slides simultaneously.

SmartArt A diagram that presents information visually to effectively communicate a message.

Snap A feature that arranges windows automatically on the left and right sides of the desktop.

Snip A screen display that has been captured and displayed by screen capture software.

Snipping Tool A Windows 7 accessory program that captures screen displays for saving or sharing.

Soft page break Inserted when text fills an entire page and continues onto the next page.

Soft return Created by the word processor as it wraps text to a new line.

Soften To blur the edges of the content in a picture to make the boundaries less prominent.

Sort Lists records in a specific sequence, such as ascending by last name or descending by employee id.

Sort Ascending Arranges a list of text data in alphabetical order or a numeric list in lowest to highest order.

Sort Descending Arranges a list of text data in reverse alphabetical order or a numeric list in highest to lowest order.

Sort row A row in the Query Design view that enables you to sort query results in ascending or descending order.

Sorting Listing records or text in a specific sequence, such as alphabetically by last name.

Sparkline A small line, column, or win/loss chart contained in a single cell.

Split form A type of form that combines two views of the same record source—one section is displayed in a stacked layout and the other section is displayed in a tabular layout.

Splitter bar A feature in Form design view that divides the form into two halves.

Spreadsheet An electronic file that contains a grid of columns and rows to organize related data and to display results of calculations.

Spreadsheet program A computer application, such as Microsoft Excel, that people use to create and modify spreadsheets.

Spyware Software that is installed from the Internet, usually without the user's permission. It can gather information for marketing purposes, and is sometimes capable of changing computer settings and recording keystrokes.

Stacked column chart A chart type that places stacks of data in segments on top of each other in one column, with each category in the data series represented by a different color.

Stacked layout form A type of form that displays fields in a vertical column and displays one record at a time.

Stacked layout report A type of report that displays fields in a vertical column.

Stacking order The order of objects placed on top of one another.

Start button A button located at the left side of the taskbar. Click the Start button to display the Start menu.

Start menu A menu that is displayed when you click the Start button. It is a list of programs, folders, utilities, and tasks.

Status bar (Office Fundamentals) The horizontal bar located at the bottom of an Office application containing information relative to the open file. (PowerPoint) Contains the slide number, the design theme name, and View buttons, in PowerPoint.

Stock chart A chart type that shows fluctuations in stock changes.

Storyboard A visual plan of a presentation that displays the content of each slide in the slide show.

Structured reference A tag or use of a table element, such as a column heading, as a reference in a formula.

Style A set of formatting options you apply to characters or paragraphs.

Subfolder A folder that is housed within another folder.

SUBTOTAL function A predefined formula that calculates an aggregate value, such as totals, for values in a range or database.

SUM function A predefined formula that calculates the total of values contained in two or more cells.

Surface chart A chart type that displays trends using two dimensions on a continuous curve.

Syntax The rules that dictate the structure and components required to perform the necessary calculations in an equation or evaluate expressions.

Tab (Office Fundamentals) Ribbon area that contains groups of related tasks. (Word) A marker that specifies the position for aligning text in a document.

Table (Access) An object in a database that stores related information. (Word, Excel, PowerPoint, Access) Organizes information in a series of records (rows), with each record made up of a number of fields (columns).

Table alignment The position of a table between the left and right document margins.

Table array The range that contains the body of the lookup table, excluding column headings. The first column must be in ascending order to find a value in a range, or it can be in any order to look up an exact value.

Table Move handle The graphical image that displays in the upper-left corner of a table and enables you to select a whole table at one time.

Table of authorities Used in legal documents to reference cases and other documents referred to in a legal brief.

Table of contents Lists headings in the order they appear in a document and the page numbers where the entries begin.

Table of figures A list of the captions in a document.

Table row A row in the Query Design view that displays the data source.

Table style The rules that control the fill color of the header row, columns, and records in a table.

Tabular layout form A type of form that displays records horizontally, with label controls across the top and the data values in rows under the labels.

Tabular layout report A type of report that displays data horizontally across the page in a landscape orientation.

Tag A file property, such as a rating, that a user can apply to a file for identification purposes.

Taskbar The horizontal bar located at the bottom of the desktop. It displays icons for open windows, a Start button, pinned icons, and a notification area.

Template A predesigned file that incorporates formatting elements, such as a theme and layouts, and may include content that can be modified.

Text One or more letters, numbers, symbols, and/or spaces often used as a label in a worksheet.

Text box An object that enables you to place text anywhere on a slide.

Text box control A control that displays the data found in a form's record source.

Text data type A data type that can store either text or numerical characters.

Text direction The degree of rotation in which text displays.

Text pane A pane for text entry that opens when a SmartArt diagram is selected.

Text wrapping style The way text wraps around an image.

Texture fill Inserts a texture such as marble, canvas, or cork into a shape.

Theme A collection of design choices that includes colors, fonts, and special theme effects used to give a consistent look to a presentation.

Thumbnail A miniature of a slide that appears in the Slides tab and Slide Sorter view.

Title bar A horizontal bar that appears at the top of each open window. The title bar contains the current file name, Office application, and control buttons.

TODAY function A predefined formula that displays the current date in a cell.

Toggle Commands such as bold and italic that enable you to switch from one setting to another.

Tone A characteristic of lighting in pictures (also called *temperature*).

Toolbar A collection of icons or items, usually displayed in a horizontal fashion, from which you can make selections.

Total row A table row that appears below the last row of records in an Excel table, or in Datasheet view of a table or query, and displays summary or aggregate statistics.

Totals query A query that contains an additional row in the design grid and is used to display only aggregate data when the query is run.

Track Changes Monitors all additions, deletions, and formatting changes you make in a document.

Transition A specific animation that is applied as a previous slide is replaced by a new slide while displayed in Slide Show view or Reading view.

Transparency The visibility of fill.

Trendline A line that depicts trends or helps forecast future data.

Type style The characteristic applied to a font, such as bold.

Typeface A complete set of characters—upper- and lowercase letters, numbers, punctuation marks, and special symbols.

Typography The arrangement and appearance of printed matter.

Unbound control A control that displays labels and other decorative design elements.

Ungrouping Breaking a combined object into individual objects, which enables them to move or act separately.

User Account Control (UAC) A Windows feature that asks a user's permission before allowing any changes to computer settings.

User interface A collection of onscreen components that facilitates communication between the software and the user.

Validation rule A property that prevents invalid data from being entered into a field.

Value A number that represents a quantity or an amount.

Value axis The chart element that displays incremental numbers to identify approximate values, such as dollars or units, of data points in the chart.

Vector graphic An object-oriented graphic based on geometric formulas.

Vertex The point where a curve ends or the point where two line segments meet in a shape.

Vertical alignment The position of data between the top and bottom cell margins.

View The way a file appears onscreen.

Visual Basic for Applications (VBA) Microsoft's programming language that is built into all of the Office products.

VLOOKUP function A predefined formula that looks up a value and returns a related result from the lookup table.

Watermark Text or graphic that displays behind text.

Web Layout view View to display how a document will look when posted on the Web.

Widow The last line of a paragraph appearing by itself at the top of a page.

Wildcard A special character used in a query to include all records that begin with a specific character or match one or more characters in the criterion of a query.

Window A rectangular bordered area of space on the desktop that represents a program, system resource, or data.

Windows Defender An antispyware program that is installed along with Windows 7.

Windows Explorer A Windows component that can be used to create and manage folders.

Windows Update A software patch, or fix, provided by Microsoft, that prevents or corrects problems. Many updates focus on security concerns.

Wizard A tool that makes a process easier by asking a series of questions, then creating a document structure based on your answers.

Word A word processing program that is included in Microsoft Office.

Word processing software A computer application, such as Microsoft Word, used primarily with text to create, edit, and format documents.

Word wrap The feature that automatically moves words to the next line if they do not fit on the current line.

WordArt Text that has a decorative effect applied.

WordPad A basic word processing program built into Windows 7.

Workbook A collection of one or more related worksheets contained within a single file.

Worksheet A single spreadsheet that typically contains labels, values, formulas, functions, and graphical representations of data.

Wrap text A formatting option that enables a label to appear on multiple lines within the current cell.

X Y (scatter) chart A chart type that shows a relationship between two variables using their X and Y coordinates. Excel plots one variable on the horizontal X-axis and the other variable on the vertical Y-axis. Scatter charts are often used to represent data in educational, scientific, and medical experiments.

X-axis A horizontal border that provides a frame of reference for measuring data horizontally on a chart.

Y-axis A vertical border that provides a frame of reference for measuring data vertically on a chart.

Zoom slider Enables you to increase or decrease the size of file contents onscreen.

INDEX

← (arrow key)
move left one cell, 315
one character to left (insertion point), 121
Return to Previous Slide/Animation, 791

↑ (arrow key)
move up one cell/line, 121, 315
Return to Previous Slide/Animation, 791

→ (arrow key)
Advance Through Slide Show, 791
move right one cell, 315
one character to right (insertion point), 121
Tab (nonprinting symbol), 177

↓ (arrow key)
Advance Through Slide Show, 791
move down one cell/line, 121, 315

1 Page Per Sheet (print setting), 148
3-D charts, 426
3-D Format (font effect), 165
3-D rotation (shape effect), 864
7×7 guideline (presentations), 772
100% stacked column chart, 425–426
(pound signs), 335
* (multiplication operator), 321
+ (addition operator), 321
– (subtraction operator), 321
.aiff (Audio Interchange File Format), 953
.asf (Advanced Streaming Format), 943
.au (UNIX Audio), 953
.avi (Audio Video Interleave), 943
.dib (Device Independent Bitmap), 921
.emf (Windows Enhanced Metafile), 921
.gif (Graphics Interchange Format), 921
.jpg/.jpeg (Joint Photographic Experts Group), 921
.mid/.midi (Musical Instrument Digital Interface), 953
.mp3 (MPEG Audio Layer 3), 953
.mpg/.mpeg (Moving Picture Experts Group), 943
.pct, 921
.pic, 921
.pict, 921
.png (Portable Network Graphics), 921
.ppsx (PowerPoint show), 765
.rtf (Rich Text format), 825
.swf (Flash Video file format), 943
.tif/.tiff (Tagged Image File Format), 921
.txt (Plain Text format), 825
.wav (Wave Form), 953
.wma (Windows Media Audio), 953
.wmv (Windows Media Video), 943
/ (division operator), 321
= (equal sign)
<= (less than or equal to), 395, 551
= (equal to operator), 395
>= (greater than or equal to), 395, 551
formulas after, 317, 321, 385

^ (exponentiation), 321
> (greater than), 395, 551
>= (greater than or equal to), 395, 551
< (less than), 395, 551
<= (less than or equal to), 395, 551
<> (not equal to), 395, 551

A

ABS function, 387
absolute cell reference, 375
Accept (Changes group), 222
Accept All Changes in Document, 222
Access (Microsoft Access 2010). See also
    databases; Microsoft Office 2010
    characteristics, 64
    /Excel, when to use, 553–554
    functions (built-in), 662–678
    Interface, 533–535
    keyboard shortcuts, 551
    as RDBMS, 560
    Ribbon, 534–535
    user interface components (Office), 64–69
    working from storage, 540
access speed, 541
accessory programs (Windows 7), 23–26
Accounting (number format style), 348
Action Center, 10, 26–27
    alerts, 10, 26–27
    icon, 9, 10, 27
active cell, 315
active voice/passive voice (presentations), 772
Add-Ins tab
    Excel, 314
    PowerPoint, 791
    Word Options category, 125
addition operator (+), 321
Address Block (Mail Merge command), 290
adjustment handle, 853
Adobe Flash Media, 943
Adobe Illustrator, 889
Advance Through Slide Show (navigation option), 791
Advanced section (Word Options category), 125
Advanced Streaming Format (.asf), 943
Advanced tab (Font dialog box), 166, 167
Aero Flip 3D, 13–14
Aero Peek, 5–6
aggregate functions, 675–678
AID field, 600, 601
Album Layout section (Photo Albums), 961–962
alerts (Action Center), 10, 26–27
Align Text Left, 178

Align Text Right, 178
alignment
    cell alignment, 346
    keyboard shortcuts, 179
    objects, 893–896
    pictures/images, 201
    tables (Word), 266
    text alignment, 178, 181
Alignment Dialog Box Launcher, 347
Alignment group
    Decrease Indent, 347
    features, 346
    Increase Indent, 347
    Merge & Center, 347
    Orientation, 346, 347
    Table Tools Layout tab, 264
    vertical/horizontal alignment settings, 346
    Wrap Text, 347
Allow Zero Length (table property type), 589
Alt+Enter (line break in cell), 316
Alt+Shift+X (Mark Entry), 239
American Psychological Association (APA) style, 232
AND operator, 618
animate audio sequence, 955
Animation Gallery, 782
Animation Painter, 781
animations, 781–782
    defined, 781
    Return to Previous Slide/Animation (navigation option), 791
    transitions and, 781–784
annotations (for slide shows), 793
antispyware, 26, 27
antivirus software. See viruses
APA (American Psychological Association) style, 232
area charts, 428–429
arguments, 382. See also functions
    in brackets, 384
    defined, 382, 662
    Function Arguments dialog box, 382, 383, 384
    IF function, 395
    nonadjacent ranges as, 386
    PMT function, 398, 663
arithmetic
    calculations (order of operations), 650
    date arithmetic, 583, 665–666
arrange objects (presentation design), 892–896
Arrow Outline Style (lines), 863
arrows. See also specific commands with arrows
    commands with arrows, 88
    scroll arrows, 120
    spin arrows (dialog box component), 15

artistic effects
    graphic editing feature, 201
    PowerPoint pictures, 928–929
ascending order (sort order), 274, 552
aspect ratio, 887
Attachment (data type), 586
audience handouts. *See* handouts
audio file formats, 953
Audio Interchange File Format (.aiff), 953
audio tools (PowerPoint media tools),
    953–956
    animate audio sequence, 955
    audio over multiple slides, 955
    audio settings, 955–956
    record/inset audio, 954
Audio Video Interleave (.avi), 943
Auto Arrange icons, 4
Auto Check for Errors (Mail Merge
    command), 290
Auto Fill, 323
AutoCaptions, 241
AutoComplete (Excel), 317. *See also*
    Formula AutoComplete
AutoFilter dialog box, 496
AutoFit Column Width (Cells group), 335
AutoFit Row Height (Cells group), 335
AutoMark command, 240
AutoNumber data type, 585, 586
AutoRecover, 145
AVERAGE function, 385
axes (charts)
    axis titles, 453–454
    formatting, 455
    types, 423

B

background
    desktop, 10–12
    pictures/images, 200, 923–924, 932–933
    worksheet (Page Setup command), 354
Background Styles gallery (PowerPoint
    themes), 834
Backstage view, 65, 66, 76–80
    exiting, 150
    Help button, 69, 70
    printing options, 79–80, 147–148
    printing worksheets, 357
    tasks, 76–80
backups, 59
    AutoRecover, 145
    database backup utility, 541, 542
    frequent, 144
    options (Word), 145–146
Banded Columns (table style option), 488
Banded Rows (table style option), 488
bar charts, 427
bar tab (tab marker), 173
Behind Text (text wrapping style), 198
bevel (shape effect), 864
bibliographies, 231. *See also* citations
bitmap images, 920
Blank Form (form tool), 699

Blank Report (report tool), 728
blue wavy line, 100, 135, 136
bold (type style), 164
bold italic (type style), 164
borders, 174–175
    cells/ranges, 348
    Page Border tab, 174, 175
    paragraphs, 174–175
    Word tables, 264
Borders and Shading dialog box, 174–175
bound control, 712
brackets, arguments in, 384
breakpoint, 396
Breaks (Page Setup command), 354
brightness (images), 200, 201, 925
Bring Forward (order objects), 893
Bring to Front option (order objects), 893
Browse Help, 37. *See also* Help and Support
bubble charts, 431–432
Bullet Library, 175, 176
bulleted lists, 175–176

C

calculated control, 713–714, 742
calculated fields, 583, 650, 651–653
Calculator (Windows 7 program), 24–25
callouts, 853
CamelCase notation, 585
Cancel (Excel window element), 314
capitalization (Change Case), 167
Capitalize Each Word (Change Case
    option), 167
Caption dialog box, 241
caption property, 589
captions, 241
Cascade Delete Related Records option, 598
Cascade Update Related Fields option, 597
category axis, 423
category labels, 422
cells. *See also* formulas; ranges
    active, 315
    alignment, 346
    borders, 348
    clearing, 317
    conditional formatting, 509–514
    dates in, 317
    defined, 315
    deleting, 334
    editing, 317
    fill color options, 348
    indenting cell contents, 347
    inserting, 333–334
    line breaks in, 316
    Merge Cells command, 263
    navigation keystrokes, 315–316
    rotating cell contents, 347
    selecting, 337
    Split Cells command, 263
    text in, 316
    times in, 317
    values in, 317
    Word tables, 262

cell addresses, 315
cell margins (Word tables), 266
cell references, 321–322
    absolute, 375
    circular, 376
    mixed, 375–376
    range names *v.*, 405
    relative, 375
    toggle (F4), 376
cells. *See also* formulas; ranges
    active, 315
    alignment, 346
    borders, 348
    clearing, 317
    conditional formatting, 509–514
    dates in, 317
    defined, 315
    deleting, 334
    editing, 317
    fill color options, 348
    indenting cell contents, 347
    inserting, 333–334
    line breaks in, 316
    Merge Cells command, 263
    navigation keystrokes, 315–316
    rotating cell contents, 347
    selecting, 337
    Split Cells command, 263
    text in, 316
    times in, 317
    values in, 317
    Word tables, 262
Cells group
    AutoFit Column Width (Format), 335
    AutoFit Row Height (Format), 335
    Column Width (Format), 335
    Delete Cells (Delete arrow), 334
    Delete Sheet (Delete arrow), 332
    Delete Sheet Columns/Delete Sheet Rows
      (Delete arrow), 334
    Hide Columns/Hide Rows (Format), 336
    Insert Cells (Insert arrow), 333–334
    Insert Sheet (Insert arrow), 332
    Insert Sheet Columns/Insert Sheet Rows
      (Insert arrow), 333
    Move or Copy Sheet (Format), 332–333
    Rename Sheet (Format), 331
    Row Height (Format), 335
    Tab Color (Format), 331
    Unhide Columns/Unhide Rows
      (Format), 336
Center
    table alignment (Word), 266
    text alignment, 178
center tab (tab marker), 173
centered text, 178
central tendency, 385
Change Case (Font group), 167
Change Shape, 856
changed lines, 221
Changes group (Review tab), 222
character spacing, 166–167
character styles, 187–188
chart area, 423

chart labels, 453–455
Chart Layouts group, 442
chart sheet, 434, 444
Chart Styles group, 443
chart titles, 453
Chart Tools contextual tab, 435, 441, 443
    Design tab, 441–445
    Format tab, 434, 435, 441
    Layout tab, 435, 451–456
charts
    area, 428–429
    bar, 427
    basics, 422–435
    bubble, 431–432
    changing chart type, 441
    changing data source/structure, 442
    column, 423–426
    creating, 432–435
    data point, 422
    data series, 422, 423
    data sources for, 432–433, 442
    defined, 422
    design, 441–445
    doughnut, 431
    elements, 451–456
    embedded, 444
    formatting, 451–456
    gridlines, 456
    layout, 442
    legends, 424, 454
    line, 427
    moving, 443
    pie, 428
    positioning, 434–435
    printing, 444
    radar, 432
    scatter (X Y), 429
    sizing handles, 434–435
    sparklines, 444–445
    stock, 430
    style, 443
    surface, 430–431
    as templates, 441
    3-D, 426
    trendlines, 456
    types, 422–432
    X Y (scatter), 429
check boxes (dialog box component), 15
Choose a SmartArt Graphic dialog
    box, 876
circular references, 376
citations, 229–231. See also sources
    bibliographies and, 231
    Citations & Bibliography group, 229, 231, 232
    footnotes/endnotes, 232
    Insert Citation feature, 229, 231
Clear All style, 188
clearing
    cell contents, 317
    conditional formatting (cells), 512
    filters (Excel tables), 497
    sparklines, 445

clip art
    defined, 99
    flip/rotate, 888–889
    grouping/ungrouping, 889–890
    modifying, 887, 889
    recolor, 891–892, 928
Clip Art Task Pane, 99, 887
    audio added from, 953
    videos added from, 944
Clip Organizer, 920, 921, 953
Clipboard (Office Clipboard), 87, 89–90
    Dialog Box Launcher, 89
    task pane, 89
Clipboard group
    Copy arrow, 339
    Paste arrow, 339–340
    tasks (Office applications), 87–90
Close button (Office interface), 65
closed shapes, 854
closing files/Office applications, 80
clustered bar chart, 427
clustered column charts, 423–424
collaborative projects (document
    revisions), 218–223. See also research
    paper
collapsed outline, 818–819
Collated (print setting), 148
Collect Data (External Data tab), 598
Color (graphic editing feature), 201
color changes (PowerPoint pictures),
    926–928
color scales, 512
Color Scales (conditional formatting
    option), 509, 511–512
Colors gallery (PowerPoint themes), 834
column charts, 423–426
    axes, 423
    clustered, 423–424
    100% stacked, 425–426
    stacked, 424–426
    3-D, 426
column headings
    as Excel window element, 315
    printing, 357
    in reports, 742
column index number, 397
Column Width (Cells group), 335
columns
    Banded Columns (table style option), 488
    deleting, 334
    First Column (table style option), 488
    freezing, 475–476
    hiding/unhiding, 336
    inserting, 333–334
    Last Column (table style option), 488
    selecting, 337
    text, 176–177, 181
    transposing, 340
    width, 334–335
    width, in forms, 700
    width, in reports, 729
    width, in Word tables, 263–264
command buttons (dialog box
    component), 15

commands, 67
    with arrows, 88
    toggles, 86, 121
comments, 218–221
    markup balloons and, 218–219
    response, 219
    view/modify/delete, 219–221
common fields, linked tables with, 583–584
Compact and Repair, 541
Comparison layout, 780
comparison operators, 395, 551, 617–618
Compatibility Checker, 146
Compatibility functions, 382
Compatibility Mode, 145
Compatibility Pack, 144
complex structured references, 498
compression (pictures/images), 200, 201,
    920, 931
conclusion (in presentation/slide), 771
conditional formatting (cells), 509–514
    clear, 512
    create new rules, 512–514
    formulas in, 513–514
    overdoing, 512
    sorting/filtering by, 514
connectors, 855
constants, 583
    date arithmetic and, 583
    in formulas, 322
constraining shapes, 854
Content with Caption layout, 780
context menu, 87
contextual spelling feature, 125, 135, 136
contextual tabs, 68, 97
continuous section breaks, 133
contrast (images), 200, 925
controls
    forms, 712–714
    reports, 742
conversions
    tables (Excel) to ranges, 486
    text to SmartArt diagram, 880
    text to tables (Word), 275
Convert Text to Table dialog box, 275
Copy, 88–90
    Ctrl+C, 69, 89
    options, 89
Copy arrow (Clipboard group), 339
    Copy, 339
    Copy as Picture, 339
copying
    queries, 619
    ranges, 338–339
    worksheets, 333
copyright
    defined, 933
    guidelines, 934–935
    infringement of, 933
Copyright Act of 1976, 934
CorelDRAW, 889
correcting pictures (PowerPoint),
    924–926
Corrections (graphic editing feature), 201
COUNT function, 386, 675

COUNTA function, 386
COUNTBLANK function, 386
Cover Page feature, 124
Create Names from Selection dialog
    box, 404
Create Source dialog box, 229, 230
Create Sparklines dialog box, 444
Create tab (Access), 535
Create Table dialog box, 485
criteria
    for data types, 616–618
    defined, 538
    null, 617
    operands, 616–617
Criteria row (Query Design view), 615
cropping, 199–200, 201, 930–931
cross-references, 243–244
Ctrl+←, 121
Ctrl+↑, 121
Ctrl+→, 121
Ctrl+↓, 121
Ctrl+A (selecting ranges), 337
Ctrl+C (Copy), 69, 89. See also Copy
Ctrl+E (align center), 179
Ctrl+End, 69, 121, 316
Ctrl+Enter (hard page break), 122
Ctrl+F (finding items), 91
Ctrl+F1 (hide/display Ribbon), 67
Ctrl+G (Go To dialog box), 316, 405, 474
Ctrl+Home, 69, 316
Ctrl+J (justify), 179
Ctrl+L (align left), 179
Ctrl+Page Down, 121
Ctrl+Page Up, 121
Ctrl+R (align right), 179
Ctrl+semicolon (current date), 317
Ctrl+Shift+Hyphen (insert nonbreaking
    hyphen), 168
Ctrl+Shift+semicolon (current time), 317
Ctrl+Shift+Spacebar (insert nonbreaking
    space), 168
Ctrl+Tab (movement within table),
    263, 787
Ctrl+V (Paste), 69, 89. See also Paste
Ctrl+X (Cut), 89. See also Cut
Ctrl+Z (undo), 69
Cube functions, 382
Currency (data type), 586
Currency (number format style), 348
Current List, 230
Custom (number format style), 349
Custom AutoFilter dialog box, 497
Custom Margins (Page Setup dialog box),
    102, 148
Customize Quick Access Toolbar menu, 66
Customize Ribbon (Word Options
    category), 125
customizing. See also Options
    chart labels, 453–455
    desktop, 10–12
    document properties, 150
    legends, 454
    page numbers, 123
    Quick Access Toolbar, 66

shapes, 857–864
sparklines, 445
taskbar icons, 6
Cut, 87
    Ctrl+X, 89
    options, 89
Cycle (SmartArt diagram type), 874

D

Dash Outline Style (lines), 863
data. See also databases
    Access table (design principles), 580–584
    information v., 533
    redundancy, 583
    sample, database skills and, 561
data analysis, quantitative, 311
data bars, 511
Data Bars (conditional formatting option),
    509, 511–512
Data group (Table Tools Layout tab), 264
data labels (chart element), 454–455
data point, 422
data series
    defined, 422
    multiple, 423
    single, 423
data sources (charts)
    changing, 442
    selecting, 432–433
data sources (recipient lists). See also Mail
    Merge feature; main documents;
    record sources
    databases as, 285–286
    fields in, 283
    header row, 283
    records in, 283, 286–287
    tables (Word) as, 283
    worksheets as, 284–285
data table, 453, 455
data types (Access), 585–586, 588–589
    Attachment, 586
    AutoNumber, 585, 586
    criteria for, 616–618
    Currency, 586
    Date/Time, 586
    field, 616
    Hyperlink, 586
    Memo, 586
    Number, 586, 589
    OLE, 586
    Text, 586, 588–589
    Yes/No, 586
Database functions, 382
Database Tools tab (Access), 535
databases (Access relational databases). See
    also forms; macros; modules; queries;
    relationships; reports; tables (Access)
    backup utility, 541, 542
    Compact and Repair, 541
    as data source (mail merge), 285–286
    defined, 533
    file management, 541–542

Get External Data - Excel Spreadsheet
    feature, 598–602
    objects, 533, 534, 537, 540
    as relational databases, 560–562
    sample data and, 561
datasets (large datasets), 474–478
Datasheet forms, 698, 699
Datasheet view (Access tables),
    535–537, 588
Date (number format style), 348
Date & Time functions, 382, 387–388
date arithmetic, 583, 665–666
date filters (Excel tables), 496–497
date formatting, 665
DATE function, 388
date functions (Access), 665–666
DatePart function, 665–666
dates
    in cells, 317
    Ctrl+semicolon (current date), 317
    /times, updating, 388
Date/Time (data type), 586
DAY function, 388
decimal places (increasing/decreasing),
    349, 387
decimal tab (tab marker), 173
Decrease Decimal, 349, 387
Decrease Indent option, 179, 347
decreasing/increasing decimal places,
    349, 387
default options, 101
Default Value (table property type), 589
Delete arrow (Cells group)
    Delete Cells, 334
    Delete Sheet, 332
    Delete Sheet Columns/Delete Sheet
    Rows, 334
Delete dialog box (cells), 334
deleting
    cells, 334
    columns, 334
    comments, 221
    fields, from forms, 700
    fields, from reports, 729
    fields, in multi-table query, 627
    icons, 3
    range names, 404
    records (Excel tables), 486
    rows, 334
    rows (Word tables), 263
    tab markers, 173
    /viewing/modifying comments, 218–221
    worksheets, 332–333
delivery tips (PowerPoint presentations),
    760, 792, 831
descending order (sort order), 274, 552
design. See also presentation design
    charts, 441–445
    slide shows/presentations, 830–834
    tables (Access), 580–584
    tables (Excel), 484–485
    worksheets/workbooks, 312–313
Design tab (Chart Tools contextual tab),
    441–445

Design view
    Access tables, 535–537, 588
    forms, 712
    reports, 741
desktop, 2–12
    background, 10–12
    customizing, 10–12
Detail section (form section), 709
Detail section (report section), 740
development (presentation development).
        See presentations
Device Independent Bitmap (.dib), 921
dialog box launcher, 67. *See also specific
        launchers*
dialog boxes. *See also* Options
    AutoFilter, 496
    Borders and Shading, 174–175
    Caption, 241
    Choose a SmartArt Graphic, 876
    Compatibility Checker, 146
    components, 15
    Convert Text to Table, 275
    Create Names from Selection, 404
    Create Sparklines, 444
    Create Table, 485
    Cross-reference, 243–244
    Custom AutoFilter, 497
    defined, 14–15, 67
    Delete (cells), 334
    Edit Relationships, 597
    Envelopes and Labels, 290
    Excel Options, 315, 316
    Find and Replace, 90–91
    Font, 87, 164–167
    Footnote and Endnote, 232
    Format Cells, 347, 348, 349
    Format Data Labels, 454–455
    Format Data Series, 451–452
    Function Arguments, 382, 383, 384
    Go To (F5 or Ctrl+G), 316, 405, 474
    Grid and Guides, 894
    Header and Footer, 784–785
    Help button, 68, 70
    Import Spreadsheet Wizard, 599, 600,
        601, 602
    Insert, 332, 333, 334
    Insert Chart, 434
    Insert Function, 314, 383
    Insert Picture, 98
    Layout, 198
    Mark Citation, 242
    Mark Index Entry, 239
    Modify Style, 188
    Move Chart, 443
    Move or Copy Sheet, 332–333
    Name Manager, 404
    Open, 77
    Page Number Format, 123
    Page Setup, 102–103, 354–357, 478
    Paragraph, 178, 179, 180
    Paste Name, 405
    Print, 15
    Save Chart Template, 441
    Screen Saver Settings, 10–11

    Show Table, 603
    Styles Pane Options, 189–190
    Symbol, 201
    Table of Figures, 242
    Table Properties, 264, 266
    Tabs, 172–173, 174
    Trim Video, 948
    Zoom, 137, 138
Direction arrow (Enter key direction), 315
directory (main document type), 282
Display for Review arrow, 222, 223
Display section (Word Options
        category), 125
displaying cell formulas, 324
distribute option (shapes), 895
division operator (/), 321
documents (Word). *See also* files; main
        documents
    comments, 218–221
    footnotes/endnotes, 232–233
    headers and footers, 131–132
    navigation (keyboard shortcuts),
        120–121
    properties, 149–150
    research paper basics, 229–233
    research paper enhancements,
        237–244
    revisions, 218–223
    saving, 144–145
    symbols inserted in, 201
    Track Changes feature, 221–223
Document Inspector, 146–147
Document Panel, 149
document productivity. *See* Mail Merge
        feature; tables (Word)
dot leaders, 173, 174
doughnut charts, 431
Draft view, 136
Draw Borders (Table Tools Design tab), 265
Drawing group, 853
duplicate records (Excel tables), 487

E

EDATE function, 388
Edit Recipient List (Mail Merge
        command), 290
Edit Relationships dialog box, 597
Edit Shape feature, 856
editing
    cell content, 317
    images/graphics, 199–201
    range names, 404
    records (Excel tables), 486
    relationships, 604
Editing group, tasks (Office applications),
        90–91
editorial styles (writing styles), 231–232
Effects gallery (PowerPoint themes), 834
e-mail messages (main document type), 282
embedded
    charts, 444
    videos, 944

End Slide Show (navigation option), 791
endnotes, 232–233
enforce referential integrity, 561, 597
Engineering functions, 382
Enhanced ScreenTips, 70
Enter (Excel window element), 314
Enter key direction, 315
envelopes
    as main document type, 282
    printing, 283
Envelopes (Mail Merge command), 290
Envelopes and Labels dialog box, 290
EOMONTH function, 388
equal sign (=)
    = (equal to operator), 395
    >= (greater than or equal to),
        395, 551
    <= (less than or equal to),
        395, 551
    formulas after, 317, 321, 385
Even Page section break, 133
Excel (Microsoft Excel 2010). *See also*
        charts; functions; Microsoft Office
        2010; tables (Excel); worksheets
    /Access, when to use, 553–554
    characteristics, 64
    paper ledgers *v.*, 321
    user interface components (Office),
        64–69
    window elements, 313–314
Excel Options dialog box
    Direction arrow (Enter key
        direction), 315
    Enable AutoComplete for cell values check
        box, 316
expanded outline, 818–819
exploded pie charts, 428
exponentiation (^), 321
Export (External Data tab), 598
Expression (table property type), 589
Expression Builder tool, 660–662, 665
expressions (formulas), 651–652
    creating, 661–662
    defined, 651
External Data tab (Access)
    description, 535
    options, 598–599

F

F4 (toggle cell references), 376
F5 (Go To dialog box), 316, 405, 474
Fade In (video playback option),
        948, 949
Fade Out (video playback option),
        948, 949
Fancy Format
    index style, 240
    table of contents style, 238
field data type, 616
field properties, 588–589
Field row (Query Design view), 615
Field Size (table property type), 589

fields. *See also* formulas; merge fields; tables
  in Access tables, 533
  AID, 600, 601
  calculated, 583, 650, 651–653
  common, linked tables with, 583–584
  in data sources, 283
  in Excel tables, 484, 486–487
  in forms, 700
  formulas as, 274
  in reports, 728–729
figures, table of, 241–242. *See also* pictures/images
file formats (PowerPoint)
  audio, 953
  graphics, 921
  video, 943
File tab (Access), 535
files. *See also* databases
  closing, 80
  database, management of, 541–542
  defined, 52
  as documents, 76
  opening, 76–79
  printing, 79–80
  properties, 34, 65
fill color (cells), 348
fill handle, 323
fills (shape fills), 858–862
Filter and Sort dialog box, 287
Filter by Form, 551
Filter by Selection, 551
Filter Records tab, 287
filters/filtering
  Access tables, 549–552
  by conditional formatting, 514
  date filters, 496–497
  defined, 287
  Excel tables, 495–497
  number filters, 496
  records (in data sources), 286–287
  text filters, 495–496
Final: Show Markup view, 222–223
Financial functions, 382, 398
find (Ctrl+F), 90–91
Find and Replace dialog box, 90–91
Find Recipient (Mail Merge command), 290
Finish & Merge (Mail Merge command), 288, 290
Finish group (Mailings tab), 288
firewalls, 26, 29–30
First Column (table style option), 488
first line indent, 179
First Record (Mail Merge command), 290
flash drive, 541
Flash Video file format (.swf), 943
flip (object manipulation), 888–889
flow chart (presentation shape), 855
Fly In Effect Options gallery, 782, 783
folders, 52
Font dialog box, 87, 164–167
Font Dialog Box Launcher, 164
Font group, 67, 86–87, 167

fonts (typeface), 86–87
  attributes, 86–87, 164–167
  symbols and, 201
  as typeface, 164
Fonts gallery (PowerPoint themes), 834
footers, 131–132. *See also* headers and footers
Footnote and Endnote dialog box, 232
footnotes, 232–233
foreground (pictures/images), 200, 923–924
foreign keys, 560, 587, 597
Form Design (form tool), 699
Form Footer section, 709
Form Header section, 709
form letters, 281–282
form sections, 709–710
form splitter bar, 697
Form tool, 694, 696, 699
form tools, 694–699
Form view, 710–711
Form Wizard (form tool), 699
Formal Format
  index style, 240
  table of contents style, 238
Format (Cells group). *See* Cells group
Format (table property type), 589
Format Cells dialog box, 347, 348, 349
Format Data Labels dialog box, 454–455
Format Data Series dialog box, 451–452
Format Page Number feature, 123
Format Painter, 87, 88
Format Shape dialog box, 860, 861, 862, 864, 887
Format tab (Chart Tools contextual tab), 434, 435, 441
formatting. *See also* styles
  axes (charts), 455
  cells (conditional formatting), 509–514
  chart elements, 451–456
  data tables, 455
  dates, 665
  graphical objects (Word), 197–201
  paragraphs, 172–181
  tables (Word), 264–266
  videos, 946–947
  worksheets, 346–349
formatting marks
  list of, 177
  Show/Hide feature and, 121
forms (Access database object), 694–701, 709–714
  column width in, 700
  controls, 712–714
  Datasheet, 698, 699
  defined, 538, 694
  Design view, 712
  fields in, 70
  form tools, 694–699
  Form view, 710–711
  Layout control, 700
  Layout view, 696, 711
  modify, 699–700
  Multiple Items, 697–698, 699
  record sources, 695–696

sections, 709–710
sketch, 696
split, 697, 699
Stacked Layout, 696
styling, 714
Tabular Layout, 696
Formula AutoComplete, 382, 383, 384, 405, 498
Formula Bar, 314
formulas, 317, 321–324, 374–376. *See also* cell references; functions
  in conditional formatting, 513–514
  constants in, 322
  defined, 317
  displaying, 324
  equal sign (=) before, 317, 321, 385
  expressions, 651–652, 661–662
  as fields, 274
  functions *v.*, 385
  green triangles (formula error), 376
  mathematical operators in, 321–324
  range names in, 403–405
  semi-selection (pointing), 374
  structured references in, 498
  syntax, 273
  text in, 395
  Word tables, 273–274
Fraction (number format style), 349
freeform shapes, 856–857
Freeze First Column, 475
Freeze Panes, 475
Freeze Top Row, 475
freezing rows/columns, 475–476
FREQUENCY function, 387
Full Screen Reading view, 136
fully justified text, 178
Function Arguments dialog box, 382, 383, 384
function ScreenTip, 383
functions, 382–398. *See also* arguments; formulas
  ABS, 387
  aggregate, 675–678
  AVERAGE, 385
  built-in (Access), 662–678
  categories, 382
  Compatibility, 382
  COUNT, 386, 675
  COUNTA, 386
  COUNTBLANK, 386
  Cube, 382
  Database, 382
  DATE, 388
  date (Access), 665–666
  Date & Time, 382, 387–388
  DatePart, 665–666
  DAY, 388
  EDATE, 388
  Engineering, 382
  EOMONTH, 388
  Financial, 382, 398
  formulas *v.*, 385
  FREQUENCY, 387
  HLOOKUP, 397–398

IF, 394–395
IIf, 664
Information, 382
inserting, 382–384
INT, 387
Logical, 382, 394–395
Lookup & Reference, 382, 396–398
Math & Trig, 382, 387
MAX, 386
Maximum, 675
MEDIAN, 385
MIN, 386
Minimum, 675
MODE.SNGL, 387
MONTH, 388
nested, 395
nested IIf, 664
NETWORKDAYS, 388
NOW, 388
PI, 387
PMT, 398, 662–663
PRODUCT, 387
RANDBETWEEN, 387
RANK.AVG, 387
RANK.EQ, 387
ROUND, 387
Standard Deviation, 675
Statistical, 382, 385–387
SUBTOTAL, 499–500
SUM, 384–385, 675
SUMPRODUCT, 387
syntax, 382
Text, 382
TODAY, 387, 388
TRIMMEAN, 387
TRUNC, 387
Variance, 675
VLOOKUP, 396–397
WEEKDAY, 388
WORKDAY, 388
YEAR, 388
YEARFRAC, 388
future value (PMT function), 663
fv (PMT function), 398

G

gadgets, 4
galleries, 68
General (number format style), 348
General section (Word Options category), 125
Get External Data - Excel Spreadsheet feature, 598–602
glows (shape effect), 864
Glow/Soft Edges (font effect), 165
Go To dialog box (F5 or Ctrl+G), 316, 405, 474
Go To option, 91
Go To Record (Mail Merge command), 290
Go to Specific Slide (navigation option), 791
gradient fill, 858, 860

grammar checker. *See* spelling and grammar checker
graphical objects (Word), 197–201. *See also* pictures/images
graphics file formats, 921
Graphics Interchange Format (.gif), 921
greater than (>), 395, 551
greater than or equal to (>=), 395, 551
green triangles (formula error), 376
green wavy line, 100
Greeting Line (Mail Merge command), 290
Grid and Guides dialog box, 894
gridlines
  chart, 456
  worksheet, printing, 357
grids, 894
Group (graphic editing feature), 201
group header/footer section (report section), 738–739, 740
grouping levels (reports), 722, 724
grouping objects, 889–890
groups, 67
guides (align objects), 894–895

H

hacking, 26
handles (sizing objects), 97, 98
handouts (audience handouts), 791
  headers/footers, 784–785
  Notes and Handouts tab, 784, 785
  printing, 795
hanging indent, 179
hard page breaks, 122
hard returns, 120
Header & Footer Tools Design contextual tab, 132, 356
Header and Footer dialog box, 784–785
header row (data source), 283
Header Row (table style option), 488
Header/Footer tab (Page Setup dialog box), 356
headers and footers
  documents, 131–132
  slides, 784–785
height
  rows, 335
  rows (Word tables), 263–264
  /width adjustment (images), 197, 201
Help (Office 2010), 69–70
Help and Support (Windows 7), 34, 37–39
Help button
  Backstage view, 69, 70
  in dialog boxes, 68, 70
  on Ribbon, 67, 69–70
hidden data values (area charts), 429
hidden text, 166, 177
Hide Columns/Hide Rows (Cells group), 336
hiding
  columns/rows, 336
  Ribbon, 67
  taskbar, 7

hierarchy, 817
Hierarchy (SmartArt diagram type), 874
Highlight Cell Rules (conditional formatting option), 509, 510
Highlight Merge Fields (Mail Merge command), 290
Highlighter (text highlighting), 167
High-Low-Close (stock chart), 430
HLOOKUP function, 397–398
Home key, 121, 316
Home tab. *See also* Clipboard group; Editing group
  Access, 535
  functionality, 67
  tasks (Office applications), 84–91
horizontal cell alignment, 346
horizontal ruler, 119
horizontal scroll bar, 119, 120
horizontal text alignment, 178
Hyperlink (data type), 586
hyphens
  as leader characters, 173
  nonbreaking, 168, 177
  regular, 177

I

icon sets, 512
Icon Sets (conditional formatting option), 509, 511–512
icons, 2–4
  Action Center, 9, 10, 27
  Auto Arrange, 4
  deleting, 3
  pinning, 8–9
  pushpin, 78
  renaming, 3
  on taskbar, 5–6
IF function, 394–395
IIf function, 664
Illustrations group, 97–99
Illustrator (Adobe), 889
images. *See* pictures/images
Import & Link (External Data tab), 598
Import Spreadsheet Wizard, 599, 600, 601, 602
importing outlines, 825–826
In Front of Text (text wrapping style), 198
In Line with Text (text wrapping style), 198
Increase Decimal, 349
Increase Indent option, 179, 347
increasing/decreasing decimal places, 349, 387
indenting
  cell contents, 347
  paragraphs, 179
Indents and Spacing tab, 172, 178, 179, 180
Indexed (table property type), 589, 598
indexed locations (searches), 35
indexes, 239–240

infographics, 852
information, data *v.*, 533
Information functions, 382
infringement of copyright, 933
input area, 313
Input Mask (table property type), 589
Insert arrow (Cells group)
   Insert Cells, 333–334
   Insert Sheet, 332
   Insert Sheet Columns/Insert Sheet
      Rows, 333
Insert Chart dialog box, 434
Insert dialog box, 332, 333, 334
Insert Function dialog box, 314, 383
Insert Merge Field (Mail Merge
     command), 290
Insert Picture dialog box, 98
Insert tab tasks (Office applications), 67,
     97–99
inserting
   captions, 241
   cells, 333–334
   citations, 229, 231
   clip art, 99
   columns, 333–334
   columns (Word tables), 263
   comments (in documents), 218–221
   cross-references, 243–244
   endnotes, 232
   footnotes, 232
   functions, 382–398
   indexes, 239–240
   media objects (in presentations), 780
   merge fields, 287–288
   multiple rows/columns (Word
     tables), 263
   objects, 97–99
   pictures, 98
   pictures (in slides), 920–922
   range names, 404–405
   /recording audio, 954
   rows, 333–334
   rows (Word tables), 263
   sparklines, 444–445
   table of authorities, 242–243
   table of contents, 237–238
   table of figures, 241–242
   tables (Word), 262–264
   worksheets, 332–333
inspectors (Document Inspector),
     146–147
INT function, 387
Interface (Access Interface), 533–535
Internet (as PowerPoint resource),
     933–935
italic (type style), 164

J

join lines, 560, 629
Joint Photographic Experts Group
     (.jpg, .jpeg), 921
Jump List, 8–9

justified text, 178
Justify (alignment option), 178

K

Kelvin (K) units, 927
kerning (Font dialog box), 166
Key Tips, 69
keyboard shortcuts (keystrokes)
   Access, 551
   alignment, 179
   document navigation, 120–121
   selecting text (Word/PowerPoint), 85
   worksheet/cell navigation, 315–316
keys
   foreign, 560, 587, 597
   primary, 536, 585–587, 598
keystrokes. *See* keyboard shortcuts

L

Label control (forms), 712
Label Wizard, 727–728
labels
   category labels, 422
   chart labels, 453–455
   data labels (chart element), 454–455
labels (mailing labels)
   defined, 727
   Envelopes and Labels dialog box, 290
   Mail Merge command, 290
   as main document type, 282
   printing, 283
   reports, 727–728
landscape orientation, 102, 131, 354
Language section (Word Options category),
     125
large datasets, 474–478
Last Column (table style option), 488
Last Record (Mail Merge command), 290
layout
   reports, 725–726
   slides, 772–773
   SmartArt diagram, 879
Layout control
   forms, 700
   reports, 729
Layout dialog box, 198
Layout tab (Chart Tools contextual tab),
     435, 451–456
Layout view
   forms, 696, 711
   reports, 741
leader characters, 173, 174
leaders (dot leaders), 173, 174
Left
   table alignment (Word), 266
   text alignment, 178
left tab (tab marker), 173
legends
   customizing, 454
   defined, 424

less than (<), 395, 551
less than or equal to (<=), 395, 551
letters (main document type), 282
Line and Page Breaks tab, 180
line break
   in cell, 316
   nonprinting symbol, 177
line charts, 427
line spacing, 179–180, 181
line thickness (points), 862
line weight, 862
lines (shapes), 854–855
Link to Previous feature, 134
linked Access tables, 583–584
linked videos, 944–945
List (SmartArt diagram type), 874
list boxes (dialog box component), 15
lists
   bulleted, 175–176
   multilevel, 175–176
   numbered, 175–176
Live Preview, 68
Lock Drawing Mode, 853
Logical functions, 382, 394–395
logical operators, 395
logical tests, 394–395
Lookup & Reference functions, 382, 396–398
lookup tables, 396–397
lookup values, 397
lowercase (Change Case option), 167
low/high values (MIN/MAX functions), 386

M

Macintosh PICT, 921
macros
   database object, 533, 534
   Trust Center and, 125
Macros & Code group, 535, 613, 614, 619
magnification. *See* Zoom slider
Mail Merge feature, 281–290. *See also* data
     sources
   commands (Mailings tab), 290
   wizard, 282, 290
mailing labels. *See* labels
Mailings tab
   Finish group, 288
   Mail Merge commands, 290
   Start Mail Merge group, 282, 283, 284,
     285, 286
main body (of slides), 771
main documents (Mail Merge), 282–283.
     See also data sources
   /data source, merging, 288–289
   selecting, 282–283
   types, 282
many-to-many relationships, 603
margins, 102
   cell margins (Word tables), 266
   custom, 102, 148
   section formatting and, 181
Margins (Page Setup command), 102, 354
Margins tab (Page Setup dialog box), 355

Mark Citation dialog box, 242
Mark Index Entry dialog box, 239
markers (tab markers), 172–174
markup
    Final: Show Markup view, 222–223
    Original: Show Markup view,
        222–223
    Show Markup feature, 220, 221
markup balloons, 218–219
Master List, 230
Match Fields (Mail Merge command), 290
Math & Trig functions, 382, 387
mathematical operators
    in formulas, 321–324
    order of precedence for, 322
Matrix (SmartArt diagram type), 875
MAX function, 386
Maximize button (Office interface), 65
Maximum function, 675
Media Elements (Microsoft), 934
media objects (in presentations), 780
media tools (PowerPoint)
    audio, 953–956
    copyright guidelines, 933–935
    Internet as resource, 933–935
    multimedia, 920
    pictures, 920–933
    video, 943–949
MEDIAN function, 385
Memo (data type), 586
memory, working from, 540
Merge & Center, 347
Merge Cells command, 263
merge fields
    defined, 282
    inserting, 287–288
Merge group (Table Tools Layout
        tab), 264
merging main documents/data source,
        288–289. *See also* Mail Merge feature
Microsoft Clip Organizer, 920, 921, 953
Microsoft Media Elements, 934
Microsoft Office 2010 (Office 2010). *See
        also* Access; Excel; PowerPoint; Word
    fundamentals, 64–70, 76–80, 84–91,
        97–103
    Help, 69–70
    Home tab tasks, 84–91
    Insert tab tasks, 67, 97–99
    Page Layout tab tasks, 101–103
    Review tab tasks, 99–101
    user interface components, 64–69
Microsoft Office Online templates, 78, 79,
        809, 810, 811
Microsoft Windows Metafile (.wmf), 921
MIN function, 386
Mini toolbar, 85–86
Minimize button (Office interface), 65
Minimize the Ribbon, 67
Minimum function, 675
mixed cell reference, 375–376
MLA (Modern Language Association)
        style, 232
Modal Dialog (form tool), 699

Modern Format
    index style, 240
    table of contents style, 238
Modern Language Association (MLA)
        style, 232
MODE.SNGL function, 387
modify
    form sections, 710
    forms, 699–700
    multi-table queries, 626–629
    objects (presentation design), 887–892
    reports, 728–730
    /view/delete comments, 218–221
Modify Style dialog box, 188
modules (Access database object), 533, 534
monospaced typeface, 164
MONTH function, 388
More button, 67, 68
Move Chart dialog box, 443
Move or Copy Sheet (Cells group), 332–333
Move or Copy Sheet dialog box, 332–333
movie files, 943
moving
    charts, 443
    footnotes/endnotes, 233
    keystrokes for (cell navigation), 315
    keystrokes for (document navigation), 121
    ranges, 338
    worksheets, 332
Moving Picture Experts Group
        (.mpg, .mpeg), 943
MPEG Audio Layer 3 (.mp3), 953
Multilevel List command, 176, 191
multilevel lists, 175–176
multimedia. *See also* media tools
    copyright guidelines, 934–935
    defined, 920
multiple data series, 423
Multiple Items form, 697–698, 699
multiple rows/columns (Word
        tables), 263
multiplication operator (*), 321
multi-table queries, 625–629
    add/delete fields in, 627
    answers with, 626
    creating, 625–626
    join line in, 629
    modifying, 626–629
    problem fix in, 628
Musical Instrument Digital Interface
        (.midi, .mid), 953

N

Name Box
    Excel window element, 314
    range selection with, 338
Name Manager dialog box, 404
naming
    icons, 3
    reports, 726
    worksheet tabs, 331
narration, 954–955

navigation
    in documents (keyboard shortcuts),
        120–121
    in/among worksheets, 315–316
    sheet tab navigation buttons, 314
    in slide shows, 791
navigation buttons (Access), 536, 537
Navigation Forms (form tool), 699
Navigation Pane, 53, 54–55
    Access, 534
    Word, 91
nested functions, 395
nested IIf functions, 664
NETWORKDAYS function, 388
New Slide button, 773
Next
    Changes group, 222
    Comments group, 221
Next Page section break, 133
Next Record (Mail Merge command), 290
nonadjacent ranges
    as arguments, 386
    defined, 337
nonbreaking hyphens/spaces, 168, 177
nonprinting formatting marks
    list of, 177
    Show/Hide feature and, 121
Normal template, 188
Normal view (PowerPoint), 761–762
not equal to (<>), 395, 551
NOT operator, 618
Notepad, 23
Notes and Handouts tab, 784, 785
Notes Pages
    printing, 795
    view, 762–763
Notification area, 5, 9–10
NOW function, 388
No/Yes (data type), 586
nper (PMT function), 398
null, 617
null criteria expressions, 617
Number (data type), 586, 589
Number (number format style), 348
number filters (Excel tables), 496
number formats, 348–349
Number group, 349
numbered lists, 175–176
Numbering Library, 176
num_periods (PMT function), 663

O

object manipulation (presentation design),
        887–896
    align objects, 893–896
    arrange objects, 892–896
    flip, 888
    grouping, 889
    guides, 894–895
    modify objects, 887–892
    order objects, 893
    rotate, 888–889
    ungrouping, 889–890

objects (database objects), 533, 534, 537, 540. *See also* forms; macros; modules; queries; reports; tables (Access)
objects (graphical), 197–201
Odd Page section break, 133
Office 2010 (Microsoft Office 2010). *See also* Access; Excel; PowerPoint; Word
  fundamentals, 64–70, 76–80, 84–91, 97–103
  Help, 69–70
  Home tab tasks, 84–91
  Insert tab tasks, 67, 97–99
  Page Layout tab tasks, 101–103
  Review tab tasks, 99–101
  user interface components, 64–69
Office Clipboard, 87, 89–90
  Dialog Box Launcher, 89
  task pane, 89
Office.com
  SmartArt diagram type, 875
  templates, 78, 79, 809, 810, 811
OLE (data type), 586
100% stacked column chart, 425–426
1 Page Per Sheet (print setting), 148
one-to-many relationships, 602–604
one-to-one relationship, 603
online Help (Windows Help and Support), 39
opaque (shape fills), 859
Open dialog box, 77
Open-High-Low-Close (stock chart), 430
opening files, 76–79
OpenType, 166–167
operands, 616–617
operating systems, 2. *See also* Windows 7
operations (order of operations), 650
operators, 616–617. *See also* comparison operators; logical operators; mathematical operators
option buttons (dialog box component), 15
Options (Word Options), 124–125
OR comparison operator, 551, 618
order objects, 893
order of operations (arithmetic calculations), 650
order of precedence, 322
orientation, 131
  landscape, 102, 131
  Page Setup command, 354
  portrait, 102, 131
  rotating cell contents, 346, 347
  section formatting and, 181
Original: Show Markup view, 222–223
orphans, 180
Outline Style (font effect), 165
Outline view
  documents, 138, 190–191
  presentations, 817–818
outlines (presentations), 795, 817–820
  collapsed, 818–819
  expanded, 818–819
  modifying, 818–819
  printing, 795, 819–820
outlines (shape outlines), 862–863

outlines (Word)
  Outline view v., 191
  in presentations, 825–826
output area, 313

P

Page Border tab, 174, 175
page breaks
  Excel, 476–477
  Word, 121–122
Page Down, 121
Page Down keystroke, 316
Page Footer section (report section), 738, 740
Page Header section (report section), 737, 740
Page Layout tab, 354–357, 476
  Page Setup group, 354
  Scale to Fit group, 354, 355
  Sheet Options group, 354, 357
  tasks (Office applications), 101–103
Page Number Format dialog box, 123
page numbers
  adding, 122–123
  customizing, 123
  section formatting and, 181
page orientation. *See* orientation
Page Setup commands, 354, 478
Page Setup dialog box, 102–103, 354–357, 478
Page tab (Page Setup dialog box), 357
Page Up, 121
Page Up keystroke, 316
Pagination section (Line and Page Breaks tab), 180
Paint, 24
paper ledgers, 321
paragraphs
  indenting, 179
  line spacing for, 179–180, 181
  orphans and, 180
  paragraph spacing for, 179–180
  widows and, 180
Paragraph dialog box, 178, 179, 180
Paragraph Dialog Box Launcher, 172, 174
paragraph formatting, 172–181
  section formatting v., 181
  tab markers, 172–174
Paragraph group, 178
paragraph styles, 187–188
parallel construction (presentations), 772
parental controls, 30
Parentheses, Exponentiation, Multiplication, Division, Addition, Subtraction (Please Excuse My Dear Aunt Sally), 322
passive voice/active voice (presentations), 772
Paste, 88–90
  Ctrl+V, 69, 89
  options, 89

Paste arrow (Clipboard group)
  Paste Special, 339–340
  previewing options, 339–340
  transposing columns/rows, 340
Paste Name dialog box, 405
Paste Options button, 339
pasting ranges, 338–339
Percentage (number format style), 349
Photo Albums (presentations), 961–962
PI function, 387
Picture (SmartArt diagram type), 875
Picture Border (graphic editing feature), 201
Picture Effects (graphic editing feature), 201
picture fill
  Format Data Series dialog box, 452
  shapes, 859
Picture Styles (PowerPoint), 929–930
Picture Styles gallery, 199
Picture Tools Format tab, 197, 199, 200, 922, 924, 925, 926, 929, 930, 931
pictures/images. *See also* clip art
  alignment, 201
  Artistic Effects, 201
  artistic effects (PowerPoint), 928–929
  background, 200, 923–924, 932–933
  brightness, 200, 201, 925
  color changes (PowerPoint), 926–928
  Color feature, 201
  compression, 200, 201, 920, 931
  contrast, 200, 925
  corrections (PowerPoint), 924–926
  Corrections feature, 201
  cropping, 199–200, 201, 929–930
  defined, 98
  editing, 199–201
  file formats (PowerPoint), 921
  foreground, 200, 922–923
  Group feature, 201
  height/width adjustment, 197, 201
  inserting, in slides, 920–922
  Position feature, 201
  PowerPoint media tools, 920–932
  recolor, 891–892, 928
  Remove Background, 200, 201
  Rotate feature, 201
  saturation, 926–927
  scanning, 921
  sharpening (PowerPoint), 924
  in slides/presentations, 920–933
  softening (PowerPoint), 924
  table of figures, 241–242
  transforming (PowerPoint), 922–933
pie chart data labels, 455
pie charts, 428
pinning, 8–9
PivotChart (form tool), 699
PivotTable (form tool), 699
placeholders (in slides), 772–773
plagiarism, 229
Plain Text format (.txt), 825
planning, for worksheet/workbook design, 312–313
playback (video playback options), 948–949

Please Excuse My Dear Aunt Sally
  (Parentheses, Exponentiation,
  Multiplication, Division, Addition,
  Subtraction), 322
plot area, 423
plus sign (+), 321
PMT function, 398, 662–663
pointing (semi-selection), 374
points (line thickness), 862
Portable Network Graphics (.png), 921
portrait orientation, 102, 131, 354
Position (graphic editing feature), 201
positioning charts, 434–435
poster frame option, 946–947
pound signs (###), 335
PowerPoint (Microsoft PowerPoint 2010).
  See also media tools; Microsoft Office
  2010; presentations; slide shows
  characteristics, 64
  text selection (shortcuts), 85
  user interface components (Office),
    64–69
  views, 761–765
PowerPoint show (.ppsx), 765
precedence (order of precedence), 322
present value (PMT function), 663
presentation design (PowerPoint)
  object manipulation, 887–896
  shapes, 852–864
  slide show design principles, 830–833
  SmartArt, 873–880
  WordArt, 873, 881–882
presentations (PowerPoint), 769–774. See
  also handouts; media tools; outlines;
  slide shows
  active voice/passive voice, 772
  assessing content, 772–773
  conclusion for, 771
  defined, 760
  delivery tips, 760, 792, 831
  development, 780–785, 810–812,
    817–820, 825–826, 830–834
  media objects in, 780
  parallel construction, 772
  Photo Albums, 961–962
  pictures in, 920–933
  planning, 769–771
  reviewing, 774
  7×7 guideline, 772
  slides added to, 825–826
  storyboards, 769–771
  templates, 810–812
  themes, 773, 833–834
  views, 761–765
Presenter view (PowerPoint), 765
Preview Results (Mail Merge command),
  290
Previous
  Changes group, 222
  Comments group, 221
Previous Record (Mail Merge command),
  290
primary keys, 536, 585–587, 598

printing
  chart sheet, 444
  charts, 444
  document properties, 150
  envelopes, 283
  highlight colors, 167
  large datasets, 476–478
  mailing labels, 283
  options (Backstage view), 79–80, 147–148
  outlines (presentations), 795, 819–820
  in PowerPoint, 793–795
  row/column headings, 357
  slides, 794–795
  worksheet gridlines, 357
  worksheets, 354–357
Print All Pages (print setting), 148
print area, 477–478
Print Area (Page Setup command), 354
Print dialog box (components), 15
Print Layout view, 136
Print One Sided (print setting), 148
print order, 478
Print Preview, 79, 741
Print Selection option, 478
Print Titles (Page Setup command), 354, 478
Process (SmartArt diagram type), 874
PRODUCT function, 387
program shortcuts. See shortcuts
programs. See software programs
proofing options
  PowerPoint Options, 774
  Word Options, 125
proportional typeface, 164
Proposal for Fair Use Guidelines for
  Educational Multimedia, 934
public domain, 933
pushpin icons, 78
pv (PMT function), 398
Pyramid (SmartArt diagram type), 875

Q

quantitative data analysis, 311
queries (Access database object)
  copying, 619
  defined, 538, 613
  multi-table, 625–629
  operands in, 616–617
  running, 619
  select, 614
  single-table, 613–621
  totals query, 677–678
Query Design view, 613, 615–616
query sort order, 617
Query Wizard, 619–621
Quick Access Toolbar, 65–66
  customize (Word Options category), 125
  Customize Quick Access Toolbar menu, 66
  Word window element, 119
Quick Styles
  on shapes, 857–858
  with SmartArt, 878
  with WordArt, 881

Quick Styles gallery
  Picture Styles gallery, 199
  SmartArt, 878
  WordArt, 881

R

radar charts, 432
RANDBETWEEN function, 387
range names, 403–405
ranges
  borders, 348
  convert tables (Excel) to, 486
  copy/paste, 338–339
  moving, 338
  nonadjacent, 337
  selecting, 337–338
RANK.AVG function, 387
RANK.EQ function, 387
rate (PMT function), 398, 663
RDBMS (relational database management
  system), 560. See also databases
Reading View (PowerPoint), 763–764
Recent Documents list, 77–78
recipient lists. See data sources
recolor process (pictures), 891–892, 928
Record Sound dialog box, 954
record sources. See also data sources
  forms, 695–696
  reports, 722
record/insert audio, 954
records
  in data sources, 283, 286–287
  in forms, 701
  in reports, 730
records (Access tables), 533
  filters, 549–552
  Shift+Enter (save changes), 541
records (Excel tables), 484–485
  adding/editing/deleting, 486
  defined, 484
  duplicate, 487
  filters, 495–497
red exclamation point (Run
  command), 619
red wavy line, 100
Redo/Replace (Quick Access Toolbar), 66
redundancy, data, 583
Reference functions, 382, 396–398
reference tables
  captions and, 241
  cross-references and, 243–244
  indexes, 239–240
  other, 241–243
  table of authorities, 242–243
  table of contents, 237–238
  table of figures, 241–242
references, structured, 498
References tab
  Citations & Bibliography group, 229,
    231, 232
  indexes and, 239–240
  table of contents feature, 237–238

referential integrity (enforce referential integrity option), 561, 597
Reflection (font effect), 165
reflections (shape effect), 864
regular (type style), 164
Reject (Changes group), 222
Reject All Changes in Document, 222
related tables (Access), 625
relational database management system (RDBMS), 560
relational databases, 560–562. *See also* databases
relational power, 561–562
Relationship (SmartArt diagram type), 874
relationships (table relationships), 553, 596–598. *See also* databases; tables
  editing, 604
  many-to-many, 603
  one-to-many, 602–604
  one-to-one, 603
Relationships window, 560–561, 596, 603–604
relative cell reference, 375
relocating footnotes/endnotes, 233
Remote Assistance, 39
Remove Background (graphic editing feature), 200, 201
remove picture background, 923–924
Rename Sheet (Cells group), 331
renaming icons, 3
renaming worksheet tabs, 331
replace, 90–91. *See also* Find and Replace dialog box
Report Design (report tool), 728
Report Footer section, 738, 740, 741
Report Header section, 737, 740
report sections, 737–741
Report tool, 721, 722–723, 728
report tools, 721–728
Report view, 741
report views, 741–742
Report Wizard, 723–727
reports (Access database object), 539–540, 721–730, 737–742
  column headings in, 742
  column width in, 729
  controls, 742
  defined, 539, 721
  fields in, 728–729
  grouping levels, 722, 724
  layout, 725–726
  Layout control, 729
  mailing labels, 727–728
  modify, 728–730
  naming, 726
  record source, 722
  report sections, 737–741
  report tools, 721–728
  saving, 726
  sketching, 722
  Stacked Layout, 723
  themes in, 729–730
  views, 741–742

Required (table property type), 589
research paper
  basics, 229–233
  enhancements, 237–244
resetting videos, 947
response comments, 219
Restore Down button (Office interface), 65
Result Type (table property type), 589
Return to Previous Slide/Animation (navigation option), 791
Reuse Slides Pane, 826
Reveal Formatting task pane, 190
Review tab
  Changes group, 222
  tasks (Office applications), 99–101
Reviewing Pane, 219, 220, 221
revision marks, 221
revisions (document revisions), 218–223. *See also* research paper
Ribbon, 67–68
  Access, 534–535
  customize (Word Options category), 125
  Help button on, 67, 69–70
  hide/display, 67
Rich Text format (.rtf), 825
Right
  table alignment (Word), 266
  text alignment, 178
right tab (tab marker), 173
rotate
  cell contents, 347
  graphic editing feature, 201
  object manipulation, 888–889
ROUND function, 387
row headings
  as Excel window element, 315
  printing, 357
Row Height (Cells group), 335
rows, 314
  Banded Rows (table style option), 488
  deleting, 334
  freezing, 475–476
  Header Row (table style option), 488
  height, 335
  hiding/unhiding, 336
  inserting, 333–334
  selecting, 337
  total, 499–500, 676
  Total Row (table style option), 488
  transposing, 340
  Word tables, 263–264
Rows & Columns group (Table Tools Layout tab), 264
ruler
  tab markers on, 173
  vertical/horizontal, 119
Rules (Mail Merge command), 290
Run command (red exclamation point), 619
running queries, 619

S

sans serif typeface, 164
saturation, 926–927
Save As command
  compatible format, 144
  files, 58
  PowerPoint show (.ppsx), 765
Save button (Quick Access Toolbar), 66
Save Chart Template dialog box, 441
Save command, 58, 144
Save section (Word Options category), 125
saved searches, 36
saving
  Access objects, 540
  documents, 144–145
  reports, 726
scale/scaling feature
  Font dialog box, 166
  Size dialog box, 197
scanning images, 921
scatter (X Y) charts, 429
Scientific (number format style), 349
Screen Saver Settings dialog box, 10–11
screen savers, 10–11
scroll arrows, 120
scroll bars (horizontal/vertical), 119, 120
Search box
  of Help and Support, 37
  on Start menu, 6, 7, 34
  in windows, 34, 35
searches, 34–36
  with document properties, 150
  expanding/narrowing, 35–36
  in Help and Support, 37–38
  indexed locations, 35
  saved, 36
  for sources, 230
section breaks, 132–135
  types, 133
  viewing, 135
section formatting, 132–134
  orientation, 102, 131
  page numbers, 122–123
  paragraph formatting *v.*, 181
sections
  form sections, 709–710
  report sections, 737–741
  for slides, 830
security (Windows 7), 26–30
"Select, then do," 84
Select All (Excel window element), 314
select queries, 614
Select Recipients (Mail Merge command), 290
Select Table dialog box, 286
selecting
  cells, 337
  ranges, 337–338
  rows/columns, 337
  text, 84–85

selection net, 858
Selection Pane, 892
semi-selection (pointing), 374
Send to Back (order objects), 893
sentence case (Change Case option), 167
serif typeface, 164
7×7 guideline (presentations), 772
shading, 174–175
   Borders and Shading dialog box, 174–175
   tables (Word), 264
Shadow (font effect), 165
shadow effects (shape effect), 894
Shape Fill gallery, 858, 859, 860, 861, 892
shapes (presentation design), 852–864
   changing, 856
   closed, 854
   connectors, 855
   constraining, 854
   creating, 852–857
   customizing, 857–864
   defined, 852
   distribute option, 895
   Edit Shape, 856
   effects, 864
   fills, 858–862
   flow chart, 855
   freeform, 856–857
   lines, 854–855
   outlines, 862–863
   Quick Styles on, 857–858
   text box, 855
   vertexes and, 856–857
Shapes Gallery, 853
sharing sources, 230
sharpening (PowerPoint picture corrections option), 924
Sheet tab (Page Setup dialog box), 357
sheet tabs. See worksheet tabs
Shift+Enter (save changes to record), 541
shortcut menus, 87–88
shortcuts (program shortcuts), 3. See also icons; keyboard shortcuts
Show Markup feature, 220, 221
Show row (Query Design view), 615
Show Table dialog box, 603
Show/Hide feature, 121
Simple Format
   index style, 240
   table of contents style, 238
Simple Query Wizard, 613
single data series, 423
single-table queries, 613–621
Size (Page Setup command), 354
Size Dialog Box Launcher
   Format Shape dialog box, 887
   Size dialog box, 197
sizing handles
   charts, 434–435
   graphical objects (Word), 197
   objects, 97, 98

sketching
   forms, 696
   reports, 722
slide layouts, 772–773
slide show (desktop background), 12
Slide Show view, 764–765
slide shows (PowerPoint), 760. See also handouts; presentation design; presentations
   annotations for, 793
   controls, 792
   design principles, 830–833
   navigation options, 791
   starting, 765
Slide Sorter view
   defined, 763
   transitions and, 783
slides. See also media tools
   adding, to presentations, 825–826
   conclusion, 771
   defined, 760
   headers/footers on, 784–785
   main body, 771
   New Slide button, 773
   pictures in, 920–933
   placeholders in, 772–773
   printing, 794–795
   Reuse Slides Pane, 826
   sections for, 831
   tables on, 781
   themes, 773, 833–834
   title slide, 771
Slides tab, 761, 762
SmartArt, 873–880
   change type, 880
   diagram types, 873–876
   modifying, 877–880
   text in, 876
   text pane, 876
   text to SmartArt conversion, 880
   theme colors, 877–878
Snap, 14
Snap object to grid feature, 894
Snipping Tool, 25–26
snips, 25–26
soft edge (shape effect), 864
Soft Edges/Glow (font effect), 165
soft page breaks, 121–122
soft returns, 120
softening (PowerPoint picture corrections option), 924
software programs. See also Access; Excel; Office 2010; PowerPoint; Word
   accessory (Windows 7), 23–26
   antivirus, 26
   firewalls, 26, 29–30
   spyware, 26
   Windows Defender, 26, 27
   Windows Firewall, 29–30
   word processing, 119–120
Sort row (Query Design view), 615
sorting
   ascending order, 274, 552

   by conditional formatting, 514
   descending order, 274, 552
   query sort order, 617
   records (in data source), 286–287
   records (in forms), 701
   records (in reports), 730
   table data (Access), 552–553
   table data (Excel), 493–494
   table data (Word), 273, 274–275
source documents. See main documents
Source Manager dialog box, 230, 231
sources, 229–231. See also citations; data sources
   Create Source dialog box, 229, 230
   creating, 229–230
   Current List, 230
   Master List, 230
   plagiarism and, 229
   searching for, 230
   sharing, 230
spaces
   in calculated field names, 653
   character spacing, 166–167
   line spacing, 179–180, 181
   nonbreaking, 168
   nonprinting symbol, 177
   paragraph spacing, 179–180
Spacing section (Indents and Spacing tab), 179, 180
sparklines, 444–445
Special (number format style), 349
spelling and grammar checker
   blue wavy line, 100, 135, 136
   contextual spelling feature, 125, 135, 136
   Office applications, 100–101
   Word, 135–136
spin arrows (dialog box component), 15
Split Cells command, 263
split forms, 697, 699
spreadsheet programs, 311, 312
spreadsheets. See also worksheets
   defined, 311, 312
   Get External Data - Excel Spreadsheet feature, 598–602
   Import Spreadsheet Wizard, 599, 600, 601, 602
spyware, 26, 27
Square (text wrapping style), 198
stacked column charts, 424–426
Stacked Layout form, 696
Stacked Layout report, 723
stacking order, 893
Standard Deviation function, 675
Start button, 5
Start Mail Merge (Mail Merge command), 290
Start Mail Merge group, 282, 283, 284, 285, 286
Start menu, 6–7
   pinning items to, 9
   Search box, 6, 7, 34
starting documents. See main documents
Statistical functions, 382, 385–387

status bar (Office applications), 69
 Excel window element, 315
 PowerPoint, 761
 view buttons, 69, 119, 138
 Word, 69, 119
 Zoom slider, 69, 70, 79, 80
Sticky Notes, 25
stock charts, 430
storage, working from, 540
storyboard template, 771
storyboards, 769–771
structured references, 498
Style Inspector, 188, 190
styles, 187–191. *See also* Quick Styles;
 templates; writing styles
 forms, 714
 index, 240
 Picture Styles (PowerPoint), 929–930
 table of contents, 238
 table styles (Excel), 487–488
 table styles (Word), 265
Styles Pane Options dialog box, 189–190
Styles Task Pane, 188
subform, 696
SUBTOTAL function, 499–500
subtraction operator (-), 321
SUM function, 384–385, 675
SUMPRODUCT function, 387
surface charts, 430–431
Symbol command, 201
Symbol dialog box, 201
symbols. *See also* formatting marks
 in documents, 201
 fonts and, 201
syntax, 273, 382, 651. *See also* expressions;
 formulas; functions

T

Tab Color (Cells group), 331
Tab Color palette, 331
Tab key
 move right one cell, 315
 nonprinting symbol (→), 177
table array, 397
Table group (Table Tools Layout tab), 264
Table Move handle, 262, 263
table of authorities, 242–243
table of contents, 237–238
table of figures, 241–242
Table of Figures dialog box, 242
Table Properties dialog box, 264, 266
table relationships. *See* relationships
Table row (Query Design view), 615
Table Style Options (Table Tools Design
 tab), 265
table styles
 Excel tables, 487–488
 Word tables, 265
Table Styles (Table Tools Design tab), 265
Table Styles Gallery, 488
Table Tools Design tab, 264–265
Table Tools Layout tab, 263–264

tables. *See also* charts
 data tables, 453, 455
 lookup tables, 396–397
 movement within (Ctrl+Tab), 263, 787
 on slides, 781
tables (Access). *See also* databases; fields;
 queries; records; relationships
 calculated fields, 583
 creating, 584–589
 as data source, 285–286
 defined, 533, 580
 design principles, 580–584
 fields, 533
 filters, 549–552
 linked, 583–584
 property types, 589
 related, 625
 sorting data, 552–553
 views, 535–537, 588
tables (Excel), 484–488. *See also* cells;
 columns; records; rows
 creating, 485–487
 date filters, 496–497
 defined, 484
 design, 484–485
 fields, 484, 486–487
 filtering data, 495–497
 number filters, 496
 sorting data, 493–494
 text filters, 495–496
tables (Word), 262–275. *See also* cells;
 columns; rows
 advanced features, 273–275
 alignment, 266
 borders, 264
 as data source, 283
 formatting, 264–266
 formulas, 273–274
 inserting, 262–264
 shading, 264
 sorting data, 273, 274–275
 styles, 265
 text to tables (conversion), 275
tabs. *See also* worksheet tabs; *specific tabs*
 contextual, 68, 97
 Ribbon, 67, 68
 tab markers, 172–174
Tabs dialog box, 172–173, 174
Tabular Layout form, 696
Tagged Image File Format (.tif, .tiff), 921
tags, 34
taskbar (Windows desktop), 4–10
 hiding, 7
 icons, 5–6
templates, 78–79. *See also* styles
 charts as, 441
 Normal, 188
 Office.com, 78, 79, 809, 810, 811
 presentation, 810–812
 storyboard, 771
text
 alignment, 178, 181
 in cells, 316
 columns, 176–177, 181

 in formulas, 395
 hidden, 166, 177
 highlighting, 167
 selecting, 84–85
 in SmartArt, 876
 text to SmartArt (conversion), 880
 text to tables (conversion), 275
Text (data type), 586, 588–589
Text (number format style), 349
Text Box control, 712–714
text boxes
 dialog box component, 15
 shape (presentations), 855
text direction, 266
Text Effects feature, 165
Text Fill (font effect), 165
text filters (Excel tables), 495–496
Text functions, 382
Text Highlight Color command, 167
Text Outline (font effect), 165
text pane (SmartArt), 876
text wrapping styles (Wrap Text
 options), 198
texture fill
 Format Data Series dialog box, 452
 Shape Fill gallery, 861
theme colors (SmartArt), 877–878
themes
 in forms, 700–701
 in reports, 729–730
 on slides/presentations, 773, 833–834
Thesaurus, 101, 774
3-D charts, 426
3-D Format (font effect), 165
3-D rotation (shape effect), 864
Through (text wrapping style), 198
thumbnails (slide miniature), 761
Tight (text wrapping style), 198
Time (number format style), 348
Time functions. *See* Date & Time
 functions
times
 in cells, 317
 Ctrl+Shift+semicolon (current time),
 317
 /dates, updating, 388
Title and Content layout, 780
title bar, 12, 65, 119, 533
title slide, 771
TODAY function, 387, 388
toggle case (Change Case option), 167
toggle Datasheet/Design views, 588
Toggle Field Codes command, 274
toggles, 86, 121
tone, 927
toolbars, 7–8
Top and Bottom (text wrapping style), 198
Top/Bottom Rules (conditional formatting
 option), 509, 510–511
total number (COUNT functions), 386
total row, 499–500, 676
Total Row (table style option), 488
totaling values (SUM function), 384–385
totals query, 677–678

Track Changes feature, 221–223
Transform option (WordArt), 881–882
transforming pictures (PowerPoint), 922–933
transitions, 781–784. *See also* animations
transparency (shape fills), 859
transposing columns/rows, 340
trendlines, 456
Trig functions. *See* Math & Trig functions
Trim Video dialog box, 948
TRIMMEAN function, 387
TRUNC function, 387
Trust Center (Word Options category), 125
Two Content layout, 780
type argument (PMT function), 398, 663
type style, 164
typeface, 164. *See also* fonts
typography, 164

U

UAC (User Account Control), 27–28
unbound control, 713
Undo
  Ctrl+Z, 69
  Quick Access Toolbar, 66
ungrouping objects, 889
Unhide Columns/Unhide Rows (Cells group), 336
unhiding columns/rows, 336
UNIX Audio (.au), 953
update date and time, 388
Update Labels (Mail Merge command), 290
UPPERCASE (Change Case option), 167
User Account Control (UAC), 27–28
user interface, 64
user interface components (Office 2010), 64–69

V

validation rule, 589
Validation Text (table property type), 589
value axis, 423
value_if_false, 395
value_if_true, 395
values
  in cells, 317
  lookup values, 397
Variance function, 675
VBA (Visual Basic for Applications), 698
vector graphics, 889
verify calculated results, 652
vertexes, 856–857
vertical cell alignment, 346
vertical ruler, 119
vertical scroll bar, 119, 120
video file formats, 943
video tools (PowerPoint media tools), 943–949

embedded videos, 944–945
format video, 946–947
linked videos, 944–945
poster frame option, 946–947
resetting video, 947
video playback options, 948–949
view buttons (status bar), 69, 119, 138
View tab, 136–138
viewing section breaks, 135
view/modify/delete comments, 219–221
views
  Access table, 535–537, 588
  Design view (Access tables), 535–537, 588
  Design view (forms), 712
  Design view (reports), 741
  Form view, 710–711
  Layout (forms), 696, 711
  Layout (reports), 741
  PowerPoint, 761–765
  Query Design, 613, 615–616
  Report view, 741
  report views, 741–742
viruses
  antivirus software, 26, 27
  firewalls and, 29
Visual Basic for Applications (VBA), 698
VLOOKUP function, 396–397
Volume-High-Low-Close (stock chart), 430
Volume-Open-High-Low-Close (stock chart), 430

W

warp options (WordArt transform category), 881–882
watermarks, 135
Wave Form (.wav), 953
Web Layout view, 138
Web Linked Lists (External Data tab), 598
WEEKDAY function, 388
widows, 180
width
  column, in forms, 700
  column, in reports, 729
  columns, 334–335
  columns (Word tables), 263–264
  /height adjustment (images), 197
wildcards, 616
window elements
  Excel, 313–314
  Word, 119
windows (Windows 7), 2
  components, 12–15
  Search box in, 34, 35
Windows 7, 2–15, 23–30, 34–39
  accessory programs, 23–26

desktop, 2–12
  as operating system, 2
  security, 26–30
Windows Bitmap, 921
Windows Defender, 26, 27
Windows Enhanced Metafile (.wmf, .emf), 921
Windows Explorer, 52–56
  defined, 52
  images (in slide show) from, 922
Windows Firewall, 29–30
Windows Media Audio (.wma), 953
Windows Media File, 943
Windows Media Video (.wmv), 943
Windows Media Video File, 943
Windows Remote Assistance, 39
Windows Updates, 29
Windows Video File, 943
wizards
  defined, 282
  Form Wizard, 699
  Import Spreadsheet, 599, 600, 601, 602
  Label Wizard, 727–728
  Mail Merge, 282, 290
  Query Wizard, 619–621
  Report Wizard, 723–727
  Simple Query Wizard, 613
Word (Microsoft Word 2010).
  See also documents; Microsoft Office 2010; Options; tables (Word)
  backup options, 145–146
  characteristics, 64
  graphical objects, 197–201
  Navigation Pane, 91
  spelling and grammar checker, 135–136
  tables, 262–275
  text selection (shortcuts), 85
  user interface components (Office), 64–69
  versatility, 118
  window elements, 119
Word 97-2003 format, 144, 145
Word Options, 124–125
word processing software, 119–120
word wrap, 119–120
  hard/soft returns and, 120
  nonbreaking hyphens/spaces and, 168
WordArt, 873, 881–882
WordPad, 23
workbooks. *See also* worksheets
  defined, 311, 312
  designing, 312–313
WORKDAY function, 388
working from memory, 540
working from storage, 540
worksheet tabs, 315
  colors for, 331
  navigation buttons, 315
  renaming, 331

worksheets. *See also* columns; rows; tables (Excel)
- background (Page Setup command), 354
- copying, 332
- as data source (mail merge), 284–285
- defined, 311
- deleting, 332
- designing, 312–313
- formatting, 346–349
- inserting, 332
- landscape orientation, 354
- managing, 330–333
- moving, 332
- navigation in/among, 315–316
- printing, 354–357
Wrap Text option, 347
- graphic editing feature, 201
- text wrapping styles, 188
writing styles (editorial styles), 231–232

X

X (close file/application), 80
X Y (scatter) charts, 429
X-axis, 423

Y

Y-axis, 423
YEAR function, 388
YEARFRAC function, 388
yellow diamond (adjustment handle), 853
Yes/No (data type), 586

Z

Zoom dialog box, 137, 138
Zoom slider, 69, 70, 79, 80, 119, 137
Zoom to Page, 79, 80, 147

SINGLE PC LICENSE AGREEMENT AND LIMITED WARRANTY

READ THIS LICENSE CAREFULLY BEFORE OPENING THIS PACKAGE. BY OPENING THIS PACKAGE, YOU ARE AGREEING TO THE TERMS AND CONDITIONS OF THIS LICENSE. IF YOU DO NOT AGREE, DO NOT OPEN THE PACKAGE. PROMPTLY RETURN THE UNOPENED PACKAGE AND ALL ACCOMPANYING ITEMS TO THE PLACE YOU OBTAINED THEM. *THESE TERMS APPLY TO ALL LICENSED SOFTWARE ON THE DISK EXCEPT THAT THE TERMS FOR USE OF ANY SHAREWARE OR FREEWARE ON TH E DISKETTES ARE AS SET FORTH IN THE ELECTRONIC LICENSE LOCATED ON THE DISK:*

1. GRANT OF LICENSE and OWNERSHIP: The enclosed computer programs ("Software") are licensed, not sold, to you by Prentice-Hall, Inc. ("We" or the "Company") and in consideration of your purchase or adoption of the accompanying Company textbooks and/or other materials, and your agreement to these terms. We reserve any rights not granted to you. You own only the disk(s) but we and/or our licensors own the Software itself. This license allows you to use and display your copy of the Software on a single computer (i.e., with a single CPU) at a single location for academic use only, so long as you comply with the terms of this Agreement. You may make one copy for back up, or transfer your copy to another CPU, provided that the Software is usable on only one computer.

2. RESTRICTIONS: You may not transfer or distribute the Software or documentation to anyone else. Except for backup, you may not copy the documentation or the Software. You may not network the Software or otherwise use it on more than one computer or computer terminal at the same time. You may not reverse engineer, disassemble, decompile, modify, adapt, translate, or create derivative works based on the Software or the Documentation. You may be held legally responsible for any copying or copyright infringement which is caused by your failure to abide by the terms of these restrictions.

3. TERMINATION: This license is effective until terminated. This license will terminate automatically without notice from the Company if you fail to comply with any provisions or limitations of this license. Upon termination, you shall destroy the Documentation and all copies of the Software. All provisions of this Agreement as to limitation and disclaimer of warranties, limitation of liability, remedies or damages, and our ownership rights shall survive termination.

4. DISCLAIMER OF WARRANTY: THE COMPANY AND ITS LICENSORS MAKE NO WARRANTIES ABOUT THE SOFTWARE, WHICH IS PROVIDED "AS-IS." IF THE DISK IS DEFECTIVE IN MATERIALS OR WORKMANSHIP, YOUR ONLY REMEDY IS TO RETURN IT TO THE COMPANY WITHIN 30 DAYS FOR REPLACEMENT UNLESS THE COMPANY DETERMINES IN GOOD FAITH THAT THE DISK HAS BEEN MISUSED OR IMPROPERLY INSTALLED, REPAIRED, ALTERED OR DAMAGED. THE COMPANY DISCLAIMS ALL WARRANTIES, EXPRESS OR IMPLIED, INCLUDING WITHOUT LIMITATION, THE IMPLIED WARRANTIES OF MERCHANTABILITY AND FITNESS FOR A PARTICULAR PURPOSE. THE COMPANY DOES NOT WARRANT, GUARANTEE OR MAKE ANY REPRESENTATION REGARDING THE ACCURACY, RELIABILITY, CURRENTNESS, USE, OR RESULTS OF USE, OF THE SOFTWARE.

5. LIMITATION OF REMEDIES AND DAMAGES: IN NO EVENT, SHALL THE COMPANY OR ITS EMPLOYEES, AGENTS, LICENSORS OR CONTRACTORS BE LIABLE FOR ANY INCIDENTAL, INDIRECT, SPECIAL OR CONSEQUENTIAL DAMAGES ARISING OUT OF OR IN CONNECTION WITH THIS LICENSE OR THE SOFTWARE, INCLUDING, WITHOUT LIMITATION, LOSS OF USE, LOSS OF DATA, LOSS OF INCOME OR PROFIT, OR OTHER LOSSES SUSTAINED AS A RESULT OF INJURY TO ANY PERSON, OR LOSS OF OR DAMAGE TO PROPERTY, OR CLAIMS OF THIRD PARTIES, EVEN IF THE COMPANY OR AN AUTHORIZED REPRESENTATIVE OF THE COMPANY HAS BEEN ADVISED OF THE POSSIBILITY OF SUCH DAMAGES. SOME JURISDICTIONS DO NOT ALLOW THE LIMITATION OF DAMAGES IN CERTAIN CIRCUMSTANCES, SO THE ABOVE LIMITATIONS MAY NOT ALWAYS APPLY.

6. GENERAL: THIS AGREEMENT SHALL BE CONSTRUED IN ACCORDANCE WITH THE LAWS OF THE UNITED STATES OF AMERICA AND THE STATE OF NEW YORK, APPLICABLE TO CONTRACTS MADE IN NEW YORK, AND SHALL BENEFIT THE COMPANY, ITS AFFILIATES AND ASSIGNEES. This Agreement is the complete and exclusive statement of the agreement between you and the Company and supersedes all proposals, prior agreements, oral or written, and any other communications between you and the company or any of its representatives relating to the subject matter. If you are a U.S. Government user, this Software is licensed with "restricted rights" as set forth in sub-paragraphs (a)-(d) of the Commercial Computer-Restricted Rights clause at FAR 52.227-19 or in subparagraphs (c)(1)(ii) of the Rights in Technical Data and Computer Software clause at DFARS 252.227-7013, and similar clauses, as applicable.

Should you have any questions concerning this agreement or if you wish to contact the Company for any reason, please contact in writing:

Multimedia Production
Higher Education Division
Prentice-Hall, Inc.
1 Lake Street
Upper Saddle River NJ 07458